BUSINESS
A PRACTICAL INTRODUCTION

BUSINESS

A PRACTICAL INTRODUCTION

Brian K. Williams

Stacey C. Sawyer

Susan Berston
City College of San Francisco

PEARSON

Boston   Columbus   Indianapolis   New York   San Francisco   Upper Saddle River
Amsterdam   Cape Town   Dubai   London   Madrid   Milan   Munich   Paris   Montreal
Toronto   Delhi   Mexico City   São Paulo   Sydney   Hong Kong   Seoul   Singapore   Taipei   Tokyo

Editorial Director: Sally Yagan
Director of Development: Stephen Deitmer
Acquisitions Editor: James Heine
Director of Editoral Services: Ashley Santora
Editorial Project Manager: Karin Williams
Editorial Assistant: Ashlee Bradbury
Director of Marketing: Maggie Moylan
Senior Marketing Manager: Nikki A. Jones
Senior Managing Editor: Judy Leale
Senior Production Project Manager:
 Karalyn Holland
Senior Operations Supervisor: Arnold Vila
Operations Specialist: Cathleen Petersen
Senior Art Director: Kenny Beck

Text Design: LCI Design
Cover Design: LCI Design
Cover Art: Tree root bar-code/Shutterstock/Robert
 Adrian Hillman; Green tree/Shutterstock/Smit
Media Editor: Allison Longley
Media Project Manager: Lisa Rinaldi
Development: Burrston House
Full-Service Project Management: S4Carlisle
 Publishing Services
Composition: S4Carlisle Publishing Services
Printer/Binder: Courier/Kendallville
Cover Printer: Courier/Kendallville
Text Font: 11/12 Times Roman

Credits and acknowledgments borrowed from other sources and reproduced, with permission, in this textbook appear on the appropriate page within text.

Many of the designations by manufacturers and sellers to distinguish their products are claimed as trademarks. Where those designations appear in this book, and the publisher was aware of a trademark claim, the designations have been printed in initial caps or all caps.

Library of Congress Cataloging-in-Publication Data
Williams, Brian K.
 Business : a practical introduction / Brian Williams, Stacey Sawyer, Susan Berston.
  p. cm.
 Includes bibliographical references.
 ISBN-13: 978-0-13-233429-7
 ISBN-10: 0-13-233429-1
 1. Business. 2. Industrial management. I. Sawyer, Stacey C. II. Berston, Susan. III. Title.
 HF1008.W547 2011
 658-dc23
                                2011037129

10 9 8 7 6 5 4 3

PEARSON

ISBN: 10:   0-13-233429-1
ISBN: 13: 978-0-13-233429-7

To BH, with profound respect for your work and appreciation for our friendship. And to Atticus, Lily, and Nicolas, with love.

—B.K.W.

To Gina and Brian Kaspar, my good friends and support system.

—S.C.S.

To my personal board of directors: Samuel, my chairman of the board, and Patty, my patient, understanding, and steadfast vice-chair. To my father for his guidance and to my precious mother, whose unconditional, forever love and devotion inspire me in all my endeavors.

—S.B.

BRIEF CONTENTS

CONTENTS

2
Ethics & Social Responsibility
Business as a Positive Force 32

6

The Entrepreneurial Spirit
Pursuing the Dream of Success in Small Business 160

10

Motivating Employees
Achieving Exceptional Performance in the Workplace   284

PREFACE

No two Introduction to Business courses are completely alike—they're as different and unique as the educational professionals who teach them. And no two Introduction to Business students are completely alike either. In order to make sure we provide a wide range of information, we've created 11 thematic areas of interest that our research has shown is important to students like you—and the future companies you may be working for.

The 11 themes highlighted in this text are:

 Business Culture & Etiquette. Explores in-depth what students need to know about today's business etiquette and the importance of knowing about different business cultures.

 Business Skills & Career Development. Practical advice on career development (including much that is applicable to nonbusiness careers) and detailed tips to help students become rising stars.

 Customer Focus. Regardless of the business sector, any student working today will need to understand and appreciate the importance of focusing on the customer.

 Earning Green by Going Green. Businesses face a new dynamic, one that poses significant challenges as well as opportunities—the need to "green" products and services. Environmentally driven businesses will represent one of the world's major forces and industries in the 21st century.

 Global Business. America's deep involvement in the world is matched by the world's involvement with us, and every year that interdependency increases. This theme endeavors to raise students' consciousness to this reality.

 Infotech & Social Media. Businesses are scrambling to integrate information technology and social media into their promotional mix. Entrepreneurs are also using it as a means to inexpensively form and launch new businesses. This theme reflects the rapidly increasing impact of this phenomenon.

 Legal & Ethical Practices. Ethical behavior and community responsibility are not just niceties. As the deplorable record from Enron to Madoff shows, they should be the very underpinnings of business, as this theme demonstrates.

 Personal Finance. Many students are lacking in experience about how to handle their personal finances. To ensure that all students receive exposure to this subject, this theme integrates it with related topics—in addition to an entire personal finance flex chapter.

Small Business & Entrepreneurs. Most students will work in small businesses and many want to *own* their own businesses. This theme addresses the issues faced by many small businesses and entrepreneurs.

 Socially Responsible Business. At what point does the pursuit of profits reach a point of detriment for the greater good? Does business have a responsibility to evaluate that balance? This theme highlights businesses that are attempting to answer these tough questions.

 A World of Constant Change. The future business landscape is rapidly being altered. This theme discusses the effects of 2007–2009 Great Recession on capital markets and regulation, as well as computers, the Internet, robotics, and the like. It also covers the impact of the changing mix of racial, ethnic, age, and gender groups in the United States and throughout the world.

Building from Student-Centered Fundamentals

Technology Focus

MyBizLab

From the first word to the last, each detail in this book was created with 21st Century students in mind. The combination of *Business: A Practical Introduction* with **MyBizLab** provides you with access to personalized learning options so you can learn at your own pace. **MyBizLab** helps you actively study and prepare material for class through chapter-by-chapter activities that focus on what you need to review and learn in order to succeed. Tools to help you in the learning process include videos, decision-making simulations (called BizSkills), and much more.

Superior Content Organization for Enhanced Learning

Shaped to address modern learning styles, this research-driven text is organized in a unique educational format that appeals to student interests and provides numerous tools for learning. Every page engages you in the material to stimulate interest in the dynamic world of business through colorful writing and storytelling, contemporary mini-cases and examples, and superb visuals. This student-centered approach to learning integrates words, pictures, and layout into a framework directed toward the varied learning styles of today's students and considers your time constraints and priorities.

Visually Appealing

We use a visually appealing layout combined with content structured in bite-size portions and include 12 learning and study tools to help you focus on, engage with, and retain what you read. The effectiveness of this pedagogical structure is supported by comparative class testing in 15 schools, in which more than 80% of students favored our approach over that of their assigned texts.

Our system works like this . . .

Reading With a Purpose

Each chapter begins with a list of section titles and the **Essential Question** to be answered about each section, a **Forecast** or overview of the chapter, and **Winners & Losers** cases, as follows.

4

Globalization
Rising to the Challenge of World Competition

After reading and studying this chapter, you will be able to answer the following essential questions:

4.1 Globalization: The Shrinking of Time & Distance
THE ESSENTIAL QUESTION: What are three developments in globalization that will probably affect me?

4.2 Why & How Companies Conduct International Trade
THE ESSENTIAL QUESTION: Why do companies expand internationally, and how do they do it?

4.3 Conditions Affecting International Trade
THE ESSENTIAL QUESTION: What factors should I be aware of that affect international markets?

4.4 International Trade: Barriers & Facilitators
THE ESSENTIAL QUESTION: What are barriers to free trade, and what international organizations are designed to promote trade?

MyBizLab Where you see MyBizLab in this chapter, go to www.mybizlab.com for additional activities on the topic being discussed.

FORECAST: What's Ahead in This Chapter
We consider the rise of the global workplace and electronic commerce, one big world market, and huge multinationals along with Internet-enabled small firms. We then discuss why countries trade; how companies enter foreign markets; and the cultural, economic, and political/legal conditions affecting trade. Finally, we describe barriers to trade, organizations promoting trade, and the major trading blocs of the world.

MyBizLab

Gain hands-on experience through an interactive, real-world scenario. This chapter's simulation entitled Going Global is located at www.mybizlab.com.

98

Essential Questions: Each chapter begins with three to six provocative, motivational **Essential Questions,** written to appeal to your concern about "How can this benefit me?" and to help you determine what's important about each section.

Forecast: The chapter opening also includes **Forecast: What's Ahead in This Chapter,** which gives you a preview of the upcoming chapter contents.

Winners & Losers cases: Most business textbooks open each chapter with a single case, often an example of success. However, students in Introduction to Business courses learn equally from examples of failure. Accordingly, we open each chapter with *two* cases—**Winners & Losers.** One case demonstrates a successful strategy pertaining to the subject of the chapter, the other a failure.

Your Call: To further involve you in these opening cases, we ask you, under **Your Call,** to do some analysis, express an opinion, or otherwise get involved in the two cases. Instructors may use the Winners & Losers and Your Call features to launch some spirited class discussion.

Easy-Learning Format with Frequent Opportunities for Concept Reinforcement

To ease reading and study, topics within the section are presented in small, bite-size portions for learning. Chapters are organized to cover each Essential Question in turn, giving you discrete amounts of information that can be easily grasped. Frequent opportunities are offered for reinforcement through judicious repetition.

The Big Idea and The Essential Question: Every section begins with The Big Idea, giving you a brief overview of the section you are about to read and highlights what's important. This is followed by The Essential Question, designed to be provocative and motivational and to address your "How can this benefit me?" concerns.

Subsection questions: Within the section are subsection headings, each followed by its own question about the material you are about to read.

Key Takeaways: Appearing in the margins at critical points, the **Key Takeaway** is a mini-summary of important material in the text.

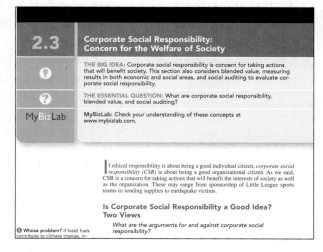

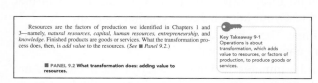

Presenting Information Effectively

Learning isn't just a matter of repetition, questions, and summaries. It is also advanced by presenting information in formats that suit various learning modes and therefore is more easily accessed. For visual learners we provide more illustrations per page than any other Introduction to Business text—with more than 370 photos and 155 figures and tables (Panels).

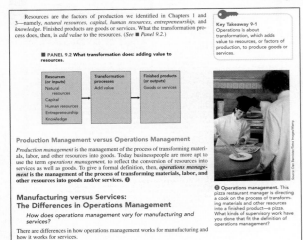

Resources are the factors of production we identified in Chapters 1 and 3—namely, *natural resources, capital, human resources, entrepreneurship,* and *knowledge.* Finished products are goods or services. What the transformation process does, then, is *add value* to the resources. (*See* ■ *Panel 9.2.*)

Key Takeaway 9-1
Operations is about transformation, which adds value to resources, or factors of production, to produce goods or services.

■ PANEL 9.2 What transformation does: adding value to resources.

Production Management versus Operations Management

Production management is the management of the process of transforming materials, labor, and other resources into goods. Today businesspeople are more apt to use the term *operations management,* to reflect the conversion of resources into services as well as goods. To give a formal definition, then, *operations management* **is the management of the process of transforming materials, labor, and other resources into goods and/or services.** ❶

Manufacturing versus Services:
The Differences in Operations Management

How does operations management vary for manufacturing and services?

There are differences in how operations management works for manufacturing and how it works for services.

❶ Operations management. This pizza restaurant manager is directing a cook on the process of transforming materials and other resources into a finished product—a pizza. What kinds of supervisory work have you done that fit the definition of operations management?

Precise Positioning of Illustrations: Instead of positioning figures and tables (Panels) at the top or bottom of the page as most texts do, we put them immediately following or adjacent to the related text discussion for maximum reinforcement and ease of reading.

Photos Closely Connected to Text Ideas: Instead of having photos free-floating or randomly placed on the page, we connect them to relevant text via circled numbers, such as ❶ or ❷. Photo captions also contain substantive content and meaningful questions to stimulate application and critical thinking.

Key Terms and Definitions Emphasized: To avoid confusion about which terms are important and what they actually mean, we print each key term in *highlighted bold italic* and its definition in **boldface.** For study purposes, we also boldface the names of important contributors to business ideas—e.g., **Adam Smith.**

Offering Context Through Prominently Displayed Examples

Examples in textbooks are often buried within the text, and thematic boxes are often positioned as sidebars and so students skip them. We do things differently. To motivate readers to give examples the attention they deserve, **we do three things: (1) clearly identify them with a design element; (2) position them within the flow of the narrative to *immediately* follow the related topic or concept; and (3) precede them with compelling headlines** that stimulate the reader's curiosity.

End-of-Chapter Resources Reinforce Key Concepts and Topics

The Learning & Skills Portfolio at the end of each chapter integrates and reinforces key concepts and topics.

- **Summary:** Each end-of-chapter Summary repeats the Essential Questions, contains abstracts of the chapter material, and includes questions to encourage deeper thinking on the key issues covered by the chapter.
- **Key Terms:** The key terms defined within each chapter are repeated, along with page numbers for ready reference to the definitions in context.
- **Pop Quiz Prep:** This feature offers brief questions you can use to further review the main topics and test your knowledge of chapter content.
- **Critical Thinking Questions:** These critical thinking questions give you the opportunity to think deeply about chapter materials.
- **Video Case:** Videos 5 to 15 minutes in length, one for each chapter, are suitable for viewing in classrooms or individually and are available at www.mybizlab.com.
- **Business Decision Cases:** These cases, based on material in business newspapers and magazines, ask you to analyze a firm's strategy and actions and then consider several "What would you do?" questions.

Want to Know More? Feature

Our research has shown that, even when not assigned to do so, some students will voluntarily access and review material on specific topics of interest. Throughout the book, called out through marginal *Want to Know More?* boxes, we provide high-interest, practical content that, if not assigned, you can explore on your own at www.mybizlab.com. Some expand on topics covered in the chapter, while others complement in-text topics by providing new information.

Sample titles:

- "Annotated History of Business Timeline"
- "Why Do Businesses Fail?"
- "Examples of Public Relations Crises"
- "How the United States Is Changing in Race, Ethnicity, & Class"
- "More about White-Collar Criminals"
- "Who Are the United States' Big Competitors?"

Emphasis on Contemporary Coverage: A Book for the 21st Century

Ours is the first completely new introductory business text written from scratch during the Great Recession and its aftermath. It is therefore the first to reflect the recession's continuing domestic and global impact. Other topics of contemporary coverage include:

- The increasing impact of **China and India** as rising economic powers
- The remarkable rise and influence of **social media**
- The **green economy** and its challenges and promises for developing industries
- The **changing demographics** among U.S. employees and consumers
- The increasing U.S. interaction with the **global economy**
- The need for **ethics and social responsibility** in a competitive marketplace

Offering Unequaled Practicality

When asked by our researchers what could make a text more valuable, Introduction to Business students were almost unanimous in their desire to see more practical information—material that helps them with career planning and workplace success. This text and **MyBizLab** help students learn, apply, and master the course concepts, as well as provide professional and career development. With these materials, students will achieve success in the course and in their careers.

In Chapter 1, we present **Seven Key Business Rules for Success** that provide useful career planning and ensure workplace success. In addition, this texts offers **Practical Action** sections, offering practical advice to help students survive and thrive in business and their careers. Examples include:

- "What Do Companies Look for in Résumés & References?"
- "Creating a Successful Business Plan: Make It Sing"
- "Surviving & Thriving in a New Job: The First 60 Days of Fitting into an Organization's Culture"
- "How to Read an Annual Report"
- "Partnering in Business with a Spouse or Boyfriend/Girlfriend: Defining Roles & Setting Limits"

MyBizLab

Want to Know More? 17-1

Key Terms & Definitions in Sequential Order to Study as You Go Along

Go to www.mybizlab.com.

■ **PANEL 1.4 Seven Key Business Rules for Success.** These are seven rules to be observed in the pursuit of business success in the 21st century.

- *Stakeholders.* Rule 1—You must meet the needs of stakeholders, those with an interest in your organization.
- *Uncertainty.* Rule 2—You must deal with constant change, including technological change.
- *Competition.* Rule 3—You must master the competitive environment to stay ahead of rivals.
- *Common economy.* Rule 4—You must deal with an interdependent global economic system.
- *Ethics.* Rule 5—You must be ethical and socially responsible.
- *Societal differences.* Rule 6—You must learn to deal with different kinds of people.
- *Self-development.* Rule 7—You must acquire the personal skills needed for business success.

MyBizLab

Online Activities and Exercises: Available at MyBizLab

Students will learn, apply, and master the course concepts through online Activities and Exercises available at **MyBizLab**. The following features can be found online at www.mybizlab.com:

- **Ethical Dilemma Cases:** These provocative cases present ethical situations that are typically based on real events. Students are asked to think about the behavior or breach of ethics that created the dilemma and then to formulate the action they would take to address it.
- **Developing Marketable Business Skills:** The five skills important for success in the world beyond school that students should achieve (as identified by **SCANS—the Secretary's Commission on Achieving Necessary Skills**) are
  1. Resource skills
  2. Interpersonal skills
  3. Information skills
  4. Systems understanding
  5. Technology ability

  To help advance these goals, we offer several potential assignments (for each chapter). Some activities may be done with impromptu student teams in the classroom and require no preparation. Others will require online or library research and some actual field work.
- **Maximizing Your Net Worth:** These are assignable exercises aimed at teaching key tenets of personal finance, from banking to credit cards to real estate to securities to personal finance software. They include creation of an online portfolio and a stock trading simulation.
- **Going to the Net! Internet Research Activities:** These optional or assignable exercises for each chapter allow you to use the Internet to research chapter-related topics to gain an increased level of understanding.
- **Getting Your Career in Gear:** This feature presents practical information related to each chapter's associated careers. Highlights include career data, the job and industry outlook, salary information, and skill requirements.

About the Authors

Brian K. Williams is married to Stacey Sawyer, and they share an avid interest in seeing college students become well educated. From their home and offices first in San Francisco and later at Lake Tahoe and nearby high-desert Nevada, they have individually or together **authored more than 25 books** (more than 60, counting revisions). Their longstanding text *Using Information Technology: A Practical Introduction* is in its 10th edition, and Williams's best-selling book with Angelo Kinicki, *Management: A Practical Introduction,* is in its 5th edition. Williams has also coauthored (with Carl Wahlstrom) a number of college success books.

A native of Palo Alto, California, he has been managing editor for college textbook publisher Harper & Row/Canfield Press in San Francisco; editor-in-chief for trade book publisher J. P. Tarcher in Los Angeles; publications and communications manager for the University of California, Systemwide Administration, in Berkeley; and an independent writer and book producer based in the San Francisco and Lake Tahoe areas. He has a B.A. in English and M.A. in Communication from Stanford University.

Stacey C. Sawyer is also an independent writer and book producer, formerly based in Monterey, California, and San Francisco and now in the Lake Tahoe area. A native of New York City and Bergen County, New Jersey, she has taught at Ohio State University and was a manager for Brooks/Cole Publishing Co. in Monterey.

She has a B.A. from Ohio Wesleyan and the University of Freiburg, Germany, and an M.A. from Middlebury College and the University of Mainz, Germany.

She is coauthor of *Computers, Communications, & Information,* a college textbook in print for 15 years, and cowriter of 10 editions of *Using Information Technology.* A social science text for Pearson Education coauthored with Williams and Carl Wahlstrom is slated for publication in mid-2012 in its 3rd edition. She is also a publishing consultant who has overseen the editing and production of many academic trade books, college textbooks, and university press books.

Susan Berston is professor of business at City College of San Francisco, with over 14 years of experience teaching business courses. Although her favorite course is introduction to business, she also teaches supervision and management, business communication, and entrepreneurship and small business. She received her M.B.A. degree in finance from the University of San Francisco and her bachelor's degree from the University of California, Berkeley in Political Science and Economics. Her professional career was spent as a sales executive with printer R.R. Donnelley & Sons Company, and upon graduating from business school she spent three years in corporate banking with Union Bank lending to middle-market companies in the San Francisco Bay Area.

Berston currently serves as a faculty advisor for Alpha Beta Gamma, an international business honor society for two-year college students studying business, and has served as faculty advisor for City College of San Francisco's Undergraduate Investment Club. Berston has earned numerous teaching awards voted upon by her students. She welcomes any and all comments about the book at *sberston@ccsf.edu*.

Acknowledgments

We could not have completed this product without the help of a great many people. The book was signed by Jeff Shelstad, with the support of Jerome Grant, president of business publishing. It came into being under the able auspices of our cheerleader, hard-working acquisition editor James Heine, to whom we are extremely grateful. James worked under the management of editorial director Sally Yagan, to whom we also must express our appreciation for her confidence in us. Editorial project manager Karin Williams kept us upbeat and motivated through the good, the bad, and the rest and is truly a top-notch professional. Warm thanks also go to Karalyn Holland, senior production project manager; Nikki A. Jones, senior marketing manager; and Kenny Beck, senior art director, as well as to Ashlee Bradbury, Allison Longley, Lisa Rinaldi, Linda Albelli, and Judy Leale.

Outside of Pearson, we were extremely fortunate to be able to work with Burrston House, a research and development firm that earlier helped develop Williams and Sawyer's well-received information technology and management texts as well as best-selling editions of a competing introductory business text. They, as we, believe very strongly in practicing *evidenced-based business,* grounding decisions in real-world data. Thus, they use extensive market research to produce contemporary learning tools and resources that carefully respond to the needs of both instructors and students. Burrston House was instrumental not only in helping to write the original proposal for our book but also in rigorously developing and testing the manuscript over the several years it took us to get this project right. Glenn and Meg Turner, Cherie Anderer, Bobbie Combs, Carlin Barmada, and especially Cathy Crow—we can't thank you enough for everything.

We are also grateful for the fine work of S4Carlisle Publishing Services and the noble efforts of senior project editor Heather Willison, one of the most organized, calm, and proficient people we've ever met. She was ably aided by talented copyeditor Joan Lyon, who saved us from misspelled company names and other embarrassments.

We would also like to thank Tom McFarland and Bob Farris for their work on the instructor's manual, Mary Stone and PreMedia Global for the test bank, and Randy Gerber and Brad Cox for the PowerPoint slides.

Susan Berston also would like to thank those colleagues, professionals, friends, and family who encouraged and supported her during what seemed at times a never-ending endeavor: Danny Grossman, Greg Maciel, Kim Bratcher, Sherri Franklin, Anne Lauck, Michael Levy, Burt Magen, Marie Rochelle Macaspac, Connie Norton, Danny Briskin, Deborah Alvarez-Rodriguez, Linda Shih, Jan Cohen, Kathleen Moynihan, Robert Sapolsky, Lisa Share, A. James Lopresti, Elisa Adams, Gary Grellman, Richard Shaw, Kira Waldman, Ella Francis, Charene Zalis, Peter Waldman, Alison Cease, Marci Schleifer, Susan Bluer, Laurie Gottlieb, Abby Kochavi, William Do, Alexander Hudzilin, Sofya Mulenok, Anastasia Bogdanova, Luis Reyes, Marie Seredkina, Kimihiro Sano, Howard Lee, Joshua Beisiegel, Kirill Ignatuev,

Yuliya Bazyleva, Jane Yue, Ophelia Clark, Arthur Rose, Pat Wille, David Dore, Beth Cataldo, Deborah Kitchin, Leslie Morales, Carole Meagher, Gina Hector, Margaret Hock, Deborah Rauchwerger, Judith Feldman, Marilyn Goodman, Manny Berston, and Patricia Stanton.

Special thanks to the following organizations: San Francisco Goodwill, MyGym Children's Fitness Center, Pet Food Express, Aegis Corte Madera, Vierra, Magen, Marcus & Deniro, LLP, Littler Mendelsohn, Wild Planet Toys, City College of San Francisco Student Counseling Center, Johnny Rockets, and Muttville Senior Dog Rescue.

Warmest thanks and appreciation go to the following individuals who provided valuable input during the developmental stages of this edition:

Maria Aria, *Camden County College*

Vondra Armstrong, *Pulaski Technical College*

Lee Ash, *Skagit Valley College*

Barry Axe, *Florida Atlantic University*

Xenia P. Balabkins, *Middlesex County College*

Robert Bennett, *Delaware County Community College*

Carl M. Bergemann, *Arapahoe Community College*

George Bernard, *Seminole State College*

Harry V. Bernstein, *Essex County College*

Susan Berston, *City College of San Francisco*

Margaret Black, *San Jacinto College*

David Braun, *Los Angeles Pierce College*

Deborah Brown, *North Carolina State University*

Barry Bunn, *Valencia C.C.–West*

Ron Capute, *Palm Beach State College–Belle Glade*

Diana Carmel, *Golden West College*

Carlene M. Cassidy, *Anne Arundel Community College*

Ronald Cereola, *James Madison University*

Barbara C. Ching, *Los Angeles City College*

Nancy Willingham Christenson, *Brevard CC–Cocoa*

Mark Clark, *Collin County Community College–Spring Creek*

Paul Eugene Coakley, Jr., *Community College of Baltimore County; Catonsville Campus*

Joy Colarusso, *Daytona State College–Daytona Beach*

Stephen W. Colyer, *Miami-Dade College–North*

Ronald Cooley, *South Suburban College*

Dean L. Danielson, *San Joaquin Delta College*

Vincent J. Daviero, *Pasco-Hernando C.C.–West*

Colleen Dunn, *Bucks County Community College*

Henry Dunn, *Stephen F. Austin State University*

Bob Farris, *Mount San Antonio College*

Janice Feldbauer, *Schoolcraft College*

William P. Frank, *Barry University*

Sofia Klopp Gill, *Palm Beach State College–Palm Beach Garden*

James R. Glover, *The Community College of Baltimore County: Essex Campus*

Mary Gorman, *University of Cincinnati*

Karen Hawkins, *Miami-Dade C.C.–Kendall*

Pamela Edwina Hawkins, *Diablo Valley College*

Dorothy Hetmer-Hinds, *Trinity Valley Community College*

John Hilston, *Brevard C.C.–Palm Bay*

Nathan Himelstein, *Essex County Community College*

Steve Hixenbaugh, *Mendocino College*

Rebecca Innerarity, *Angelina College*

Charlotte Q. Jacobsen, *Montgomery College–Rockville Campus*

Susan Kendall, *Arapahoe Community College*

Mary Beth Kerly, *Hillsborough Community College–Tampa*

Ellen L. Ligons, *Pasadena City College*

Gregory Lindeblom, *Broward Community College–South Campus*

Gregory Luce, *Bucks County Community College*

Jennifer H. Malfitano, *Delaware County Community College*

Dewith Mayne, *Central Florida C.C.–Ocala*

Lee H. McCain, *Valencia Community College–East*

Tom McFarland, *Mount San Antonio College*

Norman Pacula, *College of Marin*

Esther Page-Wood, *Western Michigan University*

Barry R. Palatnik, *Burlington County College*

Ron Pardee, *Riverside City College*

Becky Parker, *McLennan Community College*

Jack Partlow, *Northern Virginia Community College–Annandale Campus*

Hui Pate, *Skyline College*

Clifford Perry, *Florida International University*

John Patrick Phillips, *Northern Virginia Community College–Manassas Campus*

Michael Quinn, *James Madison University*

Angela J. Rabatin, *Prince George's Community College*

Nancy Ray-Mitchell, *McLennan Community College*

Julian Redfearn, *Kilgore College*

Doug Richardson, *Eastfield College*

Gayle M. Richardson, *Bakersfield College*

Maurice M. Sampson, *Community College of Philadelphia*

Christina Shaner, *Evergreen Valley College*

Anastasios V. Sioukas, *Los Angeles Valley College*

Carolyn Denise Smith, *Folsom Lake College*

Ray Sparks, *Pima Community College–East Campus*

Rieann Spence-Gale, *Northern Virginia Community College–Alexandria*

William E. Steiger, *University of Central Florida*

Dottie Kohl Sutherland, *Pima Community College (East Campus)*

Julia Sweitzer, *Lake Sumter Community College*

Shafi Ullah, *Broward College–South*

James D. Van Tassel, *Mission College*

Jim White, *North Lake College*

Carolinda Williams, *Broward College–North*

Charles D. Wyckoff, *Riverside Community College*

Gina Yaquinto, *Hillsborough C.C.–Ybor City*

Mark Zarycki, *Hillsborough C.C.–Brandon*

How to Succeed in This Course

Success in this course is based on observing four key rules:

1. **Don't delay studying.** Don't put off studying until the last minute and then try to absorb it all the night before a test ("cramming"). There's just too much to learn.
2. **Review frequently.** Repetition works. You need to read or review lectures and readings more than once.
3. **Don't cut class.** You can't learn if you're not there, especially if instructors give clues as to what will be on the test.
4. **Figure out how to use this book—starting right now.** This book has built-in learning aids. You'll come out ahead if you know how to use them.

How to Use This Book to Get an A or a B in the Course

Most textbooks provide learning aids, but *this text is structured from the first page on with different student learning styles in mind.* Accordingly, here is how you should approach this book:

- **First page of chapter:** Read the headings and "Essential Questions," then read the "Forecast." This gives you an overview.
- **Second page of chapter:** Read the "Winners & Losers" cases, which will get you into the spirit of the chapter subject matter, and read "Your Call" to make a decision. (You'll need to make lots of decisions during your career. This gives you practice.)
- **Sections within the chapter:** Read the section title, "The Big Idea," and "The Essential Question" to understand what the section is about. Then read the section itself, paying attention to the *questions beneath the subheadings* and silently trying to answer them. Look at the photos and try to answer the questions posed there.
- **Other learning aids:** Concentrate on the key terms (*yellow*) and definitions (boldface). Look at the "Key Takeaways" in the margin. Explore the "Want to Know More?" readings at **MyBizLab.** Look at the photo captions. Try the MyBizLab exercises.
- **End of chapter:** Use the Summary and Key Terms at the end of the chapter to see how well you understand the major concepts. Try answering the Pop Quiz Prep and the Critical Thinking Questions.
- **A review of everything:** After reading all the material we've recommended, reread any material you're not sure about.

If you follow this process regularly, you'll probably have at least a reasonable grasp of the material so that you need only lightly review it the night before a test. Good luck in this course. We're cheering for you!

Brian K. Williams • Stacey C. Sawyer • Susan Berston

BUSINESS

A PRACTICAL INTRODUCTION

PART 1

TODAY'S BUSINESS ENVIRONMENT: How Exceptional Businesspeople Prepare for Today's Challenges

Starting Out

Business: The Driving Force of Change

After reading and studying this chapter, you will be able to answer the following essential questions:

MyBizLab

Where you see MyBizLab in this chapter, go to www.mybizlab.com for additional activities on the topic being discussed.

FORECAST: What's Ahead in This Chapter

You learn how business benefits society, how for-profit and nonprofit organizations differ, how selling goods and services generates revenue and profits, and how the U.S. economy has evolved. We consider how businesspeople take risks and how factors of production are the building blocks of wealth. We next consider the business environment. Finally, we present our Seven Key Business Rules for Success.

WINNER: Rick Steves's Books Travel the Road to Success

Rick Steves is a backpacker who has built a business empire by writing about life on the road. His 30 travel books sell nearly half a million copies a year, and he has a tour business and a signature line of luggage. He also has TV and radio shows, and he contributes columns to newspapers. What's behind his success?

Steves took his first trip to Europe in 1969, visiting piano factories with his father, a piano importer. "I got over there and it was fascinating," Steves says. "I mean, different pop, one-armed bandits [slot machines] in the hotel lobbies . . . I mean, it was a wonderland for a 14-year-old kid."

At 18, with funds from giving piano lessons, he returned to Europe with a friend, and they toured 15 countries in 10 weeks on the cheap. Two years later, he started teaching travel classes and realized he could make travel pay.

In 1976, he started his own tour, Europe Through the Back Door (ETBD), leading seven women in a minibus around Europe. For years, he ran his travel business on a seasonal basis with a small staff in his hometown of Edmonds, Washington, and he slept down the hall in another part of the building. In 1980, he self-published the first edition of his travel skills book, *Europe Through the Back Door*.

Steves believes that cheap travel is actually better, because too much money insulates travelers from the locals. Most of his travel books incorporate this theme. ETBD also launched a travel center offering free information and selling Railpass Guides. Their tours offer 27 itineraries.

Of course, publicity generated by Steves's TV programs and travel columns has helped to build his business, which now has 60 full-time employees. Steves himself travels four months a year. "I love my work so much," he says, "I just work."[1]

LOSER: Richard Snyder's Golden Books Goes Bankrupt

Richard Snyder was a well-known figure in book publishing, having built Simon & Schuster into the largest U.S. publisher. He eventually left the company and in May 1996 became head of Golden Books, publisher of children's classics, such as *Scuffy the Tugboat*. However, in three years the $400 million firm was bankrupt. What happened?

Instead of concentrating on the core business, children's books, Snyder made plans to expand the brand—to Golden parenting books, Golden family videos, Golden play centers, Golden theme parks.

At his former company, Snyder was used to selling high-priced children's books in regular bookstores, but Golden Books sold for $1.29 and its largest customer, Walmart, treated them like any other discount goods. Snyder learned a new term, *fill rate*—the rate at which a publisher was able to keep store shelves filled. But Golden was unable to keep them filled to Walmart's satisfaction.

Snyder learned Golden Books had no sales reports at all, and then compounded the problem by firing nearly all the experienced managers because he thought they were too rigid. He admitted later that for two years he was "flying blind," operating without a good sales-report system.

Instead of concentrating on sales-report and fill-rate problems, Snyder ordered up a complex (and unworkable) new financial system and also began empire building: starting a grown-up books line, paying $81 million for a video company, looking into play centers and theme parks, and moving the headquarters at great expense from Wisconsin to New York City.

Although millions of Golden Books were selling, all the empire building drained cash. In 1998, the company went bankrupt.[2] It was later acquired by another book publisher, Random House.

YOUR CALL Believing that readers can learn from both success *and* failure, we open each chapter in this book with "Winners & Losers" cases, like this one. What points can you take away here? Is it fair to compare running a small startup business with running a large existing one? Can we draw lessons that could be applied regardless of a firm's size?

MyBizLab

1.1

Business & Profits: The Basis of Wealth

THE BIG IDEA: Business seeks to make a profit by selling goods or services to others. We distinguish for-profit organizations from nonprofit organizations and explain how businesses make money by taking in revenue.

THE ESSENTIAL QUESTION: What is business, and how are profits made?

MyBizLab: Check your understanding of these concepts at www.mybizlab.com.

How would you like to work in your career—alone or in an organization?

Most people, even most lone wolves, have a lot of help from others. Although you may end up working as a solo operator, like some salespeople, researchers, and artists, most people work with others in organizations.

Two Types of Organizations: For-Profit & Nonprofit

Even if I don't work for a for-profit organization, could I still apply the business skills I've learned?

An *organization* is a group of people who work together to accomplish a specific purpose. There are two types of organizations—*for-profit* and *nonprofit*.

For-Profit Organizations: For Making Money

A *for-profit organization* is a business—an organization formed to make money, or profits, by selling goods or services. Is a hospital a business? It can be. Are farmers and ranchers profit oriented? Most are.

When you think of businesses, think of all the for-profit organizations that are trying to *sell* you something, from Aetna Insurance to Zephyr Paintball.

Nonprofit Organizations: For Offering Products or Services

The purpose of a *nonprofit organization* is not to distribute its surplus funds, or profits, to owners but rather to further its goals. Examples are most colleges, many hospitals, and most social-welfare agencies (the Red Cross, Save the Children). Others are the United Auto Workers, the Better Business Bureau, the New York Fire Department, and the National Football League. Most nonprofits pay their employees. Some, such as the University of Massachusetts, are in the public sector; others, such as Harvard University, are in the private sector.

What You Learn about Business Is Applicable in Any Organization

The biggest difference among these two groupings is the measure of accomplishment: In for-profits, the measure generally is profit (or loss). In nonprofit organizations, money and expenses are important concerns, but success is usually measured by how effectively services are delivered.

Want to Know More? 1-1

Key Terms & Definitions in Sequential Order to Study as You Go Along

Go to www.mybizlab.com.

Examples: For a college president, one measure of accomplishment is the percentage of students who graduate. For a police chief, accomplishment might be measured by the number of crimes that are solved. Whatever the purpose, *the skills you learn to succeed in business—such as management skills—can help you achieve success in other kinds of organizations.*

The Fundamentals of What Businesses Do: Selling Goods or Services to Generate Revenue & Profits

How does a business actually make money?

What, in fact, is a business? **A *business* is any activity that seeks to make a profit by satisfying needs through selling goods or services to generate revenue.**

How the Sales of Goods or Services Produce Revenue & Possible Profits

Let's see what the parts of the foregoing definition of business mean.

Selling **is the exchange of goods or services for an agreed sum of money.** This money from sales is known as *revenue*, **the total amount of money that the selling of goods or services produces for a business during a defined period of time,** such as every 3 or 12 months.

Goods **are defined as tangible products**—things you can touch—such as food, clothing, appliances, gasoline, and books.

Services **are defined as intangible products**—things you can't touch—such as education, recreation, or health care.

What a businessperson is hoping to get out of this activity is a *profit*, **the amount of money a business makes after paying for its salaries and all other costs—that is, revenue minus expenses.** The opposite of profit is a *loss*, **which occurs when business expenses are larger than revenues.**

BRIEFING / SMALL BUSINESS & ENTREPRENEURS

How One Man Makes Inspirational Writing and Speaking a Revenue-Producing Business. Josh Shipp, 29, has a youthfulness and inspirational message that appeal to high school students and young adults.[3] Using nothing but words and ideas, how has he built a business?

As an inspirational writer, reports small-business magazine *Inc.*, he makes money by turning his ideas into *goods* that people will pay for—tangible things such as a book, DVDs, T-shirts, and high school educational materials. (The book is *The Teen's Guide to World Domination: Advice on Life, Liberty, and the Pursuit of Awesomeness*.) ❶

As an inspirational speaker, he also makes money by performing a *service*—giving speeches, at about $5,000 apiece, that people pay to hear, coming away with nothing tangible but with a possibly inspiring experience. (They often buy the book and other goods as well.)

The money realized from Shipp's sales is *revenue*—close to $2 million a year. If he spends too much on travel, production expenses, and the other costs of running a business, he might end up with a *loss*. However, by keeping expenses less than revenues, he makes a *profit*. ∎

Want to Know More? 1-2

Who Are Some Major Not-for-Profit Employers?

Go to www.mybizlab.com.

Want to Know More? 1-3

Why Do Businesses Fail?

Go to www.mybizlab.com.

❶ **Products provider.** When motivational speaker Josh Shipp gives speeches, he provides intangible products—services. When he turns his ideas into T-shirts and DVDs, he provides tangible products—goods.

Source: Courtesy of Josh Shipp Productions, LLC.

Want to Know More? 1-4

Business History 101: It's More Fascinating Than You Think

Go to www.mybizlab.com.

The New American Economy: From Goods to Services

From an economic standpoint, providing services—intangible things—is what most Americans do today. But it wasn't always so. At the time of the founding of our republic, the great majority of the workforce was employed in agriculture—that is, producing and selling goods such as food, cotton, and leather. Since then technology has made farming and ranching so efficient that today less than 2% of the population is employed in agriculture.[4]

During the late 19th and 20th centuries, the United States also evolved from an agricultural nation into an industrial one, selling manufactured goods: steel, tools, and machines—everything from ships to locomotives to automobiles to toasters. Indeed, America's industrial power became the envy of the world and made a huge difference in turning the tide toward victory during World War II.

Today, however, American business is principally concerned with developing and selling services. Indeed, during the last 50 years, jobs involving manufacturing—the production of goods—have declined, mainly because of **global outsourcing, or offshoring, the use of suppliers outside the United States, such as those in China and India, to provide labor, goods, or services.** In the United States in the last 25 years, most new jobs can be attributed to the growth in services: entertainment, health, legal, financial, educational, personal care, repair, janitorial, and other services.

BRIEFING / BUSINESS SKILLS & CAREER DEVELOPMENT

What's the Pay for Entry-Level Jobs for College Graduates in Business? Some of the fastest-growing new jobs, such as those of janitors and security guards, are lower paying than manufacturing jobs.[5] However, those that require more education and training are among the higher-paying jobs, and most of these provide services rather than goods.

In this category, recent business graduates have done very well. For 2011 college graduates entering the job market, average starting salaries ranged from $32,263 a year for those with degrees in elementary teacher education to $66,886 for those in chemical engineering. The average pay was $50,462.

Most of the entry-level salaries for graduates with business-related degrees fell in the middle range: international business $37,714, marketing/marketing management $44,432, business administration/management $46,832, accounting $50,316, finance $53,048, and economics $54,634.[6] ■

Some college education will be imperative in the years to come. "High school graduates and dropouts will find themselves largely left behind in the coming decade as employer demand for workers with postsecondary degrees continues to surge," says a report by the Center on Education and the Workforce at Georgetown University.[7] In 2018, it predicts, the number of jobs requiring at least a two-year associate's degree will outstrip the number of people qualified to fill those jobs by 3 million or more.

THE BIG IDEA: Business can raise people's standard of living and contribute to long and healthy lives and to human knowledge. It benefits society by producing useful goods and services, providing employees with paychecks and benefits, paying taxes, and donating to community causes.

THE ESSENTIAL QUESTION: How can business benefit society?

MyBizLab: Check your understanding of these concepts at www.mybizlab.com.

MyBizLab

In recent times, the United States and the world have narrowly averted what many feared would be the Second Great Depression, the largest economic downturn since the 1930s. Today we may well be living in a world where the range of financial outcomes—and risk—is much wider than normal.[8]

For many people, confidence in the business world—the system of buying and selling and trading we are used to—has been deeply shaken. With millions out of work, 10 years of stock market gains wiped out, and houses worth two-thirds or less of their former value, there have been many angry critics who say business owners and managers are greedy, ruthless, and irresponsible—and these characterizations are true in some cases.

But let's also point out that, when backed by social and legal controls to keep abuses in check, business can be a powerful force for good.[9] Let's see how. ②

② **Good business.** BigBelly Solar manufactures solar-powered trash compactors. The cans hold up to 32 gallons of compacted trash and can send text messages to a central server when the cans are full. When Arizona State University began using the devices, the daily trash pickup was reduced to once a week. Isn't this a case of business being a force for good?

Source: Courtesy of BigBelly Solar.

Business Can Improve People's Quality of Life

How can business make people's lives better?

Quality of life **expresses a society's general well-being as measured by standard of living, health care, educational opportunities, freedom, happiness, art, environmental health, and innovation.**[10] Ultimately, business can help society by enriching people's quality of life.

Raising the Standard of Living

A large part of an enhanced quality of life for individuals results from an improved *standard of living,* **defined by how many goods and services people can buy with the money they have.** About 1.3 billion of the world's 6.9 billion people are in extreme poverty, living on $1.25 a day or less, and over a billion of them go hungry every day.[11] These are largely outside the system of business, since they live at subsistence levels. By contrast, before the Great Recession of 2007–2009 at least, Americans traditionally enjoyed quite a high standard of living, in great part because of the goods, services, and paychecks business provides.

Contributing to Long & Healthy Lives & to Human Knowledge

Business research, products, and services may help to advance human development. The United Nations Human Development Index measures the average achievements in a country in three dimensions of human development: (1) life expectancy, (2) educational attainment, and (3) income. (*See* ■ *Panel 1.1.*) The top 15 countries on the index traditionally have had strong business environments and cultures, although poor worldwide economic conditions have drastically altered recent rankings. (Iceland, once 3 on the list, is now 17, and Spain, once 15, is now 20. Ireland, despite being 5 on the list, is also unwell.)

Business Supports Employee, Government, & Community Interests

What are four ways business can benefit society?

Business can advance the interests of society in four ways:

1. **Producing Goods & Services:** Food and medicine, clothing and shelter, heat and light, and other necessities of life are generally produced by businesses.
2. **Providing Paychecks & Benefits for Employees:** Typically, there are scores or hundreds of employees depending on every business owner for paychecks and benefits, such as health insurance and a pension plan.
3. **Paying Taxes to Support Government Services:** Most businesses pay taxes of some sort. (In New York, for instance, through the purchases they make, businesses pay 25% of local sales taxes outside New York City and 41% of total property taxes.)[12] Moreover, employees of the business also pay taxes. The government's ability to fund public health, social security, education, defense, and other services is based primarily on a combination of taxes paid by businesses and their employees.
4. **Donating Funds, Goods, & Services for Community Causes:** In many communities, businesses are strong supporters of charitable causes, such as donating supplies to help earthquake disaster victims, making monetary contributions to United Way, buying ads in high school yearbooks, and sponsoring Little League baseball teams. ❸

❸ **Business donations.** Companies around the world donated to the relief of 2010 Haiti earthquake victims. General Electric, for instance, provided this solar-powered water purification unit, which can treat groundwater, surface water, and recycled rainwater to produce clean drinking water. What kinds of business support of community causes have you observed?

THE BIG IDEA: Entrepreneurship means taking risks to create new products or a new enterprise. Entrepreneurship, natural resources, capital, and human resources constitute the four fundamental resources, or factors of production, needed to create wealth. Some scholars also add knowledge as a factor of production.

THE ESSENTIAL QUESTION: What are the main sources of wealth?

MyBizLab: Check your understanding of these concepts at www.mybizlab.com.

MyBizLab

Many people are satisfied with a career working for an organization, whether for-profit or nonprofit. But people like Rick Steves, described in the "Winners & Losers" at the start of this chapter, want a career that allows them to fulfill their dreams independently. The founder of Europe Through the Back Door, Steves by now is no doubt wealthy, though he often continues to travel in the near-vagabond way in which he started. This suggests the question, Who are the wealthy in America, and how did they get that way?

Want to Know More? 1-5
Who Are Some Young Billionaires?
Go to www.mybizlab.com.

The Wealthy People Next Door

How did most wealthy people make their money?

In their book *The Millionaire Next Door,* researchers Thomas Stanley and William Danko revealed some surprising facts:

- **Most wealthy people are self-employed business owners:** It's seldom inheritance, luck, advanced degrees, or even intelligence that enables people to amass fortunes. "Most of the affluent in America are business owners, including self-employed professionals," they write. "Twenty percent of the affluent households in America are headed by retirees. Of the remaining 80%, more than two-thirds are headed by self-employed owners of businesses."

- **The self-employed are more likely than the salaried to be rich:** "In America," they continue, "fewer than one in five households, or about 18%, is headed by a self-employed business owner or professional. *But these self-employed people are four times more likely to be millionaires than those who work for others*" (their emphasis).[13]

What type of business is most apt to make you a millionaire? Stanley and Danko say that the character of the business owner is more important than the kind of business in predicting level of wealth. What's interesting, however, is that the businesses of self-employed millionaires are not usually glamorous. They include such conventional occupations as janitorial-services contractor, cafeteria owner, rice farmer, pest-control service operator, liquor wholesaler, funeral home operator, and sand-blasting contractor.[14] ❹

Source: John Angelillo/UPI/Newscom.

❹ **Making money from trash.** Wayne Huizenga is a self-made billionaire (and former owner of the Miami Dolphins football team) who initially made money in a very ordinary line of work—waste management. Could you see yourself building wealth this way?

⑤ The entrepreneur. Los Angeles–based Roy Choi, former chef in New York's fancy La Bernardin restaurant, took advantage of several trends—taco trucks, multiethnic cuisine, and Twitter—to launch America's first "viral restaurants," two roving Kogi Korean taco trucks. He uses Twitter (a website that allows users to share their whereabouts with friends) to announce the ever-changing locations of the trucks, which dispense tacos stuffed with Korean food. *Newsweek* described the product's appeal as "market produce and unfamiliar proteins prepared for the authenticity-craving . . . palate and sold at recession-ready prices ($2–$7)." Can you think of a mix of unusual elements that might result in a new product?

But, of course, most self-employed people don't become millionaires, just as most employees who work for organizations such as General Electric don't become millionaires. What does it take to succeed in business? This is a foundational question we will address throughout this book.

Do Only Entrepreneurs Take Risks?

Which is more risky—being an entrepreneur or being a salaried employee?

Risk in the business realm is defined as the possibility that the owner or owners of a business may invest time and money in the enterprise and fail—that is, not make a profit.

Taking risks is what entrepreneurs do. **An *entrepreneur* is a person who sees a new opportunity for a product or service and risks his or her time and money to start a business to make a profit. ⑤**

But risk is often in the eye of the beholder. Stanley and Danko, authors of *The Millionaire Next Door,* tell the story of a professor once asking a group of 60 corporate executives the question, "What is risk?"

One replied, "Being an entrepreneur!" The other executives agreed.

Then the professor answered his own question with a quote from an entrepreneur:

What is risk? Having one source of income. Employees are at risk. . . . They have a single source of income. What about the entrepreneur who sells janitorial services to your employers? He has hundreds and hundreds of customers . . . hundreds and hundreds of sources of income.[15]

Most people prefer the security of a job and paycheck and benefits, although, as many employees found out during the severe economic downturn of 2007–2009 and its aftermath, the risk in working for a single employer is that you might be laid off. But, of course, as Stanley and Danko go on to point out, there is also a lot of risk in being a self-employed person or business owner. The difference is that, in investing money, time, and reputation, *the entrepreneur's risk is offset by the possibility of great rewards.* Indeed, the promise of high returns is the reason why entrepreneurs take the risks that they do.

Factors of Production: The Building Blocks of Wealth

What are factors of production?

Wealth isn't created out of the sheer energy and motivation of an entrepreneur alone. Whether a business is an individual pursuit by one person or an organization of thousands of employees, it relies on *factors of production*, or resources, **to create wealth—natural resources, capital, human resources, and entrepreneurship.** Some add a fifth factor: *knowledge.* (*See* ■ *Panel 1.2.*)

The Traditional Four Factors of Production

Most scholars emphasize just the first four factors of production.

Natural Resources. *Natural resources* consist of production inputs that are useful just as they appear in nature, such as land, forests, water, wind, sunlight, mineral deposits, and the like. Most natural resources can't be created; they must be mined, harvested, harnessed, or purified.

■ **PANEL 1.2 Factors of production.**

Traditional factors
- Natural resources
- Capital
- Human resources
- Entrepreneurship

Many now also add . . .
- Knowledge

Capital. *Capital* **includes the buildings, machines, tools, and technology used to produce goods and services.** As used in this sense, however, capital does not include money, although money is used to acquire buildings and other capital.

Human Resources. *Human resources* **consist of labor, the physical and intellectual contributions of a company's employees.**

Entrepreneurship. *Entrepreneurship* **is the process of taking risks to try to create a new enterprise.** Entrepreneurs are businesspeople who recognize an unmet need and use the opportunity to create a new product or service.

A Fifth Factor of Production—Knowledge

Management philosopher Peter Drucker suggested adding a fifth factor of production, *knowledge,* which he thought was the most important.[16] Knowledge has been revolutionized by the application of computers, telecommunications, and databases, which allow the entrepreneur to quickly determine new wants and needs and quickly deliver new goods and services.

Want to Know More? 1-6

Which Are the Most Profitable U.S. Companies?

Go to www.mybizlab.com.

BRIEFING / EARNING GREEN BY GOING GREEN

Factors of Production in an Entrepreneurial Furniture Business. In 2006, Seth Meyer, now 40, and John Wells, 45, started a Seattle-based business, Meyer Wells, that makes custom furniture from urban trees (production factor: *natural resources*) that have been cut down owing to disease, storms, or development.

Each furniture piece has "a distinct botanical narrative," says a *New York Times* story.[17] What differentiates the firm from other custom furniture makers is emphasis on "the big slab, furniture that could bring indoors the raw power of the environment rather than a builder's vision" (production factor: *entrepreneurship*). ❻ For instance, Meyer Wells built a wooden kitchen bar for Richard and Donna Majer with a "canyonlike crack ripping right down its middle," taken from a storm-damaged oak in their yard. "I see the beauty of the hard life the tree had," says Mrs. Majer. "And it helps me find the beauty in my own life's scars."

Source: Lydia Daniller.

❻ **Factors of production.** Meyer Wells of Seattle turns the natural resources of reclaimed urban trees into modern furniture that reflects "an intimate relationship with our materials that yields distinctive and compelling results." Although the company's residential business decreased during the recession, the growth in corporate commissions made up the difference. What would you say is the most distinctive factor of production in this business?

The firm currently has 32 employees (production factor: *human resources*). Drying, milling, design, joining, and finishing take place in an 8,000-square-foot, high-ceiling building (production factor: *capital*). Coffee and dining tables cost $3,000 to $10,000, and conference tables around $20,000. The company has been profitable from the start, with revenue reaching $850,000 in 2009.

Meyer grew up learning from his stepfather, a furniture maker; Wells made furniture in high school and once ran a one-man custom furniture shop. They depend for a steady stream of old, doomed trees not only on "tree lovers' anguished calls," says the *Times,* "but increasingly on networks with other businesses and design professionals" (production factor: specialized *knowledge*). ∎

1.4

The Business Environment: Forces That Encourage & Discourage Entrepreneurship

THE BIG IDEA: Companies operate within the business environment, which consists of economic, technological, competitive, global, and social forces that encourage or discourage the development of business.

THE ESSENTIAL QUESTION: What major forces affect the way companies and individual businesspeople operate?

MyBizLab

MyBizLab: Check your understanding of these concepts at www.mybizlab.com.

■ **PANEL 1.3 Forces in the business environment.**

Business and entrepreneurship don't exist in a vacuum. Companies both large and small operate within the ***business environment*, the arena of forces that encourage or discourage the development of business. These forces include economic, technological, competitive, global, and social.** (*See* ■ *Panel 1.3.*) Let's briefly consider these.

Economic Forces: The Tension between Freedom & Restraint

How do freedom and regulation affect business?

A continual source of tension is that between the amount of freedom allowed for people to establish and run their businesses and the amount of restraint that governments impose on business—some of which is necessary for business to be successful. Whether regulation is light or heavy affects . . .

- **Taxation:** Some countries (and states) have higher tax rates on businesses, which restricts how much companies can invest in various business programs and keep as profits.
- **Contract enforcement:** In countries that don't have strong enforcement of contract laws, businesspeople are reluctant to enter into legal relationships with other businesspeople.
- **Corruption:** Countries that don't punish corruption and bribery allow uncertainty that hurts honest businesspeople.

Technological Forces: The Effect on Productivity & Security

Can technology both improve and impede productivity?

***Technology* includes not only digital technology—computers, telecommunications, and giant data storage—but also all machines required to help a company get things done,** whether delivery vans, vending machines, or surveillance cameras. Technology can have both positive and negative effects impacting . . .

- **Productivity:** The purpose of installing any technology is to improve a company's ***productivity*, which is defined as the amount of output given the**

amount of input—such as the number of doughnuts produced for a given number of hours worked.

- **Security:** More complex technological systems can enhance productivity but they can also compromise security, such as allowing hackers to break into customer credit files.

Competitive Forces: The Influence on Customer, Employee, & Investor Satisfaction

Does competition make a difference in how customers, employees, and investors may be affected?

Having no *competitors*—**people or organizations that compete for customers or resources**—or having lots of competitors can certainly determine the amount of effort that a company is willing to put into satisfying . . .

- **Customers:** A company such as a public utility that is the only one in its industry has no particular incentive to improve service with its customers, since it knows they have nowhere else to go.
- **Employees:** A technology company trying to recruit and keep top talent will go to greater lengths if it knows there are other companies fiercely competing for that talent.
- **Investors:** A bank that is the only one in a state or country may pay its investors whatever it wants.

Global Forces: The Effect on Trade & Stability

How do global forces affect business?

Global forces—trade pacts, economic agreements, military alliances, currency exchanges, immigration policies, environmental influences, and other matters—can have a powerful influence on business in that they can affect . . .

- **Trade:** Formalized agreements, such as trade pacts, can facilitate the exchange of goods and services between nations, which in turn can affect a nation's manufacturing, employment, travel, and other policies.
- **Stability:** Wars, terrorism, recessions, currency panics, epidemics, refugee flows, and ecological changes can undermine national stability.

7 **Changing social forces.** A Latino market in Los Angeles is one sign of the explosive growth of the Hispanic population, which doubled over the past 20 years to 50 million, one out of six Americans. In the near future, the numbers of Hispanics and other racial/ethnic minorities are expected to pass the numbers of non-Hispanic whites in the United States. In what ways do you think this demographic shift will change the way U.S. businesses operate?

Social Forces: The Changes in Population

Will people from different backgrounds affect how business operates?

Changes in a country's *demographics*, **the measurable characteristics of a population,** such as gender, age, race, family composition, and the like, can change the numbers of customers and customer needs and tastes. It can also change the employee pool and skills that a company has to deal with. **7**

Source: Neil Setchfield/Alamy.

<table>
<tr><td>

1.5

</td><td>

Seven Key Business Rules: The Great Adventure of Being in Business in the 21st Century

</td></tr>
</table>

THE BIG IDEA: The general universe of changing forces suggests you will need to observe Seven Key Business Rules to be successful in today's business world: (1) You must keep an eye on 10 types of groups whose interests are affected by your firm's activities. (2) You must deal with many uncertainties. (3) You must strive to assert your competitive advantage. (4) You must operate in a global economic system. (5) You must try to stay true to your values. (6) You must deal with others who are diverse in race, ethnicity, religion, and so on. (7) You must develop superior personal skills.

THE ESSENTIAL QUESTION: What are Seven Key Business Rules to observe in pursuing business success?

MyBizLab

MyBizLab: Check your understanding of these concepts at www.mybizlab.com.

Succeeding in business today is a huge balancing act as you deal with a general universe of changing forces—economic, technological, competitive, global, and social—different from those that your parents and grandparents faced during the 20th century. Balancing these competing interests while trying to hone your professional and personal skills and operate in a responsible way suggests there are *Seven Key Business Rules for Success* you will need to observe in order to thrive, as follows. (*See* ■ *Panel 1.4.*)

> ■ **PANEL 1.4 Seven Key Business Rules for Success.** These are seven rules to be observed in the pursuit of business success in the 21st century.
>
> • *Stakeholders.* Rule 1—You must meet the needs of stakeholders, those with an interest in your organization.
>
> • *Uncertainty.* Rule 2—You must deal with constant change, including technological change.
>
> • *Competition.* Rule 3—You must master the competitive environment to stay ahead of rivals.
>
> • *Common economy.* Rule 4—You must deal with an interdependent global economic system.
>
> • *Ethics.* Rule 5—You must be ethical and socially responsible.
>
> • *Societal differences.* Rule 6—You must learn to deal with different kinds of people.
>
> • *Self-development.* Rule 7—You must acquire the personal skills needed for business success.

The observant reader will notice that the initial letters for these rules spell *success*.

Think you're up for these kinds of challenges? The purpose of this book is to help you meet them.

Stakeholders: Rule 1—You Must Meet the Needs of Stakeholders, Those with an Interest in Your Organization

Who are 10 stakeholders that I must recognize and deal with?

Businesspeople practice the art of ***management*, organizing and coordinating the activities of an enterprise according to certain policies to achieve certain objectives.** As a manager, you will operate in an organizational environment made up of various ***stakeholders*, those whose interests are influenced by an organization's activities.** The illustration below shows some principal stakeholders; you may think of some others.[18] (*See* ■ *Panel 1.5.*)

■ **PANEL 1.5 The universe of business stakeholders.**
The organization's environment.

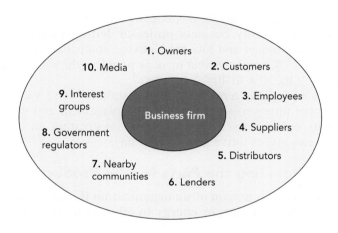

1 Owners: Hoping for Profit but Risking Loss

The *owners* of an organization are those who can claim it as their legal property. In the for-profit world, there are several forms of ownership. One familiar class of owners is ***stockholders* or *shareholders*, owners of *stock*—shares of ownership—in a company.** The goal of the owners is to make a profit, but they are risking loss—perhaps the loss of everything they've invested.

We consider types of ownership in greater detail in Chapter 5.

2 Customers: The Focus of Business

Why do experts say the first law of business is to *take care of the customer*? Because ***customers* are the people who pay to use an organization's goods or services.** Customers may be the focus of not only for-profit organizations but also nonprofit ones, such as students in colleges. A new channel for reaching out to customers is social media, such as Twitter and Facebook.[19] ⑧

⑧ **Facebook support.** Facebook, which drew more visitors than Google in 2010, is becoming a growing channel for customer support and service. It also serves well for "F-commerce"—Facebook commerce—that is, a place for customers to buy products from a company.

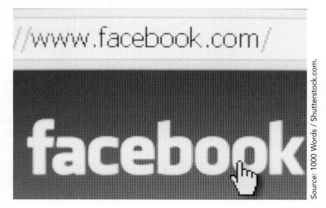

Source: 1000 Words / Shutterstock.com

BRIEFING / CUSTOMER FOCUS
Taking Care of Buyers: Amazon Pays Close Attention to "The Customer Experience." Amazon founder and CEO Jeff Bezos says he is "obsessed" with what he calls "the customer experience." Thus, whereas the average wait for customer service at Facebook has been found to be 99 minutes (rated "horrible" by users), for Amazon it is 1 minute ("excellent").

9 Customer-obsessed. Jeff Bezos, founder and CEO of Amazon.com, declares himself to be "obsessed with the customer experience." What companies can you think of that go the extra mile to do right by their customers? Do they appear to be more successful?

The company also offers an easy-to-use website, with online technology rated more error-free than those of rivals Walmart.com and Target .com.[20] It has two-day free shipping on all packages for an annual fee of just $79 and a readily available customer-service phone number. In addition, it is willing to quickly correct mistakes, even those that are not its fault. For instance, it replaced—for free and just in time for Christmas Eve—a $500 PlayStation 3 Christmas present that a customer had ordered for his son but that had disappeared after being delivered to his apartment building.[21]

Customers "care about having the lowest prices, having vast selection, so they have choice, and getting the products . . . fast," Bezos has said.[22] "And the reason I'm so obsessed with these drivers of the customer experience is that I believe that the success we have had over the past 12 years has been driven exclusively by that customer experience." **9** ■

3 Employees: The Need for Performance

Have you ever worked for a "toxic organization"? This is the name that Stanford University business professor Jeffrey Pfeffer gives to firms with high turnover and low productivity, companies that drive employees away.[23] "Companies that manage people right will outperform those that don't by 30% to 40%," he says.[24]

An example of a nontoxic organization is Men's Wearhouse, which has lower turnover—and thus lower replacement and training costs—than its competitors because it works at creating an environment in which employees thrive and want to stay.

4 Suppliers: Providing the Parts for the Product

A *supplier*, or *vendor*, **is a person or an organization that supplies raw materials, services, equipment, labor, or energy to other organizations.**

■ **Example of Suppliers: Makers of the Apple iPhone 4.** Who makes the iPhone 4, Apple's smartphone? Not Apple, but a number of Asian, American, and European companies. Samsung (South Korea), Toshiba (Japan), and Broadcom (United States) supply processors and the device's flash-memory chip. Other chips are made by German chip maker Infineon. The gyroscope is made by STMicroelectronics in Italy and France. Manufacturing and assembly is done by Foxconn in southern China. Having effective relationships with suppliers is obviously important to Apple, since the loss of even one could cause major headaches.[25] ■

5 Distributors: Directing Products to Customers

A *distributor* **is a person or an organization, such as a dealer or retailer, that helps sell goods and services to customers.** Tickets to artists' performances might be sold to you through distributors such as Ticketmaster. Distributors can be quite important in industries (such as distributors to magazine newsstands) in which there is limited competition because they have a lot of power over the price and placement of the product.

6 Lenders: Carrying the Company When Money Is Short

Businesses often rely on lenders such as banks, savings and loans, and insurance companies to give them loans when revenues are low or when they need to borrow money to finance expansion. Some entrepreneurs finance their new enterprises by using their personal credit cards for cash advances or expenses.

7 Nearby Communities: The Local Environment

Nearby communities are important stakeholders because schools and municipal governments rely on businesses for a portion of their tax base. In addition, families and merchants depend on the employee payroll for their livelihoods, and nonprofit organizations such as sports leagues may depend on them for donations.❿ When DHL Express, former competitor to FedEx and UPS, abandoned its U.S. business in 2008, its hub city of Wilmington, Ohio (population 12,000), was devastated by the loss of 8,000 DHL jobs.[26]

8 Government Regulators: Local, State, Federal, & World

Governmental regulators **are government agencies that establish rules and regulations under which organizations may operate** and in turn are often affected by these organizations. These bodies may range from local planning departments to state commissions to federal agencies and boards and even international agencies (such as the World Trade Organization, which oversees international trade).

■ **Example of Government Regulator: OSHA.** The Occupational Safety and Health Administration (OSHA), an agency of the U.S. Department of Labor, issues and enforces workplace health and safety rules to prevent work-related illnesses, injuries, and deaths. Critics have debated whether OSHA regulations add too much in the way of costs in return for the benefits, but one study found that regulated industries typically overestimated the expected cost of implementing proposed OSHA standards.[27] ■

9 Interest Groups: People with Specific Issues

The Sierra Club, the National Rifle Association, the United Auto Workers, and the Chamber of Commerce are examples of *interest groups*, or *special-interest* **groups—groups whose members try to influence businesses and governments on specific issues.** Interest groups may try to exert political influence, as in contributing funds to lawmakers' election campaigns or in launching letter-writing efforts to businesses and politicians.

10 Media: From Print to Internet

No businessperson can afford to ignore the power of news and entertainment media. These include not only newspapers, magazines, radio, and TV but also fast-moving Internet social media, such as Twitter, Facebook, and YouTube. Because the media can rapidly and widely disseminate news both bad and good, most midsized and larger businesses have a public-relations person or media department to communicate effectively with the press. In addition, top-level executives often receive special instruction on how to best deal with the media.

BRIEFING / A WORLD OF CONSTANT CHANGE
A Media Prank Hurts Domino's Pizza. Sometimes companies experience problems that come out of nowhere. In 2009, Domino's Pizza experienced a public relations nightmare when a prank video made by two Domino's employees in North Carolina appeared on YouTube. The video featured several gross-out actions, one of which involved one of the pair sticking cheese up his nose and pretending to sneeze into a sandwich he was making, using that cheese.

Domino's got high marks from crisis-management experts for responding quickly, using a consumer affairs blog, The Consumerist, whose readers

IF EVERY FAMILY IN THE U.S. SPENT AN EXTRA TEN BUCKS LOCALLY WE WOULD ALL FEEL BETTER ABOUT THE ECONOMY.

❿ **Shopping local.** Independent We Stand is a nationwide movement of independently owned local businesses that promotes the benefits of consumers shifting some of their spending from national chains to local small businesses. "You can support the cause and help revive the local economy by shopping at your friends' and neighbors' stores," says the organization. "Buy their products. Eat their food. Use their services." This activity will pump dollars into the local economy by way of taxes, payrolls, and purchases, which will provide money for schools, roads, services, and new jobs.

Key Takeaway 1-1
Stakeholders influenced by an organization include owners, customers, employees, suppliers, distributors, lenders, nearby communities, government regulators, interest groups, and the media.

Want to Know More? 1-7

Some Examples of Public Relations Crises

Go to www.mybizlab.com.

helped track down the guilty employees. It also used Twitter to reach out to the public and begin to reinstitute trust.

Lesson learned: A company needs to monitor its reputation online and respond rapidly to incidents. "Nothing is local anymore," said a Domino's spokesperson. "That's the challenge of the Web world."[28] ■

Uncertainty: Rule 2—You Must Deal with Constant Change, Including Technological Change

What kinds of change do I have to be alert for that could affect my work life?

Here's something new: "recession psychosis." Though not officially recognized by the psychiatric profession, it describes symptoms of patients suffering mentally from the 2007–2009 worldwide financial meltdown, including severe anxiety, suicidal tendencies, and "delusions of poverty." (For instance, one wealthy woman became so worried that she wouldn't have enough money to buy groceries that she refused to eat.)[29]

Twists and turns in the economy are only one of the many uncertainties that businesspeople must deal with in the 21st century. Another is the speed of information flows brought about by computers and the Internet, so that e-mail and text messaging between potential investors is nearly instantaneous, quickly driving stock values up—or down.[30] In addition, *e-commerce,* **or electronic commerce—the buying and selling of products or services over computer networks—** is revolutionizing entire industries and reshaping the very idea of what a company is. More important than e-commerce, information technology has facilitated *e-business,* **using the Internet to facilitate** *every* **aspect of running a business.**[31] We return to the subject of e-commerce in the future and discuss information technology in Flex-Chapter D.

An even more daunting uncertainty is that of climate change, which threatens not only polar bears, penguins, and marine life but also the very stability of human society.[32] Still, the crisis lends itself to great opportunities for green businesses stressing the three Ps of profit, people, and planet.[33] *Green businesses* **are those that adopt practices for the use of renewable resources and otherwise operate in ways that solve, rather than cause, both environmental and social problems.** California, for example, has found that energy-efficiency policies created nearly 1.5 million jobs from 1977 to 2007.[34] The Obama administration has called for a new era emphasizing projects embracing alternative energy sources such as wind and solar.[35] We cover climate change and green business throughout the book.

Add to these uncertainties others such as threats from terrorists, drug cartels, and computer criminals (hackers), and you can see that going forward will continue to be the "age of surprise," an era in which we will be required to adapt quickly.[36]

Competition: Rule 3—You Must Master the Competitive Environment to Stay Ahead of Rivals

What are four areas in the competitive environment I must master to be successful?

Every organization has to be actively aware of its competitors. Florist shops and delicatessens must be aware that customers can buy the same products at Safeway or Kroger. And with the Internet as a medium for selling, competition is more global than ever.

All businesses must deal with competition—Ford Motor Co. must compete not only against other U.S. automakers but also against carmakers in Europe and Asia. This means a business must constantly seek what's known as ***competitive advantage***, **the ability of an organization to produce goods or services more effectively than its competitors**.

BRIEFING / A WORLD OF CONSTANT CHANGE

U.S. Manufacturing Isn't Dead; It's Becoming More Upscale. The conventional wisdom is that "nothing is made in the United States anymore; it's all done overseas." Although the percentage of the American labor force holding manufacturing jobs in 2011 was only 9%, down from 29% in 1960, the United States still remains the world's leading manufacturer by value of goods produced. "For every $1 of value produced in China's factories," points out one writer, "America generates $2.50."[37]

What's happening is that the United States is making things that other countries can't or don't—for example, farming equipment, aircraft, medical electronics, gas turbines, and processed food—rather than TVs, toys, clothes, and other items found in retail stores. ⑪

As mentioned, the Obama administration has targeted as a major national goal the making of clean-energy equipment, such as windmills and solar panels. ■

Unless your business is the only organization serving its market, you must constantly strive for competitive advantage to realize a profit—since being profitable is, of course, the first requirement of being a for-profit business. This means an organization—and you personally—must try to stay ahead in four areas: (1) being responsive to customers, (2) making continual improvement in the quality of your product or service, (3) finding ways to deliver new or better products or services (what's called *innovation*), and (4) striving for employee efficiency.

■ **Example** of Employee Efficiency: Eliminating Secretaries Causes Managers to Be More Efficient. Today many managers—aided by their desktop computers—do much of their own correspondence and filing. Secretarial staffs have been reduced, but of course the secretarial work remains, so managers have had to learn to be more efficient. ■

Common Economy: Rule 4—You Must Deal with an Interdependent Global Economic System

What is globalization?

The "common economy" is the *global economy,* or ***globalization***—**the trend of the world economy toward becoming a more interdependent system.** *New York Times* columnist Thomas Friedman, in his book *The World Is Flat,* has pointed out the revolution by which globalization has leveled (made "flat") the competitive playing fields between industrial and emerging market countries.[38]

Among other concerns, this has led to worries about U.S. jobs disappearing to Mexico, China, and India. ⑫ Actually, the bigger employment threat to American jobs, particularly in manufacturing, is probably not foreign competition but budget cuts and improved technology at home, according to one viewpoint.[39] In fact, according to one report, foreign-based firms actually send far more office work to the United States than American companies send abroad.[40] And, in some fields, overseas competition is losing its price advantage, allowing small U.S. companies to capitalize on their home-based manufacturing, as Philadelphia clothing maker Boathouse Sports has, when rising labor and transportation costs made Asia more expensive.[41]

⑪ **Competitive advantage.** Farming equipment, such as that made by John Deere, used widely in the United States but also exported to the rest of the world, helps to keep us first in the world in manufacturing, when measured by value of goods sold. Do you think other countries could overtake the United States in making these and other "big ticket" products?

⑫ **Brain drain to India?** India-born Kunal Bahl wasn't allowed to stay in the United States when his work visa expired in 2007, so he returned home and started SnapDeal in his native country. Now the company, which offers daily discount deals of 50% to 90% in major cities in India, is on pace to top $100 million in annual revenue in 2012. Perhaps, some observers suggest, immigrants have better opportunities outside the United States, and so some foreign-born engineers and scientists have been leaving—a brain drain. Do you think the United States could ever lose its innovative spirit because of foreign competition?

The complex, ongoing challenge of globalization is covered in Chapter 4.

Ethics: Rule 5—You Must Be Ethical & Socially Responsible

How important are ethical behavior and corporate social responsibility in business?

With the pressure to make profits—or, in a down economy, even keep their jobs—businesspeople can find themselves confronting ethical dilemmas: deciding between economic performance and social performance. "It's a tough issue, choosing between being a law-abiding person and losing your job," says one lawyer, who represented a woman fired for complaining about running her boss's office football pool.[43]

But ethical behavior is a significant part of doing business, as was readily apparent in 2001 when Enron, a Houston-based energy company, shocked the American public with revelations about its irregular financial dealings, which led to tremendous losses for shareholders and employees. The company, once the seventh largest firm in the United States, ultimately went bankrupt, and several of its top executives went to prison. ⑬

Businesspeople also need to be aware of the importance of corporate social responsibility, a concern for taking actions that will benefit the interests of society as well as the organization.

Source: ROBERTO SCHMIDT/AFP/Getty Images/Newscom.

⑬ **Enron before the fall.** The corporate culture of the Texas-based energy company made it a "very arrogant place, with a feeling of invincibility," said Sharron Watkins, a vice president who warned top managers the firm was going to "implode" because of irregular accounting practices—which it ultimately did. Do you think you would be able to do the right thing in such a high-pressure, high-powered environment?

On August 10, 2010, a California federal judge called the practice "unfair and deceptive" and ordered Wells Fargo to refund $203 million in overdraft fees to California customers. The judge said that the bank had devised "a trap that would escalate a single overdraft into as many as 10 through the gimmick of processing in descending order. It then exploited that trap with a vengeance, racking up hundreds of millions off the backs of the working poor, students, and others without the luxury of ample account balances."[44]

He went on to say that Wells Fargo's dominant motive "was to maximize the number of overdrafts and squeeze as much as possible" out of customers who spent more than they had in their accounts.[45] The bank, which had collected nearly $1.8 billion in overdraft fees in California alone from 2005 to 2007, said it would appeal. ■

We return to the subject of ethics and social responsibility in Chapter 2 and throughout this book.

Social Differences: Rule 6—You Must Learn to Deal with Different Kinds of People

What trends in diversity are occurring that I should be aware of?

During the next half-century, the mix of American racial/ethnic and religious groups will change considerably, as will the nature of the American family. Some CEOs recognize that having diversity in their workforces is a matter of survival. For instance, Eric J. Foss, CEO of the Pepsi Bottling Group, argues that "our employee base needs to be reflective of our customer base. As our customers continue to become more diverse, it's important that organizationally we look like them."[46]

Scott E. Page, a professor of complex systems, political science, and economics at the University of Michigan, suggests that variety in staffing produces organizational strength. "Diverse groups of people bring to organizations more and different ways of seeing a problem," he says, "and, thus, faster/better ways of solving it." He adds: "there's certainly a lot of evidence that people's identity groups—ethnic, racial, sexual, age—matter when it comes to diversity in thinking."[47]

Clearly, the challenge to businesspeople is to be able to maximize the contributions of extremely diverse employees and to serve the needs of extremely diverse customers. ⑭

⑭ **Faces of the future.** In this ad, Intel, the California technology company, promotes the diversity of its employees. The swiftness with which the United States has become a more diverse nation—more Hispanic and Asian, more aware of multiracial identities, more tolerant of untraditional family structures—in the last two decades has stunned social observers. "By 2050, Americans will look back at the controversies around immigration," predicts sociologist Robert Lang, "controversies about diversity, and wonder what the big deal was."

BRIEFING / A WORLD OF CONSTANT CHANGE

 U.S. Social Differences in the 21st Century. Today one in three U.S. residents is a member of a racial or ethnic minority. Babies born to non-Hispanic white women declined to 53% in 2008, compared with 65% in 1990.[48] And non-Hispanic whites in the United States are projected to decrease from 67% of the population in 2005 to 47% in 2050. African Americans are projected to remain the same at 13%. Asians and Pacific Islanders are projected to increase from 5% to 9%, and Hispanics from 14% to 29%.[49]

Attitudes toward religion are changing. A survey found that 53% of Americans have changed their faiths at least once, with Catholics leaving largely because of disagreements with church teachings, and Protestants because of life changes such as marriage or moving.[50] Today, 15% of Americans check "no religion," although half of the "nones" still believe in a higher power.[51] Among those who attend religious services, 26% say they do so at more than

i **Want to Know More? 1-8**

How Is the United States Changing Demographically?

Go to www.mybizlab.com.

one place.[52] Almost three-fourths of 18- to 29-year-olds say they're more spiritual than religious.[53]

Changes are also affecting the American family. More marriages are between spouses of different races or ethnicities, with white-Hispanic marriages being the most common mixed-ethnic union.[54] Over the past 40 years, American women have outpaced men in both education and earnings growth, and, compared to 1970, a larger share of men today are married to women whose education and income exceed their own.[55] Yet 40% of births in the United States are to single mothers, a trend that is especially common in the middle class.[56]

Finally, the Great Recession has had a huge impact. Suburban homelessness has been on the rise.[57] More families have had to move in together, and divorce rates have fallen as couples stay together in homes they can't sell.[58] More children have fallen into poverty as family incomes have shrunk, more older workers have been dogged by financial worries and have been retiring early to draw on social security, and more families have been struggling to put food on the table.[59] ■

We discuss diversity and changing demographics in more detail in later chapters, such as Chapter 11.

Self-Development: Rule 7—You Must Acquire the Personal Skills Needed for Business Success

To be successful, what personal skills should I cultivate?

Becoming an effective businessperson is not just a matter of successfully managing or dealing with the larger forces we mentioned. It also means managing yourself. This means using your education and experience to develop three important skills—*ability to perform a specific job, ability to think analytically,* and *ability to interact well with people.*[60]

1 Ability to Perform a Specific Job

Rick Steves, whom we discussed in the "Winners & Losers" cases introducing this chapter, certainly has acquired the job-specific knowledge needed to function in the world of the travel industry. Gaining the ability to perform a specific job is what many people think they are in college for: to become an engineer, a nurse, a chef, or whatever. ⑮

⑮ **Self-development.** Is learning a specific kind of job the most important thing you can do in college? Actually, it's only one skill. Equally or more important are learning to think analytically and learning to interact well with people. Do you think you've already mastered these two skills or are there ways you could improve?

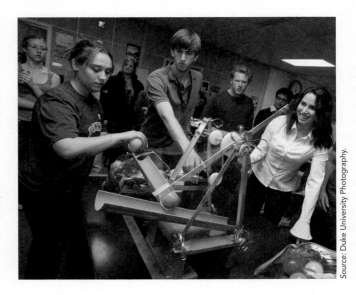

Source: Duke University Photography.

■ **Example** of Gaining Skills to Perform a Specific Job: Hotel Management.
If you were planning a career in hotel management, you would take courses in food and beverage management, marketing and tourism, human resources management, and communication, as well as do internships that required working in hotels and restaurants. ■

2 Ability to Think Analytically

Steves also has the "big picture" knowledge of all the steps required to attract customers to his travel business and to manage the various tours his firm runs. The ability to think analytically means being able to deal with problems that are *ambiguous,* a particularly important skill for business owners and top managers. Analytical thinking means being able to visualize an organization as a whole, break it down into its constituent parts, and understand how the parts work together.

Key Takeaway 1-2
Self-development consists of learning how to perform a specific job, think analytically, and interact well with people.

■ **Example** of Ability to Think Analytically: Eliminating Ambiguity at a Grocer. One of the ambiguous goals of Tesco, now Britain's leading grocer, was to do a better job of "listening to customers." Tesco executive Terry Leahy broke that goal down into specific actions. For instance, cashiers were taught to call for additional cashiers whenever more than one shopper was waiting in the checkout line. In addition, says one article, "Tesco received 100,000 queries per week from customers. Leahy's team made sure that all Tesco managers had access to customer concerns. (If you want to listen to customers, you had better make sure your managers know what they're saying.)"[61] ■

3 Ability to Interact Well with People

The ability to interact well with other people in order to get things done may well be the most difficult set of skills to master, requiring the ability to motivate, to inspire trust, and to communicate with others. Such ability is necessary for business owners and managers of all levels, and developing human-interaction skills may be an ongoing, lifelong effort.

Rick Steves has an easygoing manner, and everyone in Edmonds, Washington, knows his name. He also gets along well with the wide range of people he meets in the countries he visits. Most importantly, he is popular with his customers. Indeed, his fans seem to treat him more like a rock star than a travel writer. (They even have a name for themselves: "Rickniks.")

In nearly all respects, then, Steves had and still has what it takes to be a star—to be highly successful in business. ⑯

What about you? In the rest of this book, we hope to provide you with the tools for achieving this kind of success.

Source: Images used with permission by Rick Steves: www.ricksteves.com.

⑯ **Rick Steves.** The founder of Europe Through the Back Door clearly has learned to do the specific job of running a travel business. Equally or more important, he has learned to think analytically and to interact well with people. What other skills do you think are important to succeed in business?

*The **Practical Action** boxes, along with the **Business Skills & Career Development** and **Business Culture & Etiquette** Briefings, in this book offer practical advice about how to sharpen your career by using your college experience. We'll discuss habits, teamwork, flexibility, goal setting, networking, mentoring, voluntarism, ethics, and similar subjects.*

Maybe you don't think of college as having much to do with the "real world" of business. But it does, because it gives you an environment in which to develop certain talents that will serve you well in getting a job and being successful in your career.

Learning to Focus

"Life," says Winifred Gallagher, author of *Rapt,* "is the sum of what you focus on."[62]

Another writer says, "You can drive yourself crazy trying to multitask and answer every email message instantly. Or you can recognize your brain's finite capacity for processing information."[63]

Multitasking is shifting focus from one task to another in rapid succession. When you read this textbook while listening to music and watching TV, you may think you're simultaneously doing three separate tasks, but you're really not. "It's like playing tennis with three balls," says one expert.[64]

Today multitasking is easy and focus is hard because of all the things demanding our attention—text messages, e-mail, Twitter, Facebook, MySpace, websites, blogs, music, not to mention phone calls, radio, and TV. Plus the classroom (or online) instructor trying to get his or her points across.

To succeed in business, you need to be able to pay attention. Prospective employers look at your grades as proof of this. Will you have been focused enough to have grades you'll be proud of?

Part of going to college is learning new discipline and new habits. Here are some tips from Gallagher on learning to concentrate:[65]

- **Realize you're always making choices about your focus—and make the right ones:** "People don't realize that attention is a finite resource, like money," she says. "Do you want to invest your cognitive cash on endless Twittering or Net surfing or couch potatoing [watching TV]?" Elsewhere she adds, "Where did the idea come from that anyone who wants to contact you can do so at any time? You need to take charge of what you pay attention to instead of responding to the latest stimuli."[66] For example, to block out noise, you can wear earplugs while reading, to create your own "stimulus shelter."

- **Devote the first 90 minutes of your day to your most important task:** Writing a paper? Studying biochemistry? Make it your first task of the day, and concentrate on it for 90 minutes. After that, your brain will probably need a rest, and you can answer e-mail and texts, return phone calls, and so on. But until that first break, don't do anything else, because it can take the brain 20 minutes to refocus.

Practicing Etiquette

Etiquette—socially acceptable behavior—may seem an old-fashioned word, but learning it is crucial to business success, and it starts with your behavior in the classroom. Now's the time to practice.

Walking into class late; talking with other students; texting instead of listening to the lecture; eating, yawning, scratching, and belching—all these show disrespect to the instructor. If he or she were your boss at work, imagine what kind of performance review you would get. Discuss a bonus or promotion? Not you.

So, now's the time to begin exercising basic courtesy and manners with your instructors, just as you'll be expected to do with your boss and coworkers in business.

LEARNING & SKILLS PORTFOLIO

Summary

1.1 Business & Profits: The Basis of Wealth

THE ESSENTIAL QUESTION: *What is business, and how are profits made?*

Even if I don't work for a for-profit organization, could I still apply the business skills I've learned? There are two types of organizations, and business education is applicable to both. A for-profit organization is simply a business, an organization formed to make money, or profits, by selling goods and services. A nonprofit is designed to provide products or services to clients rather than to make a profit for owners and managers.

How does a business actually make money? A business is engaged in trying to make a profit by selling goods (tangible products) or services (intangible products). The purpose of the selling activity is to generate revenue, the total amount of money that the selling produces during a defined period of time. After the costs of salaries and other business expenses are subtracted from the revenue, the owners will know whether the business realized a profit or took a loss (when expenses are larger than revenues).

1.2 Business as Benefactor: Payoffs beyond Money

THE ESSENTIAL QUESTION: *How can business benefit society?*

How can business make people's lives better? Business can help society by enriching people's quality of life, the expression of society's general well-being as measured by standard of living, freedom, happiness, art, environmental health, and innovation. Standard of living is defined by how many goods and services people can buy with the money they have. Business has been found to contribute to the standard of living, as well as to a long and healthy life and access to knowledge.

What are four ways business can benefit society? Business benefits society by producing goods and services; providing paychecks and benefits for employees; paying taxes to support government services; and donating funds, goods, and services for community causes.

1.3 Risk, Entrepreneurship, & the Factors of Production: The Creative Fire of Business

THE ESSENTIAL QUESTION: *What are the main sources of wealth?*

How did most wealthy people make their money? Most wealthy people are self-employed business owners. The self-employed are more likely than the salaried to be rich.

Which is more risky—being an entrepreneur or being a salaried employee? Risk is the possibility that a business owner may invest time and money and fail to make a profit. Taking risks is what entrepreneurs do, people who see a new opportunity for a product or service and risk their time and money to start a business. Some entrepreneurs view salaried workers as taking more risks because they have only a single source of income whereas an entrepreneur often has several sources of income.

What are factors of production? Wealth is created from the factors of production, which consist of natural resources, capital, human resources, and entrepreneurship. Some also add knowledge. Natural resources consist of production inputs that are useful just as they appear in nature. Capital includes buildings, machines, tools, and technology used to provide goods and services. Human resources consists of labor, the physical and intellectual contributions of a company's employees. Entrepreneurship is the process of taking risks to try to create a new enterprise. The possible fifth factor, knowledge, has been revolutionized by computers, telecommunications, and databases.

1.4 The Business Environment: Forces That Encourage & Discourage Entrepreneurship

THE ESSENTIAL QUESTION: *What major forces affect the way companies and individual businesspeople operate?*

How do freedom and regulation affect business? The amount of freedom that governments allow people to run their businesses versus the amount of restraint they put on them can affect taxation, contract enforcement, and corruption.

Can technology both improve and impede productivity? Technology, whether digital or otherwise, can have both positive effects, increasing productivity, and negative effects, hindering a firm's security.

Does competition make a difference in how customers, employees, and investors may be affected? The presence or absence of competitors can determine the amount of effort a company is willing to put in to satisfy customers, employees, and investors.

How do global forces affect business? Global forces can affect trade among nations and the stability of nations.

Will people from different backgrounds affect how business operates? A country's demographics, the measurable characteristics of a population, can change customer needs as well as the pool from which a company draws employees.

1.5 Seven Key Business Rules: The Great Adventure of Being in Business in the 21st Century

THE ESSENTIAL QUESTION: *What are Seven Key Business Rules to observe in pursuing business success?*

We suggest there are Seven Key Rules for pursuing business success, abbreviated by the initial letters SUCCESS—for stakeholders, uncertainty, competition, common economy, ethics, societal differences, and self-development.

Who are 10 stakeholders that I must recognize and deal with? The universe of business stakeholders—the people whose interests are affected by the organization's activities—consists of owners (some of whom may be stockholders, owners of stocks or shares of ownership), customers, employees, suppliers (those who supply raw materials, services, and equipment to the organization), distributors (who help sell goods and services to customers), lenders, nearby communities, government regulators, interest groups (whose members try to influence businesses and governments on specific issues), and media.

What kinds of change do I have to be alert for that could affect my work life? Businesses must deal with a range of uncertainties. These include twists and turns in the economy, changes brought about by information technology and the Internet (including e-commerce, the buying and selling of products or services over computer networks), and climate change (which may provide opportunities for green businesses, those that adapt practices for the use of renewable resources and otherwise operate in ways that solve both environmental and social problems).

What are four areas in the competitive environment I must master to be successful? Most businesses must deal with competitors, people or organizations that compete for customers or resources. Firms must strive for a competitive advantage, to produce goods or services more effectively than their competitors. Four areas a firm must try to exceed in are being responsive to customers, making continual improvement in the quality of the product or service, finding ways to deliver new or better products or services, and striving for employee efficiency.

What is globalization? Globalization is the trend of the world economy toward becoming a more interdependent system.

How important are ethical behavior and corporate social responsibility in business? Ethical behavior is a significant part of doing business. So is corporate social responsibility, a concern for taking actions that will benefit the interests of society as well as the organization.

What trends in diversity are occurring that I should be aware of? During the next half century, the mix of American racial or ethnic groups will change considerably, with about half the U.S. population being made up of ethnic minorities. The largest changes will be a reduction in the number of non-Hispanic whites and an increase in the number of Asians, Pacific Islanders, and, particularly, Hispanics.

To be successful, what personal skills should I cultivate? You should use your education and experience to develop three important skills—ability to perform a specific job, ability to think analytically, and ability to interact well with people.

Key Terms

MyBizLab

business   5
business environment   12
capital   11
competitive advantage   19
competitors   13
customers   15
demographics   13
distributor   16
e-business   18
e-commerce   18
entrepreneur   10
entrepreneurship   11
factors of production   10
for-profit organization   4

global outsourcing   6
globalization   19
goods   5
governmental regulators   17
green businesses   18
human resources   11
interest groups   17
loss   5
management   15
natural resources   10
nonprofit organization   4
organization   4
owners   15
productivity   12

profit   5
quality of life   7
revenue   5
risk   10
selling   5
services   5
shareholders   15
stakeholders   15
standard of living   7
stock   15
stockholders   15
supplier   16
technology   12

Pop Quiz Prep

1. What is a nonprofit organization?
2. How is *revenue* defined?
3. How is *standard of living* defined?
4. When businesses sponsor Little League teams or help disaster victims by making monetary contributions, which method of businesses benefiting society does this illustrate?
5. According to research mentioned in this chapter, what group of people is most likely to be wealthy in America?

6. In terms of the factors of production, what are buildings, machines, tools, and technology considered?
7. How is an organization likely to behave if it has no competition?
8. How is *productivity* defined?
9. Who are the distributors of a business?
10. What is *globalization*?

Critical Thinking Questions

1. Booker T. Washington was an African American educator, author, orator, and political leader. He represented the last generation of leaders born in slavery. One hundred years ago, Washington said, "It is easily seen, that if every member of the race should strive to make himself the most indispensable man in his community, and to be successful in business, however humble that business might be, he would contribute much toward smoothing the pathway of his own and future generations."[67] Utilizing the textbook and class lectures, interpret and discuss this quote.

2. Wealth is created from the factors of production. These consist of natural resources, capital, human resources, entrepreneurship, and, according to some experts, knowledge. Using the criteria of creating wealth, rank the factors of production in order of importance. Explain your ranking.

3. As discussed in the chapter, a country's demographics (the measurable characteristics of a population such as race and age) affect customer needs as well as the pool from which a company draws employees. Discuss how the following demographic trends might have an impact on U.S. business practices, and give examples of how businesses could respond to these changes: (a) the increased number of minorities, (b) an aging workforce (baby boomers born between 1946 and 1964), and (c) the growing number of single-parent households and changing family structures.

4. A National Public Radio (NPR) article, "Defining Diversity: Beyond Race and Gender," says that diversity in the current workplace often goes beyond the traditional gender and race quotients.[68] The article states that companies now include factors such as sexual preference, disabilities, veteran status, weight, and working parent status as examples of diversity. For instance, Motorola defines diversity as including gay, lesbian, bisexual, or transgender status.[69] Abbott, a health care company, includes flexible work schedules as part of its diversity plan.[70] How would you define diversity at your school, work, or a community group in which you're involved? Is it defined differently than traditional age, gender, and race? Explain.

5. Buy Nothing Day (BND) is an international day of protest against consumerism observed by social activists. BND was founded by Vancouver artist Ted Dave and promoted by Adbusters, an anticonsumerism organization.[71] In the United States, BND is celebrated on "Black Friday," the day after Thanksgiving, which is the unofficial kickoff to the holiday shopping season and often the busiest shopping day of the year. Buy Nothing Day is officially defined as "a 24-hour moratorium on consumer spending, designed to remind both the consumer and the retailer of the true power of the buying public. It is an exercise in financial self-control. It is reclamation of consumer control of the marketplace. It is a gesture of protest for those of us who feel, all too often, as if our lives and dreams have been marketed back to us. Participate by not participating."[72] As a member of the buying public, would you be interested in participating in this? Do you think BND is effective in achieving its goal as stated above? Discuss.

VIDEO CASE
Making a Difference in Society: Saving Lives of Senior Dogs

"Can you teach an old dog new tricks?" the question is asked. With the help of many dedicated and passionate dog-loving volunteers, Sherri Franklin, founder of Muttville Senior Dog Rescue, has to date been able to find "forever homes" for over 1,300 mature furry friends. Since founding the dog rescue in 2007, Franklin has succeeded by "teaching new tricks" to San Francisco Bay Area pet owners, by convincing them that a senior rescue dog is an excellent alternative to purchasing a puppy from a puppy mill. Muttville Senior Dog Rescue defines senior dogs as those "seven years young" and more. Franklin and her volunteers believe that this maturity brings increased love, commitment, and companionship.

Muttville is a nonprofit organization. Much of its existence depends on the generosity of donors who contribute necessary funds to cover veterinary costs and supplies for dogs who might otherwise be euthanized. While Muttville's focus is to find homes for its canine kids, the jobs performed within the organization are similar to those at a for-profit company—including creating projections, financial planning, accounting, budgeting, outreach, marketing, and strategic planning. Also similar to a for-profit organization, Muttville has chosen a board of directors. The board members are individuals who are not only passionate about dogs but possess important skills such as sales, public relations, finance, accounting, strategic planning, development, and marketing.

The video highlights that Muttville has outgrown its current location, and that its volunteers and board members are working diligently on a capital campaign to raise funds to expand to a new location—in much the same way a for-profit would. The new space is needed to provide office space, to create an adoption and foster meeting "matching" space, and of course to temporarily house more dogs—all with the goal of increasing throughput and saving more precious lives. "The number of pets in need of a forever home is never in short supply," says Franklin, "and the more happy homes we can find, the closer we come to reaching our goal of saving worthy lives. Of course, it all requires an immense amount of time and planning to reach our goals, and as you may know, an incredible amount of money."

Franklin's natural resources (her dogs) land at Muttville's headquarters for two main reasons. The first is their age. Because they are older, many people find them less adoptable than the puppies with whom they compete. The second reason is that their owners are no longer able to care for them due to illness, foreclosure, or other reasons. Fortunately, Franklin's entrepreneurial spirit, innovative approach, targeted outreach, and marketing team remain committed and determined to find homes for all canine orphans—including those who are let go as a result of a difficult housing market, which has resulted in a record number of foreclosures. "When homeowners realize they cannot afford to live in the home they once saw as their 'American Dream,' unfortunately, the once-coveted and loved family pet becomes less of a priority and sadly, no longer a member of the family," says Franklin.

Franklin has created awareness of a niche market. She has increased demand (through adoptions) for these senior dogs through careful education and advocacy at outreach events and well-developed programs. One of Franklin's programs, "Seniors for Seniors," matches loving, trained, and well-behaved senior dogs in need of some TLC with loving senior companions. Kenzie, a beautiful schnauzer, has found her forever home in Santa Cruz, California, with Ivan, a retired and widowed schoolteacher who fraternizes with other dog-loving neighbors during daily walks in this beautiful ocean-side community. Kenzie has provided Ivan with immense love, pleasure, companionship, and exercise—for which he is extremely grateful. "I cannot imagine my life without my girl Kenzie," 84-year-old Ivan says lovingly, like a proud papa. These success stories are Muttville's greatest profit. Does Muttville Senior Dog Rescue wish to increase its profits by saving more senior dogs? The answer is one loud "ruff," which translates to a definitive "yes!"

What's Your Take?

1. "Quality of life" reflects a society's general well-being as measured by standard of living, freedom, happiness, art, environmental health, and innovation.[73] Ultimately, business can help society by enriching people's quality of life. Based upon the definition of quality of life, which of these measurements is most prevalent in the work that Sherri Franklin and Muttville Senior Dog Rescue perform to improve the quality of life for both dogs and humans?

2. In for-profit organizations, the measure or metric of success is generally profit (or loss). In nonprofit organizations, money and expenses are important concerns, but success is usually measured in how effectively services are delivered. Name at least five ways you would measure the success of Muttville Senior Dog Rescue.

3. An entrepreneur is a person who sees a new opportunity for a product or service and risks his or her time and money to start a business to meet this opportunity, with the ultimate goal of making a profit. Describe how Sherri Franklin can be considered an entrepreneur. What would you say are the primary differences between Franklin's "start-up" and a for-profit entrepreneurial start-up?

4. Did you know that it is illegal to abandon a pet? Think about and explain some of the reasons why owners may surrender their dogs. Which are direct results of the economy? What do you think the impact of the economy has been on animal rescue organizations like Muttville Senior Dog Rescue?

BUSINESS DECISION CASE
Apple & Google: Relationship Status Change

At one time, Google sold advertising and Apple sold hardware. This case explores how a surge in mobile device usage has changed the way users are accessing the Internet. This in turn has created a growing competition between Google and Apple in mobile computing, mobile applications (apps), and other related products.

In 2006 when the iPhone was unveiled, Google CEO Eric Schmidt was on stage with Apple CEO Steve Jobs. Google had collaborated with Apple on mapping for the iPhone, and Schmidt sat on Apple's board of directors. The companies were strategic allies, and the CEOs often spoke favorably of one another. In the next few years, however, significant changes took place in the smartphone market *and* the relationship between the two companies.[74]

Competition between the two companies began when Google announced its mobile phone and Android operating system—and when it became clear that smartphones would be the computers of the future. Soon the Google CEO gave up his seat on the Apple board of directors. The late Steve Jobs is quoted as saying, "Eric's effectiveness as an Apple board member would be significantly diminished, because he will have to recuse himself from even larger portions of our meetings." The rivalry grew when Google opened a Web-based store for apps that run on mobile devices powered by its Android software, including Motorola's Droid and HTC Corporation's Evo.[75]

Both Apple and Google are hyperfocused on the growing mobile computing market. Compared to the Web, dollars in mobile advertising are small—but studies show that more users have begun to access the Internet through their mobile devices as compared to the traditional desktop computer. Mary Meeker of Morgan Stanley predicts that within five years more users will tap into the Internet via mobile devices than desktop PCs.[76] Morgan Stanley's global technology and telecom analysts project that mobile devices will eventually outship the global netbook and notebook market, and that by 2012, smartphones will also outship the global PC market, which includes notebooks, netbooks, and desktops.[77]

It is not surprising that the race for delivering content is intensifying; the research firm Gartner projected that the revenues generated by apps would triple in 2011 to more than $15 billion, and by 2014 revenue from apps would reach $58 billion.[78] The companies are also competing for mobile advertising dollars. Borrell Associates, an advertising research and consulting firm, forecasts that spending for ads delivered by mobile applications will increase to $8.4 billion by 2015 and spending on ads delivered through a mobile browser will reach $10.9 billion.[79] As the race to deliver content intensifies, it appears that the two companies aren't as friendly as they once were.

What's Your Take?

1. Is this just a situation of capitalism and friendly competition? Do you have any ideas as to what the future holds in terms of the competitive landscape between these two companies?

2. As the competition between Apple and Google continues to intensify, do you think that Apple may decide to dump Google as the default search engine on its mobile devices? If they do, who might they turn to for search or how they would deal with search on their devices?

3. Are there any benefits for the consumer of increased competition?

4. If you were considering purchasing a smartphone (iPhone, HTC, or Blackberry), or replacing an older model, would any of the competitive issues outlined in this case be a factor in your purchase? Explain why these issues would or would not affect your decision.

5. In an effort to take greater control and to increase profits, Apple is moving to a system of delivering and billing for electronic content viewed on its devices by requiring publishers of books, magazines, and newspapers to conduct sales of content within apps, handled by the iTunes billing system.[80] Publishers are not pleased with Apple's announcement because if the only way for users to purchase electronic content, newspapers, and magazines is through the iDevice, they lose valuable information about their subscribers. Subscriber information is the lifeblood of an online seller because it is used to market and build long-term relationships, and of course, upsell or market similar products based upon information from past purchases.[81]

As a user, if you wanted to purchase content, would you have an issue if you had to do so through the content publisher's website, for example, or an iTunes store?

Briefings

Go to www.mybizlab.com for online activities and exercises related to the timely topics discussed in this chapter's Briefings, as well as additional theme-related Briefing *Spotlights* highlighting how these concepts apply in today's business environment.

In-chapter Briefing:
- A Media Prank Hurts Domino's Pizza
- U.S. Manufacturing Isn't Dead—It's Becoming More Upscale
- U.S. Social Differences in the 21st Century

Activity:
- Developing Marketable Business Skills – Forces Affecting Business

Briefing Spotlight:
- Change Is Our Business

In-chapter Briefing:
- What's the Pay for Entry-Level Jobs for College Graduates in Business?
- New College Grads Find Jobs Overseas

Activity:
- Developing Marketable Business Skills – Knowledge Workers vs. Manual Workers
- Getting Your Career in Gear – Comparing a For-Profit to a Nonprofit
- Going to the Net! – Emotional Intelligence

Briefing Spotlight:
- Drafting Your New-Grad Résumé

In-chapter Briefing:
- Taking Care of Buyers: Amazon Pays Close Attention to "The Customer Experience"

Activity:
- Developing Marketable Business Skills – Customer-Driven Business
- Developing Marketable Business Skills – Types of Stakeholders

Briefing Spotlight:
- The Customer Is King/Queen!

In-chapter Briefing:
- Factors of Production in an Entrepreneurial Furniture Business

Activity:
- Developing Marketable Business Skills – Green Initiatives
- Going to the Net! – The "Go Green" Initiative
- Going to the Net! – Home Energy Use
- Going to the Net! – The Greening of Society

Briefing Spotlight:
- The "Dollars & Sense" of Sustainability

In-chapter Briefing:
- Wells Fargo Is Ordered to Refund "Unfair and Deceptive" Overdraft Fees

Activity:
- Ethical Dilemma Case – Profits or Principles: The Booming Business of Essay Writers for Hire

Briefing Spotlight:
- Teaching Ethical Behavior

In-chapter Briefing:
- How One Man Makes Inspirational Writing and Speaking a Revenue-Producing Business

Activity:
- Going to the Net! – Are You Ready to Start a Business?

Briefing Spotlight:
- Young and Entrepreneurial

Additional Briefing Spotlights available at MyBizLab:
- BUSINESS CULTURE & ETIQUETTE
- GLOBAL BUSINESS
- INFO TECH & SOCIAL MEDIA
- PERSONAL FINANCE
- SOCIALLY RESPONSIBLE BUSINESS

2

Ethics & Social Responsibility

Business as a Positive Force

After reading and studying this chapter, you will be able to answer the following essential questions:

MyBizLab

Where you see MyBizLab in this chapter, go to www.mybizlab.com for additional activities on the topic being discussed.

FORECAST: What's Ahead in This Chapter

This chapter explains the ethical and social responsibilities of businesspeople and how organizations can promote ethical behavior. It also explains the concept of corporate social responsibility, as well as the concepts of blended value and social auditing. Finally, it describes the negative effects of bad business behavior and the benefits to stakeholders of good business behavior.

MyBizLab

Gain hands-on experience through an interactive, real-world scenario. This chapter's simulation entitled Navigating Murky Ethical Waters is located at **www.mybizlab.com**.

WINNER: Doing Right When It's Difficult

What's a true test of moral character? Could you meet it?

After 20 years as a pharmaceutical salesman for Merck & Co., in 1995 Doug Durand joined TAP Pharmaceutical Products in Lake Forest, Illinois, at a salary of $140,000, with the promise of a $50,000 bonus. As a new vice president of sales, Durand was shocked to hear his sales staff in a conference call openly discussing how to bribe urologists (with a 2% "administration fee") for prescribing TAP's prostate cancer drug, Lupron. He also learned that for years TAP reps had encouraged physicians to charge government medical programs (taxpayer funded) full price for Lupron they received free or at a discount, a tactic designed to help establish Lupron as the prostate treatment of choice.

Gradually, Durand learned that TAP, instead of using science to promote its products, relied on kickbacks and freebies—giving big-screen TVs, computers, and golf vacations to cooperating urologists. He also discovered that, though required by federal law, reps could not account for half of their Lupron samples. Terrified he might be scapegoated for the illegalities, he tried applying to other companies that had offered him jobs before TAP but found them already filled.

Eventually, Durand began to secretly document TAP's abuses and finally mailed the evidence to a friend with close ties to an assistant U.S. attorney specializing in medical fraud. The friend urged him to sue TAP for fraud against the government under the federal whistleblower program. (A whistleblower is an employee who reports organizational misconduct to the public.) It wasn't easy for him to do so. "The idea of suing as a whistleblower intimidated me," Durand said. "Nobody likes a whistleblower. I thought it could end my career."

In the end, however, he found himself believing it was the right thing to do.

Eventually he left TAP for AstraMerck and later testified against his former employees and colleagues. The result: The government went after TAP and fined it heavily.[1]

Source: www.whistleblowers.org.

LOSER: Taking Credit Where None Is Deserved

Is lying acceptable? If so, how much is allowable before it reflects poorly on your character?

William H. Swanson, chief executive officer of Raytheon, a military contractor, became known as a management sage for his *Swanson's Unwritten Rules of Management*, a folksy collection of 33 rules of business survival. Examples:

#1. *Learn to say "I don't know." If used when appropriate, it will be used often.*

#2. *Never be afraid to try something new. Remember, an amateur built an ark that survived a flood while a large group of professionals built the Titanic!*

Raytheon promoted the book on the company's website and gave away more than 300,000 copies. The magazine *Business 2.0* featured the book on its cover, and *USA Today* did a story about it.

Then came an e-mail from a San Diego chemical engineer named Carl Durrenberger, who pointed out that "nearly all of these 'unwritten rules' have indeed been written—by another author in fact, 60 years ago. Mr. Swanson has plagiarized from the little-known [1944] book *The Unwritten Laws of Engineering* by W. J. King."

It was also revealed that Swanson had pirated rules 1 through 4 from a collection known as "Rumsfeld's Rules" by U.S. Secretary of Defense Donald Rumsfeld, which were published in the *Wall Street Journal* in 2001. Rule 32, drawing a life lesson about rude treatment of waiters, was similar to something written by humor columnist Dave Barry.

Ultimately, Swanson had to issue statements of regret and apology. "I did not properly check source material," he said. "I apologize to those whose material I wish I had treated with greater care."[2]

For his failure to give credit for plagiarized material, the Raytheon directors took away almost $1 million in Swanson's 2006 compensation. The punishment might have been harsher had the board not decided that the ethical breach was "unintentional and not negligent. It was just poor judgment."[3]

Source: Photograph by Sally Lindsay.

YOUR CALL The problem of plagiarism—presenting others' work as your own—clearly isn't limited to college students writing term papers (for which they can be flunked). What would you have done in Swanson's case? Do you think the punishment fit the crime? What signals does Swanson's behavior send to Raytheon's stakeholders? Could you do the right but difficult thing that Durand did? Would it affect your opinion to know that Durand received a $77 million reward under the federal whistleblower statute? Still, you should know that when he made the decision to report TAP's behavior he was not aware that he could benefit so well financially.

MyBizLab

THE BIG IDEA: This section describes the global corporate social responsibility pyramid, which suggests a guide for thinking about moral matters. We also describe values, ethics, laws, and corporate social responsibility. We define ethical dilemmas and discuss the "holier-than-thou" effect.

THE ESSENTIAL QUESTION: What is the order of priorities for a businessperson?

MyBizLab

MyBizLab: Check your understanding of these concepts at www.mybizlab.com.

■ **PANEL 2.1 Illegal, unethical, both, or neither?** These categories show how different actions can vary in being legal and ethical.

1. **Both illegal and unethical**
   Embezzlement
   Consumer fraud
   Sexual harassment
   Cash payments to avoid taxes

2. **Legal but unethical**
   Making sleazy, short-lived products
   Canceling company retirement plan
   Avoiding taxes on U.S. revenues using offshore banks

3. **Ethical but illegal**
   Paying more despite union contract limits
   Selling raw milk for human consumption

4. **Both legal and ethical**
   Green businesses
   Consumer-friendly behavior
   Employee fringe benefits
   Community contributions

Hard economic times, such as those of the recent Great Recession, can force people to take desperate measures to find or keep a job or to attract and keep customers. How far would you go to bend the rules—to push the ethical boundaries—if your job was on the line?

Prior to deciding whether a contemplated action is appropriate, suggests Hewlett-Packard's code of business conduct, an employee should pose a simple test: "Before I make a decision, I consider how it would look in a news story."[4] Certainly in the foregoing "Winners & Losers" accounts, Doug Durand looked good in the headlines and William Swanson looked bad.

So, as you contemplate making a questionable move that might make you (or your company) amazingly rich, what kind of imagined televised news images would make you think twice? You in handcuffs and an orange prison jumpsuit? You in court as defendant in an ugly civil lawsuit? You facing shouting reporters who want to know how you feel about depleting the life savings of innocent victims—even though what you did was entirely legal?

Maybe you would be more troubled by the idea of going to jail than of looking sleazy. Not all unethical actions are illegal, after all; there are lots of nuances, as the panel at left makes clear. (*See* ■ *Panel 2.1.*) But it should be your goal to be *both* legal and ethical.

Carroll's Social Responsibility Pyramid: Profit, Law, Ethics, & Citizenship

What's a way of framing my moral priorities?

University of Georgia business-ethics scholar **Archie B. Carroll** provides a guide for thinking about such practical and moral matters. His ***global corporate social responsibility pyramid* suggests the obligations of an organization in the global economy are to make a profit, to obey the law, to be ethical, and to be a good global corporate citizen.** Some people hold that a company's first and only duty is to make a profit. However, Carroll suggests an organization's global responsibilities should have the following priorities, with profit being the most fundamental (base of the pyramid) and corporate citizenship at the top:[5]

- *Make a profit* consistent with expectations for international business. (This is called economic responsibility.)

- *Obey the law of host* countries as well as international law. (This is legal responsibility.)
- *Be ethical in its practices,* taking host-country and global standards into consideration. (This is ethical responsibility.)
- *Be a good global corporate citizen,* as defined by the host country's expectations. (This is philanthropic responsibility.)

These priorities—profit, law, ethics, and citizenship—could apply to the corporation's and its employees' business behavior in its home country as well.

Values, Ethics & Laws, & Corporate Social Responsibility

How should I distinguish among values, ethics, laws, and corporate social responsibility?

We may think we know what *values, ethics, laws,* and *social responsibility* mean, but do we? Let's take a closer look.

Values: Underlying Beliefs That Help Determine Behavior

Underlying ethical and legal systems are *values,* **the relatively permanent and deeply held underlying beliefs and attitudes that help determine people's behavior.** An example of a value is humility—the opposite of overbearing pride (hubris)—as in St. Paul's advice, "In humility count others as better than yourself."[6] Values are the underpinnings for ethical systems, as in the oath physicians take to "First do no harm" to a patient (Hippocratic oath), and legal systems, as in lawyers' pledges to uphold the law and the U.S. Constitution.

Ethics & Laws: Standards of Right & Wrong

Ethics **are principles of right and wrong that influence behavior.** *Laws* **are rules of conduct or action formally recognized as binding or enforced by a controlling authority.**

Some standards are nearly universal, such as the belief that killing is never justified except for the most important of reasons (such as self-defense). Other standards are culturally based, varying according to what a particular culture considers right or wrong. This is particularly true in international business, where what one culture considers wrong both ethically and legally is considered perfectly acceptable in another culture.

■ Example of Acts That Vary Ethically or Legally According to Culture: "Is That a Gratuity or a Bribe?" In many Latin American and Asian countries, tipping a public official is considered a gratuity, a gift, a donation, a commission, or even a consulting fee intended to reward someone for providing you with a competitive advantage or better service.

In the United States, Canada, and many parts of Europe, however, the same act is considered a kickback, grease money, a bribe, which is certainly unethical and usually illegal. An American businessperson performing such an act with a foreign official is considered to be in violation of U.S. law—specifically, the Foreign Corrupt Practices Act—although it may be perfectly legal in the host country. ■

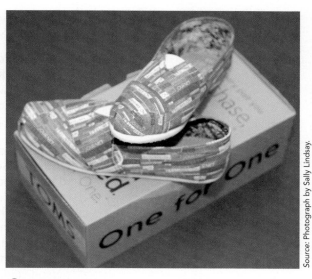

Source: Photograph by Sally Lindsay.

❶ Good corporate citizen. In 2006, American Blake Mycoskie was traveling in Argentina, where he observed that many children had no shoes to protect their feet. On returning home, he founded TOMS Shoes as a company that would—"One for One"—give a new pair of shoes to a child in need for every pair purchased. Later that year he returned to Argentina with family, friends, and staff members with 10,000 pairs of shoes made possible by TOMS customers.

Want to Know More? 2-1

Key Terms & Definitions in Sequential Order to Study as You Go Along

Go to www.mybizlab.com.

Want to Know More? 2-2

What Else Can Be Learned about Carroll's Pyramid?

Go to www.mybizlab.com.

Corporate Social Responsibility: Benefiting Society as Well as the Organization

Corporate social responsibility (CSR), **also called** *corporate citizenship,* **is a concern for taking actions that will benefit the interests of society as well as of the organization.** That is, CSR seeks to maximize a firm's positive impact on society and minimize its negative impact.

> ■ **Example** of Corporate Social Responsibility: Pepsi Stops Selling Sugary Drinks in Schools. In 2006, responding to complaints about products linked to childhood obesity, both Coke and Pepsi agreed to stop selling sugary soft drinks in U.S. schools. In March 2010, Pepsi went on to voluntarily agree to remove high-calorie sweetened soft drinks from schools for children up to the age of 18 in more than 200 other countries.
>
> The company received compliments from the Center for Science in the Public Interest. "We applaud Pepsi for its global commitment," a spokesperson said. "But shame on Coca-Cola for insisting on targeting high school students in most countries around the world."[7] ■

Corporate social responsibility, or being a good corporate citizen, rests at the top of Carroll's pyramid. This reflects global society's expectations, says Carroll, "that business will engage in social activities that are not mandated by law nor generally expected of business in an ethical sense."[8]

We discuss corporate social responsibility further in Section 2.3. First, however, let us give more consideration to ethical behavior.

Defining Ethical Dilemmas

How would I recognize when I'm in an "ethical dilemma"?

An *ethical dilemma* **is a situation in which people have to decide whether to pursue a certain action that may benefit them or their organization but that is unethical or even illegal.** In business, a frequent source of ethical dilemmas is the conflict between the competing demands to make money yet also be fair and honest in business relationships.

> **BRIEFING / LEGAL & ETHICAL PRACTICES**
> **Ethical Dilemma for the Thomas Kinkade Company: Was It "Just Business" to Exploit Gallery Owners' Faith?** Self-described "painter of light" Thomas Kinkade is a born-again Christian who uses religious themes in his art. But his company also used sharp-edged marketing and business tactics to make money from that art. Could Kinkade have found himself in an ethical dilemma between following his religious values and ways of selling his products?
>
> At a presentation for prospective Kinkade Signature Gallery owners, said the former proprietors of a Virginia gallery, Kinkade and his representatives used words such as *Christian,* *God, partner,* and *trust* to create "a certain religious environment designed to instill a special relationship of trust."[9] What the couple was not told, their attorney said, was that they would have to sell Kinkade artworks at set retail prices even while the Thomas Kinkade Co. simultaneously undercut them with its own discount sales. ❷
>
> The result was they were forced to close their gallery and lost the life savings they had invested. An appeals court ruled

❷ **Ethical conflict?** Painter Thomas Kinkade's company was ordered to pay damages to former gallery owners. They accused his company of exploiting their faith to force them into a business in which they competed unfairly with the Kinkade company itself. Do you think it's acceptable for a company to put hardball (if legal) money-making practices ahead of other considerations?

Source: s70/ZUMA Press/Newscom.

that the Kinkade company had to pay the couple $860,000 in damages plus $1.2 million in other fees and expenses, which ultimately led to the firm's bankruptcy.

Regardless of your religious beliefs, do you think hardball business practices are "just business" or "just part of the game" and therefore allowable? Or do some tactics pose an ethical dilemma for you? ∎

Behaving Badly, Behaving Well

Why might I attribute purer motives to myself than to others?

Sam Waksal, MD, founder and CEO of ImClone, a biotechnology company, learned—before the news was made public—that the U.S. government would refuse to approve ImClone's new cancer drug, a decision certain to drive down the company's stock price. Waksal quickly tried to sell $5 million of his ImClone stock, an act of insider trading for which he ultimately was sentenced to 87 months in prison and fined $3 million. **Insider trading is the illegal use of private company information to further one's own fortunes or those of family or friends.** (This was the case that affected home-décor and lifestyle guru Martha Stewart as well.)

Behaving Badly: The "Holier-than-Thou" Effect Excuses Our Own Behavior but Not Others'

What makes some businesspeople think it's acceptable to engage in such moral sleaziness—insider trading, deceptive advertising, shady banking practices, and the like? Perhaps people have a self-inflated bias about themselves, a condition known as the *holier-than-thou effect.*[10] Many of us overestimate our willingness to do what's morally right, and it can greatly influence how we judge other people's actions, such as cheating on tests. ③

Research shows people will make generous forecasts about their own moral behavior and less generous predictions about their peers'. But the negative predictions about others turn out to apply not only to others but to themselves as well.[11]

The holier-than-thou effect diminishes quickly when people become involved in the actual experience they are judging. As one writer says, "Dubious accounting practices will appear less shady to the person who has had to put a good face on a failing company."[12] In other words, is it really the situation, not moral character, that guides behavior?

Behaving Well: Treat Others as You Would Yourself

Why be ethical? Why be good? Maybe, suggests a brain study, people perform selfless acts not just for an emotional reward but because they're acutely tuned in to the needs and actions of others.[13] "And therefore," says one of the study authors, "I might want to treat them like I might want them to treat myself."[14]

When you graduate into the business world, will you do the right thing? Earning money is certainly acceptable, but many students have decided it's equally important to be ethical and socially responsible. For example, a high percentage of the 2009 Harvard Business School class graduating with master's degrees in business administration (MBA) signed the **MBA oath, a voluntary student-led pledge of intention to serve the greater good. They promised to act responsibly and ethically and refrain from advancing their "own narrow ambitions" at the expense of others.** "No one wants to have their future criticized as a place filled with unethical behaviors," said Max Anderson, a pledge organizer. He and his classmates want to learn from the ethical failures of the past, "do things differently, and accept our duty to lead responsibly."[15] Is this the way you would like to be as well?

Want to Know More? 2-3

The Inside Story on Insider Trading with ImClone, Sam Waksal, & Martha Stewart

Go to www.mybizlab.com.

Source: Suzanne Tucker, 2009/Used under license from Shutterstock.

③ **Cheating.** Obviously, students who don't do the work themselves are not learning and, research shows, they slip behind in knowledge and grades. How do you judge other students' cheating on tests? How do you judge yourself?

Want to Know More? 2-4

What Are Some Tests to Use to Determine If an Act Is Ethical?

Go to www.mybizlab.com.

Want to Know More? 2-5

What Are Some Important Details of the Harvard MBA Oath?

Go to www.mybizlab.com.

Are we a nation of cheats and liars?

David Callahan, author of *The Cheating Culture,* worries about "ordinary people's willingness to deceive others and cut corners purely to make more money or win some prize."[16] James Stewart, who wrote *Tangled Webs,* thinks there is so much high-level lying that it is "threatening to swamp the legal system, stymie the courts, and sow cynicism nationwide."[17]

Why does such unethical behavior happen? Perhaps, suggest two experts, many of us are guided by *motivated blindness.* That is, we overlook information that works against our best interests. For example, when we are busy focusing on organizational goals such as sales, they say, "the ethical implications of important decisions can fade from our minds. . . . We end up engaging in or condoning the behavior we would condemn."[18]

Motivated blindness *begins in school* and is carried into business.

School Cheating: Design for Failure

Cheating, getting unauthorized help in fulfilling graded assignments such as tests, and *plagiarism,* representing others' work as your own, are major concerns to educators—and to employers.[19]

Cheating is widespread among high school students, with 64% in one survey admitting to it, often aided by cellphones and the Internet.[20] Cheating is also an alarming problem in college, with 87% of undergraduates saying their peers at least "sometimes" plagiarize from the Web, for example.[21] It even occurs in graduate school—56% of graduate business students were found to have cheated.[22]

How do students attempt to justify this? Some may cheat on an exam and say, "I don't usually do this, but I really have to do it." They would rather cheat, that is, than show their families they got an F.[23] Whatever the motive, research shows, students who cheated and thus didn't actually do the assigned work were more likely to fail.[24]

Workplace Cheating & Lying: Will It Come Back & Wreck Your Career?

"Students don't just say 'OK I cheated in school, but now I'm in the workplace and it ends here,'" says an Arizona professor. "They are forming bad habits that carry over into the market."[25]

Slipping into major cheating and lying begins with "small infractions—illegally downloading a few songs, skimming small amounts from the register, lies of omission on taxes—and grows by increments," suggests science writer Benedict Carey. These "small infractions" can become a way of life that grows into a deliberate strategy of deception or fraud.[26]

Why do people engage in theft and fraud in the workplace? The reasons are mainly emotional:

- **Corner cutting:** People subconsciously seek shortcuts—as by cheating—more than they realize, says Carey. We constantly make choices "between short- and long-term gains, . . . between the more virtuous choice and the less virtuous one."

- **Resentment:** We justify cheating and lying because we have resentments of an authority or of a specific rule.

- **Unfairness:** "Perhaps the most powerful urge to cheat," says Carey, "stems from a deep sense of unfairness"—such as the fact that other people had advantages you did not. Still, does that give you an excuse to, say, take credit for other people's work?

- **Fear of being a chump:** The biggest fear might be of "not being smart" and "finishing out of the money." So strong is this fear that many people cheat to avoid having to deal with feeling like chumps.

THE BIG IDEA: To foster high ethical standards, a company needs to have support from top management for a strong ethical climate, hire ethical employees, and institute a code of ethics and training programs in ethics. An indicator that a firm has ethical problems is a history of whistleblowers. Public corporations must now comply with the Sarbanes–Oxley Act.

THE ESSENTIAL QUESTION: What are four ways organizations can foster high ethical standards?

MyBizLab: Check your understanding of these concepts at www.mybizlab.com.

MyBizLab

Here's a collector's item, if you can find it—the 64-page "Enron Code of Ethics." The Houston-based energy company was once the seventh largest company in the United States, but it plunged into bankruptcy after disclosure of highly irregular financial dealings, bringing tremendous losses to stockholders and employees, and prison terms to some of its highest-ranking executives.

Clearly, any company can work up some sort of code of ethics to post in the employee lunchroom. But how can we know if it is working actively to foster high ethical standards? We suggest there are three signs to look for.

1 Top Managers Strongly Support an Ethical Climate: "We're Not Just Giving Lip Service"

Is top management support really necessary?

It may be that lower-level employees will act ethically and honorably. But if top executives wink at ethical problems, look the other way, dodge them with legal loopholes, or generate public relations smokescreens, they are clearly failing to lead by example. This will make employees cynical about the loose ethical climate. Why should a clerk not steal from the office supply cabinet when the people at the top are using the company jet for personal vacation travel?[27] ④

Source: Tayhutch/Shutterstock.

BRIEFING / SOCIALLY RESPONSIBLE BUSINESS
An Ethical Top Manager at CitiMortgage Keeps People in Their Homes. A big story in the 2007–2009 recession was how the government came forward to inject billions of dollars into banks to keep them from failing. Many people complained, however, that the banks mostly used the money to shore up their reserves or pay executive bonuses rather than to rescue depositors or mortgage holders whose homes were in danger of foreclosure. Antibank feeling brought the morale of employees of financial institutions to all-time lows.

One such institution was CitiMortgage, the nation's fourth-largest mortgage lender, part of Citigroup, which received $45 billion in U.S. financial rescue

④ **Top-level example.** In June 2009, executives from four banks receiving bailout money from U.S. taxpayers were reported to have taken corporate jets for their "personal use"—code for vacation—as in flying one's family to a luxury resort in West Virginia. Knowing this, if you were a low-level bank employee, would you feel at all guilty if you phoned in "sick" to go to a ball game?

Source: Photograph by Sally Lindsay.

⑤ An ethical mortgage lender. CitiMortgage, headquartered in St. Louis, became a leader in doing everything possible to avert foreclosures. CEO Sanjiv Das exemplifies the kind of executive we could all hope to see more of. His dedication to keeping mortgage holders in their homes during hard times represents an ethical model that many other bankers failed to live up to. Do you know any businesspeople whose ethics are exceptional?

funds. Gloom among employees was augmented by the wave of foreclosure filings crippling the housing market.

Fighting these problems became the job of CitiMortgage's new CEO Sanjiv Das, appointed in 2008 to head the St. Louis–headquartered company. The India-born Das, then 47, said one of his goals was to bolster employee morale and another was to avert foreclosures. To those ends, he helped pioneer a first-of-a-kind program at the bank to help homeowners who lost their jobs by allowing them to lower mortgage payments for three months while they looked for new jobs. He also promoted loan modifications, finding a way to keep six delinquent borrowers in their homes for every one foreclosed upon. ⑤

"Our mantra to [employees] is very clear," Das said. "It's about keeping people in their homes." He drew upon his value system as the son of an Indian army officer to nurture morale by expressing purpose and integrity. "The No. 1 thing I talk about are the customers. Each day, my business is to keep them in their homes, no matter what." ■

2 The Firm Tries to Hire the Right Employees: "We Want Honest, Responsible People Working Here"

What can companies do to screen job applicants?

Few companies deliberately try to hire dishonest, irresponsible employees, but how do you screen them out? One common method is to have personality tests, but people have found ways to cheat on these.[28] Another is to run applicants through E-Verify, the federal program that allows employers to quickly check out the legal status of potential employees and remove illegal immigrants.[29] Finally, of course, they must check—really check—applicants' résumés and references. (We discuss applicant screening in considerable detail in Chapter 11.)

BRIEFING / BUSINESS CULTURE & ETIQUETTE

Who Will You Ask to Write You a Reference? (And Don't Forget to Thank Them.) Getting ready to apply for that first job? Hope you're one of those great people that companies are always looking for? The application effort can't begin too early, as you need to think about the people you will ask to write personal recommendations for you. For most students, it will be their instructors, who are frequently valued by employers for their insight into students' work habits. (And, by the way, good class attendance and participation definitely work in your favor in getting a reference.)

But here's something important to know: *Whenever people do you a favor, you need to write a note or e-mail to thank them.* Think that's obvious? Actually, many people think that "politeness and manners seem to have gone the way of the dinosaurs."[30] One woman high up in a large cosmetics company decided to refuse to help fellow alumni from her prestigious university. The reason: Over an 18-month period, she had gone out of her way to help six alumni network into new jobs. In response to all her efforts, not a single one took the time to thank her.[31]

Thus, when instructors write you references, be sure to *thank* them. By sending them a note. It's clearly the right thing to do. (And, from a purely selfish standpoint, you need to realize you may need their help again someday.) ■

3 There Are Ethics Codes & Training Programs: "We Need to Tell Employees What We Expect of Them"

What are two kinds of ethics codes?

A *code of ethics* consists of a written set of ethical standards to help guide an organization's actions. Most codes state top management's expectations for employees, offering guidance on how to treat customers, suppliers, and competitors and prohibiting conflicts of interest, bribery, and making false accounting statements. JCPenney, for instance, is well known for its code of ethics and customer service called "Penney Principles."

ⓘ
Want to Know More? 2-6
What Are "Penney Principles"?
Go to www.mybizlab.com.

Two Kinds of Ethics Codes: Compliance-Based & Integrity-Based

Ethics codes may be either *compliance-based* or *integrity-based*.

Compliance-Based Ethics Codes. *Compliance-based ethics codes* **attempt to prevent criminal misconduct by increasing control and by punishing violators.** For instance, many companies ask employees to sign nondisclosure agreements in which they acknowledge that if they leak confidential information about products under development they can be fired and even sued.

■ **Example of Compliance-Based Ethics Code: Apple, Maker of Computers and iPods.** Few companies "are more secretive than Apple," according to a *New York Times* story, "or as punitive to those who dare violate the company's rules."[32] Employees are fired for leaking news to outsiders. Everyone must sign nondisclosure agreements. Those working on priority projects must pass through a maze of security doors. When then-CEO Steve Jobs had a liver transplant in 2009, the news was kept secret until he was safely back at work.[33] ■

Integrity-Based Ethics Codes. *Integrity-based ethics codes* **attempt to enable responsible employee conduct by creating an environment that supports ethically desirable behavior.** This approach stresses a culture of fair play, honesty, and diversity and emphasizes shared accountability among employees.

■ **Example of Integrity-Based Ethics Code: Innocent, Maker of Little Tasty Drinks.** British smoothie maker Innocent—"We call them innocent because our drinks are always completely pure, fresh, and unadulterated," says the company's website—has become known not only for healthy ingredients but also for its social commitment. By giving 10% of its profits to charity, providing help to the homeless, and using recycled bottles, Innocent strives to create a culture of ethical and socially responsible behavior. In 2009, Coca-Cola acquired a minority stake in the company.[34] ■

Ethics Training & Ethics Officers

To reinforce the ethics codes, many companies provide ethics training, often presenting employees with possible ethical dilemmas they may eventually encounter. Large companies frequently have an ethics office, headed by an ethics officer. **The job of the *ethics officer* is to integrate the organization's ethics and values initiatives, compliance activities, and business conduct practices into the company's decision-making processes.** Companies with ethics officers include the Chase Corporation, Microsoft, and Yahoo. ⑥

⑥ **Yahoo and ethics in China.** In 2007, the Internet-services company hired its first chief compliance and ethics officer. This followed a board meeting in which Yahoo was criticized for cooperating with the Chinese government on censorship as well as providing information about a Yahoo Mail user, a Chinese journalist, who was arrested and sentenced to 10 years. Do you think getting an ethics officer could sometimes be a company's way of whitewashing a problem?

Source: Lou Linwei/Alamy.

Sign of Major Ethical Problems: When Insiders Blow the Whistle

Do I think of a whistleblower as being a "snitch"?

Sometimes a company develops an ethical climate the hard way—by having its dirty laundry exposed by a ***whistleblower*, an employee who reports organizational misconduct to the government or the public,** such as corruption, fraud, overcharging, waste, or health and safety problems. Doug Durand, in "Winners & Losers" at the start of this chapter, is one such example. Another is John Kopchinski, a former pharmaceutical salesman who earned more than $51.5 million for a whistleblower lawsuit against Pfizer, the world's largest drugmaker, found guilty of promoting drugs for unapproved uses and doses.[35]

Although employers have been prohibited by health and safety laws from firing employees who report workplace hazards, in earlier years about two-thirds were fired anyway.[36] Then, in 2002, the Sarbanes-Oxley Act (discussed below) became law, giving whistleblowers protection from retaliation. Still, taking the brave step of exposing corporate wrongdoing usually comes at a cost. Although the public rightfully regards whistleblowers as heroes, employers and fellow employees may consider them "snitches."

White-Collar Fraud & the Sarbanes-Oxley Reform Act

What is Sarbanes-Oxley?

Bernard Madoff was considered one of the world's most successful investors, founder of the Wall Street firm Bernard L. Madoff Investment Securities LLC. Then in December 2008, as the U.S. economy spiraled downward, Madoff confessed to his sons that his investments were all "one big lie"—not investments at all, but rather a $50 billion ***Ponzi scheme*, using cash from newer investors to pay off older ones.** (Ponzi scheme was named for Charles Ponzi, an Italian immigrant who practiced the fraud in the early 1900s, although the scheme itself is far older.) Madoff's "offenses only came to light," says one report, "because he could no longer raise the money [a consequence of the Great Recession] to keep his scheme going."[37] A few months later, the perpetrator of possibly the world's biggest fraud, then age 71, was sentenced to 150 years in prison.[38] ❼

Madoff joins a long list of business scoundrels whose names came to light in the early 21st century. Earlier there were Tyco International CEO Dennis Kozlowski (now serving prison time for grand larceny, securities fraud, and other crimes), WorldCom head Bernard Ebbers (doing 25 years for fraud), Adelphia CEO John Rigas (15 years for conspiracy and bank fraud), and former Enron chief Jeffrey Skilling (24 years for similar white-collar crimes). The various forms of deceit practiced by Skilling, Rigas, and other top-level managers generated a great deal of public outrage that ultimately led to reform legislation known as Sarbanes-Oxley.

Source: Mug Shot/Alamy.

❼ **Bernard Madoff.** Perpetrator of possibly the greatest fraud in history, Madoff was sentenced to 150 years in prison. Over a period of 25 years, he defrauded investors of between $12 billion and $20 billion. He is scheduled to be released from prison on November 14, 2159.

The *Sarbanes-Oxley Act of 2002,* often known simply as *SOX* or *SarbOx,* established protections for whistleblowers and requirements for proper financial record keeping for public companies and penalties for noncompliance. Besides protecting whistleblowers from company retaliation (providing for reinstatement and back pay for those who have been punished by their employers), the law requires a firm's chief executive officer and chief financial officer to personally certify the organization's financial reports, along with various other provisions and requirements. (*See* ■ *Panel 2.2.*)

Want to Know More? 2-8

More about White-Collar Criminals

Go to www.mybizlab.com.

■ **PANEL 2.2 Sarbanes-Oxley: Principal provisions.**

1. Protects whistleblowers (people who report company fraud to the government) from employer retaliation.

2. Provides for job reinstatement and back pay to whistleblowers who are punished by their employers.

3. Requires public corporations to institute systems for employees to anonymously report auditing and accounting issues.

4. Prohibits alteration or destruction of key audit documents under pain of severe criminal penalties.

5. Requires a firm's chief executive officer (CEO) and chief financial officer (CFO) to personally certify the organization's financial reports.

6. Prohibits CEO, CFO, and company directors from taking personal loans or lines of credit from the company.

7. Requires CEO and CFO to reimburse the company for bonuses and stock options when required by restatement of corporate profits.

8. Requires the company to have established procedures and guidelines for audit committees.

9. Establishes the Public Company Accounting Oversight Board, a five-member committee under the Securities and Exchange Commission charged with overseeing the accounting industry.

THE BIG IDEA: Corporate social responsibility is concern for taking actions that will benefit society. This section also considers blended value, measuring results in both economic and social areas, and social auditing to evaluate corporate social responsibility.

THE ESSENTIAL QUESTION: What are corporate social responsibility, blended value, and social auditing?

MyBizLab: Check your understanding of these concepts at www.mybizlab.com.

If ethical responsibility is about being a good individual citizen, *corporate social responsibility (CSR)* is about being a good organizational citizen. As we said, CSR is a concern for taking actions that will benefit the interests of society as well as the organization. These may range from sponsorship of Little League sports teams to sending supplies to earthquake victims.

Is Corporate Social Responsibility a Good Idea? Two Views

What are the arguments for and against corporate social responsibility?

It used to be that a company's most important goal was to make money pretty much any way it wanted, regardless of the consequences. Today, however, many for-profit enterprises make a point of contributing to society as well as deriving profit from it.[39]

The Case for CSR: "Companies Aren't Separate from Society"

There are three primary arguments for corporate social responsibility:

First, since businesses create some problems (such as environmental pollution), they should help to solve them; after all, companies aren't separate from the rest of society. For example, as one writer put it, "the prices people pay for gasoline, electric power, and other energy products don't reflect their true costs, among them the impact of greenhouse gases."[40] ⑧

Second, business firms often have the resources to solve problems that the nonprofit sector does not. Thus, while they have no obligation to do so, they can make a big difference if they choose to commit to major support.

Finally, being socially responsible gives companies a positive public image that can help head off government regulation.

Thus, in the opinion of economist Paul Samuelson, who recently passed away, a company should be concerned with society's welfare as well as corporate profits. "A large corporation these days not only may engage in social responsibility," he said, "it had damned well better try to do so."[41] The same, of course, could be said about small corporations and even mom-and-pop businesses.

⑧ **Whose problem?** If fossil fuels contribute to climate change, including such effects as melting ice caps, should energy companies be held accountable? What should they do by way of making amends, if anything?

Source: siloto/Shutterstock.

The Case against CSR: "Companies Should Just Make Profits"

"The social responsibility of business is to make profits," wrote the late economist Milton Friedman in a famous 1970 article.[42] "There is one and only one social responsibility of business—to use its resources and engage in activities designed to increase its profits so long as it stays within the rules of the game, which is to say, engages in open and free competition without deception or fraud." (Note the stress on "without deception"—deception, unfortunately, often being considered within fair bounds by some businesspeople.)

Friedman argued that if a firm was distracted from its mission of maximizing profits, it would fail to provide goods and services and benefit its stockholders, thereby also failing to create jobs and expand economic growth—the real social justification for the company's existence.

More and more, however, companies are finding that being socially responsible can actually enhance profits (a point we take up again in Section 2.4).

Want to Know More? 2-9
Paul Samuelson's Famous Article
Go to www.mybizlab.com.

Want to Know More? 2-10
Milton Friedman's Famous Article
Go to www.mybizlab.com.

BRIEFING / EARNING GREEN BY GOING GREEN
Subaru Proves Going Green Can Lower, Not Increase, Costs.
The conventional wisdom is that adopting environmentally friendly processes adds to the cost of doing business. But companies can do well by doing good. "No one disputes that it's expensive to cap smokestacks and process hazardous waste," observe two management scholars. "But . . . the focus shouldn't be on cleaning up and its costs—the focus should be on creating less mess to begin with."[43]

For 20 years, the Lafayette plant of Subaru of Indiana Automotive pursued green initiatives during the course of manufacturing 800 vehicles a day. "With employees at every level of the plant looking for ways to save energy, reduce waste, and generally make processes more efficient," report the scholars, "one measure of its success is a 14% reduction in electricity consumption . . . since 2000. An even bigger achievement: It has not shipped any waste to a landfill [since 2004]." ❾

Source: Photo Courtesy of Subaru of Indiana Automotive, Inc.

❾ **Subaru of Indiana Automotive.** In a state that lost 46,000 auto jobs in the last decade, Subaru has never resorted to layoffs and in fact has given workers a wage increase every year. One of the major ways the company has achieved this is through a relentless focus on recycling, reducing water use by 50%, and composting 98% of the plant's waste—paper, plastic, glass, metals, and so on. Could this approach be applied to all American industry?

Some lessons to be drawn: (1) Profits come by increasing efficiency and reducing waste, although they don't always come immediately. (2) Management leadership is vital in setting goals and getting departments to cooperate. (3) Frontline workers have to be engaged in finding ways to reduce, reuse, and recycle. (4) Suppliers must be similarly involved, as in steel suppliers providing rolls of steel of exact dimensions. (5) All wastes must be considered potential products, as in cafeteria waste being sent to a waste-to-energy power plant. (6) Green initiatives give a company competitive advantages, as in reducing costs and conserving energy. [44] ■

Blended Value: Measuring Results in Both Economic & Social Areas

Can business success be judged by other ways than profit?

"We tend to categorize value as economic or social," says Jed Emerson, a managing director of Uhuru Capital Management. "You either work for a nonprofit that creates social value or you work for a for-profit that creates economic value."[45]

In reality, however, nonprofits (which represent 7% of the U.S. gross domestic product—the total dollar value of all goods and services produced) contribute economic value too, because they create jobs and consume goods and services. Conversely, for-profits create social value, as well: They pay taxes that support local communities, produce products that better people's lives, and create jobs that keep family units stable. Emerson has proposed the yardstick of **blended value, in which the outcome of all business investments should be measured in both economic and social realms.** "There is no 'trade off' between the two," he states, "but rather a concurrent pursuit of value—both social and financial. The two operate together, in concert, at all times."[46]

Source: Ron Cortes KRT/Newscom.

⑩ **Triple bottom line.** Judy Wicks, who founded the White Dog Café in Philadelphia, believes that "Profit is a tool. The major purpose of business is to serve." More specifically, she adheres to the concept that profits are only one goal of local business; the other elements of the "triple bottom line" are the fostering of social and environmental consciousness. Do you agree with this?

BRIEFING / SMALL BUSINESS & ENTREPRENEURS

The White Dog Café Expresses Blended Value in the "Triple Bottom Line." Judy Wicks, who founded the White Dog Café in Philadelphia 28 years ago, has her own view of what business should do. "Profit is a tool," she says. "The major purpose of business is to serve."[47]

After opening her restaurant, Wicks realized she was spending so much time making it work that the only way to be socially active was through her business. Thus, the White Dog became known for buying its electricity from wind power, obtaining produce from organic farmers, and getting meat, poultry, and fish from producers practicing humane treatment of animals. Wicks also opened up the restaurant as an educational forum with guest speakers and to share ideas with competitors.

"Our customers and employees share our values," she says, "and come here for a sense of community, for a chance to be aligned with something greater than themselves." ⑩

Wicks is also cofounder of the Business Alliance for Local Living Economies, a nonprofit network established in 2001 to promote the "triple bottom line," the concept that local business should not only be profitable but also foster social and environmental consciousness. ■

Social Auditing: Evaluating Corporate Social Responsibility

How can I evaluate a company's social performance?

The obvious problem with the blended-value idea is that it is fairly easy to measure progress in financial performance but not so easy to measure social performance (such as environmental value). It has been only in the last few years that society has been grappling with environmental impacts, for example. Thus, Emerson believes, it may well take several years to learn how to adequately track and report social value.

Fortunately, there is already a tool for evaluating socially responsible business activities, and it is called *social auditing*. **A *social audit* is a systematic assessment of a company's performance in implementing socially responsible programs, often based on predefined goals.**

Some examples of the goals are as follows.

1 Corporate Policy: Positions on Political & Social Issues

Corporate policy **describes the positions a company takes on political and social issues.** Many companies take positions on environmental matters. Example: Owners of the New Belgium Brewery decided at the outset that the Fort Collins, Colorado, beer maker would be kind to the environment, and it became the first U.S. brewery to be powered entirely by wind.[48]

2 Community Activities: Sponsorship, Fund-Raising, Donations, & Other Support

Many companies contribute to the United Way, sponsor sports teams, buy ads in school newspapers, donate to museums, enable employees to volunteer time to charities, and support similar community activities. Example: Comet Skateboards of Oakland, California, is a backer of the Hood Games in East Oakland and South Central Los Angeles, community events featuring skateboarding, music, and fashion.[49] Hood Games events provide a way for youths, skateboarders, musicians, and others to perform, with events and merchandise being used to enrich the community. ⑪

3 Cause-Related Marketing: Supporting Worthy Causes

Cause-related marketing, **or simply *cause marketing,* is a commercial activity in which a business forms a partnership with a charity or nonprofit to support a worthy cause, product, or service.** Example: If you subscribe to cell-phone company CREDO Mobile, every time you make a phone call the company will make a donation to nonprofit groups like the Alliance for Climate Protection or Human Rights Watch.

4 Social Entrepreneurship: Leveraging Business for Social Change

Social entrepreneurship **is defined as innovative, social value–creating activity that can occur within or across for-profit or nonprofit sectors.** The focus is generally on creating social value rather than shareholder wealth. The activity is also characterized by innovation, or the creation of something new, rather than simply repeating existing business practices.[50]

■ **Example of Social Entrepreneurship: Acción Makes Small Loans to the Poor.** When *Fast Company* magazine named 43 entrepreneurial organizations for its 2007 Social Capitalist Award, it singled out firms working in areas such as antipoverty, literacy, and the environment that were trying to make a difference by applying free-market solutions to some of the world's oldest problems. Examples are microlending institutions such as Acción International, which provides poor clients with loans for as little as $100 with which to start businesses.[51] Another such microcredit organization is Wokai, founded by two 25-year-old San Francisco–area women to aid small entrepreneurs in China.[52] ■

Source: Warren Goldswain/Shutterstock.

⑪ **Comet Skateboards supports Hood Games.** Many companies support various community activities— at least during economic good times. Comet Skateboards is a bit unusual in supporting street competitions in minority neighborhoods, such as this one in East Oakland, California. What would be another cool thing for a company to sponsor?

Want to Know More? 2-11

What Companies Rank High for Social Responsibility?

Go to www.mybizlab.com.

Source: Christopher Crane.

⑫ **Sustainability.** Founded in 2001 by Tom Szaky, then a 20-year-old Princeton University freshman, TerraCycle is an eco-friendly innovator that converts non-recyclable or hard-to-recycle waste into over 1,500 different products, such as those shown here. People and organizations who join one of its "brigades" are paid to collect and send waste to them, such as used snack bags and drink pouches.

5 Sustainability: "Green Is Good"

Sustainability **is defined as economic development that meets the needs of the present without compromising the ability of future generations to meet their own needs.**[53] Companies large and small have launched green marketing campaigns promoting environmentally friendly causes, products, or stores.[54] ⑫ Example: By using recycled textiles in his products, Rob Anderson transformed Interface, a Georgia carpet manufacturer he founded, into the world's first billion-dollar sustainable company—"taking nothing from the earth that is not rapidly and naturally renewable, and doing no harm to the biosphere."[55]

6 Philanthropy: "Not Dying Rich"

"He who dies rich dies thus disgraced." So said 1880s steel manufacturer Andrew Carnegie, after he turned from making money to *philanthropy,* **making charitable donations to benefit humankind.** Carnegie became well known as a supporter of free public libraries, among other good works.

More recently, Microsoft's Bill Gates, one of the richest persons in the world, announced he would focus on spending billions from his foundation on health, education, and overcoming poverty.[56] In 2010, Gates and fellow philanthropist Warren Buffett were joined by director George Lucas, Oracle database billionaire Larry Ellison, and 38 other megawealthy people who pledged to donate the majority of their riches to charity.[57]

Not only individuals, but also companies practice philanthropy.

◼ **Example of Philanthropy: Mary Kay Contributes to Organizations Working to Stem Violence against Women.** The Mary Kay Foundation, created by the late cosmetics company founder Mary Kay Ash, has made donations to organizations that work to stem violence against women, awarding more than $11 million in grants to shelters for women and children in all 50 states. In 2005, it also lobbied Congress to commit more than $500 million in federal funds to combat domestic violence, sexual assault, and stalking.[58] ◼

Key Takeaway 2-2
A social audit may assess a firm's corporate policy, community activities, cause-related marketing, social entrepreneurship, sustainability, and philanthropy.

THE BIG IDEA: It might be expected that customers and the community should benefit from ethical behavior and corporate social responsibility, but this section also shows how owners, employees, and suppliers benefit as well.

THE ESSENTIAL QUESTION: In what ways do customers, owners, employees, suppliers, and the community benefit from ethics and corporate social responsibility (CSR)?

MyBizLab: Check your understanding of these concepts at www.mybizlab.com.

MyBizLab

When all is said and done, why *should* a company be ethical and socially responsible? A close look suggests there are practical reasons for doing good—reasons important to any hardheaded businessperson.

The Negative Effects of Being Bad

What are ways that illegal behavior can hurt a company?

"It takes 10 years to build up your company's reputation," says legendary investor Warren Buffett, "but 10 seconds for you to lose it."[59] Indeed, Buffett found his own reputation diminished overnight after one of his executives pocketed $3 million from trading in the stock of a chemical company Buffett's firm was acquiring.[60]

Illegal behavior can result in whopping jail sentences and fines, as we have seen. Unethical or illegal behavior can also damage not only a company's reputation but its finances as well, as follows.

High Costs of Employee Fraud

Employee fraud, which can occur because of workers' perceptions of employer unfairness, mistreatment, or management hypocrisy, costs employers about 5% of every dollar earned. Frauds by executives are particularly costly, resulting in a median loss of $723,000.[61] ⓭

Diminished Stock Price

In one survey, 74% of people polled said their perception of a company's honesty affected their decision about whether to buy its stock.[62] The announcement of certain kinds of illegalities—tax evasion, bribery, or violations of government contracts—can hurt a company's stock price, according to some research.[63] Other research shows that investments in unethical firms earn abnormally negative returns for long periods of time.[64]

Diminished Sales Growth

A company convicted of illegal activity may suffer from diminished sales growth that lasts far longer than the damage to the stock price—indeed, it may last for several years.[65]

⓭ **Fraud.** Dell Computer confessed that for four years it improperly inflated reports of financial results. The two most common fraud schemes are corruption, which the Association of Certified Fraud Examiners says occurs in 27% of all cases, and fraudulent billing schemes, which occur in 24%. Financial statement fraud is the most costly type, with a median loss of $2 million in 2008. Have you heard or read about any employee fraud happening with a firm located near you?

Source: iDesign/Shutterstock.

Want to Know More? 2-12

More about the Effects of Lawsuits

Go to www.mybizlab.com.

Damaging Lawsuits

Lawsuits resulting from a company's illegal behavior can clearly hurt its profitability. The executives and directors of former energy company Enron were sued for inflating earnings to drive up the stock price (and collect $1.1 billion in profits on the stock they personally owned).

The Positive Effects of Being Good

How do stakeholders benefit from a firm's good behavior?

There are positive—and proven—reasons for a firm to observe sound ethical and socially responsible practices.

Benefiting Customers

Ethical and socially conscious businesses may actually enjoy a competitive edge with customers. The evidence: In one survey, 80% of the people polled said they decide to buy a firm's goods or services partly on their perception of its ethics.[66] In another survey, 72% of adults said they would rather buy products and services from a company with ethical business practices and higher prices than from a company with questionable business practices and lower prices.[67] In a third survey, 76% of the people polled said they would switch from their current brand to one associated with a good cause if price and quality were equal.[68] Finally, 88% of respondents in a fourth survey said they were more apt to buy from companies that are socially responsible than from companies that are not.[69]

Benefiting Owners

In general, studies show, profitability is enhanced by a company's reputation for honesty and corporate citizenship.[70] In addition, companies that made a public commitment to ethics have been found to have a higher market value than companies that merely adopted an ethics code or those that didn't have an ethics code at all.[71]

⑭ **Ending child hunger.** ConAgra's campaign to end child hunger benefits everyone: hungry children, the company's brands, and of course ConAgra's owners—the stockholders.

Source: Courtesy of ConAgra Foods.

BRIEFING / LEGAL & ETHICAL PRACTICES

A Food Giant Benefits Its Owners by Feeding Hungry Children. American food companies have come under attack for designing foods that cause obesity, a matter that threatens sales and profitability and the owners' investments.[72] The industry responds that it has modified more than 10,000 recipes to reduce calories and changed children's TV ads to showcase healthy choices such as 100% fruit juice.[73]

Omaha-based ConAgra Foods has gone beyond these moves in backing a campaign called "Child Hunger Ends Here," using TV specials and social media and providing 250 million pounds of food to Feeding America, a group that supplies food banks. ConAgra is also donating one meal for each eight-digit package code—up to 2.5 million meals—on specially marked ConAgra brands, such as Chef Boyardee, Healthy Choice, and Marie Callender's. ⑭

Many consumers think marketing campaigns that link a company to a social cause are done "only for publicity and marketing purposes, not because they truly care about the issue," says one account.[74] However, some firms have risen above that bar—Pepsi, Tide, Nike, and Newman's Own being identified as those that "place as much importance on supporting a social cause as they place on profit." ∎

Benefiting Employees

A National Business Ethics Survey found that 79% of employees said their firms' concern for ethics was a key reason they continued to work at their respective companies.[75] This is particularly true for members of the younger generation, who, points out *BusinessWeek,* are "demanding more attention to stakeholders and seeking more from their jobs than just 9-to-5 work hours and a steady paycheck." As a result, companies such as Home Depot (which committed to building 100,000 affordable green homes and planting 3 million trees) are trying to become more socially responsible to help attract these and other workers.[76]

In addition, responsible behavior can improve the quality of a company's job applicants. In one study of 1,020 people surveyed online, 83% rated a company's record of business ethics as "very important" when deciding whether to accept a job offer (only 2% rated it "unimportant").[77]

Benefiting Suppliers

One way in which CSR-conscious companies can be beneficial is in insisting on the elimination of *sweatshop* working conditions among suppliers. **A *sweatshop* is a shop, factory, or farm in which employees work long hours at low wages— or no wages, in the case of prison or slave and some child labor—usually under environmentally, physically, or mentally abusive conditions.**

Although we may tend to think that sweatshops exist mainly in developing countries, they can also be found in the United States in some garment factories and upholstery shops and on some farms employing illegal immigrants.[78] When suppliers' standards are raised, not only do their employees benefit but so do the vendors themselves, who may attract a better client base.

Benefiting the Local & National Community

When a socially responsible company gives its employees time off for voluntary activities, supports social causes, or donates money, goods, and services, it clearly benefits the community.

■ **Example of Benefiting the Community: Hurricane Katrina Victims Benefit from Corporate Goodwill—and So Do the Donors.** After Hurricane Katrina destroyed much of New Orleans and the Gulf Coast, corporations responded generously.

Papa John's employees handed out thousands of pizzas. Emigrant Savings Bank deposited $1,000 into the account of each customer in the areas hardest hit. General Electric donated millions of dollars of cash and equipment, including a mobile power plant. Biotechnology company Amgen donated $2.5 million. Georgia Pacific sent 65 truckloads of consumer goods. Walmart donated 18 vacant buildings to relief agencies. Pfizer sent a steady stream of drugs.

While such measures certainly generate goodwill, they also serve to publicize the firms' business or products.[79] ■

Benefiting the International Community

Should a firm buy goods produced by a country employing slave labor? Should it pay bribes to get its imports through another country's borders? Should it be concerned about global climate change? By the actions it pursues, a corporation can make an important difference in such matters.

It can also benefit itself by helping to shape the laws and regulations emerging that govern corporate behavior at regional or international levels. The thinking goes: If regulation is coming anyway, "let's play a part in shaping the rules of the game and leveling the playing field."[80]

 BRIEFING / GLOBAL BUSINESS
Unilever Benefits the International Community by Addressing Important World Problems. Unilever, a $40 billion Dutch-British rival to Procter & Gamble, isn't concerned just with selling consumer

tissue, soap, and detergent. It also wants to help fight poverty, water scarcity, and the effects of climate change. For instance, the company helps women in remote Indian villages start microenterprises, finances eco-friendly "drip" irrigation for farmers, recycles waste at a toothpaste factory, operates a free community laundry in a Brazilian slum, and is reducing carbon dioxide emissions at its factories.

The reasons are not just for public relations. "Some 40% of the company's sales and most of its growth now take place in developing nations," according to *BusinessWeek*. Moreover, "as environmental regulations grow tighter around the world, Unilever must invest in green technologies or its leadership in packaged foods, soaps, and other goods could be imperiled."[81] ∎

One important consequence of the focus on good global corporate citizenship is the ***Global Compact*, a voluntary agreement established in 2000 by the United Nations that promotes human rights, good labor practices, environmental protection, and anticorruption standards for businesses.** (See ∎ *Panel 2.3.*) About 3,000 businesses (including Nike, Levi Strauss, and Hewlett-Packard) from more than 100 countries have signed the compact.[82]

∎ **PANEL 2.3 The 10 principles of the U.N. Global Compact.** These are intended to promote social and environmental principles for businesses. Why would any company refuse to sign on to and abide by these principles?

Principles	Business should . . .
Human Rights	1. support and respect the protection of internationally proclaimed human rights; and
	2. make sure that they are not complicit in human rights abuses.
Labor Standards	3. uphold the freedom of association and the effective recognition of the right to collective bargaining;
	4. uphold the elimination of all forms of forced and compulsory labor;
	5. uphold the abolition of child labor; and
	6. uphold the elimination of discrimination in employment and occupation.
Environment	7. support a precautionary approach to environmental challenges;
	8. undertake initiatives to promote environmental responsibility; and
	9. encourage the development and diffusion of environmentally friendly technologies.
Anti-corruption	10. work against corruption in all its forms, including extortion and bribery.

Source: United Nations Global Compact, www.unglobalcompact.org/AboutTheGC/TheTenPrinciples/ index.html (accessed April 25, 2011).

Interdependency in Solving Common Problems: The Threat of Global Climate Change

Is climate change forcing closer cooperation among the countries and companies of the world?

"There is really no such thing as nature untainted by people," an article in *Science* points out. Indeed, as of 1995, only 17% of the world's land area remained directly uninfluenced by humans, and the amount is surely less by now.[83]

That human footprint, most scientists believe, has contributed to what has been called "the most compelling issue of our time": *global warming,* or *global climate change,* **an increase in the average temperature of the earth's atmosphere.**[84] Scientists generally agree global warming is caused by the emission of carbon dioxide produced by the burning of fossil fuels and industrial pollutants. The foreseeable effects are nothing short of the greatest calamity: more severe hurricanes and tornadoes, more lightning and wildfires, melting glaciers, rising sea levels, crop devastation, and changing animal migrations. A 2006 report by economist Nicholas Stern found that if no action is taken to control greenhouse gas emissions, the costs and risks of climate change "will be equivalent to losing at least 5% of global GDP [gross domestic product] each year, now and forever."[85]

Can Climate Change Be Reversed?

Is it possible to reverse the serious environmental consequences from the changing climate? Irreversible effects on plants, animals, farming, and weather are already apparent. The glaciers in Glacier National Park have decreased in number from 150 to 26 since 1850. The snows of Mt. Kilimanjaro are soon to be history. Shrinking sea ice may reduce the number of polar bears by two-thirds by 2050.[86] Many scientists take the gloomy view that there may be no return.[87]

To be sure, there are some aggressive attempts to rein in energy use. For example, environment ministers in Europe, citing their moral duty to future generations, have agreed to cut greenhouse gas emissions 20% below 1990 levels by 2020.[88] As for the two largest greenhouse gas–producing countries (40% of the world's total), the United States pledged in 2009 to cut emissions 17% from 2005 levels by 2020, and China announced it would cut emissions 40% to 45% by that year.[89] Left unanswered are questions of how both nations will achieve such cuts.

BRIEFING / EARNING GREEN BY GOING GREEN

What Can Business Do to Fight Climate Change? In the United States, the U.S. Chamber of Commerce, which is supposed to represent the views of business, has been most resistant to climate change legislation.[90] However, a number of companies, including Apple and Pacific Gas & Electric, resigned from the Chamber in protest.[91] Perhaps, then, business can begin to take the lead. After years of being slow to address climate change, major corporations—including industrial giants that make products ranging from electricity to chemicals to bulldozers—have begun to call for limits on global warming emissions.[92] Five reasons for this change are shown at right. *(See* ■ *Panel 2.4.)*

One way that has been proposed to reduce emission of greenhouse gases is for the world's nations to level a global carbon tax on anyone who drives a car or uses electricity produced by fossil fuels, with some tax revenues being used to help the poor and the middle class.[93] A second system is "cap and trade," in which governments mandate limits (caps) on carbon emissions and give companies emission-reduction allowances (credits) to emit specific amounts. If a company doesn't reach its cap, it can trade its credits to other firms that need to increase their emission allowances.[94] ■

■ **PANEL 2.4 Five reasons why business has become interested in climate change.**

1. **More awareness of social responsibility.** There is a growing awareness that climate change could ruin corporate leaders who continue to deny it. Corporations have become aware that their existence, like the rest of the world, is connected to the environment.

2. **Desire to influence regulation.** Some companies believe government regulation of carbon dioxide emissions is inevitable, and they want to have a say in policy making, so as to reduce the burden on themselves.

3. **Saving on energy use.** High fuel prices punish inefficiency. Making transportation, manufacturing, and workplace heating and cooling more efficient reduces energy use and saves money—as well as reduces carbon emissions.

4. **Finding new markets.** Some companies see lucrative new markets in clean-energy technologies, such as materials used in solar cells, wind turbines, fuel cells, and lightweight automobiles, which will all become more desirable in a world in which carbon emissions carry a cost.

5. **Desire to crush competition.** Being first to market with an environmentally friendly product—as Toyota has been with its hybrid Prius, which runs on both gasoline and electricity—is a way of beating competitors.

What You Can Do: The "Civic Generation" Can Be a Force for Change

What are two ways I could be an "activist doer"?

If you're a young adult born between 1982 and 2000—part of the so-called Millennial Generation—you are an "activist doer," a member of the most civic-minded generation since those of the 1930s and 1940s, according to experts.[95]

Is there a way you can take this impulse to serve and exercise it in the business world? Let's consider how you might go about it.

Working with Companies as an Intern to Advise on Saving Energy

An *intern* **is a student or a recent graduate who undergoes supervised practical training in a business setting.** (We discuss interning further in Chapter 11.) Recently, some companies have been bringing in student interns during the summer to help them analyze their energy use under a program called the Climate Corps fellowship supported by the Environmental Defense Fund.[96]

Want to Know More? 2-13
Explore the Environmental Defense Fund's Climate Corps
Go to www.mybizlab.com.

Companies that included eBay, Hewlett-Packard, and Sony Pictures used the research and recommendations of several interns to save a total of $35 million over five years. Student John Joseph, for instance, helped Intuit, a Mountain View, California, software company, find how it could cut $500,000 a year from its energy bill through such steps as setting lights in the restrooms to turn off automatically when not in use.

Volunteering Your Services for Free

There's nothing to stop you from giving away your services. It's a good way to create goodwill that may lead to a paying job later.[97] Katherine Yaros, for instance, spent her freshman spring break from the University of Michigan–Dearborn building a wheelchair ramp so a paralyzed Detroit man could leave his home. The second year, she spent spring vacation working at a residential treatment center for troubled girls. "Volunteering is not such a casual thing anymore," says Yaros, 19. "Giving back is part of our own way of being empowered to create a positive change within the community."[98]

Summary

2.1 The Ethical & Social Responsibilities of Businesspeople: The Way You Live Matters

THE ESSENTIAL QUESTION: *What is the order of priorities for a businessperson?*

What's a way of framing my moral priorities? Archie Carroll's pyramid suggests a company or an individual should be profitable, obey the law, be ethical, and be a good corporate citizen—in that order.

How should I distinguish among values, ethics, laws, and corporate social responsibility? Values are the relatively permanent and deeply held underlying beliefs and attitudes that help determine people's behavior. Ethics are the standards of right and wrong that influence behavior. Laws are rules of conduct or action formally recognized as binding or enforced by a controlling authority. Corporate social responsibility (CSR) is a concern for taking actions that will benefit the interests of society as well as of the organization.

How would I recognize when I'm in an "ethical dilemma"? An ethical dilemma is a situation in which people have to decide whether to pursue a course of action that may benefit them or their organization but that is unethical or even illegal.

Why might I attribute purer motives to myself than to others? Illegal trading is the illegal use of private company information to further one's own fortunes or those of family or friends. People indulge in such practices perhaps because of the holier-than-thou effect: a self-inflated bias in which people make generous predictions about their own moral behavior and less generous predictions about their peers'. Some students at Harvard Business School signed an MBA oath, a voluntary student-led pledge of intention to serve the greater good rather than advance their own narrow interests.

2.2 Doing the Right Thing: How Organizations Can Promote Ethical Behavior

THE ESSENTIAL QUESTION: *What are four ways organizations can foster high ethical standards?*

Is top management support really necessary? If top managers wink at ethical problems, they fail to lead by example and make employees cynical.

What can companies do to screen job applicants? Managers check applicants by giving them personality tests, running them through E-Verify, and above all checking their résumés and references.

What are two kinds of ethics codes? A code of ethics consists of a formal written set of ethical standards guiding an organization's actions. There are two kinds of ethics codes: (1) Compliance-based codes attempt to prevent criminal misconduct by increasing control and by punishing violators.

(2) Integrity-based ethics codes attempt to enable responsible employee conduct by creating an environment that supports ethically desirable behavior. Some companies hire an ethics officer to integrate the organization's ethics and values initiatives, compliance activities, and business conduct practices into the company's decision-making practices.

Do I think of a whistleblower as being a "snitch"? A whistleblower is an employee who reports organizational misconduct to the government or the public.

What is Sarbanes-Oxley? Various kinds of business fraud inspired the Sarbanes-Oxley Act of 2002 (SOX or SarbOx), which establishes protections for whistleblowers and requirements for proper financial record keeping for public companies and penalties for noncompliance.

2.3 Corporate Social Responsibility: Concern for the Welfare of Society

THE ESSENTIAL QUESTION: *What are corporate social responsibility, blended value, and social auditing?*

What are the arguments for and against corporate social responsibility? The case for CSR is that (1) since businesses create some problems, they should help solve them; (2) business often has the resources to solve problems in ways that the nonprofit sector does not; and (3) being socially responsible gives businesses a favorable public image that can help head off government regulation. The case against CSR is that business has only one responsibility—to engage in activities designed to increase its profits so long as it engages in open and free competition without deception or fraud.

Can business success be judged by other ways than profit? The yardstick of blended value has been proposed, in which the outcome of all business investments should be measured in *both* economic and social realms.

How can I evaluate a company's social performance? One tool for evaluating socially responsible business activities is the social audit, a systematic assessment of a company's performance in implementing socially responsible programs, often based on predefined goals. Six examples of the goals are (1) corporate policy, which is the positions a company takes on political and social issues; (2) community activities a company contributes to; (3) cause-related marketing, a commercial activity in which a business forms a partnership with a charity or nonprofit to support a worthy cause, product, or service; (4) a company's social entrepreneurship, the innovative, social value–creating activity that can occur within or across for-profit or nonprofit sectors; (5) sustainability, economic development that meets the needs of the present without compromising the ability of future generations to meet their own needs; and (6) philanthropy, making charitable donations to benefit humankind.

2.4 The Payoffs from Doing Good: The Benefits to Stakeholders

THE ESSENTIAL QUESTION: *In what ways do customers, owners, employees, suppliers, and the community benefit from ethics and corporate social responsibility (CSR)?*

What are ways that illegal behavior can hurt a company? Ethical or illegal misbehavior can harm not only a company's reputation but also its finances, as in losses from employee fraud, diminished stock price, diminished sales growth, and damaging lawsuits.

How do stakeholders benefit from a firm's good behavior? Positive reasons for a firm's observing sound ethical and socially responsible practices are that it will benefit customers, owners, employees, suppliers, the local and national community, and the international community. Good corporate citizenship has resulted in the Global Compact, a voluntary agreement by the United Nations that promotes human rights, good labor practices, environmental protection, and anticorruption standards for businesses.

Is climate change forcing closer cooperation among the countries and companies of the world? Global climate change, the increase in the average temperature of the earth's atmosphere, is caused by the emission of carbon dioxide produced by the burning of fossil fuels and industrial pollutants. Irreversible effects on plants, animals, farming, and weather are already apparent. To rein in energy use, European governments have agreed to cut greenhouse gas emissions 20% below 1990 levels by 2020. The United States has pledged to cut emissions 17% and China has pledged to cut emissions 40% to 45% by that year.

What are two ways I could be an "activist doer"? One way is to become an intern—one who undergoes supervised training in a business setting—in a company where you might advise on saving energy, for instance. Another way is to volunteer your services for free as a way to create goodwill that may lead to a paying job later.

Key Terms

MyBizLab

blended value 46
cause-related marketing 47
code of ethics 40
compliance-based ethics codes 41
corporate policy 47
corporate social responsibility (CSR) 36
ethical dilemma 36
ethics 35
ethics officer 42

global climate change 53
Global Compact 52
global corporate social responsibility pyramid 34
global warming 53
insider trading 37
integrity-based ethics codes 42
intern 54
laws 35
MBA oath 37

philanthropy 48
Ponzi scheme 42
Sarbanes-Oxley Act of 2002 43
social audit 47
social entrepreneurship 47
sustainability 48
sweatshop 51
values 35
whistleblower 42

Pop Quiz Prep

1. According to the global corporate social responsibility pyramid, what priority is at the top of the pyramid?

2. What is the definition of *ethics*?

3. How do companies use E-Verify with regard to job applicants?

4. What is the nature of a compliance-based ethics code?

5. What is a common argument against corporate social responsibility?

6. What is a problem with the blended-value idea?

7. What is the Global Compact?

8. What are the potential consequences to a company for ignoring unethical or illegal behavior?

Critical Thinking Questions

1. Do you think it's ethical to surf the Web for personal use on the company's dime? What, if any, do you believe is an adequate amount of time employees should be allowed to use the Internet for nonwork-related purposes?

2. Can you give examples of companies that, in your experience, are responsible corporate citizens? How did you learn of their efforts, and specifically what are these efforts? Are you more inclined to purchase things from these types of companies?

3. In the past, were you ever motivated to purchase a product related to cause marketing, such as the Pink Ribbon Campaign or Product Red Campaign? What was the product, and was the "cause" a major decision-making factor in your purchase? If you have not purchased such a product, what types of company advertisements, if any, have you seen? Explain.

4. Do you agree that the stakeholders of a company (customers, investors, employees, banks, suppliers, and people in the community) need to know immediately when an offer of interest to purchase is made to a company? If you were an employee of a company, how soon would you want to know if the company might be sold or if there were financial troubles?

5. If you decided to donate the majority of your future riches to charity, as Bill and Melinda Gates and Warren Buffett have, what would your causes or charities be? (Bill Gates is founder and former CEO of Microsoft; Buffett is CEO of Berkshire Hathaway, which owns subsidiaries engaged in numerous business activities.)

VIDEO CASE
Patagonia: Social Responsibility & Managing Ethics

(Video running time 4:01 minutes; activity time 30 minutes)

"Would you report your company if it were illegally dumping waste on public land, even if it cost you your job?" That's the question with which this video about Patagonia begins. Headquartered in Ventura, California, Patagonia takes great pains to make sure it is not this kind of company.

Founded by Yvon Chouinard in 1972, Patagonia—named for the southernmost region of South America—designs and makes apparel and equipment for outdoor types who bike, hike, ski, fish, or surf. (You may have seen fellow students wearing Patagonia rain jackets and fleece-lined coats.) A customer's decision to buy from this company usually has to do with not only purchasing quality products but also doing business with a socially responsible and ethical global citizen, one named "Coolest Company on the Planet" by *Fortune* in 2007.

As part of its focus, Patagonia is involved in a number of environmental and wildlife campaigns, including prevention of oil drilling that may endanger animal life. Its devotion to environmental causes is demonstrated in the construction of its Reno, Nevada, distribution center, which features green design and technologies. In 2008, Patagonia won the Eco-Friendly Company of the Year award at a trade show in Munich, Germany.

In addition, Patagonia has an environmental internship program, which provides employees with up to two months' paid leave with full benefits so that they can do volunteer work with a nonprofit organization of their choice. It also belongs to the "1% for the Planet" alliance, a program in which businesses donate 1% of their sales to the preservation and restoration of the natural environment.

Finally, Patagonia is a great believer in corporate transparency. In the past, points out CEO Casey Sheahan, some executives might have considered it acceptable for a company to hide some of its less desirable activities. Now, he says, "you have to become transparent with everything you do because eventually, with the power of the Web and social media, customers are going to find out what you're doing anyway, so why not tell

them?" With this thought in mind, the company stays focused on its social responsibilities along with the quality of its products and its economic performance.

What's Your Take?

1. Discuss what is meant by the application of "transparency" in Patagonia's business practices. How is the company trying to accomplish this? Provide examples.

2. In what ways is Patagonia committed to producing products under legal, fair, safe, and humane working conditions?

3. In the video, Jill Dumain, Patagonia's Director of Environmental Analysis, states that "we started realizing as a company that what we make pollutes, and we had been known as an environmental company." What are ways the company pollutes, and what alternatives is it implementing?

BUSINESS DECISION CASE
Oprah Winfrey Not Forgotten: The Importance of Giving Back

The chapter discusses the case for and against corporate social responsibility—and the positive effects of "being good" and trying to make the world a better place. Many times, social responsibility and philanthropy are associated with companies and nonprofit organizations, but have you ever stopped to think about the difference a single individual can make? While some companies and nonprofits have tirelessly contributed to bettering society, employees, customers, and the local communities in which they operate, have you ever thought about an individual like Oprah Winfrey and the power

she possesses as a philanthropist? What is it that inspires some people to give in such profound and immense ways?

Oprah's childhood reveals much about her philanthropic roots. She has long believed that education is the door to freedom, offering a chance at a brighter future.[99] She was raised in rural Mississippi by her grandmother, who read books to her and instilled in her a love of reading, learning, and going to the library. Oprah began memorizing Bible verses and performing for her grandmother's friends at the age of three. At the age of five, she began kindergarten—already knowing how to read and write.[100] In middle school a teacher suggested that Oprah attend Nicolet High School in Glendale, Wisconsin. At Nicolet, Oprah was the only African American student, but she was later quoted as saying, "In 1968 it was real hip to know a black person, so I was very popular."[101] She went on to graduate from Tennessee State, where she earned a degree in speech and drama.[102]

Oprah is the most powerful African American woman of all time. *Forbes* magazine has calculated her net worth at $2.7 billion.[103] In 2005, she became the first African American person listed by *BusinessWeek* magazine in its top 50 philanthropists list—reportedly giving away over $300 million of her own money.[104] She is commonly touted with top billing of those celebrities who give away the largest percentage of their own money. What has propelled her to these heights and why has she given back so generously?

According to a *BusinessWeek* interview, Oprah's inspiration as a philanthropist came one Christmas at around the age of 12, when she knew there would be no gifts under the tree—or even a tree. When a trio of nuns showed up at her family's home with food and gifts (and a doll of her very own), she says, "I remember feeling that I mattered enough to these nuns—who I had never met and to this day still do not know their names—and what it meant that they had remembered me. I wasn't forgotten."[105]

Oprah's causes are related to education and empowerment. Her Angel Network, which began in 1998, has given over $80 million to various causes and nonprofits. Oprah personally donated $11 million of her own money to Hurricane Katrina victims.[106] In 2007, she spent $40 million to build the Oprah Winfrey Leadership Academy for girls in Johannesburg, South Africa. The project is meant to empower young girls to become leaders of their communities.[107] On her success, Oprah says, "What material success does is provide you with the ability to concentrate on other things that really matter. And that is being able to make a difference, not only in your own life, but in other people's lives."[108]

What's Your Take?

1. Are you aware of other celebrities who have made significant contributions as philanthropists, and if so, what are their causes?

2. It is stated that companies are not separate from society. Are celebrities separate from society? Do you think celebrities with exorbitant earnings have an obligation to society? Explain.

3. Oprah is quoted as saying, "to whom much is given, much is expected." How do you interpret this? Explain.

4. Do you think Oprah's childhood contributed to her philanthropic generosity? Had she come from different means, do you think she'd still be as generous?

Briefings   MyBizLab Activities & Cases

Go to www.mybizlab.com for online activities and exercises related to the timely topics discussed in this chapter's Briefings, as well as additional theme-related Briefing *Spotlights* highlighting how these concepts apply in today's business environment.

In-chapter Briefing: • Who Will You Ask to Write You a Reference? (And Don't Forget to Thank Them.)	**Activity:** • Developing Marketable Business Skills – Volunteering	**Briefing Spotlight:** • How Much Is Too Much?
In-chapter Briefing: • Subaru Proves Going Green Can Lower, Not Increase, Costs • What Can Business Do to Fight Climate Change?	**Activity:** • Going to the Net! – McDonald's Potato Energy & Other Best Global Practices	**Briefing Spotlight:** • Rolling Out the Green Carpet
In-chapter Briefing: • Unilever Benefits the International Community by Addressing Important World Problems	**Activity:** • Going to the Net! – The Gap's Social Responsibility Report	**Briefing Spotlight:** • Hot Steam to Cold Cash

In-chapter Briefing:
- Ethical Dilemma for the Thomas Kinkade Company: Was It "Just Business" to Exploit Gallery Owners' Faith?
- A Food Giant Benefits Its Owners by Feeding Hungry Children

Activity:
- Developing Marketable Business Skills – Technology's Impact on Ethics
- Ethical Dilemma Case – Going Mainstream & Downstream?
- Going to the Net! – National Whistleblowers Center Website

Briefing Spotlight:
- GMAC – Robo Cops or Crooks?

In-chapter Briefing:
- The White Dog Café Expresses Blended Value in the "Triple Bottom Line"

Activity:
- Going to the Net! – Social Entrepreneurs: A Hybrid of Nonprofit with For-Profit

Briefing Spotlight:
- A Guy Who Works for Peanuts

In-chapter Briefing:
- An Ethical Top Manager at CitiMortgage Keeps People in Their Homes

Activity:
- Developing Marketable Business Skills – The Toyota Recall
- Developing Marketable Business Skills – Activism or Slacktivism?
- Developing Marketable Business Skills – Two Views of Corporate Social Responsibility
- Going to the Net! – The Philanthrocapitalism of the Gates Foundation
- Going to the Net! – The 100 Best Corporate Citizens: What Makes Them the Best?

Briefing Spotlight:
- Just Good Corporate Citizens

Additional Briefing Spotlights available at MyBizLab:
- A WORLD OF CONSTANT CHANGE
- BUSINESS SKILLS & CAREER DEVELOPMENT
- CUSTOMER FOCUS
- INFO TECH & SOCIAL MEDIA
- PERSONAL FINANCE

3

Economics

How Business Builds
& Distributes Wealth

After reading and studying this chapter, you will be able to answer the following essential questions:

3.1 Freedom to Succeed—or Fail: How Economics Affects Business

THE ESSENTIAL QUESTION: *What is economics principally concerned with, and what are its two major fields?*

3.2 Three Types of Economies: Command, Free-Market, & Mixed

THE ESSENTIAL QUESTION: *How do the three different economies of the world differ from each other?*

3.3 How Free-Market Capitalism Works

THE ESSENTIAL QUESTION: *What are the basic underpinnings of the free market?*

3.4 What Businesspeople Need to Know: How to Operate Successfully within the U.S. Economic System

THE ESSENTIAL QUESTION: *What do I need to know about the U.S. economic system to operate successfully within it?*

3.5 The—Almost—Second Great Depression: The Road to a Global Economic Crisis

THE ESSENTIAL QUESTION: *What launched the Great Recession?*

MyBizLab

Where you see MyBizLab in this chapter, go to www.mybizlab.com for additional activities on the topic being discussed.

FORECAST:
What's Ahead
in This Chapter

After describing scarcity and the factors of production, we discuss communism and socialism, capitalism, and mixed economies. We consider the underpinnings of the free market: basic rights, kinds of competition, and supply and demand. We discuss major economic indicators, productivity, and the business cycle. We end by analyzing the recent global economic crisis.

MyBizLab

Gain hands-on experience through an interactive, real-world scenario. This chapter's simulation entitled Adapting to the Economic Environment is located at **www.mybizlab.com**.

WINNER: Basic Instinct—
Box Office Hit

The film *Basic Instinct* is an erotic thriller starring Sharon Stone and Michael Douglas. It was written by Joe Eszterhas, then the highest-paid screenwriter in Hollywood, and directed by Paul Verhoeven. Released in March 1992, it was made for an estimated $49 million and went on to gross $353 million worldwide. Until the success of that movie, Stone was still a relative unknown and received only $500,000 for her role.

What do studio executives do to try to ensure a movie will be a hit? Usually they try to hire "bankable" stars, high-demand actors with enough hits that they add value to a film in terms of getting it financed and the cameras rolling. Bankable stars appear on a roster called "the A list" (which then included Michael Douglas). Superstars appear on the changing "A+ list"—most recently, Will Smith, Johnny Depp, Brad Pitt, Tom Hanks, George Clooney, Will Ferrell, Reese Witherspoon, Nicolas Cage, Leonardo DiCaprio, and Russell Crowe. Less popular actors are on A, B+, B, and C lists.

The A list is based on something called the Ulmer Scale, a method devised by James Ulmer, a veteran entertainment journalist, of quantifying a star's value according to his or her successes versus failures, professional demeanor, and willingness to travel and promote films. If an actor has 100 points on the Ulmer Scale for a given film budget, that means a movie can have 100% of its financing guaranteed, based solely on that actor's participation. Both the A list and the Ulmer Scale are parts of a guide called *The Hot List,* which rates the bankability of more than 1,300 actors and 600 directors.[1]

Movie budgets and box office grosses are posted on The Numbers website. For instance, the big-budget *Titanic* (released December 1997) cost $200 million to make and grossed $2.2 billion worldwide. But *The Blair Witch Project* (1999) cost only $35,000 to make and grossed $248 million worldwide—the most profitable film ever made, based on money earned compared to money spent (return on investment).

LOSER: Basic Instinct 2—
Box Office Bomb

Why do movie studios make all those sequels—the successors to *Star Wars* (7 movies), James Bond (23), *Batman* (7), *Harry Potter* (5), *Spider-Man* (3), and so on?[2] Clearly, investors hope that the financial success of the original hit movie will be repeated. Usually sequels generate an average 27% more revenue than similar stand-alone films, but they can be duds as well.[3]

And so it was that after many years of delays, *Basic Instinct 2* finally appeared (released in March 2006, 14 years after the first film). None of the original cast and crew returned except for Sharon Stone and the producer. Costing $70 million, *Basic Instinct 2* grossed only $5 million in the United States, making it the most unprofitable film of 2006—a true box office bomb.

Even A-list stars are not invincible. In that same year, Russell Crowe struck out with *A Good Year,* Nicholas Cage with the remake *Wicker Man,* and Sean Penn with the remake *All the King's Men.* The original A-list writer and director for *Basic Instinct,* Joe Eszterhas and Paul Verhoeven, have had their flops as well, both of them receiving Razzie Awards (for Golden Raspberry—the worst) for the 1995 movie *Showgirls.* Sharon Stone herself has had several years of bombs.[4]

In extreme cases, a single film's poor performance can push a studio into financial ruin, as *Heaven's Gate* did for United Artists and *Raise the Titanic!* did for ITC Entertainment.[5]

By contrast, so-called *sleeper films* surprise everyone with their high degree of success relative to the modest expectations investors had for them. A sleeper film is an under-promoted film that becomes a hit over time through word of mouth and good publicity generated by good reviews or awards.[6] Examples are, of course, *The Blair Witch Project,* as well as *American Pie, Barbershop, Monster's Ball, My Big Fat Greek Wedding, The 40-Year-Old Virgin,* and *Paranormal Activity.* The 2006 sleeper *Little Miss Sunshine* garnered four Academy Awards and grossed $100.3 million internationally.

YOUR CALL The task of the entertainment business is to determine customers' economic *demands* and then try to *supply* the products to meet those demands. But the failure of many sequels and remakes and the success of many sleepers lend credence to famed screenwriter William Goldman's opinion that "Nobody knows anything"—that even seasoned moviemakers can't predict whether a film will be a hit or a bomb. Only 6% of Hollywood films account for the bulk of the industry's profits, according to Arthur DeVany, author of *Hollywood Economics.*[7] In other forms of the entertainment business, only 10% of recordings actually turn a profit, most new network TV shows fail, and most new books are busts.[8] If successful entertainment products are so scarce, why would anyone try to supply them?

MyBizLab

3.1 Freedom to Succeed—or Fail: How Economics Affects Business

THE BIG IDEA: Economics, which is divided into macroeconomics (in a nutshell, large economic units) and microeconomics (small units), is concerned with studying the production, distribution, and consumption of scarce goods and services. We also consider the importance of knowledge in the new economy.

THE ESSENTIAL QUESTION: What is economics principally concerned with, and what are its two major fields?

MyBizLab

MyBizLab: Check your understanding of these concepts at www.mybizlab.com.

"Nobody knows anything"—William Goldman's comment on the movie industry—applies to other kinds of businesses as well. If certainty were really possible, there would be no losers as well as winners, no bombs as well as hits, no busts as well as booms. That is why business is so much about taking *risks*.

People often want to deny the possibility of risk. Before the recent global economic crisis, for instance, many professional investors thought, in the words of one reporter, "they had found a way to increase their profits without taking on risk," using sophisticated computer financial models.[9] They received a harsh awakening in the financial bust that ushered in the 2007–2009 Great Recession.

Risks, then, are part and parcel of our free-market system. To begin to appreciate this, we need to have some understanding of economics.

Economics: Dealing with Scarcity & the Forces of Supply & Demand

What is the definition of "economics"?

A subject that economists think a lot about is *scarcity*. Air would seem to be one thing that's plentiful—as in "as free as the air we breathe"—but, of course, breathable, healthy air may well be scarce. For example, people living in areas with higher levels of air pollution have a greater risk of developing heart attacks, strokes, and other cardiovascular disease.[10] No wonder houses near a freeway or coal-burning plant are cheaper than those that are not.

Dealing with Scarcity

Want to Know More? 3-1

Key Terms & Definitions in Sequential Order to Study as You Go Along

Go to www.mybizlab.com.

***Economics* is concerned with the production, distribution, and consumption of scarce goods and services, which includes the forces of supply and demand.** Although not all economists agree, most believe *scarcity* is important to the definition. The idea is that, no matter how much of something there seems to be, all things are essentially scarce or limited—at least for some people.[11]

BRIEFING / A WORLD OF CONSTANT CHANGE
The Scarcity of Super Bowl Losers' Caps. Seconds after the clock clicks down to 00:00 in a major championship game, caps and shirts

celebrating the win instantly appear on every player on the successful team—as in "Super Bowl XLIV Champions," with the logo of the winning 2010 New Orleans Saints.

But what happens to all the hats and T-shirts made up in advance for the team that didn't win, such as the 2010 Super Bowl–losing Indianapolis Colts? The National Football League, which authorizes the production of both winning and losing hats, dictates that the losers' items must never appear on television, eBay, or any part of U.S. soil, and so the gear ends up being donated to impoverished people, usually in Africa. (The National Basketball Association also donates final playoff losers' clothing to charity; Major League Baseball destroys it.)[12]

Villagers in Ethiopia appreciate the clothing because manufactured goods of any kind are scarce. But should some of these items ever find their way back to the United States, they would enter a different world of scarcity—that of avid collectors of sports memorabilia who would pay far more than the $20 to $30 that the clothes are nominally worth. ❶ ■

Source: Photograph by Sally Lindsay.

❶ **Scarcity.** You can easily find one of these New Orleans Saints' Super Bowl XLIV winner's caps, the kind that the triumphant players don at the end of the game. But how easily could you find a "Super Bowl Champions" hat for the Indianapolis Colts, who lost the contest? How much would such a cap be worth as a collector's item?

The Forces of Supply & Demand

Scarcity has a great deal of bearing on the forces of *supply and demand.* We explore these concepts later in this chapter, but here let us simply say this:

- **Supply:** *Supply* expresses how willing and able sellers are to provide goods and services at different prices. Generally, the more scarce a product is, the more a seller will want to charge for it. And the less scarce the product, the less a seller will be able to charge.

- **Demand:** *Demand* expresses how willing and able buyers are to purchase goods and services at different prices. Generally speaking, the less scarce a product is, the less buyers will want to pay for it. And the more scarce, the more buyers will be willing to pay.

Two Major Fields of Economics: Macroeconomics & Microeconomics

How do "macroeconomics" and "microeconomics" differ?

Economics is divided into two major fields—*macroeconomics,* the study of large economic units, and *microeconomics,* the study of small units.

Macroeconomics: The Study of Large Economic Units

**Macroeconomics** **studies the economy as a whole; it concentrates on large economic units, such as the operations of a nation's economy and the effect on it of government policies and allocation of resources.** For instance, macroeconomists might study . . .

- The U.S. gross domestic product, or GDP (the total dollar value of all the goods and services produced in the United States);
- Job growth and unemployment;
- Growth in industrial production;
- The consumer price index and similar large economic indicators; and
- Which presidential administrations have a better track record in improving the U.S. economy.

ⓘ
Want to Know More? 3-2

A Comparison: Macroeconomic Performance in Democratic & Republican Administrations— Which Are Better? (You May Be Surprised)

Go to www.mybizlab.com.

Microeconomics: The Study of Small Economic Units

Microeconomics **studies the economic behavior of individual economic units, the operations of particular groups of people, businesses, organizations, and markets.** Microeconomists might be concerned with such matters as . . .

- How increases in tuition fees affect college enrollments;
- How changes in gas prices affect what size cars people buy;
- The impact of a black market on prices of legitimate goods;
- How professional sports-team monopolies affect television markets;
- The effect of coupons on consumers' buying behavior; and
- How the introduction of e-books affects book sales. ❷

The Importance of Knowledge in the New Economy

Why does specialized knowledge make a difference?

How are goods and services created? This falls within the area of ***resource development,*** **the study of how to develop the resources for creating and best utilizing goods and services.** The resources may be developed by the government (as with the interstate highway system or the Internet) or they may be developed by business (as with Apple's iPad or automakers' electric cars).

The means for developing goods and services and satisfying demand are the *factors of production,* which as discussed in Chapter 1 are . . .

- **Natural resources**—materials supplied by nature, such as land, soil, water, and minerals.
- **Capital**—the buildings and tools used to produce goods and services.
- **Human resources**—the human effort, both mental and physical, required to produce goods and services.
- **Entrepreneurship**—the process of taking risks to create a new enterprise.
- **Knowledge**—the technological expertise and practical experience that allows entrepreneurs to quickly determine new wants and needs and deliver new products.

What has become crucial in today's economic system is the fifth production factor, knowledge. As information technology does more of the work formerly done by humans, knowledge is becoming a competitive advantage. Technological change has increased the need for "knowledge workers," those with great technical skills who are good at abstract thinking and problem solving.

❷ **E-books and booksellers.** In early 2009, e-book readers like this Amazon Kindle made up 2.9% of general (trade) book sales, but by February 2011 they had grown to nearly 30%. This and other new competition (as from online sellers) has forced the big bookseller chains such as Barnes & Noble into significant losses (and Borders into bankruptcy and eventually out of existence) and caused them to reevaluate their strategies— a worthy subject of study for microeconomists.

Source: Dmitry Lobanov/Shutterstock.

🌐 BRIEFING / A WORLD OF CONSTANT CHANGE
Using Knowledge to Build a Technology for Predicting Hit Movies. Could it be that we were wrong to suggest that "nobody knows anything" about how to predict hit movies? A "knowledge work" company called Epagogix has devised a way of predicting movie hits that relies on analysis of scripts rather than on the "bankability" of any stars. Hit-movie script elements were given to a computerized system called an artificial neural network, which looks for patterns in large amounts of data. After thousands of adjustments and tests, a formula was devised that predicted the financial success of every movie analyzed.

A studio then gave Epagogix nine unreleased movies, and the scripts were analyzed without reference to the stars, director, producer, or marketing budget. On three films, the Epagogix estimates of box office gross were way off. On the remaining six, they correctly identified whether the film would make or lose money. "Had the studio used Epagogix on those nine scripts before filming started," said a studio executive, "it could have saved tens of millions of dollars."[13] ∎

Three Types of Economies: Command, Free-Market, & Mixed

3.2

THE BIG IDEA: Of the three types of economies—command (communism and socialism), free-market (capitalist), and mixed—business operates best within the framework of capitalism. All three economic systems have their own benefits and drawbacks.

THE ESSENTIAL QUESTION: How do the three different economies of the world differ from each other?

MyBizLab: Check your understanding of these concepts at www.mybizlab.com.

MyBizLab

To build a business, most people would assume, it helps to have a great deal of economic freedom. Which do you think would offer more of this: Hong Kong or the United States? Denmark or Japan?

Does it surprise you that, in the 2011 Index of Economic Freedom (by the *Wall Street Journal* and the Heritage Foundation), Hong Kong, which used to belong to the United Kingdom and now belongs to communist China, was ranked 1 on the list and the United States was ranked 9? That Denmark, with its extensive state-supported health, educational, and social welfare programs, was ranked 8, whereas Japan was ranked 20?[14] You might find *The Global Competitiveness Report 2010–2011* by the World Economic Forum also surprising, since it rated the United States as 4 (down from 2 just two years before), behind Switzerland, Sweden, and Singapore, with Finland, the Netherlands, and Denmark ranked 7 through 9. (*See* ■ *Panel 3.1.*)

As we will see, countries we may tend to think of as "socialistic" may nevertheless have strong free-market components. Let us describe the three classic kinds of economies: (1) *command economies,* (2) *free-market economies,* and (3) *mixed economies.*

1 Command Economies: Communism & Socialism

What's the difference between communism and socialism?

Command economies, or **central-planning economies, are economic systems such as communism and socialism, in which the government owns most businesses and regulates the amounts, types, and prices of goods and services.** The two principal variations of command economies are *communism* (which is in decline) and *socialism.*

Communism: All Property Is Owned by the Government

Communism is an economic system in which all property is owned by the government and everyone works for the government. The movement originated with 19th-century German philosopher **Karl Marx,** who felt that private ownership led to the exploitation of working men and women. Convinced of the need for a new economic system based on "From each according to his abilities, to each according to his needs," Marx wrote *The Communist Manifesto* in 1848.

Want to Know More? 3-3

The United States vs. the Rest of the World: Biggest Competitors to the United States

Go to www.mybizlab.com.

■ **PANEL 3.1 The World Economic Forum's country rankings for competitiveness, 2010–2011.**

1. Switzerland
2. Sweden
3. Singapore
4. United States
5. Germany
6. Japan
7. Finland
8. Netherlands
9. Denmark
10. Canada
11. Hong Kong
12. United Kingdom
13. Taiwan
14. Norway
15. France

Source: World Economic Forum, *The Global Competitiveness Report 2010–2011,* September 9, 2010, www.weforum.org/en/initiatives/gcp/Global%20Competitiveness%20Report/index.htm (accessed August 11, 2011).

Source: Bartlomiej Magierowski/Shutterstock.

❸ Shenzhen. Located immediately north of Hong Kong and one of the fastest growing cities in the world, Shenzhen became the first of China's Special Economic Zones, attracting US$30 billion in foreign investment in both fully owned and joint venture companies. Would you think a city with such a modern and distinctive landscape as being in a "communist" country?

The Rise & Continuing Fall of Communism. Marx's theories inspired the rise of various political and economic reform movements throughout Europe. The most important of these became the Communist Party, which grew out of the Russian Revolution of 1917. After World War II, communism spread throughout Eastern Europe, and in 1949 it was established as the major economic system of China. By the early 1980s, almost one-third of the world's population lived under communism, mostly in the Soviet Union and in the People's Republic of China.

Since the erosion of communism in Eastern Europe in the late 1980s and the breakup of the Soviet Union in 1991, the influence of communism has declined, particularly as Communist governments reduced control over their economies to stimulate growth. Today about one-quarter of the people of the world live in Communist countries, most of them in China.

🌐 BRIEFING / GLOBAL BUSINESS

The (Mostly) Communist Countries Today. North Korea is probably the most communist country remaining today. Four other countries—China, Vietnam, Laos, and Cuba—are also nominally communist, although some business activity is tolerated. (Cuba in 2011 actually encouraged *more* private enterprise, though not calling it that.)[15] In North Korea and Cuba, severe shortages exist—indeed, in North Korea, there is widespread starvation. In China and North Korea, slave labor also still exists.

China and Vietnam have relaxed state control of their economies in order to increase growth. For instance, China has instituted market-oriented Special Economic Zones, which are free of central government control. One such zone, Shenzhen, went from a village to 10 million people in only 20 years. ❸ American, European, and Japanese companies are seen everywhere in China (Buick is a favorite car of the Chinese).

On the other hand, Vietnam's movement toward a market economy, which began in 1986, has left many of the poor behind, struggling to pay for food and medical care.[16] The 2008 global economic crisis affected China as it did the rest of the world, and millions of workers were laid off.[17] ∎

The Drawbacks of Communism. There are three major problems with communism, as follows:

- **Central planning flaws:** In a pure communist government, decisions about what products and services to make are made by bureaucrats in a central office. Because prices set by the government are not a true indicator of supply and demand, the central planners never quite know what or how much to produce; they have to guess. With this kind of poor information, the Soviet Union continually failed to adequately anticipate and meet demands for food and housing, which led to long lines and waiting lists among citizens.

- **Lack of incentive:** Despite the Marxian promise of workers being rewarded "each according to his needs," there is no motivation for workers to work "each according to his abilities." Because workers do not benefit directly from their work and because the government taxes most of their earnings, there is no need to work hard. There is also no competition and thus no incentive to improve business decision making and to "build a better mousetrap."

- **Total government intrusion:** Government control over the economy extends (or can extend) to interference with people's private lives. Want to practice a certain religion? The government may not allow it. Want to change jobs or residence? You'll need to get government permission.

Socialism: State-Owned Industries & Redistributed Wealth

Derived from Marxist principles, *socialism* is an economic system in which some major industries are owned by the government, but smaller businesses are owned by individuals. **Much of the wealth or surplus of high incomes is redistributed by the government through social programs.** Unlike Communist countries, which (at least theoretically) have only one employer—the state—socialist countries allow citizens to work for either the government-owned industries or private businesses owned by individuals.

What, Exactly, *Is* a Socialist State? Trying to precisely identify a socialist state can be difficult, for several reasons:

- **"Socialism" in name only:** Some countries, such as Egypt, Libya, Portugal, and Sri Lanka, make references to socialism in their constitutions but do not subscribe to Marxist principles.
- **State-owned enterprises:** Socialist countries have state-owned enterprises, such as Norway's state-owned gas pipeline network. But many socialist countries also have large privately owned companies, such as Swedish Match (smoke-free tobacco products). Of course, even the United States has government-owned enterprises—the interstate highway system, for instance, or public universities—but the term *socialism* seems to suggest there is a larger proportion of governmental than of private economic activity.
- **Welfare state:** Many countries with state-owned industries provide their people with a *welfare state*—**government social services to give citizens economic security by providing for them when they are unemployed, ill, or elderly and, in some countries, providing subsidized college educations and child care.** France's social services expenditures are quite extensive; the country spends 28.4% of its gross domestic product on them. Sweden spends 27.3%. Tenth-ranked Portugal spends 22.5%. By contrast, Canada (which some people like to think is socialist, mainly because of its government-payer health care system) spends only 16.9%, the United States spends 16.2%, and Mexico spends 7.2% among 34 industrialized nations ranked by the Organisation for Economic Co-operation and Development (OECD) in 2007.[18] (*See* ■ *Panel 3.2.*)
- **High taxes:** Countries with a high level of government services may also tend to have high taxes. As a percentage of gross domestic product in 2008, Denmark's share of taxes was 48.3%, and Sweden's was 47.1%. By contrast, Canada ranked 17 (of 26 countries) at 32.2%, the United States ranked 22 at 26.9%, and Mexico was ranked 26 (last place) at 21.1%.[19] (*See* ■ *Panel 3.3.*) Americans' current federal tax burden is at the lowest level since 1958.[20]

The Benefits of Socialism. Unquestionably, socialism is attractive to many people, which is why it is found in so much of Europe, Africa, and India. Some pluses are as follows:

- **More benefits to citizens:** Citizens receive such benefits as free education even through college, fully paid health insurance, free child care, longer vacations, job security, and generous retirement packages. Thus, socialist countries tend to have lower infant mortality rates and higher adult life expectancy rates compared to many capitalist countries. (Denmark, incidentally, was found to be the happiest country in the world, according to a study by the U.S. National Science Foundation; the United States was ranked 16.)[21]
- **Less social inequality and poverty:** By taking more of wealthier people's incomes and redistributing it to poorer people through government programs, socialism reduces the amount of social inequality and poverty compared to capitalist countries.

■ **PANEL 3.2 Welfare states: Percentage of gross domestic product spent on government social services, 2007.**

1. France	|||||||||||||||||||||||||	28.4
2. Sweden	||||||||||||||||||||||||	27.3
3. Austria	|||||||||||||||||||||||	26.4
4. Belgium	|||||||||||||||||||||||	26.3
5. Denmark	|||||||||||||||||||||||	26.1
6. Germany	||||||||||||||||||||||	25.2
7. Finland	|||||||||||||||||||||	24.9
8. Italy	|||||||||||||||||||||	24.9
9. Hungary	||||||||||||||||||||	23.2
10. Portugal	|||||||||||||||||||	22.5
25. Canada	|||||||||||||	16.9
27. United States	|||||||||||||	16.2
34. Mexico	|||||||||	7.2

Source: OECD Stat Extracts, Social Expenditures, Aggregated Data, May 11, 2011, http://stats.oecd.org/Index.aspx?datasetcode=SOCX_AGG (accessed August 11, 2011).

■ **PANEL 3.3 Taxes: Total tax ratio as a percentage of gross domestic product for 26 developed countries, 2008 (provisional).**

1. Denmark	||||||||||||||||||||||||||	48.3
2. Sweden	|||||||||||||||||||||||||	47.1
3. Belgium	|||||||||||||||||||||||	44.3
4. Italy	||||||||||||||||||||||	43.2
5. France	||||||||||||||||||||||	43.1
6. Austria	|||||||||||||||||||||	42.9
7. Finland	|||||||||||||||||||||	42.8
8. Norway	||||||||||||||||||||	42.1
9. Hungary	|||||||||||||||||||	40.1
10. Luxembourg	||||||||||||||||	38.3
17. Canada	|||||||||	32.2
22. United States	||||||	26.9
26. Mexico	|||	21.1

Source: OECD, *OECD Revenue Statistics 1965–2008, 2009 Edition,* Table A, www.oecd.org/dataoecd/6/16/44126373.xls (accessed August 11, 2011).

Socialism, Denmark style. Danish (and Swedish) citizens pay the highest taxes of 26 industrialized nations. Having high taxes, however, doesn't mean the Danes are impoverished by the burden of government; in fact, their per capita income is the highest of any country in Europe—even higher than in the United States. What do you think nonsocialist countries could learn from Denmark's experience?

Source: Tupungato/Shutterstock.

The Drawbacks of Socialism. The major criticisms of socialism are as follows:

- **Problems with central planning:** Like communist countries, socialist states can face huge problems if central planners fail to correctly anticipate the right kind and quantity of goods and services to produce.

- **High taxes:** A frequent criticism of the welfare state is that it requires high taxes. Certainly, this is sometimes true, as shown by the tax rates of Denmark and Sweden, discussed earlier. On the other hand, it can be argued that these two Nordic countries, at least, have very progressive systems of taxation, which don't disproportionately burden the middle and poorer classes, and they have high-performing economies.

- **Possible "brain drain":** Some argue that socialism forces professionals and entrepreneurs to leave the country to avoid high taxes. This so-called ***brain drain, or emigration of highly skilled intellectual and technical labor to other countries in order to better their economic condition,*** could be a problem, although the evidence is mixed.

  Denmark, the country that (along with Sweden) has the highest tax rate, has reportedly had problems retaining educated young workers, who have been fleeing to other countries where taxes are lower.[22] Thus, many Danish companies, encouraged by the government, have been looking offshore to recruit talented foreign workers.

- **Less job and wealth creation:** The lack of incentives under socialism, it's argued, tends to discourage workers from working as hard as they can. Consequently, socialist countries are not as effective as capitalist countries at creating jobs or creating wealth.

- **Possible government deficits:** Some socialist-type governments in developed countries are running budget ***deficits, with spending exceeding income—*** that is, revenue from taxes. For instance, four socialist countries—Portugal, Ireland, Greece, and Spain (called PIGS)—are presently considered to be so highly indebted as to threaten the economic stability of much of the rest of Europe (the Euro zone, described in Chapter 4).

  Yet even nonsocialist countries can run a deficit. The *CIA World Fact Book 2011* ranked 172 countries with 2009 budget deficits as a percentage of gross domestic product. The nonsocialist United States ranked pretty high at 27 (budget deficit 8.3% of GDP) and the United Kingdom ranked at 22.

68   **PART 1**   Today's Business Environment

Three socialist countries were even higher—Ireland was ranked 2 (budget deficit 37.96%), Spain 24, and Greece 25. France ranked 33, Portugal 39, and Iceland 44.

Yet not all socialist countries run high deficits. Some socialist countries in 2009 ranked a lot better than the United States: Netherlands ranked 63, Austria 70, Denmark 72, Italy 74, Belgium 77, Germany 103, Finland 110, and Sweden 148 (budget deficit 1.46%).[23] Canada ranked 83.

2 Free-Market Economies: Capitalism

What is the basis of capitalism?

In a *free-market economy,* also commonly called *capitalism,* **the production and distribution of goods and services are controlled by private individuals rather than by the government.** Capitalism has traditionally been the basis of the economies of the United States, England, Japan, and several other developed countries.

What Creates Wealth? Adam Smith's Theory

Scottish economist **Adam Smith,** considered to be the founder of modern economics, was one of the first to imagine a system for creating wealth and improving the lives of everyone—from top to bottom. Whereas other thinkers believed that fixed resources had to be divided among competing groups, Smith suggested that resources could be *expanded* so that everyone could become richer. His theories were put forth in his 1776 book *An Inquiry into the Nature and Causes of the Wealth of Nations,* usually simply called *The Wealth of Nations.* ⑤

The "Invisible Hand" of the Marketplace. For capitalism to work, Smith believed, government officials should play no role in determining which products and services should be produced, how they would be priced, and how they would be distributed. Instead, Smith thought, if left alone the marketplace would operate as though guided by an *"invisible hand,"* **with individuals' drive for prosperity producing needed goods and services that would provide economic and social benefits to all.**

The Importance of Incentives: Risks and Rewards. Smith believed that if farmers, manufacturers, and business owners were allowed the freedom to earn profits from their labor, they would be motivated to work as hard as possible in order to prosper and benefit their families. Incentives, then, are extremely important. If individuals are to take big risks, there must be big rewards.

The Benefits of Capitalism

Although businesspeople would be working primarily to improve their own lives, their efforts would also, Smith suggested, produce economic benefits for others. Such benefits, he thought, would occur in three ways:

More Jobs and Incomes. Business owners would hire additional workers, providing more jobs and incomes. This benefit certainly seems to have turned out to be true. Unlike communism and socialism, which aren't as effective at creating jobs, capitalism has excelled at job creation and in raising incomes.

Businesses like Yahoo, Google, eBay, and Facebook, which didn't even exist a few years ago, have provided thousands of jobs, and the part of California in which they are located, the San Francisco Bay area, has one of the highest standards of living in the world.

⑤ **Adam Smith.** A Scottish social philosopher, he taught moral philosophy at the University of Glasgow. In his later life, he traveled throughout Europe meeting intellectual leaders, then returned home and spent 10 years writing *The Wealth of Nations.* Do you believe, as he did, that expanding resources can make everyone richer? How much do you think population growth and increased demand might have affected Smith's conclusions?

ⓘ

Want to Know More? 3-4

The Wealth of Nations

Go to www.mybizlab.com.

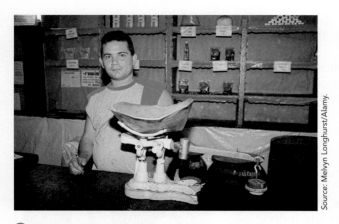

Source: Melvyn Longhurst/Alamy.

⑥ Scarcity of goods. Unlike stores in the United States, stores in Havana, Cuba, are not brimming with goods to sell. There is a toilet paper shortage, for instance, and the country has to import 60% of its food. What do you think are the primary factors in Cuba that lead to a chronic shortage of available goods?

Want to Know More? 3-5

Income Inequality: Just a Few of the Many Causes

Go to www.mybizlab.com.

Capitalism also offers the *possibility,* at least, that people can work their way up from poverty to a more comfortable life. (This is the message of the 2007 Will Smith movie *The Pursuit of Happyness,* based on the true experiences of Chris Gardner, who went from homelessness to fabulous wealth as head of his own brokerage firm. Not an ordinary story, of course, but it does happen.)

More Goods and Services. In pursuit of prosperity, the businessperson, Adam Smith thought, would produce goods and services that would benefit consumers and provide more choices. This benefit, too, seems to have been proven. During the Cold War, for example, people from communist countries who came to the capitalist countries of the West were amazed at the variety of goods in stores—and the comparison stands today in the differences between South Korea or the United States (principally capitalist) and North Korea or Cuba (principally communist). ⑥

Help for the Less Fortunate. Successful businesspeople, Smith assumed, would reach out and help the less fortunate in the community. Although there are capitalists who do not seem to want to share their wealth, many others do, as exemplified by the foundations established by such names as Rockefeller and Ford, as well as by Microsoft's Bill Gates.

Some Other Benefits: Career Choice and Entrepreneurism. Some other benefits of capitalism that Smith could have mentioned (but did not) are that people can make their own career choices. They can also become entrepreneurs and own their own businesses, make their own business decisions, and keep the profits (after taxes) that they make as business owners.

The Drawbacks of Capitalism

Despite all its benefits, capitalism can have an unhappy downside.

Not Everyone Is Suited to Competition. Capitalism can be a bruising activity, involving competition and risk. Not everyone has the drive, energy, courage, talent, education, health—or good luck—to compete successfully. Rewards can be high, but losses can be shattering.

Income Inequality. The disparity between the incomes at the top and the bottom can be considerable in a capitalist economy. Hard work is not always enough. One may work 100 hours a week and still make a relatively low wage compared to someone at the top. In 2010, the median pay package (salary, bonuses, and nonsalary income) for the chief executive of a company whose stock was listed on Standard & Poor's index of 500 stocks was $9 million. The median pay, including benefits, of private-sector workers in the United States was $40,500.[24]

Exploitation. "Greed is healthy," said stock speculator Ivan Boesky in 1985, a statement echoed in the line "Greed is good" by Michael Douglas in his Oscar-winning role of corporate raider Gordon Gekko in the movie *Wall Street.* Greed, however, can lead individuals to break the law, join in conspiracies to raise prices, and otherwise exploit others—the kind of behavior that gave rise to the phrase "cut-throat capitalism." Moreover, because under capitalism the state is not obliged to take care of the disadvantaged, the homeless, the elderly, and the sick, they must seek help on their own.

3 Mixed Economies: Publicly & Privately Owned

Why is there a trend toward mixed economies?

In their pure forms, neither command economies (communism or socialism) nor free-market economies (capitalism) have proved to be entirely satisfactory in benefiting all citizens, for the following reasons:

- **What's lacking in command economies—job creation:** Socialism, and to a certain extent communism, may have been successful at creating social safety nets for the poor, the elderly, and the disabled. However, they have not created enough jobs to keep their economies growing, forcing governments (such as some in Europe) to cut back on their welfare states.

- **What's lacking in free-market economies—social welfare:** Capitalist economies have been successful in creating jobs and boosting incomes. But they have not been effective in equalizing income differences or in taking care of citizens who have not benefited so much from free-market principles.

The result throughout the world is a trend toward ***mixed economies,* in which some resources are allocated by the free market and some resources are allocated by the government, resulting in a somewhat better balance between freedom and economic equality.**

Want to Know More? 3-6

Mixed Economies: India, Australia, Germany, & Canada

Go to www.mybizlab.com.

■ Example of a Mixed Economy: The United States. Although most businesses in the United States today are privately owned, the U.S. government owns several large enterprises, such as the Amtrak passenger-rail system and the electricity-producing Tennessee Valley Authority. (The federal government is also the largest employer in the United States.) In general, however, the economic foundation of the United States is capitalism, with the government aiding the system by promoting economic growth and social equality. ■

The principal economic systems are summarized below. (*See* ■ *Panel 3.4.*)

■ PANEL 3.4 Economic systems compared.

	Communism	Socialism	Capitalism	Mixed Economy
Country examples	North Korea, Cuba	No pure examples exist; Denmark, Sweden are closest	No pure examples exist; United States is closest	United States, United Kingdom, Canada, Mexico, Japan, China, India
Property rights and profits	All property owned by state, no profits exist	Major industries owned by state, some businesses owned by private individuals, who may earn profits	Property owned by private individuals, who may earn profits	Private business, with government regulation; some state-owned industries
Incentives*	Nonmaterial	Nonmaterial and material	Material	Nonmaterial and material
Employer	State	State or businesses	Businesses	Businesses or state
Production and investment decisions	By state officials	Major decisions by state officials	Mostly by private individuals	By private individuals and state officials
Income distribution	According to individual needs	State benefits to citizens	Income to wealth creators	Income to wealth creators, some state benefits

*Incentives consist of *material rewards*, such as money; *nonmaterial rewards*, such as status recognition; or both.

THE BIG IDEA: To operate successfully, a capitalist country must allow four basic rights—to own property, to compete, to choose freely, and to keep profits. Four kinds of free-market competition are perfect competition, monopolistic competition, oligopoly, and monopoly. Free markets depend on demand from buyers and supply from sellers to reach a market price for a good or service.

THE ESSENTIAL QUESTION: What are the basic underpinnings of the free market?

MyBizLab

MyBizLab: Check your understanding of these concepts at www.mybizlab.com.

Want to Know More? 3-7

The Global Competitive Index: Twelve Pillars of Competitiveness

Go to www.mybizlab.com.

Why would such supposedly "socialistic" countries as Sweden, Germany, Finland, the Netherlands, and Denmark be listed among the top 10 countries (along with the United States, ranked 4) in global competitiveness? (Refer back to *Panel 3.1.*) Because, according to the World Economic Forum, they scored well on "12 pillars of competitiveness" that include not only business sophistication and innovation, financial market sophistication, and technological readiness but also institutions, infrastructure, health and primary education, and higher education and training. Most countries in Latin America, by contrast, such as Brazil (ranked 58), Guatemala (78), Ecuador (105), and Paraguay (120), are ranked low because they suffer from poorly defined property rights, undue influence, inefficient government operations, and unstable business environments.[25]

We can see, then, that free-market capitalism doesn't exist in a vacuum. To operate successfully, it needs to be supported by the right kind of laws, institutions, infrastructure, and culture.

The Four Basic Rights under Capitalism

What are the four rights a country must have for a free-market economy to operate successfully?

Businesspeople in a free-market economy have four basic rights that enable them to take business risks they might otherwise be inclined to avoid. Still, these rights are not unlimited; all are restricted in certain ways by the government. The four rights, and their restrictions, are as follows:

1 The Right to Own Property

The foundation of all the other rights, the first basic right is the right to own property. That is, you can buy things—land, buildings, equipment, intellectual-property rights, and so on—and use them to generate income. You can sell them to others or pass them along to your heirs. In the United States, this right cannot be easily taken away from you. As stated in the Fifth Amendment to the U.S. Constitution, no person may be deprived of life, liberty, or *property* without due process of law.

Restrictions: In the United States, property ownership is restricted by zoning, environmental, and antifraud laws and regulations. ❼

2 The Right to Compete

You have the right to go into the marketplace and compete with other businesses according to your best judgment and skills, whatever your age, sex, race, ethnicity, or even basic qualifications.

Restrictions: The more exploitative aspects of competition are limited by antitrust, fraud, licensing, and consumer-protection legislation.

3 The Right to Free Choice

You have the right to choose what to buy and sell, where to establish your business, and where to live. Your employees are free to work for any enterprise willing to pay them what they wish.

Restrictions: The sale of certain items—drugs, alcohol, some weapons, and medical products, for example—are restricted by the government. Zoning laws restrict businesses from certain neighborhoods. Employers are prohibited by government regulations from discriminating against employees because of gender, age, race, ethnicity, or physical disability.

4 The Right to Make & Keep Profits

After using whatever production, marketing, and sales strategies you choose, you are free to earn a profit—that is, keep what is left over after you have earned your revenues and paid your expenses and taxes.

Restrictions: Your means of earning income are regulated by laws pertaining to child labor, workers' compensation, truth in advertising, workplace safety, and others. ❽ Also, revenues and profits are subject to taxation.

Four Types of Free Markets: The Varieties of Competition

How would I distinguish between the four types of free markets?

Not all competition is the same. Some markets may be so competitive (grocery stores, computers) that it's hard, as they say, to make a buck; others are less so (gas and electricity). Economists distinguish among four kinds of free markets: (1) *perfect competition,* (2) *monopolistic competition,* (3) *oligopoly,* and (4) *monopoly.*

Source: doglikehorse/Shutterstock.

❼ **Restrictive zoning.** Located 150 miles north of San Francisco on a headland surrounded by the Pacific Ocean, Mendocino (population 894) is an artists' colony and a popular site for visitors. The town's rural and historical charm is protected by strict local zoning regulations, so that, for instance, a homeowner needs to get a permit to paint the front door or mailbox. Do you think such restrictions on one's property should be allowed?

Source: Jeff Greenberg/Alamy.

❽ **A sign of OSHA.** The Occupational Safety and Health Administration (OSHA), an agency of the U.S. Department of Labor, attempts to prevent work-related injuries and illnesses by issuing and enforcing standards for safety and health in most private-sector workplaces, such as this auto repair shop. Do you think this kind of government regulation puts too much of a chokehold on employers and unnecessarily restricts their ability to compete? Would your answer be any different if you were a mechanic or shop worker?

1 Perfect Competition: Many Sellers, No Product Differences

This is the Adam Smith model. **In *perfect competition,* the market has many small sellers who sell interchangeable products to many informed buyers, and no seller is large enough to dictate the price of the product.** In this pure form, there is no government regulation.

■ **Example** **of Perfect Competition: Farmers Markets.** Only a few markets in our present economy offer these kinds of conditions. One example is farmers markets, where growers sell pretty much identical fruits and vegetables. (After all, how do you distinguish among peaches that all look pretty similar?) ■

  Monopolistic competition. TACA Airlines is a group of five Central American airlines that mainly connects to Central America, South America, and the Caribbean. If several different airlines fly from Miami to Peru, as TACA does, what makes one better than another? If prices are about the same, why, for instance, would you fly TACA, say, rather than Delta or American?

2 Monopolistic Competition: Many Sellers, Some Product Differences

Monopolistic competition is not the same as monopoly (see #4 below). **In *monopolistic competition,* the market has many sellers who sell similar products, but they have found ways to distinguish among them or buyers have perceived their products as being different.** The forms of differentiation may be slight—such as delivery time, advertising, branding, or store location—but they are sufficient to gain the seller a niche with buyers.

■ **Example** **of Monopolistic Competition: Fast-Food Restaurants.** Of course pizza, taco, and fried chicken purveyors differ from each other, but what about all those fast-food restaurants selling hamburgers? McDonald's, Burger King, Wendy's, Carl's Jr., Jack in the Box, White Castle, Sonic, In-N-Out—is there *really* any difference among them? Yes, certain fans will always go for a Big Mac over a Whopper, but most people don't see a whole lot of difference. Thus, hamburger sellers have found ways—by advertising, pricing, or "specials"—to attract buyers. Merchants running T-shirt shops, dry cleaners, gift shops, beauty salons, and convenience stores are also operating in this kind of competition. ■

3 Oligopoly: Few Sellers, Some Product Differences

In an *oligopoly,* the market has a few sellers offering similar but not identical products to many small buyers. This describes markets in which participants are required to put up huge initial investments. Thus, such a market will consist of, say, three or four medium-sized or large sellers who dominate more than half the market and who individually try to differentiate their products through marketing and branding. Usually prices tend to be in the same range, since competitors are afraid any price cuts they make would be matched by others.

⚖ BRIEFING / LEGAL & ETHICAL PRACTICES
The Oligopoly of Health Insurers in Some Markets. Oligopolies occur in such industries as airlines, soft drinks, and automobiles. Oligopoly is also legal among sellers of health insurance, but is it right?

Among private health insurers, competition is often absent, according to several studies.[26] "One or two health insurers dominate many cities," writes health care consultant Carl Mankowitz. "Their dominance allows them to dictate low provider reimbursements. But lack of competition lets them charge high premiums."[27]

Source: David R. Frazier Photolibrary, Inc./Alamy.

Source: Photograph by Sally Lindsay.

⑩ **Oligopoly?** What kind of argument could you make to justify the right of a few large health insurance companies, such as Blue Cross, to dominate particular markets? How much do you think the limited number of health insurers contributes to high premiums?

The big insurers' advantage in obtaining low rates from doctors, hospitals, and other providers, he points out, creates a hurdle that small competitors can't overcome, because they don't have enough members and so their costs can't be as low. Oligopolies thus benefit from what's known as "economies of scale"—their costs go down as they are able to serve more people. ⑩

It remains to be seen how recent health legislation will affect this arrangement. ■

4 Monopoly: One Seller Only, No Competition

In a *monopoly*, there is only one seller, and no competition. People have traditionally viewed monopolies with dread because they can operate without restraint, setting prices at whatever level they want. This is why monopolies are generally prohibited in the United States. ⑪

■ **Example** of Monopoly: Power Utilities. Monopolies in most business sectors may be illegal. But exceptions are made for power utilities—for example, California's PG&E (Pacific Gas & Electric, or "Pigs, Goats & Elephants," according to rate payers), New York's Con Edison, or Florida Power & Light. The assumption is that it would be inefficient to run competing electricity and gas connections to every house and increase energy costs. However, to prevent utilities from abusing their exclusive market power, they are closely regulated by the state. ■

The Way Free Markets Work: Demand, Supply, & Market Price

What are the important principles under which free markets operate?

Is there a market for oversized rabbits? Maybe not. But the North Koreans have been willing buyers because they hoped to use them to alleviate chronic food shortages, and a German farmer who raises 22-pound rabbits was happy to oblige them.[28] (Note the irony here—a communist state that professes not to believe in the free market haggling *in* the free market to get enough food to feed its people.)

There are many transactions that might seem somewhat peculiar. But the point of free markets is that they bring people with particular wants (buyers) together with people willing to fulfill those wants (sellers) to negotiate a price. The price tells producers how much to produce.

Demand, Supply, & Meeting of Minds

A great example of the marketplace in operation is eBay, the online auction website. All kinds of things are offered for sale (supply), from old matchbooks to houses, and all kinds of buyers log on with their own desires (demand).

Source: Photograph by Sally Lindsay.

⑪ **Monopolist?** Are professional sports leagues, such as the National Football League, considered monopolies? In effect they are, although the U.S. Supreme Court has ruled that professional sports must observe antitrust laws. (The exception is baseball, which for some reason is considered more a game than a business, and so antitrust laws supposedly do not apply.) But many owners of professional sports teams behave in monopolistic ways, setting high ticket prices and threatening to move their teams elsewhere if the cities they are in won't pay for new stadiums.

Key Takeaway 3-1
The four kinds of free markets are (1) perfect competition, (2) monopolistic competition, (3) oligopoly, and (4) monopoly.

Demand: How Much Are People Willing to Buy for What Price? *Demand* **is the quantity of products that people are willing and able to buy at various prices at a given time.** The more scarce a product is, the more it will be in demand and the higher the price people will be willing to pay for it, if they are able to—like a parched prospector in the desert willing to pay top price for a drink of water (high demand). And the less scarce the product, obviously, the less people will be willing to pay for it (low demand).

Supply: How Much Are People Willing to Produce for What Price? *Supply* **is the quantity of products that people are willing to sell at various prices at a given time.** The more scarce a product is, the more the seller will want to charge for it—like someone selling rare antiques (low supply). And the less scarce the product, the less sellers will be able to charge (high supply).

The Market Price: The Interaction of Demand & Supply. **The** *market price,* **or** *equilibrium price,* **is determined by the interaction of demand and supply.** Or stated another way, the market price of a product is determined when the quantity supplied is equal to the quantity demanded—when an *equilibrium point* between the two is reached. eBay is a great arena for buyers and sellers to meet because it is so extensive. However, a weekend garage sale or a farmer in remote Tibet offering cattle for sale to his neighbors operates essentially the same way: buyers and sellers agree on a price, and the transaction is accomplished.

Graphing Demand & Supply: Reaching the Market Price

The interaction of demand and supply can be illustrated on three graphs. (*See* ■ *Panels 3.5, 3.6,* and *3.7.*) This could be for any good or service, but we will use the example of tablet computers. (In this theoretical example, both buyers and sellers are assumed to have "perfect knowledge" about others' technology and competitive prices, so that no one has a secret advantage.)

■ **PANEL 3.5 The demand curve: illustrating demand at various prices.** This sample demand curve shows the quantity of tablet computers at various prices. The curve falls from left to right because the lower the price of tablets, the higher the quantity demanded.

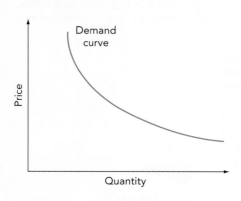

■ **PANEL 3.6 The supply curve: illustrating supply at various prices.** This sample supply curve shows the quantity of tablets for sale at various prices. The curve rises from left to right because the higher the price of tablets, the more sellers will be willing to supply them.

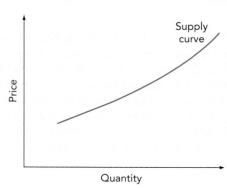

■ **PANEL 3.7 Establishing a market price (equilibrium): illustrating where demand and supply curves meet.** This graph shows that when the sample demand curve and the sample supply curve are put on the same graph, they intersect at a place where the quantity demanded and the quantity supplied are equal—the *equilibrium point*. This intersection establishes the market price—the price at which the quantity supplied to the market is equal to the quantity demanded.

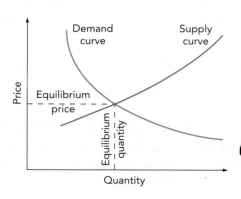

How Real Is the Demand & Supply Model?
A Word about Consumer Sovereignty

No doubt the model just described works flawlessly in an ideal world of perfect competition. It depends on the greed (or ambition, if you like) of sellers to offer more products when prices are high, and so greed serves the general interest.

The conditions of perfect competition may apply to farmers markets. They do not apply, however, in the real world of tablet computers, nor of physicians' services, theater tickets, defense-industry contracts, electric utilities, or new cars. These marketplaces in the real world are affected by other matters, as follows.

Government Influences. The government influences the marketplace in all kinds of ways. Think taxation, regulation, and import/export restrictions, to name a few, but also infrastructure development and maintenance.

> ■ **Example of Government Influence: Federal Involvement in the Economy Has a Long History.** Yale University economist Robert J. Shiller points out that even George Washington "envisioned some government involvement in the commercial system, even as he recognized that commerce should belong to the people."[29] And indeed government has had a long history of influencing the U.S. economy in beneficial ways. In the beginning, it developed highways, canals, and railroads, infrastructure that helped citizens achieve their best potential, but otherwise it let individual economic liberty prevail. ■

Incomplete Buyer-Seller Information. Buyers and sellers don't have perfect information about needs and availability. Even in the age of the Internet, not all buyers and sellers are aware of one another. And sellers may well hide essential information about the products they are selling.

> ■ **Example of Incomplete Information: Sellers Know More Than Buyers about a Car's Condition.** George Akerlof won a Nobel Prize in economics in 2001 for his work on imperfect information. He found, for example, that economic outcomes are changed when a car salesperson knows more about the condition of a vehicle he or she is selling than the prospective buyer does, so that the seller is able to misrepresent the actual condition of the car. According to reporter Louis Uchitelle, "It was an imbalance that helped to produce state 'lemon laws' that protect buyers."[30] Lemon laws are disclosure laws designed to help buyers of cars that repeatedly fail to meet standards of quality and performance. ■

Buyer-Seller Irrationality. Economics often assumes a model of rationality, with coldly calculating buyers and sellers. But, of course, our buying and selling decisions are often influenced by more irrational emotions, such as passion and envy.[31] And the brain itself may be miswired in some ways.

BRIEFING / PERSONAL FINANCE
The Irrational Desire of Preferring to Pay by Credit Card Instead of Cash. As an example of economic irrationality, Jonah Lehrer points out in *How We Decide* that the human brain has a propensity to be strongly "loss averse" in the short run but not in the long run. Many financial strategies are designed to exploit this inherent defect. "Payment with plastic fundamentally changes the way we spend money, altering the calculus of our financial decisions," Lehrer writes. "When you buy something with cash, the purchase involves an actual loss—your wallet is literally lighter. Credit cards, however, make the transaction abstract."[32]

Source: Deklofenak/Shutterstock.

If you really want to save money, then, make it so your credit cards are difficult to use. One thrifty student, for example, stores her cards in a frozen mug of water (ice) in the freezer compartment of her refrigerator. ⓬ ∎

Still, the interaction of supply and demand *is* real, if not precisely predictable or quantifiable. And the party with the upper hand is the *buyer*, otherwise known as the consumer. Consumers exercise what's called ***consumer sovereignty,*** **the idea that consumers influence the marketplace through the decisions of which products they choose to buy or not to buy.** To be successful, the producers of products must stay closely attuned to changing consumer tastes; otherwise, they risk failure.

⓬ **No-pain plastic.** It's easy to eat out frequently when payment is painless, as it seems to be when you pay with a credit card instead of cash. (The pain comes in the monthly Visa or MasterCard statement.) Do you find the convenience of using "plastic" frequently leads to overspending?

Want to Know More? 3-8
Behavioral Economics & Irrational Consumer Behavior
Go to www.mybizlab.com.

How Can Capitalism Survive?

Is regulation necessary?

In mid-2009, the U.S. Chamber of Commerce, which represents 3 million business organizations, announced it was launching a multiyear media campaign, the Campaign for Free Enterprise, to promote the virtues of the free market.[33] But you probably didn't hear the words *capitalism* and *risk taking* used in that campaign because research showed they didn't test well with average citizens.

"'Capitalism' was universally problematic," said a Chamber spokesperson.[34] Added a research professional, "There were those who associated 'capitalism' with greed and with the powerful dominating the vulnerable."[35] Those negatives weren't attached to the term *free enterprise*. As for risk taking, which is at the heart of capitalism (free enterprise), it was found that average Americans don't like the idea of business risks. "They think of a casino and someone throwing the dice," said the Chamber spokesperson.

Regulation or No Regulation?

This attitude may be a reaction to the worst effects of capitalism during the 2007–2009 recession, when banks failed and millions became unemployed, as we discuss further in Section 3.5. A free-market economy, however, clearly involves risk taking. The real question is: Can unregulated capitalism survive? It seems obvious that federal bureaucrats can't eliminate business downturns and unemployment, as was thought in the decades after World War II. Yet it also seems obvious that unfettered capitalism creates its own excesses. One longtime Wall Street economist notes that many government leaders in charge of the U.S. economy in the 1990s and early 2000s "confused the fact that market capitalism was the best economic system with the misguided notion that it was the perfect system."[36] ⓭

What Would Adam Smith Do?

Adam Smith, it turns out, was well aware of the ways that pride, envy, and other emotions influence economic decisions and their effects on the human community. Thus, according to Princeton University economist Alan B. Krueger, he "was not nearly as doctrinaire a defender of unfettered free enterprise as many of his late-20th-century followers have made him out to be," favoring some regulation and even taxes on the "luxury carriages" of the wealthy.[37] Is this a form of capitalism that you could endorse?

Source: Photo by Jeff Vanuga, USDA Natural Resources Conservation Service.

⓭ **Factory farm waste.** Large industrial farms have become the norm in the United States and are not highly regulated. Many of them generate enormous amounts of air and water pollution that we all have to endure. Do you think this type of farming is sustainable?

THE BIG IDEA: In this section, we describe the booms and busts of the business cycle, including recession and depression. We also identify and discuss three major indicators of economic conditions: the gross domestic product, the price-change indexes that measure inflation and deflation plus other indexes tracking economic stability (consumer price index, producer price index), and the unemployment rate. We also define productivity and explain how the government influences the economy through fiscal and monetary policies.

THE ESSENTIAL QUESTION: What do I need to know about the U.S. economic system to operate successfully within it?

MyBizLab: Check your understanding of these concepts at www.mybizlab.com.

MyBizLab

Four billion dollars: How big is that?

It's equivalent to 363 *tons* of *hundred*-dollar bills—which is what the United States sent to Iraq to pay for goods after the initial invasion. ("Who in their right mind would send 363 tons of cash into a war zone?" asked one congressional committee chairman.)[38]

But $4 billion is a mere drop in the bucket of the American economy, where we're talking about *really large* numbers. The total dollar value of all the goods and services produced in the United States (the gross domestic product, or GDP, as we'll describe) was well over $14 trillion in mid-2011 (actually $14.77 trillion). Fourteen trillion dollars is $14,000,000,000,000—14 followed by twelve zeros.

How do we wrap our minds around a number so huge? Suppose dollars were expressed as seconds: A million (1,000,000) seconds is 13 days, and a billion (1,000,000,000) seconds is 31 years. A trillion seconds is . . . 31,688 years![39]

With these thoughts, let's consider what businesspeople need to know to operate successfully within the framework of the U.S. economy, where gargantuan numbers are simply routine.

The Business Cycle: The Booms & Busts of Economic Activity

What are the phases of the business cycle?

People can get into a frame of mind where they think the current economic boom (or bust) that they're in will go on forever. Certainly that was the case in the run-up to the 2000–2002 stock market decline, when investors lost $7 trillion in market value. And it was the same again in the run-up to the 2007–2009 global recession, in which banks lost $4.1 trillion.[40] ⑭

But as sure as the sun rises in the morning, there is a business cycle to bring humility to even the most fanatical believer. Although it doesn't

⑭ **Reality time.** Until November 2008, when this headline appeared in the *San Diego Union-Tribune*, most investors had been lulled into complacency by a constantly rising stock market. That was shattered when in two days stocks had their worst drop since 1987, losing 10% of their value. "Normally, markets are driven by fear and greed," said one strategist. "Now it's fear and fear." The meltdown marked about the halfway point between the start and the bottom of the part of the business cycle known as the Great Recession (December 2007–June 2009).

Source: JustASC/Shutterstock.

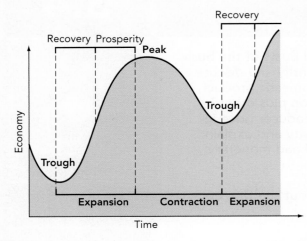

PANEL 3.8 The business cycle. This is a theoretical example. No two business cycles are alike.

repeat at regular time intervals, the *business cycle* **is the periodic but irregular pattern of ups and downs in total economic production.** Unfortunately, we often don't know quite where we are in the business cycle while we're in it. The picture becomes clear only after it's over.

Booms & Busts: The Four Phases of the Business Cycle

The business cycle is not a regular or easily predictable phenomenon, but it is a recurring pattern of economic activity, with four phases: (1) *expansion,* (2) *peak,* (3) *contraction,* and (4) *trough.* (*See* ■ *Panel 3.8.*)

Expansion: Pace of Economic Activity Speeds Up. The expansion in economic activity is triggered by a rise in investment spending, government spending, or exports, which causes an increase in GDP. The initial part of the expansion is called the *recovery* phase (because the economy is recovering from the trough). The latter part is the *prosperity* phase—the part where people say "business is booming."

Peak: Economic Activity Hits Its High. The height of prosperity, the peak, is when the expansion starts to lose steam and go into a decline or contraction.

Contraction: Pace of Economic Activity Slows Down. In the contraction phase, the pace of economic activity slows down and the GDP falls, usually triggered by falling investment, cuts in government spending, or rise in taxes, which causes decline in consumer spending. This is the part known as a *recession* or even *depression,* as we'll explain.

Trough: Economic Activity Hits Bottom. The trough is the lowest point of a business cycle, where the contraction ends—and the expansion begins again.

The number of months from trough to peak—the period of expansion—has varied from as little as 10 (March 1919–January 1920) to as long as 120 (March 1991–March 2001).[41] The "trough date" for the recent Great Recession, which started in December 2007 and lasted 18 months, was in June 2009, although its effects continued to be felt into 2010 and 2011. In late 2011, there was great fear that the country might head into a *second* recession—making the entire economic downturn a "double-dip" recession.[42]

Recession & Depression: Decline & Worse Decline

The contraction part of the business cycle is usually called a *recession,* although on rare occasions it is a *depression.*

- **Recession—two quarters of GDP decline: A *recession* is defined as two or more consecutive quarters (a quarter is three months) of decline in the GDP.** (It's apparent from this definition that economists don't know when we're in recession until *after* it has occurred.) During a recession, prices decline, consumers reduce their buying, and businesses go under, all of this leading to increased unemployment and lowered standard of living.

- **Depression—severe, long-lasting recession: A *depression* is defined as a particularly severe and long-lasting recession, accompanied by falling prices (deflation).** There are many recessions but few depressions. The last major one affecting the United States (and the world) was the Great Depression of 1929–1933.

Want to Know More? 3-9

Can You Guess How Often U.S. Business Cycles Have Occurred?

Go to www.mybizlab.com.

Want to Know More? 3-10

How Do U, V, & W Types of Recessions Differ?

Go to www.mybizlab.com.

Three Major Indicators of Economic Conditions: GDP, Price Indexes, & Unemployment Rate

What are the principal indicators I need to watch to see how well the U.S. economy is doing?

Being successful in business means you have to understand the big picture—what's going on in the national economy. Three big-picture measures of U.S. economic conditions are (1) the *gross domestic product (GDP)*, (2) the *two price-change indexes*—namely, the *consumer price index* and the *producer price index*, and (3) the *unemployment rate*.

Gross Domestic Product: Goods & Services Produced in a Year

The *gross domestic product (GDP)* **is the total value of all the goods and services that a country produces within its borders in one year.** For the United States, the GDP for 2010 was estimated by the World Bank at $14.7 trillion. This means *everything* that was produced within U.S. borders, regardless of whether the company had domestic owners (Ford, Hershey) or foreign owners (Toyota, Nestlé). Goods and services produced by governments and nonprofits are counted. However, those produced by illegal—what are often called "underground"—enterprises are not counted, such as unlawful gambling, drugs, or vice. Activities such as cash-only garage sales are also not counted.

Want to Know More? 3-11

What's the Real Difference between GDP & Real GDP?

Go to www.mybizlab.com.

Price-Change Indexes: Measuring Inflation & Deflation

Business thrives best during periods of predictability, or *economic stability,* **when (1) there are enough desirable goods and services to satisfy consumers' demands, and (2) consumers have enough money, in total, to buy what they need and want.** However, threats to economic stability are always lurking in the background, as when prices of products go up sharply or the markets are flooded with products but people are short on money and so they can't purchase them all.

Three Threats to Economic Stability: Inflation, Deflation, and Disinflation. Among the threats to economic stability, which undermine predictability and make it hard to do business, are *inflation, deflation*, and *disinflation*.

* **Inflation—when prices rise:** *Inflation* **is defined as a general increase in the prices of most goods and services.** In the United States, that would mean two things are going on: (1) there are too many dollars that are (2) trying to buy too few goods. This means your dollars lose purchasing power—you can't buy as much as you used to. ⑮

> ■ **Example** of Inflation in Brazil: Shopping Fast before Money Loses Value. American John Deal reported that when he lived in Brazil in the 1960s and 1970s, the currency was losing 30% to 40% of its value every month. "A high inflation rate," he wrote, "means you go to bed with $100 in the bank (or in your pocket) and wake up with [your money worth] $98 or $99, and on the next day you have $96, without spending a penny (well, a *centavo*). It also means when you get paid, you immediately go to the market for groceries and/or stores to purchase any basic goods you may need" before prices go up again.[43] ■

* **Deflation—when prices fall:** The opposite of inflation, *deflation* **is defined as a general decline in the prices of most goods and services.** Deflation occurs when there are too *few* dollars chasing too many goods. That is, a country is producing so many goods that there are not enough buyers for them all.

⑮ **Hyperinflation.** The United States has had periods of inflation but never hyperinflation (although it came close during the Revolutionary and Civil wars), defined as a monthly inflation of at least 50%. In 1923, a hyperinflated economy caused the German government to issue two-trillion Mark notes, such as those shown here; the highest value banknote had a face value of 100 trillion Marks. At the height of the inflation, one U.S. dollar was equal to 4 trillion German marks.

Source: World History Archive/Alamy.

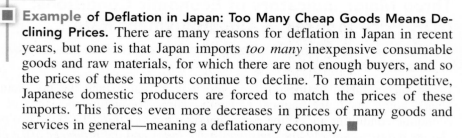

■ **Example of Deflation in Japan: Too Many Cheap Goods Means Declining Prices.** There are many reasons for deflation in Japan in recent years, but one is that Japan imports *too many* inexpensive consumable goods and raw materials, for which there are not enough buyers, and so the prices of these imports continue to decline. To remain competitive, Japanese domestic producers are forced to match the prices of these imports. This forces even more decreases in prices of many goods and services in general—meaning a deflationary economy. ■

- **Disinflation—when price increases are slowing:** A kind of in-between situation is *disinflation,* **defined as a general slowing of price increases.** That is, the inflation rate is declining. When prices are rising at a rate of 3.8% one month, but then rise at a rate of 3.6% the following month and 3.4% the month after that, that shows a pattern of disinflation.

Indexes for Tracking Economic Instability: The CPI and PPI.
How can we tell when the country has been suffering from one of these conditions? (The look is usually backward, tracking where we've been rather than where we are at the moment.) Several measures are used in the United States, such as retail sales indicators and housing starts, but two of the most important are the *consumer price index* and the *producer price index.*

- **The consumer price index (CPI)—costs of 400 consumer goods and services:** The *consumer price index (CPI)* **consists of the monthly costs of about 400 representative consumer goods and services that measure the rate of inflation or deflation.** CPI statistics are published monthly by the Bureau of Labor Statistics (BLS) in the U.S. Department of Labor. Among the "market basket" of such goods and services are the prices of food, clothing, and medical services, which are gathered by BLS employees in 56 cities and then weighted and averaged.

- **The producer price index (PPI)—prices at the wholesale level:** The *producer price index (PPI)* **is a measure of prices at the wholesale level— wholesale goods being those purchased in large quantities for resale.** The PPI is published monthly by the Bureau of Labor Statistics. Most of the data are collected through a systematic sampling of producers in manufacturing, mining, and service industries.

The Unemployment Rate: Joblessness among Active Job Seekers

The *unemployment rate* **can be defined generally as the level of joblessness among people actively seeking work.** More specifically, the unemployment rate measures people 16 years or older who are nonfarm payroll employees and who tried to find a job during the previous four weeks. In July 2011, the U.S. unemployment rate overall was 9.1% (down from the peak of 10.1% in October 2009). That was 13.9 million people out of a workforce of 153.2 million.[44] The statistics do not count *discouraged workers,* **those who have given up looking for work and have simply dropped out of the labor force.** The official counts also make no distinctions about *underemployed workers,* **those who hold jobs below their level of qualification or are working part time but want to work full time.**

There are four types of unemployment, as shown opposite. (*See* ■ *Panel 3.9.*)

Productivity: Key to Business Survival & Better Living Standards

What is productivity, and why is it important?

"For a company and for a nation," said former General Electric CEO Jack Welch, "productivity is a matter of survival."[45] It's important to a company because it

Want to Know More? 3-12

What Are Some Other Economic Indicators?

Go to www.mybizlab.com.

Want to Know More? 3-13

What's in the CPI Market Basket?

Go to www.mybizlab.com.

Key Takeaway 3-2
Three big-picture measures of U.S. economic conditions are (1) the gross domestic product (GDP), (2) the two price-change indexes—namely, the consumer price index and the producer price index, and (3) the unemployment rate.

determines whether it is profitable or even endures, and important to the nation because the more productive we are, the higher our standard of living.

What Productivity Is: More Products Created with the Resources Needed to Produce Them

Productivity **is defined as the amount of goods and services a person or organization produces given the resources needed to produce them,** such as the number of hours worked. That is, the better you are able to use your productive resources—people, technology, time, energy, and so on—to create a product, the more products you will produce; hence, the higher your productivity.

BRIEFING / EARNING GREEN BY GOING GREEN
Boosting Productivity in Junk Hauling—Applying High Tech to a Low-Tech Business. Brian Scudamore skipped his senior year in college and founded 800-GOT-JUNK? in 1989 with $700 and a beat-up old pickup truck, serving people who would pay a small fee to have their old furniture and other junk hauled away. Now it's 180 franchises throughout the United States and Canada. ⑯

Green business can be very productive, with many junk materials recycled or sold to scrap metal dealers and others. What Scudamore did was take this long-standing low-tech business and put a high-tech spin on it. As one writer described it, he added "clean shiny trucks that act as mobile billboards, uniformed drivers, on-time service, and up-front rates."[46] He also got a central call center to do all the booking and dispatch for franchise partners. All this added up to increased productivity: more services produced in proportion to the hours put in. (Can you think of some other low-tech industry where you might do this?) ■

⑯ **1-800-GOT-JUNK?** "When even the Salvation Army won't take in your tired little toaster," writes business analyst Hoover's Inc., "your huddled grass clippings, yearning to be free, who ya gonna call?" For a fee, 1-800-GOT-JUNK? will pick up any nonhazardous materials that their crews can lift and haul it to recycling centers and disposal transfer stations. About 60% of the materials it takes away are recycled or donated to local charities.

Source: Courtesy of 1-800-GOT-JUNK?

Can Productivity Improvements Be Done for Service Industries as They Were for Manufacturing?

Once an agricultural nation, the United States became a manufacturing powerhouse in the 20th century, as technological innovations made possible spectacular

Unemployment is one of the most severe problems one can encounter and can have an enormous impact.

Richard H. Price, a psychologist at the University of Michigan who studied the effects of unemployment on 756 people for two years, says that people tend to think the greatest shock is at the moment of job loss. But, he says, "it's the cascade of events that is triggered by it that causes greater and more lasting harm."[47]

The layoff leads to financial insecurity, which then causes depression, which leads to people feeling they have little control over events, which is followed by hopelessness and then sleeplessness, headaches, and chronically upset stomachs and fatigue.[48] Increases in alcoholism, separation, divorce, spousal abuse, suicide, and homicide are all associated with unemployment, especially if the joblessness lasts beyond a year.[49]

However, many people who lose their jobs are able to use the transition in powerful ways, as follows.

Explore Career Alternatives

When Mark Gozonsky lost his job as a manager for AOL, he enlisted his twin seven-year-old daughters as career counselors. "You should work in an art museum telling people stories about art, because you love art and telling stories," said one. "You should design theme-park rides so we can help you test them," said the other. "Finding out about the jobs my kids dreamed up for me was a great place to start looking for my dream job," Gozonsky said. And when he landed a job as a fifth-grade teacher, his daughters were thrilled. Inviting his children into his job search also helped him become more involved with them in a way he never anticipated.[50]

Rediscover Past Enjoyable Activities

Another exercise: Write down five anecdotes describing things you enjoyed and did well in the past, work related or not. This helps you realize that you have succeeded at things you liked—the first step in believing it could happen again.

Become Better at Looking for Work

Another activity is to simply become more adept at looking for work, as in improving interviewing skills, presentation, and focus. Finding a job seekers' club, such as WIND (Wednesday Is Networking Day) in New England, gives the unemployed a place to meet and hear advice from career counselors and other specialists. Having a session or two with a career coach can also help.

Volunteer Yourself into a Job

Sandra Erbe volunteered for a Maryland nonprofit for eight months, using her communications skills to do strategic planning and branding. When a communications job became available, she was first in line—and got the job.[51]

Follow Matthews's Job-Hunting Advice

Chris Matthews, host of MSNBC's *Hardball*, offers five pieces of advice for finding employment:[52]

- **Show up!** "Don't email. Don't phone. Show up," he advised Temple University 2011 graduates. "Put yourself in their face. If you want a job, show up for it."
- **Ask!** Ask for a job. "It comes down to looking someone in the face and telling them what you can do for them. You've got to get them to invest in you."
- **Take on investors.** "Network like a bandit," he advises. "Everyone you ask for a job, everyone you even ask for advice, becomes a stockholder in you."
- **Don't do it yourself.** "Keep your friends close. Stay in touch with your classmates. One of them might strike gold and bring you in on it."
- **Upbeat beats downbeat.** Put your best face on things. In a lousy economy, "nobody's going to ask why you're looking for a job." Thus, you need to stay positive.

gains in such industries as automobiles and electronics (think Henry Ford's assembly lines). Now much of that manufacturing has been outsourced to foreign countries and workers, as foreign competitors have shown that they can do things more cheaply. As a result, as we stated in Chapter 1, we are becoming a nation of service workers.

Unlike manufacturing, which deals with tangible products (for example, steel, cars, and food products), services deal with intangible products, such as health care, banking, education, and insurance. Services, however, tend to be more labor intensive, and this is the new frontier in productivity improvements.

Two problems exist in trying to improve productivity in services:

- **Difficulty of using technology to improve quantity rather than quality:** Productivity is concerned with quantity—more products produced with resources. But how do you use technology to improve, say, the number of guests that a bellhop can show to their rooms? Or the number of patients a lab tech might draw blood samples from in a day?

- **Difficulty of measuring productivity improvements:** Manufacturing improvements are easily quantifiable (you can easily count more cars produced in a day, for example). Service improvements aren't always as easy to count.

Even so, most economists seem to think that much of productivity growth in the United States in the 2000s—it went from a disappointing 1.5% in 1997 to 4.6% in 2002, then slid to 1.0% in 2008, then roared back to 3.9% in 2010—was mainly the result of organizations' huge investments in technology: computers, the Internet, and telecommunications advances.[53] (*See* ■ *Panel 3.10.*) After the recession hit, however, productivity was mainly achieved by cutting jobs and workers' hours and hiring experienced employees at less pay.[54] (In early 2011, the rate was 3.1%.)

Fiscal & Monetary Policies: Government's "Visible Hand" in the Business Cycle

How do fiscal and monetary policies differ?

If the free market can be considered to operate under Adam Smith's "invisible hand," maybe the government's intervention into this market could be considered a "visible hand"—because it doesn't operate in some sort of mysterious universe; rather, actual people make actual decisions that affect us all.

Because recessions and depressions are so disastrous for so many people, there has been a determined attempt by government to affect the markets in an effort to avoid economic busts and disruptions such as inflation. The principal tools the federal government uses to try to manage fluctuations in the business cycle are (1) *fiscal policy* and (2) *monetary policy*.

Fiscal Policy: Adjusting Government's Taxation & Borrowing Approaches to Achieve Economic Stability

Fiscal policy **represents the U.S. government's attempts to keep the economy stable (1) by raising or lowering taxes, or (2) through government borrowing.** With these two tools the government has the ability to infuse money into or withdraw money from the general economy, which can affect the money available to businesspeople for their own uses.

Let's consider the two parts of fiscal policy—(1) *taxation* and (2) *government borrowing.*

1. **Taxation: Will Lowering Taxes Give Business More Money to Grow?** *Taxes* **are how the government raises money to support governmental services.** States and local governments have their own taxes, but here we are concerned with federal taxes. One school of thought holds that lowering taxes will leave more money in the private economy, which business can draw on to grow. The idea is that the government will realize its benefits later in the form of taxes on higher earnings. Thus, low taxes would theoretically give a boost to the economy. On the other hand, government itself spends just as businesses do, which can also create jobs and stimulate the economy. The real point of debate between these two approaches is where money should be spent and how efficiently it is spent.

2. **Government Borrowing: Will Borrowing by the Government to Increase the Money Supply Give Businesses Access to Funds Needed for Growth?** The principal idea here is that the federal government has such enormous

■ **PANEL 3.10** Annual U.S. productivity rates for nonfarm business, 1982–2010.

Year	Rate	Year	Rate
1982	−1.1	1997	1.5
1983	4.4	1998	2.9
1984	2.0	1999	3.3
1985	1.6	2000	3.4
1986	3.1	2001	2.9
1987	0.3	2002	4.6
1988	1.6	2003	3.6
1989	0.8	2004	2.8
1990	1.8	2005	1.6
1991	1.5	2006	0.9
1992	4.0	2007	1.6
1993	0.6	2008	1.0
1994	1.0	2009	3.7
1995	0.4	2010	3.9
1996	2.6		

Source: "Major Sector Productivity and Costs Index," Bureau of Labor Statistics, May 29, 2011, http://data.bls.gov/pdq/SurveyOutputServlet (accessed August 11, 2011).

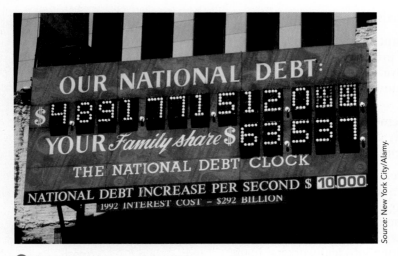

Source: New York City/Alamy.

⑰ **The national debt clock.** This huge digital counter was installed in 1989 in New York's Times Square (near an Internal Revenue Service office). The photo is, of course, out of date. As of August 15, 2011, the amount of U.S. indebtedness was over $14 trillion—specifically, $14,587,911,305,995.95. Of the $4.3 trillion in U.S. debt owned by foreign governments, China and Japan own nearly half. Who would you guess owns the rest?

Want to Know More? 3-14

Did You Know Your Share of the National Debt Is More Than Many People Earn?

Go to www.mybizlab.com.

power that it can affect the amount of money available in the national economy to borrow from. And if government borrowing shrinks the pool of money available to private borrowers, that means businesspeople will have to pay higher interest rates to borrow from whatever funds are left.

Why would government borrow? Doesn't it get enough already in taxes? Of course, government is not an abstraction: It's the sum of our congressional representatives legislating funds for defense, education, highways, social programs, and, during the recent financial crisis, bailouts and stimulus programs. Add to these the wars in Iraq and Afghanistan and tax reductions without spending cuts. The result: Government spends more than it collects in taxes, and so it has to borrow the difference (as from China). This means we have a *federal budget deficit,* or *national debt,* **the amount of money the government owes because federal spending exceeds federal revenue.** ⑰

For the past several years, government spending has exceeded government revenues, and now each man, woman, and child in the United States owes an average of $48,014. As a result of this enormous public indebtedness ($14.58 trillion as of mid-August 2011), the World Economic Forum warns that the United States may not be able to hold its place (which slipped from second to fourth) for economic competitiveness.[55]

Monetary Policy: Adjusting the Money Supply & Interest Rates to Achieve Economic Growth

Monetary policy **represents the U.S. government's attempts to manage the money supply and interest rates in order to influence economic activity.**

The part of the government responsible for doing this is the Federal Reserve System (the Fed), an independent agency that supervises banks, buys and sells foreign currencies, regulates various types of credit, and performs other functions. The Fed is headed by a chairman (currently Ben Bernanke, formerly Alan Greenspan) and board of governors, who are nominated by the president and confirmed by Congress. All national banks are required to belong to the Fed and to keep a portion of their checking and savings funds on deposit with it.

To influence economic activity, the government, through the Fed, can do two things:

Expand or Limit the Money Supply. When the Fed thinks the economy is growing too fast and threatens overexpansion and rising prices (inflation), it can reduce the supply of money available (so-called *restrictive monetary policy*). When the Fed thinks the economy is slowing down and the cost of borrowing is too high, it can make more money available to banks for businesspeople and others to use (*expansionary monetary policy*).

Raise or Lower Interest Rates. If the economy is growing too fast, the Fed can raise interest rates, making banks' money more expensive for businesses to borrow. Businesspeople will borrow less and spend less, slowing the economy. If the economy is too slow, the Fed can lower interest rates, making borrowing from banks more attractive to businesspeople.

We take up fiscal and monetary policy and the Fed in more detail in Chapter 15.

THE BIG IDEA: This section briefly compares the 1930s Great Depression and the recent Great Recession, describes the two economic bubbles (dot.com and subprime) that led to the present-day economic meltdown, and explains the failures of important financial institutions and the government's attempts to use fiscal and monetary policy to cope.

THE ESSENTIAL QUESTION: What launched the Great Recession?

MyBizLab: Check your understanding of these concepts at www.mybizlab.com.

MyBizLab

How close did the United States come to a second Great Depression in recent years? Very close, it seems. Christina Romer, head of the Council of Economic Advisors under President Barack Obama and a scholar of the Great Depression of the 1930s, believes the initial blow to confidence was far greater now than then, reports economics writer Robert J. Samuelson.[56] The differences:

Source: Pictorial Press Ltd/Alamy.

- **The first Great Depression:** Although stock prices lost a third of their value from September to December 1929, few Americans then owned stocks. In addition, home prices dropped very little. Finally, total household wealth declined only 3% from December 1928 to December 1929. ⑱

- **The almost second Great Depression:** By contrast, says Samuelson, in the Great Recession "the loss in household wealth between December 2007 and December 2008 was 17%—more than five times as large. Both stocks and homes, more widely held, dropped more. Thus traumatized, the economy might have gone into a free fall ending in depression."

In a moment we will explain how this calamity was narrowly averted, but first let's back up and set the scene.

A Tale of Two Bubbles: Dot.com & Subprime

How did technology stocks and mortgage loans contribute to two 21st-century economic bubbles?

In the waning years of the 20th century, most Americans happily enjoyed great economic stability—low unemployment, low inflation, high productivity, and a high standard of living. Then came two *economic bubbles*—**situations in which prices for securities, especially stocks, rose far above their actual value.**

The Dot.com Bubble: Overvalued Technology Stocks

The advent of the World Wide Web and the rise in popularity of Internet browsers in the 1990s sparked an entrepreneurial surge in Internet-based firms known

⑱ **Bread line.** The Great Depression began in 1929, and many people suffered greatly. Unemployment was around 25% and didn't fall below 14% until 1941. Thousands of evicted city dwellers, along with farm families and itinerant workers who fled to the cities from the countryside, combined to overwhelm municipal resources, including relief services such as bread lines and soup lines. Have you seen anything comparable during the Great Recession of the late 2000s?

as dot.com companies. Aided by low interest rates, free-flowing venture capital, and tales of overnight wealth, entrepreneurs drove speculation and stock market indexes to new heights. Then in 1999 and 2000, in an attempt to cool off the economy and head off inflation, the Federal Reserve raised interest rates six times. Stock markets plummeted, bursting the dot.com bubble.

As stocks fell and unemployment rose, the country slid into the 2001–2002 recession, which the Fed then attempted to alleviate by reducing interest rates—from 6.5% in mid-2000 to 1.25% at the end of 2002. This had the effect of flooding the economy with cheap credit and quantities of money for investment.

The Subprime Bubble: Overvalued Mortgage Loans

With so much money but with few opportunities for high returns, investors began to focus on *subprime mortgage loans,* **essentially loans to borrowers who did not qualify with mainstream lenders—borrowers with low credit scores and incomes insufficient to repay the loans.** Once a small part of the mortgage market, subprime loans caught on among both lenders and borrowers.

Borrowers: Benefiting from a Rising Housing Market. For subprime borrowers, the attractiveness of such loans lay in their easy availability, since often no proof of income, credit history, or down payment was required. As a result, all kinds of borrowers "qualified" who had no business doing so. In California, a "strawberry picker with an income of $14,000," wrote Michael Lewis, "was lent every penny he needed to buy a house for $720,000."[57]

The wave of new borrowers fueled the 2004–2007 real-estate boom, leading to a possible 250,000 more new houses being built a year than normal, according to one economist.[58] Borrowers assumed that when higher rates kicked in on their adjustable-rate loans, they could handle the higher payments by either selling their now-higher-priced houses or refinancing them at reduced rates.

Lenders: Benefiting from Bundling Loans to Sell to Investors. Banks and investment houses found they could make money not only from borrowers paying interest on their loans but also from a practice known as securitization. Developed in 1977, *securitization* **is a process of distributing risks by packaging loans together into mortgage-backed securities that can be sold to many kinds of investors.** Because of the boom in housing prices, securitized bonds (known as "collateralized debt obligations") seemed relatively low risk—the assumption being that the original mortgage borrowers would always be able to handle their loan repayment as long as the housing market went up.[59]

In 2005, however, housing prices hit their peak—and in the following years the air began to go out of the mortgage bubble. During 2006–2007, many subprime borrowers were not only unable to make their loan payments but found themselves owing more on their homes than their homes were worth ("underwater" or "upside down"). The result, from which we have yet to recover: a continuous wave of *foreclosures*—**banks repossessing and selling homes on which the borrowers could not meet their loan payment obligations**. ⑲

From Boom to Bust

The Great Recession, as mentioned, officially began December 2007—and it got worse as it went along. Through 2008, the decline in mortgage values and plunging home prices battered banks and other financial institutions. When the U.S. government, after hinting that it would not allow any major financial firms to fail—indeed, six months earlier it had rescued mortgage banker Bear Stearns—suddenly refused to bail out giant Wall Street investment bank Lehman Brothers (twice Bear's size), it "shook market confidence to its core," says one expert, "and caused people to believe the whole system could blow up."[60]

 Foreclosure. Long after the Great Recession began in late 2007, home foreclosures were still occurring at near record levels across most of the United States. From January to May 2011, almost 400,000 homes were repossessed by banks or sold at foreclosure auctions. Do you know of anyone who lost their home this way? Did your family?

Indeed, Lehman's September 15, 2008, bankruptcy triggered a near meltdown of the U.S. financial system. Stock prices collapsed, dropping by 34% a year later and destroying $14 trillion in household wealth. Banks refused to lend, even to each other. Credit markets froze, causing loan interest rates to skyrocket. General Motors and Chrysler declared bankruptcy. ㉐

A record 8.4 million jobs disappeared—three times the job losses of the dot .com bust.[61] The unemployment rate doubled to nearly 10%. And the economic crisis went global, affecting countries from Iceland and Ireland to China and Japan.[62]

The Government Intervenes: But Where Were the Regulators Originally?

What steps did the federal government take?

"Private markets for goods, services, labor, and securities do mostly self-correct," says Samuelson, the economics writer, "but panic feeds on itself. . . . In this situation, only government can protect the economy as a whole, because most individuals and companies are involved in self-defeating behavior of self-protection."[63] And indeed the federal government intervened in the economy in a major way, using tools of both fiscal and monetary policy—successfully enough, it seems, to avert a calamitous depression, but still unable to avoid the worst downturn since the 1930s.

Fighting Back

In September 2008, the U.S. Treasury Department took over Fannie Mae and Freddie Mac, lending institutions that owned half of U.S. mortgages but whose worth had plummeted 90% from a year earlier. The Fed also stepped forward with an $85 billion loan for global insurance company AIG, once the 18th-largest public company in the world, after its credit rating was downgraded. But bad news continued to roll in.

Congress acted, and on October 3, 2008, the Troubled Assets Relief Program, or TARP, was signed into law, a $700 billion program to purchase bank assets in order to strengthen the financial sector (with some money also used to bail out General Motors and Chrysler). Still, banks continued to fail at a rapid rate.[64]

㉐ **Chevy Volt.** Among the many factors that led to the collapse of General Motors and Chrysler, and their need for government-backed loans, was their failure to offer more fuel-efficient cars. A symbol of GM's rebirth is the Volt, an electric/gas hybrid that, according to the U.S. Department of Energy, achieves the equivalent of 93 miles per gallon when operating on electricity only.

ⓘ

Want to Know More? 3-15

Financial Crisis Basics: What Happened, Who Is Responsible, & How Will It Be Fixed?

Go to www.mybizlab.com.

Ultimately it took $19 trillion in public funds to save the financial system, 91% of which went mostly to banks and to supporting Fannie and Freddie. The other 9% went to U.S. citizens in the form of tax benefits, subsidies, and indirect mortgage guarantees.[65] It was left to a new presidential administration in 2009 to try to deal with high unemployment, diminished incomes, and rising poverty through an $825 billion "stimulus plan," the American Recovery and Reinvestment Act.

What Really Happened?

By mid-2011, the United States—and the world—were painfully trying to work back toward economic normalcy, and it is not clear which interventions worked best. It does seem to be clear, however, that the government's $14 trillion intervention probably staved off global collapse—and actually made money for taxpayers.[66] As for causes, some observers think that government regulators "stood idly by for years as financial firms built their houses of cards" and that "financial deregulation led directly to the financial meltdown."[67] We will return to this topic elsewhere in the book.

LEARNING & SKILLS PORTFOLIO

Summary

3.1 Freedom to Succeed—or Fail: How Economics Affects Business

THE ESSENTIAL QUESTION: *What is economics principally concerned with, and what are its two major fields?*

What is the definition of "economics"? Economics is concerned with the production, distribution, and consumption of scarce goods and services, which includes the forces of supply and demand. Scarcity has a great deal of bearing on the forces of supply and demand. Supply expresses how willing and able sellers are to provide goods and services at different prices. Demand expresses how willing and able buyers are to purchase goods and services at different prices.

How do "macroeconomics" and "microeconomics" differ? Macroeconomics studies the economy as a whole; it concentrates on large economic units, such as the operations of a nation's economy and the effect on it of government policies and allocation of resources. Microeconomics studies the economic behavior of individual economic units, and the operations of particular groups of people, businesses, organizations, and markets.

Why does specialized knowledge make a difference? Resource development is the study of how to develop the resources for creating and best utilizing goods and services. The means for developing goods and services are the factors of production—natural resources, capital, human resources, entrepreneurship, and knowledge. Knowledge is the technological expertise that is crucial in today's economic system.

3.2 Three Types of Economies: Command, Free-Market, & Mixed

THE ESSENTIAL QUESTION: *How do the three different economies of the world differ from each other?*

What's the difference between communism and socialism? Command economies, or central-planning economies, are economic systems such as communism and socialism, in which the government owns most businesses and regulates the amounts, types, and prices of goods and services. The two principal variations of command economies are communism and socialism. Communism is an economic system in which all property is owned by the government and everyone works for the government. Socialism is an economic system in which some major industries are owned by the government, but smaller businesses are owned by individuals. Much of the wealth or surplus of high incomes is redistributed by the government through social programs.

What is the basis of capitalism? In a free-market economy, also called capitalism, the production and distribution of goods and services are controlled by private individuals rather than by the government. Economist Adam Smith in 1776 said he believed that, if left alone, the marketplace would operate as if guided by an "invisible hand," with individuals' drive for prosperity producing needed goods and services that would provide economic and social benefits to all. Smith believed if business owners were allowed to earn profits from their labor, they would work hard to benefit their families and would hire others, producing economic benefits.

Why is there a trend toward mixed economies? Command economies are lacking in job creation, and free-market economies are lacking in social welfare. The result throughout the world is a trend toward mixed economies, in which some resources are allocated by the free market and some resources are allocated by the government, resulting in a somewhat better balance between freedom and economic equality.

3.3 How Free-Market Capitalism Works

THE ESSENTIAL QUESTION: *What are the basic underpinnings of the free market?*

What are the four rights a country must have for a free-market economy to operate successfully? Businesspeople in a free-market economy have four basic rights: the right to own property, the right to compete, the right to free choice, and the right to make and keep profits.

How would I distinguish between the four types of free markets? Four kinds of free markets are perfect competition, monopolistic competition, oligopoly, and monopoly. (1) In perfect competition, the market has many small sellers who sell interchangeable products to many informed buyers, and no seller is large enough to dictate the price of the product. (2) In monopolistic competition, the market has many sellers who sell similar products, but they have found ways to distinguish among them or buyers have perceived their products as being different. (3) In an oligopoly, the market has a few sellers offering similar but not identical products to many small buyers. (4) In a monopoly, there is only one seller, and no competition.

What are the important principles under which free markets operate? Free markets operate under the principles of supply and demand. Markets bring people with particular wants (buyers) together with people willing to fulfill those wants (sellers) to negotiate a price. The price tells producers how much to produce. The market price, or equilibrium price, is determined by the interaction of demand and supply. That is, the market price of a product is determined when the quantity supplied is equal to the quantity demanded—when an equilibrium between the two is reached. The party with the upper hand is the buyer, or consumer. Consumers exercise so-called consumer sovereignty, the idea that consumers influence the marketplace by deciding which products to buy or not to buy.

Is regulation necessary? A free-market economy involves risk taking, but can unregulated capitalism survive? Adam Smith favored some regulation.

3.4 What Businesspeople Need to Know: How to Operate Successfully within the U.S. Economic System

THE ESSENTIAL QUESTION: *What do I need to know about the U.S. economic system to operate successfully within it?*

What are the phases of the business cycle? The business cycle is the periodic but irregular pattern of ups and downs in total economic production. The cycle has four phases: (1) expansion, the pace of economic activity speeds up; (2) peak, economic activity hits its high; (3) contraction, economic activity slows down; and (4) trough, economic activity hits bottom. The contraction is usually called a recession, defined as two or more consecutive quarters of decline in the GDP, or rarely a depression, a severe and long-lasting recession accompanied by falling prices.

What are the principal indicators I need to watch to see how well the U.S. economy is doing? Three big-picture measures of U.S. economic conditions are as follows: (1) The gross domestic product (GDP) is the total value of all the goods and services a country produces within its borders in one year. (2) Price-change indexes, which measure threats to economic stability, measure inflation, a general increase in the prices of most goods and services; deflation, a general decline in the prices of most goods and services; and disinflation, a general slowing of price increases. Two indexes for tracking economic instability are the consumer price index, monthly costs of about 400 consumer goods and services that measure the rate of inflation or deflation, and the producer price index, a measure of prices at the wholesale level. (3) The unemployment rate measures the level of joblessness among people actively seeking work.

What is productivity, and why is it important? Productivity is the amount of goods and services a person or organization produces given the resources needed to produce them. Productivity is crucial to a firm's survival.

How do fiscal and monetary policies differ? Fiscal policy represents the U.S. government's attempts to keep the economy stable by raising or lowering taxes or through government borrowing. Two parts of fiscal policy are taxation, how the government raises money to support governmental services, and government borrowing, which can lead to a federal budget deficit or national debt when the government owes because its spending exceeds its revenues. Monetary policy represents the U.S. government's attempts to manage the money supply and interest rates in order to influence economic activity. This can be done by expanding or limiting the money supply or raising or lowering interest rates.

3.5 The—Almost—Second Great Depression: The Road to a Global Economic Crisis

THE ESSENTIAL QUESTION: *What launched the Great Recession?*

How did technology stocks and mortgage loans contribute to two 21st-century economic bubbles? Economic bubbles are situations in which prices for securities, especially stocks, rise far above their actual values. The dot.com bubble of 1999–2000 ended because of attempts to cool off fast-rising technology stocks. The subprime bubble of 2006–2007 ended when borrowers were unable to continue paying subprime mortgage loans, loans to borrowers who did not qualify with mainstream lenders. The result was a wave of foreclosures, with banks repossessing and selling homes on which buyers could not meet their obligations. This led to the Great Recession of December 2007 through June 2009, the worst downturn since the Great Depression of the 1930s.

What steps did the federal government take? The government put forth various loans, including the $700 billion Troubled Assets Relief Program to purchase bank assets in order to strengthen the financial sector.

brain drain   68
business cycle   80
capitalism   69
command economies 65
communism   65
consumer price index (CPI)   82
consumer sovereignty   78
deficits   68
deflation   81
demand   76
depression   80
discouraged workers   82
disinflation   82
economic bubbles   87
economic stability   81
economics   62

equilibrium price   76
federal budget deficit   86
fiscal policy   85
foreclosures   88
free-market economy   69
gross domestic product (GDP)   81
inflation   81
"invisible hand"   69
macroeconomics   63
market price   76
microeconomics   64
mixed economies   71
monetary policy   86
monopolistic competition   74
monopoly   75

national debt   86
oligopoly   74
perfect competition   74
producer price index (PPI)   82
productivity   83
recession   80
resource development   64
securitization   88
socialism   66
subprime mortgage loans   88
supply   76
taxes   85
underemployed workers   82
unemployment rate   82
welfare state   67

Pop Quiz Prep

1. How does scarcity generally affect supply and demand?

2. What is an issue that would be of concern to a macro-economist?

3. Under a socialist economic system, who owns businesses and industries?

4. What is a downside to capitalism?

5. What is the model of perfect competition?

6. What is meant by the term *consumer sovereignty*?

7. Which phase of the business cycle is triggered by a rise in investment spending, government spending, or exports?

8. How is *deflation* defined?

9. What is an economic bubble?

10. What is TARP?

Critical Thinking Questions

1. The four kinds of free-market competition are perfect competition, monopolistic competition, oligopoly, and monopoly. The following list contains various examples of industries, products, and services. For each, decide on its degree of competition by indicating one of these: perfect competition (PC), monopolistic competition (MC), oligopoly (O), or monopoly (M). Discuss your decisions in pairs or in groups.
   a. Wireless service providers _____
   b. Printed newspapers _____
   c. Streamed online or TV movies _____
   d. Commercial banks _____
   e. Makers of laundry detergent (Procter & Gamble and Unilever have most of the market share) _____
   f. Tomatoes and corn _____
   g. Airliner market (Boeing and Airbus) _____
   h. Online schools _____
   i. Viagra (patent expiration is 2019) _____
   j. Energy drinks _____
   k. Pet apparel _____
   l. Toothpaste _____
   m. Grapes and apples _____
   n. Beer industry (Anheuser-Busch and MillerCoors control about 80%) _____
   o. Television industry _____
   p. Automobile industry _____
   q. Diamond industry (De Beers Diamonds) _____

2. David Geffen, an American record executive, philanthropist, and film/theater producer, is quoted as saying "Happy is harder than money. Anybody who thinks money will make you happy hasn't got money."[68] What are your thoughts on this? Explain.

3. An article from the weekly news magazine *The Economist* about GDP and its impact on happiness says "capitalism is adept at turning luxuries into necessities—bringing to the masses what the elites have always enjoyed. But the flip side of this genius is that people come to take for granted things they once coveted from afar. Frills they never thought they could have become essentials that they cannot do without. People are stuck on a treadmill: as they achieve a better standard of living, they become inured to its pleasures."[69] How would you interpret this quote? Discuss.

4. Measurements of the gross domestic product (GDP) are not exact. One of the best ways to think about GDP is as a complicated estimate of the value of all the goods and services produced by a country. The GDP, however, does not include "off the books" business transactions that occur in the underground economy or black market. The black market consists of illegal activities, such as smuggling, prostitution, and drug and arms trafficking. But it also consists of legal activities in which income is not reported and consequently taxation is avoided; this is most often found in construction and service industries. In

the underground economy or black market, payments are untraceable because of issues like purely cash transactions and money laundering. What percentage of GDP would you estimate the underground economy accounts for in the United States? Do you think it's more in other countries? Explain.

5. How is customer demand affected by factors such as price, customer preferences, income, substitute products, and the price of goods that go together? For each of the products, fill in the following chart with a brief explanation of the impact of each. Does the fact that some of these products are necessities (insulin, for example, if you have diabetes) affect your answer? Explain.

	Cigarettes	Insulin	Smartphone	Designer Shoes or Sneakers	Textbook	Coffee
Price						
Customer preferences and income levels						
Is there a substitute product?						
Prices of goods that go together						

VIDEO CASE
An Economics Lesson: Gourmet Food Trucks Thrive

The mobile gourmet food truck has traveled a long way from the nostalgic days of its predecessor, affectionately known as a "roach coach," a simple catering truck that appeared at carnivals, construction sites, sporting events, office buildings, or other places lacking a cafeteria or nearby food service.[70] Mobile food trucks have been around for years. Since so many of these vehicles thrived at construction sites, today the result is a surplus of such vehicles, due mainly to dwindling business. The housing bubble and economic downturn has resulted in far fewer construction sites. Consider this: what about combining the vehicle surplus with a few great chefs (some from high-end restaurants), ordinary foodies, and a few enterprising entrepreneurs like Lindsay Laricks who are willing to take a risk in the private enterprise system? The result? The current gourmet food truck trend and all-natural Fresher Than Fresh Snow Cones.

Interestingly, economic conditions and adjusted consumer spending habits have contributed to the growth of the mobile food truck trend. In 2011, Americans are expected to spend $630 million on food from mobile vendors, up from the previous year's total of $608 million.[71] The National Restaurant Association (NRA) identified food trucks as a top trend in its most recent restaurant industry forecast.[72] The food truck trend has "shifted into high gear" as consumers have traded down and reduced restaurant visits, according to an industry veteran speaking at the NRA's annual meeting in a session entitled "The Road Ahead for Food Trucks."[73] Even in an economic recession, consumers remain committed to fun, flavor, and variety. Many pinpoint 2008 as the unofficial onset of the food truck phenomenon when the wrapped and branded vehicles rolled onto the food scene.[74] Food trucks have attracted savvy social-networking millennials (born between the mid-1970s and mid-1990s), and their market influence is widening among a number of demographics and age groups who are hopeful to try something new, like Laricks's Fresher Than Fresh Snow Cones.

What is the advantage to Laricks of selling snow cones from a truck rather than a retail location? The advantages of food trucks as a business model are many, including lower overhead, mobility, a variety of food offerings (when there are many food trucks in a single location), lower prices, great quality, their social value (when the trucks converge, so do people), and their ability to serve as test outlets for brick-and-mortar restaurant concepts.[75] In addition, advertising and promotion costs are nominal compared to those for a traditional brick-and-mortar restaurant. Social media allows Laricks to get the word out to her Kansas City customers, not only through her website which has a calendar showing the truck's whereabouts, but through Facebook and Twitter as well.[76]

On the Fresher Than Fresh website, it states: "We are Kansas City's 1st all natural snow cone stand on wheels! Our

mission is to please modern taste buds that are looking for the fun and refreshment without all the artificial stuff."[77] Laricks has resourcefully combined fresh fruit, high-quality sugars, and herbs into something gourmet and poured it over ice to create demand for the first all-natural snow cone. The forces of supply and demand and her unique flavors, like Lemon Prickly Pear, are definitely working in Laricks's favor.

What's Your Take?

1. Local support during challenging economic times is the way many small-business ideas actually come alive and survive. Part of Laricks's support came in the form of online contributions through an innovative website called Kickstarter.com. Laricks says, "I feel like I couldn't be doing this without the support that's come locally. I built all of it out of my own pocket and then realized to be completely mobile and up to code that I needed all this equipment. So I did this Kickstarter project online, which is basically 'angel investing,' like 80% of the donations were pledges that came from local people who wanted to support this and wanted something like this locally." Kickstarter is an online funding platform for entrepreneurs like Laricks with creative projects and businesses in need of financing. Go to www.kickstarter.com and discuss the categories and locations of projects available for investors to contribute to. Would you contribute to someone else's project or try to get funding for a project of your own as Laricks did?

2. Economists distinguish between four types of free markets. Based upon where Fresher Than Fresh stands (as a monopoly), what would have to occur for it to move to an oligopoly structure?

3. The four basic rights of capitalism are the right to own property, the right to compete, the right to free choice, and the right to make and keep profits. How is each of the four basic rights identified in the video?

4. The video narrator states, "Lindsay is fortunate. Her unique, Midwestern treats still sell more than enough to keep her in business. That's the nice thing about supply and demand . . . sell something people really want, they'll often buy it even during tough times." What other items can you think of that people will continue to purchase during tough times? How do the forces of supply and demand affect Laricks's sales?

5. As stated in the chapter, "Adam Smith, it turns out, was well aware of the ways that pride, envy, and other emotions influence economic decisions and their effects on the human community." What examples are seen in the video that influence economic decisions and their effects on the human community?

BUSINESS DECISION CASE
The Ivory Coast: Despite Uncertainty, the Sweetest Place on Earth

Cocoa is a powder made from cacao seeds after they have been fermented, roasted, shelled, ground, and freed of most of the fat.[78] It is the main ingredient used to make chocolate. The Ivory Coast, located in West Africa, is the world's largest producer of cocoa, and a global supplier of one-third of all cocoa,[79] valued at $3.9 billion (at current prices).[80] Cocoa exports make up almost one-third of the Ivory Coast's gross domestic product.[81] Factors affecting supply and demand of cocoa—and subsequently, its price—include weather conditions, chocolate consumption, underinvestment in cocoa farming due to high taxes and more lucrative crops, political issues (leading to an export ban), and investor speculation.

Cocoa farming in the Ivory Coast has suffered from weather conditions—as in too little rain, or a drought, which has caused a shortage. As the economy has improved, demand for cocoa by confectioners or candy makers has increased, and with a shortage a price increase usually results. In the Ivory Coast, cocoa has suffered from chronic underinvestment and high taxes, with many farmers switching to the more lucrative trade in rubber.[82] Without new planting, trees can reach their peak of productivity and this can affect production. The impact of investment and taxes on a country's crop and main export can be dramatic for a country like the Ivory Coast, relying on one-third of its GDP from the sale of cocoa exports.

Politics can have an impact as well. Exports of cocoa from the Ivory Coast came to a standstill after a presidential election where the winner called for an export ban of the commodity to "squeeze the purse strings of the incumbent who had refused to step down (the disagreement was over alleged voting fraud in the northern part of the country), after he lost."[83] Both used cocoa as a bargaining chip and tactic to threaten the other. As a result of this ban, prices were driven up by futures investors hoping to make money on the commodity under political turmoil. The export ban drove cocoa futures higher. The ban caused cocoa beans to pile up in Ivory Coast warehouses, causing transportation bottlenecks when shipments resumed.[84]

When a ban is imposed on a commodity, it causes unrest for the exporting country and its growers. Those in need of the commodity—for example, large confection companies—may end up sourcing cocoa from other countries.[85]

The biggest support of prices of any commodity is based on fear of supply constraint. As the supply goes down, prices increase and investors begin speculating. Speculation occurs when, in an effort to make a buck, investors turn to a higher-risk commodity, with hopes of an upward price shift. The effect of the political unrest is that cocoa prices jumped on the global commodity markets to levels not seen since the late 1970s, sending shockwaves throughout the cocoa-processing industry.[86] As these many factors continue to have an impact on the supply and price of cocoa, what impact will they have at the vending machine when you're craving a tasty chocolate treat?

What's Your Take?

1. When export bans are put in place, what do you think might happen to companies like Mars, makers of M&M's, Snickers, Twix, Dove, and Three Musketeers?

2. Free markets depend on demand from buyers and supply from sellers to reach a market price for a good or service. How do you interpret this statement with regard to some of the factors affecting the price of cocoa?

3. When the price for cocoa increases, can it always be attributed to a shortage of these precious beans? Explain.

4. If you took a poll, and assumed a drought in the Ivory Coast leading to a cocoa shortage, what is the maximum your friends would be willing to pay for a candy bar before choosing a substitute? What would the substitute be?

5. If you knew that more cocoa is required for the production of dark chocolate, as a candy maker, what would you research in terms of consumer preferences and tastes?

Go to www.mybizlab.com for online activities and exercises related to the timely topics discussed in this chapter's Briefings, as well as additional theme-related Briefing *Spotlights* highlighting how these concepts apply in today's business environment.

In-chapter Briefing:
- The Scarcity of Super Bowl Losers' Caps
- Using Knowledge to Build a Technology for Predicting Hit Movies

Activity:
- Developing Marketable Business Skills – Influences on Gas Prices
- Going to the Net! – Shocking Real-Time Estimates of Debt
- Going to the Net! – A Good Investment? The Forever Stamp

Briefing Spotlight:
- A Global Economy in Flux

In-chapter Briefing:
- Boosting Productivity in Junk Hauling – Applying High Tech to a Low-Tech Business

Activity:
- Going to the Net! – Green GDP

Briefing Spotlight:
- Investing in a Healthy Planet

In-chapter Briefing:
- The (Mostly) Communist Countries Today

Activity:
- Going to the Net! – Exploring Outsourcing Locations in Kenya
- Going to the Net! – Understanding Global Economic Indicators

Briefing Spotlight:
- Levi's: Old Company, New Tricks

In-chapter Briefing:
- The Oligopoly of Health Insurers in Some Markets

Activity:
- Ethical Dilemma Case – Who Is to Blame for the Housing Bubble?

Briefing Spotlight:
- Greenwashing for Dollars

In-chapter Briefing:
- The Irrational Desire of Preferring to Pay by Credit Card Instead of Cash

Activity:
- Developing Marketable Business Skills – College Tuition & Microeconomics
- Going to the Net! – Compare the Cost of an Item Today to the Year You Were Born
- Maximizing Your Net Worth – Using Credit Cards Responsibly

Briefing Spotlight:
- Good Lessons Learned the Hard Way

Additional Briefing Spotlights available at MyBizLab:

- BUSINESS CULTURE & ETIQUETTE
- BUSINESS SKILLS & CAREER DEVELOPMENT
- CUSTOMER FOCUS
- INFO TECH & SOCIAL MEDIA
- SMALL BUSINESS & ENTREPRENEURS
- SOCIALLY RESPONSIBLE BUSINESS

4

Globalization

Rising to the Challenge of World Competition

After reading and studying this chapter, you will be able to answer the following essential questions:

MyBizLab

Where you see MyBizLab in this chapter, go to www.mybizlab.com for additional activities on the topic being discussed.

FORECAST: ▶
What's Ahead in This Chapter

We consider the rise of the global workplace and electronic commerce, one big world market, and huge multinationals along with Internet-enabled small firms. We then discuss why countries trade; how companies enter foreign markets; and the cultural, economic, and political/legal conditions affecting trade. Finally, we describe barriers to trade, organizations promoting trade, and the major trading blocs of the world.

MyBizLab

Gain hands-on experience through an interactive, real-world scenario. This chapter's simulation entitled Going Global is located at **www.mybizlab.com**.

WINNER: Rich Products' Local Approach Succeeds in China

As more American companies try to conquer international markets, the successful ones are making constant adjustments to meet the new cultural and business order. "Like cultural chameleons, they're adapting to hundreds of countries, languages, and religious practices," says reporter Edward Iwata in *USA Today*.[1]

U.S. food companies began taking greater advantage of new business opportunities after the 1989 fall of the Berlin Wall signaled not only the beginning of the end of communism but also relaxation in trade restrictions. Tyson Foods now exports chicken products to Japan, Mexico, and Australia; Heinz sells ketchup in the United Kingdom and chili sauce in Scandinavia; CPC International/Best Foods does business in the Caribbean and Pacific Islands.[2]

An example of a forward-looking approach was that taken by Buffalo, New York, food manufacturer Rich Products Corporation (motto: "Caring for Customers Like Only a Family Can"), born in 1945 with the creation of the world's first non-dairy whipped topping. When Rich began marketing overseas, president William Gisel Jr. found early success in adapting products to fit local needs and lending a hand to clients needing help.

A young Chinese customer, for instance, who used Rich items in his cake shop, was just getting started and didn't have accounting skills, so Rich helped him set up an accounting system. Twenty years later that shop owner operates 800 cake shops in China and is one of Rich's most loyal customers.

Gisel encourages companies to build business by taking a "shoe-leather" approach—walking the streets and learning what people buy and where. "It means we've gone slower [than other U.S. companies pushing into China]," he says. "But I think our success rate is much better. We've never lost money from day one in international markets."[3]

LOSER: Campbell Soup's "One Size Fits All" Fails in China

Among the international food companies that have expanded their markets into China are KFC fried-chicken outlets, Starbucks, and McDonald's. In the early 1990s, Campbell Soup Co. also tried. The soup market there is huge—the Chinese eat soup more than five times a week, on average, compared to Americans' once a week. Thus, the Chinese consume about 320 billion servings each year, in contrast to only 14 billion in the United States.[4]

A big problem for Campbell, however, is that the majority of soup in China is made from scratch, which is not as common an activity in the United States. Chinese consumers also reported that they didn't like the tinny or can-like taste of prepared soups. But, says a *Wall Street Journal* story, "Campbell didn't do a lot of listening to consumers. . . . Rather than tailor soups to Chinese tastes and cooking customs, the company simply exported its condensed soups. Consumers, some wondering why they should pay for something that could be easily made from scratch, shunned the soups. Campbell pulled out."[5]

A decade later, however, the giant soup maker was back, making a serious attempt to gain some market share not only in China but also in Russia, another soup-loving nation. This time, the *Journal* reports, it employed cultural anthropologists to visit Chinese and Russian homes to study consumers' soup preparation and eating practices, and researchers conducted more than 10,000 consumer interviews and thousands of household tests.[6] It was learned that consumers still don't like ready-to-eat soups, although they seemed inclined to use soups as a base for other cooking. Accordingly, Campbell decided to introduce broths and soup bases that would help make old-fashioned soup preparation easier.

Can Campbell overcome the aversion to soup in a can? "It is like telling Americans they can have Thanksgiving in a can," writes one analyst.[7] At least this time, however, the company's trying. In 2011, it agreed to buy major ownership in a Hong Kong–based company that had distributed Campbell's broth in China since 2007.[8]

 YOUR CALL Would you agree that we are all bound by the culture we grew up in? Campbell's early venture in China is an example of *parochialism* or *ethnocentric* ("we know best") thinking, in which people see things solely through their own perspective. Rich Products has countered this by paying close attention to the locals. To avoid being blinded by your culture, what should you do to widen your perspective so that as economic power continues to steadily shift abroad you can survive in tomorrow's global marketplace?

MyBizLab

THE BIG IDEA: Globalization, the trend whereby national economies are becoming integrated into the world economy, is reflected in three developments: (1) the rise of the global workplace and e-commerce, (2) the trend of the world's becoming one big market, and (3) the rise of both big firms and quick, Internet-enabled small firms worldwide.

THE ESSENTIAL QUESTION: What are three developments in globalization that will probably affect me?

MyBizLab

MyBizLab: Check your understanding of these concepts at www.mybizlab.com.

Source: Bangalore Office India/Alamy.

❶ Independent and resourceful. This young American (*right*) is working in India. Do you think working in an overseas job would challenge you? Would it make you more adaptive and inquisitive? Would it make you more marketable? Why?

Will working overseas help advance your success? Probably. International experience demonstrates that you are probably independent, resourceful, and entrepreneurial, according to executive recruiters. ❶

People who have worked and supported themselves overseas, says a network television human resources executive, tend to be adaptive and inquisitive—valuable skills in today's workplace.[9] "Anyone with international experience will have a leg up, higher salary, and be more marketable," says the executive director of a national financial recruitment firm.[10]

Probably the best time to seek overseas experience is when you're young.

BRIEFING / BUSINESS SKILLS & CAREER DEVELOPMENT

When's the Best Time to Take a Job Abroad? If you're no longer young (halfway through your working life, say), spending a lot of time overseas may not be such a good idea. Being away from your company's U.S. headquarters may actually hinder career advancement, because being "out of sight, out of mind" may unplug you from the company's domestic social networks.[11] If you have a family, the spouse and children accompanying you may be strongly affected by "culture shock, loneliness, identity loss, and depression," according to one report.[12] Or, if your company sends you overseas without the family for a short-term assignment (several months to a year), that too can be stressful for family members.[13]

If you're young, however—go for it! Joshua Arjuna Stephens, a recent graduate of Wesleyan University in American studies, took a temporary summer position in marketing research with a Shanghai educational travel company. "I didn't know anything about China," he says. "People thought I was nuts to go not speaking the language, but I wanted to do something off the beaten track." Two years later, after stints at two other jobs, he was proficient in Mandarin and became manager for a Beijing company making online games.[14]

Scott Stapleton, formerly of Oakland, California, took a marketing position with InfoSys in India. "The job blends practical work experience with life in a developing country," says Stapleton, adding that it's "a rare opportunity to actually witness globalization."[15] ■

Globalization **is the increasing connectivity and interdependence of the world's economies, societies, and cultures because of advances in communication, technology, trade, international investment, movement of currency, and migration.**

Over the past century and a half, time and distance have effectively shrunk, producing three important global results:[16]

- The development of the global workplace and electronic commerce.
- The consolidation of many national markets into one big world market.
- The development of two opposite kinds of international business: huge firms and quick, Internet-enabled small firms.

The Development of the Global Workplace & E-Commerce

How has the world economy changed?

Thirty years ago, cellphones, pagers, fax, and voice mail barely existed. When in 1983 AT&T launched the first cellular communications system, it predicted about 1 million U.S. cellphone subscribers by the end of the century, but a mere decade later there were already 16 times that number. By mid-2011, about three-quarters of the world had cellphones.[17]

Another powerful technology is the Internet, used by over 2 billion people as of early 2011.[18] First developed in 1969, the Internet had remained mainly a technology used by academics, until 1991 when Englishman Tim Berners-Lee came up with the coding system, linkages, and addressing scheme that became the World Wide Web. In doing so, he converted the powerful communications system of the Internet from a technology used by only a few people to one that could be used by everyone.

The technology of the Web allowed the development of *e-commerce,* or *electronic commerce,* **the buying and selling of products and services through computer networks.** Total U.S. e-commerce retail sales were estimated at $47.5 billion in mid-2011.[19]

Today e-mail communications are rapidly being augmented by text messaging and social media applications (such as Twitter, Facebook, and LinkedIn) that enable access to real-time interactive worlds. This new ease of availability is greatly enhancing e-commerce.[20] **②**

We discuss the Internet thoroughly in Flex-Chapter D, "Information Technology."

SMELL LIKE A MAN, MAN.
Old Spice

Source: Procter & Gamble.

② **Twitter ads.** What's the potential marketing reach of social media? If you ask Old Spice, it's remarkable. Old Spice is a collection of men's fragrances and other products that advertises that for 71 years "we've been perfecting the art of making you more awesome by fixing your mansmell problems." Featuring ads like the ones shown at left, Old Spice attracted more than 32 million views. Have you purchased any products you've seen advertised in social media?

One Big Market: Free Trade & the Global Economy

What are the significant elements of global trade?

In the late 1980s, communism collapsed in Eastern Europe, Asian countries began opening themselves to foreign investment, and an increasing number of nations began deregulating their economies. These events led to an increase in *free trade,* **the movement of goods and services among nations without political or economic restrictions.**

The conditions have resulted in the *global economy,* **the increasing interaction of the world's economies with one another as a single market instead of in many national markets.** The global economy has intensified the rise of *multinational corporations,* **organizations with multinational management and ownership that manufacture and market products in many different countries.** Examples of such firms are General Mills, ExxonMobil, and Toyota.

Imports & Exports: The Ebb & Flow of the Global Economy

Free trade and the global economy are based on a constant stream of imports and exports.

Imports: Buying from Other Countries. When *importing,* **a company buys goods outside the country and resells them domestically.** The Apple iPhone 4, for instance, is imported from China, where it is assembled. However, its more than 100 parts come from all over the world.[21] Several countries—including China, Taiwan, South Korea, Japan, Germany, Switzerland, and the United States—contributed to its manufacture in some way. Some classic brands, such as Jaguar, that were once identified with their home countries are now made elsewhere or have foreign owners. **❸**

Source: Photograph by Sally Lindsay.

❸ Who owns Jaguar? This luxury brand of car grew out of a motorcycle sidecar company that was founded in England in 1922. In 1999, it became part of Ford Motor Co.'s Premier Automotive Group (which included other formerly foreign brands Aston Martin, Volvo, and Land Rover), but in 2008 it was acquired by Tata Motors of India. Jaguar continues to be made in England, but new manufacturing plants are being established in India. Do you think different ownership can affect the quality of a brand?

BRIEFING / SMALL BUSINESS & ENTREPRENEURS
A Los Angeles Salon Owner Imports Real-Hair Extensions from India. Is there money to be made from human hair? Many beauty salon operators think so. For instance, human hair extensions made from remy hair, which looks most natural and comes from Hindu temples in India, where women shave their heads in offerings to the gods, can cost a customer hundreds or even thousands of dollars.[22]

Sonia Seye owns Hair Universal, a Los Angeles salon that specializes in braiding hair and creating fashionable hairdos from multicolored hair extensions. Wanting to expand her business, she launched a search for a hair supplier in India. She spent six months researching suppliers online, querying prospects by e-mail, and checking them out with the Indian consulate. She then flew to India, where she met the suppliers under consideration and made her final choice. By buying direct, instead of going through middlemen, she halved her hair-extension costs, and thus is able to undercut the prices of rival salons.

The trip to India has more than paid for itself. "You don't have to be big to be global," Seye says.[23] ■

Exports: Selling to Other Countries. When *exporting,* **a company produces goods domestically and sells them outside the country.** The United States is a great exporter of American pop culture, in the form of movies, CDs, and fashion, as well as various forms of technology. "We are losing world market share relative to consumer goods," points out one economist, "but we continue to have a fairly strong hold on higher-end products like machinery, capital equipment, tractors, and aircraft, as well as chemicals and food."[24] Indeed, the United States exports an array of manufactured and agricultural goods. (*See* ■ *Panel 4.1.*) Some of our exports you'd probably never guess.

■ **PANEL 4.1 What the United States exports: a sampling.**

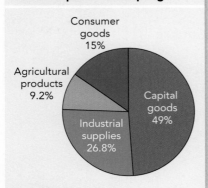

- Consumer goods 15%
- Agricultural products 9.2%
- Capital goods 49%
- Industrial supplies 26.8%

- Capital goods: transistors, aircraft, motor vehicle parts, computers, telecommunications equipment, etc.
- Industrial supplies: organic chemicals, etc.
- Consumer goods: automobiles, medicines, etc.
- Agricultural products: soybeans, fruit, corn, etc.

Source: Central Intelligence Agency, *The World Factbook*, April 26, 2011, https://www.cia.gov/library/publications/the-world-factbook/geos/us.html (accessed May 16, 2011).

Exporting U.S. Chicken Feet—A Great Chinese Delicacy. As the Chinese population has grown more prosperous, it has become the largest consumer of one peculiar U.S. export: scrumptious chicken feet. "We have these jumbo, juicy [feet] the Chinese really love," says an American poultry economist.[25]

Exports of American poultry totaled $4.34 billion in 2008, of which less than 2% was exported to China and Hong Kong. About half of this 2% was chicken feet and wings. Chicken feet are worth only a few cents a pound in the United States. However, as delicacies in China they fetch 60 to 80 cents a pound, a price that can't be matched by other foreign markets. Because U.S. poultry farmers grow birds that feature big breasts and white meat to serve American tastes, the chickens necessarily also have king-size feet.

What other things can you think of that are produced in the United States that we don't think are very important but other countries find desirable? ■

i

Want to Know More? 4-3

What Are the Most Unusual Things the United States Exports?

Go to www.mybizlab.com.

Positive & Negative Effects of the Global Economy

The economies of the world have never been more involved with each other. As technology journalist Kevin Maney once wrote, "They're tied together by instantaneous information arriving via everything from currency trading databases to websites to CNN broadcasts. Capital—the money used to build businesses—moves globally and moves in a matter of keystrokes."[26]

Positive Effects. Does a global economy really benefit the United States? U.S. exports, international trade, and U.S. workers are connected, pointed out an executive of the Inter-American Development Bank in Washington, D.C. "As consumers in other regions of the world see their income go up, they are going to be more interested in U.S. products," she said. "The bottom line is that growth of jobs and income in other countries will mean growth of jobs and income in [the United States]."[27] And indeed that was generally true for a long time.

Negative Effects. The problem with globalization is that it is disruptive, as many other nations have discovered when American corporations have attempted to move in. ❹ The reverse is also true: Global economic interdependency means that other nations may challenge the economic dominance of the United States, leading to job losses and wage stagnation for Americans. Already the United States has given up the domestic production of electronics, as manufacturing has shifted to low-wage countries.[28] A product as basic as dinnerware is now mainly produced overseas.[29] More than 300 U.S. furniture plants have closed in 10 years.[30] Issues about the quality of some imported products, such as Chinese

Source: EPA/Money Sharma.

❹ **Global disruption.** As shown here, not everyone embraces globalization. India does not allow multi-brand foreign retailers to sell directly to consumers, but they can open wholesale operations, which was what Walmart was recently trying to do. The result was a protest of several hundred Indian shopkeepers fearful that foreign-owned corporate retailers might soon undermine the small retailers in traditional marketplaces that dominate the country.

drywall containing compounds that emit toxic fumes that cause illness, continue to haunt us.[31]

Equally serious, the flows of capital and credit that sparked the boom in trade also put the world at risk when the economy faltered.[32] The troubles stemming from credit problems behind the U.S. mortgage meltdown in 2007–2008, says one account, "spread in one way or another to every part of the globe: from Iceland and Ireland to the United Kingdom and Germany, from Japan to China and Singapore, Brazil to Mexico, the Middle East to Russia."[33] In 2009, trade shrank all around the world.[34]

Despite its destabilizing aspects, the process of globalization is irreversible, if only because of the information technology and communications revolutions. "One cannot pick and choose in the package," says the former managing director of the World Economic Forum in Switzerland. "The new globality means a tremendous emphasis on speed, flexibility, versatility, and permanent change—in some respects, insecurity."[35]

The Rise of Two Kinds of International Businesses: The Big & the Quick

Why has there been a rise in huge multinationals and small, fast-moving startups internationally?

The new technologies and spread of worldwide electronic information forces things to get bigger and smaller at the same time, suggests one technology philosopher, Nicholas Negroponte. "When things want to do both but not stay in the middle . . . there will be an increasing absence of things that aren't either very local or very global."[36] Thus, we have been seeing an increase in two opposite kinds of businesses: mergers of huge companies into even larger companies, and development of small, quick-moving startup companies.

Huge Multinationals: Large Companies Merge into Larger Ones

Many big companies have tended to get bigger and to spread across borders by merging with other big companies. Some of the most famous mergers in multinationals have occurred in oil (Exxon + Mobil, Conoco + Phillips), automobiles (Porsche + Volkswagen, Chrysler + Fiat), telecommunications (Nokia + Siemens, Comcast + NBC Universal), financial services (Bank of America + Merrill Lynch), and pharmaceuticals (Roche + Genentech). We discuss mergers and acquisitions in detail in Chapter 5.

Small, Quick-Moving Firms: Startups Operate Worldwide

The Internet and World Wide Web allows almost anyone to be global, which gives small companies great advantages, as follows.

Small Companies Can Get Started More Quickly. Because anyone can list their products on a website and sell worldwide, this removes the former competitive advantages of distribution and scope that favored large companies.

■ **Example of a Startup: RVParking.com.** When in 2007 Erik Budde launched RVParking.com, a Menlo Park, California, startup offering information on where people could park their recreational vehicles, he needed Web-based workers to gather research on thousands of campgrounds and answer customer service calls. To keep costs down, he turned to an online hiring hall called ODesk, which specializes in finding computer-based workers anywhere in the world.[37] ■

Small Companies Can Change Direction Faster. Little companies can maneuver more easily and change direction faster, which gives them an advantage in terms of time and distance over large companies.

BRIEFING / SMALL BUSINESS & ENTREPRENEURS
Communications Technology Enables a 20-Person Irrigation-Equipment Firm to Operate in Three Countries. Driptech is a Palo Alto, California, irrigation-equipment company with 20 employees, seven of whom are located in China and India. Owner Peter Frykman was a Stanford University graduate student who in 2008 belonged to a group that came up with a way of making drip irrigation systems inexpensively. After testing in Ethiopia, he says, "we saw that this could help farmers across the world," and so he formed Driptech. A successful pilot program in India led to initial sales in 2009, in India and China, which in turn attracted $900,000 in funding from investors.

Presently seven Driptech employees are working in offices in Beijing and outside Mumbai, which presents a challenge for a small workforce. Fortunately, technologies like file sharing and videoconferencing allow Frykman to hand off work in the evening from California to coworkers in Asia, which he then picks up again in the morning. "If you get the rhythm right," he says, "you can really be working around the clock as an organization."[38] ❺ ■

Source: Driptech, inc.

❺ **A startup operates worldwide.** Indian farmers watch a Driptech irrigation system being installed. The American firm has only 20 employees, but communications technology allows them to operate together in three countries—the United States, India, and China. Can you think of a small worldwide business you might start that could follow this model?

Why & How Companies Conduct International Trade

THE BIG IDEA: Countries trade with each other because they are not self-sufficient and because they have resources or technology other countries want, which gives them a comparative advantage. The success of international trade is measured in the balance of trade, balance of payments, and counter-trading. Companies enter foreign markets by means of exporting and importing, franchising and foreign licensing, global outsourcing, joint ventures, and foreign subsidiaries.

THE ESSENTIAL QUESTION: Why do companies expand internationally, and how do they do it?

MyBizLab

MyBizLab: Check your understanding of these concepts at www.mybizlab.com.

An American specialist in global outsourcing—how U.S. companies can find cheaper suppliers in foreign countries—Bill Fink has a collection of old bottle stoppers, corked heads of 1940s popular figures (actor Cary Grant, English prime minister Winston Churchill). These were originally made by low-wage West Germans who were starving refugees of World War II. Later, as Germany became a high-tech nation, its high labor costs forced it to outsource such products to cheaper labor markets, beginning with the Czech Republic. But, Fink learned, as the Czech workers also became more expensive, Germany moved its outsourcing on to Budapest, Hungary. When Fink visited Hungary, however, he found factories half empty. What happened? "The damn cheap Romanians are taking our jobs," one worker said. Still, in Budapest, as in the Czech Republic and Germany, some manufacturing work remained. "The factory manager touted new custom build techniques, a lean supply chain, highly trained workers, and their proximity to Germany," Fink writes. "It was no longer cost, but value they were selling."[39]

Such is the nature of international commerce: Just when you think one country may be dominant at something, everything shifts. ❻

Source: EdBockStock/Shutterstock.

❻ **Oursourcing radiology.** A shortage of radiologists in the United States has contributed to the discipline of *teleradiology*—sending X-rays via a few keystrokes to be interpreted by radiologists in Asia and elsewhere. This activity also allows American hospitals to get a quick scan of an X-ray in the middle of the night, when a U.S. radiologist may not be on duty. How much do you think the lower fees charged by radiologists in India are contributing to this trend?

Why Countries Trade with Each Other

Why do nations trade, and what are absolute and comparative advantages?

Why should a nation bother to trade at all with other nations? Couldn't a country as wealthy as the United States supply itself from within its own borders?

Three Reasons Countries Trade

There are three principal reasons countries engage in free trade:

No Country Is Self-Sufficient. Regardless of its power, technological sophistication, or abundant natural resources, no country is completely *self-sufficient*—**able to produce by itself all of the products and services it needs or that its people want.**

Some Countries Have Natural Resources That Other Countries Want. Not every country has oil, for example, which nearly all nations need to run their economies today. Thus, Nigeria, Venezuela, Saudi Arabia, and other oil-producing nations have the advantage over non–oil-producing Japan, Switzerland, and Germany.

Some Countries Have Technology That Other Countries Want. South Korea and Germany offer sophisticated computer and automotive technology, for example, but have relatively few natural resources.

The top U.S. trading partners are shown at right. (*See* ■ *Panel 4.2.*)

Absolute & Comparative Advantage: Countries Playing to Their Strengths

It's obvious that natural and technological resources and services are not distributed evenly. Not every country has the technological know-how to launch a space program, for instance, and not every country has the right climate to have a thriving sugar-cane crop.

This leads to the distinction between the principles of absolute advantage and comparative advantage.

Absolute Advantage. An *absolute advantage* exists when one country has a monopoly on producing a product more cheaply or efficiently than any other country can. Eighteenth-century Scottish economist Adam Smith thought a country should specialize in producing products in which it had a monopoly (absolute advantage) so it could trade with other countries producing other products, so that all nations would benefit.

■ **Example of Absolute Advantage: China's Rare Earths.** China accounts for 95% to 97% of the world's supply of so-called *rare earths,* 17 minerals (with names like indium, gallium, and tellurium) crucial to high-technology products, including mobile phones, hybrid cars, and 3-D TV screens.[40] This puts China's foreign rivals at a disadvantage. This nearly absolute advantage of a country is also extremely uncommon. While absolute advantage may exist between regions (Nevada has the advantage in gold mining, but Maine has the advantage in seafood, for example), today it rarely exists on a global basis. ■

Comparative Advantage. In the real world, we are more apt to see nations having a *comparative advantage,* **meaning a country sells to other countries those products and services it produces most cheaply or efficiently and buys from other countries those it does not produce most cheaply or efficiently.** ❼

■ **Example of Comparative Advantage: GE Exports Technology.** American companies export all kinds of technological know-how. General Electric, for instance, is well known in the United States for its light bulbs, appliances, and former ownership of NBC Universal. But with about half of its revenue now coming from overseas, it is concentrating on exports in fast-growth areas such as energy equipment, health care technology, water-processing technology, and rail engines.[41] ■

Balance of Trade, Balance of Payments, & Countertrading

How is international trade measured?

How does a country know whether its trade policy is successful? There are two kinds of scorecards—the *balance of trade* and the *balance of payments.*

■ **PANEL 4.2 Top 10 U.S. trading partners, December 2010.**

Top 10 Nations for Exports of U.S. Goods	Top 10 Nations the U.S. Imports Goods From
1. Canada	1. China
2. Mexico	2. Canada
3. China	3. Mexico
4. Japan	4. Japan
5. United Kingdom	5. Germany
6. Germany	6. United Kingdom
7. South Korea	7. South Korea
8. Brazil	8. France
9. Netherlands	9. Taiwan
10. Singapore	10. Ireland

Source: U.S.Census Bureau, "Top Trading Partners," July 12, 2011, www.census.gov/foreign-trade/statistics/highlights/top/top1012yr.html (accessed August 21, 2011).

Source: Blue Jean Images/Alamy.

❼ **Comparative advantage?** If the sun's rays belong to everyone, shouldn't every country be able to compete on solar technology? However, four of the five top solar cell producers are based in China. Although the country has always had cheap labor, with solar its advantages have more to do with ready access to financing during the global economic downturn and advanced equipment for making solar cells. Still, there have been complaints alleging that China resorts to unfair competition and makes cheap products. Do you think the U.S. and Europe can compete here?

U.S. exports to:		
China	lllllll	$26.4 billion
Japan	llll	$16 billion
Germany	lll	$11.9 billion

Exports to U.S. from:		
China	llllllllllllll	$90.2 billion
Japan	lllllllll	$33.2 billion
Germany	llllll	$23.3 billion

Source: U.S. Census Bureau, U.S. International Trade in Goods & Services, www.census.gov/foreign-trade/Press-Release/current_press_release (accessed May 15, 2011).

Balance of Trade: Comparing Exports & Imports

The *balance of trade* is the value of a country's exports compared to the value of its imports as measured over a particular period of time. When the figures are added up, there may be either a *trade surplus* or a *trade deficit.*

Trade Surplus: When Exports Exceed Imports. A *trade surplus,* also called a *favorable balance of trade*, exists when the value of a country's total exports exceeds the value of its total imports. Countries prefer to export more than they import because then they have money left over to spend on other things.

Trade Deficit: When Imports Exceed Exports. A *trade deficit,* or *unfavorable balance of trade*, exists when the value of a country's total imports exceeds the value of its total exports. (*See* ■ *Panel 4.3.*) Nations dislike trade deficits because less money is left over to spend in other ways.

■ **Example** of Trade Surpluses and Trade Deficits: China versus the United States. Before 1976, the United States ran trade surpluses every year. Since then it has had trade deficits because, even though we are the world's top exporter, we have an extraordinary appetite for foreign products that are cheaper than those made in the United States. In the first three months of 2011, China shipped $90.2 billion worth of exports to the United States, but we shipped only $26.4 billion worth of exports to China.[42] Hence, in relation to their dealings with each other, China had a trade surplus, whereas the United States had a trade deficit. ■

Balance of Payments: Comparing Money In & Money Out

The balance of payments is the *overall flow* of money into and out of a country (not just payments from trade). More formally, **the *balance of payments* is determined by measuring (1) the difference between the money coming into a country (received as payments for its exports) and (2) the money going out of the country (as payments for its imports). In addition, the balance of payments takes into account (3) money flowing in and out from foreign aid, tourism, foreign investment, military investment, and other factors.**

The balance of payments may be either a surplus or a deficit.

Balance-of-Payments Surplus: When More Money Flows In. A *balance-of-payments surplus,* or *favorable balance of payments*, exists when more money flows into a country than flows out. Nations prefer this state because it means they have more money to spend.

Balance-of-Payments Deficit: When More Money Flows Out. A *balance-of-payments deficit,* or *unfavorable balance of payments*, exists when more money flows out of a country than flows in. A country in this situation is a debtor nation—as the United States is today.

Since 1976, the United States has mostly had a balance-of-payments deficit, mainly because it has bought more goods from other countries than it has sold to them (thus running a large trade deficit). China, on the other hand, has a tremendous balance-of-payments surplus, mainly because of its trade surplus—it has exported more than it has imported.

Countertrading: Bartering Goods for Goods

Sometimes other countries may wish to import certain goods but lack the currency to pay for them. In that case, the exporting country may resort to *countertrading*—that is, bartering goods for goods (or services). For example, in a 2002 Indonesia-India

Key Takeaway 4-1
A trade deficit occurs when a nation spends more on imports than it receives from its exports. A balance-of-payments deficit occurs when a nation spends more on imports, foreign aid, tourism, foreign investment, and military investment with other countries than it receives from other countries.

countertrade agreement, the Indonesian government agreed to swap crude palm oil in return for India's building 120 kilometers (74.5 miles) of railroad track in the Indonesian province of South Sumatra.

How Companies Enter Foreign Markets

What are five ways companies reach global markets?

Most companies edge into global markets, making minimal investments and taking minimal risks. Let's consider five principal ways. (*See* ■ *Panel 4.4.*)

1 Importing & Exporting: Lowest Risk

Perhaps the easiest way for a company to enter global markets is through importing or exporting.

Importing: Bringing in Foreign Products to Sell at Home. Tiptoeing into international markets may begin with importing commercial merchandise to re-sell. To begin this process, you will probably need to find an *import company*. You can get specific names by asking some small American retailers who sell the kinds of goods you are thinking of importing what import companies they use.

The most commonly used third parties in importing are (1) *customhouse brokers,* who handle U.S. customs documentation; (2) *shippers,* who consolidate freight from several companies to make full container loads, thereby reducing shipping costs; and (3) *freight forwarders*, who handle documentation and shipping both domestically and internationally.[43]

Exporting: Selling Your Product across International Borders. Exporting may be performed *indirectly*, as when a company manufactures a product (such as an airplane part) that becomes a component of some other company's product that is exported. Or it may be performed *directly*, as when the company sells in markets outside its home country.

Suppose that you're a small-business person who's decided to try to sell your product overseas. How do you go about it? Two kinds of assistance are available through *U.S. Export Assistance Centers* and *export trading companies*.

- **Export Assistance Centers—support for small business:** U.S. government–backed ***Export Assistance Centers*** **are offices located in major metropolitan areas throughout the United States that provide export assistance for small- and medium-sized businesses seeking to market their products to foreign countries.** In these offices, small-business people can receive personalized assistance from several agencies, principally the Small Business Administration (including possible help with financing), the Department of Commerce, and the U.S. Export-Import Bank.

- **Export-management companies—help in establishing trading relationships:** *Export-management companies,* or *export-trading companies*, **consist of international specialists who can help first-time exporters find foreign buyers, complete transaction documents, comply with regulations, and above all get paid.**

2 Franchising & Foreign Licensing: Moderate Risk

Franchising and licensing are similar, although franchising is used more frequently by service companies and licensing is used more often by manufacturing companies.

■ **PANEL 4.4 Five ways companies reach foreign markets: from lowest risk to highest risk.**

Method	Risk level
5. Foreign subsidiaries	Highest
4. Joint ventures	High
3. Global outsourcing	
2. Franchising and foreign licensing	Moderate
1. Importing and exporting	Lowest

i **Want to Know More? 4-4**
"Made in USA" Standard
Go to www.mybizlab.com.

8 **EAC helps NEI.** Los Angeles–based NEI Treatment Systems offers a reliable, cost-effective water treatment system for seafaring vessels. The company has credited the services of the U.S. Commercial Service of the Department of Commerce with helping it to license its technology in major shipbuilding markets in several Asian countries.

Source: Courtesy of N.E.I. Treatment Systems, LLC.

i **Want to Know More? 4-5**
Top Franchises
Go to www.mybizlab.com.

Franchising: Sharing Brand and Know-How for a Fee and Part of Profits. With *franchising,* **a company allows a foreign company to pay it a fee and a share of the profits in return for using the first company's brand name and a package of materials and services.** ❾

Companies with well-known names (Hilton Hotels, Burger King) provide the use of their names plus their operating know-how (facility design, equipment, management systems) to companies overseas in return for an upfront fee plus a percentage of the profits.

Example: America's No. 2 pizza maker (after Pizza Hut), Domino's Pizza has more than 9,000 stores in 60 markets worldwide, some company-owned, some franchise stores. It has some 4,000 stores outside the United States, including 500 in Mexico, 300 in Britain and Australia, and 200 in South Korea and Canada.

Foreign Licensing: Allowing a Company to Use Your Product for a Fee. In *foreign licensing,* **a company gives a foreign company permission, in return for a fee, to make or distribute the first company's product or service.** An American company might license a foreign company to make a product, which means that the U.S. company can make money without having to invest large sums to conduct business directly in that foreign country.

> ▣ **Example: A U.S. Publisher Licenses Book Translations.** The U.S. publisher of one of the authors (Williams) licensed a foreign publisher to produce a Chinese translation edition of his book *Management: A Practical Introduction* for use in Singapore. Two of the authors (Williams and Sawyer) were also licensed to a foreign publisher who will do a Chinese translation of their introductory computer book, *Using Information Technology.* In both cases, both the U.S. publisher and authors will receive a fee from sales of the Chinese version. ▣

3 Global Outsourcing: Moderate Risk

A common practice of many companies, *outsourcing,* or *contract manufacturing,* **is defined as using suppliers outside the company to provide goods and services.** Extending this technique, *global outsourcing,* **sometimes called** *offshoring,* **is defined as using suppliers outside the United States to provide labor, goods, or services.** ❿

❾ **Subway International franchise.** The sandwich purveyor has 34,965 restaurants in 97 countries, including two in Afghanistan, four in the Bahamas, and 2,657 in Canada. Many U.S. franchises operating abroad are devoted to fast food, but 7-Eleven has 25,000 international franchises and Curves, a fitness studio for women, has 2,000. What foreign-owned franchises can you name that are present in the United States?

Want to Know More? 4-6

What Areas of Employment Are Apt to Stay in the United States?

Go to www.mybizlab.com.

❿ **Art again imitates life.** The movie *Outsourced* (starring Josh Hamilton) developed a cult following and eventually gave birth to an NBC TV series of the same name. In the film, Hamilton and all the jobs in his department were outsourced from Seattle to India, where he was required to train his replacement in a call center. Reluctantly, he did so, but just when he succeeded, the company announced the "new" India call center had been moved to China. What jobs can you think of that are not subject to being outsourced?

As the United States struggled to put people back to work following the recession of 2007–2009, even high-tech companies were being slow to hire, because of the availability of a highly skilled labor force overseas.[44] If even computer scientists and software engineers have been vulnerable, what about people in other occupations? When U.S. multinationals, which employ a fifth of all American workers, are hiring abroad while cutting back at home, what kind of strategies should we follow to try to obtain homegrown employment?[45]

What Kinds of Jobs Are Likely to Be Sent Overseas?

Here are two ways to look at them:

- **Routine jobs:** "As soon as a job becomes routine enough to describe in a spec sheet, it becomes vulnerable to outsourcing," says a *Time* writer. "Jobs like data entry, which are routine by nature, were the first among obvious candidates for outsourcing." But even "design and financial-analysis skills can, with time, become well-enough understood to be spelled out in a contract and signed away."[46]

- **Precisely describable jobs:** "If you can describe a job precisely, or write rules for doing it, it's unlikely to survive," says economist Fred Levy. "Either we'll program a computer to do it, or we'll teach a foreigner to do it."[47] Or the foreigners will have already caught up with us, because their educational systems and industries aren't standing still.

What Kind of Jobs Will Probably Stay at Home?

Some jobs, regardless of industry, won't be sent offshore These are apt to have some of the following characteristics:[48]

- **Jobs that are geography specific:** Some transportation jobs, such as railroad jobs, can't be sent overseas because they are geography specific. Nor can certain blue-collar jobs such as plumbing, auto repair, gardening, and restaurant work. Lawyers and accountants knowledgeable about state and local laws are also probably in geographically safe occupations—at least so far.

- **Jobs involving face-to-face contact:** The job of a salesperson with a specific territory, an emergency room doctor, a hospice social worker, or a probation officer is less likely to be offshored because it involves face-to-face contact.

- **Jobs involving physical contact:** The jobs of dentists, nurses, massage therapists, physical trainers, and nursing-home aides will remain at home because they require physical contact.

- **Jobs requiring recognition of complex patterns:** Some jobs involve the human ability to recognize complex patterns, such as a physician's ability to diagnose an unusual disease. This also describes certain jobs that demand an intimate knowledge of the United States, such as coaching U.S. sports teams, marketing to American teenagers, or lobbying Congress.

Requirements for Jobs of the Future

Besides targeting one of the types of careers described above, what can you do to equip yourself for finding work at home? Consider the following:

- **Get a good education:** Although not all the jobs described in this box require a college degree, in general the more education you have, the more you are apt to prevail during times of economic change. Men and women with four years of college, for instance, earn nearly 45% more on average than those with only a high school diploma.[49]

- **Develop the ability to team with others:** "Jobs that persist are dynamic and creative and require the ability to team with others," says Jim Spohrer, a researcher at IBM. "At its heart, a company is simply a group of teams that come together to create" products.[50]

- **Develop flexibility:** "Jobs used to change very little or not at all over the course of several generations," says Spohrer. "Now, they might change three or four times in a single lifetime." Flexibility—as in being willing to undergo retraining—thus becomes important. Fortunately, as management theorist Peter Drucker pointed out, the United States is "the only country that has a very significant continuing education system. This doesn't exist anywhere else." The United States is also the only country, he said, in which it is easy for younger people to move from one area at work to another.[51]

There are three reasons for outsourcing:

- **Special resources:** The foreign supplier has resources not available in the United States, such as the availability of hardwoods found only in South American rainforests or marble found only in Italian quarries.
- **Special expertise:** The supplier has special expertise, such as how to do special weaving or how to penetrate local markets.
- **Labor costs:** The supplier's labor is cheaper than American labor—the principal reason for global outsourcing nowadays.

Does outsourcing destroy jobs at home? "Nobody seems to realize that we import twice or three times as many jobs as we export," observed management philosopher Peter Drucker. "I'm talking about the jobs created by foreign companies coming into the U.S. The most obvious [importers] are foreign auto companies. . . . We are exporting low-skill, low-paying jobs but are importing high-skill, high-paying jobs."[52] One study found that when U.S. multinationals hired lower-cost labor at foreign subsidiaries, they hired even more people in the United States to support their expanded operations.[53] Others disagree with this analysis, citing a lack of data.[54]

4   Joint Ventures: High Risk

A U.S. firm may form a ***joint venture,*** **also known as a *strategic alliance*, with a foreign company to share the risks and rewards of starting a new enterprise together in a foreign country.** In many cases, as with China until recently, the foreign country requires the U.S. company to join with a local company as a condition of doing business there.

Three advantages are as follows:

- **Local expertise:** The in-country partner provides information about products, promotion, and pricing in the local market.
- **Local base:** The local partner may offer physical facilities, trained labor, a distribution system, and government and customer contacts.
- **Outside assistance:** The U.S. company offers financial, technical, and managerial assistance to the local company.

Source: Stephan Shaver/UPI/Newscom.

哥的留下是为了姐，哥依然迷恋您着姐 谷姐

⑪ Goojje. In 2010, after Google threatened to abandon China in a dispute over cyber attacks and Web censorship, this imitator suddenly appeared, which contained a plea urging the U.S. search engine giant not to leave. At about the same time, YouTubecn.com also appeared, a copycat site offering videos from YouTube, which is blocked in China. What do you think the two U.S. technology companies should do about this?

⚖ BRIEFING / LEGAL & ETHICAL PRACTICES

General Motors Links with Shanghai Company in Joint Venture to Sell Buicks in China. Although some Americans consider Buick a grandpa's car, it has an entirely different status in China. "Buick is an expensive car, and has a very big name," says Yan Lili, 30, a corporate manager in Beijing. "I'd love to own one."[55] The difference in perception is partly because Buicks were among the first foreign cars on Chinese roads, back in the 1900s.[56] Thus, Buick's maker, General Motors, in a joint venture with Shanghai Automotive Industry Group, is able to charge about $37,000 for a Buick Regal, which sells in the United States for about $23,000.

For many years, the only way legally that foreign companies could do business in China was through joint ventures with Chinese companies. Recently, the government has allowed foreign players to acquire domestic firms, but the joint venture requirement still applies to cars.[57]

Joint ventures do have their risks, among them: (1) The in-country partner may copy the U.S. company's techniques and technology and use them in its own side ventures. ⑪ (2) The technology may become obsolete and unusable, if the in-country partner declines to upgrade. ∎

5   Foreign Subsidiaries: Highest Risk

A *foreign subsidiary* is a company in a foreign country that is totally owned and controlled by the parent company. The foreign subsidiary may be an existing company that is purchased outright, or it may be created from scratch by the parent organization. Example: Among its many, many subsidiaries, General Motors owns Adam Opel in Germany, Vauxhall Motors in England, Holden in Australia, GM Korea, and General Motors do Brasil.

The advantages of having a foreign subsidiary are as follows:

- **No sharing:** The multinational company does not need to share decision making, revenues, or profits with a foreign partner.
- **More control:** Compared with franchising and certainly with licensing, the parent company is better able to control the development and marketing of its products.
- **More in-country incentives:** Compared to exporting its products, which may involve import fees and paperwork, a multinational may actually benefit from labor guarantees, tax incentives, and low-interest loans from foreign countries wishing to encourage outside investment.

A disadvantage with foreign subsidiaries is that the parent company assumes all the risk if the product fails to catch on or if the host country's government turns against it. This is why companies tend to hire local managers with knowledge of local market conditions.

Key Takeaway 4-2
Five ways firms reach world markets: foreign subsidiaries; joint ventures; global outsourcing; franchising, foreign licensing; importing and exporting.

Want to Know More? 4-7
Fair Labor Association & Improving Factory Labor Standards
Go to www.mybizlab.com.

4.3

Conditions Affecting International Trade

THE BIG IDEA: Three conditions affect trading in global markets: (1) cultural, (2) economic, and (3) political/legal.

THE ESSENTIAL QUESTION: What factors should I be aware of that affect international markets?

MyBizLab: Check your understanding of these concepts at www.mybizlab.com.

Want to Know More? 4-8

Examples of Business Mishaps Caused by Cultural Misunderstandings

Go to www.mybizlab.com.

Scott McKain is now a frequent foreign business traveler, and he makes it a point to study the language and etiquette—politeness—of each country before traveling there. But he was not so experienced when, at age 18, while at a welcome dinner during a trade mission to Brazil, he responded to a local mayor who asked whether he was enjoying his first Brazilian meal. Because his mouth was full, McKain made an "okay" sign with his thumb and index finger. "The mayor literally dropped his jaw and fork," McKain said later. It turned out the gesture was akin to making an obscene sign with a middle finger in the United States.[58]

Cultural Conditions: Avoiding Misunderstandings

What are three cultural differences important to work?

Inexperienced North American business travelers "commit etiquette blunders more than 70% of the time when doing business abroad," says business etiquette author Ann Marie Sabath.[59] But the demand for executives who can move easily between different cultures is extremely high, and the talent pool of such executives is very small.[60] It's important, then, to understand the cultural differences before engaging in serious business deals.

Culture—**the shared set of beliefs, values, knowledge, and patterns of behavior common to a group of people**—can be very powerful. And because a culture is made up of so many nuances, visitors to another country may experience *culture shock*—**the feelings of discomfort and disorientation associated with being in an unfamiliar culture.**

How do you go about bridging cross-cultural gaps? It begins with understanding. Let's consider variations in three areas: (1) *verbal and nonverbal communication,* (2) *time orientation,* and (3) *religion.*[61]

1 Verbal & Nonverbal Communication

Although the average American believes that about half of the world can speak English, it's actually only around 20%.[62] But even if you stick to English, there are all kinds of nuances between cultures that can lead to misunderstandings. It's hard for foreigners to learn English because English has about 900,000 words, whereas French, for example, has fewer than 100,000.[63] Foreigners also find it hard to grasp sarcasm in English—a French worker took offense when a British colleague jokingly referred to a fellow Brit as "not too clever" during a telephone call. One survey found that nonnative English speakers in global corporations who were working to learn English found a number of common business activities difficult to handle in English, such as telephone calls (77%), socializing (66%), and meetings (64%).[64]

If you are trying to communicate with a speaker in one of the other 3,000 or so languages of the world, you have three options, all varying in effectiveness: speak English, use a translator, or learn the local language. (*See* ■ *Panel 4.5.*)

Nonverbal communication **consists of messages sent outside of the written or spoken word,** such as what constitutes permissible interpersonal space. Five ways in which nonverbal communication is expressed are through *personal space, eye contact, facial expressions, body movements and gestures,* and *touch.* Nonverbal communication is responsible for perhaps as much as 60% of a message being communicated.[65]

BRIEFING / BUSINESS CULTURE & ETIQUETTE

U.S.-Arab Cultural Differences—Touch & Interpersonal Space. When Crown Prince Abdullah of Saudi Arabia met with President George W. Bush in 2005 in Texas, the media recorded a sight not usually seen in the United States: two men holding hands. Men walking hand in hand is a common sight in the Middle East, and it does not carry any sexual connotation. Rather, holding hands is a sign of solidarity and kinship, the warmest expression of affection between men, according to one sociologist.[66] ⑫

Arabs also have a different comfort level with personal space. Whereas people in North America and northern Europe tend to conduct business conversations at a range of 3 to 4 feet, for Arabs it is under 1 foot. "Arabs tend to get very close and breathe on you," says one anthropologist. "The American . . . feels that the Arab is pushy. The Arab comes close, the American backs up." For Arabs, however, "breathing on people is a form of communication."[67] Once Americans understand this, they may feel more comfortable. ■

2 Time Orientation: Segmented versus Flexible

Time orientation can vary by culture. In the United States, time is usually viewed as schedule driven, precisely segmented, and limited, which is why Americans get antsy after 5 minutes on hold on the phone or more than 15 minutes in a Department of Motor Vehicles line.[68] In other cultures, however, time may be viewed as flexible and multidimensional. In Peru, for example, the national government has asked schools, businesses, and governments to stop tolerating *hora peruana,* or Peruvian time, which usually means being an hour late and has affected productivity.[69]

Source: Jim Watson/AFP/Getty Images/Newscom.

⑫ **Touching sight.** President George W. Bush and Crown Prince Abdullah of Saudi Arabia hold hands during the prince's 2005 visit to the United States. In the Middle East, holding hands is the warmest expression of affection among men. If you were a man visiting an Arab country, would you feel squeamish about doing this?

■ PANEL 4.6 Approximate numbers of current followers of some of the major world religions.

Christianity	2.1 billion
Islam	1.5 billion
Hinduism	900 million
Chinese traditional religion	394 million
Buddhism	376 million
Judaism	14 million

Source: Based on Central Intelligence Agency World Fact Book, www.cia.gov; Adherents.com, "Major religions of the world ranked by major adherents," August 7, 2007 http://www.adherents.com/Religions_By_Adherents.html (accessed August 21, 2011).

Want to Know More? 4-9

What Are Some Keys to Cultural Differences?

Go to www.mybizlab.com.

■ **Example of Different Time Orientation: Workers in a Knitware Factory Deep in Mexico.** Some Los Angeles garment makers who outsourced their knitware to a factory near Guadalajara, Mexico, found themselves challenged by a workplace culture far looser than that of the United States or even of northern Mexico.

"If they come on Monday, they're out on Tuesday. If they come on Tuesday, they're out on Wednesday," said a plant manager. Even offering a 10% bonus to those who came in every day for a week didn't always work. "These workers don't necessarily see their lives revolving around a job," says an expert at UCLA. "There's a great deal of informality that they have come to expect from factory employment. You work hard during certain periods of time, and relax during others."[70] ■

3 Religion: Can It Influence Work Values?

Although Christianity is the single largest religious group, collectively the other religious groups outnumber Christians. Whatever your religion (or lack of one), however, you need to be aware of the impact religious differences have on work. (*See* ■ *Panel 4.6.*)

■ **Example of Influence of Religion: Different Work-Related Values for Different Faiths.** A study of international students found wide variations in the primary work-related values for different religions.[71] For Catholics, it was consideration; for Protestants, employer effectiveness; for Buddhists, social responsibility; for Muslims, continuity. For you as a businessperson and manager, however, it's probably more practical to be aware of the importance of certain religious holidays, times for prayer, modes of dress (such as head scarves), types of food, and the like. ■

Economic Conditions: Infrastructure & Currency Shifts

How do a country's infrastructure and resources and currency shifts affect international business?

The economic conditions that can affect international business dealings are (1) the *infrastructure and resources,* which determine whether countries are developed or less developed, and (2) *currency shifts,* such as exchange rates.

Infrastructure & Resources: What Affects a Nation's Level of Development

The United States is the best in the world in terms of its roads, telecommunications, and health care system, right? Certainly, they are fairly sophisticated, though it's debatable whether they are the best.

Infrastructure and Resources. Telecommunications are part of a country's *infrastructure,* **the physical facilities that form the basis for its level of economic development.** Other examples are schools, roads, airports, railroads, harbors, utilities, and hospitals. Before you as a businessperson get involved in major projects in a foreign country, you should become aware of drawbacks in its infrastructure. Are the roads good enough? Are electrical systems reliable or even available? Can food be dependably refrigerated?

 BRIEFING / A WORLD OF CONSTANT CHANGE
Cellphones Improve the Infrastructure in Africa. In the United States, Canada, and much of Europe, we pretty much take the landline

phone system for granted. In other parts of the world, getting a phone installed may take weeks, even months, and then it may still be inefficient. The significance of the cellphone is that countries with underdeveloped wired telephone systems can use cellular phones as a fast way of installing better communications.

Africa has the fastest-growing cellphone market in the world, and mobile phone penetration is far greater than that of the Internet on that continent.[72] In Kenya, for instance, there are fewer than half a million landlines for 37 million people, but recently 6 million Kenyans have acquired cellphones, often reconditioned ones. Such technology gives Kenyans a chance of joining the world economy.[73] ⑬ ■

Businesspeople also need to be concerned about resources. If you want to set up an apparel plant in Malaysia, for example, you need to think about where the fabric and the sewing equipment are going to come from—whether you can get them from suppliers in that country or have to import them.

Developed versus Less-Developed Countries. It used to be that the United States, Canada, Australia, New Zealand, Japan, and the countries of western Europe were known as first-world countries. The communist nations were called second-world countries. Pretty much all the rest, especially those in the Southern Hemisphere, were known as third-world or developing countries. With the end of the Cold War, the world now seems to be divided between *developed countries* and *less-developed countries.*

- **Developed countries:** *Developed countries* **are first-world countries, those with a high level of economic development and generally high average level of income among their citizens.** Most international organizations are headquartered in developed countries. Also, about three-quarters of foreign investment has been directed toward developed countries.[74]

- **Less-developed countries:** *Less-developed countries,* **also known as** *developing countries,* **are the third-world countries, those nations with low economic development and low average incomes.** These are most countries of Africa, Asia, and Latin America, including large ones such as China, India, Brazil, and Nigeria. The economies of some less-developed countries are growing extremely fast—so fast, in fact, that the GDPs of China and India are expected to outgrow that of the United States by 2050. (*See* ■ *Panel 4.7.*)

Source: Visions of America, LLC/Alamy.

⑬ **"Hey, what's happening?"** Mobile phones enable emerging nations in Africa and elsewhere to leapfrog landline technology by avoiding having to install telephone poles and miles of wiring.

■ **PANEL 4.7 GDP projections (in billions of dollars) of top five economies in 2050.**

2011		2050	
1. U.S.	$15,051	**1.** China	$59,475
2. China	$10,656	**2.** India	$43,190
3. Japan	$4,322	**3.** U.S.	$37,876
4. India	$4,412	**4.** Brazil	$9,762
5. Germany	$3,108	**5.** Japan	$7,664

Source: Based on L. Elliott, "GDP Projections from PwC: How China, India, and Brazil Will Overtake the West by 2050," *Datablog, The Guardian,* January 7, 2011, www.guardian.co.uk/news/datablog/ 2011/jan/07/gdp-projections-china-us-uk-brazil (accessed August 15, 2011).

Less-developed countries are often characterized by high birth rates. More than 80% of babies are born in Africa and Asia. Niger has the world's highest

⑭ Growing. An example of a less-developed country, Niger in Africa has the highest fertility rate in the world, with 7.6 children per mother. What kind of foreign investment would you expect to find here?

ⓘ

Want to Know More? 4-10

Currency Converter

Go to www.mybizlab.com.

---

⑮ Pounds, dollars, and pesos, oh my. The pound (Sterling) is the currency of the United Kingdom, but eight other countries, from Egypt to Syria, also call their currencies "pounds." The currency of the United States is represented in dollars, of course, but 21 other countries, from Australia to Zimbabwe, also call their currencies "dollars." There are 165 currencies in the world, and if you go online, you can probably find the exchange rate among all of them, whether it's Iraq's dinar, Vietnam's dong, or Gambia's dalasi.

fertility rates—7.6 children per mother (compared to 1.4 in Germany, for example), because of early marriage, low use of contraceptives, and low levels of education.[75] ⑭

Currency Exchange Rates

The *currency exchange rate* is the rate at which one country's currency can be exchanged for the currencies of other countries. Among themselves, Americans buy and sell in dollars, but beyond the U.S. border they have to deal with pesos in Mexico, pounds in England, euros in Europe, and yuan in China. Because of changing economic conditions, the values of currencies fluctuate in relation to each other, so that sometimes a U.S. dollar, for example, will buy more goods and sometimes it will buy less.

BRIEFING / PERSONAL FINANCE
An American in London Dealing with Currency Exchange— How Much *Is* That Big Mac, Really? Let's pretend, for simplicity, that $1 trades equal to 1 British pound (symbolized by £1). Thus, an item that costs 3 pounds (£3) can be bought for $3. If the exchange rate changes so that $1 buys 1½ pounds, then an item that costs 3 pounds can be bought for $2 (the dollar is said to be "stronger" against the pound). If the rate changes so that $1 buys only ½ a pound, an item that costs 3 pounds can be purchased for $6 (the dollar is "weaker").[76]

In 2009, the dollar was weaker, buying only .59 of a pound, but then in mid-2010 it became stronger and would buy .69 of a pound. As this is written, the dollar is weaker again, and will buy only about .61 of a pound. Thus, staying in London became more expensive for Americans. Indeed, if you're an American living in England working for a U.S. company and paid in dollars, your standard of living went down.

To give you a sense of what an American's purchasing power is worth when $1 equals .61 British pound (or 1 pound equals $1.62)—the exchange rate in August 2011—consider these prices for various goods in New York versus London (estimated in U.S. dollars):

	New York	London
2-liter Coke	$1.98	$2.85
Big Mac meal	$6.59	$7.28
Levi's 501 jeans	$52	$108
Adidas Trainers	$80	$88
Volkswagen Golf 2.0 TD1	$21,464	$28,371

With this example you can see why it's important to understand how exchange rates work and what value your U.S. dollars actually have. ⑮

Of course, if you're a Londoner looking at this kind of currency exchange rate, it's a terrific time to visit New York.[77] ■

Two important aspects of currency exchange rates are (1) floating exchange rates and (2) devaluation.

Floating Exchange Rates: Currency Traders Determine Values. Currency values fluctuate, or "float," according to the supply and demand for various currencies in the international market. In this *floating exchange rate system,* **the values of all currencies are determined by supply and demand.** The supply and demand reflect the actions of currency traders all over the world, who create a market for currencies based on what they perceive to be the investment and trade prospects for each country.

■ **Example of How Supply and Demand Determine Currency Value: The U.S. Dollar and Currency Traders Large and Small.** In September 2007, when the U.S. housing market experienced a credit crunch that resulted in worldwide loss of confidence in the U.S. dollar, it impelled many currency traders to get out of dollars and into other currencies (such as the euro).

Many professional traders took huge losses. So also did another class of investors: middle-class Japanese housewives who, between household chores, moonlighted as amateur currency speculators. One, a Ms. Itoh, spent a sleepless week after market losses wiped out her holdings—family savings equivalent to $100,000 in U.S. dollars. She had never told her husband about her after-hours hobby.[78] ■

Devaluation: When a Currency Is Worth Less. *Devaluation* **means that a nation's currency is lowered relative to other countries' currencies.** A government will devalue its currency when it wants to make its domestic products cheaper abroad and increase the price of imports.

Example: In 2009, Vietnam decided to devalue the country's currency (the dong), by shaving 5% off its value. The effect was to make Vietnam's manufactured goods (such as textiles) cheaper than those of many other Asian countries. This was intended to accelerate a longer-term shift of manufacturing to the country, which already had the advantage of a low-cost labor force, to attract more foreign investment and to stimulate Vietnam's exports.[79]

Political & Legal Conditions: Adjusting to Other Countries' Governments & Laws

What three matters affect a country's political and legal conditions?

Whether it's taxes, trade practices, import/export regulations, patents, copyrights, product liability, or labor relations, every country has its own laws and rules. And these usually reflect (1) a country's political system, (2) its political stability, and (3) its approach to corruption and enforcement.

1 Political System: Democratic or Totalitarian?

In exporting or importing, you will have to deal with unfamiliar political systems. There are two extremes:

Democratic Systems: More Familiar to Americans. *Democratic political systems* **rely on free elections and representative assemblies.** The government is supposed to represent the society as a whole, or at least the majority of its citizens. From the standpoint of ease in doing business, democratic systems of government, such as those in western Europe, will generally seem more familiar to an American businessperson. Nevertheless, different national attitudes toward bureaucracy, monopolies, and the acceptance of "gratuities" can make it difficult to do business. (As we mentioned in Chapter 3, political systems are different from economic systems; thus, democratic *political* systems may have capitalist or socialist or mixed *economic* systems.) ⑯

Totalitarian Systems: Higher Risk? *Totalitarian political systems* **are ruled by a dictator, a single political party, or a special-membership group,** such as a handful of ruling families or a military junta (such as Cuba under Fidel Castro or Indonesia under Sukarno). The risk for you as an international businessperson is that the political tides may change and through no fault of your own you may find

⑯ **Political stability can be fragile.** On February 12, 2011, newspaper headlines exploded with the news that Egypt's longtime ruler Hosni Mubarak had been forced out in a revolt by the country's youth, aided by the military. In the aftermath, Egypt's fledgling political parties struggled to organize for a new constitution and parliamentary elections that would not be dominated by any political bloc (particularly one with a religious base) that would have unchecked influence to set the laws of the land. Many international companies are now cautious about investing in Egypt, which harms the Egyptian economy. In what ways are business and politics intertwined?

yourself somehow on the wrong side. Some governments fall in between democratic and totalitarian. Mexico, for example, regularly features free elections, but for decades it was ruled by a single political party. (A totalitarian *political* system may involve different *economic* systems—China, for instance, is a totalitarian system but permits many capitalist elements.)

2 Political Stability: What's the Risk?

Every firm contemplating establishing itself abroad must calculate its political risk—the risk that political changes will cause loss of a company's assets or impair its foreign operations. Two political risks an organization planning to do business abroad might anticipate are instability and expropriation.

Instability. Even in a developed country a company may be victimized by political instability, such as riots or civil disorders, as happened in 2011 in poorer neighborhoods of London and other English cities when thousands of young men rioted. Overseas an international company may also have to try to anticipate revolutions or changes in government. Since the end of World War II, for example, Italy has had 62 governments—that's 62 governments in 65 years.

Expropriation. *Expropriation* **is defined as a government's seizure of a domestic or foreign company's assets.** After socialist Hugo Chavez became president of Venezuela, in 2009 his government stepped up a campaign to seize land and businesses, such as a rice plant owned by Cargill, one of the United States' largest privately owned companies. The government has also taken over oil, electricity, steel, cement, and telecommunications companies.[80]

3 Approaches to Corruption & Enforcement

Whether it's called *mordida* (Mexico), *huilu* (China), or *vzyatka* (Russia), it means the same thing: a bribe. Although the United States is relatively free of such corruption, it is an acceptable practice in other countries. In African, Latin American, and newly independent states, frequent bribe paying is the norm; in Asia and the Pacific and southeast Europe, it is moderate; and in North America and the European Union, bribes are seldom paid for services. (*See* ■ *Panel 4.8.*)

■ **PANEL 4.8 Countries most affected by bribery, 2009.** Percentage of respondents reporting that they had paid a bribe in the previous 12 months. (Not all countries of the world are represented.)

- **More than 50%:** Cameroon, Liberia, Sierra Leone, Uganda
- **23–49%:** Armenia, Azerbaijan, Bolivia, Cambodia, Ghana, Indonesia, Iraq, Kenya, Lithuania, Moldova, Mongolia, Russia, Senegal, Venezuela
- **13–22%:** Belarus, Greece, Hungary, Kosovo, Kuwait, Lebanon, Nigeria, Pakistan, Peru, Romania, Serbia, Ukraine
- **7–12%:** Bosnia & Herzegovina, Chile, Colombia, Czech Republic, Hong Kong, India, Malaysia, Philippines, Thailand
- **<6% or less:** Argentina, Austria, Brunei Darussalam, Bulgaria, Canada, Croatia, Denmark, Finland, FYR Macedonia, Georgia, Iceland, Israel, Japan, Luxembourg, Netherlands, Norway, Panama, Poland, Portugal, Singapore, South Korea, Spain, Switzerland, Turkey, United States

Source: Transparency International, Report on the Global Corruption Barometer 2009, Berlin, May 2009, http://global_corruption_barometer_web.pdf (accessed May 15, 2011).

American businesspeople are prevented from participating in overseas bribes under **the 1978 *Foreign Corrupt Practices Act,* which makes it illegal for employees of U.S. companies to make "questionable" or "dubious" contributions to political decision makers in foreign nations.** While this creates a competitive disadvantage for Americans working in foreign countries in which government bribery may be the only way to obtain business, the United Nations Global Compact is attempting to level the playing field by promoting anticorruption standards for business (see p. 52 in Chapter 2).

In 2009, a dozen or so American executives and high-level employees of corporations were criminally charged with violating the Foreign Corrupt Practices Act for bribing foreign government officials or employees of state-owned companies. The U.S. Justice Department took the point of view that, to effectively deter such wrongdoing, it had to prosecute *individuals* rather than companies, which could more easily absorb big fines and a hit to their reputations.[81]

Want to Know More? 4-11

Who are the Americans Who Paid Bribes?

Go to www.mybizlab.com.

THE BIG IDEA: Barriers to free trade are tariffs, import quotas, and embargoes. Organizations promoting international trade are the World Trade Organization, the World Bank, and the International Monetary Fund. Major trading blocs are NAFTA, the EU, APEC, and Mercosur.

THE ESSENTIAL QUESTION: What are barriers to free trade, and what international organizations are designed to promote trade?

MyBizLab

MyBizLab: Check your understanding of these concepts at www.mybizlab.com.

To protect their domestic industries against foreign competition, countries often resort to *trade protectionism*—**the use of government regulations, tariffs, quotas, and embargoes to limit the import of goods and services.** The principal excuse often used is that protectionism saves jobs. Actually, most economists don't consider protectionism beneficial to international business because of what it does to the overall global trading atmosphere.[82]

Three Kinds of Trade Protectionism

What are three ways countries exert protectionism?

The three ways by which countries try to exert protectionism are via *tariffs, import quotas,* and *embargoes.*

1 Tariffs: A Fancy Name for "Taxes" on Imports

A *tariff* is a trade barrier in the form of a customs duty, or tax, levied principally on imports. There are two types of tariffs: (1) *Revenue tariffs* are designed simply to raise money for the government. (2) *Protective tariffs* are designed to raise the price of imported goods to make the prices of domestic products more competitive.

17 Chinese tires. Would you buy Chinese-made tires if they cost less than American-made tires? What if they cost the same—because the U.S. government imposed a tariff (that is, a tax)? Do you think protective tariffs are acceptable as a way of protecting jobs and our own manufacturing capacity? How important do you think it is for the United States to remain a source of manufacturing?

■ **Example of a Protective Tariff: Chinese-Made Auto Tires.** In 2009, following several years of job losses in U.S. tire plants amid a flood of imported tires, the Obama administration imposed a 35% tariff on imported Chinese tires. Although the move was cheered by American labor because it seemed to protect U.S. jobs, domestic tire makers complained the tariff—really a tax, as we mentioned—would force them to raise prices and cause them to lay off employees elsewhere in the U.S. tire business.**17**

China, for its part, threatened to retaliate by imposing tariffs on American exports of automotive products and chicken meat, increasing tensions between the two nations.[83] ■

2 Import Quotas: Limits on How Many Products Are Allowed In

An *import quota* is a trade barrier in the form of a limit on the quantity of a product that can be imported. Its purpose is to protect domestic industry by limiting the availability of foreign products.

Source: REUTERS/Nir Elias.

■ **Example** of Import Quota: Mexico Raises Quotas on Sugar. Mexico's economic ministry raised the quota for imported sugar by 300,000 tons for late 2009, reaching a total of 900,000 tons for the year. Because of a reduction in domestic production of sugar cane, Mexican officials predicted the national supply of sugar would be insufficient to satisfy the country's demand for the product. In early 2010 it had to raise the quota by another 250,000 tons because of expected shortages.[84] ■

Quotas are often designed to prevent *dumping*, **the activity of a foreign company's selling its products abroad for less—even less than the cost of manufacture—than the price of the domestic product in that market. The purpose is to drive down the price of the domestic product.** Why would any foreign company sell ("dump") products for less than they cost to make? Because it hopes to become popular with consumers in the country it's targeting. But, of course, long-standing domestic producers in that country can't compete with the invading firm's below-market prices.

3 Embargoes: Bans on Certain Import or Export Products

An *embargo* is a complete ban on the import or export of certain products.

■ **Example** of Embargo: The United States Nixes Importation of Cuban Cigars. Ever had a Cuban cigar? They're difficult to buy in the United States, since they're embargoed—illegal to import. When instituted in 1962, for the stated purpose of pressuring the communist government into being more democratic, the embargo resulted in American importers losing an estimated $1.2 billion. But the embargo cost the Cuban government and its cigar makers even more—about $70 billion.[85] ⑱ ■

⑱ **Embargoed.** Cuban cigars have been illegal to import into the United States for over a half century, although they are available for sale in Canada and Mexico. Do you think the power of business and desire for free trade will ultimately lead to a change in this embargo?

The U.S. government also tries to embargo the export of certain supercomputers and other high-tech equipment with possible military uses to countries such as China.

Organizations Facilitating International Trade

What are three organizations important in promoting world trade?

In the 1920s, tariff barriers, which were intended to save jobs, did the opposite. By depressing the demand for goods and services, they led to the loss of jobs anyway—and to the massive unemployment of the 1930s Great Depression.[86]

After World War II the advanced nations of the world realized that if all countries could freely exchange the products that each could produce most efficiently, the result would be lower prices all around. And so there began a movement to significantly remove all barriers to free trade.

The principal organizations designed to facilitate international trade are (1) the *World Trade Organization,* (2) the *World Bank,* and (3) the *International Monetary Fund.*

Want to Know More? 4-12
WTO, World Bank, & IMF
Go to www.mybizlab.com.

1 The World Trade Organization

The *World Trade Organization (WTO),* **consisting of 153 member countries, is designed to monitor and enforce trade agreements.** The agreements are based on the *General Agreement on Tariffs and Trade (GATT),* **an international accord first signed by 23 nations in 1947, which helped to reduce worldwide tariffs and other barriers.** Out of GATT came a series of negotiations, called "rounds," that resulted in the lowering of barriers. For instance, the Uruguay Round, implemented in 1996, cut tariffs by one-third.

WTO succeeded GATT as the world forum for trade negotiations and has the formal legal structure for deciding trade disputes. WTO also encompasses areas besides tariffs and trade, such as services, patent rights, and telecommunications.

Source: IMF Staff Photo/Stephen Jaffe.

⑲ The IMF meets. The IMF has become more visible in the public eye recently because of its role in shoring up some weaker European economies, including making loans to Portugal, Ireland, and Greece and considering what moves to make to assist Spain and Italy. If the IMF did not exist, how do you think global economic stability would be affected?

2 The World Bank

The World Bank was created after World War II to help the devastated countries of Europe rebuild. Today the purpose of **the *World Bank* is to provide low-interest loans to developing nations for improving health, education, transportation, and telecommunications.** The bank has 184 member nations, with most contributions coming from the United States, Europe, and Japan.

The bank has been extensively involved in working with governments and international development partners in assessing damage caused by major natural disasters, such as the tsunami that slammed into American Samoa, Samoa, and Tonga in 2009, and helping to work out reconstruction plans.[87]

3 The International Monetary Fund

Established in 1945, the International Monetary Fund is another pillar supporting the international financial community. Now affiliated with the United Nations and consisting of 185 member nations, **the *International Monetary Fund (IMF)* is designed to assist in smoothing the flow of money between nations.** The IMF operates as a last-resort lender that makes short-term loans to countries suffering from unfavorable balance of payments—most recently, Portugal, Ireland, and Greece. ⑲

Common Markets: NAFTA, EU, Mercosur, & APEC

What are four principal common markets?

A *common market,* also known as an *economic community* or a *trading bloc,* is a group of nations within a geographical region that have agreed to remove trade barriers with each other. The four major common markets are (1) the *NAFTA* nations, (2) the *European Union,* (3) the *Mercosur,* and (4) the *APEC* countries.

1 NAFTA—the Three Countries of the North American Free Trade Agreement

Established in 1994, **the *North American Free Trade Agreement (NAFTA)* is a common market consisting of the 435 million people of the United States, Canada, and Mexico.** (*See* ■ *Panel 4.9.*) The agreement is designed to eliminate 99% of the tariffs and quotas among these countries, allowing for freer flow of goods, services, and money in North America. Trade with Canada and Mexico now accounts for one-third of the United States' total world trade.

Free trade and foreign investment have certainly benefited Mexico as well. However, it has also hurt hundreds of thousands of subsistence farmers there, triggering illegal immigration of almost half a million people a year to the United States. As for the United States, more than a half million workers, mostly in manufacturing, have been certified by the U.S. government as having lost their jobs or had their hours or wages reduced because of NAFTA's shifting of jobs to the south. It's also created a significant trade deficit. However, supporters insist NAFTA ultimately will result in more jobs and a higher standard of living among all three trading partners.[88]

■ **PANEL 4.9 Map of NAFTA nations.**

Source: http://en.wikipedia.org/wiki/North_American_Free_Trade_Agreement.

2 The EU—27 Countries of the European Union

The world's largest free market is the ***European Union (EU),* which was formed in 1957 and presently consists of 27 trading partners in Europe.** (*See* ■ *Panel 4.10, next page.*)

Nearly all trade barriers have been removed, including the flow of labor between countries, making the EU a union of borderless neighbors. By 2002, such national symbols as the franc, the mark, the lira, the peseta, and the guilder had been replaced with the EU currency, the euro.

■ **PANEL 4.10 Map of EU nations.**

3 Mercosur—10 Countries of Latin America

The *Mercosur* is the largest common market in Latin America and has four core members—Argentina, Brazil, Paraguay, and Uruguay, with Venezuela scheduled to become a full member—and five associate members, Bolivia, Chile, Colombia, Ecuador, and Peru. Besides reducing tariffs by 75%, Mercosur nations are striving for full economic integration, and the alliance is also negotiating trade agreements with NAFTA, the EU, and Japan.

4 APEC—21 Countries of the Pacific Rim

The *Asia-Pacific Economic Cooperation (APEC)* is a common market of 21 Pacific Rim countries whose purpose is to improve economic and political ties. (*See* ■ *Panel 4.11.*) Most countries with a coastline on the Pacific Ocean are members of the organization, although there are a number of exceptions. Among the 21 members are the United States, Canada, and China. Since the founding in 1989, APEC members have worked to reduce tariffs and other trade barriers across the Asia-Pacific region.

■ **PANEL 4.11 Map of APEC nations.**

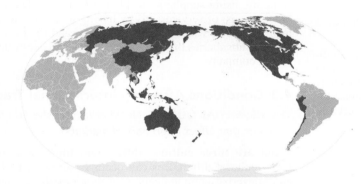

The World No Longer Revolves around the United States

How will the world's economy change in the coming years?

Key Takeaway 4-3
Some common markets: NAFTA, EU, APEC, Mercosur.

For most of the period following World War II, Americans assumed (correctly) that the world economy revolved around them. At one time, the United States was responsible for 46% of world output at market prices. Today that figure is down to 30%, and it may be headed lower as China and India grow their economies. A World Bank study suggests that fast-growing developing nations are expected to increase their share of world output from 23% today to about 33% in 2030.[89] With the weakened U.S. economy, there has even been talk of replacing the dollar with the euro as the dominant world currency, although Europe is certainly having its own economic troubles. These facts have enormous significance. To survive, Americans will have to pay ever more attention to what's happening outside the United States.

Summary

4.1 Globalization: The Shrinking of Time & Distance

THE ESSENTIAL QUESTION: *What are three developments in globalization that will probably affect me?*

How has the world economy changed? The Internet and World Wide Web have enabled the development of e-commerce, or electronic commerce, the buying and selling of products and services through computer networks.

What are the significant elements of global trade? With the collapse of communism in Eastern Europe, the opening of Asian countries to foreign investment, and the increased deregulation of several nations' economies, there began an increase in free trade, the movement of goods and services among nations without political or economic restrictions. These conditions resulted in a global economy, the increasing interaction of the world's economies with one another as a single market. The global economy intensified the rise of multinational corporations, organizations with multinational management and ownership that manufacture and market products in many different countries. Free trade and the global economy are based on a constant stream of imports and exports.

Why has there been a rise in huge multinationals and small, fast-moving startups internationally? Electronic information in the global marketplace creates both big global companies who become bigger by merging with each other and small local ones that are easy to start and can sell goods and services worldwide and maneuver faster than larger ones can.

4.2 Why & How Companies Conduct International Trade

THE ESSENTIAL QUESTION: *Why do companies expand internationally, and how do they do it?*

Why do nations trade, and what are absolute and comparative advantages? Three reasons countries engage in free trade are that no country is completely self-sufficient, some countries have natural resources that other countries want, and some countries have technology that other countries want. This suggests the distinction between absolute and comparative advantages. An absolute advantage exists when one country has a monopoly on producing a product or service more cheaply or efficiently than any other country can. A comparative advantage means a country sells to other countries those products and services it produces most cheaply or efficiently and buys from other countries those it does not produce most cheaply or efficiently.

How is international trade measured? There are two kinds of scorecards by which a country knows whether its trade policy is successful—the balance of trade and the balance of payments. (1) The balance of trade is the value of a country's exports compared to the value of its imports as measured over a particular period of time. Countries prefer to have a trade surplus, when the value of the country's exports exceeds the value of its total imports, rather than a trade deficit, which is the reverse. (2) The balance of payments is determined by measuring the difference between money coming into the country (payments for exports and revenue from tourism) and money going out (payments for imports, foreign aid, and military investment). Here, too, countries prefer a surplus rather than a deficit in balance of payments.

What are five ways companies reach global markets? Five ways that companies reach global markets, from lowest risk to highest risk, are as follows: (1) by exporting goods and services to other countries and importing goods and services from them; (2) by franchising, allowing others to use the company's brand name and services for a fee, or licensing, allowing others to make or distribute the company's product; (3) by global outsourcing, using suppliers outside the United States to provide labor, goods, or services; (4) by having joint ventures, or strategic alliances, with foreign companies; and (5) by launching foreign subsidiaries that are totally owned and controlled by the parent company.

4.3 Conditions Affecting International Trade

THE ESSENTIAL QUESTION: *What factors should I be aware of that affect international markets?*

What are three cultural differences important to work? Cross-cultural differences can occur in three areas: in verbal and nonverbal communication, in time orientation, and in religious values.

How do a country's infrastructure and resources and currency shifts affect international business? Economic conditions that affect international business are the infrastructure, or basic physical facilities, and resources, such as product materials. It is easier to do business in developed countries with higher economic development and higher average incomes than in less-developed countries. Currency exchange rates are also important, whether affected by currency traders' perceptions of a nation's prospects or by a government's devaluation to make its goods cheaper and more appealing.

What three matters affect a country's political and legal conditions? Every country's laws and rules reflect its political system, political stability, and approach to corruption. Political systems may be democratic, relying on free elections and representative assemblies, or totalitarian, ruled by a dictator or special membership group. Stable political systems are predictable, but unstable ones may lead to problems such as expropriation, or seizure of a firm's assets. Corrupt political systems are also harder to work in, and Americans paying bribes to foreigners can be prosecuted under the U.S. Foreign Corrupt Practices Act.

4.4 International Trade: Barriers & Facilitators

THE ESSENTIAL QUESTION: *What are barriers to free trade, and what international organizations are designed to promote trade?*

What are three ways countries exert protectionism? Trade protectionism, the use of government regulations to limit import of foreign goods and services that threaten domestic industries, consists of three devices: (1) Tariffs are trade barriers in the form of customs duties, or taxes, mainly assessed on imports. (2) Import quotas are limits of the numbers of a product that can be imported. (3) Embargoes are complete bans on import or export of certain products.

What are three organizations important in promoting world trade? The first organization designed to facilitate international trade is the World Trade Organization, consisting of 153 countries, which is supposed to monitor and enforce trade agreements. The second is the World Bank, which provides low-interest loans to developing countries for improving basic infrastructure. The third is the International Monetary Fund, which is designed to assist in smoothing the flow of money between nations and make short-term loans.

What are four principal common markets? There are four principal common markets, or groups of trading nations within a geographical region that have agreed to remove trade barriers. NAFTA (North American Free Trade Agreement) consists of the United States, Canada, and Mexico. The EU (European Union) is a collection of 27 countries in Europe. The Mercosur unites countries in Latin America. APEC (Asia-Pacific Economic Cooperation) is a common market of countries with a coastline on the Pacific Ocean.

Key Terms

MyBizLab

absolute advantage 107
Asia-Pacific Economic Cooperation
  (APEC) 125
balance of payments 108
balance-of-payments deficit 108
balance-of-payments surplus 108
balance of trade 108
common market 124
comparative advantage 107
countertrading 108
culture 114
culture shock 114
currency exchange rate 118
democratic political systems 119
devaluation 119
developed countries 117
dumping 123
e-commerce 101
embargo 123

European Union (EU) 124
Export Assistance Centers 109
exporting 102
export-management companies 109
expropriation 120
floating exchange rate system 118
Foreign Corrupt Practices Act 121
foreign licensing 110
foreign subsidiary 112
franchising 110
free trade 102
General Agreement on Tariffs and
  Trade (GATT) 123
global economy 102
global outsourcing 110
globalization 101
import quota 122
importing 102
infrastructure 116

International Monetary Fund
  (IMF) 124
joint venture 112
less-developed countries 117
Mercosur 125
multinational corporations 102
nonverbal communication 115
North American Free Trade Agreement
  (NAFTA) 124
outsourcing 110
self-sufficient 106
tariff 122
totalitarian political systems 119
trade deficit 108
trade protectionism 122
trade surplus 108
World Bank 124
World Trade Organization (WTO) 123

Pop Quiz Prep

1. Generally speaking, when is the best time to seek overseas work experience?
2. How is the term *free trade* defined?
3. When does a trade surplus exist?
4. What is the least risky way for a U.S. company to edge into global markets?
5. What is an example of nonverbal communication?
6. What is expropriation?
7. What is an embargo?
8. How does the World Bank work to facilitate international trade?

Critical Thinking Questions

1. The fast-food culture of quick, convenient, and cheap, which started in the United States, has entered the cultures of many nations. McDonald's has more than 32,000 restaurants worldwide serving nearly 64 million people in over 110 countries. McDonald's has posted increases in same-store sales (a statistic in the retail industry to compare sales of stores that have been open for a year or more) for 30 consecutive quarters since early 2003. Even during

the depths of the recession in 2008, same-store sales rose by 6.1%.[90] What factors do you think have contributed to the growth of fast-food companies worldwide? Would you prefer to eat at an American fast-food restaurant while traveling abroad? Explain.

2. As its name suggests, microlending began as the act of disbursement of small loans to people living in extreme poverty, typically entrepreneurs, who are locked out of the banking system due to their lack of collateral or creditworthiness. The idea is to help them start or expand small businesses that generate income.[91] With a microloan, Parbati Karki of Nepal purchased a Jersey cow five years ago. She now has two cows and sells 18 liters of milk daily—earning enough to build a new house with her income and her husband's earnings.[92] With the lure of repayment rates over 90%, commercial banks and other investors from international markets have moved into microfinance. This has led to questions of whether it is ethical to capitalize on the poorest people on earth. What are your thoughts?

3. In "Secrets, Lies, and Sweatshops," *BusinessWeek* writer Peter Engardio profiles an inspection at a factory in China that supplies pens and highlighters to Walmart.[93] Discovered in an audit, the factory has been cited with its third offense for paying its 3,000 workers less than the minimum wage. Under Walmart's labor rules, a fourth offense would end the relationship. According to Engardio, this factory, like others, hires "consultants" to help factories create authentic-looking records and double sets of books

for such audits. What are your thoughts about the growing business of coaching mid-level factory managers and workers to mislead auditors?

4. Bottled water barely existed as a business 30 years ago in the United States.[94] Today it has grown to a $15 billion a year industry.[95] Huge multinational companies are jumping on the bandwagon and making billions of dollars on water they simply extract from the ground, pour into a plastic bottle, slap a label on, and sell at competitive prices.[96] Examples of these companies include Aquafina (owned by Pepsi), Dasani (Coke), Perrier (Nestlé), Evian, and Fiji Water, among hundreds of others. In your opinion, what are the benefits and drawbacks of bottled water?

5. Electronic waste (e-waste), defined as discarded consumer electronics such as computers, mobile phones, television sets, and refrigerators, is a growing international problem.[97] According to the Environmental Protection Agency, the United States produces an estimated 50 million tons of e-waste annually, including 30 million computers and 100 million phones.[98] Unless these products are properly collected and materials recycled, many developing countries (where the products are sent for disposal) face hazardous e-waste mountains, with consequences for the environment and public health. Many of the products contain contaminants such as lead, cadmium, beryllium, and flame retardants. What factors have contributed to the growth of electronic waste worldwide and the growth of the electronic waste recycling business? What are the environmental and social benefits of reuse and refurbishing?

Cases

Go to MyBizLab

The Mini: A Mega-Mini Comeback in the United States

The video profiles the overwhelming popularity of the Mini, a British automobile owned by BMW Group. The Mini, produced in Oxford, England, was reintroduced in the United States in 2002. In its first year, the company sold 25,000 cars. Mini describes its customers as possessing a "Mini mindset," and the video reveals the difference in selling strategies employed in each of Mini's global markets. Watch the video to see how a car withdrawn from the U.S. market close to 50 years ago has created what fans of all ages refer to as "Mini-Mania."

Despite its overwhelming popularity over the last decade or so in the United States, you may not have ever heard of British Motor Corporation (BMC). The Mini, first produced by BMC in 1959, went on to become an icon in the 1960s.[99] All four of the Beatles (John Lennon, Paul McCartney, Ringo Starr, and George Harrison) owned a Mini. The most famous Mini was Harrison's psychedelic version which appeared in the 1967 film *Magical Mystery Tour*.[100]

The Mini was developed in reaction to a world crisis and conflict called the Suez Canal, which reduced oil supplies and

left the United Kingdom to resort to what was called "petrol rationing" (petrol is short for petroleum).[101] At about the same time, in the early 1960s, the U.S. automobile market began to change as the entry of foreign competitors (from Europe and

Japan) caused the share of automakers Ford, Chrysler, and General Motors (known as "The Big Three") to slide significantly.[102] On top of that, an oil embargo in the 1970s made smaller Japanese imports even more compelling to Americans. With a brief (and not very successful) stint in the American market, the Mini was allegedly withdrawn because it did not meet U.S. emissions and safety standards instituted in 1968, and it was never updated to meet the more rigorous regulations.[103]

In a 1982 abstract by Norman Fieleke, then vice president and economist of the Federal Reserve Bank of Boston, he discussed the "growing internationalization of the automobile industry," which was symbolized by what he called the "world car."[104] "The world car is a car designed for consumers across the world, and typically assembled from parts produced in diverse locations," he wrote. "It is just one more illustration—albeit a very dramatic one—of the gainful division of labor across national boundaries that is permitted by international trade."

Fieleke went on to say, "One important reason for the recent decline in U.S. auto production was the abrupt rise in the price of gasoline, which shifted purchases away from large U.S. cars toward small cars offering higher mileage per gallon. Since foreign producers were already making such cars for their own markets, they were able to expand their exports to the U.S. market quickly." Rather than "sudden, ingenious innovations," the gains of the foreign producers in the U.S. automobile market resulted from the petrol rationing described above, and thus, the demand for smaller cars.[105] In 1958, a year before the Mini was produced, just 8% of the cars sold in the United States were imports, and over half of those sold were Volkswagen Beetles.

Even with the previous "big car culture" in America, Mini-mania has made its mark among an "eclectic group of buyers possessing a Mini-mindset." As recent gas prices continue their unpredictable ride, BMW has produced a stylish and certainly greener alternative to the gas guzzling SUVs crowding the roads less than a decade ago. Might you one day be a member of one of the over 300 Mini clubs worldwide?[106]

What's Your Take?

1. How does the concept of import and export explained in the chapter explain the situation of increasing manufacture of imported car brands in the United States (for example, BMW in Spartanburg, South Carolina) and many American car companies producing their cars in places like Mexico and Canada?

2. How is the concept of comparative advantage applied at BMW (Mini)?

3. How do the purchasing patterns and decision-making processes of U.S. consumers differ from those outside the United States, and what has Mini done to deal with these differences in the United States?

4. Approximately 10,000 Minis were exported to the United States between 1960 and 1967.[107] Discuss the impact government regulations had on the company, and why they stopped exporting to the United States. What changed when the company began to sell their cars in the United States in 2002?

BUSINESS DECISION CASE
Outsourcing Health Care & Medical Tourism: Is a Trip to an Exotic Country Included in Your Health Benefits?

Outsourcing is on the rise for many types of U.S. businesses, but outsourcing health care? Yes—it's called medical tourism. Performing surgery overseas in places like the Philippines, India, Singapore, or Thailand can save a company 75% compared to performing the same surgery in the United States. The industry is expected to grow as the baby boomer population swells and companies look to lower their health care costs.

It often makes more financial sense to have surgery in India than in the United States—even after the cost of airfare. For example, in the United States, knee surgery can cost up to $50,000, while the same surgery in India runs about $10,000. Heart surgery, which in the United States can cost in excess of $100,000, costs one-tenth of that amount in India. Surprisingly, many of the doctors performing these overseas operations have been trained in the United States.[108]

Medical tourism has typically been for (1) America's medically uninsured that are unable to pay for the high cost of procedures in their home country or (2) those choosing cosmetic or elective surgery, typically not covered by insurance. However, with health care costs on the rise, U.S. companies have been looking into medical tourism as a viable option for their employees.

For instance, in an effort to reduce health care expenses, Hannaford Brothers (owned by a European company), an operator of supermarkets in New England and New York, began offering employees in need of knee and hip replacements the option of traveling to Singapore for surgery.[109] Hannaford worked with insurer Aetna to pay 100% of the patient costs, and the company even agreed to pick up the tab for the airfare. All deductibles and copayments were waived. Not surprisingly, some companies remain skeptical about medical tourism until it becomes more mainstream.

As baby boomers (born between 1948 and 1964) continue to age, U.S. health insurance companies, eager to outsource whatever they can to cut costs, will likely turn more often to medical tourism. BlueCross BlueShield of South Carolina, for example, has created a medical-tourism unit, Companion Global Healthcare, that helps arrange travel and care for patients at 18 internationally accredited hospitals in 10 countries, including Thailand, Costa Rica, Ireland, Turkey, and Taiwan.[110] However, some insurance companies are reluctant to allow policyholders overseas, owing to lack of credentialing. The number of hospitals that are credentialed is growing as the industry learns it is crucial that the overseas providers have the credentials to show that they can offer comparable care to their U.S. counterparts. The Joint Commission International (JCI) is an American nonprofit that accredits medical facilities outside the United States. There were 76 JCI-accredited hospitals overseas in 1995, and by 2009 there were more than 300 in 39 countries.[111]

Health care companies that would profit from growth in the medical tourism industry have taken steps to increase their share of the business, particularly those in India, Thailand, and the Philippines.[112] Indian hospital operator Fortis Healthcare (with 46 hospitals in India), in an effort to build its reputation in the medical tourism business, purchased a large stake in Singapore-based Parkway Holdings, which has some of Asia's best doctors and hospitals.

There is little doubt that this is a growing industry. Singapore hosted 410,000 "medical travelers" in 2009, while Bumrungrad Hospital in Thailand also received 400,000 foreign patients that year, according to Patients Beyond Borders, a Boston-based agency advocating global medical tourism.[113] Is it time for a vacation, a little elective surgery, or both?

What's Your Take?

1. The U.S. insurance industry is heavily promoting medical tourism to reduce medical bills. If your employer offered this option, and if the quality of the care was comparable, would you consider? Please explain.

2. Do you think someone with a low deductible would spend up to $2,000 for a plane ticket and travel 24 hours to have a hip or knee replacement? (A deductible is the amount that must be paid out of pocket by the insured before an insurer will assume paying expenses.) If you needed specialized surgery, what incentives would you need to do this?

3. What are some patient issues or risks that could arise from medical tourism? State examples.

4. Do you think it is unethical for a U.S. health insurance company to encourage an individual they insure to go overseas to save money? As a cost containment measure, do you believe that both a company and its employees benefit?

Briefings

MyBizLab Activities & Cases

Go to www.mybizlab.com for online activities and exercises related to the timely topics discussed in this chapter's Briefings, as well as additional theme-related Briefing *Spotlights* highlighting how these concepts apply in today's business environment.

In-chapter Briefing:
- Cellphones Improve the Infrastructure in Africa

Activity:
- Developing Marketable Business Skills – Climate Change & Individual Energy Use

Briefing Spotlight:
- Turning the Outsourcing Tables

In-chapter Briefing:
- U.S.-Arab Cultural Differences—Touch & Interpersonal Space

Activity:
- Going to the Net! – Cultural Compatibility Test on WorldBusiness-Culture.org

Briefing Spotlight:
- For Women, Not Business as Usual

In-chapter Briefing:
- When's the Best Time to Take a Job Abroad?

Activity:
- Get Your Career in Gear – Exploring Career Paths in International Business

Briefing Spotlight:
- No English, No Jobs

In-chapter Briefing:
- Exporting U.S. Chicken Feet—A Great Chinese Delicacy

Activity:
- Going to the Net! – Export Assistance Program

Briefing Spotlight:
- The Shadow Economy

In-chapter Briefing:
- General Motors Links with Shanghai Company in Joint Venture to Sell Buicks in China

Activity:
- Ethical Dilemma Case – Outsourcing at the Drive-Through

Briefing Spotlight:
- No Bribes Allowed

In-chapter Briefing:
- An American in London Dealing with Currency Exchange—How Much *Is* That Big Mac, Really?

Activity:
- Developing Marketable Business Skills – Comparative Advantage of a College Degree

Briefing Spotlight:
- Income Hide-and-Seek

In-chapter Briefing:
- A Los Angeles Salon Owner Imports Real-Hair Extensions from India
- Communications Technology Enables a 20-Person Irrigation-Equipment Firm to Operate in Three Countries

Activity:
- Going to the Net! – Inc. Magazine Profiles 30 Top Entrepreneurs Under 30

Briefing Spotlight:
- India's Entrepreneurial Women's Movement

Additional Briefing Spotlights available at MyBizLab:

- CUSTOMER FOCUS
- EARNING GREEN BY GOING GREEN
- INFO TECH & SOCIAL MEDIA
- SOCIALLY RESPONSIBLE BUSINESS

5

Forms of Ownership

Business Enterprises Great & Small

After reading and studying this chapter, you will be able to answer the following essential questions:

5.1 Basic Forms of Business Ownership: Sole Proprietorships, Partnerships, Corporations, & Cooperatives

THE ESSENTIAL QUESTION: *Which of the four basic forms of business ownership would best suit a business I might start?*

5.2 Franchises: A Special Form of Ownership

THE ESSENTIAL QUESTION: *What are franchises, and how might I benefit or not benefit by owning a franchise?*

5.3 Mergers & Acquisitions: Paths to Business Expansion

THE ESSENTIAL QUESTION: *If I wanted to expand my company, what are the ways to do it?*

MyBizLab

Where you see MyBizLab in this chapter, go to www.mybizlab.com for additional activities on the topic being discussed.

FORECAST: What's Ahead in This Chapter

This chapter first considers four basic forms of business ownership: sole proprietorships, partnerships, corporations, and cooperatives. Next we consider types of franchises and trends in franchising. Finally, we discuss how businesses can grow themselves through mergers and acquisitions, including types of mergers, hostile takeovers, leveraged buyouts, and employee buyouts.

WINNER: Wayne Huizenga: A Billionaire through Acquisitions

Merging or acquiring companies is a classic way of building a business—and perhaps a personal fortune. Here's how one man, listed as one of *Forbes* magazine's 400 richest Americans (net worth $2.1 billion), did it.

Wayne Huizenga (pronounced "*High*-zing-a") was born in a Chicago suburb in 1937. He moved to Florida in his teens, where he worked driving a truck and pumping gas after school and on weekends. After army service and some college, he went to work for a garbage collection company. Huizenga would drive the truck from 2:30 a.m. until noon, then knocked on doors to drum up business.

Within two years, he bought his own truck and branched out, growing his firm to 40 trucks locally, then merging with another business to form Waste Management Inc. (WMI). Shortly thereafter, the company offered its stock to the public and used its buying power to acquire nearly 150 local and regional garbage services. In the course of growing WMI into the largest waste disposal company in the United States, Huizenga hit upon his model for success: Find and acquire companies in a fragmented, pedestrian industry filled with small, undercapitalized operators but with a steady cash flow, then put together a company with a national presence.

Huizenga began to apply this formula to other industries. He bought a bottled water company, then acquired 16 more bottlers. Then he and two partners bought 35% of Blockbuster Video, and in four years grew it from 19 stores to 1,654, finally selling out to Viacom for $8.4 billion in stock. Next he created AutoNation, the first nationwide automobile dealer. Then he created Extended Stay America, growing it to nearly 500 hotels. Having sold WMI earlier, he reentered the waste management business by creating Republic Services and growing it into the third-largest waste management company in the United States before merging it with WMI.

What is the key to Huizenga's success? "He focuses on service industries, mostly those that have recurring income: dumpster rental, trash collection, video rental, etc.," says one account. "There's no big manufacturing plant, and the emphasis is on customer service."[1]

LOSER: AOL & Time Warner: "The Worst Merger in History"

In a so-called merger of the century, in January 2000 the No. 1 online portal service, AOL (America Online), headed by Steve Case, purchased old-line publishing conglomerate Time Warner, whose CEO was Gerald Levin, for $164 billion. The two companies became a new entity named AOL Time Warner. At the time, this was the biggest corporate merger in history, with both companies together worth $290 billion.

Case envisioned a revolution in both new media and old. He saw a combined company so influential in news and entertainment and on the Internet that it would touch every consumer's life. Case predicted that the cross-pollination of AOL's pervasive Internet presence with Time Warner's well-known news and entertainment brands—*Time, Sports Illustrated,* and *People* magazines; music and book divisions; movie divisions Warner Bros. and New Line Cinema; and cable systems—would equal unprecedented prosperity.[2]

Two years later, AOL Time Warner had lost more than $150 billion of the 2000 market value. "That means," said one commentator, "an amount equal to the whole value of pre-merger AOL is up in smoke. Truly staggering."[3] The "merger of the century" had become "the worst merger in history."

What happened? Some observers say the purchase came at the end of the "dot.com bubble," when technology companies were overvalued and Case understood "his run was over and that it was time to trade in his stock certificates for those of a company that had genuine assets."[4] Once merged, the AOL division began to grapple with decelerating subscriber growth and increasing competition from high-speed Internet service providers.[5] The notion that the merger would inspire the company's businesses to collaborate never happened, as these divisions continued to operate in old ways.[6] "Time Warner," wrote Case, "has proven to be too big, too complex, too conflicted, and too slow-moving—in other words, too much like a conglomerate—to seize new opportunities."[7]

In response to the huge loss, the company dropped the "AOL" from its name and removed Case as executive chairman. In 2005 he resigned from the board.

YOUR CALL Is the problem in growing companies through mergers and acquisitions all about managing size? Is it about vision? Focus? Leadership? What do you think Wayne Huizenga would have done if he had been in Steve Case's place in 2000 in order to profit from AOL?

MyBizLab

THE BIG IDEA: We describe four basic forms of business ownership, each of which has its benefits and drawbacks. (1) Sole proprietorships, usually one-person businesses, are the most common. (2) Partnerships, involving two people or more, may be a general partnership, a limited partnership, a master limited partnership (MLP), or a limited liability partnership (LLP). (3) Corporations, whether a mom 'n' pop store or a world Goliath, may be a C or S corporation, a limited liability company (LLC), or a B (for benefit) corporation. (4) Cooperatives can be formed by user members who pool their resources for their mutual benefits.

THE ESSENTIAL QUESTION: Which of the four basic forms of business ownership would best suit a business I might start?

MyBizLab

MyBizLab: Check your understanding of these concepts at www.mybizlab.com.

When Angela Ford, while on the staff of another company, started her Chicago-based real estate and property company, TAG Worldwide, she worried that new customers might perceive it to be the one-person, part-time business that in fact it was. After all, as management lecturer Eric Siegel of the Wharton School of the University of Pennsylvania says, "Perception in the marketplace is a significant factor to success."

To create the impression of a large company, Ford lined up an answering service that used live operators, so that when customers called the TAG number—actually, Ford's home phone—the operators would answer "Let me see if she's available," then try her cellphone. "If I could take the call, I would," Ford says. A few years later Ford was running the company full time, had added several employees, and doubled revenue every year.[8]

Small businesses like TAG—businesses with 100 employees or less—are the primary engine for creating jobs in the United States, creating 46.7% of new jobs compared to only 28.2% for large companies with over 1,000 workers (based on statistics from a 13-year period, 1992–2005).[9] Even nationwide firms like Staples and Waste Management Inc. started out small, often as single-person operations. Here we discuss the various forms of ownership that companies take, from simplest to most complex, then consider how they can grow through mergers and acquisitions. We describe the following four forms:

- Sole proprietorships
- Partnerships
- Corporations
- Cooperatives

The percentage of U.S. businesses that are sole proprietorships, partnerships, and corporations are shown at left. (*See* ■ *Panel 5.1.*)

■ **PANEL 5.1 Forms of business ownership.**

Number of Firms: Percentage

Sole proprietorships (nonfarm)	‖‖‖‖‖‖‖‖‖‖‖‖‖‖‖‖‖‖‖‖‖‖ 72%
Partnerships	‖‖ 9.6%
Corporations	‖‖‖‖‖‖ 18.2%

Total Receipts: Percentage

Sole proprietorships (nonfarm)	‖ 3.9%
Partnerships	‖‖‖‖‖ 13.6%
Corporations	‖‖‖‖‖‖‖‖‖‖‖‖‖‖‖‖‖‖‖‖‖‖‖‖‖‖ 82%

Source: Statistical Abstract of the United States 2011, Table 743, www.census.gov/compendia/statab/2011/tables/11s0744.pdf (accessed August 25, 2011).

Note there are many more sole proprietorships and partnerships than corporations, but corporations provide the great majority of total revenues.

Sole Proprietorships: One-Owner Businesses

What is a sole proprietorship, and what are its major benefits and disadvantages?

The oldest and simplest form of business ownership—and, at 72%, certainly the largest—is the **sole proprietorship, a business owned, and typically managed, by one person.** Many retail establishments, small service businesses, home-based businesses, and farms are sole proprietorships.[10] ●

Source: Photo by Robert Gross.

BRIEFING / BUSINESS SKILLS & CAREER DEVELOPMENT
A Minority-Owned Public Relations Firm.

When Robert Smith, 31, of Rockton, Illinois, couldn't find a job in his chosen field as a paralegal, he decided to take a risk by starting a child-support collection agency, Robert Smith & Associates. While promoting that business, he discovered he had a gift for publicity. "I was bitten by the bug," he said.

Smith started his public relations firm from his kitchen table as a sole proprietorship to advise companies wanting to influence minority customers, especially African Americans and Hispanics. He first used computers at the public library, opening a free e-mail account, to help him attract and serve his early customers. Once revenue began to flow, he was able to begin acquiring his own office equipment, buying used PCs for $450, then a cellphone and a $700 copier. Seven years after starting, he was anticipating billings of half a million dollars for the year.[11] ■

❶ **Home-based business.** Ann Peterson runs her company, Mundo Images, out of her home in Buffalo, New York. She produces English- and Spanish-language greeting cards featuring her own dramatic photography as well as resonating quotations she has collected for years. A portion of the profits from her cards, which sell in 27 states and Canada, goes to environmental charities. What do you think are the biggest challenges of starting and running a one-person business from your home?

Five Benefits of Being a Sole Proprietorship

There are at least five advantages to being a sole proprietorship. You can or may . . .

1. **Start Up the Business with Ease.** You might have to obtain a business license. After that, it's pretty much your choice what equipment to buy, announcements to make, and office to rent—or whether to work out of your home.

2. **Make All Your Own Decisions.** You have no boss over you (or rather you have several bosses—they're called "customers"); you run your own show. You decide what to charge, whom to hire, and how to grow your business, if you wish. You may even allow employees who are parents to take care of their children at work, for example. Unlike corporations with their stockholders, you don't need to share information with anyone (unless you're trying to get a loan and need to show a banker your financial picture).

3. **Keep All the Profits.** No matter how much you make, you don't have to share your earnings with anyone else—except the IRS, of course.

4. **Keep Your Taxes Relatively Simple.** Your profits are taxed just once, at your personal income rate.

5. **End the Business with Ease.** Decide you no longer want to operate your business? You can simply stop. You don't need the permission of anyone else.

Five Drawbacks of Being a Sole Proprietorship

You may experience the exhilaration of independence when you're starting up the business, but after a while many small-business people begin to feel weighed

> ℹ️ **Want to Know More? 5-1**
> **Key Terms & Definitions in Sequential Order to Study as You Go Along**
> Go to www.mybizlab.com.

Source: Greg Miller.

❷ Losses. When Jan Lee retired from IBM with a nest egg of $100,000, she decided to open a diet and exercise center in Hawthorn Woods, Illinois. She chose to open a franchise. Including franchise fees, her initial startup costs were over $100,000. Besides using her savings, she also took out a loan against her house. The business was not a success. Eventually she lost not only her business, but her house and her marriage. Even if you choose a form of business that protects you from personal liability, you can still lose your house if you've borrowed against it. Would you put your home at risk in order to open a business?

❸ Small-business time stress. Renee Wood, shown here with some sympathy gifts she sells, found it was nearly impossible to take a vacation. Is this the kind of sacrifice you'd be willing to make in order to be your own boss?

Source: Hazelton Photography.

down by the endless responsibilities. There are at least five disadvantages to being a sole proprietor. You may or will . . .

1. **Have Unlimited Financial Liability—Your Personal Possessions Are at Risk.** Perhaps the major disadvantage of being a sole proprietor is that you have *unlimited liability*—**that is, any debts or damages incurred by the business become the responsibility of the business owner.** This is a serious business risk because the law holds there is no difference between your business assets and your personal assets, so you might be called upon to empty your bank account and sell your car, house, or other possessions to satisfy business debts. ❷ If someone sues you in a business dispute, you might lose everything you own.

2. **Have Limited Financial Resources and Few Fringe Benefits.** Most sole proprietorships are small scale, which means they have limited financial resources. They also don't have the borrowing power of large organizations and are frequently limited to the owner's personal credit. In addition, the kind of *fringe benefits*—**such as vacation pay, sick leave, health benefits, and pension plans, which provide benefits beyond base wages**—that you might be used to having in large organizations may be few or nonexistent, since they have to be paid for out of whatever revenues you make.

3. **Have Management Problems.** Maybe you have the talent to practice your trade—run a hair salon, fitness studio, car-repair shop, or whatever. But do you have the managerial discipline to keep records, meet IRS deadlines, withhold and record various federal and state taxes from your employees' paychecks, and so on? Do you have the necessary marketing skills, human resources skills, and purchasing skills? Lots of small-business people don't have such management expertise and can't pay enough to attract professional managers to do it for them.

4. **Be Overstressed about Time.** Most sole proprietors put in long hours and are reluctant to take vacations—because they feel there is no one to turn the business over to. Indeed, to be a small-business person is to be running flat out all the time, even while you're supposedly on holiday, where you may be constantly checking your e-mail and text messages.

BRIEFING / SMALL BUSINESS & ENTREPRENEURS
A Small-Business Owner Finally Takes a Vacation. Renee Wood of Geneva, Illinois, owns the Comfort Company, which sells sympathy gifts for people to give the newly bereaved. She found after five years on the business treadmill that her life was out of balance. "Your business is your baby," she says. "You really don't believe someone would come in there and handle it with care." ❸

As a result, she had never taken a vacation, and so had missed spending time with her four children. Finally, however, she was able to go on leave because she took on an employee she trusted to run the business in her absence. Even so, she stayed in touch during her five-day trip by using a handheld computer to do as much customer service as she could.[12] ∎

5. **Not Be Able to Sell or Pass along the Business.** Although some sole proprietors are able to sell the business to someone or pass it along to their heirs as part of their estate, for many people the business is retired or dies when they do. If you have a unique skill of, say, building custom-made guitars, it's hard for someone else to take over.

With these kinds of burdens, is it any wonder that some sole proprietors try to find a partner with whom they can share the load? This brings us to the second form of business—partnerships.

Partnerships: Two or More Owners

What are the benefits and drawbacks of being a partnership?

A *partnership* **is a business owned and operated by two or more persons as a voluntary legal association.** "The right partner is not a friend or relative who simply wants to get in on the action," says one article, "but someone who is going to strengthen your financial position when purchasing the business, add expertise in running the business, or both."[13] Of course, there are many partners who don't fit this description, such as married couples who run a home business—a difficult feat for many.[14] ❹

An important part of setting up a partnership is to have a *partnership agreement,* which, among other things, spells out how breakups or changes will be handled. (We describe setting up "articles of partnership" in another few paragraphs.)[15]

Source: Jonathan Sprague/Redux.

Types of Partnerships: General, Limited, Master Limited, & Limited Liability

There are four basic types of partnerships:

- **General Partnership: Partners Share Business Profits and Liabilities.** In a *general partnership,* **two or more partners are responsible for the business and share profits, liabilities, and management responsibilities.** The partners need not be equal; one, for instance, may invest a sum of money but have no involvement in day-to-day business operations. Some partners are "silent partners"; their participation is kept hidden from the public.

- **Limited Partnership: Some Partners Have Less Liability and Responsibility.** A *limited partnership* **has one or more general partners plus other, limited partners who contribute only an investment but do not have any management responsibility or liability.** That is, limited partners have *limited* liability, which is based on the amount they have invested in the company.

- **Master Limited Partnership (MLP): The Partnership Acts Like a Corporation, Selling Stock.** In a *master limited partnership (MLP),* **the partnership acts like a corporation, selling stock on a stock exchange, but it is taxed like a partnership, paying a lesser rate than the corporate income tax.**

- **Limited Liability Partnership (LLP): The Partnership Limits the Risk of Loss of Personal Assets.** In a *limited liability partnership (LLP),* **the liability of each partner—and the risk of losing personal assets—is limited to just his or her own acts and omissions and those of his or her directly reporting employees.** Thus, if another of your partners in your LLP firm is guilty of negligence or malfeasance, your own personal assets are not at risk. (In many states, however, this limitation in risk of loss of personal assets does not extend to certain contract situations involving creditors, leases, and bank loans.)

An LLP is not to be confused with an LLC (limited liability company), which we discuss later in this chapter.

Four Benefits of Being a Partnership

Partnerships have some of the same advantages as sole proprietorships, and they are also in many ways better, mainly because having more people put up money means the company can do more things.

There are at least four advantages to being involved in a partnership. You can or may . . .

1. **Start Up the Business with Relative Ease.** It's almost as easy to start up a partnership as it is a sole proprietorship. However, you should probably get a lawyer to draw up *articles of partnership,* **a legal agreement that (a)**

❹ **Working together.** There are lots of benefits of going into a partnership with someone you know—friend, spouse, or boyfriend/ girlfriend. Rachel and Andy Berliner of Petaluma, California, founded Amy's Kitchen (named for their baby) in 1987 and built it into a leading frozen-food brand catering to vegetarians. In the early years the couple struggled with the pressures of financing, delivery schedules, marketing, and an accident that ruined 100,000 vegetable and tofu potpies. Do you think your relationship could survive such business stresses for so many years?

Want to Know More? 5-2

What Does a Partnership Agreement Look Like?

Go to www.mybizlab.com.

Want to Know More? 5-3

What's a Good Example of a Master Limited Partnership?

Go to www.mybizlab.com.

Key Takeaway 5-1
Partnerships may be general, limited, master limited, or limited liability.

⑤ Launching a foreign company.
Robin Chase's first company, Boston-based Zipcar, shook up the U.S. auto rental industry by offering a subscription-based, pay-by-the-hour system. She eventually stepped down as CEO and became a transportation consultant. However, the lure of entrepreneurship brought her back to the hourly car rental business, but this time in Paris. Privately financed, Buzzcar was launched in 2011 and, unlike the Zipcar concept, uses people's own cars. They rent them out to neighbors through Buzzcar via a location-based, smartphone app. What factors might make starting a new business in a foreign country more challenging?

Want to Know More? 5-4

How Do You Form a Partnership?

Go to www.mybizlab.com.

defines the role of each partner in the business, (b) specifies how much money each is to invest, and (c) specifies the buy/sell arrangements if one or both partners die or if one wants to get out of the arrangement. But if you don't have articles of partnership, in every state except Louisiana partnerships are covered by the *Uniform Partnership Act,* which defines general principles of ownership, sharing of profits and losses, and rights to participate in managing the business.

2. **Have More Financial Resources.** Having more people involved in the startup means you will have more money to cover expenses. You may also have a better chance at getting bank financing. Thus, you might be able to start a more ambitious enterprise than you would as a sole proprietor. ⑤

3. **Have More Managerial and Other Expertise.** With the right kind of partners, you will have one or more people to draw on for specialized skills, more managerial involvement, and ways to divide the work so that all of you can have some time off.

4. **Keep Your Taxes Relatively Simple.** Your profits will be taxed as the personal income of each partner, just as it is with sole proprietorships.

Three Drawbacks of Being a Partnership

If you were (or are) in a marriage or serious relationship, do you think it could survive the stresses of the two of you running a small business together? The same question applies to a partnership that's not also a love relationship. (We consider this further in the Practical Action box on the page opposite.)

There are three disadvantages to being in a partnership. You may or will . . .

1. **Experience Personality Conflicts or Other Disagreements among Partners.** Limited partners have no say in operating the business, but general partners do, so it's important that they be able to resolve differences. You and the other owners need to determine who can handle money, authorize payments, hire and fire employees, and so on. How are profits to be divided up? What if your partner invested more money, but you are investing more hours in running the operation—should you both be equally compensated? These questions are, of course, best addressed in the articles of partnership before the business opens its doors the first day. But what happens downstream if there are severe personality conflicts?

2. **Have Unlimited Liability.** If you're a general (not limited) partner, you are equally responsible with other general partners for debts and damages incurred by the company, even if the fault is theirs, not yours. Thus, like a sole proprietor, you are at risk for losing your personal possessions—house, car, and so on—if you are sued or file for bankruptcy.

3. **Have Difficulty Ending or Changing the Partnership and Can't Pass the Business Along.** As with a sole proprietorship, you can't usually pass along your share of the business to your heirs. If you leave the business, normally your share is sold to another general partner or partners. If you want to stay with the business but change partners—get rid of one, add another—it may be difficult. If you want to take your money out, you may find your partners are unwilling to buy you out. Once again, it's best to spell out such contingencies in advance in the articles of partnership.

Is it possible that by going into business by yourself or with a partner you are actually exposing yourself to the risk of losing everything you own should something go horribly wrong? Perhaps the way to avoid this hazard is to consider incorporating.

Corporations: From Mom 'n' Pops to World Goliaths

What are the differences among the four types of corporations?

We tend to think of corporations as huge organizations of colossal power—world Goliaths like ExxonMobil or General Motors, with thousands of employees, millions of shareholders, offices throughout the world, and a 20-person board of directors. But many individuals, including mom 'n' pop businesses, are also incorporated—and for good reason: the owners can protect their personal property if the corporation runs up debts, loses a lawsuit, or goes bankrupt. Indeed, most U.S. corporations are small businesses.

Types of Corporations: C, S, LLC, & B

There are a great many kinds of corporations. (*See* ■ *Panel 5.2, next page.*) However, if you were to elect to form your new business as a corporation rather than as a sole proprietorship or partnership, you would have four choices:[18]

The C Corporation: Any Number of Owners, Two Levels of Taxation. A *C corporation* **is a state-chartered entity that pays taxes and is legally distinct from its owners.** (A *charter,* or *corporate charter,* is a certificate issued by the state that contains such information as the scope of the business and the amount of money invested.) As an owner, you might risk losing the amount of money you invested in the corporation, but you wouldn't have to worry about losing your car, house, or other personal possessions.

The C corporation is the traditional form of corporation favored by most big businesses and is apt to have a great many owners (shareholders), most of whom don't work for it. If you are an owner of a C corporation, your profits are taxed twice. At the corporate level, taxes are paid on profits; then, all or part of those

Key Takeaway 5-2
Three conventional corporations are C, S, and LLC. B is uncommon.

■ PANEL 5.2 Different kinds of corporations: a mini-glossary.

Corporation	Definition
Privately held (or closed)	Ownership is restricted to a small group of investors
Publicly held (or open)	Shares can be easily bought and sold by investors
Domestic	Operates in the state in which it is incorporated
Foreign	Operates in states other than the one in which it was incorporated
Alien	Operates in the United States but is incorporated in another country
Multinational	Operates in several countries
Subsidiary	Most stock owned by another corporation
Professional	Operated by owners offering professional services (e.g., medicine, law); not publicly traded
Nonprofit	Doesn't seek personal profit for its owners
Employee-owned	Employees own stock in corporation that employs them
Government-owned	Formed and operated by federal or state government for specific purpose
Quasi-public	Public utility with approved monopoly providing basic public services

profits are typically distributed to shareholders as dividends, where they are taxed again as part of personal income.

The S Corporation: Up to 100 Owners, Only One Level of Federal Taxation. An *S corporation* **is a corporation with no more than 100 owners (shareholders), but, like a partnership, the owners are taxed only at the personal (not corporate) level.** (It may still be subject to a state tax.) As with C corporations, the owners have little or no liability for the debts of the business.

An S corporation can provide its owners with both salaries and distributions (profits). "The government will levy a 15.3% self-employment tax on owners' salaries, but not on distributions," one business writer points out. "So there is a financial incentive to keep salaries as low as possible . . . and pay yourself more in distributions."[19]

The Limited Liability Company (LLC): One Level of Federal Taxation, Little or No Liability. A *limited liability company (LLC)* **combines the tax benefits of a sole proprietorship or partnership—one level of tax—with the limited liability of a corporation.** In most states, an LLC is available to single-member businesses as well as to larger groups. An LLC has the additional benefit of being free of the legal requirements that govern corporations, including annual reports, director meetings, and shareholder requirements.[20] ❻

The B Corporation: A "Benefit Corporation" Legally Required to Adhere to Socially Beneficial Practices. The newest form of corporation is the *B corporation,* **or "benefit corporation," whose corporate charter legally requires that the company adhere to socially beneficial practices,**

❻ **LLC.** Many small-business people, such as doctors, lawyers, and accountants, but also others, such as restaurant owners, structure their business as an LLC. If you were starting your own business, do you think you would form it as an LLC? Why?

Source: Photograph by Sally Lindsay.

1206
CHARLES J. FELDMAN CLU
CHARTERED FINANCIAL CONSULTANT

BUSINESS AND ESTATE PLANNING
CONSULTANTS, INC.

FELDMAN WEALTH ADVISORY, LLC

JOSEPH M. FELDMAN, CFP
CERTIFIED FINANCIAL
PLANNERS ™ professional

such as helping communities, employees, consumers, and the environment. ❼ A goal of B corporations is to obtain tax breaks from various levels of government, such as that granted by the city of Philadelphia. In 2010, Maryland became the first state to legally recognize B corporations. The B-corporation idea was created by B Lab, a nonprofit organization dedicated to using business to solve social and environmental problems, which also evaluates businesses for compliance with B-corporation goals.[21]

Five Benefits of Being in a Corporation

There are at least five advantages to setting up your business as a corporation. You can or may . . .

1. **Have Little or No Liability.** Probably the chief advantage of corporations is that, when set up properly, they leave the owners with little or no personal liability to lawsuits, debts, or bankruptcy. If the corporation is sued for producing faulty products and has to declare bankruptcy, for instance, the most the owners can lose is the amount they invested in the company; they won't lose their personal property, such as home and car.

2. **Get Possible Tax Breaks.** If you're the owner of a small business, being incorporated gives you "the possibility of tax breaks that may mean the difference between success and failure," as one book states.[22] For example, you may be able to deduct more health benefits and medical-related expenses than you would be able to as a sole proprietorship or partnership.

3. **Have Far More Financial Resources.** A corporation can sell ownership shares to any number of people—perhaps hundreds of thousands of shareholders, in the case of large C corporations. Thus, it is able to raise more investor money than a sole proprietorship or partnership ever could, giving it a major advantage in its ability to discover, make, and market more products or services. Typically corporations also find it easier to obtain bank loans and individual loans (by issuing bonds). We discuss stocks and bonds in more detail in Chapter 17.

4. **Have Far More Managerial and Other Expertise.** With its larger sums of money, a corporation is in a far better position than a sole proprietorship or partnership to find managerial, professional, and other talent, as well as to acquire buildings, equipment, and even other companies that can give it more power in the marketplace.

5. **More Easily Sell Ownership Shares and Continue the Life of the Business.** Unlike being the owner of a sole proprietorship or co-owner of a partnership, being in a corporation makes it easier to sell your share of ownership (as in putting your C-corporation stock up for sale). You can also be fairly assured that your ownership in the corporation will outlive you, so that, if you wish, you can transfer that ownership to your heirs.

Four Drawbacks of Being in a Corporation

There are four disadvantages to being in a corporation, even if you are a lone individual or one of a few individuals weighing whether to incorporate rather than make your business a sole proprietorship or partnership. You may or will . . .

1. **Have to Deal with Startup and Ongoing Costs and Paperwork.** Each state (plus the District of Columbia) has its own set of corporation codes. You contact the secretary of state in the state in which you want to incorporate and, for fees ranging up to $300, file incorporation documents. (*See* ■ *Panel 5.3.*) You may also have to pay a county recording fee or meet a publishing requirement. You will need to complete IRS forms. Once incorporated, you will need to file various compliance forms, reports, and tax returns. Complicated? No wonder so many business owners hire a professional to help with all this.

Source: Photograph by Sally Lindsay.

❼ **B corporation.** Method (branded small-M "method") Products is a certified B-for-benefit corporation that offers personal care and other products. The San Francisco firm tries to operate in a values-driven manner, says its website, "building social and environmental benefit into its products and everything it does." Being a B corporation helps build that purpose "into the legal backbone of the company so that those values will never be compromised." Do you agree this legal structure will lock in the firm's particular focus?

■ **PANEL 5.3 Applying for incorporation.**

The application you submit to a state official (usually the secretary of state) for incorporation must include the following:

1. Name and address of the corporation
2. Principal business purposes
3. Type of stock and number of shares to be issued
4. The corporation's minimum capital
5. Methods for transferring shares of stock
6. Names and addresses of directors
7. Duration of the corporation (usually perpetual)

Want to Know More? 5-5

How Do You Form a Corporation?

Go to www.mybizlab.com.

BRIEFING / LEGAL & ETHICAL PRACTICES

Incorporating a Small Business in Nevada. Two states, Delaware and Nevada, make it easy to incorporate, no matter what state you live in or are doing business in. With Nevada, for instance, you can go online and find a service company or professional that, for a fee of $700 or so, will handle all the necessary filings with state offices. For another slight yearly fee, they will also send you regular e-mails reminding you when you have to do something—such as file annual reports or hold annual meetings—in order to keep your corporation in compliance with the law.

You need not be a Nevada resident to file for incorporation there. Many people pick that state for incorporation because it has no state income tax. ■

2. **Be Taxed Twice.** Your corporation will have to pay taxes on the profits it receives before they are distributed (as dividends) to the shareholders. Then each shareholder will have to pay personal income taxes on the payments he or she receives from the corporation. By contrast, the owner of a sole proprietorship or partnership is taxed only once. (The exception for corporations, as we mentioned, is that income for S and LLC firms is taxed only once at the federal level.) Corporate returns can be quite complex, and a businessperson is well advised to enlist the help of a certified public accountant.

3. **Have to Publicly Disclose Financial Information.** Publicly (but not privately) held corporations must disclose to the Securities and Exchange Commission a wide range of financial data: earnings, financial condition, product offerings, and qualifications of top managers and directors. Although this helps investors, it also alerts competitors to sensitive information about the company.

4. **Have Difficulty Ending the Corporation.** Once a corporation is established, it's somewhat difficult to terminate it because of the amount of paperwork required.

Cooperatives: Limiting Power of Each Shareholder

What is a cooperative?

A *cooperative,* or a *co-op,* is a corporation owned by its user members, who have pooled their resources for their mutual benefit. The purpose of a co-op, such as a retail cooperative, is not so much to make a profit as to provide a service to its members.

There are some 467,000 cooperatives in the United States today, ranging from student-owned college bookstores, to rural electric utilities, to food cooperatives, to hardware stores. While many cooperatives are small storefronts, others are quite large, including some Fortune 500 companies such as Ace Hardware, with 4,530 stores.[23] Ace and the citrus supplier Sunkist, another cooperative (6,500 members), consist of small businesses that have banded together for purchasing and marketing clout. Generally speaking, the shareholders in a cooperative elect their own board of directors, who then hire managers to run the company.

BRIEFING / LEGAL & ETHICAL PRACTICES

A Rural Town Abandoned by National Chains Forms a Cooperative Department Store. When the local JCPenney store closed its doors, residents of rural Ely, Nevada (population 4,041), were faced with having to drive 190 miles just to buy a pair of shoes. Other retailers, such as Walmart, which typically won't serve markets under 50,000 people, rebuffed Ely's overtures.

Ely decided to take cues from other communities that had lost national retailers, such as Powell, Wyoming, which formed community-owned department stores. Ely formed its own cooperative corporation, the Community Owned Mercantile Project Inc., known as Garnet Mercantile, and raised more than $400,000 by selling 880 shares of stock to local and statewide investors. To prevent anyone getting too much control, no one was allowed to buy more than 20 shares.

Using fixtures donated by JCPenney, Garnet Mercantile opened in 2004 and is still in operation. Backers of the store contend the key to its success is its ability to tailor its goods to the needs of the community, as opposed to the generic, centralized buying of a chain.[24] **8** ■

Source: Courtesy of Garnet Mercantile.

8 **Garnet Mercantile.** This cooperative department store in Ely, Nevada, is an example of the approach rural communities have been taking when they lose their local big chain store. Would you buy shares in such a business?

The four *principal* forms of business ownership we just discussed are compared below. (*See* ■ *Panel 5.4.*)

■ **PANEL 5.4 The four principal forms of business ownership.**

Type of business ownership and number of owners	Financial risk if the firm is sued or files for bankruptcy	Advantages of this form of ownership You may or will be able to . . .	Disadvantages of this form of ownership You may or will . . .
Sole proprietorship: One owner	**Unlimited financial liability:** Owner at risk of losing personal possessions (e.g., house, car)	1. Start up the business with ease 2. Make all your own decisions 3. Keep all profits 4. Keep your taxes relatively simple 5. End the business with ease	1. Have unlimited financial liability 2. Have limited financial resources and few fringe benefits 3. Have management problems 4. Be overstressed about time 5. Not sell or pass along the business
Partnership: Two or more owners	**Unlimited financial liability:** Any general (not limited) partner is at risk of losing personal possessions	1. Start up the business with relative ease 2. Have more financial resources 3. Have more managerial and other expertise 4. Keep your taxes relatively simple	1. Experience personality conflicts or other disagreements among partners 2. Have unlimited financial liability 3. Have difficulty ending or changing the partnership and can't pass the business along
Corporation: Unlimited number of owners; for S corporations, up to 100 owners	**Little or no liability:** Owners can lose amount they invested in the company, but not personal possessions	1. Have little or no liability 2. Get possible tax breaks 3. Have far more financial resources 4. Have far more managerial and other expertise 5. More easily sell ownership shares and continue the life of the business	1. Have to deal with startup and ongoing costs and paperwork 2. Be taxed twice 3. Have to publicly disclose financial information 4. Have difficulty ending the corporation
Cooperative: Unlimited number of owners	**Little or no liability:** Owners can lose amount they invested in the company, but not personal possessions	1. Have little or no liability 2. More easily sell ownership shares and continue the life of the business 3. Be protected against a single shareholder's dominance 4. Find the organization more resilient because it's less prone to take risks	1. Find decision making may take too long 2. Find it's difficult to get bank financing 3. Experience squabbling among members 4. Find that the organization never makes a profit

💡 **THE BIG IDEA:** Franchises, in which you get help starting a business, are of three types: business-format, product-distribution, and manufacturing franchises. There are at least five benefits and five drawbacks to owning a franchise.

❓ **THE ESSENTIAL QUESTION:** What are franchises, and how might I benefit or not benefit by owning a franchise?

MyBizLab

MyBizLab: Check your understanding of these concepts at www.mybizlab.com.

If you drive through the outskirts of many growing towns in the United States, what do you see? 7-Eleven. Denny's. Burger King. Dunkin' Donuts. Hallmark. Holiday Inn. Jiffy Lube. If the new parts of town look so much alike, blame it partly on the explosion not only in chains but also in franchises, where appearances are often tightly controlled. Yet franchises represent one important way you can get into business. ❾

Franchises: Help in Starting a Business

What's the difference between a franchisor and a franchisee?

A *franchise* **is an arrangement in which a business owner allows others the right to use its name and sell its goods or services within a specific geographical area.** Starting a small business can be a risky, time-consuming endeavor. However,

❾ **College Hunks Hauling Junk.** Started in 2003 by a pair of college students, this Tampa, Florida, trash removal company grew into a national franchise. In 2011 it merged with 1-800-JUNK-USA, a well-known nationwide waste management and recycling company. The biggest thing franchises, such as Denny's and Applebee's, have going for them is their familiarity. Do you like to experiment with new eating places? Or do you feel more comfortable eating at a restaurant that is recognizable nationwide?

Source: Courtesy of College Hunks Hauling Junk.

the effort may be reduced considerably if you as a *franchisee,* **the buyer of a franchise,** are helped in establishing your business by a *franchisor,* **the business owner that gives others the rights to sell its products or services.** You can set up a franchise as a sole proprietorship, partnership, or corporation.

The largest franchise industries in the United States are fast-food restaurants, followed by retail sales, services, automotive, restaurants, maintenance, building and construction, retail-food, and lodging.[25] One study estimated 784,802 of just one type of franchise (the business-format franchise, defined in the following section) in the United States in 2011.[26]

BRIEFING / SMALL BUSINESS & ENTREPRENEURS

Jersey Mike's Sub Sandwich Shop Develops a Small Business into a Franchisor. Could you take a small business and franchise it? Peter Cancro, now 53, did. Cancro grew up on the New Jersey Shore and during summers worked at Mike's Subs. When vacationers swelled the population, "We probably made 1,000 subs a day," he said later.

At age 17 he learned the owners wanted to sell the sandwich shop, and he knocked on doors to raise money and used the help of a former football coach and banker to get a bank loan to buy the business. Later he found that summer customers would ask him to wrap subs to take cross-country. That gave him the idea to sell franchises. The firm started in 1987 and now has franchises in over 400 locations.

Any words of wisdom? "I've learned how critical the right location is for a retail store," Cancro says, "and that it's important to find out the revenues of other businesses in the area. I've also learned how important training is." Aspiring entrepreneurs, he concludes, "should know that running a business will be more work than they ever realized."[27] ■

⑩ A tough purchase. Chipotle Mexican Grill has almost 700 stores, but only eight are franchises! Why? Chipotle's Food with Integrity program has very strict requirements regarding suppliers, so much so that the company is now reluctant to give up any control in this area to new franchisees. Do you think Chipotle's tight controls will discourage or enhance company growth?

Types of Franchises

Which type of franchise might most interest me?

All kinds of businesses have been successfully franchised—from banks to fast-food restaurants, from convenience stores to real-estate agencies, from fitness studios to dating services, from porta-potties to funeral homes. There is even a company called DoodyCalls that franchises the business of cleaning yards of dog poop.[28] In general, however, franchises may be categorized as three types: (1) *business-format,* (2) *product-distribution,* and (3) *manufacturing.* (See ■ Panel 5.5.)

Business-Format Franchise: Using a Franchisor's Name & Format

Most of the more visible franchises you see, such as McDonald's, Starbucks, and Jiffy Lube, are examples of a business-format franchise. **A *business-format franchise,* or *chain store* or *franchise outlet,* allows a franchisee to use the trade name and format of a franchisor, following guidelines for marketing and pricing the product.** ⑩

Product-Distribution Franchise: Selling a Franchisor's Trademarked Product

Jeep, Mercedes, Exxon, and Shell are examples of a ***product-distribution franchise,*** **also known as a *distributorship,* in which a franchisee is given the right to sell trademarked products purchased from the franchisor.**

■ **PANEL 5.5 Three kinds of franchises.**

Type of Franchise	Examples
Business-format franchise: Chain store or franchise outlet	AAMCO Dunkin' Donuts H&R Block Merry Maids Motel 6
Product-distribution franchise: Distribute product	ARCO Baskin-Robbins Buick John Deere
Manufacturing franchise: Make and distribute product	A&W Root Beer Closets by Design Eureka Woodworks Invisible Fence

Want to Know More? 5-6
Popular Franchises Don't Come Cheap!
Go to www.mybizlab.com.

Manufacturing Franchise: Making a Product Using a Franchisor's Formula

Coca-Cola and Pepsi-Cola bottlers are examples of franchisees who have acquired a ***manufacturing franchise,*** **in which franchisees are given the right to manufacture and distribute a certain product, following a formula or using supplies purchased from the franchisor.**

Five Benefits of Owning a Franchise

What are five ways I might benefit by owning a franchise?

There are both advantages and disadvantages to owning a franchise. (*See* ■ *Panel 5.6.*) Among the attractions are that you may or will be able to . . .

1 Own Your Own Business & Be Your Own Boss . . . to Some Extent

Buying a franchise allows you to own your own business and, to some extent, be your own boss. Note, however, that the franchisor will require you to observe certain rules and regulations that most independent businesspeople don't have to follow.

2 Start Your New Enterprise with Some Name Recognition

It's hard to open up a new business under your own name. It's far easier to do so under a trademarked name that's recognized around the country or the world: Starbucks. Taco Bell. Marriott. H&R Block. Kwik-Copy. The UPS Store.

3 Follow Someone Else's Proven Formula for Doing Business

When you acquire a franchise, you're investing in a business that probably has already successfully proven itself, especially if it's one of the well-established brands, such as Holiday Inn. This can help lower the risk of failure.

4 Receive Marketing Support

Besides name recognition, your franchise will probably also receive marketing and advertising support from the franchisor. If you're new to the hamburger business, you may not be able to afford TV advertising, but the fees you pay as a franchisor will enable McDonald's, Wendy's, Burger King, and Jack in the Box to do it for you.

5 Receive Management & Financial Support

Examples of the support that franchisors make available to franchisees include market research, on-site location studies, help in leasing or building and decorating your store or office, training (as at McDonald's Hamburger University), technical assistance, and help in ordering supplies. Many will also help you in operating your new business during the first 6 to 12 months. In addition, many franchisors offer financial assistance to their franchisees, such as help with spacing out payment of the franchise fee and extending credit on materials and supplies.

Five Drawbacks of Owning a Franchise

What are ways owning a franchise might turn out badly?

Investing in a franchise sounds like an ideal way to start a business without having to suffer the uncertainties of most new small-business people. Is it? There are at least five disadvantages to owning a franchise. You may or will . . .

1 Need to Come Up with a Large Initial Franchise Fee & Other Startup Costs

The average franchise fee runs from $20,000 to $30,000.[29] Fees vary depending on the business concept, generally starting at less than $10,000 for mobile and home-based businesses and ranging up to $6 million for a lodging franchise. (Unbelievably, a DoodyCalls franchise costs as much as $59,030.)[30] ⓫

In addition, you'll need to have a net worth that will satisfy the franchisor's requirements plus working capital to support any ongoing expenses that can't be covered by revenues. This is on *top of costs*—perhaps huge costs—for legal services, insurance, licenses, inventory, equipment, rent, signage, construction, landscaping, and employee training and salaries. You should not, therefore, underestimate how much you'll need for all the startup costs.[31] ⓬

2 Need to Share Your Sales with the Franchisor

Besides paying the franchisor an initial franchise fee, you will also probably need to pay your franchiser *royalties*—**a percentage of your sales**—generally 4% to 6% of sales before taxes and other expenses—even if you're unprofitable.[32]

3 Have to Endure Close Management by the Franchisor

If you've gone into business to be your own boss, you may be frustrated and disappointed by the franchisor's rules, orders, and regulations. The franchisor can even terminate your franchise if you fail to meet certain standards. You may also have to share high advertising costs. Don't forget you're in a legally binding long-term relationship, and the average length of an initial franchise contract is 10.6 years.[33] If you decide to get out, the franchisor even has approval rights over who you can sell your franchise to.

4 Possibly Have to Deal with Shady Practices by the Franchisor

Although most franchisors are honest, you have to be aware of those who aren't. Some smaller, lesser-known franchisors may give promise-the-moon sales presentations, overcharge you for supplies, and assess fees for unnecessary training. Some try to make their money just on the fees from selling franchises to new prospects and do not spend any money on helping their existing franchisees.[34]

5 Possibly Be Disappointed in the Payoff of Your Franchise

The franchisor's sales and profit projections will probably be optimistic, so you should consult with other franchisees before you buy. Franchises are often promoted as being a safer bet than other kinds of business, but there is reason to question that. One well-known study of more than 20,000 new businesses started in a four-year period in the 1990s found that 35% of franchise units had gone out of business compared with 28% of independents.[35]

Usually the higher your original investment, the higher the return on that investment, but this is not always the case. Thus, you should check with competing franchisees in the same industry before deciding which company to go with. "Franchises typically yield earnings of at least 30% of their total investment annually, which you could reasonably expect to reach by your third year," says one source. "The ultimate goal is to clear at least a six-figure income, but it may take a few years to reach this level."[36]

Source: Photograph by Sally Lindsay.

⓫ **Want to be a Hilton?** Suppose you've built a hotel and want it to carry the Hilton name. Here's what Hilton's website says being a franchisee will cost you: Initial fee: $85,000 for the first 275 guest rooms and suites, $300 for each one over that. Also 9.75% of monthly room revenue. Also 3% of food and beverage revenue. Interested?

Source: Courtesy of Nerds! We Can Fix That.

⓬ **Computer repair franchise.** Acquiring a Nerds franchise is considerably cheaper than acquiring a Hilton. The franchise fee is only $6,950, which can be financed with $999 down and $220 monthly payments. The company says it can help the franchisee solve particular problems, such as "system crashes, viruses, firewalls, and networking issues with multiple computers." When it comes to purchasing a franchise, do you think there's a strong relationship between price and the risk of failure?

Want to Know More? 5-7

How Common Is Franchise Fraud?

Go to www.mybizlab.com.

Want to Know More? 5-8
What's Most Important When Evaluating a Franchise?
Go to www.mybizlab.com.

13 Starbucks franchisee and franchisor. Multimillionaire Earvin "Magic" Johnson *(left)*, retired professional basketball player (with the Los Angeles Lakers), is hardly typical of racial minority franchisees. In 1988, Johnson formed a joint venture with Starbucks and its CEO Howard Schultz *(right)* called Urban Coffee Opportunities. The company's primary goal was to locate stores in diverse urban and suburban neighborhoods, bringing quality products and services to minority communities as well as providing economic opportunities. Ultimately, this venture grew to over 100 stores, at which time Starbucks elected to purchase and make them part of the company-owned portfolio.

■ **PANEL 5.7 Some franchise companies with high minority participation.**

Industry Type and Company	Percent Minority Participation
Food service	
Denny's	52.1%
Jack in the Box	68.6%
Church's Chicken	74.8%
Maintenance	
Anago Cleaning Systems	76.9%
Status Building Solutions	80.5%
Bonus Building Care	90.6%

Source: Based on R. Bond and L. Yu, "50 Top Franchises for Minorities," USA Today, November 5, 2010, p. 7B.

Trends in Franchising

What are some principal trends in franchising?

Among trends affecting franchising are the following:

Home-Based Businesses

Late-night TV is full of commercials suggesting that you can "make thousands of dollars running your business from home." Indeed, there are many enterprises, such as direct mail, that can be run out of a home office. Working at home need not mean feeling isolated. Some franchisees are now connected to each other by e-mail, allowing them to share information.

Many home-based franchisees use websites to generate a portion of their sales via e-commerce. Before buying in, however, you really need to investigate the franchisor for the possibility of a scam.

■ **Examples of Scams: Launching Home-Based Businesses.** Two scams to be alert for are (1) those in which someone promises to pay you as an employee to do certain tasks (craft assembly, envelope stuffing) and (2) those that promise to help you start your own home-based business (network marketing, medical billing, "make money with your computer," or whatever).[37] Most of these are not franchise related. ■

Minorities & Franchising

Minorities (African American, Hispanic, Asian American, Indian American, and so on) are said to own over 15% of U.S. franchises, up from 5% to 6% in 2000.[38] **13** Minority franchises can be found in a wide range of industries, with the most popular being fast-food restaurants and cleaning-services companies. (*See* ■ *Panel 5.7.*) However, companies seeking minority franchisees also include AIM Mail Centers, Anytime Fitness, Cruise Planners, Kiddie Academy, Liberty Tax Service, Pop-A-Lock, Pronto Auto Insurance, and Starwood Hotels & Resorts.[39]

■ **Example of Active Search for Minorities: Straw Hat Restaurants Targets Indian Americans.** In 2010, when banks were curtailing loans, the Straw Hat pizza chain was having trouble finding prospective franchisees who could qualify financially. It decided to focus on Indian Americans because they were less likely to need a loan. As one article explains, "the [Indian] culture fosters moral and financial support among friends and relatives." Also, Indians have close ties to their community and a "strong service-oriented mentality," two mandates for new Straw Hat franchisees.[40] ■

Going International

Some franchisors have tried moving into the international arena, competing in countries from which their own products ultimately descended—with mixed results. Starbucks, for instance, has introduced five stores in Austria, the birthplace of the coffeehouse tradition ever since the Turkish invaders left in 1683. Taco Bell has twice opened stores in Mexico, but failed to catch on.

THE BIG IDEA: Companies grow through internal expansion, by increasing sales and capital investment. Or they grow through external expansion, through merging with or acquiring other companies. Companies use mergers as shortcuts to growth, to acquire managerial expertise, to save money, and for tax benefits. The three types of mergers are horizontal, vertical, and conglomerate. Some mergers involve hostile takeovers. There are also merging borrow-and-buy strategies such as leveraged buyouts and employee buyouts.

THE ESSENTIAL QUESTION: If I wanted to expand my company, what are the ways to do it?

MyBizLab: Check your understanding of these concepts at www.mybizlab.com.

MyBizLab

Once you've established your business, how do you grow it? Minneapolis-based furniture retailer Room & Board, Inc., which consists of just a dozen stores in seven states and Washington, D.C., "has a devoted base of customers who rave about its hip design and customer service on message boards and blogs," says a *BusinessWeek* story.[41] Because of the retailer's popularity, founder John Gabbert frequently receives overtures from investors urging him to take their money and put it into a vigorous program of expansion. Gabbert routinely turns them down. He believes staying small is the best way to maintain the chain's customer-focused culture and to continue to work effectively with the small U.S. manufacturers who supply 90% of its products. Growth will be at R&B's own comfortable pace. ⑭

However, other businesspeople believe the route to success lies in expanding as rapidly as possible. How is this done?

How to Grow: Internal & External Expansion, Mergers, & Acquisitions

What are the paths to expansion?

There are two ways to grow your company:

- **Internal expansion:** You can grow through *internal expansion*—namely, by **increasing sales and capital investment.** This was the route Starbucks took, opening stores in market after market.

- **External expansion:** Another path is through *external expansion*—a **company merges with or buys another company or companies.** This is the way that feeds so many headlines in the business press, as we saw in the "Winners & Losers" at the beginning of this chapter.

There are two types of external expansion—*mergers* and *acquisitions:*

- **Merger—joining two companies together:** A *merger* occurs when two **firms join to form a new firm.** Most are like the marriages of two willing partners, but some are forced marriages (hostile mergers).

Source: Room & Board.

⑭ **Expand this?** Room & Board's furniture and home furnishings are mainly handmade and mostly made in the United States. Prices are on the high end, but the retailer has a loyal base of customers. Despite being urged to expand quickly by opening lots of new stores, CEO John Gabbert is content to grow revenues patiently and deliberately. Is this a strategy other kinds of businesses could successfully emulate?

- **Acquisition—buying another company: An *acquisition* occurs when one company buys another one.** This is like the ones we mentioned in the "Winners & Losers" case in which Wayne Huizenga built his wealth.

Why Mergers & Acquisitions Occur

What are four reasons mergers and acquisitions occur?

Mergers and acquisitions occur for at least four reasons: (1) *as a shortcut to growth*, (2) *to acquire particular management talent (and remove competition)*, (3) *to save money*, and (4) *to reduce taxes*. Let's consider the differences.

Shortcut to Growth: Acquiring Rather Than Developing a Capability

A frequent reason one firm will merge with or acquire another is so that it can quickly gain a capability—such as a technology (Lenovo acquiring IBM's PC line) or customer base (Alcatel's joining with Lucent Technologies)—that otherwise would take a lot of time to build from scratch.

Source: Photo Edit/Alamy.

■ **Example of Acquisition as Shortcut to Growth: Google Buys YouTube.** In late 2006, Google, the Internet search firm, bought online video-sharing website YouTube for $1.65 billion in stock.[42] ⑮ Google felt justified in paying the steep price because developing a similar site on its own might have taken years. ■

⑮ **Owned by Google.** Google has had an aggressive course of expansion, not only through internal development but also through acquisition of existing companies, such as YouTube for $1.65 billion in stock. Do you think this is an example of a company overpaying to acquire capabilities that it might well have developed on its own?

Management Talent: Acquiring Managerial Expertise

A firm that lacks management expertise in one area may merge with or acquire another firm to get the management talent it lacks. This also has the effect, of course, of diminishing the competition.

■ **Example of Acquiring Managerial Talent: Chase Manhattan and J. P. Morgan.** Chase Manhattan Bank took over commercial investment bank J. P. Morgan in late 2000 because Chase wanted to expand its business of asset management and management of very-high-net-worth clientele, which Morgan was known for. Morgan's management also "had a leg up in terms of European mergers and acquisitions advisory activities," said one analyst. "Chase's equity activity was pretty limited."[43] ■

Saving Money: Consolidating Operations to Reduce Costs

When two companies come together, they can consolidate and reduce similar operations, such as human resources departments or payroll operations, and handle more employees, more products, or more customers at reduced cost.

■ **Example of Merging to Save Money: Sirius and XM Satellite Radio.** The 2009 merger of Sirius Satellite Radio (where Howard Stern was the leading star) and XM Satellite Radio (which offered *Oprah & Friends*) was anticipated to save the combined company billions of dollars, since they could combine and reduce parallel operations.[44] (This is known as achieving "economies of scale," as we discuss later in the book.) ■

Tax Benefits: Acquiring an Unprofitable Firm to Reduce Taxes

Sometimes a very profitable firm will merge with a firm that is unprofitable or has a tax loss that can be carried forward to reduce the taxes on the earnings of the combined new company.

The Three Types of Mergers: Horizontal, Vertical, & Conglomerate

How do horizontal, vertical, and conglomerate mergers differ from one another?

Mergers are of three types: (1) *horizontal*, (2) *vertical*, and (3) *conglomerate*. Let's consider the differences.

Horizontal Mergers: Same Industry, Same Activity

In a ***horizontal merger*, two companies merge that are in the same industry and perform the same activity.**

> ■ **Example of a Horizontal Merger: Whole Foods and Wild Oats.** In 2007, upscale popular grocery chain Whole Foods Market, which offers all-natural and organic foods, purchased its smaller rival Wild Oats Markets, which sells similar products. The combined entity would have controlled about 11% of the natural foods market.[45] Concerned about loss of competition, antitrust regulators at the Federal Trade Commission got Whole Foods to sell off some of its Wild Oats stores.[46] ■

Vertical Mergers: Same Industry, Different Activities

In a ***vertical merger*, two companies merge that are in the same industry but each performs a different activity.**

> ■ **Example of a Vertical Merger: Federal Express and Flying Tiger Line.** Formed in 1945, Flying Tiger Line, was named after the Flying Tigers fighter unit of World War II. It became the world's largest cargo airline in the 1980s, operating scheduled cargo service to seven continents. In 1989, it was acquired by cargo shipper Federal Express (now FedEx Corp.), which until then mainly served the continental United States, as a way of expanding its international operations. ■

> **ⓘ Want to Know More? 5-9**
>
> **What Are the Antitrust Implications of Mergers?**
>
> Go to www.mybizlab.com.

Conglomerate Mergers: Different Industries, Different Activities

In a ***conglomerate merger*, two companies merge that are in different industries and each performs different activities. ⑯**

> ■ **Example of a Conglomerate Merger: FedEx and Kinko's.** Whereas FedEx started out ferrying air cargo, Kinko's (named for founder Paul Orfalea's kinky hair) began in 1970 as a photocopy shop near the University of California, Santa Barbara, and expanded into a nationwide chain of stores. Kinko's was bought by FedEx in 2004 for $2.4 billion to become the corporation's retail arm to provide a range of business services as well as FedEx shipping—and so FedEx could compete with UPS, which had acquired the Mailboxes copying and shipping stores. ■

Unfriendly Mergers: Hostile Takeovers

What is a hostile takeover, and how can it be stopped?

Many mergers and acquisitions are friendly arrangements.[47] But some are unfriendly to the point of viciousness. These are known as ***hostile takeovers*, situations in**

Source: Kimihiro Hoshino/AFP/Getty Images/Newscom.

⑯ **Conglomerate merger.** Microsoft CEO Steve Ballmer *(left)* shakes hands with Skype CEO Tony Bates during an announcement in May 2011 in San Francisco. The software giant acquired the Internet phone service company so that it could have a bigger presence in an online arena dominated by Google and Facebook. Do you think this is a good strategy?

which an outsider—often called a "corporate raider"—buys enough shares in a company to be able to take control of it against the will of the corporation's top management and directors.

BRIEFING / EARNING GREEN BY GOING GREEN

Maxxam Acquires Pacific Lumber in a Hostile Takeover. Is a green policy always good for a company? Perhaps it is if the firm's type of ownership allows it to always protect its assets. That wasn't the case with Pacific Lumber Co. on California's North Coast.

For over 100 years, a family named Murphy owned and operated the company, engaging in "sustainable forestry" even before there was such a term. By 1985, thanks in part to its century-old practice of slow, steady logging, it owned three-quarters of the world's remaining ancient-growth redwood forests.

But a decade earlier, in a fateful move, Pacific went from being privately owned to being publicly owned—family members decided they could make more money by offering shares to the public. But this meant that anyone could become a stockholder. And in 1986, against the family's wishes, Texas financier and corporate raider Charles Hurwitz and a company named Maxxam, in which he was chief stockholder, borrowed $800 million against Pacific Lumber's forest assets (in a "leveraged buyout," a mechanism we describe in the next section) to finance a hostile takeover of the lumber company.

Ironically, until that time Pacific Lumber had operated virtually debt-free. In order to repay the debt, Maxxam then began an aggressive policy of clearcutting, and now there are almost no ancient-growth redwood trees left. In early 2007, in great part because of its debt obligations, Pacific Lumber filed for bankruptcy.[48] **⓱** ■

i
Want to Know More? 5-10
Shady Business Dealings?
Charles Hurwitz & Maxxam
Go to www.mybizlab.com.

Tender Offers & Proxy Fights: Ways to Launch a Hostile Takeover

Two ways by which hostile takeovers are launched are by (1) a *tender offer* or (2) a *proxy fight.*

Tender Offer: Offer Shareholders Above-Market Price for Their Stock. With a *tender offer,* an outsider seeking to take over a company directly contacts the company's shareholders and offers to buy their stock at a price that

⓱ Hostile takeover. Once the owner of three-quarters of the world's old-growth redwood trees, Pacific Lumber of Scotia, California, was forced into an unwilling marriage with Maxxam, Inc. by a corporate raider. To pay off the debt that was acquired to effect the takeover, the new corporate entity was obliged to raise money by clearcutting most of its redwood holdings. Do you think hostile takeovers usually have negative results?

Source: Richard Wong/Alamy.

exceeds the present market price. The raider hopes to get enough shareholders to sell that he or she can gain control of the company.

● **Proxy Fight: Urge Shareholders to Vote for the Raider's Directors.** *Proxy* is the authority to act for another. If you're a shareholder in a company, you may be sent a proxy form to sign authorizing someone else, usually the company's management, to cast your vote at a shareholder meeting. Sometimes there is a so-called *proxy fight*—a struggle between opposing forces seeking to represent your vote.

In a *proxy fight,* the outsider contacts shareholders and urges them to vote for the raider's hand-picked candidates for the board of directors. If the raider's directors are voted in (and they are in the majority), they can then force out the company's existing top management.

"White Knights" & "Poison Pills": Ways to Resist a Hostile Takeover

When a company's top managers find out a hostile takeover is being attempted, they are apt to resist fiercely, knowing they may well lose their jobs if the takeover is successful. Besides trying to thwart the raider's proxy fight by using their company's resources to lobby shareholders to back their own slate of directors, they may employ strategies of resistance, such as (1) try to locate a *white knight* or (2) launch a *poison pill* to make the company less attractive.

Finding a "White Knight": Locating a More Acceptable Buyer. The technique of **locating a *white knight* is to find a buyer for the company who is more acceptable to management.**

■ **Example of a White Knight: Pharmaceutical Wars—Merck Loses Out in Acquisition of Schering to Bayer.** In 2006, Merck KGaA was trying to get ● to the top position in the German drug industry by acquiring rival Schering AG. But Merck called off its plans after Bayer AG came in as a white knight, beating Merck's acquisition price.[49] ■

Launching a "Poison Pill": Taking on More Debt to Make the Company Less Attractive. In the technique of **launching a *poison pill,* the managers take actions designed to make the stock less attractive to the potential buyer**—that is, force the company to take on large amounts of debt to make the firm less attractive to the raider.

Borrow-&-Buy Strategies: Leveraged Buyouts & Employee Buyouts

How do leveraged buyouts and employee buyouts work?

In most mergers, the acquiring company uses cash produced by its other businesses to finance the acquisition. However, there are two borrow-and-buy strategies for financing an acquisition: (1) the *leveraged buyout* and (2) the *employee buyout.*

Leveraged Buyout (LBO): Borrowing against the Assets of the Firm Being Acquired

In a *leveraged buyout (LBO),* **one firm borrows money to buy another firm. The purchaser uses the assets of the company being acquired as security for the loan being used to finance the purchase.** This was the strategy that Charles ● Hurwitz and Maxxam used to buy Pacific Lumber. This financial strategy may work fine if earnings continue to grow and the debt is paid off. But if things go wrong, the debt can become a crushing burden—as it did for Pacific Lumber.

ⓘ
Want to Know More? 5-11
Examples of a "White Knight" & a "Poison Pill"
Go to www.mybizlab.com.

Source: Photocome/Newscom.

⓭ **Poison pill promiser.** Jerry Yang was CEO of Yahoo when in 2008 Microsoft made an unsolicited bid to acquire the Internet company for $44.6 billion. Yang threatened to exercise a "poison pill" unless the bid was raised—which Microsoft did, but Yahoo rejected that, too. (Yahoo stockholders, who thought it was a great deal, were furious.) The poison pill Yang alluded to was a 2001-enacted "stockholder rights plan" under which if any company bought 15% or more of Yahoo stock (as a step toward a takeover), existing shareholders would have the right to buy extra shares. This would have the effect of substantially diluting the stock ownership of the group attempting the takeover.

Want to Know More? 5-12

Who's Next? Family Business & Succession Planning

Go to www.mybizlab.com.

■ **Example of an Empire Built from LBOs: Spectrum Brands' Rise and Fall.** Over a 12-year period beginning in the 1990s, using money from several leveraged buyouts, the conglomerate that came to be known as Spectrum Brands acquired a variety of businesses, from Rayovac batteries and Hot Shot insecticide to Remington electric shavers and United Pet dog chews. Although Spectrum soared in value for a time, ultimately business reversals—failures in the battery business and rising gas prices—forced the company to face the fact that it had too much debt and had to perform too much of a balancing act.[50] ■

Employee Buyout: Borrowing against Employees' Assets to Create an Employee-Owned Firm

In an *employee buyout,* **a firm's employees borrow money against their own assets, such as their houses or their pension funds, to purchase the firm from its present owners; the employees then become the new owners of the firm.**

■ **Example of an Employee Buyout: The Tribune Company.** In 2007, the Tribune Company—owner of the *Chicago Tribune,* the *Los Angeles Times,* and a few TV stations—was acquired by its employees (under what's known as an employee stock ownership plan, or ESOP). This gave employees incentive to make the company more efficient and figure out ways to stop it from losing money.[51] (The company was later sold to a billionaire investor, Sam Zell.) ■

LEARNING & SKILLS PORTFOLIO

Summary

5.1 Basic Forms of Business Ownership: Sole Proprietorships, Partnerships, Corporations, & Cooperatives

THE ESSENTIAL QUESTION: *Which of the four basic forms of business ownership would best suit a business I might start?*

What is a sole proprietorship, and what are its major benefits and disadvantages? A sole proprietorship is a business owned and typically managed by one person. Five benefits of being a sole proprietorship are that you can (1) start up a business with ease, (2) make all your own decisions, (3) keep all the profits, (4) keep your taxes relatively simple, and (5) end the business with ease. Five drawbacks of being a sole proprietorship are that (1) you may or will have unlimited financial liability, so your personal possessions are at risk for any debts or damages incurred by the business; (2) you may have limited financial resources and few fringe benefits, such as vacation pay, sick leave, and health benefits; (3) you have to have the

management discipline to run the business; (4) you may be overstressed about time; and (5) you may not be able to sell or pass along the business.

What are the benefits and drawbacks of being a partnership? A partnership is a business owned and operated by two or more persons as a voluntary legal association. There are four types of partnerships. (1) In a general partnership, two or more partners are responsible for the business and share profits, liabilities, and management responsibilities. (2) A limited partnership has one or more general partners plus other, limited partners who contribute only an investment but do not have any management responsibility or liability. (3) In a master limited partnership (MLP), the partnership acts like a corporation, selling stock on a stock exchange, but it is taxed like a partnership, paying a lesser rate than the corporate income tax. (4) In a limited liability partnership (LLP), the liability of each partner—and risk of losing personal assets—is limited to just his or her own acts and omissions and those of his or her directly reporting employees.

Four advantages of being in a partnership are that you can or may (1) start up the business with relative ease, using a legal agreement called articles of partnership; (2) have more financial resources; (3) have more managerial and other expertise; and (4) keep your taxes relatively simple. Three drawbacks are that you may or will (1) experience personality conflicts or other disagreements among partners, (2) have unlimited liability, and (3) have difficulty ending or changing the partnership and not be able to pass along the business to your heirs.

What are the differences among the four types of corporations? Corporations can be large businesses, but most are small. If you incorporate your business, you have four choices. (1) A C corporation is a state-chartered entity that pays taxes and is legally distinct from its owner; this type is favored by most big businesses. (2) An S corporation has no more than 100 owners (shareholders), but, like a partnership, the owners are taxed only at the personal, not corporate, level. (3) A limited liability company (LLC) combines the tax benefits of a sole proprietorship or partnership—one level of tax—with the limited liability of a corporation. (4) The charter of the B corporation, or "benefit corporation," legally requires that the company adhere to socially beneficial practices, such as helping communities, employees, consumers, and the environment.

Five benefits of being a corporation are that you can or may (1) have little or no liability, (2) get possible tax breaks, (3) have far more financial resources, (4) have far more managerial and other expertise, and (5) be able to more easily sell ownership shares and continue the life of the business. Four drawbacks are that you may or will (1) have to deal with start-up and ongoing costs and paperwork, (2) be taxed twice, (3) have to publicly disclose financial information, and (4) have difficulty ending the corporation.

What is a cooperative? A cooperative is a corporation owned by its user members, who have pooled their resources for their mutual benefit. The purpose of a cooperative is not so much to make a profit as to provide a service to its members.

5.2 Franchises: A Special Form of Ownership

THE ESSENTIAL QUESTION: *What are franchises, and how might I benefit or not benefit by owning a franchise?*

What's the difference between a franchisor and a franchisee? A franchise is an arrangement in which a business owner allows others the right to use its name and sell its goods or services within a specific geographical area. A franchisor is the business owner that gives others the rights to sell its products or services. The franchisee is the buyer of the franchise.

Which type of franchise might most interest me? Franchises may be categorized as three types. (1) A business-format franchise allows a franchisee to use the trade name and format of a franchisor, following guidelines for marketing and pricing the product. (2) A product-distribution franchise is one in which a franchisee is given the right to sell trademarked products purchased from the franchisor. (3) In a manufacturing franchise, franchisees are given the right to manufacture and distribute a certain product, following a formula or using supplies purchased from the franchisor.

What are five ways I might benefit by owning a franchise? Five attractions of owning a franchise are that you may or will be able to (1) own your own business and be your own boss (to some extent), (2) start your new enterprise with some name recognition, (3) follow someone else's proven formula for doing business, (4) receive marketing support, and (5) receive management and financial support.

What are ways owning a franchise might turn out badly? Five disadvantages of owning a franchise are that you may or will (1) need to come up with a large initial franchise fee and other startup costs, (2) need to share your sales with the franchisor, (3) have to endure close management by the franchisor, (4) possibly have to deal with shady practices by the franchisor, and (5) possibly be disappointed in the payoff of your franchise.

What are some principal trends in franchising? Among trends affecting franchising are an increase in home-based businesses, more franchises being acquired by minorities, and more franchisors trying to move into the international arena.

5.3 Mergers & Acquisitions: Paths to Business Expansion

THE ESSENTIAL QUESTION: *If I wanted to expand my company, what are the ways to do it?*

What are the paths to expansion? Two ways to grow a company are through internal expansion—that is, by increasing sales and capital investment—or by external expansion—when a company merges with or buys another company or companies. Two types of external expansion are mergers and acquisitions. A merger occurs when two firms join to form a new firm. An acquisition occurs when one company buys another one.

What are four reasons mergers and acquisitions occur? (1) A merger or an acquisition can occur as a shortcut to growth—by acquiring rather than developing a capability. (2) It can also occur as a means of acquiring managerial talent. (3) It can happen to save money, by consolidating operations to reduce costs. (4) Finally, it can be a way to reduce taxes.

How do horizontal, vertical, and conglomerate mergers differ from one another? Mergers are of three types. (1) In a horizontal merger, two companies merge that are in the same industry and perform the same activity. (2) In a vertical merger, two companies merge that are in the same industry but each performs a different activity. (3) In a conglomerate merger, two companies merge that are in different industries and each performs different activities.

What is a hostile takeover, and how can it be stopped? Hostile takeovers are situations in which an outsider ("corporate raider") buys enough shares in a company to be able to take control of it against the will of the corporation's top management and directors. Hostile takeovers are launched in two ways. With a tender offer, an outsider seeking to take over a company directly contacts the company's shareholders and offers to buy their stock at a price that exceeds the present market price. In a proxy fight, the outsider contacts shareholders and urges them to vote for the raider's hand-picked candidates for the board of directors. Two ways firms resist a takeover are by locating a "white knight," a buyer for the company who is more acceptable to management, or by launching a "poison pill," taking actions designed to make the stock less attractive to the potential buyer.

How do leveraged buyouts and employee buyouts work? There are two borrow-and-buy strategies by which a company may finance an acquisition. In a leveraged buyout (LBO), one firm borrows money to buy another firm. The purchaser uses the assets of the company being acquired as security for the loan being used to finance the purchase. In an employee buyout, a firm's employees borrow money against their own assets, such as their houses or their pension funds, to purchase the firm from its present owners; the employees then become the new owners of the firm.

Key Terms

acquisition 150
articles of partnership 137
B corporation 140
business-format franchise 145
C corporation 139
conglomerate merger 151
cooperative 142
employee buyout 154
external expansion 149
franchise 144
franchisee 145
franchisor 145

fringe benefits 136
general partnership 137
horizontal merger 151
hostile takeovers 151
internal expansion 149
leveraged buyout (LBO) 153
limited liability company (LLC) 140
limited liability partnership (LLP) 137
limited partnership 137
manufacturing franchise 146
master limited partnership (MLP) 137
merger 149

partnership 137
poison pill 153
product-distribution franchise 145
proxy fight 153
royalties 147
S corporation 140
sole proprietorship 135
tender offer 152
unlimited liability 136
vertical merger 151
white knight 153

Pop Quiz Prep

1. What is the largest form of business ownership?
2. What is a benefit of being a corporation?
3. McDonald's and Starbucks are examples of which type of franchise?
4. What is a benefit of owning a franchise?

5. What is an example of internal expansion?
6. Which type of merger can be described as two companies merging that are in the same industry but each performs a different activity?

Critical Thinking Questions

1. You and a classmate have talked about becoming partners in an event-planning business after graduation. What types of questions should the two of you address to determine compatibility in forming a partnership?
2. When starting a business, the needs of the businessperson and the kind of business are major considerations when deciding the best form of ownership. Discuss whether a sole proprietorship, partnership, or corporation is the best form of ownership for the following new businesses: dry cleaning and laundry, hair and nail salon, local print and copy shop, microbrewery, and a law firm. Explain.
3. Levi Strauss, founder of the world's most famous denim jeans company, made his fortune in the California Gold Rush as the maker of sturdy pants. Levi Strauss & Co. is privately held by the descendants of the family of Levi Strauss, and shares of company stock are not publicly

traded. What are the advantages and disadvantages of keeping Levi Strauss & Co. under family control rather than selling stock to the public?
4. Your friend is in a quandary, and she needs your help. She cannot decide whether to start an independent business from scratch or to purchase a franchise. Help her decide by educating her on the advantages and disadvantages of each. Which route would you recommend for your friend?
5. Identify whether the following mergers and/or acquisitions are horizontal, vertical, or conglomerate: Disney and Pixar, Pfizer and Warner Lambert, General Electric and Smiths Aerospace, Flint Media Group and Torda Ink Manufacturer, Coca Cola and Glaceau (vitamin water), Berkshire Hathaway and Benjamin Moore Paint, eBay and PayPal, and Sirius and XM Radio.

VIDEO CASE
Owning a Slice of the Action: A Domino's Pizza Franchise

There are various forms of ownership a business can choose. Sole proprietorships (single-owner businesses), partnerships (two or more owners), and corporations (legally distinct, state-chartered entities) are common forms of ownership. A franchise is a special form of business ownership. With this arrangement the franchisor (or business owner) allows others (its franchisees) the right to use its name and sell its goods or services within a specific geographic area. Most companies do not begin as franchises, but over time, the owners decide that the franchising form of ownership does not require a huge investment, and with the right partners, it's a cost-effective and profitable way to expand. Franchises can be profitable for the franchisees as well, especially if they own more than one franchise of the brand. Many fast-food and pizza restaurants are franchise owned.

Domino's Pizza is a franchise. It has over 9,000 franchised and company-owned stores in the United States and more than 70 international markets.[52] Over 90% of Domino's Pizza stores are owned by franchisees, and the remaining 10% are owned by Domino's Pizza, Inc. Some Domino's franchisees own three or more locations.

Domino's, the second largest franchised pizza chain to Pizza Hut, was started in Michigan in the 1960s by two brothers when they bought a small pizzeria called Dominick's.[53] Today, Domino's Pizza, a strong global brand, employs over 145,000 people worldwide.[54] In 1998, the company was sold to a private equity firm, Bain Capital, by one of its original owners, Tom Monaghan, for over $1 billion. In 2004, the company went public. It trades on the New York Stock Exchange under the ticker symbol DPZ.[55] In a 2009 survey by market research firm Brand Keys, Domino's ranked first in convenience and price. But for consumer taste preferences among national chains, Domino's was last—tied with Chuck E. Cheese's.[56,57] In December of that year, as described in the video, Domino's announced plans to reinvent its pizza. It began a self-deprecating ad campaign in which consumers were filmed criticizing the pizza's quality, and chefs were shown developing the new product.[58] While enthusiastically embraced by many franchisees, the launch of the "new and inspired" pizza was controversial for franchise owners who felt the old pizza was just fine.

For the new recipe, Domino's tested dozens of cheeses, 15 sauces, and 50 crust-seasoning blends over two years. The final primary changes include a garlic-seasoned crust; a sweeter, bolder tomato sauce with herbs and a red pepper kick; and 100% real mozzarella shredded cheese flavored with a hint of provolone.[59] "We're basically relaunching Domino's Pizza," says Russell Weiner, chief marketing officer. "The entire company has been involved in this," Weiner continued. "From our CEO to our franchisees; from our supply chain division to our supply partners; from our product development team to our marketers—everyone has had a hand in reinventing our pizza."[60]

J. Patrick Doyle, current CEO of Domino's Pizza, views the pizza redesign effort as having a positive impact on its first full-year results, stating, "We're a new Domino's. In the U.S., our decision to improve our pizza, and the success that resulted from it, allowed us to build a new base of customers and a stronger base of business from which to grow." The company's domestic sales for the first full year since its redesign grew almost 10%, and its international sales grew almost 7%.[61] It remains to be seen if the company can keep up its momentum to maintain its "slice" of the fiercely competitive pizza delivery franchise business, but so far, results look promising.

What's Your Take?

1. Assume you are interested in purchasing a "slice of the pie" by investing in a Domino's Pizza franchise. Compare and contrast the benefits of owning a Domino's franchise (listed in the chapter) to starting a pizza delivery business from scratch.

2. It took considerable time and effort to get all the franchisees on board with the "new and inspired" pizza. Scott Hinshaw, executive vice president of franchise operations, describes the process: "We brought some key franchisees in and we had showed them the product, how we were going to get there, what it was going to cost to make the food. Once we got their buy-in, we took it to the advisory boards and then we took it to the marketplace." Russell Weiner, chief marketing officer, adds: "We spend a lot of time going out to our franchisees on road shows and conference calls, trying to let them know the reasons why we are doing things." What does this suggest about the culture, openness, and transparency at Domino's?

3. Scott Hinshaw, executive vice president of franchise operations, states: "Our franchisees are entrepreneurs, and they have great ideas and suggestions and recommendations. Our franchisees know the best way to make money is not to cut and save, it's to reinvest and drive top-line sales." What do you think he means by this?

4. Domino's "Operate to Own" program allows prospective entrepreneurs and owners to experience the organization before investing. The franchise information part of the Domino's website reads: "Think about it . . . if you've never owned a business before, what better way to prepare yourself than to learn how to successfully operate our business before buying our business! Follow the path of more than 90% of our franchisees and learn to run and operate a store, or supervise multiple stores, before investing in your own."[62] Why do you think Domino's requires that its prospective franchisees run and operate a store or supervise multiple stores before investing in one of their own? From the standpoint of a franchisee ready to own and operate a store right away, do you believe Domino's is taking a chance with this one-year requirement?

5. Research and discuss some of the requirements for owning a Domino's Pizza franchise. This can be found on the Domino's Pizza website and other franchising opportunity websites. Would you be interested in becoming a Domino's franchise owner? According to your research, what are the pros and cons?

Model of Success: Green Bay Packers, Super Bowl XLV Champions— A Nonprofit Professional Sports Team Owned by Its Fans

This case explores the Green Bay Packers, the only publicly owned nonprofit organization in the National Football League (NFL). This form of ownership is to some a working model for a better way to organize and administer an organization in what has become the turbulent world of professional football.

In 1923, the Green Bay Packers were nearly bankrupt and close to extinction. Out of desperation, the team held a stock sale and reached out to their small, local community of Green Bay, Wisconsin. The community came to their rescue. Today the Packers have 112,158 shareholders who own 4.7 million shares of the only publicly traded franchise in the NFL.[63] Interestingly enough, the shareholders receive no cash dividends or even discount tickets to the games—only a piece of paper saying they are part owners of the Green Bay Packers. Their support is based on love and devotion to their team and the surrounding community. The people of Green Bay did get the best return on their investment they could ever ask for—between 1923 and 2011 the Packers won four NFL Super Bowls.[64]

In direct violation of current league rules, which stipulate a limit of 32 owners of one team and one of those owners having a minimum stake of 30%, the Packers model of ownership was "grandfathered" when the NFL current ownership policy was created in the 1980s. Thus, the Packers form of ownership is exempt from NFL rules.[65]

Many people think organizing the Packers as a nonprofit organization is a better approach to professional sports. In an age of greed, soaring player salaries, threats of work stoppages, lockouts, and talk of season cancellations over squabbles related to contracts, this form of ownership is simply immune to all of that. Green Bay lacks a single, all-powerful money- and ego-oriented owner and instead has an executive committee that oversees the team's day-to-day operations. Committee members serve voluntarily, except for the president, who represents the team at league meetings. The goal of the Packers' board of directors is to remain financially solvent and competitive on the field. As a result, this form of wholly owned community ownership doesn't risk lockouts as the other franchise owners do. In his book *Bad Sports: How Owners Are Ruining the Games We Love*, David Zirin makes the case for Packers-style ownership by stating that "Green Bay is a dangerous example for [sports] owners because the franchise proves the argument for public ownership in practice."[66]

The dominant form of team ownership in the NFL is called a franchise, and the teams are arguably not purchased out of civic duty. In many cases, franchise owners are motivated by profits and are wealthy individuals. An example is Paul Allen, cofounder of Microsoft, who owns the Seattle Seahawks. Many owners are successful businesspeople and former corporate leaders who have traded their corner office for an NFL stadium. If your home team was organized as a franchise, do you think you'd be interested in being part owner?

What's Your Take?

1. What benefits are there to the Green Bay Packers model of ownership?

2. Do you think this model could ever be duplicated today?

3. With the Green Bay Packers, there are no billionaire owners. The fans consider themselves owners, and they are personally invested in the team. Their dividend is not dollars but victory and pride in their team and community. Now that you know the ownership structure of the Packers, would attending a Green Bay Packers football game be different?

4. What drawbacks, if any, are there to this type of ownership?

5. The majority of teams in the NFL are franchises owned by an individual. What advantages do you see to this form of ownership?

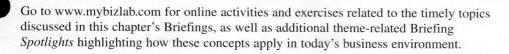
Go to www.mybizlab.com for online activities and exercises related to the timely topics discussed in this chapter's Briefings, as well as additional theme-related Briefing *Spotlights* highlighting how these concepts apply in today's business environment.

In-chapter Briefing:
- A Minority-Owned Public Relations Firm

Activity:
- Get Your Career in Gear – Exploring a Career as a Franchisor

Briefing Spotlight:
- Skillfully Starting Your Own Business

In-chapter Briefing:
- Maxxam Acquires Pacific Lumber in a Hostile Takeover

Activity:
- Developing Marketable Business Skills – Starting a Slow Food Mobile Catering Business on Campus

Briefing Spotlight:
- Driven to Go Green

In-chapter Briefing:
- Incorporating a Small Business in Nevada
- A Rural Town Abandoned by National Chains Forms a Cooperative Department Store

Activity:
- Developing Marketable Business Skills – Coco Chanel's Empire Demise
- Ethical Dilemma Case – Investors in a Fury About Full & Fair Auction Process for Clothing Retailer J. Crew

Briefing Spotlight:
- It's All In the Family

In-chapter Briefing:
- A Small-Business Owner Finally Takes a Vacation
- Jersey Mike's Sub Shop Develops a Small Business into a Franchisor

Activity:
- Going to the Net! – Famous Entrepreneurial Partnerships

Briefing Spotlight:
- There's an Art to Starting a Business

Additional Briefing Spotlights available at MyBizLab:

- A WORLD OF CONSTANT CHANGE
- BUSINESS CULTURE & ETIQUETTE
- CUSTOMER FOCUS
- GLOBAL BUSINESS
- INFO TECH & SOCIAL MEDIA
- PERSONAL FINANCE
- SOCIALLY RESPONSIBLE BUSINESS

6

The Entrepreneurial Spirit

Pursuing the Dream of Success
in Small Business

After reading and studying this chapter, you will be able to answer the following essential questions:

MyBizLab

Where you see MyBizLab in this chapter, go to www.mybizlab.com for additional activities on the topic being discussed.

FORECAST:
What's Ahead in This Chapter

We discuss entrepreneurship, its innovators, the characteristics of entrepreneurs, and how small-business people and entrepreneurs differ. We consider the contributions of small business and describe some home-based and Web-based businesses. We show how to start or buy a small business, write a business plan, and get financing. We discuss why small businesses fail and how to improve their chances.

MyBizLab

Gain hands-on experience through an interactive, real-world scenario. This chapter's simulation entitled Getting Your Business off the Ground is located at **www.mybizlab.com**.

WINNER: Facebook—"Focus on Building Things"

In early 2004, a Harvard psychology student named Mark Zuckerberg turned his photo-illustrated class directory, known as the "facebook," into a website that allowed anyone with a Harvard e-mail address to join and to create a profile, consisting of a photograph and personal information. Facebook quickly became popular, attracting students from other campuses.

"By luck or design," says one account, "Zuckerberg had tapped into a powerful yearning: the desire of hundreds of ambitious and impressionable young people to establish themselves and make friends in an unfamiliar environment. . . . The site quickly became a platform for self-promotion, a place to boast and preen and vie for others' attention as much as for their companionship."[1] In less than a year, it had grown to 1 million users, and Zuckerberg and his two cofounders moved the company to Palo Alto, California, to contact venture capitalists (big-bucks investors).

In 2005, Facebook opened its doors to high school students, and in 2006 it admitted working adults. In late 2007, instead of creating services, it borrowed a technique from Microsoft and launched a "platform" that allowed people unaffiliated with the company to build online services operating within its website. Now Facebook offers thousands of services, such as online storage, horoscopes, photo slideshows, and full-length songs.[2] Some problems cropped up: The site slowed at times as it struggled to handle the surge in traffic. The company introduced a service that let users track what their friends were doing, which resulted in thousands of protests about violation of privacy.[3] Yet revenues began to pour in, as Facebook delivered highly tailored ads to individuals and their networks of friends.[4]

In 2006, Yahoo offered $1 billion to buy Facebook, but was turned down. Finally, in 2007, 1.6% of Facebook was sold to Microsoft for $240 million.[5] But Zuckerberg (who became *Time* magazine's 2010 Person of the Year) is uninterested in buyouts. "People are constantly trying to put us in a bucket," he has said. "Are we trying to sell the company? . . . For me and a lot of people around me, that's not really what we focus on. We're just focused on building things."[6]

LOSER: Friendster—"Potential Unmet"

Friendster is a social networking website created in Mountain View, California, in 2002 by Jonathan Abrams, a computer programmer then in his early 30s. In the wake of a failed relationship, Abrams devised the technology as a way to meet women. Six months after its founding, Friendster had signed up 3 million registered users. Half a year later, Google offered Abrams $30 million for the startup—a deal that might be worth $1 billion today.[7] Hoping for megawealth like that acquired by the Yahoo and Google founders, Abrams rejected Google. But no further offers materialized.

What went wrong? First, the company loaded its board with venture capitalists, primarily men in their 50s, who were far older than the site's target audience. They had little feel for the product and appointed top managers who were much like themselves. As Friendster became more popular, its overwhelmed website became slower, so that one of its Web pages took as long as 40 seconds to download. Yet the board devoted its time talking not about the performance problem but about potential competitors and advertising deals and adding new features, such as Internet phone services.

CEO Abrams was replaced with a series of other executives, each of whom changed the firm's direction and none of whom stayed long. The company did not add new features to compete with copycat social networking sites such as MySpace, which were adding features like blogs and ways of organizing around favorite bands. Friendster users could link only to a relatively short chain of acquaintances, whereas MySpace was open and much simpler and encouraged users to do much as they pleased.[8] Abrams, said one reporter, had "the distinction of founding a company that is shorthand for potential unmet."[9]

In the United States, Friendster was quickly passed by other social networks. It stayed relevant in Asia, however, and in 2009 was acquired by a Malaysian e-commerce company for $100 million. But it never caught up with its rivals. In August 2011, top-ranked Facebook averaged 700 million and second-ranked Twitter 200 million unique visitors a month. Friendster, number 15 in social networks, had 4.9 million.[10]

YOUR CALL What can we learn from the Facebook/Friendster experience? Did Friendster miss its window of opportunity? In refusing to sell out to bigger companies, is Facebook risking extinction as social networking becomes a contest between megafirms? Or did a 2011 $500 million infusion of cash from Goldman Sachs (in return for the opportunity to buy shares) and others make this unnecessary?[11] If you were a prospective entrepreneur with a revolutionary idea, what lesson would you draw?

MyBizLab

THE BIG IDEA: A person may found a small business just to make a living. Or he or she may be an entrepreneur hoping it will become a high-growth enterprise. People become entrepreneurs sometimes out of necessity but usually in search of opportunity. Entrepreneurship is expressed through three kinds of innovators: classic entrepreneurs, intrapreneurs, and entrepreneurial teams. Entrepreneurs have four characteristics that differentiate them from others in business.

THE ESSENTIAL QUESTION: Do I have what it takes to be a small-business entrepreneur?

MyBizLab

MyBizLab: Check your understanding of these concepts at www.mybizlab.com.

Source: Shafer Vineyards.

❶ Two-career success. During his first career, John Shafer was a great success, rising to the position of vice president and chief financial officer of a major Chicago-based publishing company. In the mid-1970s, seeking different challenges, he abandoned corporate life to become a California grape grower and winery owner. Today Shafer Vineyards is one of the Napa Valley's most successful and innovative wineries. How much do you think prior career achievement contributes to entrepreneurial success?

How unsatisfied are most Americans with their current jobs? Back in 2007, before the onset of the recent Great Recession (when many workers were grateful to even *have* a job), a survey found that . . .

- 67% of working adults thought about quitting their jobs "regularly" or "constantly"
- 72% wanted to resign to start their own business.[12] ❶

Many, perhaps most, people want to find a comfortable, secure job in a big company—although in today's world such "secure, comfortable" jobs are getting harder to find. Others yearn to own their own small business in order to have more control over their future. Those in the second group would be encouraged to learn, from another survey, that . . .

- 84% of small-business owners were happy running their own show
- 73% said they would encourage others to start a business
- 83% said they would start their business over again, given the chance.[13] (A later survey found 71% would do so, despite the recession.)[14]

Would you consider starting a business? You might need the two attributes of the antelope-like African gazelles: *speed* and *agility*. Gazelles, as one writer has termed successful small-business adventurers, "have mastered the art of the quick. They have internal approaches and fast decision-making approaches that let them move with maximum agility in a fast-changing business environment."[15]

Being a Small-Business Owner versus Being an Entrepreneur

What's the difference between small-business owners and entrepreneurs who start out with small businesses?

After they retired, Peter Gutter (pronounced "Gooter") and his wife, Michael, formed Gutter Pairs Etc. in Carson City, Nevada, as a small home-based business to sell collectible stamps. Earlier both had enjoyed collecting stamps as a hobby, and the new business was just intended to keep them busy and help them get stamps from countries (China, Russia) they were particularly interested in. As their client base expanded, they learned to manage a number of mail and phone lists, as well as to obtain business licenses and pay sales taxes in nine states in which they operated. At present, the business is in its 25th year—and the Gutters are still operating out of their home, still just a two-person business.[16]

Are the Gutters just a couple of small-business people? Or are they something more than that—a pair of business entrepreneurs? Some might call them *micropreneurs*—**those who take the risk of starting and managing a business that remains small (often home-based), lets them do the kind of work they want to do, and offers them a balanced lifestyle.**[17] Most business scholars, however, tend to make a distinction between . . .

- Small-business owners who want to stay small and make a living, and
- Entrepreneurs who begin as small businesses and hope to grow into something larger.

Of course, both types are engaged in *taking risks,* a condition underlying all business. And also some businesses that started out as "a way to make a living" may expand in entrepreneurial ways.

Small-Business Owners: "I Just Want to Make a Living"

In Chapter 5, we defined small business as having "100 employees or less." In this book, when we say "small business," that's the figure we generally mean. A firm with 500 employees or less is also used in some definitions of small business, but in other discussions that is said to constitute a midsize business.

However, according to the Small Business Administration, **a *small business* is defined by the U.S. government as a business that is (a) independently owned and operated, (b) is not dominant in its field of operation, and meets certain criteria set by the SBA for (c) number of employees and (d) annual sales revenue.** Under this definition, you could be running a 1,500-employee factory making solar panels, and you would still be considered small.

Many small-business owners are simply looking to make a living—those who own pizza parlors, beauty salons, liquor stores, pool-cleaning companies, lawn-care services, and the like. They may even have slightly unusual kinds of businesses, like Gold Prospecting Adventures in California's gold country.

BRIEFING / SMALL BUSINESS & ENTREPRENEURS
The Shock Brothers' Small Business—Gold Prospecting Adventures. Can you get rich panning for gold in California? Lots of people think so—especially since, as of August 2011, its price had more than doubled in 2½ years. But the Shock brothers—Brent, 59, and Bryant, 56, founders of Gold Prospecting Adventures, a gold-panning shop in Jamestown, California—know better. "Guys call me up all the time and say, 'How can I get enough gold to pay my bills?'" says Brent. "I tell 'em, sell doorknobs or shovels. The merchants were the ones who really made the money in that last big gold rush of 1849. . . . We just remind them that prospecting is very hard work. It's best to think of it as a great hobby."

The Shocks are happy to show customers how to do gold panning and sell them pans and shovels. Occasionally they do some prospecting themselves, but they're not getting rich. Still, says Bryant, "We do OK overall throughout the year."[18] ❷

Although the Shock brothers might hope for riches, they would seem to be mainly small-business people who are just hoping to get by. ∎

Want to Know More? 6-1

Key Terms & Definitions in Sequential Order to Study as You Go Along

Go to www.mybizlab.com.

❷ **Golden opportunity?** Brent Shock, of Gold Prospecting Adventures, in his gold-panning shop in Jamestown, California. He and his brother, Bryant, make a living as small-business owners but aren't getting rich. Could you be content with having a business like this?

Source: Lacy Atkins/San Francisco Chronicle/Corbis.

Entrepreneurs: "I Want to Build a High-Growth Business"

Another class of small-business people is not satisfied with simply making a living. This consists of *entrepreneurs,* **business owners who, in the classic meaning of** the term, see a new opportunity for a product or service and start firms that may lead to a high-growth business—those who become the "millionaires next door," as we called them in Chapter 1.

 BRIEFING / SMALL BUSINESS & ENTREPRENEURS
Chef-Owner Mourad Lahlou's Entrepreneurial Small Business— Aziza, New Moroccan Cuisine. The jet-black tattoos on the Moroccan-born restaurant entrepreneur's chest and arms represent thoughtful reflections of his life's story. "Each of these pinpoint an important moment that I don't want to forget," says Mourad Lahlou, 40. One is the word *Strength*, inked at a time when he felt he needed it most. He also shaved his head in remembrance of his late grandfather, who took him to the food markets in Morocco. Lahlou emigrated to the United States at age 17.

Now chef-owner of San Francisco–based Aziza, Lahlou says that "every Moroccan place in America is the same. And it works—that's the problem. So [the cuisine] hasn't really evolved in the last 30 years." Although Lahlou is basically self-taught and hasn't cooked in any restaurant other than his own, at Aziza he has become a pioneer of modern Moroccan cooking, blending traditional foods with local fresh ingredients and contemporary technique. "He's taken it into the 21st century," says a knowledgeable Moroccan food expert. "That's something even the Moroccans haven't done."[19]

Spending nearly every minute of his time in the kitchen has paid off for Lahlou and Aziza, which has been awarded a coveted Michelin star, symbol of dining excellence. This and a victory on the TV reality show *Iron Chef* have also attracted the food world's attention, leading to a 13-part TV cooking series and accompanying cookbook. ■

Do you have what it takes to start up a new *enterprise,* **an endeavor in which the primary motive is to make a profit?** Which would it be—a small business that makes you a decent living? Or a small business that, with enough entrepreneurial drive, might grow into something huge?

Three Types of Entrepreneurs

Which of three entrepreneurial types would I want to be?

■ **PANEL 6.1 Three entrepreneurial types.**

1. Classic entrepreneur: sees a new opportunity for a product or service and starts a firm that can lead to a high-growth business.

2. Intrapreneur: works inside an existing organization and sees an opportunity for a product or service and mobilizes the organization's resources to try to realize it.

3. Entrepreneurial team: group of people with different kinds of expertise who form a team to create a new product.

Entrepreneurship—**the process of taking risks to try to create a new business—** has received a lot of admiring attention in the business press and on television. However, says business columnist Rhonda Abrams, many people base their choice of entrepreneurial role models more on TV than reality. For instance, the entrepreneur most inspiring to American women is Oprah Winfrey, chosen by 66% in one survey. For men it was real-estate tycoon Donald Trump with 38% and *Playboy* founder Hugh Hefner with 34%.[20] In 2009, teenagers ranked (the late) Steve Jobs the most admired entrepreneur, followed by Oprah.[21]

But the entrepreneurial spirit is expressed in all kinds of ways. However the dream is pursued, the true entrepreneur "always searches for change, responds to it, and exploits it as an opportunity," according to the late management philosopher Peter Drucker.[22]

We distinguish among three entrepreneurial types: (1) *classic entrepreneurs* (usually known simply as *entrepreneurs*), (2) *intrapreneurs,* and (3) *entrepreneurial teams.* (See ■ *Panel 6.1.*)

1 Classic Entrepreneurs—Individuals Starting Up Their Own Firms: "I See a Way to Build a High-Growth Business"

The classic entrepreneur meets the definition we gave above for *entrepreneur*. A *classic entrepreneur* **is an individual who sees a new opportunity for a product or service and starts a firm that can lead to a high-growth business.**

■ **Example of a Classic Entrepreneur: Andrew Rollert Founds SpotScout to Find Parking Spaces.** Today, "you shouldn't have to look for a parking space anymore," says Andrew Rollert, 32, founder of SpotScout, being tested in Boston, New York, and San Francisco. ❸

With SpotScout, Rollert hopes drivers using cellphones can reserve private garage and driveway parking spaces and also swap public parking spaces in real time, with vacant spaces going to the highest bidder.[23]

Will the idea work? No one knows. That's the thing about being an entrepreneur: There's usually a great deal of risk. ■

2 Intrapreneurs—Individuals Creating New Ideas as Company Employees: "I See an Opportunity for My Employer"

An *intrapreneur* **is someone who works inside an existing organization who sees an opportunity for a product or service and mobilizes the organization's resources to try to realize it.** This person might be a researcher or scientist but could also be a manager who sees an opportunity to create a new venture.

❸ **Entrepreneur.** SpotScout founder Andrew Rollert demonstrates how the SpotScout service allows drivers to find waiting parking spaces on their cellphones. Are you capable of taking a wild idea and trying to turn it into a new business?

BRIEFING / A WORLD OF CONSTANT CHANGE
Intrapreneur Seamus Blackley Dreams Up Microsoft's Xbox. A game designer whose last big project, a dinosaur-shooting game, bombed in the marketplace, Seamus Blackley joined Microsoft in early 1999. During an airplane flight, he visualized a new idea for creating a videogame console using personal computer technology. Banding together with three Microsoft engineers, Blackley helped design a console that used the best PC graphics and microprocessor technologies but that hooked up to a TV set and was easier to use than a PC.

Then Sony announced its forthcoming PlayStation 2 console, and Microsoft founder Bill Gates decided his company should enter the game console business. As development proceeded, however, disputes threatened to sideline the project. There were disagreements over whether to wait to bring out the Xbox until after the Sony launch, whether to include a hard-disk drive, and whether to have Microsoft or various PC makers manufacture the machines. At one point Blackley had to deal with Microsoft president Steve Ballmer yelling, "You're going to lose the company a lot of money!"

Eventually, Blackley got the go-ahead, and the Xbox was launched in late 2001.❹ "I think I succeeded," says Blackley, "because I had nothing to lose." As a first-year employee, "I had no baggage."[24] ■

❹ **Xbox.** Launched in 2001, the Xbox was developed internally at Microsoft by Seamus Blackley and others. It sold 24 million units worldwide by 2006. Do you think entrepreneurial ideas such as the Xbox are more easily conceived and developed inside or outside the corporate culture?

Want to Know More? 6-2

How Did the IBM Skunkworks Develop the PC?

Go to www.mybizlab.com.

3 Entrepreneurial Teams—Company Groups Developing Ideas: "I Can Join with Others to Develop a New Product"

An *entrepreneurial team* is a group of people with different kinds of expertise who form a team to create a new product. One variant is the *skunkworks,* a team whose members are separated from the normal operation of an organization and asked to produce a new, innovative project. The skunkworks is the device that IBM used to bring its first IBM Personal Computer to market, doing so in only 12 months, skirting the company bureaucracy.

> **BRIEFING / SMALL BUSINESS & ENTREPRENEURS**
> **A Recession-Decimated Hot-Tub Maker Creates Entrepreneurial Teams to Find New Products to Make.** Bob Hallam's Dimension One Spas, of Vista, California, maker of spas (hot tubs), had been in existence for 32 years when the Great Recession produced a crisis: As the U.S. housing market collapsed, consumers became less inclined to put forth $15,000 for a luxury item such as a spa. At that point, Hallam, who owns his own factory, began thinking about what other products Dimension One might make. He called together some of the company's more creative staff members to brainstorm possibilities—a team he called "007," for the seven possibilities it came up with, including urinals and horse trailers. Hallam okayed development of one idea, a soft bathtub.
>
> That, it turned out, was not nearly enough, and Hallam was forced to institute pay cuts and layoffs. He then created a new entrepreneurial team involving his director of business development and an engineer and told them to focus on new product ideas. Eventually they identified several possibilities: making parts for an electric vehicle company, manufacturing bulletproof vests and helicopter landing pads for the military, crafting wind-turbine parts for wind power companies, and producing stand-up paddleboards for a surfboard company.
>
> Hallam knows not all the initiatives will hit pay dirt, but if just one takes off, he can begin to rebuild his company. "It's the tipping-point approach," he says. "Go down the road little by little until something shows promise, and then dump in the [development] money."[25] ■

How Do People Become Entrepreneurs? Opportunity versus Necessity

What's the difference between opportunity entrepreneurs and necessity entrepreneurs?

People who become individual entrepreneurs, classic entrepreneurs operating outside a traditional company's environment, do so for two different reasons—*opportunity* and *necessity*.[26]

Opportunity Entrepreneurs: "I Burn to Pursue Success"

Most entrepreneurs are *opportunity entrepreneurs,* **those who are ambitious and start their own businesses in a voluntary pursuit of opportunity.** Like chef Mourad Lahlou, they are driven to pursue their own vision of success.

Necessity Entrepreneurs: "I Need to Replace Lost Income"

Others are *necessity entrepreneurs,* **people who suddenly must earn a living and are simply trying to replace lost income.** Examples are laid-off workers, divorced homemakers, discharged military people, and some recent college graduates.[27] The number of self-employed people grows about 2% to 3% a year when the economy is good. In 2008, a recessionary year, the number of people working for themselves jumped 8.1%.[28] Entrepreneurial activity increased 6%.[29]

■ **Example of a Necessity Entrepreneur: Laid-Off Marketer Starts Korean Condiment Business.** A layoff from a marketing job at a financial services firm "forced me to take the jump" into entrepreneurship, says Lauryn Chun, 40.[30] She embarked on a completely new venture, Mother-in-Law's Kimchi, the traditional Korean spicy pickled cabbage condiment, which is sold online. ■

Do You Have What It Takes to Be an Entrepreneur? Four Characteristics

Do I have the four characteristics of an entrepreneur?

Entrepreneurs seem to have psychological characteristics that make them different from those who want to become company managers:[31]

1 High Self-Confidence & Belief in Personal Control

Managers need to be self-confident and to think they have personal control of their destinies. To paraphrase British poet William Ernest Henley—"I am the captain of my fate, the master of my soul." This is even more so for entrepreneurs, who need the confidence to act decisively. ❺

2 High Need for Achievement & Action Orientation

Managers are motivated more by promotions and organizational rewards of power and perks. Entrepreneurs are motivated to execute their ideas and realize financial rewards. They are also more action oriented, wanting to get things done as quickly as possible.

3 High Tolerance for Ambiguity & Risk

Managers need to be able to make decisions based on unclear or incomplete information. Entrepreneurs must have even more tolerance for ambiguity because they are trying things they haven't done before. They also need to be willing to take risks, even personal financial risks, in the pursuit of new opportunities.

4 High Energy Level

Managers may have to put in long hours in order to rise to the top of an organization. But entrepreneurs are willing to invest even more time and energy.

Want to Know More? 6-3
Are You the Entrepreneurial Type?
Go to www.mybizlab.com.

Key Takeaway 6-2
Entrepreneurs are high in self-confidence, need for achievement, tolerance for ambiguity and risk, and energy level.

Source: Erin Patrice O'Brien.

❺ **"Captain of my fate."** In 1997, at age 23, Alison Schuback of Dallas was in an automobile accident that left her with traumatic brain injuries and wheelchair bound—and with mountains of medical bills. Determined to pay them off herself, she invented a transparent, washable bib for adults with disabilities and launched a company to sell it. The company ran out of cash, but then Schuback, through a PBS reality show, *Everyday Edisons,* came to the attention of a Fortune 500 executive who was prepared to back her. The product is now available as the Invisibib Protective Vinyl Bib. Schuback herself was named Entrepreneur of the Year for 2008 by *Inc.* magazine.

THE BIG IDEA: We discuss the contributions that small business makes in the United States, some home-based and Web-based businesses, some challenges of running a small enterprise, and some considerations involved in buying a small business.

THE ESSENTIAL QUESTION: How important is small business, and what newer types might interest me?

MyBizLab: Check your understanding of these concepts at www.mybizlab.com.

When Jimmy Au, who is five feet two, arrived in Hawaii from Hong Kong as a student, he supported himself by selling custom suits door to door. After a time, he noticed that most of his customers were short men and realized he had discovered an untapped market. Although there are hundreds of stores in the United States specializing in clothes for "big and tall" men, there are few designer-clothing retailers for short men (many of whom are forced to shop in children's clothing departments). After moving to southern California, Au opened a succession of stores catering to short men, finally culminating in 2005 with an upscale store in Beverly Hills—Jimmy Au's For Men 5'8" and Under. "The store is scaled down," Au says. Ceilings are low, clothing racks and mannequins are small, and even the chairs are made shorter.[32] ⑥

As this example shows, a small business need not be uninteresting, even if its owners are not particularly motivated to pursue high growth.

Source: Javier Plaza.

⑥ **Small** business. Jimmy Au *(left)*, with son Alan, operates a business that is small in more than one sense: a family-owned store serving short men. There are all kinds of apparel businesses catering to people whose shapes and abilities fall outside the norm. Can you think of any?

The Contributions of Small Business

How does the United States benefit from small business?

"Small business is the backbone of America," you hear it said. Is this true? If small business is defined as companies employing 500 people or less, the statistics suggest that U.S. small businesses . . . [33]

- **Represent most employers and employ half of U.S. workers:** Small firms with fewer than 500 employees represent 99.7% of the 29.6 million businesses in this country. They employ over half of U.S. workers.
- **Provide more new jobs:** Small businesses generated 64% of net new jobs annually over the 15 years ending in 2008.
- **Provide more first jobs:** Small firms provide the first job for most entrants to the labor force.
- **Are often the innovators in their fields:** Small innovative firms produce 13 times more patents per employee than large patenting firms. Small firms are twice as innovative per employee as larger firms.

■ **Example** of Small-Business Innovation—and Failure: A Lake Tahoe Lodge Aimed at Snowboarders. The Block was introduced in 2007 as a new kind of Lake Tahoe, California, lodge to serve a niche market by catering to snowboarders. As one writer described it, "With graffiti paint jobs, iPod-compatible stereos, beer-proof rubber floors, top-line videogame consoles, or even full-size arcade games, rooms at The Block . . . don't resemble [those in] other ski-town motels."[34]

The backer, Rogue Ventures, found private investors to finance the deal. Unfortunately, The Block was forced to close after a few years when it failed to make enough money to pay $200,000 in taxes to the city of South Lake Tahoe. ■

Some Types of Small Businesses: Home-Based & Web-Based

What are some considerations I need to know about running home-based and Web-based businesses?

Small businesses are found in every sector of the American economy: farming, manufacturing, construction, wholesaling, retailing, services, and high technology. About 53% of new small businesses begin in the home, financed on less than $10,000, many starting with leased or used equipment.[35]

With today's portable technology, some people, known as *bedouins* (pronounced "bed-u-ins") after the nomadic Arabs who wandered freely in the desert, don't have even a home office. They just roam from café to café, using laptops and cellphones to conduct business and paying for their "office space" and wireless Internet access by buying coffee and muffins.[36] ❼

Source: Lev Olkha/Fotolia LLC.

❼ **High-tech "bedouins."** Some small-business people, such as those in sales, prefer to operate out of coffeehouses and cafés rather than offices. Does this appeal to you? (Some café owners have started limiting hours per customer, especially around mealtimes, because bedouins tend to tie up tables.)

Home-Based Businesses: Running Your Own Show from Home

There are a great many businesses that can be started at home. Indeed, about half of a recent *Inc.* magazine's 500 fastest-growing small businesses were started at home. The average startup cost was only $25,000, and many were started with $5,000 or less.[37]

■ **Example** of a Business That Started at Home: Karen Frost Creates the Ergo Baby Carrier. Karen Frost of Maui, Hawaii, was a 41-year-old first-time mother when her baby came along in 2001. She discovered that none of the existing baby slings and pouches on the market kept her son as close to her body as possible while also being comfortable. So Frost invented her own version, hand-sewing the first 50 carriers in her home before she found a manufacturer in China.[38] Today, Ergo Baby Carrier is a company with a global presence. In 2010, Connecticut-based Compass Diversified Holdings agreed to acquire it for $91 million.[39] ■

Home-Based Businesses: Some Possibilities. Many home-based businesses are one- or two-person operations, from clothing boutiques to interior decorators to website developers.[40] (Beware, however, of those schemes advertised on television promising lucrative at-home jobs with little training.) Among the possible opportunities for earning money from home using the Internet, for example, are the following:[41]

- **Freelance work:** Writers, programmers, designers, administrative assistants, even engineers and business professionals can find opportunities by going to certain freelance websites.

Want to Know More? 6-4

Some Online Networking Connections for Small-Business People

Go to www.mybizlab.com.

• **Direct sales:** Many companies have programs for selling from home via the Internet.

• **Customer service:** Not all customer service has been outsourced to India. Many companies (such as JetBlue) hire people with experience to do this from home, provided you have a computer, landline, and quiet environment. A virtual concierge, for instance, handles errands and inquiries.

• **Transcription service:** Doctors, lawyers, and others hire people to work at home transcribing audio recordings. You'll need good English and typing skills.

• **Tutoring:** You may be able to do online teaching, particularly if you've had teaching experience.

Some websites that may be helpful are shown at left. (*See* ■ *Panel 6.2.*)

The Challenges of Working at Home. Working at home has certain challenges, such as trying to manage your time and keep your work life and personal/family life separate. Basically, one article advises, you need to "make it a point to look and act professional—even though there's no one around to judge."[42] Some suggested rules:

• **Dress for work:** Some people do just fine dressed in their pajamas, but others find that taking a shower and putting on office clothes gives them the discipline they need.

• **Set a routine and stick to it:** You should get to your desk at about the same time every day, check your e-mail, contact your clients, and perform your work just as you would in an office.

• **Keep work and family stuff on separate computers:** You don't want other family members getting in your way or accessing unauthorized websites on your business computer.

• **Interact with other professionals:** To stay in touch, e-mail other professionals who work from home, or arrange to get out and have lunch with them once in a while. This is known as ***networking,*** **the process of establishing and maintaining connections with professionals and managers in your field to help you advance in your career.**

■ **Example of How Some Small-Business Home-Based Professionals Connect with Others: The Ladieswholaunch.com Networking Site.** Christina Carthanassis is president of ChristabellesCloset.com in New York, which sells designer clothes and accessories from the closets of the rich. She likes to go to *www.ladieswholaunch.com,* a business networking website that allows small-business women to network and find resources. "You can ask for advice from other women who have had similar experience," she says.[43] ■

Web-Based Businesses: Using a Website to Build a Business

Many small businesses have become successful based on little more than a website and a business concept.

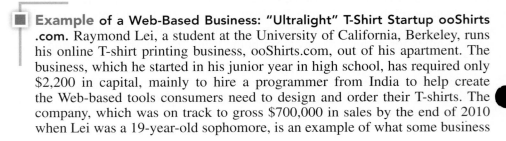

■ **Example of a Web-Based Business: "Ultralight" T-Shirt Startup ooShirts.com.** Raymond Lei, a student at the University of California, Berkeley, runs his online T-shirt printing business, ooShirts.com, out of his apartment. The business, which he started in his junior year in high school, has required only $2,200 in capital, mainly to hire a programmer from India to help create the Web-based tools consumers need to design and order their T-shirts. The company, which was on track to gross $700,000 in sales by the end of 2010 when Lei was a 19-year-old sophomore, is an example of what some business

8 Making money exclusively from a website. Raymond Lei of ooShirts and one of his products. The World Wide Web has generated many new ways of making money, especially for small businesses. With this method, could you start a small business out of a college dorm room or a spare bedroom at home?

observers call an "ultralight" startup, requiring little investment. **8** "When my friends talk to me about wanting to get jobs," says Lei, "I tell them they'd be better off to start a company."[44] ■

Among the things that make launching a Web-based business easy are the following:

- **Simple and reliable servers:** Web servers, the computers that host the websites, have become simple and reliable enough that they can run on their own, without a lot of fussing and hand-holding.
- **Speedy wireless networks:** Connections to fast wireless networks have become widespread among smartphones and tablet computers, so that it is easier to go online and use powerful applications over the Web.[45]
- **A sophisticated economic infrastructure:** Many websites make money in three ways: (1) via Google's small ads placed on a site's Web pages, (2) by selling big banner ads, and (3) through affiliated marketing, in which other websites pay to have customers sent to them.[46]
- **Facebook tools for reaching local customers:** Among other things, you can create a Facebook page for your business and migrate your fans from a personal page onto the new business page.[47]

Owning Your Own Business: Buy or Start?

Why would I buy rather than start a business?

How do most business owners get into their businesses? According to one survey of 201 business owners with annual revenues of $10 million or more . . .

- 52% started their own business
- 18% purchased their business from a non-family member
- 11% took over the business from a family member
- 5% inherited a family business
- 14% used other means.[48]

Let's consider the possibility that you might want to buy an existing business rather than start up a new business from scratch.

The founders of Integration Appliance in Palo Alto, California, knew they would have to stretch every dollar. So they came up with a "bring your own chair" hiring policy. In that startup, ratty and uncomfortable chairs became signs of a sleek, frugal operation.[49]

Frugality. That's a good word for any new business. "Starting a business is an adventure," says entrepreneur James Currier. "It can build your character as you build the business. . . . Having an austere environment helps get your team into that mindset." Currier started his Internet company, Tickle, in a dank, drafty basement in Cambridge, Massachusetts, with a computer perched on bricks to stay dry during rainstorms. He sold Tickle in 2004 for $100 million.[50]

It's amazing what you can do to launch a business on the cheap. Some ideas:[51]

- **Bartering for supplies and services:** When Tricia Ballad of Bloomington, Indiana, started her Web hosting business, Hosting SPOC, with little cash, she saved money by trading services with other businesses. For instance, in return for legal services, Ballad gave her lawyer computer services. When Kim Francis of Columbus, Ohio, started her consulting business, KAF Enterprises, she acquired websites by swapping design of brochures and bookkeeping services with another company.

- **Inexpensive phone and fax:** For a few dollars a month, companies such as EVoice and Kall8 provide toll-free numbers.

- **Cheap website, hosting, and blogging services:** Companies like Homestead Technologies and Yahoo provide inexpensive Web services. Yahoo even has cheap blogging programs.

- **Business cards and brochures:** VistaPrint is an online store where budget-conscious customers can design and order business cards, brochures, and other printed materials for not much money. You can even get some business cards free.

Want to Know More? 6-5

How Can I Evaluate & Buy an Existing Business?

Go to www.mybizlab.com.

Buying a Small Business

Assuming you have the money, it shouldn't be too hard to find a business to buy, right? ❾ Maybe it's not so easy. Brad Bottoset, a business broker, says he devotes a lot of time to searching for qualified business owners interested in selling their businesses. "In my experience," he says, "for every 100 phone calls I make, I'll be able to get through to the owner approximately 60% of the time. During these conversations, about 5% may actually be seriously contemplating selling their business. Unfortunately, only a very low percentage of them, approximately 30%, will have a business that will be attractive to a potential buyer."[52]

Source: Photograph by Sally Lindsay.

❾ **For sale.** Do you think it's easier to take over an existing business than to build one from scratch—assuming the business is worthwhile? How should you analyze a business you're considering buying so you can help make the right decision?

If finding a worthwhile business to buy is so frustrating, why bother? There are two reasons:

- **To reduce uncertainty:** When you take over a successful business, the previous owner has obviously dealt with and overcome most of the risks.
- **To generate profits more quickly:** When you step into an existing well-run enterprise, presumably you should be able to get profits fairly quickly. With a startup, you might have to wait several years.

Looking Over & Negotiating for an Existing Business

There are a lot of steps to take when sizing up a business to buy, once you've located a good prospect. Here are some things to think about:

- **How does the business work? How does the industry work?** You'll need to develop an understanding of everything you can about the business and the industry it's in: the products, the customers, the pricing, the employees, the competition, the cost of doing business, and so on.
- **Why is the owner selling, and what does he or she want to do next?** You'll need to find out why the owner is willing to sell. You'll also want to learn what the owner's future plans are. (Will it be to open up a competing business?)
- **Is the price right?** The owner may have high expectations about what the business is worth. You'll certainly want to look carefully at the books, probably with the help of a financial consultant, to find out what the business is truly worth.

BRIEFING / INFO TECH & SOCIAL MEDIA
An Entrepreneur Buys a Blog Devoted to Funny Cat Pictures & Builds a Web Empire. Sometimes it's not possible to get the foregoing questions answered when you're buying a business that's relatively untested. Such was the case for Ben Huh, a 32-year-old entrepreneur, when in 2007 he became aware of I Can Has Cheezburger?, a blog devoted to silly cat pictures paired with quirky captions submitted by readers. The blog had linked to Huh's own pet blog—and immediately made it crash from a wave of new visitors.

Sensing a business opportunity, Huh put up $10,000 of his savings and obtained financing from investors and purchased the website for $2 million from the Hawaiian bloggers who started it. "It was a white-knuckle decision," he said later. "I knew that the first site was funny, but could we duplicate that success?"[53] ⑩

Huh expanded the oddball Cheezburger blog into an empire that now includes 53 sites. The Cheezburger Network attracted 15 million unique visitors in June 2011, 55% of them in the United States.[54] ∎

Selling Your Business

What are some reasons I might want to sell my business?

Some entrepreneurs and business owners sell their businesses because that's what they (and their investors) wanted to do all along—to make a killing. Perhaps their product becomes wildly popular (as MySpace did early on), and so they are able to make a profitable exit and move on. However, other people sell their businesses for less glorified reasons: they've been whipped by their competitors, they've inherited a firm they have no interest in running, they have health problems, and so on. Regardless, in every case, the sellers should hire a business lawyer, accountant, and other advisors to help them obtain the best deal.[55]

Source: Photo courtesy of Cheezburger.com.

⑩ **I Can Has Cheezburger?** Assuming you could come up with $10,000 of your own money and get $2 million from investors, would you have rolled the dice like entrepreneur Ben Huh and bought a blog devoted to "lolcats"—silly cat pictures linked to humorous reader-submitted captions? How would you have expected to make money with this?

Want to Know More? 6-6

What Are the Things I Should Know about Selling My Business?

Go to www.mybizlab.com.

Starting Up: From Idea to Business Plan

THE BIG IDEA: If you want to start a business, you need to sort out your ideas, and then get some relevant training and experience. Whether you buy or start a business, you should probably write a business plan, although not all startups have one.

THE ESSENTIAL QUESTION: If I wanted to start a company, how should I go about it?

MyBizLab: Check your understanding of these concepts at www.mybizlab.com.

Every year millions of people follow their dreams of independence by starting a business. How do they start? Usually with an *idea*.

It Begins with an Idea

What are some ways to come up with a business idea?

There are all kinds of ways to come up with a business idea. For example, you can . . .

- Simplify an existing product
- Enhance an existing product
- Take a product from one market and adapt it to another market
- Change materials used in a product to make it less expensive
- Take a product with multiple features and spin off one feature
- Combine two or more products. ⑪

⑪ **Combining products.** Popchips were developed in 2007 by Keith Belling (*above*) and Pat Turpin (*right, in warehouse*) as a cross between a potato chip and a rice cake. The product is made by popping potatoes like popcorn, using no oil in the popping process and producing a healthier product. What kind of widely differing ideas can you think of that might be fused together to form a new concept in business?

Source: popchips.

BRIEFING / EARNING GREEN BY GOING GREEN

Restoring Buildings Using Green Materials. Architect and urban redeveloper Guy Bazzani moved from the West Coast back to his hometown of Grand Rapids, Michigan, and set up Bazzani Associates in 1994. The firm, in one description, "specializes in restoring old buildings, [using] techniques and tools including green roofs that are covered with plants, storm water management systems, and environmentally friendly building materials."[56] The business strategy, then, is one of enhancing an existing product or of changing materials used in a product to make it less expensive.

Bazzani's customers discovered that his green buildings would save them 40% to 50% in annual energy costs when compared to a traditionally constructed facility. "When I came back here," says Bazzani, "I thought I'd stay a couple of years and return to California. But my green business took off. When people come to me, I'm their first choice, a locally owned business that can produce value." ■

Three further observations we might make. The business idea . . .

- Should involve something you like to do, if possible, and are pretty good at doing
- Should satisfy some sort of need in the marketplace
- Should exploit a niche—offer a distinctive product or service, not the same kinds of things easily available to customers in local stores. Indeed, this is a key element in making a small business successful, particularly with Web-based businesses.[57]

Some of these principles underlie the following example.

BRIEFING / CUSTOMER FOCUS

Plenty of Fish, an Online Dating Site, Begins as a One-Person Web-Based Business. "It's like my own personal toy," says Markus Frind of Vancouver, British Columbia, where he operates Plenty of Fish (at plentyoffish.com), a dating website. Ranked among the top 100 busiest websites in North America, Plenty of Fish generates traffic that would normally require a team of employees to keep it going, but Frind began it by himself, with occasional help from his girlfriend, Annie Kanciar. ⑫

The basis for the site's success is that it is free, whereas most dating sites charge $20 to $40 a month. Frind also keeps things simple, with modest graphics that he designed himself. The site runs on Microsoft software on a half dozen servers a few miles away. Frind makes money via the three means described previously: Google small text ads, banner ads, and affiliated marketing. The business itself was run out of a spare room in his apartment, but recently moved to an office building.[58] ■

⑫ **Worth plenty of bucks.** Considered to be the first successful *free* dating website, Plenty of Fish was founded by Markus Frind, shown playing with his girlfriend. Frind's business idea satisfies the criteria of being something he likes doing, satisfying a market need, and exploiting a niche—being free in a universe of pay-to-play dating services.

Source: Jeff Minton/Outline Gallery/Corbis.

Learning about Business, Getting Experience

What's the logical way to prepare to start my own firm?

Let's say you come up with an idea for a restaurant that not only serves good food but also allows you to promote social and cultural causes. That's what Judy Wicks, who opened the White Dog Café in Philadelphia 24 years ago (see p. 46), wanted to do.[59] So did Sean O'Hair, owner of Record Street Café in Reno, Nevada. Both used or use their establishments to be socially active, as in having guest speakers or promoting certain musicians.

First, however, they had to learn about business and get experience. O'Hair, for instance, was a university instructor who had burned out on teaching. After he bought his restaurant he had to learn on the job about staffing, food costs, recipes, bookkeeping, permits, and taxes. "The first months were really difficult," says O'Hair. "I was convinced I knew more and could do more than I ended up being able to do."[60]

Is there a better way? Probably. Rather than start cold, maybe you should gradually immerse yourself in the startup process by acquiring training and experience, as follows:

Step 1: Read about Business—& Your Prospective Business

You're already doing some of this by taking this course and reading this book. That is, you are learning about basic business principles, which you'll expand on in later business courses, if you desire. Once you discover an industry or area in which you might like to launch a startup, you should do further detailed reading about that.

Step 2: Talk to Knowledgeable People— Mentors & Trade Associations

Next you should talk to people already knowledgeable about the particular business you want to go into. Two sources of expert knowledge are *mentors* and *trade associations*.

Source: Photo Credit of The Boston Beer Company.

⓭ Mentor. Jim Koch heads the Boston Beer Company, maker of award-winning Samuel Adams beers, but he finds time to lend his expertise to aspiring and existing micro-brewers. For example, he helped a former teacher and firefighter transform their hobby of handcrafted ales into a nationwide brand through their Oceanside Ale Works in Oceanside, California.

Mentors. A *mentor* **is an experienced person who coaches and guides lesser-experienced people by helping them understand an industry or organization's culture and structure.** Usually we think of mentors as being supervisors or experienced people in an organization with which we are newly employed. However, it's possible to get a mentor to help you understand the workings of the new business you're trying to get going. ⓭

If you can't find a private mentor, you should be aware that the Small Business Administration (discussed in the next section) offers mentors through SCORE—**the *Service Corps of Retired Executives*, consisting of retired executives who volunteer as consultants to advise small-business people.** SCORE advisors can, for example, help you figure out a five-year financial plan for your business. SCORE is supplemented by the ***Active Corps of Executives (ACE)*, composed of executives who are still active in the business world but have volunteered their time and talents.**

Trade Associations. No matter what kind of business you're trying to get into, there's probably a trade association for it, since there are nearly 40,000 such associations.[61] A *trade association* **consists of individuals and companies in a specific business or industry organized to promote common interests.** A trade association can provide research data, training, certification programs, and links to others in your prospective field.

Step 3: Get Experience

The next step is to get some experience. Perhaps you could work part time in your area of interest while you're still a student, as in an internship or co-op job (a job that combines classroom instruction with practical work experience). Or after graduation you could go to work in that area for a couple of years, in effect apprenticing yourself to a manager or entrepreneur who can teach you the ropes.

Once you're ready to go out on your own, the first thing to do is to write a business plan for the venture you anticipate starting or buying.

ⓘ

Want to Know More? 6-7

Could I Start a Business While Still in School?

Go to www.mybizlab.com.

Writing a Business Plan

Do I need to write a business plan? Why or why not?

Brian Allman, 17, saw a simple vending machine for sale at Sam's Club and bought it for $425 from personal savings. With that he started a small vending-machine business, Bear Snax Vending, stocking the machine and four others he added later with popular candy such as Skittles, M&Ms, and Snickers. His route includes small to mid-size businesses.[62]

What did Allman do by way of initial planning for his business? Not much, it seems. And sometimes that's the case with entrepreneurs, even those far older than 17. However, the best advice is that *you should write a business plan.* A ***business plan*** **is a document that outlines a proposed firm's goals, the methods for achieving them, and the standards for measuring success.**

Why Write a Business Plan?

There are three important reasons for writing a business plan before you actually start a new business venture:

Creating a Business Plan Helps You Get Financing: "If You Want Us to Invest Our Money, Show Us Your Plan." The most compelling reason for doing a formal business plan is to have the information lenders and investors, whether your parents or a bank, will want to see before they invest in your startup. The bigger the sum of money you are asking investors to put at risk, the more elaborate your business plan will have to be. (We explain the various ways to finance a business in Section 6.4.) ⓴

Creating a Business Plan Helps You Think through Important Details: "Don't Rush Things; It's Better to Get the Strategy Right." In most cases, business ideas don't have to be rushed to market, and it typically takes businesses a long time to get established anyway. So if you're at all serious about your future business, you might as well take the three or four weeks (or more) that it takes to write a business plan to think your ideas through.

Having a Business Plan Suggests Your Company Will Succeed: "Firms without Business Plans Are More Likely to Fail." Western Reserve University professor Scott Shane researched 396 entrepreneurs in Sweden and found that a greater number of firms that failed never had a formal business plan.[63]

How Do You Conceptualize a Business Plan?

There are thousands of books on the subject of business plans. (A search of Amazon.com turned up 39,025 books with the words *business plan* in the title.) But you need not let this fact intimidate you.

Questions to Ask before You Write a Business Plan. In general, before you write such a document, you need to answer the following questions:

- **What's the basic idea behind my business?** How would you explain your proposed business to someone? What need does the business fill? That is, what is the ***business model***—**the need the firm will fill, the operations of the business, its components and functions, as well as its expected revenues and expenses?**[64]

Source: Christopher Robbins/Photodisc/Thinkstock.

 "I have a plan . . ." Writing a business plan not only focuses your ideas for your prospective enterprise, it also provides a document that lenders or investors can evaluate. Here an entrepreneur is making a pitch to a group of venture capitalists, who have read his business plan but have questions that need answering. Have you ever seen a business plan?

ⓘ

Want to Know More? 6-8

Is There a Ready-Made Form for a Business Plan?

Go to www.mybizlab.com.

- **What kind of industry am I entering, and how is my idea different?** Is the industry highly competitive? How would your business be different from those of competitors?
- **How will I market to customers?** Who are your customers, how will you market your products or services to them, and what will you charge?
- **What qualifies me to run this business?** What is your background that qualifies you to start up and operate this business?
- **How do I propose to finance the business?** Will you be getting loans from your family or financing it with savings, credit cards, or bank loans? What kind of returns do you propose to give investors?

Company Name and Other Factors. Take some care in coming up with a name for your business. (Shouldn't a company called "Sierra Restroom Solutions"—yes, this is a real firm—have worried about the unintended pun in its name?) Go online to check that it isn't registered with someone else. Make sure the name reflects your company's purpose.

Business plans usually include the following components: (1) an executive summary, (2) introduction, (3) marketing, (4) manufacturing, (5) management team, (6) legal plan, and (7) financing plan. These are described in the Practical Action box on the page opposite. **⑮**

Is It Really Necessary to Create a Formal Business Plan? The Reasons Why Not

Creating a business plan is always desirable and clearly takes work. Indeed, the steps outlined in a business plan are unavoidable, even if you don't do a formal plan. But "formal" does not necessarily mean long and detailed. Outlining your objectives on a paper napkin is still a business plan. In any case, we encourage you to make the effort.

That said, you need to know that a business plan is not always necessary. The arguments:

You May Need to Act Fast to Get the Business Going. Many business concepts are transitional in nature. By the time you spend weeks or months writing a 60-page business plan, the best opportunity may be gone.

You May Be Able to Get Financing without a Full Formal Plan. You might be able to pitch investors with just an informal 5- or 10-page summary or a PowerPoint presentation that simply outlines your business model and basic financial projections.[65]

Many Firms Have Done Well without a Business Plan. In one study, 41% of *Inc.* magazine's 1989 list of fastest-growing private firms didn't have a business plan and 26% had only rudimentary plans.[66] A follow-up study by *Inc.* in 2002 found the percentage without a plan remained much the same.

i

Want to Know More? 6-9

What Are Some Examples of Successful Business Plans?

Go to www.mybizlab.com.

Source: Business Plan Pro is a product of ©Palo Alto Software.

⑮ Business plan software. Considered the world's best-selling business plan software, Business Plan Pro features over 500 sample business plans, along with expert advice and built-in financial formulas.

In writing a business plan, which may be 20 to 60 pages long, you should assume that your prospective lenders, investors, or other readers have evaluated or are evaluating many other people's business plans as well. Thus, your job is to make yours as attractive as possible—*to make it sing.*[67]

1. **Executive Summary—"Here's What My Venture Proposes to Do and Its Promise for Success."** This 1- to 10-page section (which you should write last) provides a short description of your product or service, its market potential, and what distinguishes it from competitors. This is the place to really sell your idea to your reader.

2. **Introduction—"Here Is the Product or Service I Intend to Provide."** This section describes the general nature of the industry you propose to compete in, the product or service you will offer, its unique characteristics, and why customers will want and benefit from it.

3. **Marketing—"This Describes My Target Market, the Competitors, My Marketing Strategy, and Projected Sales."** Here you describe the market you are going into; your competitors; your strategy for identifying, contacting, and servicing customers; advertising plans; pricing; and projected sales. If your venture is a retail business, provide an analysis of the store's location, including vehicle and pedestrian traffic patterns, and the ages and socioeconomic status of projected customers.

4. **Manufacturing—"This Describes Where and How the Products Will Be Made."** If your venture is making a product, this section should describe how the product will be made, in what location, the equipment and labor required, and inventory and quality-control methods.

5. **Management—"This Describes My Management Team."** This section discusses the background and qualifications of you and others who will manage the organization. If you can't show that your team has the necessary expertise, then name consultants you will call upon for help. Describe the firm's directors, other investors, the management style that will be employed, and the compensation proposed for executives.

6. **Legal—"This Discusses the Legal Entity the Firm Will Assume Plus the Permits, Licenses, and Insurance Needed."** Here you discuss the legal plan for the business, whether sole proprietorship, partnership, corporation, or whatever. You should also describe licenses, permits, and insurance that will be needed and name the attorney who will handle your legal matters.

7. **Financing—"Here Is My Financial Plan, Including Projected Revenue and Expenses, Break-Even Point, and Funding Required."** In this section, you get into the numbers: your expected revenue and expenses every year for the first five years, your month-by-month cash flow for the first two years, and when you expect the firm to break even (that is, when sales reach the point that your revenues will equal your costs). State what funds you need and will need in the future. Offer best-case and worst-case scenarios for each of these, and avoid rosy promises.

8. **Cover Letter—"This Letter Describes the Business Plan Attached and Its Most Attractive Aspects."** After you write the executive summary, write a one-page cover letter, directed to your reader by name. Use different phrasing to briefly summarize your business venture and its most attractive features. This letter goes in the package as the first sheet on top of your business plan. Later you may wish to write a follow-up letter.

6.4

MyBizLab

Getting Financing

THE BIG IDEA: We describe eight potential sources of funds for financing new businesses.

THE ESSENTIAL QUESTION: What are various ways of financing my new business?

MyBizLab: Check your understanding of these concepts at www.mybizlab.com.

Source: Trujillo Paumier.

16 Self-financing. While in college in 2002 at the University of Colorado at Boulder, Nathan Seidle was tinkering with an electronics project and discovered how expensive components were. So he decided to max out his credit card and set up SparkFun Electronics to import and sell cheap, high-quality parts from Bulgaria. Eight years later, the mail order electronics retailer's annual revenue was $18.7 million. Can you think of a better way to use a credit card?

Every November, Meg and Gary Hirshberg have headed south from New Hampshire to New York to celebrate Thanksgiving with her mother and three brothers. While anticipating a joyful reunion, Meg has also usually felt a surge of anxiety—because all four of her family members have invested heavily in the Hirshbergs' new company, Stony Yogurt. "And I knew that soon after our arrival, the conversation would turn to the fate of their cash," she writes. "*Profits?* Not even close. . . . *Cash burn?* Lots of that."

Fortunately, she reports, these discussions are for the most part supportive. But this story does raise a point: "Building a business requires sacrifices," she observes. "When the business is funded by relatives, those sacrifices may include the carefree family gathering, the casual lunch with a sibling, and the lighthearted phone chat with Mom and Dad."[68]

Financing a New Enterprise: Eight Sources of Funds

If I were launching a new business, how would I finance it in the first year or two?

Would you approach your family to help fund your new enterprise? If not, where else? There are eight possibilities for financing: (1) *personal savings, credit cards, and second mortgages;* (2) *family and friends;* (3) *supplier and barter arrangements;* (4) *financial institutions;* (5) *Small Business Administration–backed loans;* (6) *angel investors and venture capitalists;* (7) *public stock offerings;* and (8) *other.*[69]

1 Personal Savings, Credit Cards, & Second Mortgages

A mom-and-pop business may often be financed by . . . mom and pop themselves. That is, entrepreneurs often fund their new enterprises from their personal savings or, alternatively, by maxing out their credit cards, taking a second mortgage on their homes, or taking money out of their retirement plans. These methods, of course, can represent a gamble, for if the business doesn't succeed, then they have even *less* personal financial security. Still, it needs to be noted that lenders often insist you put up a sizable sum yourself, such as 30% of startup costs, as proof of your commitment to the new business. **16**

2 Family & Friends

Two other popular sources of funds for entrepreneurs—indeed, for 90% of all startups—are family and friends.[70] Family members can range from those in the immediate family to an extended chain of relatives.

■ **Example of Entrepreneur Funding: Indian American Families Find Niche in the Hotel Industry.** Indian Americans make up only 5% of the U.S. population, but they own an astonishing 40% of all lodging properties in the United States and more than 50% of low-budget hotels and motels, according to the Asian American Hotel Owners Association, which is made up mostly of Indians.[71] "Indians say that operating a hotel suits their family-oriented culture," says one account. "Owning a hotel provides immigrants with a place to live, and children and the extended family help run the business. And when they go into business for themselves, Indians rely on the financial backing and support of the Indian community. That invariably assures success."[72] ⓱ ■

Source: Courtesy of Dinu Patel.

3 Supplier & Barter Arrangements

Suppliers can help with financing your small business in three ways:

Short-Term Credit. A supplier might provide you with short-term credit, giving you 30 to 45 days to pay for supplies or services.

Extended-Payment Plan. With heavy-duty equipment, such as trucks and computers, the supplier may give you an extended-payment arrangement, allowing you three to five years to pay for purchases.

Barter Arrangements. *Barter*—**to trade goods or services without the exchange of money**—is, as mentioned earlier, another option, as in trading your old Ford F-150 pickup to a roofer for replacing your restaurant's roof.[73]

4 Financial Institutions

Financial institutions consist of banks, savings and loans, and credit unions. Although normally reluctant to make loans to startups, they may do so if you have a good credit history or can offer some collateral, property to secure the loan such as your house. In the recent recession, even good customers found loans hard to get. Best advice: Get to know some bank loan officers and try to educate them about your business.[74]

5 Small Business Administration–Backed Loans

If you don't qualify for a loan with your bank, you might be able to get a bank loan that is guaranteed by the *Small Business Administration (SBA),* **the principal U.S. government agency charged with aiding small businesses by providing help in financing, management training, and support in securing government contracts.** The SBA has about 1,000 Small Business Development Centers across the United States, which provide free, in-depth counseling.[75] Although the SBA doesn't usually make direct loans, it guarantees a great many loans made to small businesses. The Small Business Investment Company (SBIC) program is a public/private partnership designed to give small businesses access to capital. For instance, Staples, the office supply store, was started with SBA backing.

6 Angel Investors & Venture Capitalists

Angel investors **are defined as individuals who invest their own money in a private company, typically a startup.** These are people who already have a lot of money and want to make more by getting into a business with high growth potential.[76] (For examples, look up Garage.com at www.garage.com.)

⓱ **Family and friends.** Indian Americans have been able to make a great impact on the lodging industry in the United States in part because individuals are able to call upon family and friends for assistance, including financial help. Could you count on family members for financial assistance and to pitch in when needed to help you launch a new business?

Want to Know More? 6-10

More about the Small Business Administration

Go to www.mybizlab.com.

Venture capitalists **are generally companies, not individuals, that invest in new enterprises in return for part ownership of them**—perhaps as much as 60% ownership. Venture capital firms blossomed in California's Silicon Valley during the dot.com boom of the late 1990s.[77] However, they actually provide very little financing for most small businesses, being drawn mainly to software, medical devices, biotech, green technology, and Internet-specific enterprises.[78]

7 Public Stock Offerings: Should You Sell the Business?

The expression ***"going public"* means that a privately owned company becomes a publicly owned company by issuing stock for sale to the public.** A public stock offering would not be a method of financing a startup, but it might be done for a small company that has attained a substantial measure of success. Indeed, public stock offerings are usually the means by which angel investors and venture capitalists hope their early investment will result in earning them a fortune (as was done by backers of Yahoo and Google).

8 Other Funding Sources

There are many other sources of funds for new businesses. Many entrepreneurs take second jobs to stay afloat.[79] Others obtain small loans, "microloans" of $500 to $35,000, run through organizations such as the Women's Initiative for Self-Employment or Prosper.com, a peer-to-peer lending group.[80] Some organizations grant funds to women in small business; others help minorities trying to start up new enterprises. Finally, some small-business people have even turned to their customers and communities for funding in hard times.[81]

Want to Know More? 6-11

How Can I Find Out More about Enterprise Zones?

Go to www.mybizlab.com.

Other Support: Incubators & Enterprise Zones

How might incubators and even enterprise zones be of help to building a business?

All along the way in planning your business, you can avail yourself of other forms of support, as follows.

Incubators

An *incubator* is a facility that offers small businesses low-cost offices with basic services, such as secretarial and accounting services and legal advice.[82] Some incubators are sponsored by state and local economic development departments. ⑱

⑱ **Incubator.** The San Francisco Bay Area is well known for business incubators, many associated with information technology startups. What's unusual about nonprofit La Cocina is that it focuses on mentoring low-income and immigrant women entrepreneurs to jumpstart and grow their own food businesses by offering them kitchen space and technical assistance.

Enterprise Zones

An *enterprise zone* is a specific geographic area in which government tries to attract business investment by offering lower taxes and other government support. Some are known as *urban enterprise zones,* because they are located in economically distressed areas in the industrial or commercial parts of cities. In Colorado, for instance, a businessperson who locates in an enterprise zone can get an investment tax credit, a job training tax credit, a new business facility tax credit, a vacant building rehabilitation tax credit, and many other such benefits.

La COCINA
Cultivating Food Entrepreneurs

Source: Courtesy of La Cocina.

Achieving Success in a Small Business

THE BIG IDEA: This section describes five reasons why small businesses fail and gives some suggestions for improving the chances of success.

THE ESSENTIAL QUESTION: How can I avoid failure and keep my business healthy?

MyBizLab: Check your understanding of these concepts at www.mybizlab.com.

MyBizLab

"In San Francisco," wrote Scott Hauge of Small Business Advocates in that city, "it can take visits to 14 separate departments to start or expand a small business. It can take months to get the proper permits and cost thousands of dollars to meet the necessary regulations." Hauge was writing to a local newspaper to urge voter support of a local ballot proposition that would bring together those 14 departments into a one-stop shop where small businesses could go to handle most of their needs.[83]

Hauge touches on one reason why small businesses may fail—dealing with excessive government paperwork. But there are other reasons, too.

Why Small Businesses Fail

Why might my business not succeed?

Small businesses are more apt to fail than big businesses are. Often this is because they are taking more risks—selling products that are new and untried. But there are also at least five other reasons, as follows:

1 Inadequate Management Skills

Some entrepreneurs undertake a new business—opening a bed and breakfast inn, for example—without having had any actual experience in that line of work before. ⑲ Or they may be experienced at one aspect of a business—research and development, for instance, or sales and marketing—but know nothing about planning and cost control. Or, especially important, they don't manage their *cash flow*—that is, the incomings and outgoings of money.

2 Lack of Financial Support

Often new ventures are seriously underfunded and don't have the deep pockets to ride out an economic downturn or other money problems. In addition, small businesses face two other financial difficulties:

Lack of Credit. Traditionally, banks have been reluctant to lend money because new firms have no track record, although many a fledgling business has been financed through personal credit cards.

Unfavorable Economies of Scale. *Economies of scale* refers to the savings realized from buying materials or manufacturing products in large

Source: Anyka/Shutterstock.

⑲ **Bed and breakfast.** Many people have found the notion of running a B&B in some beautiful area an attractive idea. How many, do you think, are prepared for the actual hard work of operating a seasonal business that requires being constantly available and frequently coping with sometimes difficult customers?

quantities. Big businesses can buy materials in bulk, thus reducing the cost of producing each product they make. Small businesses don't have the financial clout to do this.

3 Difficulty Hiring & Keeping Good Employees

Small businesses often don't have the money to attract and keep good employees. Or employees leave because the firm is so small that there are no opportunities for growth and promotion. Some firms cope with this problem by offering employees partial ownership, as a restaurant owner might to a valued chef.

4 Aggressive Competition

An entrepreneur who takes a chance on a new business and then experiences success may be rewarded not only with profits but also with competitors entering the market who diminish those profits. Or he or she may have unknowingly or unwisely entered a market that is already full of cut-throat competition.

5 Government Paperwork

Big businesses can afford to hire specialists to deal with government permits and keep government-mandated records concerning payroll deductions, taxes, expenses, safety violations, compliance with environmental regulations, and similar matters. Small-business people can find themselves drowning in such paperwork, costing them time and money, delaying their efforts, and risking penalties and fines for missing important deadlines.

Key Takeaway 6-3
Small businesses fail because of faulty management, financing, and employees, as well as too much competition and paperwork.

How to Keep a Small Business Healthy

What can I do to help my business survive?

Staying in business means constantly staying on your toes. Some suggestions:

1 Keep Good Records & Know When to Ask for Help

At the very beginning, you should get an accountant or bookkeeper to help you set up your records on sales, expenses, payroll, inventory control, taxes, profits, and other financial matters. A computer-based accounting system such as QuickBooks can be invaluable. When something goes awry, know when to put out a call for help—to pay for a consultant. Having a good lawyer also helps.

2 Stay in Tune with Your Customers

Serving your customers has to be considered your reason for existence. Your advantage as a small-business person is that you are better able to know your customers than big businesses are and make adaptations when their needs change. The best way to keep customers happy is to sell a quality product or service at a fair price.

3 Learn How to Manage Employees

You may pay your employees less and offer fewer benefits compared to big businesses, but you do have an essential advantage: You can keep them happier by treating them with respect, listening to their ideas, and trying to make their work interesting and challenging. We discuss this further in Chapter 10.

Summary

6.1 Small Business & Entrepreneurship: The Art of the Quick

THE ESSENTIAL QUESTION: *Do I have what it takes to be a small-business entrepreneur?*

What's the difference between small-business owners and entrepreneurs who start out with small businesses? Small business in this book is one with 100 employees or less. However, the U.S. government defines a small business as one that is independently owned and operated, is not dominant in its field of operation, and meets certain criteria set by the Small Business Administration for number of employees and annual sales revenue. Entrepreneurs are business owners who see a new opportunity for a product or service and start firms that may lead to a high-growth business.

Which of three entrepreneurial types would I want to be? Entrepreneurship is the process of taking risks to try to create a new business. There are three entrepreneurial types. (1) A classic entrepreneur is an individual who sees a new opportunity for a product or service and starts a firm that can lead to a high-growth business. (2) An intrapreneur is someone who works inside an existing organization who sees an opportunity for a product or service and mobilizes the organization's resources to try to realize it. (3) An entrepreneurial team is a group of people with different kinds of expertise who form a team to create a new product. One variant is the skunkworks, a team whose members are separated from the normal operation of the organization and asked to produce a new, innovative project.

What's the difference between opportunity entrepreneurs and necessity entrepreneurs? Opportunity entrepreneurs are those who are ambitious and start their own businesses in a voluntary pursuit of opportunity. Necessity entrepreneurs are people who suddenly must earn a living and are simply trying to replace lost income.

Do I have the four characteristics of an entrepreneur? Entrepreneurs seem to have the following psychological characteristics that make them different from those who want to become company managers: (1) high self-confidence and belief in personal control, (2) high need for achievement and action orientation, (3) high tolerance for ambiguity and risk, and (4) high energy level.

6.2 The World of Small Business

THE ESSENTIAL QUESTION: *How important is small business, and what newer types might interest me?*

How does the United States benefit from small business? The statistics suggest that U.S. small businesses constitute the world's third-largest economy, represent most employers, provide more new jobs, provide more first jobs, and are often the innovators in their fields.

What are some considerations I need to know about running home-based and Web-based businesses? About 53% of new small businesses begin in the home, financed on less than $10,000. Home-based businesses cover freelance work, direct sales, customer service, transcription service, and tutoring. Using a website to build a Web-based business requires simple and reliable servers and a sophisticated economic infrastructure for making money by placing ads.

Why would I buy rather than start a business? People may buy a small business, rather than start it from scratch, in order to reduce uncertainty and generate profits more quickly. When buying a business, you should ask how the business works, how the industry works, why the owner is selling, and is the price right.

What are some reasons I might want to sell my business? You might sell to earn a lot of money or because you've been beaten by competitors, you have no interest in running the firm, or you have health problems.

6.3 Starting Up: From Idea to Business Plan

THE ESSENTIAL QUESTION: *If I wanted to start a company, how should I go about it?*

What are some ways to come up with a business idea? You might think about simplifying or enhancing an existing product, moving it from one market to another, changing the materials used in it, taking one feature of a product, or combining two or more products.

What's the logical way to prepare to start my own firm? First, you should read about business in general and your prospective business. Second, you should talk to knowledgeable people, such as mentors and members of trade associations. Third, you should get some preliminary experience.

Do I need to write a business plan? Why or why not? A business plan is a document that outlines a proposed firm's goals, the methods for achieving them, and the standards for measuring success. Three reasons for writing a business plan are it helps you get financing, it helps you think through important details, and it tends to be associated with success. To conceptualize a business plan, you need to first ask questions, such as what is the basic idea behind my business, what kind of industry am I entering and how am I different, how will I market to customers, what qualifies me to run this business, and how do I propose to finance the business. Some reasons for not creating a formal business plan are that you may need to act fast to get the business going, you may be able to get financing without a full formal plan, and many firms have done well without a business plan.

6.4 Getting Financing

THE ESSENTIAL QUESTION: *What are various ways of financing my new business?*

If I were launching a new business, how would I finance it in the first year or two? Eight possible sources of funding for a new business are (1) personal savings, credit cards, and second mortgages; (2) family and friends; (3) supplier and barter arrangements; (4) financial institutions; (5) Small Business Administration–backed loans; (6) angel investors and venture capitalists; (7) public stock offerings; and (8) other.

How might incubators and even enterprise zones be of help to building a business? Other forms of support are incubators, facilities that offer low-cost offices with basic services; and enterprise zones, geographical areas offering lower taxes and other government support to attract business investment.

6.5 Achieving Success in a Small Business

THE ESSENTIAL QUESTION: *How can I avoid failure and keep my business healthy?*

Why might my business not succeed? Some businesses fail because they are taking more risks, but other reasons are inadequate management skills, lack of financial support, difficulty hiring and keeping good employees, aggressive competition, and government paperwork.

What can I do to help my business survive? Some suggestions for staying in business are keep good records and know when to ask for help, stay in tune with your customers, and learn how to manage employees.

Key Terms

MyBizLab

Active Corps of Executives (ACE) 176	entrepreneurs 163	opportunity entrepreneurs 166
angel investors 181	entrepreneurship 164	Service Corps of Retired Executives 176
barter 181	"going public" 182	skunkworks 166
business model 177	incubator 182	small business 163
business plan 177	intrapreneur 165	Small Business Administration (SBA) 181
classic entrepreneur 164	mentor 176	trade association 176
economies of scale 183	micropreneurs 163	venture capitalists 182
enterprise 164	necessity entrepreneurs 166	
enterprise zone 182	networking 170	
entrepreneurial team 166		

Pop Quiz Prep

1. IBM used a skunkworks to bring its first Personal Computer to market in only 12 months, skirting the company bureaucracy. This is a variant of which type of entrepreneurship?

2. People who are ambitious and start their own businesses in voluntary pursuit of a prospect are considered which type of entrepreneur?

3. Why are small businesses (companies employing 500 people or fewer) called the "backbone of America"?

4. What percentage of new small businesses begin in the home, and what is the typical startup cost?

5. How does SCORE help small businesses?

6. What is a business plan?

7. Which sort of funding for a new enterprise involves trading goods or services without the exchange of money?

8. In the context of new businesses, what is an incubator?

9. How do economies of scale affect small businesses?

10. What is an advantage that small businesses have compared to big businesses with regard to employees?

Critical Thinking Questions

1. After taking an entrepreneurship class as one of your electives, you've been bitten by the bug (a way of saying you have become passionately interested in something). As a junior, you are considering leaving college to launch a business. After all, there are many famous entrepreneurs (Mark Zuckerberg of Facebook, the late Steve Jobs of Apple, and Bill Gates of Microsoft) who never finished college. What are the arguments for and against leaving school to launch your new business venture?

2. Compare and contrast the difference between a small-business owner and an entrepreneur by evaluating the types of businesses in which each is typically involved. Would you be more interested in a small business that makes you a decent living or a small business that, with enough entrepreneurial drive, might grow into something huge?

3. Small businesses fill a niche in the market by providing goods and services not provided by larger companies or by finding a need and filling it. In your community, can you find an example of a small-business owner who found a need and filled it? Discuss what is unique about this business.

4. The Internet has leveled the playing field and allowed small businesses to compete against larger ones regardless of location. As online retail sales in the United States continue to increase, is it important for small businesses to incorporate e-business or e-commerce into their strategies in order to remain competitive in the marketplace? Discuss.

5. What would you guess a "mompreneur" is? Look it up. What do you think might be some of the reasons for being one, and the benefits? Would it work for other groups too?

VIDEO CASE
Extreme Entrepreneurship: No Toying Around at Wild Planet

In 2010, First Lady Michelle Obama launched her comprehensive *Let's Move* initiative aimed at solving the problem of childhood obesity through healthy, affordable food, and a focus on becoming more physically active.[84] Wild Planet Entertainment, a toy company, has strived to align its goals to this initiative and has worked to bring physical activity to the forefront of the toy industry, according to Kim Bratcher, Wild Planet's director of public relations.[85]

The company, whose toys are distributed in more than 50 countries through mass retail stores,[86] plans to expand the options for physical fun in the toy aisle, and says that currently two-thirds of the company's new releases are movement based.[87] The company recognizes that good health greatly contributes to a child's happiness. During the product concept and design stage of its new products, Wild Planet understands quite well how play can be a major component of a healthy lifestyle.[88] The packaging on its Speed Slider, Freeze Ball, and Balance Bender products features wording like "Healthy Heart" or "Strong Body," and the company has designed each of its Hyper Game toys to align with the U.S. Department of Health and Human Service's *Let's Move* campaign.[89] Its Torx brand focuses on aim, energy, strategy, and skill, and is targeted at tween boys (between the ages of 9 and 12), for whom the company sees the value in incorporating physical activity into games. If seeing, hearing, recording and storing evidence is for the "investigator to be" in your family, the company has produced a line of toys aptly named "Spy Gear." Products include a motion-activated digital camera, an undercover recording device, and a super sleek safe (as in storing money), and a laser-pointing pen.

Its founder Danny Grossman was a former Mattel International executive (maker of Barbie and Hot Wheels) and an unconventional CEO. He was once an aggressive advocate for human rights in the Soviet Union, serving as a foreign service diplomat in Leningrad[90]—the inspiration of his popular Spy Toy line. Like most small businesses, privately held Wild Planet was financed by Grossman with savings and a few family members. The company has grown to over $40 million in annual revenues since its inception in 1993. Wild Planet is now at a point where it can use its equity to bankroll new product line ideas—and the company continues to have hit after hit.

What's Your Take?

1. Wild Planet Toys is a growing company dedicated to developing nonviolent, innovative products that appeal to both parents and kids. Why do you think the company is intent on having its toys appeal not only to kids, but also to their parents?

2. Describe the creativity and flexibility at Wild Planet toys. Do you think most toy companies (some of whom are volumes larger) have the same sort of corporate culture as Wild Planet? Give examples.

3. Review, from the chapter, the four characteristics of what it takes to become an entrepreneur: high confidence and belief in personal control, high need for achievement and action orientation, high tolerance for ambiguity and risk, and high energy level. Which would you say apply to someone like Grossman who came from a larger toy company (Mattel) and decided to strike out on his own?

4. How does a classic entrepreneur who starts up his or her own firm and sees a way to build a high-growth business differ from the other two types of entrepreneurs—intrapreneurs and entrepreneurial teams?

BUSINESS DECISION CASE
Big Love in India: An Online Group Dating Website Finds Its Place in India's Changing Social Culture

This case explores social and cultural change in India and the launch of a group dating website by three twentysomethings. Originally intended for twentysomethings in the United States, the site has unexpectedly become the largest group dating website in India.

If you're in your twenties, you've probably been on enough awkward dates—maybe a few of which have been facilitated through online dating websites. Niche online dating websites continue to grow. There are online dating websites for Jewish singles, gays and lesbians, Christian singles, single parents, farmers in search of other farmers, geeks, fitness-minded singles, single seniors, Silicon Valley executives, millionaires, Apple (as in iPod, iPad) fanatics, Trekkies (*Star Trek* and sci-fi fans), and pet lovers. It only takes "clicking" with one Mr. or Ms. Right on that first date, correct? Think again.

In 2008, three young men in Manhattan started Ignighter .com, a group dating website for people in their twenties. If this reminds you of high school, you're right. The site allows users to create groups and meet other like-minded groups to arrange mass hangouts. The site promotes itself on the basis of safety in numbers, and with some of the media attention on the danger of Craigslist meetups; some may feel safer in a group setting. Think of this too—the odds of hitting it off with someone increase. If you don't hit it off with one person in the group, talk to another, or another.[91]

The founders of Ignighter.com initially began the site for the U.S. market, and by hosting parties, putting up flyers, and pushing the site on Facebook they enticed a good number of people to sign up. In April 2009, while evaluating the traffic to the site, they noticed thousands of users being added in Singapore, Malaysia, India, and South Korea.[92] As the traffic continued to increase, particularly from India—in places like New Delhi, Mumbai, Hyderabad, and Chennai—the founders changed the focus of the site to an Indian group dating site. Ignighter.com now boasts almost 2 million users—and as many users in India are signing up in a week as those who signed up in a year in the United States. The company recently closed a $3 million round of funding led by venture partners and angel investors in both the United States and India. Ignighter was picked by TechStars camp as among the top ten best startups out of 400 entries received each year.[93]

The site works like this: Friends come together to create a group profile (much like an individual profile on a traditional online dating website). Here pictures of the group are posted, along with details about the group's interests and where they like to hang out. Once a profile is created, groups can be matched with other groups based upon specified criteria. Groups can also search for others based upon location or mood. The messaging system allows your group to send messages to another group. If sparks fly between two people once the group meets, they're on their own (the website doesn't facilitate one-on-one communication). In addition, an iPhone app that uses GPS allows your group to find other groups close to your current location. The benefit is that the pressure of one-to-one dating is removed, and these young entrepreneurs have "married" technology with real-world benefits of group activities. Would you and your friends post a group profile on this website? Is dating less scary when there is strength in numbers?

What's Your Take?

1. It's not unusual for a startup to shift gears after realizing greater growth potential elsewhere. Do you think that such a refocus is common for entrepreneurs and startups in general? Why?

2. How would you explain the large numbers of twentysomethings going to Ignighter.com in light of the fact that in India, arranged marriages have been the norm for centuries?

3. While other online sites in India are focused on marriage (matrimonial websites), what do you think the goal of the Ignighter.com users might be?

4. How successful do you think this company will be in light of the fact that the three founders have never been to India? How would you recommend overcoming these cultural blind spots?

5. Who are Ignighter.com's competitors, and do they pose a threat?

Briefings

MyBizLab Activities & Cases

Go to www.mybizlab.com for online activities and exercises related to the timely topics discussed in this chapter's Briefings, as well as additional theme-related Briefing *Spotlights* highlighting how these concepts apply in today's business environment.

In-chapter Briefing:
- Intrapreneur Seamus Blackley Dreams Up Microsoft's Xbox

Activity:
- Developing Marketable Business Skills – Small Businesses Incorporating E-Business into Their Strategies

Briefing Spotlight:
- Small Town, Big Payoff

In-chapter Briefing:
- Plenty of Fish, an Online Dating Site, Begins as a One-Person Web-Based Business

Activity:
- Going to the Net! – Using SurveyMonkey to Learn More about and Connecting with Customers

Briefing Spotlight:
- TOMS Shoes: Heart and Sole

In-chapter Briefing:
- Restoring Buildings Using Green Materials

Activity:
- Developing Marketable Business Skills – Slate NYC: Eco-Friendly Dry Cleaning in New York City and Beyond

Briefing Spotlight:
- Ecopreneurism

In-chapter Briefing:
- An Entrepreneur Buys a Blog Devoted to Funny Cat Pictures & Builds a Web Empire

Activity:
- Going to the Net! – Kleiner Perkins: The Top Dog of Venture Capital Firms

Briefing Spotlight:
- It's Not Just About Me

In-chapter Briefing:
- The Shock Brothers' Small Business—Gold Prospecting Adventures
- Chef-Owner Mourad Lahlou's Entrepreneurial Small Business—Aziza, New Moroccan Cuisine
- A Recession-Decimated Hot-Tub Maker Creates Entrepreneurial Teams to Find New Products to Make

Activity:
- Developing Marketable Business Skills – *Inc.* Magazine's Coolest Products from the 2011 Coolest College Startup List

Briefing Spotlight:
- Start Me Up

Additional Briefing Spotlights available at MyBizLab:

- BUSINESS CULTURE & ETIQUETTE
- BUSINESS SKILLS & CAREER DEVELOPMENT
- GLOBAL BUSINESS
- LEGAL & ETHICAL PRACTICES
- PERSONAL FINANCE
- SOCIALLY RESPONSIBLE BUSINESS

7

Management & Leadership

Realizing Exceptional Results

After reading and studying this chapter, you will be able to answer the following essential questions:

MyBizLab

Where you see MyBizLab in this chapter, go to www.mybizlab.com for additional activities on the topic being discussed.

FORECAST: What's Ahead in This Chapter

We consider the four functions of management: (1) planning, (2) organizing, (3) leading, and (4) controlling. We discuss the hierarchy of top, middle, and supervisory managers and how managers make decisions. We then consider planning, its benefits, vision and mission statements, and strategic, tactical, and operational planning. Finally, we discuss organizing, leading, and controlling.

MyBizLab

Gain hands-on experience through an interactive, real-world scenario. This chapter's simulation entitled Plan for Success is located at **www.mybizlab.com**.

WINNER: Apple's Steve Jobs

In November 2009, Steve Jobs appeared on the cover of *Fortune* magazine as the "CEO of the Decade." Why him? An article blurb explained: "Apple's imperious, brilliant CEO transformed American business."[1]

Jobs, who died in 2011, had been identified with Apple since he cofounded it in 1976. He was fired in the 1980s (over differences with a new CEO he himself had hired), was invited to return in 1997, and became permanent CEO in January 2000. The company, worth about $5 billion in 2000, jumped in value to about $317 billion in 2011, exceeding that of ExxonMobil.

What was the secret to Jobs's success? Said Oracle CEO Larry Ellison, "He's really in pursuit of . . . technical and aesthetic perfection."[2] Added *Fortune* writer Adam Lishinsky: "He may not pay attention to customer research, but he works slavishly to make products customers will buy. He's a visionary, but he's grounded in reality too, closely monitoring Apple's various operational and market metrics. . . . The rare pairing of micromanagement with big-picture vision is a Jobs hallmark."[3]

Jobs recognized that gorgeous design could differentiate Apple's computers from rivals' bland products, and he was intensely involved in those details. He also controlled the details of the message about a product, rehearsing "over and over every line he and others utter in public about Apple," said Lishinsky. He was careful to guard against overexposure, usually speaking only when he had products to announce. This had the effect of building a frenzy of suspense and speculation in the media that paid off in a lot of free advertising.

Equally important, Jobs had a knack for innovation and "pouncing at the right moment," as when he used his years in exile from Apple to found the computer animation studio Pixar, later sold to Disney. After his return to Apple, he launched the breakthrough iMac followed by the iTunes music software, the Mac OS X operating system, the first Apple retail stores, the first iPod, and the first iPad.

Over this period, then, Jobs reshaped not only personal computers but also movies, telecommunications, and music—as well as the worlds of retail and design. And he and Apple created billions in shareholder wealth.

Source: Kimihiro Hoshino/AFP/Getty Images/Newscom.

LOSER: Microsoft's Steve Ballmer

For Microsoft, the same 12 years was a different story. Founder Bill Gates stepped aside in 2000 and handed over the job of CEO to his longtime second in command, Steve Ballmer. At that time, says observer Daniel Lyons, "Microsoft was still the meanest, mightiest tech company in the world, a juggernaut that bullied friends and foes alike and which possessed an operating-system franchise [Windows] that was practically a license to print money."[4]

Twelve years later, Windows was still running on 90% of personal computers, Microsoft Office dominated desktop applications, and revenue had nearly tripled, from $23 billion to $62 billion. But Microsoft's stock had dropped from $120 to $24 a share, while Apple's had increased 750%. And the company was being overtaken in new markets.

Apple created the iPod, the iTunes store, and the iPhone; Microsoft responded with the Zune music player and its own new stores, but they have not caught on. Google came out of nowhere to dominate Internet search and e-mail (with Gmail) and created its own operating system, Android, for mobile devices; Microsoft brought out its Bing search engine and then its mobile-devices software platform, Windows Mobile, both of which have been overshadowed by others. Amazon.com grew to dominate online retail, started a cloud computing business, and launched the Kindle e-reader; Microsoft brought out its own cloud-computing service four years later.

How did Microsoft lose its edge? Lyons thinks that Ballmer is smart about business but is a nontechie and also was distracted by battles with antitrust regulators. The Vista operating system was released with so many problems that it took engineers three years to undo the mess. Finally, Ballmer allowed Microsoft to "become bureaucratic and lumbering," Lyons says, so that it was unable to respond quickly and catch up with new rivals. Meanwhile a new generation of Internet startups—Facebook, YouTube, Twitter—have taken root.

Ballmer hopes that the 2009 Windows 7 operating system will be a "once-in-a-lifetime reset." But in 2011, Windows' market share was starting to slip.

Source: Courtesy of Microsoft®.

YOUR CALL Management, said one pioneer of management ideas, is "the art of getting things done through people."[5] Do you think there can be many styles of effective management that can get things done through people? What if during the last 10 years, Ballmer had headed Apple and Jobs had headed Microsoft? In the end, do you think management and leadership styles really affect results?

MyBizLab

THE BIG IDEA: Managers are needed to make an organization more effective and more efficient. Management has four functions: *planning, organizing, leading,* and *controlling.* It has three levels: *top, middle,* and *supervisory.* Managers make decisions by identifying problems, thinking up alternative solutions, evaluating alternatives, selecting a solution, and implementing and evaluating the solution chosen.

THE ESSENTIAL QUESTION: Why are managers needed, what do they do, what are their levels, and how do they make decisions?

MyBizLab

MyBizLab: Check your understanding of these concepts at www.mybizlab.com.

■ PANEL 7.1 The four functions of management. As a manager, you need to do *planning, organizing, leading,* and *controlling* to accomplish the firm's goals. Although shown here in sequential order, all four functions should happen *concurrently.*

As a manager, you need to do . . .

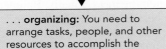

. . . **planning:** You need to set goals and decide how to achieve them

↓

. . . **organizing:** You need to arrange tasks, people, and other resources to accomplish the work

↓

. . . **leading:** You need to motivate people to work hard to achieve the organization's goals

↓

. . . **controlling:** You need to monitor performance, compare it with goals, and take corrective action as needed

↓

. . . **so as to accomplish the firm's goals.** You need to do these tasks to achieve the organization's goals *effectively* and *efficiently*

Could you run a business organization without managers? Couldn't you and your friends establish a democratically run enterprise in which everyone just pitches in, all members contribute their own specialized talents toward creating and selling a product, and all members vote on every decision?

The Need for Management: To Achieve Effectiveness & Efficiency

Are managers really necessary? Why?

Certainly democratic ways of running companies have been tried. (Contractor South Mountain Company of Martha's Vineyard, Massachusetts, is managed by 17 worker-owner employees.)[6] But imagine how long it could take to get major decisions made. An organization might stumble along for a while without managers, but eventually it will find it needs them if it is to deliver a quality product on time—that is, to achieve its goals *effectively* and *efficiently.*

- **Effectiveness—realizing goals:** Effectiveness is about the ends. **To be *effective* means to achieve results, to realize the firm's goals by making the right decisions and executing them successfully.**
- **Efficiency—the means of realizing goals:** Efficiency is about the means. **To be *efficient* means to use people, money, raw materials, and other resources wisely and cost-effectively.**

The Four Things Managers Must Do

What are the four functions I'm supposed to perform as a manager?

We defined *management* briefly in Chapter 1, but let's expand it here. **Management is the pursuit of organizational goals effectively and efficiently through (1) planning, (2) organization, (3) leading, and (4) controlling the organization's resources.** (*See ■ Panel 7.1.*)

Let's consider each of these four functions, using the example of Jeff Bezos and Amazon.com.

1 Planning: "What Are My Goals & How Do I Achieve Them?"

***Planning* is defined as setting goals and deciding how to achieve them.** In a for-profit organization, one of these goals is to satisfy customers. Thus, top executives must plan the right strategy to achieve this goal.

■ **Example of Planning: Internet Retailer Amazon.com.** In 1994, Jeff Bezos left a successful career on Wall Street with a plan to use the World Wide Web to launch an online retail bookseller. Based in Seattle, his company, Amazon.com, has the goal of being "earth's most customer-centric company, where people can come to find and discover anything they may want to buy online." The entrepreneur made two important decisions early on: (1) He decided to specialize in selling books first (and move on to other products later). ❶ (2) He decided to forgo early opportunities to turn a profit in order to build a "customer-centric" company—that is, develop a base of satisfied customers. ■

Source: Photograph by Sally Lindsay.

❶ **Box of books?** Amazon.com started out with a very deliberate plan: specialize in selling books first, then move on to other products. It also decided to work on building a base of satisfied customers. How well do you think the plan has worked so far? What major online competitors for Amazon can you name?

2 Organizing: "How Do I Arrange Tasks, People, & Other Resources to Get Things Done?"

***Organizing* is defined as arranging tasks, people, and other resources to accomplish the work.** Thus, the company must design a structure and establish conditions for achieving the goal of satisfying customers.

■ **Example of Organizing: Amazon.com.** As part of the strategy of concentrating on customers first, Bezos believes in "conserving money for things that matter," as in saving on office furniture by making desks out of cheap wooden doors atop sawed-off two-by-fours. He has also tried to create, in one description, "a decentralized, disentangled company where small groups can innovate and test their visions independently of everyone else."[7]

A great deal of effort has been put into boosting sales by making the website as customer centered as possible. For instance, beginning in 1995, Amazon pioneered letting customers post reviews about products on its site, playing "a central role in the change in consumer behavior by being the first successful Web retailer to embrace customers' views," says one account.[8] In 1999 it unveiled Wish Lists, allowing people to share their favorite products, and in 2006 it created discussion hubs that enable consumers to talk about a wider range of topics, such as yoga or *Harry Potter*. By assembling one of the world's largest collections of customer opinions, Amazon has built a website with a leading source of product reviews, which lure even more viewers to the site. ■

ℹ **Want to Know More? 7-1**

Key Terms & Definitions in Sequential Order to Study as You Go Along

Go to www.mybizlab.com.

3 Leading: "How Do I Motivate People to Work to Achieve Important Goals?"

***Leading* is defined as motivating, directing, and otherwise influencing people to work hard to achieve the organization's goals.** Leading means establishing a vision and a mission for the company and then communicating and guiding others to realize the organizational goals.

■ **Example of Leading: Amazon.com's Jeff Bezos.** Bezos's public image is as a quirky, goofy geek with a famous booming laugh. But he is the founder of Amazon, of course, and companies tend to do well when founders remain with the firms they created. The reasons: their personal fortunes are tied to the company stock, they don't usually risk long-term performance for the short, they

🔑 **Key Takeaway 7-1**
Managers pursue organizational goals through planning, organization, leading, and controlling.

know their industries, and they have learned to fight in the early years.[9] Bezos's focus on growing market share over profits has made Wall Street uneasy, and indeed Amazon continued to post net losses in the early years. But Bezos has been blessed not only with great good luck but also with boundless optimism. ❷

He also combines a contradictory decision-making style that shows a focus on numbers and spreadsheets where quantitative data really matter yet also a willingness to take nervy gambles. For decisions that can be backed by facts, "the most junior person in the company can win an argument with the most senior person," says Bezos.[10] For other decisions, those that can't be backed by data—such as whether to allow third parties to compete with Amazon by selling products on Amazon's website—Bezos relies on his senior executives, whom he often recruits from larger companies. ■

4 Controlling: "How Do I Monitor Performance, Compare It with Goals, & Take Corrective Action?"

***Controlling* is defined as monitoring performance, comparing it with goals, and taking corrective action as needed.** That is, controlling means determining what actually occurs while trying to meet the organization's goals.

■ **Example** of Controlling: Amazon.com. The business is always watching its numbers and tinkering with procedures to continue to keep costs down and extend market share. For instance, when the company's stock price declined, Amazon took corrective action by cutting costs, laying off employees, and closing a distribution center. The company posted its first full-year profit in 2003. Over a five-year period, the company's shares zoomed 245%. ■

We expand on the four functions of planning, organizing, leading, and controlling in the rest of this chapter.

❷ **Jeff Bezos of Amazon.com.** Bezos is known for his quirky personality, resourcefulness, numbers orientation, and willingness to take big chances. Do these qualities contribute to superior leadership abilities? How essential do you think these characteristics were to Bezos's and Amazon's survival and ultimate success?

■ **PANEL 7.2 The three levels of management: top, middle, and supervisory.**

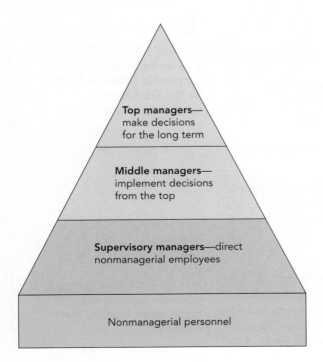

Top managers—make decisions for the long term

Middle managers—implement decisions from the top

Supervisory managers—direct nonmanagerial employees

Nonmanagerial personnel

Pyramid Power: The Three Levels of Management

What are the three levels of management?

In the traditional view of management, managers are arranged in a pyramid-like organization, with one layer sitting at the top and two or more layers of managers beneath. In this model, managers fall into three levels: *top, middle,* and *supervisory.* (*See* ■ *Panel 7.2.*) The pyramid is the classic model of management organization, but it is only one of many management models. We discuss others in Chapter 8.

1 Top Managers: Those Who Make Decisions for the Long Term

***Top managers,* the highest level of management, make long-term decisions about the overall direction of the organization and establish the objectives, strategies, and policies for it.** These are key executives with titles such as *chief executive officer (CEO), chief operating officer (COO), president,* and *senior vice president.* In 2007, the national median salary for a CEO with 500 to 5,000 employees was $500,000, and $849,375 for those at companies with more than 5,000 employees.[11] In 2010, median compensation for CEOs at 200 major companies was $9.6 million.[12]

2 Middle Managers: Those Who Implement Decisions from the Top

Middle managers **implement the policies and plans of the top managers above them and supervise and coordinate the activities of the supervisory managers below them.** Middle managers have titles like *general manager, division manager, plant manager,* and *branch sales manager.* Depending on industry and company size, annual salaries may be $42,000 to $212,000.

3 Supervisory Managers: Those Who Direct Nonmanagerial Employees

Supervisory managers **make short-term operating decisions, directing the daily tasks of nonmanagerial personnel.** The job titles in this group are on the order of *department head, foreman* or *forewoman, team leader,* or *supervisor.* Their salaries run around $40,000 a year or more.

What Managers Do: Practical Decision Making

What steps should I take as a manager to reach a decision?

Regardless of level, all managers *make decisions.* **A** *decision* **is a choice made from among available alternatives.** *Decision making* **is the process of identifying and choosing alternative courses of action.** Typically there are four phases involved in making a practical decision. (*See* ■ *Panel 7.3.*)

1 Identify the Problem or Opportunity: What's Wrong? What's Possible?

Managers find no shortage of ***problems,*** **or difficulties that impede the achievement of goals.** Technology glitches. Staff turnover. Customer complaints. And so on.

Creative managers also often find *opportunities*—**favorable circumstances that present possibilities for progress beyond existing goals.** You need to look past the parade of daily problems and try to actually do *better* than the goals your boss expects you to achieve. When a competitor's top software engineer unexpectedly quits, that creates an opportunity for your company to hire that person.

2 Think Up Possible Solutions: Brainstorming Ideas

Bright ideas are a firm's greatest competitive resource. After you've identified the problem or opportunity and determined its causes, you need to come up with possible solutions. The more creative and innovative the alternatives, the better. One way to achieve this is through *brainstorming,* **in which individuals or members of a group generate multiple ideas and alternatives for solving problems.**

3 Weigh Alternative Solutions & Select One: Are They Effective, Feasible, & Ethical?

Each alternative needs to be evaluated not only according to cost and quality but also according to whether it is effective, feasible, and ethical.

Is It Effective? A proposed solution needs to be evaluated to be sure it is effective—that is, not just "good enough" but the best under the circumstances.

Is It Feasible? A proposed solution may not be feasible for a variety of reasons: The top decision makers or customers won't accept it. Time is short. Costs are high. Technology isn't available. Company policies don't allow it. The action can't be reversed if there's trouble.

i

Want to Know More? 7-2

Why Would Anyone Want to Be a Middle Manager?

Go to www.mybizlab.com.

■ PANEL 7.3 **The four phases of practical decision making.**

Phase 1: Identify the problem or opportunity.

↓

Phase 2: Dream up possible solutions.

↓

Phase 3: Weigh alternative solutions and select one.

↓

Phase 4: Implement the solution, then evaluate it.

Want to Know More? 7-3

Are Today's Teens & Young Adults More Apt to Believe in Lying & Cheating?

Go to www.mybizlab.com.

Source: Feverpitch/Shutterstock.

Is It Ethical? At times a proposed alternative will seem to be right on nearly all counts. However, if it isn't ethical, you shouldn't give it a second look. ❸

Billionaire investor Warren Buffett is reported to have said, "When you hire someone, you look for brains, energy, and integrity, and if they don't have the third, integrity, you better watch out, because the first two will kill you."[13]

4   Implement & Evaluate the Solution Chosen

With some decisions, implementation can be quite difficult. When one company acquires another, for instance, it may take months to consolidate the departments, accounting systems, inventories, and so on.

❸ **Ethical considerations.** When making a decision about whether to go with a proposed alternative, ethics should certainly be a consideration. How often do you think businesspeople really consider ethics in day-to-day decision making?

Successful Implementation. For implementation to be successful, you need to do careful planning (especially if reversing an action will be difficult) and you need to consider how the people affected will feel about the change (inconvenienced, insecure, or even fearful, all of which can trigger resistance).

This is why it helps to give employees and customers some leeway during a changeover in business practices.

Evaluation. You need to follow up and evaluate the results of the decision. If the action is not working, you need to consider whether to give the new action more time, change it slightly, try another alternative, or start over.

We show how this process works in the following Briefing.

❹ **More customer friendly?** Based on your book-buying habits, Amazon's website will recommend similar titles of interest, a traditional service of independent booksellers. But over the last 13 years, little stores were undermined by superstores like Borders, which now has been flattened by Amazon. These events have "made people long for a little bookstore," says Anne Patchet, a novelist and bookseller. The Annapolis Bookstore & Café, located near the U.S. Naval Academy, specializes in maritime and sailing books. In the era of Amazon and e-books, is this strategy realistic?

BRIEFING / SMALL BUSINESS & ENTREPRENEURS
Jeff Bezos's Major Decision: What Kind of Company Should Amazon Be? In Chapter 6, we emphasized that the initial decisions you make can be crucial, as Jeff Bezos demonstrated when creating and launching Amazon.[14]

(1) *Determining the problem or opportunity:* After reading a report that projected annual growth of e-commerce at 2,300%, Bezos made a list of 20 products that he thought could be sold on the Internet.

(2) *Thinking up alternative solutions:* Bezos then narrowed the list of products to those five he felt were most promising: CDs, computer hardware, computer software, videos, and books.

(3) *Evaluating alternatives and selecting a solution:* Bezos settled on selling books as his initial product, owing to the large market for reading material, the low price that could be offered, and the large number of titles available. He chose Seattle as the company headquarters for its high-tech workforce and closeness to a large book distributor.

(4) *Implementing and evaluating the solution:* Amazon's website debuted in July 1995 with a searchable database of over 1 million titles. After customers found the desired title, they were given the option of ordering the book with a credit card and having it delivered in a few days. It quickly became clear, however, that books could be shipped directly from wholesalers and publishers to Amazon and then immediately forwarded to customers, so that investing in a large warehouse was unnecessary. Within a month, Amazon had filled orders from all 50 states and 45 other countries.

With the basic concept of Amazon deemed a success, Bezos and his staff then began to focus on making the website as customer-friendly as possible. ❹ ■

Source: Photograph by Sally Lindsay.

Do you think smart people, experienced people, people in authority usually make rational decisions? A peek at reality:

- **Smart people:** Doctors and nurses who attended seminars via videoconference were more likely to be influenced by the charisma (personal magnetism) of the presenter than were people who were face to face with the presenter.[15] Maybe, then, dealing with people in the real world rather than the online world leads to better judgments.

- **Experienced people:** Project managers with more than 10 years of experience were found to miss more deadlines, create more errors, and generate higher costs than less-experienced colleagues—probably, says one scholar, because "the more experience we have, the more overconfident we get."[16]

- **People in authority:** Board members from gender and racial minorities might be expected to reduce corporate "group think" (uncritical thinking), but they often don't—perhaps because they are usually from the same educational and class background as white male directors. In any case, says one writer, diversity can't always overcome the "enormous pressure to agree with those sitting around the table with you."[17]

Education, sophistication, and experience don't disqualify people from doing things that are against their best interests. So, how can you make better decisions? Some tips:

- **How can I know when it's time to make a decision?** Should you decide now or should you wait? How do you know when you're keeping an open mind or just procrastinating ("analysis paralysis")? One expert on decision making suggests the time to decide is *now* if you can answer "yes" to the following questions:[18] *Do I have a reasonable grasp of the problem? Would I be satisfied if I chose one of the existing alternatives? Would it be unlikely that I could come up with a better alternative if I had more time? Could the best alternatives disappear if I wait?*

- **How can I know if my decision might be biased?** Some biases to look out for:

  Am I considering actual evidence or hanging on to my prior beliefs? This is called the *prior-hypothesis bias.* You need to be tough-minded and weigh the evidence, not look for data to support your prior beliefs.

  Am I being too cocky? This is the *overconfidence bias.* As we said, this could be a problem for decision makers with lots of experience.

  Are events connected or are they just chance? This is the *ignoring randomness bias.* Don't attribute trends to a single random event—a one-time spike in sales, for example.

- **How can I make tough choices?** Most daily decisions are small, says a management consultant, but the larger ones, where more is at stake, can be truly painful. Some ways to make decision making easier:[19]

  Gather facts, but not all possible facts, and don't delay decision making. You need to get enough data on which to make a decision but not overdo the fact gathering. Postponing decisions about small problems may simply make them large ones. Waiting rarely improves the quality of even big decisions and, in fact, can result in losing money, time, and peace of mind or missing opportunities.

  When overwhelmed, narrow your choices. Sometimes there are many good alternatives, and you can simplify decision making by eliminating some options.

  Realize you can't always have a positive outcome. Going through a well-reasoned process of choosing among alternatives increases the chances of success, even if you can't be assured of a positive outcome.

Planning: You Set Goals & Decide How to Achieve Them

THE BIG IDEA: Planning helps you (1) cope with uncertainty, (2) think ahead, (3) coordinate activities, and (4) check on your progress. Managers shape their plans on the basis of vision statements (what the company wants to become) and mission statements (what the company's fundamental purposes are). Top managers develop strategic plans, middle managers develop tactical plans, and supervisory managers develop operational plans. All these plans specify goals (broad, long-range targets) and objectives (specific, short-term targets). Performing a SWOT analysis—identifying a company's strengths, weaknesses, opportunities, and threats—can help establish strategic planning. Managers should also do contingency planning.

THE ESSENTIAL QUESTION: What are the benefits of planning, and what is the planning process?

MyBizLab

MyBizLab: Check your understanding of these concepts at www.mybizlab.com.

All companies must find ways to respond to rapidly changing markets, and sticking with one business strategy may be a sure path to failure. As a manager, how should you meet this challenge? You could copy competitors or find unexplored niches to exploit. You could produce standardized offerings at low cost (as in fast-food restaurants). You could connect clients to other people (as with eBay). You could apply customized expertise to clients' problems (as law firms do).[20]

Whatever approach you take, all involve planning. We describe . . .

- Four benefits of planning
- Vision and mission statements
- Strategic, tactical, and operational planning
- Goals and objectives
- Assessing your competitive position with SWOT analysis
- Contingency planning

⑤ Planning. It's often hard to take the time to do, say, a five-year plan when your job is to meet the weekly and monthly objectives. But what could happen if you don't devote time to planning?

Source: Yuri Arcurs/Shutterstock.

Why Plan? Four Benefits

How does planning help a manager?

As we stated earlier, *planning* is defined as setting goals and deciding how to achieve them. When you make a plan, you make a blueprint for action that describes what you need to do to realize your goals. ⑤

You can always hope you'll muddle through the next time a natural disaster strikes, or you could try to plan for it (stock up on flashlight batteries and nonperishable food, for instance). Managers face similar choices. Should you wing it through every crisis or have a plan in place?

The benefits of planning are . . .

1 Planning Helps You Cope with Uncertainty

Don't like unpleasant surprises? Most of us don't. That's why planning for various (including unpleasant) possible events is necessary.

2 Planning Helps You Think Ahead

The product you are offering at some point may well achieve maturity, and sales will begin to drop. Thus, you need to plan beyond your present work circumstances, so that you can quickly move to the next stage.

3 Planning Helps You Coordinate Activities

A plan defines the responsibilities of various departments and coordinates their activities for the achievement of common goals—so that the right hand knows what the left hand is doing.

4 Planning Helps You Check on Your Progress

How well is your work going in an organization? You won't know unless you have some way of checking your progress. You need to have some expectations of what you're supposed to do—in other words, a plan.

The Basis for Planning: Vision & Mission Statements

How do vision and mission statements differ?

"Everyone wants a clear reason to get up in the morning," says journalist Dick Leider. "As humans we hunger for meaning and purpose in our lives."[21] An organization has a purpose, too—a vision. And the vision should suggest the direction in which the organization should go—the mission. From these are derived the organization's goals and objectives. (*See* ■ *Panel 7.4.*)

The Vision: "This Is What We Want to Become"

A *vision statement* describes the company's vision, the long-term goal of what the organization wants to become. A vision "should describe what's happening to the world you compete in and what you want to do about it," says one *Fortune* article. "It should guide your decisions."[22]

An example of a vision statement, from Ford Motor Company, is:

> To become the world's leading consumer company for automotive products and services.

Other examples of vision statements are shown at right. (*See* ■ *Panel 7.5.*)

The Mission Statement: "These Are Our Fundamental Purposes"

A *mission statement* is a statement of the organization's fundamental purposes. The mission statement identifies the goods or services the organization provides and will provide and the reasons for providing them.

■ PANEL 7.4 **Making plans.** What an organization wishes to become is expressed in a *vision statement*. Its fundamental purposes are expressed in a *mission statement*. From these are derived *strategic planning*, then *tactical planning*, and finally *operational planning*. The purpose of each kind of planning is to specify *goals* and *objectives*.

Vision statement: "What do we want to become?"
↓
Mission statement: "What are our fundamental purposes?"
↓
Strategic planning: Done by top managers for the next 1–5 years
Goals, objectives
↓
Tactical planning: Done by middle managers for the next 6–24 months
Goals, objectives
↓
Operational planning: Done by supervisory managers for the next 1–52 weeks
Goals, objectives

■ PANEL 7.5 **Vision and mission statements.**

Vision statements

- **Amazon:** "Our vision is to be earth's most customer centric company."
- **Clothing maker Patagonia:** "We prefer the human scale to the corporate, vagabonding to tourism, and the quirky and lively to the toned-down and flattened out."
- **Marriott Hotels:** "Our vision is to be the world's leading provider of hospitality services."
- **Handicrafters website Etsy:** "Our vision is to build a new economy and present a better choice."

Mission statements

- **Amazon:** "To build a place where people can come to find and discover anything they might want to buy online."
- **Clothing maker Patagonia:** "Build the best product, cause no unnecessary harm, use business to inspire and implement solutions to the environmental crisis."
- **Marriott Hotels:** "Our commitment is that every guest leaves satisfied."
- **Handicrafters website Etsy:** "To enable people to make a living making things, and to reconnect makers with buyers."

An example of a mission statement, also from Ford, is:

We are a global, diverse family with a proud heritage, passionately committed to providing outstanding products and services.

Other mission statements are shown on p. 199. *(See ■ Panel 7.5.)*

Three Types of Planning for Three Levels of Management: Strategic, Tactical, & Operational

What are the three levels of planning, and who does it?

Clear, inspirational vision statements and mission statements mark the start of the planning process. Once these are developed, it is top management's job to do *strategic planning*. The strategic priorities and policies are then passed down the organizational pyramid to middle management, which needs to do *tactical planning*. Middle managers then pass these plans along to supervisory management to do *operational planning*. Each type of planning has different time horizons, although the times overlap, since the plans are somewhat elastic.

Strategic Planning by Top Managers: 1 to 5 Years

Top managers make long-term decisions about the overall direction of the organization. The CEO, the vice presidents, and the division heads need to pay attention to the competitive environment outside the organization, being alert for long-run opportunities and problems. These executives must be future oriented, dealing with uncertain, highly competitive conditions.

Using their mission and vision statements, top managers do **strategic planning—determining the organization's long-term goals for the next 1 to 5 years with the resources they anticipate having.** "Strategic planning requires visionary and directional thinking," says one authority.[23] It should communicate not only general goals about growth and profits but also ways to achieve them.

■ **Example of Strategic Planning: Ford Motor Company Gets Ready for a New Era in Truck Engines.** To continue dominating the market for large pickup trucks, which generates much of its overall profit, and still meet new federal environmental regulations, Ford's top management decided on the major goal of bringing out a new Super Duty pickup, to go on sale in spring 2010. Its most prominent feature was to be a new diesel engine with state-of-the-art antipollution technology, superior fuel economy, and no significant maintenance required before 300,000 miles.

Bob Fascetti, Ford's chief engineer of big engines, was handed a nearly impossible schedule: 30 months, a year faster than usual. He gave the assignment to Adam Gryglak, chief diesel engineer.[24] ■

Tactical Planning by Middle Managers: 6 to 24 Months

Middle managers implement the policies and plans of the top managers above them and supervise and coordinate the activities of the supervisory managers below them. In for-profit organizations, middle managers are the functional managers and department managers. Their decisions often must be made without a base of clearly defined informational procedures, perhaps requiring detailed analysis and computations.

Middle managers do **tactical planning, determining what contributions their work units can make with their existing resources during the next 6 months to 2 years.** Often the top and supervisory managers will have a hand in developing the tactical plans.

Want to Know More? 7-4

If You Become a Supervisor, What Will Your Responsibilities & Activities Involve?

Go to www.mybizlab.com.

Source: Roy Ritchie.

6 The new engine guy. Middle manager Adam Gryglak, Ford's chief diesel engineer, and his Project Scorpion team, drew up a tactical plan to develop a new truck engine in only 30 months. This was accomplished in part by having a "skunkworks" away from Ford's main tech center and outside the usual reporting arrangements.

■ **Example of Tactical Planning: Ford's "Project Scorpion" to Develop a New Engine.** Ford normally has a strict product-development hierarchy, but diesel engineer Adam Gryglak realized he'd never meet his deadline following the usual process. So in October 2006 he put together a team of engineers and, with his boss's permission, moved them out of Ford's tech center in Dearborn, Michigan, to get away from the close scrutiny and second-guessing of top management. (This is the arrangement known as a "skunkworks," with reporting outside of usual channels, that we mentioned in Chapter 6.) He called the project Scorpion, after the heavy metal band the Scorpions. **6**

Away from the atmosphere of rigidity, Gryglak's team felt free to experiment. For instance, Ford usually forces suppliers to adapt their technology in hundreds of small ways to Ford's specifications, which means lots of reworking. But with time short, the engineers learned to trust their suppliers more, as in letting the German company Bosch work on the engine's antipollution device with minimal reengineering. ■

Operational Planning by Supervisory Managers: 1 to 52 Weeks

The supervisory managers are the managers at the bottom of the pyramid who direct the daily tasks of nonmanagerial personnel. Some of their decisions may be predictable ones that follow well-defined procedures, but others require using independent judgment.

Following the plans of middle and top managers, supervisory managers do ***operational planning,*** **determining how to accomplish specific tasks with existing resources within the next 1-week to 1-year period.**

Employees may take part in formulating operational plans, as may middle managers.

■ **Example of Operational Planning: Ford's Project Scorpion.** Some of Gryglak's engineers acted in supervisory capacities, responsible for different details of the truck engine's development. For instance, some working on the goal of increasing fuel efficiency finally led Team Scorpion to decide to build the engine out of a lighter material.

Key Takeaway 7-2
Three types of planning are strategic, tactical, and operational.

Scorpion's approach (the team approach, discussed in Chapter 8) also had another payoff: Specialists used to working only with fellow specialists became more familiar with what other engineers were up to. "We saved months by knowing hourly what the other guys were thinking and what their problems were," said a veteran engineer. "The result was that the engine fit into the truck perfectly the first time, and that almost never happens." ■

Goals & Objectives

What's the difference between a goal and an objective?

Whatever its type—strategic, tactical, or operational—the purpose of planning is to achieve a goal. A **goal is a broad, long-range target that an organization wishes to attain.** An *objective* **is a specific, short-term target designed to achieve the organization's goals.**

■ **Example of Goals and Objectives: Construction Contractors and Subcontractors.** In construction, a company called a prime contractor wins the work, such as building an office complex, which would be considered the *goal*. The prime contractor then contracts out to subcontractors the individual building activities, which could be considered the *objectives*—grading the site, pouring the foundation, erecting the steel frame, performing the electrical work, and so on. ❼ ■

Source: John Korpics.

❼ **Higher goals.** Completed in 1931, New York City's famous Empire State Building has 102 floors, representing enormous energy costs. In 2008, the building's owners began a five-year green refurbishing, with the *goal* of reducing energy use by 38% and saving $4.4 million a year. An important *objective* toward that goal: replace the existing windows, all 6,500 of them, with solar-efficient panes, as this worker is doing on the 61st floor.

Assessing Your Competitive Position for Strategic Planning: SWOT Analysis

How would SWOT help me figure out a strategic plan?

Strategic planning often starts with a ***SWOT analysis,*** **which is a description of the strengths (S), weaknesses (W), opportunities (O), and threats (T) affecting the organization.** A SWOT analysis should provide senior management with a realistic picture of their organization in relation to its internal and external environments so they can better establish strategy in pursuit of its mission.

The SWOT analysis has two parts: inside matters and outside matters—that is, a picture of *internal strengths and weaknesses* and a picture of *external opportunities and threats. (See* ■ *Panel 7.6.)*

■ **PANEL 7.6 A SWOT analysis.** Examples of strengths, weaknesses, opportunities, and threats for a hypothetical company.

Internal Strengths—S	**Internal Weaknesses—W**
Examples: Technology leader, seasoned management, cost advantages, energy-reduction technology, etc.	Examples: Outdated facilities, weak implementation strategy, missing key skills, etc.
External Opportunities—O	**External Threats—T**
Examples: Diversify into related services, compete in new markets, capitalize on complacency of competitors, etc.	Examples: Growing consumer power, government regulatory pressure, changing buyer tastes, spike in fuel costs, etc.

Toyota Takes a Look at Itself—A Hypothetical SWOT Analysis.
If in 2011, Toyota Motor Corp. were to do a SWOT, it might find the following:[25]

Internal strengths: World's biggest carmaker. Manufacturing system known for quality and efficiency. Cars enjoy reputation for quality and reliability. Toyota RAV4 top pick 4 out of 5 years by *Consumer Reports*. Toyotas perform well in dependability.

Internal weaknesses: Recalls of 12 million vehicles worldwide for problems involving floor mats and sticky accelerators drive down market share. Rust problems on frames of older Tundra pickups. Underused plants in Japan. Weak earnings forcing various cuts, as in company's famed research-and-development budget.

External opportunities: Loyal customers. Many GM, Chrysler, and European cars are not as reliable. Chance to make smaller cars for young urbanites with cramped parking spaces. Chance to be cutting edge with gas-electric hybrids.

External threats: Currency-exchange rates (yen versus dollar) reduce Toyota profits. Combined, more Honda and Nissan cars sold in the United States than Toyotas sold in the United States. Toyota buyers are getting older. Volkswagen passes Toyota in global sales. Honda and Subaru still strong. Ford brands just about caught up with Toyota in Power quality survey. Reliability of European cars improving. ■

Other Plans: Contingency

What's a contingency plan?

***Contingency planning* is the creation of alternative hypothetical courses of action that a company can use if its original plans don't prove workable.** The scenarios present alternative combinations of different factors—economic, competitive, budgetary, and so on—to anticipate changes in the environment. Because the scenarios look anywhere from two to five years into the future, they are usually written in rather general terms. Contingency planning not only equips a firm to prepare for uncertainty and even emergencies, it also gets managers thinking *strategically.*

❽ What are the odds? In a defining picture from the March 2011 Japanese tsunami disaster, this 100-foot pleasure boat wound up on the roof of a two-story building in Otsuchi. Crisis planning is a special type of contingency planning. In a world in which nearly anything can happen, how much "what if" should be realistically put into a crisis or contingency plan?

AlixPartners Creates Doomsday Contingency Plans for (Currently) Profitable Companies. For more than two decades, AlixPartners made money by leading turnarounds of companies in trouble, some of them near bankruptcy. But in early 2009, as the United States and the world sank further into recession and credit dried up, chief executive Fred Crawford started hearing from a different set of potential clients: healthy firms suddenly worried about the future. "They're not used to dramatic slowdowns in demand, to customers going bankrupt or not paying them," he said. "Some well-run companies are being snuck up on."[26]

AlixPartners is now in the business of creating doomsday contingency plans for still-profitable companies to help them cope with possible economic reversals. ❽

Managers who used to be focused on growth may be ill-prepared for dealing with flagging sales, leaning on clients to pay bills, laying off employees, and canceling product lines. But Crawford suggests that if clients have projected a 5% drop in revenues in their next-year budget, they should refigure it for a 15% drop. "Every company should be ready to pull the trigger on a plan that imagines a scenario worse than they could ever predict," he says. ■

Source: Hideo Kurihara/Alamy.

THE BIG IDEA: Organization charts represent traditional hierarchical management arrangements and show both authority (vertically) and specialization (horizontally). To be successful, managers need to develop their skills in three areas: technical, conceptual, and human.

THE ESSENTIAL QUESTION: What do organization charts show, and what three skills do managers need?

MyBizLab: Check your understanding of these concepts at www.mybizlab.com.

Prior to its merger with Southern Pacific, the Union Pacific railroad had so many fatal accidents that in 1997 the Federal Railroad Administration (FRA) sent inspectors to UP's Omaha headquarters, where they learned UP's structure seemed to discourage teamwork and communication. In fact, the top-down, military-style organization had its roots in the post–Civil War era, when executive ranks were staffed with former combat-hardened officers. "When something happened," said a UP vice president explaining the attitude of leading by fear, "you pulled out your gun and shot the guy in charge of the territory." Said the head of the FRA of UP's dysfunctional working arrangements, "They were separated from each other in a way that almost guaranteed problems."[27] That culture began to change after the UP-SP merger in 1999.

The Organization Chart

What does an organization chart show?

Though traditional, a pyramid-style hierarchy of top, middle, and supervisory managers need not be unworkable, as Union Pacific's was, and many companies are based on this arrangement. Hierarchical organizations are frequently represented in an *organization chart,* **a box-and-lines illustration of the formal lines of authority and the official positions or work specializations.** (*See* ■ *Panel 7.7.*)

■ **PANEL 7.7 An organization chart.** This basic type of chart shows both the formal lines of authority and the work specialization. (Other kinds of charts are described later.)

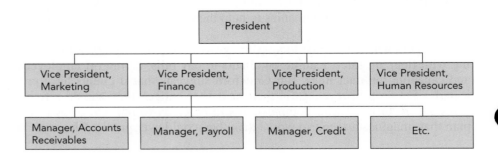

The organization chart provides two kinds of information about the company's structure: (1) the vertical hierarchy of authority, and (2) the horizontal specialization.

Vertical Hierarchy of Authority: Who Reports to Whom

A top-to-bottom scan of an organization chart shows the *vertical hierarchy,* the chain of command, who officially communicates with whom. In a simple two-person organization, the owner might communicate with just an assistant. In a complex organization, the president might talk principally to the vice presidents, who talk to the assistant vice presidents, and so on.

Horizontal Specialization: Who Specializes in What Work

A side-to-side scan of the organization chart shows *horizontal specialization,* the different jobs or work specialization. The husband-and-wife partners in a two-person advertising firm might agree that one is the "inside person," handling production and research, and the other is the "outside person," handling sales, client relations, and finances. A large firm might have vice presidents for each task—production, marketing, finance, and so on.

The Skills That Star Managers Need

To be a top-notch manager, what skills should I develop?

One researcher found that through education and experience managers acquire three principal skills: *technical, human,* and *conceptual.*[28]

1 Technical Skills: The Ability to Perform a Specific Job

***Technical skills* consist of the job-specific knowledge needed to perform well in a specialized field.** Having the requisite technical skills seems to be the most important for supervisory managers.

> ❾ **Judy McGrath.** As chair and CEO of MTV Networks, McGrath mastered the three principal skills— technical, human, and conceptual— that all managers need. Which of these skills do you think you've developed the most so far?

■ **Example of Technical Skills: Judy McGrath of MTV Networks.** Judy Mc-Grath was 26 when she arrived in New York with an English degree. After a period of writing articles for women's magazines, she was hired to create promotional material for MTV, eventually rising to CEO, a position from which she retired in May 2011.❾ MTV, which was launched as a music video channel in 1981, now comprises TV channels, websites, and wireless services. In her climb up the management ladder, McGrath clearly acquired the specific knowledge needed to function in the world of TV and digital entertainment. But technical expertise is more important at lower levels, and when she rose to the top she could rely on others for this. ■

2 Human Skills: The Ability to Interact Well with People

Perhaps the hardest set of skills to master, ***human skills* consist of the ability to work well in cooperation with other people to get things done.** These skills—the ability to motivate, to inspire trust, and to communicate with others—are necessary for managers at all levels.

■ **Example of Human Skills: Judy McGrath.** McGrath "is known for her skillful management of talent and the chaos that comes with a creative enterprise," reports a business magazine article. "Judy's ability to concentrate on people" is intense, says an MTV executive. Even as a busy top executive, she tried to listen to everyone, from interns to vice presidents, then offer advice. This approach helped foster a company culture of inclusiveness, creativity, and risk taking.[29] ■

Want to Know More? 7-5

What Are Some Examples of Conceptual Skills & Why Are They Important for Managers?

Go to www.mybizlab.com.

Key Takeaway 7-3
Managers need technical, human, and conceptual skills.

3 Conceptual Skills: The Ability to Think Analytically

Conceptual skills **consist of the ability to think analytically, to visualize an organization as a whole and understand how the parts work together.** Conceptual skills are particularly important for top managers, who must deal with problems that are ambiguous but that could have far-reaching consequences.

■ **Example of Conceptual Skills: Judy McGrath.** During McGrath's career at MTV, she showed she had the "big picture" ability to stay on top of her job. Most nights she lugged a bagful of scripts and tapes home and exchanged Blackberry messages with executives well past midnight. She networked constantly with entertainment industry executives and stars, but also read widely—everything from *U.S. Weekly* to the Samuel Beckett novel *Malone Dies.* "Judy was the only person I ever worked with who knew as much about great literature as what was going on between East Coast and West Coast rappers," a former MTV executive said. "I always thought her intuitive appreciation of storytelling and characters was an enormous secret weapon."[30] ■

How the Mix of Skills Changes as One Rises to the Top

It's important to know that *the required mix of skills changes as one rises through the organization, from supervisory manager to middle manager to top manager—* generally from *less technical* to *more conceptual.* ⑩ Thus . . .

- A supervisor needs more technical skills, a fair amount of human skills, and fewer conceptual skills.
- A middle manager needs roughly an even distribution of each skill.
- A top manager needs more conceptual skills, a fair amount of human skills, and fewer technical skills.

Source: Sally Ryan/The New York Times/Redux.

⑩ **Upward bound.** The mix of management skills changes the higher one rises in the organization. In the informal environs of Silicon Valley technology companies, it's often hard to tell managers from subordinates, as in these offices at Groupon, the online coupon firm that promotes entertainment, food, and shopping deals through its popularity with consumers. Do you have the right mix of skills to rise to the top?

THE BIG IDEA: Leaders cope with change, whereas managers cope with complexity. Three styles of leadership, ranging from boss centered to employee centered, are autocratic, participative, and free-rein. Transactional leaders are concerned with getting people to do ordinary things; transformational leaders are concerned with getting them to do exceptional things. There are four key things that transformational leaders do.

THE ESSENTIAL QUESTION: How do leaders and managers differ, and what are the different types of leaders?

MyBizLab: Check your understanding of these concepts at www.mybizlab.com.

MyBizLab

W hen you as a manager *direct* or *order* someone to do something, is that the same as *leading?* Certainly that has been a time-honored way by which managers got employees to do things. And it's still the preferred way of managing low-skill workers, such as those in farming, fast-food restaurants, and dry cleaning.

But, as the heading above suggests, leadership is really about *motivating* people. Nowadays, therefore, particularly with so-called **knowledge workers—people who work primarily with information or who develop and use knowledge in the workplace,** such as scientists, engineers, and database administrators—managers strive to empower employees. ***Empowerment*** **means employees share management responsibilities, including decision making.** This means that leading has become a much more subtle process than it was in the days when a manager could simply say "Do this!" ⓫

Source: Photo by Brian Ach.

Leader versus Manager: Dealing with Change versus Dealing with Complexity

What's the difference between leaders and managers?

Although we see the words *leader* and *manager* seemingly used interchangeably, management scholar John Kotter suggests they are different: *Leaders* cope with *change*, he says, whereas *managers* cope with *complexity*.[31]

How Leaders Cope with Change

Business has become so volatile and competitive that it's no longer enough for a company to get by on just making minor improvements. What's required are leaders who can deal with great changes by creating a vision and strategic plan and inspiring others to rally around common goals.

Leaders cope with change in three ways: (1) by determining what needs to be done and setting a direction through planning and budgeting; (2) by communicating the new direction so that people can align behind it; and (3) by motivating and inspiring people by appealing to human needs, values, and emotions to keep them moving ahead in spite of obstacles.

⓫ **Management sharing.** Danny Meyer, shown here with partners Paul Bolles-Beaven *(left)* and chef Michael Romano *(center)*, is founder of Union Square Hospitality Group in New York, which owns several restaurants, including the flagship Union Square Café shown here. Considered to be one of the best restaurateurs in the United States, Meyer frequently brings his chefs into ownership positions and empowers each staff member to do whatever is required to achieve a positive experience for all patrons. How would it change your job motivation if you became part owner?

How Managers Cope with Complexity

Today's organizations, especially multinationals, can be incredibly complex. Good management is essential, therefore, to keep them from slipping into chaos.

Managers cope with complexity in three ways: (1) by planning and budgeting, setting targets and specifying the resources and means for achieving them; (2) by organizing, creating the necessary structure and hiring the people to fulfill the jobs; and (3) by controlling and problem solving, monitoring results and solving problems as they arise.

You Need Not Be a Manager to Be a Leader

Key Takeaway 7-4
Managers cope with complexity, leaders cope with change.

Want to Know More? 7-6
What Are Some Other Leadership Styles?
Go to www.mybizlab.com.

While it's possible to be a manager without being a leader, it's also true that you can be a leader without being a manager—that is, showing the way through your own example and motivating others to do their best. Indeed, any employee can lead. In today's business most efforts are *team* efforts (as we discuss in Chapter 8): everyone has to work together to achieve common goals.

Leadership Styles: From Boss-Centered to Employee-Centered Leadership

What are three common styles of leadership?

Researchers have looked at all kinds of leaders to see what kind of *traits,* or characteristics, they have in common, but most results do not seem to be reliable.[32] Some leaders are kind and empathetic, and some are unkind and arrogant, and both types may get results.

Similarly, there are different *styles,* or ways authority is used, that characterize leaders, although no single type works best for any given set of circumstances. Three common leadership styles are (1) *autocratic,* (2) *participative (democratic),* and (3) *free-rein (laissez-faire).*[33] They range along a continuum from boss-centered leadership to employee-centered leadership.

Autocratic Leadership: "Do This Because I Said So!"

***Autocratic leaders* make decisions without consulting others.** This "my way or the highway" style tends to work in hierarchical organizations with a militaristic orientation, such as the U.S. Army or some branches of law enforcement, but it can also be effective in less formal kinds of organizations where focus and determination are important.

■ **Example of Autocratic Leadership: Martha Stewart.** Autocratic leadership is sometimes quite successful, as with style guru Martha Stewart, who built Martha Stewart Living Omnimedia with personal attention to every detail. "Whether you liked her or not," says one account, "she was meticulous and demanding."[34] It could be argued that this style allowed her to flourish in a competitive environment such as the entertainment industry. ⑫ ■

Participative (Democratic) Leadership: "Let Me Get Your Thoughts on What to Do"

***Participative leaders,* also called *democratic leaders,* delegate authority and involve employees in their decisions.** This style involves a good deal of communication—requiring the leader to have good listening skills and empathy—between the leader and the led. Although it may not increase effectiveness, it usually enhances job satisfaction.

Source: lev radin/Shutterstock. Source: lev radin/Shutterstock.

⑫ **Two autocratic leaders.** Television personalities Martha Stewart *(The Martha Stewart Show)* and Donald Trump *(The Apprentice)* also built business empires partly by exercising an autocratic leadership style. Martha Stewart Living Omnimedia is devoted to media-lifestyle products. The Trump Organization is mainly concerned with real estate and Trump Entertainment Resorts operates casinos and hotels. Do you think autocratic managers typically set and demand higher performance standards?

■ **Example of Participative Leadership: Herman Miller Furniture's D. J. Pree.** The Herman Miller office furniture company, headed by the late D. J. Pree (and his sons Hugh and Max, who succeeded him), was a pioneer in participative leadership (or participative management), allowing employees to share in decision making and profits. In 1950, employees were given opportunities to structure their workloads and comment on corporate decision making. In 1983, the company introduced an employee stock-ownership program.[35] ■

Free-Rein Leadership Style: "Here's the Goal, Do What You Want to Achieve It"

The opposite of autocratic leaders, *free-rein leaders,* **also known as** *laissez-faire leaders,* **set objectives, and employees are relatively free to choose how to achieve them.** This style of leadership is often successful with professionals such as research scientists, doctors, and computer engineers.

■ **Example of Free-Rein Leadership: Intuit's Steve Bennett.** Steve Bennett, former CEO of Intuit, the Mountain View, California, maker of Quicken and TurboTax software, seems to be an example of a free-rein leader. "We want everyone to aim for what we call True North objectives—or better short-term as well as long-term results—and we want everyone to feel enthused and connected at work," he said.[36] Thus, he told his managers to create a "psychological contract" with their subordinates, describing what is expected, how well they are performing, and what they must do to get ahead. ■

What Style Works Best?

How well a particular style works depends on the people and the situation, as well as the company's mission and strategy. For instance, autocratic leadership works well in many newspaper newsrooms—it helped the *New York Times* win several

Source: Courtesy of United Scrap Metal.

⓭ **Successful leadership.** CEO Marsha Serlin and her son Brad, chief operating officer, who head up United Scrap Metal near Chicago, practice a kind of participative leadership. For instance, before they are interviewed by the Serlins, job applicants are screened by rank-and-file employees sorting scrap metal in the yard to see whether they will fit into the family atmosphere. Brad takes his subordinates' opinions seriously and is willing to scuttle an application on their say-so. We learn more about United Scrap Metal in Chapter 10.

journalism awards.[37] Participative leadership doesn't work well with low-skill or low-motivated employees, but it does with others, especially educated professionals in small groups. Free-rein leadership works well with highly skilled and motivated employees. ⓭

Some leaders will vary the styles depending on who they're dealing with—whether it's a new employee, for example, or an old hand who knows more about a process than they do. "Some people think you either have a demanding, command-and-control style or you have a nurturing, encouraging style," says Jim McNerney, former chairman and CEO of 3M. "I believe you can't have one without the other."[38]

Transactional versus Transformational Leaders

What leader would I be, transactional or transformational?

Two positive traits of a good leader are what are called *transactional* and *transformational* leadership behaviors. One is concerned with getting people to do *ordinary* things, the other with getting people to do *exceptional* things.

Transactional Leadership: Promoting a Well-Run Organization

Transactional leadership **focuses on creating a smooth-running organization, motivating employees to meet performance goals.** Transactional leaders are concerned with setting goals, clarifying employee roles, providing rewards and punishments related to performance, and monitoring progress.[39] If the transactional leader's steady pursuit of order, stability, and performance goals sounds dull, it is nevertheless essential to a well-run organization. Several studies have found that self-effacing, diligent, conscientious types who have good execution and organizational skills make the best managers.[40]

■ **Example** of Transactional Leadership: Jacqueline Kosecoff of Prescription Solutions. The CEO of Prescription Solutions, which manages prescription drug benefits of commercial, Medicare, and government health plans, Jacqueline Kosecoff has a three-pronged approach to leadership.

The first is "coming up with the concept for a product or service to offer," she says. "And then you have to make sure that the entire team believes in that concept and understands it." The second prong is execution. "You often hear people say, 'The devil's in the details,'" says Kosecoff. "I think it's the divine." The third prong is measurement. "We measure when we're succeeding," she says. "And we also measure where we're not succeeding" and then try to fix it.[41]

Nothing about Kosecoff's leadership style or philosophy seems particularly flashy. But it has produced solid results. ■

Transformational Leadership: Promoting Vision, Creativity, & Exceptional Performance

Transformational leadership **focuses on inspiring long-term vision, creativity, and exceptional performance in employees.** It strives to promote high levels of commitment and loyalty that can produce significant organizational change. Transactional leaders appeal to followers to put the interests of the organization ahead of their own self-interests.

Four Key Things That Transformational Leaders Do

Transformational leaders act in four ways to create changes in followers' goals, values, and beliefs.[42]

1. **They Inspire Motivation by Promoting a Grand Design: "Let Me Present an Overarching Vision for the Future."** Transformational leaders offer a grand design or ultimate goal for the organization that serves as a beacon of hope and common purpose. The vision attracts commitment and energizes employees by promoting high ideals and creating meaning in employees' lives.

■ **Example** of Inspirational Motivation: Tero Ojanperä of Nokia. Tero Ojanperä, executive vice president of Finnish phone maker Nokia, has a magnetism described in a 2009 *Fast Company* article as "a cross between Andy Warhol mystic and James Bond villain."[43]

Ojanperä likes to point out that the company used to make "great car tires and also great rubber boots." Now, he says, Nokia "will quickly be the world's biggest entertainment media network." When his audience snickers, Ojanperä says, "That's okay. Laugh. That's what people did when we said we were going to be the biggest cellphone company in the world—back when we were making car tires and rubber boots."

Is magnetic and enthusiastic leadership enough to carry a company through perilous times? When the *Fast Company* article appeared, Nokia still held first place in world market share for cellphones. The following year, however, it fell to third place behind Apple and Samsung.[44] The company is now working furiously to switch its phones from its own Symbian software and run Microsoft Windows Phone software to avoid being left behind in the fast-moving mobile phone industry. ■

ⓘ **Want to Know More? 7-7**

Who Are Some of History's Most Transformational Business Figures?

Go to www.mybizlab.com.

⑭ **Transformational.** Tero Ojanperä, executive vice president of services and developer experience for Finnish smartphone maker Nokia, is considered a transformational figure. But even a company led by powerful, enthusiastic executives can find itself lagging if its business strategy is outmoded. Once number 1 in mobile phone market share, Nokia is now scrambling to climb back from number 3 (behind Apple and Samsung). What transformational leaders can you think of?

Source: Jo Yong hak/Reuters.

Want to Know More? 7-8

What Is Your Leadership Style? Take This Online Quiz

Go to www.mybizlab.com.

Want to Know More? 7-9

What Are Some of the Top-Ranked Undergraduate Management Programs?

Go to www.mybizlab.com.

2. **They Inspire Trust by Expressing Their Integrity: "We All Want to Do What's Right."** Transformational leaders model desirable values by displaying high ethical standards, even making personal sacrifices for the good of the organization, thus inspiring trust in their employees.

> ■ **Example of Expressing Integrity: Anna Roddick of the Body Shop.** The late Anna Roddick, founder of eco-friendly grooming-and-cosmetics firm the Body Shop, opposed animal testing and encouraged fair trade, environmental awareness, and respect for human rights. ■

3. **They Actively Encourage Employee Development: "You Have the Opportunity to Excel Here."** These leaders encourage their followers to grow and excel by empowering them, giving them more responsibility and challenging work, and providing individualized mentoring.

> ■ **Example of Encouraging Individual Growth: Kim Jordan of New Belgium Brewing Company.** Based in Fort Collins, Colorado, New Belgium Brewing Company gives every employee who has worked there five years a free trip to Belgium, the country whose beer tradition the U.S. company strives to follow. New Belgium also encourages employee ownership and staff participation in strategic planning and budgeting. "People are engaged and committed," Jordan says.[45] ■

4. **They Communicate a Strong Sense of Purpose: "There Are Great Challenges That We Can Conquer Together."** Transformational leaders communicate the organization's strengths, weaknesses, opportunities, and threats so that employees develop a strong sense of purpose and learn to view problems as personal challenges to be overcome.

BRIEFING / EARNING GREEN BY GOING GREEN
Nike's Mark Porter Communicates a Strong Sense of Purpose. CEO Mark Porter of Nike, who started with the athletic equipment and apparel company 30 years earlier as a footwear designer, demonstrates that "designing with both technology and sustainability in mind can transform everyone's performance," according to one report.[46] The technology—specifically Nike Flywire superlightweight shoes "stitched cable-style with threads stronger than steel"—proved itself at the Olympics.

Nike also announced its Considered initiative, which has the goal of making every pair of sneakers meet green standards (reduced waste and toxins, designed for easy recycling) by 2011. ⑮ "To us, this is a long-term commitment that will put us in a better, more competitive position," says Porter. "For example, to reduce waste, we've created this new modular design, with component parts that can be interchanged not only for aesthetic purposes but for functional purposes as well." ■

⑮ **Green purpose.** Nike CEO Mark Porter strongly communicated his desire to have every pair of sneakers meet green standards. The Air Generate MSL Men's Training Shoe follows this direction, with scrap waste from the cutting operation used for components of the shoe.

Source: Photograph by Sally Lindsay.

THE BIG IDEA: Control is needed for at least six reasons: it can help you deal with changes and uncertainties, become aware of opportunities, detect errors and irregularities, increase productivity or add value, deal with complexity, and decentralize decision making and facilitate teamwork. Four control process steps are (1) establish standards, (2) monitor performance, (3) compare performance against standards, and (4) take corrective action, if needed.

THE ESSENTIAL QUESTION: How does control work, and how should I use it to be an effective manager?

MyBizLab: Check your understanding of these concepts at www.mybizlab.com.

MyBizLab

Control is monitoring performance, comparing it with goals, and taking corrective action as needed. Thus, control—answering the question, "Are we on track?" or making sure that performance meets goals—is concerned with achieving productivity and realizing results.

Why Control Is Needed: Six Reasons

Is control really a necessary management function? Why?

There are six reasons why control is important. Control can help you . . .

1 Deal with Changes & Uncertainties

All businesses must deal with changes and uncertainties: New competitors. Changing customer tastes. New technologies. Altered laws and regulations. Control systems can help you anticipate, monitor, and react to these shifting circumstances.[47]

■ **Example of Dealing with Changes: Starbucks Changes Its Growth Strategy.** Before the recent recession, Starbucks tried to grow by expanding the number of stores (coffeehouses) in the United States. Falling short of its goals, the company decided in early 2011 to alter its strategy and try to achieve growth by selling consumer products in grocery stores, tripling the number of Starbucks stores in China (to 1,500 by 2015), and expanding further in digital media.[48] ⓰ ■

2 Become Aware of Opportunities

Controls can help alert you to opportunities you might otherwise not have noticed. Some examples: New overseas markets. Hot-selling product lines. Competitive prices on materials. Changing population trends.

⓰ **Tea or coffee?** Starbucks is betting on being able to alter the drinking habits of some Chinese by tripling the number of its stores in China by 2015. What role do you think the control function plays in the company's China strategy?

Source: Zhang Yang/TAO Images Limited/Alamy.

Source: Ted's Montana Grill.

Authentic American Dining

⑰ **Opportunity.** If restaurants are among the most wasteful energy users in the world, isn't there an opportunity here for a "people, planet, profit" approach? That is, you serve people good food. You recycle everything and employ strong energy-control measures. You make a reasonable profit. That's the approach taken by media mogul Ted Turner and his partner with Ted's Montana Grill, whose motto is "Eat great. Do good." Is this a reasonable strategy for mom 'n' pop restaurants?

BRIEFING / EARNING GREEN BY GOING GREEN

Becoming Aware of Opportunities—Ted Turner's Montana Grills Offer Green Grub. Restaurants are the retail world's largest energy users, with a restaurant using five times more energy per square foot than any other commercial building.[49] Moreover, nearly 80% of commercial food service energy dollars are in inefficient cooking, holding, and storage, and a typical restaurant also generates 100,000 pounds of garbage per year, more than almost any other retail business.

Media entrepreneur Ted Turner and restaurateur George McKerrow Jr. saw an opportunity in such numbers. Their casual dining chain of Ted's Montana Grill, founded in 2002, is designed to leave a smaller impact on the environment. In these places, "you won't find a plastic straw or cup," says one account. "The straws are made from biodegradable paper. The menus are printed on 100% recycled paper. Even the cups are cornstarch."[50]

The chain now consists of 46 restaurants in 16 states, and Turner hopes the effort will inspire other restaurant owners to think about energy use and waste. "Imagine the implications for global warming if we get the whole restaurant industry to go green," he says. ⑰ ∎

3 Detect Errors & Irregularities

Customer dissatisfaction. Employee turnover. Cost overruns. Manufacturing defects. Accounting errors. All such matters may be tolerable in the short term, but if left to fester they can bring down an organization.

∎ **Example of Detecting Errors and Irregularities: Discovering Computer Crime.** "Cybercriminals are actively probing corporate networks for weaknesses," says a 2011 account, and "businesses face unprecedented pressure to let everyone know when they've been hacked."[51] As of midyear, there were 251 publicly acknowledged data breaches, according to the nonprofit Privacy Rights Clearinghouse.

Internet hackers invade the accounts of thousands of credit card holders and steal only a few pennies from each—amounts not usually missed by the consumers but worth thousands of dollars to the hackers. Thus, security software that monitors charge accounts for small, unexplained deductions can be a worthwhile control strategy. ∎

4 Increase Productivity, Eliminate Waste, Reduce Costs, or Add Value

Control systems can increase productivity, eliminate waste, reduce labor costs, and decrease materials costs. In addition, they can add value to products or services, making them more attractive to customers.

∎ **Example of Increasing Productivity and Adding Value: Electronic Stability Control Lowers SUV Deaths.** Death rates for drivers of sport-utility vehicles used to be high (82 per million vehicles for 1999–2002 models), a significant source of concern to insurance companies. But the rates have dropped an amazing 66% for recent models (28 per million vehicles for 2005–2008 models). These numbers come from a study by the Insurance Institute for Highway Safety, which found that installing stability control—which uses brakes and engine power to keep SUVs on the road—made a tremendous difference.[52] ∎

5 Deal with Complexity

Different product lines, different customer bases, different company cultures—all are complexities that must be dealt with. When one company merges with another, these differences may suddenly become important. Controls help managers integrate and coordinate these disparate elements.

■ **Example** of Dealing with Complexity: Macy's Reads the Numbers and Goes from a Nationwide Merchandising Approach to a Local Approach. Macy's has had to deal with two incidents of massive complexity. The first occurred in 2006, when it acquired and pulled together several retail chains—Marshall Field's, Robinsons-May, Kaufmann's, and other local stores. It then tried to meld them into one chain under the name of Macy's and to harness them with a single national strategy.

But when control numbers showed the new organization losing money, CEO Terry Lundgren altered the strategy. In 2007, he changed course from a one-size-fits-all national approach to a "going local" approach, tailoring merchandise in local stores to suit local tastes.[53] ■

6 Decentralize Decision Making & Facilitate Teamwork

Managers can use controls to decentralize decision making at the company's lower levels and encourage employees to work as a team.

■ **Example** of Decentralizing Decision Making and Facilitating Teamwork: Whole Foods Market. In contrast to most retail companies, where ordering decisions are made high up, employees are hired by supervisors rather than fellow employees, and everyone's paycheck is secret, at Whole Foods each store organizes itself into eight teams, compensation is tied to team rather than individual performance, and performance reports and pay are open to all. Each team is tasked with improving the food for which it is responsible and is given great responsibility in hiring, firing, shelf stocking, and responding to consumers. The success of this approach is seen in the stock price—up from $2.13 in 1991 to $37.07 in 2010.[54] ⑱ ■

⑱ Teamwork. Whole Foods employees are organized into eight teams per store, with each team given great responsibility for performance and each individual compensated for the team's performance. If you're an ambitious go-go type of person, do you think this arrangement would hamper your individual chances of recognition and success?

Source: o44/Zuma Press/Newscom.

Taking Control: Four Steps in the Control Process

What are the control process steps I need to be aware of?

Generally control systems follow the same steps, although they may be modified to fit individual situations. The four ***control process*** steps are **(1) establish standards; (2) monitor performance; (3) compare performance against standards; and (4) take corrective action, if needed.** These steps are illustrated at right. (*See* ■ *Panel 7.8.*)

1 Establish Standards: "What Is the Desired Outcome?"

A ***control standard*** is **the desired performance level for a given goal.** Standards can be set for almost anything, although they are more easily measured when they are made quantifiable. For-profit organizations might have standards of financial performance, employee hiring, manufacturing defects, percentage increase in market share, percentage reduction in costs, number of customer complaints, and return on investment. More subjective standards, such as level of employee morale, can also be set, although they may have to be expressed more quantifiably, using measurements such as reduced absenteeism and fewer sick days.

■ **PANEL 7.8 Steps in the control process.**

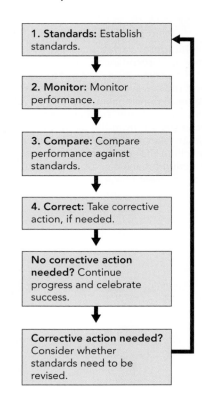

1. **Standards:** Establish standards.

2. **Monitor:** Monitor performance.

3. **Compare:** Compare performance against standards.

4. **Correct:** Take corrective action, if needed.

No corrective action needed? Continue progress and celebrate success.

Corrective action needed? Consider whether standards need to be revised.

⑲ Performance monitoring. As a boss you could sit in your office and keep tabs on the work by receiving reports by e-mail and phone. Or you could go out into the workplace and observe and ask questions—"management by walking around (MBWA)," as this manager is doing. Do you think some employees would consider the MBWA approach confrontational and the equivalent of "looking over their shoulder"?

Source: Marcin Balcerzak/Shutterstock.

Source: Andresr/Shutterstock.

⑳ Range of variation. Short for *magnetic resonance imaging*, an MRI machine uses a magnetic field and radio waves to create detailed three-dimensional image "slices" of the human body, such as the nervous system from the spine to the brain. Manufacturing an expensive machine that performs such a critical function means it's not possible to have a great range of variation.

2 Monitor Performance: "What Is the Actual Outcome?"

The next step in the control process is to measure performance—for example, by number of products sold or units produced. Less quantifiable activities, such as new patents applied for by a research scientist, may be measured by opinions expressed in peer reports.

Performance measures draw on three sources: (1) written reports, such as computerized printouts; (2) oral reports, such as subordinates' weekly verbal statements of accomplishments; and (3) personal observations, such as those made by a manager walking around the factory floor ("management by walking around"). ⑲

3 Compare Performance against Standards: "How Does the Actual Differ from the Desired?"

The next step compares measured performance against the standards established. Performance that exceeds standards becomes an occasion for handing out bonuses, promotions, and other rewards. When performance is below standards, managers need to ask whether the deviation from performance is significant. The greater the deviation, the greater the need for action.

How acceptable the deviation is depends on the *range of variation* built in to the standards set in step 1. For instance, a range of 3% to 4% error is considered acceptable in political polling, but only 0% error is supposed to be acceptable in actual voting, where there is supposed to be no range of variation—where, as the expression goes, "every vote counts." In machining parts for a high-end automobile such as a Bentley, the range of variation is less tolerant than when machining parts for a motorbike. ⑳

4 Take Corrective Action, If Needed: "What Changes Are Necessary to Obtain Desirable Outcomes?"

There are three possible scenarios:

- Make no changes.
- Recognize and celebrate positive performance that meets or exceeds the standards set by bestowing rewards—whether it's a verbal "job well done" or more substantial payoffs such as raises, bonuses, and promotions in order to reinforce good behavior.
- Correct negative performance by examining the reasons why and taking appropriate action. Sometimes the standards are unrealistic and need to be altered. Sometimes employees haven't been given the resources for achieving the standards. And sometimes employees may need more attention and direction from management.

Summary

7.1 Management: What It Is, How You Do It— The Four Essential Functions

THE ESSENTIAL QUESTION: *Why are managers needed, what do they do, what are their levels, and how do they make decisions?*

Are managers really necessary? Why? Managers help an organization achieve its goals effectively and efficiently. To be effective means to achieve results, to realize the firm's goals by making the right decisions and executing them successfully. To be efficient means to use people, money, raw materials, and other resources wisely and cost-effectively.

What are the four functions I'm supposed to perform as a manager? Management is defined as the pursuit of organizational goals effectively and efficiently through (1) planning, (2) organization, (3) leading, and (4) controlling the organization's resources. Planning is defined as setting goals and deciding how to achieve them. Organizing is defined as arranging tasks, people, and other resources to accomplish the work. Leading is defined as motivating, directing, and otherwise influencing people to work hard to achieve the organization's goals. Controlling is defined as monitoring performance, comparing it with goals, and taking corrective action as needed.

What are the three levels of management? The three levels of management are top, middle, and supervisory. Top managers, the highest level of management, make long-term decisions about the overall direction of the organization and establish the objectives, strategies, and policies for it. Middle managers implement the policies and plans of the top managers above them and supervise and coordinate the activities of the supervisory managers below them. Supervisory managers make short-term operating decisions, directing the daily tasks of nonmanagerial personnel.

What steps should I take as a manager to reach a decision? A decision is a choice made from among available alternatives. Decision making is the process of identifying and choosing alternative courses of action. Typically there are four phases associated with making a practical decision. Phase 1 is to identify the problem or opportunity. Problems are difficulties that inhibit the achievement of goals. Opportunities are situations that present possibilities for exceeding existing goals. Phase 2 is to dream up possible solutions, using brainstorming, in which individuals generate multiple ideas and alternatives for solving problems. Phase 3 is to weigh alternative solutions and select one, weighing each alternative not only according to cost and quality but also according to whether one is effective, feasible, and ethical. Phase 4 is to implement the solution, then evaluate it.

7.2 Planning: You Set Goals & Decide How to Achieve Them

THE ESSENTIAL QUESTION: *What are the benefits of planning, and what is the planning process?*

How does planning help a manager? Planning helps you cope with uncertainty, think ahead, coordinate activities, and check on your progress.

How do vision and mission statements differ? A vision statement describes the long-term goal of what the organization wants to become. A mission statement is a statement of the organization's fundamental purposes.

What are the three levels of planning, and who does it? Using mission and vision statements, top managers do strategic planning—they determine what the organization's long-term goals should be for the next 1 to 5 years with the resources they expect to have available. Middle managers do tactical planning—they determine what contributions their departments or similar work units can make with their given resources during the next 6 months to 2 years. Supervisory managers do operational planning—they determine how to accomplish specific tasks with available resources within the next 21-week to 1-year period.

What's the difference between a goal and an objective? Whatever its type, the purpose of planning is to achieve a goal. A goal is a broad, long-range target that an organization wishes to attain. An objective is a specific, short-term target designed to achieve the organization's goals.

How would SWOT help me figure out a strategic plan? The starting point for establishing strategic planning is often a SWOT analysis, which is a search for the strengths (S), weaknesses (W), opportunities (O), and threats (T) affecting the organization. A SWOT analysis should provide senior management with a realistic understanding of their organization in relation to its internal and external environments so they can better formulate strategy in pursuit of its mission.

What's a contingency plan? Contingency planning is the creation of alternative hypothetical courses of action that a company can use if its original plans don't prove workable.

7.3 Organizing: You Arrange Tasks, People, & Other Resources to Get Things Done

THE ESSENTIAL QUESTION: *What do organization charts show, and what three skills do managers need?*

What does an organization chart show? Hierarchical organizations are frequently represented in an organization chart, a box-and-lines illustration showing the formal lines of authority and the organization's official positions or work specializations. The organization provides two kinds of information about the company's structure: the vertical hierarchy of authority and the horizontal specialization.

To be a top-notch manager, what skills should I develop? Managers acquire three principal skills. Technical skills consist of the job-specific knowledge needed to perform well in a specialized field. Human skills consist of the ability to work well in cooperation with other people to get things done. Conceptual skills consist of the ability to think analytically—to visualize an organization as a whole and understand how the parts work together.

7.4 Leading: You Motivate People to Work to Achieve Important Goals

THE ESSENTIAL QUESTION: *How do leaders and managers differ, and what are the different types of leaders?*

What's the difference between leaders and managers? Leadership is really about motivating people, particularly with so-called knowledge workers—people who work primarily with information or who develop and use knowledge in the workplace. Managers strive to empower such employees; empowerment means employees share management responsibilities, including decision making. The difference between managers and leaders is that leaders cope with change, whereas managers cope with complexity.

What are three common styles of leadership? Three styles are autocratic, participative, and free-rein. Autocratic leaders make decisions without consulting others. Participative leaders delegate authority and involve employees in their decisions.

Free-rein leaders set objectives, and employees are relatively free to choose how to achieve them.

What leader would I be, transactional or transformational? Two kinds of leadership behavior are transactional and transformational. Transactional leadership focuses on creating a smooth-running organization, motivating employees to meet performance goals. Transformational leadership focuses on inspiring long-term vision, creativity, and exceptional performance in employees. Transformational leaders inspire motivation by promoting a grand design for the organization, inspire trust by expressing their integrity, actively encourage employee development, and communicate a strong sense of purpose.

7.5 Controlling: You Monitor Performance, Compare It with Goals, & Take Corrective Action

THE ESSENTIAL QUESTION: *How does control work, and how should I use it to be an effective manager?*

Is control really a necessary management function? Why? There are six reasons why control is important. Control can help you (1) deal with changes and uncertainties; (2) become aware of opportunities; (3) detect errors and irregularities; (4) increase productivity, eliminate waste, reduce costs, or add value; (5) deal with complexity; and (6) decentralize decision making and facilitate teamwork.

What are the control process steps I need to be aware of? The four control process steps are (1) establish control standards, the desired performance level for a given goal; (2) monitor performance; (3) compare performance against standards; and (4) take corrective action, if needed.

Key Terms

MyBizLab

Pop Quiz Prep

1. How is the *controlling function of management* defined?
2. Someone with the title "department head" falls under which category of employee?
3. What does a mission statement do?
4. What is the time frame for strategic planning?
5. What does a glance up and down an organization chart show?
6. Star managers need technical, human, and conceptual skills. Generally speaking, how do these needs vary with management level?

7. What is the relationship between leading and managing?

8. What kind of behavior would you expect from autocratic leaders?

9. Can a control standard be subjective?

10. What is the final step of the control process?

Critical Thinking Questions

1. The most frequently asked question about leadership is whether leaders are born or made. It turns out that maybe it's a little of both. Based upon what you know to be the qualities of a leader, what do you think? Please explain.

2. A micromanager is someone who closely observes or controls the work of his or her subordinates or employees. Micromanagement is a result of impatience and the desire for more expediency. The most common reason for micromanagement has to do with the manager's focus on detail, emotional insecurity, and doubts about employee competence. Discuss the impact that micromanagement can have on employees in a professional work environment and what possible solutions you could suggest for employees subjected to this type of management.

3. You may have heard it before—companies evaluate prospective employees, in addition to required skills and résumé, upon personality and "fit." A culture is basically the personality of an organization, and while it's hard to express, it's easy to sense whether you might fit in. Based upon your personality, what do you think would be the right organizational culture for you? Discuss.

4. The control function of management allows a company to become aware of opportunities it might not have otherwise noticed, such as new overseas markets, hot-selling product lines, competitive prices on materials, and changing population trends. For each of these opportunities, give a "real life" example of how the control function has created opportunities for a company.

5. The graduate school you've wanted to attend since before you started college has wait-listed you. As the time draws near for you to notify the other schools to which you have been accepted, you realize that your wait-list status and chances of acceptance to your first-choice school appear to be slim. What is your contingency plan, and how would you deal with this situation using some of the functions of a manager?

VIDEO CASE
Triple Rock Brewing Company Management Insist on a Relaxed Work Setting

Triple Rock Brewing Company is located in Berkeley, California, adjacent to the University of California campus. The video features short interviews with the restaurant's general manager, chef, and bartender, depicting what can result from an environment of collaborative teamwork, employee empowerment, and an obsessive focus on quality and the customer experience. Each relays the importance of their part in the planning and organizing that goes into running an efficient operation resulting in happy employees and even sometimes, happier customers.

Jesse Sarañina, general manager of Triple Rock Brewing Company, insists on a relaxed work setting. This laid-back environment is what keeps the customers coming back, and it is equally important that the employees feel relaxed while performing their work. "I give everybody the responsibility and room to relax and be themselves, and to have fun doing what they're doing," he says. His goal is for every customer walking through the door to enjoy themselves, and he feels that it starts with a relaxed environment, an outgrowth of confident and well-trained employees. From the "front of house" management, to servers, to bartenders, to the chef—the teamwork and value of the employee and customer is part of the culture. "We operate on mutual respect," he adds. His overall responsibilities involve not just managing day-to-day operations, but being acutely aware of conceptual thinking, which helps when brainstorming ideas to continuously grow the business.

Jim Humberd is the chef at Triple Rock, and he emphatically believes that planning and organizing is the key to success of the customer and employee experience. For the kitchen to operate correctly, he emphasizes, "it takes planning ahead—anticipating level of volume, how busy or slow it is going to be." On Tuesday, Humberd likes to begin planning some of the food items for the busiest day of the week, Thursday. "You must be ready ahead of time," he continues, "so it's understanding how long it takes to complete the work and have the right people in place to execute 'the service' for the day." He believes that planning ahead not only serves the customer well, but instills more faith in the staff about the decision-making process. He believes the management function of planning allows his staff (servers) to accomplish their work by having the food and tools they need.

Humberd also emphasizes the importance of the leading function of management. "A manager should have the ability to understand people and all different types of people and different types of scenarios. The challenge is to tap into each person every day." He is passionate when it comes to understanding his employees and providing them with tools to motivate.

As a manager, Sarañina expresses the uncertainty the job can bring, "with all of the many variables that come into play each day," and the skills needed to "script the scenario in my head beforehand so that I can use my experience to deal with it appropriately." This type of decision making allows Triple Rock to be proactive when dealing with the many uncertainties of running a production facility (brewery) and providing a quality service and product. The importance of making good decisions using timely information is evidenced in the video.

In conclusion, Sarañina states that "an [employee] must possess an unwavering dedication to the job." "Complacency," he states, "is the biggest killer in management. If you slide into a point of complacency, and you're there just to get a paycheck, then you're not looking out for the business and growing the business." To learn more about this company, and see their real-time "Beer Board Cam" and what their product line consists of, go to www.triplerock.com.

What's Your Take?

1. What type of management style does Glenn Pitman, the bartender, employ? Would you want to work for a manager like him?

2. What type of culture do you think exists in this work environment, and is this a culture you could see yourself a part of? What are the positives or negatives of this type of culture? Discuss.

3. Which of the three employees interviewed (general manager, chef, or bartender) has the most difficult job? Why?

4. What emphasis does Sarañina, the general manager, place on the control function and defining a standard?

5. Discuss how the video conveys employee empowerment. Can you give an example?

BUSINESS DECISION CASE
Is Middle Management as We Know It Becoming Extinct? Or Does It Need a Revival?

Is the middle-level manager becoming obsolete or extinct? This case explores the rise of instant communication technologies and questions whether the new technology has become a replacement for the general manager. Or is this just an oversimplification of the functions of a manager?

Lynda Gratton is a professor of management practice at the London Business School and author of a number of influential management books. In an article for the *Harvard Business Review* entitled "The End of the Middle Manager," she states, "new technology has itself become the great general manager." She goes on to say, "Moreover, skilled teams are increasingly self-managed. . . . There is little competitive advantage left in being a jack-of-all-trades when your main competitor might be Wikipedia." In her work, she is leading an international business consortium focused on the future of the workplace. Gratton believes that the old-school middle manager is an endangered species. So, you might ask, "What does the middle-manager of the future look like?"[55]

The case for the obsolescence of the middle-level manager has to do with the current generation of workers called Millennials or Generation Y—those born between the mid-1970s and 1999. Gen Y workers prefer not to be closely supervised. Many grew up as "latchkey kids" and, as children of the current Baby Boom Generation, they are used to making decisions on their own. (A latchkey kid is a child who returns from school to an empty home because his or her parent or parents are away at work.) This generation sees little value in reporting to a middle manager who simply tracks what they do—particularly when they feel that much of what the middle manager accomplishes can be done by themselves, by their peers, or by using technology. In the midst of automated corporate systems and controls, some come to question the value of a middle-level manager. The rise of instant communication technologies made possible through use of the Internet, such as e-mail, texting, and instant messaging and new media used through websites like YouTube and social networking sites like Facebook and Twitter, may explain the Millennials' reputation for being somewhat peer-oriented due to easier facilitation of communication through technology.[56] Millennials' preference to interact with peers and

technology is not surprising when you consider they came of age during the computer and Internet revolution.

It is not only with Millennials that technology has affected the role of the middle manager. Because the technology revolution has allowed companies to interact with their customers and employees very differently, the role of the middle manager has changed with this trend. Technology allows virtual teams around the globe to work and collaborate, thus changing the nature of human interaction and communication. But does this trend suggest that the functions of managers no longer are needed?

The idea that technology can allow those doing the "real" work to connect in ways a manager has yet to do can be seen by the middle management cuts that have been ongoing over the last decade. Cutting out middle management has larger cost savings than one might think. The savings are not only in the salaries of those individuals but also in the time and energy expended by their subordinates and upper management to interact with them.[57] It is not surprising then, that middle managers are being let go and replaced by either technology or a less expensive employee. Could that less expensive employee be a Gen Y by chance?

What's Your Take?

1. Do you agree that Millennials want more personal leadership and mentoring and less "middle management"? If you're unsure of the answer, discuss what type of leadership you would prefer in the workplace.

2. Does Gratton's research suggest that managers could be replaced with a tweet? (A tweet is a post or status update using Twitter.) Do you think this seems like an oversimplistic view of the responsibilities of a middle manager?

3. What should a middle-level manager do to deal with this perceived obsolescence? Discuss your ideas.

4. What types of technology exist to manage remote employees? In what ways can a manager use technology to be a better manager for Millennials?

Go to www.mybizlab.com for online activities and exercises related to the timely topics discussed in this chapter's Briefings, as well as additional theme-related Briefing *Spotlights* highlighting how these concepts apply in today's business environment.

In-chapter Briefing:
- AlixPartners Creates Doomsday Contingency Plans for (Currently) Profitable Companies

Activity:
- Developing Marketable Business Skills – Climate Change & Individual Energy Use
- Going to the Net! – Cash in Your Border's Gift Cards!
- Going to the Net! – Larry Page, Google Co-founder, Is Promoted from within to CEO

Briefing Spotlight:
- Big Change, Big Risk

In-chapter Briefing:
- Nike's Mike Porter Communicates a Strong Sense of Purpose
- Becoming Aware of Opportunities—Ted Turner's Montana Grills Offer Green Grub

Activity:
- Developing Marketable Business Skills – Losing Sight of a Firm's Main Focus

Briefing Spotlight:
- Four for 2011

In-chapter Briefing:
- Toyota Takes a Look at Itself—A Hypothetical SWOT Analysis

Activity:
- Developing Marketable Business Skills – Discuss Robert Nardelli's Leadership Style at Home Depot, a Global Home Improvement Specialty Retailer

Briefing Spotlight:
- A Taste for Success

In-chapter Briefing:
- Jeff Bezos's Major Decision: What Kind of Company Should Amazon Be?

Activity:
- Developing Marketable Business Skills – Interview a Small Business Owner to Learn More about Management Styles in a Small Business Environment

Briefing Spotlight:
- Managing Entrepreneurial Prosperity

Additional Briefing Spotlights available at MyBizLab:

- BUSINESS CULTURE & ETIQUETTE
- BUSINESS SKILLS & CAREER DEVELOPMENT
- CUSTOMER FOCUS
- INFO TECH & SOCIAL MEDIA
- LEGAL & ETHICAL PRACTICES
- PERSONAL FINANCE
- SOCIALLY RESPONSIBLE BUSINESS

8

The Effective Organization

Being Change Oriented in a Hyperchanging World

After reading and studying this chapter, you will be able to answer the following essential questions:

MyBizLab

Where you see MyBizLab in this chapter, go to www.mybizlab.com for additional activities on the topic being discussed.

FORECAST: What's Ahead in This Chapter

We consider the need for companies to adapt to change, the four areas of change, and three ways change is implemented. We then discuss the informal side of an organization, its culture, and the formal side, its structure. Finally, we discuss the importance of networks and teamwork in enhancing organizational performance.

WINNERS & LOSERS

COMPANY CULTURES

WINNER: Creative Adaptation at Nucor Steel

Maybe you've never heard of U.S. steelmaker Nucor Corporation, but it gained renown in the late 1980s for paying the majority of workers according to performance and for having a natural close-knit *culture*—shared beliefs and values among employees.

The payoff: when the electrical grid at Nucor's steelmaking plant in Hickman, Arkansas, failed, electricians came in from other Nucor plants as far away as Alabama and North Carolina—without being asked and with no direct financial incentive. The electricians were following team norms. They came because, as *BusinessWeek* stated, "Nucor's flattened hierarchy and emphasis on pushing power to the front line lead its employees to adopt the mindset of owner-operators."[1]

Nucor's culture grew out of a former CEO's insight that employees would make extraordinary efforts if treated with respect, given real power, and rewarded richly. Instead of following the command-and-control model typical of most businesses, Nucor executives motivate their frontline people by "talking to them, listening to them, taking a risk on their ideas, and accepting the occasional failure," says *BusinessWeek*.

Good work is rewarded—production of defect-free steel can triple a worker's pay—but bad work is penalized, with employees losing bonuses they normally would have received. Executive pay is linked to team building, with bonuses tied not just to the performance of a particular plant but to the entire company's performance. There is not only healthy competition among facilities and shifts but also cooperation and idea sharing. The result: until the recent economic downturn affected all steelmakers, Nucor was highly profitable, producing a 387% return to shareholders in five years. Following the recession, in the first part of 2011 its profits jumped fivefold.

LOSER: Dell Computer—A One-Trick Pony?

Dell Inc. became a success story through one core idea: becoming a lean, mean direct sales machine. Using the slogan "Direct from Dell," it made personal computers cheaply by being super-efficient in acquiring and assembling components and selling them directly to consumers via the Internet.

In 2006, however, sales began to decline as competitors stepped up their efforts and markets shifted away from some of Dell's key advantages. Instead of adapting, Dell stuck to its old way of doing things, cutting costs to the point that, critics say, the company compromised customer service and possibly product quality. Said a rival, "They're a one-trick pony. It was a great trick for over 10 years, but the rest of us have figured it out and Dell hasn't plowed any of its profits into creating a new trick." Even back in 2003, Dell revealed the limits of its business model. "There are some organizations where people think they're a hero if they invent a new thing," said CEO Kevin Rollins. "Being a hero at Dell means saving money."[2]

The limitations of this viewpoint were revealed in the extent to which new ideas were discouraged at Dell. Says one former manager, "You had to be very confident and thick-skinned to stay on an issue that wasn't popular. A lot of red flags got waved—but only once." Adds Geoffrey Moore, author of a book on innovation, "Dell's culture is not inspirational or aspirational. This is when they need to be imaginative, but [Dell's] culture only wants to talk about execution."[3]

Valued at $100 billion in 2005, Dell was worth only $30 billion by 2009 and the same the next year. In 2010, CEO Michael Dell scrambled to change almost everything about the company he had founded, trying to establish a culture of flexibility, customer service, innovation—and employee motivation.[4]

Source: Michael Sears/MCT/Newscom.

Source: Lou Linwei/Alamy.

YOUR CALL Although Nucor and Dell both function and compete in a hyper-changing world, their *organizational cultures*—shared beliefs and values that guide the behavior of the companies' members—are remarkably different. In both companies, the thinking of groups dominates, but in Dell's case the bias of groups has been counterproductive. If you were chairman Michael Dell, who originally founded the company in his University of Texas dorm room, what could you do to break the restrictive culture? As for Nucor, can you think of any industries and types of businesses in which the steelmaker's model for strengthening team norms would not work very well? Could struggling manufacturing companies, automakers, airlines—and certain computer makers—respond better to customers if their cultures were made to resemble Nucor's?

MyBizLab

THE BIG IDEA: To recognize the need for change, it helps to be aware of five stages of organizational decline. Four areas of an organization in which change is often needed are with people, technology, strategy, and structure. Three steps for implementing change are to recognize problems and opportunities and devise solutions, gain allies by communicating your vision, and overcome employee resistance and empower and reward them in order to achieve progress.

THE ESSENTIAL QUESTION: What areas of an organization often need changing, and how can I implement changes?

MyBizLab

MyBizLab: Check your understanding of these concepts at www.mybizlab.com.

Source: Jeff Greenbog/Alamy.

❶ IBM job fair. By 2050, there will be fewer white faces in the American workforce and there will probably be more women. In addition, more U.S. citizens are likely to be working abroad. Do you consider yourself flexible enough to deal with great numbers of people outside your own race, ethnicity, gender, religion, and nationality?

"Today's youth are coming of age in a world undergoing an unprecedented transformation powered by multiple technological revolutions," says futurist Edward Cornish. "These technological advances, all occurring simultaneously, are overturning the world's economies and undermining long-established institutions, careers, and lifestyles."[5]

Massive computing power, digital networks, huge data storage, and widespread use of smartphones and other handheld devices are upending our lives and our organizations. But technology is only one transformational factor. Others are increased globalization, major demographic and migration shifts, energy and water shortages, "green" issues, and more workforce diversity.[6] ❶

In times past, when organizations were smaller, the marketplace was relatively stable, and the stern male boss modeled the patriarchal society at large, rigid and authoritarian organizations made sense. With the present constant upheavals, the traditional approaches no longer work—and many companies have been caught flat-footed, as we describe next. The resulting failures have shown the need for organizational change in both informal and formal ways, as we discuss in the rest of this chapter.

How Do You Recognize the Need for Change? Collins's Five Stages of Organizational Decline

What are the five stages organizations tend to go through when they go into decline?

Xerox. IBM. Disney. Nordstrom. Boeing. Nucor. Merck. Hewlett-Packard. Texas Instruments. Pitney Bowes. What do such different companies have in common?

"Each took at least one tremendous fall at some point in its history and recovered," says Jim Collins, researcher of enduring great companies.[7] The former Stanford professor and author of *Good to Great* and *Built to Last*, Collins's most recent book is *How the Mighty Fall and Why Some Companies Never Give In*.[8]

Collins's research shows that institutional decline goes through five stages. The stages—which are largely self-inflicted—are as follows:[9]

1 Hubris Born of Success: "We're So Great We Can Do Anything"

Stage 1, Hubris Born of Success, begins when a company develops arrogance, or what the ancient Greeks called *hubris*—"We're so great, we can do anything!" That is, its employees begin attributing the company's success to their own superior qualities and lose understanding about the underlying factors that created that success. As a former Motorola top executive says, "Success is one of the biggest impediments to growth. It can reinforce a traditional way of doing things."[10]

2 Undisciplined Pursuit of More: "Let's Apply Our Genius to Areas beyond Our Core Business"

The hubris of Stage 1 leads to Stage 2, the Undisciplined Pursuit of More—more of whatever those in power define as "success," such as more growth or more acclaim. Here companies begin *overreaching,* making undisciplined leaps into areas where they cannot be great, taking actions inconsistent with their basic values, or outstripping their resources, leading them to ignore their core business.

3 Denial of Risk & Peril: "Our Setbacks Are Just Temporary"

In Stage 3, Denial of Risk and Peril, internal warning signs begin to increase, but managers explain away disturbing data by suggesting that difficulties are "temporary" or "not that bad." In this stage, says Collins, "leaders discount negative data, amplify positive data, and put a positive spin on ambiguous data."

4 Grasping for Salvation: "We Need a Magic-Bullet Solution to Keep Us Going"

In Stage 4, the perils of the previous stage reach the point of throwing the company into a sharp decline that is visible to all. At that point, managers may begin Grasping for Salvation. Such desperate reaches, Collins says, may include "a bold but untested strategy, a radical transformation, . . . a hoped-for blockbuster product, a 'game-changing' acquisition, or any number of other silver-bulleted solutions." Usually these don't work. "Leaders atop companies in the late stages of decline," says Collins, "need to get back to a calm, clear-headed, and focused approach."

5 Capitulation to Irrelevance or Death: "It's the End of the Line"

The longer a company remains in Stage 4, grasping for magical silver bullets, the more likely it will slip downward into Stage 5, Capitulation to Irrelevance or Death. In this final stage, the company may be sold, left to shrivel into utter insignificance, or allowed to die—go bankrupt. ❷

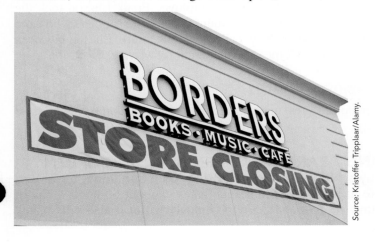
Source: Kristoffer Tripplaar/Alamy.

Want to Know More? 8-1
Key Terms & Definitions in Sequential Order to Study as You Go Along
Go to www.mybizlab.com.

Key Takeaway 8-1
Collins's stages of institutional decline: Hubris Born of Success. Undisciplined Pursuit of More. Denial of Risk and Peril. Grasping for Salvation. Capitulation to Irrelevance or Death.

❷ **Capitulation.** In July 2011, Borders announced it would close its doors and sell off its assets of books, CDs, and other products. The nationwide chain fell victim to competition from online booksellers and e-readers but also to poor management decisions—such as paying Amazon to run the Borders website, thereby depriving it of a chance to build its own digital strategy and giving Amazon access to its customers.

Want to Know More? 8-2

What Are Some Recent U.S. Business Failures & Why?

Go to www.mybizlab.com.

Organizational decline is "harder to detect but easier to cure in the early stages; easier to detect but harder to cure in the later stages," says Collins. But the scary part, he says, is that companies don't *visibly* fall until Stage 4. That is, "companies can be well into Stage 3 decline and still look and feel great, yet be right on the cusp of a huge fall."

Even so, with this kind of road map to decline in hand, Collins thinks, companies that are skidding downhill may still be able to reverse course—as did some of the famous companies mentioned at the start of this section.

■ **PANEL 8.1 People changes.** Managers may need to implement four kinds of people changes.

Changes in perceptions. Employees might feel wages are too low. Managers might be able to counter by showing, however, that the company's benefits are highly competitive within the industry.

Changes in attitudes. In traditional blue-collar industries, workers may feel that it is natural to have an adversarial relationship between labor and management. Managers may need to show why this point of view doesn't advance the interests of either side.

Changes in skills. Upgrading skills can be difficult, especially when globalization and technology can change how business is done. Will employees resist training? What training techniques work best?

Changes in performance. What incentives actually work to improve people's performance? Should a company pay the gardeners who maintain its grounds by the hour? By the square yard? By the total job? Will one way cost less but lead to fast, sloppy work? Will one result in manicured grounds but cost too much?

Areas in Which Change Is Often Needed

What four areas tend to need organizational changes?

Successful change to avert decline doesn't just happen. To make an organization perform better, managers need to initiate the change. The four areas in which change is most apt to be needed are *people, technology, strategy,* and *structure.*

1 People: Changing Employees' Minds & Performance

Even in a small organization, changes may be required in employee perceptions, attitudes, skills, or performance. (*See* ■ *Panel 8.1.*)

2 Technology: Changing Machines & Processes

A major area of change for many organizations is **technology, defined as any machine or process that gives an organization a competitive advantage in changing materials used to produce a finished product.** The technology need not be computerized, although today it often is.

BRIEFING / INFO TECH & SOCIAL MEDIA
Twitter, Facebook, & Other Social Media Change the Approach to Customer Service. Technologies that some managers once viewed as employee distractions—e-mail, instant messaging, even access to the Internet itself—have since been adopted to advance business purposes. The latest example is in the use of Twitter, Facebook, and other networking sites.

A survey of technology executives found that 54% of companies prohibit employees from using social-media sites at work. The downside, however, is that this rule could stifle the creativity of employees using these sites to help their employers.[11] Indeed, says the CEO of one technology company, more forward-looking executives "now recognize that the Web is no longer about shopping and information, it's about collaboration and cooperation."[12] In fact, Comcast employee Frank Eliason took the initiative in 2008 to use his own Twitter account to contact customers who were tweeting about service problems. Now called Famous Frank, Eliason has been credited with turning around Comcast's reputation for service. ❸ ■

twitter

Source: Courtesy of Twitter, Inc.

❸ **The Twitter revolution.** When a Comcast employee, Frank Eliason, realized that a lot of public complaints were being sent over Twitter, it changed the culture of the company, which now routinely monitors the social medium for complaints and to engage with customers. "Famous Frank" himself now has 11 people working under him simply to respond to Comcast information coming in on Twitter. In what ways could small business use Twitter?

3 Strategy: Changing Company Direction

Shifts in economics, popular tastes, or other factors may force companies to have to change their strategy.

BRIEFING / EARNING GREEN BY GOING GREEN
Best Buy's New Strategy—"Bring Us Your Junk." The Best Buy store in Roseville, Minnesota, takes in about 60 items a day of such junk as outmoded TVs and desktop computers. But it also sells plenty

of new electronics—flat-screen TVs, iPhones, netbooks—to the people bringing in junk. Best Buy began offering such free recycling at the urging of staffers and customers interested in environmental sustainability.

CEO Brian Dunn constantly monitors focus groups, social media, and websites for input. "One of my roles as CEO is to be the chief listener," Dunn says. "I don't believe that . . . there are a few really smart people at the top of the pyramid that make all the strategic decisions. It is much more about being all around the enterprise, and looking for people with great ideas and passionate points of view that are anchored to the business and connected to things our customers care about."

As a result, Best Buy has adopted the strategy of being a good corporate citizen, which includes not only offering recycling but also promoting employee diversity, monitoring foreign suppliers for worker exploitation, and offering college scholarships to teenagers.[13] ■

Source: Nick Carr/ScoutingNY.com.

4 Socially responsible. Best Buy's E-cycle massive recycling program seems to be expensive to run, but the electronics chain benefits from a reputation as a champion of green environmental policy, a focus on service, and a new way to get customers into the stores. Why shouldn't every business do this?

4 Structure: Changing the Management Hierarchy

One way to stimulate performance is to change an organization's structure. At Nucor, for instance, the recent trend is to eliminate several middle layers of management—"flatten the hierarchy"—and use electronically linked work teams. We discuss structure and teams later in this chapter.

> **Key Takeaway 8-2**
> Areas in which change is often needed: people, technology, strategy, structure.

How Are Changes Implemented?

What are three steps for implementing positive change?

If you're going to not just survive but *prevail* as a businessperson, it's important to know how to make positive change happen. Briefly, there are three steps.

Recognize Problems & Opportunities & Devise Solutions

Change begins when you recognize a problem that needs solving or an opportunity.

Gain Allies by Communicating Your Vision

Once you've decided how you're going to handle the problem or opportunity, you need to start developing and communicating your *vision*—to create a picture of the future and paint in broad strokes how your innovation will be of benefit.

Overcome Employee Resistance, & Empower & Reward Them to Achieve Progress

Once you've got the blessing of your managerial superiors, then you need to overcome the resistance of the people reporting to you. You'll need to hand out periodic rewards—recognition, celebrations, bonuses—for tasks accomplished.

> ***i***
> **Want to Know More? 8-3**
> **What Are Some Ways to Overcome Employee Resistance to Change?**
> Go to www.mybizlab.com.

THE BIG IDEA: The study of organizational culture is the study of the shared beliefs and values within an institution. The culture is expressed through heroes, stories, symbols, and rites and rituals. Culture gives employees an organizational identity, facilitates collective commitment, promotes social-system stability, and shapes behavior by helping employees make sense of their surroundings.

THE ESSENTIAL QUESTION: How does an organization express its culture, and why is culture important?

MyBizLab

MyBizLab: Check your understanding of these concepts at www.mybizlab.com.

Just as a human being has a personality—such as fun-loving, warm, disorganized, competitive, hard-working, uptight, or frantic—so an organization has a "personality" too, only it's called its *culture*. This is the "social glue" that binds members of the organization together. In order to initiate change in organizations, we must begin to understand their cultures.

Organizational Culture: A Firm's "Social Glue"

What is the meaning of "organizational culture"?

Organizational culture, **sometimes called** *corporate culture,* **consists of the shared beliefs and values that develop within an organization and guide the behavior of its members.**[14] The sources of the culture may represent the strong views of the founders, the effects of competitors, the reward systems that have been put in place, and so on. A culture can differ considerably from one organization to the next, with varying emphases on treatment of employees, teamwork, rewards, rules and regulations, and conflict and criticism.

Culture is communicated to company employees in several ways, not only through such surface manifestations as manner of dress, office layout, and slogans but also through *heroes, stories, symbols,* and *rites and rituals.*

Heroes: Exceptional People Embodying the Firm's Values

As we use the term in the business sense, **a** *hero* **is a person whose accomplishments embody the values of the organization.** The accomplishments of heroes, past and present, are told and retold to motivate other employees to do the right thing.

BRIEFING / BUSINESS SKILLS & CAREER DEVELOPMENT

Anne Mulcahy Becomes a Hero to Xerox. What does it take to save a company—and, incidentally, to realize career success? In 2001, Xerox Corporation had declined to a Stage 4 situation, Grasping for Salvation. It had $19 billion in debt and only $100 million in cash, and faced the prospect of bankruptcy. Anne Mulcahy had worked for Xerox for nearly a quarter century when she became chief executive. "Some observers," says Jim Collins, "questioned whether this insider . . . would have the ferocious will needed to save the company."[15]

They needn't have worried. Mulcahy drew inspiration from a book about adventurer Ernest Shackleton, who rescued his men after their ship was crushed by Antarctic ice in 1916. For two years, Mulcahy didn't take a single weekend off. She cut $2.5 billion from the company cost structure and closed a number of its businesses. She resisted advice that Xerox file for bankruptcy. She also refused to cut research and development, believing that long-term health depended on long-term investment in new products. Five years after she became CEO, the company reported a profit of more than $1 billion. And in 2008, *Chief Executive* magazine named Mulcahy "CEO of the Year."

What does it take to become a company culture hero like Mulcahy? (She's now retired.) Lots of determination and hard work. ❺ ■

Stories: Oral Histories about the Firm's Achievements

A *story* **is a narrative based on true events, which is repeated—and sometimes embellished upon—to emphasize a particular value.** Stories are oral histories that are repeated by members about incidents and important players in the organization's history.

🖱 **BRIEFING / SMALL BUSINESS & ENTREPRENEURS**
The Baker's Story—Giving a Six-Time Felon One Last Chance at Redemption. In 2004, recovering crystal meth addict Dave Dahl got out of prison for the fourth time. His brother, Glenn, despite Dave's having repeatedly broken his trust before, decided to give him one last chance at participating in the family health-food company, AVB (an insider joke that stands for "A Very Big") Corporation of Portland, Oregon. In August 2005, the firm introduced what was then called Dave's Bread, but sales were only modest. Then, at Dave's suggestion, the word "Killer" was added to the label. At a local farmers market, 200 loaves sold out instantly. Eventually there were 16 types of high-end organic Dave's Killer Bread.

AVB Corporation has since taken the story of Dave's redemption and used it for marketing purposes—to drive sales by reaching out to a hipper, alternative kind of consumer. The bakery designed the bread bag with a cartoon of buff, long-haired Dave playing his electric guitar and featuring his confession of finding peace after 15 "long and lonely" years in prison. He healed himself, he wrote, by "practicing my guitar, exercising, and getting to know myself—without drugs. A whole lot of suffering has transformed an ex-con into an honest man who is doing his best to make the world a better place . . . one loaf of bread at a time." ❻

Portland media began to pay attention, families of ex-cons wrote letters, and patrons lined up at supermarket demonstrations to get a glimpse of Dave. Today Dave's story has made him a celebrity, AVB sells 300,000 bread loaves every week, and the firm has $35 million in annual sales—a 1,000% increase since 2005.[16] ■

Symbols: Objects & Events Conveying a Firm's Important Values

A *symbol* **is an object, act, quality, or event that conveys meaning to others.** Symbols are meant to convey an organization's most important values.

■ **Example** of Symbols: T-5 Restaurants Express JetBlue's Values. JetBlue Airways says its brand values are "nice, smart, fresh, stylish, and witty." Embodying some of these qualities, its unusual (for an airline) 40-plus restaurants

❺ **Xerox hero.** When Anne Mulcahy was named CEO of Xerox Corporation, no one was more surprised than Mulcahy herself. "I took on this position feeling equal parts excitement and dread," she recalled in remarks to a Stanford University audience. "I certainly hadn't been groomed to become a CEO. I didn't have a very sophisticated financial background, and I had to make up for my lack of formal training. I had to make up for it with intense on-the-job learning." Do you think you could have turned around a company of this size coming from a background in sales and human resources, as Mulcahy had?

❻ **A felon's story.** AVB Corporation's Dave's Killer Bread bread bag, featuring Dave Dahl's story. Can you recall any obvious cultural stories or symbols from the jobs you've worked at?

Source: Creatas Images/Thinkstock.

7 Rites and rituals. Many companies have ceremonies to increase employee morale. In some small firms, for instance, the president takes a person out for lunch on his or her birthday. What kinds of public events honoring employees would you like to see in a business?

Key Takeaway 8-3
Manifestations of culture: heroes, stories, symbols, rites and rituals.

Want to Know More? 8-4

What Are Some Good & Bad Kinds of Corporate Cultures?

Go to www.mybizlab.com.

in T-5, the JetBlue Terminal in New York's JFK airport, feature Spanish tapas, lobster tempura, Kobe steak, and affordable organic fare. The sports bar features 48 brands of beer on tap. Occasionally $1,000 bottles of wine are sold.[17] Consumables, yes, but symbols nevertheless. ■

Rites & Rituals: Celebrating Important Occasions

Rites and rituals **are the activities and ceremonies, planned and unplanned, that celebrate important occasions and accomplishments in the organization's life.** 7

■ **Example of Rites and Rituals: Alaskan Cruises as Performance Awards.** Radio Shack has several times taken 100 of its top dealers and franchisees and their spouses on Alaskan cruises as part of the company's annual business performance award program. Cruises, it's felt, provide a more memorable experience than cash awards do.[18] ■

How Culture Influences an Organization's Members

What are four ways an organization's culture could affect me and other employees?

The culture of the organization you work for can have a powerful influence on your and other employees' behavior and thereby affect the organization's success. Four possible effects are . . .

1 Goal Understanding: "I Understand What the Organization Does"

An organization's culture helps employees understand, first, why the organization does what it does and, second, how it intends to accomplish its long-term goals. For example, 3M, the diversified technology company, sets goals stating that 25% to 30% of annual sales must come from products that are only 5 years old or less. 3M sets expectations for innovation by having an internship and co-op program, which provides 30% of the company's new college hires.[19]

2 Organizational Identity: "I Know What the Company Wants to Do"

Well known for making Post-it notes, 3M traditionally built innovation into its culture, encouraging experimentation, allowing mistakes, and prohibiting destructive criticism. Employees were allowed to operate with a lot of autonomy, spending up to 15% of their time pursuing personal research interests.[20] The result was a culture that produced many hit products, including masking tape, Scotchgard, and optical films for coating computer screens.

3 Collective Commitment: "I'm Proud to Be Part of This Company"

One of 3M's proclaimed values is to be "a company that employees are proud to be part of." Thus, one manager says he has stayed for 27 years "because, quite frankly, there's no reason to leave. I've had great opportunities to do different jobs and to grow a career. It's just a great company." 3M's culture of collective commitment has resulted in less than 3% turnover among salaried employees.

When you begin a new job, you should go into it with a sense of urgency and make the first 60 days count. Things to do:[21]

Make a Good First Impression— in Seven Seconds

Fox News CEO Roger Ailes believes that the period in which to make a good first impression is in the first seven seconds, when people are already starting to make up their minds about you. This is the period when you need to "amp it up." "When meeting someone for the first time, concentrate on one thing: your energy level," he says. "If you don't demonstrate energetic attitude on your first day, you're already screwing up."[22] Be warm and open, which makes you look strong and unafraid.

Be Pleasant to Be Around

"Be enjoyable to be around," says one career coach. "People prefer to work with those who make their lives more pleasant. They'll often prefer a likable person even over a more competent one."[23] Indeed, you should be nice to everyone, even when it's not expedient.

Get to Know People and Learn about the Organization

During the initial days, introduce yourself to a few new people and try to have lunch with them. Learn how the organization works, what the boss is like, what the company's culture encourages and discourages. Your role here is not to charm people but to listen.

Make It Easy for Others to Give You Feedback

Ask your boss, coworkers, and subordinates to give you feedback about how you're doing. Be prepared to take unpleasant news gracefully. "Don't get defensive," advises Lois P. Frankel, author of *Overcoming Your Strengths*. "It's not other people's job to tell you how to correct your performance."[24] At the end of 30 days, have a meeting with your boss to find out how you're doing. And review how your job differs from the initial job description and what opportunities you might pursue.

Learn How to "Manage Upward"

"It's not what your manager can do for you," says Mark Tutton in *CNN.com*, "but what you can do for your manager."[25] Better still, anticipate what your boss needs, don't ask. Be self-sufficient and respectful of your boss's time.[26] If he or she is a bad boss given to verbal attacks or unwarranted criticism, learn to not react strongly to the annoying behavior, to remind yourself that "it's not about you."[27]

Get Something Done

Performance reviews for new hires generally take place at 60 to 90 days, so be sure to have accomplished enough to show your boss your potential. Cure your perfectionism and overcome procrastination. Pick projects that are neither too complex nor too easy.

4 Social-System Stability: "I Feel I'm Treated Fairly Here"

Social systems within organizations are more stable when conflict and change are managed so that employees feel they are in a positive work environment. At 3M, social stability is encouraged via such methods as promoting from within and hiring capable college graduates.

THE BIG IDEA: The six basic structural characteristics of an organization are (1) authority, accountability, and responsibility; (2) division of labor; (3) hierarchy of authority; (4) span of control; (5) delegation; and (6) centralization versus decentralization of authority.

THE ESSENTIAL QUESTION: What are six characteristics of an organization's structure?

MyBizLab: Check your understanding of these concepts at www.mybizlab.com.

The understanding in the military that "Taps" will be played at a veteran's funeral is a matter of *culture,* an informal aspect of an organization. The understanding that junior officers report to senior officers is a matter of *structure,* a formal aspect of an organization. To effect change in organizations, you need to understand both their informal and their formal aspects.

Organizational structures have several characteristics, as follows:

1 Authority, Accountability, & Responsibility

How are these three characteristics defined?

Authority has to do not with a manager's personality but with his or her defined place in the organization. With authority goes accountability and responsibility.

Authority: Making Decisions & Giving Orders to Subordinates

Authority **is the legitimacy an organization confers on managers in their power to make decisions, give orders, and utilize resources.** If you're serving in the military, it's expected that you will obey orders or else risk court martial and imprisonment. In civilian organizations, you are still expected to accept that a higher-level manager has a legitimate right to give orders, but the consequences of disobeying are less serious—you're risking merely being demoted or fired.

Accountability: Reporting & Justifying Results to Superiors

Managers are given authority because they are held accountable for getting things done. *Accountability* **means managers must report and justify their work results to managers above them.**

Responsibility: Obligation to Perform Assigned Tasks

With managerial authority goes responsibility. *Responsibility* **is the obligation to perform the tasks assigned to you.** As a low-level hamburger flipper, you have little authority but also little responsibility—just keep cooking those burgers. A manager, however, has greater responsibilities.

Sometimes managers aren't given enough authority to accomplish their responsibilities, making their jobs quite difficult. At other times, managers are given a lot of authority but not enough responsibility, so that they may become dictatorial and even abusive toward their employees.

2 Division of Labor: Work Specialization

How is division of labor defined?

***Division of labor,* or *work specialization,* means that different parts of a task are done by different people.** With division of labor, specialists can perform the different parts of complex work, resulting in greater efficiency. ❽ Even a husband-and-wife patio-building firm could have work specialization. The wife, for instance, might handle marketing and financial matters, and the husband might direct construction crews—or the roles might be reversed.

Source: joyfull/Shutterstock.

❽ **Division of labor.** The people who work in fancy restaurants, such as sous chefs, pastry chefs, and wine stewards, are usually trained to perform specialized tasks. If you were starting up your own upscale restaurant, which key skills would you feel confident you could do yourself? If hiring a head chef, what skills would be essential?

3 Hierarchy of Authority: The Chain of Command

What is the hierarchy of authority?

The *hierarchy of authority,* or *chain of command,* is an arrangement for making sure that work specialization produces the right result—that the right people do the right things at the right time.

To get a particular task done, there must be managers, people with the authority to direct the work of others. Without levels of authority—president, vice president, assistant vice president, and so on—managers would have to consult with all the people in their areas, making it difficult to get anything done.

4 Span of Control: Narrow versus Wide

How do narrow and wide spans of control differ?

The *span of control* refers to the number of people reporting to a particular manager. It is exercised in two forms, *narrow* and *wide.*

Narrow Span of Control: Manager Has Few People Reporting

A *narrow span of control* means a limited number of people are reporting to a manager. Two vice presidents reporting to a president is an example of narrow span of control. When an organization has many levels with narrow spans of control, we say that it is *tall.*

In general, when managers must be closely involved with their subordinates, as when the management duties are complex, they are advised to have a narrow span of control. This is why presidents tend to have only a handful of vice presidents reporting to them.

Wide Span of Control: Manager Has Many People Reporting

A *wide span of control* means several people are reporting to a manager. A president who has nine vice presidents reporting to him or her would be an example of a wide span of control. Supervisory managers directing subordinates with similar work tasks may tend to have a wide span of control.

Today's management style tends to emphasize lean management staffs and more efficiency, which means that spans of control need to be as wide as possible while still providing adequate supervision. Wider spans also fit in with the trend toward allowing workers greater autonomy in decision making. An organization with only a few levels with wide spans of control is said to be *flat.*

The benefits and drawbacks of narrow versus wide spans of control are shown below. (*See* ■ *Panel 8.2.*)

■ PANEL 8.2 **Narrow and wide spans of control: benefits and drawbacks.**

	Narrow span of control	Wide span of control
Benefits	More managerial control	More employee freedom to make decisions
	Closer supervision	More responsiveness to customers
	Greater specialization	Faster decision making
Drawbacks	Less employee freedom to make decisions	Less managerial control and input
	Less responsiveness to customers	Loss of supervision
	Delayed decision making	Less specialization

ⓘ

Want to Know More? 8-5
How Well Do You Delegate?
Go to www.mybizlab.com.

5 Delegation: Line versus Staff Positions

How can I tell line from staff positions?

***Delegation* is the process of assigning work to subordinates.** The purpose of delegation is to allow managers to become more efficient by giving some of their work to others. A surprising number of managers fail to realize that delegation is an important part of their job, and so they tend to take on too much work for themselves.

Regarding the delegation of authority and responsibility, organization charts distinguish between two positions, *line* (solid line) and *staff* (dashed line). (*See* ■ *Panel 8.3.*)

■ PANEL 8.3 **Line and staff.** Line positions are identified with solid lines, staff positions with dashed lines.

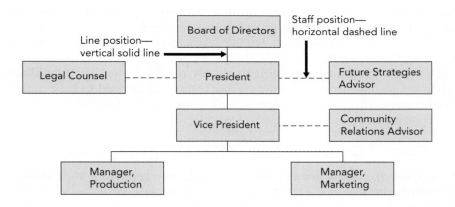

Line Positions: Jobs That Have Decision-Making Authority

***Line managers* are involved directly in an organization's goals, have authority to make decisions, and usually have people reporting to them.** Examples of line managers are the president, the vice presidents, the director of human resources, and the head of accounting and finance. Line positions are indicated on an organization chart by a *solid line*—usually a vertical line.

There are many reasons why managers fail to delegate. An excessive need for perfection. A fear that others will think them lazy. A wish to keep the fun parts of the job. A belief that only they should handle "special," "difficult," or "unusual" matters. A reluctance to let subordinates take risks or fear that they won't deliver. A concern that the subordinates will show them up by doing a better job.

However, to accomplish more, you must do *less,* not do everything faster. Managers who find themselves often behind, always taking work home, doing their subordinates' work for them, and constantly having to give employees approval before they can act are clearly not delegating well. How do you decide when to delegate and when not to? Here are dos and don'ts:

- **Do Delegate Routine and Technical Matters:** Try to let subordinates do the routine tasks and paperwork. Try to let experts handle technical matters.
- **Do Match the Tasks Delegated to Your Subordinates' Skills and Abilities and Help Them Grow:** Try to make your assignments appropriate to the training, talent, skills, and motivation of your employees, all the while recognizing that delegation involves some risk that things won't always get done to your satisfaction. When possible, let subordinates solve their own problems and try new things that will help them grow in their jobs.
- **Don't Delegate Emergencies or Confidential or Personnel Matters:** By definition, an emergency is a crisis for which there is little time for solution, and you should handle this yourself. Also you should handle any tasks that are confidential or that involve the evaluation, discipline, or counseling of subordinates.
- **Don't Delegate Special Tasks That Your Boss Asked You to Do—Unless You Have His or Her Okay:** If your supervisor gives you a special assignment, such as attending a particular meeting, don't delegate it unless you have permission to do so.

Staff Positions: Jobs That Are Advisory

Staff personnel **have advisory duties; they provide advice, recommendations, and research to line managers.** Examples of staff people are legal counsels, strategic planning advisors, and other specialists. Staff positions are indicated on the organization chart by a *dashed* or *dotted line*—usually a horizontal line.

6 Centralization versus Decentralization of Authority

How do centralization and decentralization differ?

The matter of centralization versus decentralization of authority is concerned with the question: who makes the important decisions in an organization?

Centralized Authority: Big Decisions Made by Higher Managers

When important decisions are made by higher-level managers, that is called *centralized authority.* Nearly all organizations, no matter what their size, have at least some authority concentrated at the top of the hierarchy. Lots of big firms are centralized, but small firms—those with fewer than 100 employees—are likely to be the most centralized. ❾

❾ **Centralized authority.** Most of us have experience with McDonald's only at the retail level, but the company itself operates with top-down centralization of authority, which includes its operation of Hamburger University, its management training center in Oak Brook, Illinois. Centralized authority is important because the principal contributor to McDonald's success is its insistence on standardization and uniform procedures. What would the company be like if it flattened its hierarchy and dispersed authority?

Source: Used with permission from McDonald's Corporation.

Decentralized Authority: Big Decisions Made by Lower Managers

When decisions are made by middle-level and supervisory-level managers, that is called *decentralized authority.* Here, obviously, power has been delegated throughout the organization.

BRIEFING / A WORLD OF CONSTANT CHANGE

Cisco's Failed Experiment of 48 Decentralized "Management Councils." Cisco Systems, $36 billion maker of telecommunications gear, tried an ambitious expansion into 30 different markets simultaneously, from Flip video cameras to multimillion-dollar data centers. To do this, in 2005 CEO John Chambers put in place an unusual management system of 48 interlocking "councils," so managers could make decisions without having to wait for his approval.[28] The hope was to spur cooperation among units.

Did it work? Apparently not. Instead, the council-based structure created a slow-moving bureaucracy. "By requiring employees to petition groups of people for department budgets, the councils slowed decision making," says one account. "It left managers without full control of units."[29] The company now has just three management councils. ∎

The benefits and drawbacks of centralization versus decentralization are shown below. (*See* ∎ *Panel 8.4.*)

∎ PANEL 8.4 **Centralization and decentralization: benefits and drawbacks.**

	Centralization	Decentralization
Benefits		
	More control by top management	More decision autonomy by lower managers
	Less duplication of effort	Faster decision making
	More efficient procedures	More responsiveness to customers
	Greater specialization	Higher employee morale
Drawbacks		
	Less decision authority by lower managers	Less control by top management
	Delayed decision making	More duplication of effort
	Less responsiveness to customers	Fewer streamlined procedures
	Lower employee morale	Less specialization

THE BIG IDEA: Organizations can be arranged into four basic types of structures: functional, divisional, hybrid, and matrix.

THE ESSENTIAL QUESTION: How would I describe the four main types of organizational structures?

MyBizLab: Check your understanding of these concepts at www.mybizlab.com.

MyBizLab

The characteristics just described are used to form some sort of organizational structure made up of various *departments*. **Departmentalization is the dividing up of an organization into smaller units, or departments, to facilitate management.** There are four principal departmental arrangements: (1) *functional,* (2) *divisional,* (3) *hybrid,* and (4) *matrix.*

1 Functional Structure: Grouping by Occupational Specialties

What is a functional structure?

In a *functional division,* **people performing similar activities or occupational specialties are put together in formal groups,** such as production, marketing, and similar departments, each headed by a vice president (VP), who reports to the company's president. (*See ▪ Panel 8.5.*)

This arrangement has many benefits, which is why so many companies use it, but it also has some drawbacks. (*See ▪ Panel 8.6.*)

▪ **PANEL 8.5** Functional divisions: arrangements by occupational specialties.

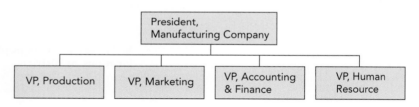

▪ **PANEL 8.6** Functional departmentalization: benefits and drawbacks.

Benefits	Drawbacks
Workers grouped by specialization—e.g., skill or resource use	Employees in a department may tend to think alike
Specialization saves costs, improves efficiency	Employees may become narrow specialists
Employees able to develop skills in depth	Department's priorities may be put before firm's priorities
Resources and expertise centralized in one place	Departments may not communicate well with one another
Specialists can easily coordinate within the department	Company may respond less quickly to outside changes
Management able to more easily direct department activities	Development of well-rounded managers more difficult

2 Divisional Structure: Grouping by Purpose

What are five types of divisional structures?

In a *divisional structure,* employees are grouped by purpose: customer groups, geographic regions, work processes, products, or industries.

Customer Divisions: Grouping by Common Customers or Customer Groups

Customer divisions group activities around common customers or customer groups. For instance, an insurance company might be structured with divisions for serving customers in need of different kinds of insurance. (*See* ■ *Panel 8.7.*)

■ PANEL 8.7 **Customer divisions: arrangements by customer groups.**

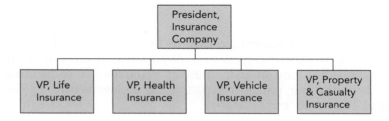

Geographic Divisions: Grouping by Regional Sites or Areas

Geographic divisions group activities around defined regional sites or areas. This arrangement is frequently used by government agencies, such as the Federal Reserve System, which has 12 separate districts around the United States. But a railroad might also use geographic divisions. Geographic divisions are frequently used by companies that operate globally. (*See* ■ *Panel 8.8.*)

■ PANEL 8.8 **Geographic divisions: arrangements by regional locations or districts.**

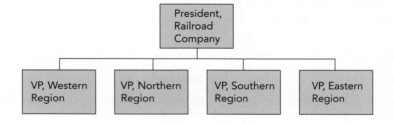

Process Divisions: Grouping by Work Specialization

A variant on the functional division, *process divisions* group activities around work processes. Some companies find it convenient to group according to the different kinds of work that go into making and selling a product. A book publisher, for instance, might have editorial, production, sales and marketing, and business departments. (*See* ■ *Panel 8.9.*)

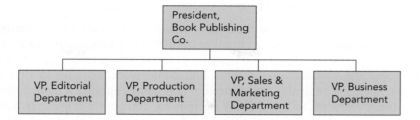

Product Divisions: Grouping by Similar Products or Services

Product divisions **group activities around similar products or services.** For instance, the Boeing Company, the second largest aircraft and defense company in the world, has three principal divisions—helicopters, commercial airplanes, and integrated defense systems. (*See* ■ *Panel 8.10.*)

■ PANEL 8.10 **Product divisions: The Boeing Company.**

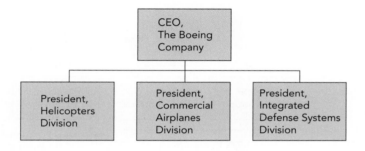

Industry Divisions: The Conglomerate Structure

A large-scale variant on the product-division structure is the conglomerate structure. **A** *conglomerate* **is a large company that is doing business in different, often quite unrelated areas.** For example, United Technologies Corporation, which is concerned with technology for the building and aerospace industries, is made up of seven divisions: Pratt & Whitney (aircraft engines), Otis (elevators and escalators), Carrier (heating and air conditioning), Sikorsky (helicopters), UTC Fire & Security, Hamilton Sundstrand (aerospace systems and industrial products), and UTC Power (fuel cells).[30] **The** *conglomerate structure* **groups divisions around similar businesses or industries.** (*See* ■ *Panel 8.11.*)

■ PANEL 8.11 **Conglomerate structure: divisions by industry.**

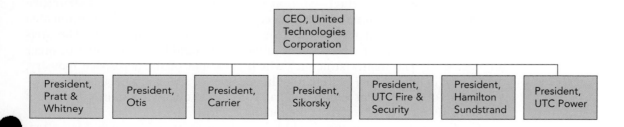

Want to Know More? 8-6

What Is the Purpose of a Hybrid Structure & How Well Does It Work?

Go to www.mybizlab.com.

3 Hybrid Structure: Both Functional & Divisional

How would I describe a hybrid organizational structure?

The third organizational form is the **hybrid structure, in which an organization uses functional and divisional structures in different parts of the same organization.** Owing to "the difficulty of working globally with a centralized functional structure and the communication gaps that come from working in divisional" structures, says one analysis, "most modern companies employ a hybrid structure that combines elements of each."[31] By using both, companies hope to balance the economies of scale (cost savings) that come from centralization with the local efficiency that comes with decentralization.

There are all different kinds of possible hybrid structures. One example could be Ford Motor Company, which at the top rung of the hierarchy is organized into huge global geographic divisions, beneath which are functional divisions; beneath that could be product divisions. (*See* ■ *Panel 8.12.* The actual Ford global organizational chart is considerably more complicated.)

■ **PANEL 8.12 Hybrid structure.** Hypothetical example of Ford Motor Company.

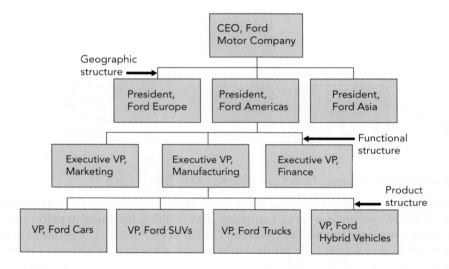

4 Matrix Structure: Vertical & Horizontal Command Structures in a Grid

What's the definition and purpose of a matrix structure?

A fourth organizational form is the **matrix structure, which combines, in grid form, the functional chain of command and the divisional chain of command—usually product—so that there is a vertical command structure and a horizontal command structure.** Here the *functional* structure remains the organization's normal divisions (Marketing, Finance, and so on). The *divisional* structure is usually by product (although it could be by customer or other arrangement). The matrix structure, which came out of the aerospace industry, works best in temporarily pulling together people for special projects, such as development of a particular automobile, as Ford did to create the Taurus and might theoretically have done to create the Fusion Hybrid.

Ford's functional structure could be the departments of Finance, Marketing, Production, and Engineering, each headed by a vice president; this reporting arrangement is vertical. The divisional structure might be by project or product (cars), each headed by a project manager; this reporting arrangement is horizontal. Thus, an employee would report *permanently* to the VP of Engineering but *temporarily* to the Project Manager for Ford Fusion Hybrid. (*See* ■ *Panel 8.13.*)

■ **PANEL 8.13 Matrix structure.** Hypothetical arrangement Ford might use to develop the Fusion Hybrid.

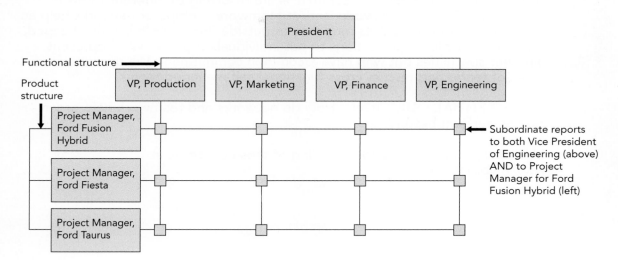

You might think that employees reporting to two managers would have conflicts (and sometimes they do). However, workers are assigned to a project on a *temporary* basis, during which time they report to the project manager only. Once their work is finished, they return to reporting to their functional manager.

The benefits and drawbacks of matrix structures appear below. (*See* ■ *Panel 8.14.*)

Key Takeaway 8-4
Principal departmental arrangements: functional, divisional, hybrid, matrix.

■ **PANEL 8.14 Matrix structures: benefits and drawbacks.**

Benefits	Drawbacks
Allows managers to use firm's resources more effectively	May not be a long-term solution to development problem
Gives managers flexibility in assigning right workers to projects	Can be expensive and complicated to execute
Can lead to innovative solutions in product development	Employees may be confused about who they report to
Encourages cooperation among different specialists	Project members may have communication problems

THE BIG IDEA: To deal with hyperchanging conditions and eliminate organizational functional barriers, companies are resorting to different forms of organization involving networks and/or teamwork. Computer networks help an organization contract out its functions to outside firms, which can be changed. Teamwork enables organizations to put individuals together who represent different specialties but who have a common commitment. We describe four types of teams and discuss cross-functional self-managed teams.

THE ESSENTIAL QUESTION: How do networks and teamwork help organizations perform better?

MyBizLab

MyBizLab: Check your understanding of these concepts at www.mybizlab.com.

The point of developing an effective organization is not just to survive. As Jim Collins (of Section 8.1) says, it is to make a distinctive impact on the world. And the point of the efforts discussed in this chapter is to help the organization realize this by dealing with hyperchange.

The matrix structure just described suggests a new reality: companies are having to devise new ways of organizing themselves to be able to respond quickly and effectively to changing conditions. One way to eliminate organizational functional barriers is to use computer *networks*—specifically the Internet. Another way is to use *teamwork.*

Organizations Using Networks: Core Companies Linked to Outside Firms

What is distinctive about a virtual organization?

A ***virtual organization,*** or *networked organization,* **consists of a company with a central core that is connected by computer network, usually the Internet, to outside independent firms, which help the core firm achieve its purpose.** The benefit of such a networked entity is *flexibility:* The core company can outsource various processes or functions to outside companies—any one of which can be changed when necessary. For example, a construction company that does bridge building might set up a network with several specialized companies to do the design, engineering, fabrication, and so on. (*See* ■ *Panel 8.15, opposite page.*)

A company operating as a virtual organization is called a *virtual corporation* or even a *hollow corporation,* because its core company retains processes essential to its operation (such as strategic decision making and marketing) while outsourcing other processes (such as design or distribution), thus appearing to "hollow out" the organization. To its customers and others, however, the virtual corporation appears to be a single, unified organization, perhaps operating from a single location.

A variation on the virtual organization is the ***modular structure,*** **in which a firm assembles pieces, or modules, of a product provided by outside contractors.** The difference here is that the organization is outsourcing pieces of a *product*

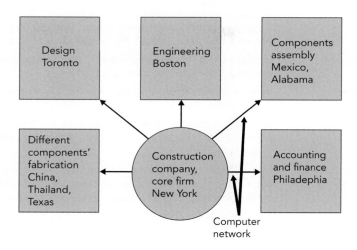

■ **PANEL 8.15 Virtual organization.** Example of a U.S. construction company specializing in bridge building outsourcing functions to other companies, connected by computer network.

rather than, as is true in virtual organizations, outsourcing certain *processes* (such as design or distribution).

> ■ **Example** of Modular Structure: How RIM Made the BlackBerry Torch. The BlackBerry Torch smartphone is made by Research In Motion (RIM), a Canadian company. However, it is assembled in Mexico from components made in the United States, South Korea, Japan, Germany, Switzerland, and the United Kingdom.[32] The power-management chip, for instance, is made by Texas Instruments in the United States, but memory chips are made by Samsung in South Korea. ⑩ ■

Organizations Using Teamwork: Benefiting from Common Commitment

What is the definition of a team?

If different drivers stop at the scene of a car accident and try to interact with each other to offer assistance, what do you call them? And when an ambulance crew arrives, what do you call it? The first is a group; the second is a team.

"The essence of a team is common commitment," say management consultants Jon R. Katzenbach and Douglas K. Smith. "Without it, groups perform as individuals; with it, they become a powerful unit of collective performance."[33] **A team, then, is defined as a small group of people with complementary skills who are committed to common performance goals and a common approach to realizing them, for which they hold themselves mutually accountable.**[34]

There are many good reasons why teamwork is favored by today's management, as shown on the next page. (*See* ■ *Panel 8.16.*)

Different Kinds of Teams: Action, Production, Project, & Advice

How do the four types of teams differ?

There are many kinds of teams engaged in collective work requiring coordinated effort. In *virtual teams,* for instance, members interact with each other via computer network to collaborate on projects.

Source: Photograph by Sally Lindsay.

⑩ **Smartly built smartphone.** An example of modular structure, the BlackBerry Torch smartphone, a Canadian product, is constructed in Mexico of parts made in many other countries, from the United States to South Korea. If you think there should be more U.S. manufacturing jobs, how would you handle the modular structure approach to fabrication and assembly of your company's product?

■ **PANEL 8.16 Why teamwork is important.**

The Improvements	Examples
Increased productivity	American Apparel sewing workers trained in teamwork and paid by number of garments produced by their team instead of individually tripled output from 30,000 to 90,000 pieces a day, with only a 12% increase in workers.
Increased speed	Guidant Corp., maker of life-saving medical devices, halved the time it took to get products to market.
Reduced costs	Boeing used teamwork to develop the 777 at costs far less than normal.
Improved quality outcomes	Training surgery personnel in teamwork at 74 Veterans Administration hospitals resulted in 18% fewer surgery-related deaths.
Reduced destructive internal competition	Men's Wearhouse fired a salesman who wasn't sharing walk-in customer traffic with other salespeople, and total clothing sales volume among all salespeople increased significantly.
Improved cohesiveness, reduced absenteeism	Isola Fabrics restructured production into a teamwork system that resulted in decline of absenteeism rates of 28% for the summer and 39% for the winter.

Source: Based on A. Kinicki and B. K. Williams, *Management: A Practical Introduction*, 4th ed. (New York: McGraw-Hill/Irwin, 2009), p. 407.

Want to Know More? 8-7

More about Cross-Functional Work Teams

Go to www.mybizlab.com.

Basically, however, there are four types of teams, whose names reflect their purpose: *action, production, project,* and *advice.*

Action Teams: For Tasks Requiring High Coordination among Trained Specialists

We are quite accustomed to thinking of teams in terms of sports. Sports teams are called *action teams,* because they work on tasks (winning games) that require a high degree of coordination among people with specialized training (such as the pitcher, catcher, or outfielder). Other examples of action teams: hospital surgery teams, airline cockpit crews, police homicide investigation teams.

Production Teams: For Performing Day-to-Day Operations

Production teams are charged with performing the day-to-day operations in an organization. Examples: cabin crews, maintenance crews, data processing groups, manufacturing product-assembly teams.

Project Teams: For Doing Creative Problem Solving

Project teams work to do creative problem solving. Often this is done by temporary teams of knowledgeable workers who meet long enough to solve a specific problem and then disband, such as the Ford truck engine team. Other examples: task forces, planning teams, engineering teams, development teams, research groups. Any of these could be a virtual team—one that does all work online.

Advice Teams: For Providing More Information

Advice teams give managers a broader base of information on which to make decisions. Examples: committees, review panels, research teams.

Cross-Functional Self-Managed Teams

What is a team that is both cross-functional and self-managed?

To give you an idea of how teams work, consider cross-functional self-managed teams, with routine activities formerly performed by supervisors now performed by team members. ***Cross-functional self-managed teams* are defined as groups of workers with different skills who are given the authority to manage themselves.** *Cross-functional* means the team is made up of workers with different specialties and expertise. *Self-managed* means the traditional clear-cut distinction between manager and managed is blurred as nonmanagerial employees are delegated greater authority over planning, scheduling, monitoring, and staffing and granted increased autonomy. The idea, of course, is to increase productivity and employee quality of work life. The benefits and drawbacks of such teams appear below. (*See* ■ *Panel 8.17.*)

■ **PANEL 8.17 Cross-functional self-managed teams: benefits and drawbacks.**

Benefits	Drawbacks
Bring more expertise	More training required
Boost innovation and productivity	Possible conflicts, disorganization
Higher employee morale, less boredom and apathy	Unclear leadership roles

Summary

8.1 Adapting Organizations to Tomorrow's Marketplace

THE ESSENTIAL QUESTION: *What areas of an organization often need changing, and how can I implement changes?*

What are the five stages organizations tend to go through when they go into decline? Institutional decline goes through five stages, according to Jim Collins: Hubris Born of Success, Undisciplined Pursuit of More, Denial of Risk and Peril, Grasping for Salvation, and Capitulation to Irrelevance or Death.

What four areas tend to need organizational changes? Four areas in which change is most apt to be needed are people, whose minds and employee skills may need changing; technology, any machine or process that enables an organization to gain a competitive advantage in changing material used to produce a finished product; strategy; and structure or management hierarchy.

What are three steps for implementing positive change? The steps are recognize problems and opportunities and devise solutions, gain allies by communicating your vision, and empower and reward employees to achieve progress.

8.2 The Informal Side of an Organization: Culture

THE ESSENTIAL QUESTION: *How does an organization express its culture, and why is culture important?*

What is the meaning of "organizational culture"? Organizational culture—the shared beliefs and values that develop within an organization and guide members' behavior—is communicated through heroes, stories, symbols, and rites and rituals.

What are four ways an organization's culture could affect me and other employees? The culture could help employees understand the organization's goals and how to accomplish them, provide an organizational identity, establish collective commitment, and help achieve social-system stability.

8.3 The Formal Side of an Organization: Structure

THE ESSENTIAL QUESTION: *What are six characteristics of an organization's structure?*

How are authority, accountability, and responsibility defined? Authority refers to the rights inherent in a managerial position to make decisions, give orders, and utilize resources. Accountability means managers must report and justify work results to managers above them. Responsibility is the obligation you have to perform the tasks assigned to you.

How is division of labor defined? The first characteristic of an organization's structure is division of labor: different parts of a task are done by different people.

What is the hierarchy of authority? The hierarchy of authority is an arrangement for making sure that the right people do the right things at the right time.

How do narrow and wide spans of control differ? The span of control—the number of people reporting to a given manager—can be narrow, with a limited number reporting, or wide, with several people reporting.

How can I tell line from staff positions? Delegation is the process of assigning managerial authority and responsibility to managers and employees lower in the hierarchy. Line managers have authority to make decisions and usually have people reporting to them. Staff personnel have advisory functions.

How do centralization and decentralization differ? In centralized authority, important decisions are made by higher-level executives; in decentralized authority, they are made by middle-level and supervisory-level managers.

8.4 Organizational Structures: Four Principal Types

THE ESSENTIAL QUESTION: *How would I describe the four main types of organizational structures?*

What is a functional structure? In departmentalization—the dividing up of an organization into smaller units to facilitate management—the first structure is the functional division: people with similar occupational specialties are put together in formal groups.

What are five types of divisional structures? In a divisional structure, employees are grouped by purpose: customer groups, geographic regions, work processes, products, or industries (the conglomerate structure, for large companies doing business in different, quite unrelated areas).

How would I describe a hybrid organizational structure? In the hybrid structure, an organization uses functional and divisional structures in different parts of the same organization.

What's the definition and purpose of a matrix structure? A matrix structure combines, in grid form, the functional chain of command and the divisional chain of command so that there is a vertical command structure and a horizontal command structure.

8.5 Networks & Teamwork: Two Ways Organizations Respond to Changing Conditions

THE ESSENTIAL QUESTION: *How do networks and teamwork help organizations perform better?*

What is distinctive about a virtual organization? A virtual organization is a company with a central core linked by computer network to outside independent firms, which help the core firm achieve its purpose.

What is the definition of a team? A team is a small group of people with complementary skills who are committed to common performance goals and a common approach, for which they hold themselves mutually accountable.

How do the four types of teams differ? Action teams require high coordination among trained specialists, production teams perform day-to-day operations, project teams do creative problem solving, and advice teams provide managers with a broader base of information.

What is a team that is both cross-functional and self-managed? Cross-functional self-managed teams are groups of workers with different skills who are given the authority to manage themselves.

Key Terms

accountability 234
authority 234
centralized authority 237
conglomerate 241
conglomerate structure 241
corporate culture 230
cross-functional self-managed
   teams 247
customer divisions 240
decentralized authority 238
delegation 236
departmentalization 239

division of labor 235
divisional structure 240
functional division 239
geographic divisions 240
hero 230
hierarchy of authority 235
hybrid structure 242
line managers 236
matrix structure 242
modular structure 244
narrow span of control 235
organizational culture 230

process divisions 240
product divisions 241
responsibility 234
rites and rituals 232
span of control 235
staff personnel 237
story 231
symbol 231
team 245
technology 228
virtual organization 244
wide span of control 235

Pop Quiz Prep

1. Which stage of institutional decline is associated with a company attributing its prosperity and good fortune to its own superior qualities and losing understanding about the underlying factors that created it?

2. You've begun creating a picture of the future, showing others how your way of handling a problem will be of benefit. Which step in the process of implementing change does this illustrate?

3. How is *corporate culture* defined?

4. In terms of an organization's corporate culture, what are symbols?

5. How is the *span of control* defined?

6. What is a benefit of decentralization?

7. In which organizational structure are people with similar occupational specialties put together in formal groups?

8. What is a drawback to functional departmentalization?

9. What is a virtual organization?

10. What is an example of a production team?

Critical Thinking Questions

1. In 1995, Pixar produced its first computer-animated feature film, *Toy Story*. Fifteen years later *Toy Story 3* became the highest-grossing animated film of all time at $1 billion.[35] When *Harvard Business Review* interviewed Ed Catmull, CEO of Pixar, he emphasized that the secret to the company's creative edge is spending time with people who are "different than oneself professionally," and how doing so will always be useful and intellectually stimulating.[36] He went on to say, "Silos occur and smart thinking slows down because we stick to our cubicles for too much time in a row." The term 'silo' is often used in large organizations to reflect how teams and or business units don't share knowledge. The very reason for these silos is the fear that sharing knowledge will result in less power for the leaders within the silos.[37] What type of organizational structure and corporate culture would you assume exists at Pixar?

2. When companies develop arrogance, or what the ancient Greeks called *hubris*, adopting a "we're so great, we can do anything" attitude, they begin attributing their success to their own superior qualities and lose understanding about the underlying factors that created their success. One such example can be cited with Borders, the book retailer. Give an example of a company that currently exhibits hubris—or a company that has failed as a result of too much hubris. Discuss.

3. On a *Harvard Business Review* blog, Rob Cross—an associate professor of management in the McIntire School of Commerce at the University of Virginia—explores the impact of social media in the workplace. He found that bigger is not better when it comes to the size of your network and that activities related to social media such as

Facebook can consume up to 90% of a typical workweek. The authors concluded that social media tools are "as likely to actually hurt performance and engagement as they are to help—if they simply foist more collaborative demands on an already-overloaded workforce."[38] In what ways can collaborative technologies such as social media diminish efficiency and innovation at work? In what ways can it improve efficiency and innovation? What recommendations would you have when using social media in the workplace?

4. A company's culture is conveyed to its employees through its heroes, stories, symbols, rites, and rituals. In this regard, a hero is someone whose accomplishments embody the values of an organization. For example, in the 1980s, Roberto Goizueta shook up the culture at Coca-Cola to focus more on the customer and in the process increased Coke's market capitalization more than 30-fold.[39] Are there any heroes that come to mind as you've read about different organizations? Choose one person (can be from a nonprofit organization), and explore and discuss how that person's accomplishments are used to motivate employees, past and present.

5. Executive development is a type of training for top executives to inspire them and allow them to gain skills and competencies. Jack Welch, former CEO of General Electric, had a unique methodology of attracting "A" performers. It entailed annually grading each manager as an A, B, or C performer. Grades were based solely on the person's performance—and that of his or her work-group—against preestablished, quantifiable, and objective goals. Welch promoted the A players, let the C players go, and put the B players on notice to either raise their performance to an A or be sent packing with the C group. He sent each participant that would be attending his session of General Electric's Executive Development Course (EDC) the following question to consider: "What are your thoughts on just what makes up an A, B & C player?" If you were an attendee of General Electric's Executive Development Course, how would you prepare to answer this question for Mr. Welch? Do you agree with his approach to attracting A players?

Cases

Go to MyBizLab

VIDEO CASE
Herman Miller: From Office Environment to Healing Environment

This video shows the innovative and collaborative teamwork at furniture maker Herman Miller, and why *Fast Company* magazine listed them as "Most Innovative" in a recent year.

Have you ever heard of the "Marshmallow Sofa" or the "Aeron" chair? These design classics are made by Herman Miller, a 100-year-old furniture maker based in western Michigan. The company began in 1923 as Star Furniture,[40] making high-quality, traditional-style bedroom suites, and was one of the first to produce products in what has become the modern furniture movement. The line of furniture made by Herman Miller in the 1940s and 1950s is some of the most influential in modern design. The company has been making furniture for so long, it claims, some of their cutting-edge styles are now retro classics.

Today, the company makes cutting-edge ergonomic furniture and has sold 6 million units of the Aeron (which sells for $750), their best-selling chair, yielding over $3 billion in sales. The Aeron, once a status symbol of the dot.com executives, has become a mainstay in both home and office environments. Herman Miller's product line includes (and yes, some of it is still manufactured in the United States) office and health care furniture and accessories such as office and institutional seating; small office, home office, and residential furniture; and filing and storage products. Herman Miller has influenced more than just the furniture that goes into a workplace. While working with Herman Miller, Bob Propst invented the cubicle, allowing for an open office environment and, as a result, a significant shift in communication and collaboration. This

popularized the modern office layout, allowing offices to be easily moved or added to allow for efficient use of floor space.

In 2010, Herman Miller achieved a spot as "Industry Leader," for the 23rd year in a row, in *Fortune* magazine's annual list of "Most Admired Companies." How has an office furniture company achieved such high status and regard? Simply put: its people and corporate culture.

Herman Miller's success can in part be attributed to its servant leadership style. The servant leadership style encourages the qualities of listening, empathy, healing, awareness, persuasion, conceptualization, foresight, stewardship, growth, and community building. These qualities are celebrated at Herman Miller.

The design company is structured around the various geographic markets served, and a matrix organization goes across that. Management at Herman Miller conveys a mission and vision to all employees, an important part of which is to empower each employee to "get work done in whatever fashion makes sense to produce the most innovative and creative solutions." Project teams are used to carry a product from inception to delivery, and the company's employees pride themselves on learning both collectively and individually by mistakes made. According to the employees, they also wouldn't have it any other way.

The company is acutely aware of how important it is for people to get along, and that criterion is part of its employee review, hiring, and team-building processes. The company's project teams are allowed autonomy, which the company believes is crucial, or else "they risk losing their way or infighting." The company balances the need for autonomy with accountability with its open communication and clear articulation of its vision and goals. Management is the glue that holds the teams together; and while the teams are largely self-managed, management is aware of what is occurring companywide and able to react quickly when problems arise.

What sets Herman Miller apart from its competitors is its consummate drive to encourage employee innovation—this shows in its state-of-the-art and ergonomic office furniture design and solutions presiding in offices and healing environments worldwide.

What's Your Take?

1. What are the two parts of the performance review that are discussed in the video, and what does this tell you about the company's culture?

2. In 1950, the company instituted a program of participative management. In 1983, it instituted an employee stock ownership program. Today all employees with one month of service are entitled to own stock in the company. As of July 1999, 16% of all outstanding shares in Herman Miller were held by employee-owners. What do you think has earned this company a coveted spot on *Fortune* magazine's "100 Best Companies to Work For" list? What other things would you say make this company unique?

3. According to the video, what are the most valued skills a Herman Miller employee possesses, and what will make or break a person's success at this company?

4. Herman Miller prides itself on its sustainable business practices, which go beyond compliance with environmental regulations to include pursuing prevention of pollution and elimination of waste of any kind; implementing technologies to efficiently use energy resources; designing products, processes, and buildings for the environment; and promoting environmental knowledge and awareness. Go to the company's website and review its "Environmental Advocacy" page. What are some innovative initiatives that set this company apart?

5. How do you think the leadership at Herman Miller has responded to the economic downturn that has resulted in downsizing by major corporations and thus decreased demand for office furniture? What ideas would you have in response to this if you were on the Herman Miller management team?

BUSINESS DECISION CASE
New Corporate Culture: Office Romance on the Rise & Out of the Closet

This case explores the topic of love in the workplace, and questions the effectiveness and value of a written policy banning workplace dating. While such a policy is perfectly legal, many companies say that establishing a written policy sends a negative message of an organizational culture that many employees might see as micromanaging and imposing rules into their personal lives.

Imagine that you're in your twenties and you've started your first job after college. Your company is full of singles around your age, and the culture promotes working closely in teams. For instance, there are team-building activities aimed at creating strong working relationships, and social events to attend, designed to foster the company's casual, informal, collaborative work culture. To your knowledge, there are no rules against dating a coworker—and you've heard there are some couples in the company. In such a culture, it's difficult to ignore those relationships that can develop into more than "just coworkers."

There's no doubt that each year, many people find love in the workplace. The 2010 Office Romance Survey by Vault Career Services found that almost 60% of respondents reported having participated in some form of workplace romance. Of those, 41% admitted to an ongoing but casual relationship, 35% to a random office hookup, and 40% to a long-term, serious relationship, with 19% reporting having met their spouse/partner at work.[41] It's not surprising that such a large percentage of people become romantically involved with work colleagues. After all, we spend many of our waking hours at work, and often find common ground and support with coworkers. In fact, Michelle and Barack Obama met at work. (She was his superior.)

Some companies have established a written policy prohibiting workplace romance; however, since human nature cannot be controlled, it's likely that such a policy will remain unenforceable.[42] Researchers have found that employers realize that trying to stamp out office romance is like standing in front of a speeding train. "The office keeps coming up as No. 1" in surveys as the best place to meet a mate, leading bosses to conclude they "have to be cool about it," says Janet Lever, a professor of sociology at California State University, Los Angeles, and longtime researcher on office romance.[43] Many companies with a young workforce have come to accept the inevitable, and Cisco Systems, for example, doesn't encourage or discourage consensual relationships between employees. Relationships between supervisors and subordinates, however, are "frowned upon" and may result in a transfer or reassignment, the policy says.

Why do companies care about office romance? What is their concern? After all, we're all adults, even after a breakup, right? Not always. According to a survey by the Society for Human Resource Management, messy breakups are the biggest pitfall of office romance: 67% of 493 employers surveyed cited them as a significant problem, often because of the possibility of retaliation by scorned or disappointed lovers. Another issue is the impact on coworkers, many of whom are encouraged to take sides or to become sounding boards for the scorned. In a smaller work environment, some may feel victim to bias and favoritism, and others may feel left out or excluded when the lovebirds disappear during lunch for some private time during the workday.

There are other liabilities for the company such as sexual harassment lawsuits which may stem from dating relationships gone sour. As someone who advises on sexual harassment issues, Mark Kluger, an employment lawyer, makes it clear to management: "If it's heard through the grapevine, the employer must look into it. Gossip is recognized by the courts as a means of information to the employer. If [a manager] knew of some of the behavior, or should have known because it was all over as gossip, [the manager] could be liable."[44]

To ward off any potential harassment charges, some companies are using a consensual relationship agreement, also called a "love contract," created by Gary Mathiason of employment firm Littler Mendelson in San Francisco. These contracts spell out that the relationship between employees is consensual, mutually agreeable, and unrelated to company matters, and that any relationship dispute will be settled outside of a lawsuit through arbitration.[45] So, the next time your heart skips when you bump into that "someone" in the mailroom, should you begin searching for a new job, or simply linger, take a chance, and open your mail there?

What's Your Take?

1. How would you feel about working at a company where there was a policy against intraoffice dating? Do you think this type of policy crosses over into dictating people's personal lives?

2. What rules do you think companies should have about office dating?

3. Does a company's culture affect the rules around intraoffice dating? Explain.

4. What advice would you give to a coworker whose office romance has gone bad?

5. What do you think about the "love contract," which actually was devised for senior-level executives in the entertainment industry?

6. Some companies, like Southwest Airlines, encourage in-house relationships. Why do you think a company would encourage in-house dating?

Briefings   MyBizLab Activities & Cases

Go to www.mybizlab.com for online activities and exercises related to the timely topics discussed in this chapter's Briefings, as well as additional theme-related Briefing *Spotlights* highlighting how these concepts apply in today's business environment.

In-chapter Briefing:
- Cisco's Failed Experiment of 48 Decentralized "Management Councils"

Activity:
- Developing Marketable Business Skills – Borders Books & Its Borderline Organizational Decline
- Going to the Net! – Change through People, Technology, Strategy, & Structure

Briefing Spotlight:
- Organizational Evolution

In-chapter Briefing:
- Anne Mulcahy Becomes a Hero to Xerox

Activity:
- Developing Marketable Business Skills – Does Teamwork Compensate for Skill?
- Developing Marketable Business Skills – Authority, Accountability, & Responsibility: A Student's Experience
- Get Your Career in Gear – Do You Think You Want to Climb the Corporate Ladder?

Briefing Spotlight:
- Small Business Job Hunting

In-chapter Briefing:
- Best Buy's New Strategy— "Bring Us Your Junk"

Activity:
- Going to the Net! – New Belgium, Maker of Fat Tire Amber Ale, Counts Its Carbon Footprint

Briefing Spotlight:
- Survival of the Greenest

In-chapter Briefing:
- Twitter, Facebook, & Other Social Media Change the Approach to Customer Service

Activity:
- Developing Marketable Business Skills – Virtually Speaking about Amazon .com & Dell
- Going to the Net! – Work Whenever & Wherever You Want? Really?

Briefing Spotlight:
- Caution: Social Intelligence is Watching

In-chapter Briefing:
- The Baker's Story—Giving a Six-Time Felon One Last Chance at Redemption

Activity:
- Developing Marketable Business Skills – Culture: The Informal Side of a Small Business

Briefing Spotlight:
- If the Shoe Fits

Additional Briefing Spotlights available at MyBizLab:

- BUSINESS CULTURE & ETIQUETTE
- CUSTOMER FOCUS
- GLOBAL BUSINESS
- LEGAL & ETHICAL PRACTICES
- PERSONAL FINANCE
- SOCIALLY RESPONSIBLE BUSINESS

9 Operations Management
Generating Quality Products & Services

After reading and studying this chapter, you will be able to answer the following essential questions:

9.1 **Operations Management: How Goods & Services Are Produced**

THE ESSENTIAL QUESTION: *What is the process for obtaining high-quality goods and services?*

9.2 **Production Processes: Improving Production Techniques**

THE ESSENTIAL QUESTION: *What are the various types of production processes and technologies, old and new?*

9.3 **Operations Management Planning: Designing & Managing Production Operations**

THE ESSENTIAL QUESTION: *What factors should a business consider for effective production operations?*

9.4 **Quality Assurance: Producing Better Products & Services**

THE ESSENTIAL QUESTION: *How do top companies improve the quality of their products or services?*

MyBizLab

Where you see MyBizLab in this chapter, go to www.mybizlab.com for additional activities on the topic being discussed.

FORECAST:
What's Ahead in This Chapter

Operations management is about converting materials, labor, and other resources into goods and/or services. We discuss continuous versus intermittent conversion processes, how operations processes add value, the history of production, and ways of improving production. We then consider operations management planning and quality control.

MyBizLab

Gain hands-on experience through an interactive, real-world scenario. This chapter's simulation entitled Improving a Business is located at **www.mybizlab.com**.

WINNER: Ritz-Carlton Soars

The Ritz-Carlton Hotel Company, a luxury chain of 61 hotels with 35,000 employees that is a subsidiary of Marriott International, has long been heralded for the consistency of its service. First-year managers and employees receive 250 to 310 hours of training, some of it at the Leadership Center, where Ritz managers share their secrets. The president meets each employee at a new hotel to ensure he or she understands Ritz-Carlton's standards for service, which are intended to create the aura that will attract luxury travelers. The chain has also developed a database that records the preferences of more than 1 million customers, so that each hotel can anticipate guests' needs.[1]

Every manager and frontline employee carries a laminated card with 12 service values guidelines. (No. 10: "I am proud of my professional appearance, language, and behavior." No. 1: "I build strong relationships and create Ritz-Carlton guests for life.") The purpose of these is to make sure every employee, from valet to front-desk attendant to housekeeper to waiter, is warm, friendly, courteous, and eager to make the guest's stay memorable. The point is to create a strong emotional engagement between staff and guests.

The service values are reinforced every day when employees from every department gather for a 15-minute meeting (called the "lineup") to discuss problems, guest experiences, and ways to improve service. Then time is spent telling the "wow story" of the day—the same story is shared across hotels in 21 countries—which singles out a Ritz-Carlton employee who went well beyond the call of duty. (Example: A family carrying specialized eggs and milk for their allergic son found the food had spoiled upon their arrival at a Ritz. The executive chef remembered a particular store in another country that sold them and arranged with his mother-in-law to buy them and have them flown in.)

The everyday 15-minute training of the lineup not only recognizes employees for their commitment but also reinforces the service values and staff enthusiasm.

LOSER: Toyota Slips

Originally the "Toyota Way," as practiced at Toyota Motor Corporation, stressed continuous improvement (*kaizen*) and eliminating waste (*muda*). Dedicated to maintaining quality, the Toyota Way, says one report, "mandates planning for the long term; highlighting problems instead of hiding them; encouraging teamwork with colleagues and suppliers; and, perhaps most important, instilling a self-critical culture that fosters continuous and unrelenting improvement."[2]

However, in the 1990s the company launched a drive to become the world's largest automaker, embarking on aggressive overseas expansion and doubling its overseas plants. The focus on cost reduction intensified to the point that the virtue became a vice. Suppliers were continually pushed to design parts 10% cheaper and 10% lighter. Common parts were used in most Toyota models, acquired from outside companies instead of trusted longtime Japanese suppliers.[3]

From 2000 to 2010, U.S. driver complaints to the National Highway Traffic and Safety Administration about "vehicle speed control" issues soared, with 11.7% of faulty vehicle components identified as Toyota's.[4] Then came widely publicized problems with sticking gas pedals or floor mats that could jam pedals, prompting 12 million recalls worldwide and suspension of the sales and production of eight models in the American market.[5] The blow to Toyota's vaunted reputation for quality was severe. "When your whole deal was quality, every mistake is a big deal," said a manufacturing expert.[6]

"I fear the pace at which we have grown may have been too quick," said Toyota's CEO, grandson of the company's founder, in later testimony before a U.S. congressional committee. "Priorities became confused, and we were not able to stop, think, and make improvements as much as we were able to before."[7]

Although a later U.S. investigation found no flaws in Toyota electronics, the gas pedal and floor mat problems that caused jammed accelerators caused the company's share of the U.S. auto market to fall to 15.2% from 16.6% in the first nine months of 2010.

Source: Roussel Photography/Alamy.

Source: Photograph by Sally Lindsay.

YOUR CALL "Every single industry changes and, eventually, fades," writes marketer Seth Godin. "Just because you made money doing something a certain way yesterday, there's no reason to believe you'll succeed at it tomorrow."[8] Do you agree? Is it possible to have profitability and quality *and* have growth? Do you think it is harder or easier to provide quality services, as Ritz-Carlton attempts to do (which means dealing with issues such as intangibility, variability, and involvement of the customer in the production process), than to provide quality goods, as Toyota attempts to do?

MyBizLab

9.1 Operations Management: How Goods & Services Are Produced

THE BIG IDEA: Production or operations is any process that takes basic resources and converts them into finished products—inputs into outputs. Operations management is the management of the process of converting resources into goods and/or services. Manufacturing businesses and service businesses differ in their operations management.

THE ESSENTIAL QUESTION: What is the process for obtaining high-quality goods and services?

MyBizLab: Check your understanding of these concepts at www.mybizlab.com.

How do you provide higher-quality goods and services in the most productive way? The answer to this question requires that we look at how goods and services are actually developed.

Operations, Production, & Operations Management: What They Are, How They Work

What terms are used to describe how goods and services are produced?

Got milk? those ads ask, showing some celebrity with a white smear of milk over the upper lip. When you "get" milk, does it come straight from a cow's udder? Or do you buy it in a container at a store?

If it's the second way, the milk went through a *transformation*—the original cow's milk was screened, pasteurized, and put into a carton or bottle. The terms *production* or *operations* are about transformation processes.

Production or Operations: Transforming Resources into Finished Products

Production or operations refers to any process that takes basic resources and transforms them into finished products—inputs into outputs, whether grapes into wine or electronic parts into cellphones. (*See* ■ *Panel 9.1.*)

■ **PANEL 9.1 Transformation processes: converting basic resources into finished products.**

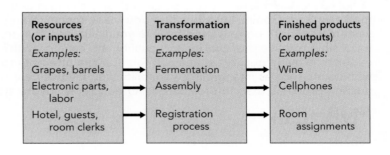

Want to Know More? 9-1
Key Terms & Definitions in Sequential Order to Study as You Go Along.
Go to www.mybizlab.com.

Resources are the factors of production we identified in Chapters 1 and 3—namely, *natural resources, capital, human resources, entrepreneurship,* and *knowledge.* Finished products are goods or services. What the transformation process does, then, is *add value* to the resources. (*See* ■ *Panel 9.2.*)

■ **PANEL 9.2 What transformation does: adding value to resources.**

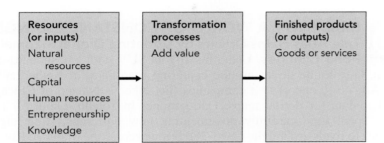

Production Management versus Operations Management

Production management is the management of the process of transforming materials, labor, and other resources into goods. Today businesspeople are more apt to use the term *operations management,* to reflect the conversion of resources into services as well as goods. To give a formal definition, then, **operations management is the management of the process of transforming materials, labor, and other resources into goods and/or services.** ❶

Manufacturing versus Services: The Differences in Operations Management

How does operations management vary for manufacturing and services?

There are differences in how operations management works for manufacturing and how it works for services.

Manufacturing Businesses: Producing Goods

Manufacturing businesses, which mainly deal with *things,* produce goods; they convert raw materials into finished products.

❶ **Operations management.** This pizza restaurant manager is directing a cook on the process of transforming materials and other resources into a finished product—a pizza. What kinds of supervisory work have you done that fit the definition of operations management?

BRIEFING / EARNING GREEN BY GOING GREEN
Metal Management Shreds Scrap Metal to Make New Steel.
Where do steel and other metals for those Japanese cars we drive come from? Quite likely from us—the United States.

There are two ways to make steel: create it from iron ore and coke, or melt down used steel and recycle it into new steel. Metal Management of Newark, New Jersey, is America's first nationwide scrap yard and recently went global by merging with a worldwide metal-recycling company in Australia. The CEO of Metal Management, Daniel Dienst, who formerly worked on Wall Street, saw the potential in the scrap metal industry and the soaring demand for metals, largely the result of the industrial growth of China, India, and other developing nations.

Metal Management is in the business of converting what were once finished products—old cars, refrigerators, and other metal junk—by sorting and shredding them into material for making recycled steel. Thus, the finished product again becomes raw material, which the Japanese and others will make into *new* finished products, such as cars to be exported to the United States. ■

Service Businesses: Performing Services

Service businesses, which deal mainly with *people,* perform services; they convert people's unmet needs into satisfied needs.

Want to Know More? 9-2

What Are Some Intriguing Service Businesses?

Go to www.mybizlab.com.

Want to Know More? 9-3

How Does the Census Define Services & What Is NAICS?

Go to www.mybizlab.com.

BRIEFING / A WORLD OF CONSTANT CHANGE
Tele Atlas Helps Drivers by Updating Digital Mapmakers on Road Changes. Using his Toyota SUV with a dashboard-mounted laptop, Guy Vitale drives around capturing road data for Netherlands-based Tele Atlas NV, one of two companies (the other is Navteq of Chicago) that supplies data for digital maps. One summer in Toledo, Ohio, for instance, Vitale spent time carefully documenting new on-ramps, street signs, and changes to roads around the new I-280 bridge across the Maumee River. Other employees drive around and update the company's database with other new road details, from speed limits to new interchanges.

The Tele Atlas data will appear as navigation aids in cars and mobile devices carrying GPS (global positioning system) devices, as well as online services like Google Maps. If you've ever been misled by an erroneous digital map, you know how valuable this service is. And as the market for GPS devices grows, people will use them not only for basic navigation, says one report, but also for "traffic updates, fuel prices, and tools for people to track each other's whereabouts." ■

PRACTICAL ACTION
Transforming Your Own Work: Becoming More Efficient

Since in the workplace your own labor is part of some transformational process (turning inputs into outputs), your bosses depend on you to be efficient. Some tips:

- **Reduce procrastination:** Today about 26% of Americans think of themselves as chronic procrastinators, up from 5% in 1978. Why the increase? Too many tempting diversions.[9] But putting off addressing important problems can make you feel completely overwhelmed.

- **Reduce multitasking:** Multitasking (texting while walking, chatting on the phone while driving, and so on) is the enemy of concentration. Indeed, says one researcher, high multitaskers "are lousy at everything that's necessary for multitasking. They're suckers for irrelevancy. Everything distracts them."[10] Like an athlete, then, you should work on maintaining your focus.

- **Increase checklists:** There is so much information in the world that it is easy to overlook essentials. The answer? Checklists. "Not only are checklists a help, they are required for success," says the author of *The Checklist Manifesto.* "There may be no field or profession where checklists wouldn't be tremendously beneficial."[11]

Production Processes: Improving Production Techniques

THE BIG IDEA: Form utility is the value that people add in converting resources into finished products. Two ways of adding value are by breaking down resources or combining resources to create finished products. Production processes may be continuous (ongoing) or intermittent (as needed). Historically production processes have been changed by the introduction of mechanization, standardization, assembly lines, automation, and mass production. More recently, production processes have been improved through the use of computerized design and manufacturing, flexible manufacturing, lean manufacturing, and mass customization.

THE ESSENTIAL QUESTION: What are the various types of production processes and technologies, old and new?

MyBizLab: Check your understanding of these concepts at www.mybizlab.com.

MyBizLab

Although most readers of this book either are already working in or will find careers in services, most ideas about production processes are based on manufacturing, and later extended to service businesses. What are the commonalities of the various production processes? What's required to convert eggs to eggnog, tin to tin cans, newsprint to newspapers? Or indifferent hotel guests to happy guests? Let's consider this.

Form Utility: How Operations Processes Add Value

What is form utility, and what are two ways of adding value in converting resources into finished products?

Form utility **is the value that people add in converting resources—natural resources, capital, human resources, entrepreneurship, and knowledge—into finished products.** The way that operations processes add value to resources and convert them into products is *by changing their form.* Two ways of adding value are to break down raw materials or combine raw materials. For instance, a cow's milk may be separated out, producing cream. Or it may be combined with sugar and other ingredients to produce ice cream. ❷

Breaking Down Materials: Analytic Transformation

The process in which resources are broken down to create finished products is known as *analytic transformation.* All kinds of materials are made into new forms by breaking the original substance down further, using chemical or mechanical means. Gold ore is crushed, separated, and smelted into pure gold. Chickens are butchered into breasts, legs, and other parts. A new building may be divided into offices, retail shops, condos, and apartments.

❷ **Changing the form.** In Chapter 2, we showed a purse that is one of the 1,500 finished products New Jersey eco-company TerraCycle makes from used drink pouches, snack bags, and other hard-to-recycle materials. How is the transformation done? Here the base "fabric" is generated by running Oreo cookie wrappers through a fusion machine. The process of converting useless waste materials into new materials or products of better quality is called *up-cycling.* Do you own any up-cycled items?

Source: Christopher Crane.

Combining Materials: Synthetic Transformation

The process in which resources are combined to create finished products is called *synthetic transformation.* Gold may be combined with silver to make jewelry, for instance. Chicken may be combined with vegetables to make a casserole. Buildings may be combined with streets to make a housing development. (Another term, *assembly processes,* describes the processes in which components are put together, as in electronics and automobile manufacturing.)

Continuous versus Intermittent Conversion Processes

How would I identify a continuous production process as opposed to an intermittent process?

Whether for manufacturing or for services, production processes are either *continuous* or *intermittent*.

Continuous Processes: Ongoing

A *continuous process* **is a production process in which goods or services are turned out in a long production run on an ongoing basis over time.** Chemical plants, nuclear plants, and oil refineries, which shut down only rarely, are examples of continuous production processes, but they are not the only ones.

Source: Eric Gevaert/Shutterstock.

❸ Bread line. Loaves of bread are transported through one of Oroweat's continuous process bakeries. Founded in North Hollywood, California, in 1932, and known for its use of whole grains, Oroweat Bakeries is now part of Bimbo Bakeries USA, with operations in several states. The process of making Oroweat is high automated, requiring a large investment in equipment. What do you think a new, independent bakery would need to do to compete with a big operation like this?

■ **Example** of **Continuous Process: Oroweat Bread.** Whole wheat loaf bread made by Oroweat Bread, found on many supermarket shelves, is the result of continuous process, in which the same baking materials are steadily converted into the same type of bread around the clock. ❸ ■

Intermittent Processes: As Needed

An *intermittent process* **is a production process in which finished goods or services are turned out in a series of short production runs and the machines are changed frequently to make different products.** Garment makers, for instance, frequently shut down their factories to retool them to handle different clothing styles. Loads of concrete are also made on an on-demand basis, and between orders the equipment and concrete trucks have to be cleaned.

■ **Example** of **Intermittent Process: Biggest Little Cake Shoppe.** Located in Reno, Nevada, the Biggest Little Cake Shoppe offers wedding cakes, birthday cakes, custom cakes, and desserts for all occasions. Here the production is short-run (one or two cakes perhaps) and the cake-making machinery is frequently cleaned up and set up again—representing an intermittent process. ■

A Short History of Production

What are five significant technology changes that improved efficiency in production?

Even before the Industrial Revolution, producers were concerned with increasing the efficiency of transforming resources into finished products. Ancient copper miners in Wales, for instance, used unpaid children to help extract ore from hard-to-reach places. The great Michelangelo used apprentices and helpers to paint the ceiling of the Sistine Chapel.

Then came the Industrial Revolution in 18th-century England, and later America, which introduced a series of technology changes that improved efficiency: (1) *mechanization,* (2) *standardization,* (3) the *assembly line,* (4) *automation,* and (5) *mass production.*

1 Mechanization: Using Machines to Replace Labor

The first development was ***mechanization,* the use of machines to do the work formerly performed by people.**

■ **Example of Mechanization: The Cotton Gin.** Before the invention of the cotton gin, the greatest difficulty in processing cotton was separating the seeds from the cotton, which made the process extremely labor intensive. Although earlier gins had been available, Eli Whitney is credited with inventing a cotton gin in 1794 that came to be the basis for expanding cotton farming in the South before the Civil War.[12] ■

2 Standardization: Using Uniform Parts

Hand in hand with mechanization was the development of ***standardization,* the use of uniform parts that could be easily interchanged with similar parts.** This eliminated the need for handcrafting every product, and reduced the need to employ experienced craft workers.

■ **Example of Standardization: Interchangeable Gun Parts.** Eli Whitney is also credited with inventing a gun (musket) with standardized, interchangeable parts, although in fact the idea predated him. Nevertheless, the concept of interchangeable parts made possible Henry Ford's assembly line, described next. ■

3 Assembly Line: Series of Specific Tasks

Taking the concept of standardization further, the factory ***assembly line* consists of a series of steps for assembling a product, each step using the same interchangeable parts and each being performed repetitively by the same worker.**

■ **Example of Assembly Line: Henry Ford.** Although Henry Ford did not invent the assembly line, he saw its possibilities and was one of the first to have a moving assembly line, which used conveyor belts to move an automobile under construction past a series of work stations, where workers used standardized parts in the car's assembly. ④ ■

Source: Everett Collection Inc/Alamy.

④ **Some assembly required.** Ford's assembly line, developed over the years 1908 to 1913, was initially inspired by the overhead trolley used in Chicago meat packing houses—the "disassembly line," where animal carcasses were butchered as they moved along a conveyor. Ford Model Ts like this one came down the line in 3-minute intervals, so that cars could be built much faster than previously. The efficiency allowed Ford to drop the price of its Model T from $825 in 1908 to $575 in 1912, leading to the widespread popularity of the automobile in American society. Have you ever worked in an assembly-line operation?

Source: Glow Images/Newscom.

⑤ Robot world. A welding robot sends up a shower of sparks as it spot-welds a component to the body of a General Motors SUV moving down the production line. Robots have had a huge impact on manufacturing, displacing many workers, but they also affect service industries, such as banking, with its automated teller machines (ATMs).

Key Takeaway 9-2
Five technology changes in production are mechanization, standardization, assembly line, customization, and mass production.

Want to Know More? 9-4
What Are Some Other Examples of Mass Production in Services?
Go to www.mybizlab.com.

4 Automation: Minimal Human Intervention

Gradually, in order to increase output and profits, manufacturers began trying to reduce the role of manual labor on their production lines, striving to use ***automation*, using machines as much as possible rather than human labor to perform production tasks.** Particularly interesting is the field of ***robotics*, the use of programmable machines, or *robots*, to manipulate materials and tools to perform a variety of tasks.** Robots are used for everything from building cars to harvesting alfalfa to doing nuclear inspections to fighting oil-well fires.

■ **Example** of Automation: Factory Robots at GM Lansing Plant. In 2001, General Motors opened its most state-of-the-art automobile assembly plant in Lansing, Michigan. The plant uses robots, conveyors, and other equipment to assemble a variety of vehicles, from two-seat sports cars, to four-door sedans, to pickup trucks, as well as left-hand and (for overseas consumption) right-hand drive cars. In the body shop, 338 programmable welding robots perform 2,163 welds per vehicle. The plant employs about half the labor force of other GM plants.[13] ⑤ ■

5 Mass Production: Production of Great Quantities

Mechanization, standardization, assembly lines, and automation have made possible reduction of production costs and the development of ***mass production*, the production of uniform goods in great quantities.** Mass production is used all the time to produce goods, of course (such as cars, jeans, and canned soups), but it is also possible for services, where the goal is to produce a predictable experience.

■ **Example** of Mass Production of Services: How Four Seasons Hotels Hire Employees Who Give Great Service. The upscale Four Seasons hotel chain is not the only hotel operator (besides Ritz-Carlton) to track customer histories and preferences in order to deliver great service, but how do they manage to mass-produce this experience? Company founder Isadore Sharp discovered that the way to get the best employees was to "hire for attitude, not skill," then train the new hires thoroughly and treat them with the respect he expects them to show the hotel's guests.

Job applicants are first subjected to at least four rounds of interviews, the last one by top managers, with interviewers trying to answer the question, "Are you an innately friendly, happy person?" Says regional vice president Thomas Gurtner, "I can teach you to be a doorman or a bellman or a bartender. But if your mama didn't teach you to be nice, then I can't either."[14] ■

Improving Production: Use of CAD/CAM/CIM, Flexible Manufacturing, Lean Manufacturing, & Mass Customization

How would I describe four kinds of technologies developed in recent times to increase productive efficiencies?

In recent years, companies have stepped up their production efficiencies by adopting new forms of technology. They are *CAD/CAM/CIM, flexible manufacturing systems, lean manufacturing,* and *mass customization*.

1 CAD, CAM, & CIM: Computer-Aided Design, Computer-Aided Manufacturing, & Computer-Integrated Manufacturing

Computers have now become a well-established technology in improving production. Three types of computer technologies are abbreviated *CAD, CAM,* and *CIM:*

CAD—Computer-Aided Design: Using Computers to Design Products. *Computer-aided design (CAD)* **programs are used to design products, structures, civil engineering drawings, and maps.** One advantage of CAD software is that the product can be drawn in three dimensions and then rotated on the computer screen, so that the designer can see all sides. ❻

CAD programs help architects design buildings and workspaces and help engineers design cars, planes, electronic devices, roadways, bridges, and subdivisions. Examples of CAD programs that are available to beginners and that can be used on microcomputers are Autosketch, AutoCAD, Turbocad, and CorelCAD.

CAM—Computer-Aided Manufacturing: Using Computers to Manufacture Products. *Computer-aided manufacturing (CAM)* **is the use of computers in the manufacturing process.** CAM systems allow products designed with CAD to be input into an automated manufacturing system that makes products.

CIM—Computer-Integrated Manufacturing: Uniting CAD with CAM. Originally, CAD systems didn't have the software to communicate directly with CAM systems. That changed with the introduction of *computer-integrated manufacturing (CIM),* **systems in which computer-aided design is united with computer-aided manufacturing.** Often these may be integrated through computer networks linking several departments or contractors.

❻ **CAD at work.** The piston rod being held by this designer was designed on the screen of this computer-aided design system, where the image could be drawn in 3-D and rotated on the screen. Later the design was transmitted to other systems (CAM or CIM) for manufacture of the actual part.

■ **Example of CIM Use: The Fashion Industry.** CIM systems brought a whirlwind of enhanced creativity and efficiency to the fashion industry. Some CAD systems, says one writer, "allow designers to electronically drape digitally generated mannequins in flowing gowns or tailored suits that don't exist, or twist imaginary threads into yarns, yarns into weaves, weaves into sweaters without once touching needle to garment."[15]

CIM systems then input the designs and specifications into CAM systems that enable robot pattern-cutters to automatically cut thousands of patterns from fabric with minimal waste. Previously the fashion industry worked about a year in advance of delivery; CIM has cut that time to 8 months—a competitive edge for a field that feeds on fads. ■

Want to Know More? 9-5

What Are Some Examples of CAD, CAM, & CIM?

Go to www.mybizlab.com.

2 Flexible Manufacturing Systems: Machines for Multiple Tasks

A *flexible manufacturing system (FMS)* **is a facility that can be modified quickly to manufacture different products.** Thus, for example, a manufacturer need not take down an existing assembly line for a certain line of cars and reconstruct it to build other vehicles. Instead, with an FMS, a change in the kind of product can be handled just by sending a few signals to the computer.

■ **Example of Flexible Manufacturing System: Nissan's Multiple-Vehicle Production Line.** At the Canton, Mississippi, Nissan factory, pickup trucks, minivans, and sport utility vehicles can all be sent down the same assembly line. Robotic welding machines can be programmed to put weld spots in different places for different vehicles. Robotic painting machines can be programmed to paint different kinds of vehicles one after the other without pause.[16] ■

3 Lean Manufacturing: Using Fewest Resources

Lean manufacturing **is the production of products by eliminating unnecessary steps and using the fewest resources, as well as continually striving for**

7 Lean manufacturing. Shelter Systems is a Westminster, Maryland, manufacturer of wood structural building components, such as this roof truss. Within the plant, the lumber storage and retrieval system moves lumber in only one direction, traveling in straight lines, from saw to assembly to loading dock. Lumber can also be stored, sorted, and accessed in both horizontal and vertical space, ensuring that 80% of the lumber stored is no more than 25 feet from the saw it's cut at. The system's ergonomic design also allows a single worker to operate each machine and to retrieve lumber without ever having to lift a single piece.

improvement. Thus, waste is completely eliminated to the extent possible, labor is pared to the minimum, machines use the fewest moving parts, rejected products are considered unacceptable, and materials are delivered as closely as possible to the time when they are needed (just-in-time system).

Lean manufacturing was honed by Japanese companies such as Toyota, which identified all the steps in the production process and eliminated unnecessary ones. The automaker also used teamwork to examine problems and fix them as soon as they appeared. Finally, supplies were obtained from vendors only as they were needed in the factory (just-in-time system).[17]

Lean manufacturing isn't a miracle solution to a company's problems. For instance, during an economic slump it is hard for a lean factory to cut jobs because workers in such operations are so highly specialized that each one is vital to keeping things running smoothly.[18] **7**

BRIEFING / A WORLD OF CONSTANT CHANGE

Starbucks Takes on "Lean" Techniques. Can lean techniques be applied to service companies? In 2009, feeling the pressure of the recession and growing competition, Starbucks, which had built its success on being an "anti-fast-food" business, decided to behave more like its mainstream competitors and adopt "lean" techniques to speed up customer service.

In the future, managers advised, coffee beans were to be kept on top of the counter instead of underneath so the baristas didn't have to bend over, and bins were color-coded so they could find a particular roast without having to read labels. In addition, different colored tape was also to be used to quickly differentiate between pitchers of soy, nonfat, or low-fat milk.[19]

A year later, however, harried baristas were being told to slow down because customers complained the chain had "reduced the fine art of coffee

8 Fast or friendly? How would you like that latte—delivered quickly in a batch with other customers' orders or delivered with careful attention to your individual tastes? Starbucks thought it could help its bottom line by practicing lean techniques but ran into customer complaints about taking the romance out of coffee making. If you just want a fast cup of coffee on your way to work, where would you go?

Source: Jeff Greenberg/Alamy.

making to a mechanized process with all the romance of an assembly line," according to one report.[20] Baristas were told to stop making multiple drinks at the same time and focus instead on making no more than two drinks at a time. They were also supposed to steam milk for each drink separately rather than steaming an entire pitcher to be used for several beverages. **8**

While the lean techniques introduced earlier had improved the company's profitability, clearly they didn't all add up to a "fulfilling customer experience." ■

4 Mass Customization: Using Mass Production to Produce Individualized Products

When a tailor creates a one-of-a-kind suit, it is a *customized,* or individualized, product—the opposite of a mass-produced product, such as a suit you would buy at Macy's. However, new technologies have allowed the development of ***mass cus-tomization,*** **using mass production techniques to produce customized goods or services.** All kinds of products and services are now being produced to match individual customer needs and tastes, from clothes to cars to computers.[21]

BRIEFING / CUSTOMER FOCUS
TasteBook Uses Mass Customization to Manufacture Per-sonalized Cookbooks. Founder of the online photography service Ofoto, Kamran Mohsenin observed that customers took pride in making personalized calendars and books. With TasteBook.com, he took the idea one step further, allowing users to create personalized hardcover cookbooks.

For $34.95, cooking enthusiasts can go online and draw on CondéNet's Epicurious.com, a database of 25,000 recipes, to assemble a customized book of 100 recipes. The website also accommodates customers who want to incorporate their own or others' recipes. In addition, the process allows them to put their own title on the cover, as well as select from a variety of cover images, such as a bowl of cherries or corn on the cob.[22] ■

Mass customization has also been applied to services. For example, luxury hotels such as the Ritz-Carlton and Four Seasons constantly update their databases on individual guests so that local hotel staffs know the guests' individual preferences (such as favorite drinks) and can serve them accordingly.

Want to Know More? 9-6

What Are Some Other Kinds of Mass Customization?

Go to www.mybizlab.com.

THE BIG IDEA: To effectively design and manage production operations, business organizations need to consider facility location, facility layout, purchasing and supply-chain management, inventory and just-in-time systems for storing supplies, materials requirement planning and enterprise resource planning for purchasing and business organization, and Gantt and PERT charts for scheduling.

THE ESSENTIAL QUESTION: What factors should a business consider for effective production operations?

MyBizLab

MyBizLab: Check your understanding of these concepts at www.mybizlab.com.

As a businessperson, you not only need to design the goods and/or services you are selling, you also need to design the operations for producing them: where to locate your office, store, or factory; how to lay it out; how materials will be purchased and delivered; and so on. Thus, in this section we describe (1) *facility location*, (2) *facility layout*, (3) *purchasing and inventory*, (4) *supply-chain management and just-in-time systems*, (5) *materials requirement planning and enterprise resource planning*, and (6) *scheduling tools—Gantt and PERT charts*.

Facility Location: Selecting a Place for Your Company's Operations

What are four reasons an organization might locate its business facility in a particular place?

Facility location **is the process of selecting a location for company operations,** whether it's an office, a store, a gas station, a warehouse, a factory, or a cattle ranch. The kind of location, of course, will depend on the type of business and its special requirements—an apparel factory will have different needs from a cement plant, a gambling casino, a factory-outlet store, an import-export firm, an artichoke farm, and so on. ❾ However, there are four factors that often are important business considerations: *availability and cost of resources, nearness to suppliers, nearness to customers,* and *tax relief and local government support*.

❾ **Facility location.** In times past, industries were often located near their energy and supply sources. Steel mills were originally built in Pittsburgh, for example, because iron ore, coal, and limestone were available locally and nearby rivers could take away the heavy steel. Can you think of any industry that would benefit by being near a power source such as this wind farm?

Source: Brian A Jackson/Shutterstock.

1 Availability & Cost of Resources: Materials, Energy, & Labor

It's clear that the factors that principally influence the production process—materials, energy, labor, money, knowledge, and entrepreneurship—affect a facility's location. Consider materials, energy, and labor:

How Materials & Energy Affect Facility Location. Obviously, many businesses have to be located where the raw materials exist—silver mines, banana plantations, wind-powered utilities, and so on. Sometimes companies will locate facilities near particular sources of material resources or energy not because they have to but because it makes the most economic sense.

■ **Example** of Locating a Facility Near Resources: Google Builds Huge Server Farm on the Columbia River. Google, the search engine company, was expected to have 800,000 server computers by 2011. The company has built a sprawling server "farm," or data center, 80 miles east of Portland, Oregon, on the banks of the Columbia River. Why in that remote place? Because of the availability of cheap power from dams along the Columbia; water for cooling plants, which are essential because of the searing heat produced by so much computing power; and a large surplus of fiber-optic networking, a legacy of the dot.com boom. Microsoft and Yahoo have also set up shop in the region.[23] ■

How Labor Affects Facility Location. Although people seem to readily migrate all over the world to obtain work, businesses still clearly choose to locate their facilities in particular areas and countries—because the labor is inexpensive, because the labor force is highly skilled, because upper-level managers want to live there, or because of the quality of life there.

- **Inexpensive labor:** Inexpensive labor is the reason that automakers with union plants in Michigan relocated their manufacturing plants to nonunionized areas such as Mexico. It is also the reason that call centers have been moved from Boston to North Dakota or India. (We discussed outsourcing for cheap labor in great detail in Chapter 4.)

- **Highly skilled labor:** Technology companies such as Apple, Hewlett-Packard, and Intel grew up in Silicon Valley—the high-tech area south of San Francisco—because of a particular confluence of factors (university research, highly educated population). But why do they stay there when the real estate is so expensive? The answer: that's where the high-skill talent is, from software engineers to network administrators to financing specialists. ⑩

- **Wishes of upper-level managers:** Sometimes facilities are located in a particular place simply because top managers want to live there. For instance, the headquarters of certain hedge funds are located in prosperous suburbs of Connecticut near New York City because that's where the founders live.

- **Quality of life:** Companies may pick a particular area for their facility because of the quality of life—low crime, good schools, pleasant weather, and the like. Many firms have relocated to the Research Triangle Park near Durham and Raleigh, North Carolina, because of high education levels, good weather, and similar benefits.

Source: imagelab/Shutterstock.

⑩ **Wanted: smart people.** The southern part of the San Francisco Bay Area was originally called Silicon Valley because of the large number of silicon chip manufacturers located there, such as Intel and AMD. In 2011, even though the United States suffered high unemployment elsewhere, high-tech employers in the area were struggling to find enough educated professionals to meet job demands. Why do you think the United States isn't producing enough qualified computer engineers?

2 Nearness to Suppliers

Why did Henry Ford locate his automobile plant in Michigan? Because it was close to supplies of iron ore and the coal needed to turn it into steel. Locating production facilities near suppliers helps reduce the costs of shipping supplies and leads to better communication.

■ **Example** of Locating a Facility Near Suppliers: Ford's River Rouge Plant. Perhaps the most famous auto factory in the world, Ford Motor Company's River Rouge Plant is located in Dearborn, Michigan, where the Rouge and Detroit rivers meet. This site allows iron ore and coal to be easily delivered by boat. Measuring 1.5 miles wide by 1 mile long, the plant has its own docks, interior railroad track, electricity plant, and ore-processing facility. The Rouge, as it is called, is able to turn raw materials into vehicles within this single complex.[24] ■

3 Nearness to Customers: Reducing Time to Market

The benefit of locating a production facility close to customers is that it can reduce *time to market*—**the length of time it takes from a product being conceived until it is available for sale.**

■ **Example** of Locating a Facility Near Customers: General Motors in China. After China moved from rigid communism to a hybrid form of capitalism, in 1998 General Motors reintroduced Buick, a symbol of luxury in China in the 1930s, by opening a Buick factory in Shanghai. Now GM is hoping to gain acceptance for another of its brands, having recently opened a Chevrolet plant in Yantai, near Chinese consumers.[25] ■

4 Tax Relief & Local Government Support

Some states have more favorable tax treatment of companies than other states do. Nevada, for instance, has no warehouse tax, which makes that state a good place for companies storing products for shipment. In order to provide local jobs, many local governments also provide tax benefits, zoning changes, and other financial incentives. Some cities have special enterprise zones, as described in Chapter 6.

Want to Know More? 9-7

What Are Some of the Other Ways Government Supports Small Business?

Go to www.mybizlab.com.

Facility Layout: Arranging Your Production Resources

What are three options for layouts for producing goods?

***Facility layout* is the physical arrangement of equipment, offices, rooms, people, and other resources within an organization for producing goods or services.** The arrangements can be similar for delivering both goods and services.

The three principal facility layouts for producing goods are *product layout*, *process layout*, and *fixed-position layout*.

1 Product Layout: The Assembly-Line Arrangement

In the *product layout*, equipment and tasks are arranged into an assembly line—a sequence of steps for producing a single product. This method, of course, is the classic way by which automobiles are manufactured, but it's also used for making household appliances. (*See* ■ *Panel 9.3*.)

■ **PANEL 9.3 Product layout: pickup truck assembly plant.** Product layouts are usually set up to produce only one kind of product at a time.

| Frame, wheels, and drive train | Install engine | Install steering and seats | Install cab, hood, truck bed | Install doors and windows |

2 Process Layout: Work Grouped by Function

In the *process layout*, similar work is grouped by function. A cabinet maker or machine shop, for example, might perform work in one room before the product is moved to another department for finishing work. Or a hospital might perform x-rays in one department, patient examinations in another, and surgery in another. (*See* ■ *Panel 9.4*.)

■ **PANEL 9.4 Process layout: body work shop.** Groups of employees work on a similar function in a single department.

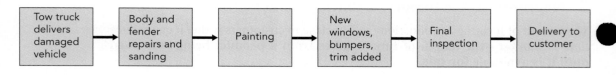

Tow truck delivers damaged vehicle → Body and fender repairs and sanding → Painting → New windows, bumpers, trim added → Final inspection → Delivery to customer

3 Fixed-Position Layout: Equipment & Labor Transported to Production Site

In the *fixed-position layout*, **materials, equipment, and labor are transported to one location.** This is certainly the case for a nuclear power plant, a dam, or an airport. But it's also true for most buildings. (*See* ■ *Panel 9.5*.)

■ **PANEL 9.5 Fixed-position layout: building a restaurant.** Different employees, equipment, and materials move from one work area to another.

(6) Roofing
(5) Electrical work
(4) Plumbing and heating
(3) Rough carpentry
(2) Foundation
(1) Grading

(7) Windows and doors
(8) Finish carpentry
(9) Flooring
(10) Painting
(11) Signage
(12) Parking lot paving

Purchasing & Inventory: Getting & Storing the Best Resources

What are two strategies for lining up suppliers, and what is inventory?

Purchasing **is the activity of finding the best resources for the best price from the best suppliers to produce the best goods and services.** The Internet, of course, has made it much easier for a company to search for the best suppliers and best price—just as the Net makes it easier for the suppliers to scout for possible customers.

Dealing with Suppliers: Two Strategies

There are two strategies for dealing with suppliers—*use a lot of suppliers* or *use just a trusted few*.

The First Strategy: Use Many Suppliers to Ensure Constant Resources. Some companies will deal with many suppliers, reasoning that if one of them fails in some way or charges too high a price, another will be able to deliver the resources needed at the right price. This strategy has been popular in the past.

The Second Strategy: Use a Few Trusted Suppliers to Ensure Reliability. More recently, companies tend to deal with just a few suppliers, believing there will be more reliability and fewer chances proprietary secrets will be revealed.

■ **Example of Supplier Strategies: Kodak.** In the late 1990s, Kodak's Worldwide Purchasing Group was highly decentralized, and a huge supply base of 3,500 suppliers accounted for 80% of the company's spending. Over a three-year period, Kodak revised its supplier system, integrating many processes and reducing suppliers down to 877 companies, cutting procurement costs by $1 billion.[26] ■

i

Want to Know More? 9-8

What Are the Best Ways to Deal with Suppliers?

Go to www.mybizlab.com.

Inventory & Inventory Control: Keeping the Goods in Stock

When you buy household supplies—soap, toilet paper, towels, and the like—where do you store them? Businesses face the same problem—only more so, because resources are constantly used up by the production process or by sales to

Source: Stan Kujawa/Alamy.

⑪ **Small-business inventory.** Even a one-person guitar maker must keep enough woods, strings, and other materials on hand to be able to make instruments—plus enough guitars to sell to customers. Keeping the stock organized and updated can require a good deal of time and organization. Imagine the challenge of inventory supply and control in large companies, such as Walmart or Home Depot.

customers. The question of storing supplies (or products resulting from the production process) is known as an inventory problem. ⑪

Inventory **is the name given to goods kept in stock to be used for the production process or for sales to customers.** Makers of acoustic guitars have to store special woods. Shoe stores have to store shoes. In both cases, there are problems with *inventory control*—**the system for determining the right quantity of resources and keeping track of their location and use.** Guitar woods, for instance, may need to be stored in special climate-controlled conditions. Shoe stores have to cover the widest variety of sizes and fashions.

Supply-Chain Management & Just-in-Time Systems: Storing the Supplies That Suppliers Supply

What is supply-chain management, and how is JIT often a better way to handle inventory?

You can visualize the movement of supplies into a production facility as representing a long chain involving many suppliers—a *supply chain*. In this view, one company's output becomes another company's input. The JCPenney dress shoes you might buy were supplied by shoemaking factories, which in turn were supplied by leather tanners, which in turn were supplied by cattle ranchers—all representing the supply chain.

Supply-Chain Management: Integrating Production from Suppliers to Customer

Many businesses now engage in a process known as *supply-chain management,* **in which companies produce goods and services by integrating many facilities, functions, and processes, from suppliers to customers.** This requires that suppliers be much more involved in the design process. We gave an example of supply-chain management with Kodak earlier. We return to the subject of supply-chain management in Chapter 15.

Source: J. IRWIN/ClassicStock/Alamy.

⑫ **Just-in-time product.** Harley-Davidson shipped 206,000 motorcycles in 2008. That's a lot of motorcycle parts. If Harley tried to store all those parts under its own roof, it's easy to imagine how difficult—and expensive—it would be to keep track of them. Having parts delivered precisely when needed, or just in time (JIT), puts the burden on the supplier. Can you think of reasons why JIT might not work for some manufacturers?

Just-In-Time: Let Supplies Be Delivered Just as They're Needed

Holding a storeroom or warehouse full of inventory can be expensive. Many businesses, therefore, now rely on a concept called *just-in-time (JIT) inventory control,* **in which only minimal supplies are kept on the organization's premises and others are delivered by the suppliers on an as-needed basis.** Once a JIT system is established, all resources should be continuously flowing, with suppliers connected electronically to ensure everyone knows when materials will be needed.

■ **Example of Just-in-Time System: Harley-Davidson.** After the Harley-Davidson Motorcycle Company instituted a JIT system for delivering motorcycle parts on an as-needed basis, inventory levels went down by 75%, productivity went up by 50%, and the percentage of motorcycles coming off the line completed went from 76% to 99%.[27] ⑫ ■

JIT doesn't work for all situations. For instance, it's not effective if demand varies throughout the year, if a firm has a diverse product line, if businesses underestimate the quantities of supplies needed, or if suppliers can't locate close by or make deliveries on time or otherwise meet the whims of their clients.

MRP & ERP: Using Computers to Deliver the Right Resources to the Right Place at the Right Time

What are two technologies for managing resources?

Purchasing and supply-chain management has been much enhanced by the use of computers. This has developed into two kinds of systems, *materials requirement planning (MRP)* and *enterprise resource planning (ERP).*

Materials Requirement Planning: Using a Bill of Materials to Deliver the Right Materials on Time to the Right Place

Like JIT, *materials requirement planning (MRP)* **is a computer-based method of delivering the right amounts of supplies to the right place at the right time for the production of goods. It uses what is known as a *bill of materials,* which is essentially a list of materials that go into the finished product.** This list is programmed into a computer that already contains the customer's order (for example, 500,000 cellphones) so that the right kinds of materials can be delivered in the right quantities at the right time.

Enterprise Resource Planning: Integrating All Business Processes across the Entire Company

Want to Know More? 9-9

What Are Some Good Examples of ERP?

Go to www.mybizlab.com.

MRP is concerned with organizing the materials to go into a single product. ERP is concerned with the firm's entire enterprise. *Enterprise resource planning (ERP)* **is a computer-based system that collects and provides information about a company's entire enterprise, including identifying customer needs, receipt of orders, distribution of finished goods, and receipt of payment.**

Most of today's ERP applications are offered by software vendors such as SAP and Oracle Applications, which have the applications on their own computer systems and allow companies to access them via the Internet.

Scheduling Tools: Gantt & PERT Charts

How could Gantt and PERT charts help handle schedules?

Scheduling **is the act of determining time periods for each task in the production process.** Two tools used by managers in the scheduling process are *Gantt charts* and *PERT charts.*

Gantt Charts: Visual Time Schedules for Work Tasks

Developed by **Henry L. Gantt,** Gantt charts are useful for graphically indicating deadlines. **A *Gantt chart* is a kind of time schedule—a specialized bar chart that shows the relationship between the kind of work tasks planned and their scheduled completion dates.** (*See* ■ *Panel 9.6.*)

■ **PANEL 9.6 Gantt chart for designing a cellphone app.** Visual chart of tasks done and the time planned for remaining tasks to develop a cellphone app.

Stage of development	Week 1	Week 2	Week 3	Week 4	Week 5	Week 6
Review other cellphone apps	‖‖‖‖‖‖‖‖‖‖‖					
Get content info for your app		‖‖‖‖‖‖‖‖‖‖				
Learn app programming tools		‖‖‖‖‖‖‖‖‖‖	‖‖‖‖‖‖‖‖‖‖			
Create cellphone app				///////////	///////////	/////
"Publish" app online						/////////

‖‖‖‖‖‖‖‖‖‖ Done   /////////// To be done

There is nothing difficult about creating a Gantt chart. You express the time across the top and the tasks down along the left side. Indeed, you could use this device in college to help schedule and monitor the work you need to do to meet course requirements and deadlines (for papers, projects, and tests).

A number of personal computer software packages can help you create and modify Gantt charts, such as CA-SuperProject, Microsoft Project Manager, Sure-Trak Project Manager, and TurboProject Professional.

A Gantt chart may be used to compare planned time to complete a task with actual time taken to complete it, so that you can see how far ahead or behind schedule you are for the entire project. This enables you to make adjustments so as to hold the final target date.

PERT Charts: Identifying Best Sequence of Production Activities

Although a Gantt chart can express the interrelations among the activities of relatively small projects, it becomes cumbersome and unwieldy when used for large, complex projects. More sophisticated management planning tools may be needed, such as PERT charts. A **_PERT chart_—PERT stands for _program evaluation and _review _technique—is a diagram for determining the best sequencing of tasks.** Managers use PERT to analyze the tasks involved in completing a project and estimate the minimum time needed to complete each task, as well as the total time for the project. (*See* ■ *Panel 9.7.*)

■ **PANEL 9.7 PERT chart for setting up an art/photography show.** This shows the time (in weeks) involved in finding art/photography submissions, an exhibit hall, and judges; judging the submissions; and presenting awards.

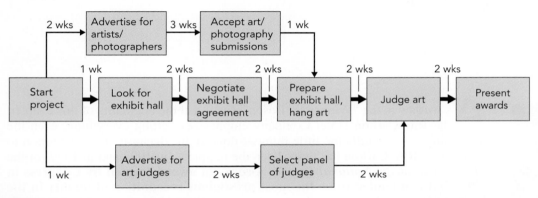

Critical path—sequence that takes longest to complete—indicated by

Using a PERT chart in a production process involves the following steps:

1. **Identify the Tasks.** You identify the tasks required in the production process.
2. **Arrange Tasks in Order.** You arrange the tasks in the order in which they must take place.
3. **Estimate Time for Each Task.** You estimate the time needed to complete each task.
4. **Diagram the Task Sequences and Times.** Using these steps, you draw a PERT diagram (called a PERT network). You can then compute the *critical path.*
5. **Compute the Critical Path. In a PERT chart, the _critical path_ is the sequence of tasks that takes the longest time to complete.** In other words, the critical path will tell you the time expected to complete the project.

Key Takeaway 9-3
Operations management tools: facility location and layout, purchasing and inventory, supply-chain management and JIT systems, MRP and ERP, Gantt and PERT charts.

Quality Assurance: Producing Better Products & Services

THE BIG IDEA: Total quality management (TQM) is dedicated to continuous quality improvement, training, and customer satisfaction. It begins with the concept of quality, the total ability of a product or service to meet customer needs, and quality assurance, the strategy for minimizing errors by managing each stage of production. Three quality assurance techniques are the ISO 9000 series, statistical process control, and Six Sigma.

THE ESSENTIAL QUESTION: How do top companies improve the quality of their products or services?

MyBizLab

MyBizLab: Check your understanding of these concepts at www.mybizlab.com.

⑬ Award winning. The Ritz-Carlton Hotel Company has twice been recognized with the Malcolm Baldrige National Quality Award for providing top-quality service. Have you had any experience with a company that does things so well that you think they would qualify for this award?

Want to Know More? 9-10

Who Else Has Won the Baldrige Award?

Go to www.mybizlab.com.

As we saw in the "Winners & Losers" section at the beginning of this chapter, the Ritz-Carlton Hotel Company emphasizes getting everything, even the little things—*especially* the little things—done right. Because of this attention to excellence, Ritz-Carlton has twice been the recipient (in 1992 and in 1999) of the ***Malcolm Baldrige National Quality Award,*** **an award created by Congress in 1987 that is intended to be the most prestigious recognition of quality in the United States.** Baldrige awards are given annually to U.S. organizations in manufacturing, service, education, health care, and small business. ⑬

The Baldrige award was created when U.S. managers in the early 1980s became aware that three-fourths of Americans were telling survey takers that the label "Made in America" no longer represented craftsmanship. Indeed, U.S. consumers were saying they considered products made overseas, especially in Japan, equal to or better in quality compared to U.S.-made products. Much of the drive for quality improvements in Japanese products came from American consultants **W. Edwards Deming** and **Joseph M. Juran,** whose work led to the commitment to quality known as total quality management.[28]

Total Quality Management: Seeking Continual Improvement

What is total quality management, and what are its four components?

Quality **refers to the total ability of a product or service to meet customer needs.** The term refers to not only giving customers what they want but also reducing defects and errors before and after the product or service is delivered to them.

Whereas once quality inspections were done by a separate department at the end of a production line, today, in a strategy known as quality control, it is implemented throughout the entire process. ***Quality assurance*** **is defined as the process of minimizing errors by managing each stage of production.** Among other techniques, it relies on statistical sampling to locate errors by testing some of the items in a production run.

Source: Courtesy of The Ritz-Carlton Hotel Company, L.L.C.

TQM: What It Is

The work of Deming and Juran has led to a strategic commitment to quality known as total quality management. **Led by top management and supported throughout the organization,** *total quality management (TQM)* **is a comprehensive approach dedicated to continuous quality improvement, training, and customer satisfaction.**

The Four Components of TQM

There are four components of TQM, as follows:

1. **Continuous Improvement Is Considered a Priority.** TQM companies make small, incremental improvements an everyday priority in all areas of the organization. Continually improving everything a little bit at a time enables a TQM company to achieve long-term quality, efficiency, and customer satisfaction. ⑭

2. **Every Employee Needs to Be Involved.** TQM companies see that every employee is involved in the continuous improvement process. This means that workers must be empowered and trained to find and solve problems. The goal is to build teamwork, trust, mutual respect.

3. **TQM Companies Learn from Customers, and Their Employees Learn from Other Employees.** Successful companies pay attention to the people who use their products or services—the customers. Within the companies, employees listen and learn from other employees outside their own work areas.

4. **Accurate Standards Are Used to Identify and Eliminate Problems.** TQM organizations are always alert to how competitors do things better, then try to improve on them—an activity known as benchmarking. *Benchmarking* **is a process by which a company compares its performance with that of high-performing organizations.** For instance, Xerox Corporation has used benchmarking to measure its products and practices against companies recognized as industry leaders.

Source: Courtesy of Andy's Painting.

⑭ **Not governed by size.** Andy's Painting of Moorestown, New Jersey, demonstrated that you don't have to be a multibillion-dollar company to apply the standards and practices of TQM. In fact, owner Andy Yaman uses TQM as his primary form of advertising and to successfully distinguish his company from hundreds of competitors in his geographical area. What do you think are the primary challenges of implementing TQM in a small company?

Want to Know More? 9-11

What Are Some Prominent Examples of TQM Industry Usage & Who Is William Deming?

Go to www.mybizlab.com.

Three Quality-Control Techniques: ISO 9000, Statistical Process Control, & Six Sigma

How would I describe the three principal quality-control techniques?

Companies now use a number of quality-control techniques to continually try to improve products and services. Here we discuss three of them: the *ISO 9000 series, statistical process control,* and *Six Sigma.*

ISO 9000 Series: Meeting Standards of Independent Experts

If you're a purchasing agent for Goodyear Tire and Rubber Company in Akron, Ohio, how can you tell if the synthetic rubber you're buying overseas is adequate? If you're a sales rep for Pfizer, the pharmaceutical company, how will your overseas clients know that your products have the characteristics they want?

Of course, buyers and sellers can rely on a company's past reputation or personal assurances. A better system was developed in 1979, when the International Organization for Standardization (ISO), based in Geneva, Switzerland, created a set of quality standards known as the 9000 series. These have been called "a kind of Good Housekeeping seal of approval for global business," in one description.[29] The *ISO 9000 series* **consists of quality-assurance procedures companies** must install—in purchasing, manufacturing. inventory, shipping, and other areas—that can be audited by "registrars," or independent quality-assurance experts. The goal of these procedures is to reduce flaws in manufacturing and to improve productivity, which requires stringent employee training. Companies also are required to document the procedures and comply with key ISO management standards, such as traceable changes and easy reporting. Most companies use software systems such as DocBase Direct, a Web-delivered document and forms management system.

The ISO 9000 designation is now recognized in 100 countries, and many manufacturing corporations around the world are insisting that suppliers have ISO 9000 certification.

■ **Example of ISO 9000 Certification: Overland Products.** "You close some expensive doors if you're not certified," says Bill Ekeler, general manager of Overland Products, a Nebraska tool-and-die-stamping firm.[30] In addition, because the ISO process forced him to analyze his company from the top down, he found ways to streamline manufacturing processes that improved his profitability. ■

Statistical Process Control: Testing with Periodic Random Samples

All kinds of products require periodic inspection during their manufacture: beer, hamburger meat, flashlight batteries, and so on. The method often used for this is *statistical process control,* **a statistical technique that uses periodic random samples from production runs to see if quality is being maintained within a standard range of acceptability.** If quality is not acceptable, production is halted to allow corrective action.

■ **Example of Statistical Process Control: The Printing of This Book.** As the pages of this book were being printed, instruments called densitometers and colorimeters were used to measure ink density and trueness of color, taking samples of printed pages at fixed intervals. This is an ongoing check for quality control. ■

Six Sigma: Data-Driven Ways to Eliminate Defects

"The biggest problem with the management technique known as Six Sigma is this: It sounds too good to be true," says a *Fortune* writer. "How would your company like a 20% increase in profit margins within one year, followed by profitability over the long-term that is *ten times* what you're seeing now? How about a 4% (or greater) annual gain in market share?"[31]

What is Six Sigma, and is it really this miraculous? Developed by Motorola in 1985, *Six Sigma* **is a rigorous statistical analysis process that reduces defects in manufacturing and service-related processes.** ⑮ By testing thousands of variables in everything from product design to manufacturing to billing, a company using the process tries to improve quality and reduce waste to the point where errors nearly vanish.

Sigma is the Greek letter that statisticians use to define a standard deviation. The

Want to Know More? 9-12

What Are Some Examples of the Use of ISO 9000?

Go to www.mybizlab.com.

Want to Know More? 9-13

What Is ISO 14000?

Go to www.mybizlab.com.

⑮ **Competitive edge?** Can the standards and process of Six Sigma represent a competitive edge? Many companies certainly believe they do, and consulting companies such as eXample conduct training and certification programs throughout the world. Shown here are the graduates of a recent session in Bangalore, India.

Source: eXample Consulting Group – Enabling Excellence! www.eXampleCG.com.

higher the sigma, the fewer the deviations from the norm—in other words, the fewer the defects. The attainment of Six Sigma means there are no more than 3.4 defects per million products or procedures. Six Sigma means being 99.9997% perfect. By contrast, Three Sigma or Four Sigma means settling for only 99% perfect—the equivalent of a utility failing to deliver electricity about 7 out of 730 hours in a month. Or a major airport failing to land about 3 planes out of 340 landings in a day.[32] "Six Sigma gets people away from thinking that 96% is good, to thinking that 40,000 failures per million is bad," says the vice president of a consulting firm.[33]

Six Sigma is not necessarily perfect, since it cannot compensate for human error or control events outside a company. Still, it lets managers approach problems with the assumption that there's a data-oriented, tangible way to solve them.[34]

> **Key Takeaway 9-4**
> Three quality-control techniques: ISO 9000, statistical process control, Six Sigma

In Rotterdam, Holland, Club Watt captures customers' gyrations on the dance floor to generate electricity for powering the club's light show.[35] Other businesses have also discovered that "going green" pays off.

Issues of sustainability and climate change have businesses focusing not only on green inventions and products but also on improved internal operations and business practices. With this new awareness, other institutions are following suit by offering training for green jobs, covering everything from engineers developing alternative fuels to people working in recycling plants.

- **Training programs:** Various programs offer training and internships in green construction, energy efficiency, and solar panel installation. An example is the Oakland, California, Green Job Corps.[36]
- **Community colleges:** Two-year colleges are at the forefront in offering certification programs for

"everything from wind technicians to solar cell designers to energy auditors," according to a *Fortune* article.[37]

- **Four-year colleges:** Many colleges and universities are offering degrees in environmental studies, environmental science, environmental management, bioengineering, and energy resources engineering. Arizona State University, for example, offers bachelor's degrees in sustainability.[38]
- **Business schools:** Conventional business graduate schools such as Stanford and Harvard have begun offering courses leading to MBAs in sustainable business practices. In addition, there are experimental schools such as Presidio School of Management in San Francisco that offer Green MBAs that focus on the "triple bottom line" of people, planet, and profit.[39]

Summary

9.1 Operations Management: How Goods & Services Are Produced

THE ESSENTIAL QUESTION: *What is the process for obtaining high-quality goods and services?*

What terms are used to describe how goods and services are produced? Production or operations refers to any process that takes basic resources and converts them into finished products. Operations management is the management of the process of transforming materials, labor, and other resources into goods and/or services.

How does operations management vary for manufacturing and services? Manufacturing businesses deal with things; they convert raw materials into finished products or goods. Service businesses deal mainly with people; they convert people's unmet needs into satisfied needs.

9.2 Production Processes: Improving Production Techniques

THE ESSENTIAL QUESTION: *What are the various types of production processes and technologies, old and new?*

What is form utility, and what are two ways of adding value in converting resources into finished products? Form utility is the value that people add in converting resources, by changing their form, into finished products. In analytic transformation, resources are broken down to create finished products. In synthetic transformation, resources are combined to create finished products.

How would I identify a continuous production process as opposed to an intermittent process? A continuous process is a production process in which goods or services are turned out in a long production run on an ongoing basis over time. An intermittent process is a production process in which finished goods or services are turned out in a series of short production runs and the machines are changed frequently to make different products.

What are five significant technology changes that improved efficiency in production? The first, mechanization, was the use of machines to do the work formerly performed by people. The next was standardization, the use of uniform parts that could be easily interchanged with similar parts. The assembly line consisted of a series of steps for assembling a product, each step using the same interchangeable parts and each being performed repetitively by the same worker. Automation is the use of machines (such as robots) rather than human labor to perform production tasks. Mass production is the production of uniform goods in great quantities.

How would I describe four kinds of technologies developed in recent times to increase productive efficiencies? The

four technologies are CAD/CAM/CIM, flexible manufacturing systems, lean manufacturing, and mass customization. CAD (computer-aided design) consists of computer programs to design products, structures, civil engineering drawings, and maps. CAM (computer-aided manufacturing) is the use of computers in the manufacturing process. CIM (computer-integrated manufacturing) unites CAD and CAM. A flexible manufacturing system (FMS) is a facility that can be modified quickly to manufacture different parts. Lean manufacturing is the production of products by eliminating unnecessary steps and using the fewest resources, as well as continually striving for improvement. Mass customization is use of mass production techniques to produce customized goods or services.

9.3 Operations Management Planning: Designing & Managing Production Operations

THE ESSENTIAL QUESTION: *What factors should a business consider for effective production operations?*

What are four reasons an organization might locate its business facility in a particular place? (1) Availability and cost of resources—materials, energy, and labor. (2) Nearness to suppliers. (3) Nearness to customers. (4) Tax relief and local government support.

What are three options for layouts for producing goods? Facility layout is the physical arrangement of equipment, offices, rooms, people, and other resources within an organization for producing goods or services. The three principal facility layouts for producing goods are (1) product layout, with equipment and tasks arranged into an assembly line—a sequence of steps for producing a single product; (2) process layout, in which similar work is grouped by function; and (3) fixed-position layout, with materials, equipment, and labor being transported to one location.

What are two strategies for lining up suppliers, and what is inventory? Two strategies for dealing with suppliers are to use many suppliers to ensure constant resources or use a few trusted suppliers to ensure reliability. Inventory is the name given to goods kept in stock to be used for the production process or for sales to customers.

What is supply-chain management, and how is JIT often a better way to handle inventory? In supply-chain management, companies produce goods and services by integrating many facilities, functions, and processes, from suppliers to customers. In just-in-time (JIT) inventory control, only minimal supplies are kept on the firm's premises and others are delivered by the suppliers when needed.

What are two technologies for managing resources? Materials requirement planning (MRP) is a computer-based method of delivering the right amounts of supplies to the right place at the right time for the production of goods. Enterprise resource planning (ERP) is a computer-based system that collects and provides information about a company's entire enterprise, including identifying customer needs, receipt of orders, distribution of finished goods, and receipt of payment.

How could Gantt and PERT charts help handle schedules? A Gantt chart is a specialized bar chart that shows the relationship between the kind of work tasks planned and their scheduled completion data. A PERT (program evaluation and review technique) chart is for determining the best sequencing of production activities.

9.4 Quality Assurance: Producing Better Products & Services

THE ESSENTIAL QUESTION: *How do top companies improve the quality of their products or services?*

What is total quality management, and what are its four components? The Malcolm Baldrige National Quality Award,

created by Congress in 1987, is the most prestigious recognition of quality in the United States. Quality refers to the total ability of a product or service to meet customer needs. Quality assurance is the process of minimizing errors by managing each stage of production. Total quality management (TQM) is a comprehensive approach dedicated to continuous quality improvement, training, and customer satisfaction. The four components of TQM are (1) make continuous improvement a priority, (2) get every employee involved, (3) listen to and learn from customers and employees, and (4) use accurate standards to identify problems.

How would I describe the three principal quality-control techniques? The ISO 9000 series consists of quality-assurance procedures companies must install that can be audited by independent quality-assurance experts. Statistical process control uses periodic random samples from production runs to see if quality is being maintained within a standard range of acceptability. Six Sigma is a rigorous statistical analysis process that reduces defects in manufacturing and service-related processes.

Key Terms

analytic transformation 259
assembly line 261
automation 262
benchmarking 275
bill of materials 271
computer-aided design (CAD) 263
computer-aided manufacturing (CAM) 263
computer-integrated manufacturing (CIM) 263
continuous process 260
critical path 273
enterprise resource planning (ERP) 272
facility layout 268
facility location 266
fixed-position layout 269
flexible manufacturing system (FMS) 263

form utility 259
Gantt chart 272
intermittent process 260
inventory 270
inventory control 270
ISO 9000 series 275
just-in-time (JIT) inventory control 271
lean manufacturing 263
Malcolm Baldrige National Quality Award 274
mass customization 265
mass production 262
materials requirement planning (MRP) 271
mechanization 261
operations 256
operations management 257

PERT chart 273
process layout 268
product layout 268
production 256
purchasing 269
quality 274
quality assurance 274
robotics 262
robots 262
scheduling 272
Six Sigma 276
standardization 261
statistical process control 276
supply-chain management 270
synthetic transformation 260
time to market 267
total quality management (TQM) 275

Pop Quiz Prep

1. What is the definition of operations management?
2. How does operations management differ for manufacturing and services?
3. What is an example of analytic transformation?
4. How is *standardization* defined?
5. In which facility layout are materials, equipment, and labor transported to one location?
6. What is just-in-time inventory control?
7. What is quality assurance?
8. Which quality-control technique requires the involvement of independent quality-assurance experts, or registrars?

Critical Thinking Questions

1. Levis Strauss and Company claims it will be using 21% less water during the manufacturing of its jeans.[40] Can you find examples of other companies that claim to be using more eco-friendly processes or a green manufacturing approach?

2. You have decided to start a small café near campus serving coffee and pastries, and you need to select suppliers. Discuss how you will select suppliers for your new venture and what factors will influence your selection.

3. Look at the label of any outer garment you happen to be wearing. This can be your sweater, hat, hoodie, T-shirt,

shirt, jacket, or pants. Where is the garment manufactured? What type of production process (continuous or intermittent) and facility layout would you assume for this garment? If you are in a classroom environment, is anyone wearing an item made in the USA?

4. Have you ever filled out a customer satisfaction survey because you were dissatisfied? If not, when was the last time you experienced service that fell short? What were the reasons, and what improvements would you recommend?

5. How is the production of services different from the production of goods?

Cases   Go to MyBizLab

Blackbird Guitars—"Big Sound, Small Body"

In 2005, Joe Luttwak, outdoor adventure traveler, decided to build a guitar he could take anywhere. Together with co-designer Kyle Wolfe, he founded Blackbird Guitars. The San Francisco–based company created a high-quality portable—streamlined, lightweight, durable, and less bulky than traditional guitars—without compromising sound or quality.

Blackbird caters to professionals and others who have always wanted a portable, compact, high-quality string instrument. Many of the Blackbird guitar models were inspired during Luttwak's days working at Ferrari in Italy. At Blackbird, he has transferred the unparalleled Ferrari quality and technology to his passion for making guitars. The development of the company's first product, the Rider, weighing less than three pounds, took two years. "Part mountain dulcimer, part F1 race car," Blackbird guitars are high-performance instruments built one by one for the road.

Blackbird uses advanced manufacturing early in the process, including foam molds and three-dimensional computer-aided design (CAD). A CAD model is created of the guitar including all its parts (even down to the fret markers on the neck of the guitar) so that every dimension is fine-tunable for superb playability, action, and tone.[41]

Luttwak began to generate as many concepts as possible, using the encouragement and feedback of many guitar-making luminaries in the San Francisco Bay Area.[42] What sets this company apart is its unparalleled and obsessive attention to detail and quality. Its products take several years to design. If a guitar isn't right, the team won't risk their reputation by having it go out the door. Each guitar is made using a unique blend of technology and craftsmanship on a very intermittent basis, one by one, turning out about 200 instruments a year (all of which sell out quickly). The instrument is tested and tweaked and the company describes its production process as "an elegant blend of old-world craftsmanship with the latest 3D CAD design innovation, robotic front-end process, and small-scale fabrication technologies." The company emphasizes quality over quota, evident in its small annual production and slow, intentional growth. It is clearly a strategy that works. While some of their

competitors have gone out of business, the demand for Blackbird guitars continues to grow.

Blackbird guitars are distinguished from competitors' models by their hollow uni-body (all one piece) shell. This eliminates the weak and sound-absorbing joints traditionally found with other guitars. The strong and stiff carbon fiber structure gives the guitar a lightweight and durable advantage over competitors.

A guitar made after a Formula 1 race car? Blackbird even produces a Ferrari version of the carbon fiber guitar sporting a Maranello Red interior, a red A string, complete with a Scuderia emblem (Ferrari logo) on the head. According to Luttwak, "Great acoustic guitar construction, like great race car construction, benefits from stiff and ultra light materials. Using carbon fiber, like Ferrari's Formula 1 race cars, for the guitar's uni-body design produces an instrument that sounds better and is much more durable than any travel guitar available today." Get ready to be serenaded by someone with a Blackbird guitar on your next camping trip under the great starry skies.

1. Go to the blackbirdguitars.com website and discuss the technology used to create this unique instrument. What type of production process would you call this? How is computer-aided design utilized?

2. When an employee at Blackbird is out ill or delivery of supplies is late, what impact does this have on the company? How is this handled when it happens?

3. How would you describe the product development process? How about the production process? How long does it take?

4. How would you say Blackbird Guitars differentiates itself from traditional guitar makers? How much of this is in the production process?

5. Do you believe Blackbird Guitars could increase output without compromising the quality and craftsmanship for which they are known? What type of production would have to take place?

6. What concepts learned in this chapter are shown in the video?

BUSINESS DECISION CASE
My Coworker Is a Robot

This case explores the issue of robots in an office and hospital environment, and discusses how mobile telepresence robots are projected to save billions of dollars for the health care industry in Japan.

In the 1980s, the automobile industry underwent a major transformation with the introduction of robots that performed jobs once completed by humans. Automobile makers use robots to perform welding chores and other repetitive tasks that humans find gruesomely boring; the robots execute these jobs highly efficiently, with very few complaints, and even fewer injuries. Over 50% of all robots in use today are in automobile manufacturing.[43] However, with changing demographics, mobile robots have begun finding new homes in familiar places like the office, hospital, and home. Some of the robots look like computers on wheels, quickly becoming part of the new office and hospital landscape.

Mobile robots, also known as telepresence robots, are being tested around workplaces. They allow employees in remote locations to stay engaged and connected from afar. Mobile telepresence allows a user to take control of the robot remotely and wander around an office, interacting with coworkers and gauging their reactions through the built-in camera and microphone as if they were in the same room.[44] This may sound similar to Skype; however, where Skype is a stationary, more static way of communicating one on one, the more interactive robot conveniently wheels itself around from room to room or cubicle to cubicle.

Does this sound like a chapter from a sci-fi novel? It works like this: Try to picture yourself at work, sitting in your cubicle. Your manager's face wheels by on a 15-inch flat screen, attached to a pole. By the way, your manager is physically located in another part of the country. His robot "stand-in" is wheeling by on his way to a meeting you will be attending in a few minutes. At Mozilla (maker of Firefox, an open-source Web browser) in Menlo Park, California, situations like this are already common. The company has been testing robots made by Willow Garage of Menlo Park, which can be controlled remotely with a PC and Wi-Fi to run errands, chat, and attend meetings. Another advantage of the technology is that it saves the company money on costly business trips.

Mobile telepresence robots are also being tested as "caregivers" in assisted living facilities and as continuous in-home monitoring devices for elderly individuals who choose to live independently but need some assistance. The robots assist with cleaning chores, teach new skills using number and word games, and provide reminders to take medications—and they also provide an important sense of security. It has been suggested that the robots might reduce the feeling of isolation that the elderly often feel when living alone. With the first of 76 million baby boomers turning 65, and having higher life expectancy than any other generation, companies may have found a home (and a demand) for their robots.

Demographic changes in Japan suggest that this country may be a promising market for telepresence robots. Japan's aging population and low birthrate point to a looming shortage of workers; additionally Japan's elder care facilities and hospitals are already competing for nurses. These changes and the associated needs they create have not escaped Toyota's notice. In 2010, the company, which runs Toyota Memorial Hospital in Toyota City, Japan, began selling "Toyota Partner Robots" after extensive field trials. The idea of robotic nurses drew additional support when Japan's Machine Industry Memorial Foundation estimated the country could save 2.1 trillion yen (about $21 billion) in health care costs each year using robots to monitor the nation's elderly.[45] With the service sector continuing to grow, do you see a day when we as humans will embrace our ever-reliable robotic coworkers?

What's Your Take?

1. How would you feel with a robot in your office environment or as your supervisor? Do you see a time when you will work side by side with a robot or have one helping you care for your grandmother or helping clean the dishes?

2. What type of resistance would there be if robots were placed in an assisted living facility for elders? Do you think different age groups will respond to the use of these robots differently?

3. With projected $21 billion cost savings from using robots in a health care environment, it isn't surprising that the concept is gaining momentum in Japan. What are the safety issues with the increased use of robots?

4. How does using Skype differ from using robots? Do you have experience using Skype, and, if so, how was it utilized?

5. If you had the option, would you prefer to travel to a location for a meeting or roll up your robot to the meeting?

Go to www.mybizlab.com for online activities and exercises related to the timely topics discussed in this chapter's Briefings, as well as additional theme-related Briefing *Spotlights* highlighting how these concepts apply in today's business environment.

In-chapter Briefing:
- Tele Atlas Helps Drivers by Updating Digital Mapmakers on Road Changes
- Starbucks Takes on "Lean" Techniques

Activity
- Going to the Net! – Minimal Human Intervention at BMW's Robotic Facility in Germany

Briefing Spotlight
- Toyota Operations after Japan Earthquake & Tsunami

In-chapter Briefing:
- TasteBook Uses Mass Customization to Manufacture Personalized Cookbooks

Activity:
- Developing Marketable Business Skills – Why Are Companies Moving toward Flexible Manufacturing and Customer-Driven Production Process?
- Going to the Net! – Taking Delivery When Needed: Just-in-time Inventory at Dell
- Going to the Net! – J.D. Powers' Ranking of Customer Service Champions

Briefing Spotlight:
- Mass Customization: The Impact on Operations of "Having It Your Way"

In-chapter Briefing:
- Metal Management Shreds Scrap Metal to Make New Steel

Activity
- Going to the Net! – Green Manufacturing: Calculating a Product's Carbon Footprint during Production

Briefing Spotlight
- Beer Maker SABMiller Tracks Its Water Footprint

Additional *Briefing Spotlights* available at MyBizLab:

- BUSINESS CULTURE & ETIQUETTE
- BUSINESS SKILLS & CAREER DEVELOPMENT
- GLOBAL BUSINESS
- INFO TECH & SOCIAL MEDIA
- LEGAL & ETHICAL PRACTICES
- PERSONAL FINANCE
- SMALL BUSINESS & ENTREPRENEURS
- SOCIALLY RESPONSIBLE BUSINESS

10

Motivating Employees

Achieving Exceptional Performance in the Workplace

After reading and studying this chapter, you will be able to answer the following essential questions:

MyBizLab

Where you see MyBizLab in this chapter, go to www.mybizlab.com for additional activities on the topic being discussed.

FORECAST:
What's Ahead in This Chapter

This chapter discusses how to motivate people to perform well. We describe 11 theories of motivation, showing how each one is used today and how it can benefit you as a manager. Beyond the theory, we also consider nonmonetary kinds of motivation, such as being nice and being an effective listener.

WINNER: United Scrap Metal Employees Love Their Jobs

"I wouldn't work anywhere else," says José Ruiz, 41, who has been employed for 15 years at United Scrap Metal on the outskirts of Chicago. USM's 24-acre yard is filled with mounds of scrap metal—pipe, steel beams, twisted car parts—where workers hand-sort the materials into categories for melting down at nearby foundries. "It is tedious, backbreaking, and hazardous duty," says one account.[1]

How does this grimy business keep workers from constantly checking want-ads? A principal reason is the family atmosphere created by CEO Marsha Serlin, 56, and her son Brad, 38, who is chief operating officer. One worker, who became the first full-time worker 25 years ago, estimates that he has recruited 30 relatives.

But knowing someone at USM is just the start. All applicants go through at least three interviews. In the first round, Brad screens for people who "play well with others," who are involved with community groups, and have good personal chemistry. In the second and third rounds, applicants meet with rank-and-file members of a particular department, who do an evaluation for likability as well as other skills; the CEO has final say-so. After hiring, the training process ensures that employees have a sense of connection to the company beyond their specific job. Even front-office hires must spend five weeks sorting pipe and counting soda cans.

Finally, there are the perks: bonuses, retirement plan, flextime for family obligations, an annual $2,000 tuition-reimbursement program, onsite English-language classes, health insurance coverage.

The result: in an industry in which employee turnover averages nearly 30% a year, USM's rate is just 7.5%. About 90% of the 115 workers have been with the company at least five years, and 49% have been around ten or more. The low turnover rate represents substantial savings: keeping a single yard worker a year or more costs about $3,500 less than hiring a new one. "Holding on to people has added to our bottom line," says Brad.

Source: holbox/Shutterstock.

LOSER: Allpoints Equipment Employees Rob Their Company

Do ordinary employees steal from their employers? Research suggests nearly any worker may in some situations.[2] One expert suggests most employees who steal from work are honest in other areas. But when stealing, he says, "there is a sense of entitlement and they don't think they are hurting anyone. Many feel angry and entitled to steal from work because of perceived feelings of being victimized or not being appreciated."[3]

What do you do if employees are taking from you? That's what CEO Alan Bridges of Tampa, Florida, had to think about. Since 1992, when he founded Allpoints Equipment, which sells racks, forklifts, and other warehouse supplies, he found he'd been robbed on nearly 50 occasions by people who worked for him.[4]

An accounting employee paid her home electricity bill out of Allpoints funds. A finance executive included his family vehicles in the firm's auto insurance plan. One worker stole $24,000 worth of equipment and scrap from a job site. When discovered, the workers were fired, of course, but Bridges was shocked at the extent of the criminality. Perhaps he should not have been: the average business loses the equivalent of 6% of revenue to fraud each year. And if employees feel not only unmotivated but also frustrated or dissatisfied about some aspect of the workplace, it can go a lot higher.

Many employees think they are entitled to the things they steal, figuring the company can well afford it. Some experts believe that employee theft represents workers' attempts to even the score when they feel that they haven't been treated fairly by their organizations.[5]

Bridges instituted a new accounting system and cross-trained employees so more than one worker now looks at the financials. He also spot-checks Allpoints' books. Employees are made to sign out company tools before taking them to job sites. Job applicants' credit histories are checked to look for debt problems.

Finally, Bridges had a frank discussion with his staff, explaining how employee theft was bad for morale and the bottom line, affecting their salaries and perks.

Source: Lenvert Konuk/Shutterstock.

YOUR CALL Will treating employees well make them produce more and keep them from stealing? Or does it matter what kind of perks they have—you have to watch out for slackers and thieves anyway? Your views about workers and their motivations may determine how productive they will be. At Allpoints, Bridges took steps to improve his controls in order to reduce theft and also talked to employees about the problem. Can you think of steps he might take to improve employee motivation? Do you think this would have an effect on the theft problem?

MyBizLab

Motivating for Performance

THE BIG IDEA: Motivation consists of the psychological processes that inspire people's goal-directed behavior. People's needs motivate them to perform specific behaviors in pursuit of certain goals for which they receive rewards, both extrinsic and intrinsic, that feed back and satisfy the original need. We describe five reasons motivation is important in business.

THE ESSENTIAL QUESTION: Why should I be motivated to study motivation?

MyBizLab: Check your understanding of these concepts at www.mybizlab.com.

W hat would make you rise early to make sure you got to work on time—and to work hard when you got there? Subsidized cafeterias? Free all-day snacks? On-site dry cleaning? Nearby child care plus summer camp for your kids? In-office physicians, hairdressers, Pilates instructors?

Believe it or not, these are among the benefits or perquisites (perks) available to employees at SAS, pronounced *sass,* the world's largest privately held software business. Based in Raleigh, North Carolina, SAS has been a regular presence for 14 years on *Fortune* magazine's list of "Best Companies to Work For" (No. 1 in 2010 and 2011).[6]

This "paragon of perks," in the magazine's description, is the brainchild of CEO Jim Goodnight, whose motives are not solely charitable. "My chief assets," he says of his employees, "drive out the gate every night. My job is to make sure they come back." The result: annual turnover of 2% in 2009, compared to a software industry average of 22%.

Want to Know More? 10-1

Key Terms & Definitions in Sequential Order to Study as You Go Along.

Go to www.mybizlab.com.

Motivation: What Lights Your Fire?

How does motivation work, and why is it important?

Why do you do the things you do? And why do others do what *they* do? Answer: Most people are motivated to fulfill their needs (or wants). And you as a future businessperson need to understand this process if you are to successfully guide employees to accomplish what you want.

Motivation: What It Is, How It Works

Motivation **consists of the psychological processes that induce people to pursue goals.** Although its actual operation is complex, the basic model of motivation is simple: you have certain *needs* that *motivate* you to perform specific *behaviors* to try to attain a certain *goal* for which you receive *rewards* that *feed back* and satisfy the original need. Here's an example:

BRIEFING / BUSINESS SKILLS & CAREER DEVELOPMENT
A Motivational Mind Game for Success. Want to make more money (*need*)? Would that impel (*motivate*) you to find a technique for working

more effectively without working more hours (*behavior*)? If it works, the technique will provide you with more money (*goal, reward*) and inform you (*feedback*) that working more productively without working more hours will fulfill your need for more money in the future.

You might, then, try this mind-game technique from Krissi Barr, founder of Barr Corporate Success, a business consulting firm in Cincinnati. "If I think something is going to take me an hour," she says, "I give myself 40 minutes. By shrinking your mental deadlines, you work faster and with greater focus."[7] ■

Two Types of Rewards: Extrinsic & Intrinsic

What is the difference between extrinsic and intrinsic rewards?

Rewards are of two types—*extrinsic* and *intrinsic*. Briefly, extrinsic is the money you get when you build and sell a boat; intrinsic is the feeling of accomplishment you get from building the boat.

You can use both to encourage your employees (and yourself) to better work performance. Consider the extrinsic and intrinsic rewards of starting up a green business, as described in the two Briefings that follow.

Extrinsic Rewards: Satisfaction in Receiving Pay or Recognition from Others

An *extrinsic reward* is the payoff, such as money or recognition, a person receives from others for performing a particular task. An extrinsic reward is an external reward. The payoff comes from the reward given to you as recognition for an accomplishment. Praise, pay raises, and promotions are examples of extrinsic rewards.

 BRIEFING / EARNING GREEN BY GOING GREEN
The Extrinsic Rewards of Investing in Green Energy: Making Money. A strong reason for investing in a startup company specializing in green energy or renewable energy is simple: to make money. Thus, in recent times, new "clean technology" companies—in solar, wind, biofuels, and the like—gained favor among investors because they didn't require as much cash to start as oil and gas exploration and promised big financial payoffs later.[8]

Makers of recycled and eco-friendly building materials are also jumping into green technology, and home builders are being drawn to green building even while construction spending as a whole has plunged owing to the recession. "While the rest of the [construction] industry has retreated," says one investor, "green construction has actually grown."[9] ❶ ■

 Key Takeaway 10-1
Extrinsic rewards: satisfaction in payoffs. Intrinsic rewards: satisfaction in accomplishments.

Want to Know More? 10-2

There Are Some Great Green Jobs Out There.

Go to www.mybizlab.com.

Source: Photograph by Sally Lindsay.

❶ **Green construction.** Designed by the architectural firm of Grimm + Parker and built by Hess Construction, Great Seneca Creek Elementary School in Montgomery County, Maryland, was the first school in the state to receive a LEED (Leadership in Energy and Environmental Design) Gold rating. It was also the first in the United States to be certified by the Green Building Council. Over its life, the school's green design will save over 30% in energy and 40% in water consumption.

Source: Courtesy of Green Clean Institute.

❷ Green Clean. To serve and facilitate the desire within the business community to go green, new organizations such as the Green Clean Institute (GCI) have been established to provide environmental education and training in such areas as building and office maintenance. What do you think managers see as the true benefits of engaging the services of companies like GCI?

Want to Know More? 10-3

Top 10 Colleges with "Go Green" Degree Programs.

Go to www.mybizlab.com.

Intrinsic Rewards: Satisfaction in Accomplishing the Task Itself

An *intrinsic reward* is the satisfaction, such as a feeling of accomplishment, a person receives from performing the particular task itself. An intrinsic reward is an internal reward; the payoff comes from pleasing yourself, such as the satisfaction you feel inside when you get an A in a course.

BRIEFING / EARNING GREEN BY GOING GREEN
The Intrinsic Rewards of Investing in Green Energy: Gaining Feelings of Accomplishment. Certainly there is money to be made in going green. But would it make you feel even better to know the investments you made—including the career you chose—helped to save the planet? That feeling is an example of intrinsic reward.

Not every college student is interested in just making a lot of money (extrinsic rewards). In one survey of 1,023 students enrolled at four-year colleges, a high percentage said they wanted "socially responsible" jobs—49% wanted to work for a socially responsible corporation, 38% for government service, and 34% for a nonprofit organization or foundation.[10]

Green entrepreneurs run businesses that provide green products and services. Green consultants provide consulting services to paying clients. Education varies, but (as mentioned in Chapter 9, Practical Action box) some colleges are adding green studies and others even offer a "Green MBA."[11] ❷ Michael Richmond, director of the Green Clean Institute, says green consultant and entrepreneur is "likely the business career of the decade."[12] Many companies are also encouraging green jobs and the hiring of eco-managers such as sustainability officers and green supervisors, and the number is sure to grow in the near future.[13]

Want to follow your bliss, perhaps by finding a socially responsible kind of career? "In this time of economic chaos," says one business coach, people "may realize that if they are going to live with uncertainty, and work like crazy to secure their livelihood, . . . they might as well pursue something they care about deeply." That would be the ultimate form of intrinsic reward.[14] ∎

Why Is Motivation Important?

As a future businessperson, you can see there are at least five reasons why it's important to motivate the employees in your organization.[15] You want to stimulate in talented prospective workers the desire to come to work for your company. You want the people you hire to show up for work—and to show up on time. You want good people to stay with your organization, in good times and bad. You want employees who will do more than work just hard enough to avoid being fired, who will give you high productivity. Finally, you want employees who will give more than just the standard effort, who will be good organizational citizens and represent your company well in the community. These motivations are summarized below. (*See* ∎ *Panel 10.1.*)

∎ **PANEL 10.1 Five reasons why it's important to motivate employees.**

You want employees to . . .

1. **Join.** You want to motivate talented prospective workers to hire on with you.

2. **Show up.** You want employees to be motivated to come to work—to show up on time.

3. **Stay.** You don't want good people to leave.

4. **Perform.** You want them to be motivated to be highly productive.

5. **Do extra.** You hope they will be good organizational citizens and perform extra tasks beyond the regular call of duty.

Motivation Theory

THE BIG IDEA: We describe a number of motivational theories that offer different perspectives that may help us: scientific management, the "Hawthorne effect," Maslow's hierarchy of needs, Herzberg's two-factor theory, job enrichment theory, McGregor's Theory X and Theory Y, Ouchi's Theory Z, Vroom's expectancy theory, Adams's equity theory, goal-setting theory and management by objectives, and reinforcement theory.

THE ESSENTIAL QUESTION: What can I learn from motivation theory to help explain why people want to succeed?

MyBizLab: Check your understanding of these concepts at www.mybizlab.com.

MyBizLab

"Why do people behave the way they do?" is the question underlying many of the social sciences—and often there is no agreement on the answer. Here we consider 11 possible perspectives on motivation and productivity. No one theory provides all the solutions, so there is a good reason for looking at each one.

1 Taylor's Scientific Management: Improving Productivity by Studying Work Methods

How does scientific management get people to produce more?

In the early 20th century, labor was in such short supply that managers were hard pressed to raise the productivity of their workers. This inspired the rise of *scientific management*, **which emphasized the scientific study of work methods to improve the productivity of individual workers.** Its two chief proponents were Frederick W. Taylor and the team of Frank and Lillian Gilbreth.

Frederick Taylor & the Principles of Scientific Management

Engineer **Frederick W. Taylor,** known as the "Father of Scientific Management," believed managers could increase worker productivity by applying four principles: (1) Evaluate a task by scientifically studying each part of the task. (2) Carefully select workers with the right abilities to perform the task. (3) Give those workers the training and incentives to do the task and to use proper work methods in doing so. (4) Use scientific principles to plan the work methods and to help workers to do their jobs.[16]

Taylor based his system on *time-motion studies,* **in which he broke down each worker's job into basic physical motions and then trained workers to use the methods of their best-performing coworkers.** In addition, he suggested employers institute a *differential rate system,* in which the more efficient workers earned higher wages than the less efficient ones. ❸

Note that all this has more to do with *productivity* than with *motivation.* Still, Taylor believed that raising production could increase profits to the point where labor and management would no longer have to quarrel over them.

❸ **The uses of scientific management.** Frederick W. Taylor's studies, performed in 1881, helped companies improve efficiencies in worker movement. Some of his ideas live on in the training given to UPS drivers to help them do their job with the least wasted motion. Are there any routine activities that you do that could be improved by this kind of study?

Source: David R. Frazier Photolibrary, Inc./Alamy.

Frank & Lillian Gilbreth & Industrial Engineering

Frank and Lillian Gilbreth were a husband-and-wife team of industrial engineers who expanded on Taylor's motion studies to develop their *principle of motion economy,* **in which every job could be broken down into a series of elementary motions.** For instance, they were able to identify 17 motions (each one called a *therblig—Gilbreth* spelled backwards with the *t* and *h* transposed) in the task of a bricklayer, analyzing each motion to make it more efficient.

■ **Example of the Use of Scientific Management: What's the Best Way to Clean a Hotel Room?** A hotel housecleaner may be expected to whip 16 to 30 rooms into spick-and-span shape during an eight-hour shift. Vacuuming, dusting, mopping, making beds, and so on, may be expected to take about 20 to 24 minutes per room, according to time-motion studies. Making a neatly tucked bed should take no more than 3 minutes.

The work can be physically demanding. Thus, a housekeeper at the Westin in downtown Seattle, for example, must be taught "how to bend properly, in a way that is easier on your body," according to one hotel executive.[17] All such times and procedures are based on step-by-step observations, as devised by scientific management. ■

The Practical Significance of Taylor & the Gilbreths Today

As is clear from the previous example, the contributions of Taylor and the Gilbreths live on. Their beliefs that work was amenable to a rational approach—that application of the scientific method, time-motion studies, and job specialization could boost productivity—are in evidence every time you observe fast-food workers, airline baggage handlers, or race-car pit crews. ❹

Since the Taylor/Gilbreth time, however, work has mostly evolved from the manual to the intellectual. Consequently, the theory has evolved so that managers now often must think more about how *motivation* affects productivity.

❹ **Time and motion.** In an event in which split seconds count, race-car pit crews are trained to gas up cars and swap tires in well-rehearsed motions developed after analyses that follow the steps of scientific management. What other activities could benefit from Taylor's and the Gilbreths' findings?

Source: Dean Siracusa/Transtock Inc./Alamy.

2 Mayo & the Supposed "Hawthorne Effect": Giving Employees Added Attention to Improve Productivity

How does the Hawthorne effect work?

The *Hawthorne effect* is the name given to a Harvard research group's conclusion that employees worked harder if they received added attention—if they thought managers cared about their welfare and that supervisors paid special attention to them.

The *Hawthorne studies* began with an investigation by **Elton Mayo** and his associates in the 1920s at Western Electric's Hawthorne (Chicago) plant, which began by looking into whether workplace lighting level affected worker productivity. In later experiments, the investigators altered other variables, such as wage levels, rest periods, and length of workday. Because worker performance varied but tended to increase over time, the Mayo team hypothesized the effort came about because employees received added attention (and special attention) from managers.

The Practical Significance of the Hawthorne Studies

The Hawthorne studies were later criticized for being poorly designed and not having enough empirical data to support the conclusions. Nevertheless, they succeeded in drawing attention to the importance of *motivation*—of how managers using good human relations, not just offering money, could improve worker productivity. This in turn led to the so-called *human relations movement* in the 1950s and 1960s, which focused more on psychological motivation rather than work steps in increasing productivity.

Want to Know More? 10-4
What Happened at Hawthorne?
Go to www.mybizlab.com.

3 Maslow's Hierarchy of Needs: Meeting Unsatisfied Employee Wants

What are the five needs in Maslow's hierarchy?

The **human relations movement** proposed that better human relations could increase worker productivity. One of its key theorists, Brandeis University psychology professor **Abraham Maslow,** in 1943 put forth a theory of motivation called the hierarchy of human needs, in which he suggested that needs are never completely fulfilled, that our actions are aimed at fulfilling the unsatisfied needs higher in the hierarchy.

The Maslow Hierarchy

Maslow's hierarchy of needs theory **proposes that people are motivated by five levels of needs, ranging from low to high: (1) physiological, (2) safety, (3) social, (4) esteem, and (5) self-actualization.**[18] The five needs are explained—with workplace examples—in the illustration below. (*See* ■ *Panel 10.2.*)

■ PANEL 10.2 **Maslow's hierarchy of needs.**

5. **Self-actualization need—the highest-level need:** Need for self-fulfillment: increasing competence, using abilities to the fullest. *Workplace example: sabbatical leaves to further personal growth.*

4. **Esteem need:** Need for self-respect, status, reputation, recognition, self-confidence. *Workplace examples: bonuses, promotions, awards.*

3. **Social need:** Need for love, friendship, affection. *Workplace examples: office parties, company bowling teams, management retreats.*

2. **Safety need:** Need for physical safety, emotional security, avoidance of violence. *Workplace examples: health insurance, job security, work safety rules, and pension plans satisfy this need.*

1. **Physiological need—the most basic human physical need:** Need for food, clothing, shelter, comfort, self-preservation. *Workplace example: these are covered by wages.*

BRIEFING / SOCIALLY RESPONSIBLE BUSINESS
Fulfilling Higher-Level Needs—One Man Tries to Strike a Balance between Safety & Higher-Level Needs. Often people will strive to fulfill higher needs, such as self-actualization, without sacrificing needs lower in the hierarchy, such as safety or physiological needs. For instance, Peter Grant is an African American executive who has worked quietly behind the scenes to recruit and encourage the hiring of more than

3,500 minorities at one large financial institution—his own form of self-actualization. Through the years he has asked every person he hired to promise to bring other minorities along. With this strategy, he achieved his goal of hiring more people of color without making big waves within his company and sacrificing his need to stay employed.

Grant is an example of a "tempered radical," Stanford organizational behavior professor Debra Meyerson's term for people who work to strike a balance between what they believe in and what the system expects.[19] In this way, they fulfill their physiological or safety needs while also striving to fulfill their self-actualization needs. ■

The Practical Significance of Maslow's Ideas

In *Peak: How Great Companies Get Their Mojo from Maslow,* Joie de Vivre hotel chain founder Chip Conley describes how he used Maslow's theory to build employee and customer loyalty.[20] For instance, when company revenues were falling after the 9/11 attacks, he stabilized his workforce of line-level employees by maintaining salary levels and not resorting to layoffs. With their security needs met, employees could focus on work rather than possible loss of income.

However, research does not clearly support Maslow's ideas. "There are still very few studies that can legitimately confirm (or refute) it," one scholar writes. "It may be that the dynamics implied by Maslow's theory of needs are too complex to be . . . confirmed by scientific research."[21]

4 Herzberg's Two Kinds of Motivating Factors: Dealing with Employee Satisfaction & Dissatisfaction

Do employee dissatisfaction and satisfaction spring from the same needs?

In the 1960s, psychologist **Frederick Herzberg** interviewed 203 accountants and engineers to determine what made them happy and unhappy about their jobs.[22] Job *satisfaction,* he found, was more frequently associated with achievement, recognition, characteristics of the work, responsibility, and advancement. Job *dissatisfaction* was more often associated with working conditions, pay and security, company policies, supervisors, and interpersonal relationships.

From these survey results came Herzberg's *two-factor theory,* **which proposed that work dissatisfaction and satisfaction arise from two different factors—work satisfaction from higher-level needs he called** *motivating factors,* **and work dissatisfaction from lower-level needs he called** *hygiene factors.* (*See* ■ *Panel 10.3.*) The motivating factors resemble Maslow's higher-level needs (self-actualization, esteem, social), and the hygiene factors resemble Maslow's lower-level needs (safety, physiological).

Motivating Factors: "What Will Make Employees Satisfied?"

The higher-level needs, *motivating factors,* or simply *motivators,* are factors associated with job *satisfaction*—such as achievement, recognition, responsibility, and advancement—all of which affect the rewards of work performance. Motivating factors—challenges, opportunities, recognition—must be instituted, Herzberg believed, to spur superior work performance.

 Example of Motivating Factors: Giving Recognition. "The best thing management can do for any employee is to let them know how much we appreciate their hard work," says the CEO of a Houston marketing firm. "You

Want to Know More? 10-5
What Is McClelland's Acquired Needs Theory?
Go to www.mybizlab.com.

■ **PANEL 10.3 Herzberg's factors for job satisfaction and dissatisfaction.** Motivation factors can be used to create more work satisfaction. Hygiene factors can cause work dissatisfaction, but changing them may have little motivational effect.

Motivating factors (causing work satisfaction)

Achievement

Recognition

The work itself

Responsibility

Advancement and growt

Neutral area: neither satisfied nor dissatisfied

Hygiene factors (causing work dissatisfaction)

Pay and security

Working conditions

Interpersonal relationships

Company policy

Supervisors

get back so much."[23] Accordingly, her company gives its workers half a day off on Fridays on a rotating basis. Other motivators: bringing surprise breakfasts, lunches, and ice cream sundaes into the office, plus twice-yearly staff recognition awards. ■

Hygiene Factors: "Why Are Employees Dissatisfied?"

The lower-level needs, *hygiene factors* **are factors associated with job** *dissatisfaction*—**such as salary, working conditions, interpersonal relationships, and company policy—all of which affect the job environment in which people work.**

■ **Example of Hygiene Factors: Work Environment and Benefits.** Although 97% of workers think financial compensation is one of the most important rewards of the workplace, it's not the main reason employees change jobs, according to one survey (done before the recent recession, at which point jobs became harder to find).

The top two reasons for changing jobs were growth and advancement in potential for higher earnings (30%) and time and flexibility (23%), all *motivating factors*. Lesser reasons were financial compensation (22%), culture and work environment (22%), and benefits (12%), all *hygiene factors*.[24] Changing the hygiene factors, then, would probably not increase worker motivation much or make them satisfied with their existing jobs. ■

The Practical Significance of Herzberg's Research

Herzberg's research suggests that a company should first eliminate sources of employee dissatisfaction, making sure that pay levels, working conditions, and employment policies are reasonable. It should then concentrate on spurring motivation by providing opportunities for recognition, responsibility, achievement, and personal growth. ❺

❺ **Satisfied employee.** Investment adviser Edward Jones has been on *Fortune* magazine's prestigious list of "100 Best Companies to Work For" for 12 years, including the No. 2 position in 2010 and No. 11 in 2011. The company has made diversity a priority and is trying to bring people of color into a workforce that is 93% white. Which of Herzberg's factors does this represent—motivating or hygiene?

5 Job Enrichment: Fitting Jobs to People

How would I benefit by job enrichment?

Which works best—fitting people to jobs or fitting jobs to people? There are times when either is appropriate.

Fitting People to Jobs: The Technique of Job Simplification

Fitting people to jobs is the approach often taken with jobs involving routine tasks. The notion assumes that people will adapt to any work situation. Still, this means the jobs must be tailored so that nearly anyone can do them.

For managers the challenge becomes "How can we make the worker most compatible with the work?" One way is through *job simplification,* **which involves reducing the number of tasks a worker performs.** Stripping a job down to its simplest elements enables a worker to focus on doing more of the same task, increasing his or her efficiency.

■ **Example of Fitting People to Jobs: Harvesting Lettuce.** You don't work at "picking lettuce"; it's "cutting lettuce." That's what journalist Gabriel Thompson found out when he spent two months harvesting lettuce in Yuma, Arizona.

"Cutting lettuce requires an immense amount of skill," Thompson reports. "A cutter bends down, grabs a head of lettuce with one hand while making

a quick cut at the base of the stem with an 18-inch knife. Next, he lifts the lettuce to his stomach and makes a second cut, trimming the trunk and shaking the outer leaves to the ground. Still holding the blade, he bags the lettuce in a quick motion from a packet that hangs from his belt. The entire process should take only a few seconds, but my first head of lettuce took several minutes."[25] Each cutter is responsible for more than 3,000 heads a day. ⑥

In some kinds of agriculture (wheat, oranges), technology makes harvesting easier. That's not available for lettuce. "I'd come home with a red face, swollen hands and feet, and a throbbing back that was never quite aligned correctly," Thompson writes. ∎

⑥ **Fitting people to jobs.** There are no modern machines to help these workers cut lettuce in California's lettuce fields, which are harvested the old fashioned-way—by humans stooped over using 18-inch knives. Can you think of other kinds of production in which people have to be adapted to the job rather than jobs adapted to people?

Fitting Jobs to People: The Techniques of Job Enlargement & Job Enrichment

Fitting jobs to people rests on the idea that people are underutilized at work and that they want more variety, challenges, and responsibility. In this approach, an outgrowth of Herzberg's theory, the main challenge for managers is "How can we make the work most compatible with the worker so as to produce both high performance and high job satisfaction?"

Two techniques used to fit jobs to people involve (1) *job enlargement* and (2) *job enrichment.*

Job Enlargement: Making a Job More Varied. *Job enlargement* **consists of increasing the number of tasks in a job to improve employee satisfaction, motivation, and quality of production.** For instance, the job of installing windshields on an automobile production line could be enlarged to also include installation of other car windows. Or maybe headlights.

By itself job enlargement won't have a lasting impact on job performance, since working at two boring jobs instead of one doesn't add up to much challenge. One answer to this is *job rotation,* **in which an employee is moved from one job to another,** to help alleviate boredom.

Job Enrichment: Putting More Motivating Factors into a Job. Job enrichment is the practical application of Herzberg's motivator–hygiene theory of job satisfaction. Specifically, *job enrichment* **consists of creating a job with motivating factors such as recognition, responsibility, achievement, stimulating work, and advancement.**

Unlike job enlargement, which gives employees additional tasks of similar difficulty, job enrichment entails giving employees more responsibility. Thus, employees might take on chores normally performed by supervisors.

∎ **Example of Job Enrichment: Expanding Employee Discretion in Hotel Work.** Hotels and restaurants typically replace two-thirds of their workers in a year (at least in nonrecessionary times). To keep good staff members, managers of the Hotel Carlton in San Francisco give employees more leeway in handling their jobs.

For instance, Theophilus McKinney, who oversaw the front desk, "was allowed to wear the funky shoes he favored and to rearrange the reception phones so they were easier to answer," according to one account. McKinney was also permitted to shift his hours to the evening "when more guests were around so he could focus on thinking up ways to keep them happy—such as buying cakes or flowers for those with birthdays or honeymoons."[26] ■

Source: Mike Greenslade/Alamy.

According to proponents of job enrichment, there are five core job characteristics that affect workers' motivation and performance, as follows:

- **Skill variety: "How many different skills does my job require?"** *Skill variety* describes the extent to which a job requires a person to use a wide range of different skills. Example: The skill variety required by a restaurant chef is higher than that for a dishwasher.

- **Task identity: "How many different tasks are required to complete the work?"** *Task identity* describes the extent to which a job requires a worker to perform all the tasks needed to complete the job from beginning to end. Example: The task identity for a craftsperson making a custom surfboard is higher than it is for a worker who just makes scores of standard molded fiberglass boards. ⑦

- **Task significance: "How many other people are affected by my job?"** *Task significance* describes the extent to which a job affects the lives of other people, whether inside or outside the organization. Example: An emergency room doctor has higher task significance than an orderly changing sheets on hospital beds.

- **Autonomy: "How much discretion does my job give me?"** *Autonomy* describes the extent to which a job allows an employee to make choices about scheduling different tasks and deciding how to perform them. Example: A traveling salesperson has more leeway in planning which accounts to call on than someone sitting by the phone taking orders.

- **Feedback: "How often do I find out how well I'm doing?"** *Feedback* describes the extent to which workers receive clear, direct information about how well they are performing the job. Example: A salesperson receives immediate feedback on how many of his sales calls result in orders. An engineer working on new weapons systems may go years before learning how effective her performance has been.

The Practical Significance of Ideas about Job Enrichment

These five core characteristics are thought to affect a worker's motivation because they affect three critical psychological states:

- Meaningfulness of work
- Responsibility for results
- Knowledge of results

That is, the more that workers (1) feel that they are doing meaningful work, (2) feel that they are responsible for outcomes of the work, and (3) have knowledge of the

⑦ **Task identity.** Some jobs—custom surfboard making, perhaps—require a worker to perform all the tasks needed to complete the project from beginning to end. This means the job has strong task identity. Have you ever held such a job? Do you prefer doing all aspects of a job rather than just one or two parts of it?

Key Takeaway 10-2
Five key job characteristics affecting job enrichment: skill variety, task identity, task significance, autonomy, feedback.

Want to Know More? 10-6

What Are Some of the Best Ways to Motivate Top Performers?

Go to www.mybizlab.com.

actual results of the work and how they affect others, then the more likely they are to have four favorable work outcomes:

- High motivation
- High performance
- High satisfaction
- Low absenteeism and turnover

6 McGregor's Theory X & Theory Y: Treating Employees Differently

Which most resembles your own view of worker behavior—Theory X or Theory Y?

Having been a college president (of Antioch College in Ohio), **Douglas McGregor** came to realize that it was not enough for managers to try to be liked; they also needed to be aware of their attitudes toward employees. Basically, McGregor suggested in his classic book, *The Human Side of Enterprise,* these attitudes could be either "X" or "Y."[27]

Theory X: The Pessimistic View about Employees

Representing a pessimistic, negative view of workers, ***Theory X* assumes workers to be irresponsible, resistant to change, lacking in ambition, hating work, and preferring to be led rather than to lead.** This theory seems to support the notion of offering *extrinsic rewards* for good performance—namely, managers offering pay raises, promotions, and other symbols of recognition. ⑧

Theory Y: The Optimistic View about Employees

Representing the point of view of the human relations movement, ***Theory Y* makes the positive assumption that workers are capable of accepting responsibility, self-direction, and self-control and of being imaginative and creative.** Thus, Theory Y supports the notion of offering *intrinsic rewards* for good performance—that is, the rewards should be related to the job itself and the sense of accomplishment the employee realizes from it.

Theory Y leads to the concept of ***empowerment,* in which management makes employees more involved in their jobs by giving them the authority and responsibility to make decisions.** When empowering employees, managers need to find out from them what the company's problems are, help them create solutions by setting expectations and establishing standards, let them implement the solutions, and follow up with periodic evaluations.

Source: Mehmet Dilsiz/Shutterstock.

⑧ **Theory X?** Is there a better way than shown here to get good performance from an employee? It may depend on whether you think most employees are natually motivated to do well, or hate work and resist change.

The Practical Significance of Theory X/Theory Y

The Theory X/Theory Y perspective may or may not be true (it is an assumption), but the principal contribution it offers is helping managers avoid the trap of the *self-fulfilling prophecy.* This is the idea that if a manager expects a subordinate to act in a certain way, the worker may very well act that way, thereby confirming the manager's expectations: the prophecy that the manager made is fulfilled. The Theory Y approach also stresses the importance of designing jobs so that they are more interesting and offer employees more freedom in developing their own ideas.

7 Ouchi's Theory Z: Combining Japanese & American Management Approaches

Why would I want to work for a Theory Z company?

Developed by UCLA management professor **William Ouchi** (pronounced *oh-chi*), who studied management approaches in Japan and the United States, ***Theory Z is a motivational approach that emphasizes involving employees at all levels, giving them long-term job security, allowing collective decision making, emphasizing slow evaluation and promotion procedures, and treating workers like family.*** (See ■ *Panel 10.4.*)

The Basis for Theory Z: Blending Japanese & American Management Approaches

Despite its title, Theory Z has nothing to do with Theory X/Theory Y. Ouchi arrived at his management philosophy during the Asian economic boom of the 1980s, when Japanese companies seemed to be outperforming U.S. firms.

In those days, the Japanese stressed lifetime employment, consensual decision making, individual responsibility within a group context, and nonspecialized career paths. Americans emphasized short-term employment, individual decision making, individual responsibility, and specialized career paths.

Recognizing that the Japanese cultural traditions couldn't be easily grafted onto American business practices, Ouchi proposed his Theory Z as a combination of approaches from both cultures. The theory thus focuses on increasing employee loyalty and work motivation by providing workers with jobs that strongly focus on their well-being.

> **Example** **of Theory Z: SAS Focuses on Employee Well-Being.** At the start of this chapter, we mentioned that the North Carolina software company SAS boasts a laundry list of benefits for employees, which has vastly limited turnover. Among them is a working environment that supports family and culture, such as high-quality child care at $420 a month, unlimited sick days, a summer camp for children, and family nights at the rodeo, circus, and Monster Jam Trucks. "People do work hard here," says one employee, "because they're motivated to take care of a company that takes care of them."[28] ■

The Practical Significance of Theory Z

Whereas McGregor's Theory X and Theory Y reflect perceptions of how management views employees, Ouchi's Theory Z considers how employees view management. Theory Z assumes that employees value a working environment supporting family, culture, and traditions and that they have a desire to work hard, are competent to make informed decisions, want to have cooperative relationships, and are knowledgeable about various issues in the company.

■ **PANEL 10.4 Characteristics of Theory Z.**

1. Long-term employment
2. Collective decision making
3. Collective responsibility (individual responsibility within a group context)
4. Slow evaluation and promotion
5. Implicit, informal control with explicit, formalized control measures
6. Moderately specialized career paths
7. Concern for the total person, including his or her family

8 Reinforcement Theory: Behavior Modification

How does reinforcement work?

Pioneered by **Edward L. Thorndike** and **B. F. Skinner,** reinforcement is concerned with how the consequences of a certain behavior affect that behavior in the future.[29] ***Reinforcement theory* suggests that behavior with positive consequences tends to be repeated whereas behavior with negative consequences tends not to be repeated.** The use of reinforcement theory to change human behavior is called *behavior modification.*

How Reinforcement Theory Works

In reinforcement theory, there are four types of responses (consequences) that cause a given behavior to be repeated or inhibited. Both positive reinforcement and negative reinforcement will increase (reinforce) the behavior, while both extinction and punishment will decrease the behavior.

Positive Reinforcement. This is the use of positive consequences to encourage desirable behavior, such as managers' use of praise, more money, recognition, and awards to reward accomplishments. Example: On the cooking reality show *Hell's Kitchen,* winning teams are rewarded with fancy shopping trips or dinners.

Negative Reinforcement. This is the removal of unpleasant consequences following a desired behavior. Example: *Hell's Kitchen* winners are spared from the dirty work of cleaning up the kitchen, which losing teams are forced to do. ❾

Extinction. This is the withholding or withdrawal of positive rewards for undesirable behavior, so that the behavior is less likely to occur in the future. Example: An employee who sends frequent, repeated e-mails about unimportant matters to his or her manager will eventually stop if the manager withholds attention by failing to respond.

Punishment. This is the application of negative consequences to stop or change undesirable behavior, such as managers' use of reprimands, reduction in pay, suspension, and termination. Example: A manager might punish an employee who is repeatedly late to work by docking his or her pay.

❾ Negative reinforcement. Aspiring chefs who are winners at a particular task on the TV cooking reality show *Hell's Kitchen,* starring celebrity chef Gordon Ramsay *(center),* are spared from cleaning up a dirty kitchen. This "reward" is intended to make them work harder on the next task. Do you think this is more motivating than the positive rewards they receive, such as dinner in a fancy restaurant or free shopping in upscale stores?

Source: Handout/KRT/Newscom.

BRIEFING / SOCIALLY RESPONSIBLE BUSINESS
Using Reinforcement to Improve Accountability & Integrity. Software engineer Firinn Taisdeal of Walnut Creek, California, designed a social event database, now called LinkUp Central, that for a $5-a-month membership fee offers its San Francisco Bay Area members 12,000 member-hosted group events per year, from rock climbing to theater. But he discovered that events were being ruined by "flakes," as he called them, who didn't show up.

So he modified the database to chart patterns of flakiness—an accountability system that works on the principle of positive and negative reinforcement. Thus, if people RSVP for events but don't show up, their "reliability threshold" goes down. With some events, such as restaurant dinners, guests can sign up only if they have a reliability index of 50% or more. "By changing their behavior over time," says one report, "people can improve their ratings."[30] ∎

The Practical Significance of Reinforcement Theory

Reinforcement theory offers some practical applications for managing employees, whether you want to increase desirable behaviors or reduce undesirable behaviors.

To encourage desirable behaviors, you should be clear about exactly what behavior is desired, you should reward only desirable (not undesirable) behavior, you should hand out rewards as soon as possible, and you should recognize that different people respond to different rewards. ❿

To reduce unwanted behavior, you should be clear about what behavior is undesirable, punish only undesirable behavior, give reprimands as soon as possible, administer the punishment in private, and be sure to tell employees what they are doing right as well as doing wrong.

9 Vroom's Expectancy Theory: Meeting Employee Expectations

What are three calculations I might make before deciding to work hard at something?

Introduced by **Victor Vroom,** a business school professor at the Yale School of Management, *expectancy theory* **proposes that people are motivated by (1) how strongly they want something, and (2) how likely they think they are to get it.**[31] That is, assuming they have choices, people will make the choice that promises them the greatest reward if they think they can get it.

Three Calculations of Expectancy Theory

What determines how willing you are to work hard at tasks important to your company's success? The answer, according to Vroom, is: you will do what you *can* do when you *want* to. Your motivation, Vroom suggests, involves three assessments or calculations, which he labeled expectancy, instrumentality, and valence:

- **Assessment 1** (*expectancy*): "Will I be able to accomplish a certain task?"
- **Assessment 2** (*instrumentality*): "If I accomplish the task, what kind of reward will I get?"
- **Assessment 3** (*valence*): "How much do I want the reward?"

These relationships are shown below. (*See* ■ *Panel 10.5.*) All three assessments must be answered positively for a person to be motivated.

❿ **Use of reinforcement.** C.D. Moody, CEO of Moody Construction of Lithonia, Georgia, is a highly successful builder of schools and churches. He motivates his employees by handing out inspirational books such as John C. Maxwell's *The 21 Irrefutable Laws of Leadership.* (Law No. 3: "Leadership develops daily, not in a day.") Moody follows up with positive discussions that encourage them to apply what they've read and makes clear the types of behavior that lead to success and rewards.

Source: Courtesy of C.D. Moody Construction Company, Inc.

■ **PANEL 10.5 Expectancy theory: the three assessments or calculations.**

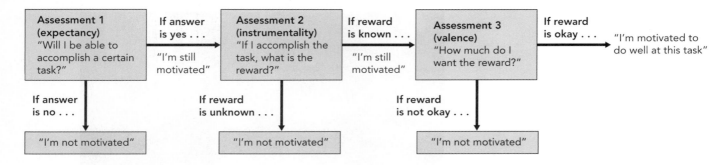

■ **Example** of Expectancy Theory: Financial Incentives for Quitting Smoking. The concept of assessment 2 (instrumentality)—"If I accomplish the task, what is the reward?"—can be seen in practice by considering pay-for-performance compensation for giving up smoking. In an experiment with nearly 900 smokers employed by General Electric, it was found that 15% given financial incentives were smoke-free after a year, compared with 5% of those who weren't eligible for cash rewards.

The study rewarded employees for making incremental achievements: $100 for completing a smoking-cessation course, $250 for abstaining from cigarettes for 6 months, and $400 more for being smoke-free after a year—inducements totaling $750. "People are drawn to tangible things," says a researcher on the study.[32] ■

The Practical Significance of Expectancy Theory

Expectancy theory suggests that when attempting to motivate your employees you should ask the following questions:

What Rewards Do My Employees Value? As a businessperson, you should get to know your employees and determine what rewards they value, such as bonuses or awards.

What Are the Job Objectives and the Performance Level I Want? You need to define the performance objectives and figure out what behavior you want so you can tell your employees what they need to do to attain the rewards.

Are the Rewards Linked to Performance? Employees must be made aware that a certain kind of high performance within a defined period of time will result in specific kinds of rewards. If high-performing employees aren't rewarded, they may leave or slow down and affect the performance of other employees.

Do My Employees Believe I Will Deliver the Right Rewards for the Right Performance? Your employees must believe that you have the ability and the will to give them the rewards you promise for the performance you are requesting. This is about your credibility. (Moral: Don't promise something you can't deliver.) ⑪

10 Adams's Equity Theory: Treating Employees Fairly

What are the three elements I look at in determining whether I am being paid fairly?

The perception of fairness can be a big issue in organizations. For example, how would you feel if you performed the same amount of work as someone who has more years of experience, but he or she is paid more? Is that fair?

Source: Peter Smith.

⑪ **Promises, promises.** One trait employees respect is believability. If you say you're going to deliver the right rewards, will you do so?

Equity theory **focuses on employee perceptions as to how fairly they think they are being treated compared to others.** Developed by psychologist **J. Stacey Adams,** equity theory is based on the idea that employees are motivated to seek fairness in the rewards they expect for task performance.[33] Clearly, this is an important matter. Experts believe that employee theft, for example, which costs American business billions every year (reportedly $18.7 billion in 2009), represents employees' attempts to even the score when they perceive that they haven't been treated fairly by their organizations.[34] Another way employees "get back" at organizations is by underperforming.

The Elements of Equity Theory: Comparing Your Contributions & Returns with Those of Others

The key elements in equity theory are *contributions* (also called *inputs*), *returns* (also called *outputs*), and *comparisons*.

Contributions—"What Do You Think You're Putting In to the Job?"
The *contributions* that people perceive they give to an organization are their time, effort, training, experience, intelligence, creativity, seniority, status, and so on.

Returns—"What Do You Think You're Getting Out of the Job?"
The *returns* are the rewards that people receive from an organization: pay, benefits, praise, recognition, bonuses, promotions, status perquisites (corner office with a view, say, or private parking space), and so on.

Comparisons—"How Do You Think Your Ratio of Contributions and Returns Compares with Those of Others?"
Equity theory suggests that people compare the *ratio* of their own returns to contributions against the *ratio* of someone else's contributions to returns. When employees compare the ratio of their contributions and returns (rewards) with those of others, they then make a judgment about fairness. Either they perceive there is *equity*—they are satisfied with the ratio and so they don't change their behavior; or they perceive there is *inequity*—they feel resentful and act to change the inequity.

The Practical Significance of Equity Theory

According to Adams, employees who feel they are being underrewarded will respond to the perceived inequity by reducing their contributions, trying to change the returns they receive, distorting the inequity, and the like. (*See ■ Panel 10.6.*) Employees who feel they are being treated fairly are more likely to support organizational change and to cooperate in group settings and less likely to turn to the courts or arbitration to remedy real or imagined wrongs.

Three lessons that can be drawn from equity theory are as follows:

Employees' Perceptions Matter. Probably the most important lesson is this: no matter how fair managers think the organization's policies, procedures, and reward systems are, the individual employees' *perception* of those factors is what matters.

Employees' Participation Helps. Allowing employees to participate in important decisions can greatly benefit both managers and employees. For example, employees are more satisfied with their performance appraisal when they are allowed to state their opinions during their appraisal review.

Having an Appeal Process Helps. When employees are allowed to appeal decisions affecting their welfare, they are more apt to believe that management treats them fairly. Perceptions of fair treatment promote job satisfaction and commitment and reduce absenteeism and turnover.

Want to Know More? 10-7

What Is Meant by a "Psychological Contract" in an Organization?

Go to www.mybizlab.com.

■ **PANEL 10.6 Equity theory: how employees try to reduce inequity.**

- *They will reduce their contributions:* They will do less work, take longer breaks, leave early on Fridays, and call in "sick" on Mondays.

- *They will try to change the returns or rewards they receive:* They will lobby their supervisor for a raise or they will steal company supplies or equipment.

- *They will distort the inequity:* They will exaggerate their work efforts and complain they're not paid what they're worth.

- *They will change the object of comparison:* They may compare themselves to another person instead of the original one.

- *They will leave the situation:* They will quit, transfer, or shift to another group.

11 Goal-Setting Theory & Management by Objectives

What are the three key elements of goal-setting theory?

Developed by psychologists **Edwin Locke and Gary Latham** in the 1980s, ***goal-setting theory* proposes that employees can be motivated by goals that are specific and challenging but achievable.** Locke and Latham assert that the goal-setting process is certainly natural, but that it is useful only if two things happen—people *understand* the goals and *accept* them. What's needed, then, is to set the right goals in the right way.[35]

Three Desirable Qualities Goals Should Have

As we saw in Chapter 7, a goal is different from an objective. A *goal* is a broad, long-range target that an organization wishes to attain; an *objective* is a specific, short-term target designed to achieve the organization's goals. To result in high motivation and performance, according to goal-setting theory, goals must have three qualities: they must be *specific, challenging,* and *achievable.*

Specific—"Goals Need to Be Measurable." Goals such as "Sell as many laptops as you can" or "Be cheery to customers" are too vague and therefore have no effect on motivation. Instead, goals need to be specific—usually meaning *quantitative,* rather than qualitative (which are more difficult to measure). A supervisor, for example, may be asked to boost his or her workgroup's revenues by 20% and to cut absenteeism by 20%, both specific, measurable goals. ⑫

Source: Glen Jones/Shutterstock.

⑫ **Specific goals.** Goals work best when they are specific, such as: "Reduce absenteeism by 20%," which can be helped when managers require lower-level employees to punch a time clock at the beginning and end of each shift. What kind of specific goals do you set when it comes to doing your schoolwork?

Challenging—"Goals Need to Spur Higher Performance." A goal should not be just something nearly anyone can reach ("Show up for work every day"), since that isn't very motivating. Rather it should be challenging ("Show up for work on time at least 90% of the time"), which will motivate people to concentrate on the right target and apply themselves toward achieving higher performance.

Achievable—"Goals Need to Be within Workers' Capabilities." Goals can't be unattainable. Thus, if you want your Spanish-speaking staff to suddenly begin servicing customers who speak English, you have to train your staff in some English. Managers always need to make sure employees have additional training, if necessary, to achieve challenging goals.

Key Takeaway 10-3
Goals should be specific, challenging, and achievable, according to goal-setting theory.

Management by Objectives: The Four-Step Process for Motivating Employees

First suggested by management philosopher **Peter Drucker,** management by objectives has become popular among managers in both business and government largely because of its emphasis on converting general objectives into specific ones for all members of an organization.[36] ***Management by objectives (MBO)* is a four-stage process in which (1) a manager and an employee jointly set objectives for the employee, (2) the manager develops an action plan for achieving the objective, (3) the manager and employee periodically review the employee's performance, and (4) the manager makes a performance appraisal and rewards the employee according to results.** (*See* ■ *Panel 10.7.*)

The purpose of MBO is to *motivate* rather than control subordinates. Thus, managers must act like coaches, helping their employees to set and attain goals, including actively involving them in setting goals and engaging in the appraisal process.

For MBO to be successful, three things have to happen:

The Commitment of Top Management Is Essential. "When top-management commitment [to MBO] was high," said one review, "the average gain in productivity was 56%. When commitment was low, the average gain in productivity was only 6%."[37]

MBO Must Be Applied throughout the Entire Organization. The program has to be put in place organizationwide. That is, it cannot be applied in just some departments; it has to be done in all of them.

Objectives Must "Cascade" Down through the Organization. MBO works by *cascading* objectives down through the organization; that is, objectives are structured in a *unified hierarchy,* becoming more specific at lower levels of the organization. Top managers set general organizational objectives, which are translated into divisional objectives, which are translated into departmental objectives. The hierarchy ends in individual objectives set by each employee.

The Practical Significance of Goal-Setting Theory

The benefits of setting goals are that a manager can tailor rewards to the needs of individual employees, clarify what is expected of them, provide regular reinforcement, and maintain equity.

When developing employee goals, you should not only make sure the goals are specific, challenging, and achievable but also make sure they (1) are set jointly with the employee, (2) are measurable, and (3) have a target date for attainment. Finally, make sure (4) that you give feedback so that employees know of their progress—and don't forget to reward people for doing what they set out to do.

■ PANEL 10.7 The four stages of management by objectives (MBO).

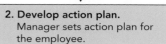

1. **Jointly set objectives.** Manager and employee meet and jointly set objectives for the employee.

2. **Develop action plan.** Manager sets action plan for the employee.

3. **Jointly review performance.** Manager and employee periodically review the employee's performance.

4. **Performance appraisal and rewards.** Manager makes a performance appraisal and rewards the employee according to results.

How Forward-Looking Companies Motivate Their Employees: Perks, Benefits, Listening, & Praise

THE BIG IDEA: Some companies have discovered that keeping employees loyal and happy, by offering important job perks and frequently surveying them, can pay off not only in less employee turnover but also in loyal and happy clients. Another important motivator is praise, but different generations have different expectations about praise.

THE ESSENTIAL QUESTION: What are some of the primary ways firms motivate employees?

MyBizLab

MyBizLab: Check your understanding of these concepts at www.mybizlab.com.

There are all kinds of ways to motivate employees. Some of the more conventional methods, such as compensation, benefits, promotions, and the like, are described in Chapter 11. Here let's consider some nonmonetary methods.

What Students Say They Want in a Job

What are the three qualities students worldwide say they want most in a job?

Employees who can work independently, solve problems, and take the initiative are apt to be the ones who will leave if they find their own needs aren't being met. What would you guess those needs are?

PricewaterhouseCoopers, the international consulting and accounting firm, surveyed 2,500 university students in 11 countries to see what they wanted in a career.[38] The results:

- **The need for balance between life and work:** The survey found that 57% named as their primary career goal "attaining a balance between personal life and career." In other words, they don't want to give their lives to their jobs.
- **The need to learn additional skills:** Younger workers who watched their parents undergo the trauma of being laid off during the recession are particularly apt to want a job that helps them gain additional skills that will give them more opportunities to earn a living in the future.
- **The need to do something that matters:** Students said they want to work for an organization that makes them feel that what they do matters. They want to commit not just to a corporation but to their fellow team members or to their profession.

Treating Employees Well

What are some nonmonetary ways of keeping employees?

As we saw with software maker SAS earlier in this chapter, many companies have discovered the bottom-line benefits of keeping employees happy.

⓭ **Well treated.** Exuberant Southwest Airlines staffers are rewarded every year with a Halloween party at the Dallas headquarters. The firm expects employees to work very hard and do tasks outside their usual job descriptions. Do you think such "above and beyond" productivity can be traced to the company's free-wheeling culture?

Some other companies that think the same way: Southwest Airlines; W. L. Gore & Associates, maker of Gore-Tex clothing; and consumer products maker S. C. Johnson & Son. ⓭ Here's another:

BRIEFING / CUSTOMER FOCUS

Clients Like Ad Firm's Happy Employees. An independent global creative agency with offices in London, New York, and Buenos Aires known for its offbeat ads, strong employee loyalty, and rapid growth and earnings promotes its corporate culture by printing business cards with each staffer's mother portrayed on them. That's because the firm is named *Mother,* and it has discovered an important principle: happy, loyal employees also make for happy, loyal customers. ⓮

Mother provides not only a fun-loving culture but also such perks as a small daily "self-improvement bonus" (about $2) applicable to gym memberships and yoga classes, two types of weekly massages, free hot lunches, winter ski trips, three-month sabbaticals, and days off for birthdays and the day after Mother's Day.

Turnover among both employees and clients is low: only 10% of the staff leaves every year (compared to 19% among competitors), and most customers—including Coca-Cola and Unilever—have been with Mother throughout the firm's 15-year existence. Clients stay because, says one, they like an ad shop "with a highly motivated, happy workforce . . . because we get better work out of it."[39] Loyal staffers, clients find, also provide stable teams and solid relationships. ▪

There is a whole class of incentives to motivate employees that can be expressed simply as: *treat employees well,* some examples of which follow.

⓮ **What would Mother do?** Producer of advertising and other creative services, Mother offers a fun-loving culture and employee perks that have led not only to happy employees but to happy clients. Could this formula work at increasing productivity at huge firms such as General Electric?

Learning Opportunities

Learning opportunities can take two forms. Managers can help workers build skills by matching them with coworkers that they can learn from, allowing them, for instance, to "shadow" workers in other jobs or be in interdepartmental task forces. In addition, companies can establish programs of tuition reimbursement to enable employees to do part-time study at a college or university.

Work-Life Benefits

Work-life benefits, according to Kathie Lingle, an executive with KPMG, an accounting and consulting firm, are programs "used by employers to increase

Source: Morgan Lane Photography/Shutterstock.

15 Home work. Allowing people to work at home can result in more, not less, productivity. Do you agree this option should be given not just to high performers but to lesser ones as well, so as to allow them to cope with family matters that could help them be better workers?

i

Want to Know More? 10-8

Take the Kiersey Temperament Sorter® Personality Test.

Go to www.mybizlab.com.

i

Want to Know More? 10-9

How Well Do You Listen?

Go to www.mybizlab.com.

16 Praise from the top. No doubt a performance award would stimulate your motivation to do better. What if the recognition was from your *country*? France awards the prestigious Meilleur Ouvrier de France to individuals judged best at what they do, such as recipient Josiane Deal, a cheese maker, shown here with husband and partner Christian.

Source: Courtesy of Josiane Deal.

productivity and commitment by removing certain barriers that make it hard for people to strike a balance between their work and personal lives."[40] Besides alternative scheduling, work-life benefits include employer help with daycare (including on-site child-care centers), domestic-partner benefits, job-protected leave for new parents, and provision of technology such as mobile phones and laptops to enable parents to work at home.[41]

Lingle emphasizes that work-life benefits "are not a reward, but a way of getting work done." After all, some employees are low performers simply because of a lack of work-life balance, with great demands at home. "If you only give these 'rewards' to existing high performers," she says, "you're cutting people off who could, with some support, be high performers." **15**

Being Nice

What does "being nice" mean? It could mean reducing managerial criticism, becoming more effusive in praising subordinates, and writing thank-you notes for exceptional performance.

Unfortunately, according to one study, employers spend too little time showing workers that they matter, as evidenced in lack of communication by managers with employees and by a lack of interest in new ideas and contributions.[42] Another survey found that a majority of employees feel underappreciated. Forty percent of employees who rated their boss's performance as poor said they were likely to look for a new job; only 11% of those who rated it excellent said they would.[43]

Because employee satisfaction with their supervisors is closely linked to motivation and job satisfaction, managers need to think about how their behavior affects their subordinates.[44] "It's extraordinary how often it is the small and often banal gestures that are the most meaningful," says one expert. "People will often say things like, 'I'm not really happy, but not yet prepared to jump ship because my boss was really good to me when my mother was sick.'"[45] Employers can offer breaks or other opportunities for people to mix and socialize to promote personal relationships in the workplace, which most employees are concerned about.

The Benefits of Listening

How can listening be helpful?

Some companies realize the importance of just *listening*. American Express, Abbott Laboratories, and Yum Brands (parent of fast-food restaurants KFC, Taco Bell, Pizza Hut, and Long John Silver's), for example, have a practice of listening to employees to track their engagement.

■ **Example of Listening: A KFC Manager Surveys His Staff Frequently.** One KFC restaurant manager surveys his staff of about 20 every three months to address problems, solicit ideas for improvement, and bolster their commitment to their jobs. Yum says restaurants that have adopted quarterly surveys also score high on customer evaluations for cleanliness, accuracy, and speed.[46] ■

Praise: One of the Most Important Motivators

What's the right way to praise?

For most employees, one of the most important motivators is *praise*. People over 60 tend to like formal awards presented publicly, such as certificates and medallions. Middle-aged people prefer being praised with self-indulgent treats, such as free massages and high-tech gadgets. Employees under 40 require more stroking. Indeed, says Bob Nelson, who advises companies such as Walt Disney and Hallmark Cards on praise issues, young people want near-constant feedback. "It's not enough to give praise only when they're exceptional," he says, "because for years they've been getting praise just for showing up."[47] **16**

"Is it them or is it me?"

How often have you wondered, when someone has shown a surprising response to something you said, "How did *that* miscommunication happen?" Barriers to communication are of many kinds—physical, cultural, organizational, and language—some of which you might not be able to do much about. Personal barriers, however, are more susceptible to change.

To communicate well on a personal level, you need to learn how to . . .

Listen with Understanding

Listening, *really* listening, is the most valuable communication skill. We all have a natural tendency, according to psychologist Carl Rogers, to judge others' statements from our own point of view (especially if we have strong feelings about the issue).[48] To really listen with understanding, you have to imagine yourself in the other person's shoes.

Or, as Rogers and his co-author put it, you have to "see the expressed idea and attitude from the other person's point of view, to sense how it feels to him, to achieve his frame of reference in regard to the thing he is talking about."[49] One way to gain perspective is to write three viewpoints about a tough work situation.[50]

Receive & Give Criticism Well

We all need to learn to both receive and give criticism well. One way to think about this is to grasp the difference between criticism and feedback. Criticism, notes psychologist Leon Seltzer, is judgmental and accusatory, whereas feedback focuses on providing information to motivate the other person to reconsider his or her behavior.

Criticism often includes advice and commands that make the other person angry, whereas feedback tries to prompt a discussion about the benefits of change.[51] One baseball coach found the best way to criticize players was not to tell them what they did wrong but to ask them to analyze what they thought they could have done better.[52]

Receive & Give Compliments Well

We all crave compliments, even if we have trouble accepting them graciously. "Yet we remember the good ones, and the bad ones, for a very, very long time," says one writer.[53] (Example of a bad one: "You certainly dress well . . . for a fat man." Oops.)

Some tips for receiving compliments: Just say thank you; don't be self-deprecating. Also, don't worry about complimenting the other person in return. Tips for giving compliments: Be specific. (Example: "That sweater really brings out the color of your eyes," not "You look pretty/handsome today.") Make your compliment neither too big nor too small. Tell the person how he or she has positively affected you.[54]

Apologize When Necessary—& Apologize Appropriately

We all offend someone sometimes, and we need to take responsibility for our mistakes by making our apologies, which permits us to have a future relationship with the person we offended. It's said that women are sometimes too quick to apologize, hoping to make uncomfortable situations go away, but that men are often reluctant to apologize at all, because they feel it puts them in a weakened position.[55]

An apology should be sincere and should be done in person. (E-mail or texting may be used for very minor incidents.) Some apologies are not apologies at all, such as "I want to apologize." Nor are "I'm sorry if you were offended" or "I'm sorry if I hurt your feelings," which imply that the offended party is just too sensitive. A true apology should "take the focus off yourself and keep it on your counterpart," advises communications consultant Holly Weeks.[56]

More about apologizing can be found at Apology-pros.com, PerfectApology.com, and ThePublicApology.com.

Avoid Participating in Workplace Gossip

"It might be human nature to think an unkind thought about a coworker," says Shayla McKnight, a technical service assistant for an online printing company, "but it's a choice whether or not to actually say it."[57] McKnight's company actually has a no-gossip policy, but you might not be so lucky, so you should adopt your own policy.

Gossiping and talking behind people's backs can lead to negative attitudes and backstabbing. By avoiding gossip, you avoid having to take sides and foster a greater sense of teamwork.

Unearned praise is condescending and destructive, in the opinion of management consultant Jerry Pounds, and it's not necessary to coddle young people by giving them kudos just for coming to work on time.[58] More important, perhaps, is for managers to provide guidance and mentoring—telling people when they're on track.

A couple of tips for praising properly without overdoing it:[59]

- **Use descriptive praise:** Don't tell an employee he or she is "wonderful" or "a genius," since it offers no direction. Instead, provide some descriptive details. Example: "Everyone was listening so attentively when you gave your report. And the statistics you found really drove home your point."

- **Don't use e-mail to "mass praise":** Eye-to-eye praise is best, but it's okay to use e-mail or texting from time to time to send an employee an artfully composed sentence of praise. However, don't send mass praise to a hundred employees. If everyone gets kudos, no one will feel special.

One survey asked 1,625 workers and job seekers, "What aspect is important when your employer communicates with you?" Among the top four answers (multiple responses were allowed): Giving insights on how to be more effective (52% of respondents). Showing how to fit into the company's vision (47%). Explaining the company's vision (45%). Engaging on a personal level (41%).[60]

LEARNING & SKILLS PORTFOLIO

Summary

10.1 Motivating for Performance

THE ESSENTIAL QUESTION: *Why should I be motivated to study motivation?*

How does motivation work, and why is it important? Motivation consists of the psychological processes that induce people to pursue goals. The model is: People have certain needs that motivate them to perform specific behaviors to try to attain a certain goal for which they receive rewards that feed back and satisfy the original need.

What is the difference between extrinsic and intrinsic rewards? An extrinsic reward is the payoff, such as money, a person receives from others for performing a particular task. An intrinsic reward is the satisfaction, such as a feeling of accomplishment, a person receives from performing the particular task itself.

10.2 Motivation Theory

THE ESSENTIAL QUESTION: *What can I learn from motivation theory to help explain why people want to succeed?*

How does scientific management get people to produce more? Scientific management emphasized the scientific study of work methods to improve the productivity of individual workers. Its two chief proponents were Frederick W. Taylor and the team of Frank and Lillian Gilbreth. Taylor believed worker productivity could be accomplished by applying four principles, which were based on time-motion studies, in which a worker's job was broken down into basic physical motions and then workers were trained to use the methods of the best performers. The Gilbreths expanded on Taylor by developing the principle of motion economy, in which every job could be broken down into a series of elementary motions.

How does the Hawthorne effect work? The Hawthorne effect is the name given to a Harvard research group's conclusion that employees worked harder if they received added attention—if they thought managers cared about their welfare and that supervisors paid special attention to them.

What are the five needs in Maslow's hierarchy? The human relations movement proposed that better human relations could increase worker productivity. One of its key theorists was Abraham Maslow, whose hierarchy of needs theory proposes that people are motivated by five levels of needs ranging from physiological to safety to social to esteem up to self-actualization.

Do employee dissatisfaction and satisfaction spring from the same needs? Frederick Herzberg's two-factor theory proposed that work dissatisfaction and satisfaction arise from two different factors—work satisfaction from higher-level needs he called motivating factors (such as achievement, recognition) and work dissatisfaction from lower-level needs he called hygiene factors (such as pay, working conditions).

How would I benefit by job enrichment? Job simplification, which involves reducing the number of tasks a worker performs, fits people to jobs. Job enlargement, which consists of increasing the number of tasks in a job to improve employee satisfaction, motivation, and quality of production, fits jobs to people. Job enrichment consists of building into a job such motivating factors as responsibility, achievement, recognition, stimulating work, and advancement. According to proponents of job enrichment there are five job characteristics that affect workers' motivation and performance: skill variety, task identity, task significance, autonomy, and feedback.

Which most resembles your own view of worker behavior— Theory X or Theory Y? Douglas McGregor thought that managers ought to be aware of their attitudes toward employees: either Theory X, which makes the negative assumption that workers are irresponsible, are resistant to change, lack ambition, hate work, and prefer to be led rather than to lead, or Theory Y, which makes the positive assumption that workers are capable of accepting responsibility, self-direction, and self-control and of being imaginative and creative. Theory Y leads to the concept of empowerment, in which management makes employees more involved in their jobs by giving them the authority and responsibility to make decisions.

Why would I want to work for a Theory Z company? William Ouchi proposed Theory Z, a motivational approach that emphasizes involving employees at all levels, giving them long-term job security, allowing collective decision making, emphasizing slow evaluation and promotion procedures, and treating workers like family.

How does reinforcement work? Reinforcement theory, as pioneered by Edward L. Thorndike and B. F. Skinner, suggests that behavior with positive consequences tends to be repeated whereas behavior with negative consequences tends not to be repeated.

What are three calculations I might make before deciding to work hard at something? According to expectancy theory, introduced by Victor Broom, the three calculations are expectancy, instrumentality, and valence. That is, will I be able to accomplish the task, what is the reward, and how much do I want it?

What are three elements I look at in determining whether I am being paid fairly? Equity theory, developed by J. Stacey Adams, focuses on employee perceptions as to how fairly they think they are being treated compared to others. It looks at contributions, returns, and comparisons.

What are the three elements of goal-setting theory? Edward Locke and Gary Latham developed goal-setting theory, which suggests that employees can be motivated by goals that are (1) specific and (2) challenging but (3) achievable. An aspect of goal theory, suggested by Peter Drucker, is management by objectives (MBO), in which (1) managers and employees jointly set objectives for the employee, (2) managers develop action plans, (3) managers and employees periodically review the employee's performance, and (4) the manager makes a performance appraisal and rewards the employee according to results.

10.3 How Forward-Looking Companies Motivate Their Employees: Perks, Benefits, Listening, & Praise

THE ESSENTIAL QUESTION: *What are some of the primary ways firms motivate employees?*

What are the three qualities students worldwide say they want most in a job? Students in 11 countries told survey takers the three qualities they seek in work are to attain work-life balance, to expand their skills, and to allow them to feel they matter.

What are some nonmonetary ways of keeping employees? Three incentives are thoughtfulness, offering work-life benefits, and providing skill-building and educational opportunities.

How can listening be helpful? Listening to employees can help track their engagement.

What's the right way to praise? Different employees prefer to be praised in different ways—people over 60 prefer formal awards, middle-aged people prefer self-indulgent treats, and people under 40 need lots of stroking. Managers need to provide guidance and mentoring—telling people when they're on track.

Key Terms

empowerment 296
equity theory 301
expectancy theory 299
extrinsic reward 287
goal-setting theory 302
Hawthorne effect 290
human relations movement 291
hygiene factors 293
intrinsic reward 288

job enlargement 294
job enrichment 294
job rotation 294
job simplification 293
management by objectives (MBO) 303
Maslow's hierarchy of needs theory 291
motivation 286
motivating factors 292

principle of motion economy 290
reinforcement theory 298
scientific management 289
Theory X 296
Theory Y 296
Theory Z 297
time-motion studies 289
two-factor theory 292

Pop Quiz Prep

1. A manager comes up with an innovation that will reduce her department's carbon footprint by more than 30% each year. What is an example of an extrinsic reward for the manager's performance?

2. Why is motivation important?

3. According to Maslow's hierarchy, what is the lowest level of human needs?

4. What is meant by the term *job enrichment*?

5. What is an example of a work-life benefit?

6. What would be the most effective way to praise a middle-aged employee?

Critical Thinking Questions

1. Most people work principally for the money (extrinsic reward), but some are lucky enough to find rewards in the work itself (intrinsic rewards) such as building a home or being a musician, a teacher, an actor, or a clothing designer. What kind of work would you find intrinsically rewarding? Do you believe that you should "do what you love" when choosing a career?

2. As a student, think about the times when you were self-motivated to study and learn and the times when you were not. What motivated you? Was fear ever a motivator, and if so, did it improve your performance? Describe the situation.

3. If you are presently working, or have worked in the past, discuss the motivation techniques used by the company you worked for. Were the techniques effective, and if so, how? If they were not, please discuss why. If you have not worked before, please discuss the motivation techniques used by your teachers.

4. If you were paid $1,000 for each final grade of an A and $500 for a B, do you think you would try harder in your classes? If money (or scholarships) were offered for academic success, would this make a difference in your motivation level?

5. When employees compare the ratio of their contributions (inputs) and returns (rewards) with those of others—either coworkers within the organization or others in similar jobs outside it—they then make a judgment about fairness. Discuss a situation in which you compared the ratio of your contributions and returns with others, and whether there was equity or inequity. Did you change your behavior as a result? (Panel 10.6 has some insight of how employees try to reduce perceived inequity.)

Cases

Go to MyBizLab

VIDEO CASE STUDY

Zappos—Motivating Employees through Company Culture

Tony Hsieh, founder and chief executive officer of Zappos, an online shoe and apparel seller, is a new generation of CEO, whose top priority is his commitment to employee happiness. "If you get the culture right, you don't need to worry about a lot of the things companies spend their time worrying about," he states in the video. Published in June 2010, his first book, *Delivering Happiness: A Path to Profits, Passion, and Purpose*, outlines his path from a young boy starting a worm farm and taking apart computers to starting Zappos. At the heart of Zappos' success lies its corporate culture. The video depicts many examples of the unique and fun atmosphere of "work hard, play hard," which Hsieh has created.

Given the fact that hourly Zappos employees make on average a little less than $25,000 a year (less than industry average), the unique corporate culture must be working. The core values at Zappos are lived in a tried-and-true manner every day by the leader himself, who reports that his "unified happiness theory" involves establishing balance among four basic human needs: perceived progress, perceived control, relatedness, and a connection to a larger vision.[61]

Hsieh claims that the success of Zappos lies in the virtue of not just hanging a plaque on the wall but leading by example, and being willing to hire and fire based upon these values. The executive team, who refer to themselves as "monkeys," couldn't agree more. The fun and zany Zappos family core values, which all 1,800 employees embrace, include things like "Be Humble," "Build Open and Honest Relationships with Communication," and "Create Fun and a Little Weirdness."

Hsieh is committed to making sure that the Zappos culture remains strong and employees remain happy, even with the 2009 acquisition by e-commerce giant, Amazon.com. In an *Inc.* magazine article entitled, "Why I Sold Zappos," Hsieh states, "I think we're proof that a company doesn't need to lose itself as it grows bigger—or even after it gets acquired."[62]

An important aspect of the Zappos culture is the relationships between employees. It is so essential that the company has begun tracking the number and strength of cross-departmental relationships. Hsieh explains, "When employees log into their computers, we ask them to look at a picture of a random employee and then ask them how well they know that person—the options include "say hi in the halls," "hang out outside of work," and "we're going to be longtime friends." Hsieh's hope is that more employees can become close friends.

Hsieh's obsession with employee happiness—often referred to by Zappos' board of directors as "Tony's social experiments," or "Tony's pet project"—has caused some disagreement.[63] While Hsieh believes that getting the culture right is what creates the heart and soul of a business, the board prefers a more conservative approach of profitability first, and then doing nice things for the employees with the profits.[64] The board says that Tony's social experiments are good for PR, but advises that Hsieh should spend less time worrying about employee happiness, and more time selling shoes if he wants to move the company forward.

Hsieh, who has continued to lead the company after the 2009 acquisition, believes in a quasi-religious way that "a company can accomplish lots by motivating, but can accomplish even more by inspiriting employees to a bigger vision that they are passionate about." Can you see yourself "creating fun and a little weirdness" as a Zappos employee?

What's Your Take?

1. Without knowing the exact generational composition of the Zappos workforce, if you were to assume it consisted primarily of baby boomers (those born between 1948 and 1964), do you think the "work hard, play hard" culture would be as effective for motivational purposes? Do you think this culture is a fit for a multigenerational workforce?

2. On a *Harvard Business Review* blog, Bill Naylor, founder of *Fast Company* magazine says, "After a week or so in this immersive experience, though, it's time for what Zappos calls 'The Offer.' The fast-growing company says to its newest employees: 'If you quit today, we will pay you for the amount of time you've worked, plus we will offer you a $2,000 bonus.'"[65] What is their rationale for this and does it surprise you that only 2% to 3% of the people take the offer, while the other 97% say "no deal" to the instant cash?[66]

3. Psychologist Frederick Herzberg believed that to spur superior work performance, motivating factors like challenges, opportunities, and recognition must be instituted. Which of Herzberg's theories are at work at Zappos? How is it that employees who sell shoes over the phone at industry wages are so motivated? Explain.

4. Discuss what makes the employee training at Zappos different.

5. What makes the interview process at Zappos different? What is of utmost importance for recruiters at Zappos when choosing a candidate?

BUSINESS DECISION CASE
Pets in the Workplace: Increased Employee Engagement or Barking?

In today's challenging economic environment, companies are searching for new and innovative ways to keep employees engaged and productive—without, of course, having to compensate them with increased salary and wages. Companies know that a happy employee is more likely to stay with the organization, so it is worth finding creative ways to make an employee's workday more enjoyable—and more fruitful.

One creative way that some companies are trying to increase motivation is by allowing employees to bring their canine kids (dogs) to the workplace. "Companies hire in-house masseuses to in-house chefs. Why not take this step and allow people to bring a companion that's really important to them in their lives?" argues Phil Carpenter, vice president of marketing at Simply Hired, an online jobs database company that has added an option for job-seekers to select a dog-friendly company.

Companies are becoming more aware of the importance of a work-life balance—and pets, more than ever before, are considered part of the American family. The American Pet Products Association (APPA) 2009–2010 National Pet Owners Survey found that pet ownership is at its highest level ever, with 77.5 million households in the United States owning at least one pet—62% of all households, up 12% over the last decade.[67] Recession or no recession, industry experts estimate Americans spent $47.7 billion in 2010 on goods and services for their feathered, furry, and scaly friends, up from $45.5 billion in 2009.[68] Other examples of the growing importance of pets are that people make provisions in their wills for their pets, plan vacations around pets, hire dog walkers and dog sitters, and even place their pampered pets in doggie daycare while at work. A survey by Simply Hired and Dogster, an online site, found that a third of dog owners would take a 5% pay cut to take their pets to work, two-thirds would work longer hours, and half would switch jobs.[69]

With these statistics, it is not surprising that interest in bringing pets to work is growing. Companies that have allowed pets into the work environment have reported success; they have found that allowing pets in the office creates a more productive work environment, increases morale, lowers absenteeism, allows employees to bond and get along, relieves stress, and reduces or eliminates doggie daycare and pet-sitting costs—which in turn results in greater employee happiness. Additionally, a study by the American Pet Products Manufacturers Association found that pets provide more benefits to companies than management classes,[70] and thousands of companies participate in "Take Your Dog to Work Day," which encourages pet adoption while celebrating the great companions dogs make.[71]

While the positive aspects of dogs in the workplace are many, there are those who do not want dogs in the workplace, regardless of studies showing increased morale and productivity. The reasons vary: Some people just don't like animals; others are allergic. Some find they are distracting, they smell, and they demand attention. Some may feel that those with dogs are less productive due to frequent dog walks and bathroom breaks. Besides that, one small accident can be a deal breaker, and chewing is out of the question. What about you? If you are a pet owner, would you like to bring your treasured and loved canine kid to the workplace? Would it be a deciding factor for you when choosing a job?

What's Your Take?

1. What are some of the pros and cons of allowing dogs in the workplace? Have teams debate this with one team for dogs in the workplace, and another against.

2. The Occupational Safety and Health Administration (OSHA) does not have standards that prohibit the presence of pets in the workplace. Do you think there are safety risks associated with pets in the workplace?

3. Do you believe that offering the benefit or perk of bringing dogs to work will improve employee retention? Explain.

4. More than 400 companies have listed themselves as dog friendly, including Google. Do you think this can pay off in a competitive market? Is there a possibility that allowing dogs would cause some people to not want to work at such a company?

5. Not everyone loves dogs. Some people love cats. And some people are not animal lovers and do not see a place for dogs at work. To respect the needs of those who don't like pets, what rules would you suggest your organization put in place if a policy of dogs at work was allowed?

Briefings   MyBizLab Activities & Cases

Go to www.mybizlab.com for online activities and exercises related to the timely topics discussed in this chapter's Briefings, as well as additional theme-related Briefing *Spotlights* highlighting how these concepts apply in today's business environment.

In-chapter Briefing:
- A Motivational Mind Game for Success

Activity:
- Developing Marketable Business Skills – Interview a Supervisor or Manager
- Developing Marketable Business Skills – Goal-Setting Theory: Three Desirable Qualities for Goals
- Get Your Career in Gear – Training & Development Specialists & Managers
- Going to the Net! – Achievement? Relationships? Power? Take the Thematic Apperception Test
- Going to the Net! – Rypple.com: Feedback Junkies Ask, "Got Feedback?"
- Going to the Net! – Perkfinder: How to Find Companies That Will Give You What You Want Most

Briefing Spotlight:
- Know What Motivates You & Be Ready for Reinvention

In-chapter Briefing:
- Clients Like Ad Firm's Happy Employees

Activity:
- Going to the Net! – "I'm Sorry!" Learning the Importance of How & When to Apologize to Your Customers

Briefing Spotlight:
- Nordstrom Culture: Motivating Employees for Customer Focus

In-chapter Briefing:
- The Extrinsic Rewards of Investing in Green Energy: Making Money
- The Intrinsic Rewards of Investing in Green Energy: Gaining Feelings of Accomplishment

Activity:
- Going to the Net! – Companies Providing Eco-Friendly Employee Incentive Programs

Briefing Spotlight:
- The Reusable Bag: An Intrinsic or Extrinsic Reward?

In-chapter Briefing:
- Fulfilling Higher-Level Needs—One Man Tries to Strike a Balance between Safety & Higher-Level Needs
- Using Reinforcement to Improve Accountability & Integrity

Activity:
- Going to the Net! – What Makes a Company One of the 100 Best?

Briefing Spotlight:
- Scotts Miracle-Gro Motivates Employees to Be Healthy

Additional *Briefing Spotlights* available at MyBizLab:

- A WORLD OF CONSTANT CHANGE
- BUSINESS CULTURE & ETIQUETTE
- GLOBAL BUSINESS
- INFO TECH & SOCIAL MEDIA
- LEGAL & ETHICAL PRACTICES
- PERSONAL FINANCE
- SMALL BUSINESS & ENTREPRENEURS

11

Human Resource Management

Getting the Right People for Business Success

After reading and studying this chapter, you will be able to answer the following essential questions:

11.1 Finding Great People: Building Human Capital

THE ESSENTIAL QUESTION: *Why is human resource management important, and how are needs determined?*

11.2 Laws Affecting Human Resource Management

THE ESSENTIAL QUESTION: *To avoid exposing myself and my organization to legal liabilities, what areas of the law do I need to be aware of?*

11.3 Recruiting, Selection, Orientation, Training, & Development

THE ESSENTIAL QUESTION: *How do firms get the best people and train them to do their best work?*

11.4 Performance Appraisals

THE ESSENTIAL QUESTION: *How should I handle employee evaluations, and how should I handle evaluations of me?*

11.5 Compensating, Promoting, & Disciplining

THE ESSENTIAL QUESTION: *How can I reward and discipline the people who work for me?*

MyBizLab

Where you see MyBizLab in this chapter, go to www.mybizlab.com for additional activities on the topic being discussed.

FORECAST: What's Ahead in This Chapter

This chapter describes the activities for planning for, attracting, developing, and retaining an effective workforce. We discuss laws affecting human resource management. We describe recruiting, selecting, orienting, and training, then move on to appraising, compensating, promoting, and disciplining employees. We also consider different ways of motivating employees.

WINNER: Costco, with 24% Employee Turnover

Costco Wholesale (107,200 full-time and part-time U.S. employees) is a chain of warehouse stores founded in Seattle in 1983 and now with 424 stores in the United States and Puerto Rico. Its business model focuses on selling a few (rather than multiple) brands of bulk-packaged products at high volume to businesses and individuals. Compared to Walmart and other big-box stores, it tends to attract more affluent shoppers. It charges a yearly member fee and spends no money on advertising.

Costco pays retail cashiers $15.47 an hour. Indeed, non-supervisory wages range between $11.57 and $15.47 per hour, high enough to enable employees to buy homes and take vacation trips.[1] In addition, 96% of eligible workers are covered by company health insurance—higher than average. Although a few of the stores are unionized, the great majority are not.

Does this affect shareholder earnings? (Sales were $76.3 billion at the end of its fiscal year on August 31, 2010, of which $1.3 billion was net profit.) "From the perspective of investors," said one stock analyst, "Costco's benefits are overly generous. Public companies need to care for shareholders first." Another analyst says that at Costco "it's better to be an employee or customer than a shareholder."[2] The more favorable employee benefits lead to a less favorable stock price for Costco compared with Walmart.

However, Costco chief executive Jim Sinegal rejects the assumption that discount stores must pay poorly and skimp on benefits. "I happen to believe," he says, "that in order to reward the shareholder in the long term, you have to please your customers and workers."[3]

As a result of the generous pay and benefits, Costco has only a 24% annual employee turnover. It's been calculated that a 10% reduction in employee turnover can yield a 20% savings on labor costs. Thus, Costco's labor costs amount to only 7% of its annual sales, a very low percentage.

Source: Photograph by Sally Lindsay.

LOSER: Walmart, with Up to 70% Employee Turnover

Walmart Stores, founded in Bentonville, Arkansas, in 1962 and now totaling more than 4,300 stores domestically, is the United States' largest employer, with 2.1 million employees (called "associates"). Sales were $419 billion at the end of its fiscal year January 31, 2011—50% more than its five closest competitors combined.

The part of Walmart that directly competes with Costco is the members-only Sam's Club, which has 609 warehouse stores in the United States and is second largest to Costco in sales, earning $49.4 billion in 2010.[4] To execute its well-known business strategy of "Always low prices" (though not all its prices are the lowest), Walmart has traditionally paid an hourly wage—currently $8.50 an hour, or a range of $7.64 to $11.06 on average—that is similar to that of competitors such as Target.[5]

The company's total benefits package has frequently lagged behind. At one time, Walmart used to say less than 10% of employees lacked health insurance (now it is less than 5.5%), but the system of premiums and deductibles made it difficult for low-wage employees to afford such insurance.[6]

Walmart has reportedly locked out workers overnight and hired illegal immigrants to mop its floors. The company has been sued for discrimination and for limiting medical care to injured employees.[7]

"Where you stand on Walmart," says one account, "seems to depend on where you sit. If you're a consumer, Walmart is good for you. If you're a wage earner, there's a good chance it's bad. If you're a Walmart shareholder, you want the company to grow. If you're a citizen, you probably don't want it growing in your backyard."[8]

The result of its employment policies: Walmart's annual employee turnover rate is 50%—one report says as high as 70% for employees in their first year.[9] A 50% turnover means that Walmart's labor costs amount to 12% of its annual sales, compared with Costco's 7%.

Source: Photograph by Sally Lindsay.

YOUR CALL Is it possible to treat employees right and still make money? Consider: Both companies have appeared on *Fortune* magazine's annual "Most Admired Companies" list, which is based on profitability to investors. In the last decade, Walmart has been ranked number 1, 2, 9, and 11 on the list. Costco has been ranked 21, 22, 28, 29, and 32. Ironically, however, Costco has never appeared on another *Fortune* list—that of "100 Best Companies to Work For," whereas Walmart has appeared on it twice (ranked #80 in 2001 and #66 in 1999). Does this mean that *other* companies have gotten better about taking care of employees while also achieving profitability?[10]

MyBizLab

11.1 Finding Great People: Building Human Capital

THE BIG IDEA: Human resource management consists of the activities managers perform to plan for, attract, develop, and retain an effective workforce. Determining the human resources needed consists of understanding current employee needs and predicting future employee needs.

THE ESSENTIAL QUESTION: Why is human resource management important, and how are needs determined?

MyBiz**Lab** **MyBizLab:** Check your understanding of these concepts at www.mybizlab.com.

For many people seeking employment, the problem of choosing between a Costco and a Walmart pales beside the principal problem brought about by the Great Recession of 2007–2009 and its aftermath—namely, having a job at all.

With unemployment at a 25-year high, the job market has not been kind to recent college graduates. New degree holders have found themselves competing for work not only with fellow classmates but also with laid-off experienced workers, financially strapped retirees, and still-unemployed college grads from previous years. The tough economy has forced them to consider alternative possibilities: taking part-time jobs, taking jobs that don't fit their majors, starting their own businesses, becoming unpaid interns to gain experience, and continuing on in school.

Yet new graduates also have a number of advantages.[11] Often they can work cheaper than more experienced employees. They may be more flexible, willing to travel frequently or to relocate to less desirable cities. They can be open-minded about contemplating different career possibilities.

And if you're still in college, you're in a great position to do some planning that will help you in your initial job search.

BRIEFING / BUSINESS SKILLS & CAREER DEVELOPMENT
Preparing Now for Your First Post-College Job. Is the job market still difficult? If so, consider the following advice.

Get ready now. A freshman or sophomore can start building an appealing résumé by doing unpaid work—volunteering for college and community activities and performing entry-level business tasks for free. You can also expand your network of helpful acquaintances by meeting guest speakers, alumni, friends of your parents, and so on.

Learn how to market yourself. The key to getting the first job is to learn how to promote and transfer your college skills and activities to the professional world. Whether your major is finance or accounting, English or philosophy, tailor your strengths to the particular job description of the position you're seeking.[12]

Be willing to adjust your expectations. "Most people don't develop careers related to their majors anyway," says business writer Alexandra Levit. "For your first position, adjust your expectations and look for something that allows you to master the transferable skills that will serve you well no matter what future path you decide to pursue."[13]

We offer further advice on job seeking throughout the rest of this chapter. ∎

Want to Know More? 11-1
Key Terms & Definitions in Sequential Order to Study as You Go Along
Go to www.mybizlab.com.

Human Resource Management: Managing an Organization's Most Important Resource

How would I define human resource management?

"Attracting, retaining, and developing great people is sometimes the only way our organizations can keep up with the competition across the street or around the globe," says Susan Meisinger, president and CEO of the Society for Human Resource Management.[14]

The measure of an organization's value, then, is not just the worth of its property, plant, and equipment but also its *people*— what's known as the firm's **human capital, the productive potential of employee experience, knowledge, and actions.** In today's hypercompetitive environment, a key concern of most organizations— especially ones with knowledge workers, such as Yahoo, eBay, and Apple— is *staffing,* **the recruitment, hiring, motivating, and retention of valuable employees.**

Once upon a time, you applied for a job at a door marked "Personnel Department." Now the sign usually says "Human Resources Department," and the change is not just cosmetic; it is meant to signal the importance of people in a company's success. *Human resource (HR) management* **consists of the activities managers perform to obtain and maintain an effective workforce to assist organizations in achieving goals.**

Although talking about people as "resources" might seem to put them at the same level as financial resources and material resources, in fact people are an organization's most important resource. Indeed, companies ranked first on *Fortune*'s annual list of "100 Best Companies to Work For," such as software maker SAS in 2010 and 2011, have discovered that putting employees first has been a principal reason for their success. ❶ Other "Best Companies" ranked No. 1: data storage firm NetApp in 2009, search engine company Google in 2008 and 2007, pharmaceutical firm Genentech in 2006, Wegmans Food Markets in 2005. ❷

Determining the Human Resources Needed

How do I understand present and future job needs?

Does a particular job really require a college degree? How can business managers avoid hiring people who are overqualified (and presumably more expensive) or underqualified (and thus not as productive) for a particular job?

Job Analysis, Job Description, & Job Specification

To get the best employees for the future, managers need to understand their employee picture today. This requires doing a *job analysis,* then writing a *job description* and *job specification.*

Job Analysis: Figuring Out the Job. The purpose of *job analysis* **is to determine the basic elements of a job, using observation and analysis.** Here the manager interviews job occupants about what they do, observes the flow of work, and learns how results are accomplished.

Job Description and Job Specification: Defining the Job. Once the elements of a job are understood, a manager can write a *job description,* **which outlines what the holders of the job do and how and why they do it.** Next comes a *job specification,* **which describes the minimum qualifications people must have to perform the job successfully.** By entering a job description and

❶ **One of the 100 best.** Every year *Fortune* magazine publishes a list of the "100 Best Companies to Work For" in the United States. In 2010 and 2011, first on the list was North Carolina software maker SAS, which has tried to institute a culture of "trust between our employees and the company." In-house gyms, pools, and physician and on-site medical services are just some of the benefits that SAS offers to keep employees happy.

❷ **Employee and customer friendly.** Ranked No. 3 on *Fortune*'s 2010 and 2011 lists of "100 Best Companies to Work For" (and No. 1 in 2005), Wegmans Food Markets are considered customer friendly because they are employee friendly. (Among the perks: company-provided health screenings and flu shots.) Here an executive chef fills the Chef's Case with ready-to-heat, ready-to-eat meals in a setting meant to look and feel like a European open-air market.

Source: Ted Foxx/Alamy.

③ Integrad. The UPS driver training center near Washington, D.C. combines technology, hands-on experience, and real-time feedback. Trainees are taught the prescribed "340 methods" compiled over the years as part of job analysis and job description of the most efficient ways to perform a UPS driver's job.

i

Want to Know More? 11-2

What Are the Cutting-Edge Jobs of the Future?

Go to www.mybizlab.com.

specification with their characteristics into a database, an organization can do computer-searching for candidates by matching keywords on their résumés with the keywords describing the job.

BRIEFING / A WORLD OF CONSTANT CHANGE

Job Analysis & Description for UPS Drivers. UPS has specialized job analysts who ride with drivers and time how long it takes to deliver a load of packages and what problems are encountered (traffic jams, vicious dogs, intended recipients not home, and so on).[15]

Based on the job analyses, UPS establishes standards for its drivers that set projections for the number of miles driven, deliveries, and pickups. For instance, drivers are taught to walk at a "brisk pace" of 2.5 paces per second, except under icy or other unsafe conditions. However, because conditions vary depending on whether routes are urban, suburban, or rural, standards vary for different routes.

Most of the 99,000 UPS drivers in the United States are former package sorters, but they must meet certain standards, such as hold safe driving records and be in good health. They must also attend and graduate from Integrad, an 11,500-square-foot training center near Washington, D.C., where they practice UPS-prescribed "340 methods" shown to save seconds and improve safety.[16] ③ ■

Predicting Future Employee Needs

Job descriptions change and new jobs are created. Who could have visualized an "e-commerce accountant" 10 years ago, for example? Thus, predicting future employee needs means managers need to consider two questions:

1. **What Kind of Employees Will Help Achieve the Firm's Vision?** Although you might assume your company won't change much, it's better to assume that it will. Thus, as a manager you need to understand the firm's vision and strategic plan so that you can hire the right people to realize them.

2. **Where Can Such Employees Be Found?** You can look for future employees among the best trained and motivated of your present staff, thinking what extra training they might need. Or you can recruit from outside, concentrating on what talent is and will be available in your industry's and geographical area's labor pool, the training of people graduating from various schools, and the like.

■ **Example** of Predicting Future Employee Needs: Looking for "Green" Businesspeople. With more businesses emphasizing sustainability, how is your firm to go about doing this? After building "green" into the company's vision, you might look for suitable employees on campuses offering sustainability degrees or green MBAs.[17] ■

THE BIG IDEA: Four areas of human resource law you need to be aware of are labor relations, compensation and benefits, health and safety, and equal employment opportunity.

THE ESSENTIAL QUESTION: To avoid exposing myself and my organization to legal liabilities, what areas of the law do I need to be aware of?

MyBizLab: Check your understanding of these concepts at www.mybizlab.com.

MyBizLab

Whatever the nature of your business, in the United States it has to operate within the environment of American law. Four areas you need to be aware of are (1) *labor and unions,* (2) *compensation and benefits,* (3) *workplace health and safety,* and (4) *equal employment opportunity.*

Some of the most important laws are summarized on the next page. (*See* ■ *Panel 11.1.*)

1 Labor & Unions: General Employee Rights

How do laws affect employee well-being?

Early laws concerned with employee welfare had to do with unions, and they are still important. The 1935 Wagner Act created the **National Labor Relations Board, which enforces procedures allowing employees to vote to have a union and the rules for collective bargaining. *Collective bargaining* consists of negotiations between management and employees in disputes over compensation, benefits, working conditions, and job security.**

The 1947 Taft-Hartley Act allows the president of the United States to prevent or end a strike that threatens national security. In 1981, Ronald Reagan invoked Taft-Hartley to order striking air controllers back to work. In 1997, Bill Clinton probably had the authority to use Taft-Hartley to force striking UPS workers to return to their jobs, but he refused to do so. In 2002, George W. Bush invoked the act to avert a shutdown of 29 West Coast ports.

2 Compensation & Benefits: Pay, Pensions, & Perks

What legislation affects employee compensation and retirement and health benefits?

The 1935 Social Security Act created the U.S. retirement system. The 1938 *Fair Labor Standards Act* established a federal minimum wage (in 2011 it was $7.25 an hour) and a maximum workweek (now 40 hours a week), along with banning products from child labor. Executive, administrative, and professional employees who earn salaries rather than hourly wages are exempt from overtime rules. The 1993 Family and Medical Leave Act requires employers to allow employees to take up to 12 weeks of unpaid leave for childbirth, adoption, or family emergency.

■ **PANEL 11.1 Some important recent U.S. federal laws and regulations protecting employees.**

Year	Law or Regulation	Provisions
Labor and Unions		
1974	Privacy Act	Gives employees legal right to examine letters of reference concerning them
1986	Immigration Reform & Control Act	Prohibits employers from hiring illegal immigrants
1988	Polygraph Protection Act	Limits employer's ability to use lie detectors
1988	Worker Adjustment & Retraining Notification Act	Requires organizations with 100 or more employees to give 60 days notice for mass layoffs or plant closings
2003	Sarbanes-Oxley Act	Prohibits employers from demoting or firing employees who raise accusations of fraud to a federal agency
Compensation and Benefits		
1974	Employee Retirement Income Security Act (ERISA)	Sets rules for managing private pension plans
1993	Family & Medical Leave Act	Allows 12 weeks of unpaid leave for medical and family reasons, including for childbirth, adoption, or family emergency
1996	Health Insurance Portability & Accountability Act (HIPAA)	Allows employees to switch health insurance plans when changing jobs and receive new coverage regardless of preexisting health conditions; prohibits group plans from dropping ill employees
Workplace Health and Safety		
1970	Occupational Safety & Health Act (OSHA)	Sets and enforces workplace safety standards
1985	Consolidated Omnibus Budget Reconciliation Act (COBRA)	Requires an extension of health insurance benefits after termination
2010	Patient Protection & Affordable Care Act	Employers with more than 50 employees must provide health insurance
Equal Employment Opportunity		
1963	Equal Pay Act	Prohibits pay differences based on gender for performing equal work
1964, amended 1972	Civil Rights Act, Title VII	Prohibits discrimination in employment decisions such as hiring, pay, and promotion based on race, color, religion, national origin, or sex
1967, amended 1978 and 1986	Age Discrimination in Employment Act (ADEA)	Prohibits discrimination of employees over 40 years old; restricts mandatory retirement
1978	Pregnancy Discrimination Act	Broadens discrimination to cover pregnancy, childbirth, and related medical conditions; protects job security during maternity leave
1990	Americans with Disabilities Act (ADA)	Prohibits discrimination against employees with physical or mental disabilities or chronic illness; requires employers to make "reasonable accommodation" for employees with disabilities
1991	Civil Rights Act	Amends and clarifies Title VII, ADA, and other laws; permits suits against employers for punitive damages in cases of intentional discrimination

3 Workplace Health & Safety: Standards for Employee Well-Being

What laws regulate workplace conditions?

From cotton mill workers breathing lint to miners risking tunnel cave-ins, industry has always had dirty, dangerous jobs. Since 1970, with the passage of the Occupational Safety and Health Act (OSHA), there has grown a number of laws prohibiting organizations from forcing employees to endure hazardous working conditions. Among the safety regulations brought about by OSHA: required guards on machinery with moving parts (such as snowblowers and chainsaws); maximum exposure limits to certain chemicals; extended use of personal protective equipment, such as gloves and respirators; and rules regarding exposure to asbestos. Later laws extended health coverage for employees, most notably the 2010 Patient Protection and Health Care Act, President Barack Obama's signature health care legislation.

4 Equal Employment Opportunity: Banning Bigotry

What three concepts are covered by EEO laws?

Attempts to reduce discrimination in employment based on racial, ethnic, and religious bigotry and gender stereotypes began with Title VII of the Civil Rights Act of 1964. This law created the ***Equal Employment Opportunity (EEO) Commission*, which is charged with enforcing antidiscrimination and other employment-related laws.** Title VII applies to all organizations or their agents engaged in an industry affecting interstate commerce that employ 15 or more employees, including contractors doing business with the U.S. government. Other laws were added later preventing discrimination against older workers and people with physical and mental disabilities.

Three important areas covered by EEO laws are *discrimination, affirmative action*, and *sexual harassment.*

Discrimination

***Discrimination* is judged to happen when people are hired or promoted—or denied hiring or promotion—for reasons not relevant to the job,** such as skin color, gender, religion, or national origin. People who have been discriminated against may sue for back pay and punitive damages.

Affirmative Action

***Affirmative action* aims at achieving equality of opportunity within an organization.** To try to make up for past discrimination in employment, affirmative action programs actively try to find, hire, and develop the talents of people from groups traditionally discriminated against. Steps include active recruitment, removal of prejudicial questions in interviews, and creation of minority hiring goals, but they do not include hiring quotas, which are illegal.

Sexual Harassment

***Sexual harassment* consists of unwanted sexual attention that creates an adverse work environment.** ❹ Offensive acts range from physical nonsexual contact, unwanted touching, suggestive remarks, unwanted dating pressure, and sex-stereotyped jokes to obscene gestures, sexually oriented

❹ **Is this sexual harassment?** Is it sexual harassment when men ogle a woman's body without her knowing it? Should any type of sexually suggestive remarks be tolerated in an office setting? Is mild flirtation acceptable?

Source: Stockbyte/Thinkstock.

Want to Know More? 11-3

Unwanted Attention: Five Biggest Sexual Harassment Cases in the United States

Go to www.mybizlab.com.

posters and graffiti, sexual propositions, obscene phone calls, and threats of retaliation unless sexual favors are given.

Whether the harassment is done by someone of the opposite sex or the same sex, a manager or a coworker—or even a company outsider—it is still illegal. Women are not the only victims; indeed, sexual harassment claims made by men doubled from 8% of all claims in 1990 to 16% in 2009.[18]

There are two types of sexual harassment, *hostile environment* and *quid pro quo.*

Source: Chris Rout/Alamy.

Hostile Environment Harassment: Offensive or Intimidating Workplace.

In a *hostile environment* type, the person being sexually harassed experiences an offensive or intimidating work environment but doesn't risk economic harm. According to one survey, 38% of women said they heard sexual innuendo, wisecracks, or taunts at the office, up from 22% the year before.[19] Another growing problem is bullying on the job, experienced by 37% of workers, both male and female.[20] **5**

Quid Pro Quo Harassment: Risk of Economic Injury.

In *quid pro quo* harassment, the victim of unwanted sexual attention is put in the position of jeopardizing being hired for a job or obtaining job benefits or opportunities unless she or he implicitly or explicitly goes along with the unwanted behavior.

5 Bullying. Whether done by supervisors or by other employees, workplace bullying leads to feelings of defenselessness and humiliation among the bullied. Cursing, unwarranted criticism, and imposing unrealistic deadlines are all forms of bullying. Is it illegal? Not usually, unless it involves harassment based on race, religion, disability, and the like. But it definitely affects workplace morale and productivity.

Key Takeaway 11-1
Four areas of business legislation: labor and unions, compensation and benefits, workplace health and safety, equal employment opportunity.

BRIEFING / LEGAL & ETHICAL PRACTICES
Sexual Harassment Case Costs FedEx Big-Time. After 11 years of working for Federal Express in San Leandro, California, dispatcher Charlotte Boswell, a single mother, resigned in 2001, saying the company had created a hostile work environment.

Boswell said her boss "had hugged and kissed her and other female employees at staff meetings for many months and gave preferential treatment to those who went along," according to one account. When she objected, she "was punished with delayed paychecks, bad schedules, and unwarranted criticism, and was eventually assigned a shift that she couldn't work because she had to take care of a disabled child."[21]

In 2007, a jury concluded that Boswell's resignation had been coerced and awarded her $3 million—$300,000 for lost earnings, $250,000 for emotional distress, and $2.45 million in punitive damages for FedEx's violating her rights. A judge later cut her punitive damages to $300,000, the maximum under federal law, but a U.S. circuit court later gave Boswell the right to a new trial on punitive damages under California law, which has no dollar limit. ■

Most companies now recognize they are at risk legally when supervisors are allowed to embarrass and humiliate their employees, let alone inflict retaliation and force them to quit. Some rules of avoidance are shown below. (*See* ■ *Panel 11.2.*)

■ **PANEL 11.2 Guidelines for preventing sexual harassment.**

Don't . . .

• Request or suggest sexual favors for rewards related to work or promotion.

• Do uninvited touching, hugging, or patting of someone's body.

• Create sexual pictures or displays or written notes of a sexual nature.

• Make suggestive jokes of a sexual nature, demeaning remarks, or obscene gestures or sounds.

THE BIG IDEA: Companies recruit qualified applicants for jobs from both inside and outside the organization. Selecting the best person is done by reviewing candidates' application forms, résumés, and references; doing interviews, either structured or unstructured; and screening with ability, personality, and other kinds of employment tests. Three ways newcomers are helped to perform their jobs are through orientation, training, and development.

THE ESSENTIAL QUESTION: How do firms get the best people and train them to do their best work?

MyBizLab: Check your understanding of these concepts at www.mybizlab.com.

MyBizLab

Trying to get hired, not always easy in the best of times, became even more difficult during the Great Recession, when there were six job seekers for every job opening. But even prior to the downturn, points out Harvard economist Lawrence Katz, the hiring process became more protracted, as human resource departments became more professional and employers had to diversify and justify their hiring processes to meet affirmative action and civil rights laws.[22] In addition, employer offshoring of jobs and investment in labor-saving technologies resulted in reduced opportunities for employment within the United States.[23]

For new college graduates, says a college director of career services, this means they can't be casual about their search—they must "bring their A game to the job market," with their networking, résumé, cover letter, and interviewing skills being top-notch.[24] ❻

Let's see how you can develop that game.

Source: Champlain College/Stephen Mease.

❻ **The A game.** How strong are your job-hunting skills—your networking, résumé, and interviewing skills? The Great Recession and the years afterward have meant job hunters need to bring their "A game" to the employment market. What grade would you give your game right now?

The Recruiting Process:
How Companies Look for Qualified Applicants

How do internal and external recruiting differ?

Recruiting **is the process by which companies find and attract qualified applicants for jobs open.** Of course, companies want to find people whose characteristics, abilities, and skills are best suited to the organization—who are, in a word, *qualified.*

Recruiting is of two types: *internal* and *external.*

1 Internal Recruiting: When Companies Hire from the Inside

It's usually a lot easier to find a job once you're on the inside of an organization. In fact, most vacant positions in organizations are filled through internal recruitment, especially promotions.[25] ***Internal recruiting*** **is what companies do when they make employees already working for the organization aware of job openings.**

The principal avenue by which companies let employees know of job openings is through ***job postings,*** **putting information about job vacancies on company websites, break-room bulletin boards, and newsletters.** Companies also rely on referrals by current employees.

Internal recruitment has advantages and disadvantages:

Advantages. Compared to external recruiting, internal recruiting has three advantages for companies: (1) It fosters greater effort and loyalty because employees realize that staying put with the organization and working hard may result in more opportunities. (2) The standard recruiting process—advertising, interviewing, and so on—is less expensive. (3) Internal candidates are already known to the organization and so there is less risk they won't work out.

Disadvantages. There are three disadvantages: (1) Internal recruitment limits the pool of fresh talent and different viewpoints. (2) It leads employees to assume that longevity and seniority alone will lead to promotion. (3) When a job is filled, the person filling it leaves another job to be filled within the organization.

Want to Know More? 11-4
How Can Job Boards Be Useful?
Go to www.mybizlab.com.

2 External Recruiting: When Companies Hire from the Outside

External recruiting **is what companies do in trying to attract job applicants from outside the organization.** They might list job vacancies through newspaper ads, Craigslist, or career websites such as Monster.com. They might contact employment agencies, executive recruiting firms (so-called head hunters), college job-placement offices, technical training schools, or union hiring halls; and they might participate in job fairs. In general, it is more difficult for small firms to recruit qualified people than it is for big firms. Still, there are many things that small employers can do.[26] (*See* ■ *Panel 11.3, opposite page.*)

Advantages. To an employer, two advantages of recruiting from outside the organization are that applicants may have (1) specialized knowledge and experience and (2) fresh viewpoints.

Disadvantages. Two disadvantages are: (1) hiring from outside is more expensive and takes longer than internal recruiting, and (2) the risks are higher because the persons hired are less well known.

■ **PANEL 11.3 How small businesses can recruit qualified employees.**

Besides using conventional sources to locate and attract possible employees, small-business owners may try the following approaches:

- **Offer an appealing environment:** Small businesses can offer an environment where employees can have an impact that they can't in large firms. They can also offer appreciation, flexible schedules, close connection to the product, and (perhaps) more frequent promotions and raises.

- **Use Facebook, social networking, and other Internet tools:** Posting job openings on Facebook, LinkedIn, Twitter, and the like can reach job seekers in ways that conventional ads cannot. Employers can also post job openings on career websites such as Monster.com.

- **Try word of mouth:** Small-business owners can seek referrals through employees, customers, friends, and relatives and also ask them to spread the word about job vacancies.

- **Advertise to walk-ins:** Employers can post job notices at the front of the firm's building or in the lobby to alert walk-ins.

- **Post notices at educational institutions:** High schools, vocational and technical schools, and colleges and universities are excellent sources for all sorts of employees.

- **Use publicity in local media:** Local newspapers and other media are always on the lookout for stories about community businesses. A firm's press release announcing new developments can also mention that the company is hiring.

Getting Noticed by Prospective Employers: Online Networking, Personal Networking, Internships, & Transition Jobs

Particularly if you're on the outside looking in, it's important that you develop the less formal ways of getting noticed by potential employers rather than relying just on the avenues described above. (Only about 6% of jobs are filled by candidates recruited through ads, for example.)[27] Four methods for doing this are via *online networking, personal networking, paid or unpaid internships,* and *transition jobs.*

Online Networking: Linking Up Digitally. In general, *networking* **is the process of interacting with others outside and inside the organization in order to build relationships.** Digital technology has led to *online networking,* or *social networking,* **use of online communities that allow members to share personal or professional interests, photos, videos, stories, and ideas with other members.**

Today Americans spend nearly a quarter of the time they're on the Internet, or about 6 hours a month, on social-networking sites, such as Facebook, Twitter, YouTube, and LinkedIn.[28] Prospective employers also scan these sites, as well as their own company websites.[29] If you join only one such site, it should be LinkedIn, the best-known site for connecting job vacancies and job hunters.[30] **7**

Source: digitallife/Alamy.

7 LinkedIn. A business-related social networking site, LinkedIn reportedly has 120 million users spread over 200 countries and territories and adds a new member about every second. Students can use LinkedIn apps Career Explorer to follow the employment footsteps of real people and Company Pages to find connections to any given company. Why do you think a business networking site like LinkedIn is so popular?

BRIEFING / BUSINESS CULTURE & ETIQUETTE

Taking Control of Your Digital Reputation. An important part of online networking is managing your reputation. "Your digital life is just like real life," says marketing expert Larry Weber. "That's why you must be very conscious of what you put online. What's online is a very important part of the way people are hired."[31]

Weber suggests you use such sites as LinkedIn (or Indeed.com or Plaxo) for your professional résumé and business networking, and Facebook to connect only with people you know well, such as friends and family.

In addition, clean up your Facebook page and other profiles by deleting controversial content and photos, getting rid of off-color comments and references to drinking and drug use, and becoming aware of how to use your Facebook privacy settings to limit your networks. Always assume that employers *will* scan your social-networking sites prior to considering you for an interview.[32] ■

Personal Networking: Talking to Real People. Digital networking only gets your foot in the door; talking to real people is still the best way to get a job. Online ties represent "just a starting point," says networking consultant Scott Allen. "You still need some kind of relationship."[33] Well-connected people are successful not because of whom they know, says University of Chicago sociologist Ronald Burt, but because they are able to engage, fit in, and communicate well with diverse groups of people.[34]

ⓘ

Want to Know More? 11-5

What Is a Good Strategy for Networking?

Go to www.mybizlab.com.

BRIEFING / BUSINESS SKILLS & CAREER DEVELOPMENT

How to Go About Networking. "The trouble is," says business columnist Alina Tugend, "networking brings up many of the same emotions as dating—fear of rejection, fear of looking like an idiot, fear of overstepping boundaries, fear of failing."[35] Thus, you need to do "the pre-work of networking," says Career Pro president John O'Connor. "What do you want to get out of your network? How do you want to be perceived by others? What do you have to offer others? Answer these questions first, then take a disciplined approach and make a plan by reaching out."[36]

Practice your "elevator speech"—how you can sell yourself in as short a time as an elevator ride—and find a way to make yourself stand out in a crowd. Then dress professionally and go out and attend events frequented by others in your field of interest, asking the people you meet not for job leads but for thoughts on the direction of your job search. ■

⑧ Intern at work. Internships have benefits for both sides. The intern gains valuable career-related experience, an up-close view of how a company works, and an inside track to job offers. The company becomes better acquainted with a prospective employee than it could through the normal job application process. Isn't this also a good way for an organization to develop potential future employees?

Source: Jim West/Alamy.

Paid or Unpaid Internships: Planned, Supervised Work to Advance Your Career. An *internship* **is an opportunity for college students—and even out-of-work professionals—to obtain career-related experience by doing supervised work in their future fields.** According to one survey, 50% of graduating students in 2008 were found to have held internships, up from 17% in 1992.[37] More and more, internships are seen as not just desirable but necessary parts of a student's résumé, since a significant percentage of interns are later offered full-time positions with the companies they worked for. ⑧

Most internships are probably at small companies and nonprofits rather than large public corporations, according to Internships.com, a placement service.[38] Thus, many students tap family connections, some do their own "guerrilla marketing" (employing imaginative techniques to reach employers), and others adjust the type of work they are seeking.[39] Some students have created internships out of thin air by simply e-mailing marketing or human resource directors at organizations of interest to them.[40]

Although some internships pay a modest salary, many others are unpaid. Unfortunately, some students hungry for experience simply can't afford to work for no pay, which means internships become a perk for the privileged.[41] Still, in recent economic hard times, even older laid-off workers have applied for unpaid internships, to gain new skills and expand their networks.[42] (Incidentally, a poll by the Society for Human Resource Management found that 70% of its members preferred to hire a candidate who did an *unpaid* internship *in* their field compared to a candidate who worked in a *paid* position *outside* of their field.)[43]

Want to Know More? 11-6

What Are Some Ways to Get an Internship?

Go to www.mybizlab.com.

BRIEFING / BUSINESS SKILLS & CAREER DEVELOPMENT

Creating Your Own Internship—How a Future Celebrity Chef Got Started. David Chang, who was to become founder of the celebrated Momofuku restaurant group in New York City, went to culinary school and then started his cooking career at Mercer Kitchen in New York as a line chef. Then he heard about a new restaurant, called Craft, and decided he really wanted to work there.

"I put in a call to the chef de cuisine, Marco Canora," Chang writes, "who told me he didn't have room or a need for my services 'unless I wanted to answer the phones.' So on my days off from Mercer Kitchen, I answered phones at Craft. . . . The glimpse I got into the kitchen life there—the dedication of the cooks, the talent, the quality of the ingredients—kept me answering the phones and bothering Marco every single day for a chance to peel carrots and clean mushrooms. . . .

"My determination paid off. I found a way into the kitchen by working for free in the mornings: chopping mirepoix [mixed finely diced vegetables], cleaning morels [mushrooms], doing menial but essential tasks. . . . When they opened for lunch, I graduated to paid kitchen slave and, eventually, to cook."[44] ■

Transition Jobs: Being among the Employed—The Group Most Attractive to Potential Employers. If you can't find a job in your targeted field, you could try taking any one of a number of *transition jobs*, which are usually lower paid and thus easier to land.

Transition jobs are often filled by **contingent workers, or temporary workers, employees who are hired for a short time to supplement a company's permanent workforce.** Contingent workers are often taken on to provide extra labor during peak-load times—to process extra mail and packages at Christmas, to handle crowd control at college football games, or to prepare tax returns at tax time.

These employees include on-call workers, part timers, seasonal workers, independent contractors, and "temps"—temporary workers from employment agencies such as Kelly Services or Manpower. Students are often used as contingent workers. However, the contingent workforce also includes professionals and experts—contract computer programmers, substitute teachers, "rent-a-judge" jurists, on-call nurses and physicians, even work-for-hire CEOs.

Besides helping you pay your bills and avoid a large unemployment gap on your résumé, says career-advice writer Denene Brox, "transition jobs put you . . . into the ranks of the employed, the group most attractive to potential employers."[45] In addition, they help you build transferable skills (such as communications and project management skills) and do networking with customers and clients you interact with, who might be useful in helping you make your next move.

Key Takeaway 11-2
Four ways for job applicants to attract employer attention: online networking, personal networking, internships, transition jobs.

The Selection Process: How Companies Choose the Best Person for the Job

What are the three kinds of tools used to select employees?

"Any time you hire a new employee, you take a gamble," says one business writer. The purpose of the next step for employers, then, is to perform an exercise that will reduce that gamble. This is the **selection process, which screens job applicants to hire the best candidate.** Three types of selection tools are *background information, interviewing,* and *employment tests.*

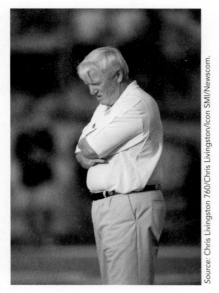

 You did what? George O'Leary, currently head football coach at the University of Central Florida, in 2001 was briefly head coach at the University of Notre Dame. He was asked to resign after it was discovered that his résumé had multiple embellishments, among them a claim to a master's degree from a nonexistent institution ("NYU-Stony Brook University"). Have you ever "embellished" or "shaded" your résumé or a job application?

Want to Know More? 11-7

What Are Some Good Strategies for Writing Résumés & Cover Letters?

Go to www.mybizlab.com.

Want to Know More? 11-8

How Can You Get Extra Help from Your References?

Go to www.mybizlab.com.

1 Background Information: Résumés, Applications, Reference Checks, Credit Checks, & Checks on Legal Status

Résumés and application forms provide basic background information about job applicants, such as citizenship, education, work history, and certifications. Some companies resort to computer prescreening, which job seekers must pass before obtaining an in-person interview. Macy's, for instance, requires applicants to undergo an 8- or 10-minute screening, using a phone's keypad to answer multiple-choice questions.

Are Résumés and Applications Honest? Unfortunately, a lot of résumés consist of exaggerations, misstatements, and even full-blown fabrications. Indeed, one 2003 report found that 53% of all job applications contain some kind of inaccurate information.[46] In a 2004 survey of human resource professionals, 61% said they "often" or "sometimes" found inaccuracies in résumés.[47] Common misrepresentations include past job titles, salary history, length of employment, inflated accomplishments, and gaps in employment histories.

BRIEFING / LEGAL & ETHICAL PRACTICES

Would You Tell These Kinds of Lies on Your Résumé? People do all kinds of fibbing on their résumés, such as the following:

Education. Applicants may pretend to hold a degree (or advanced degree) they don't actually have. RadioShack CEO David Edmondson, for instance, had to resign after he was discovered to have falsely claimed on his résumé to hold degrees in psychology and theology.[48] One study reported that 41% of education records showed a difference between the information provided by an applicant and that provided by the educational institution.[49]

Employment histories, ages, salaries, and job titles. People often lie to cover gaps in employment history, although there are straightforward ways to handle this, as by highlighting length of service instead of employment dates.[50] People also lie about their ages for fear of seeming to be too experienced (hence expensive) or too old.[51] Finally, people embellish their salary histories, job titles, and achievements on projects.[52] ∎

Effective Résumés and Cover Letters. There are many ways to prepare your résumé (or résumés—you can have different ones, adapted for specific jobs) that will show your experience in your best light, and you should make it a point to study the various methods. In addition, whether you send a potential employer your résumé via regular mail or via e-mail, it should be accompanied by a cover letter.

"Cover letters are a graceful way to introduce yourself, to convey your personality, and to impress a hiring manager with your experience and your writing skills," says one article.[53] The letter should be customized as much as possible, using the hiring manager's name and referring to the employer's products or services. It also can be used to frame issues such as an incomplete college degree, job-hopping history, or periods of unemployment.

Reference Checks. Companies now routinely check résumés or hire companies that do so, such as one that contracts with most major universities to glean their student databases for basic information. Unfortunately, many employers don't give honest assessments of former employees, fearing negative comments may produce a lawsuit by former workers and positive comments may produce lawsuits by new employers whose new hires fail. Because honest references are so hard to get, candidates are now being scrutinized more carefully for character and candor during the interview process.[54]

Credit Checks. Consumer advocates say it's unfair to base hiring decisions on credit histories (particularly when so many workers are unemployed and can't

Source: Proformascreening.com.

⑩ Résumé checking. Located in Purcellville, Virginia, Proforma Screening Solutions provides employers with background screening of potential and existing employees. Would you say it's even more important to the success or failure of a small firm with few employees to do intensive background screening of potential hires?

pay creditors). But one head of a firm that runs background checks for businesses says "credit reports can be valuable—particularly if the job includes fiduciary responsibilities."[55]

Sixty percent of employers (including the U.S. government) run credit checks on at least some job applicants, according to a 2011 survey.[56] Some employers apparently use evidence of huge credit card balances and late payments as signs that people haven't made good decisions, although there is no indication that poor credit history is tied to subpar workers.[57] Thus, you should be prepared, if necessary, to explain your credit picture to a potential employer, as, for instance, outlining the percentage of debt involving student loans. (For students who graduated in 2007–2008 with a bachelor's degree from a private, nonprofit college, the median debt was $22,380.)[58]

Checks on Legal Status. As the numbers of undocumented (illegal) workers have risen, employers have been required to verify the U.S. citizenship of job applicants.[59] Use of E-Verify, the federal program that allows employers to quickly check the legal status of potential employees, has increased significantly, although perhaps half of illegal workers still slip by the system.[60] ⑪

More and more job seekers are also being required to explain their criminal records or are seeking to have their arrests or convictions expunged, when possible.[61] In 2007, it came out that the foundation that runs online encyclopedia Wikipedia had failed to do a basic background check on its chief operating officer Carolyn Doran, who had not disclosed that she had once been convicted of drunken driving and fleeing a car accident.[62]

2 Interviewing: Unstructured or Structured

Once applicants have cleared all the foregoing hurdles, they face the commonly used selection technique known as interviewing, which may take place face to face, by videoconferencing, on the phone, or—as is increasingly the case—via the Internet.[63] To help deter bias, interviews can be designed, conducted, and evaluated by a committee of three or four people.

Interviewing may be either *unstructured* or *structured*.

The Unstructured Interview—Unsystematic, Conversational Questions. In an ***unstructured interview***, the interviewer simply asks applicants probing questions in a conversational way; there are no identical, fixed questions asked of all applicants and no systematic scoring of answers.

Source: John Moore/Getty Images.

⑪ Illegals. In 2009–2010, Immigration and Customs Enforcement (ICE) officials fined New Jersey business owners $640,000 for use of undocumented workers. The agency conducts surprise raids where they check forms that document a person's eligibility to work in the United States. The federal program E-Verify is a voluntary program that employers can use to screen for illegal workers. What would you do if you discovered a valued employee was an illegal?

Want to Know More? 11-9

How Should You Handle Telephone & Virtual Interviews?

Go to www.mybizlab.com.

This technique may well be used by managers in a small business, but because the impressions are subjective and apt to be influenced by the interviewer's biases, it is susceptible to legal challenge. Hence, unstructured interviews are almost never used in big businesses or in governmental organizations.

The Structured Interview: Systematic, Identical Questions. In the *structured interview,* **the interviewer asks each applicant the same identical, fixed questions and rates their responses according to some standard measure,** such as a five-point rating scale ranging from "excellent" to "poor."

In some structured interviews (known as *situational interviews*), applicants are asked to focus on a hypothetical situation. Example: "What would you do if you saw two of your employees arguing loudly in the work area?" The idea is to learn if the applicant can handle difficult situations that may arise on the job.

In other structured interviews (known as *behavioral-description interviews*), applicants are asked to talk about what they have actually done: Example: "What was the best idea you ever sold to a supervisor, teacher, peer, or subordinate?" This question is designed to assess the applicant's ability to influence others.

3 Employment Tests: Performance, Ability, Personality, & Other

From a legal standpoint, *employment tests* **consist of any procedure used in the employment selection decision process.** This includes not only traditional paper-and-pencil, performance, and physical-ability tests but also application forms, interviews, and educational and experience requirements.[64]

Among the most common employment tests are . . .

- **Performance tests:** These measure performance on actual job tasks, such as typing; ⑫
- **Ability tests:** These measure physical abilities, such as strength and stamina, or mechanical skills;
- **Personality tests:** These measure personality traits, such as sociability, adjustment, independence, and need for achievement;
- **Other tests:** Examples are tests for lies (using polygraphs) and for drugs (a new test is the hair test, which can detect drug use for a period of up to 90 days).[65]

With any kind of employment test, two important legal considerations are *reliability* and *validity.*

Reliability: Measuring Things Consistently. *Reliability* **expresses how well a test measures the same thing consistently,** so that an individual's score remains about the same over time, assuming the characteristics being measured also remain the same.

Validity: Being Free of Bias. *Validity* **means the test measures what it purports to measure and is free of bias.** If a test is supposed to predict performance, then a person's actual performance should reflect his or her score on the test. Invalid tests can create legal problems if they are ever challenged in court.

Orientation, Training, & Development

How does orientation work, and how are training and development different?

Orientation and training are important because starting a new job can produce a lot of uncertainty and anxiety, in part because, depending on the job, a new hire can

Source: Bloomberg via Getty Images.

⑫ **Super-performance test.** At the Google India Code Jam, young programmers compete to see who will be the most brilliant software coder in South and Southeast Asia and win a $6,900 prize. More important, they may win a coveted job offer at one of Google's research and development centers. Normally, Google's hiring process is a seven-stage process that can take months, but the Code Jam can serve as a shortcut. Most performance tests, such as typing, probably aren't this stressful. Have you had to take any kind of test to get a job?

Want to know how to blow your job interview? Consider the top five interviewer turnoffs, according to one study of 1,910 interviewers: (1) Not learning about the job and/or the organization—this is the biggie. (2) Being arrogant. (3) Showing up late. (4) Not asking any questions. And (5) not speaking professionally.[66]

This suggests an important principle for job hunters: "Sweat the small stuff."[67] Let's see what this means.

Before the Interview: Do Your Homework about the Company & Interviewer

Using the Web and any other aids (press releases, annual reports), find out as much as possible about the company, the job opening, and the person interviewing you—including how to pronounce his or her name. (Phone the receptionist to find out.)

Write out and rehearse answers to the kinds of questions you're apt to be asked. Examples: "Why should we hire you?" "What are your three greatest strengths and three greatest weaknesses?" "What do you like and dislike about your present boss?" "Do you work better alone or in a team?" "How have you handled a difficult situation with a coworker?" "When and how have you gone above and beyond the call of duty?" "Describe an unpopular decision that you implemented and how you handled it."[68]

Dress Appropriately, Be Early, & Look Alert

In a survey of its members by the Society for Human Resource Management, 28% said they decide not to hire someone within the first 5 minutes of a job interview and another 30% within the first 15 minutes.[69] Thus, you can see that first impressions are important.

Dress as if you were working for the company—suit and tie or conservative dress if it's an old-line company, or pressed jeans and jacket if it's a startup. Be sure you're neat, clean, and presentable—hair of reasonable length, shoes shined, and no heavy makeup, perfume, or jewelry.

Find out the exact location of the interview and arrive 10 minutes early (time it the day before, if necessary). If you're going to be late, call the interviewer.

Announce yourself 10 minutes ahead of your appointed time. Greet the interviewer warmly and confidently, shake hands, and address him or her by name. Wait to be invited to sit down. Look alert and interested.

During the Interview, Act Relaxed, & Be Honest & Enthusiastic

Prior to the start of the interview, "Prepare to engage in small talk," says the vice president of Robert Half International, "which helps to break the ice . . . and also demonstrates your ability to make conversation with potential clients, coworkers, and executives."[70] The small talk, which takes about 3 minutes and gives you a chance to establish rapport, can be about objects in the interviewer's office. You can also ask penetrating questions that show you've done your homework on the company and the industry.

During the interview itself, always maintain an upbeat attitude, never apologize, be enthusiastic, and emphasize your strong points. "Be honest about your background and experience," advises one article. "Don't make excuses or blame schools, employers, or fellow workers, if a past weakness or failure comes up. Explain the situation and what you learned from it."[71]

If the interviewer brings up salary, then it's appropriate to discuss it; otherwise, it's better to bring it up in a follow-up conversation.

Be Prepared to Manage Multiple Interviews

You may be asked to do "multi-interviews"—interview with people in various departments, each of whom may want to learn something different. You should learn to tailor responses to fit the circumstances. Try to collect business cards, and when time permits jot down notes about each contact.[72]

After the Interview: Write a Thoughtful Follow-Up Letter

"Your post-interview correspondence should deliver a sales pitch far more compelling than a simple thanks," writes Joann Lublin.[73] You should link your skills to solving specific workplace problems, describe relevant achievements, and allay any qualms the interviewer may have shown. Offer to make yourself available for any follow-up interviews.

accomplish only 60% as much in the first three months as an experienced worker can.[74] Thus, employers have found it's better to give new job holders some help rather than let them learn erroneous habits that may be hard to correct later.[75]

Orientation: The First 30 to 90 Days on the Job

After an applicant is offered and has accepted the job, he or she begins the process of *orientation,* **which is designed to help the newcomer fit smoothly into the job and the organization.** In a large organization, orientation may be a formal, established process. In a small business, it may be so informal that employees find themselves having to make most of the effort themselves. ⑬

The first 30 to 90 days of the initial socialization period is designed to give a new employee the information he or she needs to be effective—namely, . . .

⑬ **Orientation.** If you go to work for a big organization, whether for-profit or nonprofit, you may be expected to attend orientation sessions, such as classes on the company's mission, operations, and important rules. With small organizations, you may have to become oriented by simply asking questions of your supervisor and coworkers. Have you had either or both kinds of experiences?

⑭ **FedEx training.** How important is employee training to an organization's success? FedEx believes it's crucial, spending almost 3% of its annual expense budget to make certain its employees are well-schooled in performing their assigned tasks. Some new employees receive as much as 14 weeks of training. Do you know of another company with similar commitment to training? If so, how is their performance?

- **The job routine**—what is required in the job for which he or she was hired, how the work will be evaluated, and who the immediate coworkers and managers are.
- **The organization's mission and operations**—the purpose, products, operations, and history of the organization.
- **The work rules and employee benefits**—procedures and matters of law (such as those prohibiting sexual harassment) affecting work operations that every employee should be made aware of, plus the benefits to which employees are entitled, such as health plan.

Training & Development: Helping Employees Fill Gaps in Knowledge

Quite often new employees lag behind in knowledge, which needs to be filled by *training and development,* **steps taken by the organization to increase employee performance and productivity.**

Training refers to improving the abilities of technical and operational employees—X-ray technicians, electronics technicians, and computer network administrators, for example—to better do their jobs in the present. *Development,* or *management development,* refers to improving the abilities of professionals and managers—nurses, accountants, lawyers, and managers of all levels—to help them better do their jobs in the future. ⑭

Two types of training and development are *on-the-job* and *off-the-job:*

On-the-Job Training. *On-the-job training* **takes place in the workplace while employees are working at job-related tasks.** Three types of on-the-job training are *shadowing, apprenticeship,* and *job rotation.*

- **Shadowing—watching more experienced employees:** *Shadowing* means that an employee being trained on the job learns skills by watching more experienced employees.
- **Apprenticeship—working with experienced employees:** An *apprenticeship* is a training program in which a new employee works with an experienced employee to

master a particular craft, such as electrician or plumber. Often such programs are sponsored by trade unions.

* **Job rotation—making employees well rounded:** *Job rotation* consists of rotating employees through different assignments in different departments to give them a broader picture of the organization.

Want to Know More? 11-10

What Is a Learning Organization?

Go to www.mybizlab.com.

Off-the-Job Training. *Off-the-job training* consists of classroom programs, videotapes, workbooks, online distance learning programs, and similar training tools. One specific type is *vestibule training,* off-the-job training in a simulated environment.

■ **Example** of Vestibule Training: Use of Simulators. Simulators, or computer-generated "virtual reality" devices, are applied to a great deal of training. For instance, to train bus drivers, they are used to create lifelike bus control panels and various scenarios such as icy road conditions. They are also used to train pilots on various aircraft and to prepare air-traffic controllers for equipment failures. ■

Mentoring: Guiding Newcomers

Mentoring **describes the process in which an experienced employee, the** *mentor,* **supervises, teaches, and provides guidance for a less-experienced employee, the** *mentee* **or** *protégé.* If you can find an experienced employee to be your organizational sponsor and help you understand and navigate the organization's culture and structure, it can be a great assist to your career. **⑮** One survey of 4,561 respondents from 42 countries found that 46% felt that coaching or mentoring had a great impact and 45% felt it had a moderate impact on their success.[76]

What's the best way to go about acquiring a mentor—or mentors? (You might want to have more than one.) Some advice:[77]

Source: Ryan McVay/Digital Vision/Thinkstock.

⑮ Mentor and mentee. Have mentors or counselors/advisors helped you in making good choices in college? What characteristics do you think would make an effective mentor?

Make a Plan and Pick Your Own Mentor. Before you begin contacting people to be mentors, assess where you want to go and what skills and knowledge you need to get there, so that you'll know the kind of help you need. Before approaching prospective mentors, call their administrative assistants, explain what you want to do, and ask what their bosses are like to work with. Find out a convenient time to approach them.

Choose Anyone You Can Learn from, and Look for Someone Different from You. A mentor need not be a seasoned manager higher up in the organization. He or she can also be a peer—someone at your own level. Look for someone who is different from you in personal style, who will challenge you, and who will help you be more objective.

Want to Know More? 11-11

More about Mentoring.

Go to www.mybizlab.com.

Show Your Prospective Mentor That You Can Provide Extra Effort. "Mentoring is a two-way street," says Anne Hayden, senior vice president of Metropolitan Life Insurance Company. "The person being mentored gets help, advice, and coaching, and the person doing the mentoring generally gets extra effort—someone very committed to working on special projects or on assignments that maybe don't fall within the boxes on the organizational chart."[78]

When you first meet, establish the rules for how frequently you will meet and when and where, such as whether it will be in the office, over lunch, or at the gym. You should meet at least once a month and in between stay in touch by phone and e-mail.

THE BIG IDEA: Performance appraisals, assessing employee performance, and providing employee feedback, may be formal or informal, objective or subjective. Appraisals may be by managers but also by coworkers, subordinates, customers, or the employees themselves. Giving evaluations requires tact, and dealing with negative reviews from your boss requires clarity and toughness.

THE ESSENTIAL QUESTION: How should I handle employee evaluations, and how should I handle evaluations of me?

MyBizLab: Check your understanding of these concepts at www.mybizlab.com.

If you're a member of the generation born after 1977, you are used to instant-feedback videogames, rapid-fire texting, instant messaging, and tweeting, which feeds your desire for fast results.[79] As a consequence, in the workplace you tend to want "frequent and candid performance feedback," according to one survey, and having your managers provide "detailed guidance in daily work" is very important to you.[80]

Letting you know how you're doing on the job is part of ***performance appraisal*, which consists of a manager's assessing an employee's performance and providing feedback.** These days, students themselves often write performance appraisals—in the evaluations they give college faculty about their teaching and grading policies.

Performance appraisals, or performance reviews, have two purposes: First, they help employees understand how they are doing in relation to objectives and standards; here the manager must *judge* the employee. Second, they help employees in their training and personal development; here the manager must *counsel* the employee.[81]

16 "How am I doing?" Do performance appraisals work? Some scholars think not—that they are skewed by whether you and your boss share similar characteristics, such as gender and race. Do you think if you were a manager judging a subordinate you could be fair-minded regardless of your employee's demographic differences?

Source: Polka Dot/Thinkstock.

Types of Performance Appraisals: Formal versus Informal, Objective versus Subjective

How do I distinguish between formal and informal, objective and subjective performance appraisals?

Many performance reviews are worthless, in the opinion of UCLA management professor Samuel Culbert, co-author of *Get Rid of the Performance Review!*[82] One reason is that they are often dictated by a date on the calendar rather than need. Another is that they are "one-sided, boss-dominated" assessments that come down to whether your superior "likes" you.[83]

Stanford University business professor Jeffrey Pfeffer also believes most performance appraisals are ineffective. Often "gender and race affect reviews," he says, "with evaluations more positive for underlings whose managers share their social demographic." In addition, political skill "helps individuals put a gloss on their performance that ensures a higher rating."[84] As for negative evaluations, supervisors who are office bullies have been known to use performance reviews to undermine workers.[85] **16**

How to Prepare for a Performance Review. Companies vary in their approach to performance appraisals. "At some companies, negative comments on performance reviews are uncommon, so anything that's not glowing is cause for concern," points out one business writer. "Other companies give every worker areas for improvement."[86] Thus, it's important that you know how the process works at your company.

In addition, before a review you should write a summary of your achievements for your boss, if not asked to do so as part of the company's process. "There's an art to doing that," says Janet Civetelli of Bridgeway Career Development. "You don't want to be too apologetic, but you also don't want it to appear you've never thought about anything to improve on."[87] Thus, any time you mention a weakness you could say what you plan to do about it. ▪

Not everyone thinks performance reviews should be abolished. Stanford management professor Robert I. Sutton believes they are typically done badly but can be valuable if properly executed.[88] Let's see how this might be accomplished.

Formal versus Informal Performance Appraisals

Performance appraisals may be of two types—*formal* or *informal*.

Formal Appraisals: Scheduled Evaluations. *Formal appraisals,* **which are conducted at scheduled times of the year, are based on pre-established performance measures.** Formal appraisals are the equivalent of you, a student, receiving a grade on a midterm test and a grade on a final test, and weeks may go by in which you are unaware of your actual progress in the course.

Informal Appraisals: Unscheduled Evaluations. *Informal appraisals,* **which are conducted at unscheduled times, consist of less rigorous indications of employee performance.** Informal appraisals are the equivalent of a professor giving students occasional unscheduled pop quizzes and short papers or of you dropping into the instructor's office to talk about your work; you have more frequent feedback about your performance. ⓱

Source: Stuart Forster/Alamy.

⓱ Informal appraisal. Whereas formal performance appraisals may be scheduled events, involving a sit-down between boss and employee every 3, 6, or 12 months, informal appraisals are more spontaneous. Your supervisor may see you passing by and suggest you drop into his or her office to talk about how things are going. Which type of appraisals, formal or informal, frequent or annual, would be most effective with you? Why?

Objective versus Subjective Performance Appraisals

Whether formal or informal, appraisals may be either *objective* or *subjective:*

Objective Appraisals: Evaluation According to the Employee's Numbers. *Objective appraisals* **are based on facts and often based on numbers related to employees**—numbers of products sold, of expenses charged, of complaints by customers, or whatever applies. Sometimes the numbers are set according to *management by objectives* (see Chapter 10), which encourages employees to adopt behavior that will produce specific results—such as, for a salesperson, aiming for a 15% increase in customer orders during the next three months.

Two benefits of objective appraisals are . . .

- **They measure results:** It doesn't matter if two car salespeople have different personalities (one is easygoing and warm, the other fretful and hyper) if each sells about the same number of Fords and Lincolns.

- **They are harder to challenge for bias:** It is harder for employees evaluated under objective appraisals to claim bias on the grounds of racial, gender, or age discrimination if all employees are judged by the same quantitative methods.

 Trait appraisal. Subjective performance appraisals may be based on a manager's perceptions of a subordinate's traits, or subjective attributes, such as "initiative" or "leadership." Do you think such important characteristics can be determined by casual observation?

Key Takeaway 11-3
Performance appraisals may be formal or informal, objective or subjective.

i

Want to Know More? 11-12

What Is the Society for Human Resource Management?

Go to www.mybizlab.com.

Subjective Appraisals: Evaluation According to the Manager's Perceptions. Objective results don't tell the full story about most employees. Thus, most companies supplement objective appraisals with *subjective appraisals,* **which represent a manager's perceptions of a subordinate's traits or behaviors.**

- **Trait appraisals—looking at subjective attributes:** *Trait appraisals* are ratings of such subjective attributes as "attitude" and "initiative." Trait evaluations are easy for managers to create and use, but their accuracy is questionable because the appraisals are affected by the manager's personal bias. ⑱

- **Behavioral appraisals—looking at observable performance:** *Behavioral appraisals* measure specific, observable aspects of performance—on-time attendance, for instance—although making the evaluation is still somewhat subjective. Example: One device, the *behaviorally anchored rating scale (BARS),* rates employee performance according to scales of specific behaviors, such as "always early for work" (5 points) to "frequently late" (1 point).

Other Evaluators besides Managers Who Can Report on Employee Performance

Besides the manager, who else could provide appraisal information about an individual employee?

Most performance appraisals are done by managers, of course. However, to provide different perspectives, sometimes managers ask other people who are knowledgeable about particular employees to give additional information. They include reports by *coworkers, subordinates,* and *customers* and by the *individual employees* themselves.

Reports by Coworkers, Subordinates, & Customers

Coworkers and subordinates often see different aspects of an individual's performance than a manager does. Such information shouldn't be used for evaluation, but it can be useful for development.

Hotels, restaurants, and automobile-dealer service departments are among the organizations that ask customers for their appraisals of employees.

Reports by Employees about Themselves

How would you rate your own performance in a job, knowing that it would go into your personnel file? Probably the bias would be toward the favorable. Even so, *self-appraisals* motivate employees to become involved in the evaluation process and may make them more receptive to feedback about areas needing improvement.

BRIEFING / BUSINESS SKILLS & CAREER DEVELOPMENT

Honest Self-Assessments Are Important. A salesman in an industry in which it takes as long as 2 years to make a large sale has been on the job only 6 months when asked to do a self-evaluation as part of his first performance review. Because he hasn't much quantitatively to report and thus can't meet the performance appraisal's objective criteria, he's thinking of giving himself an A-plus in all the self-ratings. "I think I've been highly productive," he writes a business advice columnist, "getting in to see clients, including people who'd dropped when my predecessor had this job."[89]

The columnist suggested that the salesman's giving himself all top grades "seems to signal a lack of self-criticism and an inability to assess oneself clearly." At the least, the salesman was advised, he should give himself "less than the full rating on some scales [because] it will add more credibility to the scales where you do give yourself a high score." An alternative would be to skip the numeric ratings altogether if they seemed inappropriate given his short time with the company, and to offer his supervisor a narrative evaluation describing the progress made with various clients. ■

Source: Photograph by Sally Lindsay.

Reports by Everybody: The 360-Degree Assessment

In a technique called **360-degree assessment, employees are appraised not only by their managers but also by their coworkers, subordinates, and sometimes customers or clients,** thus providing several perspectives. Typically in this kind of assessment an employee chooses 6 to 12 other people to fill out anonymous forms, the ratings are tabulated, and the employee and his or her manager go over the results to develop a long-term plan for the employee's performance goals.

 360-degree assessment. Managers are not the only ones who can give performance appraisals. They may ask your coworkers to do so as well. Software such as Rypple can also be employed to obtain anonymous feedback from managers, coworkers, or anyone else. Would you be comfortable putting questions about your performance out there for anonymous responses?

BRIEFING / BUSINESS SKILLS & CAREER DEVELOPMENT

Using Social Networking–Style Systems to Help with 360-Degree Assessment. A relatively new approach takes a page from social networking websites. Rypple is software that, according to business writer Jena McGregor, "lets people post Twitter-length questions about their performance in exchange for anonymous feedback." For example, an employee might post the question "How can I run meetings better?" and e-mail it to managers, coworkers, or anyone else; short, anonymous responses are then collected and sent back.

Accenture offers Performance Multiplier, a Facebook-like program that enables employees to post status updates, photos, and two or three weekly goals that can be viewed by colleagues. The intent is to induce users to constantly document and adjust their goals, whether weekly or quarterly, "making performance feedback a much more real-time and ongoing process," says McGregor.[90] ⑲ ■

Grading Employees on the Curve: "Rank & Yank"

How do forced ranking performance review systems work?

A number of companies (General Electric, Ford, Intel) use so-called *rank and yank* evaluation systems, which resemble those students are accustomed to when being graded in a college course. More formally called **forced ranking performance review systems, these are systems in which all employees within a business unit are ranked against one another, and grades are distributed along some sort of bell curve.** (*See* ■ *Panel 11.4.*) **Top grade earners are then rewarded with bonuses and promotions, and low grade earners are warned or dismissed.**[91]

■ **PANEL 11.4 Bell curve.**

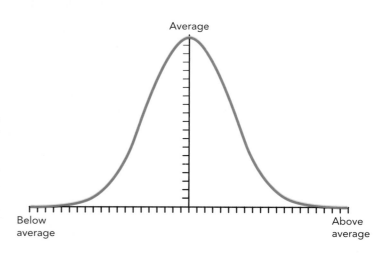

The purpose of this system is to identify and remove poor performers (such as the bottom 15%) and to reward excellent performers (such as the top 15%) according to a predetermined compensation curve. Every year, 10% of General Electric's managers are assigned the bottom grade, and if they don't improve, they are yanked—told to leave the company.

Rank and yank won't work if it is imposed on an organization without preparation, since pitting employees against one another can hurt morale, productivity, and loyalty. There may also be legal problems, as some employees have complained that forced ranking has a disparate effect on particular groups of employees, such as certain minorities.[92]

Giving & Receiving Effective Performance Feedback

How should managers give feedback, and how should employees respond?

The whole point of performance appraisal, of course, is to help an employee deliver better job performance. Let's see how this can work—from the manager's point of view and from the employee's point of view.

How Managers Should Handle Appraisal Feedback: "What's the Best Way to Counsel an Employee?"

Whether doing a formal (scheduled) appraisal or informal (unscheduled) appraisal, most managers are not comfortable delivering criticism. If you have to go over a performance review with an employee, think of yourself as an athletic *coach:* Your purpose is not to find fault, which may only undermine your players' confidence. Rather, your purpose is to show them how to improve.

Following are some tips:

Take a Problem-Solving Approach. When giving feedback, treat the employee with respect and avoid criticism. Describe to the employee how he or she is performing well and not well and give evidence. Example: Don't say (to a kitchen worker) "You're holding that knife wrong" (avoid the word *wrong*). Say "If you hold it with your index finger at the side and chop with a rocking motion, you can go much faster."

Use Facts Rather Than Impressions, and Be Specific. Facts should always be used rather than impressions. Be specific in describing performance and desired improvements. Managers are sometimes advised to keep diaries about specific incidents so they won't have to rely on their memories (and so that their evaluations will be more lawsuit-resistant). Example: A beer-delivery driver might be told, "There were only three complaints last month from people who didn't receive their orders on time compared with five the month before. Let's see if we can get them down further this month."

Get the Employee's Ideas. Don't make it a one-way conversation; get the employee's own ideas. Example: Don't say "You've got to get here on time every day." Say "What changes do you think could be made so that your station is covered when customers start calling?"

Frank Cordaro, 56, of Ontario, New York, had had years of good performance reviews, but then he received one bad review from a new manager. "It played hell with my physical health, my mental health, too," he said. He ended up taking medication to cope with the anxiety and stress at work.[93]

Some advice for dealing with a negative performance review ⑳:

Take Time to Think about the Review before You React

"Generally when we get bad news, we need some time alone to marinate in it and let the gravity of the feedback sink in," says Paul Shrivastava, management professor at Bucknell University. "It's probably a good idea to give yourself time to process the review before you react, just so you don't do something you might regret."[94]

Ask Your Manager for Details about the Criticism

It's certainly acceptable to ask the boss for more information, but, says Teri Hires, executive with a Minneapolis leadership consulting firm, you shouldn't sound accusatory, so it won't sound like you're challenging the manager's judgment.

In addition, she advises, your follow-up questions should focus on what went wrong and how you could improve. Two good questions are "Can you tell me how that behavior was exhibited?" and "If I were doing this right, what would it look like?" "When you take the boss's feedback as a given and focus on what you can do next," says Hires, "it shows that you're willing to make things work."[95]

If you disagree with the substance of the review, disagree respectfully.

If the facts are wrong, refute them calmly and try to provide evidence that demonstrates what actually happened.

Move Forward, Do an Action Plan, & Provide Frequent Status Reports

To move forward and regain credibility, meet with your manager and work out a step-by-step checklist for improvement. "Move forward," says John Robinson, a Tampa, Florida, employment lawyer. "Outline your action plan and show how you're going to rise above it and move on. Outline how you see your future at the company and what you'll contribute."[96]

Then you should deliver frequent status reports to keep your boss advised on what you're doing. You should also request periodic meetings to discuss your overall development. "Going out of your way to show your manager that you've heard the criticisms and you're ready to take them seriously speaks volumes about how committed you are to long-term success," says Ronald Mitchell, CEO of a New York career coaching company.[97]

Source: © Catchlight Visual Services / Alamy.

⑳ **Bad news.** How do you think you would handle a negative performance review? What would you do if you thought it was inaccurate or unfair?

THE BIG IDEA: As a businessperson, you will need to manage compensation, which includes base pay (wages or salaries), benefits, and incentives. You must also deal with the movement and replacement of employees, as by promoting, transferring, suspending, demoting, laying off, or firing.

THE ESSENTIAL QUESTION: How can I reward and discipline the people who work for me?

MyBizLab

MyBizLab: Check your understanding of these concepts at www.mybizlab.com.

In hard economic times, it may be cheaper to trim hours or pay than to slash staff, since layoffs often cost more than you think (as we'll explain).[98] In addition, financially pinched companies often are forced to squeeze employee benefits.[99]

But even in the worst of times, there are always some companies that continue to provide the best compensation as well as to promote their top talent.

Compensation: Base Pay, Benefits, & Incentives

Which kind of compensation would motivate me best?

The principal reason most people work, of course, is for *compensation*. But compensation is more than money. ***Compensation* has three categories: base pay, benefits, and incentives.** Depending on the industry or organization, one category may be more important than another. For instance, in education, health and retirement benefits may outweigh a modest base pay. In a technology startup, base pay and benefits may be adequate, but the real payoff comes later in incentives such as bonuses or stock options.

Base Pay: Wages or Salaries

***Base pay* consists of the basic wage or salary workers are paid for doing their jobs.** The base pay is arrived at by looking at the prevailing industry pay levels, what competitors are paying in a given location, whether the jobs are unionized, whether the jobs are hazardous, and the employees' rank and experience.

Benefits: Nonwage or Nonsalary Compensation

***Benefits,* or *fringe benefits* or *perquisites* ("perqs" or "perks"), are nonwage or nonsalary forms of compensation paid for by the organization for its employees.** Examples are paid holidays, vacations, sick leave, family leave, insurance (health, dental, life), and pension plan, as well as discounts on company merchandise, country club membership, and so on. Some top executives negotiate a so-called ***golden parachute,* an employment agreement that guarantees a key executive lucrative severance benefits if control of the company changes hands followed by management shifts.** ㉑

Benefits make up a sizeable share of an organization's costs. Wages and salaries accounted in 2011 for nearly 70% of a worker's cost to the

㉑ **He's golden.** During the tenure of CEO Mark Hurd, Hewlett-Packard's stock doubled in value. Yet, for falsifying expense reports, the board of directors demanded and received his resignation. However, the same board reportedly awarded him a "golden parachute" that topped $40 million—$12.2 million in severance pay plus millions more in stock and stock options. In what circumstances do you think golden parachutes should apply, if any?

Source: Dai Sugano/MCT/Newscom.

employer; the other 30% consisted of benefits and supplemental pay, according to the U.S. Bureau of Labor Statistics. Earlier the U.S. Chamber of Commerce found employee benefit costs to be even higher—42.7% of payroll costs in 2007, with medical benefit costs (at 12.7%) constituting the largest part.[100] (*See ■ Panel 11.5.*)

■ **PANEL 11.5 How much U.S. civilian workers cost.** The average total cost of wages and benefits for a U.S. civilian worker in June 2011 was $28.13 an hour, of which 70% (specifically 69.4%), or $19.81, was wages or salaries; the remaining 30% was the cost of benefits and supplemental pay.

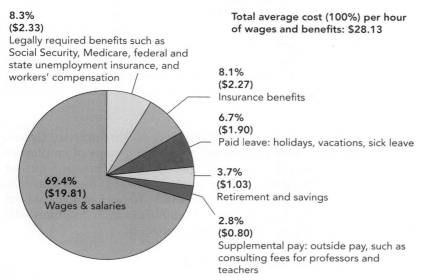

8.3% ($2.33)
Legally required benefits such as Social Security, Medicare, federal and state unemployment insurance, and workers' compensation

Total average cost (100%) per hour of wages and benefits: $28.13

8.1% ($2.27)
Insurance benefits

6.7% ($1.90)
Paid leave: holidays, vacations, sick leave

69.4% ($19.81)
Wages & salaries

3.7% ($1.03)
Retirement and savings

2.8% ($0.80)
Supplemental pay: outside pay, such as consulting fees for professors and teachers

Source: Bureau of Labor Statistics, "Employer Costs for Employee Compensation—June 2011," *Economic News Release,* September 8, 2011, www.bls.gov/news.release/ecec.nr0.htm (accessed September 27, 2011).

Incentives: Inducements to Employee Productivity

Many organizations offer *incentives,* **such as commissions, bonuses, profit-sharing plans, and stock options, to induce employees to be more productive or to attract and retain top performers.** For incentive plans to work, rewards must satisfy individual employee needs, must be agreed upon by employee and manager, must be linked to performance, must be measurable, and must be perceived by the employee as being believable, fair, and achievable. A good deal of criticism about executive pay—huge bonuses for failing CEOs, for example—is that the whopping rewards are not linked to performance.

Some of the most well-known incentive compensation plans are *pay for performance, bonuses, profit sharing, stock options,* and *gainsharing.*

Pay for Performance: Paying According to Results. Also known as *merit pay,* *pay for performance* **bases pay on the employee's work results.** Different salaried employees might get different pay raises, promotions, and other rewards depending on their overall job performance.

One standard pay-for-performance plan is payment at a *piece rate,* **in which employees are paid according to how much output they produce.** The piece rate method is often used with agricultural workers picking fruits and vegetables. Another is the *sales commission,* **in which salespeople are paid a percentage of the earnings the company made from their sales.** Thus, the more they sell, the more they are paid.

Bonuses: Paying for Achieving Specific Performance Objectives. *Bonuses* **are cash awards given to employees who achieve particular performance objectives.** Unlike commissions, bonuses are not computed simply as a

㉒ Competitive compensation?
What type of incentive program can small, independent businesses like Termini Bakery, a classic family-owned Philadelphia bakery, offer employees to be competitive and generate loyalty?

Source: Courtesy of Susan Berston.

Key Takeaway 11-4
Types of incentive compensation plans: pay for performance, bonuses, profit sharing, stock options, gainsharing.

percentage of sales but also may be calculated according to the employee's rank in the organization and years of employment.

Profit Sharing: Paying with Part of a Company's Profits. *Profit sharing is sharing a percentage of the company's profits with employees.* Shares are apportioned to individual employees according to such criteria as performance, attendance, and lateness. ㉒

Stock Options: Paying with Company Stock Bought at a Lower Price. With *stock options,* **key employees are given the right to buy stock at a future date for a discounted price.** The motivator here is that employees holding stock options will supposedly work hard to make the company's stock rise so that they can make a larger profit when they sell their shares obtained at a cheaper price. Example: In more prosperous times, when fast-food and restaurant employee turnover sometimes reached 300% a year, Starbucks was able to hold its annual turnover to a mere 60% by giving stock options to all employees who worked 20 or more hours a week.[101]

Gainsharing: Paying According to Cost Savings and Productivity Gains. *Gainsharing* **is the distribution of savings or "gains" to groups of employees that reduced costs and increased measurable productivity.** Perhaps a quarter of Fortune 1000 companies have adopted the arrangement.[102] Mike's Carwash, named one of 2009's top small workplaces by the *Wall Street Journal,* paid out $569,000 in gainsharing the previous year to 437 employees in 37 locations who had been challenged to beat targets set at the corporate level.

Other Inducements: Altering Work Hours

Can a company slice and dice the 24 hours in a day, seven days a week, in ways that can better motivate employees? Among the alternative work schedules:

Part-Time Work: Less Than 40 Hours. *Part-time work* **is any work done on a schedule less than the standard 40-hour workweek.** Some part-time workers, such as some temporary workers, actually want to work 40 hours or more but can't find full-time work. Other workers work part time by choice, and that can include programmers, market researchers, lawyers, even top executives.

Flextime: Flexible Working Hours. *Flextime,* **or flexible time, consists of flexible working hours, or any schedule that gives an employee some choices in working hours.** Flextime hours, as when an employee is allowed to start and finish, say, an hour earlier or an hour later than the normal shift, can help organizations attract and keep employees who need to take care of children or elderly parents or who wish to avoid heavy commuting times. The main requirement is that the employee be at work during certain "core" hours, so as to be available for meetings and consultations.

Compressed Workweek: 40 Hours in Four Days. In a *compressed workweek,* **an employee works a full-time job in less than five days of standard 8- or 9-hour shifts.** The most common arrangement is a 40-hour week performed in four days of 10 hours each, which can offer employees three (instead of two) consecutive days off. While this can offer employees more leisure time, the disadvantages are possible scheduling problems, unavailability of an employee to coworkers and customers, and fatigue from long workdays.

Job Sharing: Two People Split the Same Job. In *job sharing,* **two people divide one full-time job.** Usually, each person works a half day, although there can be other arrangements (working alternate days or alternate weeks, for example). As with a compressed workweek, job sharing provides employees with more personal or leisure time. The disadvantage is that it can result in communication problems with coworkers or customers.

Telecommuting: Work-at-Home Arrangements. Some employees have always been allowed to work at home, away from the office, but modern technology (e-mail, fax machines, personal computers, the Internet) and overnight-delivery services now make this arrangement much more feasible. **Working at home with telecommunications between office and home is called *telecommuting*.** ㉓ The advantages to employers are increased productivity because telecommuters experience less distraction at home and can work flexible hours.

Moving & Replacing Employees within the Organization: Promotions, Transfers, Disciplining, & Dismissals

What are the forms of employee replacement or dismissal?

As you go forward in your career, the skills that will mean the most for success are not so much the technical—the ones that actually enable you to perform the work, such as engineering or accounting—but rather the so-called *soft skills:* communication, collaboration, problem solving, conflict resolution, and adaptability.[103] (*See* ■ *Panel 11.6.*) Both as an employee and as a manager, these will help you navigate the ways people move within an organization: being promoted, transferred, disciplined, and dismissed.

1 Promotion: Moving Upward

Apart from awarding raises and bonuses, one of the principal ways managers recognize a person's superior performance is through *promotion*—moving the employee to a higher management job within the company.

Before this act can take place, however, managers must ask three questions: (a) *Is the promotion fair?* The step upward must be deserved, not the result of favoritism, as through nepotism (favoring relatives) or cronyism (favoring friends). (b) *Is the promotion nondiscriminatory?* The manager cannot discriminate against other employees similar in rank for reasons of race, gender, age, physical ability, religion, or pregnancy. (c) *Will nonpromoted employees be resentful, and how should they be handled?* Some workers left behind may resent the promotion and need to be counseled about their performance and their future opportunities. ㉔

㉓ **Telecommuting.** Telecommuters have benefited from information technology to be able to work at home while still being closely connected to coworkers, managers, and customers. Some people, however, dislike being away from the office "community." Would this be a problem for you?

■ PANEL 11.6 Five "soft skills" for success.

Can you . . .

1. **Communicate?** Can you do a typo-free résumé, explain a problem, write a coherent memo, make a persuasive presentation?

2. **Collaborate?** Can you work effectively as part of a team?

3. **Problem-solve?** Can you analyze a problem, interpret data, suggest possible solutions?

4. **Resolve conflicts?** Can you negotiate win-win solutions with others?

5. **Adapt?** Can you keep on learning and expand your skills to keep up with the company's needs?

㉔ **Congratulations!** One thing managers need to think about when promoting individuals is how to deal with coworkers left behind—especially when the newly promoted employee might even be their new boss. If you were making the promotion, what "soft skills" would you employ with the nonpromoted employees?

2 Transfer: Moving Sideways

Transfer is movement of an employee sideways within the company to a different job with *similar responsibility,* as from sales manager in Chicago to sales manager in Miami, or from product manager to quality-control manager.

Three reasons for transferring an employee are as follows: (a) *The transfer broadens an employee's experience.* If you're being groomed for a management career in the hotel industry, for instance, you might be transferred from reservations and the front desk to convention sales, to give you a wider range of experience. (b) *The transfer solves an organizational problem.* If you've developed a reputation for problem solving, your bosses might transfer you from convention sales to catering if that department was being badly managed. (c) *The transfer keeps an employee motivated.* If you're feeling burned out with your present job or unhappy with coworkers, you might ask for a transfer to another department or geographical location.

3 Disciplining: Suspensions & Demotions

Disciplining is punishing an employee, often for a poor performance appraisal, usually by suspending or demoting that employee.

If you have been sloppy about handling the finances of the hotel's catering operations, you might be given a warning or reprimand and then *suspended*—temporarily removed from your job (with or without pay) while the company investigates the situation and figures out what to do with you.

Or you might be *demoted*—have your current responsibilities and pay taken away—and reduced from catering manager down to simple catering employee. (During the Great Recession, as companies downsized, resulting in fewer higher-level management positions, many employees had to accept demotions.)

4 Dismissal: Laying Off, Downsizing, or Firing

Cutting jobs might seem to be the fastest and easiest way to get a company through economic hard times, but the costs can be high. Loss of morale among surviving employees. Loss of future leaders. Reduced ability to attract top talent. Decline in stock price, if Wall Street views the dismissals as a troublesome sign. Significant rehiring costs and delays when the economy picks up.[104] Far better, then, if a company can reduce hours or pay. Indeed, says one account, "a 5% salary cut costs less than a 5% layoff because there are no severance payments."[105]

Still, sometimes companies may have to resort to *dismissals,* in which employees are temporarily or permanently removed from employment. Dismissals consist of three categories of removals, as follows:

Layoff: Temporary Dismissal, Possible Rehiring Later. The phrase *being laid off* tends to suggest that a person has been dismissed *temporarily*—as when an appliance manufacturer doesn't have enough orders to justify keeping its production employees—and may be recalled later when sales improve.

Downsizing: Permanent Dismissal, No Rehiring Later. A *downsizing* is a *permanent* dismissal; there is no rehiring later. An appliance maker discontinuing a line of washing machines or on the path to bankruptcy might permanently let go of its production employees.

Firing: Permanent Dismissal "for Cause." The phrase *being fired*, with all its euphemisms and synonyms—being "terminated," "separated," "let go," "canned"—tends to mean that a person was dismissed *permanently "for cause,"* the cause being unsatisfactory performance as documented in the performance appraisal, absenteeism, sloppy work habits, breaking the law, and the like.

In all states except Montana, employers operate under the legal doctrine of *at-will employment,* or *employment at will,* **in which the employer is free to dismiss any employee for any reason at all—or no reason—and the employee is equally free to quit work.** (Exceptions are some whistleblowers and people with employment contracts, such as a union's collective bargaining agreement. Dismissals are also prohibited when they involve discrimination on the basis of gender, skin color, and so on.)

It used to be that managers could use their discretion about dismissals. Today, however, because of the changing legal climate, steps must be taken to avoid employees suing for "wrongful termination." That is, an employer has to carefully *document* the reasons for dismissals. (*See* ■ *Panel 11.7.*)

■ **PANEL 11.7 The ethical, sensitive, sensible way to handle a dismissal.**

- **Give the employee a chance to straighten out.** If the employee has been discovered to have a problem with absenteeism, alcohol/drug dependency, or the like, tell that employee what's wrong with his or her performance, then set up a plan for improvement (which might include counseling). Or if an employee has a bad fit with the company—a by-the-book style, say, that's at odds with your organization's flexible, fast-moving culture—have a conversation and give the employee time to find a job elsewhere.

- **Document the reasons.** If the employee doesn't improve, make sure you document all the problems and the steps leading up to the dismissal. And make sure all your procedures are *legal*.

- **Don't delay.** Even if you feel sorry for the employee, don't carry him or her along and delay the dismissal. Your first obligation is to the organization.

- **Be aware of the devastating effects.** The person being let go can experience a dismissal as severely as a divorce or a death in the family. Dismissals can also negatively affect those remaining with the company, leading to layoff survivor sickness, which is characterized by anger, depression, fear, guilt, risk aversion, distrust, vulnerability, powerlessness, and loss of motivation.

- **Offer help in finding another job.** Letting a long-standing employee go with only a few weeks of severance pay not only hurts the person being dismissed but will also hurt the organization itself, as word gets back to the employees who remain. Knowledgeable employers offer dismissed employees assistance in finding another job.

Summary

11.1 Finding Great People: Building Human Capital

THE ESSENTIAL QUESTION: *Why is human resource management important, and how are needs determined?*

How would I define human resource management? Human capital is the economic or productive potential of employee knowledge, experience, and actions. Most organizations are concerned with staffing, the recruitment, hiring, motivating, and retention of valuable employees. Human resource (HR) management is what managers do to plan for, attract, develop, and retain an effective workforce.

How do I understand present and future job needs? To hire future employees for a job, managers first need to do a job analysis to determine the basic elements of the existing job, using observation and analysis. This can be developed into a job description summarizing what the job holder does and why. Finally, a job specification can be developed to describe the minimum qualifications needed for the job. To predict future employee needs, managers must ask what kind of employees will help achieve the firm's vision and where they can be found.

11.2 Laws Affecting Human Resource Management

THE ESSENTIAL QUESTION: *To avoid exposing myself and my organization to legal liabilities, what areas of the law do I need to be aware of?*

How do laws affect employee well-being? The first such laws had to do with unions, such as the Wagner Act establishing the National Labor Relations Board, which enforces procedures whereby employees may vote to have a union and for collective bargaining. Collective bargaining consists of management-employee negotiations about disputes over compensation, benefits, working conditions, and job security.

What legislation affects employee compensation and retirement and health benefits? The Social Security Act established the U.S. retirement system. The Fair Labor Standards Act established a federal minimum wage.

What laws regulate workplace conditions? The Occupational Safety and Health Act and other laws require employers to establish safe working conditions and health coverage for employees.

What three concepts are covered by EEO laws? The Equal Employment Opportunity (EEO) Commission enforces laws pertaining to discrimination in hiring or promoting people, affirmative action to achieve equality of opportunity within an organization, and sexual harassment leading to an adverse work environment.

11.3 Recruiting, Selection, Orientation, Training, & Development

THE ESSENTIAL QUESTION: *How do firms get the best people and train them to do their best work?*

How do internal and external recruiting differ? In internal recruiting, firms try to locate and attract candidates for job vacancies by making existing employees in the organization aware of job openings through bulletin-board notices and company websites. External recruiting is what companies do in trying to attract job applicants from outside the organization. They might list job vacancies online, contact college or technical school job-placement offices, work through employment agencies or executive recruiting firms, and so on.

What are the three kinds of tools used to select employees? The selection process for screening applicants for the best candidate has three tools. The first is checking background information by reviewing résumés and applications, checking references, doing credit checks, and checking on legal status. The second tool is interviewing, which may be unstructured, with the interviewer simply asking applicants probing questions in a conversational way, or structured, with the interviewer asking each applicant the same identical, fixed questions and rating their responses according to some standard measure. The third selection tool involves use of employment tests, such as performance, ability, and personality tests.

How does orientation work, and how are training and development different? After being hired, applicants are put through orientation—informed about the job routine, company mission and operations, work rules, and employee benefits—to help them fit into the job and the organization. To increase their productivity, employees are also given training (for technical and operational employees) and development (for managers and professionals). This may be through on-the-job training via shadowing (watching experienced employees), apprenticeship, or job rotation through different assignments. Or it may be through off-the-job training, such as vestibule training, using simulators. Employees also learn from mentoring, guidance by a more experienced employee.

11.4 Performance Appraisals

THE ESSENTIAL QUESTION: *How should I handle employee evaluations, and how should I handle evaluations of me?*

How do I distinguish between formal and informal, objective and subjective performance appraisals? In performance appraisals, managers assess an employee's performance and provide feedback. Appraisals may be formal, conducted at specific times and based on preestablished performance measures. Or they may be informal, conducted on an unscheduled basis with less rigorous indicators. Objective appraisals are based on facts and are often numerical. Subjective appraisals are based on a manager's perceptions of an employee's traits or behaviors.

Besides the manager, who else could provide appraisal information about an individual employee? Employees can do self-appraisals of their own performance. In a 360-degree assessment, employees are appraised not only by their managers but also by their coworkers, subordinates, and customers or clients.

How do forced ranking performance review systems work? In these systems, all employees within a business unit are ranked against one another. Grades are distributed along some sort of bell curve. Top grade earners are rewarded with bonuses and promotions; low grade earners are warned or dismissed.

How should managers give feedback, and how should employees respond? Managers should take a problem-solving approach, use facts rather than impressions, be specific, and get the employee's input. Employees should take time to think before reacting, ask for details about any criticism, and move forward by doing an action plan and providing frequent status reports.

11.5 Compensating, Promoting, & Disciplining

THE ESSENTIAL QUESTION: *How can I reward and discipline the people who work for me?*

Which kind of compensation would motivate me best? Compensation consists of base pay, or basic wage or salary; benefits, or nonwage forms of compensation; and incentives, such as commissions, pay for performance, bonuses, profit-sharing plans, and stock options. Other inducements are allowing employees to alter work hours, as by doing part-time work, flextime, compressed workweeks, job sharing, and telecommuting.

What are the forms of employee replacement or dismissal? Forms of employee replacement are promotion, transfer, suspension, demotion, and dismissal—by laying off, downsizing, or firing.

Key Terms

MyBizLab

Pop Quiz Prep

1. How is *human capital* defined?
2. What is a job specification?
3. Why might a U.S. president decide to invoke the Taft-Hartley Act?
4. When an employee is subjected to unwanted dating pressure and suggestive remarks in the workplace, what is occurring?
5. What is an advantage that external recruiting has over internal recruiting?
6. If you are going to participate in an unstructured interview, what should you expect?
7. What is an example of an objective appraisal?
8. What takes place in 360-degree assessments?
9. What is a golden parachute?
10. How does gainsharing work?

Critical Thinking Questions

1. Do you know your credit score? A future employer might want to. A Society for Human Resource Management (SHRM) survey reported that 60% of employers check the credit history of at least some job applicants.[106] Are employee credit checks an invasion of privacy? Are there some jobs with a legitimate reason to check on an applicant's credit? Do you think it is fair to base a hiring decision on someone's credit score?

2. Some companies have a policy of not giving a full, formal reference but will only confirm dates of employment and position. Unfortunately, this lack of positive input may hurt job prospects for a stellar employee. Conversely, withholding negative input can help a subpar performer. What are your thoughts about a company policy that only allows confirmation of dates and position? Do you think this policy is fair? What are the risks associated with previous employers sharing information about poor job performance?

3. Ronald Zarella, now retired CEO of Bausch & Lomb, claimed that he had an MBA from New York University's Stern School of Business. He did attend the program from 1972 to 1976, but never earned his MBA, a fact not checked by his employers. Once the discrepancy was discovered, Bausch & Lomb had Zarella forfeit over $1.1 million in bonus money, but he remained with the company because "he brought too much value to the company and its shareholders to fire him completely."[107] What would you have done if you were on the board of directors at Bausch & Lomb? What are common misstatements and exaggerations on résumés? Why do you think these types of "fibs" are so common?

4. The use of tests and other selection procedures can be an effective means of determining which applicants or employees are most qualified for a particular job (for example, accounting). However, use of such tools can violate the federal anti-discrimination laws if an employer intentionally uses them to discriminate based on race, color, sex, national origin, religion, disability, or age or if they disproportionately exclude people in a protected group, unless the employer can justify the test or procedure under the law.[108] In 1971 the Supreme Court upheld this statute in *Griggs v. Duke Power*, in which Duke Power was found guilty of refusing promotions to a protected class (in this case, African Americans) by implementing promotions standards that included a high school diploma and passing scores on two tests (many of the African Americans employed there did not have high school diplomas and/or passing test scores)—one intellectual and the other mechanical—neither of which was related to job performance. What tests can you name that are job related and necessitate measuring performance prior to hiring a candidate?

5. Most sexual harassment complaints filed with the Equal Employment Opportunity Commission (EEOC) are by women, but the number filed by men is increasing. In 1992, 9.1% of sexual harassment claims were filed by men, and in 2010, the percentage was 16.4%.[109] It has been argued that as women achieve greater workplace success, power, and respect, some have also begun to adopt the behavior of their male counterparts—abusing the power and influence of their elevated status.[110] How do you explain the increase in claims by men? Do you agree that women's increasing status and power in the workplace is a contributor?

Cases

Go to MyBizLab

VIDEO CASE STUDY
Joie de Vivre Hospitality—Creating an Emotional Connection

Chip Conley, executive chairman/chief creative officer and founder of Joie de Vivre Hospitality, says, "Our goal is to create landmark destinations full of soul and personality. . . . Some in the hotel world say they are in the business of 'selling sleep,' we're in the business of creating dreams." At age 26, with an MBA from Stanford University, and without any intention of becoming a conventional CEO, he started his company. Its mission statement, written collaboratively with employees, is "Creating opportunities to celebrate the joy of life."[111] The video depicts the culture Conley has cultivated at Joie de Vivre, and the importance of customer satisfaction, employee engagement, and a feeling of safety and care for each and every employee—especially important during tough economic times. Joie de Vivre is America's second largest boutique hotel company, with 40 unique hotels, day spas, and restaurants. Each property creates a unique experience for its guests. Unlike large

cookie-cutter hotel chains, where every room is identical regardless of location, Joie de Vivre attempts to make an emotional connection with its guests by catering to a psychographic (lifestyles, values) rather than a demographic (gender, age, income, and so on).

Conley insists on having five adjectives that describe each property. The properties range in flavor from its first hotel in 1987, the Phoenix, catering to the funky, hip, young-at-heart, irreverent, and adventurous, to the Hotel Vitale with more of an urbane, revitalizing, modern, fresh, and nurturing feel, to the Hotel Rex in New York, which is worldly, sophisticated, literate, artistic, and clever.[112]

Using Maslow's hierarchy of needs, Conley shares in his book, *PEAK: How Great Companies Get Their Mojo from Maslow*, a unique formula for success based upon this theory of needs—one of which, survival, is discussed in the video. After the dot-com bust in 2001, one of the worst times ever for Bay Area hoteliers, Conley made sure his frontline employees were safe from job cuts. He is adamant about operating in an environment free of fear and discusses the hazardous impact fear can have on an organization.

In September 2010, Conley stepped down as CEO of Joie de Vivre when Geolo, the private equity arm of the John A. Pritzker family, bought a controlling stake in Joie de Vivre Hospitality. Conley plans to stay involved as executive chairman/chief creative officer. With Geolo's backing, Joie de Vivre will purchase $300 million to $500 million of hospitality assets over the next five years. That expansion will bring Joie de Vivre outside California for the first time, and will increase the number of hotels in the company's portfolio from 34 to around 50 hotels by 2015.[113]

Conley is a firm believer that the success of his hotels, now and in the future, is attributed primarily to his employees. He continues to believe firmly that the reasons people stay at their jobs have less to do with financial incentives and more to do with being part of something special—something that exists at Joie de Vivre Hospitality.

What's Your Take?

1. According to Chip Conley, what is the primary reason people stay at their current job, even when given an opportunity to make more money elsewhere? Do you agree? How do most businesses lose sight of this?

2. According to the video, what perks does Joie de Vivre offer that are meaningful to employees? What dual purpose do the perks serve?

3. What is a good lesson about "the pyramid," according to Conley in the video? Do you agree?

4. According to Conley, why is fear not a good motivator?

BUSINESS DECISION CASE
Stink over Ink? Victims of Tattoo Layoffs

Benjamin Amos, a seven-year veteran at a Dallas-area Starbucks, was fired when the store manager told him the regional and district managers did not like his tattoos. Amos was hired with the permanent tatoos already in place and adhered to the company's dress code to keep them covered while working. After he was fired, Amos filed a lawsuit against the company under Title VII of the Civil Rights Act of 1964 for gender discrimination. Why gender discrimination? The lawsuit alleges that there were several female employees with tattoos at the same Starbucks location who were not discharged.[114] "Employers are allowed to impose dress codes and appearance policies as long as they do not discriminate on race, color, religion, age, national origin or gender," said Diane Amos, (not related), a public affairs specialist at the Equal Employment Opportunity Commission.[115]

As tattoos have become more mainstream, increased numbers of employees are challenging companies for the legality of appearance-related policies. As exhibited in the Starbucks lawsuit, it is crucial that companies exercise consistency when adhering to these policies. The policies must apply to all workers—and a company cannot pick and choose among employees to whom the policies apply.

Company policies about visible tattoos vary. While California-based grocer Albertsons forbids tattoos, Bank of America, operating in a far more formal and established financial services industry, is more forgiving. Bank of America is "Open to all mods that aren't extreme. Extreme is based on branch manager's preference, and there is no official corporate policy."[116] Policies exist, says Tom Williams, a spokesman for Walmart, because they help customers feel comfortable.[117] What can be an "offensive" tattoo to one person may not be to another, and it is this kind of judgment that creates the gray area. Because there is so much subjectivity around what is considered offensive, some companies have adopted a "better safe than sorry" approach.

There are as many different reasons for getting a tattoo as there are people getting them. Many view tattoos and body piercings as art form and as personal expression—similar to the choice one makes when choosing jewelry and clothing. "In ancient cultures, body modification was a rite of passage from youth to adulthood," says one commentary. It symbolized bravery, strength, and tribal affiliations—in fact, it became your identification.[118] Can an employee be discriminated against because of, or asked to hide something that represents, a religious or cultural ritual? This has yet to be challenged in court.

In January 2008, a survey conducted online by Harris Interactive estimated that 9% of 18- to 24-year-olds, 32% of 25- to 29-year-olds, and 25% of 30- to 39-year-olds have tattoos. Men are just slightly more likely to have a tattoo than women (15% versus 13%).[119] With these kinds of statistics, it may be time for companies to revisit their dress code rules.

Do you think it will take some time until judgments, attitudes, and perceptions about individuality and self-expression change, and companies are willing to take more of a risk to protect their employees at the expense of possibly offending their customers? So, for now, you may ask, "All this stink over ink?" What do you think?

What's Your Take?

1. Do you think employees with tattoos should be protected under any of our nation's employment laws? What exceptions might there be to this?

2. Why do you think employers may choose to have a dress code that requires that body art (tattoos) be covered? Are there certain jobs where visible tattoos are more acceptable?

3. Do you think Amos's gender discrimination lawsuit against Starbucks alleging violations of Title VII of the Civil Rights Act of 1964 is justified? Starbucks's argument was that male tattoos are "more aggressive" and perceived differently than female tattoos? Do you agree? Do you perceive tattoos on males differently than those on females?

4. Have you ever worked with someone bearing piercings, multicolored hair, and/or tattoos? If so, how were they perceived? Have you ever felt judged because of your unique style and individual expression in terms of hair, clothing, body piercings, or body art?

5. If tattoos have reached critical mass (gone mainstream), do you think it is time for companies to revisit and revise their dress code policies? How realistic do you think dress codes are in this day and age?

Briefings   MyBizLab Activities & Cases

Go to www.mybizlab.com for online activities and exercises related to the timely topics discussed in this chapter's Briefings, as well as additional theme-related Briefing *Spotlights* highlighting how these concepts apply in today's business environment.

In-chapter Briefing:
- Job Analysis & Description for UPS Drivers

Activity:
- Going to the Net! – The Power of a Company's Board of Directors & Their Impact on Leadership Changes

Briefing Spotlight:
- Survivor's Guilt and High Unemployment

In-chapter Briefing:
- Taking Control of Your Digital Reputation

Activity:
- Developing Marketable Business Skills – Job Title: All Flash, No Cash?
- Going to the Net! – What Is the Culture of Safety at Federal Express?

Briefing Spotlight:
- Social Media Using "Netiquette" at Work

In-chapter Briefing:
- Preparing Now for Your First Post-College Job
- How to Go About Networking
- Creating Your Own Internship—How a Future Celebrity Chef Got Started
- How to Prepare for a Performance Review
- Honest Self-Assessments Are Important
- Using Social Networking–Style Systems to Help with 360-Degree Assessment

Activity
- Developing Marketable Business Skills – Doing More with Less: Are We All Overworked?
- Developing Marketable Business Skills – The Confusion of Employment-at-Will
- Developing Marketable Business Skills – Reverse Mentoring
- Get Your Career in Gear – Careers for Human Resource Professionals
- Going to the Net! – Got Job? Go to Monster.com
- Going to the Net! – Go to EEOC.gov & See What It Takes to File a Claim
- Maximizing Your Net Worth – What Are You Worth?

Briefing Spotlight
- The Art of Schmoozing for Your Career & Beyond

In-chapter Briefing:
- Sexual Harassment Case Costs FedEx Big-Time
- Would You Tell These Kinds of Lies on Your Résumé?

Activity:
- Ethical Dilemma Case – Facebook: The New Background Check

Briefing Spotlight:
- A Pump-Friendly Workplace & New Law for Nursing Moms

Additional *Briefing Spotlights* available at MyBizLab:
- CUSTOMER FOCUS
- EARNING GREEN BY GOING GREEN
- GLOBAL BUSINESS
- INFO TECH & SOCIAL MEDIA
- PERSONAL FINANCE
- SMALL BUSINESS & ENTREPRENEURS
- SOCIALLY RESPONSIBLE BUSINESS

12

Marketing

Creating Successful Customer Relationships with Desirable Products

After reading and studying this chapter, you will be able to answer the following essential questions:

MyBizLab

Where you see MyBizLab in this chapter, go to www.mybizlab.com for additional activities on the topic being discussed.

FORECAST:
What's Ahead in This Chapter

This chapter describes marketing, how it evolved, and the types of products. It considers the influences on consumers that affect their buying behavior. It also looks at marketing strategy and the types of markets. It discusses why new products are created and the 4-P strategies of the marketing mix. It then considers marketing research and the marketing environment.

MyBizLab

Gain hands-on experience through an interactive, real-world scenario. This chapter's simulation entitled Market Research Matters is located at **www.mybizlab.com**.

WINNERS & LOSERS
WHO KNOWS MARKETING?

WINNER: Apple's Product Design Leads to Customer Loyalty

Apple, maker of iPods, iPhones, and iPads, surpassed Microsoft in 2010 to become the No. 1 technology company and by October 2011 had just edged past Exxon Mobil to become the largest company in terms of value of company shares. It was also moving more strongly into business markets and expanding heavily overseas.[1] What led to this success?

It's not as though Apple hasn't made mistakes. In fact, it's made a lot of them. Who now remembers the Apple Mac G4 Cube, a sleek but pricey computer introduced in 2000 that had cracks on its top, which didn't affect performance but did bother Apple's aesthetic-loving consumers?[2] What about the dismal-selling Apple TV, with its big hard drive for storing lots of movies and music (and costing $229), now quietly overhauled into a $99 device that stores everything up on some sort of "cloud" on the Internet?[3]

Then there's the iPhone 4, which had a design flaw in its external antenna, built into the phone's frame and prone to interference from normal handling by users. Apple has a penchant for secrecy that has actually been a boon to stimulating customer speculation and curiosity about new products.[4] But in the case of the iPhone 4, Apple's secretiveness and refusal to admit a mistake turned into a public relations negative that damaged investor confidence.[5]

Still, iPhone 4 sales have soared, with demand outstripping Apple's production capacity. Why is this? "The reason is design," suggests former *BusinessWeek* journalist Jay Greene. The smartphone continues to sell "because Apple's decade-long focus on design has bought it significant goodwill among consumers. . . . Apple's customers are willing to cut the company some slack because of its reputation."[6] Design here is not simply about aesthetics. "It's not just what it looks like and feels like," Apple's late CEO, Steve Jobs, has said. "Design is how it works."[7]

LOSER: Microsoft Mishandles Its Offerings in Smartphones

Microsoft has also been a technology powerhouse, its hefty stock price reflecting the dominance of the company's Windows and Office programs among most users' computers for nearly two decades. It has also not been shy about innovation, introducing many new products.

Indeed, Microsoft was an early entrant in the fledgling smartphone software market, offering the Windows Mobile operating system, designed to run on handsets by Motorola, HTC, and Samsung Electronics. Then Apple came out with its first iPhone, offering touchscreen interface and mobile Web surfing. Microsoft's Windows Mobile, by comparison, "seemed outdated and difficult to use," says one report.[8]

Recognizing that smartphones were a high-growth category, Microsoft in 2008 began rewriting Windows Mobile. The overhaul took so long that handset makers began to turn to another smartphone operating system, Android from Google. In May 2010, Microsoft also brought out its own mobile phone line, the Kin One and Kin Two, which garnered positive reviews. However, potential consumers complained the Kin wasn't able to upload photos to services such as Twitter. The phone was discontinued just 18 days after its announcement.

In November 2010, Microsoft unveiled its new Windows Phone 7, which one prominent reviewer declared to be novel and attractive but inexplicably lacking in key features (video calling, visual voice mail, copy and paste) common on other phones.[9] Others called Phone 7 "too little, too late" and said "too much about it seems dictated by business considerations rather than user experience."[10]

"After years of making software for cumbersome, poorly designed phones," observed Jay Greene, "Microsoft hasn't engendered much goodwill with the public."[11]

 YOUR CALL Do Apple's products really offer more value? Are Microsoft's that bad? Isn't marketing of a product really just about giving it a lot of exposure and putting out positive news about it? Or do you think marketing goes to the heart of how a product is built and how useful it is made for consumers? What kind of marketing would make customers willing to overlook a product's shortcomings, as they apparently did with the iPhone 4 but did not with the Kin? How do you think Windows Phone 7 will do?

MyBizLab

THE BIG IDEA: Marketing is the activity, set of institutions, and processes for creating, communicating, delivering, and exchanging offerings that have value for customers, clients, partners, and society at large. Marketing evolved over four eras: the production, selling, marketing concept, and customer relationship eras. Value is an important part of marketing. Companies market products, product lines, and a product mix.

THE ESSENTIAL QUESTION: What is marketing, how has it evolved, and what exactly are companies marketing?

MyBizLab: Check your understanding of these concepts at www.mybizlab.com.

Aren't new-car promotions basically all alike? So what could an ad agency do to call attention to the new Mitsubishi Outlander Sport, aimed at young consumers?

The answer, the agency executives decided, was to set up an outdoor course on which people could do an *online* test drive of the actual vehicle from anywhere in the country by using the arrow keys on their computer keyboards.

Piloting the vehicle for 90 seconds at up to 20 miles an hour, participants could watch their progress from a webcam mounted on the driver's seat and with a camera operator following their movements. Mechanisms powered by compressed air turned the steering wheel, shifted the transmission, and operated the brakes. Drivers could steer a route over a course the size of several football fields that took them over 12 white emblems on the pavement indicating the vehicle's features (although some drivers just drove around as they wished).

Mitsubishi officials were thrilled with the event, which enlisted 5,000 participants. "This program has gained wide acceptance from our dealer body, consumers, and the general public," said a company vice president, "not only improving brand awareness, but also driving consumer traffic" to dealerships.[12]

And that suggests a great deal about what marketing is supposed to do.

Want to Know More? 12-1

Key Terms & Definitions in Sequential Order to Study as You Go Along

Go to www.mybizlab.com.

Marketing: The Most Current Definition

What is the best definition of marketing?

According to the American Marketing Association, **marketing is the activity, set of institutions, and processes for creating, communicating, delivering, and exchanging offerings that have value for customers, clients, partners, and society at large.**[13] Marketing is practiced by both . . .

- **For-profit organizations:** We see marketing being practiced everywhere by profit-oriented firms to deliver goods (Tide, Wrangler, Chevrolet) and services (Hilton, Verizon, H&R Block).

- **Not-for-profit organizations:** But we also see marketing used more and more by not-for-profits, whether *private-sector organizations* like Harvard University, the Presbyterian Church, the Red Cross, the Sierra Club, or the American Cancer Society, or *public-sector organizations* like the University

❶ Not-for-profit ad. This Sierra Club ad promotes switching from burning coal, which has been linked to increased asthma attacks and other disorders, to cleaner energy sources. Some sponsors of not-for-profit advertising, particularly advocacy ads like this one, have to pay print, TV, and other media to run the ads. With other not-for-profits, such as the Red Cross, the media may feature their ads for free.

CHICAGO'S COAL-BURNING POWER PLANTS HAVE A NEW FILTER.

HIS NAME IS PETER.

Source: Sierra Club™.

of Nebraska, the state of Michigan, the U.S. Postal Service, the U.S. Marines, or the U.S. Treasury. Ads from nonprofits promote everything from buying U.S. savings bonds to picking up litter. ❶

How Marketing Evolved: Four Periods

What are the four periods of marketing?

In the United States, marketing has evolved over four periods from the 1700s to the present: the *production era,* the *selling era,* the *marketing concept era,* and the *customer relationship era.* (See ■ *Panel 12.1.*)

■ **PANEL 12.1 Four eras: the evolution of marketing in the United States.**

Production era
‖‖‖

               Selling era
               ‖‖‖‖‖‖‖‖‖‖‖‖‖‖‖‖‖‖‖‖‖‖‖‖‖

                          Marketing concept era
                          ‖‖‖‖‖‖‖‖‖‖‖‖‖‖‖‖‖‖‖‖‖‖‖‖‖‖‖

                                  Customer relationship era
                                  ‖‖‖‖‖‖‖‖‖‖‖‖‖‖‖‖‖‖‖‖‖‖‖‖

1860 1870 1880 1890 1900 1910 1920 1930 1940 1950 1960 1970 1980 1990 2000 2010 2020

1 The Production Era, 1700s to 1920s: Produce as Many Goods as Possible

From the beginning of Europeans arriving on the shores of the North American continent until the 1920s, the emphasis was on production. **The *production concept* emphasized producing as many goods as possible because there was an unlimited demand.** In the new (to Europeans) country, producers were small time (farmers, tradesmen), goods were handmade and scarce, demand was high, and goods were bought as soon as they were available. In short, the era of the production concept represented a *seller's market*—**a market in which there is more demand for products than there is supply.**

Examples: Oil, which is in tremendous demand today, fits the definition of a product marketed under the production concept. So does certain seafood that is hard to get, such as abalone and wild caviar. So, unfortunately, do bulletproof cars in countries terrorized by carjackings and ransom abductions.[14]

2 The Selling Era, 1920s to 1950s: Use Creative & Aggressive Sales Techniques to Sell Products

Early in the 1900s, production underwent a dramatic change, as mass-production techniques such as assembly lines began to crank out more and more goods. This period led to a *buyer's market*, **in which there were more products available than there were buyers.** This in turn led to the *selling concept*, **which emphasized high-powered sales techniques to sell products.**

Example: The selling concept prevailed until the 1950s, but practitioners of the approach linger on today in those aggressive TV salespeople who exhort you to "COME ON DOWN THIS WEEKEND AND GET THE BEST DEAL IN . . . [cars, furniture, whatever]!"

3 The Marketing Concept Era, 1950s to 1990s: Focus on Customers, Service, & Profitability

Some firms still operate on one of the preceding concepts, but most have moved on. The next period, which held sway after World War II, emphasized the three-part *marketing concept*, **which focuses on customer satisfaction, service, and profitability.** Consider these three parts:

Customer Satisfaction: "We Need to Give Buyers What They Expect from Us." Learning what customers want and giving it to them isn't a unique idea, but it's surprising how many firms emphasize promotion or sales instead. *Customer satisfaction* **is the concept of offering a product to please buyers by meeting their expectations.** The most successful American businesses owe their status to doing a close reading of what customers want and providing them with it. ❷

Focus on Service: "Everyone, from CEO to Stock Clerk, Should Focus on Customer Service." Firms that successfully employ the marketing concept integrate their approach so that everyone in the organization—from top management to the lowest stock clerk—focuses on the same goal of satisfying the customer. This is why you may see managers at local supermarkets step up and help with bagging groceries during busy periods at the checkout counters. The "not my job" attitude doesn't work here.

Emphasis on Profitability, Not Sales: "We Need to Concentrate on the Products That Are Most Profitable." Successful firms focus on offering the goods and services that are most profitable, not on offering the entire range of products and not on total sales. Should gasoline dealers offer free road maps, windshield cleaning, and oil and tire-pressure checks? Once upon a time they did. But they found most customers were willing to do those services themselves, and so the retailers focused on what was profitable: selling gasoline, food, and drinks.

🔍 BRIEFING / CUSTOMER FOCUS

Marketing Technology to Boomers. Baby Boomers (those born between 1946 and 1964) have long passed the ages of 18 to 34, the age group long coveted by marketers because they were thought to be ripe for establishing lifetime brand loyalty. But, says one savvy advertising executive, marketers "forget that people over 50 still have dreams."[15] They also have money to spend.

Boomers are actually among the biggest buyers of new technology. Indeed, recently they spent on average $850 on their latest home computers, $50 more than any other group.[16] For instance, Chris Bonney, 58, of Virginia Beach owns an iPhone, iPod, and iMac (and probably by now also an iPad). This is because he feels Apple's marketing speaks to his interests "and not to my age." Clearly, Apple is trying to apply parts of the marketing concept—focusing on customer satisfaction, service, and profitability. ❸ ▪

Source: Photograph by Sally Lindsay.

❷ **Customer-satisfaction ad.** Customer feedback represents the other half of the customer satisfaction equation. How often have you ignored a company's invitation to critique its products and services or express your preferences? Typically, businesses take this type of feedback very seriously, so it's important for consumers to fulfill their role in the relationship.

❸ **The marketing concept.** The fastest growing group using social networking is adults ages 65 and older, followed by those 50 to 64. How would you go about trying to market to this group?

Source: Goodluz/Shutterstock.

4 The Customer Relationship Era, 1990s to the Present: Focus on Using Customer Information to Satisfy Their Expectations

The marketing concept has led to a further refinement known as the relationship management concept. ***Customer relationship management (CRM)* emphasizes finding out everything possible about customers and then using that information to satisfy and even exceed their expectations in order to build customer loyalty over the long term.**

BRIEFING / CUSTOMER FOCUS

Using Social Media to Target College Students' Wants & Needs. Discretionary spending by the 19 million full- and part-time college students in the United States was expected to be $76 billion in 2010, up from $61 billion in 2006.[17]

Marketers have learned that students aren't much influenced by old-style marketing techniques such as posters and ads on dorm room door handles. More effective is to get brands incorporated into the college lifestyle through the efforts of other students. West Virginia senior Gina Damato, for instance, works for trendy clothing retailer American Eagle Outfitters by using Facebook to promote free car-to-dorm room help on move-in day and handing out free flip-flops. There are around 10,000 paid student reps like Damato on campuses nationally.

"Much of their work is via social media, such as relevant Facebook updates and targeted tweets on Twitter," says one account. "It is detail-oriented marketing intricately tuned in to things vital and specific to student bodies at each of the nation's 4,100 colleges and universities—and in many cases to the individual student."[18] American Eagle, Apple, and Red Bull try to induce students, particularly freshmen, to develop brand loyalties by reaching them mostly (but not exclusively) where they live: on their cellphones and laptops. ■

Key Takeaway 12-1
Four marketing periods: production era, selling era, marketing concept era, customer relationship era.

Delivering Value: When Customers Perceive a Better Relationship with Your Product versus Others' Products

What does the word "value" mean in marketing?

What is it that companies are marketing? According to the official definition we gave earlier in this chapter, firms are concerned with producing and delivering *offerings that have value*—for customers, clients, partners, and society at large. ***Value* is defined as a customer's perception that a certain product offers a better relationship between costs and benefits than competitors' products do.** Note that we used the word *perception*—it is not the actual value of one product compared to another, but rather how the customer *perceives* that value.

■ **Example of Value: Paper versus Digital Textbooks.** The text you are reading is probably available in both paper and digital form. Yet despite college students' comfort with laptops and cellphones, most have analyzed cost versus convenience and decided that traditional textbooks offer more value than digitized (and cheaper) versions, when they are available. "E-textbooks are good," says one student, "but it's tempting to go on Facebook, and it can strain your eyes." Moreover, many students "are reluctant to give up the ability to flip quickly between chapters, write in the margins, and highlight passages," reports one account, although some software allows students to use e-textbooks that way.[19] ■

Products, Product Lines, & Product Mixes: What Organizations Have to Offer

How would I distinguish among products, product lines, and product mixes?

Whatever the type of marketing, the point is to get consumers to buy or use the organization's products. All organizations carry some sort of *product(s)*, and some have *product lines* and *a product mix*. Most for-profit organizations try not to rely on a single product, instead offering a number of products so as to better survive wide swings in demand.

Product: A Good or Service That Can Satisfy Buyers' Needs

A *product* is a good (which is tangible) or service (intangible) that can satisfy customer needs. A product can be almost anything: goods such as tomato soup, motorcycles, hearing aids, or houses, or services such as auto insurance, plumbing repair, Internet connection, hotel stay, or college education. We explain the types of products in Chapter 13.

Product Line: A Group of Products Designed for a Similar Market

A *product line* is a collection of products designed for a similar market or that are physically similar. Examples: Campbell Soup Company sells not only tomato soup but also a product line of other condensed soups: mushroom, minestrone, and so on. State Farm offers not only auto but also life, home, and health insurance.

Product Mix: The Combination of All Product Lines

A *product mix* is the combination of all product lines that a firm offers. Examples: Campbell offers condensed soups, Chunky soups, Kids soups, and so on, as well as a product mix that includes Supper Bakes meal kits, Pace sauces, Prego Italian sauces, Swanson broth, and Pepperidge Farm cookies. ❹ State Farm offers not only insurance but also mutual funds, banking, loans, and credit cards.

Source: The TABASCO® marks, bottle and label designs are registered trademarks and servicemarks exclusively of McIlhenny Company, Avery Island, Louisiana 70513. www.TABASCO.com.

❹ **Hot shots.** In 1868, Edmund McIlhenny invented a fiery red concoction he called Tabasco pepper sauce, made from oak-aged red peppers, vinegar, and salt. More than 140 years later, the Louisiana-based McIlhenny Company is still owned and operated by the same family, and Tabasco pepper sauce is sold in over 165 countries and territories around the world. The Tabasco brand Family of Flavors now includes six products alongside the Original Red Sauce, among them: Garlic, Sweet & Spicy, Habanero, Chipotle, Jalapeño-based Green, and a Buffalo Style hot sauce. Can you think of any other line of products that is this enduring?

Consumer Buying Behavior

THE BIG IDEA: The consumer buying process consists of five steps by which consumers make decisions: problem recognition, information search, evaluation of alternatives, purchase decision, and postpurchase evaluation. Factors influencing consumer buying behavior are culture and subculture, social class, reference groups, personal image, and situational matters.

THE ESSENTIAL QUESTION: How are consumers influenced to buy?

MyBizLab: Check your understanding of these concepts at www.mybizlab.com.

MyBizLab

James Thomas's company, Black Box, has done a thriving business in selling skateboards, sneakers, and T-shirts because, as a professional skateboarder, he knows that his customers belong to a very anti-establishment group. Thus, he has refused several offers to sell his company, for the same reason he won't display his products anywhere but in skateboard shops. The reason: he understands his market and knows boarders hate sellouts who betray their rebel subculture.[20]

The Consumer Buying Process: Five Steps in Making Decisions

How does the consumer buying process work?

Thomas is one of many of today's marketers who are keenly interested in **con-sumer buying behavior, the behavior shown by consumers in considering and buying various products.** Essentially, this activity consists of five decisions the consumer makes when considering whether to buy a product, as follows. (See ■ *Panel 12.2.*)

**1 Problem Recognition:
"I Realize I Have a Problem to Resolve"**

Here you discover you have a problem or need that needs to be addressed, such as hunger. Example: You feel the need for companionship.

**2 Information Search:
"I've Got to Find a Solution to My Problem"**

Here you do some sort of search for a solution to your problem. Example: You decide to join various social clubs to meet someone, look through newspaper and Craigslist relationship ads, and go online to check dating services.

**3 Evaluating Alternatives:
"I'll Weigh the Pros & Cons of the Products Available"**

After gaining information on competing products, you consider the benefits and drawbacks of each. Example: You look at websites of various dating services to see which appeal to you.

■ **PANEL 12.2 The process of consumer buying behavior.**

1. Problem recognition: "I realize I have a problem to resolve."

↓

2. Information search: "I've got to find a solution to my problem."

↓

3. Evaluating alternatives: "I'll weigh the pros and cons of the products available."

↓

4. Purchase decision: "I'll choose this one or not choose at all."

↓

5. Postpurchase evaluation: "I'm happy/unhappy with my purchase, and will/will not buy a similiar one in the future."

4 Purchase Decision:
"I'll Choose This One or Not Choose at All"

Finally, you make your decision—to choose between eHarmony (because it advertises that compatibility is its core tenet), Match.com (because it has websites in 20 countries), and PlentyOfFish (because it's cheaper).

5 Postpurchase Evaluation: "I'm Happy/Unhappy with My Purchase, & Will/Will Not Buy a Similar One in the Future"

Marketers hope you will be satisfied with your purchase and might be inclined to repeat your choice in the future. On the other hand, you might suffer unhappiness, "buyer's remorse," for having bought something that you perceive later to be too expensive, too shoddy, lacking other products' features, not delivering on its promises, and so on. Thus, you may decide the online dating service you chose simply isn't yielding the relationship matches you hoped for.

Factors Influencing Buying Behavior

What are five factors influencing how I buy things?

Throughout the buying process, the consumer is influenced by various factors, from global to personal, from general to specific, some of them as follows:

Source: Photo: Joey Muellner. Ad: Jamie Thomas & Black Box Dist., LLC.

Culture & Subculture: The Influence of Values & Attitudes

Our ideas about ways of doing things, passed along to us from earlier generations of whatever nationality we are (culture) and the ethnic, religious, age, educational, gender, and other groups we belong to (subculture), influence our buying decisions. Your buying tastes in clothes, for instance, represent these influences. ❺

Social Class: The Influence of Our Socioeconomic Group

Our choices are also affected by our social class, whether lower, middle, or upper. The cars and houses people buy, for instance, reflect their income levels.

❺ **The influence of subculture.** Iconic skateboarder Jamie Thomas started skating professionally in 1992 at age 18 and two years later started a small clothing company, which became Zero Skateboards. That company and two others, Fallen Footwear and Mystery Skateboards, are now part of Thomas's larger firm, Black Box Distribution. It's easy to see what subculture influences buyers of Thomas's products. Can you think of other subcultures that would want different types of T-shirts—maybe saying "Taylor Swift" or "Oakland Raiders"?

Reference Groups: The Influence of Groups We Identify With

We are also affected by those special groups we belong to or identify with: family, friends, fellow students, coworkers, music lovers, fraternity/sorority members, and so on. If you're an athlete, for example, you may favor the kind of footwear worn by other athletes, rather than, say, those in country music bands.

Personal Image: The Look We Wish to Project

A lot of us want to project a certain image, based on the products we buy. This is why marketers often recruit sports stars and other celebrities to promote products.

Situational Matters: The Effects of Timing, Moods, Impulse, Expectations, & So On

All kinds of other things affect our buying decisions: timing, moods, impulse, expectations, advertising, pricing, and beliefs about a product.

Want to Know More? 12-2
What Is Customer Lifetime Value (CLV)?
Go to www.mybizlab.com.

BRIEFING / SOCIALLY RESPONSIBLE BUSINESS

Is It Ethical to Exploit Consumers' Misguided Beliefs? Can fake pills do magical things? Indeed, they can. A fake pill, or placebo ("pla-*see*-boh"), is a dummy pill with no active chemicals in it, which may affect a person—as by reducing pain—simply because he or she *believes* it can. Equally interesting is that a fake pill that costs $2.50 will *work better* at reducing some users' pain than one that costs 10 cents. That is, expensive fake is more convincing than cheap fake.[21]

Such was the result of an experiment involving 82 men and women who rated the pain caused by electric shocks applied to their wrists. Half the participants had read that the pill, supposedly a newly approved prescription pain reliever, was priced at $2.50 each; the other half read that it had been discounted to 10 cents. The dummy pills had a strong pain-relieving effect in both groups. But *significant* pain relief was reported by 85% of those using the expensive pills, compared with only 61% on the cheaper pills.[22]

"It's all about expectations," says researcher and behavioral economist Dan Ariely.[23] But would it be ethical for a maker of pain pills to exploit consumers' beliefs by putting a high price on the pills? ■

The five factors are shown below. (*See* ■ *Panel 12.3.*)

■ PANEL 12.3 **Influences on consumer decision making.**

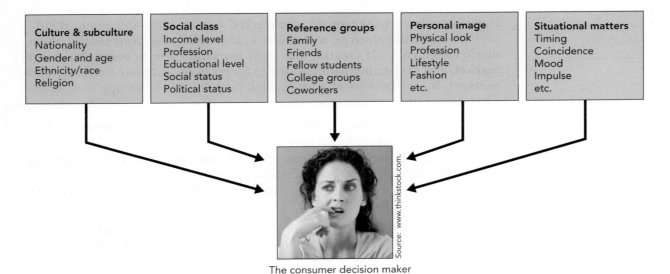

Culture & subculture	Social class	Reference groups	Personal image	Situational matters
Nationality	Income level	Family	Physical look	Timing
Gender and age	Profession	Friends	Profession	Coincidence
Ethnicity/race	Educational level	Fellow students	Lifestyle	Mood
Religion	Social status	College groups	Fashion	Impulse
	Political status	Coworkers	etc.	etc.

Source: www.thinkstock.com.

The consumer decision maker

12.3 | Marketing Strategy & Types of Markets

THE BIG IDEA: A marketing strategy is a plan for identifying the target market among market segments (groups), creating the right marketing mix, and dealing with the external environment. Marketers targeting consumers may market to geographic, demographic, psychographic, benefit, or user-rate segments and may also resort to niche marketing and one-to-one marketing. Business-to-business marketers classify business markets into geographic, customer-based, and product-use-based segments. Not-for-profit organizations frequently employ marketing.

THE ESSENTIAL QUESTION: How are markets classified?

MyBizLab

MyBizLab: Check your understanding of these concepts at www.mybizlab.com.

Marketing, which begins with learning who your customers are and what they need and want, may be of three types:

- For-profit marketing to consumers
- For-profit marketing of businesses to other businesses
- Not-for-profit marketing

Developing a Marketing Strategy

How should I begin to develop a marketing strategy?

How do you begin to understand your market? It starts with—this is important!—having a **marketing strategy, a plan for (1) identifying the *target market* among market segments, (2) creating the right *marketing mix* to reach that target market, and (3) dealing with important forces in the *external marketing environment*.** Buyers or users of a product fall into all kinds of groups, or *segments*. Thus, a marketing strategy relies on . . .

- **Market segmentation, dividing a market into groups whose members have similar characteristics or wants and needs**.
- ***Target marketing strategy,* consisting of marketing directly to such segments—the *target market*.** Marketers don't have endless resources. Thus, they need to direct their efforts toward people who are most likely to buy their products. (*See* ■ *Panel 12.4.*)

Let's first consider market segmentation. We consider the marketing mix in Section 12.4 and the external marketing environment in Section 12.5.

Want to Know More? 12-3

Marketing Strategy & Michael Porter

Go to www.mybizlab.com.

■ **PANEL 12.4 Target marketing strategy.** Attributes of a well-defined target market.

People in the target market . . .

1. Have a particular need that the firm can serve.
2. Are not already served by too many competitors.
3. Have enough money to afford the firm's product.
4. Have decision-making power to buy the product.
5. Have access to the product.

For-Profit Marketing to Consumers: Goods & Services for Personal Use

What are five types of market categories for individual or household consumers?

The **consumer market** consists of all those individuals or households that want goods or services for their personal use. These are all the products you buy every day, from toothpaste to insurance to downloaded songs.

Consumers fall into five *segments,* or groups: *geographic, demographic, psychographic, benefit,* and *user rate.*

Want to Know More? 12-4

Geodemography: PRIZM Neighborhood Clusters.

Go to www.mybizlab.com.

Geographic Segmentation: Dividing the Market by Location

Geographic segmentation **categorizes customers according to geographic location.** Examples: A nationwide retailer of hiking boots would tend to advertise more in Colorado (with its Rocky Mountain trails) than in New York City. Makers of tortillas would promote their products more in Texas (with its large Hispanic population) than in Minnesota.

Demographic Segmentation: Dividing the Market by Age, Gender, Income, & So On

Demographic segmentation **consists of categorizing consumers according to statistical characteristics of a population, such as gender, age, income, education, social class, ethnicity, and so on.** Clothing, of course, is segmented first by gender, then by age, then by income level.

> **BRIEFING / A WORLD OF CONSTANT CHANGE**
>
> **Harley-Davidson Markets to Female Bikers.** Who's buying Harley-Davidson motorcycles? A big consumer market is middle-aged men with time and money to spend. But Harley is trying hard to woo another important market, as well—middle-aged women.[24]
>
> "Put a plant out there to say you are female-friendly," advised Delia Passi, a marketing consultant offering tips on selling to women at a Harley-Davidson dealers convention. American women are the fastest-growing part of the motorcycle business, buying more than 100,000 machines a year and making up about 12% of customers (compared with 4% in 1990). ❻
>
> Harley-Davidson runs a website aimed at women (harley-davidson.com/womenriders) and is advertising in women's magazines. It is also selling more clothes, colorful garb with rhinestones rather than standard black and orange. ∎

Psychographic Segmentation: Dividing the Market by Psychological Characteristics, Values, & Lifestyles

Psychographic segmentation **consists of categorizing people according to lifestyle, values, and psychological characteristics,** such as frugal versus free spending, or rebel versus conservative.

> **BRIEFING / EARNING GREEN BY GOING GREEN**
>
> **Where Are the Supporters of the Environment?** What sort of people are inclined to support green values? Students, women over 50, progressives would seem to be obvious candidates. Actually, about two-thirds of Americans tell pollsters they are sympathetic with or active in the environmental movement. But, says one report, "it has proved tough to get the

Source: J.W. Alker/imagebroker/Alamy.

❻ **The driver's seat.** Women are no longer an unusual consumer to Harley-Davidson; in fact, they are the fastest-growing demographic group in the motorcycle business. Especially for a business that is maturing, as Harley's is, it's very important to develop additional customers from new or different demographic groups. How many women do you know who ride their own bikes, or would like to?

Source: Photo courtesy of Reverb, www.Reverb.org.

Who acts green? The eco-conscious Dave Matthews Band works actively with a nonprofit group, Reverb (www.reverb.org), to educate and engage concertgoers through an interactive Eco-Village at the band's shows. Recently Reverb and other founding members (the Dave Matthews Band, Willie Nelson, Sheryl Crow, Linkin Park, Warner Music Group, and others) launched Green Music Group to bring about environmental change within the music industry and around the globe. Do you think other industries can be influenced to promote sustainable values?

Key Takeaway 12-2
Five consumer segments: geographic, demographic, psychographic, benefit, user rate.

Want to Know More? 12-5
Market Segmentation: Values & Lifestyles Segmentation.
Go to www.mybizlab.com.

average consumer to make even relatively simple changes, like using energy-efficient light bulbs."[25] How to make the environmentally inactive become active? The secret isn't financial incentives or giving more information. It's tapping into feelings of *guilt*—by using the "everyone's doing it" argument.

To find out who could be induced to "act green," researchers tested two placards in hotel bathrooms. One was headlined "Help Save the Environment" and urged guests to "Show your respect for nature" by reusing towels to save on laundry energy expenditures. The other was headed "Join Your Fellow Guests in Helping Save the Environment" and stated that 75% of guests were reusing towels. Travelers exposed to the second sign were 25% more likely to reuse their towels. **7** ∎

Benefit Segmentation: Dividing the Market by Benefits That People Seek in a Product

Benefit segmentation **consists of categorizing people according to the benefits, or attributes, that people seek in a product,** such as style versus economy, or safety versus speed, or high-tech versus low-tech features, or even help for kinky hair over straight hair.

∎ **Example of Benefit Segmentation: Ouidad's Specialized Hair Care Products.** Lebanon-born Ouidad Wise had a tough time conquering her hard-to-tame curls while growing up. From this experience came her Ouidad ("*Wee*-dod") hair care products and frizz-reducing hair-cutting technique (called "carving and slicing") designed for women with wavy, kinky, or curly hair. One advantage of her business, now worth millions: Women with curly hair buy more styling products than do women with straight hair.[26] ∎

User-Rate Segmentation: Dividing the Market by Frequency of Customer Usage

User-rate segmentation **consists of categorizing people according to volume or frequency of usage,** as with heavy users versus light users.

Example: There are about 80 million gun owners in the United States, but many use their firearms rarely or not at all. Handgun and rifle makers therefore find more success advertising in gun, hunting, and outdoor-sports magazines rather than in more mainstream publications.

Taking Segmentation Even Further: Niche Marketing & One-to-One Marketing

Segmentation can be taken even further through two other processes: (1) *niche marketing* and (2) *one-to-one marketing.*

Niche Marketing: Dividing Marketing Segments into Microsegments.
Niche marketing **consists of dividing market segments even further, to microsegments for which sales may be profitable.**

BRIEFING / SMALL BUSINESS & ENTREPRENEURS
Practicing Niche Marketing: Using Blogs to Sell Paintings of Bluegrass Musicians. When watercolor artist Robert Yonke wanted to promote his paintings of bluegrass musicians, he sent pitches to three online bluegrass blogs, asking them to review or post photos of his art. The bloggers wrote about Yonke's work, and he began receiving orders. Blogs have become a great way for businesses to find market niches.[27]

Niche marketing can be practiced by any size of firm, small or large. One article suggests "Companies need to stake out unique market *sweet spots,* those areas that resonate so strongly with target consumers that they are willing to pay a premium price, which offsets the higher production and distribution costs associated with niche offerings."[28] ∎

One-to-One Marketing: Reducing Market Segmentation to Individual Customers. *One-to-one marketing* **consists of reducing market segmentation to the smallest part—individual customers.** Marketers need to do intensive research to gain deep understanding of a customer's preferences and keep detailed records on customer interactions. Examples: High-end applications are sales of expensive real estate, boats, and cars, where a salesperson may collect all kinds of information about a wealthy prospect, then craft a custom sales pitch. Common uses are online recommendations for books and movies by Amazon.com based on consumers' previous purchasing or viewing histories.

For-Profit Marketing to Businesses: Goods & Services for Business Use

What are three market segments that businesses may target in marketing to other businesses?

The *business market* or *business-to-business (B2B) market,* **also known as the** *industrial* **or** *organizational market,* **consists of those business individuals and organizations that want business goods and services that will help them produce or supply their own business goods and services. ❽**

Business markets can be classified into three categories: *geographic, customer-based,* and *product-use-based.*

Geographic Segmentation: Dividing the Market by Location

As with the consumer version, the business version of *geographic segmentation* consists of categorizing customers according to their geographic location. Industries are often grouped in certain geographical areas.

Examples: The part of the San Francisco Bay Area near Palo Alto that has been dubbed Silicon Valley hosts such well-known information-technology companies as Google, Yahoo, Facebook, Apple, Intel, Oracle, and Sun Microsystems. Another example is the Oil Patch, parts of Texas, Oklahoma, and Louisiana, where a lot of petroleum is produced.

Customer-Based Segmentation: Dividing the Market by Customer Characteristics

Resembling demographic segmentation for consumers, in the business market *customer-based segmentation* **consists of categorizing business customers according to such characteristics as size, industry type, and product/service-related attributes.**

Source: Courtesy of Xerox Corporation.

❽ **B2B marketing.** "We focus on translating and delivering Ducati's global publications," says this Xerox ad. "So they don't have to." This business-to-business pitch stresses that the Ducati motorcycle company can focus its energies on building amazing bikes for both road use and racing because Xerox is authoring, translating, and delivering Ducati's handbooks and technical manuals.

Want to Know More? 12-6

Five Ways for B2B Companies to Engage on Facebook.

Go to www.mybizlab.com.

BRIEFING / BUSINESS SKILLS & CAREER DEVELOPMENT
General Mills Sales Reps Call on Different Types of Industries. Want to rise to the top of a big organization? Then it helps to know that lots of CEOs started out in the sales department. One place you might consider, for instance, is doing sales for General Mills, the food company known for such brands as Cheerios, Yoplait, Betty Crocker, and Häagen-Dazs. This firm is always looking for sales rep candidates who have a bachelor's degree,

Key Takeaway 12-3
Business markets: geographic, customer-based, product-use-based.

preferably in business administration, marketing, finance, management, economics, or liberal arts.

One of the company's sales divisions, the Bakeries & Foodservice division, has three main business channels. The Foodservice channel sells branded food products to hospitals, institutes of higher education, K–12 schools, hotels, business and industry cafeterias, and commercial restaurants. The Convenience channel sells retail products with customized packaging and General Mills branded items to convenience stores across the United States. The Bakery/Restaurant channel sells mixes and frozen dough products to supermarkets and retail and wholesale bakeries, as well as customized products to quick-service restaurants such as KFC, McDonald's, and Pizza Hut.[29] ▩

Product-Use-Based Segmentation: Dividing the Market by Customer Use of the Product

Product-use-based segmentation **categorizes business customers according to how they will use the seller's product.** Example: A manufacturer of GPS (global positioning system) devices might divide its target market into, say, long-haul trucking companies, taxi-cab companies, delivery companies (pizza, flowers), home health care services, security companies, and so on.

Not-for-Profit Marketing

Do not-for-profit organizations also do marketing?

Not-for-profits—whether private sector, such as churches, charities, and environmental organizations, or public sector, such as governmental organizations—also frequently employ marketing. **9**

Source: Courtesy of Burston House, Ltd.

9 Not-for-profit marketing. Located near Lake Tahoe, Nevada's oldest town of Genoa hosts the Genoa Cowboy Poetry & Music Festival, featuring western music and poetry readings. The money raised helps pay for the town's historic buildings and its operations. What kind of nonprofit events attract your interest and support?

▩ **Example** of Not-for-Profit Marketing: From "Think Pink" to "Pure Michigan" to "NBA Cares." The Think Pink campaign, sponsored by the Breast Cancer Awareness Foundation, urges the public to support Breast Cancer Awareness month "in October and all year long, by seeking out companies that donate to breast cancer research."

Several Michigan towns have helped to sponsor the "Pure Michigan" commercials, which *Forbes* magazine declared to be one of the "all-time 10 best tourism promotion campaigns worldwide." (One TV commercial shows Michigan vineyards while a voice intones: "With more than 70 wineries the harvest has never been better. Let's all raise a glass to Pure Michigan. Your trip begins at *michigan.org*.")

The NBA Cares public service announcements are sponsored by the National Basketball Association. One TV spot features athletes such as the Houston Rockets' Yao Ming (now retired) and Shane Battier supporting the league's global community outreach initiative that addresses important social issues such as education, youth and family development, and health and wellness. ▩

THE BIG IDEA: Companies have to develop new products for four important reasons. Doing such development requires doing initial research and identifying the target market. This information becomes the basis for determining the marketing mix, which consists of four key strategy considerations—the "four Ps" of product, pricing, place, and promotion.

THE ESSENTIAL QUESTION: Why develop new products, how is it done, and what are strategy considerations?

MyBizLab: Check your understanding of these concepts at www.mybizlab.com.

My BizLab

"Don't look back," said legendary ballplayer Satchel Paige (1906–1982). "Something might be gaining on you."

This sentiment also expresses an important reason why a company should produce new products, but it is only the first of four reasons, as follows.

Why Develop New Products: Four Reasons

What are four justifications for developing new products?

A *new product* is defined as a product that either (1) is a significant improvement over existing products or (2) performs a new function for the consumer. New products (which may be new to the company, if not necessarily the marketplace) are the lifeblood of any company and of the free-market system.

Four reasons a company should introduce new products are . . .

1 To Stay Ahead of or Match the Competition

History is full of examples of companies that thought they were dominant in their fields and failed to recognize how important a competitor's development was.

Example of a Company That Failed to Match Its Competition: Levi Strauss. In 1997, Levi Strauss was jolted awake when its market share slid, as competing designers and retailers introduced jeans products by other manufacturers to serve the high and low ends of the market. "By the time the growth stall had become evident," says one analysis, "the company found itself with an expensive retail strategy and a product line that was out of step with both ends of the denim jeans market."[30] (Since then, Levi has made an aggressive comeback.) ⑩ ■

2 To Continue to Expand Revenues & Profits

Some small businesses (pushcart vendors, yarn shop owners, perhaps) may be content to have the same earnings every year. But other businesses need to grow to continue rewarding shareholders. And to do that, they need to introduce new products.

⑩ **Competition.** Where there was once just Levi, Wrangler, or Lee to choose from in jeans, now there are all kinds of designer jeans makers. What makes you choose one brand over another?

Source: IS0266J1C/Image Source/Alamy.

⑪ Adding new products to expand revenues. Typical of the evolution of videogames away from consoles to social networks, YoVille was acquired by Zynga in 2008 from independent developers, in a successful move to add new product that could generate new revenues. The first of Zynga's profitable -Ville series (CityVille, FarmVille, FrontierVille), YoVille allows Facebook or Myspace members to visit anyone in their virtual apartment or in places like YoDepot, Diner, Nightclub, and so on. Do you think any large entertainment business could survive *without* acquiring or developing new products?

Source: Photograph by Sally Lindsay.

■ **Example** of a Company Division That Failed to Significantly Expand Revenues and Profits: Walt Disney's Videogame Group. In January 2011, Walt Disney Company laid off nearly a third of the roughly 700 workers in its money-losing Interactive Media Group, in which it had invested heavily (it was the only division in the red). Videogames are a growth market, but Disney had concentrated on the console game business—"a category with some of the highest production budgets and greatest risks in the games business," says one report.[31] However, weak sales in console videogames brought on by the emergence of games on mobile phones and on Facebook had forced Disney to reevaluate its strategy. ⑪ ■

3 To Fill Out a Product Line

If you produced only knives and spoons, wouldn't you want to produce forks as well? Many companies need to flesh out their product lines.

■ **Example** of a Company That Failed to Market an Expanded Product Line: Revlon. In 2006, hoping to increase its revenues among an aging population, Revlon introduced its Vital Radiance cosmetics line aimed at older women. Because of marketing missteps, the campaign flopped horribly, causing $70 million in losses. "It didn't incorporate the well-known Revlon brand name, hired unrecognizable models as spokeswomen, and cost more than consumers cared to spend," says one account. "By contrast, the antiaging makeup lines by Procter & Gamble's Cover Girl and L'Oréal's namesake brand respectively featured celebrity spokeswomen Christie Brinkley and Diane Keaton."[32] ■

4 To Take Advantage of an Opportunity

"Strike while the iron is hot" is a familiar phrase. Companies may capitalize on new social or economic trends. Or they may miss the moment, as Schwinn Bicycle Company did.

■ **Example** of a Company That Failed to Exploit Opportunities: Schwinn. Formed in 1895, Schwinn was a successful brand by 1970 and had introduced such innovations as the ten-speed bike. But in the late 1970s, three trends occurred that Schwinn failed to exploit: lightweight ten-speeds, BMX bikes, and mountain bikes (which Schwinn dismissed as simply a California fad). By 1992, Schwinn was in bankruptcy.[33] (The company reorganized, but never regained its market prominence.) ■

The Marketing Process, with the Marketing Mix: The 4-P Strategy—Product, Pricing, Place, & Promotion

What is the marketing process, and what is the 4-P strategy, the building blocks of marketing?

Once a firm has determined that it needs a new product, the next challenge is . . .

- First, to conduct *research* to determine opportunities and challenges;
- Second, to identify the *target market*; and,
- Third, to determine the strategies for the *marketing mix*.

The marketing process is shown in the diagram at right. (*See* ■ *Panel 12.5.*)

The **marketing mix consists of the four key strategy considerations called the four Ps:** *product, pricing, place,* **and** *promotion* **strategies.** Specifically, the marketing mix involves (1) developing a *product* that will fill consumer wants, (2) *pricing* the product, (3) distributing the product to a *place* where consumers will buy it, and (4) *promoting* the product. All these blended together constitute a marketing program.

Let's see how the marketing process works.

Conducting Research & Determining the Target Market: "Is There an Opportunity & a Group of Buyers for Our Possible Product?"

The marketing process begins with conducting a survey or research (*marketing research,* as we explain in the next section) to determine whether there's a market for the product the company is considering producing. That research should help to establish the target market for the product.

▣ BRIEFING / EARNING GREEN BY GOING GREEN

Is There a Market for an Off-Campus Electric-Car Charging Station? Automakers are beginning to offer electric cars for the American (and world) market, but a limiting factor is the lack of an infrastructure of charging stations.[34] Is there an opportunity here for an enterprising firm—perhaps one involving you and some friends—to establish a charging station near your college campus and collect a fee from users? Are collegians, with their interest in "going green" and generally short commuting patterns, apt to be early users of short-range electric vehicles?

Your group begins by doing a preliminary survey of the neighborhoods around your campus to see if there are any existing charging stations. You check with the city building department to see if permits have been issued for any in the near future. You learn how much electric-car chargers cost. You investigate how much is available in government subsidies, tax credits, and grants to help fund the operation. You look at electricity costs.

In trying to identify your target market, you look in campus and nearby parking lots to see how many existing electric vehicles you can find. You research how affordable electric cars are or will be to members of the campus community. You check with electric-car dealers to see if they offer campus discounts. You do a door-to-door survey in college offices and dorms and among off-campus commuter students to see if they'd be inclined to buy an electric vehicle.

All these constitute the beginning steps in the marketing process: identifying an opportunity, doing some initial research, and determining your target market of campus users. ■

■ **PANEL 12.5 The marketing process, including the four Ps.**

> **Conduct research**
> What are the opportunities and challenges for a new product?
>
> ↓
>
> **Determine target market**
> Toward what kind of market segment are we directing our product?
>
> ↓
>
> **1. The Product Strategy**
> How do we design and test a product that will best meet consumer wants and needs?
>
> ↓
>
> **2. The Pricing Strategy**
> How do we determine the right price to set for the product?
>
> ↓
>
> **3. The Place Strategy**
> How do we place (distribute) the product in the right locations?
>
> ↓
>
> **4. The Promotion Strategy**
> How do we communicate the benefits of the product?

ⓘ

Want to Know More? 12-7

What Does the American Marketing Association Do?

Go to www.mybizlab.com.

The next steps in the marketing process involve the marketing mix—the 4-P strategy.

1 The Product Strategy: "How Do We Design & Test a Product That Will Best Meet Consumer Wants & Needs?"

A marketing program starts with designing and developing a *product*—a good, service, or idea intended to satisfy consumer wants and needs. The designers must consider shape, size, color, brand name, packaging, and product image. Product strategy is considered at length in Chapter 13.

In reaching these decisions, a company needs to consider such matters as how well the product differs from other products. It also may do *concept testing* and *test marketing* to get a sense of consumer likes and dislikes.

Concept Testing. *Concept testing* **is marketing research designed to solicit initial consumer reaction to new product ideas.** That is, you might go out among the population you've identified as your target population and *ask* them if they think your potential product is a good idea. ⑫

Test Marketing. *Test marketing* **is the process of testing products among potential users.** That is, you *try out* a sample of the potential product among the target population to see what they think of it.

Source: FocusTechnology/Alamy.

⑫ **Concept testing.** Is it a good idea? The Prius Plug-in Hybrid was only a concept test designed to ascertain consumer interest when this photo was taken. Toyota hoped that these admiring observers would become buyers and users when the car became available at participating dealers in March 2012. Do you think college students are interested in purchasing hybrid vehicles?

■ **Example** of Developing Product Strategy: How Can an Electric-Car Charging Station Be Designed to Meet Consumer Needs? The product being considered is a charging station that, for a fee, will offer electric-car drivers an opportunity to recharge their vehicles.

You begin by doing *concept testing:* You ask potential consumers—students, faculty, staff—on your campus whether they might use your plug-in service, now or in the near future.

Later you do *test marketing:* You lease a few $2,500 chargers, set them up in a corner of an off-campus parking lot, and put a sign out front with a try-out of your business name ("The Charger Kings: Electric cars plug in here. Low rates"). ■

2 The Pricing Strategy: "How Do We Determine the Right Price to Set for the Product?"

Pricing **is figuring out how much to charge for a product—the price, or exchange value, for a good or service.** The price of a product can depend on whether you have competitors, whether you need to offer low prices to get customers in the door, and the like. We discuss pricing strategy in Chapter 13.

■ **Example** of Developing Pricing Strategy: What Kind of Payment Should an Electric-Car Charging Business Seek for Its Services? Your company, the Charger Kings, will want to make enough to cover its costs: parking lot rental, electricity, metering devices, and advertising. Presumably users would pay their fees by running their credit or debit cards through the metering device that measures the amount of electricity used. Since it's a new business and electric cars are not yet in wide use, you'll need to keep charging fees low—at least in the first year. One of the appeals of electric vehicles, after all, is that they not only produce less environmental pollution but also cost less to run than gasoline- or diesel-powered vehicles. ■

3 The Place Strategy: "How Do We Place (Distribute) the Product in the Right Locations?"

● **Placing, or *distribution,* is the process of moving goods or services from the seller to prospective buyers.** Why do so many pizza parlors do home delivery but hamburger purveyors don't? Perhaps the reason lies in their distribution strategy (pizzas can be kept warm, but hamburger buns get mushy). We discuss distribution strategy in detail in Chapter 14.

■ **Example of Developing Place Strategy: Where Should an Electric-Car Charging Station Be Located?** The Charger Kings' first location needs to be close enough to campus that electric-car users can easily walk to work or class. The parking lot needs to have enough room to accommodate drivers for 1 to 12 hours or even overnight. There must be either enough chargers available to serve most users or a system by which an attendant can switch a charger from one car to another. ■

4 The Promotion Strategy: "How Do We Communicate the Benefits of the Product?"

Promotion **consists of all the techniques companies use to motivate consumers to buy their products**—techniques such as advertising, public relations, publicity, personal selling, and other kinds of sales. What technique works better to make you sign up for a magazine subscription—a subscription solicitation card that falls out of the pages of a magazine or a pitch from a neighbor child who hopes to go on an educational trip if he or she sells enough subscriptions? Such are the promotion strategies available to marketers. We discuss promotion strategy in detail in Chapter 14.

● ■ **Example of Developing Promotion Strategy: How Should an Electric-Car Charging Station Be Publicized?** The Charger Kings should promote its location in a number of ways: by sending flyers to electric-car dealerships, by putting ads in the campus newspaper, by posting notices on campus bulletin boards, by Twittering, by having a highly visible sign in front of its place of business, and so on.

Later, if your business takes off, you can expand it to other off-campus locations and intensify the promotional effort. ⑬ ■

Source: David Young-Wolff/Alamy.

⑬ **Charging for charging.** If the 4-P strategy of the marketing mix—product, pricing, place, and promotion—proves successful, the Charger Kings (discussed in the text) will be able to expand its business to several electric-car charging stations. Do you think this could be a viable business? Do you have an idea or business concept that you think is well suited to the 4-P strategy?

THE BIG IDEA: Marketing research, part of the process of determining the 4-P marketing mix, is a four-step process of gathering and analyzing data about problems relating to marketing products, aiming to provide accurate information to marketers. Besides the marketing mix, marketing strategy must take into account the external marketing environment, which consists of seven outside forces.

THE ESSENTIAL QUESTION: How does marketing research work, and what is the external marketing environment?

MyBizLab

MyBizLab: Check your understanding of these concepts at www.mybizlab.com.

D o marketers really know how to appeal to our deepest needs? Not always. A. K. Pradeep, author of *The Buying Brain* and a neuromarketer—a specialist in the application of neuroscience to buying behavior—points out that "Most ads are designed by guys for guys. The woman, though, is responsible for a trillion dollars in spending. She is the primary shopper."[35]

Marketing expert Martin Lindstrom, author of *Buyology,* notes there are many times when promotions don't work. (Cigarette warning labels, for instance, actually stimulate activity in the part of a smoker's brain linked to cravings.) "Eight out of 10 products launched in the United States are destined to fail," he says. "Roughly 21,000 new brands are introduced worldwide per year, yet history tells us that more than 90% of them are gone from the shelf a year later."[36]

A lot of marketing is done simply by hunch. But there's a better way. It's called use of *marketing research.*

Want to Know More? 12-8

The Best U.S. Undergraduate Marketing Programs

Go to www.mybizlab.com.

Marketing Research: Getting Accurate Information to Make Marketing Decisions

What are the steps in the marketing research process?

For a marketing program to be successful, it depends on something crucial: accurate information. Accurate information is the province of **marketing research, the systematic gathering and analyzing of data about issues relating to the marketing of goods and services.** Among other things, marketing research can tell you what consumers think about your firm's products, how satisfied they are with them compared with competitors', the effectiveness of your ads, what the sales potential is of new products, and what price changes might do to sales.

The marketing research process consists of four basic steps. (*See ■ Panel 12.6.*) They are . . .

1 Define the Problem: Clarify the Question to Be Answered

What is the present problem? What are the opportunities? What information is needed? How should we collect and analyze data? These are part of step 1.

■ **PANEL 12.6 The steps in marketing research.**

1. **Define the problem:** Clarify the question to be answered.

2. **Collect facts:** Use published data or interviews, observation, experimentation, and focus groups to get information.

3. **Analyze the data:** Use statistical tools to determine the facts.

4. **Take action:** Implement the best solution.

■ **Example** of Defining the Problem: What's a Better Way to Promote Paint? Most TV commercials for interior paint typically emphasize quality and color selection and show homeowners in blue jeans and flannel shirts using rollers to apply paint to walls. But people hate to be reminded of all that work. Accordingly, paint manufacturer Valspar decided to ask: Is there a better way to promote paint to consumers?[37] ■

2 Collect Facts: Use Published Data or Interviews, Observation, Experimentation, & Focus Groups to Get Information

Marketing research draws upon two kinds of data—*secondary* and *primary*. Most market researchers start with secondary data because it's cheaper and easier, although it has some disadvantages. (*See* ■ *Panel 12.7.*)

Secondary Data: Information Developed by Others. *Secondary data* **is information acquired and published by others.** Examples: U.S. Census Bureau data, various government publications, newspapers, magazines, academic journals, Internet searches, and blogs are all examples of secondary data sources.

Primary Data: Information Derived from Original Research. *Primary data* **is data derived from original research,** such as that which you might conduct yourself. Examples: Direct observation, interviews, surveys, questionnaires, customer comment cards, and concept testing are all different sources of primary data. Some other important sources:

- **Focus groups:** *Focus groups* **are small groups of people who meet with a discussion leader and give their opinions about a product or other matters.** For example, various professors in different parts of the country read the manuscript for this textbook, then met in focus groups with a discussion leader representing the publisher to talk about it.
- **Databases:** *Databases* **are integrated collections of data stored in computer systems.** In big companies, databases can be huge—so-called *data warehouses*—and allow market researchers to perform *data mining,* do computer searches of the data to detect patterns and relationships, such as customer buying patterns.

    Recently databases have been used to track individuals' purchasing and craft Web ads tailored to their specific interests, although 61% of consumers in one poll said they didn't like this intrusion on privacy.[38]
- **Neuromarketing:** A newer tool, *neuromarketing* **is the study of how people's brains respond to advertising and other brand-related messages by scientifically monitoring brainwave activity, eye tracking, and skin response.**

■ **Example** of Collecting Facts: How Do People Really Visualize the Experience of Painting a Wall? Market researchers for Valspar, the paint manufacturer, evidently did a lot of primary research that relied on surveys, interviews, and focus groups. What did they find out?

Most consumers consider painting "an emotional journey with lots of highs and lows," and the act of rolling on paint is certainly not the high point. "Consumers talk about what they feel when they finish the project, and that's a sense of pride and accomplishment," says Valspar's director of marketing. "They say, 'I feel like an artist,' and 'I feel a sense of freedom and joy.'" ■

■ **PANEL 12.7 Respective advantages of using secondary and primary data for research.**

Secondary Data	Primary Data
Cheaper and easier to obtain	More expensive and harder to obtain
Open to competitors	Belongs to you exclusively
May not fit your needs	Can be tailored to your needs
May be out of date	Is up to date

Want to Know More? 12-9

What Are Primary & Secondary Sources That Marketers Use?

Go to www.mybizlab.com.

Want to Know More? 12-10

How Does Neuromarketing Work?

Go to www.mybizlab.com.

3 Analyze the Data: Use Statistical Tools to Determine the Facts

Once data has been gathered, marketing researchers need to consider whether it needs to be treated further to make it useful. It may need *editing,* **or checking over to eliminate mistakes.** It may require the application of *data analysis,* **subjected to statistical tools to determine its significance.**

> ■ **Example** of Analyzing Data: What Did Marketers Conclude from Data about Consumers' Comments about Painting? After applying editing and statistical tools, Valspar market researchers analyzed the data and realized that they were principally dealing with consumers' imagination and emotions with regard to paint. As the company's marketing director noted, "They ladder up to a lot of high-level emotional benefits, and that's what we're trying to tap into." ■

4 Take Action: Implement the Best Solution

Finally, with all the data and analysis in hand, the decision makers must decide how to use it—to determine the best solution and how it should be implemented.

Key Takeaway 12-5
Marketing research steps: define problem, collect facts, analyze data, take action.

> ■ **Example** of Taking Action: Using the Results of Marketing Research to Do a Different TV Commercial Promoting Paint. Building on the researchers' findings about the "emotional benefits" of doing interior painting, a recent Valspar commercial showed a couple guiding a blank wall resembling a drive-in movie screen through various spectacular landscapes, with the wall assuming the colors of the backdrops, "from the incandescent green of flora near a waterfall to the warm tan of a hayfield to the reddish brown of a mountain setting," in one description.[39] ■

⓮ **Environmental scanning.** Marketers need to scan the world around them to identify trends that may affect their marketing program, such as increased racial and ethnic diversity, along with changing attitudes and values among customers. What do you think are some big trends that will affect you and your career?

The Marketing Environment: Outside Factors That Influence Marketing Programs

What kinds of things in the wider world can affect a marketing program?

As we mentioned in Section 12.3, marketing strategy involves (1) identifying the *target market,* (2) determining the right *marketing mix,* and (3) dealing with the *external environment*—specifically the ***external marketing environment,* the outside forces that can influence the success of marketing programs. These forces are (1) global, (2) economic, (3) sociocultural, (4) technological, (5) competitive, (6) political, and (7) legal and regulatory.**

To understand this environment, marketing managers working on marketing strategy need to do ***environmental scanning*—look at the wider world around them to identify what matters can affect the marketing program.** ⓮ Marketers usually can't control the external environment, but they need to understand how they are hindered or aided by it. (*See* ■ *Panel 12.8 on the next page.*)

Source: Kathy deWitt/Alamy.

The external marketing environment, the marketing mix, and the target market. Companies generally cannot control the marketing environment, but they can control the marketing mix.

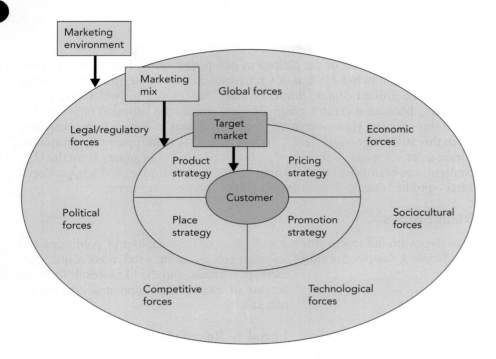

Global Forces

Global forces consist of influences brought about by all our global interconnections. Example: The U.S. national palate is changing—Americans want hotter, mintier, more flavorful foods—influenced by intense flavors from places such as Latin America, China, and Thailand.[40] ⑮

Economic Forces

Economic forces—recessions, inflation, and the like—certainly affect consumers' buying power and willingness to buy. Example: The recent Great Recession, with its vanished jobs, foreclosed homes, and destroyed savings, had a tremendous impact on retail sales.

Sociocultural Forces

Sociocultural forces include cultural changes reflecting customs, beliefs, and lifestyles of groups that differ in social class, ethnicity, age, and so on. Example: Members of the generation known as the Millennials (also as Gen Y, Net Generation, and Echo Boomers), born between 1981 and 2000, are found to be optimistic, civically engaged, self-confident, team oriented, close to parents, and technology focused. Members of the Silent Generation, born 1925 to 1945, are friendly, professional, conciliating, and trust credentialed expertise, according to some research.[41]

Technological Forces

Technological forces consist of influences both highly visible that affect retailing (such as the introduction of smartphones) and less visible that affect manufacturing and distribution (such as factory robots), which change the nature of delivering goods and services. Example: Users of Android cellphones have struck fear into

Source: Arena Creative/Shutterstock.

⑮ **Global influence.** The U.S palate has been influenced by many forms of international cuisine, such as spicy Thai food, which started becoming popular in the United States in the 1970s. The food is considered flavorful because it tries to balance the four basic taste senses: sweet, sour, salty, and bitter. What global forces have changed the way your family lives and the products it buys?

the hearts of retailers because consumers can walk into a store such as Best Buy, see a product they like, then type the model number into an app that compares Best Buy's price with those of other retailers, find a cheaper product, and order it immediately via the phone from a competitor.[42]

Competitive Forces

Competitive forces consist of the actions of competing firms, industries, or countries. Example: Goldwind USA is a Chinese-owned company that makes wind turbines for the United States. Some say the firm should be welcomed to the United States because it creates green jobs and speeds the adoption of renewable energy in this country. However, others see it as a threat to American workers and profits in this still-burgeoning field.[43] Indeed, the 2011 bankruptcy of a prominent California solar company, Solyndra, that was the recipient of grants from the U.S. government was blamed on undercutting in pricing of similar products produced in China—products heavily subsidized by the Chinese government.

Political Forces

Political forces are influences that occur because of the decisions of politicians and public officials. Example: Subsidies for green power—solar, wind, wave action, geothermal, biomass, and the like—result from the actions of elected and appointed government officials.

Legal & Regulatory Forces

Legal and regulatory forces consist of laws and government regulations designed to protect consumers and restrain anticompetitive business behavior. Example: In late 2010, President Obama signed into law the Food Safety Modernization Act, the most major legislation of its kind since the 1930s. The Food and Drug Administration will now be allowed to do a mandatory recall of tainted food when a company fails to voluntarily recall the contaminated product upon the agency's request.[44]

16 Energy subsidies. Can geothermal plants like this one in Iceland—which use the natural heat of the earth to drive steam power plants or electric turbines—provide an alternative to oil, which is in high demand by U.S. major economic competitors in China, India, and Europe? Is geothermal too localized to attract the interest of U.S. business and if so should it be subsidized?

Source: Chris Pole/Shutterstock.

i
Want to Know More? 12-11

What Are Some Other Examples of the External Marketing Environment?

Go to www.mybizlab.com.

The World of Marketing: Onward to the 4-Ps

What kinds of coverage are offered in Chapters 13 and 14?

Students find marketing one of the most interesting subjects in business, perhaps because they are exposed to it so directly in their own lives. Indeed, you may find that marketing offers some great career possibilities.

In the next two chapters we explore the very core of marketing—the 4-Ps—as follows:

- Chapter 13 discusses product and price—that is, product development and pricing.
- Chapter 14 covers place and promotion—that is, distribution and advertising, sales, and other forms of promotion.

Many companies track your mouse clicks to find out what you're clicking on, gathering clues about tastes and preferences—a valuable source of data for marketers, though a point of concern to privacy advocates.[45] Conversely, however, consumers are increasingly using the Internet to communicate with, and about, the companies they do business with. Here's what's available to you.

Protests by E-Mail

Think advertisers don't read protesters' e-mail? Actually, most e-mail complaints carry a lot of power. "The explosion of Internet, e-mail, and blogs means every complaint gets magnified and gets spread much more quickly," says one fashion magazine editor. "They can make a lot more noise than before, even if it isn't the prevailing view."[46] **17**

Corporate Blogs Allowing Unfiltered Comments

Lots of companies have corporate blogs—General Motors, Dell, and Boeing, for example—with polished material promoting their products. More recently, however, they have been striving for authenticity, in which buyer-bloggers are free to write in their own voice, free from corporate censorship. Walmart, for instance, established Check Out (checkoutblog.com), which, in one description, became "a forum for unvarnished rants about gadgets, raves about new videogames, and advice on selecting environmentally sustainable food."[47]

Source: Laura Segall.

17 I hear you. Ben Bethel, owner and general manager of the Clarendon Hotel in Phoenix, constantly keeps up with guests' e-mail comments. Do you think the type of business makes a difference when determining whether and how quickly it should respond to instantaneous feedback? Why?

Consumer Blogs That Review Products

Many food lovers have created their own blogs to review foods and beverages, ranging from frozen dinners to energy drinks. (Examples: HeatEatReview.com, IAteAPie.net, typetive.com/candyblog.) Food companies court these sites, even when reviews are negative (one said meat inside a bread pocket looked like BandAid strips), to try to build publicity.[48]

Independent Websites Providing Feedback for Customer Complaints

Besides blogs, the Internet provides unhappy customers with sound-off sites (Yelp, Epinions) and dedicated customer-service sites (PlanetFeedback, Complaints.com, and Get Satisfaction).

Get Satisfaction (getsatisfaction.com) enables consumers to post feedback about their experiences with any company they choose, and the company is encouraged to visit the site and respond publicly. "All this venting can bring about some productive results—happier customers, resolved disputes," says one account.[49]

An Online Community of Users

Etsy.com is an online marketplace for handmade goods made by 130,000 artisans and crafters, who sell their wares on its site. Etsy uses the social networking concept to enable its customers to interact with other customers, encouraging dialogue and embracing outside sites, in order to build positive exposure and encourage customer loyalty. For instance, it touts and links to the outside social-networking site created by Etsy fans at We Love Etsy.

Summary

12.1 Marketing: What It Is, How It Evolved

THE ESSENTIAL QUESTION: *What is marketing, how has it evolved, and what exactly are companies marketing?*

What is the best definition of marketing? Marketing, which is practiced by both for-profit and not-for-profit organizations, is the activity, set of institutions, and processes for creating, communicating, delivering, and exchanging offerings that have value for customers, clients, partners, and society at large.

What are the four periods of marketing? The production era (1700s to 1920s), in which there was more demand for goods than supply available, emphasized producing as many goods as possible. The selling era (1920s to 1950s), when more products were available than buyers, emphasized high-powered sales techniques to sell products. The marketing concept era (1950s to 1990s) focused on customer satisfaction (pleasing buyers by meeting their expectations), service, and profitability. The customer relationship management era (1990s to now) emphasizes learning everything possible about customers, then using it to satisfy, even exceed, their expectations so as to build long-term customer loyalty.

What does the word "value" mean in marketing? Firms try to deliver offerings that have value—customers' perception that a certain product offers a better relationship between costs and benefits than competitors' products do.

How would I distinguish among products, product lines, and product mixes? A product is a good (tangible) or service (intangible) that can satisfy customer needs. Some firms offer a product line, a group of products designed for a similar market or that are physically similar, and a product mix, the combination of all their product lines.

12.2 Consumer Buying Behavior

THE ESSENTIAL QUESTION: *How are consumers influenced to buy?*

How does the consumer buying process work? Steps taken by customers in the consumer buying process are problem recognition, information search, evaluation of alternatives, purchase decision, and postpurchase evaluation.

What are five factors influencing how I buy things? They are culture and subculture, social class, reference groups, personal image, and situational matters (such as timing and moods).

12.3 Marketing Strategy & Types of Markets

THE ESSENTIAL QUESTION: *How are markets classified?*

How should I begin to develop a marketing strategy? Marketing is of three types: for-profit marketing to consumers, for-profit marketing of businesses to other businesses, and not-for-profit. A marketing strategy is a plan for (1) identifying the target market among market segments, (2) creating the right marketing mix to reach that target market, and (3) dealing with important forces in the external marketing environment. Thus, a marketing strategy relies on market segmentation, dividing a market into groups whose members have similar characteristics or wants and needs, and on target marketing strategy, consisting of marketing directly to such segments—the target market.

What are five types of market categories for individual or household consumers? The first type of marketing is for-profit marketing to consumers, all those individuals or households that want goods or services for their personal use. Five kinds of segmentation, or customer grouping, are by (1) geographic location; (2) demographic characteristics, such as gender, age, or income; (3) psychographic, grouping according to lifestyle, values, and psychological characteristics; (4) benefit, grouping according to the attributes people seek in a product; and (5) user-rate segmentation, grouping people according to volume or frequency of usage. Two further refinements are niche marketing, which divides market segments into microsegments, and one-to-one marketing, which reduces segmentation to individual customers.

What are three market segments that businesses may target in marketing to other businesses? The second type of marketing is for-profit marketing to businesses, which segments markets according to (1) geographic location; (2) customer-based traits such as size, industry type, and product/service-related attributes; and (3) product-use-based segmentation, categorizing business customers according to how they will use the seller's product.

Do not-for-profit organizations also do marketing? Not-for-profits—whether private sector, such as churches, charities, and environmental organizations, or public sector, such as governmental organizations—frequently employ marketing.

12.4 The Marketing Process: The 4-P Marketing Mix

THE ESSENTIAL QUESTION: *Why develop new products, how is it done, and what are strategy considerations?*

What are four justifications for developing new products? A new product is one that either is a significant improvement over existing products or performs a new function for the consumer. Four reasons a firm should introduce new products are (1) to stay ahead of or match the competition, (2) to expand revenues and profits, (3) to fill out a product line, and (4) to exploit an opportunity.

What is the marketing process, and what is the 4-P strategy, the building blocks of marketing? The marketing process begins with conducting research and determining the target market for an opportunity and group of buyers for the seller's possible product. The marketing process then proceeds to the 4-P marketing mix. (1) The product strategy, the design and development of a product, uses concept testing to research consumer reaction to new product ideas and test marketing of products among potential users. (2) The pricing strategy determines pricing or how much to charge for a product. (3) The place, or distribution, strategy determines the process of moving goods or services from seller to buyers. (4) The promotion strategy determines the techniques for motivating consumers to buy products.

12.5 Marketing Research & the Marketing Environment

THE ESSENTIAL QUESTION: How does marketing research work, and what is the external marketing environment?

What are the steps in the marketing research process? Marketing research is the systematic gathering and analyzing of data about issues relating to the marketing of goods and services. It consists of four steps: (1) Define the problem. (2) Collect facts, using secondary data acquired and published by others, or primary data derived from original research such as focus groups, mining of databases, or neuromarketing studies of brain responses to advertising. (3) Analyze the data, editing out mistakes and subjecting it to statistical tools. (4) Take action to effect the best solution.

What kinds of things in the wider world can affect a marketing program? Marketing strategy can be affected by outside forces in the external marketing environment: global, economic, sociocultural, technological, competitive, political, and legal and regulatory.

Key Terms

MyBizLab

benefit segmentation 364
business market 365
business-to-business (B2B) market 365
buyer's market 356
concept testing 370
consumer buying behavior 359
consumer market 363
customer relationship management (CRM) 357
customer satisfaction 356
customer-based segmentation 365
data analysis 374
databases 373
demographic segmentation 363
distribution 371
editing 374

environmental scanning 374
external marketing environment 374
focus groups 373
geographic segmentation 363
market segmentation 362
marketing 354
marketing concept 356
marketing mix 369
marketing research 372
marketing strategy 362
neuromarketing 373
new product 367
niche marketing 364
one-to-one marketing 365
pricing 370

primary data 373
product 358
product line 358
product mix 358
production concept 355
product-use-based segmentation 366
promotion 371
psychographic segmentation 363
secondary data 373
seller's market 355
selling concept 356
target marketing strategy 362
test marketing 370
user-rate segmentation 364
value 357

Pop Quiz Prep

1. During which era of marketing was the emphasis on creating as many goods as possible due to an unlimited demand?

2. What is meant by the term *product mix*?

3. What is the final step in the process of consumer buying behavior?

4. What is an example of a situational matter that influences consumer decision making?

5. When consumers are divided by their gender, age, income, social class, and so on, what type of market segmentation is taking place?

6. According to customer-based segmentation in the business market, how are business customers categorized?

7. What are the "four Ps" of the marketing mix?

8. How is test marketing conducted?

9. What is *secondary data*?

10. How is neuromarketing conducted?

Critical Thinking Questions

1. The five steps of the consumer buying process are problem recognition, information search, evaluation of alternatives, purchase decision, and postpurchase evaluation. Think of a large purchase you've recently made. Did you follow the steps of the consumer buying process when deciding? Evaluate each step and discuss whether you passed through each step or stage during your purchase decision. If you did not, which steps were skipped and why?

2. After Russell Simmons, cofounder of Def Jam Records, made a deal with Courvoisier (a liquor company) to promote their cognac brand among hip hop fans, Busta Rhymes

recorded the song "Pass the Courvoisier." Think of products you typically purchase. Was your buying behavior ever influenced by the factors described in the chapter (culture, social class, reference groups, personal image, situation matters) or by lyrics in a song? Discuss.

3. Marketing fast food to children is controversial because studies show that fast food has been a contributor to childhood obesity. On the www.retireronald.org website (referring to Ronald McDonald, the McDonald's clown), it says, "Using the underfunding of the nation's schools as a marketing opportunity, McDonald's conceived 'Mc-Teacher's Night,' a fundraising program that puts teachers behind the register for a night. In exchange for their free labor, McDonald's donates a percentage of the evening's profits to the local school." What are your thoughts about this marketing strategy?

4. Education, like occupation, is often associated with socio-economic status. Come up with a list of ten products and services that people who are highly educated are likely to purchase. Do you think your purchases will differ once you earn your college or graduate degree? How?

5. Red Bull is an example of a successful social media campaign. "To mark one million fans on Red Bull's Facebook page," according to one description, "the caffeine pushers hid hundreds of free cans of the popular energizing thirst quencher all over the USA, posting clues to their locations on the Internet. Cans could be found anywhere from under a tree to atop a fence. Social media meets real life!"[50] What are your thoughts on the effectiveness of social media campaigns? Are you aware of any others? Discuss in small groups.

Cases

Go to MyBizLab

VIDEO CASE STUDY
Sales at Jones Soda: Sometimes Fizzy, Sometimes Flat

Jones Soda, a Seattle-based premium soda company, has had some ups and downs competing against behemoths Coca-Cola and PepsiCo. Jones's unique marketing roots for its funky colored and oddly named sodas have focused on skateboard and tattoo counterculture types in their teens and twenties. The question remains as to whether Jones can regain its fizz after a "few spills." Through its "alternative distribution," the company has created awareness for its brand at places like clothing and music stores, sporting equipment shops, comic book stores, skate parks, and tattoo parlors, where they gave their soda away. The company still employs two Jones Soda RVs which travel the West and East Coasts of North America "handing out soda and talking to the people on the street."[51]

Jones Soda differentiates itself in several ways. Unlike rivals Coke and Pepsi, all of Jones's products are made with pure cane sugar instead of high-fructose corn syrup, and the machinery required for this retrofit cost Jones Soda in excess of $1 million.[52] Jones offers a unique interactive user experience. Customers can participate in customizing their soda bottle label by sending in their picture and special ordering the beverage; MyJones is a customizable 12-pack of bottles on which a buyer can feature a personal picture and message.[53] The direct "one unit at a time" relationship is truly unique and innovative. In addition, the company picks photos of customers and features them on its own bottles for large-scale distribution.

Another way that Jones sets itself apart from the "big guys" is that the company, like Ben and Jerry's, has coined a number of truly unique names and matching themes like "Turkey and Gravy" for Thanksgiving. To commemorate the Seattle Seahawks' 2007 season, Jones offered a limited-edition Seahawks pack including flavors like Perspiration, Sports Cream Natural Field Turf, Dirt, and Sweet Victory. Jones is the official drink of the Seattle Seahawks.

Jones's grassroots efforts and ability to connect with its target market brought initial overwhelming success. Unfortunately, its decision to expand the target market to the average supermarket shopper (mass distribution) was not as effective as the company's previous grassroots approach of targeting die-hard loyalists through alternative distribution channels. The company realized its mistake and since the video was made, Jones has a new CEO and a focused turnaround strategy for targeting typical shoppers. The company has signed an agreement to distribute six-packs of its soda throughout 3,800 U.S. Walmart locations, and recently received $10 million in financing.[54]

Jones Soda has also been diversifying its product line for its target market. It has relaunched an energy drink, appropriately named for this demographic, called "WhoopAss," which will allow Jones to expand its product mix of existing soft drinks, noncarbonated beverages, energy drinks, and candy. In addition, the company has licensing agreements to produce flavored lip balm and frozen soda pops. The company's slogan, which appears on most of its products, is "Run with the little guy . . . create some change," and indeed the company continues to do just that.

What's Your Take?

1. A study shows that 12-year-olds who drank soft drinks regularly were more likely to be overweight than those who didn't. In fact, for each additional daily serving of sugar-sweetened soft drink consumed during the nearly two-year study, the risk of obesity jumped by 60 percent.[55]

As the public's awareness of increasing obesity continues, what is Jones Soda doing to deal with this?

2. Discuss the "faulty market research" referred to in the video, and how it happened. What are your thoughts?

3. The "one unit at a time" direct-to-consumer relationship that Jones enjoys is unique in the industry. Can you think of any other companies that have a similar relationship?

4. As discussed above, Jones has taken steps to maintain and grow its market share. If you were named CEO of Jones Soda, what additional steps would you suggest?

BUSINESS DECISION CASE
Can Coarse Language, Sexuality, & Nudity Be Effective Marketing Techniques to Sell Denim?

(15 minutes)

If you were a marketer, what would you do to sell denim? Levi Strauss & Company created a slogan for their Curve ID women's jeans that stated "All A—es Were Not Created Equal." It appeared on billboards and in magazines and store windows—with the slang term for derriere included.[56] "Meanwhile, the 'Booty Reader' ad for Old Navy features two mannequins talking about, well, their booties," says Charlotte Cowles, in an article entitled, "Denim ads are too 'crude' for *The Wall Street Journal*."[57] In July of 2010, after a seven-year hiatus, Abercrombie and Fitch released its quarterly shrink-wrapped "magazine" called *A&F Quarterly,* which is shrink-wrapped, is only given to customers 18 years and older, and includes nudity and sexual images.[58] Calvin Klein has been accused of crossing the line between fashion and pornography using underage children, claiming the ads reflect the "independent spirit" of young people. In 1980, he featured a 15-year-old Brooke Shields purring "Nothing comes between me and my Calvins."[59]

What do you think of these advertisements? Do you find them attention grabbing? Offensive? Both? Even advertising and branding experts are split on whether using slang and coarser language is effective. For example, seasoned advertising executive Dean Crutchfield said that the Levi's ad was successful if it got attention, "It's fresh. Not that many other people are using it, so you're going to stand out."[60] However, Susan Credle, chief creative officer of well-known ad agency Leo Burnett, warned that not only could customers be offended but it could even make the company look "desperate."[61] She also added that she could not recall such strong language being used in mainstream media in quite some time.[62]

Using sexual and controversial images and ideas in advertising is not new; after all, the first step in an advertisement's effectiveness is getting people to pay attention to it. However,

according to the Media Awareness Network, a nonprofit organization that promotes understanding of the effects of media, "there is a new conservatism among consumers, who are fed up with X-rated images hawking everything from beer to video games. In continuing to push the envelope, designers like Calvin Klein may find that they have pushed the patience of their consumers too far."[63] Calvin Klein is a master of shock, awe, and sales. "Jeans are about sex," Klein himself once said.[64]

Companies feel they need to stand out in a challenging economy and fiercely competitive denim market, and each brand claims it has received overwhelmingly positive response and few complaints. What are your thoughts? Would you feel embarrassed walking by one of these billboards with your grandmother?

What's Your Take?

1. Do you think that these ads make the brands look desperate?

2. Do you agree that there is a new conservatism among consumers—that people "are fed up with X-rated images hawking everything from beer to video games"? Explain.

3. Why do you think companies take a chance using sexual images in advertising, and do you think they're aware that their messages could offend people?

4. Can you think of companies who promote their denim jeans in a less controversial way? Or companies who choose to promote similar types of apparel to this demographic in a way that doesn't involve using sexual images, coarse language, or nudity?

Go to www.mybizlab.com for online activities and exercises related to the timely topics discussed in this chapter's Briefings, as well as additional theme-related Briefing *Spotlights* highlighting how these concepts apply in today's business environment.

In-chapter Briefing:
- Harley-Davidson Markets to Female Bikers

Activity:
- Developing Marketable Business Skills – Staying Ahead of Competition with Free Shipping

Briefing Spotlight:
- The "Coffice" & the Growing Mobile Business Population

In-chapter Briefing:
- General Mills Sales Reps Call on Different Types of Industries

Activity:
- Get Your Career in Gear – Careers for Marketing Managers

Briefing Spotlight:
- Do You Want Fries with That Shake?

In-chapter Briefing:
- Marketing Technology to Boomers
- Using Social Media to Target College Students' Wants & Needs

Activity:
- Developing Marketable Business Skills – Customer Evangelism? Students as Product Ambassadors for JetBlue
- Developing Marketable Business Skills – Is There Simply Too Much Choice?
- Going to the Net! – Target Market
- Going to the Net! – Niche Marketing & 1-to-1 Marketing
- Going to the Net! – Take the Values & Lifestyle (VALS) Survey
- Going to the Net! – Robb Report Magazine: "Your Global Luxury Resource"
- Going to the Net! – Package Shipping for Consumers vs. Business

Briefing Spotlight:
- Hair Growth: "Blow on the Go" Style Salons

In-chapter Briefing:
- Where Are the Supporters of the Environment?
- Is There a Market for an Off-Campus Electric-Car Charging Station?

Activity:
- Developing Marketable Business Skills – Greener Shopping: Local Mom & Pops or Online?

Briefing Spotlight:
- Psychographic Segmentation: Kimpton Hotels' Sustainability Campaign Targets Eco-Friendly Travelers

In-chapter Briefing:
- Practicing Niche Marketing: Using Blogs to Sell Paintings of Bluegrass Musicians

Activity:
- Developing Marketable Business Skills – Market Research: Opening a Vegetarian Restaurant Near Campus

Briefing Spotlight:
- Using Demographic Segmentation to Sell a Personal Finance Solution

In-chapter Briefing:
- Is It Ethical to Exploit Consumers' Misguided Beliefs?

Activity:
- Going to the Net! – Halos for Companies with the Best Cause Marketing Campaigns

Briefing Spotlight:
- Starbucks: Would You Like a Latté with That Job?

Additional *Briefing Spotlights* available at MyBizLab:

- BUSINESS CULTURE & ETIQUETTE
- GLOBAL BUSINESS
- INFO TECH & SOCIAL MEDIA
- LEGAL & ETHICAL PRACTICES
- PERSONAL FINANCE

13 Product & Pricing Strategies

Offering Great Products That Meet Consumers' Wants & Needs

After reading and studying this chapter, you will be able to answer the following essential questions:

13.1 The Start of Product Strategy: Determining the Total Product Offer

THE ESSENTIAL QUESTION: *If I want to develop a product, what do I need to understand before I begin?*

13.2 Innovation, the Product Life Cycle, & the New-Product Development Process

THE ESSENTIAL QUESTION: *Why is product innovation necessary, and how is it done?*

13.3 Product Differentiation: Creating Product Differences by Branding & Packaging

THE ESSENTIAL QUESTION: *In what ways are branding and packaging used to differentiate a product?*

13.4 Pricing Strategies: What Will Customers Pay?

THE ESSENTIAL QUESTION: *How is pricing important, and what are the various pricing strategies?*

MyBizLab

Where you see MyBizLab in this chapter, go to www.mybizlab.com for additional activities on the topic being discussed.

FORECAST: ▶ What's Ahead in This Chapter

This chapter considers consumer versus business markets, innovation, the product life cycle, and the new-product development process, or how to design a product to meet buyers' needs. We discuss how a product is differentiated from competitors' products, using branding and packaging. Finally, we describe various pricing strategies.

MyBizLab

Gain hands-on experience through an interactive, real-world scenario. This chapter's simulation entitled Pricing Strategies & Objectives is located at **www.mybizlab.com**.

WINNERS & LOSERS

DEVELOPING A NEW PERSONAL FINANCE TOOL

WINNER: Mint.com Builds a Successful Brand

Big companies like Coca-Cola and 3M think up, screen, and develop ideas for new products all the time—often for many products, since the chances of any one succeeding are very low. For small-business startups, however, the risks are even higher, because often the firm develops just *one* product.

Such was the case for Mint.com, a website that helps users in the United States and Canada organize and track their finances, bills, and investments. The product is free, and the company makes its money from ads on the site.

The idea for Mint.com came to Aaron Patzer in 2005 while the entrepreneur was catching up on his personal budgeting. He realized he was in for an afternoon of tedious accounting-type work poring over bank statements, filling in missing entries, and categorizing scores of purchases. "All this just to get the answer to one, seemingly simple question: How much did I spend this month? And on what?"[1]

For two years, Patzer, who has a computer science background, developed and carefully tested technology that automatically identifies and organizes a user's purchases in nearly any bank or credit account, and transactions with nearly any brokerage or retirement account. The program featured an easy, intuitive user interface. In September 2007, Mint.com was launched as an online service that allows users to automatically monitor their bank accounts, credit cards, investments, and bills and to track whether they are exceeding their average spending. They also can get money-saving advice and promotional offers based on their individual finances.[2]

Two years after launch, Mint.com, located in Mountain View, California, had over 1.5 million users, had helped users track nearly $200 billion in purchases, and attracted the attention of major national media, according to the company's website. In November 2009, Mint was acquired by Intuit, makers of Quicken and Turbo Tax, for $179 million.

Source: Mint.com.

LOSER: Wesabe Fails Despite Being a "First Mover"

Marc Hedlund and Jason Knight founded Wesabe (apparently a made-up name) in Berkeley, California, in December 2005 to "help consumers budget their money and make better financial decisions," according to a *New York Times* article.[3] Although Wesabe was not the first website to help people manage their personal finances, it could be considered a "first mover"—that is, it had the competitive advantage that a company has when it is first to enter a particular market. In its initial year, it signed up 150,000 members.

Like Flickr and del.icio.us, Wesabe relied for its success on assembling a community of users and on features such as user-added "tags," descriptors to facilitate searching without dependence on premade categories. In addition, wrote Hedlund, "we tried to automatically aggregate and store all of our users' financial accounts on the Web. . . . Most especially, we tried to learn from the accumulated data our users uploaded and make recommendations for better financial decisions based on that data."[4]

Ten months after Wesabe's founding, Mint.com appeared. In September 2007, Mint won the TechCrunch40 award for being the best of 40 new startups. From then on, says Hedlund, Wesabe was considered second-best, as its rival was able to attract more users and better venture financing. In July 2010, the Wesabe site was switched off.

What went wrong? First, Mint.com certainly had a better name. Second, Wesabe passed on using an existing automatic financial data aggregation service (which Mint chose to use, allowing it to get started earlier) and tried to create its own technology. Third, says Hedlund, "Mint focused on making the user do almost no work at all, by automatically editing and categorizing their data," whereas Wesabe tried to educate its users to understand their data by making them do a high degree of work (using tags, for instance).

Source: Photograph by Sally Lindsay.

 YOUR CALL "God is in the details," said architect Ludwig Mies van der Rohe, arguing for restraint in design. He also said "Less is more" and "It is better to be good than to be original." Could following these bits of advice have saved Wesabe? Do you think it's possible to change consumer behavior, as Wesabe was attempting to do (get consumers to understand their finances better)? Or do you think it's better just to settle for making users happy quickly, as Mint.com evidently did? What other advice would you give to someone who is trying to develop a new product?

MyBizLab

THE BIG IDEA: All the factors that prospective buyers evaluate in a product are called the total product offer. The products themselves may be developed for consumer or business markets, which have different characteristics.

THE ESSENTIAL QUESTION: If I want to develop a product, what do I need to understand before I begin?

MyBizLab

MyBizLab: Check your understanding of these concepts at www.mybizlab.com.

E ver heard of OK Soda? What about Choglit or Surge? These products lie in the Coca-Cola Company's "graveyard of beverage busts," as *BusinessWeek* put it.[5] Indeed, the chances of new products failing are extremely high—86% don't make it.[6]

Successful products are those that are introduced in a timely way, are significantly different from other products, and have discernible performance or price advantages. Companies that create successful products usually have a product-development system, one that encourages many ideas, screens them quickly, and ensures rigor so that only the soundest ideas come to market.

The point, of course, is to deliver *value*—what, as we said in Chapter 12, the consumer perceives as a superior relationship between costs and benefits in your firm's product compared with competitors' products. This isn't always easy: individual buyers don't evaluate a product's benefits in the same way, so it may be difficult to design one that satisfies many different consumers.

This chapter covers the first two of the 4-Ps in the marketing mix—that is . . .

- **The product strategy—"How do we design and test a product that will best meet consumer wants and needs?"** A marketing program begins with designing and developing a *product* that consumers will want. We discuss product strategy in the first part of this chapter.

- **The pricing strategy—"How do we determine the right price to set for the product?"** *Pricing* is figuring out how much to charge for a product—the price, or exchange value, for a good and service. We discuss pricing in the last section of this chapter.

The last two of the 4-Ps, place and promotion, are described in Chapter 14.

The Total Product Offer: Determining How Potential Buyers Evaluate a Product

What is a total product offer, and what are the kinds of markets for which it is intended?

Want to Know More? 13-1

Key Terms & Definitions in Sequential Order to Study as You Go Along

Go to www.mybizlab.com.

The ***total product offer,*** **also known as the** *value package,* **is all the factors that potential buyers evaluate in a product when considering whether to buy it.** These are all the factors, tangible and otherwise, that shoppers consider before buying a product or service. When you're shopping for a cantaloupe, there might not be many factors: price, smell, feel, and store reputation, perhaps. Other products embody lots of factors.

The Total Product Offer of the Toyota Prius. What parts of the total product offer induce consumers to buy a car? Advertising may be one, but a host of others may influence them as well. Brand? Reputation? Comfort? Price? Power? Speed? Color? Electronics? Financing? Warranty? Availability? For the Toyota Prius, the gasoline-electric hybrid, these aspects figured in the total product offer, but the most distinctive feature has been fuel economy. "The current car," says a 2011 report, "which starts at $22,800, has long been a gas-mileage wonder. It is government-rated at 51 miles a gallon in city driving, 49 mpg on the highway."[7] Despite Toyota's recall problems, the company sold 140,928 Priuses in 2010, outselling the Ford Mustang two to one.

Now Toyota is taking advantage of the brand to expand Prius into a whole line of gasoline-electric vehicles, including a plug-in version that will go up to 13 miles on electricity after only a two-hour charge—a key part of the value package. ■

As a marketer, you have to put yourself in the shoes of potential buyers and figure out what will be in your total product offer. ❶ A total product offer draws on a list of components such as those shown at right. (*See* ■ *Panel 13.1.*)

IT'S TIME FOR TEXAS A&M

Source: © 2011, Texas A&M University.

Consumer versus Business Markets: The Personal versus the Industrial

How do markets for individual/household consumers differ from those for business?

The two major markets that exist are the *consumer market* and the *business market.* A furniture maker, for example, might make desks and chairs to go into (1) suburban dens and bedrooms (consumer) and (2) offices (business).

Consumer Markets: Goods & Services for Personal Use

The *consumer market* **consists of all those individuals or households that want goods or services for their personal use.** For instance, a kitchen appliance maker might make food processors for home kitchens.

Consumer goods and services fall into four general classes. They are . . .

Convenience: Those Purchased Frequently and Easily. *Convenience goods and services* **are those inexpensive products that people buy frequently and with little effort,** such as candy, milk, and gum. "Convenience" does not mean they are available only in convenience stores. You probably can also find them in supermarkets and mass merchandisers (particularly up front near the registers, where they may tempt impulse buyers). Convenience goods and services are best marketed by making them easily available and by giving them the right kind of image, since with these items many consumers are relatively indifferent to price.

Examples: Convenience stores such as 7-Eleven, Circle-K, and am-pm sell bottled water, candy bars, hot dogs, potato chips, newspapers, aspirin, Band-Aids, gasoline, and so on that make up convenience goods. Banks serve the same function for convenience services, offering checking and savings accounts.

❶ **What's the total product offer?** Like marketers of other products, universities and colleges must present a total product offer to recruit students. What were the components offered by your college that made you choose it over other institutions of higher learning?

■ **PANEL 13.1 Possible components of a total product offer.**

- Advertising image
- Availability
- Brand name
- Consumer's prior experience
- Convenience
- Financing
- Guarantees
- Internet access
- Maker's reputation
- Packaging
- Price
- Product labeling
- Retailer's environment
- Service
- Warranty

② Comparing for value. Price-Grabber.com is a price comparison service, just one of a number of websites consumers can access to quickly compare the value, quality, and style of various shopping goods and services, such as wi-fi tablets. What are the advantages and short-comings of this type of shopping?

Source: Photograph by Sally Lindsay.

Shopping: Those Purchased after Consumers Make Comparisons. *Shopping goods and services* **are more expensive products that people buy after comparing for value, price, quality, and style.** Shopping goods and services are best marketed through the right combination of price, quality, and service. ②

Examples: Sears, Macy's, and JCPenney carry a mix of product lines, such as different clothing lines, that invite price and quality comparisons. Financial services firms such as Merrill Lynch and insurance companies such as Met Life offer similar choices in services, such as different stocks and bonds.

Specialty: Those Requiring Special Effort to Purchase. *Specialty goods and services* **are usually much more expensive products that buyers seldom purchase or that have unique characteristics that require people to make a special effort to obtain.** Most buyers of specialty products won't accept substitutes and will go out of their way to make sure they've got the right brand. These kinds of goods and services are best marketed to special groups of potential consumers through advertising.

Examples are $200,000 Porsche, Ferrari, and Lamborghini sports cars. So is the $45,000 Louis Vuitton Tribute Patchwork Bag, a luxury specialty good that is usually advertised in glossy print media.[8]

Unsought: Those Products Consumers Are Not Aware of or Interested In. *Unsought goods and services* **are those that people have little interest in, are unaware of, or didn't think they needed.** The marketing for these kinds of

Key Takeaway 13-1
Four classes of consumer goods and services: convenience, shopping, specialty, unsought.

goods and services depends on what they are, whether acne cream, towing services, emergency clean-up services, or home warranties.

Obviously whether a particular good or service falls into a particular category varies for different buyers, with some buying their easily available coffee beans at the closest store (convenience) and others driving across town to buy their cherished brand at the one-and-only store that sells it (specialty).

Business Markets: Goods & Services for Firms Providing Goods & Services

The *business market* or *business-to-business (B2B) market* consists of those businesses that want ***industrial goods,* or *business goods,* products used to produce other products.** Types of business products include *installations, capital items, accessory equipment, raw materials, component parts, process materials, supplies,* and *business services. (See ■ Panel 13.2.)*

Want to Know More? 13-2

More about B2B/Industrial Goods

Go to www.mybizlab.com.

■ PANEL 13.2 **Business product classifications.**

Category	Definition	Examples
Installations	Large capital purchases	New buildings, heavy machinery
Capital items	Large, long-lasting equipment	Industrial robots, long-haul tank trucks
Accessory equipment	Smaller, more mobile equipment	Computers, copiers, desks
Raw materials	Basic materials for making principal product	Steel, wood, oil, wool, corn
Component parts	Finished or nearly finished products for making principal product	Computer chips, batteries, switches, tires
Process materials	Materials for making principal product not readily identifiable in that product	Industrial glue, food preservatives
Supplies	Goods to help make, but not become part of, principal product	Paper, printer ribbons, cleaning agents
Business services	Services used in operations	Legal, financial, research, online

THE BIG IDEA: Innovation is a necessary and ongoing part of business, and an innovation may vary from slight to radical: continuous, dynamically continuous, and discontinuous. Constant innovation is required because products go through a life cycle of introduction, growth, maturity, and decline. New products are developed in a six-stage process: idea generation, screening, analysis, development, test marketing, and commercialization.

THE ESSENTIAL QUESTION: Why is product innovation necessary, and how is it done?

MyBizLab

MyBizLab: Check your understanding of these concepts at www.mybizlab.com.

What are the leading innovations of the last 30 years? According to a panel of judges at the University of Pennsylvania's Wharton School, the top five are the *Internet* (including broadband and the World Wide Web), *PC and laptop computers, mobile phones, e-mail,* and *DNA testing and sequencing.*[9]

Each of these has clearly changed the world and raised our standard of living. But an innovation need not be that transformational to be considered an innovation. Simply stated, **an *innovation* is a product that customers perceive as being newer or better than existing products.** Examples of past innovative products range from the vacuum cleaner (1907) to Velcro (1954) to the Searle birth control pill (1960) to the Toyota Prius hybrid (2003).[10]

For anyone interested in marketing strategy, understanding how the process of innovation works is important for at least three reasons:

- **Product obsolescence:** Existing products become obsolete as consumers' needs change or competitors add better features.
- **Frequent failure of new products:** Constant innovation is necessary because most new products your company introduces will not be accepted by enough consumers to be successful.
- **Long development time:** Some products take years to take shape. Indeed, a product under development may be so wildly ahead of its time as to seem impractical today. (Think self-steering cars.)

How New Is New? Continuous, Dynamically Continuous, & Discontinuous Innovation

What are the three types of innovation?

Most innovative products are not radically new. Indeed, the degree of newness can be ranged along a continuum, as follows. (*See* ■ *Panel 13.3, opposite page.*)

Continuous Innovation: Modest Improvements

Continuous innovation **represents modest improvements to an existing product to distinguish it from competitors; they require little consumer behavior change.** These are the "slight tweaks" that companies make in a product, such as giving it a new color, size, or packaging.

Continuous innovation	Dynamically continuous innovation	Discontinuous innovation
"Slight tweaks"— generally modest improvements to an existing product	"Quite new"—marked changes to an existing product	"Brand new"—totally new product that creates major changes in the way we live

Slightly new ⟶ Radically new

■ **Example of Continuous Innovation: Changing the Campbell's Soup Label.** In 1999, after 102 years, the Campbell Soup Company decided to enhance the soup label on its can to appeal to time-pressed shoppers and enable them to choose a soup more easily. Five colored banners were added, reading "classic," "fun favorites," "special selections," "great for cooking," or "98% fat free." In addition, each label showed a photo of the soup in a bowl.[11] ■

Dynamically Continuous Innovation: Marked Changes

Dynamically continuous innovation **represents marked changes to an existing product that require a moderate amount of consumer learning or behavior change.** E-book readers and electric cars might be in this category.

BRIEFING / LEGAL & ETHICAL PRACTICES

Are "Toning Shoes"—a Dynamically Continuous Innovation— Too Risky? What kinds of shoes are so innovative that they come with an instructional booklet and DVD? So-called *toning shoes* are redesigned athletic footwear that, in one description, "are supposed to tone muscles, promote healthy weight loss, and improve the posture of those who walk, work, or shop in them."[12] Introduced in 2007, the shoes—which often have rounded soles to stretch the wearer's leg muscles with each stride—represent dynamically continuous innovation because they require users to learn to walk or run all over again by changing their gait.

Although athletes (such as former NFL quarterback Joe Montana) may swear by them, some doctors worry about out-of-shape patients coming to them with inflamed Achilles tendons resulting from the shoes. So far, the shoes are considered perfectly legal. Despite some wearers' injuries, do you think it's ethical for a manufacturer to continue making this apparel, provided buyers are given adequate warnings? ■

Discontinuous Innovation: Brand New

Discontinuous innovation **means the product is totally new, radically changing how people live.** Such innovations are more than just new inventions. As the Wharton School academics at the start of this section said of the top innovations of the last 30 years, they create more opportunities for growth and development and have problem-solving value. The full list of the Wharton top 30 discontinuous innovations is shown on the next page. (*See* ■ *Panel 13.4.*)

Level of Innovation: Key to Type of Marketing Strategy

Understanding these three levels of innovation helps marketers develop the right kinds of marketing strategies to go along with a product. For instance, a classic strategy with a new product representing dynamically continuous innovation is to launch it at a reduced price in a limited-time offer.

■ **PANEL 13.4 Discontinuous innovation: Top 30 innovations of the last three decades.**

1. Internet, broadband, WWW (browser and html)
2. PC/laptop computers
3. Mobile phones
4. E-mail
5. DNA testing and sequencing/ Human genome mapping
6. Magnetic Resonance Imaging (MRI)
7. Microprocessors
8. Fiber optics
9. Office software (spreadsheets, word processors)
10. Non-invasive laser/robotic surgery (laparoscopy)

11. Open source software and services (e.g., Linux, Wikipedia)
12. Light emitting diodes
13. Liquid crystal display (LCD)
14. GPS systems
15. Online shopping/ecommerce/ auctions (e.g., eBay)
16. Media file compression (jpeg, mpeg, mp3)
17. Microfinance
18. Photovoltaic Solar Energy
19. Large scale wind turbines
20. Social networking via the Internet

21. Graphic user interface (GUI)
22. Digital photography/ videography
23. RFID and applications (e.g., EZ Pass)
24. Genetically modified plants
25. Bio fuels
26. Bar codes and scanners
27. ATMs
28. Stents
29. SRAM flash memory
30. Anti retroviral treatment for AIDS

Want to Know More? 13-3

More about the Top 30 Innovations

Go to www.mybizlab.com.

The Product Life Cycle: Four Stages

How would I summarize the product life cycle?

A *product life cycle* **is a model that graphs the four stages that a product or service goes through during the "life" of its marketability: (1) introduction, (2) growth, (3) maturity, and (4) decline.** The product life cycle is a useful concept for figuring out long-range sales, profitability, and new ways to extend the life of a product (as by reducing the price, figuring out new uses, modifying the product, or broadening the target market).

The rise and fall of the product life cycle—which can vary a great deal in time, from weeks to decades, depending on the product (short in the case of this year's fashion line, long in the case of the development and use of a jetliner)—is represented on the page opposite. (*See* ■ *Panel 13.5.*)

1 Introduction: Getting the Product to Market

The *introduction stage* **is the stage in the product life cycle in which a new product is introduced into the marketplace.** This is the stage that is heavy on startup costs for production, marketing, and distribution. Managers have to concentrate on building inventory and staff without loss of quality. With sales usually low during this period, the product is probably losing the company money. There is also the huge risk that the product may be rejected in the marketplace.

BRIEFING / A WORLD OF CONSTANT CHANGE
Is the United States Ready for a "Credit Card Phone"? As an example of Life Cycle Stage 1, introduction of a product, would you want to use your smartphone instead of a credit or debit card to pay for parking meters, fast food, and retail products? It's being done in other countries, such as Japan. Such "mobile payments" are just now being launched in the United States.[13]

For instance, Wells Fargo is testing a program in which consumers could use a Nokia phone to make mobile payments at restaurants and elsewhere.[14]

■ PANEL 13.5 **The product life cycle.** Length of time varies by product. Managers use this cycle to create marketing strategies for each stage.

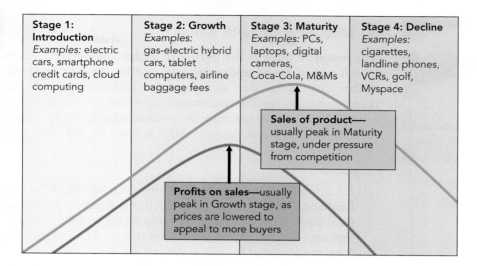

Stage 1: Introduction	Stage 2: Growth	Stage 3: Maturity	Stage 4: Decline
Examples: electric cars, smartphone credit cards, cloud computing	*Examples:* gas-electric hybrid cars, tablet computers, airline baggage fees	*Examples:* PCs, laptops, digital cameras, Coca-Cola, M&Ms	*Examples:* cigarettes, landline phones, VCRs, golf, Myspace

Sales of product— usually peak in Maturity stage, under pressure from competition

Profits on sales—usually peak in Growth stage, as prices are lowered to appeal to more buyers

Google, too, hopes to make the smartphone the "wallet of the future."[15] The service "would let users buy milk and bread by waving their mobile phones against a register at checkout," says one report.[16] Apple, Visa, and PayPal are also exploring this technology.

What do you think the chances are that smartphone credit cards will succeed in the United States? ■

2 Growth: Demand Increases

The *growth stage*, which is the most profitable stage, is the period in which customer demand increases, the product's sales grow, and later competitors may enter the market. At the start, the product may have the marketplace to itself, and demand for it may be high. Managers need to worry about getting sufficient product into the distribution pipeline, maintaining quality, and expanding the sales and distribution effort. All the while, competitors are rushing to get their products to market.

BRIEFING / A WORLD OF CONSTANT CHANGE

Growth of the Kindle E-Book. An instance of Life Cycle Stage 2, growth, is demonstrated by the Kindle, which was launched by Amazon in the United States in November 2007. By late 2008, sales of the e-book reader were so hot that it completely sold out over Christmas, with available secondhand units going for twice the $359 retail price.[17] Amazon brought out the Kindle 2 in early 2009, followed by the large-screen Kindle DX ($489) in the summer.

In February 2010, the Kindle seemed to be on a world-beating path to growth, with 68% of the digital book market. Already, though, competition was appearing in the form of the Sony Reader, the Barnes & Noble Nook, and other rivals. "The market for digital readers is getting increasingly crowded," said a *Wall Street Journal* story, "and price-slashing has become the norm."[18]

Then, in early 2010, Apple's Steve Jobs announced the birth of a tablet-style touchscreen computer called the iPad, which, unlike the single-purpose Kindle, was a multipurpose device. The iPad, pointed out technical journalist Walter Mossberg, offered not only a variety of e-reading apps but also "has

Source: Tyler Olson/Shutterstock.

③ Mature products. The length of time can vary for the life cycle of different products. Both laptops and jetliners are in their mature stages, but the commercial airliner does not seem to be headed toward decline. How long do you think it will be before it does? Can you think of other goods that seem to defy the typical product life cycle?

Source: Mars Evis/Shutterstock.

④ In decline. First marketed in 1992, Hummer was a civilian version of the military Humvee. The brand was purchased in 1998 by General Motors, which produced three variations: the Hummer H1, based on the Humvee, and the H2 and H3 models, which were smaller. The Great Recession and rise in gas prices caused GM to question the Hummer's viability, and in 2010 it stopped making any more of the vehicles and withdrew it from the market.

prompted many of its owners to use it instead of their laptops for everything from e-mail and social networking to games and Web surfing."[19] ∎

3 Maturity: Growth Slows

The *maturity stage* is the period in which the product starts to fall out of favor and sales and profits start to level off. In this phase, sales slow as competition makes inroads. At this point, managers need to concentrate on reducing costs and instituting efficiencies to maintain the product's profitability. Sometimes they can extend the life of the product by tinkering with its various features. ③

∎ **Example of Products in Maturity: The Kindle, PCs, and Laptops.** By early November 2010, the Kindle's portion of total market sales fell to 47%, from a high of 68%. Most of that was taken by the iPad, which rose to 32%. (The Sony Reader accounted for 5%, the Nook for 4%.)[20]
Kindle joined two other electronic products reaching maturity: personal computers and laptops. By 2013, according to Gartner, a market research company, the number of smartphones will surpass PCs by 1.82 billion. Forester Research predicts that 82 million Americans will be using tablet computers like the iPad by 2015.[21] ∎

4 Decline: Withdrawing from the Market

The *decline stage* is the period in which the product falls out of favor, and the organization eventually withdraws it from the marketplace. The product loses popularity, and managers sound the bugle for retreat, scaling down relevant inventory, supplies, and personnel. ④ While this phase may mean withdrawal of support for the old product, it need not shut down the organization. Much of the same expertise will be required to support new endeavors.

In electronics, products rise and fall in a relatively short time, with video recorder/players and personal digital assistants, for instance, now showing steep declines. But decline happens all the time in other areas as well.

∎ **Example of Products in Decline: Myspace, *ER*, and Golf.** Mismanagement and strategic blunders caused Myspace to fall from being one of the most popular websites on earth to practically an afterthought, says one article.[22] The fictional medical TV series *ER* ran for 15 years, but was canceled as fans moved to other medical shows such as *House* and *Grey's Anatomy*.[23] In the United States, at least, the sport of golf has declined, with core golfers (those playing eight rounds or more per year) down 3% to 4.5% every year since 2006—perhaps because so many Americans simply don't have the time.[24] ∎

In Chapter 14 (Panel 14.13), we show how different marketing strategies can be applied during different phases of the product life cycle.

Six Stages in Developing a New Product

How should a firm go about developing a product?

The lifeblood of most firms is the constant creation of new products. Thus, companies like 3M (famed for its Post-it notes, among many other products) churn out thousands of ideas for new products every year in hopes of producing a winner. The process they follow consists of six steps. (*See* ■ *Panel 13.6.*)

Each step must be approved by management before proceeding to the next step, so that funds and resources won't be wasted.

1 Idea Generation: Collecting Product Ideas from All Sources

Idea generation **is coming up with new product ideas, ideally by collecting ideas from as many sources as possible.** Companies may develop new products internally by listening to employees or through research-and-development departments. Or they may get ideas from customers, suppliers, and competitors. Quantity counts, since research suggests that only one idea in 3,000 will end up making money.[25]

2 Product Screening: Eliminating Unfeasible Product Ideas

Product screening **is elimination of product ideas that are not feasible,** because they don't fit the company's product mix, are too expensive, will take too long to execute, or won't generate enough sales. Many ideas don't survive this stage.

3 Product Analysis: Estimating the Proposed Product's Profitability

Product analysis **is doing cost estimates to calculate the product's possible profitability,** taking into account cost of materials, production expenses, impact of competitors, and potential sales.

4 Product Development: Producing a Prototype, a Preliminary Product Version

Product development **is the production of a** *prototype* **of the product, a preliminary version, so the company can see what the product will look like.** Some prototypes cost a lot of money and take considerable time. General Motors builds futuristic "concept cars" that never go beyond a single model. ➎

5 Test Marketing: Trying Out the Product in Selected Markets

Test marketing **is the introduction of a new product in a limited form to selected geographical markets to test consumers' reactions.** When Frontier Airlines of Denver introduced service to Reno, Nevada, it did it on a limited basis to see how consumers would respond.

6 Commercialization: Doing Full-Scale Production & Marketing of the Product

Commercialization **is the full-scale production and marketing of the product,** using information learned during test marketing. A big question in this final stage is distribution: whether to roll out the product gradually in selected geographical areas, or roll it out nationwide all at once.

Example: Pacifico beer was first introduced in states like Arizona and California, reflecting the brand's origin in Baja California, Mexico. The national push was to come later, utilizing the beer's website (mexicoviapacifico.com) and brand-oriented video clips.[26]

Commercialization of a new product represents the first, or introduction, stage in the product life cycle.

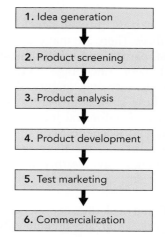

■ **PANEL 13.6 Stages in developing a new product.**

1. Idea generation
↓
2. Product screening
↓
3. Product analysis
↓
4. Product development
↓
5. Test marketing
↓
6. Commercialization

ⓘ

Want to Know More? 13-4

Amazon's Product Development Process: Start with the Customer & Work Backward

Go to www.mybizlab.com.

Source: zhu difeng/Shutterstock.

➎ **Prototype.** General Motors may have given up on the Hummer, but they are continuously developing "concept cars" for testing and to assess consumer reaction. Most of these experimental cars never go into production. Why do you think going to this trouble and expense is useful to automakers?

As we saw, product development begins with *idea generation*. There are many ways to stimulate conceptualization, particularly when brainstorming with others: Defer judgment. Encourage wild imagination. Be visual. Go for quantity over quality. Build on others' ideas.[27] Most of these suggestions are in accord with the observation of two Stanford business creativity researchers, Michael Ray and Rochelle Myers: "The less judgment the more curiosity, and the more curiosity the more creativity."[28] The takeaway: *Destroy judgment, create curiosity.*

The Voice of Judgment (VOJ)

"If you lack the confidence to create," write Ray and Myers, "you are undoubtedly tuned into the Voice of Judgment that all of us have within. . . . This judgment condemns, criticizes, attaches blame, makes fun of, puts down, assigns guilt, passes sentence on, punishes, and buries anything that's the least bit unlike a mythical norm."[29]

Do You Have a Fixed or a Growth Mindset?

Some of us are more rigid than others. Stanford research psychologist Carol Dweck says people generally approach challenges with one of two mindsets.[30]

People with *fixed mindsets* tend to thrive or feel good "when things are safely within their grasp. If things get too challenging—when they're not feeling smart or talented—they lose interest," Dweck says. They stay interested in difficult material only when they do well right away. If it isn't a testimony to their intelligence, they can't enjoy it.

People with the *growth mindset* thrive when they're stretching themselves. They maintain a high level of interest even when they find the work very challenging.

Mindlessness versus Mindfulness

Fortunately, a person with a fixed mindset can develop a growth mindset, but it means developing some self-awareness and taking chances. One barrier to being flexible is *mindlessness*, which is characterized by three attributes, according to Harvard psychology professor Ellen Langer.[31]

The first attribute is "entrapment in old categories," in which we think there is only one way of doing things, although usually there isn't.[32] The second is "automatic behavior," in which we take in and use limited signals from the world instead of being open to new information. The third is "acting from a single perspective," as when we assume that other peoples' motives and intentions are the same as ours.[33]

The opposite of mindlessness is *mindfulness*—being open to novelty, alert to distinctions, sensitive to different contexts, aware of multiple perspectives. Developing mindfulness means consciously adapting, being oriented in the present.

Emotional Blocks to Creativity

What are the blocks to your creativity, if any? To start developing your growth mindset, see the statements below.[34]

SOME EMOTIONAL BLOCKS TO CREATIVITY:
What Does Your VOJ Say?

1. I'm afraid of making a mistake, of risking, of failing.
2. I can't tolerate ambiguity; I have "no appetite for chaos."
3. I prefer to judge ideas, not generate them.
4. I'm unable to relax, incubate, or "sleep on it."
5. I strongly need to succeed quickly . . .
6. . . . Alternatively, if I find a problem lacks challenge, it doesn't engage my interest.
7. I can't seem to access areas of imagination within me.

Based on James L. Adams, *Conceptual Blockbusting.*

THE BIG IDEA: Product differentiation is designing a product different enough from competitors to attract consumers. An important part of it is establishing a brand, whether brand name, brand mark, or trademark. Unlike generic (unbranded) products, brands may be national or private, family or individual. Branding has four goals: to publicize the company name, differentiate its products from competitors', get repeat sales, or make entering new markets easier. The importance of a brand is judged by brand equity, the factors people associate with a brand name, and brand loyalty or level of commitment, whether awareness, preference, or insistence. Packaging also is important for protecting and promoting a product.

THE ESSENTIAL QUESTION: In what ways are branding and packaging used to differentiate a product?

MyBizLab: Check your understanding of these concepts at www.mybizlab.com.

MyBizLab

Verizon, Häagen-Dazs, Google, and Twitter—well-known brand names all, collectively worth billions of dollars in marketing value.

Where did such names come from? Verizon and Häagen-Dazs were simply made up. Google was the founders' misspelling of the numerical term *googol* (which means 1 followed by 100 zeros). Twitter, according to a company spokesman, was "the result of a brainstorm between a small group of employees at Odeo, the San Francisco podcasting startup, where Twitter initially began as a side project. They came up with possible names, including 'Jitter' and 'Twitter,' and put them in a hat." Twitter won.[35] ❻

Notice something about these names? They are all somewhat *odd*. That's what it takes for a product or a company to stand out in the global marketplace these days, according to a corporate naming expert.[36] Indeed, branding and naming are so important to companies that there are now probably some 50 naming firms worldwide. Their principal concern is differentiation, whether of companies or of products.

***Product differentiation* is the attempt to design a product in a way that will make it be perceived differently enough from competitors' products that it will attract consumers.** Of course, the kind of differentiation will depend on what kind of goods and services are involved and what kinds of markets.

Two important ways to differentiate a product are through . . .

- **Branding:** a unique name, symbol, and/or design
- **Packaging:** a unique covering or wrapping

Brands, Brand Names, Brand Marks, & Trademarks: Creating a Unique Identity for a Product

How would I define "brand," and how would I describe the three classes of brands?

Burmashave. Selectric. Falstaff. Nash. A shaving cream, a typewriter, a beer, a car. Famous in their day, now gone. That's what happens with brands that have outlived

Source: Photograph by Sally Lindsay.

❻ **What's in a name?** Do you think the popularity of Twitter is attributable to its quirky name? Or is it all derived from its convenient technology? If you were starting your own business, would you favor an unusual moniker or something more common or traditional, such as the family name? Why?

Want to Know More? 13-5

What Makes a Brand Name Successful?

Go to www.mybizlab.com.

their service, as we saw with the product life cycle. But some old brands just keep going on and on: Arm & Hammer (founded 1846). Campbell's Soup (1869). Levi's (1873). Quaker Oats (1901). Jeep (1941).

A *brand* **is a unique name, symbol, or design that identifies an organization and its product or service.** Many firms have a *brand manager,* **or** *product manager,* **to be responsible for the key elements of the marketing mix—product, price, place, and promotion—for one brand or one product line.**

Brands fall into three general classes:

Brand Names: Brands Expressed as Words, Letters, or Numbers

Brand names **are those parts of a brand that can be expressed verbally, such as by words, letters, or numbers.** Wheaties, Yahoo!, NBC, A1 Steak Sauce, and 3-in-1 Oil are examples.

Brand Marks: Brands That Cannot Be Expressed Verbally

Brand marks **are those parts of a brand that cannot be expressed verbally, such as graphics and symbols.** Examples: McDonald's golden arches, the Nike swoosh, the Mr. Peanut symbol, the Wells Fargo stagecoach, the Shell seashell sign.

Trademarks: Brands Given Exclusive Legal Protection

Trademarks **are brand names and brand marks, and even slogans, that have been given exclusive legal protection** (often indicated by a special ™ sign for "unregistered trademark" or ® for "registered trademark"). Examples: *UPS®, United Parcel Service®,* and *Big Brown®.* Or the dating service Chemistry.com's slogan: *Come as you are.*™ There are also unregistered service marks. Companies often sue other firms for using brand names or marks that are too close to their own. (*See* ■ *Panel 13.7.*)

■ PANEL 13.7 Types of trademarks.

Symbols and Meanings	Use
™ Unregistered trademark	To promote or brand goods
SM Unregistered service mark	To promote or brand services
® Registered trademark	Allows lawsuit for trademark infringement

Want to Know More? 13-6

How Do Brands Lose Their Trademark Status?

Go to www.mybizlab.com.

Different Types of Brands: Manufacturer's & Private-Label, Family & Individual

How would I distinguish the four different types of brands from one another?

In times past, supermarkets offered low-priced *generic* or *unbranded* products—such as toilet paper, cooking oil, and wine labeled simply "Red Table Wine"—that were sold in plain packaging with minimal labeling and given little or no advertising. Today most generic products have given way to private-label brands, as we'll discuss.

In contrast to generic products, brands hold out the promise of quality (or at least of familiarity). There are four principal categories of brands, of contrasting types—*manufacturer's* versus *private-label, family* versus *individual.*

Manufacturer's Brands: For Products Distributed Nationally

Manufacturer's brands—**also called** *national* **or** *producer brands,* **or even** *global brands* **when extended worldwide—are those attached to products by companies that distribute nationwide or even worldwide.** Examples (just to take some brand names with the letter *x* in them): Excel, Ex-lax, Lexis, Lexus, Netflix, Nextel, Paxil, Paxon—and thousands of other names.

Private-Label Brands: For Products Distributed by One Store or Chain

Unlike manufacturers' brands, *private-label brands*—**also known as** *private,* *store,* **and** *dealer brands*—**are those attached to products distributed by one**

store or a chain. Examples: Sears offers Kenmore appliances, Craftsman tools, and Diehard batteries. Staples offers its own brand of paper, staples, and other office supplies. Safeway has its O Organics private-label foods.

Private brands are generally lower priced than national brands and consumers may consider them less prestigious (although this is not the case with Sears).

Family Brands: Giving All Company Products the Same Brand

With *family brands,* **the same brand name is given to all or most of a company's products.** Kellogg puts most of its breakfast cereals under one brand: Kellogg's Cornflakes, Kellogg's Rice Krispies, Kellogg's Frosted Flakes, and so on. Wineries also take this approach. The idea with family branding is to build on the consumer's recognition of an existing brand to give credibility to the brand extensions. ❼

Source: Photograph by Sally Lindsay.

Individual Brands: Giving Different Company Products a Different Brand

Unlike family brands, with *individual brands,* **different brand names are given to different company products.** Examples: General Motors has different names—and tries to have different identities—for its car and truck lines: Chevrolet, Buick, Cadillac, and GMC. Indeed, within each product line there is further branding: Chevrolet cars have the Aveo, Cobalt, Corvette, HHR, Impala, and Malibu. Each brand is aimed at a different kind of consumer.

Co-Branding: Brands of Two Noncompeting Products Are Combined

Sometimes two companies or entities will get together and combine their brands, in hopes of advancing the interests of both. This is known as *co-branding,* **two noncompeting products link their brand names together for a single product.** Target combines with Visa to offer a credit card. Subaru produces a car model with the name L.L. Bean on it, identified with the Maine clothier. In a way, sports stadiums and ballparks have also been doing this when selling their naming rights to big companies, as with American Airlines Arena (Dallas), Staples SportsCenter (Los Angeles), and AT&T Park (San Francisco).

❼ **Family branding.** Breakfast cereals from Post Foods strive for different identities through variation in their packaging designs—the box of Honey Bunches of Oats is assuredly different from that of Fruity Pebbles—but all are linked through the family name Post, which is prominently displayed.

Key Takeaway 13-2
Four types of brands: manufacturer's, private-label, family, individual.

Want to Know More? 13-7
Individual Brands at Marriott
Go to www.mybizlab.com.

What Is Branding Supposed to Do? Four Goals

What are four reasons brands are valuable?

Why have brands taken on such importance that companies will spend enormous sums to protect them? Four reasons brands are valuable are . . .

1 To Publicize the Company Name & Build Trust

Through branding, a company is able to expose its name to consumers and build trust in its products. Consumers are apt to pay more for a product they have confidence in, as opposed to an unknown or generic product.

2 To Differentiate the Company's Product from Competing Products

Having a well-known brand is especially valuable for differentiating a product when there are only a handful of competitors. There are all kinds of small moving companies, for example, but for long-distance moves consumers are apt to pick from the well-known brands: Allied, Atlas, Bekins, Mayflower, North American,

United, Wheaton. The same is true of toothpaste: People often choose among Colgate, Crest, Gleem, and Pepsodent.

3 To Get Repeat Sales

The more you liked the last camping equipment you bought from REI, the more apt you are to buy from them again. If you liked your last stay at a Hilton hotel, the more probable you will stay with them in the future.

i

Want to Know More? 13-8

Ten Principles of Strong Brands

Go to www.mybizlab.com.

4 To Make Entering New Markets Easier

When a company with high brand recognition introduces new products, it doesn't have to start from scratch in trying to convince customers that it has credibility.

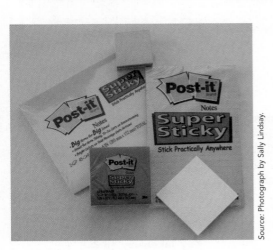

Source: Photograph by Sally Lindsay.

■ **Example** of How a Recognized Brand Eases the Way for New Products: Post-it Notes Helps Introduce Super Sticky Notes. 3M's Post-it Notes were originally designed for offices and found their way into people's homes by way of the workplace. In mid-2010, 3M decided to go after the home and educational arena for a variation on Post-its called Super Sticky Notes. ⑧

A commercial showed a Jack Russell terrier jumping and fixing his teeth into an orange note with a drawing of a bone affixed several feet above on a kitchen wall, then hanging suspended by it. "Post-it Super Sticky Notes hold on stronger, and longer, but of course remove cleanly," said a voiceover. Clearly, the universality of 30-year-old Post-it Notes made the introduction of Super Sticky Notes much easier.[37] ■

⑧ **Leveraging the brand.** Launched in the 1970s, Post-it Notes have been used in offices for years. Now 3M, its manufacturer, hopes to capitalize on the familiarity of the brand with a derivative designed for home and education use, Post-it Super Sticky Notes. Do you think this product line will survive or can be adapted as we continue the move to a paperless society?

Judging the Value of a Brand: Brand Equity & Brand Loyalty

What is brand equity, and what are the three degrees of brand loyalty?

How attached are people to brands? That is the question that marketers try to answer with the concept of brand equity. **Brand equity is the marketing and financial value derived from the combination of factors that people associate with a certain brand name,** such as emotions, images, and loyalty.

Brand loyalty is commitment to a particular brand—the degree to which consumers are satisfied with a product and will buy it again. There are three degrees of loyalty: (1) *awareness,* (2) *preference,* and (3) *insistence.*

Brand Awareness: People Recognize the Product

The lowest level of loyalty, *brand awareness* **means that consumers recognize the product.** People not into power tools might nevertheless recognize the name Black & Decker. People who don't buy makeup still are familiar with the name Avon.

Brand Preference: People Use the Product Habitually

The next level of brand loyalty, *brand preference* **means that consumers habitually buy the product if it is easily available, but will try alternatives if they can't find it.** For example, you may regularly use Crest toothpaste but don't object to buying Colgate if you can't find Crest.

Brand Insistence: People Will Accept No Substitutes

The highest level of loyalty, **brand insistence means that consumers insist on the product; they will accept no substitutes.** Apple apparently inspires this kind of loyalty, as does Harley-Davidson. Zealous football fans—supporters of the Oakland Raiders or Green Bay Packers, say—maintain their fan loyalties (and continue to buy the team's jacket and other products) even after they, the fans, have moved across the country.

Highly popular brands often bring forth **knockoff brands, illegal imitations of national brand-name products.** Sometimes it's an outright counterfeit, such as fake (and cheap) "Rolex" watches and "Hermès" scarves sold out of attaché cases by low-paid immigrants on Fifth Avenue in New York. Sometimes the knockoff features a name that is close to but not the same as the original: "Roleks" instead of Rolex or "Hermèz" instead of Hermès. ❾

Source: paul prescott/Shutterstock.

Packaging: Protecting & Promoting a Product

What are five functions of packaging?

What pizza has a little red hat on the pizza box? What cigarettes have a picture of a desert animal on the pack? What U.S. airline has our national colors—red, white, and blue—on its planes? (Answers: Pizza Hut, Camel, American Airlines.) All these are various kinds of packaging, an important part of branding.

Packaging **is the covering or wrapping around a product that protects and promotes the product.** Packaging has five functions:

1 To Protect the Product

Packaging protects the goods inside, preventing them from spoilage (as with mayonnaise) or damage (eggs) or tampering (Tylenol). Some packaging is also intended to protect children *from* the product, such as aspirin and rat poison.

2 To Help Consumers Use the Product

Packaging can make it easier for buyers to use the product. Examples: Many products—sugar, olive oil, detergents—provide spouts for pouring. Some dry laundry soaps come with measuring scoops. Now some plastic squeeze bottles of catsup and mustard are packaged upside down, with spouts on the bottom. Some packaging provides a bonus use, such as jelly jars that can be used later for drinking glasses.

3 To Provide Product Information

Packaging can provide information about the contents of the package. Food packages list nutrition information. Drug packages provide dosages and medical warnings. Packaging on DVDs provides information about music, performers, and the like. Power tool packages carry warranties.

❾ **Knockoffs.** Many people can't tell the difference between an imitation product and the real thing, as with these (presumably phony) handbags being sold on a street corner. However, if a crucial car part made overseas was masquerading as an American brand-name part, wouldn't you want to know before it was installed in your car?

Want to Know More? 13-9
What Is the Fair Packaging & Labeling Act?
Go to www.mybizlab.com.

Want to Know More? 13-10
Waste Hierarchy & Product & Package Development
Go to www.mybizlab.com.

Want to Know More? 13-11

Decisions, Decisions: *Consumer Reports* Magazine

Go to www.mybizlab.com.

4 **To Indicate Price & Universal Product Code**

Small stores may still just put price stickers on their packages, and in some instances the product itself (such as books) carries a preprinted price. Most packages, however, carry *universal product codes (UPCs),* **bar codes printed on the package that can be read by bar code scanners.** UPCs allow retail stores to change the prices within the store's computer system, as well as to keep track of which products sell and which don't and to reorder products when they run low.

5 **To Promote the Product & Differentiate It from Competitors**

Package designers put a lot of thought and effort into picking typography, colors, and graphics that will attract the casual eye and distinguish the product from the packages of competing products. Think Kodak film, Wheaties cereal, Pennzoil motor oil, Absolut vodka (the distinctive bottle), and so on. ❿ The packaging may also describe the benefits of the product.

■ **Example of Distinctive Packaging: At Cold Temperatures, Mountains Turn Blue on Coors Light Bottles and Cans.** To know that a beer is cold "when you reach into the fridge at home or at a convenience store on a hot August afternoon is meaningful," says Tim Sproul, an advertising creative director who works on Coors Light beer promotion.[38] The idea of "cold beer insurance" was designed into new packaging launched by Colorado-based MillerCoors in 2007. Temperature-sensitive labels on Coors Light beer bottles featured mountains that turned blue when, in the Coors slogan, it's "as cold as the Rockies." In 2009, the concept was extended to Coors Light cans. (The bottles start to turn blue at 46 degrees Fahrenheit and turn fully blue at 42 degrees. For cans, it is 48 and 44, respectively.)

The packaging and its accompanying advertising was designed to make Coors Light "synonymous with 'cold' and help differentiate the brand from competitive brews," says a *New York Times* article.[39] The brand image work was successful enough that Coors Light edged out Miller Light, making it number 3 behind best-selling Bud Light and Budweiser. ■

Source: Photograph by Sally Lindsay.

❿ **Distinctive packaging.** Some packages are so unusual that they become collectors' items. Assuming you liked the taste, wouldn't you remember to buy this Vermont Maple Syrup brand again the next time you saw it on a shelf?

THE BIG IDEA: Pricing, the second of the 4-Ps, is figuring out how much to charge for a product. Pricing is supposed to make a profit, match or beat the competition, attract customers, make products affordable to certain people, and create prestige. An essential part of pricing is using break-even analysis to determine the revenue needed to cover the costs of making a product. The three principal pricing strategies are cost pricing, target costing, and competitive pricing. Six other pricing strategies are price skimming, penetration pricing, discounting, everyday low pricing, bundling, and psychological pricing. Credit terms are another purchasing inducement.

THE ESSENTIAL QUESTION: How is pricing important, and what are the various pricing strategies?

MyBizLab: Check your understanding of these concepts at www.mybizlab.com.

MyBizLab

One more blessing (or curse) of the Internet: It has relentlessly driven down prices by enabling consumers to easily do price-comparison shopping on similar products. To fight against this race to the bottom, some online retailers are trying new tactics—including simply eliminating prices on e-commerce sites for televisions, cameras, jewelry, and the like. Thus, "to see how much these items cost," says one reporter, "shoppers must add the merchandise to their shopping carts—in effect, taking it up to the virtual register for a price check."[40] Such is the new world of pricing, the second of the 4-Ps of marketing.

Pricing, we said, is figuring out how much to charge for a product—the price, or exchange value, for a good or service. In this section, we discuss five aspects:

- What pricing is supposed to do—the goals
- Covering your costs—break-even analysis
- Principal strategies
- Alternative strategies
- Credit terms

What Pricing Is Supposed to Do: Five Possible Goals

What are five objectives when assigning prices to things?

There are several ***pricing objectives,* or goals, that product producers—as well as retailers and wholesalers—hope to achieve in pricing products for sale.** Five of the most popular objectives (some of which may overlap) are . . .

1 To Make a Profit

Achieving a *target return on investment* is simply fancy language for making a profit, a specified yield on the investment. For example, a firm might specify a 15% return on investment. ⓫

⓫ **Profitable.** Most products are price sensitive—but not all. Want a last-minute ticket to the Super Bowl? It might cost you $5,000—a huge increase from their original $600 to $1,200 face value. If you were setting the price for Super Bowl tickets, what factors would you need to take into account to maximize the NFL's profit? What characteristics are shared by other products that seem to be immune from competitive pricing?

Source: Jeff Greenberg/Alamy.

⑫ Loss leaders. Walmart boasts of its "everyday low prices," but some prices are better deals than others. Loss leaders—products priced at or below cost—are often promoted at the front of the store to draw customers in so they may buy other goods. Do you tend to assume that loss leaders reflect a store's pricing in general?

⑬ World's priciest shops. Rodeo ("ro-day-o") Drive in Beverly Hills, California, may be the most expensive three-block shopping district in the world, known for celebrated clothiers Armani, Gucci, Christian Dior, and others. With prestige pricing, customers tell themselves, "Yes, it's expensive, and I'm worth it." Have you ever paid a lot for something simply because you wanted to pamper or reward yourself?

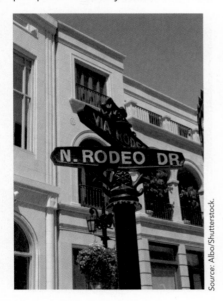

2 To Match or Beat the Competition

Many companies set prices simply to meet their competitors' prices. Example: Two gas stations, a Shell and a BP, occupying the same intersection may raise and lower gasoline prices to keep up with each other. (This might have no effect on luring drivers who hold one or the other brand's credit card, but it will probably influence the motorists who have other means to pay.)

3 To Attract Customers

Attracting customers—also known as "driving traffic"—is, of course, a principal function of pricing, which is why retailers often hold sales. Sometimes stores will use certain products as ***loss leaders,*** **products advertised at or below cost to attract customers.** ⑫ Low pricing can also be used to increase ***market share,*** **the percentage of the market of total sales for a particular product or good.**

BRIEFING / SOCIALLY RESPONSIBLE BUSINESS
Does Ikea's Inexpensive Furniture Put the Planet at Risk?
Low prices have helped Ikea, the international home products company, to attract customers in the market for inexpensive, ready-to-assemble Scandinavian furniture. But is low pricing always a good thing? Ellen Ruppel Shell, author of *Cheap: The High Cost of the Discount Culture,* suggests that low prices may exact their own price on the planet.[41] Ikea, she says, buys much of its wood in Eastern Europe and far eastern Russia, "where wages are low, large wooded regions remote, and according to the World Bank, half of all logging is illegal."[42] This deforestation contributes to global warming, she argues, thus threatening the planet.

The company's head replied that Ikea is taking steps, such as employing monitors, to avoid doing business with illegal foresters. Still, Ruppel Shell thinks that Ikea and other discount retailers "have abandoned their principles in pursuit of rock-bottom prices," according to one account, and "she is angry with the rest of us for supporting them."[43]

What do you think? Could companies' fixation on offering bargains ultimately be hurting the environment? ∎

4 To Make Products More Affordable to Certain People

Low pricing can be used not only to attract customers but also to make goods or services more widely available for those who otherwise would not be able to afford them.

∎ **Example of Pricing to Make Products Widely Affordable: Prices for Children and Seniors.** Some small businesses, such as restaurants and movie theaters, have less expensive prices for children and seniors, or lower prices during less popular hours. The "blue plate special" refers to the special rates on dinners for senior citizens during normal predinner hours. Public institutions—public transportation, museums, state parks—often post lower prices for people under age 12 and over 65 than for those in between. The purpose is to make products more affordable to people who may not have as much income. ∎

5 To Create Prestige

For some products, such as certain cars, clothes, perfumes, and watches, setting a higher price can be used to create an image of high quality or prestige. ⑬

BRIEFING / PERSONAL FINANCE

Pricing to Create Prestige—Does High-Priced Wine Really Taste Better? Winemakers price certain wines high to create a sense of prestige in potential buyers' minds. But is the wine itself necessarily better? Or is it just what you think? Maybe this is knowledge you can put to personal use.

Baba Shiv, professor of marketing at Stanford Graduate School of Business, is an expert in the field of "decision neuroscience," which uses brain scans to see how people react to products. In one study reported by Shiv and colleagues, subjects were told they'd be tasting different wines, one priced at $5, one at $45. They were then given the exact same wine to sip through a tube while undergoing brain scans in a magnetic resonance imaging (MRI) scanner, the kind of machine used to diagnose brain tumors.

The study showed, according to one article, that a region of the brain linked to pleasure "was more active when the subject thought he or she was drinking the more expensive wine." In other words, the *price* of a product can influence, in the researchers' phrase, "experienced pleasantness."[44] ■

Key Takeaway 13-3
Objectives of pricing: make profit, match competition, attract customers, make products affordable, create prestige.

Determining the Revenue Needed to Cover Costs: Break-Even Analysis

How does break-even analysis work?

Shouldn't the price you as a businessperson set on your product or service at least cover the costs of providing it? Of course. Pricing, therefore, begins with an exercise known as break-even analysis for doing a future "what-if" scenario of costs, prices, and sales for a particular product. ***Break-even analysis* is a way of identifying how much revenue is needed to cover the total costs of developing and selling a product.**

Specifically, its purpose is to find the ***break-even point*—the point at which sales revenues equal costs; that is, at which there is no profit but also no loss.**

The break-even point involves (1) fixed costs and (2) variable costs.

Fixed Costs: Expenses That Don't Change

***Fixed costs,* or *total fixed costs,* are expenses that don't change regardless of how many products are made or sold.** Fixed costs are those you have to pay out on a regular basis, such as weekly or monthly. Examples: The rent and insurance on your manufacturing facility and the equipment inside it usually don't change much, and so are considered fixed costs.

Variable Costs: Expenses That Change According to Number of Products Produced

***Variable costs* are expenses that vary depending on the numbers of products produced.** Examples: The costs of materials and labor required, which will change if more items are produced, are variable costs.

Computing Break-Even Point: Using Fixed Costs & Variable Costs

The formula for computing the break-even point is as follows:

$$\text{Break-even point} = \frac{\text{Fixed cost}}{\text{Price of 1 unit} - \text{Variable cost of 1 unit}}$$

BRIEFING / SMALL BUSINESS & ENTREPRENEURS

A Pizza Restaurant Uses Fixed & Variable Costs to Calculate the Break-Even Point. Suppose you, small-business owner of Hipster's Storefront Pizza, pay $200,000 per year in *fixed costs* for rent and insurance, pizza ovens and other kitchen equipment, and furniture in your pizza restaurant. And suppose you have $2 per pizza in *variable costs* for labor and for pizza and other ingredients. To achieve the *break-even point*, you need to sell 100,000 pizzas a year at $4 each. That is:

$$\text{Break-even point} = \frac{\$200{,}000}{\$4 - \$2} = \frac{\$200{,}000}{\$2} = 100{,}000 \text{ pizzas}$$

Source: Luiz Rocha/Shutterstock.

⑭ **Break-even.** Running a pizza restaurant—how hard could it be? Plenty hard, actually, if you don't understand your costs. The failure of owners and managers to work through the crucial details associated with correctly pricing their products has been the ruin of many businesses, especially small ones. The first lesson: pricing your product begins with computing your break-even point.

Any pizza sold for under $4, then, won't achieve the break-even point.

Note that the break-even analysis does not provide you with a *profit,* for which you would have to add more money—a dollar more on the price, say—which is above and beyond your fixed and variable costs. Note also that break-even analysis has nothing to do with the prices charged by your competitors, who may have figured out how to make pizzas for less than $4 apiece. ⑭ ■

Principal Pricing Strategies: Three Approaches

How would I explain cost pricing, target costing, and competitive pricing?

There are three principal strategies for pricing a product or service. They are . . .

1 To Cover Costs of the Product & Profit: Cost Pricing

Some companies favor *cost pricing,* **in which the cost of producing or buying the product—plus making a profit—is the primary basis for setting price.**

We demonstrated this kind of pricing in the pizza break-even analysis example above, in which we determined the cost of making each pizza, then added a $1 profit.

Strictly speaking, this approach to pricing ignores market forces, such as the efforts of competitors to undercut you.

2 To Meet Optimum Pricing, Profit, & Production Goals: Target Costing

Unlike cost pricing, target costing considers market forces. In *target costing,* **a company starts with the price it wants to charge, figures out the profit margin it wants, then determines what the costs must be to produce the product to meet the desired price and profit goals.** This is the method used by Nike Shoes and by Starbucks: the companies find out the price consumers are willing to pay, determine the desired profit, then figure out what they will have to pay to make the product—and if they can't get the production costs low enough, the product won't get made.

■ **Example of Target Costing: Isuzu Motors.** Japanese automakers (and many other Japanese companies) often do market research to find the optimum market price. They then determine their profit margin and calculate how they can hold down materials, labor, and manufacturing costs to still be able to make a competitive, profitable product. ■

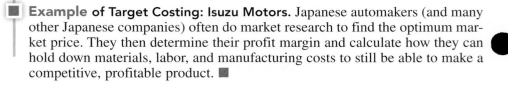

3 To Compete with Rivals: Competitive Pricing

In *competitive pricing,* **price is determined in relation to rivals, factoring in other considerations such as market dominance, number of competitors, and customer loyalty.**

■ **Example of Competitive Pricing: Cellphone Calling Plans.** The competition between AT&T, Sprint, Verizon Wireless, and T-Mobile is brutal. Each one aggressively prices its calling plan options in relation to competitors—and forcefully promotes the results in the media. ■

Alternative Pricing Strategies: Six Other Approaches

How would I distinguish among six alternative pricing strategies?

Besides the three foregoing principal strategies, there are six alternative pricing strategies. These are . . .

1 To Price the Product High When There's Little Competition: Price Skimming

To recover its high research and development costs on a product, a company may resort to *price skimming,* **setting a *high* price to make a large profit; it can work when there is little competition.** Naturally the big profits will quickly attract competitors.

■ **Example of Price Skimming: Amazon's Kindle.** When it was introduced in November 2007, the Kindle e-book reader was priced at $399. Then, as Amazon began to experience competition not only from other e-book readers (such as Barnes & Noble's Nook) but also tablet PCs (Apple's iPad) and even smartphones, the company gradually dropped the price. By 2011, the smaller Kindle was down to $79. ⓯ ■

2 To Price the Product Low to Attract Lots of Customers & Deter Competitors: Penetration Pricing

Penetration pricing **is setting a *low* price to attract many customers and deter competition.** This pricing strategy is designed to generate customers' interest and stimulate them to try out new products. Example: Hewlett-Packard used penetration pricing when it introduced its DeskJet color printer. Two years later, when it had a high market share, it dropped the price even lower—by half.

3 To Set Regular Prices for Products but Then Offer Special Sales to Undercut Competitors: Discounting

Discounting, **or** *high-low pricing,* **is assigning regular prices to products but then resorting to frequent price-cutting strategies, such as special sales, to undercut the prices of competitors.** A drawback of this strategy is that customers may tend to wait for the sales to do their shopping.

■ **Example of Discounting: Department Store Sales.** Sears, Macy's, JCPenney, and even upscale department stores such as Neiman Marcus and Saks Fifth Avenue periodically hold sales, both to attract customers and to clear out inventory. These may be called white sales, red tag sales, January sales, or some other name.⓰

Goliath, meet David.

The all-new NOOK. The Simple Touch Reader™.
Smaller, lighter, and twice the battery life of Kindle™™
"Blows the current Kindle out of the water." —ZDNET, 05/24/2011
Touch the all-new NOOK at your neighborhood Barnes & Noble or NOOK.com

Only $139.

nook
by Barnes & Noble

READ FOREVER™

⓯ **Starting high.** When Amazon had the market for e-book readers mostly to itself, it could afford to price its Kindle at the high price of $399. However, the strategy of price skimming attracted competitors, such as the Nook from Barnes & Noble, forcing prices down. Would you be willing to pay an extra $25 for the color feature offered by Nook?

⓰ **Discounted!** A regular feature of retail life, sales come with all kinds of promotional handles: *red-tag, white, special, pre-Christmas, post-Christmas, winter clear-out,* and so on. In a red-tag sale at a furniture store, the deals are promoted with tags or stickers affixed to discounted items. In your experience, how powerful is this type of pricing strategy as an incentive to buy?

A recent development is *personalized discounting,* in which, using computers, a store such as Sam's Club will offer bargains tailored to each member, based on that member's buying history.[45] ■

4 To Price Products Lower Than Competitors' & Have No Special Sales: Everyday Low Pricing

Unlike discount pricing, *everyday low pricing (EDLP)* **is a strategy of continuously setting prices lower than those of competitors and then not doing any other price-cutting tactics such as special sales, rebates, and cents-off coupons.** Example: Walmart might have been the first to undercut the traditional department stores (Macy's, JCPenney) by having an EDLP policy, but others quickly followed suit: Costco, Kmart, Home Depot, Lowe's, and Dollar Stores.

5 To Price Two or More Products Together as a Unit: Bundling

Bundling **is the practice of pricing two or more products together as a unit,** such as a burger, fries, and soft drink (Burger King); a shirt and tie (Men's Wearhouse); or a washer and dryer (Sears). At the height of the Great Recession, when careful, reluctant consumers forced retailers to lower their prices again and again, stores began to resort to bundling to clear store shelves. "Buy a laptop, get a free printer, ink cartridges—and paper," as one industry analyst explained.[46]

6 To State Prices in Odd, Not Even, Dollar or Cents Amounts to Make Products Seem Less Expensive: Psychological Pricing

Psychological pricing, **sometimes called** *odd-even pricing,* **is the technique of pricing products or services in odd rather than even amounts to make products seem less expensive.** This is the technique in which a used car is advertised for $5,999 instead of $6,000 or pizza for $11.99 instead of $12.00. However, there are other aspects of psychological pricing as well. "When we look at prices, we make judgments in a fraction of a second," explains Cornell University marketing professor Manoj Thomas. "We read from left to right. We anchor our judgment on the first thing we see."[47]

■ **PANEL 13.8 Psychological pricing.** How prices are set for psychological advantage.

- Round numbers (e.g., $450,000) signal *quality or prestige,* whereas precise numbers (e.g., $451,435) suggest a *lower-priced good or bargain.*

- Buyers focus on the first digit of a price, so $4,999 *seems far cheaper* than $5,000.

- People tend to subconsciously interpret precise numbers as being smaller than round ones.

- If you cut your asking price, make it easy for buyers to *calculate the discount;* otherwise, they may perceive only a small difference (e.g., cut from $595,395 to $580,395, not to $578,495).

BRIEFING / PERSONAL FINANCE
Psychological Pricing Uses Fact That Precise Numbers Seem Cheaper Than Round Numbers. Although we all know that $11.99 is barely less than $12, retailers continue to use this tactic. Why? Because it works! This is knowledge you can use to sharpen your own personal finance skills.

However, there are other aspects of psychological pricing as well. Which costs more—a house priced at $450,000 or a house priced at $451,435? According to Cornell research that looked at 27,000 real estate transactions, many people say the precise price ($451,435) is *less expensive,* even though it is not. The reason, it's suggested, is that we tend to use precise numbers for small amounts and round numbers (those with lots of zeros) for large ones. Thus, sellers of a house can make prospective buyers perceive the price is smaller than it is by replacing zeros with other digits.[48] ■

Some other aspects of psychological pricing are shown at left.[49] (*See* ■ *Panel 13.8.*)

Credit Terms: Another Inducement

How can credit terms be used competitively?

TV is full of them—commercials such as "NO PAYMENTS UNTIL 2013!" Or, "72 MONTHS TO PAY!" And so on.

Credit can certainly be used as part of a company's pricing marketing strategy to stimulate business. A firm can . . .

- Offer credit terms with no (or small) down payment, as in a car dealer's commercial jingle—"One-ninety-nine down delivers your next car at Diamond Motors."
- Offer a zero interest rate for a period of time, as for a year.
- Extend the time period of payments.
- Lower interest rates for preferred or prompt-paying customers.
- Offer a discount for early-paying customers.

This concludes our discussion of the first two of the 4-Ps—product and pricing. In the next chapter we consider place (distribution) and promotion.

Want to Know More? 13-12

Buy Now, Pay Later: Impact of Credit Inducements in Advertising

Go to www.mybizlab.com.

LEARNING & SKILLS PORTFOLIO

Summary

13.1 The Start of Product Strategy: Determining the Total Product Offer

THE ESSENTIAL QUESTION: *If I want to develop a product, what do I need to understand before I begin?*

What is a total product offer, and what are the kinds of markets for which it is intended? The total product offer is all factors potential buyers evaluate in a product when considering buying it.

How do markets for individual/household consumers differ from those for business? The consumer market, composed of all individuals or households wanting goods or services for personal use, consists of four classes of consumer goods and services: (1) convenience, or inexpensive products that people buy frequently and with little effort; (2) shopping, or more expensive products people buy after comparing for value, price, quality, and style; (3) specialty, or very expensive products with unique characteristics that buyers must make a special effort to obtain; and (4) unsought, or products people have little interest in, are unaware of, or didn't think they needed. The business market consists of those businesses that want industrial goods, products used to produce other products.

13.2 Innovation, the Product Life Cycle, & the New-Product Development Process

THE ESSENTIAL QUESTION: *Why is product innovation necessary, and how is it done?*

What are the three types of innovation? An innovation is a product that customers perceive as being newer or better than existing products. Innovation is necessary because of product obsolescence, frequent failure of new products, and long development time for some products. Three types of innovation are (1) continuous innovation, modest improvements to an existing product in order to distinguish it from competitors and requiring little consumer behavior change; (2) dynamically continuous innovation, marked changes to an existing product that require a moderate amount of consumer behavior change; and (3) discontinuous innovation, a totally new product, radically changing how people live.

How would I summarize the product life cycle? A product life cycle consists of the four stages a product goes through during its "life" of marketability: (1) introduction—a new product is introduced to the marketplace; (2) growth—customer demand increases, the product's sales grow, and later competitors may enter the market; (3) maturity—the product starts to fall out of favor, and sales and profits level off; and (4) decline—the product falls out of favor and is withdrawn.

How should a firm go about developing a product? The six stages in developing a new product are (1) idea generation, coming up with new product ideas; (2) product screening, elimination of product ideas that are not feasible; (3) product analysis, doing cost estimates to calculate the product's possible profitability; (4) product development, building of a product prototype, a preliminary version; (5) test marketing, introduction of a new product in limited form to test consumer reactions; and (6) commercialization, full production and marketing.

13.3 Product Differentiation: Creating Product Differences by Branding & Packaging

THE ESSENTIAL QUESTION: *In what ways are branding and packaging used to differentiate a product?*

How would I define "brand," and how would I describe the three classes of brands? Product differentiation is the attempt, using branding and packaging, to design a product so it will be perceived differently from competitors' products and will attract consumers. A brand is a unique name, symbol, and/or design that identifies an organization and its product or services. A firm may have a brand manager responsible for the key elements of the marketing mix—product, price, place, and promotion—for a brand or product line. Three classes of brands are brand names, which can be expressed verbally, as by words, letters, or numbers; brand marks, which cannot be expressed verbally, such as graphics and symbols; and trademarks, which are brand names and brand marks with exclusive legal protection.

How would I distinguish the four different types of brands from one another? Manufacturers' brands are those attached to products by firms that distribute nationwide or worldwide. Private-label brands are those attached to products distributed by one store or chain. Family brands are those in which the same brand name is given to all or most of a company's products. Individual brands are different brand names given to different company products. Sometimes two companies will do co-branding, linking two noncompeting products' brand names together for one product.

What are four reasons brands are valuable? The reasons are to publicize the company name and build trust, to differentiate the company's product from competing products, to get repeat sales, and to make entering new markets easier.

What is brand equity, and what are the three degrees of brand loyalty? Brand equity is the marketing and financial value derived from the combination of factors that people associate with a certain brand name. Three degrees of brand loyalty, or commitment to a particular brand, are (1) brand

awareness—consumers recognize the product; (2) brand preference—consumers habitually buy the product but will try alternatives if they can't find it; and (3) brand insistence—consumers will accept no substitutes.

What are five functions of packaging? Packaging, the covering or wrapping that protects and promotes a product, has five functions: to protect the product, help consumers use it, provide information about it, indicate price and universal product codes, and promote the product.

13.4 Pricing Strategies: What Will Customers Pay?

THE ESSENTIAL QUESTION: *How is pricing important, and what are the various pricing strategies?*

What are five objectives when assigning prices to things? Five pricing objectives marketers hope to achieve in pricing products are (1) achieve a target return on investment, or make a profit; (2) match or beat the competition; (3) attract customers, as by using low pricing (loss leaders) to increase market share; (4) make products more affordable to certain people; and (5) create prestige.

How does break-even analysis work? Break-even analysis is a way of identifying how much revenue is needed to cover the total costs of developing and selling a product. It tries to find the break-even point, where sales revenues equal costs and there is no profit but also no loss. To do so, marketers must determine fixed costs, expenses that don't change regardless of how many products are made or sold, and variable costs, expenses that vary depending on the numbers of products produced.

How would I explain cost pricing, target costing, and competitive pricing? In cost pricing, the cost of producing the product—plus making a profit—is the primary basis for setting price. In target costing, a firm starts with the price it wants to charge, figures out the profit it wants, then determines what the costs must be to produce the product to meet those goals. In competitive pricing, price is determined in relation to rivals, factoring in other considerations such as market dominance, number of competitors, and customer loyalty.

How would I distinguish among six alternative pricing strategies? Price skimming, setting a high price to make a large profit, can work when there is little competition. Penetration pricing is setting a low price to attract many customers and deter competition. Discounting is assigning regular prices to products but then resorting to frequent price-cutting strategies, such as special sales. Everyday low pricing (EDLP) is a strategy of continuously setting prices lower than those of competitors and then not doing any other price-cutting tactics. Bundling is the practice of pricing two or more products together as a unit. Psychological pricing is the technique of pricing products or services in odd rather than even amounts to make products seem less expensive.

Key Terms

brand 398
brand awareness 400
brand equity 400
brand insistence 401
brand loyalty 400
brand manager 398
brand marks 398
brand names 398
brand preference 400
break-even analysis 405
break-even point 405
bundling 408
co-branding 399
commercialization 395
competitive pricing 407
consumer market 387
continuous innovation 390
convenience goods and services 387
cost pricing 406
decline stage 394
discontinuous innovation 391

discounting 407
dynamically continuous
    innovation 391
everyday low pricing (EDLP) 408
family brands 399
fixed costs 405
growth stage 393
idea generation 395
individual brands 399
industrial goods 389
innovation 390
introduction stage 392
knockoff brands 401
loss leaders 404
manufacturer's brands 398
market share 404
maturity stage 394
packaging 401
penetration pricing 407
price skimming 407

pricing objectives 403
private-label brands 398
product analysis 395
product development 395
product differentiation 397
product life cycle 392
product manager 398
product screening 395
prototype 395
psychological pricing 408
shopping goods and services 388
specialty goods and services 388
target costing 406
target return on investment 403
test marketing 395
total product offer 386
trademarks 398
universal product codes (UPCs) 402
unsought goods and services 388
variable costs 405

Pop Quiz Prep

1. How is the *total product offer* defined?
2. What items would be classified as convenience goods and services?
3. Which degree of innovation is characterized by marked changes to an existing product that require a moderate amount of consumer learning or behavior change?
4. Which is the most profitable stage of the product life cycle?
5. McDonald's golden arches, the Nike swoosh, and the Shell seashell sign are examples of what?

6. Zealous baseball fans who move across the country and continue to root for the New York Mets and buy the team's merchandise are displaying what?
7. A business has $300,000 a year in fixed costs and variable costs of $1 for each widget it produces. If it charges $3 per widget, what is its break-even point?
8. How does competitive pricing work?

Critical Thinking Questions

1. It's hard to turn a corner these days without seeing a billboard or advertisement for an iPad or a tablet computer. Consider the components of a total product offer, or the factors that potential buyers evaluate in a product when considering whether to buy it: advertising image, availability, brand name, consumer's prior experience, convenience, financing, guarantees, Internet access, maker's reputation, packaging, price, product labeling, retailer's environment, service, and warranty. What parts of the total product offer would induce you to buy an iPad or a tablet computer?

2. In 2008, Tata Motors introduced the world's most inexpensive car, called the Nano. The car was introduced in India to meet the increased demand among those able to achieve urban prosperity and freedom. The Nano is a small four-seater in the shape of an egg, with a list price in the $3,000 range.[50] Can you surmise what Tata's pricing strategy was when it introduced this car, and would you be reluctant to purchase a "no-frills" vehicle like this if it had been for sale in the United States?

3. "Cupidtino" (a hybrid of the words *Cupid* and *Cupertino*, a city in California where Apple is headquartered) is a micro-niche dating website started by Mel Sampat, a former program manager at Microsoft.[51] The cupidtino.com website states: "Diehard Mac & Apple fans often have a lot in common—personalities, creative professions, a similar sense of style and aesthetics, taste, and a love for technology. We believe these are enough fundamental reasons for two people to meet and fall in love, and so we created the first Mac-inspired dating site to help you find other Machearts around you."[52] Do you agree that Apple fans have a lot in common? Do you think our product purchases and brand loyalties truly reflect who we should date and have a relationship with?

4. Amazon and eBay have both released a free price comparison app for the iPhone that allow users to quickly compare in-store prices with the prices of products on Amazon.com and eBay. By snapping a photo, scanning a bar code, or speaking or typing in the name of a product, the app gives you information as to whether the product is cheaper at

the brick and mortar store or on the website. The app even allows users the option to purchase the item for delivery in a single click.[53] What impact does this have on the retailer whose bar code is being scanned? Would you use this pricing app? What limitations are there?

5. The word *freemium* (derived from the words *free* and *premium*) is a business model and pricing strategy popular among Web startups that offer a product or basic service free of charge with the option to upgrade at a cost.[54] The goal is to get users to try a product first, and then later to subscribe to a premium or enhanced version of the basic product or service at a cost.

What are some of the benefits of a freemium model? Please give examples of companies offering the freemium business model. What similarities do these companies have? Explain.

Cases

VIDEO CASE STUDY
Smashburger: "Does America Need Another Hamburger Joint?"

The Smashburger video opens with the question, "Does America need another hamburger joint?" According to Tom Ryan, founder of Smashburger, there *is* plenty of room for another burger joint. Smashburger began in 2007 with $15 million of initial funding from Consumer Capital Partners, a private investment firm. Smashburger's name comes from the fact that each burger is "smashed" on the grill for ten seconds to sear in the flavors and juices.

Smashburger is managed by two industry veterans, Tom Ryan and David Prokupek. Ryan, founder and chief concept officer, has 20 years of experience in marketing, branding, consumer research, and concept/product development for package goods and restaurant/retail companies, including Quiznos (where he serves on the board of directors), McDonald's (previous EVP worldwide chief concept officer), and Long John Silver's. Prokupek, CEO and chairman, also serves as managing partner and chief investment officer of Consumer Capital Partners, the company providing the initial funding for this startup.

Ryan's experience in product development is apparent in Smashburger's diversified menu offering "something for everyone." "It doesn't feel like a fast food restaurant," comments Ryan, who has developed menu items that include fresh ingredients and gourmet sides such as rosemary, olive oil, and garlic French fries; veggie frites (flash-fried asparagus spears, green beans, and carrot sticks); fried pickles; and sweet potato fries and salad offerings.[55]

According to Ryan, Smashburger provides the sort of ambiance not generally found at fast-food restaurants—a place with "pizazz" that has quality ingredients, real silverware, modern seating, table service, upscale table baskets, mood lighting, and "cool music in the background."

Ryan states that one aspect of the unique, differentiating concept of Smashburger is its pricing strategy. While doing market research, Ryan says he found a "market gap" in what consumers were looking for in a burger place—a speedy service level with quality ingredients. In a fast-food environment, quality can be compromised for speed of service. "If the price is too high, there isn't enough service to justify the cost, and if it's too low, you can't deliver the food quality you want," Ryan states. Smashburger's pricing strategy is to juggle speed with quality—to price a gourmet burger, both in size and ingredients, for under $10 (their burgers start at $5.99) at a speed

similar to that at McDonald's. Additionally, unlike competitors' bundled pricing, the whole family can enjoy the a la carte menu items by mixing and matching.

Prokupek believes that Smashburger has achieved its goal by providing a good value with premium pricing. "Start a little higher," he says, "because it's easier to go down in price, but not back up." And so far, Smashburger's premium price strategy has been nothing but a smashing success. Does America need another Smashburger? Apparently so—the company continues to expand by adding franchises.

What's Your Take?

1. What concepts from the chapter are shown in the Smashburger video?

2. What differentiators did Tom Ryan use to justify Smashburger's premium pricing? What challenges were there when deciding upon this pricing structure?

3. How would you answer the question asked in the opening of the video, "Does America need another hamburger joint?" Discuss.

4. How does Smashburger justify debundling as its pricing structure in comparison to its competitors' combo pricing? What challenges were there when justifying this pricing?

5. What are your priorities when eating at a fast-food burger place? (If you do so rarely or not at all, ask three friends what their priorities are when eating fast food.)

Choice: "More Is Better" or "Less Is More"?

Have you ever felt stuck trying to make a choice when you are purchasing something as simple as toothpaste, orange juice, shampoo, a pair of jeans, or even milk? Do you ever feel like you spend twice as long searching for something on the Internet because there are so many options? And how do you choose among 900 cable channels when deciding what to watch on TV? If the dazzling array of choices presented to you for even simple decisions sometimes leaves you feeling stymied, you are not alone.

A well-known consumer behavior study conducted in 1975 by Sheena Iyengar showed how "too much choice" can have an impact on the sale of a product. Iyengar and her students set up a jam (as in jelly) tasting booth at a California gourmet market. Customers were offered a selection of 6 to 24 jams, and each customer was given a promotional "dollar off" coupon to encourage purchase of the jam. Surprisingly, while more customers stopped at the booth when there was a larger assortment (60% compared to 40% for a smaller assortment), more customers bought jam when the smaller assortment was offered (30% for the small, and only 3% for the large).[56] Does presenting fewer options lessen the angst over decision making?

In his book, *The Paradox of Choice: Why More Is Less*, author Barry Schwartz concludes that too much choice causes anxiety and can lead to depression. "A bewildering array of choices floods our exhausted brains, ultimately restricting instead of freeing us," he says.[57] Despite these findings, many consumer product companies ignore the fact that too much choice isn't always a good thing, because to them, more products (resulting in more product lines and product mixes) potentially translate into increased profits. With the lure of profits and goals of increasing brand recognition, these companies continue to create different flavors, forms, colors, package sizes, and added ingredients. Comments a *Wall Street Journal* reporter, "is it really customers they're thinking about when they roll-out the 94th variety of toothpaste or the 116th type of household cleaner?! I don't think so."[58]

Some companies have embraced the idea that shopper confusion and anxiety can actually decrease sales. In 2009, Glidden Paints decided to reduce its palette of wall colors from over 1,000 down to 282.[59] In-N-Out Burger is a classic example of a "less is more" approach with their smaller menu that focuses on quality. Even Walmart is considering the depth (think: product line) and breadth (think: product mix) of product assortment choices.[60]

Apple cut out nearly all choice when they introduced MacBook Pro—over five total products, there are fewer than ten choices.[61] But wait a minute. Can you even decide with as few as ten choices?

What's Your Take?

1. Do you agree with the argument that the vast number of choices actually limits our freedom because of the amount of time it takes to make a decision? Discuss the relationship between choice and the amount of time you spent on a recent purchase.

2. Have you ever tried to decide about a purchase only to leave undecided and frustrated? Has trying to make a choice about a purchase ever caused you anxiety? If so, explain the type of purchase it was.

3. What products have you purchased recently where you experienced way too much choice and had difficulty deciding? If you don't ever have this problem, explain why.

4. Consumer behavior consultant Philip Graves, author of *Consumer.ology,* has compiled the following list of some of the reasons consumers have a difficult time making a choice:

   - "Difficulty choosing between similar options.
   - Difficulty selecting any one option as the better.
   - Confusion over which product variable or attribute to attach most importance to.
   - Anxiety about how they will feel about a choice they're inclined toward, knowing that a particular (and also attractive) alternative was available at the time they chose.
   - Customers may simply run out of energy (studies show cognitive processes burn glucose in a similar way to physical exercise)."[62]

Have you ever had a difficult time deciding because of any of the factors listed, and if so, what was the impact on your decision?

Go to www.mybizlab.com for online activities and exercises related to the timely topics discussed in this chapter's Briefings, as well as additional theme-related Briefing *Spotlights* highlighting how these concepts apply in today's business environment.

In-chapter Briefing:
- Is the United States Ready for a "Credit Card Phone"?
- Growth of the Kindle E-Book

Activity:
- Developing Marketable Business Skills – McDonald's: Burgers Flip & Some Products Flop
- Going to the Net! – Product Life Cycles: Pet Products, Gluten-Free Foods, & Typewriters

Briefing Spotlight:
- Netflix Price Change Backfires, Customers Rant

In-chapter Briefing:
- The Total Product Offer of the Toyota Prius

Activity:
- Going to the Net! – Forget the Milk! Bag or Box with Your Cereal?

Briefing Spotlight:
- UsedCardboardBoxes .com Owner Thinks Outside the Box

In-chapter Briefing:
- Are "Toning Shoes"—a Dynamically Continuous Innovation—Too Risky?

Activity:
- Ethical Dilemma Case – Knockoffs: Is Imitation Really Sincerest Form of Flattery?

Briefing Spotlight:
- Subway to Sandwich Makers: "The Word FOOTLONG is Ours!"

In-chapter Briefing:
- Pricing to Create Prestige—Does High-Priced Wine Really Taste Better?
- Psychological Pricing Uses Fact That Precise Numbers Seem Cheaper Than Round Numbers

Activity:
- Maximizing Your Net Worth – The Automobile Purchase Decision: Don't Bite Off More Than You Can Chew

Briefing Spotlight:
- Beware Sly Offers That Are Really a Bank's Tactic to Recover Fees

In-chapter Briefing:
- A Pizza Restaurant Uses Fixed & Variable Costs to Calculate the Break-Even Point

Activity:
- Developing Marketable Business Skills – Interview a Small-Business Owner Regarding Pricing Strategies

Briefing Spotlight:
- "Goo-Goo-Ga-Ga": The Sound of Babies Providing Feedback for Product Development

In-chapter Briefing:	**Activity:**	**Briefing Spotlight:**
• Does Ikea's Inexpensive Furniture Put the Planet at Risk?	• Going to the Net! – Thirsty for More Profits with Ethos Water?	• IDEO.org Provides Sanitation Solutions in Ghana

Additional *Briefing Spotlights* available at MyBizLab:

• BUSINESS CULTURE & ETIQUETTE
• BUSINESS SKILLS & CAREER DEVELOPMENT
• CUSTOMER FOCUS
• GLOBAL BUSINESS
• INFO TECH & SOCIAL MEDIA

14 Distribution & Promotion Strategies

Managing for Efficient Supply Channels & Persuasive Communication

After reading and studying this chapter, you will be able to answer the following essential questions:

MyBizLab

Where you see MyBizLab in this chapter, go to www.mybizlab.com for additional activities on the topic being discussed.

FORECAST: What's Ahead in This Chapter

This chapter describes the last two of the 4-Ps of marketing—namely, place (distribution) and promotion. We discuss ways products are distributed and the intermediaries—wholesalers, agents and brokers, and retailers—who handle them. We explain how supply chains and logistics work. We cover the tools, goals, and strategies of promotion.

Gain hands-on experience through an interactive, real-world scenario. This chapter's simulation entitled Promoting a Product is located at **www.mybizlab.com**.

WINNER: Netflix Succeeds with "Clicks & Mail"

Netflix was created in 1997 in Scotts Valley, California, after one of its founders, Reed Hastings, misplaced a videotape of *Apollo 13* that he had rented and the video store charged him a six-weeks-late fee of $40. He realized he had a better idea in allowing video rental consumers to pay a monthly subscription rate, with unlimited due dates and no late fees. Users would place orders via the Internet and receive and return their videos by mail.

By 2005, however, Netflix was being written off by business experts as unlikely to survive. Netflix is "not a sustainable business," one analyst said. Successful Internet businesses, in his opinion, tended "to have a brick-and-mortar component." In other words, they had physical retail stores.[1]

Certainly Netflix had plenty to worry about in its competitors. Not only did it appear it might have to go head to head with Blockbuster, a 5,000-store chain founded in 1986, but it was also rumored that Walmart would launch video subscriptions by mail and that Amazon.com would also enter the market. Fortunately, Blockbuster delayed its entry into mail delivery, Walmart started but then withdrew this service, and Amazon skipped it altogether, instead going directly to video on demand.

However, Netflix's "first mover" status enabled it to take actions that put its competitors at severe disadvantage. For instance, writes San Jose State University business professor Randall Stross, Netflix engineers were able to bring operating costs down by secretly modifying standard bar-code sorting machines "to handle the odd-shaped envelopes used for DVDs. The machines read the DVD bar code that peeks through the window on the envelope, print the address, then send the envelope to the appropriate ZIP code bin for bulk mailing—dashing through 5,000 envelopes."[2]

Back in 2005, Netflix stock was trading in the $11 range. Six years later it was up to $191.

LOSER: Blockbuster Fails with "Clicks & Mortar"

In 2005, when Netflix looked most vulnerable, Blockbuster was riding high. Analysts considered it a "category killer," according to financial writer James Surowiecki. That is, it was the kind of business that killed off all competition in a category "by stocking a near-endless variety of products that small retailers couldn't match."[3] Category killers were expected to take over Web e-commerce the way they had taken over suburban shopping centers. Unlike new Internet companies, Blockbuster "had customer expertise, sophisticated inventory management, and strong brands." Thus, it was thought, the video-rental chain would "be able to offer customers both e-commerce and physical stores—'clicks and mortar.'"

Blockbuster was so invested in physical stores that it didn't recognize the importance of Web commerce, which it long dismissed as a "niche market." Thus, it took the chain almost three years after introducing its online store to integrate its bricks and clicks in a 2006 program that allowed users for a flat rate to rent unlimited videos ordered online and return them to a store instead of via mail. However, says Surowiecki, "the allure of this was lost on most people." The plan also forced the company to raise subscription prices, alienating many users.[4] In addition, Blockbuster spent "lots of money and time integrating an entirely new information-technology system into the one its stores already had."[5]

Long after Netflix demonstrated that a computerized "recommendation engine" could provide more personalized service than a store clerk could, Blockbuster continued to pour money into its physical stores. This reflected decisions of a staff that couldn't believe the old days were over, as well as reluctance to scrap a costly existing structure.

Then came the final straw: A competitor, Redbox, appeared with vending machines offering new rentals for just a dollar. In September 2010, Blockbuster declared bankruptcy.

Source: Photograph by Sally Lindsay.

Source: Chris Green/Shutterstock.

 YOUR CALL As the above rivalry shows, the ostensibly mundane subject of the third of the 4-Ps—place, or distribution—needs a marketer's full attention. With hindsight we can see what Blockbuster should have done. But what should Netflix do now? In late 2011, the company abruptly raised its prices and announced two business approaches to try to force its customers to choose among DVD by mail (to be called Quikster), access to online streams (to remain as Netflix), or both. The move incurred the loss of over a million wrathful customers, the company's stock plummeted, and Netflix abandoned its plans.[6] Was the company moving too fast? Or is it true that, in Surowiecki's words, "Sometimes you have to destroy your business in order to save it"?[7]

MyBizLab

The Distribution Mix: Marketing Channels

THE BIG IDEA: The third and fourth of the 4-Ps of the marketing mix are place (distribution) and promotion. Place is concerned with distribution channels, intermediaries, the distribution mix, and the distribution strategy. Distribution channels may be consumer or industrial, and they may involve such intermediaries as agents and brokers, wholesalers, and retailers, who add value to the products they handle. Three kinds of distribution strategy are intensive, selective, and exclusive.

THE ESSENTIAL QUESTION: What are the means of distributing products between producers and consumers?

MyBizLab: Check your understanding of these concepts at www.mybizlab.com.

Jeff Bezos created the online bookstore Amazon.com in Seattle in 1995, and in its initial days everyone did everything.

"When we started out," Bezos said later, "we were packing [books] on our hands and knees on these cement floors. One of the software engineers that I was packing next to was saying, 'You know, this is really killing my knees and my back.' And I said to this person, 'I just had a great idea. We should get kneepads.' And he looked at me like I was from Mars. And he said, 'Jeff, we should get packing tables.' We got packing tables the next day, and it doubled our productivity."[8]

The 4-P Marketing Mix Continued: Place (Distribution) Strategy & Promotion Strategy

How would I define the third and fourth of the 4-Ps of the marketing mix?

Packing tables might be the last thing on your mind when you think about marketing, but you can see how they might be an important, if undramatic, part of distribution, or place, one of the 4-Ps of the marketing mix. We covered the first two of the 4-Ps, product and pricing, in Chapter 13. In the present chapter we discuss . . .

* **The place strategy—"How do we place (distribute) the product in the right locations?"** *Placing,* or *distribution,* we said, is the process of moving goods or services from the seller to prospective buyers. We discuss distribution in the first half of this chapter.

* **The promotion strategy—"How do we communicate the benefits of the product?"** *Promotion* consists of all the techniques that companies use to motivate consumers to buy their products. We discuss promotion in the second half of this chapter.

Distribution Channels, Intermediaries, the Distribution Mix, & the Distribution Strategy

What are four important things to consider in moving a product from producer to consumer?

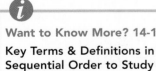

Want to Know More? 14-1

Key Terms & Definitions in Sequential Order to Study as You Go Along

Go to www.mybizlab.com.

Whatever your company's product, you need to figure out how to move it from the producer to the user, or consumer. This means you need to determine four things: (1) What *distribution channels* are available to us? (2) What *intermediaries,* or wholesalers and retailers, are in these channels? (3) What *distribution mix,* or combination of channels, should we use? (4) What should be our *distribution strategy*?

1 What Distribution Channels Are Available to Us?
Systems for Conveying Goods to Customers

A *distribution channel,* **also known as a *marketing channel,* is a system for conveying goods or services from producers to customers.** Example: T-shirts with slogans on them might move from producer to wholesaler to retailer to consumer. Or they might be marketed via the Internet directly to the consumer.

2 What Intermediaries Are in the Channels?
Agents/Brokers, Wholesalers, & Retailers

Intermediaries, **or *marketing intermediaries,* are the people or firms that move products between producer and customers.** They consist of *agents or brokers, wholesalers,* and *retailers.*

Agents and Brokers: Connecting Buyers and Sellers. *Agents* **and** *brokers* **are specialists who bring buyers and sellers together and help negotiate a transaction.** Examples: Real estate agents negotiate between house sellers and buyers. Grain brokers negotiate deals between farmers and grain buyers, such as Kellogg's, the cereal maker.

Wholesalers: Sellers to Resellers. *Wholesalers,* **also known as *middlemen,* are intermediaries who sell products (1) to other businesses for resale to ultimate customers or (2) to institutions and businesses for use in their operations.** ❶ Example: Makers of breakfast cereal, such as Kellogg's, sell products to wholesalers, who in turn sell them to grocery stores, such as Bunker Hill Market, a corner store in Boston.

Retailers: Sellers to Final Customers. *Retailers* **are intermediaries who sell products directly to customers.** Example: Bunker Hill Market sells Kellogg's Cornflakes directly to you.

3 What Distribution Mix Should We Use?
The Combination of Channels Available

The *distribution mix* **is the combination of distribution channels a company uses to get its products to customers.** For example, a producer might sell its products directly to the consumer or use all the intermediaries just described.

4 What Should Be Our Distribution Strategy?
The Plan for Moving Products to Customers

The *distribution strategy* **is the overall plan for moving products from producer to customers.**

BRIEFING / SMALL BUSINESS & ENTREPRENEURS
Distribution Strategy for an Entrepreneur's "Recipe Deck." A San Francisco woman writes to a business columnist that she has just self-published a "recipe deck," a boxed set of beautifully designed cards with recipes and tips for entertaining. "How do I find a distributor?" she asks.

Source: Richard B. Levine/Newscom.

❶ **Between catch and plate.** The Fulton Fish Market is a Bronx, New York, wholesale seafood market that is one intermediary in the distribution chain between the crews on fishing vessels who catch the fish and the restaurant or grocery that makes it available to you.

🔑 **Key Takeaway 14-1**
Four keys to distribution: channels, intermediaries, mix, and strategy.

Among the channels proposed by business writer Ilana DeBare: Besides selling directly to consumers herself and approaching local retailers, the woman could work with independent sales representatives, some of whom operate showrooms in regional marts like the San Francisco Giftcenter & Jewelry Mart. Or she could rent a booth at a trade show such as the San Francisco Gift Fair, which draws both sales reps and retail buyers.

She could also do a Web search for companies to warehouse and ship the recipe cards.[9] Out of such pieces of information, DeBare suggests, the woman should be able to determine a distribution strategy. ■

Types of Distribution Channels: Consumer & Business

What are six types of distribution channels?

We describe six types of distribution channels—four for consumer goods and services, two for business goods and services. (*See* ■ *Panel 14.1.*)

■ PANEL 14.1 **Six types of distribution channels.**

Consumer: Distribution channels for consumer goods and services

No intermediaries	Producer →→→→→→→→→→→→→→→→→→→→→→→→→→ Consumer			
1 intermediary	Producer →→→→→→→→→→→→→→→→→→→→ Retailer →→ Consumer			
2 intermediaries	Producer →→→→→→→→→→→→→ Wholesaler →→ Retailer →→ Consumer			
3 intermediaries	Producer →→ Agent/broker →→ Wholesaler →→ Retailer →→ Consumer			

Business: Distribution channels for business goods and services

No intermediaries	Business producer →→→→→→→→→→→→→→→→→→ Business user
1 or more intermediaries	Business producer →→ Agent or wholesaler →→ Business user

❷ **Flower District.** The Flower District of Downtown Los Angeles, the country's largest flower marketplace, is a six-block area of nearly 200 wholesale flower dealers. Flowers come from as far away as India (roses), Ecuador (carnations), and Thailand (orchids). Florists, event planners, and others who qualify can purchase goods at wholesale prices for resale to consumers, but during certain hours markets are also open to the public. What are the logistical challenges of transporting such a perishable product as flowers from all over the world?

Source: Photo courtesy Bloomin' News, Los Angeles Flower Market of the American Florists' Exchange, Ltd.

Distribution Channels for Consumer Goods & Services

There are four types of distribution channels for consumer goods and services, which range in intermediaries from zero to three (or even more).

No Intermediaries: Producer to Consumer—Direct Channel. A *direct channel* **is a distribution channel in which a producer sells directly to consumers,** using mail order, telemarketing, the Internet, and TV ads. Examples for goods are jewelry craftspeople who sell directly to customers at street fairs, small farmers selling at farmers' markets, and Dell Computer selling directly to customers. For services, an airline (producer) will sell you (consumer) a ticket directly, whether at the airport counter or via the airline's website.

One Intermediary: Producer to Retailer to Customer. This is a common form of distribution. As a goods example, Ford (producer) sells cars to dealers (retailers), who will sell to you (consumer). Or Coca-Cola (producer) sells soft drinks to 7-Eleven (retailer), which in turn sells them to you (consumer). For services, an airline (producer) may sell a block of tickets directly to Orbitz or Travelocity (wholesalers/retailers), who in turn sells a ticket to you (consumer).

Two Intermediaries: Producer to Wholesaler to Retailer to Consumer. In Los Angeles, flower growers (producers) bring their wares to the Flower District (site of various wholesalers), where florists (retailers) come to pick out their selections, which they ready for sale to consumers. ❷

Three Intermediaries: Producer to Agent/Broker to Wholesaler to Retailer to Consumer. Agents bring buyers and sellers together, for which they charge a fee, but at no point do they own the goods. A French winery (producer), for example, might convey, but not sell, wines to a U.S. company (agent or broker), which in turn conveys them to a wine distributor (wholesaler), which in turn sells wines to wine stores (retailers). For services, an airline (producer) will deal with a travel service (agent), who will help you (consumer) acquire a ticket.

Distribution Channels for Business Goods & Services

There are two types of distribution channels for business goods and services:

No Intermediaries: Business Producer to Business User. This direct distribution operates the same for businesses as for consumers. A rubber maker, for example, might sell directly to tire companies such as Goodyear.

One or More Intermediaries: Business Producer to Agent or Wholesaler. A Canadian forestry company that produces paper from wood pulp might sell huge rolls of paper to a paper merchant, who then sells it to newspaper or book printers.

    Incidentally, if intermediaries are eliminated, their functions must still be provided. For instance, if there's no wholesale wine broker to warehouse wine, the winemaker or the retail stores will have to do it.

Key Takeaway 14-2
Possible number of intermediaries: For consumers, 0, 1, 2, or 3. For businesses, 0 or 1 or more.

How Do Intermediaries Add Value to a Product?

Are intermediaries really needed? How do they add value to the products they handle?

It's a staple of ads from producers who sell directly to the public: "CUT OUT THE MIDDLEMAN, AND SAVE SAVE SAVE!!" Don't the middlemen—that is, intermediaries such as wholesalers and retailers—add to the final cost of the product? Actually, they probably help *lower* consumer prices. After all, most of us can't afford to travel to Michigan to buy cars from Ford or to Oregon to buy running shoes from Nike. Intermediaries add value by saving you time and money, for instance, or by doing some tasks better than you could.

    In Chapter 9, we talked about how operations processes add value to resources and convert them into products by changing their form. Intermediaries add value—or, as economists call it, ***utility*, want-satisfying ability**—to products by making them more useful or accessible to consumers. There are six ways to do this. (*See* ■ *Panel 14.2.*)

    Intermediaries add value by affecting . . .

1 Form: Changing Materials into Useful Products

Producers certainly provide form utility, changing raw materials into useful products, but so sometimes do intermediaries such as retailers, when they combine materials into useful products. Examples: A delicatessen makes you an off-the-menu sandwich to your specifications. Best Buy partner Velocity Micro builds custom-designed gaming systems and PCs.

2 Location: Selling Products Where People Want Them

Making products more available in location—that is, putting them *where* people want them—is a second way intermediaries add value. Example: Intermediaries move apples from orchards to stores, making it easier for you to shop for them.

■ **PANEL 14.2 Six ways intermediaries add value to products.**

Type of Value (Utility) Added	What It Means
1. Form utility	Changing raw materials into useful products
2. Location utility	Making products available where convenient
3. Time utility	Making products available when convenient
4. Information utility	Providing helpful information
5. Ownership utility	Helping customers acquire products
6. Service utility	Providing helpful service

Source: Jamie Pham Photography/Alamy.

③ Time and location. In a typical tweet, the Los Angeles–based Shrimp Pimp food truck used Twitter to notify "shrimpsters" that the truck would "be in Marina del Rey for lunch . . . 5454 Beethoven, 11:30–2:30. Come get a Victoria or Greek sandwich!" Do you think food trucks add more kinds of value to their products than restaurants in fixed locations?

3 Time: Selling Products When People Want Them

Making products more available at times *when* people want them is a third way intermediaries add value. Example: 7-Eleven and many other convenience stores are open 24 hours a day, seven days a week, so you can visit them anytime. ③

4 Information: Providing Knowledge about Products

Intermediaries provide information to help consumers make intelligent buying decisions about products, further adding value. Newspaper ads, for example, provide information about food availability, prices, and sales.

5 Ownership: Helping Customers Acquire the Products

Intermediaries add value by offering good credit terms and speedy delivery and installation. Sears and other sellers of household appliances routinely offer financing and delivery and installation of washers and dryers.

6 Service: Helping Customers Use the Products

Finally, intermediaries add value by providing service after the sale and showing consumers how to use the product. Example: A bicycle shop might show the buyer of a new bike how to change gears, repair tires, and so on and provide free service to tighten cables, chains, and the like within the first 30 days of the sale.

Distribution Strategies: Three Kinds of Market Coverage—Intensive, Selective, or Exclusive

How would I distinguish among distribution strategies?

How do you know which distribution channel is best? That depends on the kind of product you have and how many customers you want to expose it to. The general rule is: *Make the product available in whatever number of locations, great or small, are needed to satisfy customers.*

There are three kinds of distribution strategies, which are known as forms of **market coverage, or product distribution among locations.** They are (1) *intensive,* (2) *selective,* and (3) *exclusive.*

Intensive Distribution: "Let's Distribute as Widely as Possible"

Intensive distribution **means the product is distributed among as many locations as possible.**

■ **Example** of Intensive Distribution: Soft Drinks. If you own a Coca-Cola bottling plant, you want to distribute the beverage in many places—grocery, convenience, and liquor stores, as well as vending machines, ballparks, movie theaters, and college cafeterias. ■

Selective Distribution: "Let's Distribute Where the Product Will Get Special Attention"

In *selective distribution* **a product is distributed in preferred locations, where it will get special attention.** This strategy is used for clothes, furniture, and appliances.

BRIEFING / A WORLD OF CONSTANT CHANGE

How Selective Distribution of Luxury Goods Has Changed. Louis Vuitton handbags. Gucci shoes. Prada dresses. At one time these luxury goods from family-owned firms could be found only in upscale boutique stores in the fashion districts of New York, Paris, or Milan (exclusive distribution, described in the next section). Now, writes Dana Thomas in *Deluxe: How Luxury Lost Its Luster,* these and other luxury goods have evolved into a $157-billion-a-year mass market, whose products are sold at the nearest mall—the "corporatization of luxury."

The result is that they now lack the exclusivity, and often the quality craftsmanship, that gave them the elegant reputation that made them so desirable in the first place.[10] Even in mall stores, however, they are given selective—that is, preferential—distribution that gives them special attention. ■

Exclusive Distribution: "Let's Distribute in a Limited Way"

Exclusive distribution **means the product is distributed in only a few locations,** as was once the case for Gucci and Prada and is still for luxury cars.

■ **Example** of Exclusive Distribution: Expensive Cars. If you're the producer of quarter-million-dollar sports cars, such as Lamborghinis or Ferraris, you'll want to distribute them just to car dealers in wealthy areas such as Beverly Hills, California, or Palm Beach, Florida. ❹ ■

Source: Max Earey/Shutterstock.

❹ **Exclusivity.** You're not likely to see one of these Lamborghinis (about $202,000; 219 mph top speed) in the drive-thru lane at Dunkin' Donuts. Of the 30 Lamborghini dealerships in the United States, half are in well-off areas of California, Florida, and New York/New Jersey. There is one also in Honolulu, where the speed limit on the freeway—one of the world's shortest and busiest—is 60 mph. Do you suppose people buy cars like this mainly because they like the engine performance?

THE BIG IDEA: Intermediaries between producers and consumers consist of wholesalers, agents and brokers, and retailers. Wholesalers may be manufacturer-owned, full-service merchants, or limited-function merchants. Agents are intermediaries who tend to maintain long-term relationships with the people they represent; brokers are usually hired on a temporary basis. Retailers may be store retailers, such as product-line retailers, bargain retailers, and shopping centers; or nonstore retailers, such as vending machines, direct selling, direct marketing, video marketing, and online retailing.

THE ESSENTIAL QUESTION: How do the principal intermediaries differ from one another?

MyBizLab

MyBizLab: Check your understanding of these concepts at www.mybizlab.com.

Source: Courtesy of Famous Dave's of America.

⑤ Chocolate-covered bacon. Charlie Torgerson and Randy Jernberg joined forces with chocolatier Mary Leonard to offer this sweet-and-salty treat at the Minnesota State Fair. Pig Lickers™ consist of premium bacon coated with rich melted dark chocolate and are served cold. About 60,000 pieces were dipped for the most recent state fair. Yum.

Chocolate-covered bacon: It sounds terrible, but it tastes just right, says Joseph Marini III, a fourth-generation candy maker who sells the bacon bonbons from his store at the Santa Cruz Boardwalk in California. The Famous Dave's booth at the Minnesota State Fair also offers Pig Lickers™, dark chocolate–covered bacon pieces sprinkled with sea salt.[11] ⑤

What if Marini decided to go national? Then he would have to think about such basics as transportation, storage, sales, and advertising. In other words, he'd have to get involved with *intermediaries*—wholesalers, agents and brokers, and retailers. Let's consider these matters.

Wholesalers: Selling to Institutions or Retailers

What are the different types of wholesalers?

Wholesalers sell products (1) to other businesses for resale to ultimate customers or (2) to institutions and businesses for use in their operations. Retailers, by contrast, sell products directly to customers.

The three principal types of wholesalers are (1) *manufacturer-owned wholesalers*, (2) *full-service merchant wholesalers*, and (3) *limited-function merchant wholesalers*.

1 Manufacturer-Owned Wholesalers: The Producers Do All the Selling & Distribution

A *manufacturer-owned wholesaler* is a wholesale business that is owned and operated by a product's manufacturer. Some manufacturers want to do this to maintain full control over the selling and distribution of their products or because it costs them less than using independent wholesalers.

 BRIEFING / SOCIALLY RESPONSIBLE BUSINESS
Applying High Tech So Buyers Can Use Their Mobile Devices to Trace a Food's Source. What explains the rapidly growing popularity of farmers markets? Maybe it's the ability to look at the products and talk directly to the producers who are selling them.

In the wake of a 2006 deadly *E. coli* outbreak stemming from tainted spinach, consumers told the food industry they wanted to know where their food was coming from—they wanted to find out who was growing their greens. Thus, fresh food producers such as Sun World, which owns or controls most of the chain of production and distribution of its produce, starting with growing operations, decided they had to go high tech to build public confidence.

Sun World, Driscoll's berries, and other produce companies adopted a fresh food traceability system that let people use a computer or their mobile device, in one description, "to trace the source of fruits and vegetables, communicate with farmers, and even find out whether a particular product is on a government recall list."[12] A clamshell box of Sun World grapes, for example, carries a sticker with a HarvestMark code from YottaMark, a Redwood City, California, technology company that created the HarvestMark fresh food traceability solution. A consumer at Costco, say, can punch the code into the HarvestMark website or scan it with the company's free mobile phone application. In a second, he or she will have a history of the farm and contact information with the grower and intermediaries. "It's like putting the farmer in your kitchen," says a YottaMark spokesman. ⑥ ∎

⑥ Trust but verify. California-based Sun World, a major distributor of fruits and vegetables, places these special stickers on many of its products. With the right app (available free from the company), customers can scan the sticker with their smartphones to ascertain a food's growth and distribution history. What other products would you like to see use this tracking system?

Source: Photo courtesy of HarvestMark ©2011 YottaMark, Inc.

Two types of manufacturer-owned intermediaries are the *manufacturer's branch office* and the *manufacturer's sales office.*

Manufacturer's Branch Office: "We Sell Products and Carry Inventory." A *manufacturer's branch office* **is an office that is owned and managed by a manufacturer that not only has offices for sales representatives but also carries an inventory from which the staff can fill orders.** Examples: Car dealers and tire sellers generally are of this type.

Manufacturer's Sales Office: "We Sell Products but Don't Carry Inventory." A *manufacturer's sales office* **is an office that is owned and managed by a manufacturer and that has offices for sales representatives who sell products that are delivered at a later time.** Carpet makers, for example, may have showrooms where salespeople can show products, which are delivered to customers later from a separate warehouse.

2 Full-Service Merchant Wholesalers: Independents Take Over the Products & Provide All Services

A *full-service merchant wholesaler* **is an independently owned firm that takes title to—that is, becomes owner of—the manufacturer's products and performs all sales and distribution, as well as provides credit and other services.** Example: Beer distributors are one of these types.

3 Limited-Function Merchant Wholesalers: Independents Take Over the Products but Provide Only Some Services

A *limited-function merchant wholesaler* **is an independently owned firm that takes title to—becomes owner of—the manufacturer's products but performs only selected services,** such as storage only.

Three common types of limited-function wholesalers are (1) *rack jobbers,* (2) *cash-and-carry wholesalers,* and (3) *drop shippers.*

Rack Jobber: "We Provide Shelves of Products in Stores." A *rack jobber* **is a limited-function wholesaler who furnishes products and display racks or shelves in retail stores and shares profits with retailers.** Example: A candy vendor might put shelves of candy and gum in gas stations and split the profits. Magazines are often placed by rack jobbers. ⑦

⑦ Rack jobber's job. A magazine rack jobber enters into an agreement with a magazine publisher to market its publications to small markets, convenience stores, truck stops, and similar locations through strategically placed store racks. The jobber maintains the inventory and reports sales to the store manager, who pays the jobber for the merchandise sold, after subtracting the store's commission. Paperback books, novelties, and sweets are also distributed by jobbers.

Source: Photograph by Sally Lindsay.

Cash-and-Carry Wholesaler: "We Sell to Walk-in Customers Paying Cash." A *cash-and-carry wholesaler* is a limited-function wholesaler that sells mainly to small retailers, who come to the wholesaler, pay cash for a product, and carry it out ("cash and carry"). Nowadays such wholesalers take bank credit cards, but they don't offer financing or later-payment options. Staples and Costco are examples of stores that sell to small retailers (as well as to the general public).

Drop Shipper: "We Take Orders and Arrange for Shipment." A *drop shipper* is a limited-function wholesaler who owns (has title to) the products, but does not have physical custody of them. Rather, the drop shipper takes orders and has the producer ship the product directly to the customer. Sand, coal, lumber, and other bulky goods are often handled by drop shippers.

Agents & Brokers: People Who Bring Buyers & Sellers Together

What do agents and brokers do, and how do they differ?

Agents and brokers are specialists who bring sellers and buyers together and help negotiate a transaction. Their value to a manufacturer or producer is their knowledge of markets and their experience in merchandising.

How Do Agents Differ from Brokers?

What's the difference between agents and brokers?

- **Agents:** *Agents* tend to maintain long-term relationships with the people they represent. Examples: *Sales agents* (or *manufacturer's agents*) represent several manufacturers in one territory (but not competing products).
- **Brokers:** *Brokers* are usually hired on a temporary basis. Their relationship with the buyer or the seller ends once the transaction is completed. Example: Wine-grape brokers are hired by vineyards to sell a particular crop to the best-paying winery.

Some agents and brokers operate at the retail level, such as real-estate agents working for Coldwell Banker or RE/MAX and stockbrokers working for Merrill Lynch or Charles Schwab.

What Makes Agents & Brokers Different from Wholesalers & Retailers?

Why do we put agents and brokers in a special category, treating them neither as wholesalers nor as retailers? Here's why:

- Agents and brokers don't own—take title to—the products they handle.
- They usually don't carry inventory or provide credit.
- They earn fees or commissions (a percentage of the sales transaction) rather than profits.

Store Retailers: Selling to Ultimate Consumers

What are the two principal types of store retailers?

"When the going gets tough, the tough go shopping," according to the old joke. Where do most of us go? To retailers, of course, the intermediaries who sell products directly to ultimate customers. Here we discuss *store retailers*. In the next section we discuss *nonstore retailers*.

Store Retailers: Product-Line Retailers & Bargain Retailers

The roughly 2.3 million store retailers in the United States range from those with broad product lines, such as department stores and supermarkets, to bargain retailers, such as discount stores and warehouse clubs. (*See* ■ *Panel 14.3.*)

■ **PANEL 14.3 Types of retail stores.**

Type of Retailer	Description	Examples
Product-line retailers		
Department store	Sells a variety of products (e.g., furniture, clothes) in departmentalized sections	Bloomingdale's, JCPenney, Macy's, Nieman Marcus, Nordstrom, Saks Fifth Avenue, Sears
Supermarket	Sells mostly food and some nonfood products in specialized departments	Albertson's, Kroger, Piggly Wiggly, Publix, Safeway, Trader Joe's, Whole Foods, Winn-Dixie
Supercenter	Giant store selling wide variety of unrelated products	Kmart Super Centers, Super Target, Walmart Supercenters
"Category killer"	Sells huge variety of one type of product (may drive out smaller competitors)	Best Buy, Home Depot, Lowe's, Office Depot, Staples, Toys "R" Us
Convenience store	Sells staple convenience foods and other goods at convenient location/hours	AMPM, Circle K, 7-Eleven, gas station minimarts
Specialty store	Sells variety of goods in a narrow range	AutoZone, Barnes & Noble, Bath and Body Works, Foot Locker, Gap, IKEA, Radio Shack, Rite Aid, Victoria's Secret, Walgreens, Williams-Sonoma
Bargain retailers		
Discount store	Sells wide variety of merchandise at substantial price reductions	Dollar Stores, Dollar Tree, Grocery Outlet, Kmart, Target, Walmart
Warehouse club	Large, warehouse-style store selling food and general merchandise at discount prices	Costco, Sam's Club
Outlet store	Manufacturer-owned store selling discontinued or flawed products at discount	Burberry Outlet, Burlington Coat Factory, Liz Claiborne, Marshalls, Nike Outlet, Nordstrom Rack, TJ Maxx
Second-hand store	Sells used merchandise	Goodwill, Salvation Army

■ **Example of Store Retailers: Pushcarts and Kiosks—from Hot Dogs to Cellphones.** Most of us think of store retailers as being in buildings, but some specialty retailers operate from pushcarts, ranging from those selling hot dogs on the streets of New York to those selling belts and scarves in the walkways of shopping malls. Others operate from kiosks, ranging from outdoor drive-by booths selling lattes and cappuccinos to indoor stands in shopping centers selling cellphones. ■

Shopping Centers: From Strip Malls to Super-Regional Centers

Any and all of the above retail stores can be found in a shopping center, of course. Shopping centers can range from a strip mall of three stores along a major roadway to a regional shopping center, which has 1 to 5 anchor stores, such as supermarkets or department stores, and 40 to 175 specialty stores. There are also super-regional shopping centers, with more than 100 stores, including several department stores. The largest in the United States is the Mall of America in Bloomington, Minnesota, with more than 400 stores. ⑧

⑧ **The megamall.** Opened in 1992 near Minneapolis–St. Paul, the Mall of America is the second largest shopping center in North America (after the West Edmonton Mall in Alberta, Canada) and has 40 million visitors a year. How do you think online retailing will affect such huge walk-in shopping centers?

Source: Alamy.

Nonstore Retailers: From Vending Machines to Online Shopping

What are the principal types of nonstore retailers?

***Nonstore retailers* sell merchandise in ways other than through retail stores.** Even 10 years ago there were many forms of nonstore retailing, but the Internet has vastly expanded the possibilities.

Vending Machines: Push-Button Selling of Convenience Goods

Coin-operated *vending machines* selling convenience goods, such as candy and sodas, have been around seemingly forever. Now, of course, such push-button or lever-operated machines not only accept paper money and credit cards and make change but also sell a great many other kinds of products.

■ **Example of Vending Machine Products: Japan and Other Countries.** The Japanese have been particularly inventive with vending machines, which sell everything from beer to underwear to potted plants. Some vending machines in Japan can be accessed through cellphones. Among other products available in these machines: books (United Kingdom), gemstones (Australia), fish bait (Spain), even gold bars (Abu Dhabi). ■

Direct Selling: Door-to-Door Sales, House-Party Sales, & Multilevel Marketing

One of the oldest forms of nonstore retailing, ***direct selling* consists of face-to-face selling directly to customers in their homes or where they work.** Three types are *door-to-door, house-party,* and *multilevel marketing.*

Door-to-Door Selling: Face to Face with Individuals. This form, in which salespeople call directly on people at their homes or workplaces, has been successfully employed by sellers of brushes (Fuller Brush), cosmetics (Avon, Mary Kay), and vacuum cleaners (Hoover, Electrolux).

House-Party Selling: Face to Face with Groups. In this form, pioneered by Tupperware, a host has friends and acquaintances in for a "party" with refreshments, in return for a gift from a sponsor, who then does a sales presentation.

Multilevel Marketing: Selling Products & Recruiting Sellers. One variant of direct selling is ***multilevel marketing (MLM),* in which independent businesspeople, or distributors, sell products both on their own and by recruiting, motivating, supplying, and training others to sell those products, with the distributors' compensation being based on both their personal sales and the group's sales.** When a distributor has many "downliners," as they are called, working for him or her, clearly the compensation can be significant. Some multi-level marketing companies are Avon, Amway, and May Kay Cosmetics.

BRIEFING / LEGAL & ETHICAL PRACTICES

Weighing the Risks of Multilevel Marketing. MLM works on two levels, says business columnist Rhonda Abrams.[13] *Single-level sales* consist of your efforts selling a product, for which you get paid, either for your time or as a sales commission. *Multilevel programs* consist of you recruiting other participants, so you make money not only on your sales but also on the sales of the people you recruit.

Two drawbacks of MLM are: (1) You have to pay for the products and services you sell, plus samples and training materials and seminars. (2) You'll be advised to sell to your family and friends, which essentially turns them into "prospects," changing the personal relationship.

In addition, says Abrams, "MLM programs rank high on the list of fraud schemes."[14] Plaintiffs in a lawsuit against Fortune Hi-Tech Marketing accused the MLM company of being a "pyramid scheme" because salespeople are rewarded primarily for recruiting, not for product sales.[15] ■

Direct Marketing: Direct Mail, Catalog Marketing, & Telemarketing

Different from direct selling, **direct marketing is not done face to face but consists of selling directly to customers using mail or telephone.** There are three types of direct marketing: *direct mail marketing, catalog marketing,* and *telemarketing.* (We consider *online marketing* separately.)

Direct Mail Marketing: Letters, Brochures, and Pamphlets. *Direct mail marketing* **consists of mail promotions—letters, brochures, and pamphlets sent through the postal service to customers.** The names of consumers are culled from lists of target audiences that have been identified as likely prospects for specific products.

Catalog Marketing: Mail-Order Catalogs. *Catalog marketing,* **or** *mail-order marketing,* **consists of mailing customers catalogs, from which they may choose merchandise to be ordered via mail, telephone, or online.** The classic mail-order seller was Sears, whose Big Book catalog was mailed to up to 60 million customers a year, but it folded this operation in 1992 after years of losses. Today firms such as L.L. Bean and J. Peterman continue with catalog sales.

Telemarketing: Telephone Sales. Short for "telephone marketing," *telemarketing* **consists of using the telephone to sell products directly to customers.** Most of these systems use automated dialing, followed by either a recorded message or a sales pitch from a live person. Many customers who object to having their dinners interrupted by "junk phone calls" have put their numbers on the free National Do Not Call Registry (www.donotcall.gov).

Video Marketing: TV Shopping Channels & Programs

Best represented by QVC and the Home Shopping Network, *video marketing* **is marketing to consumers on television, either through special cable TV channels or through certain programs on regular TV channels.** In this form of non-store marketing, consumers are given a sales pitch by a TV salesperson and urged to call a toll-free number or go to a certain website to place their order.

⑨ Mail-order catalogs. Despite the growth in online shopping, catalogs are certainly not disappearing. Why? Many postal customers like receiving these free promotional pieces for particular areas of interest. Go online, urges one of several websites, and you can "request hundreds of free mail order catalogs, from apparel to woodworking." Some are even from overseas. Interested?

Source: Photograph by Sally Lindsay.

Want to Know More? 14-2
The Wheel of Retailing
Go to www.mybizlab.com.

Want to Know More? 14-3
Telemarketing Foe: The National Do Not Call Registry
Go to www.mybizlab.com.

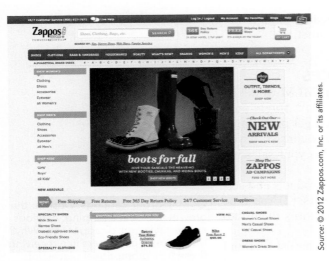

Source: © 2012 Zappos.com, Inc. or its affiliates.

Online Retailing: Electronic Catalogs, Virtual Storefronts, & Cybermalls

Online retailing, **or** ***electronic retailing,*** **is nonstore retailing of products directly to consumers using the Internet.** 🔟 New "e-tailers" such as online bookseller Amazon.com paved the way for this kind of retail marketing, and they were followed by conventional retailers, such as Barnes & Noble. Purveyors of services, such as Travelocity and Priceline, joined them, and new kinds of businesses such as Internet Auto also sprang up.

Three types of online retailing are shown below. (*See* ■ *Panel 14.4.*)

🔟 **Online shoes and apparel.** Owned by Amazon.com, Zappos (a variation on the Spanish word for shoes, *zapatos*) is the world's largest online shoe store, but it is not limited to footwear. There are currently about 50,000 variations of shoes in the Zappos inventory, including hard-to-find sizes and styles. Other products are clothing, eyewear, purses, and watches. How many customers would you guess are repeat buyers? (Answer: 75%.)

■ **PANEL 14.4** **Some types of online retailing.**

Type of Retailing	Description	Examples
Electronic catalogs (online catalogs)	Internet-based presentations of a retailer's products, including price and ordering information. The catalogs also offer the marketer 24-hour, worldwide exposure and the ability to show or describe products and to change prices and products quickly.	Tower Hobbies shows 8,000 radio-controlled vehicle products. Sears provides in-depth descriptions of 1,500 items.
Virtual storefronts (digital storefronts)	Internet-based stores that allow customers to view and order merchandise via their own computers. They offer product photos, company history, and special offers.	Four Seasons hotels show 3-D photos of their hotel rooms, plus offer maps to their locations and provide a history of the organization.
Cybermalls (virtual malls)	Internet sites that resemble shopping centers or department stores, allowing consumers to access a variety of stores.	The BlackHills.com Virtual Mall in South Dakota lists business categories, such as Adventure, Livestock, Saloons.

Want to Know More? 14-4

Greenwashing

Go to www.mybizlab.com.

BRIEFING / EARNING GREEN BY GOING GREEN

How Do You Know Eco-Friendly Claims Are True? Companies of all sorts have discovered that building a marketing strategy around sustainability can be a tremendous advantage.[16] The result is that there has been an explosion of eco-friendly seals and certificates on packaging—but not always a lot of verification.[17] The Federal Trade Commission has revised its "Green Guides" to try to distinguish *greenwashing*—misleading marketing about the environmental benefits of a product—from legitimate green products.

The environmental marketing firm TerraChoice offers a list of what it calls the "six sins of greenwashing."[18] Among the sins: "Hidden trade-off—Promotion of one aspect of a product as environmentally friendly while its negative impact is obscured." "No proof—environmental claims that can't be easily verified." Other sins may be found at http://sinsofgreenwashing.org/findings/the-seven-sins. ■

THE BIG IDEA: Physical distribution, the movement of all products from manufacturer to final buyer, involves a supply-chain sequence of suppliers and logistics, the details of transportation and warehousing that make distribution happen. Transportation may be by air, road, rail, water, or pipeline, with each having its own advantages. Warehousing may be simple storage of products for long periods of time or distribution storage for short periods of time.

THE ESSENTIAL QUESTION: What are supply chains and logistics, and how are transportation and warehousing involved?

MyBizLab: Check your understanding of these concepts at www.mybizlab.com.

"We tend to be the rogues of the airline world," says Tony Baca, a Boeing 747 cargo pilot. "The [passenger] airline pilot is all prim and proper. We're not. It's a whole different culture."[19]

Baca is a "freight dog," one of the on-call, hell-for-leather freight-cargo aviators so in love with flying that they're willing to endure terrible hours, bad food, lack of sleep, and third-world suicidal runways to ferry goods—car parts, videogames, canceled checks, roses, donor organs, whatever—to destinations anywhere in the world. Transporting goods would seem to be a very dull part of marketing, but that's not how a lot of pilots and truck drivers see it. For them, the king-of-the-road (or skies) cowboy culture endures.

Physical distribution **consists of all the activities required to move products from the manufacturer to the final buyer.** This is concerned with such questions as . . .

- **Order processing:** How quickly should orders be processed and products shipped?
- **Transportation:** How fast or how cheaply should goods be moved? What kind of transport—truck, train, plane, and so on—is best?
- **Storage:** Do we need to warehouse products at any stage? Where? Who should handle them?

Supply Chains & Logistics: Moving Products to the Final Buyers

What is supply-chain management, and how does the concept of logistics fit into it?

Getting products into the hands of customers involves a *supply chain,* **the sequence of suppliers that contribute to creating and delivering a product, from raw materials to production to final buyers.** (*See* ■ *Panel 14.5.*)

■ **PANEL 14.5 The supply chain.**

1. Raw materials
2. Suppliers' plants
3. Manufacturers
4. Wholesalers
5. Retailers
6. Consumers

🌐 **BRIEFING / GLOBAL BUSINESS**
The Supply-Chain Journey of an Ethan Allen Couch. A Discovery Channel documentary about today's China, *The People's Republic of Capitalism,* traces the supply-chain path of an expensive Pratt sofa made and sold by Ethan Allen.

Source: Photograph by Sally Lindsay.

⓫ The long supply chain. Fiji Water is not only transported from the remote Pacific island, but the raw materials for its distinctive square-shaped bottles must also travel thousands of miles to the bottler. The company is trying to reduce the carbon emissions arising from its long supply chain: ocean freight (23% of its carbon footprint), bottling (20%), and distribution (17%), as well as production of raw materials for packaging (29%). Still, many consumers are become increasingly aware that for energy efficiency it's hard to beat ordinary tap water, which is produced locally (and is also often purer than bottled water). When energy costs rise, what are the implications for lengthy supply chains like those for Fiji Water?

Want to Know More? 14-5
Bar Codes & Smart Tags
Go to www.mybizlab.com.

Cotton grown in North Carolina is sent to a fabric plant in China, where it is designed and weaved. That material is then shipped to an upholstery plant in Maiden, North Carolina, where factory workers using both handwork and computer technology construct the covering and part of the frame for the couch. A factory in China contributes part of the furniture's wooden base, which is sent to the North Carolina plant, where workers assemble the complete couch. After the sofa is inspected for quality, it is packed up, put on a truck, and sent to Long Beach, California, where it is put on a ship to China.

In China, furniture is distributed to one of Ethan Allen's 14 store locations—in this particular case, a store in Chongqing. The store delivers the Pratt couch to a wealthy Chinese couple, who paid the equivalent of $40,000 U.S. for it (in the United States, it would sell for $1,900).[20]

Can such long supply chains continue to endure? ⓫ Actually, increased fuel prices have already forced simplifications or cutbacks.[21] ■

Supply-Chain Management: The Strategy of Moving Materials & Products

With so many suppliers, kinds of transport, and materials, how do businesspeople control all this? This is the province of *supply-chain management,* **the strategy of planning and coordinating the movement of materials and products along the supply chain, from raw materials to final buyers.**[22]

Logistics: The Tactics of Moving Materials & Products

If supply-chain management is concerned with *strategy,* logistics is concerned with *tactics*—the actual movement of products. That is, *logistics* **consists of planning and implementing the details of moving raw materials, finished goods, and related information along the supply chain, from origin to points of consumption to meet customer requirements.** Often this requires sophisticated computer hardware and software to determine how to do it as efficiently and as cost-effectively as possible.

Logistics involves several forms of movement, of both goods and services *and* information, as shown opposite. (*See* ■ *Panel 14.6.*)

Transportation Trade-Offs: What's the Best Choice—Cheap, Fast, or Reliable?

What are five ways of transporting materials and products through the supply chain, and what are their benefits?

The five main ways of transporting materials and products through the supply chain are via (1) *rail,* (2) *road,* (3) *pipeline,* (4) *water,* or (5) *air.*[23] All businesspeople, great and small, should be aware of the trade-offs, opposite. (*See* ■ *Panel 14.7.*)

Rail Transport: Trains Are Best for Large, Bulky Items

Especially good for shipping bulky cargos—coal, wheat, automobiles—over long distances on a relatively energy-efficient basis, railroads handle the greatest volume of domestic goods in the United States, about 40%. Railroads have gone "piggyback," carrying truck trailers on special railcars, and "fishyback," carrying containers from oceangoing container ships.

Road Transport: Trucks Can Go Almost Anywhere

The benefit of trucks is that they can go practically anywhere and they can deliver goods door to door, which makes them the most flexible and convenient form of transport. The major drawback is that trucks are relatively expensive compared to the next three modes of transportation.

■ PANEL 14.6 **Four types of logistics.**

Type	Description	Example
Inbound logistics: movement from suppliers to producers	Involves bringing raw materials, packaging, other goods and services, and information from suppliers to producers	Book publishers bring together the materials from authors, illustrators, photographers to a production department for editing, typesetting, rendering, etc., to ready for the printer and binder.
Materials handling: movement of goods to and from and within producer's facilities	Movement of goods may be (1) within a warehouse, (2) from warehouses to factory floor, and (3) from factory floor to various workstations	Book printers and binders bring together electronically prepared plates, paper, and cover materials and prepare published books.
Outbound logistics: movement from producer to consumers	Involves managing the movement of finished products and information from producers to business buyers and final consumers	Published books are moved from the book bindery to a warehouse and then out to bookstores, such as Barnes & Noble.
Reverse logistics: movement from consumers back to producer	Involves bringing defective or unwanted products returned by consumers back to the producer or manufacturer for further handling, such as repair or recycling	Booksellers return their unsold books to publishers, who then sell them on secondary markets or destroy them.

■ PANEL 14.7 **Transportation modes compared.** Choosing among cost, speed, and reliability.

Mode	Percentage of U.S. Domestic Volume (Ton-Miles, 2006)	Cost	Speed	On-Time Dependability	Flexibility in Handling	Frequency of Shipments	Availability in Different Locations
Rail	40.0%	Average	Average	Average	High	Average	Extensive
Road	27.9%	High	Fast	High	Average	High	Very extensive
Pipeline	20.0%	Low	Slow	High	Very low	High	Very limited
Water	12.1%	Very low	Very slow	Average	Very high	Very low	Limited
Air	0.3%	Very high	Very fast	High	Low	Average	Average

Pipeline Transport: Pipelines Are Efficient for Liquids & Gas

You might not think of pipelines as transportation, but they are a surprisingly important kind of conveyance, moving about 20% of the total volume of U.S. domestic goods. Although the products they carry—liquids, such as oil, petroleum, or water, and natural gas—move a slow 3 to 4 miles an hour, they move steadily 24/7, mostly unaffected by weather or labor problems, making pipelines the cheapest mode of transportation.

Water Transport: Ships & Barges Are Cheapest but Slowest

Besides using planes, there is no other way to transport materials and finished goods to and from overseas points than by ship. However, within the inland waterways and the Great Lakes of the United States, ships and barges also are used to transport heavy, bulky cargos, such as sand, grain, and scrap metal, as well as standardized containers. Although water-borne transport is slow, it is also the cheapest method outside of pipelines.

Air Transport: Planes Are Fastest but Most Expensive

The primary benefit of shipping freight by plane is speed, which makes air freight appropriate for perishable products, such as seafood and flowers, and items that may be needed quickly, such as medicines. UPS and FedEx have their own fleets of planes for carrying overnight-delivery parcels and cargo, but many passenger airlines also carry freight cargo in addition to passengers' luggage in their holds. However, air freight is the most expensive form of transportation.

Combined Transport Modes: Intermodal Shipping & Containerization

Intermodal shipping, **which combines use of several different modes of transportation,** has become widespread, so that many railroads, for instance, have merged with trucking, air, and shipping companies to provide complete source-to-destination delivery.

Intermodal shipping goes hand in hand with *containerization,* **in which products are packed into 20- or 40-foot-long (by about 8-foot square) containers at the point of origin and retrieved from the containers at the point of destination.**[24] In between, the container may, for example, travel by truck to a ship, cross the ocean, be unloaded directly onto a dock, be placed on a railroad flatcar, transported by train across the country, and be unloaded onto a truck for delivery to the final destination.

A single container, incidentally, may be made up of several different, smaller cargos put together by a *freight forwarder,* **an organization that bundles many small shipments together into a single large shipment for more cost-effective transportation.** As you might expect, computers and software are a necessity in keeping track of all the parts and schedules of this complicated operation.

⑫ Materials handling. How efficiently goods are handled in warehouses can have a substantial impact on a company's profit. By effectively moving materials about, a company can reduce breakage and spoilage, expand the useful capacity of its storage facilities, and make its transport system more efficient. A key component of this, called *unit loading,* is to combine smaller boxes and containers into larger, standard-size ones (often stacking them on pallets, or skids) for more efficient handling.

Source: Dmitry Kalinovsky/Shutterstock.

Warehousing: Storing & Distributing Goods

What's the difference between storage warehouses and distribution centers?

Warehousing **is the element of physical distribution that is concerned with storage of goods.** Warehouses may be owned by the manufacturer (private warehouses) or be independently owned, storing goods for many companies (public warehouses). As mentioned in Panel 14.6, **the physical handling of goods to and from and within warehouses is called** *materials handling*. ⑫

Warehouses are of two types, as follows:

Storage Warehouses: For Long-Term Storage

Storage warehouses **provide storage of products for long periods of time.** Example: This type of warehouse is used by producers of seasonal products, such as agricultural items, garden furniture, or Christmas merchandise.

Distribution Centers: For Short-Term Storage

Distribution centers **provide storage of products for short periods of time for collection and distribution elsewhere.** Example: This type of warehouse is used by retailers such as Safeway or Rite-way that need to rapidly process goods from many places, mixing them up in different combinations to be put in trucks and shipped to individual stores.

THE BIG IDEA: The fourth of the 4-P marketing mix, promotion is concerned with motivating consumers to buy products. The promotion mix must consider how to select among the tools of advertising, public relations, personal selling, and sales promotion to yield a unified strategy of integrated marketing communication. The goals of promotion are to inform, to persuade, and to remind. Two different promotional strategies are pull and push.

THE ESSENTIAL QUESTION: What are the concepts of the promotion mix and integrated marketing communication, and what are the goals of promotion?

MyBizLab: Check your understanding of these concepts at www.mybizlab.com.

MyBizLab

I n 2005, Andrew Fischer, 20, of Omaha, went on eBay and offered to auction his forehead as space for a temporary tattoo advertisement for one month. Green Pharmaceuticals' SnoreStop won with a $37,375 bid, and Fischer and his inked forehead appeared in scores of newspapers and websites, as well as on national TV programs such as *Good Morning America*. "For 40 grand, I don't regret looking like an idiot for a month," Fisher told a reporter. "But it's not like the most fun thing in the world to walk around with a big ad on your face."[25] ⑬

There is almost no limit to the kinds of efforts that companies will make to bring their products to the attention of consumers. Let's now consider *promotion*, the fourth and final strategy component in the 4-P marketing mix.

Source: Green Pharmaceuticals, Inc.

⑬ **He has a head for advertising.** College student Andrew Fischer volunteered to wear a temporary ad for an antisnoring product on his forehead for a month for $37,375. That would certainly pay for a lot of college. Do you think this raised SnoreStop sales? Would you be willing to display a forehead ad for something bizarre for a longer time and less money?

Promotion, the Promotion Mix, & Integrated Marketing Communication

How would I define "promotion mix" and "integrated marketing communication"?

Promotion, as we defined it, consists of all the techniques that companies use to motivate consumers to buy their products. It's all about how to inform, persuade, and influence consumers to make a buying decision.

Two important concepts underlying promotion are a company's (1) *promotion mix* and (2) *integrated marketing communication.*

The Promotion Mix: The Combination of Tools Used to Promote a Product

The ***promotion mix*** is the combination of tools that a company uses to promote a product, selecting from among four promotional tools: (1) advertising, (2) public relations, (3) personal selling, and (4) sales promotion. We explain these tools in Sections 14.5 and 14.6. How these elements are used depends on the promotional strategy. (*See* ■ *Panel 14.8.*)

■ **PANEL 14.8 The four promotional tools.**

Promotional Tool	Relationship between Seller and Buyer(s)
Advertising	Paid, nonpersonal communication
Public relations	Unpaid, nonpersonal communication
Personal selling	In-person face-to-face communication
Sales promotion	Short-term incentives to stimulate consumer buying and dealer interest (e.g., coupons, rebates, trade shows)

Source: Photograph by Sally Lindsay.

⑭ Integrated marketing. Red Bull, despite some questions about its health effects, is the most popular energy drink in the world. Its promotional slogan is "Red Bull gives you wings." It also has an aggressive international advertising campaign, aimed at young males, using sponsored activities ranging from free-style motocross to break dancing to art shows. It is also prominent on Facebook, as shown here.

Integrated Marketing Communication: A Comprehensive, Unified Promotional Strategy

Integrated marketing communication combines all four promotional tools to execute a comprehensive, unified promotional strategy. Thus, everything from radio commercials to store-window displays, from print ads to YouTube videos, from direct-mail pieces to T-shirt images—all are designed to present a consistent message from all sources.⑭

■ **Example of Integrated Marketing Communication: NASCAR Seeks More Youth Fans.** The National Association for Stock Car Auto Racing (NASCAR) plans to get more young people interested in racing by, among other things, expanding its education platform into schools; pushing to be included in more movies, TV shows, and music; and making increasing use of digital and social media.²⁶ ■

The Goals of Promotion: Informing, Persuading, & Reminding

What are three goals of promotion?

Promotion has three goals: to *inform,* to *persuade,* and to *remind.*

1 Informing: Telling Prospective Consumers about the Product

The first promotional priority is to *inform* people about a product, because they won't buy something they know nothing about. Consumers need to be told what the product is, how to use it, where to buy it, and perhaps how much it costs.

> **BRIEFING / BUSINESS SKILLS & CAREER DEVELOPMENT**
> **Business Cards Can Be Made Informative to Prospective Consumers.** Business cards can be very effective promotional tools. If you are selling a service, your card needs to contain not only your contact information but also a statement that sums up what you do—for example, *Bill Bojangles. Providing quality dance instruction since 1999.*²⁷
> One successful car salesman dispensed his business cards very liberally, tacking them to all kinds of bulletin boards, slipping them under car windshield wipers, even throwing them up in the air by the handful while sitting in the stands at football games. ■

2 Persuading: Inducing Consumers to Buy the Product

The second priority is to *persuade* consumers to buy the product, to differentiate the product from competitive products, to say what the unique features are. We can see how this works by taking a look at the psychology of *infomercials,* **extended TV commercials ranging from 2 (short form) to 28.5 (long form) minutes that are devoted exclusively to promoting a product in considerable detail.**²⁸ One product frequently promoted in infomercials is the Snuggie, the oversized fleece blanket with sleeves.²⁹ Another is the Slap Chop vegetable slicer.

Want to Know More? 14-6
Ten Most Popular Infomercials
Go to www.mybizlab.com.

3 Reminding: Keeping Consumers Aware of the Product

The last priority is to *remind* consumers about the existence and benefits of the product.

Examples: An in-your-face television commercial that blared "HeadOn! Apply Directly to the Forehead!" (repeated three times) drove sales of the HeadOn headache remedy to new heights. Along Interstate 90 in South Dakota, scores of billboards advertising Wall Drug, the drugstore and mega-tourist attraction that is the principal industry in the town of Wall, lure as many as 20,000 visitors on a summer day. In the skies over many NFL football games, the hovering Goodyear blimp reminds spectators of the existence of Goodyear rubber products. Repetition is a standby of promotion everywhere.

Promotional Strategies: Push versus Pull

How is push strategy different from pull strategy?

Two quite different promotional strategies are often used: (1) *push* and (2) *pull*.

The Push Strategy: Aimed at Wholesalers & Retailers

The ***push promotional strategy*** **is aimed at wholesalers and retailers, to encourage them to market the product to consumers.** That is, the consumer doesn't request the product; rather, a good or service is "pushed" out to consumers through methods such as ads on websites or mailing of samples (such as tea). For example, some insurance companies market their policies to insurance agents, who in turn "push" them to consumers.

The Pull Strategy: Aimed at Consumers

The ***pull promotional strategy*** **is aimed directly at consumers, to get them to demand the product from retailers.** That is, the consumers request the product; the product is "pulled" through the distribution channel. Ads and other promotional techniques are used to entice the consumer to ask for the product. For example, GEICO TV ads try to induce you to buy an insurance policy directly from the company. ⑮

Why the difference? Whereas the push strategy is concerned with generating immediate results, the pull strategy tries to create long-time loyal consumers by developing a certain standard for the brand.[32]

⑮ **Pull strategy.** GEICO, whose TV ads feature the gecko, uses just the pull strategy, marketing its insurance policies directly to consumers. Can you think of instances of push strategies?

Source: Copyrighted image was reprinted with permission from GEICO.

Want to Know More? 14-7

What Are Some Push & Pull Strategies?

Go to www.mybizlab.com.

THE BIG IDEA: The first of four kinds of promotion, advertising, or paid non-personal communication by an identified sponsor, uses various media to inform an audience about a product. Public relations is the second kind of promotion. Three types of advertising are brand advertising, institutional advertising, and public service advertising. There are six kinds of advertising strategies: information, reminder, persuasive, competitive, direct action, and fear appeal. Advertising media include newspapers and magazines, television and radio, direct mail, outdoor media, the Internet, and other media, the selection of which involves such considerations as reach, frequency, continuity, and cost. Whereas advertising is paid coverage of a product, publicity is unpaid coverage. Handling publicity is part of public relations, which is concerned with creating and maintaining a favorable image.

THE ESSENTIAL QUESTION: How are advertising and public relations important in marketing?

MyBizLab: Check your understanding of these concepts at www.mybizlab.com.

Want to Know More? 14-8

How Do Advertising & Propaganda Differ?

Go to www.mybizlab.com.

For the movie *Up in the Air,* the writer and director wanted to use a real hotel brand for the frequent flyer character (played by George Clooney), and so the studio made a deal with Hilton Hotels. The hotel chain not only made sure details such as staff uniforms and shuttles were portrayed correctly, it also provided free sets, free lodging for the crew, and free promotion of the film on in-room TVs and on plastic room keys.[33]

Hilton's activities in this instance represent an example of **product placement, in which sellers of a product pay to have that product prominently placed in a TV show or film so that many people will see it.**[34] Payment can take several forms: straight payment, which can run as high as millions of dollars and provide films with significant financing; barter arrangements, as was done with Hilton Hotels; and help in marketing the film, as Hilton also did.[35]

Product placement is an example of **advertising, defined as paid nonpersonal communication by an identified sponsor (person or organization) using various media to inform an audience about a product.** Let's explore this subject, to which most of us receive continuous exposure.

Types of Advertising: Brand, Institutional, & Public Service

How would I describe the different types of advertising?

In general, advertising can be categorized as one of three types: *brand advertising, institutional advertising,* and *public service advertising.*

1 Brand Advertising: Promoting Specific Brands to Ultimate Consumers

Brand advertising, also called *product advertising,* **consists of presentations that promote specific brands to ultimate consumers.** You see such advertising on TV

Source: Image courtesy of OXO.

⑯ Brand advertising. OXO is a manufacturer of innovative and high-quality kitchen utensils and housewares. Staples is the world's largest office supply retailer. The two successful companies have collaborated in this ad to promote the fact that the OXO brand is now being offered in a world of office products—exclusively by Staples.

⑰ Public service advertising. The New York City Office of Recycling Outreach and Education advertises Stop 'N' Swap events—exchanges of portable, recyclable items—and other recycling services and programs. Nonprofits often prepare ads and public service announcements, which may be carried for free by the media.

and in magazines. Example: "XF: This is the new Jaguar" is the simple statement of a magazine car ad. ⑯

2 Institutional Advertising: Promoting an Organization's Image

Institutional advertising **consists of presentations that promote a favorable image for an organization.** The idea is to create goodwill and build a desirable image for a company or institution rather than to sell specific products. Example: "Investing in education. Our idea of a winning formula" is a print ad from computer chip maker Intel, promoting the fact that Intel Schools of Distinction rewards programs are proven to raise classroom performance.

One kind of institutional advertising, *advocacy advertising,* **is concerned with supporting a particular opinion about an issue.** Example: The American Clean Skies Foundation, whose mission is to educate the public about the environmental benefits of using natural gas as well as wind, solar, and other renewables to replace sources of energy that cause more pollution, ran an ad with the caption: "What are we waiting for? Put American natural gas to work for America now."

3 Public Service Advertising: Promoting Social Causes

Public service advertising **consists of presentations, usually sponsored by nonprofit organizations, that are concerned with the welfare of the community in general.** Such ads are often presented by the media free of charge. ⑰

Example: "When you help the American Red Cross, you help America." Another example: "There's a special joy in getting our hands dirty when it helps keep our land beautiful" reads an ad seeking volunteers to spruce up public lands.

Advertising Strategies: From Informational to Fear Appeals

What are six kinds of advertising approaches used to influence audiences?

Ads can also be classified by the strategies they take—that is, the approaches or appeals used to try to influence the audience. There are six distinct approaches: *informational, reminder, persuasive, competitive, direct action,* and *fear appeal.*

1 Informational Advertising: Providing Straightforward Knowledge

Informational advertising **provides consumers with straightforward knowledge about the features of the product offered,** such as basic components and price. For example, an ad from Rosetta Stone, "the world's leading language-learning software," describes such features as its "dynamic immersion" technique, its voice-recognition technology to help with more accurate pronunciation, and its adaptive software that tracks progress and customizes every lesson. It also describes the price and money-back guarantee.

2 Reminder Advertising: Keeping the Product Visible

Reminder advertising **tries to remind consumers of the existence of a product.** Example: Most people already know that DHL is (along with FedEx and UPS) a worldwide delivery service. A magazine print ad (that contains a mail-in survey card) invites consumers to receive a free overnight shipment credit in return for completing a brief four-question survey about their DHL use.

3 Persuasive Advertising: Stimulating Desire for the Product

Most advertising is *persuasive advertising,* **which tries to develop a desire among consumers for the product;** that is, the ad is not merely informational. Among the ways of doing this are to tout the *price or value* of the product, the product's *sexy image,* or the product's *association with celebrities.*

18 Got milk? Ashley Tisdale, actress (as the cheerleader Savannah Monroe in TV's *Hellcats*) and singer (*Headstrong, Guilty Pleasure*), in her first "Got Milk?" print ad. The long-running (since 1993) advertising campaign sponsored by dairy interests to get consumers to drink more milk regularly features celebrities from sports, media, and entertainment and has over 90% awareness in the United States, according to the "Got Milk?" website. Are paid celebrity endorsements more likely to get your attention than other promotion strategies? Why?

R-E-Charge! got milk?

See why Ashley Tisdale thinks milk is worth cheering for at RefuelWithChocolateMilk.com

Source: ZCVA WENN Photos/Newscom.

■ **Example of Persuasive Advertising: Using Value, Sexiness, and Celebrities to Develop Consumer Desire.** Hewlett-Packard advertises its HP Officejet inkjet printers as offering superior value because they "deliver professional color printing at a cost that's up to 50% lower per page than laser printers." Sexy blond female models appear sitting on the windshield, feet on the hood, of a convertible in a Dolce & Gabbana clothing ad. Actress Salma Hayek appears in a Campari liquor ad, and tennis star Roger Federer appears in a Rolex watch ad. The long-running "Got Milk?" campaign also features celebrities. **18** ■

4 Competitive Advertising: Comparing & Contrasting Products

Competitive advertising, **which is also called *comparative advertising,* promotes a product by comparing it more favorably to rival products.** Examples: Insurance companies GEICO and Progressive each continually run TV ads comparing their prices with those of their supposedly more expensive competitors. Hertz rental-car ads point out that if you "bring back the car without a full tank, you won't get hosed." That is, Hertz promises that, unlike its competitors, it will not charge you prices higher than those of ordinary gas stations for topping off your rental car when you return it with the gas tank partly empty.

5 Direct-Action Advertising: Stimulating the Immediate Purchase of a Product

Direct-action advertising **attempts to stimulate an immediate, or relatively immediate, purchase of a product through such devices as one-day sales,**

one-time promotions, or announcements of a special event. You see direct-action advertising principally offered in newspapers and on local TV channels, such as Macy's or JCPenney's Fourth of July weekend three-day sales.

6 Fear-Appeal Advertising: Using Worry about Loss or Harm to Sell a Product

Fear-appeal advertising **attempts to stimulate the purchase of a product by motivating consumers through fear of loss or harm.** Examples: This approach is used to sell everything from acne cream to life insurance to fire extinguishers to, perhaps, even health food.

Advertising Media: From Newspapers to the Internet

What are the things an advertiser must consider in selecting the mix of media?

Advertising permeates the American—and global—business system. It is done by retailers trying to influence consumers, by manufacturers trying to get wholesalers and retailers to carry their products, and by manufacturers trying to get other manufacturers to buy their products. It can be local, as with grocery-store ads; national, as with new-car ads; or cooperative, as when national companies share ad costs with local merchants and wholesalers.

Advertising media **are the variety of communication methods for carrying a seller's message to prospective buyers.** These consist of ads in print media (newspapers, magazines), electronic media (television, radio), direct mail, outdoor media (billboards, transit ads), Internet (Web ads), and other (Yellow Pages, telephone calls, special events, sidewalk handouts, special store displays, movie trailers, and so on).[36] (*See* ■ *Panel 14.9.*)

The advantages and disadvantages of different kinds of advertising media are shown below. (*See* ■ *Panel 14.10.*)

■ **PANEL 14.9 Share of ad spending by medium, December 2009.**

Media Type	Percent
Cable TV	22.9%
Network TV	20.6%
Local TV	16.4%
National magazines	15.0%
Internet	6.9%
Local newspapers	5.7%
Hispanic TV	2.7%
Local radio	2.5%
Syndicated TV	2.2%
Outdoor	1.6%
National newspapers	1.4%
National Sunday supplement	1.2%
Network radio	0.8%
Coupons	0.4%
Local magazines	0.1%
Local Sunday supplement	0.0%

Source: Based on data from The Nielson Company, AdAcross, Marketing Charts, March 22, 2010, www.marketingcharts.com/print/share-of-ad-spending-by-medium-december-2009-12352 (accessed October 30, 2011).

■ **PANEL 14.10 Advantages and disadvantages of different advertising media.**

Media Type	Advantages	Disadvantages
Newspapers	Good market coverage; inexpensive; local market coverage; geographic selectivity	Short life span; limited color options; cluttered pages; declining readership
Magazines	Can target specific audiences; good reproduction and color; long life of ads	Expensive; long lead time; limited demonstration possibilities
Television	Wide reach; good impact; uses sight, sound, and motion; great creative opportunities	High costs for production and air time; short exposure time; short message life; can be skipped with digital recorders
Radio	Low cost; immediacy; good for local markets; can target specific audiences	No visuals; short message life; listeners can't keep ad
Direct mail	Can target specific audiences; delivers lots of information; ads can be saved	High cost; delivery delays; consumers may reject as junk mail
Outdoor	Highly visible; repeat exposure; low cost; focus on local market	Limited message; general audience
Internet	Inexpensive; interactive; always available; global reach	Consumers may reject as spam

Creating a Media Plan: Developing Media Strategy

***Media planning* is the process of choosing the exact kinds of media to be used for an advertising campaign.** This means selecting the target audience and determining the best media by which to reach them. Many college students, for instance, prefer texting and Facebook, but they also may read the campus newspaper.

Media Buying: What Are the Considerations?

Often advertisers will come up with a media plan that involves a mix of media, such as having ads in newspapers, on the radio, and on the Internet. How do you decide which media to buy? There are four considerations: *reach, frequency, continuity,* and *cost.*

Reach: How Many People Will Be Reached at Least Once? *Reach* is the number of people within a given population that your ad will reach at least once.

Frequency: How Often Is Each Person Exposed to the Ad? *Frequency* is the average number of times each member of the audience is exposed to an ad.

Continuity: What Is the Timing of the Ads? *Continuity* is timing of the ads, how often they appear or how heavily they are concentrated within a time period.

Cost: What Is the Cost of Reaching 1,000 People? *Cost per thousand (CPM)* is the cost a particular medium charges to reach 1,000 people with an ad.

There is also another factor to consider: Digital media such as the Internet have upended the old categories, shifting ad dollars away from traditional media, including TV, newspapers, and magazines. ⑲

Source: Photograph by Sally Lindsay.

⑲ **Magazine advertising.** Print ads look "increasingly quaint these days in the ever-more-flashy world of social, mobile, TV, and cinema," says an *Adweek* article. But there were 10 magazine ads in 2011 that will really make you sit up and take notice. To see them, go to www.adweek.com/adfreak/10-great-magazine-ads-dont-just-sit-there-looking-pretty-132401.

Want to Know More? 14-9
New Media Marketing Examples
Go to www.mybizlab.com.

The Great Upheaval: Ads Move to "New Media"

Advertisers and marketers are expected to spend more than $144.9 billion on online ads by 2014, making online advertising a big business.[37] "New media" include online ads, websites, e-direct marketing, and ads on cellphones. They also include ads on store-based TV screens, videogames, and digital video recorders, as well as TV and movie product placements.

Publicity & Public Relations

How do publicity and public relations differ?

Whereas advertising is paid media coverage of a firm's products, ***publicity* is defined as unpaid coverage by the mass media about a firm or its products.** Because publicity is presented in a news format—as when a newspaper takes a company's press release and rewrites it into a news article—consumers are apt to see this kind of promotion as more credible than advertising. A ***press release,* or *news release* or *publicity release,* is a brief statement written in the form of a news story or a video program that is released to the mass media to try to get favorable publicity for a firm or its products.**

Publicity has a downside, however: because the firm doesn't pay for publicity, the treatment of an event is outside its control and so there can be bad publicity

Reaching potential customers used to be simple. Now, the array of new media provides marketers with a wealth of choices. Here are some of them:

Online Ads

The leader in online search ads is Google, which owned 83% of the paid search business in 2010, although Bing and Yahoo Search are increasing their share.[38] Besides displaying ads, the advantage of these sites is that they generate sales as customers click through to a sponsor's site.[39] Advertisers can track everything from the number of clicks an ad receives from a certain zip code to how long a person watches a video clip on a specific site.[40]

Business Websites

An alternative to telephone-book Yellow Pages ads, websites are a way for small businesses to attract customers. Online advertising companies such as Yodle, Weblistic, WebVisible, and ReachLocal are available to help manage such sites.[41] You can also list your product on websites such as eBay, Etsy, and Imagekind.[42]

Social Networking Websites

Many companies have increased their ad spending on social networking websites such as Facebook, MySpace, Twitter,

Gowalla, Foursquare, Loopt, Scvngr, Bebo, and Buzznet. Some firms even have their own social media, such as Dove's site for women, Dove's campaign for beauty.[43]

Blogs

Another marketing alternative for small businesses is the blogosphere, although blogging requires a large time commitment and some writing skills. Consultants, for instance, may be able to attract clients through their blogs. You can find blogs relevant to your field by searching on sites such as Technorati.com or Blogsearch.[44]

E-Mail Marketing

E-mail can be used to publish online newsletters, sponsor contests, publicize special promotions, and drive traffic to a firm's website.[45]

Other: Web Videos, Cellphones, & Virtual Reality Sites

With the arrival of broadband to home computers has come the arrival of online videos, which in turn has attracted advertisers.[46] Cellphones are also becoming an increasingly popular site for ads.[47] Finally, marketers are also taking ads on a three-dimensional reality game, Second Life, where they can demonstrate how their products work.

(Buick car sales are down in the United States) as well as good publicity (Buick car sales are up in China). Another drawback is that firms have no control over whether the media will use a particular news release or when and where it will appear (on the front page? back on page C-27?). Once an article has appeared, it is also (unlike an ad) not likely to be repeated.

Handling publicity is part of the job of a company's public relations department. **Public relations (PR) is concerned with creating and maintaining a favorable image of the firm, its products, and its actions with the mass media, consumers, and the public at large.** Thus, PR departments try to stay tuned to public attitudes, institute programs that are in the public's interest, and inform the public (through the mass media) about these programs. Sometimes PR departments try to obtain favorable news coverage by holding a **press conference, calling media representatives to a press briefing at which they announce new information.**

Source: Everett Collection Inc/Alamy.

 Press conference. English footballer David Beckham (who plays for the Los Angeles Galaxy in Major League Soccer) and his wife Victoria, singer and fashion designer, appear at a press conference at Macy's Herald Square in New York to trumpet the release of Beckham Signature Fragrance, available for both men and women.

---

i

Want to Know More? 14-10

Small Business Blogging: Powerful Conversations

Go to www.mybizlab.com.

THE BIG IDEA: Personal selling, the third kind of promotion, is face-to-face communication to influence customers. The fourth kind, sales promotion, is short-term marketing to stimulate dealer effectiveness and consumer buying. Three basic tasks associated with personal selling are creative selling, order processing, and sales support. Seven steps in the personal selling process are prospecting, qualifying, approaching the customer, presenting the product, handling objections, making the sale, and following up. Sales promotion can be business-to-business promotion, as through trade shows, or business-to-consumer promotion, using such techniques as bonuses, coupons, contests, sweepstakes, premiums, and so on. We also describe guerrilla marketing and word-of-mouth marketing.

THE ESSENTIAL QUESTION: How could I use personal selling and sales promotion to benefit a product?

MyBizLab

MyBizLab: Check your understanding of these concepts at www.mybizlab.com.

THE #1 NEW YORK TIMES BESTSELLER

"The quintessential rags-to-riches American dream story—amazing and inspirational."
—San Francisco Chronicle Book Review

The PURSUIT *of* HAPPYNESS

The LIFE STORY that inspired the MAJOR MOTION PICTURE

CHRIS GARDNER
WITH QUINCY TROUPE

Source: Photograph by Sally Lindsay.

㉑ Persistence. Chris Gardner overcame seemingly insurmountable odds to establish himself as a stockbroker even while homeless and caring for his young son, Christopher Jr. Now a millionaire entrepreneur and motivational speaker, Gardner demonstrated his determination and resilience early on by making 200 sales calls before leaving the office—every day. Is your career success important enough for you to make an effort equal to Gardner's?

Self-made millionaire Christopher Gardner struggled during the 1980s with homelessness while raising his toddler son, which became the basis for the 2006 movie *The Pursuit of Happyness,* starring Will Smith. While living on the streets of San Francisco by night, Gardner worked in the Dean Witter Reynolds stock brokerage training program by day. He would arrive at the office early and stay late, persistently making cold calls—the hardest kind of selling there is—to prospective clients, with the goal of making 200 calls a day. Eventually he received his stockbroker's license and went on to great success.[48]

What would make anyone willing to make 200 sales calls a day? "It's passion," Gardner says. "Passion is everything. In fact, you've got to be borderline fanatical about what you do."[49] ㉑

Personal Selling: Establishing a Relationship between Seller & Buyer

When is personal selling appropriate, and what are the three tasks associated with personal selling?

Maybe you don't have this kind of passion to be "world class at something," as Gardner did. But are you able to put yourself in other people's shoes, to solve customers' problems? Can you work without a lot of close supervision? Do you have the energy and ambition to persevere in the face of rejection—provided there are superior rewards? Then maybe you'll thrive in personal sales.

Personal selling **is face-to-face communication and promotion to influence customers to buy goods and services.** Personal selling involves establishing a personal link between seller and buyer, a kind of "professional intimacy" and climate of trust, particularly in relationship marketing.

When Is Personal Selling Appropriate?

Personal selling is more expensive than other kinds of selling (such as tele-marketing, direct marketing, and Internet sales) because it requires so much training, time, and often money for travel and lodging and, perhaps, entertainment of prospective customers. Thus, this kind of selling isn't appropriate for all situations.

Personal selling works best when the product is (1) somewhat expensive, (2) somewhat complex, and (3) aimed at a few customers located close together. Thus, big-ticket items, from boats to diamond rings to mainframe computers, are good candidates for personal sales. So are products that require some explanation or special handling, such as cars (with their financing and trade-in arrangements), musical instruments, bridal gowns, and life insurance. And traveling salespeople tend to avoid rural, desert, or mountainous areas where populations are sparse.

The Sales Tasks: Creative Selling, Order Processing, & Sales Support

Three basic tasks associated with personal selling are (1) *creative selling,* (2) *order processing,* and (3) *sales support.*

Creative Selling: Persuading Buyers to Buy Products. *Creative selling* **is the selling process in which salespeople determine customer needs, then explain their product's benefits to try to persuade buyers to buy the product.**

A real-estate salesperson, for example, has to find out from clients the location, size, and price range of the house they want, then drive them around to various houses that are on the market. This kind of selling can require a considerable investment of time and energy, as well as empathy and patience on the part of the salesperson. ㉒

Order Processing: Taking Orders and Seeing to Their Handling. A far easier task than creative selling, *order processing* **consists of receiving customer orders and seeing that they are handled correctly and that the product is delivered.**

Example: Soft drink truck drivers, who are considered salespeople, call on customers to check their supplies, take orders for more supplies, and then see to their delivery.

Sales Support: Facilitating the Sales Effort. *Sales support* **consists not of selling products but of facilitating the sale by providing supportive services,** such as finding new customers, building goodwill, and providing follow-up services after the sale.

So-called *missionary salespeople,* for example, call on existing customers and provide them with product samples and information. Pharmaceutical companies, for instance, have salespeople who call on doctors, pass out free drug samples, and explain their benefits.

Source: Christian Kieffer/Shutterstock.

㉒ **"It doesn't have enough bedrooms."** Selling real estate, a form of creative selling, can be an intense experience, since this couple may not be satisfied until they've looked at 40 houses or more. For the real estate salesman shown here, the trick is to get a firm understanding of the prospective buyers' needs, then do his best to find a house that meets those needs—not always possible. If the agent makes only about $2,500 on a sale, how many hours should he devote to this couple?

The Seven Steps in the Personal Selling Process

If I were doing personal selling, what steps would I follow with a customer?

The personal selling process—by which we mean the creative selling process—consists of a carefully planned sequence of seven activities: (1) *prospecting,*

1. **Prospecting**
Identifying potential customers

↓

2. **Qualifying**
Determining if prospects have authority to buy and ability to pay

↓

3. **Approaching customers**
Making the initial contact

↓

4. **Presenting the product**
Telling about the product

↓

5. **Handling objections**
Answering the prospect's questions

↓

6. **Making the sale**
Making trial close and actual close

↓

7. **Following up**
Staying in touch with customers and solving problems

(2) *qualifying,* (3) *approaching the customer,* (4) *presenting the product,* (5) *handling objections,* (6) *making the sale,* and (7) *following up.* These steps are shown at left. (*See* ■ *Panel 14.11.*)

1 Prospecting: Identifying Potential Customers

Prospecting* is the process of identifying potential customers, who are called *prospects. First, salespeople must have *product knowledge*—know the features and prices of their products, as well as those of competitors' products—so they will know what kind of customers they are looking for. Second, successful salespeople (except those in retail stores) spend a lot of time on *preparation*—finding their customers and learning as much as they can about them before making their first visit.

Finding customers may be done through *referral, endless-chain,* or *cold-call* techniques.

The Referral Technique: Getting Help from Satisfied Customers. The *referral sales prospecting technique* consists of asking satisfied customers to provide names of potential customers or to contact them on behalf of the salesperson. This technique clearly is the easiest way to find new buyers, and it also gives the salespeople and their products more credibility.

Example: If you run a pool-cleaning service, you might ask some of your most satisfied customers if they would mind endorsing you to their pool-owning friends.

The Endless-Chain Technique: Asking a Sales Prospect to Provide Names of Other Prospects. The *endless-chain sales prospecting technique* consists of asking each sales prospect to provide the salesperson with some names of other prospects who might be interested in the product.

Example: A house painter might ask his or her customers for the names of nearby neighbors who might want their homes painted. This technique can be useful even if the first prospect hasn't even bought or used your product.

The Cold-Call Technique: Calling on Prospects without Introduction. The most difficult prospecting technique, **the *cold-call sales prospecting technique* consists of calling on prospects with whom you have had no previous contact and to whom you do not have any kind of introduction.**

Example: If you're selling magazine subscriptions, you could simply start walking through a neighborhood knocking on doors, to see if you can get someone interested. This is the hardest prospecting technique, of course. It is also apt to be the least successful.

2 Qualifying: Determining Whether Prospects Have Authority to Buy & Ability to Pay

If a young child answers the door, does he or she have the authority or money to buy a magazine subscription from you? Probably not. The second step in personal selling, then, is *qualifying*—**determining if the prospect has the authority to buy and the ability to pay.**

Example: If you're selling complex computer systems, you would probably want to ascertain that your prospective client is someone with authority in the Information Systems Department (not, say, the Human Resources Department).

3 Approaching Customers: First Impressions Count

The *approach* consists of the initial contact with the customer, whether by letter, phone, or personal visit. In most kinds of *business-to-consumer (B2C) sales,* such

With the approach step, clearly this is the time when first impressions really count. The first impression is affected by three things: how you *look,* how you *act,* and what you *say.*

How You Look: Clothes, Cards, & Cars

Within 3 minutes of meeting someone new, people form an opinion about where the future of the relationship is headed, according to one study.[50] Thus, if your first contact is an in-person visit, make sure you're dressed appropriately (jeans are okay for calling on a surfboard shop, not for a financial institution). Make sure your business card has a professional look and that the car you drive, if any, is not a rent-a-wreck.

How You Act: Attitude & Behavior

If on your first meeting with anyone, as we saw Fox News CEO Roger Ailes advise in Chapter 8, you only have

7 seconds before people start forming an opinion about you, then the first requirement is to amp up your energy level.[51] Of course, you should also present yourself as courteous and considerate.

What You Say: A Few Well-Chosen Words

After briefly greeting the prospect and introducing yourself, you should have some carefully chosen words that will pique his or her interest and draw attention to how your product will be of benefit.

Example: "Hi, my name is Chris, and my company is Christopher Marketing Services. You don't know me from a sack of potatoes, but I'd like to give you some important information that could vitally affect your business."[52]

---

as retail-store sales (where most sales take place), not much prospecting and qualifying is required; the first step in personal selling begins with the approach, where you simply ask the customer, "Hello, how may I help you today?" to show you're there to assist them. With other kinds of sales, such as *business-to-business (B2B) sales,* or with certain kinds of B2C retail selling such as automobiles or musical instruments sales, you may need to qualify people as a step in the personal selling process.

4 Presenting the Product: The Canned versus the Need-Satisfaction Approach

In the sales presentation, you cover your product's features, use, advantages over competing products, and finally the price. You may be aided by free product samples, PowerPoint slides, letters of praise (testimonials) from satisfied users, and a demonstration of how the product is used.

You might approach the presentation in one of two ways—canned or need satisfaction.

The Canned Presentation. The *canned presentation* uses a fixed, memorized selling approach to present the product. This may be an aid for beginning salespeople, but it's an inflexible approach.

The Need-Satisfaction Presentation. The *need-satisfaction presentation* consists of determining customer needs and then tailoring your presentation to address those needs. This is by far the more preferred approach these days.

5 Handling Objections: Turning Questions into Opportunities

In most sales situations, the prospective customer will raise a few objections, or at the very least have some questions, and you should prepare to have answers for

Source: FancyVeerSet3/Alamy.

23 Handling objections. The real test of this salesman's skill is how he deals with objections. Prospects may resist for all kinds of reasons: they misunderstood the presentation, they hate making decisions, they are reluctant to do something new, the price is too high, and so on. If you get into sales, handling objections should be a crucial part of your training. It's also valuable information to have as a consumer, so you can see what techniques salespeople are employing.

Key Takeaway 14-5
Personal selling: prospecting, qualifying, approaching, presenting, handling objections, closing, and following up.

24 Starpoints. The Starwood Preferred Guest program enables frequent visitors to the hotel chain to accumulate points and get rewards, such as free stays at 875 hotels and resorts, as well as room upgrades. If you were a customer, would this "loyalty program" be enough to make you preferentially choose Starwood? What if you had a couple of bad experiences?

these. Sometimes these can be addressed by introducing others in your company, such as your manager or technical experts. **23**

Frequently, the customer will object to the price, want a discount, or inquire about making monthly payments. Salespeople are better off if they can finish their explanation of the product's features, which may impress the buyer enough that price is less of an objection. In any case, all objections and questions should be viewed as opportunities for strengthening your relationship.

6 Making the Sale: The Trial Close & the Actual Close

After you have worked to present all features, answer all questions, and overcome all objections, there comes the time to *make the sale*. Sometimes customers find it difficult to make the final decision, and you have to help them along. Two ways to do this are by making a *trial close* and then the *actual close*.

The Trial Close: Testing the Customer's Willingness to Buy. The *trial close* **is a question or statement that tests the prospect's willingness to buy.** Prospects may give off signs that indicate they are ready to buy, such as asking about delivery dates or payment plans. At that point, the salesperson can ask such questions as "Would you want 5 or 10 boxes?" or "Would you want to put that on a credit card?" This puts the burden on the prospect of rejecting the sale.

The Actual Close: Asking for the Order. In the *actual close,* **the salesperson concludes the presentation by asking the prospect to purchase the product—** that is, asking for the order. For example, you might say, "Here's the contract, and we'll need your signature here and here."

7 Following Up: Staying in Touch with the Customer

Once the sale is made, you need to do *follow-up*—thank your customers for the order, stay in touch with them to make sure they're happy with the product, help solve any problems, and demonstrate that you care about maintaining a long-term relationship. Even retail-store salespeople can benefit from doing follow-up phone calls, especially if they are selling expensive items. Following up is important because it can generate further sales later on or lead to referrals with new customers.

Sales Promotion: Short-Term Marketing to Stimulate Dealer Effectiveness & Consumer Buying

What kinds of sales promotion techniques are available?

What if you had accumulated so many Starwood Hotels & Resorts "loyalty points" (for frequent stays with that chain) that your rewards consisted of choosing between

Source: Photograph by Sally Lindsay.

(1) spending six nights at the Starwood's luxury hotel on the Champs-Elysees in Paris or (2) spending one night with John Travolta and the cast of *Hairspray* at the film's New York premiere? **24** (The real couple faced with this difficult choice, a Southern California restaurant owner and his wife, chose to hang out with Travolta.)

It used to be that hotels could simply give away hotel rooms to loyal guests who had accumulated mountains of points. But in the good times of 2007, before the Great Recession hit, according to the *Wall Street Journal,* they had to offer "the option to spend their points on a wide array of unique experiences—from weightless space flight to cooking lessons from star chefs."[53]

Point systems are one of many inducements that businesses use as part of their sales promotion to build business. ***Sales promotion* is defined as short-term marketing incentives to stimulate (1) dealer interest and (2) consumer buying.** The first is B2B; the second is B2C.

Trade Promotion: Business-to-Business Promotion

Business-to-business (B2B) sales promotion, also known as *trade promotion,* is intended to stimulate dealer interest. The devices used include trade shows, conventions, catalogs, and special printed materials for salespeople. **A *trade show* is a gathering of manufacturers in the same industry who display their products to their distributors and dealers.** Examples: Makers of furniture, boats, electronics, medical appliances, security gear, outdoor equipment, and many other products hold such shows every year.[54]

Consumer-Oriented Sales Promotion: Business-to-Consumer Promotion

Business-to-consumer (B2C) sales promotion is extremely varied. Some of the more common devices used are bonuses (such as two products for the price of one), catalogs, cents-off promotions, contests, games, and lotteries. Some businesses even offer free gas to fuel sales.[55] More specialized promotion techniques are shown below. (*See* ■ *Panel 14.12.*)

Want to Know More? 14-11

Coupon & Groupon Marketing

Go to www.mybizlab.com.

■ **PANEL 14.12 Consumer-oriented sales promotion techniques.**

Coupons	Pieces of paper entitling holders to a discount price on a product
Demonstrations	Demonstrations in which salespeople show how products work
Event marketing	Staged, public promotion featuring product, with consumers active participants in event
Point-of-purchase displays	Product displays or ads placed in retail stores where buying decision is made
Premiums	Gifts or prizes provided free to consumers who buy a specific product or accumulate points
Rebates	Potential refunds by the manufacturer to the consumer
Samples	Small product samples given away for free
Sweepstakes	Contests in which prizes are awarded on the basis of chance

Guerrilla Marketing & Word-of-Mouth Marketing

How do guerrilla marketing and word-of-mouth marketing work?

What if you don't have much money to promote your product? Sometimes the best kind of promotion relies on innovation and imagination rather than big budgets. Two variations are *guerrilla marketing* and *word-of-mouth marketing.*

Guerrilla Marketing: Innovative, Unusual, & Low-Cost Methods

Guerrilla marketing **consists of innovative, low-cost marketing schemes that try to get customers' attention in unusual ways.** This could range from handing out samples to throwing a party to paying people to (as mentioned earlier) wear ads as temporary tattoos.[56]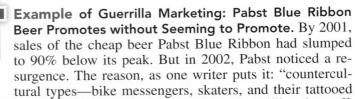

■ **Example of Guerrilla Marketing: Pabst Blue Ribbon Beer Promotes without Seeming to Promote.** By 2001, sales of the cheap beer Pabst Blue Ribbon had slumped to 90% below its peak. But in 2002, Pabst noticed a resurgence. The reason, as one writer puts it: "countercultural types—bike messengers, skaters, and their tattooed kin—in hipster redoubts like Portland, Oregon, had taken to swilling the stuff. When asked why, they would praise Pabst for its nonimage, for the fact that it seemed to care little about selling."[57]

Pabst understood that aiming a bunch of aggressive commercial messages at this kind of audience would be a sure turnoff. Instead it put its budget into bike messenger contests, skateboarder movie screenings, and the like, keeping its logo small and pretending to look like a beer of "social protest." Pabst's low-key attitude inspired deep passion in its fans. ■

Word-of-Mouth Marketing: People Telling Others about Products

Do you often go to a movie because your friends raved about it? That's an example of *word-of-mouth marketing,* **a promotional technique that relies on people telling others about products they've purchased or firms they've used.** Sometimes marketers resort to *buzz marketing,* **using high-profile entertainment or news to get people to talk about their product.** Another variant is *viral marketing,* **in which companies pay people to promote their products to others,** as through Internet chat rooms and blogs.

■ **Example of Word-of-Mouth Marketing: Focus Wealth Management Invites People to Lunch.** Focus Wealth Management, a Middleburg, Virginia, investment advisory firm, promoted itself by drawing up a list of area professionals, such as attorneys and accountants, who would be likely to encounter their ideal client type. Then the Focus top executives started inviting at least two of them to lunch each week, to talk about the services they provided and the kind of client they were looking for.[58] ■

Applying Different Marketing Strategies to Different Stages of the Product Life Cycle

How are marketing strategies varied for different product life-cycle stages?

As we mentioned in Chapter 13 in our discussion of the product life cycle, different marketing strategies can be applied during different life cycle stages—introduction, growth, maturity, decline. (See ■ *Panel 14.13, opposite page.*)

㉕ **Guerrilla bike.** On February 6, 2008, 75 brightly painted orange bicycles like this one were placed around New York City, illegally chained to city property, such as poles and trees. The bicycles were part of a guerrilla marketing campaign by fashion firm DKNY that coincided with the city's Fashion Week. Those who looked closely at the bikes found a DKNY logo. The company argued, however, that it was trying to promote cycling, not its clothes. If you encountered something like this, what would be your reaction?

Want to Know More? 14-12
Guerrilla & Word-of-Mouth Marketing
Go to www.mybizlab.com.

Product Life-Cycle Stages

Marketing Strategies	Introduction Stage	Growth Stage	Maturity Stage	Decline Stage
	Low sales; few or no profits; little compensation	*Fast-growing sales; high profits; more competitors appear*	*Peak sales; slowing profits; maximum number of competitors*	*Falling sales; low profits or even losses; declining number of competitors*
Product strategy	Present market-tested products, limited assortment	Further improve product or expand product line to widen appeal to new segments	Simplify product lines, segment markets more carefully, possibly redesign packaging	Decide whether to eliminate product; develop ideas for new products
Price strategy	High price (skimming) to recover costs or low price (penetration pricing) to attract large number of customers	May need to adjust price to meet competitors' prices	Further adjust price to maintain market share	May reduce price, if product can still be profitable, or even increase price
Place (distribution) strategy	Selective distribution to targeted market segment; use of wholesalers, dealers	Expand distribution	Distribute through as many outlets as possible; offer incentives to wholesalers, dealers	Narrow distribution to most profitable markets
Promotion strategy	Aim promotion at dealers to carry product and at first-time buyers	Adjust ads and other promotion to encourage brand loyalty	Promote product's differences and benefits to attract new users and hold on to old ones	Decrease focus of promotion to loyal customers

■ **Example of Promotion Strategy Applied to a Mature Product: "You Never Forget Your First Subaru."** Although car models change, the Subaru Forester is a mature brand. A TV commercial that tries to attract new users and hold on to old ones opens (to background music "Powerful Stuff" by Sean Hayes) with a man and his wife meeting old friends at a high school reunion. The man looks across the room and sees an attractive woman entering with her husband. Both express recognition: they were high school sweethearts.

After several quick flashbacks showing the man and the girlfriend in their younger years driving an older Subaru Forester, the scene switches back to the present. The man and his present-day wife, in their new Subaru Forester, pull into their garage, driving past the old Forester in the driveway. The wife walks past the older vehicle on her way to the house. The man follows her, then dawdles a bit. He looks at the old Forester and smiles. Voiceover: "It's true. You never forget your first Subaru."[59] ■

This concludes our discussion of marketing. In the next chapter, we move on to financial resources.

LEARNING & SKILLS PORTFOLIO

Summary

14.1 The Distribution Mix: Marketing Channels

THE ESSENTIAL QUESTION: *What are the means of distributing products between producers and consumers?*

How would I define the third and fourth of the 4-Ps of the marketing mix? Place, or distribution, strategy is about moving products from seller to buyers. Promotion strategy is about motivating consumers to buy a firm's products.

What are four important things to consider in moving a product from producer to consumer? It is important to consider (1) distribution channels—the systems for conveying products from producers to buyers; (2) intermediaries—the people or firms in the channels, such as agents and brokers who bring buyers and sellers together, wholesalers who sell products to other businesses for resale to customers or to firms for use in their operations, or retailers who sell products directly to customers; (3) distribution mix—the combination of possible distribution channels; and (4) distribution strategy—the overall plan for moving products to customers.

What are six types of distribution channels? For consumers, there may be zero intermediaries between producer and consumers, one intermediary (retailer), two (wholesaler, retailer), or three (agent/broker, wholesaler, retailer). For businesses, there may be no intermediaries or one or more between the business producer and business user.

Are intermediaries really needed? How do they add value to the products they handle? Intermediaries add value (utility) by affecting form, location, time, information, ownership, and service—changing materials into useful products, selling products where and when people want them, and helping customers understand, acquire, and use products.

How would I distinguish among distribution strategies? Three kinds of market coverage, or product distribution among locations, are intensive (many locations), selective (some preferred locations), and exclusive (few locations).

14.2 Intermediaries: Wholesalers, Agents & Brokers, & Retailers

THE ESSENTIAL QUESTION: *How do the principal intermediaries differ from one another?*

What are the different types of wholesalers? Manufacturer-owned wholesalers are owned and operated by their product's manufacturer. Independently owned full-service merchant wholesalers become owners of the manufacturer's products and provide full services. Limited-function merchant wholesalers become owners of the manufacturer's products but perform only selected services.

What do agents and brokers do, and how do they differ? They connect buyers and sellers and help negotiate a sale. Agents tend to maintain long-term relationships with the people they represent; brokers are usually hired on a temporary basis.

What are the two principal types of store retailers? They are (1) product-line retailers—department stores, supermarkets, and convenience stores; and (2) bargain retailers—discount stores and warehouse clubs.

What are the principal types of nonstore retailers? They include vending machines, direct sellers (door-to-door, house-party, and multilevel marketing), direct marketing (such as catalog marketing and telemarketing), video marketing (such as TV shopping channels), and online retailing (such as virtual storefronts).

14.3 Physical Distribution: Supply Chains & Logistics

THE ESSENTIAL QUESTION: *What are supply chains and logistics, and how are transportation and warehousing involved?*

What is supply-chain management, and how does the concept of logistics fit into it? Supply-chain management is planning and coordinating movement of materials and products along the supply chain, the sequence of suppliers that contribute to creating and delivering a product, from raw materials to production to final buyers. Logistics implements the movements of such materials, goods, and related information.

What are five ways of transporting materials and products through the supply chain, and what are their benefits? Rail is best for large, bulky items; road (trucking) for delivering goods almost anywhere; and pipelines for liquids and gas. Transport over water is the cheapest but slowest; air transport is fastest but most expensive. Intermodal shipping combines several transport modes, helped by use of shipping containers.

What's the difference between storage warehouses and distribution centers? Storage warehouses store products for long periods; distribution centers store products only for distribution elsewhere.

14.4 The Promotion Mix: Tools, Goals, & Strategies

THE ESSENTIAL QUESTION: *What are the concepts of the promotion mix and integrated marketing communication, and what are the goals of promotion?*

How would I define "promotion mix" and "integrated marketing communication"? The promotion mix is all the tools a firm uses to promote a product—advertising, public relations, personal selling, and sales promotion. Integrated marketing communication combines all four tools to execute a unified promotional strategy.

What are three goals of promotion? The goals of promotion are to inform, persuade, and remind customers about a product.

How is push strategy different from pull strategy? Push promotional strategy encourages wholesalers and retailers to market a product; pull strategy tries to get consumers to demand the product from retailers.

14.5 Advertising & Public Relations

THE ESSENTIAL QUESTION: *How are advertising and public relations important in marketing?*

How would I describe the different types of advertising? Brand advertising promotes specific brands to ultimate consumers, institutional advertising promotes a favorable image for an organization, and public service advertising promotes community welfare.

What are six kinds of advertising approaches used to influence audiences? Informational advertising provides straightforward information about product features. Reminder advertising reminds consumers of a product's existence. Persuasive advertising tries to spur consumer desire for a product. Competitive advertising compares a product favorably to rival products. Direct-action advertising tries to stimulate immediate purchase of a product, using one-time sales, promotions, or special events. Fear-appeal advertising tries to stimulate buying via consumers' fears of loss or harm.

What are the things an advertiser must consider in selecting the mix of media? An advertiser's media plan chooses the appropriate communication methods for carrying the seller's message, weighing reach, frequency, continuity, and cost.

How do publicity and public relations differ? Publicity is unpaid coverage by the mass media about a firm or its products. Public relations tries to create a favorable image for a firm.

14.6 Personal Selling & Sales Promotion

THE ESSENTIAL QUESTION: *How could I use personal selling and sales promotion to benefit a product?*

When is personal selling appropriate, and what are the three tasks associated with personal selling? Personal selling works best when the product is somewhat expensive, somewhat complex, and aimed at a few customers close together. The three tasks of personal selling, face-to-face promotion, are (1) creative selling—determine customer needs and explain product benefits; (2) order processing—receive customer orders and deliver the product; and (3) sales support—provide supportive services after the sale.

If I were doing personal selling, what steps would I follow with a customer? Identify customers, determine if they're qualified to buy, approach them, present the product, handle objections, make the sale, and follow up.

What kinds of sales promotion techniques are available? Two kinds of sales promotion techniques are (1) trade promotion, as in using trade shows and conventions to stimulate dealer interest; and (2) business-to-consumer promotion, as in using catalogs to interest buyers.

How do guerrilla marketing and word-of-mouth marketing work? Guerrilla marketing uses innovative, low-cost schemes to get customers' attention. Word-of-mouth marketing induces people to tell others about products.

How are marketing strategies varied for different product life-cycle stages? Strategy for each of the 4-P's might need adjustment depending on whether the product is being introduced, is growing, or is in maturity or decline.

Key Terms

MyBizLab

Pop Quiz Prep

1. What role do brokers play in the distribution of goods?
2. What is an example of a product that is likely to be exclusively distributed?
3. What is *direct marketing*?
4. How do agents differ from brokers?
5. What is *supply-chain management*?
6. How are distribution centers used?
7. What does integrated marketing communication do?
8. How does the push promotional strategy work?
9. How does direct-action advertising work?
10. In terms of media buying, what is continuity concerned with?
11. When does personal selling work best?
12. What is *viral marketing*?

Critical Thinking Questions

1. Do you remember seeing four different GM vehicles with "starring roles" in the movie *Transformers*? Each model transforms into a battle-raging robot that fights the bad guys to save mankind from the destruction of their planet. The four models playing "good guy" roles in the movie include a Chevrolet Camaro, a Hummer H2, a GMC pickup truck, and an economical Pontiac Solstice convertible.[60] Product placement, which is growing in popularity, is when manufacturers pay to have their products shown or used in movies and television programs for exposure. According to *Product Placement News*, "Experts say that getting a car to play the star role in films—like the Transformers—can cost more than $10 million."[61] And companies do so out of the belief that viewers will want the same cars that they see actors driving. Morgan Spurlock of *Super Size Me* fame was able to finance his movie *The Greatest Movie Ever Sold* through product placement; he landed POM Wonderful, a pomegranate juice company, as the major financer of his film.[62,63] What are your thoughts about the effectiveness of product placement, and can you remember specific examples in movies, on TV, or elsewhere? Is there a trend in the types of products that are used in movies, music videos, and videogames?

2. As more and more athletes (and politicians) deal with scandals over torrid extramarital affairs, steroid use, and dogfighting, public relations experts are called in to reassemble public images disparaged by the media. For instance, Tiger Woods hired Ari Fleischer, former press secretary for George W. Bush, to help with his large-scale PR issues and loss of sponsorships. Consultants and public relations people agree that reassembling a tattered public image is basically a three-step process: Show genuine remorse, avoid becoming overexposed, and demonstrate that you've changed your ways.[64] Regarding rehabilitating Michael Vick's image after the dogfighting scandal, publicity agent Glenn Selid said, "He can't overdo it, and it can't seem rehearsed."[65] What is the role of a public relations firm when it comes to dealing with crisis management within an organization? If it has to do with an individual's actions (which it typically does), do you agree with the three-step process outlined?

3. When retailers feel pressure to take steps to increase immediate purchases, the result to the consumer is promotion clutter. To the consumer, it feels like promotions are everywhere, including newspapers, end-of-aisle displays in stores, magazines, online, with packaging, via e-mail, and so on. Individually or in groups, brainstorm and come up with a list of ten promotions. Discuss where you saw each and the type of promotion (sample, coupon, refund, premium, point-of-purchase, attached to a product, featured in

an ad, sweepstakes, and event sponsorships). If you acted on any of the promotional offers, please describe why. Use the box to help organize your answers

Promotion	Where Seen	Type of Promotion	Action

4. A sample is a product given to a consumer in an attempt by the producer to induce purchase. Physicians appreciate samples from drug representatives, which can be used advantageously for patients to start therapy immediately, test tolerance to a new drug, or reduce the total cost of a prescription.[66] In addition to samples, one major drug company held happy hours with members of the Los Angeles Lakers where "high prescribing" physicians were routinely invited to watch Lakers home games at a luxury suite. The drugmaker also paid for golf outings, samba dance events for Hispanic doctors, tickets to the Los Angeles Philharmonic, and liquor for physicians to induce them to increase their prescriptions and to reward them for doing so.[67] Have you ever received a sample to induce you to buy something? What are your thoughts about the pharmaceutical industry's age-old promotional practice of giving samples to physicians? How would you feel if you knew that your doctor was given lavish gifts for prescribing a particular drug to you and others? Do you think such gift-giving is ethical? Is this just an extension of giving out free samples, or an entirely different situation?

5. A 2011 study by Carnegie Mellon University's Green Design Institute found that shopping online reduces energy consumption and carbon emission by 35% compared to the traditional retail shopping model.[68] Have you ever thought about this as a positive benefit of purchasing goods online? What is your motivation when purchasing goods online?

VIDEO CASE

Michael Levy of Pet Food Express "Delivers" Food, Supplies, & Community Support

With currently over 41 retail locations, it is no accident that Michael Levay, CEO, has built Pet Food Express into the eighth largest pet specialty retailer in the United States.[69] The chain sells pet food and supplies, offers low-cost vaccinations, and offers self-service pet washes in most of its stores—a place where pet owners can get their pets "shiny and new."[70]

Pet Food Express acquires the products sold in its stores through a number of distribution channels. First, it has its own product line which it sells directly to consumers through its stores (no intermediaries). Secondly, it works with and buys directly from certain manufacturers, so it is the one intermediary between manufacturer and consumer. In addition, Pet Food Express works with wholesalers, agents, and brokers who represent hundreds of different pet supply products and companies that have varying distribution channels for getting their products to consumers (two or more intermediaries).

A company can have an incredible distribution network, as Pet Food Express does, but to be successful it also must promote its products with knowledgeable sales associates. The sales associates at Pet Food Express are focused on educating customers and sharing product knowledge so customers can determine what is best for their beloved family members. Pet Food Express has passionate, pet-loving employees who see their jobs as not only work, but also a commitment to a lifestyle and culture of bettering the lives of pets. According to the company website, "It is our employees' love and passion for pets that sets them apart and inspires them to do whatever it takes to earn the trust of their customers and make them happy."[71]

Besides distributing pet food and supplies, Pet Food Express also "distributes" significant support and assistance to Northern California animal shelters, pet rescues, schools (to help with fund-raising efforts for rescues), police department K9 programs, and a number of other pet-related causes. The website defines its focus. "What won't you find at Pet Food Express? We don't sell animals. Instead, we provide more support and assistance to Northern California shelters and rescues than any other retailer so that they can do the honorable job of finding pet-parents for millions of otherwise homeless animals."[72]

This philanthropic work combined with knowledgeable salespeople sets Pet Food Express apart in a competitive retail environment and a growing market for pet supplies. The company fosters an environment that has helped earn awards such as "Best Bay Area Pet Shop," "Best Place to Work 2010," and "Best Pet Supply Store in the U.S. 2010."[73] Whether sponsoring adoptions, offering low-cost vaccination clinics and dog training classes, or providing a state-of-the-art self-service pet

wash at its stores, this is one company willing to not only talk the talk, but walk the dog walk too.

What's Your Take?

1. Intermediaries add value to a product through the following utilities: form, location, time, information, ownership, and service. Which of the utilities apply to the value offered by Pet Food Express? Name an example for each utility.

2. Why would someone choose to shop at Pet Food Express as compared to a larger general retailer who happens to sell pet supplies and products, along with other items such as clothing, toys, and home goods? Some pet supply stores advertise themselves as "direct sellers" or "wholesalers" to create a perception of low price owing to fewer intermediaries. Do you think all pet owners shop solely on the basis of price?

3. The "My Mutt Program" at Pet Food Express helps raise funds for pet rescues and pet shelters in each of the communities where its stores are located. Through the program, customers donate a minimum of $250 to a nonprofit rescue or shelter of their choice. Pet Food Express then hires a professional photographer and photographs the donor's adorable critter. A life-sized picture of the animal is placed in a Pet Food Express window location of the owner's choice for six months (or one year for a $500 donation). How do you think the "My Mutt Program" gives Pet Food Express publicity?

4. What prompted Pet Food Express to decide to manufacture and produce some of its own products? What are the benefits for retailers in producing their own products?

Should Walmart Force Its Suppliers to Comply with Its Green Goals?

An emerging trend in supply-chain management is that suppliers and large purchasing corporations are beginning to realize the commercial benefits resulting from collaborating with suppliers for their environmental initiatives.[74] Walmart has reached out to over 100,000 of its suppliers to "ask" for help to reduce carbon emissions by 20 million metric tons by 2015.[75] Some accuse the hyper-big-box retailer of pushing its "environmental agenda" onto its suppliers and customers, calling it "regulatory vigilantism."[76]

The Environmental Defense Fund, whose mission is "to preserve the natural systems on which all life depends,"[77] will collaborate with Walmart in identifying projects, quantifying reductions, and ensuring that proper procedures and protocol will be followed to reach their lofty 2015 goal.[78]

Walmart is not demanding compliance from its suppliers in reducing carbon emissions; however, suppliers have complained that there does seem to be an underlying threat that if they don't, and don't show measurable results, they could get the boot.[79] Additionally, the big-box retailer has been accused of shifting its responsibility onto its suppliers and customers. Some argue that what Walmart is requesting and requiring goes beyond what is required by law and that it is unfair to put this pressure on suppliers, many of whom are already under pressure to keep prices at rock bottom while meeting their own carbon footprint reduction program.[80] Walmart argues that because of the sheer number of suppliers, "their carbon footprint is many times larger than the company's operational footprint, and represents a more meaningful opportunity to reduce emissions."[81] Some environmental organizations welcome this perceived heavy-handed approach as a stand that more behemoth corporations should be taking.

Walmart has seen early success with some of its environmental initiatives. For example, the company has focused on saving energy, and saving customers money through focusing on laundry. "Since heating water accounts for approximately 90 percent of the total energy consumed per load of laundry, we have increased the percentage of clothing labeled "Machine Wash Cold" from 37% to 74%."[82] Another initiative to reduce the company's carbon footprint involves reducing packaging. Walmart has begun to carry only concentrated laundry detergent in their stores, which results in smaller containers using less plastic. As a result of Unilever's concentrated laundry detergent called All Small & Mighty, Walmart expects to save more than 95 million pounds of plastic resin, conserve more than 400 million gallons of water, reduce the consumption of 520,000 gallons of diesel fuel, and reduce the need for 125 million pounds of cardboard.[83] It is not only with laundry products that the positive impact of reducing packaging can be seen; Walmart's collaboration with food giant General Mills eliminated 500 trucks on the road each year through a 20% reduction of General Mills' package size of Hamburger Helper.[84]

Are two brains better than just one? Are hundreds of thousands of suppliers working to make the earth a better place through supply-chain management better than just one hyper-big-box retailer?

What's Your Take?

1. What would you do if you were a supplier desperate to keep Walmart's business—and if the reduction in your carbon footprint resulted in higher prices for your company? Do you think there's a possibility that suppliers, in an effort to reduce costs, might increase the exploitation of their workers to keep the business profitable?

2. On its website, Walmart discusses its new focus on laundry by stating, "This change was prompted through consultation with the United States Federal Trade Commission to clarify labeling laws, and then working with our suppliers to test cold water washing's effectiveness. If just 5% of our customers switch to washing their clothes in cold water, they could reduce GHG [greenhouse gas] emissions by an estimated 2 million tons per year. Each customer who switches can also save around $124 per year on their energy bills."[85] Are you surprised to find out that you could save up to $124 a year on your utility bill by switching to washing your clothes in cold water? Would you expect to learn this type of information from a big-box retailer or your utility company? Explain.

3. According to the Walmart website, their carbon footprint reduction represents "one and a half times the company's estimated global carbon footprint growth over the next five years and is the equivalent of taking more than 3.8 million cars off the road for a year." Can you name actions companies are taking to reduce their carbon footprint?

4. Do you believe that Walmart is using its clout for a good cause by "suggesting" compliance from its suppliers in reducing carbon emissions? Is it ethical for a company to imply that its practices should be the same for others?

5. What changes in packaging have you seen with the products you purchase, and have you ever chosen a product for its eco-friendly packaging? Have you noticed a change in packaging at either online or brick-and-mortar retailers where you shop?

Briefings

MyBizLab Activities & Cases

Go to www.mybizlab.com for online activities and exercises related to the timely topics discussed in this chapter's Briefings, as well as additional theme-related Briefing *Spotlights* highlighting how these concepts apply in today's business environment.

In-chapter Briefing:
- How Selective Distribution of Luxury Goods Has Changed

Activity:
- Developing Marketable Business Skills – Geolocation & Marketing Madness

Briefing Spotlight:
- Virtual Product Placement: Avoiding Fast-Forwarding with New Ads in Old Reruns

In-chapter Briefing:
- Business Cards Can Be Made Informative to Prospective Consumers

Activity:
- Developing Marketable Business Skills – The Rewards & Rejection with Personal Selling
- Get Your Career in Gear – Advertising, Marketing, Promotions, Public Relations, & Sales Managers

Briefing Spotlight:
- Supply Chain Management: Globally Organizing Many Moving Parts

In-chapter Briefing:
- How Do You Know Eco-Friendly Claims Are True?

Activity:
- Going to the Net! – Reverse Vending Machines by PepsiCo Disperse Rewards, Not Soda

Briefing Spotlight:
- Saving Fuel, Reducing Carbon Footprint with Aluminum Pallets

In-chapter Briefing:
- The Supply-Chain Journey of an Ethan Allen Couch

Activity:
- Developing Marketable Business Skills – Supply Shocks: Japan Tsunami's Impact on U.S. Companies & the Global Supply Chain

Briefing Spotlight:
- With $80 Billion in Cash, Apple Maintains Supply Chain Dominance

458 **PART 4** Marketing: Building Satisfying Relationships with Customers

In-chapter Briefing:
- Weighing the Risks of Multilevel Marketing

Activity:
- Ethical Dilemma Case – Slotting Fees: Extracting Cash for Valuable Real Estate on Shelves
- Going to the Net! – "Secret Connectors" & Word-of-Mouth Marketing
- Going to the Net! – Gender Stereotypes in Vintage Advertisements
- Going to the Net! – Unintentional Viral Marketing: Groupon's Super Bowl Ad
- Going to the Net! – Procter & Gamble's Emotional Appeal

Briefing Spotlight:
- Audi and Competitive Advertising

In-chapter Briefing:
- The "Buy This Now!" Psychology of Infomercials

Activity:
- Maximizing Your Net Worth – Identifying Wants vs. Needs

Briefing Spotlight:
- Personal Finance and the Perils of Persuasive Advertising

In-chapter Briefing:
- Distribution Strategy for an Entrepreneur's "Recipe Deck"

Activity:
- Going to the Net! – Justin Bieber, an Entrepreneurial Success: "Never Say Never"

Briefing Spotlight:
- Marketing Mix: T-Shirts and Social Media

In-chapter Briefing:
- Applying High Tech So Buyers Can Use Their Mobile Devices to Trace a Food's Source

Activity:
- Developing Marketable Business Skills – Small Business, Small Steps

Briefing Spotlight:
- Have a Pepsi with Your Hummus?

Additional Briefing Spotlights available at MyBizLab:

- BUSINESS CULTURE & ETIQUETTE
- CUSTOMER FOCUS
- INFO TECH & SOCIAL MEDIA

15

Accounting & Financial Statements

Power in the Numbers

After reading and studying this chapter, you will be able to answer the following essential questions:

MyBizLab

Where you see MyBizLab in this chapter, go to www.mybizlab.com for additional activities on the topic being discussed.

FORECAST:
What's Ahead in This Chapter

This chapter describes two aspects of financial information—accounting and financial statements. We discuss the users of accounting, both inside and outside a company; the two major categories of accounting, managerial and financial; and the six steps in the accounting process. We discuss the three important financial statements—balance sheets, income statements, and statements of cash flows. We conclude with ratio analysis and four types of financial ratios.

MyBizLab

Gain hands-on experience through an interactive, real-world scenario. This chapter's simulation entitled Financial Management is located at **www.mybizlab.com**.

WINNERS: Small Firms Get Great Bank Loans

During the Great Recession of 2007–2009, loans were hard to get. So what was a small business to do?

Century Negotiations is a North Huntington, Pennsylvania, consumer-debt settlement firm whose revenues were $8 million in 2010. In 2005, CEO David Leuthold started having his financial records audited as a check on his own bookkeeping accuracy. The audit, a formal evaluation of a firm's books, was done by a certified public accountant (CPA), an independent professional.

Although the audit cost him $8,000, Leuthold said the action paid off when next year he applied for a $100,000 line of credit—a loan arrangement in which a bank allows a customer to borrow up to a prespecified amount to meet short-term cash needs. "The bank required audited financial statements," Leuthold says. Although he thinks he might have been able to get the loan without the audit, he believes it was given on much more favorable terms. "We had what they wanted, so it was definitely worth it," he says.[1]

Indeed, Leuthold's experience is supported by a study that found that audited businesses had better chances of getting a loan on better terms—especially in a recession—than those not audited.[2] Thus, for example, for $1 million in debt, an audited business could save about $6,900 a year as a result of lower interest rates, about half a percentage point lower than that required for a nonaudited business.

But is it worth spending $5,000 to $75,000 (depending on a firm's size and finances) for a CPA's audit just to reassure a bank that a company's financial records are correctly prepared and based on verified business data?[3] After all, the CPA could simply do a cheaper, unaudited financial statement review, although it might not result in such favorable loan terms for the client.

At the heart of this is the idea of limiting a bank's *risk*. Banks (at least at this level) "love when you have audited financials," says one CPA, "because they view it as a form of insurance."[4]

LOSERS: Sophisticated Investors Say They Didn't See Fraud

It will take years for accountants and lawyers to go through the finances of Ponzi scheme fraudster Bernard Madoff to recover whatever is left of the $50 billion he supposedly acquired. As we described in Chapter 2, Madoff, now serving 150 years in prison, operated for 16 years by paying off older investors with cash from new ones.[5]

Now the court-appointed trustee, Irving Picard, who is trying to recover lost billions for the clients Madoff swindled, is arguing that some of the initial investors should have taken a "let the buyer beware" (*caveat emptor*) approach. Thus they "deserve to lose not only the fictitious profits they received, but should also lose their original investment," according to one report. The reasoning: "They were sophisticated investors who should have known that Mr. Madoff was running a Ponzi scheme."[6]

Investors who put in more than they took out are entitled to damages, Picard thinks, but not those who took out more dollars than they invested. One group that benefited is the Fred Wilpon family, owner of the New York Mets, which would owe about $1 billion in restitution. Others are Madoff's long-standing private banker, JPMorgan Chase, and Sonja Kohn, a financier at the center of a network of hedge funds that invested heavily in the scheme.[7]

Is there something to Picard's argument that financially sophisticated investors like these should have been suspicious from the beginning that Madoff was a fraud? The imprisoned "wizard of lies" himself does not say that any particular bank or fund knew about or was an accomplice in his scheme. But, according to reporter Diana Henriques, who interviewed him in prison, "he cited a failure [by investors] to conduct normal scrutiny."[8]

In civil lawsuits, Henriques goes on, Picard "has asserted that executives at some banks expressed suspicions about Mr. Madoff for years, yet continued to do business with him and steer their clients' money into his hands." Wasn't this ignoring basic commonsense precautions against taking big risks?

YOUR CALL

You can see why accountants and auditors are important. Madoff's company actually had an accounting firm—one with only three employees and located in a strip mall, which should have been "a giant red flag," says *Time* magazine.[9] But some of the nation's largest accounting firms also signed off on Madoff's investment funds, and "it's surprising that the auditors for these various funds didn't identify that the underlying assets were not there," says one expert. "You would think that is something they test."[10] Why was this? How would you check that an investment fund was fair and reliable—and real?

MyBizLab

THE BIG IDEA: Accounting measures, classifies, analyzes, and communicates financial information to people inside and outside a company. Insiders are company owners, managers, and employees. Outsiders are investors, lenders, suppliers, and the government. The two major categories of accounting are managerial, which provides certain kinds of information to inside users, and financial, which provides other kinds of information to outside users. There are also private accountants, who work inside one firm, and public accountants, who work for any number of firms. Finally, there are not-for-profit accountants, who work for governments and nonprofits.

THE ESSENTIAL QUESTION: If I were a career accountant, what would I be doing?

MyBizLab: Check your understanding of these concepts at www.mybizlab.com.

MyBizLab

Can running a complex enterprise be reduced to a spreadsheet? Two answers: (a) Yes—because if you're not watching the numbers, you can be blind-sided.[11] (b) No—because conditions may change, rendering financial analysis misleading.[12]

Despite the possibility that conditions may change, financial information is extremely important. And the way to start is by understanding accounting principles. There is power in numbers. Accounting shows how a company is performing, and managers use such information to gauge a firm's financial health and make relevant decisions.

The Users of Accounting Information: Inside & Outside the Company

If I were an accountant, who would be the ultimate consumers of the work I created?

Accounting is the measuring, classifying, analyzing, and communicating of financial information to help people inside and outside a company make good financial decisions. Accounting differs from *bookkeeping,* which is basically the recording of a firm's financial transactions.

Users of accounting information exist both inside and outside a firm.

Inside Users: Managers & Employees

It is certainly true that some companies, usually small ones, have been run for a time with the top managers not having a true understanding of their financial operations. This is why some crooked employees are able to get away with loot-ing company accounts for months or even years before they are caught. However, managing a firm successfully requires that you know how to read the "dials and gauges" that reflect its financial health.

Want to Know More? 15-1

Key Terms & Definitions in Sequential Order to Study as You Go Along

Go to www.mybizlab.com.

The two inside users of accounting information are . . .

- **The firm's managers:** Managers need it to make plans and to guide the firm.
- **The firm's employees:** Employees use it to see if the firm is profitable, if they'll keep their jobs, if retirement accounts are healthy. But accounting information can also be used to *motivate employee performance*.

BRIEFING / LEGAL & ETHICAL PRACTICES

Using Open-Book Management to Share Accounting Information with Employees. Is there anything illegal or unethical about a company being open with its employees about its financial status—its projections, costs, expenses, and (heaven forbid) even salaries? No, there's not. In fact, suggests John Case, former editor-in-chief of *Inc.* magazine, companies work better when they share financial information with their staffs.

In *The Open-Book Experience*, Case describes how 100 companies, from multi-billion-dollar printing company RR Donnelley down to Bagel Works Inc., have empowered employees and increased earnings through "open-book management."[13] The approach includes three principles: The first is to create a *transparent* company, in which everyone, not just top managers, sees and understands the real numbers. The second is creation of a system of *joint accountability,* which holds everyone responsible for his or her part in the firm's performance. The third is to give people a *stake in their success*.

The open-book management approach means employees have to be taught how to read accounting and financial statements. But the goal makes sense: to help them feel, think, and act like owners. ❶ ■

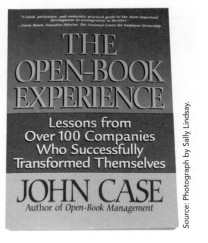

❶ **Open book management.** John Case's theory is that employees do better when they see themselves as partners in the business rather than as just hired hands. Thus, they need all relevant information about the company they are working for—profit, inventory, cash flow, and so on. They must also share in the company's prosperity. Do you agree? What if the company loses money?

Source: Photograph by Sally Lindsay.

Outside Users: Stockholders, Lenders, Suppliers, & the Government

Outsiders also need accounting information. Chief among them are . . .

- **Stockholders:** Stockholders and other outside investors need the information to see how well the firm is doing and whether it is profitable.
- **Lenders:** Banks and similar institutions need it to evaluate the company's financial health and credit rating.
- **Suppliers:** Vendors, who may extend credit, need such data.
- **Government agencies:** Authorities such as the Internal Revenue Service need such information to ensure tax revenues are collected. Regulators such as the Securities and Exchange Commission need it to confirm legal compliance and to approve issues of new stocks and bonds.

Companies whose stock is publicly traded are required to provide accounting information to outsiders on a routine basis. But even privately held companies will need to make such data available if they are seeking more investors, a bank loan, or a line of credit from a supplier.

The types of users and the uses to which they put accounting information are summarized at right. (*See* ■ *Panel 15.1.*)

■ **PANEL 15.1 Users of accounting information.**

Users	Uses
Stockholders, investors	Evaluate firm's financial health
Managers	Plan, set goals, control
Employees	Reassurance, motivation
Lenders, suppliers	Evaluate credit ratings
Government agencies	Confirm taxes, regulatory compliance

The Practitioners of Accounting: Managerial & Financial

If people asked me to define "managerial" and "financial" accounting, what would I tell them?

Counterparts (more or less) to inside users and outside users, accounting is divided into two major categories: *managerial accounting* and *financial accounting*.

1 Managerial Accounting: Providing Information to Inside Users

Managerial accounting is concerned with preparing accounting information and analyses for managers and other decision makers inside an organization. Managerial accountants prepare budgets, analyze the costs of production and marketing, determine whether departments are staying within their budgets, and similar matters. A company's finance department uses revenue and cost explanations to make budget determinations. Production managers use sales forecasts to set production levels. Marketing managers use accounting information to evaluate the impact of promotion strategies.

Example: An accountant for a new-home builder might analyze costs of materials (for the kitchen—granite versus tile counters, say, or cherrywood versus pine cabinets) to arrive at the production costs of a house. ❷

❷ Managerial accounting. Building even one luxury home requires assembling many different materials, scheduling different delivery times, and hiring many kinds of construction expertise. And, of course, the funds have to be in place—from investors and from lenders—to make it all happen, and costs must be controlled wherever possible. If you were an accountant working for a builder of 100 houses, all at the same time, what would be your biggest concern?

Source: Peter Weber/Shutterstock.

2 Financial Accounting: Providing Information to Outside Users

Financial accounting is concerned with preparing accounting information and analyses primarily for people outside the organization: stockholders, government agencies, creditors, lenders, suppliers, unions, customers, consumer groups, and so on.

Example: Every three or six months, financial accountants usually prepare three financial statements—the *balance sheet,* the *income statement,* and the *statement of cash flows*—that indicate the firm's financial health, as we will describe in Section 15.3.

Private versus Public Practitioners: Serving One Organization versus Serving Many

If I were beginning an accounting career, which would I rather be—a private or a public accountant, and why?

Practitioners of accounting are either private or public accountants, though a single organization might employ both simultaneously.

1 Private Accountants: In-House Employees

Private accountants, also called *corporate accountants,* are in-house accountants working for a single organization, whether for-profit or nonprofit. A private accountant might be on the payroll of American Airlines or JCPenney, for example, or a salaried employee of the Internal Revenue Service or Massachusetts General Hospital.

Some private accountants receive special certification as CMAs or CIAs, as follows:

Certified Management Accountant (CMA). Private accountants certified as CMAs are *certified management accountants,* which means they have passed a two-day examination, held by the Institute of Management Accountants, that tests their knowledge of managerial accounting and business.

Certified Internal Auditor (CIA). An *audit* is a formal evaluation of a client's financial records to determine their fairness and reliability. Private accountants may perform internal audits of an organization's records to determine

Want to Know More? 15-2

What Are the Requirements for Being a CMA or CIA?

Go to www.mybizlab.com.

that they follow proper accounting procedures and financial reporting. Some private accountants may be certified as CIAs, or **certified internal auditors,** which means they hold a bachelor's degree, have had two years of internal auditing experience, and have passed an examination given by the Institute of Internal Auditors. CIAs help businesses maintain control over their finances.

2 Public Accountants: Serving Many Clients for a Fee

Public accountants provide accounting services to clients on a fee basis. A client might be an individual or a for-profit or nonprofit organization. Public accountants may work as individual practitioners or they may join (usually as a CPA, discussed next) an accounting firm, such as one of the so-called Big Four accounting firms. (*See* ■ *Panel 15.2.*)

Many public accountants (and private accountants as well) are professionally licensed as **certified public accountants (CPAs), which means they have met certain requirements for education and experience and have passed a series of examinations established by the American Institute of Certified Public Accountants.** Today there are 450,000 CPAs in the United States.

Three principal services provided by CPAs are (1) *independent audits,* (2) *tax accounting,* and (3) *management advisory services.*

Independent Audits: Providing Unbiased Review of Financial Information. Many CPAs work as **external auditors,** public accountants who audit, or review, clients' financial information to see whether it was prepared under generally accepted accounting principles (GAAP—discussed in Section 15.2) and fairly presents the financial position of the firm. Such audits are called **independent audits because they are done by firms that are independent of the company being audited and therefore are presumed to provide outsiders with an unbiased opinion about the truth of the financial data being reviewed.**

⚖ BRIEFING / LEGAL & ETHICAL PRACTICES

Arthur Andersen Fails to Be Independent—and Fails as a Company. At one time the top accounting firms were known as the Big Five. But then one of them, Arthur Andersen, became the supposedly independent auditor for Houston energy giant Enron, whose irregular financial dealings caused tremendous losses, bringing the formerly No. 7 largest U.S. company to its knees. However, Andersen had become so dependent on Enron fees that it failed to maintain its neutrality and did not alert analysts and stockholders to the irregularities. Had it publicly admitted its accountability, Andersen might have averted a federal indictment and the loss of its 60 biggest U.S. clients, followed by bankruptcy.[14] ❸

Andersen and others' culpability led to the enactment of the *Sarbanes-Oxley Act of 2002,* regarding proper financial record keeping, as we described in Chapter 2. ■

Tax Accounting: Focusing on Tax Preparation and Tax Planning. Another specialty is **tax accounting, in which the CPA, trained in tax law, concentrates on preparing tax returns and doing tax planning.** The point, of course, is to minimize the client's taxes to the extent legally allowed. Because tax law is complex and ever changing, tax accountants must constantly upgrade their knowledge—given the crucial role they play for their clients.

■ **PANEL 15.2 The Big Four international accounting and professional services firms.**

Firm	2010 Revenues (in U.S. billion dollars)	Employees
Deloitte Touche Tohmatsu	$26.57	170,000
Pricewaterhouse-Coopers	$26.56	162,700
Ernst & Young	$21.25	140,964
KPMG	$20.63	137,835

Source: Scott J. Ferrell/Congressional Quarterly/Alamy.

❸ **Independent? Really?** Joseph F. Berardino, CEO of accounting firm Arthur Andersen, stated in his testimony before Congress in 2001 that bankrupt energy firm Enron might have violated securities laws. Andersen was criticized for failing in its role as an independent auditor because it depended on Enron to generate hefty consulting fees. In 2002, after being found guilty of criminal charges for mishandling the auditing of Enron, Andersen gave up its licenses to practice as Certified Public Accountants. Once one of the Big Five accounting firms, now it exists only nominally.

Management Advisory Services: Helping to Resolve Business Problems. *Management advisory services* **are specialized accounting services that CPAs offer business managers to resolve different kinds of problems,** whether it's designing accounting systems, doing production scheduling, assisting in corporate mergers, or doing financial planning.

Not-for-Profit Accountants: Working for Governments & Nonprofits

Can not-for-profit accountants do more good, and why could that be a great career?

Not-for-profit accountants, **who work for governments and nonprofit organizations, perform the same services as for-profit accountants—except they're concerned primarily with efficiency, not profits.** Let's consider the two types of clients.

Source: Oleg Golovnev/Shutterstock.

Government Accountants: Determining Where Tax Money Goes

Think of all the stories you've heard about corruption in and related to government—as, for example, has been the case with overcharging by civilian contractors in Iraq. Actually, it could be worse, were it not for the professionalism of government accountants. This includes the accountants in the *Government Accountability Office (GAO),* **the investigative arm of Congress charged with examining matters relating to the receipt and payment of public funds.** ❹

❹ **Where's this stuff going?** Government accountants at the Government Accountability Office (GAO), which is *nonpartisan,* track how taxpayer money is being spent, such as the appropriate disposal of obsolete government technology. A lot of old electronic gear, the GAO says, is sent to countries unable to do safe recycling and disposal. To see programs at "high risk" for waste, fraud, and abuse, go to www.gao .gov/press/high_risk_list_2011feb16 .html. See anything that upsets you?

Want to Know More? 15-3

What Does the Government Accountability Office Do?

Go to www.mybizlab.com.

Key Takeaway 15-1
Accountants may work as private (CMA, CIA) or public (CPA) accountants and also not-for-profit accountants.

BRIEFING / BUSINESS SKILLS & CAREER DEVELOPMENT
Working for the Government Accountability Office. What does a GAO accountant do? Every year the office issues an updated road map confronting mismanagement, waste, abuse, and fraud—whether in the collection of oil and gas royalties, in taxes owed, in finding savings in weapons systems, in cracking down on improper billing for Medicare and Medicaid, or in tackling problems in information security.

In 2003, says GAO head Gene Dodaro, the office expanded the high-risk area of information security "to include critical elements—like power distribution, water supply, telecommunications, and emergency services." It is also "creating a national and federal research and development agenda for improving cybersecurity."[15] ▪

Whether employed at the federal, state, or local level, government accountants work to provide their executives, legislators, civil servants, citizens, special-interest groups, and so on with accurate information about how tax money is being raised and spent. Government accounting standards are set by the Governmental Accounting Standards Board.

Not-for-Profit Accountants: Aiding Contributors by Providing Financial Transparency

Not-for-profit organizations consist of universities, colleges, churches, hospitals, labor unions, political parties, special-interest organizations, and philanthropic organizations such as the Red Cross, the Boy Scouts, and the Special Olympics. The most important task for not-for-profit accountants is not only to determine if the organization is staying within its budget but also to provide *financial transparency*—that is, give contributors a clear picture of where their money is going.

Want to Know More? 15-4

What Kind of Training Is Required for Forensic Accountants?

Go to www.mybizlab.com.

Forensic Accountants: Financial Sleuths

Why might I like being a forensic accountant?

"Thanks to the popularity of some criminal dramas, the word 'forensic' might cause you to think about the process of working a crime scene," says one writer.[16] But here we're not considering DNA, bloodstains, and fingerprints. **Forensic accountants investigate suspected crimes within the field of finance,** such as fraud. They investigate financial crimes, give expert testimony in court trials, and perform work related to civil disputes. As might be expected, scores of forensic accountants have been employed trying to trace the money that disappeared at Bernard L. Madoff Investment Securities. Because fraud is unfortunately a growth industry, career prospects for forensic accountants are excellent.

Want to Know More? 15-5

What Is "Green Accounting"—Environmental Management Accounting?

Go to www.mybizlab.com.

The Effect of Information Technology on Accounting

Have computers changed accounting? How?

Once bookkeeping and accounting was a tedious business of recording transactions by hand in journals, then transferring the data, again by hand, to ledgers. Information technology—computers, accounting software, and the Internet—has vastly speeded up and simplified much of this work.

Small businesses, for example, typically use an accounting program such as Intuit QuickBooks, Simply Accounting, Peachtree Complete Accounting, Sage BusinessVision Accounting, or Microsoft Office Small Business Accounting, all of which run on personal computers.[17] ❺ Large businesses use programs from SAP, Oracle, and Computer Associates, which run on more sophisticated computers. All such programs free accountants to use their time and training more productively, as in doing financial analysis.

Tax-preparation software also helps to make tedious tasks less frustrating and time consuming. Three leading personal tax-preparation programs are TurboTax, H&R Block at Home, and TaxAct.[18]

❺ **Small-biz money management.** Since its original publication, Intuit's QuickBooks software has appealed to small-business owners who lack formal accounting training. In the early 2000s, it began offering versions that met the standards of professional accountants, as well as industry-specific alternatives. If small businesses are using QuickBooks, do you think they still need the services of a CPA? Why?

Source: Intuit, Inc.

THE BIG IDEA: Accounting relies on standards known as generally accepted accounting principles to ensure that financial statements are relevant, reliable, consistent, and comparable. The accounting process involves six activities that may be summarized as collect, record, classify, summarize, report, and analyze. That is, find and sort records, put daily transactions in journals, put journal entries in categories in a ledger, test the accuracy of the ledger by running a trial balance, issue financial statements, and assess the firm's financial condition, using ratio analysis.

THE ESSENTIAL QUESTION: How would I describe the six parts of the accounting process to an interested person?

MyBizLab

MyBizLab: Check your understanding of these concepts at www.mybizlab.com.

Accountants. Will just about anyone do?

Not any more. If you're a businessperson, you need to find an accountant who understands what you do—who knows that being a manufacturer, say, is different from being a doctor.[19] Whatever an accountant's specialty, however, he or she begins with certain accounting principles that start out the same way.

Generally Accepted Accounting Principles: Relevance, Reliability, Consistency, & Comparability

What are the standards underpinning how accounting is supposed to work? How could they change?

In almost every line of work or discipline there are "bibles" or standards as to how things ought to work, whether it's pavement standards in road building or punctuation standards in publishing. Accounting has its own standards—the *generally accepted accounting principles (GAAP),* **a set of accounting standards used in the preparation of financial statements to ensure that they are (1) relevant, (2) reliable, (3) consistent, and (4) comparable.** When financial statements are consistent and comparable, users can compare them with earlier statements from the same company and with statements from other companies. (*See* ■ *Panel 15.3.*)

The legal authority for GAAP standards rests with two organizations:

- **The SEC:** The *Securities and Exchange Commission (SEC)* **is a federal agency that regulates the various stock exchanges,** among other things. (We discuss the SEC in detail in Chapter 17.)
- **The FASB:** Interestingly, the SEC delegates the primary responsibility for GAAP to a private body, the *Financial Accounting Standards Board (FASB),* **a private, self-regulating organization that establishes, evaluates, and enforces the principles used in financial accounting.**

■ **PANEL 15.3 The goals of GAAP.** The four qualities that generally accepted accounting principles try to ensure in financial statements.

A Financial Statement Should Be . . .	This Means the Information Should . . .
Relevant	Help users understand the company's financial status and financial performance.
Reliable	Be accurate, objective, and verifiable.
Consistent	Always be based on the same assumptions and procedures (and any changes must be clearly explained).
Comparable	Allow users to compare it (1) with other firms' information and (2) at different times.

Recently, the SEC moved to allow some large American companies to begin using international accounting standards—known as the *International Financial Reporting Standards (IFRS)*—established by the International Accounting Standards Board, starting in 2010. It urged that all publicly traded American companies be required to follow such standards by 2016.[20] The purpose of this is to move the world toward one set of standards, making it easier for investors to compare companies operating in different countries. It would also make it easier for companies to raise investment funds (capital) in whatever market seemed most attractive. Indeed, under international standards, U.S. companies would be able to report higher earnings. Clearly, though, it will mean some significant changes in U.S. accounting rules.

The Six Steps of the Accounting Process

If someone asked me what the six phases of the accounting process are, how would I answer?

The ***accounting process* consists of six activities that result in converting information about individual transactions into financial statements that can then be analyzed.** The purpose of the process, which is diagrammed at right, is to determine which financial documents are affected and how. (*See* ■ *Panel 15.4*.)

1 Collect: Find & Sort Records of Business Transactions

The accounting process begins by collecting the results of bookkeeping—that is, the records of all relevant business transactions: sales invoices, cash receipts, travel records, shipping documents, and so on. Today many or most of these transactions exist as computerized data. The transactions are analyzed by the bookkeeper and sorted into meaningful categories according to various financial strategies, some of which involve ways of reducing tax obligations.

2 Record: Put Daily Transactions in Journals, Using Double-Entry Bookkeeping

The bookkeeper then records financial data from the original transaction documents in a ***journal,* a record book or part of a computer program containing the daily record of the firm's transactions,** including a brief description of each.

The format for recording each journal entry is known as ***double-entry bookkeeping* because each transaction is recorded in two different accounts to make sure each adds up to the same amount,** as a check on errors. Thus, if a bookkeeper enters $9.49 in one place but mistakenly puts $9.94 in another, when the two accounts don't produce the same total that will be a tip-off that an error occurred.

■ **Example** of Double-Entry Bookkeeping: Single Entry versus Double Entry. If you run a bicycle repair shop, a *single-entry* bookkeeping transaction to repair a tire would look as follows:[21]

Date	Service or Sale	Revenues	Expenses
Feb 6	Tire repair	30.00	

A *double-entry* bookkeeping entry would look like this:

Date	Accounts	Debit	Credit
Feb 6	Cash	30.00	
	Revenue		30.00

1. Collect
Find and sort records of relevant business transactions.

2. Record
Put daily transactions in journals, using double-entry bookkeeping.

3. Classify
Put journal entries in categories in a ledger.

4. Summarize
Test the accuracy of ledger data by running a trial balance.

5. Report
Issue financial statements: *balance sheet, income statement,* and *statement of cash flows.*

6. Analyze
Assess the firm's financial condition, using ratio analysis.

With double-entry bookkeeping, notice that for each debit there is an equal and opposite credit. Thus, the total of all debits must equal the total of all credits. If they don't, it's obvious an error was made. Recording each transaction as both a debit and a credit keeps the books in balance, as we'll discuss with the balance sheet and accounting sheet. ■

3 Classify: Put Journal Entries in Categories in a Ledger

Suppose you want to know what your firm's travel expenses were for the past month. The daily journal records will show these expenses scattered throughout, but not all lumped together. That is the purpose of the bookkeeper's transferring (usually on a monthly basis) journal entries to a *ledger,* **a specialized record book or computer program that contains summaries of all journal transactions, accumulated into specific categories.** The ledger is divided into accounts, such as cash, inventories, and receivables, as we will explain.

4 Summarize: Test Ledger Data Accuracy by Doing a Trial Balance

At the end of every accounting period (every three months, say), the bookkeeper does a check for accuracy. This is known as running a *trial balance,* **making a summary of all the data in the ledgers to see if the figures are accurate, or balanced.** *Balanced* means both columns in the double-entry format have similar totals—they balance each other.

5 Report: Issue Financial Statements

Once the bookkeeper has the correct figures, he or she (or the accountant) can use that summarized data to issue three reports, or financial statements—the *balance sheet,* the *income statement,* and the *statement of cash flows*—as we will describe in Section 15.3. Most companies prepare computer-generated financial statements every month, three months (quarterly), or six months (semiannually). Financial reports may also be tied to two other matters—the organization's *fiscal year* and the release of its *annual report.*

The Fiscal Year. Financial reports are required of all publicly traded companies at the end of the firm's *fiscal year,* **the 12-month period designated for annual financial reporting purposes.** This period may coincide with the end of . . .

* **The calendar year:** The standard year, January 1 to December 31.
* **The U.S. government's fiscal year:** October 1 to September 30; for firms with government contracts, financial reports may appear sometime after September 30.
* **A particular industry's natural cycle:** In agriculture, for example, it is September 1 to August 31 (when the harvest is over).

The Annual Report. After the fiscal year-end, a firm issues an ***annual report,*** **showing its financial condition and outlook for the future.** ❻

❻ **Annual reports.** Classy covers, inspiring photos, lofty ideals—all are features of annual reports, particularly those of Fortune 1000 firms. The real truth—indeed, the real drama—is probably in the numbers and in the footnotes. Do you think you can be considered financially literate if you don't know how to read annual reports?

Source: Photograph by Sally Lindsay.

6 Analyze: Assess the Firm's Financial Condition, Using Ratio Analysis

With the financial statements in hand, the accountant can then make an assessment of the company's financial condition. The principal means for making this evaluation is *ratio analysis,* as we also discuss in Section 15.3.

Key Takeaway 15-2
The steps in the accounting process are collect, record, classify, summarize, report, and analyze.

PRACTICAL ACTION
How to Read an Annual Report

Every publicly traded company is required by the Securities and Exchange Commission (and the state in which the company is registered) to provide annual reports to shareholders and the public. These documents may be obtained with all their colorful photos and fancy graphic design from the firm's investor relations department or in basic text form from the SEC's website, www.sec.gov.

Not all annual reports are alike, but all contain a corporate profile, letter from the chairperson, auditor's report, and financial statements—balance sheet, income statement, and cash flow statement.[22] But if you're contemplating investing in a company, don't read the annual report from front to back, like a novel. Instead, try going about it this way:

Read the Auditor's Report First

The *auditor's report* or *certified public accountant's opinion letter* may be located toward the middle or end of the annual report. This is the section that summarizes the conclusions of an independent accountant, who has checked the report for accuracy. Jane Bryant Quinn, business commentator for the *CBS Morning News* and former columnist for *Newsweek,* suggests you read this section first. You should watch for the words "subject to," which means the financial report "is clean *only* if you take the company's word about a particular piece of business, and the accountant isn't sure you should."[23]

She suggests you also look at the *footnotes,* which will tell you why, for example, earnings are up (maybe it's only because of a windfall that won't happen next year—bad news) or down (perhaps because of a change in accounting—could be good news).

Read the Letter from the Chairperson

Next, suggests Quinn, you should go to the front of the annual report, to the letter from the chairperson. This is supposed to tell you how the company fared during the past year and why. "Keep an eye out for sentences that start with 'Except for . . .' and 'Despite the . . .' They're clues to problems." The chairperson's letter should also give you insights into the company's future.

Get to the Numbers: Balance Sheet, Income Statement, & Cash Flow Statement

We explain the three most important financial statements—balance sheet, income statement, and cash flow statement—in the next section. Here let us suggest what you should look for in these statements in an annual report.[24]

- **The balance sheet:** This shows the firm's assets and liabilities. The assets are listed in order by how easily they can be converted into cash. The liabilities list how much the firm owes other businesses (accounts payable), income taxes payable, and long-term debt.
- **The income statement:** This shows the net sales, cost of goods sold, and expenses and their bottom line in terms of net income or net loss for the year. You can compare the income statements from year to year to see how the company is doing.
- **The cash flow statement:** This category, which indicates the inflow and outflow of money, shows how the firm got and used cash.

Compare from Year to Year

There's much more to reading an annual report, but this will provide the basis. The main thing, however, is to learn how to compare the various categories from year to year and learn why they change.

THE BIG IDEA: Financial statements, periodic reports that show where a company's money came from, where it went, and where it is now, are of three types: (1) A balance sheet reports a firm's financial condition by specifying its assets, liabilities, and owners' equity. (2) An income statement shows a firm's revenues, expenses, and resulting profit or loss. (3) A statement of cash flows reports a firm's cash receipts and disbursements related to its operating, investing, and financing activities, to arrive at a cash balance.

THE ESSENTIAL QUESTION: What are the three important financial statements?

MyBizLab

MyBizLab: Check your understanding of these concepts at www.mybizlab.com.

---

7 Fiscally and socially responsible. Mike Hannigan *(left)* and Sean Marx head up Give Something Back Office Supplies of Oakland, California. The firm's profits may be used for social purposes, but the firm's success depends in great part in staying on top of its numbers. Can you think of firms in which these are reversed—selfish use of profits, sloppy tracking of finances?

Source: Courtesy of Give Something Back Office Supply.

Key Takeaway 15-3
Keep in mind there are three types of financial statements, and remember what they are.

One of the latest trends in business is *management by data*, in which firms try to stay ahead of their rivals by collecting more information and managing it better.[25] In particular, this means managing their *financial data*.

BRIEFING / SOCIALLY RESPONSIBLE BUSINESS
A Financially Conscious Business with an Unusual Purpose. Some CEOs spend their firms' earnings on luxuries. Not Mike Hannigan and Sean Marx, founders of the largest privately owned office supply company on the West Coast. Its name: Give Something Back Office Supplies. **7**

The Oakland firm was started in 1991 with the idea of using "the marketplace to create wealth on behalf of the community," says Hannigan. Says Marx: "I loved the idea of being able to combine what I do for work with improving the quality of life in the world I live in."[26] Donations, which topped $500,000 in 2010, go to recipients ranging from Guide Dogs for the Blind to Stand Against Domestic Violence.

However, the 88-employee firm has to perform like any other company, competing on price and service and constantly watching the numbers. Thus, it is a serious user of financial statements. ■

Financial statements are periodic reports that show where a company's money came from, where it went, and where it is now. They *show you the money!*[27] **Three types of financial statements are (1)** *balance sheets,* **(2)** *income statements,* **and (3)** *statements of cash flows.* Let's consider these.

The Balance Sheet: What We're Worth, How We Got There

What is the "accounting equation," and how is it represented in detail on a balance sheet?

Accountants employ what is known as the *accounting equation* to determine what a firm is worth. The *accounting equation* is: **Assets = Liabilities + Owners' equity.** Applied to you as an individual, here's what this means:

- **Assets:** Assets are what you have of value (cash, vehicles, and so on).
- **Liabilities:** Liabilities are what you owe (student loans, other debts).

- **Owners' equity:** Owners' equity is the amount of your investment plus earnings—your net worth after you sell assets and pay debts.

The accounting equation underlies the *balance sheet* and *income statement* (explained next). **The *balance sheet* reports a firm's financial condition at a given time by showing its assets, liabilities, and owners' equity.** It is called a *balance sheet* because it shows a balance between a firm's (a) *assets* and (b) *liabilities* plus *owners' equity*, as for retailer Best People Inc. (*See* ■ *Panel 15.5.*)

Let's consider the three concepts of *assets, liabilities,* and *owners' equity.*

Key Takeaway 15-4
The accounting equation is: Assets = Liabilities + Owners' equity. It is the basis for the balance sheet and the income statement.

Want to Know More? 15-6

What Can You Learn from a Balance Sheet?

Go to www.mybizlab.com.

BEST PEOPLE INC.
Balance Sheet, Year ending December 31

ASSETS

① Current assets

Cash	$ 39,120	
Marketable securities	4,000	
Accounts receivable	75,000	
Merchandise inventory	176,000	
Subtotal: All current assets		$294,120

② Fixed assets

Land	$ 30,000	
Buildings and improvements	200,000	
Less: Accumulated depreciation	(15,000)	
	185,000	
Equipment and vehicles	90,000	
Less: Accumulated depreciation	(12,000)	
	78,000	
Furniture and fixtures	80,000	
Less: Accumulated depreciation	(4,000)	
	76,000	
Subtotal: All fixed assets		369,000

③ Intangible assets

Goodwill	40,000	
Subtotal: All intangible assets		40,000
TOTAL ASSETS		**$703,120**

LIABILITIES

④ Current liabilities

Accounts payable	$ 50,840	
Notes payable	16,000	
Subtotal: All current liabilities		$ 66,840

⑤ Long-term liabilities

Notes payable	$ 80,000	
Bonds payable	60,000	
Subtotal: All long-term liabilities		$140,000
TOTAL LIABILITIES		**$206,840**

⑥ OWNERS' EQUITY

Common stock	$361,280	
Retained earnings	135,000	
TOTAL OWNERS' EQUITY		**$496,280**
TOTAL LIABILITIES AND OWNERS' EQUITY		**$703,120**

■ **PANEL 15.5 A balance sheet for hypothetical electronics retailer Best People Inc.** The numbers in circles at the left are used to help explain the various parts, starting on the next page. The relationship between liabilities and owners' equity is an important consideration to creditors and investors.

1 Assets: "What Things of Value Do We Own?"

An *asset* **is anything of value that is owned by a firm.** Examples: Buildings, land, supplies, inventories, cash, money owed to the firm, patents, and trademarks are all assets.

Assets are of three types: *current, fixed,* and *intangible.*

❶ **Current Assets: Things That Can Be Converted into Cash within One Year.** *Current assets* **are defined as items that can be converted into cash within one year.** This includes not only cash itself (currency and coin), of course, but also *marketable securities, accounts receivable,* and *merchandise inventory.*

- **Marketable securities:** *Marketable securities* **are stocks, bonds, government securities, and money market certificates, which can be easily converted to cash.**
- **Accounts receivable:** *Accounts receivable* **is the total amount owed to a firm from customers who have purchased goods or services on credit.**
- **Merchandise inventory:** *Merchandise inventory* **is merchandise that is being held for resale to customers.**

The essential characteristic of current assets is their *liquidity;* **they are easily converted into cash,** whereas assets such as land and buildings are not.

❷ **Fixed Assets: Things That Are Held for a Long Time.** Often called "property, plant, and equipment," *fixed assets* **are items that are held for a long time and are relatively permanent,** such as land, buildings and improvements, equipment and vehicles, and furniture and fixtures. Fixed assets are expected to be used for several years.

Accumulated depreciation **is the reduction in value of assets to reflect their wearing down or obsolescence over time.**

❸ **Intangible Assets: Valuable Assets That Aren't Physical Objects.** *Intangible assets* **are assets that are not physical objects but are nonetheless valuable, such as patents, trademarks, and goodwill.** *Goodwill* **is an amount paid for a business beyond the value of its other assets,** based on its reputation, customer list, loyal employees, and similar intangibles.

BEST PEOPLE INC.
Balance Sheet, Year ending December 31

ASSETS

❶ **Current assets**	
Cash	$ 39,120
Marketable securities	4,000
Accounts receivable	75,000
Merchandise inventory	176,000
Subtotal: All current assets	$294,120
❷ **Fixed assets**	
Land	$ 30,000
Buildings and improvements	200,000
Less: Accumulated depreciation	(15,000)
Equipment and vehicles	90,000
Less: Accumulated depreciation	(12,000)
Furniture and fixtures	80,000
Less: Accumulated depreciation	(4,000)
Subtotal: All fixed assets	$369,000
❸ **Intangible assets**	
Goodwill	40,000
Subtotal: All intangible assets	$ 40,000
TOTAL ASSETS	**$703,120**

2 Liabilities: "What Are Our Debts to Outsiders?"

A *liability* **is a debt owed by a firm to an outside individual or organization.** Examples: Vendors may deliver supplies but not insist on immediate payment, allowing the firms 30 or 60 days, say, to pay their bills. Banks may loan farmers money to enable them to operate, but want to be paid after the crop has been harvested and sold. Employees who have provided labor but not yet been paid also represent a debt to the firm.

Liabilities are of two types: *current* and *long-term.*

4 Current Liabilities: Payments Due within One Year or Less. *Current liabilities* **are obligations in which payments are due within one year or less.** The most common current liabilities are *accounts payable* and *notes payable.*

- **Accounts payable:** *Accounts payable* **is money owed to others that the firm has not yet paid.** If the company has not yet paid its electricity bill this month, that debt belongs in accounts payable.

- **Notes payable:** *Notes payable* **is money owed on a loan based on a promise (either short-term or long-term) the firm made.** If you arranged a bank loan, for example, you would be obligated to pay it back by a prearranged date.

5 Long-Term Liabilities: Payments Due in One Year or More. *Long-term liabilities* **are obligations in which payments are due in one year or more,** such as for a long-term loan from a bank or insurance company. Two common long-term liabilities are *notes payable* and *bonds payable,* **long-term liabilities that represent money lent to the firm that must be paid off.**

3 Owners' Equity: "What Is Our Value If We Were to Sell Our Assets & Pay Off Our Debts?"

6 *Owners' equity,* **or** *stockholders' equity,* **represents the value of a firm if its assets were sold and its debts paid.** Owners' equity is considered important because it is used to indicate a company's financial strength and stability. Before making loans to a company, for example, lenders want to know the amount of owners' equity in it.

Owners' equity consists of (1) *common stock* and (2) *retained earnings.*

LIABILITIES	
4 Current liabilities	
Accounts payable	$ 50,840
Notes payable	16,000
Subtotal: All current liabilities	$ 66,840
5 Long-term liabilities	
Notes payable	$ 80,000
Bonds payable	60,000
Subtotal: All long-term liabilities	$140,000
TOTAL LIABILITIES	**$206,840**
6 OWNERS' EQUITY	
Common stock	$361,280
Retained earnings	135,000
TOTAL OWNERS' EQUITY	**$496,280**
TOTAL LIABILITIES AND OWNERS' EQUITY (assets minus liabilities plus owners' equity)	**$703,120**

Common Stock: The Most Basic Form of Ownership in a Firm. As we explain later (Chapter 17), *common stock* is a particular kind of stock. For now let's just say it represents the most basic kind of ownership in a firm.

Retained Earnings: Earnings Retained by a Firm for Its Use, Not Paid as Dividends. *Retained earnings* **are net profits minus dividend payments made to stockholders; that is, they are earnings retained by a firm for its own use**—for buying more land and buildings, say, or acquiring other companies. (*Dividends,* which we discuss in Chapter 17, are part of a company's profits that are distributed to stockholders.)

Want to Know More? 15-7

What Are Other Lines That May Appear on Balance Sheets?

Go to www.mybizlab.com.

The Income Statement: What Our Revenue & Expenses Were & the Resulting Profit or Loss

What are the four parts of an income statement?

As mentioned, the accounting equation (Assets = Liabilities + Owners' equity) is also used to compute a firm's income statement. **The** *income statement,* **once known as the** *profit-and-loss statement,* **shows a firm's revenues and expenses for a particular time period and the resulting profit or loss.** The income statement has

Want to Know More? 15-8

What Can You Learn from an Income Statement?

Go to www.mybizlab.com.

four principal parts: (1) *sales revenue*, (2) *cost of goods sold*, (3) *operating expenses*, which lead to the bottom line of (4) *net income*. (See ■ Panel 15.6.)

■ **PANEL 15.6 Income statement.** The income statement may be for any period of time—week, quarter, or year.

BEST PEOPLE INC.
Income Statement, Year ending December 31

❶ Sales revenue		
Gross sales		$280,000
Less: Sales returns and allowances		(1,500)
Net sales		278,500
❷ Cost of goods sold		
Less: Cost of goods sold		(154,500)
Gross profit		124,000
❸ Operating expenses		
Selling expenses		
Salaries for salespeople	42,800	
Advertising expenses	4,500	
Supplies	4,500	
Total selling expenses	51,800	
Administrative expenses		
Administrative salaries	27,000	
Supplies	10,000	
Depreciation—office equipment	4,178	
Insurance	2,400	
Rent	7,000	
Light, heat, power	2,920	
Total administrative expenses	53,498	
Total operating expenses		(105,298)
Net operating income (before taxes)		18,702
Less: Income tax expense		(2,805)
❹ Net income (after taxes)		$ 15,897

1 Sales Revenue: "What Were the Net Sales of Our Merchandise?"

❶ **Sales revenues are the funds received from the sales of goods and services during a certain period.** The figure of interest to us is arrived at by taking *gross sales* and subtracting *sales returns and allowances*, to arrive at *net sales*.

BEST PEOPLE INC.
Income Statement, Year ending December 31

❶ Sales revenue	
Gross sales	$280,000
Less: Sales returns and allowances	(1,500)
Net sales	278,500
❷ Cost of goods sold	
Less: Cost of goods sold	(154,500)
Gross profit	124,000

Gross Sales: Total Revenue from All Products Sold. *Gross sales* are the funds received from all sales of the firm's products.

Sales Returns and Allowances: Refunds to Customers. *Sales returns* are products that customers return to the company for a refund. *Allowances* are partial refunds to customers for damaged products they choose to keep, not return.

Net Sales: Gross Sales Minus Returns and Allowances. *Net sales* is the money resulting after sales returns and allowances are subtracted from gross sales.

2 Cost of Goods Sold: "How Much Did It Cost to Acquire, Make, or Provide the Merchandise?"

❷ *Cost of goods sold* **is the cost of producing a firm's merchandise for sale during a certain period.**

Knowing net sales and cost of goods sold, you are now in a position to determine the gross profit. **The *gross profit*, or *gross margin*, is the amount remaining after the cost of goods sold is subtracted from the net sales.**

3 Operating Expenses: "What Were Our Selling & Administrative Expenses?"

❸ *Operating expenses* **are selling and administrative expenses.**

Selling Expenses: Costs of the Sales Effort. *Selling expenses* are all the expenses incurred in marketing the firm's products, such as salespeople's salaries, advertising, and supplies.

Administrative Expenses: Costs of General Business Operations. *Administrative expenses* are costs incurred for the general operation of the business, such as salaries, supplies, depreciation, insurance, rent, and utilities.

4 Net Income—the Bottom Line: "What After-Tax Profit or Loss Did We Wind Up With?"

❹ *Net income,* **the firm's profit or loss after paying income taxes, is determined by subtracting expenses from revenues.** Net income is an important measure of company success or failure. **❽**

❸ **Operating expenses**		
Selling expenses		
Salaries for salespeople	42,800	
Advertising expenses	4,500	
Supplies	4,500	
Total selling expenses	51,800	
Administrative expenses		
Administrative salaries	27,000	
Supplies	10,000	
Depreciation—office equipment	4,178	
Insurance	2,400	
Rent	7,000	
Light, heat, power	2,920	
Total administrative expenses	53,498	
Total operating expenses		(105,298)
Net operating income (before taxes)		18,702
Less: Income tax expense		(2,805)
❹ **Net income (after taxes)**		**$ 15,897**

❽ Ale and hearty. How much do you think Brewery Ommegan, which brews Belgian-style ales in Cooperstown, New York, paid for this beer-making equipment? Launching a pub with beers and ales provided by others is expensive enough. Starting a brewery is an entirely different ballgame—and considerably more expensive. What kind of net income do you think could be realized from such an operation?

Source: Vespasian/Alamy.

The Statement of Cash Flows:
How Money Came & Went

What can I learn about a company's operations from a statement of cash flows?

The *statement of cash flows* reports over a period of time, first, the firm's cash receipts and, second, disbursement related to the firm's (1) operating, (2) investing, and (3) financing activities, which leads to the bottom line of (4) the cash balance. (*See* ■ *Panel 15.7*.)

■ **PANEL 15.7 Statement of cash flows.**

BEST PEOPLE INC.
Statement of Cash Flows, Year ending December 31

❶ Cash flow from operating activities

Cash received from customers	$450,000
Cash paid to suppliers and employees	(270,000)
Interest paid	(15,000)
Income tax paid	(13,500)
Cash interest and dividends received	4,500
Net cash from operating activities	$156,000

❷ Cash flow from investing activities

Proceeds from sale of plant assets	$12,000
Payments for purchase of equipment	(30,000)
Net cash from investing activities	$(18,000)

❸ Cash flow from financing activities

Proceeds from issuance of short-term debt	$ 9,000
Payment of long-term debt	(21,000)
Payment of dividends	(45,000)
Net cash from financing activities	$(57,000)
Net increase in cash	$ 81,000
Cash balance at beginning of year	(6,000)

❹ Cash balance at end of year $ 75,000

Want to Know More? 15-9

What Can You Learn from a Statement of Cash Flows?

Go to www.mybizlab.com.

1 Operating Activities: "What Were the Incomes & Costs of Running Our Business?"

❶ *Cash flows from operating activities* reflect income from sales and other income and payments for salaries, interest, taxes, and so forth. These are the ordinary costs of running a business.

2 Investing Activities: "How Much Did We Earn from Our Investments?"

❷ *Cash flows from investing activities* reflect the cash received from selling long-term assets, cash spent on buying equipment, and other investment activities.

3 Financing Activities: "How Well Did We Do from Our Loans to Others, Payment of Debt, & Our Stock Transactions?"

❸ *Cash flows from financing activities* reflect the inflows and outflows of borrowed funds and long-term debt, sales of new stock, and payment of dividends.

4 Cash Balance: "How Much Money Is Available at the End of the Year?"

❹ *Cash balance* is the balance in the firm's cash account at the end of the year. Analyzing and understanding cash flow is vital to the success of any firm, since many failed businesses blame their financial distress on inadequate cash flow.

THE BIG IDEA: Ratio analysis is an important type of financial analysis that is used to evaluate variables in a financial statement. Four types of financial ratios are liquidity ratios, to determine how well a firm can pay its liabilities as they come due; activity ratios, to see how well the firm manages its assets to generate revenue; debt to owners' equity ratios, to determine how much the firm relies on borrowing to finance its operations; and profitability ratios, to see how good the firm's profits are in relation to its sales, assets, or owners' equity.

THE ESSENTIAL QUESTION: What is ratio analysis, and what are four types of financial ratios?

MyBizLab: Check your understanding of these concepts at www.mybizlab.com.

MyBizLab

Accountants don't just prepare financial statements. They also *analyze* the financial data to provide the firm's managers and investors with a better understanding of financial performance. One way of doing so is through *ratio analysis.* (Two other ways are horizontal analysis and vertical analysis, which can be used to compare financial statement numbers and ratios over a number of years.)

Ratio analysis uses one of a number of financial ratios—such as liquidity, activity, debt to owner's equity, and profitability—to evaluate variables in a financial statement. Ratio analysis can be used to analyze a firm's performance (1) compared to its stated objectives and (2) compared to that of similar firms.

We discuss four types of financial ratios in this section.

> **Want to Know More? 15-10**
> **What Are Horizontal Analysis & Vertical Analysis?**
> Go to www.mybizlab.com.

Liquidity Ratios: How Well Can We Pay Our Liabilities as They Come Due?

What are two important liquidity ratios?

Liquidity ratios measure a firm's ability to meet its short-term obligations when they become due. They are of interest to anyone who wants to know whether a firm is able to pay its short-term debts on time. Two important liquidity ratios are . . .

- The *current ratio*, and
- The *acid-test* (or *quick*) *ratio*.

■ **Example of Current Ratio: With a Ratio Exceeding 2.0, Best People Inc. Is a Great Loan Candidate.** The *current ratio* consists of current assets divided by current liabilities.

For Best People, the balance sheet (page 473) shows current assets of $294,120 and current liabilities of $66,840. When the first number is divided by the second, it produces a ratio of 4.40. That is,

$$\text{Current ratio} = \frac{\text{Current assets}}{\text{Current liabilities}} = \frac{\$294,120}{\$66,840} = 4.4$$

MyBizLab

Gain hands-on experience through an interactive, real-world scenario. This chapter's simulation entitled OBM and Financial Statements is located at www.mybizlab.com.

This means the company has $4.40 in assets for every $1 in liabilities. Since anything above 2.0 (the average such ratio for all industries) is considered healthy, on the basis of the current ratio the Best People electronics business appears to be doing very well. Bankers being asked to make a short-term loan or extend a line of credit will be impressed. ■

■ **Example of Acid-Test Ratio: Best People Beats the Standard Ratio of 1.0.** The *acid-test ratio,* or *quick ratio,* consists of cash + marketable securities + receivables, all divided by current liabilities.

Best People's balance sheet (page 473) shows $39,120 in cash, $4,000 in marketable securities, and $75,000 in accounts receivables, totaling $118,120. The current liabilities are $66,840. Thus,

$$\text{Acid-test ratio} = \frac{\text{Cash} + \text{Marketable securities} + \text{Receivables}}{\text{Current liabilities}} = \frac{\$118,120}{\$66,840} = 1.77$$

With a ratio of 1.77, Best People certainly beats the conventional acid-test ratio of 1.0. If it were lower than 1.0, Best People might have to boost its cash by borrowing from a high-cost lender, obtaining additional cash from investors, reducing dividend payments to stockholders, or selling inventory cheap. ■

Activity Ratios: How Well Do We Manage Our Assets to Generate Revenue?

What is the purpose of activity ratios?

Activity ratios, or efficiency ratios, are used to evaluate how well management uses a firm's assets to generate revenue. That is, they express how well a company can turn its assets (such as inventory) into cash to pay its short-term debts. Activity ratios include the *accounts receivable turnover ratio* and the *total asset turnover ratio,* but here let's consider the *inventory turnover ratio,* which measures the number of times a company sells its inventory in a year's time. The more frequently a firm can sell its inventory, the greater its revenue.

⑨ Too much obsolete inventory? Inventory turnover ratios can help a firm discover how well it is managing its inventory. Electronics retailer Best People seems to need improvement here.

Source: moodboard/Alamy.

■ **Example of Inventory Turnover Ratio: Is Best People's Inventory Obsolete?** The *inventory turnover ratio* consists of: cost of goods sold in one year divided by the average value of the inventory.

Best People's income statement (page 476) shows costs of goods sold was $154,500. Although for simplicity's sake we did not show the average inventory on that statement, it is determined by adding the inventory value at the end of last year to the inventory value at the end of the previous year and dividing by 2, which is $73,000. Thus,

$$\text{Inventory turnover ratio} = \frac{\text{Costs of goods sold}}{\text{Average inventory}} = \frac{\$154,500}{\$73,000} = 2.11$$

Inventory turnover ratios vary by industry and by company, with Nike, for example, turning over its inventory about 4.5 times a year and Starbucks 14.7 times a year. A high ratio may indicate efficiency. A low ratio, as seems to be the case with Best People, may indicate too much obsolete inventory or a need to sharpen buying strategy. ⑨ ■

Debt to Owners' Equity Ratios: How Much Do We Rely on Borrowing to Finance Our Operations?

How are debt to owners' equity ratios useful?

Debt to owners' equity ratios are measures of the extent to which a company uses debt, such as bank loans, to finance its operations. If a firm takes on too much debt, it may have problems repaying borrowed funds or paying dividends to stockholders.

■ Example of Debt to Owners' Equity Ratio: Best People Is Not Overloaded with Debt. The *debt to owners' equity ratio* consists of total liabilities divided by owners' equity.

Best People's balance sheet (page 473) shows that total liabilities were $206,840 and total owners' equity was $496,280. Accordingly,

$$\text{Debt to owners' equity ratio} = \frac{\text{Total liabilities}}{\text{Owners' equity}} = \frac{\$206,840}{\$496,280} = 41.7\%$$

With a ratio of 41.7% (nearly 42%), this means that Best People has borrowed nearly $42 for every $100 the owners have provided. The more the debt approaches 100%, the more difficult it will be for the company to borrow money from lenders. For now, Best People seems to be in reasonably good shape. ■

Profitability Ratios: How Good Are Our Profits in Relation to Our Sales, Assets, or Owners' Equity?

What three things do profitability ratios measure?

Profitability ratios are used to measure how well profits are doing in relation to the firm's sales, assets, or owners' equity. Three important profitability ratios are *return on sales (profit margin), return on assets,* and *return on owners' equity.*

■ Example of Three Profitability Ratios: Calculating Return on Best People's Sales, Assets, and Owners' Equity. Best People may know what its net income is after taxes—$15,897, according to the income statement (page 476). To determine how well the firm is using its resources, this number is put into three equations, as follows:

Return on sales, or *profit margin,* is net income divided by sales:

$$\text{Return on sales} = \frac{\text{Net income}}{\text{Net sales}} = \frac{\$15,897}{\$278,500} = 5.7\%$$

This means for every $100 in sales, the firm had a profit of $5.70. Between 4% and 5% is considered a reasonable return, so in its return on sales, Best People is certainly doing better than most.

Return on assets is net income divided by total assets:

$$\text{Return on assets} = \frac{\text{Net income}}{\text{Total assets}} = \frac{\$15,897}{\$703,120} = 2.26\%$$

A return of $2.26 on every $100 invested in assets is quite a low return, which suggests Best People is not using its assets very efficiently.

Return on owners' equity, also called *return on investment (ROI),* is net income divided by owner's equity:

$$\text{Return on owners' equity} = \frac{\text{Net income}}{\text{Owners' equity}} = \frac{\$15,897}{\$496,280} = 3.2\%$$

The company thus generates only $3.20 for every $100 invested in the business. Since the average for business in general is 12% to 15%, Best People is obviously a disappointment to its owners (investors or stockholders). Clearly, the firm's top managers will have to pay better attention to the business if they are to keep their jobs. ∎

Now that you've been grounded in accounting and financial statements, you are well prepared to move on to the study of financial management and other important money matters in Chapter 16.

LEARNING & SKILLS PORTFOLIO

Summary

15.1 Accounting: Users & Practitioners

THE ESSENTIAL QUESTION: *If I were a career accountant, what would I be doing?*

If I were an accountant, who would be the ultimate consumers of the work I created? Accounting is the measuring, classifying, analyzing, and communicating of financial information to help people inside and outside a company make good financial decisions. Inside users are the firm's managers and employees; outside users include stockholders, lenders, suppliers, and government agencies.

If people asked me to define "managerial" and "financial" accounting, what would I tell them? Managerial accounting is concerned with preparing accounting information and analyses for firm insiders, such as managers. Financial accounting is concerned with preparing accounting information and analyses for people outside the firm—stockholders, government agencies, creditors, lenders, suppliers, and so on.

If I were beginning an accounting career, which would I rather be—a private or a public accountant, and why? A private accountant, an in-house accountant working for a single organization, may be a certified management accountant (CMA), who has passed an examination held by the Institute of Management Accountants. Or he or she may be a certified internal auditor (CIA), who holds a bachelor's degree, has two years of internal auditing experience, and has passed an exam given by the Institute of Internal Auditors. An audit is a formal evaluation of a client's financial records to determine their fairness and reliability. Public accountants, who provide accounting services to clients on a fee basis, are often licensed as certified

public accountants (CPAs), who have met certain education requirements and passed exams given by the American Institute of Certified Public Accountants. CPAs may provide independent audits, tax accounting, or management advisory services.

Can not-for-profit accountants do more good, and why could that be a great career? Not-for-profit accountants, who work for governments and nonprofit organizations, are more concerned with efficiency than with profits. They may work for the Government Accountability Office (GAO), the investigative arm of Congress charged with examining matters relating to the receipt and payment of public funds, and for universities, churches, hospitals, political parties, and philanthropic organizations.

Why might I like being a forensic accountant? Forensic accountants investigate suspected crimes within the field of finance, such as fraud.

Have computers changed accounting? How? Computers, accounting software, and the Internet have vastly speeded up and simplified much of the tedious tasks of accounting.

15.2 The Accounting Process: Six Steps for Analyzing an Organization's Finances

THE ESSENTIAL QUESTION: *How would I describe the six parts of the accounting process to an interested person?*

What are the standards underpinning how accounting is supposed to work? How could they change? The generally accepted accounting principles (GAAP) are standards used in the preparation of financial statements to ensure they are relevant, reliable, consistent, and comparable. The authority of the GAAP rests with the Securities and Exchange Commission (SEC), a federal agency that regulates various stock exchanges, and the Financial Accounting Standards Board (FASB), a private, self-regulating organization that establishes, evaluates, and enforces the GAAP.

If someone asked me what the six phases of the accounting process are, how would I answer? The six activities—collect, record, classify, summarize, report, and analyze—result in converting information about individual transactions into financial statements that can be analyzed. The steps are as follows: (1) Find and sort records of relevant business transactions. (2) Put daily transactions in journals, a record book or computer program containing the daily record of the firm's transactions, using double-entry bookkeeping, in which each transaction is recorded in two different accounts to act as a check on errors. (3) Put journal entries in categories in a ledger, a specialized record book or computer program that contains summaries of all journal transactions, accumulated into specific categories. (4) Test the accuracy of the ledger data by running a trial balance, making a summary of all data in the ledgers to see if the figures are accurate. (5) Issue financial statements, summaries of all transactions occurring during a single point in time, at the end of the organization's fiscal year, the 12-month period designated for annual financial reporting purposes—and for the annual report, which shows the firm's financial condition and outlook for the future. (6) Assess the firm's financial condition, using ratio analysis (described below).

15.3 Financial Statements & Financial Analysis: The Vocabulary of Accounting

THE ESSENTIAL QUESTION: *What are the three important financial statements?*

The three financial statements are balance sheet, income statement, and statement of cash flows.

What is the "accounting equation," and how is it represented in detail on a balance sheet? The accounting equation is: Assets = Liabilities + Owners' equity. The balance sheet reports a firm's financial condition at a given time by showing its assets, liabilities, and owners' equity. (1) An asset is anything of value that is owned by a firm. Assets may be current, fixed, or intangible. Current assets are items that can be converted into cash within one year (such as marketable securities, stocks, bonds, government securities, and money market securities); accounts receivable, the total amount owed to a firm from customers who have purchased goods or services on credit; and merchandise inventory, merchandise that is being held for resale to customers. Fixed assets are items that are held for a long time and are relatively permanent, such as land and buildings. Intangible assets are assets that are not physical objects but are nonetheless valuable, such as patents, trademarks, and goodwill. (2) A liability is a debt owed by a

firm to an outside individual or organization. Liabilities may be current or long-term. Current liabilities are obligations in which payments are due within one year or less. The most common current liabilities are accounts payable, money owed to others that the firm has not yet paid, and notes payable, money owed on a loan based on a promise the firm made. Long-term liabilities are obligations in which payments are due in one year or more. Notes payable and bonds payable are two common long-term liabilities that represent money lent to the firm that must be paid off. (3) Owners' equity represents the value of a firm if its assets were sold and its debts paid. Owners' equity consists of common stock and retained earnings (net profits minus dividend payments made to stockholders).

What are the four parts of an income statement? The income statement shows a firm's revenues and expenses for a particular time period and the resulting profit or loss. It has four principal parts: (1) Sales revenues are the funds received from the sales of goods and services during a certain period. It is arrived at by taking gross sales (funds received from all sales of the firm's products) and subtracting sales returns and allowances to arrive at net sales. (2) Cost of goods sold is the cost of producing a firm's merchandise for sale during a certain period. (3) Operating expenses are selling and administrative expenses. (4) Net income or net loss is the firm's profit or loss after subtracting expenses and taxes from revenues.

What can I learn about a company's operations from a statement of cash flows? The statement of cash flows reports over a period of time, first, the firm's cash receipts and, second, the firm's operating, investing, and financing activities, which leads to the bottom line of the cash balance.

15.4 Using Financial Analysis to Dig Deep: Ratio Analysis

THE ESSENTIAL QUESTION: *What is ratio analysis, and what are four types of financial ratios?*

Ratio analysis uses one of a number of financial ratios to evaluate variables in a financial statement.

What are two important liquidity ratios? Liquidity ratios such as the current ratio and the acid-test ratio measure a firm's ability to meet its short-term obligations when they become due.

What is the purpose of activity ratios? Activity ratios are used to evaluate how well management uses a firm's assets to generate revenue.

How are debt to owners' equity ratios useful? Debt to owners' equity ratios are measures of the extent to which a company uses debt, such as bank loans, to finance its operations.

What three things do profitability ratios measure? Profitability ratios are used to measure how well profits are doing in relation to the firm's sales, assets, or owners' equity.

accounting 462
accounting equation 472
accounting process 469
accounts payable 475
accounts receivable 474
accumulated depreciation 474
activity ratios 480
annual report 470
asset 474
audit 464
balance sheet 473
bonds payable 475
bookkeeping 462
certified internal auditor (CIA) 465
certified management accountant (CMA) 464
certified public accountant (CPA) 465
cost of goods sold 476
current assets 474
current liabilities 475
debt to owners' equity ratio 481
double-entry bookkeeping 469

external auditor 465
financial accounting 464
Financial Accounting Standards Board (FASB) 468
financial statement 472
fiscal year 470
fixed assets 474
forensic accountant 467
generally accepted accounting principles (GAAP) 468
goodwill 474
Government Accountability Office (GAO) 466
gross profit 477
income statement 475
independent audit 465
intangible assets 474
journal 469
ledger 470
liability 474
liquidity 474
liquidity ratios 479

long-term liabilities 475
management advisory services 466
managerial accounting 464
marketable securities 474
merchandise inventory 474
net income 477
notes payable 475
not-for-profit accountant 466
operating expenses 477
owners' equity 475
private accountant 464
profitability ratios 481
public accountant 465
ratio analysis 479
retained earnings 475
sales revenue 476
Securities and Exchange Commission (SEC) 468
statement of cash flows 478
tax accounting 465
trial balance 470

Pop Quiz Prep

1. How is *managerial accounting* defined?
2. What is the difference between for-profit and not-for-profit accountants?
3. What is the FASB?
4. How does the bookkeeper run a trial balance?
5. What is the accounting equation?

6. What does the income statement represent?
7. What is the current ratio for a firm with current assets of $2 million and current liabilities of $0.5 million?
8. Which kind of ratios evaluate how well management uses a firm's assets to generate revenue?

Critical Thinking Questions

1. The term "bean counter" is often used in jest and sometimes negatively to describe an overly zealous or fastidious accountant.[28] It is possible that the description was inspired by fervent kitchen inventory takers who insisted on counting every bean in a bag or every potato in a sack. Discuss characteristics of how an accountant needs a certain attention to detail, and what can happen when there is too much attention to detail.

2. The Sarbanes-Oxley Act of 2002 (covered in Chapter 2) establishes requirements for proper financial reporting and record keeping, and minimizes the possibilities of financial misrepresentation at publicly held companies. Unfortunately, there are no such requirements in place for smaller, privately held companies. Should there be controls in place for these companies? If so, who should be in charge of the oversight of such practices? What type of fraud do you think small businesses commonly face?

3. There are many reasons for the failure of retailer Circuit City, but one, according to Helen Bulwik, a retail consultant, was basic inventory management. "They had been unable to move their inventory," she says. "That backlog left the company paralyzed, unable to buy fresh product or pay off its existing debts."[29] What is the risk of slow moving inventory and what can a company do if inventory is not selling? How do you think inventory value is calculated for an electronics retailer?

4. Open-book accounting is an extension of open-book management principles that encourages companies to share financial information (sometimes including salaries) with all employees, and give them the opportunity to directly profit from the company's performance.[30] The goal is to help employees feel, think, and act like owners. How does open-book accounting result in profit for employees? Do you agree with this practice? What are its downsides?

5. To ensure success, human asset accounting, also referred to as human resource accounting, takes into consideration the value and role people play in the organization, which includes the replacement cost of people and the role the organization plays investing in its people.[31] How would you apply the concept of human asset accounting to Apple since the death of its CEO, Steve Jobs?

VIDEO CASE
POPS Diner: Accounting for Food, Fuel, & Fizz

Every business uses accounting information to make important decisions, and POPS Diner, which boasts the largest retail selection of bottled soda anywhere in the United States,[32] is no exception. POPS is a futuristic gas station, restaurant, and soda pop store (they offer over 400 brands) located on the famous Route 66 in Arcadia, Oklahoma.[33] The diner is designed with "equal parts Americana, New Age, and Soda Pop," and boasts a 66-foot-tall steel pop bottle sculpture that is lit up "ala Times Square."[34] The motto of POPS is "Food, Fuel, Fizz." POPS was named one of *Travel and Leisure* magazine's top 50 "must see" U.S. attractions.[35]

How did this "futuristic icon" and unique piece of Americana come about? Aubrey McClendon, chief executive officer, chairman, and cofounder of Chesapeake Energy Corporation, came up with the idea to open a "cool" gas station next to a nearby tree farm he owns in Arcadia.[36] He teamed up with a well-known architect to design this not-so-ordinary roadside stop.[37] POPS, which opened in August 2008, sold 66,000 bottles of soda pop within its first two months,[38] which translates to an average of about 1,100 bottles a day—now that's a lot of transactions to make and record.

Accounting, often called "the language of business,"[39] or the "organizing of monetary information,"[40] is the vehicle through which companies like POPS report financial information to various people and groups within and outside of their organization. There are two main types of accounting: management and financial.

Accounting that POPS reports to people within its organization is called management accounting. This type of accounting is used to provide information to employees, managers, owners, and auditors as a basis for making decisions related to marketing, production, and finance. For POPS this would be activities like pricing the sodas, determining wages, formulating order sizes, and determining units of equipment needed. Managers need to have a pretty good understanding of what the numbers say in order to make good decisions.[41]

Accounting information that POPS provides to those outside of the organization is called financial accounting.[42] Those "outside" of the organization include shareholders, investors, creditors such as banks (who provide loans), vendors (who offer trade credit), and government agencies (for tax-reporting purposes).[43] POPS is required to submit important financial information to the government when the company files its taxes, to creditors such as banks to continue to receive financing, to its investors, and to vendors and suppliers (the many companies who supply the soda pop and other items sold).

As sales remain fizzy for this major tourist destination in the U.S. heartland, the "bottle counters" at POPS continue to taste the sweetness while realizing the importance of accounting information to manage and control its finances and resources. After all, 400 varieties of soda is a lot to look after.

What's Your Take?

1. Go to the POPS website (www.pops66.com) to learn about the various businesses within this iconic roadside attraction. Based on what you have learned from watching the video and exploring the POPS website, what types of items would you assume might be found on its balance sheet?

2. According to the text, the accounting process involves six activities: collect, record, classify, summarize, report, and analyze. Based on what you know about its business, give an example of how POPS would engage in each of the activities.

3. Discuss why it is important for the owner of a new business like POPS (or any business, for that matter) to understand accounting. What are some possible consequences for a business owner lacking a proper understanding of accounting?

4. Accounting is more than just keeping records for annual tax reporting. It allows businesspeople to make important decisions. List some of the decisions that the people at POPS might make using accounting information.

5. Based upon what you have learned in the case and the video, and drawing on some of the common ratios used to analyze a business, what assumptions would you make about POPS' (1) liquidity, (2) inventory turnover, and (3) debt ratios? Do you believe the inventory turnover ratio varies for each variety of soda sold?

Hollywood Accounting: Creative, but Not So Glamorous for Writers & Actors

My Big Fat Greek Wedding made a big fat profit of $20 million, but despite this, Tom Hanks sued Gold Circle Films, co-financier of the movie, alleging that he is owed an agreed-upon percentage share of net profits—which wasn't paid.[44] Actors and writers are paid a percentage (called royalties) of net profits.

"Hollywood accounting" is a hot topic in Hollywood, and although the term may sound glamorous, it is anything but that to the many writers and actors who feel they aren't getting the earnings they are contractually entitled to. In a recently leaked Warner Brothers (creator of the *Harry Potter* movies) accounting statement, the studio alleged that the film *Harry Potter & the Order of the Phoenix*, grossing $938 million, was still $167 million "in the hole."[45]

There are many other similar lawsuits in Hollywood over the way net profits are "calculated." The accounting reports by the film studios do not follow and generally disregard the generally accepted accounting principles (GAAP). The reported net profit can be a complex document (unique to each studio) explaining the accounting methodology employed by the studio. This has some writers and actors (who are paid royalties on net profits) fuming over the alleged "accounting" practice.

The simplified version of the explanation according to industry insiders is that "Hollywood sets up a separate corporation for each movie made, with the intent that the corporation will take on losses on the project. After the corporation is set up, the film studio charges the film corporation an exorbitant fee making up for the bulk of the expense leading to the 'loss.' The end result is that the studio still rakes in the cash, but for accounting purposes the film is considered a money "loser"—which matters quite a bit for anyone who is supposed to get a cut of the profits."[46]

Take the film *Fahrenheit 911*, for example. Michael Moore sued producers of the film, claiming that profits were diverted rather than paid to him based upon an agreed upon 50-50 split, which would have amounted to $2.7 million in profits. This is the first time Moore has ever sued anyone in his 20-year career, and he is accusing the Weinstein brothers (who formed Fellowship Adventure Group to distribute the film) of "deceptive accounting practices," and "Hollywood accounting tricks."[47]

At the heart of the issue is the controversial way in which movie costs are calculated. The industry budgets and records profits for film projects in such a way that expenditures are inflated. The net profit isn't stated accurately; it is actually deflated, which is not full and accurate accounting.[48] Part of how the expenditures are inflated has to do with how overhead is calculated. Overhead refers to fixed costs and includes items such as production, distribution, and marketing. Unfortunately, a long held tradition in Hollywood is that these costs really do not relate to actual costs and can be calculated more on a percentage basis (percentage of sales, for example), without regard for actual costs.

Believe it or not, the accounting practices employed are "legal." The issue at the center of this controversy is the meaning of the term *net profit*, and how it is calculated. Most know the definition of net profit to be revenues minus expenses, but beyond this, there are certain industries—and the movie business is one of them—where there needs to be a special language to explain when revenue is recognized and expenses are incurred.[49] According to motion picture lawyers Joseph Hart and Philip Hacker, "It is somewhat surprising to the layperson, then, to learn that the reports to net-profit participants by studios do not follow Generally Accepted Accounting Principles. Instead, these rules are disregarded, and the reported net profit follows a complex document which explains the accounting methodology employed by the studio."[50] Statistically speaking, it is said that even the blockbuster films in Hollywood do not show a net profit, and that less than 5% actually do. Unbelievable? While it is not at all entertaining for the actors, that's Hollywood!

What's Your Take?

1. Why do you think film producers continue to go through the process of making writers and lower-level actors and filmmakers feel they have a stake in the game? Do you see any other alternatives to this sort of deal making?

2. In an article entitled, "Hollywood Accounting Losing in the Courts," the writer discusses how more and more film companies are losing legal battles similar to the cases discussed above. Do you think the studios are in for a glut of lawsuits as their "accounting tricks" are exposed? Discuss.

3. Knowing what you now know about Hollywood accounting, if you were a Hollywood actor or writer, how would you go about constructing your contract or agreement with the film producer?

4. Some compare the antics of Hollywood accounting to the hush nature of salaries in corporations. In an article entitled, "We Call It Martian Accounting," the author states: "The studio doesn't want it to get out that it paid, say, George Clooney $15 million for his last movie, lest Denzel Washington ask for the same amount. Similarly, Renée Zellweger may not want people to know that she did her last role for $4 million, lest the studios try to hold her to that price again."[51] Do you agree that this is part of the explanation of Hollywood accounting?

Go to www.mybizlab.com for online activities and exercises related to the timely topics discussed in this chapter's Briefings, as well as additional theme-related Briefing *Spotlights* highlighting how these concepts apply in today's business environment.

In-chapter Briefing:
- Working for the Government Accountability Office

Activity:
- Get Your Career in Gear – Rosy Outlook for Accounting & Auditing Careers

Briefing Spotlight:
- Forensic Accountants: White-Collar Financial Sleuths

In-chapter Briefing:
- Using Open-Book Management to Share Accounting Information with Employees
- Arthur Andersen Fails to Be Independent—and Fails as a Company

Activity:
- Developing Marketable Business Skills – Accounting Fraud & Dell Computers
- Developing Marketable Business Skills – "And the Winner Is . . .": Public Accountants & the Oscars
- Ethical Dilemma Case – Government Accountability Office Investigates the Exporting of Toxic Waste
- Going to the Net! – Biggest Corporate Accounting Scandals . . . Ever!

Briefing Spotlight:
- Cynthia Cooper: A Courageous Internal Auditor

In-chapter Briefing:
- A Financially Conscious Business with an Unusual Purpose

Activity:
- Going to the Net! – Triple Bottom Line: Social, Environmental, & Economic Performance

Briefing Spotlight:
- Audits: Not Just for Financial Performance

Additional Briefing Spotlights available at MyBizLab:

- A WORLD OF CONSTANT CHANGE
- BUSINESS CULTURE & ETIQUETTE
- CUSTOMER FOCUS
- EARNING GREEN BY GOING GREEN
- GLOBAL BUSINESS
- INFO TECH & SOCIAL MEDIA
- PERSONAL FINANCE
- SMALL BUSINESS & ENTREPRENEURS

16 Financial Management

A Basic Guide to Finances, Money, & Banking

After reading and studying this chapter, you will be able to answer the following essential questions:

MyBizLab

Where you see MyBizLab in this chapter, go to www.mybizlab.com for additional activities on the topic being discussed.

FORECAST: What's Ahead in This Chapter

This chapter describes financial management and financial planning—forecasting, budgeting, and financial controls; the four reasons firms borrow money; and sources of short-term and long-term financing. We also consider money, beginning with a discussion of the money supply and how money gets into the banking system. We then describe banks and nonbanks, and how depositors are protected. Finally, we describe regulation and deregulation.

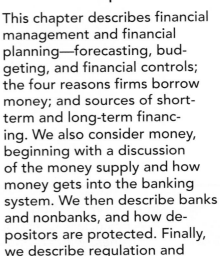

MyBizLab

Gain hands-on experience through an interactive, real-world scenario. This chapter's simulation entitled Financial Management is located at **www.mybizlab.com**.

WINNER: Live Oak Succeeds by Lending to Veterinarians

When the 2008 financial crisis hit and loans and credit dried up, veterinarian Marla Litchenberger of Glendale, Wisconsin, was turned down by six banks for a loan to build an emergency animal clinic. "As a startup, no one wanted to finance us," she says. "The economy was very bad."[1]

Then she was recommended to Live Oak Bank of Wilmington, North Carolina, and within a few months received a $2 million loan and began construction on the Milwaukee Emergency Center for Animals and Specialty Services. "Live Oak wasn't more accepting of startups than other lenders," says reporter Emily Maltby in the *Wall Street Journal*, "but it was more attuned to the specific needs of animal hospitals. The bank's portfolio [range of investments] is 92% made up of loans to veterinarians."[2] (Remaining loans are to only two other groups—dentists and pharmacists.)

Centuries ago banks were often started for the purpose of making loans to a particular industry. Some were known as "merchant banks," which offered a blend of access to growth capital and trusted advice.[3] Although most now serve a broad range of customers, their past specialties survive in such names as Farmers Bank, Mechanics Bank, or Manufacturers Bank and Trust Company.

Today Silicon Valley Bank in Santa Clara, California, caters to information technology and biotech firms. Borel Private Bank helps lawyers set up their practices. Citi Private Bank offers specialty loans for purchasing art. The advantages of specialty banks, of course, is their knowledge of particular industries. Thus, loan officers can advise on business plans, monitor how cash flows in and out, and spot instances of mismanagement.

In 2010, Live Oak was ranked third of the nation's top 10 Small Business Administration lenders by gross loan volume.[4]

Source: Courtesy of Live Oak Bank.

DOWNEY SAVINGS

LOSER: Downey Financial Fails with Adjustable Home Loans

When the financial history of the early 21st century is written, one of the most interesting aspects will be the way lenders found creative ways to make money. Some of these methods, unfortunately, led to the 2008 disastrous failures of such well-known financial institutions as Bear Stearns, Fannie Mae, Freddie Mac, Merrill Lynch, and others, necessitating a $700 billion U.S. government economic rescue.

How did it happen? The story can be found in the practices of such institutions as the Downey Financial Corporation, a big California savings and loan. Downey was founded right after World War II by Maurice McAlister, who officially resigned as CEO in 2008 after the company's shares plummeted 90% in a year. (The firm filed for bankruptcy.)

"At the heart of Downey's troubles," says one account, "are so-called option adjustable-rate mortgages, some of the riskiest home loans ever created. With option ARMs, lenders like Downey offered homebuyers temptingly low initial interest rates and let them choose how much to pay each month. The less borrowers paid, the more the lenders tacked onto the balance."[5]

The strategy worked fine as long as home prices kept rising, and by 2007, 69% of Downey's residential loans were option loans. Then house prices and the economy started to deteriorate, homeowners became unable to pay higher payments as ARMs reset interest rates upward, and Downey found itself saddled with huge numbers of bad loans whose buyers had simply stopped paying.

Downey could have diversified into other consumer loans, from credit cards to auto loans, but McAlister apparently believed that he had no choice but to do as he did. "You play the market," he said, "and practically . . . all the bankers were playing the same game."

Source: Photograph by Sally Lindsay.

YOUR CALL There were ample warnings in 2006 that a financial meltdown might be coming.[6] Why didn't Downey CEO McAlister see them? One reason was that Downey was a family-controlled firm that for decades suffered from manager turnover, so it grew out of touch with changing times. Of course, hundreds of other, nonfamily-type lenders with different structures were equally blind. Still, weren't the numbers there for all to see? Live Oak clearly survived, perhaps by virtue of its specialization. However, today specialized lenders are considered risky by bank regulators, "especially in light of the financial fallout that resulted from too-high concentration of loans in the real-estate market," says Maltby. If you were a banker looking to specialize, which industries do you think would be the safest to make loans to and the most recession-proof?

MyBizLab

THE BIG IDEA: Financial management is the job of acquiring funds for a firm and managing them to accomplish the firm's objectives. An important aspect is the risk-return trade-off, balancing the firm's risk with expected returns from its investments. A financial plan, a firm's strategy for reaching its financial goals, has three parts: (1) *forecasting*, predicting revenues, costs, and expenses; (2) *budgeting*, a detailed plan for estimated revenues and expenses for the period; and (3) *financial controls*, in which revenues and expenses are compared to the budgeted figures.

THE ESSENTIAL QUESTION: What is financial management, and what are the parts of a financial plan?

MyBizLab

MyBizLab: Check your understanding of these concepts at www.mybizlab.com.

*F*inance, or *corporate finance*, is the business function of obtaining funds for a company and managing them to accomplish the company's objectives. Finance activities include establishing budgets and financial controls, determining long-term investments, analyzing cash flows, planning the expenditure of funds, and managing the firm's financial risks.

BRIEFING / SMALL BUSINESS & ENTREPRENEURS

The Biggest Mistakes Startups Make. New business owners often have energy and passion for their products and services, says Kevin Kerridge, director of Bermuda-based insurer Hiscox Ltd., which surveyed 500 U.S. small-business owners. But they seem to have some disturbing failings.

"Owners said they lacked a sufficient understanding of taxes, financing, and credit—and hiring and firing—before launching the business," reports a *Wall Street Journal* account.[7] In other words, besides being naïve about staffing matters, they didn't anticipate the importance of managing finances. ■

Financial Management: What It Is, Why It's Important

What does a financial manager do, what is the risk-return trade-off, and why is financial management important?

The job of acquiring and managing funds is called *financial management*. Let's see what this involves.

The Job of Financial Manager & the Risk-Return Trade-Off

Who practices financial management? **The people responsible for planning and controlling the acquisition and uses of funds are called *financial managers*.** The top such manager in a firm often holds the title of *chief financial officer (CFO)*. Other titles you may encounter are the *vice president for financial management*, the *treasurer*, and the *controller*, who often report to the CFO. Of course, in a small firm, this job is probably done by the owner.

Want to Know More? 16-1

Key Terms & Definitions in Sequential Order to Study as You Go Along

Go to www.mybizlab.com.

Central to the job of financial management is ***risk-return trade-off***, in which financial managers continually try to balance the firm's investment risk with the expected return, or payoffs, from its investments.

BRIEFING / SMALL BUSINESS & ENTREPRENEURS

The Risk-Return Trade-Off of Small-Business Owners Who Can't Pay Their Taxes. It's the end of March and you as a small-business owner suddenly realize you don't have enough money to pay your income taxes. What do you do? Dip into credit cards? (Expensive.) Divert payroll tax money? (You could be liable.) Raid your retirement account? (You might pay penalties.) Consider an installment-payment program with the IRS? (You'll have to pay penalties and interest.)[8]

All these are possible solutions, but all involve various risks and different returns. To find the best solution, you have to do your research and crunch the numbers. ■

The Importance of Financial Management: Solvency & Efficiency

Many a business has closed its doors simply because managers weren't paying sufficient attention to its finances. Thus, there are a number of essential responsibilities that a financial manager oversees. (*See ■ Panel 16.1.*)

- **Oversee bill payment:** He or she has to make sure the company is paying its bills and paying them on time (so as not to be charged interest) but not too early (so that the firm's money can be used for investment).
- **Oversee collection of money owed:** The manager is also responsible for making sure the firm collects money owed to it by customers.
- **Minimize taxes:** He or she must also keep up with tax-law changes so as to advise managers on what decisions to make to minimize tax payments.
- **Monitor accounting:** Finally, the manager, or a subordinate, should examine the accounting department's accounts to make sure they are accurate and free of improprieties.

All these activities have two purposes. The first is *solvency*—being able to pay debts when they become due. The second is *efficiency*—managing money in the optimum way. The end goal, of course, is *profitability*.

Financial Planning: Forecasting, Budgeting, & Financial Controls

How would I distinguish among the three parts of a financial plan— forecasting, budgeting, and financial controls?

A ***financial plan*** is a firm's strategy for reaching its financial goals. It has three parts: (1) forecasting, (2) budgeting, and (3) financial controls. A financial plan may be as short as 1 month or as long as 10 years. Most short-term lenders are interested in 1-year financial plans, but long-term investors such as stockholders care more about long-range financial plans, such as 5 years or more.

1 Forecasting: "How Do We Predict How the Company's Money Will Come & Go?"

Forecasting **is predicting revenues, costs, and expenses for a certain period of time.** There are three types of forecasts—*cash flow, short-term,* and *long-term.* (*See ■ Panel 16.2.*)

■ **PANEL 16.1 What do financial managers do?** Unlike accountants, who record financial details and prepare financial statements, financial managers interpret these reports and suggest strategies for improving the firm's financial performance and enhancing profitability.

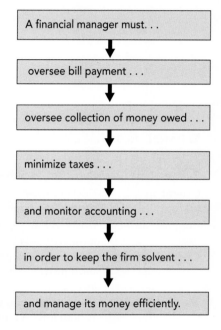

A financial manager must. . .

↓

oversee bill payment . . .

↓

oversee collection of money owed . . .

↓

minimize taxes . . .

↓

and monitor accounting . . .

↓

in order to keep the firm solvent . . .

↓

and manage its money efficiently.

■ **PANEL 16.2 Three types of forecasts.**

Forecast Type	Predictions for . . .
Cash flow	1–3 months
Short-term	4–12 months
Long-term	1, 5, or 10 years

Cash Flow Forecasts: Predictions about Money Flows in the Next 1 to 3 Months. A *cash flow forecast* is a prediction about how money will come into and go out of a firm in the near future, usually within the next 1 to 3 months. Such forecasts are based on anticipated sales and on anticipated expenses.

Short-Term Forecasts: Predictions for the Next Year or Less. Based in part on cash flow forecasts, a *short-term forecast* is a prediction about how money will come into and go out of a firm during the next 4 to 12 months.

Long-Term Forecasts: Predictions for the Next 1, 5, or 10 Years. A *long-term forecast* is a prediction about how money will come into and go out of a firm during the next 1, 5, or 10 years. Long-term forecasts may be varied to reflect different long-range strategic plans.

2 Budgeting: "What Are Our Expected Revenues & Expenses?"

■ **PANEL 16.3 Principal types of budgets.**

Budget Type	Purpose: To Show . . .
Operating budget	Costs to meet sales and production goals
Capital budget	Costs to buy expensive long-term assets
Cash budget	Cash in and out for each month and the full year
Master budget	Preceding budgets tied together for a particular period

The second part of a financial plan is budgeting. **A *budget* is defined as a detailed financial plan showing estimated revenues and expenses for a particular future period, usually one year.** That is, a budget indicates expected revenues and, based on those expectations, allocates resources throughout the company. Thus, it helps managers identify specific resources needed to achieve company goals and, in terms of the planning/organizing/leading/controlling managerial functions, is both a planning and control tool.

The four principal types of budgets, which are based on short-term and long-term forecasts, are (1) *operating budgets,* (2) *capital budgets,* (3) *cash budgets,* and (4) *master budgets.* (*See* ■ *Panel 16.3.*)

Operating Budgets: For Predicting Sales and Production Goals and the Costs Required to Meet Them. *Operating budgets* **identify a firm's sales and production goals and specify the costs required to meet those goals.** The sales budget indicates the number of units of products that the firm expects to sell and the total sales revenue it hopes to realize. Based on the sales budget, the other operating budgets indicate the labor, materials, and other costs required to produce that number of products and to sell them. ❶

❶ **Budget for bon bons.** Even a small candy factory and retail store should have an operating budget that includes sales and production goals and describes the costs of meeting them. Presumably that would cover a whole lot of sugar.

Capital Budgets: For Predicting Purchase of Long-Term Assets. *Capital budgets* estimate a firm's expenditures for purchasing long-term assets that require significant sums of money, such as buildings, machinery, and equipment. A capital budget covers a year's time, although it can be projected years into the future.

Cash Budgets: For Predicting Cash Shortages or Surpluses during the Year. *Cash budgets* forecast cash inflows and outflows for a stated period, usually one to three months. The purpose of cash budgets is to show management where it may have cash shortages or surpluses throughout the year so that managers can anticipate when they may have to borrow money, when to repay, and so on. An example of a cash budget is shown below. (*See* ■ *Panel 16.4.*)

■ PANEL 16.4 **Example of a cash budget.**

	June	July	August
BEST PEOPLE INC. Three-Month Cash Budget			
Projected monthly sales	$105,000	$120,000	$110,000
Collections			
Cash sales	$ 23,000	$ 26,000	$ 18,500
Credit sales	$ 87,000	$ 99,000	$ 96,000
Total monthly cash collections	$110,000	$125,000	$114,500
Disbursements			
Wages and salaries	$ 33,750	$ 37,500	$ 59,500
Supplies and materials	22,000	20,000	21,000
Rent, utilities, insurance	13,000	13,000	13,000
Taxes	3,500	3,500	3,500
Other expenses	6,000	4,300	7,500
Total monthly cash payments	$ 78,250	$ 78,300	$104,500
Cash budget			
Excess or deficit of cash for month	$ 31,750	$ 46,700	$ 10,000
Beginning cash balance	(3,000)	0	0
Total cash	$ 28,750	$ 46,700	$ 10,000
Less minimum cash balance ($10,000)	(10,000)	(10,000)	(10,000)
Cash available for short-term investment	$ 18,750	$ 36,700	$ 0
Total cash balance at end of month	$ 0	0	0

Capital budgets and cash budgets are called *financial budgets,* because they concentrate on the company's financial goals and the resources needed to achieve them.

Master Budgets: For Pulling Together the Other Budgets into an Overall Plan of Action. *Master budgets* tie together the above three budgets—operating, capital, and cash budgets—to present the company's overall plan of action for a particular time period.

3 Financial Controls: "How Do Our Actual Revenues & Expenses Compare with Those We Budgeted?"

The third part of a financial plan is monitoring, a process known as *financial control,* in which a company from time to time compares its actual revenues and expenses with those predicted in its budget. The purpose of this monitoring process is to identify deviations from the financial plan so that corrective action can be taken.

Key Takeaway 16-1
A financial plan has three parts: (1) forecasting, (2) budgeting, and (3) financial controls.

16.2

Finding Funds to Keep the Firm Operating

THE BIG IDEA: Firms borrow money to manage their ordinary business activities, to extend credit to their customers, to have enough product available to sell, and to make major investments.

THE ESSENTIAL QUESTION: If I were a financial manager, why would I want my firm to borrow money?

MyBizLab: Check your understanding of these concepts at www.mybizlab.com.

W hy, you might ask, can't a firm simply finance its ongoing operating costs out of its profits? Sure, you understand that in the first year or two of a startup the new company might have to run its operations on borrowed money. But after that, can't the managers just exercise some financial discipline, save money from their profits, and pay their expenses as they go along?

Why Firms Borrow Money: Four Reasons

Why do firms think they have to borrow money?

There are four reasons why companies, large as well as small, often need to obtain financing. They need funds for *managing everyday business activities, extending credit to their customers, keeping enough product (inventory) available,* and *making major investments.*

2 Zero interest! The "0% interest" sign on the window shows the lengths to which this used car dealer will go to get customers to buy its cars—namely, "We will loan you the money to buy the car and we won't charge you any interest." But the car seller itself *will* have to pay interest on the funds it borrowed from the bank to loan to car customers. Is this a reasonable arrangement? What are the implications for the selling price of the car?

1 Funds for Managing Everyday Business Activities: "We Need Money to Operate Right Now"

Farmers make money once a crop is sold—in the fall. But they plant their crops in the spring and harvest them in the summer, and for both of these seasons they may not have the money to cover equipment, labor, and so on. Thus, they need to borrow money to cover day-to-day operations during those periods, until they can sell the crops in the fall, when they can repay the loans. Other businesses also have to borrow short-term funds, ranging from toymakers (who realize most revenue at Christmas) to building contractors (who get paid when the jobs are done) to law firms (who must wait for settlement in a case).

But businesses borrow money for other reasons as well. For instance, as we will see, they can borrow money at low interest rates and invest it in ways that will give them higher returns.

Source: Photograph by Sally Lindsay.

2 Funds for Extending Credit: "We Need to Loan Our Customers Money So They Can Buy Our Products"

How often have you seen TV ads that advertise "Low interest rates!" or "No loan repayment until next year!" These suggest just how often businesses rely on credit to enable their customers to buy their products. **2**

A drawback, of course, is that a company may find it has a significant percentage of its assets tied up in credit (think car dealers, most of whose customers may still be paying off their car loans, or department stores, such as JCPenney, which have store credit cards), which means it needs to have an active collection arm. Many business-to-business firms also feel they have to offer discounts for customers who pay early.

3 Funds for Keeping Enough Product Available: "We Need to Have Sufficient Inventory to Serve Our Customers"

Some companies, such as Walmart, don't carry a lot of inventory beyond what's actually on the shelves, because their suppliers monitor inventory levels and restock as needed. But for many businesses, this arrangement is not possible—it takes time to resupply, so they need to have a lot of products on hand, or their customers will become dissatisfied. ❸

> ■ **Example of Use of Funds for Keeping Product Available: How a Big Order May Affect You.** Suppose you own an e-commerce website where the typical order is $50 to $100. Then a corporation approaches you about an order that could be over $100,000. How do you gear up for it? How do you finance it? Do you ask the customer for half the money for the order up front and half on delivery? Or for full payment up front?
>
> If the corporation issues a purchase order and, as is typical, seeks terms such as paying you in 30 or 60 days, that's great for their cash flow but not yours. So you may have to borrow. Such are the problems of a small business.[9] ■

❸ **Taking orders.** Salespeople at a gift show at New York City's Jacob K. Javits Convention Center take orders for products. Small wholesalers frequently will use the orders taken at trade shows like this one to borrow funds to purchase the inventory they need—as opposed to purchasing and holding inventory in advance.

4 Funds for Making Major Investments: "We Need to Borrow Money to Acquire Long-Term Assets"

Most ordinary consumers can't buy big-ticket items (cars, houses) without credit. Companies have their own big-ticket items that require they get loans—for land, buildings, equipment, even intellectual property such as patents or copyrights.

Such important expenditures are known as ***capital expenditures,* major investments in tangible or intangible assets.** Tangible assets, you'll recall, are defined as land, buildings, and equipment. Intangible assets are patents, copyrights, and trademarks.

Want to Know More? 16-2

Examples of Capital Expenditures for Google, Apple, & Pepsi

Go to www.mybizlab.com.

>  **BRIEFING / SMALL BUSINESS & ENTREPRENEURS**
> **Capital Expenditures for a Drum Maker.** In the 1950s, drummer Remo Belli borrowed $2,300 from his parents to open a store called Drum City in Los Angeles. Most drumheads then were made of animal skins, a challenge to keep taut in humid weather. Belli devised a new synthetic drumhead using Mylar, patented it, and started Remo Inc.
>
> His first drum-making factory, 500 square feet, quickly gave way to another one of 1,000, then 3,000, then 6,000 square feet. The current plant is more than 200,000 square feet.
>
> How did Remo finance these capital expenditures? "I rarely went to the bank," Belli says. "There were enough people out there who were very comfortable helping us out. . . . DuPont, maker of Mylar, bought [company] shares. Two of our best customers bought shares."[10] ■

Key Takeaway 16-2
Firms borrow funds for (1) everyday activities, (2) giving customers credit, (3) stocking inventory, and (4) making major investments.

THE BIG IDEA: To serve the four purposes mentioned in the previous section, companies need to look at short-term and long-term financing. Sources of short-term financing are trade credit, short-term loans, factoring, and commercial paper. Sources of long-term financing are long-term loans, debt financing, and equity financing. Financial managers need to think about financial leverage, using borrowed funds to increase the firm's rate of return, and the cost of capital, the rate of return a firm must earn to cover the cost of generating funds.

THE ESSENTIAL QUESTION: If I ever have to find money for my company, what should I do?

MyBizLab MyBizLab: Check your understanding of these concepts at www.mybizlab.com.

In general, loans are of two types: short-term and long-term. Let's consider these.

Sources of Short-Term Financing: Trade Credit, Short-Term Loans, Factoring, & Commercial Paper

If I were a small-business person needing money right away, what kind of sources would I look at?

Four principal kinds of short-term financing are *trade credit, short-term loans, pledging and factoring,* and *commercial paper.*

1 Trade Credit: Buy a Product, Get a Bill, Pay Later

An important source of short-term credit for most firms, **trade credit is short-term financing by which a firm buys a product, then receives a bill (an invoice) from the supplier, then pays it later,** usually in 30 to 90 days. ❹

This may sound no different from the way you operate when getting and paying for electricity, for instance. However, businesses operate under different conditions.

Terms of trade refers to the conditions the supplier (seller) gives the buyer when offering short-term credit. The length of time for which the supplier (seller) extends credit is known as the *net period*.

▮ **Example of Net Period: What Does "2/10, Net 30" Mean?** When a bill specifies "net 30 days," that means the supplier extended credit for 30 days. When an invoice says "2/10, net 30," that means the buyer can take a 2% discount for paying the bill within 10 days, but in any case must pay within 30 days.

Early payments of this sort can add up to significant savings over a year's time. But if you don't pay early to get the discount, you might as well wait until the end of the 30-day period to get as much cost-free credit as possible. ▮

Trade credit can take different forms, but one of the most familiar is the *promissory note,* **a written contract prepared by the buyer who agrees to pay the**

Source: T.M.O.Buildings/Alamy.

❹ **Trade credit user.** A small-business person, such as the operator of this toy store, would find it difficult to maintain inventory, especially in peak selling times such as the Christmas season, without the short-term financing of trade credit. The process of buying toys from wholesalers, with invoices coming afterward, and the payments due 30 to 90 days later, gives a small retailer the opportunity to stock many items without having to pay for them up front.

seller a certain amount by a certain time. Promissory notes are often used in the jewelry business.

2 Short-Term Loans: Family & Friends, Banks & Finance Companies, & Credit Cards

Just as you may have to seek a short-term loan when your cash reserves are low, so do financial managers, particularly those in small businesses. Companies may need to borrow short-term funds to pay unexpected bills or to buy additional inventory.

Whether short-term or long-term, a loan may be *secured* or *unsecured.*

- **Secured loans:** A *secured loan* **means that the borrower pledges some sort of asset, such as personal property, that is forfeited if the loan is not repaid.** Whether it's a car, jewelry, or piece of land, **the asset that is pledged to secure the loan is known as** *collateral,* **and it can be seized by the lender if the borrower does not repay the loan.**

- **Unsecured loans:** An *unsecured loan* **means the borrower does not pledge some sort of asset as collateral.** Lenders normally make unsecured loans only to people they have known a long time.

The way lenders make money, of course, is by charging interest on their loans. The *interest rate* **is the price paid for the use of money over a certain period of time,** so that, for instance, if someone loans you $100 for a year at a 10% interest rate, you would owe them $10 (plus repayment of the $100).

The sources of short-term loans are principally *family and friends, banks and finance companies,* and *credit cards.*

Family and Friends: Borrowing from Those You Already Know. Suppose you've started your own small business. You've encountered an unexpected cash crunch because your distributors haven't paid you on time and yet you need to pay your suppliers if they are to continue making your product. What do you do? Call your folks, a brother or sister—or a friend? Many a small-business person has done exactly this to get a short-term loan. ❺ Often such loans work out just fine, although they may well be structured in an informal way, with no written contract. At other times they can lead to misunderstandings and trouble and disrupt important relationships. Better, then, to arrange the loan by putting it in writing, with specific repayment terms, to keep things aboveboard.[11]

🖱 **BRIEFING / SMALL BUSINESS & ENTREPRENEURS**
Friends Help Eileen Fisher Get Her Clothing Line Going. Eileen Fisher, now 60, started her namesake company in New York in 1984 because "I hated shopping. There were too many choices." She wanted to make chic, simple clothes that made getting dressed easy.

A jewelry-maker friend suggested Fisher take over his booth at a trade show where buyers came to acquire clothes for their stores. With three weeks to produce her clothing line and $350 in the bank, she created some simple clothes that could be mixed and matched, modeled on some she'd seen in Japan. Eight stores made small orders totaling $3,000, and buyers made suggestions for improvement, which she followed for a second show, where she sold $40,000 worth and received orders for more.

Fisher says she took the stack of orders to a bank to borrow money to make them. "They laughed. 'How do we know that these are real orders? Or that these stores are creditworthy?' I had no idea. So I borrowed money from friends and did the order in shifts . . . Since the orders were COD [cash on delivery], the money from the first batch paid for the second batch."[12]

ⓘ **Want to Know More? 16-3**

How Do Other Trade Credit Arrangements Work, Such as Open Account & Trade Acceptance?

Go to www.mybizlab.com.

Source: Datacraft - Q × Q images/Alamy.

❺ **Family support.** One of the most frequently used sources for short-term loans by small-business owners are family members, although without written agreements such loans can sometimes lead to misunderstandings and resentments. Have you ever borrowed from a relative and then found the relationship changed because of "the money thing"?

Today her modular line is available in department stores and 55 EILEEN FISHER stores. In 2006, she gave 31% of the $320 million company to her 875 employees. **⑥** ■

Banks and Finance Companies, and Three Types of Loans: Line of Credit, Revolving Credit, and Transaction Loan. Banks—specifically those called *commercial banks*, such as Bank of America and Wells Fargo—are a popular source of funding, being a source of loans for around half of all small businesses. Another source is ***commercial finance companies*, organizations willing to make short-term loans to borrowers who can offer collateral,** such as property. Such companies (such as General Electric Capital Corporation) are willing to assume higher loan risks in return for charging higher interest rates.

Source: Courtesy of EILEEN FISHER.

⑥ With the help of friends. The EILEEN FISHER store on North State Street in Chicago represents part of a clothing apparel empire that began with the namesake owner borrowing funds from friends to manufacture some initial small orders. What are some of the advantages and potential disadvantages of such a transaction?

Three types of loans available from these organizations are the following:

- **Line of credit—how much can be lent at what terms: In a *line of credit*, a bank specifies how much it is willing to lend the borrower during a specified period of time,** such as $250,000 at a certain interest rate over a 12-month period. Having a line of credit makes it easier for borrowers to obtain funds, although it's important for them to be on time with repayments in order to keep their credit ratings up and to avoid having the amount of the line of credit reduced.

- **Revolving credit agreement—loaning up to the credit limit: A *revolving credit agreement* resembles a line of credit, except that the bank guarantees the loan and is obligated to loan funds up to the credit limit.** Banks usually limit the terms of the agreement to 1 to 3 years and charge interest on the unpaid balance.

- **Transaction loan—credit for a specific purpose: A *transaction loan* is credit extended by a bank for a specific purpose,** such as for constructing a new store or stocking up on new inventory for the season.

Source: John Macdougall/AFP/Getty Images/Newscom.

⑦ The Google guys. When this photo was taken in 2004 in Frankfurt, Germany, Sergey Brin (*left*) and Larry Page were riding high as the founders of the fantastic success that is Google, which they had established in the mid-1990s partly with credit cards while they were Stanford graduate students. Would you take a chance on wrecking your credit rating by financing a risky startup with your personal credit cards?

Credit Cards: The Last Resort. Want to launch a small startup company? Back when Visa, MasterCard, and American Express were flooding mailboxes with credit card offers, some entrepreneurs found it convenient to use multiple cards to fund new enterprises.

Some owners of small businesses also use credit cards, such as the American Express gold card, to cover ongoing operating expenses. Although having a credit card means you don't run the risk of rejection, as might happen when you apply for a bank loan, you need to use it carefully, since interest rates and late-payment penalties can be high.[13] **⑦**

BRIEFING / SMALL BUSINESS & ENTREPRENEURS
Using Credit Cards to Start a Business. Robin and John Sauve took on $40,000 in credit card debt in order to start Barkley Logistics, which arranges merchandise shipments and deliveries of time-sensitive materials such as promotional flyers. The money was used to buy the assets of Robin's failed former employer, Premier Logistics of Enfield, Connecticut.

Robin "reasoned that if things didn't work out, she could still sell the company's assets, find a new job, and pay off her credit cards," says one account.[14] Going forward, however, she found she had to take on even *more* debt to help the firm survive. This meant putting the family's personal assets on the line as collateral to acquire a bank line of credit.

Such are the risks of being a small-business owner. ■

3 Accounts Receivable: Pledging & Factoring

As we mentioned, accounts receivable is the total amount owed to a firm from customers who have purchased goods or services on credit. There are two ways firms can make use of their accounts receivable to generate short-term funds: by borrowing against them, known as *pledging,* or by selling them, known as *factoring.*

Pledging: Using Accounts Receivable as Collateral for a Loan. In the activity known as *pledging accounts receivable,* **a firm uses its accounts receivable as collateral, or security, to obtain a short-term loan,** as from a commercial bank. As receivables are collected, the firm repays the loan along with interest. In this case, the firm is liable for the entire loan, even if some of its customers default.

Factoring: Selling Accounts Receivable to a Financial Institution. In the activity known as *factoring accounts receivable,* **a firm sells its accounts receivable at a discount to a financial institution** (which is known as a "factor"). Thus, a department store might sell $100,000 worth of receivables for $95,000, a discount of 5%.

Factoring is an expensive way for firms to get a short-term infusion of funds, but it provides an avenue for small businesses that may not qualify for other kinds of loans. This is especially the case if the firm is willing to reimburse the factor for any nonpaying or slow-paying accounts. As you might expect, the amount of factoring increased during the Great Recession.

4 Commercial Paper: Unsecured Short-Term Promissory Notes Issued by Large Corporations

Substitutes for bank loans, *commercial paper* **consists of unsecured, short-term promissory notes over $100,000 issued by large banks and corporations** such as Charles Schwab and GE Capital. They are also issued by insurance companies, pension funds, public utilities, and state and local governments. They usually become due in 30 to 90 days (and no longer than 270 days), but interest rates are less than those charged by commercial banks. Because the notes are unsecured, they are issued mainly by large institutions.

Sources of Long-Term Financing: Long-Term Loans, Debt Financing, & Equity Financing

> *If I needed to get money for the long term for my company, where would I go?*

Short-term financing can help a company meet current operating needs, but long-term financing is needed when the company decides to make major investments, such as buying real estate or another company. Three sources of long-term financing are *long-term loans, debt financing,* and *equity financing.*

1 Long-Term Loans: Borrowing from Financial Institutions

Companies often receive long-term loans—loans generally requiring repayment in 3 to 7 years, although they may be as long as 20 years—from commercial banks, life insurance companies, pension funds, and commercial finance companies. Long-term loans require the borrower to sign a *term-loan agreement,* **a promissory note indicating specific installments, such as monthly or yearly, for repayment.** Because of the length of time, lenders usually insist that the firm have a good credit rating, that the loan be backed by collateral (such as real estate or

Key Takeaway 16-3
Key sources of short-term loans are family and friends, banks and finance companies, and credit cards.

Want to Know More? 16-4

Components of a Term Loan Agreement

Go to www.mybizlab.com.

8 **Still, a good credit rating.** In 2010, badly maintained Pacific Gas & Electric natural-gas pipelines blew up and destroyed dozens of homes in the San Francisco–area suburb of San Bruno. Even so, debt-rating service Moody's said the California utility's credit rating was unaffected by the neglect and resulting blast, making PG&E a good candidate for long-term loans. Further investigation may alter that analysis.

9 **Prospective IPO?** In the summer of 2011, the financial community buzzed with rumors that San Francisco–based Zynga, maker of social games such as CityVille and Farmville, would strive to raise $1 billion in an initial public offering. That rumor was followed by another that suggested Zynga would delay its IPO because of poor market conditions. If Zynga's IPO occurred under less-than-optimum market conditions, in what ways do you think the company might suffer?

(i)

Want to Know More? 16-5

Some Famous IPOs: Google & Others

Go to www.mybizlab.com.

---

equipment), and that the firm pay a higher interest rate than they would for a short-term loan. **8**

2 Debt Financing: Issuing Bonds, Secured & Unsecured

If a company is unable to obtain a long-term loan, it may try to issue corporate *bonds,* **contracts between issuer and buyer in which the purchase price represents a loan by the buyer and for which the issuing firm pays the buyer interest.** (Governments, whether domestic or foreign, or whether federal, state, or local, can also issue bonds, such as the U.S. government savings bond.) **The terms of the lending agreement are known as *indenture terms*.**

We discuss bonds in more detail in Chapter 17, but here let us simply note that bonds may be *secured* or *unsecured*.

Secured Bonds: Backed by Collateral. *Secured bonds* **are backed by some form of the firm's collateral, such as real estate or equipment.** A firm that fails to pay interest on its bonds is at risk of having its collateral seized.

Unsecured Bonds: Backed by the Firm's Reputation. *Unsecured bonds,* **or *debenture bonds,* are backed only by the reputation of the firm issuing the bonds.** Only companies with strong reputations can issue unsecured bonds.

3 Equity Financing: Selling Stock, Retaining Earnings, & Receiving Venture Capital

Equity financing involves selling ownership in the firm. This may be done in three ways: (1) by *selling stock,* (2) by *retaining earnings and reinvesting them in the firm,* and (3) by *receiving venture capital.*

Selling Stock: Private Placements versus Public Offerings. Selling stock means selling ownership shares (called *stock*) in a firm. This can be done in two ways—by means of *private placements* or *public offerings.*

- **Private placements:** *Private placements* **involve selling stock to only a small group of large investors,** such as insurance companies and pension funds.

  - **Public offerings:** *Public offerings* **involve selling stock to the general public in securities markets.** When a company sells stock to the general public for the first time, it is called an *initial public offering,* or *IPO.* **9**

Firms may find they can sell stock more cheaply when they sell it privately, because there is less government regulation involved.

Retaining Earnings: Reinvesting Profits in the Firm. As mentioned, *retained earnings* are net profits minus dividend payments made to stockholders. That is, they are earnings retained by a firm for its own use—for buying more land and buildings, for example, or acquiring other companies. This type of equity financing, which provides more flexibility and less risk, is often used by small-business firms.

Receiving Investment Capital: Getting Money from Wealthy Individuals and Institutions in Exchange for Ownership. *Venture capital* consists of funds acquired from wealthy individuals and institutions that invest in promising startups or emerging companies in return for their giving up some ownership. Some venture capitalists often provide management expertise as well.

Want to Know More? 16-6

Who's Behind Those Startups? Some Famous Venture Capitalists

Go to www.mybizlab.com.

Financial Leverage & Cost of Capital: Using Borrowed Funds to Increase the Rate of Return

What is the ultimate purpose of a firm's borrowing money?

Key Takeaway 16-4
Key sources of long-term financing are long-term loans, debt financing, and equity financing.

Maybe you're the sort of person who would rather not be in debt. Or maybe you're willing to use debt—such as taking on student loans—for *strategic purposes,* such as to finance your education because you think it will pay off with a higher income later.

That's the way company financial managers think. They are guided by the principle of *financial leverage,* **or simply** *leverage,* **the technique of using borrowed funds to increase a firm's rate of return.** The idea here is to make sure that (a) the company's earnings remain higher while (b) its interest payments remain lower, which (c) increases the rate of return on the firm's owners' investment. (A company with lots of debt is called "heavily leveraged.")

This means a financial manager must pay attention to the *cost of capital,* **the rate of return a firm must earn to cover the cost of generating funds in the marketplace.** Stated another way, the cost of capital is the overall percentage costs of the funds used to finance a firm's assets.

An example of financial leverage versus equity financing is shown below. (*See* ■ *Panel 16.5.*)

■ **PANEL 16.5 Example of leverage versus equity financing.**

Financial Leverage: Raise $250,000 90% by Selling Bonds (Debt) and 10% by Selling Stock (Equity)		Equity Financing: Raise $250,000 100% by Selling Stock (Equity)	
Sales of bonds and/or stock			
Sell bonds (@10% interest)	$225,000		
Sell common stock	25,000	Sell common stock	$250,000
Subtotal: Sales of bonds and stock	$250,000	Subtotal: Sales of stock	$250,000
Earnings from company revenue			
Earnings	$100,000	Earnings	$100,000
Less: 10% bond interest	(22,500)		
Total earnings less bond interest	$ 77,500	Total earnings	$100,000
Differences in return to company owners			
Return to company owners		Return to company owners	
Total earnings less bond interest divided by	$ 77,500	Total earnings divided by	$100,000
Common stock sales equals	$ 25,000	Common stock sales equals	$250,000
Percent return to owners:	**310%**	**Percent return to owners:**	**40%**

Sooner or later, if you're a small-business owner, you'll probably need to get a loan. How to improve your chances? The common advice is to have a sound business plan.[15] Make sure your credit report is accurate. Rent rather than own the building you're in. Have some of your own money invested in your business.

You can also try some money sources other than banks, as follows.

Social Finance: Peer-to-Peer Lending

Learning that there were $89 billion in person-to-person loan transactions in the United States, Asheesh Advani thought he had a great idea in forming a company, CircleLending, that specialized in "social finance"—charging fees to organize and process loans among family and friends. "It capitalizes on the connectedness of individuals," he says.

Indeed, the firm became so successful that in 2007 it was acquired by the British conglomerate Virgin Group and renamed Virgin Money USA.[16] By September 2008, it had grown 75% in the preceding 11 months.

By November 2010, however, Virgin had pulled the plug on its U.S. operation. Unlike other peer-to-peer lenders, says a social lending blogger, "Virgin Money specialized in organizing people who already had an existing relationship," such as family or friends.[17] (Similar organizing services still exist: LendFriend, LoanBack, WikiLoan, for example.) True peer-to-peer lenders can be found through Lending Club or Prosper. (For more information on peer-to-peer lending, go to www.sociallending.net.)

Fan Funding: Money for Creative Projects

If you're an artist who wants to take on an ambitious project, such as making a new video or recording a new album, you might try doing what other artists often do: Ask your fans to fund you.

"The band Marillion reportedly raised $725,000 by pre-selling its *Anoraknophobia* double-CD album before it was ever recorded," says one account. "Jill Sobule raised more than $80,000 from about 500 fans to record her *California Years* album."[18]

Early fan-funding sites, such as Kickstarter, solicit donations to fund creative projects, but now some such sites, such as FashionStake.com, are offering customers a chance to invest as well.[19]

Community-Supported Agriculture Programs Applied to Other Businesses

In traditional community-supported agriculture (CSA) programs, customers pay local farmers a lump sum at the start of the year in exchange for regular deliveries of fruits and vegetables. Now the CSA model has been adopted to nonproduce businesses: yarn CSAs, winery CSAs, soap CSAs, bacon CSAs, even art CSAs (you get monthly "art-in-a-box" installments).

"In the past five years," says an *Inc.* article, "LocalHarvest.org, a database of local businesses around the country, has seen CSAs triple to 3,732."[20] ❿

Source: Community Supported Art Logo by Chad Nestor.

❿ **Community supported.** The CSA movement began with community-supported agriculture and extends even to community-supported art. What other products do you think could be marketed in a similar way?

Money: What It Is, How It's Controlled

THE BIG IDEA: Money, the medium of value used to pay for goods and services, has the useful benefits of portability, divisibility, durability, uniqueness, and stability. Money has three functions: it acts as a medium of exchange, as a store of wealth, and as a standard of value. Money comes from the money supply, the amount of money the Federal Reserve System (the Fed) makes available. The money supply has two definitions (M1 and M2), with M2 the most frequently used. The Fed decides how much U.S. currency to make available to banks and also how much money to loan banks. The Fed controls the money supply through three policy tools: the reserve requirement, open-market operations, and the discount rate. The Fed also clears checks between different banks.

THE ESSENTIAL QUESTION: What are money and the money supply, and how does money get into the banking system?

MyBizLab: Check your understanding of these concepts at www.mybizlab.com.

MyBizLab

Lots of people are irrational about money. For instance, there is a herd instinct that makes investors feel more secure in investing just like everyone else does. "We are social animals who feel safer in numbers," says financial planner Carl Richards. "We take comfort in doing what everyone else is doing, and in the back of our minds we know that even if we are wrong, at least we will be wrong with a bunch of other people."[21]

However, if you're going to work in business, it's important to take a nonherd approach to finances. You have to set aside fear and greed and look at the numbers. If you aren't used to dealing with finances, you can be easily tripped up. Therefore, let's take a systematic look at money so that you'll know how to deal with it most effectively in business.

What Money Is: Five Characteristics & Three Functions

What are the characteristics and functions of money?

***Barter*, the trading of goods and/or services for other goods and/or services,** with little or no money changing hands, is a time-honored way for the cash-strapped to do business. Since the Great Recession began, barter-exchange systems such as International Monetary Systems (IMS) have reported a major jump in membership and in barter transactions.[22] ⓫ For instance, contractor Charles Keogh, an IMS

Source: Courtesy of Southern Barter Club, Inc.

⓫ **Barter club.** "Barter is recession proof, barter saves you cash," says the website of the Southern Barter Club, based in Buford, Georgia. SBC members trade accounting, contracting, dental, medical, hotel, restaurant, and many other services. Do you think bartering will become more popular in the near future? Why?

Want to Know More? 16-7

How Does Barter Work?

Go to www.mybizlab.com.

member, agreed to paint a house for $1,000 in cash and $4,000 in IMS "trade dollars" or credit, which could be applied to vacations, dining, dental care, and other goods or services offered by participants.

Normally, however, people pay for things by using *money*—perhaps using ivory tusks or animal pelts, as was once done, or nowadays maybe gold or precious stones. More commonly, however, you would use coins and currency (or checks or credit cards, which represent them). All these are examples of **money, defined as any medium of value that is generally accepted as payment for goods and services.**

The Five Characteristics of Money

Why don't people do bartering more? Because money—whatever its form—offers the following useful benefits: (1) *portability,* (2) *divisibility,* (3) *durability,* (4) *uniqueness,* and (5) *stability.*

Portability: "I Can Carry It in My Pocket." Even a bag of coins is easier to carry around than items that people barter in some parts of the world, such as goats or cassava roots.

⑫ Divisible. A young man breaks down some big bills into smaller ones, with the help of a restaurant counterman. Divisibility is a characteristic of money, whether it's dollars, euros, pesos, or other currency.

Source: Courtesy of Susan Berston.

Divisibility: "I Can Easily Break Big Bills Down into Smaller Ones." How do you break down a goat and make change? You can't. Or if you could, how would you decide how much each part was worth? There's no problem, however, about breaking down a $5 bill, whether it's into five $1 bills, ten 50-cent pieces, twenty quarters, and so on. ⑫

Durability: "The Material Won't Deteriorate Quickly." The things a person might barter with, such as goats and turnips, can't be guaranteed to last. But deep-sea divers still turn up gold and silver coins from sunken ships that went down centuries ago. U.S. paper dollar bills generally last 12 to 18 months and coins 30 years or more.

Uniqueness: "This Can't Be Easily Copied or Counterfeited." There is much the U.S. Treasury will tell you about how paper money is made—but not everything. That's because latest-generation color copiers make it easy for people to duplicate the appearance of paper money. To thwart this and other kinds of counterfeiting, officials redesigned new bills with larger portraits that are off-center and threads throughout that appear under ultraviolet light. And then there are the things they can't tell you about.

Stability: "This Has the Same Value to Everyone." If you hand over a dollar bill to a friend, you know that he or she has the same understanding of its value as you do. The same cannot be said when you hand over your goat.

The Three Functions of Money

Money has three functions: It acts as (1) a *medium of exchange,* (2) a *store of wealth,* and (3) a *standard of value.*

Medium of Exchange: "I Don't Have to Barter; Using Money Is Easier." Money is a **medium of exchange, meaning that it makes economic transactions easier and eliminates the need to barter.** Example: Let's go shopping. You take the herd of goats, I'll take a wad of bills.

Store of Wealth: "I Can Save This for Some Time." Money acts as a **store of wealth, meaning that people can save it until they need to make new**

purchases. Example: Whether saved as cash under a mattress or in a no-interest bank account, the money will still be available to you the next time you need it—unlike, perhaps, goats or turnips.

● **Standard of Value: "I Can Use This as a Common Way to Compare How Much Things Are Worth."** Money acts as a *standard of value*, **or** *unit of account*, **meaning that it can be used as a common standard to measure the values of goods and services.** Example: Money allows you to measure the difference between a $6,000 used car and a $2,000 used motorcycle, or the worth of a $10,000 diamond and a $5,000 emerald.

The Money Supply: What It Is

What are the definitions of the money supply?

Who produces U.S. *currency,* **or government-issued coins and paper money?** Coins are produced by the U.S. Mint, which is under the U.S. Treasury Department and which has production facilities in Denver, Philadelphia, San Francisco, and West Point. Paper money is produced by the Bureau of Engraving and Printing, also under the U.S. Treasury, at facilities in Washington, D.C., and Fort Worth, Texas. Both coins and bills are delivered to the Federal Reserve and its branches, as we'll discuss.

But currency represents only about 37% of all media of exchange in the United States. A better question to ask is: *What is the U.S. money supply?*

The United States' *money supply* **is defined as the amount of money the Federal Reserve System makes available for people to buy goods and services. The money supply is customarily referred to in two ways—as M1, the narrowest measure, or M2, a more generous and more commonly used measure.**

● Note there are several parts to this definition—the *Federal Reserve System, M1,* and *M2.*

The Federal Reserve System: The U.S. Government's Bank for Bankers

Formed in 1913, the *Federal Reserve System,* **called** *the Fed,* **is the central bank of the United States and controls the U.S. money supply,** through ways we'll explain shortly. The central bank in any country is the bank at which other banks can keep their funds and from which they can borrow. Thus, the Fed can be considered the government's "bank for bankers," as we'll make clear. ⓭

⓭ **Federal Reserve bank.** The Philadelphia bank shown here is headquarters for one of the 12 Federal Reserve districts in the Federal Reserve System. Do you know where the headquarters bank for your district is located?

M1, the Narrowest Measure: Quick-Access Money—Currency, Checks, & So On

M1, **the narrowest definition of the money supply, is defined as money that can be accessed quickly and easily,** such as currency, traveler's checks, bank checking account balances, and the balances in other so-called *demand deposit* accounts. A *demand deposit* **is a commercial bank's or other financial institution's checking account, from which you may make withdrawals at any time.**

M2, a Broader Measure: M1 plus Slower-Access Money— Savings, Mutual Funds, & So On

● *M2,* **a broader definition of the money supply, is defined as (1) money that can be accessed quickly and easily (that is, M1) AND (2) money that takes more time to access,** such as small *time deposits,* various savings accounts, certificates

Want to Know More? 16-8

The Federal Reserve's Way of Keeping Track of the Money Supply or Money Stock

Go to www.mybizlab.com.

of deposit, money market accounts, and mutual funds. *Time deposits* **are defined as bank funds that can't be withdrawn without notice or transferred by check.** Examples are savings accounts when banks require advance written notice prior to withdrawal. In other words, people have to make some sort of transaction before they can use these M2 assets in ways that resemble M1 money.

The two kinds of money supply are shown below. (*See* ■ *Panel 16.6.*)

■ **PANEL 16.6 Two different measures of the money supply: M1 and M2 (June 2011).** M2 is the most commonly used measure. Numbers are expressed in billions.

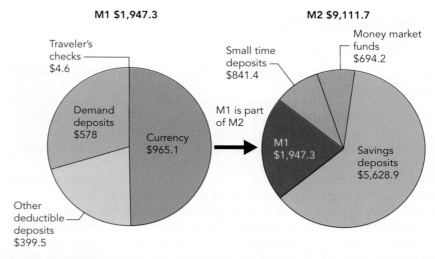

Source: Federal Reserve Bank, *Federal Reserve Statistical Release,* July 14, 2011, www.federalreserve.gov/releases/h6/Current (accessed July 14, 2011).

⑭ **Fed chairman.** Ben Bernanke, on leave as a professor of economics at Princeton University, was appointed by President George W. Bush as chairman of the Council of Economic Advisors, then as chairman of the U.S. Federal Reserve System. He was confirmed for a second term as chairman of the Fed after being nominated by President Barack Obama. Under his leadership, the Fed has had to respond to the problems of the Great Recession and its aftermath.

Source: Danita Delimont/Alamy.

How Money Is Created: The Role of the Fed & Commercial Banks

How do the Federal Reserve and commercial banks work to create money?

To understand how money is created, we need to understand how the Federal Reserve System is structured. Then we need to understand how the commercial banks work with it.

The Fed's Board of Governors & 12 Reserve Banks

The Fed has a number of parts, the most important of which are the following:

The Board of Governors. The Fed is run by a *board of governors,* consisting of seven members appointed by the president for 14-year terms, which overlap one another. The chairman, currently Ben S. Bernanke, appointed by President George W. Bush to succeed Alan Greenspan, works with the president's administration to formulate economic policy. ⑭ The board's most important function is to set *monetary policy,* using interest rates and other tools to control the money supply and the supply of credit in the economy, as we'll explain. (We first discussed monetary policy, and also fiscal policy, in Chapter 3.)

Federal Reserve Banks. The Fed is made up of 12 administrative districts, each with its own Federal Reserve bank. Each reserve bank is responsible for providing the member banks in its district with sufficient currency—for example, when these banks need more cash to serve customers during the Christmas holidays. (*See* ■ *Panel 16.7.*)

■ **PANEL 16.7 The 12 Federal Reserve districts and their headquarters.**

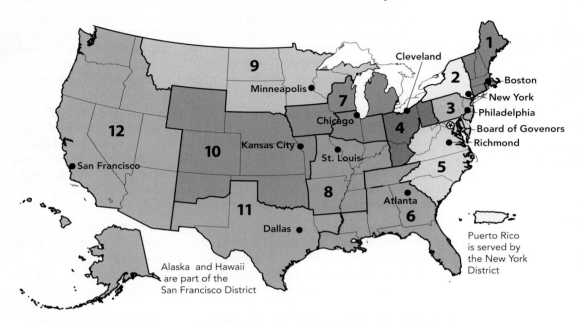

The Fed's Member Banks

Federal Reserve banks serve member commercial banks within their districts. **A *commercial bank* is a federal- or state-chartered profit-seeking financial institution that accepts deposits from individuals and businesses and uses part of them to make personal, residential, and business loans.** All commercial banks are *chartered,* meaning they have received government permission to operate, either from the federal government (national banks) or an individual state (state banks). All nationally chartered commercial banks are Fed members, as are some state-chartered banks.

Getting Money to the Banks

The Federal Reserve helps get money to commercial banks in two ways:

Making Currency Available. The Fed decides how much currency to make available. That is, it determines how much currency to produce (and how much to destroy, as in taking old bills out of circulation). It does this through its individual Federal Reserve banks, which provide their member banks with sufficient amounts of coins and paper money to run smoothly. The amounts might vary during different times of year, as, for instance, when people make more withdrawals during the summer for vacations or during December for Christmas shopping.

Making Loans Available. Member banks that need money can also get loans from their Federal Reserve banks, loans on which they pay interest, the interest rate being determined by the Fed. The banks in turn make money by making loans to their customers.

How the Fed Controls the Money Supply: Three Tools

What are three ways the Fed controls the money supply?

Why does the money supply need to be controlled? That is, why can't the Fed just leave the same amount of money in circulation (allowing for replacement of worn currency)?

■ PANEL 16.8 **Recent U.S. inflation.** Over the last 40 years the United States has experienced a steady and positive decline in the economy's CPI, which measures the rate of inflation. What do you think this trend indicates regarding the Federal Reserve's management of the money supply?

Consumer Price Index (CPI)

Years	Average Annual Increase (%)
1971–1980	8.10
1981–1990	4.48
1991–2000	2.66
2001–2010	2.35

Source: U.S. Department of Labor.

Want to Know More? 16-9

Reserve Requirements from the Federal Reserve Website

Go to www.mybizlab.com.

Consider two scenarios:

- **If there's too much money in the money supply—the road to inflation:** If the Fed injects too much money (say, twice as much) into the money supply, but the amount of goods and services remains as before, this situation could lead to inflation—too many dollars chasing too few goods. That is, more people could borrow dollars and use them to compete for the available products, pushing the prices up. (*See* ■ *Panel 16.8.*)

- **If there's too little money in the money supply—the road to deflation and recession:** If the Fed reduces the amount of money in the money supply (by half, say), it could lead to deflation—too few dollars available to buy an oversupply of goods and services. This might lead to a recession, costing people jobs and slowing economic growth. That is, people would find it harder to borrow dollars, and more products would become available than dollars to purchase them, forcing prices down.

Thus, by adjusting the money supply in response to changing economic conditions, the Fed can, it hopes, somewhat keep prices from wildly going up and down, which in turn affects economic growth and employment rates.

To regulate the money supply, the Fed uses three policy tools: (1) the *reserve requirement,* (2) *open-market operations,* and (3) the *discount rate.*

Tool 1: Reserve Requirement—Specifying Percentage of Cash Banks Must Hold in Deposits (Used Infrequently)

The Federal Reserve, through its reserve requirement, controls the rate at which a bank can make loans, although the technique is rarely used. The **reserve requirement is the percentage of total checking and savings deposits that a bank must keep as cash in its vault or in a non-interest-bearing deposit at its regional Federal Reserve bank.** When banks are required to put *more* of their money into the Fed (or their vault), it *reduces* the money supply, so that the bank has less to lend to its customers. When banks are required to put *less* money into the Fed, it *increases* the money supply, so the bank has more to lend customers.

Although banks are supposed to reserve an amount equal to between 3% and 10% of the funds they have in checking and savings accounts, they have found ways to avoid this.

BRIEFING / LEGAL & ETHICAL PRACTICES

How Banks Have Evaded the Reserve Requirement, Using Computer Programs to Transfer Depositors' Money. The reserve requirement says a bank must reserve as cash (as vault cash or in a Federal Reserve bank account) 3% to 10% of whatever funds it has in ordinary checking or savings accounts, called transaction accounts. But money market accounts (explained later in this chapter) aren't defined as such accounts.

What banks have done, then, is use computer programs to temporarily (with their depositors' prior agreement) transfer funds from customers' transaction accounts to money market accounts, so that the bank's required reserve ratio could go from, say, 10% to zero. Thus, banks were able to use more funds for loans such as the subprime mortgage loans we described in Chapter 3, which helped bring on the Great Recession.

As a result, says a report by the Federal Deposit Insurance Corporation, one bank used this technique to "reduce its required reserves from $788,000 in August 2000 to $48,000 in August 2001, a period when deposits at the institution rose by $36 million."[23]

Should banks have been allowed to do this? ■

Although there is always a reserve requirement, the money supply can be controlled by changing the rate; still, this is an infrequently used tool by the Fed.

Tool 2: Open-Market Operations—Buying & Selling U.S. Government Bonds to Increase/Decrease Bank Reserves (Used Frequently)

A more commonly used tool is *open-market operations,* **in which the Federal Reserve controls the money supply by buying and selling U.S. Treasury securities, or government bonds, to the public.** When the Fed *sells* more bonds to the public, the money it takes in payment is withdrawn from circulation, which decreases the money supply. When the Fed *buys* more bonds from the public, the money it pays out gets into circulation, increasing the money supply.

When the Fed uses open-market operations, it employs the *federal funds rate,* the Fed-set rate banks charge when they lend each other money overnight.

Tool 3: Discount Rate—Specifying the Interest Rate on Fed Loans to Member Banks (Used Only with Tool 2)

The *discount rate* **is the interest rate at which the Federal Reserve makes short-term loans to member banks.** When the Fed *raises* this interest rate, banks are less motivated to borrow from it, which reduces the number of loans they can make to their customers. When the Fed *lowers* this interest rate, it encourages banks to borrow more money, which increases the funds available to loan to their customers.

The three tools used by the Fed to control the money supply are summarized below. (*See* ■ *Panel 16.9.*)

Want to Know More? 16-10

Federal Reserve Discount Rate Window

Go to www.mybizlab.com.

■ **PANEL 16.9 Three Fed tools for controlling the money supply.**

Tool & Frequency of Use	Policy Decision	Effect on the Economy
1. Reserve requirement— Infrequently used	• Increase percentage of deposits banks must reserve as cash	• Reduces money supply, raises interest rates, slows economic growth
	• Decrease percentage of deposits banks must reserve as cash	• Increases money supply, lowers interest rates, speeds up economic growth
2. Open-market operations— Frequently used	• Fed sells bonds to the public	• Reduces money supply, raises interest rates, slows economic growth
	• Fed buys bonds from the public	• Increases money supply, lowers interest rates, speeds up economic growth
3. Discount rate— Used only with Tool 2	• Fed increases rate it charges banks for loans	• Reduces money supply, raises interest rates, slows economic growth
	• Fed decreases rate it charges banks for loans	• Increases money supply, lowers interest rates, speeds up economic growth

How the Fed Clears Checks between Different Banks

The Fed devotes a great deal of time and effort toward processing checks between different banks. If you write a $50 paper check on your Boston Wells Fargo bank account to your sister and she deposits that check into her own Wells Fargo account in Dallas, it's easy for the bank to reduce your account by $50 and raise hers by $50. But if your sister's account is with a *different* bank—say, Bank of America in Dallas—a different clearing process occurs. Looking at this time-consuming process, you can see why banks (and the Fed) would like you to stop using paper checks and go digital. (*See* ■ *Panel 16.10.*)

■ **PANEL 16.10 How a paper check clears.**

Boston ➡ Dallas	**1.** You write a $50 check from your Boston Wells Fargo account and send it to your sister in Dallas.
↓	
Dallas B of A	**2.** Your sister deposits your Wells Fargo check in her Bank of America branch in Dallas.
↓	
Dallas FRB	**3.** Bank of America sends that check to the closest Federal Reserve bank, which also happens to be in Dallas.
↓	
Boston FRB	**4.** The Dallas Federal Reserve branch sends your sister's check to your Federal Reserve bank, which is in Boston, for collection.
↓	
Boston Wells Fargo	**5.** The Boston Federal Reserve bank then sends the check to your local branch of Wells Fargo in Boston for withdrawal.
↓	
Boston FRB	**6.** Your Wells Fargo then authorizes the Boston Federal Reserve bank to deduct $50.
↓	
Dallas FRB	**7.** The Boston Federal Reserve bank pays $50 to the Dallas Federal Reserve bank.
↓	
Dallas B of A	**8.** The Dallas Federal Reserve bank credits $50 to your sister's account in the Dallas Bank of America.

⓯ **Overseas ATM.** Vietnam Bank for Industry and Trade (VietinBank), which is 70% owned by the government of Vietnam, has issued a co-branded MasterCard international smart card. Since Americans traveling in Europe have sometimes had difficulty finding ATMs that would accept their magnetic-strip credit cards, what do you think your chances are with this machine? For safety's sake, in what form should you carry money when traveling overseas?

Source: David R. Frazier Photolibrary, Inc./Alamy.

The Era of E-Cash: Money Goes Digital

What are some new technologies for handling money?

Today money consists of digital blips on an electronic screen, with many transactions done via *e-cash,* or *electronic cash*—**money held, exchanged, and represented in electronic form and transacted over the Internet.**

Electronic Money

For consumers, banking is now a 24/7 service, with always-available ATMs (automated teller machines) and *electronic funds transfer systems (EFTSs),* **computerized systems that move funds from one institution to another over electronic links,** allowing online bill paying, automatic deposit systems, and on-line banks offering (at least in Europe) same-day money transfers.[24]

Debit Cards, Smart Cards, & Cellphones

The old magnetic-strip credit card has morphed not only into a *debit card,* **which allows you to immediately transfer money from your bank account to pay for purchases electronically,** but also into a *smart card*—**a plastic card with built-in microprocessor and memory chips that can combine the functions of credit, debit, phone, bridge-toll, and (as in Germany) national-health-care cards.** ⓯ Indeed, the newest evolution is the cellphone that can double as a credit card that can "talk" to payment terminals (and, among other things, can be used to pay for parking time on a new generation of wireless parking meters).[25]

Banks & Other Financial Institutions

THE BIG IDEA: The banking system consists of (1) banks—commercial banks, savings institutions (savings and loans and mutual savings banks), and credit unions; and (2) nonbank institutions offering some banking services—insurance companies, pension funds, finance companies, and brokerage firms. Three different government organizations, abbreviated FDIC, SAIF, and NCUA, offer financial protection for money in banks, savings and loans, and credit unions.

THE ESSENTIAL QUESTION: How do banks differ from nonbanks, and how do they protect depositors?

MyBizLab: Check your understanding of these concepts at www.mybizlab.com.

MyBizLab

Thomas Jefferson "hated commerce, he hated speculators, he hated the grubby business of getting and spending (except his own spending, of course, which eventually bankrupted him)," writes historian John Steele Gordon. "Most of all, he hated banks, the symbol for him of concentrated economic power."[26]

Should we share Jefferson's attitude—especially now that we know banks have figured so much in bringing on the world's recent economic distress?

Let's see what banks do. We will distinguish among five categories of financial institutions:

- Commercial banks
- Savings institutions
- Credit unions
- Nonbanks—insurance companies, pension funds, finance companies, and brokerage firms
- Investment banks

Commercial Banks: Full-Service Banks

What are commercial banks and their services, and how do banks make money?

A *commercial bank*, as we said earlier in this chapter, is a federal- or state-chartered profit-seeking financial institution that accepts deposits from individuals and businesses and uses part of them to make personal, residential, and business loans. A commercial bank is sometimes called a *full-service bank*.

There are around 1,700 commercial banks in the United States, ranging in size from the Big Three—Bank of America, JP Morgan Chase, and Citigroup—to small community banks, and they are probably the most important of our financial institutions.[27] In its most basic business, the way a bank makes a profit is to take in more in interest on the loans it makes than it pays out in interest to depositors and in operating costs; however, banks have other ways of making money, as we'll see. ⑯

Want to Know More? 16-11
Commercial Banks Survive
Go to www.mybizlab.com.

⑯ **Commercial bank.** At the end of 2007, the so-called Big Three commercial banks—Bank of America, JP Morgan Chase, and Citigroup—collectively held 21.4% of U.S. bank deposits. Then came the 2008 economic meltdown and the failure of several important financial institutions (Washington Mutual, Wachovia), and suddenly the Big Three controlled 31.3% of deposits. B of A, headquartered in Charlotte, North Carolina, later found itself in many legal disputes over faulty mortgages and foreclosures that threatened its No. 1 status.

Source: Kevin Foy/Alamy.

Types of Deposit Accounts: Checking, Savings, NOW, Money Market Accounts, & Certificates of Deposit

As a depositor, you have a choice of a number of bank accounts with a commercial bank, as follows:

Checking Accounts: Accounts That Pay No Interest and Allow Check Writing. A traditional *checking account* allows you to deposit money in a bank account and then write checks on that account. It does not pay any interest and generally requires you to pay a monthly service fee, plus additional fees if you write more checks in a month than the account allows. And, of course, if you write a check for which you have insufficient funds, the bank will charge a penalty fee for that.

Savings Accounts: Accounts That Pay Low Interest and Don't Allow Check Writing. A *savings account,* otherwise known as a *time deposit,* is a bank account that pays low interest and doesn't allow check writing. In order to get access to your money in a savings account, you may have to visit a bank or an ATM (if you don't do online banking), making it less convenient than simply writing a check. Still, the funds are accessible enough that savings accounts are known as "near money."

NOW Accounts: Minimum-Balance Accounts That Pay Interest and Allow Unlimited Check Writing. A *NOW* (for "negotiable order of withdrawal") *account* is an account that pays interest and allows you to write an unlimited number of checks, but you have to maintain a minimum monthly balance, such as $1,000. An account requiring an even higher minimum balance (such as $5,000) but paying more interest is called a *Super-NOW account.* ⑰

Source: Courtesy of Burston House, Ltd.

⑰ **Comparison shopping.** When starting a business you will need a good banking relationship. As with many other services, it pays to shop and compare when selecting a bank and to get thoroughly acquainted with the bank's management and services. Some are much more oriented toward businesses of certain sizes. When prospecting for a bank, what questions should you ask?

Money Market Accounts: Accounts That Pay Brokerage-Competitive Interest and Offer Some Check Writing. Designed to enable banks to compete with money market accounts offered by brokerage firms, *money market accounts* are bank accounts that offer interest rates competitive with those of brokerage firm money market funds, but they require higher minimum balances and limit check writing to as few as three per month.

Certificates of Deposit: Savings Accounts That Pay Interest upon a Certificate's Maturity Date. A *certificate of deposit (CD)* is a savings (time deposit) account that pays interest upon the certificate's maturity date. The depositor agrees not to withdraw funds until that date (there is a penalty for early withdrawal). Interest rates vary depending on market conditions and length of time on the certificate, which can vary from three months to many years.

■ **Example of How Banks Attract Depositors: The Interest-Rate War.** In 2008, as the battered economy dried up sources of credit, U.S. banks engaged in a heated race to shore up their funding sources by attracting new depositors. "In the past 15 years, there's been nothing like this," said one observer. "The level of competitive intensity is unprecedented right now."[28]

The average rate on a one-year certificate of deposit jumped from 2% in May to 2.61% in October. Small banks, such as Virginia Commerce of Arlington, Virginia, were offering CDs with interest rates as high as 4.5%. (Three years later, as the recession wound down, the rate was 0.48%.) ■

Key Takeaway 16-6
Types of deposit accounts: checking, savings, NOW, money market accounts, and certificates of deposit.

How Commercial Banks Make Money: Loan Interest, Fees for Services, & Fees from Other Financial Products

Banks make money in three ways: (1) by *charging interest on loans,* (2) by *charging fees for other services,* and (3) by *offering other financial products.*

Interest on Loans. As mentioned, banks make money by charging higher interest rates on loans than they pay out in interest rates to depositors. Loans may be personal loans, business loans, real-estate loans, construction loans, and home mortgage loans.

Fees for Services. Banks also make money by charging fees for services, ranging from credit cards to overdraft protection (customers get loans at reasonable rates if they write checks for which they have insufficient funds). ⑱

Fees from Other Financial Products. In recent years, banks have found other ways to make money, offering life insurance and brokerage services. (See ■ *Panel 16.11.*)

Fee Schedule *(Effective January 10, 2011)*

Account Closed *(by mail or within 90 days)*	$20.00
Account Transfer	
Via Telephone/Customer Service	$5.00
ACH Block Service	$20.00 per month
(non-personal accounts only)	
ATM/Visa® Check Card	
Inquiry at foreign ATM*	$2.00
Withdrawal at foreign ATM*	$2.00
*A fee (surcharge) may also be charged by the owner of the foreign ATM.	
ATM Surcharge Refund Program *(per month)*	$15.00
International Visa® Transaction Fee¹	
Single currency transaction	0.80%
Multiple currency transaction	1.00%
Mini Statement *(ATM)*	$2.00
Cash Handling *(per roll/pack, business customers only)*	$0.20
Collection Item	
Domestic	$20.00 + correspondent fee
Foreign	$40.00 + correspondent fee
Court Order/Garnishment/Writ/Levy	$250.00
Deposit/Loan Account Assistance *(per hour)*	$25.00
Minimum	$10.00
Deposit Item Returned	$15.00
Direct Connect for Quicken®/QuickBooks® — Business	
Monthly fee	$15.00
Dormant Account *(no activity for 2 years)*	
Customers of MD Branches	
If balance is ≤$50.00	$10.00 prorated monthly
If balance is >$50.00	$20.00 prorated monthly
Customers of PA and WV Branches	$10.00 per month
Customers of NJ Branches	$5.00 per month
EDI Translation Fax Charge *(per month)*	$25.00
Escheat Fee	$75.00
(where permitted by law and not to exceed state limits)	
Excess Transaction	$20.00

Overdraft Fees/S...
Fees assessed per ...
available funds in ...
in person withdraw...
payment, such as ...
Paid Overdraft ...
Return Overdra...
Overdraft Swee...
(includes tran...
and lines of cr...
Overdraft Daily ...
Per day after ...
Personal Money (...
Retirement Accou...
Safe Deposit Box ...
Contact your lo...
Drilling ...
Inventory...
Key Replaceme...
Late Charge...
Statements *(per st...*
Copy of Full Sta...
Copy of Stateme...
Duplicate Stater...
Instant Money ...
Undeliverable S...
Check Images o...
Stop Payment ...
Travelers Checks ...
Standard...
Checks for two ...
Wire Transfer — I...
Wire Transfer — I...
Wire Transfer — I...

Personal

⑱ **Bank fees.** Can you read the fine print? When establishing a banking relationship, you really need to. This typical fee schedule lists 49 different charges a bank can levy for various services. Do you think most banks generate more of their revenues from loans or fees?

Savings Institutions: Savings & Loans & Mutual Savings Banks

What is the difference between savings and loans and mutual savings banks?

Savings institutions—savings and loan associations and mutual savings banks, as well as federal savings banks—are another part of the banking sector.

1 Savings & Loan Associations: For Home Mortgage Loans

***Savings and loan associations (S&Ls)* are financial institutions that accept deposits and were originally intended to make loans primarily for home mortgages.** In recent years, however, they have also ventured into life insurance, mutual funds, and consumer loans. Still, more than 70% of their loans are for home mortgages. S&Ls are owned by shareholders.

2 Mutual Savings Banks: Depositor-Owned Savings Institutions

***Mutual savings banks* are for-profit financial institutions similar to savings and loans, except that they are owned by their depositors rather than by shareholders.**

Credit Unions: Depositor-Owned Financial Cooperatives

What's distinctive about credit unions?

***Credit unions* are depositor-owned, nonprofit financial cooperatives that offer a range of banking services to their members.** Members of credit unions, which usually pay relatively higher interest rates, by law must share certain occupations or memberships in certain organizations, such as universities, corporations, unions, or government agencies.[29]

■ **PANEL 16.11 Some services offered by commercial banks.**

Automated teller machines (ATMs)

Automatic bill payment

Brokerage services

Certified checks

Checking accounts

Credit cards

Currency exchange

Debit cards

Direct deposit

Financial counseling

Individual retirement accounts (IRAs)

Life insurance

Loans

Notary services

Online banking

Overdraft protection

Safe deposit boxes

Smart cards

Trust services

Traveler's checks

Source: Kevin Foy/Alamy.

⑲ Nonbank. Although Merrill Lynch was acquired by Bank of America in 2008, the brokerage firm is considered a nonbank institution. Formerly, nonbanks, which also include insurance companies, pension funds, and finance companies, did not accept deposits, as banks did, but now some nonbank institutions do.

Want to Know More? 16-12

Credit Unions: Depositor Owned & Democratic

Go to www.mybizlab.com.

Nonbanks: Other Financial Institutions

How would I distinguish among the four kinds of nonbanks?

Nonbanks **are financial institutions—insurance companies, pension funds, finance companies, and brokerage firms—that offer many of the same services as banks provide. Formerly they did not accept deposits; today, however, some of them do.** ⑲

1 Insurance Companies: Investing Funds from Policyholders

Insurance companies **are nondeposit companies that accept payments (called** *premiums***) from policyholders—individuals or firms who have purchased insurance policies that guarantee financial protection in the event something goes wrong.** The process that insurance companies use to determine who should be insured is called *underwriting.* Because many insurance companies collect more in premiums than they pay out in insured losses (claims) or operating expenses, they typically invest any excess funds in stocks, real estate, and other assets.

2 Pension Funds: Investing Retirement Contributions

Pension funds **are nondeposit institutions that provide retirement benefits to workers and their families.** Such funds are set up by employers and funded by steady contributions from employers and employees. Pension funds tend to invest in long-term conservative assets such as common stock or government securities.

3 Finance Companies: Making High-Interest Loans to Individuals & Businesses

Finance companies **are nondeposit companies that make short-term loans at higher interest rates to individuals or businesses that don't meet the credit requirements of regular banks,** such as college students or businesses with no credit history. *Consumer* finance companies lend to individuals; *commercial* finance companies lend to businesses.

4 Brokerage Firms: Offering Stocks & Bonds & High-Interest Bank Accounts

Brokerage firms, **otherwise known as** *securities investment dealers,* **are companies that buy and sell stocks and bonds for individuals and now compete with banks by offering high-interest-rate combination checking and savings accounts.** Some commercial banks have joined forces with brokerages, as when

Key Takeaway 16-7
Nonbanks: insurance companies, pension funds, finance companies, and brokerage firms.

Bank of America took over Merrill Lynch in 2008. We discuss brokerage firms further in Chapter 17.

Investment Banks: Institutions for Raising Capital & Handling Mergers & Acquisitions

How did an investment bank used to differ from a commercial bank?

A commercial bank is an institution that accepts deposits and makes loans to individuals and businesses. An ***investment bank,*** **by contrast, is a financial institution that deals primarily with raising capital, structuring corporate mergers and acquisitions, and handling securities.**

The big names in investment banking were the powerhouse Wall Street firms Bear Stearns, Goldman Sachs, Lehman Brothers, Merrill Lynch, and Morgan Stanley. ⑳ In the past, the activities of investment banks were differentiated from other banks by 1933 legislation, the *Glass-Steagall Act,* that prohibited commercial banks from giving customers advice on stocks or underwriting them, activities that were reserved for brokerage firms and investment banks. That all changed with the 1999 *Financial Services Modernization Act,* or Gramm-Leach-Bliley Act, which did away with the separation between commercial banks and investment banks and the restrictions on the integration of banking, insurance, and stock trading imposed by Glass-Steagall.

One result of the new law was that investment banks engaged in what commentator Robert Kuttner calls "complex financial engineering"—creating so-called *credit default swaps* and other instruments known as derivatives.[30] These are blamed for being the "exotic and opaque" securities that undid the financial system in 2008, as we'll describe.

How Your Money Is Protected

What government agencies are protecting my money in banks, S&Ls, and credit unions?

During the Great Depression, the American banking system "went into convulsions," in the words of one writer. About 9,000 banks failed between 1930 and 1933 and hundreds of others were closed by the Roosevelt administration in its early days.[31] As a result, bank deposit insurance and other policies were adopted to protect depositors. The three major sources of protection are the *Federal Deposit Insurance Corporation,* the *Savings Association Insurance Fund,* and the *National Credit Union Administration.*

Source: Nicholas Roberts/AFP/Getty Images/Newscom.

⑳ **Investment bank.** In 2007, venerable Lehman Brothers was the fourth largest investment bank in the United States (behind Goldman Sachs, Morgan Stanley, and Merrill Lynch). On September 15, 2008, the 158-year-old firm went bankrupt, the result of failed investments in mortgage securities. This was the largest bankruptcy in U.S. history. What do you think the failure of Lehman Brothers indicated about its management at the time and the firm's ability to assess investment risks?

1 Protection for Banks: The Federal Deposit Insurance Corporation

The *Federal Deposit Insurance Corporation (FDIC)* **is an independent agency of the U.S. government that insures bank deposits.** Before the financial crisis of September 2008, the FDIC insured individual depositors' accounts up to $100,000. After the meltdown, it was temporarily, and later permanently, raised to $250,000. (IRAs and other retirement accounts qualify for added protection.)[32] The FDIC covers mostly commercial banks.

BRIEFING / PERSONAL FINANCE

Staying Alert to Be Sure You Don't Lose Money with Your FDIC Insurance. "No one has ever lost a dime of FDIC-insured deposits," says *USA Today* business writer Sandra Block.[33] Technically that's true. Yet Emeryville, California, depositor Fran Quittel thought she was protected when she heard IndyMac Bank had failed. She had both business checking and business savings with the bank, and because each held less than the $100,000 limit guaranteed by the FDIC at the time, she thought she was fine. Unfortunately, the two accounts *together* totaled over $100,000 and shared a single taxpayer ID number. As a result, she lost half of everything over the $100,000 limit.[34] ■

2 Protection for S&Ls: The Savings Association Insurance Fund

The *Savings Association Insurance Fund (SAIF),* **which is now part of the FDIC, insures depositors with accounts in savings and loan associations.** It insures up to $250,000 per depositor per bank. Previously it was known as the Federal Savings and Loan Insurance Corporation, established in 1934 during the Great Depression.

3 Protection for Credit Unions: The National Credit Union Administration

The *National Credit Union Administration (NCUA)* **is an independent federal agency that provides up to $250,000 insurance coverage per individual per credit union.**

Do these efforts really protect us? Certainly they're far better than the absolute lack of safeguards that existed during the Great Depression. In that time, about 10,000 of 25,000 banks went belly-up, and depositors lost every penny.[35] **㉑**

Source: Library of Congress, Prints & Photographs Division [reprod number LC-DIG-ggbain-08923].

㉑ Bank run. A great deal of the financial damage caused by the Great Depression of the 1930s was caused by bank runs, when depositors, fearing that their savings institution was about to fail, rushed to withdraw their deposits—fanning panic among other bank customers and spurring further withdrawals, leading to the bank's collapse. Even with deposit insurance in place, what events do you think might trigger a bank run today?

THE BIG IDEA: The banking system has cycled through swings in regulation and deregulation and financial panics, and is much more globally integrated today. After the Great Depression of 1929, which was followed by increased regulation, there was no panic for nearly 60 years. The 1980s and 1990s saw more deregulation and greater willingness of financial institutions to take on risk, such as use of financial instruments called derivatives. When coupled with a rise in easy credit and increased subprime loans to high-risk borrowers, derivatives led to overconfidence and speculative excess. A surge in mortgage defaults led to the worldwide financial crisis of 2008.

THE ESSENTIAL QUESTION: How has the banking system changed, and why did it get in trouble in recent years?

MyBizLab: Check your understanding of these concepts at www.mybizlab.com.

MyBizLab

Except for the 60-year period following the Great Depression, roughly every 20 years in American history, points out historian John Steele Gordon, we've had a financial panic—in 1819, 1836, 1857, 1873, 1893, 1907, 1929, 1987, and 2008.[36] 22 If most people approach finance with a mixture of greed and fear, during panics fear prevails—and with it cries for more regulation.

The Early Trend toward Regulation

Why was there no financial panic for 60 years after 1929?

Source: Photograph by Sally Lindsay.

After the 1907 panic, officials realized the financial system could not survive without some regulation, and the Federal Reserve System was created. However, fearing a single strong central bank would be too powerful, they created not one U.S. bank but 12 separate, weakly coordinated banks. As a result, says Gordon, what began as an ordinary recession in 1929 became the catastrophic Great Depression because the Federal Reserve was unable to do its job.

In 1934, therefore, the Fed was reorganized as a strong central bank. "That is a principal reason there was no panic for nearly 60 years after 1929," says Gordon, "and the crash of 1987 had no lasting effect on the American economy." Other legislation pushed through in the wake of the Great Depression resulted in bank deposit insurance and tighter regulation of financial markets. As mentioned, the Glass-Steagall Act prohibited banks from giving customers advice on stocks or underwriting them.

22 **The panic of 2008.** The bubble in housing prices burst in 2006, beginning a long period of decline in which borrowers were no longer able to make their mortgage payments or refinance their home loans, leading to increased defaults. In September 2008, the situation exploded into a full-blown financial panic. Even three years later a recovery in housing sales still hadn't hit its stride. What is the picture as you read this?

The Trend toward Deregulation & Risky Investments

How did we get to a culture allowing excessive risk?

In the 1980s and 1990s, as memories of the Great Depression faded, the pendulum swung toward deregulation. Former Senator Phil Gramm of Texas, a champion

Derivatives:
Financial contracts
Financial contracts that "derive" their value from certain assets (e.g., stocks, loans, interest rates, commodities, market indexes, mortgages). An investor contracts to pay a set price in return for the right to take profits later if the asset's value rises.

The story: The assets underlying the derivatives that ultimately destroyed the financial system were mortgage-backed securities.

↓

Mortgage-backed securities:
Assets underlying the contracts
Securities that bundle multiple mortgages into one, which is sold to investors. This security can be bundled with others into a second security—which may include other types of instruments, including risky subprime mortgages. These can become third-level securities—and so on, to four or five levels.

The story: Mortgage-backed securities were snapped up because of the high returns sparked by the sizzling housing market, made possible by easy credit.

↓

Credit default swaps:
Supposed "insurance" against mortgage defaults
Types of contracts that act like insurance to protect investors against default, as could happen with risky mortgages and mortgage-backed securities. They are not classified as "credit default *insurance*" because insurance regulations require institutions to set aside enough reserves to cover possible defaults.

The story: When the housing market crashed, insurers (such as AIG) were liable for mortgage-default payments for which they did not have reserves—bringing on the financial collapse.

of deregulation, intensively pushed laws that he said were intended to unshackle business from needless restraints. Among other things, says one account, "he led the effort to block measures curtailing deceptive or predatory lending," which critics felt contributed to the tidal wave of home foreclosures in the 2000s.[37] Other efforts led to weakened controls and monitoring by government regulators, creditors, accounting systems, and rating agencies, among others. Finally, in 2004, the Securities and Exchange Commission agreed to exempt the nation's five largest investment banks—Bear Stearns, Goldman Sachs, Lehman Brothers, Merrill Lynch, and Morgan Stanley—from a regulation limiting the amount of debt they could take on. This unlocked billions of dollars for investment.[38]

With deregulation came another trend: the greater willingness of financial institutions—and individuals—to take on risk.[39] This led to the use of complex financial instruments known as *derivatives*, which, along with *mortgage-backed securities* and *credit default swaps*, encouraged risky investment practices. A *derivative* **is a financial contract that "derives" its value from a wide range of sources, including stocks, loans, and market indexes. Investors pay a set price in return for possible profits later.**[40] (*See* ■ *Panel 16.12*.)

These instruments required the use of computers, which led, says one critic, to "financial products that were so complex that we now don't know how to value them."[41] The result of such financial engineering, says another writer, was that "clever and well-paid people created a host of complex debt instruments that were then sold to other clever and well-paid people who were similarly misemployed—with catastrophic results."[42]

The Beginning of the 2008 Crash

How did subprime loans lead to financial trouble?

The final nail in the financial system's coffin was the wide availability of cheap credit. Loans known as *subprime loans*—**loans for people with blemished or limited credit histories, which carried a higher rate of interest than prime loans to compensate for increased credit risk**—were extended to people less likely to repay them. Millions of borrowers bought homes, thinking they could sell them if they got into trouble. Also, as in 1929, says finance professor Lawrence Kryzanowski, "people thought the good times were going to go on forever. And then very quickly, they stopped."[43]

First, the holders of subprime loans found they could no longer make their mortgage payments after the interest rates on such loans reset at higher rates. Then mortgage defaults started rising, and the economy began to stall. In March 2008, Bear Stearns, once the country's fifth-largest investment bank, failed because its investors no longer believed it could repay its loans. "Even worse," says one report, "investors concluded the bank no longer could stand behind the complex agreements it had with other financial institutions."[44] The company was forced into a hastily arranged merger with JP Morgan Chase.

There followed a tsunami of financial events. In September 2008, the federal government took over mortgage giants Fannie Mae and Freddie Mac. Two weeks later, Lehman Brothers, a 158-year-old investment bank crippled with heavy investments in failed mortgage securities, filed for bankruptcy. Hours later the well-known investment firm Merrill Lynch agreed to be taken over by Bank of America. A day later the Federal Reserve agreed to lend insurer AIG $85 billion. Other institutions—Washington Mutual, Wachovia—also failed. Every financial instrument relied on by investors—except possibly for Treasury bills—came under severe pressure.[45]

Links to the Global Financial System

Why did the U.S. economic downturn affect the world?

Three days after President George W. Bush signed the October 3, 2008, $700 billion law to rescue failing U.S. financial institutions, investors were so fearful that the amount would prove insufficient that stock markets began plunging around the world. First it was markets in Tokyo, then in Hong Kong and Mumbai (Bombay), followed by Moscow, Frankfurt, Paris, and London. "This is global," said one financial strategist, "and this is the downside of globalization."[46]

A week earlier, European leaders had regarded the massive financial difficulties as a "made in America" problem, but it quickly became apparent that European banks had embraced many of the same risky practices and in fact had exposed themselves to even higher levels of debt than American banks had.[47] As the crisis spread, small economies like Iceland had to nationalize banks and seek bailouts from the International Monetary Fund (described in Chapter 4). In three months, the currencies of Iceland, South Africa, Hungary, Poland, Turkey, Mexico, Colombia, and South Korea lost more than 25% of their value.[48] Hoping to prevent a run on their banks, the governments of Austria, Sweden, Denmark, the United Kingdom, Greece, Italy, France, and Iceland raised or eliminated the ceiling on deposit insurance.[49] **❷❸**

How did the crisis, which started in the United States, go global? Many investors, relying on optimistic assumptions, had purchased the complex debt packages known as derivatives from U.S. financial institutions, then used these securities as collateral to borrow more money. Instead of spreading the risk, however, when these securities started performing badly, fear spread around the world. And, comments financial consultant David M. Smick, the complexity and sheer size of the global financial market made it "unbelievably fragile."[50]

Source: u99/ZUMA Press/Newscom.

❷❸ Crisis in Iceland. An island of only 320,000 people (equal in population to Toledo, Ohio), Iceland had seen its bank assets jump fivefold from 2004 to 2008. In the 2008 financial crisis, all three of the country's major commercial banks collapsed, which threatened to drag the country into national bankruptcy. Every Icelander owed the equivalent of $276,622 in debt.

The Question of Confidence

Are feelings of confidence influenced by recent events?

"It's all about confidence, stupid," writes *Newsweek* financial columnist Robert J. Samuelson. "Every financial system depends on trust. People have to believe that the institutions they deal with . . . will perform as expected."[51] In 2008, the United States—and the world—were in a full-blown crisis of confidence because investors and financial managers lost that trust.

Prior to August 2007, when the crisis first occurred, overconfidence contributed to years of speculative excess. Paul Slovic, an expert in the psychology of risk, points out that when the good times are rolling—when bankers are making millions selling mortgage-backed securities, for instance—"the sense of risk is depressed. You don't look as hard for warning signs."[52] Yale economist Robert Shiller adds, "One thing we know about human behavior is that our memory is influenced by recent events."[53] Thus, we get caught up in the emotion of the moment. During good times, then, says business writer Joe Nocera, "a kind of unshakable euphoria takes over, and we just can't imagine it's ever ending. Similarly, when times are bad, fear and loathing capture our imagination, and we find it equally impossible to see a glimmer of hope."[54]

Although the final story on the Great Recession has yet to be written, we would do well to keep these observations in mind as we move on to our next major financial subject—securities and investing.

Summary

16.1 Financial Management & Financial Planning

THE ESSENTIAL QUESTION: *What is financial management, and what are the parts of a financial plan?*

What does a financial manager do, what is the risk-return trade-off, and why is financial management important? Finance is the business function of obtaining funds for a company and managing them to accomplish the company's objectives. The job of acquiring and managing funds is called financial management. The people responsible for planning and controlling the acquisition and uses of funds are called financial managers. Central to the job of financial management is risk-return trade-off, in which financial managers continually try to balance the firm's investment risk with the expected return, or payoffs, from its investments. A financial manager is responsible for paying bills, collecting money, minimizing taxes, and monitoring accounting.

How would I distinguish among the three parts of a financial plan—forecasting, budgeting, and financial controls? A financial plan is a firm's strategy for reaching its financial goals. (1) Forecasting is predicting revenues, costs, and expenses for a certain period of time. There are three types of forecasts: cash flow (1 to 3 months), short-term (4 to 12 months), and long-term (1, 5, or 10 years). (2) A budget is a detailed financial plan showing estimated revenues and expenses for a particular future period, usually one year. The four types of budgets are operating budgets (costs to meet sales and production goals), capital budgets (costs to buy expensive long-term assets), cash budgets (cash in and out for each month and the full year), and master budgets (the preceding budgets tied together for a particular period). (3) In the process of financial control, a company compares its actual revenues and expenses with those predicted in its budget.

16.2 Finding Funds to Keep the Firm Operating

THE ESSENTIAL QUESTION: *If I were a financial manager, why would I want my firm to borrow money?*

Why do firms think they have to borrow money? They need funds for managing everyday business activities, extending credit to their customers, keeping enough product (inventory) available, and making major investments.

16.3 Getting Short-Term & Long-Term Financing

THE ESSENTIAL QUESTION: *If I ever have to find money for my company, what should I do?*

If I were a small-business person needing money right away, what kind of sources would I look at? Four sources of short-term financing are trade credit, short-term loans, pledging

and factoring, and commercial paper. (1) Trade credit is short-term financing by which a firm buys a product, then receives a bill from the supplier, then pays it later. Terms of trade are the conditions the supplier gives the buyer when offering short-term credit. One form of trade credit is the promissory note, a written contract prepared by the buyer who agrees to pay the seller a certain amount by a certain time. (2) Short-term loans may be secured (the borrower pledges some asset that is forfeited if the loan is not repaid) or unsecured (no asset is pledged). The sources of short-term loans are family and friends, banks and finance companies, and credit cards. Three types of loans are a line of credit, revolving credit agreement, and transaction loan. (3) Firms can make use of their accounts receivable, amounts customers owe them, by borrowing against them (known as pledging) or selling them (known as factoring). (4) Commercial paper consists of unsecured short-term promissory notes over $100,000 issued by large corporations.

If I needed to get money for the long term for my company, where would I go? Three sources of long-term financing are long-term loans, debt financing, and equity financing. (1) Long-term loans require the borrower to sign a term-loan agreement, a promissory note indicating specific installments for repayments. (2) Debt financing consists of a firm's issuing corporate bonds, contracts between issuer and buyer and for which the issuing firm pays the buyer interest. Bonds may be secured bonds, backed by the firm's collateral, such as real estate or equipment, or unsecured bonds, backed by the firm's reputation. (3) Equity financing involves selling ownership in the firm by selling stock, retaining earnings and reinvesting them in the firm, and receiving venture capital (funds acquired from wealthy individuals in return for some ownership).

What is the ultimate purpose of a firm's borrowing money? Financial managers are guided by the principle of financial leverage, the technique of using borrowed funds to increase the firm's rate of return. Such managers pay attention to the cost of capital, the rate of return a firm must earn to cover the cost of generating funds in the marketplace.

16.4 Money: What It Is, How It's Controlled

THE ESSENTIAL QUESTION: *What are money and the money supply, and how does money get into the banking system?*

What are the characteristics and functions of money? Money is any medium of value that is generally accepted as payment for goods and services. Five characteristics of money are portability, divisibility, durability, uniqueness, and stability. The three functions of money are that it acts as a medium of exchange, a store of wealth, and a standard of value.

What are the definitions of the money supply? Currency is government-issued coins and paper money. The U.S. money supply is the amount of money the Federal Reserve System makes available for people to buy goods and services and is referred to in two ways: as M1 (the narrow definition), money that can be accessed quickly and easily, and M2 (the more common measure), which is M1 plus money that takes more time to access. M1 is currency, traveler's checks, bank checking account balances, and demand deposit accounts. M2 is M1, small time deposits, money market funds, and savings deposits.

How do the Federal Reserve and commercial banks work to create money? The Federal Reserve (Fed), run by a board of governors, consists of 12 districts, each with its own Federal Reserve bank, which serve commercial banks, banks that accept deposits and make loans to individuals and businesses. The Fed helps get money to these banks by making currency and loans available.

What are three ways the Fed controls the money supply? Too much money in the money supply could lead to inflation; too little could lead to deflation. To avoid these extremes, the Fed uses three policy tools. (1) The reserve requirement specifies how much money a bank must keep to lend to customers. (2) With open-market operations, the Fed buys and sells government bonds to the public, which has the effect of increasing or decreasing the money supply. (3) By raising or lowering the discount rate, the interest rate at which the Fed makes short-term loans to member banks, it affects how motivated banks are to borrow money.

What are some new technologies for handling money? Many transactions are done by e-cash, with money represented in electronic form. There are electronic funds transfer systems, computerized systems that move funds from one institution to another via electronic links. There are also debit cards, which in some countries have become microprocessor-based smart cards, with expanded functions.

16.5 Banks & Other Financial Institutions

THE ESSENTIAL QUESTION: *How do banks differ from non-banks, and how do they protect depositors?*

What is commercial banks and their services, and how do banks make money? Among five categories of financial institutions, commercial banks are government-chartered institutions that accept deposits and use them to make loans. Types of deposit accounts include checking, savings, NOW, money market, and certificates of deposit. Commercial banks make money by charging interest on loans, charging fees for other services (such as overdraft protection), and offering other financial products.

What's the difference between savings and loans and mutual savings banks? Savings and loan associations (S&Ls) accept deposits; they started out making loans for home mortgages but have now expanded. Mutual savings banks are like S&Ls but are owned by depositors rather than shareholders.

What's distinctive about credit unions? These are depositor-owned and nonprofit financial institutions that offer loan services to certain restricted members.

How would I distinguish among the four kinds of nonbanks? Nonbanks are financial institutions that offer many bank services. They formerly did not accept deposits (but now do). They include insurance companies, pension funds, finance companies, and brokerage firms.

How did an investment bank used to differ from a commercial bank? Investment banks deal primarily with raising capital, structuring corporate mergers and acquisitions, and handling securities.

What government agencies are protecting my money in banks, S&Ls, and credit unions? The three major sources of protection are the Federal Deposit Insurance Corporation, which insures bank deposits; the Savings Association and Insurance Fund, which insures S&L depositors; and the National Credit Union Administration, which covers credit loan depositors.

16.6 The Changing Banking Environment: Regulation, Deregulation, & Financial Panics

THE ESSENTIAL QUESTION: *How has the banking system changed, and why did it get in trouble in recent years?*

Why was there no financial panic for 60 years after 1929? The Federal Reserve, first created after 1907 as 12 weakly coordinated banks, was reorganized as a strong central bank. Also legislation was passed to more tightly regulate financial markets and to cover depositors with bank deposit insurance.

How did we get to a culture allowing excessive risk? In the 1980s and 1990s, regulations curtailing deceptive lending were weakened, as was monitoring by government regulators, and the five largest investment banks were no longer limited in the amount of debt they could take on. This led to the use of complex financial instruments known as derivatives, which along with mortgage-backed securities and credit default swaps, encouraged risky investment practices.

How did subprime loans lead to financial trouble? High-interest subprime loans were made to people with blemished credit histories, who could no longer repay the loans after interest rates on the loans were reset. Then mortgage defaults started rising, leading to the collapse of Bear Stearns in 2008. The failure of other financial institutions followed.

Why did the U.S. economic downturn affect the world? After a $700 billion bank rescue law was instituted in October 2008, investors feared it would not be enough and stock markets around the world began plummeting. The risky derivatives backed by subprime loans started in the United States, but the practices were also embraced by banks in other countries, which began to fail.

Are feelings of confidence influenced by recent events? In 2008, bankers and financial managers lost people's trust, creating a full-blown crisis of confidence, which affects many ordinary investors today.

Key Terms

Pop Quiz Prep

1. What is the end goal of a financial manager's activities?
2. A cash flow forecast deals with what time frame?
3. A toymaker realizes most of its revenue at Christmas, and must borrow short-term funds earlier in the year to support its operation. This is an example of a firm borrowing money for which reason?
4. What is an example of a tangible asset?
5. What does "3/7, net 60" mean?
6. What is the definition of *collateral*?
7. What are *time deposits*?
8. What happens when the Federal Reserve raises the discount rate?
9. How does a NOW account work?
10. Is there a limit to the size of a bank account insured by the FDIC?
11. According to the text, there has been a financial panic in America roughly every how many years?
12. What is a *derivative*?

Critical Thinking Questions

1. With over 35 years of consecutive sales, Walgreen Co., a pharmacy and consumer goods retailer, in addition to its companywide ethics policy, has an additional code of ethics for all senior financial officers, including the CEO, the CFO, and the controller. The code includes items such as: "I provide accurate, complete, objective, relevant, timely and understandable disclosure in reports and documents that the company files with or submits to the Securities and Exchange Commission" and "I achieve responsible use of and control over all assets and resources employed or entrusted to me."[55] In the post-Enron, post–bank bailout era, do you agree that top financial officers and CEOs should be held to a higher ethical standard by signing a separate ethics policy?

2. In a *New York Post* article entitled "Plastic's Now Off the Menu," the writer states, "Cash is king at local restaurants and bars struggling with a tight economy and small profit margins. To avoid paying credit-card fees and—shhh—maybe fudge income numbers for the tax collector—some merchants are treating credit cards as if they aren't worth the recycled plastic they're made of. In those places, cold

cash is the only way to buy a hot meal."[56] Have you ever enjoyed a meal in a restaurant only to find that when the check arrived, they did not accept credit cards and inevitably, you didn't have enough cash on hand? Think about what you did. Why do you think some restaurants have a cash-only policy? What impact, if any, might a cash-only policy have on a business? Explain.

3. One source of business financing may be to look to those you already know (and love). Suppose you were a business owner in need of a short-term loan due to an unexpected cash crunch. If you decided to ask a friend or family member for help, what would be the best way to structure such a loan arrangement? Why do you suppose "friends and family" borrowing has grown in popularity?

4. One of the benefits of owning stock in a company is receiving dividends. A company is not legally required to pay dividends to its shareholders. If you were a shareholder, would this be a consideration in your decision to purchase a company's stock? What other benefits of owning stock in a company might a shareholder receive in lieu of dividends? Why do you think some companies choose not to pay dividends to their shareholders?

5. Part of the review process lenders use to evaluate a borrower involves quantitative (numbers) analysis and qualitative (character) analysis. The five Cs of credit, which incorporate both, consist of *character* (trustworthiness or reputation) of the borrower, *capacity* (borrowing history and track record of repayment of previous obligations), *capital* (how well capitalized a company is and how much money is invested), *collateral* (while cash flow is of paramount importance, a bank will evaluate a secondary source of repayment or the value of its assets to secure the loan), and *conditions* (what are the current economic conditions, and how is the company managing?). In small groups, compare and contrast the five Cs and discuss whether you believe some are more important than others. Do you think the five Cs are increasingly important during more difficult economic times?

VIDEO CASE
Money: More Than Just What Banks Lend

A bank is just like any other business, but its product is money. A bank's clients consist of individuals (like you) and organizations such as small businesses, nonprofits, or large corporations. To make a profit, using their customers' deposits, banks sell money—that is, they loan money for a fee. Banks make a profit on the interest they charge on loans because that interest is higher than the interest they pay on depositors' accounts. The interest rate a bank charges its borrowers depends on both the number of people who want to borrow and the amount of money the bank has available to lend. The reserve requirements, or how much money the bank has to have on hand relative to how much it can lend, is set by the Federal Reserve and varies according to the dollar amount of net transaction accounts held at that institution.[57] For banks with over $58.8 million in deposits, the reserve requirement is 10%.[58]

Banks provide loans to businesses for everyday business activities such as extending credit to customers, purchasing inventory, and making major investments and large purchases like equipment and buildings. The hope is that if a business is able to purchase inventory and equipment used in the production of its product, it can increase its profits by selling more product and hiring more employees to help create and manage the sale of even more product. Simply put, the loans banks provide businesses give them the opportunity to grow.

Banks also provide loans to individuals for a variety of reasons, such as to help people purchase homes. Recently, making home loans has been risky business, as many banks were not able to get that money back (repaid) during the recession. The video explains, "When the regulations governing banks relaxed, some banks got sloppy and made bad loans to prospective home buyers who could not afford them." Banks also make money from individuals by charging fees for services like checking accounts, ATM access, and overdraft protection. As you may have experienced, recently these types of fees have risen as banks seek to boost profits in the wake of the mortgage meltdown.

There are many different types of banks. There are retail banks (offering checking, savings, CDs, safe deposit boxes, auto and home loans), commercial banks (offering loans for large and small businesses), investment banks (helping companies go public, for example), and even online banks. BancFirst, a commercial bank, is Oklahoma's largest state-chartered bank. It has more than 100 service locations in 50 communities across Oklahoma. The bank provides a full range of banking services to retail customers and small to medium sized businesses. Calling itself a "super community bank," BancFirst prides itself on managing its banking offices on a decentralized basis, which means each branch office makes decisions based upon specific customers' needs (where demographics vary by location)—and independent of what someone at corporate headquarters may think. This allows them to be responsive to customer needs in each location. For example, a rural branch may cater to different types of customers from those banking with a large metropolitan branch.

Community banks like BancFirst facilitate local business activity through their borrowing, lending, and other activities. BancFirst provides a substantial share of banking services in rural and smaller cities throughout Oklahoma. This is an example of the important role played by banks serving as relationship and information managers with smaller customers and family businesses within the communities where they operate.

What's Your Take?

1. Free checking, offered by banks to lure new customers, surged in popularity in the last decade but is rapidly coming to an end as banks attempt to restore profits through increased fee schedules.[59] Combine that with low interest rates (on deposits), difficult-to-understand fee schedules, and account balance requirements, and choosing a bank has become even more challenging. What factors were included in your decision when choosing a bank? Have you been mostly satisfied with your decision? Why or why not? Discuss.

2. Money is defined as any medium of value that is generally accepted as payment for goods and services.[60] Barter, the trading of goods or services for other goods or services (with no money changing hands), is a way of replacing money as the method of exchange. Barter is common during times of monetary crisis.[61] Have you ever bartered with someone, and if so, what did you barter and how did you determine the value of the exchange? Explain.

3. Through TARP (Troubled Asset Relief Program), the government purchased an interest in certain troubled companies and financial institutions using taxpayer money in exchange for agreements that allowed those companies to buy back those shares with interest later.[62] Discuss the pros and cons of emergency-type government bailouts. You may do further research on this topic to learn more.

4. Over the centuries, there have been many substitutes for money accepted as payment—gold, silver, copper, nickel, animal skins, chocolate bars, cigarettes, precious gems, and so on. Some, of course, have worked better than others.

Which substitutes for money do you think have worked best? Thinking about the characteristics of money (portable, divisible, durable, unique, and stable), why have some substitutes been the most successful? Discuss.

BUSINESS DECISION CASE
Pawnshop: Lender of Last Resort? Not Necessarily So

Pawnshops, which conjure up images of seedy storefronts in bad parts of town, were once thought of as a shady lender of last resort for the down and out. With the subprime meltdown and housing market downturn, banks tightened their credit standards. Individuals who were suddenly out of work and short of cash to cover short-term expenses found themselves turned away by banks unwilling to risk additional loan defaults. Enter a different kind of secured loan business—the pawnshop. According to the National Pawnbrokers Association (NPA), the United States has over 13,000 pawnshops, many of which experienced a rise in traffic from individuals seeking secured short-term loans without the hassle of credit checks and reporting required by traditional banks.[63]

Believe it or not, "pawning" was the leading form of consumer credit in the United States until the 1950s.[64] This type of lending is featured weekly on a reality TV show called *Pawn Stars*, which profiles the colorful world of the pawn business with three generations of the Harrison family at the Gold and Silver Pawn Shop in Las Vegas, Nevada.[65] Pawnshops are frequented by those using their pawned items as collateral in exchange for a short-term loan.[66] While the traditional typical pawnshop customer has a household income of about $29,000 a year, operators around the country have reported a surge in new activity fueled by middle- and upper-middle-class customers under financial pressures like job losses and stock-market losses.[67]

Pawnbroking as a business is essentially one of the world's oldest and simplest forms of banking.[68] Pawnshops, most of which are small and independently owned, are similar to banks who extend loans to their clients. However, with a pawnshop, the customer's item is kept as collateral for a loan, with the value of the item used to determine the loan amount—typically quite small.[69] The customer agrees to loan payments, including an interest rate, regulated by each state (in Texas, for example, 3% per month is the maximum that can be charged). If the customer defaults on the agreed-upon payments, or fails to pick up the item within a specified period of time (in many cases, 30 to 180 days), the shop sells the item(s) to recoup the loan value.

Another benefit during a credit crunch is that if the borrower defaults on the loan, it isn't reported to a credit agency nor is there a collections process—so the possibility of a customer with blemished credit is avoided. Instead, the pawnshop simply keeps the item and sells it to recover the loan amount. So, in addition to acting as a bank, a pawnshop owner is also a seller of commonly used items left as collateral, which include jewelry, watches, flat-screen TVs, guitars, keyboards, and power tools. The pawnbroker or pawnshop owner benefits not only by charging interest on the loan, but also from selling the item at a profit. You may be surprised to learn that over 80% of pawnshop customers repay their loans and reclaim their items.[70]

The shops are regulated in accordance with state laws and require a license. At the federal level, they follow rules that apply to entities designated as financial institutions such as the Truth in Lending Act and IRS regulations.[71] As Congress continues to investigate and increase regulation of the financial-services industry, "alternative banks" such as pawnshops may come under stricter regulatory controls.[72]

The pawnshop industry isn't without its share of controversy. Critics of the industry advocate for harsh crackdowns on lenders charging high interest rates, and allege that the pawnshops create repayment difficulties for those most in need. For example, interest rates work out to between 50% and 250% a year.[73] Critics also see the business as "quick cash" and a repository for stolen goods. Advocates, however, argue that lenders provide short-term loans to those in need with fewer requirements than traditional lenders. A lender of last resort? Maybe in the past, but not in this economy.

What's Your Take?

1. What is your perception of pawnshops, and do you have personal experience or know anyone who has ever taken possessions to a pawnshop? There are several popular reality shows about pawnshops including *Pawn Stars* and *Hardcore Pawn*.[74] What is it about these programs that have made them so popular?

2. It has been argued that by serving the need of an unbanked population (those without access to banks or financial services, or without an account at a bank), estimated to be 7.7% of the U.S. population or 17 million people,[75] the industry provides a much-needed service of short-term loans. Do you agree?

3. Can you think of additional benefits besides the ones discussed that might lead an unbanked customer to utilize a pawnshop? You may find it helpful to think about what a customer may be wanting to avoid.

4. Compare and contrast the pawnshop industry (what you know from reading the case and from any previous knowledge or further research) to a traditional bank. What fees does a pawnshop owner incur that a bank does not?

5. When someone is robbed or burglarized, the police often encourage the victims to visit local pawnshops (or flea markets) to look for their stolen goods. How do you think pawnshops deal with the issue of suspected stolen goods? What steps might pawnshops take to protect themselves from taking stolen goods?

Go to www.mybizlab.com for online activities and exercises related to the timely topics discussed in this chapter's Briefings, as well as additional theme-related Briefing *Spotlights* highlighting how these concepts apply in today's business environment.

In-chapter Briefing:
- How Banks Have Evaded the Reserve Requirement, Using Computer Programs to Transfer Depositors' Money

Activity:
- Ethical Dilemma Case – Banks Fight Back: Federal Reserve Bans ATM & Debit Card Overdraft Fees

Briefing Spotlight:
- Counterfeiters, Listen Up: U.S. Government Unveils a Unique "Benjamin"

In-chapter Briefing:
- Staying Alert to Be Sure You Don't Lose Money with Your FDIC Insurance

Activity:
- Going to the Net! – Peer-to-Peer Lending: With a Little Help from My Friends
- Going to the Net! – A Hands-On Exercise to Learn How Credit Card Companies Profit from Our Debt
- Maximizing Your Net Worth – Risk-Tolerance Quiz

Briefing Spotlight:
- The Bank of Mom and Dad Copes with Boomerang Kids

In-chapter Briefing:
- The Biggest Mistakes Start-ups Make
- The Risk-Return Trade-Off of Small-Business Owners Who Can't Pay Their Taxes
- Capital Expenditures for a Drum Maker
- Friends Help Eileen Fisher Get Her Clothing Line Going
- Using Credit Cards to Start a Business

Activity:
- Developing Marketable Business Skills – Strapped for Cash: Small Business Owners Ask, "Can You Spare a Little Change?"

Briefing Spotlight:
- A Matchmaker for Small Business and Lenders

Additional Briefing Spotlights available at MyBizLab:

- A WORLD OF CONSTANT CHANGE
- BUSINESS CULTURE & ETIQUETTE
- BUSINESS SKILLS & CAREER DEVELOPMENT
- CUSTOMER FOCUS
- EARNING GREEN BY GOING GREEN
- GLOBAL BUSINESS
- INFO TECH & SOCIAL MEDIA
- SOCIALLY RESPONSIBLE BUSINESS

17 Securities Markets

Investing for the Future

After reading and studying this chapter, you will be able to answer the following essential questions:

MyBizLab

Where you see MyBizLab in this chapter, go to www.mybizlab.com for additional activities on the topic being discussed.

FORECAST:
What's Ahead in This Chapter

This chapter is about various securities—money market instruments, bonds, and stocks—and other investments: mutual funds, exchange-traded funds, and commodities. We also describe how to buy and sell securities. Finally, we discuss five investment strategies.

PARNASSUS INVESTMENTS®

WINNERS: Can You Thrive with Socially Responsible Firms?

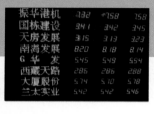

LOSERS: Can You Avoid Firms That Rip Off Investors?

Jerome Dodson is manager of a mutual fund, a group that brings together money from many people and (for a fee) invests it—in this case, in the stocks of so-called small-cap companies. These are firms with a "small capitalization" of $1 billion to $10 billion in shareholder value. In the five years ending November 2010, his Parnassus Small-Cap Fund had an 8.9% yearly return on its investments, significantly beating the norm for small-company stocks.[1]

How does Dodson do it? He tries to buy stocks in companies according to three criteria: (1) The stocks are cheap. (2) The companies' businesses are strong. (3) The firms are socially responsible.

Cheap stocks means that the market capitalization is one-third or more below Dodson's estimate of their real value.

Strong businesses are those with strong balance sheets—low debt, lots of cash—and ongoing competitive advantages.

Socially responsible businesses are those that treat their employees right and respect the environment, which means they are less likely to be sued, fined, or discovered to have practiced accounting fraud. Dodson screens out firms from the alcohol, tobacco, gambling, and weapons-contracting industries, as well as companies that generate electricity from nuclear power.[2]

Among the kinds of companies Dodson has acquired shares in are hardware and software companies with names such as Electronics for Imaging, Brocade Communications Systems, and Mentor Graphics. The fund is also heavily invested in health care, industrial materials, and telecommunications.

According to fund-watcher Morningstar in March 2011, $10,000 invested a year earlier would be worth $13,779 and the same amount invested 5 years earlier would have grown to $16,531.[3]

China's economic boom has attracted great numbers of American investors to Chinese companies, not only to the largest but also to those in the small-cap category. Many of these smaller companies trade their stock on major U.S. stock exchanges, such as the New York Stock Exchange and NASDAQ, which give companies credibility with investors.

However, according to *New Yorker* financial writer James Surowiecki, while some of these Chinese small-cap companies "are indeed thriving enterprises, more than a few seem to be specialists in a less savory business: ripping off investors."

For instance, RINO International, which claims to be a maker of environmental-protection equipment, became a kind of personal bank for its chairman and chairwoman (a married couple), who got a $3.5 million loan without even a signed loan document. Companies like RINO, says another report, "have tiny revenue numbers, creative accounting practices, and poor management practices."[4]

When accused of fraudulent accounting, RINO admitted "that two of its manufacturing contracts didn't actually exist, and that its financial statements couldn't be relied on," reports Surowiecki. After the company failed to provide more information, it was removed (delisted) from NASDAQ. Its stock declined 90% from its high.

How do such dubious companies get listed in the first place? In a technique called a reverse merger, they buy U.S. companies with a stock-exchange listing but few actual assets, then change the name. Thus, they get the credibility of being on a major exchange without having to be checked out by it. "And once you're on an exchange," says Surowiecki, "it takes a lot to be kicked off."

"The bottom line," concludes another report, "is that Chinese small caps are ridiculously risky."[5]

Source: Courtesy of Parnassus Investments.

Source: Idealink Photography/Alamy.

YOUR CALL Just like people, stocks—and the companies whose value they represent—can be good or bad, virtuous or evil. So-called socially responsible investments don't always provide the greatest return, but the Parnassus Small-Cap Fund certainly does well. Single small-cap stocks powered by a new supercycle of emerging market growth in Asia may be highly profitable, but clearly RINO is anything but. Not all mutual funds are successful, nor all single stocks risky. What can you take away from these "Winners & Losers" cases? What do they suggest you need to learn? Do you think you could become a pretty good stock picker after a month of study? After a year? What would you look for in a company whose stock you are considering buying?

MyBizLab

THE BIG IDEA: Securities markets may be primary, where new issues are first sold to investors, or secondary, where existing securities are traded by investors.

THE ESSENTIAL QUESTION: Which of the two securities markets would I be more likely to be involved with?

MyBizLab

MyBizLab: Check your understanding of these concepts at www.mybizlab.com.

Billionaire investor Warren Buffett, head of Omaha-based Berkshire Hathaway and third wealthiest person in the world in 2011, is so successful that $1,000 invested with him in 1956 was worth $27.6 million at the end of 2006.[6] His personal fortune gained $9 billion in 2009, a recession year.[7] ❶ What is his secret?

Buffett's approach is to analyze stacks of annual reports and other company financial documents. According to one report, he looks for a record of "high returns on equity capital, low debt, and a consistent, predictable business with sustainable advantages—like Coca-Cola's soft-drink franchise."[8] Stated another way, he takes time and care to study the facts before making an investment decision.

Is this the style of most investors—men or women? Actually, there may be evidence of some differences between the sexes.

BRIEFING / PERSONAL FINANCE

Do Males & Females Have Different Investment Styles? Were raging hormones among the world's financial traders, most of whom are men, responsible for sending global markets rocketing upward in the mid-2000s—and then crashing down to launch the Great Recession?

Rising levels of testosterone, the hormone of male aggressiveness, may have heavily influenced London traders during market booms, suggests a research paper.[9] That alternated with cortisol, a steroid that helps deal with stress, during market busts. Thus, it's possible men tend to trade aggressively—more than women do—simply because they're men. Women have only a fraction of the percentage of testosterone that men do.

Men tend to be "frazzled, frenetic day traders, with their ties askew, hair on end, and eyes bleary," suggests financial writer LouAnn DiCosmo.[10] "Patience and good decision making help set women apart here." Adds a *New York Times* writer, "Women trade much less often than men, do a lot more research, and tend to base their investment decisions on considerations other than just numbers."[11] As a result, according to one study, women's collections of investments on average gain 1.4% more than men's, and single women's do 2.3% better than single men's.[12] Is the bottom line, as the headline on DiCosmo's article reads, that "Warren Buffett Invests Like a Girl"? What do you think? ■

❶ **The Sage of Omaha.** Warren Buffett is the chairman, CEO, and primary shareholder of Berkshire Hathaway, a conglomerate holding company headquartered in Omaha, Nebraska. From 2000 to 2010, the company's stock produced a return of 76%, at a time when the S&P index of 500 stocks lost 11%. Buffett has pledged to give away 99% of his fortune to philanthropic causes.

Source: Kent Sievers/Omaha World Herald/PSG/Newscom.

Whether you are Warren Buffett or an average investor, you are the holder of a *portfolio,* **the collection of securities representing a person's investments.** *Securities* **are financial instruments such as stocks and bonds.** *Stocks* represent shares of ownership in a company; *bonds* are certificates that demonstrate a person has lent money to a company or government agency.

Securities are sold in two types of financial markets:

- The primary securities market
- The secondary securities market

Want to Know More? 17-1

Key Terms & Definitions in Sequential Order to Study as You Go Along

Go to www.mybizlab.com.

The Primary Securities Market: Where New Issues Are First Sold to Investors

How are new stocks and bonds sold?

The *primary securities market* **is the financial market in which new security issues are first sold to investors.** The money derived from the sale of the stocks or bonds goes to the issuer.

When a corporation's stock is offered for sale for the first time, it is called an *initial public offering (IPO).* Corporations and governments also raise money by issuing bonds, as when local governments sell bonds to finance sewers and streets. New stock and bond offerings are regularly announced in sober-looking black-and-white ads (called *tombstones*) in business publications such as the *Wall Street Journal* and *Investor's Business Daily.*

New stocks and bonds may be sold in two ways: (1) through *investment bankers,* and (2) through *open auctions.*

1 Selling through Investment Bankers: Stocks & Bonds

Most new issues of stocks and bonds are sold through *investment bankers,* **companies that engage in buying and reselling new securities,** such as Goldman Sachs and Morgan Stanley or large financial institutions such as Bank of America. **The activity of buying new issues of stocks or bonds from issuing corporations and reselling them to the public is known as** *underwriting*.

If the investment banker fails to sell part of the issue or if the price falls during the distribution of the securities, the investment banker takes a loss, which means the investment banking firm bears most of the risk. Often several such firms will get together as a so-called *syndicate* to share the risk on a particular issue.

Besides locating buyers for the issue, the investment banker helps the issuing corporation or government get approval from the Securities and Exchange Commission and market the securities to *institutional investors*—**large and powerful organizations such as pension funds and insurance companies, which invest their own or others' money**—as well as to small investors through brokerage offices.

BRIEFING / A WORLD OF CONSTANT CHANGE

Should Tech Start-Ups Raise Money through an IPO or Private Investors? Popular Internet radio service Pandora filed for an initial private offering (IPO) in February 2011 that would raise $100 million. The European on-demand music service Spotify, on the other hand, is reportedly raising the same amount from private equity investors to help come to the United States.[13] Why might private investors be better than an IPO?

Most of today's well-known technology firms raised the cash they needed to finance their growth through an IPO. Apple's IPO on December 12, 1980, was $22 a share. It raised more capital, $17.9 billion, than any IPO since Ford in 1956 and instantly created more millionaires—about 300 investors and employees—than any company in history. Google's IPO on August 19, 2004, at $85, raised $1.67 billion.

Today, however, tech start-ups—such as Facebook, Twitter, and Yelp—are probably more inclined to turn to private investors rather than IPOs for the cash they need to grow. The reason: fewer hassles. Public companies have to deal with the expectations of financial analysts and shareholders and need to comply with public company regulations such as the Sarbanes-Oxley Act (see Chapter 2), with its tougher standards for boards, management, and accounting firms.[14] ■

Want to Know More? 17-2

How Do People Bid for Treasury Securities?

Go to www.mybizlab.com.

2 Selling through Open Auctions: U.S. Treasury Securities

Most securities sold through open auction are U.S. Treasury securities. Short-term securities are auctioned weekly; longer-term securities are auctioned once a month or once every three months. Investors participate in auctions either directly through the Treasury or through investment firms and banks.

The Secondary Securities Market: Where Existing Issues Are Bought & Sold by Investors

Why might I want to participate in the secondary securities market?

The *secondary securities market* is the financial market in which existing stocks and bonds are bought and sold by investors. These markets, such as the New York Stock Exchange, the NASDAQ stock market, and even foreign stock exchanges, are ones you might very well participate in yourself. The original issuers of the securities are usually not involved and do not share in the proceeds from the sale. ❷

The principal reason people participate in the secondary securities market, of course, is the prospect of making money—that is, realizing a substantial *capital gain,* **the term given for the profit made by selling a security for a price that is higher than the price the investor paid for it.**

Example: If in 1998 you'd had $100,000 and used it to buy 3,298 shares of Apple stock (for $99,995, at $30.32 a share), 10 years later it would have been worth $1,997,797—a substantial capital gain. Of course, a stock may well lose money, resulting in a *capital loss.*

In the rest of this chapter, we discuss different kinds of investments with which you might become involved—either as a financial manager or personally:

- Money market instruments
- Bonds
- Stocks
- Mutual funds
- Exchange-traded funds
- Commodities

❷ **Secondary securities market.** More and more Americans invest not only in U.S. stock markets but also in foreign exchanges, such as the Hong Kong Stock Exchange, with its electronic trading floor. What might motivate you or deter you from trading stocks on a foreign exchange?

Do you know your investment objectives? Your investment posture will depend on the following criteria:

Goals: "What Kind of Returns Do I Want over What Period of Time?"

How much money do you want to accumulate in your lifetime? The younger you are, the more time you have. If you're 20, retiring at age 55 may seem almost unattainable, but you'll find that actually the years will fly by. Putting $10 a week into a stock market mutual fund averaging an annual return (appreciation) of 8%, for example, when compounded over 35 years, will produce $100,000.

Available Funds: "How Much Could I Afford to Invest Regularly?"

How much can you spare for investing? Many students graduate with several thousand dollars in student-loan and credit-card debt, and certainly those should be paid off first. (When in 2008 Barack Obama was elected president at age 47, he and his wife, Michelle, were only 4 years out of paying off their credit-card debt.) Still, even if you could manage only $25 a month for investment, that's a positive start.

Liquidity: "How Quickly Might I Have to Withdraw Funds from My Investments?"

Suppose you have a major emergency and need to find some quick cash. Do you have the kinds of investments, such as stocks and bonds, that you can sell quickly? Or is most of your money tied up in, say, real estate, which may take a long time to sell?

Taxes: "How Do My Investments Affect My Taxes?"

Different kinds of investments have different kinds of tax consequences. For instance, gains you make investing in municipal bonds are likely to be tax-free.

Risk: "How Well Could I Tolerate the Loss of My Investment?"

The younger you are, the more risks you can probably afford to take—because if your investment fails, you'll still have a number of years to make it up. If, however, you're 5 years away from retirement, you'll want to have your money in safe investments—perhaps paying only slight interest. Still, all investments involve some risk, and generally the riskier the investment, the greater potential for higher returns. This is why many financial advisors recommend a diversified investment program.

Two opposite approaches to risk are *speculation* and *asset allocation.*

- **Speculation: Taking high risks in anticipation of making great profits:** *Speculators* are investors who are willing to make high-risk investments for the possibility of realizing great profits. Investors who bet on future prices of commodities—raw materials and agricultural products, such as gold, oil, and coffee beans—fall in this category.

- **Asset allocation: Shifting investments to adapt to the current financial environment:** More in the spirit of diversification is the strategy known as *asset allocation,* in which you shift the investments to adapt to the current financial environment. For example, when the economy is good and the stock market is moving upward, you might divide your investments into 75% stocks, 20% bonds, and 5% money market funds. If the stock market plummets, you might turn your investments into 15% stocks, 50% government securities, and 35% money market funds.

THE BIG IDEA: Securities are of three types: money market instruments, bonds, and stocks. Money market instruments are short-term IOUs issued by governments, corporations, and financial institutions. Bonds are long-term IOUs issued by them. Bonds may be rated in various ways, and they may pay off in different ways. Stocks are units of ownership in corporations, and there are two kinds—common stock and preferred stock. There are various ways to determine what a stock is worth, and there are different exchanges, or arenas, in which to buy and sell stocks.

THE ESSENTIAL QUESTION: What are the differences in the three types of securities, and when would I invest in them?

MyBizLab: Check your understanding of these concepts at www.mybizlab.com.

Source: David Young-Wolff/Alamy.

❸ **Stock market blowup.** On September 15, 2008, newspapers headlined the previous day's shocking loss of 500 points on the Dow Jones stock index—the worst slide since the 9/11 terrorist attacks in 2001—and the erasure of $700 billion in shareholder wealth. The trigger was the bankruptcy of storied Lehman Brothers and the essentially forced sale of Merrill Lynch to Bank of America. Would such losses turn you away from stocks for a long time?

"If you are risk averse, retired, or nearing retirement, or just hate the thought of losing money, you probably view stocks as the financial equivalent of an atomic bomb," says financial writer Adam Shell. "You know what could happen to your nest egg if the stock market blows up."[15] ❸ Certainly that's the lesson many people took away from the Great Recession, which destroyed stock investments. (But if you'd stayed in the market, the stocks came back. For a while, at least.)

Most portfolios should have at least *some* stocks, but investors who want to avoid substantial risk may prefer a no-stock portfolio. One way is to load up 90% on bonds, with perhaps 10% in money market (cash) investments. At the end of this chapter, we will reveal just how successful a strategy this is.

Let's now distinguish among the three types of securities—*money market instruments (cash investments)*, *bonds*, and *stocks*.

Money Market Instruments: Short-Term IOUs from Governments, Corporations, & Financial Institutions

Why would I ever want to invest in money market instruments, and what are they?

Money market instruments, or cash investments, are short-term IOUs, debt securities that mature within one year, which are issued by governments, large corporations, and financial institutions. The *maturity date* is the date that the issuer of a money market instrument or bond must repay the principal entirely. The lender pays the borrower interest for use of the money. Examples are U.S. Treasury bills, bank certificates of deposit, and commercial paper.

Money market instruments are very conservative, easily converted into cash, and considered extremely safe, which also means that their returns are significantly lower than those of most other securities. One way to gain access to money market securities is through money market mutual funds. **Treasury bills (T-bills), short-term obligations of the U.S. Treasury with a maturity period of one year or less (typically 3 months),** may be purchased directly from the U.S. government.

Bonds: Long-Term IOUs from Governments, Corporations, & Financial Institutions

What are the different bonds, bond-rating systems, and ways bonds pay off?

Bonds are long-term IOUs issued by governments and corporations, contracts on which the issuer pays the buyer interest at regular intervals.

Bonds have certain characteristics:

- **Denominations and principal:** Bonds are issued in *denominations*, in multiples of $1,000, which represent the amount of debt. U.S. Treasury bonds, for instance, appear in denominations ranging from $1,000 to $5,000. The denomination expresses the *principal*, or face value, of the bond.

- **Maturity date and interest rate:** Upon the bond's **maturity date, the issuing organization is legally required to repay the bond's principal in full to the bondholder.** The maturity date may range up to 50 years. The bond issue also indicates the *interest rate*, or percentage of the bond's value, that is to be paid to the bondholder.

In the United States, bonds are of four types: (1) *government bonds*, (2) *municipal bonds*, (3) *corporate bonds*, and (4) *securities from financial institutions*.

Source: K. Geijer/Fotolia LLC.

❹ **Bonds.** The government paper bond shown here, Series EE, ceases paying interest in 30 years from the date it was issued. It can be bought in denominations of $50 through $10,000, and the purchase price is one-half its denomination. What types of investors favor investing in bonds? What advantages do bonds have over stocks?

1 Government Bonds: U.S. Treasury Notes & Bonds

Government bonds, bonds sold by the U.S. Treasury, consist of treasury notes and treasury bonds.

- **Treasury notes:** Sold in minimum denominations of $1,000, *treasury notes* mature in 10 years or less from the date of issue.

- **Treasury bonds:** Sold in denominations of $1,000 and $5,000, *treasury bonds* mature in 25 years or more. EE Savings bonds mature in 30 years. ❹

2 Municipal Bonds: Obligations Issued by State & Local Governments

Municipal bonds, bonds issued by state and local governments and agencies, consist of revenue bonds and general obligation bonds.

- **Revenue bonds:** *Revenue bonds* are used to pay for public projects that will generate revenue, such as toll bridges.

- **General obligation bonds:** *General obligation bonds* are used by tax-levying government agencies to pay for public projects that will not generate revenue, such as road and school construction.

An attractive feature of municipal bonds is that typically they are tax-exempt; that is, investors do not pay taxes on the interest they receive.

3 Corporate Bonds: Secured & Unsecured Bonds from Big Businesses

Corporate bonds, bonds issued by businesses as a source of long-term funding, consist of secured and unsecured bonds.

- **Secured bonds:** *Secured bonds* are backed by pledges of assets (collateral) to the bondholders.

- **Unsecured bonds:** *Unsecured bonds*, or **debenture bonds, are bonds for which no assets are pledged as collateral;** they are backed only by the issuing company's reputation.

4 Securities from Financial Institutions: Mortgage Pass-Through Securities

Mortgage pass-through securities, **bonds sold by financial institutions, are backed by a pool of mortgages whose monthly mortgage payments are "passed" from mortgagers "through" the issuers to the investors in the security.** Once popular because they provided monthly income but seemed relatively safe (because the underlying mortgages were supposedly insured), mortgage pass-throughs became victims of the 2008 financial meltdown along with other mortgage-backed bonds.

Ratings for Bonds: From Investment-Grade Quality to Junk

One factor that determines the price of a bond is its *bond rating,* **which measures the quality and safety of a bond, indicating the likelihood that the debt issuer will be able to meet scheduled repayments, which dictates the interest rate paid.** Bond ratings are determined by three bond-rating agencies, Standard & Poor's, Moody's Investors Service, and Fitch Ratings. Bonds are rated from AAA (Standard & Poor's, Fitch) or Aaa (Moody's), the top rating, down to D, which means the issuer is currently in default. (*See* ■ *Panel 17.1.*)

■ **PANEL 17.1 Bond rating.** Ratings from the two principal rating services, Standard & Poor's and Moody's, are based on the risk a bond issuer will default—not meet scheduled interest payments and repayment of principal.

Standard & Poor's	Moody's	What the Ratings Mean	Risk of Default
		Investment-grade bonds	
AAA	Aaa	Highest quality	Lowest default risk
AA	Aa	High quality	
A	A	Upper medium grade	
BBB	Baa	Medium grade	
		Speculative-grade (junk) bonds	
BB	Ba	Lower medium grade	
B	B	Speculative	
CCC, CC	Caaa	Poor	High default risk
C	Ca	Highly speculative	
D	C	Lowest grade	In default

Bonds are divided according to risk into *investment-grade bonds* and *speculative-grade (junk) bonds.*

- **Investment-grade bonds:** *Investment-grade bonds* **are bonds that are relatively safe, with a low probability of default; they have a bond rating of BBB or above.**
- **Speculative-grade bonds:** *Speculative-grade bonds,* **or** *junk bonds,* **are high-risk bonds with a greater probability of default; they have a bond rating of BB or lower, but in exchange for the higher risk, they pay about 50% more interest than investment-grade bonds.**

Key Takeaway 17-1
Bonds may be government (federal or state) bonds, municipal bonds, corporate bonds, or securities from financial institutions.

BRIEFING / LEGAL & ETHICAL PRACTICES

Were Bond-Rating Agencies Honest When Rating Mortgage-Backed Securities? The high assessments Moody's and Standard & Poor's gave to securities backed by subprime mortgage loans—home mortgage loans made to relatively poor borrowers who were likely to fail—were supposed to assure investors that their money should be safe. But after the mortgage market collapsed, it turned out these agencies knew about the weaknesses but failed to downgrade shaky securities from their AAA ratings.[16]

One possible reason: Critics say the agencies were paid by the very firms whose debt they were rating, and high ratings made it easier for such firms to sell the securities to the public. "When the referee is being paid by the players," said one congressman, "no one should be surprised when the game spins out of control."[17] Can we be sure now that these agencies, which are still influential, deserve our confidence?[18] ⑤ ∎

Source: Kurt Brady/Alamy.

⑤ **Conflict of interest?** One cause of the 2008 financial crisis, critics say, was that banks were able to choose and pay their rating agency, such as Standard & Poor's or Moody's Investor's Service, which gave favorable ratings to troubled mortgage-backed securities. During the 2010 sweeping overhaul of the financial regulatory system, however, attempts to erase this conflict of interest were removed from the legislation, leaving in place the same risky system. How much should the possibility of this conflict of interest lessen the credibility of these rating agencies?

The Varied Ways Bonds May Pay Off: Callable, Serial, Sinking-Fund, & Convertible Bonds

At some point, all bonds reach their maturity dates and must be paid off, or *redeemed* or *retired*. There are various ways bonds may be paid off, as represented by the following four types of bonds: (1) *callable*, (2) *serial*, (3) *sinking-fund*, and (4) *convertible*.

Callable Bonds: Bonds That May Be Paid Off Early. "Normally, a bond is a very simple investment instrument," observes *Forbes* writer Eric Petroff. "It pays interest until expiration and has a single, fixed lifespan. It is plain and safe. The callable bond, on the other hand, is the exciting, slightly dangerous cousin of the regular bond."[19]

Callable bonds **are bonds in which the issuer may call them in and pay them off at a prespecified price before the maturity date.** "Callable bonds have two potential lifespans," points out Petroff, "one ending at the original maturity date and the other at the callable date." Call provisions must be specified when the bond is issued.

∎ **Example** How a Callable Bond Works: When Interest Rates Drop. As a bondholder, you need to be aware that a bond issuer may be apt to call the bond when interest rates drop. For example, if you have a 30-year callable bond at 7% interest and after a few years interest rates drop to 5%, the issuer may recall your bonds because the debt could be refinanced at the lower interest rate. And if interest rates move to 10%, the issuer will do nothing, as the bond will be relatively cheap compared to market rates. ∎

Serial Bonds: Bonds That Mature on Different Dates. *Serial bonds* **are bonds that mature at different dates.** For example, a company might issue $50 million in bonds that mature over 30 years, but after 20 years $5 million in bonds will mature each year until all bonds are repaid. The concept of serial bonds, which helps the issuer avoid a cash flow problem (which could happen if all bonds were to mature in the same year), is popular with state and municipal governments.

Sinking-Fund Bonds: Bonds for Which Funds Are Saved for Paying Off on Maturity. *Sinking-fund bonds,* **or** *prefunded bonds,* **are bonds in which the issuer makes annual deposits to a bank to accumulate funds for paying off the bonds on maturity.** Both issuers and investors like this arrangement because

MICROSOFT CORP

OVERVIEW	
Price:	106.60 **1**
Coupon (%):	5.300 **2**
Maturity Date:	8-Feb-2041
Yield to Maturity (%):	4.877
Current Yield (%):	4.972
Fitch Ratings:	AAA **3**
Coupon Payment Frequency:	Semi-Annual
First Coupon Date:	8-Aug-2011
Type:	Corporate
Callable:	No

1 Price is quoted as percentage of bond's face value.

2 Coupon rate is bond's interest rate.

3 Risk associated with this bond.

Source: Based on Yahoo! Finance, http://bonds.yahoo.com (accessed October 27, 2011).

Key Takeaway 17-2
Four ways bonds pay off: as callable, serial, sinking-fund, or convertible.

6 **Paper stock certificate.** This was the stock certificate issued when MicroStrategy had its initial public offering in 1998 (4 million shares at $12 each). The firm, located in Tysons Corner, Virginia, provides integrated reporting, analysis, and monitoring software that helps leading organizations make better business decisions every day.

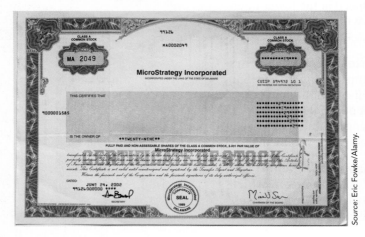

Source: Eric Fowke/Alamy.

it provides an orderly manner of paying off bond issues and it reduces the chances that bonds won't be repaid.

Convertible Bonds: Bonds That Can Be Converted to Common Stock. A category of bonds that only corporations can issue, ***convertible bonds* are bonds that can be converted into the issuing corporation's common stock.** The advantage here is that bondholders can weigh which is worth more—the interest paid out on the bond or the value of the corporation's stock—and opt for whichever is more profitable. We describe common stock in the next section.

An example of a bond quotation that appeared on Yahoo! Finance for Microsoft appears at left. (*See* ■ *Panel 17.2.*)

The advantages and disadvantages to corporations in issuing bonds are summarized below. (*See* ■ *Panel 17.3.*)

■ **PANEL 17.3 Advantages and disadvantages to corporations of raising money by issuing bonds rather than stock to raise funds.**

Advantages	Disadvantages
When issuing bonds, a firm pays interest, but it expects to earn more in profit from the use of the proceeds from the bond's sale than it's paying out.	Bonds increase the firm's debt.
Issuing bonds instead of stock does not change the firm's ownership, so any gains remain with the present owners.	
The debt incurred from issuing bonds is temporary because bonds are usually repaid.	
Interest paid on bonds is deductible from the firm's tax return.	The firm is legally obliged to pay interest, or bondholders can sue to force repayment.
Bonds can be repaid before the maturity date, if they are callable bonds.	The firm must repay the bond's face value by the maturity date, which can lead to cash flow problems.
Bonds can be converted to common stock, if they are convertible bonds.	

Stocks: Units of Ownership in Corporations

How can I judge the worth of a stock, and how do I distinguish between common and preferred stock?

***Stocks* represent shares of ownership in a company.** When corporations attempt to raise money by selling stock, it is called *equity financing,* as we discussed in Chapter 15. If you own stock, you might own a ***stock certificate,* a paper certificate listing the shareholder's name, name of the issuing company, number of shares you hold, and type of stock being issued.** **6** However, today most stock is held electronically; owners don't have a paper certificate.

How Much Is a Share of Stock Worth? Par Value, Market Value, Book Value, Dividends, & Stock Splits

To determine the value of a stock you own, you need to understand the terms (1) *par value*, (2) *market value*, (3) *book value*, (4) *dividends*, and (5) *stock splits*.

Par Value: Face Value of a Share of Stock. If you do own a stock certificate, you will see it lists a ***par value,*** **the face value of a share of stock, an arbitrary figure set by the issuing corporation's board of directors.** The par value is used mainly for bookkeeping purposes. The par value is not to be confused with *market value* or *book value.*

Market Value: The Price a Stock Currently Sells For. The ***market value*** **is the price at which a stock is currently selling.** You can find out a stock's market value by going online or looking at newspaper stock listings.

Book Value: Total Shareholders' Equity Divided by Number of Shares. To determine a stock's ***book value,*** **a company subtracts its liabilities from its assets, and the resulting figure, the shareholders' equity, is then divided by the number of shares available of the stock.** Investors find it helpful to know a stock's book value because it is usually less than market value. Thus, when a stock's market value falls to near its book value, some investors think that means the stock is underpriced and therefore it is a good time to buy.

Dividends: Profits Distributed to Stockholders. ***Dividends*** **are part of a company's profits that are distributed to stockholders.** Dividends, which are declared by the corporation's board of directors and usually paid on a quarterly basis, may be made in the form of cash or as additional shares of stock. Not all companies pay dividends.

Stock Splits: Increase in Number of Shares. **In a** *stock split,* **a company divides its existing shares into multiple shares. Because the total value of outstanding shares remains the same while the number increases, the value of each share is reduced.** This is generally a move that companies make when they think a stock is priced too high and want to make it more affordable to investors. There is no immediate economic advantage to shareholders, since the overall value of the company remains the same. However, stocks often seem to increase in price fairly rapidly after a split.

❚ **Example** **of a Stock Split: Apple Computer Shares Split Two-for-One.** On June 21, 2000, the company then still known as Apple Computer (in 2007 "Computer" was dropped from the name) split its shares by two-for-one, when the stock was trading for about $100 a share. Thus, after the split, each stockholder got two shares valued at $50 each for each $100 share. These $50 shares grew in value to about $90 on February 28, 2005, when the company split them two-for-one again replacing each share with two $45 shares. ❼ ❚

❼ Should Apple split its stock again? Apple stock has split three times, most recently in 2005, to the resounding benefit of shareholders. Some investors suggested in mid-2011 that the company was long overdue for another split. After all, the firm had more cash on hand than the U.S. government. Really!

Source: David Young-Wolff/Alamy.

🔑 **Key Takeaway 17-3**
To understand what a stock is worth, you should understand par value, market value, book value, dividends, and stock splits.

8 **Stockholders' meeting.** Rick Waggoner, then chairman and CEO of General Motors, addressed stockholders at the annual meeting June 6, 2006, in Wilmington, Delaware. Though trying to be somewhat upbeat, he warned that U.S. auto sales were likely to see further losses and attempts to cut supplier costs would fall short. But GM's troubles only deepened, and three years later it declared bankruptcy. When a publicly traded firm such as GM declares bankruptcy, do you think the CEO and board of directors should be forced to resign?

Source: Tom Mihalek/EPA/Newscom.

Common Stock versus Preferred Stock

Corporations may issue two kinds of stock—*common* and *preferred*.

Common Stock: Stockholders Have Voting Rights but Get Last Claim on Dividends and Assets. With *common stock,* **stockholders are able to vote on major company decisions, but they get (1) last claim on the company's dividends and (2) last claim on any remaining assets if the company goes out of business and its assets are sold.**

Common stock means all shareholders hold stock in common. These stockholders have some say in the firm's big decisions, such as electing directors to the board or acquisition of another company. **8** However, they risk losing all their investment if the company is forced out of business because they will be last in line, after all the other creditors, to claims on the firm's remaining assets.

Preferred Stock: Stockholders Have No Voting Rights but Get First Claim on Dividends and Assets. With *preferred stock,* **stockholders are not able to vote on major company decisions, but they get (1) preferred, or first, claim on the company's dividends and (2) first claim on any remaining assets if the firm goes bankrupt and its assets are sold.**

A drawback of being a preferred stockholder is that the dividend you receive is fixed, no matter how profitable the firm is. Thus, preferred stock is considered to be quite similar to a bond, since both have (1) a face (or par) value and (2) a fixed rate of return. Generally, a stock increases more in value than a bond, although either one, of course, can also lose in value.

The advantages and disadvantages to corporations in issuing stock are summarized below. (See ■ Panel 17.4.)

■ **PANEL 17.4 Advantages and disadvantages to corporations of issuing stock rather than bonds to raise funds.**

Advantages	Disadvantages
When issuing stock, a firm shares its ownership, but does not increase its debt.	Stockholders may be able to vote to change ownership of the company.
Unlike bondholders, stockholders don't have to be repaid their investment.	Any gains that are shared as dividends must be shared beyond present owners to newer stockholders.
The firm can reinvest its earnings, because it is not legally required to pay dividends.	Any dividends are paid from profit after taxes and are not deductible on the firm's tax return.

Stock Markets: Domestic & Foreign Marketplaces for Securities

What are the types of stock markets, and what are the four arenas of stock trading?

When you think of stock markets, do you think of frantic brokers in funny smocks shouting and frantically waving their hands in the air? Could you be right?

Types of Stock Markets: Trading Floor versus Electronic Network

A **stock market, or stock exchange, is a financial marketplace where members buy and sell stocks.** Stock markets are secondary markets; their purpose is to act as a location for *trading,* or buying and selling, of securities already issued by firms. Stock markets are generally of two types—*trading floor* and *electronic communications networks*:

Floor-Based Exchanges. In so-called *trading floor exchanges,* **there is a trading floor or big room where buying and selling of securities is done face to face.** Some of the people on the floor are *brokers,* **who for a commission will execute buy and sell orders for stock placed by other people and organizations.** Buy and sell orders are transmitted to particular locations on the trading floor, where traders (brokers) bid against one another as in an auction.

Electronic Communications Networks. In *electronic communications networks (ECNs),* **buyers and sellers are linked electronically, in a telecommunications network, so that securities trading is done electronically** rather than face to face.

U.S. Stock Markets: Four Arenas for Trading

There are several stock exchanges operating in the United States, as follows.

The Largest Trading Arena: The New York Stock Exchange—for the Largest and Best-Known Companies. When many people think of the stock market, they think of **the world's largest stock exchange, the floor-based** *New York Stock Exchange (NYSE),* often called "the Big Board," which has been in existence since 1792. ❾ The NYSE lists about 3,800 stocks (both common and preferred) and averages about 45% of all the stock trading done in the United States. Companies listed on the NYSE tend to be the oldest, largest, and best-known of American companies, such as Exxon, Walmart, and General Electric. The NYSE also features a computer-based system, called NYSE Direct+, for matching and directing buy and sell orders and bypassing brokers, so that trades are executed within seconds.

❾ **The NYSE floor.** The New York Stock Exchange was formed in 1792 by two dozen brokers who had been meeting outdoors under a buttonwood tree on Wall Street to trade securities. In 2011, the parent of the NYSE agreed to be acquired by Deutsche Boerse, the operator of the Frankfurt stock exchange in Germany. The century-old trading floor shown here is located at New York's Wall and Broad Streets.

Source: Stan Honda/AFP/Getty Images/Newscom.

BRIEFING / GLOBAL BUSINESS

A German Company Buys the New York Stock Exchange. In existence for 220 years, the New York Stock Exchange would seem to be that most American of American names. However, in 2007 it merged with Euronext, a European-wide stock exchange based in Amsterdam, to become NYSE Euronext. Then in 2011 it agreed to merge with Deutsche Boerse, which operates the stock exchange in Frankfurt, Germany. If the deal clears all regulatory hurdles on both sides of the Atlantic, the new firm (which has no new name yet) would be 60% owned by Deutsche Boerse and would be the world's largest financial company.

What lies behind the move? The technology-led globalization of markets, suggests *Wall Street Journal* columnist L. Gordon Crovitz.[20] Market information is no longer confined within four walls. "Markets grew more efficient as technology digitized information and distributed it in real time," he says. "Now, most trading of shares in NYSE companies happens elsewhere, through high-frequency electronic exchanges in places like Lenexa, Kansas, and Birmingham, Alabama." In addition, he says, the NYSE is no longer an important source for raising capital for companies because many successful companies prefer to remain private to avoid the regulatory burdens imposed on publicly owned companies. ■

⑩ **Regional stock exchange.** Founded in 1832, the Boston Stock Exchange is the third oldest stock exchange (after the NYSE and the AMEX) in the United States. It was acquired in 2007 by NASDAQ. You can take a self-guided tour of the regional exchange, which is open 8 a.m. to 7 p.m. weekdays. What advantages, if any, do regional stock exchanges provide investors?

Source: Michael Dwyer/Alamy.

The Second-Largest Trading Arena: NASDAQ—a Nationwide Electronic System. The second-largest stock market in the world after the NYSE is the **NASDAQ (pronounced "naz-dak"), a nationwide electronic communications system that enables member securities dealers to buy and sell securities online**. NASDAQ, which used to stand for the National Association of Securities Dealers Automated Quotations, lists about 2,250 companies, many of them prominent high-tech firms, such as Microsoft, Apple, Intel, Dell, and Google.

The Third Trading Arena: Other Markets—the American Stock Exchange, Regional Stock Exchanges, and the Over-the-Counter Market. Besides the NYSE and the NASDAQ, several other stock markets exist in the United States.

- **The American Stock Exchange:** Another floor-based stock exchange located in New York is the *American Stock Exchange (AMEX)*. It lists about 1,000 stocks (for both U.S. and foreign companies), mainly those of midsized growth companies.

- **Regional stock exchanges:** There are also a few regional stock exchanges, such as those located in Boston, Philadelphia, Chicago, San Francisco, and Los Angeles. ⑩ These regional exchanges were originally created to trade shares in regional companies, but they now list the securities of many large national companies as well.

- **The over-the-counter market:** The *over-the-counter (OTC) market* **is an organization of several thousand securities brokers that trade stocks that are not listed on the organized stock exchanges.** The OTC has no trading floor but uses a nationwide electronic system.

The illustration at left shows a stock quote for Microsoft as it appeared on Yahoo! Finance. (*See* ■ *Panel 17.5.*)

The Fourth Trading Arena: Small Investors Using Electronic Communications Networks. For a long time, securities trading was mainly done by securities brokers and other "middlemen"—in floor exchanges, using electronic networks, or both—and often trading was limited to institutional investors buying and selling large blocks of stock.

However, the arrival of computer-based ECNs, which directly link sellers and buyers quickly and cheaply, has speeded up transactions and lowered trading costs, thereby making it possible for small, individual investors to more easily engage

■ **PANEL 17.5 Example of stock quotation for Microsoft.**

Microsoft Corporation (NasdaqGS: MSFT)
26.93 ↑ 0.34 (1.26%) 10:30AM EDT

Last Trade:	26.92	Day's Range:	②	26.65 - 27.18
Trade Time:	10:15AM EDT	52wk Range:		23.65 - 29.46
Change:	↑ 0.33 (1.26%)	Volume:		15,954,250
Prev Close:	26.59	Avg Vol (3m):		66,252,300
Open:	27.12	Market Cap:		226.50B
Bid: ①	26.93 x 21000	P/E (ttm): ③		9.79
Ask: ①	26.94 x 1700	EPS (ttm):		2.75
1y Target Est:	31.92	Div & Yield: ④		0.80 (3.00%)

① Bid: highest price a buyer (bidder) is willing to pay. Ask: highest selling price asked.

② Highest and lowest price for the stock during the day.

③ Price/earnings ratio—price of stock divided by firm's per-share earnings.

④ Dividend & yield—annual dividend as a percentage of the price per share.

Source: Based on Yahoo! Finance, http://finance.yahoo.com/q?s=MSFT (accessed October 27, 2011).

in trading and to eliminate the middlemen. This development was perceived as a threat by the NYSE and NASDAQ, and in 2005 these two organizations quickly moved to acquire their own ECNs. NYSE acquired Archipelago, and NASDAQ bought INET. With more trades taking place on ECNs, it may be a short time before the NYSE abandons the trading floor.

Key Takeaway 17-4
Floor exchanges are giving way to electronic exchanges.

Foreign Stock Markets

During the 2008 financial crisis, American investors would awaken to see whether prices on foreign stock exchanges had gone up or down during the night—those in London, Paris, Frankfurt, Zurich, Helsinki, Mumbai, Hong Kong, Taiwan, Sydney, and Buenos Aires, as well as Toronto and Mexico City. And they often found that the stock prices in these foreign exchanges echoed the hopes and fears of investors in the *American* markets—proof again that we live in a global economy.

Regulating Securities: The Securities & Exchange Commission

How does the Securities & Exchange Commission regulate the buying and selling of securities?

As we mentioned in Chapter 15, the *Securities and Exchange Commission (SEC)* is a federal agency that regulates the various U.S. (but not foreign) stock exchanges, among other things. The agency was created by the Securities Act of 1933, which attempted to correct trading excesses leading up to the Great Depression.

The SEC requires sellers of stocks and bonds to . . .

Provide Investors with Full Disclosure of Financial Facts

All publicly traded companies with at least 500 shareholders and $10 million in assets must fully disclose to investors all the essential facts about stocks, bonds, and other securities that they need to make informed buy and sell decisions.

Register with the SEC & Provide Prospectuses & Reports

All such publicly traded companies and all securities brokers and dealers must register with the SEC, and before they issue a new security they must provide interested investors with a prospectus. **A *prospectus* is a detailed written description of a new security, including information about the issuing company and its top management.** (Thus, even if you express interest in buying a new security immediately, the seller must first send you a prospectus.) In addition, companies and individuals must file several reports with the SEC every year, such as the annual report. All such reports are available to the public.

Avoid Taking Advantage of Inside Information

The Securities Act also took steps to reduce the opportunity of securities buyers and sellers to commit fraud. Most particularly, it prohibits them from engaging in *insider trading,* which, as we said in Chapter 2, is the illegal use of private company information to further one's own fortunes or those of family or friends. ⑪

⑪ **Insider trading.** In 2011, a federal grand jury convicted billionaire Raj Rajaratnam on 14 counts of perhaps the largest hedge-fund insider trading case. The founder of the Galleon Group was alleged to have netted $63.8 million over seven years. Rajaratnam exchanged inside information with corporate insiders in wiretapped telephone conversations. He was sentenced to 11 years in prison.

Source: m57/ZUMA Press/Newscom.

THE BIG IDEA: Investing begins with selecting a broker, either full-service or discount, and learning how to issue buy or sell orders: market, limit, and discretionary. Keeping up with the market means following leading stock market indicators, such as Dow Jones, Standard & Poor's 500, NASDAQ Composite, and Wilshire 5000. In addition, you should learn to track your investments through newspapers or financial websites.

THE ESSENTIAL QUESTION: How do I start buying and selling securities?

MyBizLab

MyBizLab: Check your understanding of these concepts at www.mybizlab.com.

If you begin to get into buying and selling securities, are you taking the first steps into the high-stakes world of Gordon Gekko, the financier played by Michael Douglas in *Wall Street* (1987) and *Wall Street: Money Never Sleeps* (2010)? Probably not so much (though it's possible). Let's see how to get started.

Selecting a Broker, & Buying & Selling Securities

What broker is best, and how do I make buy and sell orders?

The process of actually trading in securities is fairly straightforward.

Choosing a Broker: Full-Service or Discount?

Ordinary investors are not allowed to trade securities on the exchanges. Thus, you'll need the services of a *broker*, or *stockbroker*, an agent who charges a fee or commission for executing orders by investors to buy and sell stocks and bonds. The broker will place your order with a member of a stock exchange, who will negotiate the price of the transaction at the exchange and who then will report back (usually within seconds) to your broker the results of the transaction.

Brokers generally work for *full-service* or *discount* brokerage firms.

⑫ Full-service broker. Want personal advice, brokerage research, more investment products, and guidance about possible investment opportunities? Full-service brokers offer this, but they're expensive. And the brokers are compensated by the frequency with which you trade, not the gains in the values of your stocks. Thus, you may be advised to trade when actually you shouldn't.

Source: Courtesy of Edward Jones.

Full-Service Brokers: For Investors Who Like Lots of Help. *Full-service,* or *traditional, brokers* offer, generally through the client's own personal broker, a wide range of investment-related services, not only execution of trades but also investment research, advice, and tax planning. Examples of such firms are A. G. Edwards, Morgan Stanley Dean Witter, and Merrill Lynch. A full-service broker might charge $50 or even $150 to execute a trade. ⑫

Discount Brokers: For Online Investors Who Like to Do Things Themselves. *Discount brokers* execute the buy and sell orders indicated by clients—who are generally online investors doing their own research—but don't offer advice and tax planning. Customers don't have their own personal broker, but place their trades through the first available broker online. Examples of discount brokers are E-Trade, Ameritrade, and TD Waterhouse. A discount broker might charge $8 to $30 to execute a trade.

Are There Still Differences? The Distinctions Blur. Recently, both types of brokers have tried to attract customers by offering what their opposite numbers have offered, with the full-service brokers charging less for commissions and the discount brokers offering more services. Thus, when you're considering what broker to use, make a point of going to the different websites and finding out what the fees are, minimum account balances required of you, what the research data and tools look like, and how fast the firm promises to execute trades. ⓭

i
Want to Know More? 17-3
What Are the Differences to Look for When Lining Up a Broker?
Go to www.mybizlab.com.

Buying & Selling Securities: Putting in the Order

What are two options when doing a buy or sell order?

When you contact your broker (whether by phone or online) and say you want to buy or sell a particular security, you need to state how many shares you want. You also need to set the conditions for your order. The three most common are *market orders, limit orders,* and *discretionary orders.*

Source: David J. Green - lifestyle themes/Alamy.

⓭ **How fast are trades executed?** Day traders rapidly buy and sell stocks throughout the day in hopes of increasing their gains. Thus, the speed with which orders are executed is an important matter. When checking out a brokerage firm, whether full-service or discount, this is one of the first questions day traders must get answered.

Market Order: "Buy or Sell at the Best Price Now Possible"

In a **_market order,_ you tell your broker to buy or sell a particular security at the best available price.** Market orders can usually be carried out within five minutes. There is a risk, however, that you may buy at a slightly higher or sell at a slightly lower price than you were hoping for.

Limit Order: "Buy Below or Sell Above Only a Certain Price"

In a **_limit order,_ you tell your broker to buy a particular security only if it is less than a certain price or to sell it only if it is above a certain price.** Specifying that the transaction be done only above or below a specific price is a particularly useful kind of order to give when the market is volatile—is fluctuating wildly. Limit orders are good for one day only.

i
Want to Know More? 17-4
What Are Stop Orders & Open Orders?
Go to www.mybizlab.com.

Discretionary Order: "Use Your Professional Judgment about When to Buy or Sell"

You might use a limit order when you worry your broker might buy a stock for more than you think it's worth or sell it for less than you think it's worth. By contrast, with the **_discretionary order,_ you trust the broker's professional experience and judgment and leave it to him or her to decide the right time and price for buying or selling a security.** (But if the decision is wrong, you can't hold the broker legally responsible.)

i
Want to Know More? 17-5
What Are Buying on Margin & Selling Short?
Go to www.mybizlab.com.

Keeping Up with the Market

What are the four major stock market indicators I need to follow, and how do I track my own investments?

Most investors want to keep up with their investments, and the Internet makes it easy to do so. Here we tell you (1) how to track the markets in general, using stock indexes, and (2) how to keep watch on specific securities.

The Leading Stock Market Indicators: Dow Jones, S&P 500, NASDAQ, & Wilshire 5000

Source: SeanPavonePhoto/Shutterstock.

Want to Know More? 17-6

What Are Other Market Indexes?

Go to www.mybizlab.com.

Key Takeaway 17-5
The leading U.S. market indexes are the Dow Jones, S&P 500, NASDAQ, and Wilshire 5000.

Stock market indicators **are indexes of stock market prices of groups of stocks that are related in some way.** In the United States, the most well known is the Dow Jones Industrial Average; in London, it is the FTSE 100 ("Footsie"); and in Tokyo, it is the Nikkei 225. Let's consider the principal stock market indicators in the United States: (1) the *Dow Jones Industrial Average,* (2) the *Standard & Poor's 500,* (3) the *NASDAQ Composite Index,* and (4) the *Wilshire 5000.*

The Dow Jones Industrial Average: General Measure of U.S. Stock Price Movements. The *Dow Jones Industrial Average (DJIA),* **or "the Dow," a general measure of the movement of U.S. stock prices, is an index of the average of prices of the stocks of 30 large corporations,** including Boeing, Coca-Cola, General Motors, Intel, and Walt Disney. Developed in 1884 by Charles Dow, editor of the *Wall Street Journal,* the Dow is the number broadcast on regular radio and television newscasts. Periodically the stocks in the index are changed to reflect changes in the U.S. economy, with, for example, pharmaceutical and technology companies replacing manufacturing companies.

The Standard & Poor's 500: A Broader, More Representative Index. Because the Dow Jones contains only 30 stocks, many professional investors consider it unrepresentative. Thus, they may pay more attention to the *Standard & Poor's 500 (S&P 500),* **an index of stock prices for 500 major corporations in a range of industries.** (It tracks 400 industrial, 40 financial, 40 public utility, and 20 transportation stocks.) Unlike the Dow, the S&P 500 also weighs stock prices to reflect the total market value of each stock, considered by many investors to be a more accurate way of computing an index.

The NASDAQ Composite Index: Leading Indicator for Tech Stocks. Also frequently quoted (along with the Dow) on daily TV newscasts, the *NASDAQ Composite Index* **tracks not only domestic but also foreign common stocks traded on the NASDAQ exchange.** ⓮ As we mentioned earlier, the NASDAQ lists many high-tech firms such as Microsoft and Google.

The Wilshire 5000 Index: The "Total Stock Market Index." The incorrectly named *Wilshire 5000 Index,* which actually includes around 6,500 stocks, is an index that covers the stocks traded on the New York Stock Exchange and the American Stock Exchange, and actively traded stocks on the NASDAQ. The Wilshire 5000 is referred to as "the total stock market index."

Tracking Specific Securities: How to Get Price Quotes

If you've purchased a particular stock or bond (or mutual fund or ETF, discussed next), how do you find out what it's worth on a day-to-day basis? You can always look in the business section of a newspaper, such as the *Wall Street Journal*'s Money & Investing section. It covers price quotations for government bonds in a table called Treasury Issues and for stocks under listings for the New York, American, and NASDAQ stock exchanges. Alternatively, you can go online to a financial website such as Yahoo! Finance (http://finance.yahoo.com) or Google Finance (http://finance.google.com). Then you go to the "Get Quotes" box, and type in the company name or *stock symbol* (for example, AXP for American Express, obtainable from a symbol-lookup website).

Other Investments: Mutual Funds, Exchange-Traded Funds, & Commodities

THE BIG IDEA: One of the most popular investments, mutual funds are diversified investments by pools of investors, who like the many choices of funds at an economical price, the varied degrees of risk, and the professional management. Exchange-traded funds are collections of stocks that are traded on an exchange, but investors have more convenience in their trading times and the fees are lower than they are for mutual funds. Commodities trading is much more risky than the previous two kinds of investments. It involves using futures contracts to buy a specific amount of a commodity, or raw material, at a certain price on a certain date.

THE ESSENTIAL QUESTION: Why would I be attracted to investing in mutual funds, exchange-traded funds, or commodities?

MyBizLab: Check your understanding of these concepts at www.mybizlab.com.

MyBizLab

One of the most important principles that many financial advisors recommend is a strategy of *diversification*—**choosing securities in such a way that a loss in one investment won't have a devastating impact on your total portfolio.** Of course, you can try to do this yourself. But mutual funds and exchange-traded funds are easier ways to achieve this.

Mutual Funds: Diversified Investments by Pools of Investors

Why should I buy shares in a mutual fund?

A *mutual fund* **is a fund operated by an investment company that brings together money from many people and invests it in an array of diversified stocks, bonds, or other securities.** The investors share in the returns in proportion to their contributions.

Mutual funds may be purchased through certain brokerages, such as Charles Schwab and Merrill Lynch. The largest mutual fund families are American Funds, Vanguard, and Fidelity.

The benefits to investing in mutual funds are . . .

1 They Offer Many Choices at an Economical Price

There are around 8,000 mutual funds in the United States today, each with different investment priorities and strategies. They may be broadly categorized as stock funds, bond funds, money market funds, and hybrid funds (stocks and bonds). Some of the most popular types of funds are shown at right. (*See* ■ *Panel 17.6.*)

As far as charges, funds are of two types:

- **Load funds: With *load funds*, you pay a commission every time you purchase shares.** This is usually between 3% and 5%, but sometimes as high as 8.5%.

■ **PANEL 17.6 Some popular types of mutual funds.**

Fund	Invests in . . .
Balanced	diversified common stocks, preferred stocks, and bonds
Global	foreign and U.S. securities
Growth	stocks in rapidly growing companies
Income	securities paying high dividends and interest
Index	stocks in market index such as S&P 500
International	foreign securities
Money market	commercial paper, CDs, T-bills, etc.
Sector (or specialty)	companies within specific industries
Socially responsible	companies meeting certain standards such as ethical behavior and environmental protection

- **No-load funds:** With *no-load funds,* **you pay no sales charges at all.** However, the investment company may charge a management fee (perhaps between 0.25% and 2%) to cover operating costs.

2 They Vary in the Degree of Risk

Whatever your investment goals and strategy, you will no doubt find a fund that offers a level of risk you can live with. For example, some *sector funds*, such as those specializing in technology, biotechnology, or energy, may offer the possibility of high returns but be very risky. *Index funds,* on the other hand, which automatically follow the moves in a market index such as the S&P 500, reflect long-term averages and so are considered lower risk. Index funds, incidentally, are a good way for newcomers to begin an investment program.

3 They Are Run by Professional Managers

Except for index funds, mutual funds are run by professional managers who keep up with the industries and companies in which their funds have bought stock. This saves you the effort of doing this kind of investigation yourself.

The Fidelity Select Technology fund offers a mix of technology stocks, and the data provided in a quote for it is shown below. (*See* ■ *Panel 17.7.*)

■ **PANEL 17.7 Example of a quote for Fidelity Select Technology mutual fund.**

FIDELITY SELECT TECHNOLOGY

Net Asset Value: ❶	90.96	Prev Close:	90.96
Trade Time:	Oct 26	YTD Return*: ❸	-13.97%
Change: ❷	⬆0.16 (0.18%)	Net Assets*:	2.04B
		Yield*: ❹	N/A
			* As of 30-Sep-11

❶ Price at which this fund may be purchased (the market value essentially).

❷ Increase in the net asset value (NAV) from the close on the previous day.

❸ Year-to-date return—percentage increase since the start of the year.

❹ Fund's earnings distributed to investors as percentage of the NAV.

Source: Based on Yahoo! Finance, http://finance.yahoo.com/q?s=FSPTX (accessed October 27, 2011).

Exchange-Traded Funds: Collections of Stocks Traded on Exchanges throughout the Day

What does an exchange-traded fund do that a mutual fund does not?

Mutual funds are collections of stocks, as we've seen, and a mutual fund can be traded on an exchange, just like an individual stock. However, regulations limit the trading of mutual funds only to the *end* of the trading day.

By contrast, an *exchange-traded fund (ETF)* **is, like a mutual fund, a collection of stocks that is traded on an exchange; however, unlike a mutual fund, it can be traded *throughout* the trading day.** Today there are perhaps 1,000 ETFs, all managed by trained specialists, just like mutual funds.

Like mutual funds, ETFs offer investors a way to spread the risk of owning securities and to have them managed by professional specialists. Additional benefits to investing in an ETF are . . .

You Can Trade an ETF More Conveniently

For trading purposes, an ETF is more convenient than a mutual fund, since you can buy shares in an ETF at any time of the trading day, not just at the end.

Fees Are Lower Than They Are for Mutual Funds

ETFs charge fees, but they are usually much lower than those charged by mutual funds. Also, unlike mutual funds, ETFs don't require any minimum initial investment.

Want to Know More? 17-7
How Does an ETF Differ from a Mutual Fund?
Go to www.mybizlab.com.

Commodities Trading: Risky Trading in Raw Materials

What are futures contracts and commodity exchanges?

Got an appetite for risk? The kind of investing in which you could make a lot of money but in which most people, perhaps 85% to 90%, lose money?[21] Then maybe you're a candidate for *commodities trading,* **trading in raw materials and agricultural products used to produce other goods,** such as metals (gold), gasoline, wheat, soybeans, coffee beans, and pork bellies (slabs of bacon). The main requirement for survival, it seems, is having thorough knowledge of the goods being sold and the market environment, along with a sense of caution about not risking too much on any one trade. ⑮

The main two components of commodities trading are *futures contracts* and *commodity exchanges.*

Source: Russell Gordon/Danita Delimont/Alamy.

⑮ **Commodities traders.** Traders at the Chicago Board of Trade, established in 1848, signal their buy/sell wishes for over 50 kinds of options and futures—including those for corn, soybeans, cattle, metals, and oil. Seem exciting? Actually, the good traders find commodities trading boring. It's the losers who look to it for the adrenaline rush. Why do you think it's desirable to have a separate exchange for trading commodities?

Futures Contracts: Agreements to Buy Commodities at a Set Price in the Future

The main expertise that most commodity traders bring to their work is knowing how to set up a *futures contract,* **making an agreement with a seller or broker to buy a specific amount of a commodity at a certain price on a certain date.** For example, believing that the price of petroleum usually keeps rising, airlines make deals to buy vast supplies of jet fuel in future years at lower prices. (However, if the price of petroleum goes *down,* an airline may be stuck having to buy millions of gallons of jet fuel at the *higher* price it contracted for.)

Commodity Exchanges: Arenas for Buying & Selling Raw Materials

A *commodity exchange* **is a security exchange in which futures contracts are bought and sold.** Examples are the Chicago Board of Trade, the world's largest grain exchange, and the Chicago Mercantile Exchange, where commodities such as butter, eggs, pork bellies, and lumber are traded. (Note that traders don't actually take physical possession of, say, great numbers of eggs; their intent is to sell the contract for a higher price.)

Want to Know More? 17-8
How Would Commodities Trading Work for a Particular Commodity?
Go to www.mybizlab.com.

THE BIG IDEA: Investors have several choices in investment strategy, including buying and holding, investing for income, investing for growth, value investing, and market timing. There are also different mixes of stocks, bonds, and cash.

THE ESSENTIAL QUESTION: Which investment strategy would be best for me?

MyBizLab: Check your understanding of these concepts at www.mybizlab.com.

Want to Know More? 17-9

What Is Program Trading?

Go to www.mybizlab.com.

"Just as most people consider themselves above-average drivers," says financial writer Jason Waggoner, "most people also consider themselves to be above-average investors."[22] Overconfident stock traders tend to be frequent traders, which raises trading costs and leads to lower returns.[23] One study found that pension-fund investments would have performed better "if the managers had gone on a 12-month vacation and never made a single trade."[24]

Here, then, is an area where investors are probably served best by being humble, keeping their costs low, not buying stocks because they're in the news, and remembering that, as Waggoner puts it, "predicting the market is hard, uncertain work. Most people don't do it well."[25]

Five Investment Strategies

What are the five best-known investment approaches?

There are five general strategies of investing you might consider, ranging more or less from the safest to the riskiest, as follows:

Want to Know More? 17-10

How Does Starting to Invest While Young Put You Ahead?

Go to www.mybizlab.com.

1 Buying & Holding: "I Want an Attractive Return over the Long Haul without Having to Constantly Track My Investments"

In the *buying and holding investment strategy,* you invest in a diversified and broad range of securities and (mostly) leave them alone to build for several years.

This strategy is suitable for anyone who is young enough to invest for the long term and patient and tough enough to ride out the inevitable market downs as well as ups. Buying and holding is also a strategy for people who don't want to be bothered with constantly watching the progress of individual stocks.

2 Investing for Income: "I Want a Steady Flow of Income, Even Though the Value of the Investments Won't Increase Much"

Investing for income focuses on getting the highest **yield, or income from securities, calculated by dividing dividend or income by the market price.**

This is a good strategy if you're an older person looking for long-term income to finance your retirement or children's college educations. Thus, you might be advised to buy low-risk securities that have predictable payouts—bonds, which pay a stated amount of interest every year, or preferred stock, which usually pays a regular fixed dividend. Or you might buy **blue-chip stocks, preferred or common stocks of big, reputable companies, which also usually pay regular dividends.** The downside, however, is that these kinds of safe investments aren't apt to increase much in market value.

3 Investing for Growth: "I Want to Increase My Wealth Fast & Am Willing to Take Risks"

Investing for growth is concerned with maximizing wealth by buying **growth stocks, stocks issued by small, innovative new companies in hot industries,** such as information technology or alternative energy.

The expectation here is that the stock price will increase rapidly. However, this strategy involves a lot of risk, and stock prices tend to be more *volatile*—to increase quickly but also fall quickly. Clearly, you wouldn't want to follow this strategy if you're about to retire and can't risk losing your investment.

4 Value Investing: "I'm Willing to Risk My Time & Money Hunting for Undervalued Stocks That Might Become Profitable"

In *value investing,* investors try to find stocks that are undervalued in the market, believing that other investors will eventually buy these stocks as well, increasing their market value and driving up the stock's price.

This is a strategy for *active* investors of any age—and we do mean active, since it requires a lot of research and analysis. In addition, the downside is that a lot of other investors are also looking for undervalued stocks, and if you are late getting in, you may find the price of the stock has already been driven up.

5 Market Timing: "I'm Willing to Take Big Risks & Pay Very Close Attention to Buy Low & Sell High for Quick Profits"

Do you believe we're in a *bull market*—that stock prices are going to rise? Or are we in a *bear market*—stock prices are going to decline? If you really can develop a sense for this, you could become a market timer.

Market timing may be the most difficult of all investment strategies, since it involves the powers of prediction: trying to make a fast profit by buying a stock at a low price and selling it at a high price within a short time. This is a strategy for *extremely active* investors with a strong stomach for risk and a familiarity with various analytical tools for tracking stock prices. In addition, because it involves frequent trading, investors need to have enough money to pay all the brokerage fees and commissions required in making those trades.

Your Own Portfolio

What's the best mix of securities for my personal portfolio?

Earlier in this chapter, we discussed having a no-stock portfolio—an "extremely conservative" investment approach. How does this compare to other strategies— "extremely aggressive" or "balanced"? The returns for a 10-year period are shown at right. (*See* ■ *Panel 17.8.*)[26] It's all about risks and returns: A no-stocks portfolio may avoid big stock downturns but mean smaller long-term returns. Having mostly stocks ("extremely aggressive") may risk loss in a market bust but provide bigger returns. And then there's in between ("balanced").

We discuss personal investing further in Flex-Chapter E, "Personal Finance."

■ **PANEL 17.8 Returns for 10 years on three different portfolios of stocks/bonds/cash asset mixes.** It's all about risk versus returns.

Extremely conservative = 0% stocks, 90% bonds, 10% cash

Balanced = 60% stocks, 30% bonds, 10% cash

Extremely aggressive = 90% stocks, 0% bonds, 10% cash

Strategy	Average Annual Return
Extremely conservative	||||| 5.4%
Balanced	||||||| 8.5%
Extremely aggressive	||||||||| 10%

LEARNING & SKILLS PORTFOLIO

Summary

17.1 The Two Kinds of Securities Markets: Primary versus Secondary

THE ESSENTIAL QUESTION: *Which of the two securities markets would I be more likely to be involved with?*

How are new stocks and bonds sold? Securities—financial instruments such as stocks and bonds—are on two financial markets, primary and secondary. The primary securities market is the one in which a corporation's new security issue is first sold as an initial public offering (IPO) to investors. New stocks and bonds may be sold in two ways: (1) through investment bankers, companies that engage in buying and reselling (underwriting) new securities, often to institutional investors, large organizations such as pension funds and insurance companies; and (2) through open auctions, as is done with U.S. Treasury securities.

Why might I want to participate in the secondary securities market? The secondary securities market is the financial market in which existing stocks and bonds are bought and sold, such as the New York Stock Exchange. Investors participate in this market to try to get a substantial capital gain—selling a security for a lot more than they paid for it.

17.2 Securities: Money Market Instruments, Bonds, & Stocks

THE ESSENTIAL QUESTION: *What are the differences in the three types of securities, and when would I invest in them?*

Why would I ever want to invest in money market instruments, and what are they? Money market instruments are short-term IOUs, debt securities that mature within one year; they are issued by governments, large corporations, and financial institutions. These may be bought through money market mutual funds. Treasury bills (T-bills), short-term obligations of the U.S. Treasury, may be purchased directly from the U.S. government.

What are the different bonds, bond-rating systems, and ways bonds pay off? Bonds are long-term IOUs issued by governments and corporations, contracts on which the issuer pays the buyer interest at regular intervals. Bonds have a maturity date, when the issuing organization is legally required to repay the bond's principal in full to the bondholder. In the United States, bonds are of four types: (1) U.S. Treasury notes and bonds; (2) revenue bonds and general obligation bonds issued by state and local governments and agencies; (3) corporate bonds, secured bonds and debenture bonds issued by businesses; and (4) mortgage pass-through securities issued by financial institutions. The quality and safety of a bond is indicated by a bond rating issued by a bond-rating agency such as Standard & Poor's or Moody's. Bonds are divided according to risk into investment-grade bonds, which are relatively safe, and speculative-grade (junk) bonds, which are riskier but pay higher interest. Bonds may pay off in four ways: as callable

bonds (which may pay off at a prespecified price before the maturity date), as serial bonds (mature at different dates), as sinking-fund bonds (issuer makes annual deposits to a bank to pay off the bonds on maturity), and as convertible bonds (convertible into the corporation's common stock).

How can I judge the worth of a stock, and how do I distinguish between common and preferred stock? Stocks represent shares of ownership in a company. Par value is the face value of a stock; market value is the price at which a stock is currently selling; dividends are part of a company's profits that are distributed to shareholders; stock splits occur when a company divides its existing shares into multiple shares. Two types of stock are common and preferred. With common stock, stockholders have voting rights but get last claim on dividends and assets if the company is sold. With preferred stock, stockholders have no voting rights but get first claim on dividends and assets.

What are the types of stock markets, and what are the four arenas of stock trading? Stock markets, places where members buy and sell stocks, may be trading floor exchanges, rooms where buying and selling is done face to face, or electronic communications networks (ECNs), where trading is done electronically. Four arenas for trading are the floor-based New York Stock Exchange, the nationwide electronic system called NASDAQ, other markets (the floor-based American Stock Exchange, regional stock exchanges, the over-the-counter market), and small investors using electronic communications networks. There are also foreign stock markets.

How does the Securities & Exchange Commission regulate the buying and selling of securities? The SEC requires sellers of stocks and bonds to provide investors with full disclosure of financial facts, to register with the SEC and provide a prospectus (detailed description of new security) and several reports, and to avoid taking advantage of inside information (insider trading).

17.3 Buying & Selling Securities

THE ESSENTIAL QUESTION: *How do I start buying and selling securities?*

What broker is best, and how do I make buy and sell orders? A stockbroker is an agent who charges a fee for executing orders by investors to buy and sell stocks and bonds. Full-service brokers offer a wide range of investment-related services; discount brokers only execute buy and sell orders.

What are two options when doing a buy or sell order? Three conditions an investor may set on an order are market order, telling the broker to buy or sell a particular security at the best available price; limit order, buying only if it is less than a certain price and sell only if above a certain price; and discretionary order, telling the broker to act on his or her professional judgment.

What are the four major stock market indicators I need to follow, and how do I track my own investments? The leading indicators or indexes of market prices are the Dow Jones Industrial Average, the Standard & Poor's 500, the NASDAQ Composite Index, and the Wilshire 5000 Index. Investments may be tracked through newspaper business sections or online.

17.4 Other Investments: Mutual Funds, Exchange-Traded Funds, & Commodities

THE ESSENTIAL QUESTION: *Why would I be attracted to investing in mutual funds, exchange-traded funds, or commodities?*

Why should I buy shares in a mutual fund? Mutual funds offer many choices at an economical price, vary in the degree of risk, and are run by professional managers. In this approach, an investment company brings together many investors and invests in an array of diversified securities; diversification means choosing in such a way that a loss in one investment won't devastate other parts of an investor's portfolio (collection of stocks).

What does an exchange-traded fund do that a mutual fund does not? Unlike a mutual fund, the shares of stocks in an exchange-traded fund can be traded throughout the trading day, not just at the end, and fees are lower.

What are futures contracts and commodity exchanges? Commodities trading is trading in raw materials and agricultural products used to produce other goods. The two main components are a futures contract, making an agreement with a seller or broker to buy a specific amount of a commodity at a certain price on a certain date, and commodity exchanges, a security exchange where futures contracts are bought and sold.

17.5 Investment Strategies

THE ESSENTIAL QUESTION: *Which investment strategy would be best for me?*

What are the five best-known investment approaches? Well-known strategies are as follows: (1) Buying and holding is investment in diversified securities and not selling them for several years. (2) Investing for income focuses on getting the highest income (yield). (3) Investing for growth emphasizes buying growth stocks, those issued by small, innovative new companies. (4) Value investing looks for stocks that are undervalued in the market. (5) Market timing is trying to buy a stock at a low price and sell it at a high price in a very short period of time, a strategy for very active investors.

What's the best mix of securities for my personal portfolio? There is no one best approach. Whether you take an aggressive, balanced, or conservative approach depends on your preferences and your tolerance for risk.

Key Terms

MyBizLab

Pop Quiz Prep

1. How is *underwriting* defined?
2. As an investor, if your primary concern is how quickly you might be able to withdraw funds from your investments in case of an emergency, what is your top priority?

3. What are *money market instruments*?
4. Speculative-grade bonds have what level of bond rating?
5. When you place a market order, what are you telling your broker to do?

6. What is the Dow Jones Industrial Average?

7. How do mutual funds and exchange-traded funds (ETFs) differ?

8. What are *no-load funds*?

9. If investors are willing to risk time and money hunting for undervalued stocks that might become profitable, which investment strategy are they following?

10. If you are an older person looking to finance your retirement or your children's college education, which investment strategy would be appropriate?

Critical Thinking Questions

1. Think about whether you would choose a full-service brokerage firm (such as Merrill Lynch or Morgan Stanley) or a discount brokerage firm (such as Charles Schwab or Ameritrade) when considering investing for a long-term goal such as retirement or your children's college. Compare and contrast the different services provided by each, and the value each provides. What would your choice be now? Do you think your choice might change in the future?

2. Socially responsible investing (SRI) is an investment strategy where an investor achieves both financial gain and social good by investing in companies that have a positive impact on society. There are many different SRI agendas, including corporate practices promoting positive treatment of employees, the environment, human rights, diversity, alternative energy use, and the avoidance of companies with objectionable products or processes, which for some may be weapons, defense, gambling, alcohol, or tobacco.[27] What are the advantages and disadvantages of investing in this way? What type of SRI agenda would you choose?

3. In his popular personal finance book, *A Random Walk Down Wall Street,* economist Burton Malkiel, argues that investors can't consistently beat the market and says that "a blindfolded monkey throwing darts at a newspaper's financial pages could select a portfolio that would do just as well as one carefully selected by experts."[28] In 1988, the *Wall Street Journal* decided to see if Malkiel's theory would hold up, and created the dartboard contest, where *Wall Street Journal* staffers, acting as the monkeys, threw darts at a stock table, while investment experts picked their own stocks.[29] What do you think the overall result was when the experts and the monkeys were compared? What do you think it takes to pick winning stocks? You may do some research to learn more about the dartboard contest.

4. For an investor, asset allocation is a balancing act. Asset allocation depends on the ability to tolerate risk, investment goals, and time frame. It involves adjusting the percentage of each investment (for example, stocks, bonds, money market funds) to balance risk, taking into consideration the current financial environment. How would a 24-year-old choose an investment, considering age and asset allocation? What about a 60-year-old? Does risk tolerance decrease with age? Explain.

5. Evaluate each of the five investment strategies discussed in the chapter (buying and holding, investing for income, investing for growth, value investing, and marketing timing), and discuss which is right for you. Explain.

Cases

Go to MyBizLab

VIDEO CASE
Capital Advisors: A Dynamic Approach to Risk Management

In the text and other activities, you have gained an understanding of the concept of risk and its relationship to investing. In this video, you will learn about a company called Capital Advisors and how this company and other financial planning and investment companies can help you manage risk to get the return that you want.

Capital Advisors provides financial planning and investment strategy services to a wide range of customers. The company believes in a "changing and dynamic approach to risk management,"[30] taking into consideration that the risk-reward trade-off is not static over time.[31] Its website states, "Capital Advisors provides structure for the financial assets of individuals and institutional investors. The process begins with an efficient plan that documents the investment objectives and risk constraints for the portfolios we manage. The outcome of

our planning process dictates which investment strategy offers the tightest match with the investment goals and risk tolerance of every client portfolio."[32] After reading this case, you should understand the approach taken by Capital Advisors, and other similar companies, so that if you wish to invest your hard-earned money, you will have the tools to decide if such a company will be helpful to you.

Capital Advisors helps individuals and institutions manage their financial assets. Financial assets refer to stocks, bonds, bank deposits, and the like—assets that can easily be converted into cash.[33] They differ from physical assets, which are real estate and personal property (art, furniture, jewelry, and collectibles). Capital Advisors helps "provide structure" by creating a plan that includes an analysis of the investment objectives and risk tolerance of an individual or institutional investor. Institutional investors are often large organizations who—like an individual, but with far larger pools of money—invest in stocks, real estate, and other investment assets. Examples include a bank, insurance company, pension fund, hedge fund, mutual fund, or retirement fund.

Capital Advisors' goal for its clients is to make the "the tightest match." This refers to matching a client's risk tolerance to the client's investment goals. For example, as Channing Smith, director of equity strategies, states in the video, a person nearing retirement may be less tolerant to risk, mainly because there is less time to recover from a loss. When a person nears retirement, preserving assets becomes increasingly important. In comparison, a younger person has more time to recover from a loss. Because of the time horizon for each, Capital Advisors may advise the near-retiree to purchase a safer, less risky investment like bonds, whereas the student may be advised to purchase stocks or equities.

And last, after considering risk tolerance and investment goals, a client portfolio ideally should represent a collection of investments or securities representing an individual's or institutional investor's investments. What is your attitude toward risk?

What's Your Take?

1. Assume you are the owner of the floral company in the video, and you wish to "expand big time." What method of financing would you choose, and why? Which factors would you consider when choosing your financing method? Explain.

2. Channing Smith of Capital Advisors states, "A savings account is safe and perfect for emergencies and short term needs, but the concept of building wealth means you truly have to make your money work for you." In what situations do you think the safety of a savings account makes sense, and what is meant by his statement of "make your money work for you"?

3. On the Capital Advisors website, it reads: "Every healthy advisor-client relationship begins with trust. At Capital Advisors, three decades of experience working with clients reinforces our understanding that we must execute three responsibilities to earn and maintain our clients' trust, including: Understand the unique investment objectives and risk constraints of every client portfolio, execute an investment strategy appropriate for those objectives and constraints, and measure and report on the results." What do you think the "measure and report" part of this statement means? How would you like to be updated about your portfolio's results and strategies if you were to hire Capital Advisors? Whose obligation is it to decide upon the strategy and changes to implement?

4. "We construct clients' bond portfolios around one of three core designs: A 'Liquidity' strategy for clients seeking low volatility and ready access to capital; an 'Income' structure intended to maximize monthly cash flows; and an 'Aggregate' approach that strikes a balance between liquidity and income objectives," reads the Capital Advisors website. The best design for an individual depends on a variety of factors; age and dependents are two important ones. Which of these core designs do you think makes the most sense for a 25-year-old woman who is a head of household with two young children? What about when she is 40? What about 55?

BUSINESS DECISION CASE
Day Trading: Risky Business

Once considered controversial by traditional investors and money managers furious about the flood of money into the market and the wild day-to-day fluctuations and market volatility it caused, day trading has become an accepted practice. Day trading refers to the buying and selling of financial instruments (stocks, currencies, futures, or other assets) within the same trading day, in hopes of a gain. Day trading was popularized in the early 1990s when a New Yorker named Harvey Houtkin began monitoring the delays between breaking news events and the adjustment of prices by certain dealers.[34]

Think about what you might have made if you had purchased some shares of each of the following stocks just in that one day, and then sold them: On its first day of trading in 1995, Netscape stock doubled in price. Yahoo shares rose 154% on its 1996 offering. Theglobe.com shot up to $97 from $9 in its first day of trading in 1998. Due to these well-publicized stock

price increases and the factors discussed in this case, day trading has become a widespread practice with people often hoping to "make a quick buck."

Houtkin realized that the financial markets are not completely efficient (market efficiency suggests that at any given time, prices fully reflect all available information on a particular stock and/or market).[35] The more efficient a market is, the faster it reacts to new information.[36] He realized that quick profits can be generated when trading (rapidly buying and selling) from the small, yet incremental movements in stock within a single day. By doing so, he opened the floodgates to hordes of new independent traders making connections to exchanges. News stories of office workers trading at their desks, retiring by age 30, or leaving their jobs to trade full time became widespread.[37] Many investors who bought these stocks in the morning, and sold in the afternoon, made more than a 400% return.[38]

Most will agree that day trading has become popularized with the ease of opening up a brokerage account, electronic communication networks, software with real-time market data and information, and, of course, some knowledge. Because of the dot.com boom, many became interested in the stock market after reading about and hearing stories about "average people" who were able to retire after day trading.

The activity of day trading first benefited from the creation of NASDAQ in 1971, dramatically changing the face of how stocks were traded. NASDAQ is a virtual stock exchange where orders are transmitted electronically. In addition, the costs of trading were reduced significantly as online brokerage firms encouraged the creation of individual electronic networks where market information could be shared. With several securities markets, investors were able to find the best prices on given stock picks, and purchase and trade them instantaneously with real-time price information. Electronic trading systems—capable of performing what are known as basket trades, in which several hundred securities are bought and sold in a single transaction—were tailor-made for the day-trading world, in which traders frequently buy and sell thousands of stocks in a single day.

Gregory J. Millman, writing in *Barron's*, compared day traders to "a swarm of maggots, insisting that, while they may be loathsome, day traders do a good job of eating away at the market's 'diseased tissue,' those 'inefficiencies that slow and sicken markets.'"[39] Regardless of these sentiments, day trading has become a widely accepted practice —and a source of income for many. Are you ready to open a brokerage account and purchase some trading software?

What's Your Take?

1. Day trading used to be dominated by financial firms and professional investors and speculators, but today day traders range from professional investors to everyday folks who trade at home (and some, of course, while on the job). Do you think day traders are similar to gamblers? If so, in what way?

2. In a *New York Times* article entitled, "Day Trading Still Alive, Outsourced to China," the writer describes a company called Swift Trade, a pioneer of outsourced day trading, who has set up 1,500 traders in China, engaging in "rapid-fire" stock trading with the world's most powerful investment houses in New York, London, and Tokyo. The Swift Trade owner says, "Our clients—they open an office, give us the money and then hire people to trade for them. That's our structure." If the traders make a profit, they keep between 10% and 50%, with the rest split between the trading firm and the investor. (If the traders produce a loss, they risk the firm's clients and possibly their own jobs.)[40] Is this what the future of day trading looks like? Discuss.

3. What type of information system, tools, and software do you think a day trader needs to make accurate, split-second decisions? You may do some research, if needed, to answer the question in greater detail.

4. Discuss the following quote from the Securities and Exchange Commission website which states, "Day traders rapidly buy and sell stocks throughout the day in the hope that their stocks will continue climbing or falling in value for the seconds to minutes they own the stock, allowing them to lock in quick profits. Day trading is extremely risky and can result in substantial financial losses in a very short period of time." Do you believe the claims of easy profits?[41] Or do you think caution is in order? Read the SEC's day-trading tips at www.sec.gov/investor/pubs/daytips.htm and discuss your thoughts.

Briefings   MyBizLab Activities & Cases

Go to www.mybizlab.com for online activities and exercises related to the timely topics discussed in this chapter's Briefings, as well as additional theme-related Briefing *Spotlights* highlighting how these concepts apply in today's business environment.

| **In-chapter Briefing:**
• Should Tech Startups Raise Money through an IPO or Private Investors? | **Activity:**
• Going to the Net! – Apple Stock Shock: Steve Job's Departure | **Briefing Spotlight:**
• Virtual Annual Shareholder Meetings |

| **In-chapter Briefing:**
• A German Company Buys the New York Stock Exchange | **Activity:**
• Going to the Net! – Foreign Investments? U.S. Companies Invest Overseas for You | **Briefing Spotlight:**
• Global Exchange Traded Fund Just for Social Media |

In-chapter Briefing:
- Were Bond-Rating Agencies Honest When Rating Mortgage-Backed Securities?

Activity:
- Developing Marketable Business Skills – Robin Hood: Stealing from the Rich in Hollywood
- Ethical Dilemma Case – "Pump & Dump" Schemes: Fraudsters Create Online Stock Fraud

Briefing Spotlight:
- Stock Tipsters: Harmless or Harmful?

In-chapter Briefing:
- Do Males & Females Have Different Investment Styles?

Activity:
- Developing Marketable Business Skills – Change of a Lifetime
- Developing Marketable Business Skills – Diversification & Risk
- Going to the Net! – Think Crock Pot: "Set It & Forget It" Lifecycle Fund
- Going to the Net! – The Dow Jones as a Benchmark?
- Going to the Net! – Virtual Investing: Try before You Buy
- Going to the Net! – Recent & Filed Initial Public Offerings: LinkedIn & Groupon
- Going to the Net! – Steering Clear of Shady Investments
- Maximizing Your Net Worth – Creating an Investment Plan

Briefing Spotlight:
- Financial Smarts Decline with Age

Additional Briefing Spotlights available at MyBizLab:

- BUSINESS CULTURE & ETIQUETTE
- BUSINESS SKILLS & CAREER DEVELOPMENT
- CUSTOMER FOCUS
- EARNING GREEN BY GOING GREEN
- INFO TECH & SOCIAL MEDIA
- SOCIALLY RESPONSIBLE BUSINESS
- SMALL BUSINESS & ENTREPRENEURS

GLOSSARY

Terms and definitions printed in italic are considered business slang or jargon.

360-degree assessment Also called a *360-degree feedback appraisal,* employees are appraised not only by their managers but also by their coworkers, subordinates, and sometimes customers or clients.

401(k) plan For for-profit employers; is a program that allows an employee to contribute (up to a maximum amount) his or her pretax dollars into a savings plan, which is then allowed, through compounding, to grow in wealth tax free until the employee makes a withdrawal.

403(b) plan For nonprofit employers; is a program that allows an employee to contribute (up to a maximum amount) his or her pretax dollars into a savings plan, which is then allowed, through compounding, to grow in wealth tax free until the employee makes a withdrawal.

Above-board *Honest and open.*

Absolute advantage Exists when one country has a monopoly on producing a product or service more cheaply or efficiently than any other country can.

Accountability Managers must report and justify work results to managers above them.

Accounting The measuring, classifying, analyzing, and communicating of financial information to help people inside and outside a company make good financial decisions.

Accounting equation Assets = liabilities + owners' equity.

Accounting process Six activities that result in converting information about individual transactions into financial statements that can then be analyzed.

Accounts payable Money owed to others that the firm has not yet paid.

Accounts receivable The total amount owed to a firm from customers who have purchased goods or services on credit.

Accumulated depreciation The reduction in value of assets to reflect their wearing down or obsolescence over time.

Acquisition When one company buys another company.

Active Corps of Executives (ACE) Organization composed of executives who are still active in the business world but have volunteered their time and talents.

Activity ratios Also known as *efficiency ratios;* ratios are used to evaluate how well management uses a firm's assets to generate revenue.

Actual close When a salesperson concludes a sales presentation by asking the prospect to purchase the product.

Actuarial tables Calculations of the number of specific events that are predicted to occur in a future year.

Administrative law Also called *regulatory law,* consists of rules and regulations made by administrative agencies—boards, commissions, and agencies at all levels of government (federal, state, and local).

Advertising Paid nonpersonal communication by an identified sponsor (person or organization) using various media to inform an audience about a product.

Advertising media The variety of communication devices for carrying a seller's message to prospective buyers.

Advocacy advertising A type of institutional advertising that is concerned with supporting a particular opinion about an issue.

Affirmative action Policy that focuses on achieving equality of opportunity within an organization.

Agency shop Workplace in which workers must pay the equivalent of union dues, although they are not required to join the union.

Agents and brokers Specialists who bring buyers and sellers together and help negotiate a transaction.

American Federation of Labor (AFL) A federation of independent craft unions that banded together to pursue fundamental labor issues rather than a broad political agenda.

Analytic transformation The process in which resources are broken down to create finished products.

Angel investors Individuals who invest their own money in a private company, typically a startup.

Annual report Issued by a firm after the fiscal year end, this shows its financial condition and outlook for the future.

Annuity A contract in which an insurance company agrees to make regular payments to a person, either for a fixed period or until the person dies.

Antitrust law Consists of laws designed to keep markets competitive by deterring big businesses from driving out small competitors.

Antivirus software A utility program that scans all disks and memory to detect viruses.

App Short for *application,* an application software program, usually for a mobile device, such as a smartphone or tablet.

Appellate courts Courts that review cases appealed from lower courts, considering questions of law but not questions of fact.

Application software Software that has been developed to solve a particular problem for users—to perform useful work on specific tasks or to provide entertainment. Examples are Microsoft Word or Excel.

Apprenticeship A training program in which a new employee works with an experienced employee to master a particular craft.

Arbitration The process in which a neutral third party, an *arbitrator,* listens to both parties in a dispute and makes a decision that the parties have agreed will be binding on them. Arbitrators are often retired judges.

Articles of partnership A legal agreement that (a) defines the role of each partner in a business, (b) specifies how much money each is to invest, and (c) specifies the buy/sell arrangements if one or both partners dies or if one wants to get out of the arrangement.

Artificial intelligence (AI) Consists of a group of technologies used for developing machines to emulate human qualities, such as learning, reasoning, communicating, seeing, and hearing.

Asia-Pacific Economic Cooperation (APEC) A common market of 21 Pacific Rim countries whose purpose is to improve economic and political ties.

Assembly line A manufacturing approach that uses a factory assembly line consisting of a series of steps for assembling a product, each step using the same interchangeable parts and each being performed repetitively by the same worker.

Asset Anything of value that is owned by a firm.

At-will employment Also called *employment at will,* employment in which the employer is free to dismiss any employee for any reason at all—or no reason—and the employee is equally free to quit work.

Audit A formal evaluation of a client's financial records to determine their fairness and reliability.

Authority The rights inherent in a managerial position to make decisions, give orders, and utilize resources.

Authorization card A card signed by a worker that designates a certain union as the worker's bargaining agent.

Autocratic leaders Leaders who make decisions without consulting others.

Automation Using machines as much as possible rather than human labor to perform production tasks.

B corporation Short for *benefit corporation;* a corporation whose corporate charter legally requires that the company adhere to socially beneficial practices.

Back door *An unethical or dishonest action.*

Bait and switch *Advertising low-priced products that are actually not available.*

Balance of payments Determined by measuring (1) the difference between the money coming into a country (received as payments for its exports) and (2) the money going out of the country (as payments for its imports). In addition, the balance of payments takes into account (3) money flowing in and out from foreign aid, tourism, foreign investment, military investment, and other factors.

Balance of trade The value of a country's exports compared to the value of its imports as measured over a particular period of time.

Balance sheet Statement of a firm's financial condition at a given time by showing its assets, liabilities, and owners' equity.

Balance-of-payments deficit Also known as *unfavorable balance of payments,* exists when more money flows out of a country than flows in.

Balance-of-payments surplus Also known as favorable *balance of payments,* exists when more money flows into a country than flows out.

Ballpark estimate *An approximate number; a rough estimate.*

Bandwidth An expression of how much data—text, voice, video, and so on—can be sent through a transmission medium in a given amount of time.

Bang for the buck *The return on invested money.*

Bankruptcy The legal means of relief for debtors no longer able to meet their financial obligations.

Bargaining unit The particular union that will represent a certain group of employees.

Barter The trading of goods and/or services for other goods and/or services.

Base pay Consists of the basic wage or salary paid workers in exchange for doing their jobs.

Batting average *Indicates the percentage of time that someone or something is successful.*

Bear market *Circumstance in which the stock market or other forms of investment are declining in value and investors believe they will continue to do so.*

Benchmarking A process by which a company compares its performance with that of high-performing organizations.

Benefit segmentation Marketing concept that consists of categorizing people according to the benefits, or attributes, that people seek in a product.

Benefits Also called *fringe benefits* or *perquisites* ("perqs" or "perks"), nonwage or nonsalary forms of compensation paid for by an organization for its employees.

Best practices *Procedures or methods that have been shown to be the most effective.*

Bill of materials Essentially, a list of materials that go into the finished product.

Biometric authentication devices Devices that authenticate a person's identity by comparing his or her physical or behavioral characteristics with digital code stored in a computer system.

Blended value Idea that the outcome of all business investments should be measured in *both* economic and social realms.

Blue-chip stocks Preferred or common stocks of big, reputable companies, which also usually pay regular dividends.

Blue-skying *An exercise in which any possibility or strategy is put forth and considered.*

Bond rating Measures the quality and safety of a bond, indicating the likelihood that the debt issuer will be able to meet scheduled repayments, which dictates the interest rate paid.

Bonds Long-term IOUs issued by governments and corporations, contracts on which the issuer pays the buyer interest at regular intervals.

Bonds payable Long-term liabilities that represent money lent to the firm that must be paid off.

Bonuses Cash awards given to employees who achieve specific performance objectives.

Book value A company subtracts its liabilities from its assets, and the resulting figure, the shareholders' equity, is then divided by the number of shares available of the stock.

Bookkeeping Recording of a firm's financial transactions.

Bottom line *The last line in a financial statement that shows income or loss; the main or essential point.*

Boycott Also called a *primary boycott,* a labor tactic in which the union persuades its members and customers to refuse to buy a company's services or goods.

Brainstorming Process in which individuals or members of a group generate multiple ideas and alternatives for solving problems.

Brand A unique name, symbol, and/or design that identifies an organization and its product or services.

Brand advertising Also called *product advertising,* consists of presentations that promote specific brands to ultimate consumers.

Brand awareness Consumers recognize the product.

Brand equity A combination of factors that people associate with a certain brand name.

Brand insistence Consumers insist on the product; they will accept no substitutes.

Brand loyalty Commitment to a particular brand—the degree to which consumers are satisfied with a product and will buy it again.

Brand (or product) manager A manager in many firms who is responsible for the key elements of the marketing mix—product, price, place, and promotion—for one brand or one product line.

Brand marks Those parts of a brand that cannot be expressed verbally, such as graphics and symbols.

Brand names Those parts of a brand that can be expressed verbally, such as by words, letters, or numbers.

Brand preference Consumers habitually buy the product if it is easily available, but will try alternatives if they cannot find it.

Breach of contract When one party fails to follow the terms of a contract.

Break-even analysis A way of identifying how much revenue is needed to cover the total costs of developing and selling a product.

Break-even point The point at which sales revenues equal costs; that is, at which there is no profit but also no loss.

Bricks-to-clicks *The establishment of a website by a traditional company in order to remain competitive.*

Broadband Used to transmit high-speed data and high-quality audio and video.

Brokerage firms Otherwise known as *securities investment dealers,* companies that buy and sell stocks and bonds for individuals and now compete with banks by offering high-interest-rate checking and savings accounts.

Brokers Some of the people on the trading floor who for a commission will execute buy and sell orders for stock placed by other people and organizations.

Budget A detailed financial plan showing estimated revenues and expenses for a particular future period, usually one year.

Bull market *Circumstance in which the stock market or other forms of investment are increasing in value and investors think they will continue to grow.*

Bundling The practice of pricing two or more products together as a unit.

Business Any activity that seeks to make a profit by satisfying needs through selling goods or services to generate revenue.

Business cycle The periodic but irregular pattern of ups and downs in total economic production.

Business environment The arena of forces that encourage or discourage the development of business. These forces include economic, technological, competitive, global, and social.

Business intelligence (BI) system One of several software applications designed to analyze a firm's data and help it discover complex relationships and derive useful insights.

Business law The legal framework in which business is conducted.

Business market or **business-to-business (B2B) market** Also known as the *industrial* or *organizational market,* consists of those business individuals and organizations that want business goods and services that will help them produce or supply their own business goods and services.

Business model The need the firm will fill, the operations of the business, its components and functions, as well as its expected revenues and expenses.

Business owner's policy (BOP) Insurance that protects a business owner against various kinds of liability, as well as damage to business property.

Business plan A document that outlines a proposed firm's goals, the methods for achieving them, and the standards for measuring success.

Business-format franchise A chain store or franchise outlet that allows a franchisee to use the trade name and format of a franchisor, following guidelines with regard to marketing and pricing of the product.

Buyer's market A market in which there were more products available than there were buyers. This in turn led to the selling concept, which emphasized high-powered sales techniques to sell products.

Buzz marketing Using high-profile entertainment or news to get people to talk about a product.

C corporation A state-chartered entity that pays taxes and is legally distinct from its owners.

Callable bonds Bonds in which the issuer may call them in and pay them off at a prespecified price before the maturity date.

Call on the carpet *To discipline or reprimand for unacceptable actions or performance.*

Canned presentation A fixed, memorized selling approach to present the product.

Cannibalize a business *Loss of sales due to the introduction of a similar product or opening of a new outlet within the same company.*

Capital Includes the buildings, machines, tools, and technology used to produce goods and services.

Capital budgets Used to estimate a firm's expenditures for purchasing long-term assets that require significant sums of money.

Capital expenditures Major investments in tangible or intangible assets.

Capital gain The return made by selling a security for a price that is higher than the price the investor paid for it.

Capitalism The production and distribution of goods and services are controlled by private individuals rather than by the government.

Card check A process whereby a majority of workers sign what are known as "cards" in favor of establishing a union. However, the process does not involve the use of the National Labor Relations Board.

Cash budgets Used to forecast cash inflows and outflows for each month and for the entire year.

Cash flow forecast A prediction about how money will come into and go out of a firm in the near future, usually within the next 1 to 3 months.

Cash-and-carry wholesaler A limited-function wholesaler that sells mainly to small retailers, who come to the wholesaler, pay cash for a product, and carry it out ("cash and carry").

Catalog marketing Also known as *mail-order marketing*, consists of mailing customers catalogs, from which they may choose merchandise to be ordered via mail, telephone, or online.

Cause-related marketing Also called *cause marketing;* a commercial activity in which a business forms a partnership with a charity or nonprofit to support a worthy cause, product, or service.

Center stage *A position of great prominence or importance.*

Centralized authority When important decisions are made by higher-level executives.

Certificate of deposit (CD) A savings (time deposit) account that pays interest upon the certificate's maturity date.

Certification Officially recognized by the National Labor Relations Board as the authorized bargaining agent for a group of employees.

Certified internal auditors They hold a bachelor's degree, have had two years of internal auditing experience, and have passed an examination given by the Institute of Internal Auditors.

Certified management accountants A certified management accountant has passed a two-day examination, held by the

Institute of Management Accountants, that tests their knowledge of managerial accounting and business.

Certified public accountants (CPAs) CPAs have met certain requirements for education and experience and have passed a series of examinations established by the American Institute of Certified Public Accountants.

Change agent *A clever title for a consultant (or employee) who sees himself as a catalyst for improvement. Often involves encouraging the adoption of new technologies.*

Chapter 7 bankruptcy Forces debtors to turn over their assets to a court-appointed trustee, who divides them among the creditors.

Chapter 11 bankruptcy A process that allows companies to reorganize and continue functioning while paying creditors a significant portion of their debts.

Chapter 13 bankruptcy Allows individuals and small businesses with unsecured debts of less than $336,900 and secured debts of less than $1,010,650 to repay their creditors under a court-approved plan.

Civil cases Concerned with duties and responsibilities between individuals or between citizens and their governments.

Claim A notice by the insured to the insurer that payment is expected to cover the loss.

Classic entrepreneur An individual who sees a new opportunity for a product or service and starts a firm that can lead to a high-growth business.

Clayton Act (1914) Intended to prohibit exclusive dealing, tying contracts, and interlocking directorates.

Client/server network Consists of *clients,* which are devices (often microcomputers) that request data and services, and a *server,* which is a centralized computer—often a powerful microcomputer, but it could be a mainframe—used to supply data and services.

Climbing the corporate ladder *To move up in the hierarchy of a business/corporation.*

Closed shop An employer may hire only workers for a job who are already in the union.

Closed shop agreement A company agrees that it will hire only current union members for a given job.

Cloud computing This basically means any computer or mobile device with Web access can obtain computing resources—processing, storage, messaging, databases, and so on—from data centers around the world.

Co-branding Two noncompeting products link their brand names together for a single product.

Code of ethics A formal written set of ethical standards guiding an organization's actions.

Cold call sales prospecting technique Consists of calling on prospects with whom one has had no previous contact and to whom one does not have not any kind of introduction.

Collateral The asset that is pledged to secure a loan, and it can be seized by the lender if the borrower does not repay the loan.

Collective bargaining Negotiations between management and employees about disputes over compensation, benefits, working conditions, and job security.

Command economies Also known as *central-planning economies,* these are economic systems such as communism and socialism in which the government owns most businesses and regulates the amounts, types, and prices of goods and services.

Commercial bank A Federal- or state-chartered profit-seeking financial institution that accepts deposits from individuals and businesses and uses part of them to make personal, residential, and business loans.

Commercial finance companies Organizations willing to make short-term loans whose borrowers can offer collateral.

Commercial paper Consists of unsecured, short-term promissory notes over $100,000 issued by large corporations.

Commercialization The full-scale production and marketing of a new product.

Commodities trading Trading in raw materials and agricultural products used to produce other goods.

Commodity exchange A security exchange in which futures contracts are bought and sold.

Common law Also called *unwritten law* or *case law,* consists of laws made by judges ruling on cases brought before their courts.

Common market Also known as an *economic community* or a *trading bloc,* a group of nations within a geographical region that have agreed to remove trade barriers with each other.

Common stock Stockholders are able to vote on major company decisions, but they get (1) last claim on the company's dividends and (2) last claim on any remaining assets if the company goes out of business and its assets are sold.

Communications technology Electromagnetic devices and systems for communicating over distances.

Communism An economic system in which all property is owned by the government and everyone works for the government.

Comparative advantage A country sells to other countries those products and services it produces most cheaply or efficiently and buys from other countries those it does not produce most cheaply or efficiently.

Compensation There are three parts: (1) base pay, (2) benefits, and (3) incentives.

Competitive advantage The ability of an organization to produce goods or services more effectively than its competitors.

Competitive advertising Also called *comparative advertising,* this promotes a product by comparing it more favorably to rival products.

Competitive pricing Price is determined in relation to rivals, factoring in other considerations such as market dominance, number of competitors, and customer loyalty.

Competitors People or organizations that compete for customers or resources.

Compliance-based ethics codes Codes that attempt to prevent criminal misconduct by increasing control and by punishing violators.

Compressed workweek This is when employees perform a full-time job in less than five days of standard eight- (or nine-) hour shifts.

Computer A programmable, multiuse machine that accepts data—raw facts and figures—and processes it into information that can be used.

Computer-aided design (CAD) Programs used to design products, structures, civil engineering drawings, and maps.

Computer-aided manufacturing (CAM) Use of computers to manufacture products.

Computer-integrated manufacturing (CIM) Systems in which computer-aided design is united with computer-aided manufacturing.

Concept testing Marketing research designed to solicit initial consumer reaction to new product ideas.

Conceptual skills The ability to think analytically, to visualize an organization as a whole, and understand how the parts work together.

Conglomerate A large company that is doing business in different, quite unrelated areas.

Conglomerate merger Two companies merge that are in different industries and each performs different activities.

Conglomerate structure Divisions are grouped around similar businesses or industries.

Congress of Industrial Organizations (CIO) A union of both skilled and unskilled workers organized by industry.

Consideration A promise to do a desired act or refrain from doing an act one is legally entitled to do in return for something of value, such as money.

Consumer buying behavior The behavior shown by consumers in considering and buying various products.

Consumer Finances Protection Bureau (CFPB) An independent agency housed in the Federal Reserve with its own budget and director and the authority to prevent or correct financial abuses.

Consumer market Consists of all those individuals or households that want goods or services for their personal use.

Consumer price index (CPI) Consists of monthly statistics of about 400 representative consumer goods and services that measure the rate of inflation or deflation.

Consumer sovereignty The idea that consumers influence the marketplace through the decisions of which products they choose to buy or not to buy.

Consumer-protection law A law concerned with protecting the rights of buyers in relation to sellers.

Containerization Products are packed into 20- or 40-foot-long (by about 8-foot square) containers at the point of origin and retrieved from the containers at the point of destination.

Contingency planning The creation of alternative hypothetical courses of action that a company can use if its original plans do not prove workable.

Contingent workers Temporary workers or employees who are hired for a short time to supplement a company's permanent workforce.

Continuity Timing of ads, how often they appear, or how heavily they are concentrated within a time period.

Continuous innovation Represents modest improvements to an existing product in order to distinguish it from competitors; such improvements require little consumer behavior change.

Continuous process A production process in which goods or services are turned out in a long production run on an ongoing basis over time.

Contract A legally enforceable agreement between two or more parties about a specific matter. It follows, then, that *contract law* is concerned with what constitutes a legally enforceable agreement.

Control process Steps that include (1) establishing standards; (2) monitoring performance; (3) comparing performance against standards; and (4) taking corrective action, if needed.

Control standard The desired performance level for a given goal.

Controlling Monitoring performance, comparing it with goals, and taking corrective action as needed.

Convenience goods and services Those inexpensive products that people buy frequently and with little effort.

Convertible bonds Bonds that can be converted into the issuing corporation's common stock.

Cookies Little text files—such as one's log-in name, password, and preferences—left on one's hard disk by some websites visited. The websites retrieve the data when visited again.

Cooking the books *A fraudulent attempt to falsify company records.*

Cooling-off period For certain critical industries, such as transportation, the President of the United States can order striking workers to return to work while the union and management continue negotiations.

Cooperative Also called a *co-op*, a corporation owned by its user members who have pooled their resources for their mutual benefit.

Copayments or **copays** Fixed fees that subscribers must pay for the use of specific medical services.

Copyright A document that protects ownership rights for the creators of literary, musical, dramatic, artistic, scientific, and similar works.

Corporate bonds Bonds issued by businesses as a source of long-term funding, they consist of secured and unsecured bonds.

Corporate policy Policy that describes the positions a company takes on political and social issues.

Corporate social responsibility (CSR) Also called *corporate citizenship;* a concern for taking actions that will benefit the interests of society as well as of the organization.

Cost of capital The rate of return a firm must earn to meet the lenders' and shareholders' expectations.

Cost of goods sold The cost of producing a firm's merchandise for sale during a certain period.

Cost per thousand (CPM) This is the cost a particular medium charges to reach 1,000 people with an ad.

Cost pricing The cost of producing or buying the product—plus making a profit—that is the primary basis for setting price.

Cost-of-living adjustment (COLA) clause During the period of the contract, a clause that ties future wage increases to increases in the cost of living.

Countertrading Bartering goods for goods (or services).

Cowboy *A worker who is difficult to supervise.*

Craft union A union representing skilled workers with a common trade or craft.

Creative selling The selling process in which salespeople determine customer needs, then explain their product's benefits to try to persuade buyers to buy the product.

Credit score The measure of a person's credit risk, which is calculated from a person's credit reports using a standardized formula.

Credit unions Depositor-owned, nonprofit financial cooperatives that offer a range of banking services to their members.

Criminal cases Cases concerned with breaking laws of regulating behavior.

Cross-functional self-managed teams Groups of workers with different skills who are given the authority to manage themselves.

Culture The shared set of beliefs, values, knowledge, and patterns of behavior common to a group of people; can be very powerful.

Culture shock The feelings of discomfort and disorientation associated with being in an unfamiliar culture.

Currency Government-issued coins and paper money.

Currency exchange rate The rate at which one country's currency can be exchanged for the currencies of other countries.

Current assets Items that can be converted into cash within one year.

Current liabilities Obligations in which payments are due within one year or less.

Customer divisions Activities are grouped around common customers or clients.

Customer relationship management (CRM) This emphasizes finding out everything possible about customers and then using that information to satisfy and even exceed their expectations in order to build customer loyalty over the long term.

Customer satisfaction The concept of offering a product to please buyers by meeting their expectations.

Customer-based segmentation Consists of categorizing business customers according to such characteristics as size, industry type, and product/service-related attributes.

Customers Those who pay to use an organization's goods or services.

Damages The monetary settlement a court awards to a party injured by a breach of contract.

Dashboard Like the instrument panel in a car, a key indicator of business statistics that organizes and presents information in a way that is easy to read.

Data Consists of the raw facts and figures that are processed into information.

Data analysis Data subjected to statistical tools to determine its significance.

Data mining The computer-assisted process of sifting through and analyzing vast amounts of data in order to extract hidden patterns and meaning and to discover new knowledge.

Data warehouse A central repository for the data that an enterprise's various business systems collect.

Databases Integrated collections of data stored in computer systems.

Debenture bonds Bonds for which no assets are pledged as collateral; they are backed only by the issuing company's reputation.

Debit card Allows one to transfer money between accounts.

Debt to owners' equity ratios Measures of the extent to which a company uses debt, such as bank loans, to finance its operations.

Decentralized authority A type of authority in which decisions are made by middle-level and supervisory-level managers.

Decertification Workers can vote to take away the union's right to represent them.

Decision A choice made from among available alternatives.

Decision making The process of identifying and choosing alternative courses of action.

Decision support systems (DSSs) Computer-based information systems that provide relevant information to help managers make decisions.

Decline stage The period in the product life cycle in which the product falls out of favor, and the organization withdraws from the marketplace.

Deductible The specified amount that a policyholder must pay toward a loss before the insurer will pay anything.

Deep dive *To explore an issue or subject in-depth.*

Deficits In an economy, when spending exceeds income.

Deflation When prices fall; a general decline in the prices of most goods and services.

Delegation The process of assigning managerial authority and responsibility to managers and employees lower in the hierarchy.

Demand The quantity of products that people are willing and able to buy at various prices at a given time.

Demand deposit A commercial bank's or other financial institution's checking account, from which one may make withdrawals at any time.

Democratic political systems Rely on free elections and representative assemblies.

Demographic segmentation Consists of categorizing consumers according to statistical characteristics of a population,
such as gender, age, income, education, social class, ethnicity, and so on.

Demographics The measurable characteristics of a population.

Denial-of-service (DoS) attack Consists of making repeated requests of a computer system or network, thereby overloading it and denying legitimate users access to it.

Departmentalization The dividing up of an organization into smaller units, or departments, to facilitate management.

Deposit institutions Financial institutions that accept deposits that can be withdrawn on demand and that offer loans and mortgages.

Depression A particularly severe and long-lasting recession, accompanied by falling prices (deflation).

Deregulation The scaling back, or relaxation in enforcement, of laws and administrative rules that seemed to restrain competition.

Derivative A financial contract that "derives" its value from a wide range of sources, including stocks, loans, and market indexes. Investors pay a set price in return for possible profits later.

Devaluation A nation's currency is lowered relative to other countries' currencies.

Developed countries First-world countries with a high level of economic development and generally high average level of income among their citizens.

Direct channel A distribution channel in which a producer sells directly to consumers.

Direct mail marketing Consists of mail promotions—letters, brochures, and pamphlets sent through the postal service to customers.

Direct marketing This is not done face to face but consists of selling directly to customers using mail or telephone.

Direct selling Consists of face-to-face selling directly to customers in their homes or where they work.

Direct-action advertising Attempts to stimulate an immediate, or relatively immediate, purchase of a product through such devices as one-day sales, one-time promotions, or announcements of a special event.

Disability insurance Designed to replace half or two thirds of a worker's lost income when he or she cannot work due to illness or accident.

Disaster-recovery plan A method of restoring information-processing operations that have been halted by destruction or accident.

Discontinuous innovation The product is totally new, radically changing how people live.

Discount brokers Execute the buy and sell orders indicated by clients—who are generally online investors doing their own research—but do not offer advice and tax planning.

Discount rate The interest rate at which the Federal Reserve makes short-term loans to member banks.

Discounting Also called *high-low pricing*, assigning regular prices to products but then resorting to frequent price-cutting strategies, such as special sales, to undercut the prices of competitors.

Discouraged workers Workers not counted in unemployment statistics; they include those who have given up looking for work and have simply dropped out of the labor force.

Discretionary order An order in which the customer trusts the broker's professional experience and judgment and leaves it to him or her to decide the right time and price for buying or selling a security.

Discrimination Occurs when people are hired or promoted— or denied hiring or promotion—for reasons not relevant to the job.

Disinflation When price increases are slowing.

Distribution The process of moving goods or services from the seller to prospective buyers.

Distribution centers Provide storage of products for the short periods of time for collection and distribution elsewhere.

Distribution channel Also known as a *marketing channel*, a system for conveying goods or services from producers to customers.

Distribution mix The combination of distribution channels a company uses to get its products to customers.

Distribution strategy The overall plan for moving products from producer to customers.

Distributor A person or an organization, such as a dealer or retailer, that helps sell goods and services to customers.

Diversification Choosing securities in such a way that a loss in one investment will not have a devastating impact on one's total portfolio.

Dividends Part of a company's profits that are distributed to stockholders.

Division of labor or **work specialization** When different parts of a task are done by different people.

Divisional structure Employees are grouped by purpose: customer groups, geographic regions, work processes, products, or industries.

Dodd-Frank Wall Street Reform and Consumer Protection Act Legislation that affects all federal financial regulatory agencies and the entire American financial services industry.

Double-entry bookkeeping In accounting, the format for recording each journal entry; each transaction is recorded in two different accounts to act as a check on errors.

Dow Jones Industrial Average (DJIA) Also known as *"the Dow,"* a general measure of the movement of U.S. stock prices, and an index of the average of prices of the stocks of 30 large corporations.

Drill down *To dig deeper or get into the finer and more minute details of a situation or scenario.*

Drop shipper A limited-function wholesaler who owns (has title to) the products, but not physical custody of them; rather, the drop shipper takes orders and has the producer ship the product directly to the customer.

Dumping The practice of a foreign company exporting products abroad at a lower price than the price in the home market—or even below the costs of production—in order to drive down the price of the domestic product.

Dynamically continuous innovation Represents marked changes to an existing product that require a moderate amount of consumer learning or behavior change.

E-business Using the Internet to facilitate every aspect of running a business.

E-cash Also called *electronic cash;* money held, exchanged, and represented in electronic form and transacted over the Internet.

E-commerce, or electronic commerce The buying and selling of products and services through computer networks.

Economic bubbles Situations in which prices for securities, especially stocks, rose far above their actual value.

Economic stability When (1) there are enough desirable goods and services to satisfy consumers' demands, and (2) consumers have enough money, in total, to buy what they need and want.

Economically feasible premium A premium that must be priced low enough to be affordable to the insured, but substantially less than the face value of the policy.

Economics The production, distribution, and consumption of scarce goods and services, which includes the forces of supply and demand.

Economies of scale Refers to the savings realized from buying materials or manufacturing products in large quantities.

Editing Checking over to eliminate mistakes.

Electronic communications networks (ECNs) Buyers and sellers are linked electronically, in a telecommunications network, so that securities trading is done electronically rather than face to face.

Electronic funds transfer systems (EFTSs) Computerized systems that move funds from one institution to another over electronic links.

Embargo A complete ban on the import or export of certain products.

Employee benefits The benefits that employers extend to their workers in addition to their regular compensation.

Employee buyout Practice in which a firm's employees borrow money against their own assets, such as their houses or their pension funds, to purchase the firm from its present owners; the employees then become the new owners of the firm.

Employment tests Consist of any procedure used in the employment selection decision process.

Empowerment Giving employees the authority and responsibility to make decisions to allow them more involvement in their jobs.

Encryption The process of altering readable data into unreadable form to prevent unauthorized access.

Endless-chain sales prospecting technique Consists of asking each sales prospect to provide the salesperson with some names of other prospects who might be interested in the product.

Enterprise An endeavor in which the primary motive is to make a profit.

Enterprise resource planning (ERP) A computer-based system that collects and provides information about a company's entire enterprise, including identifying customer needs, receipt of orders, distribution of finished goods, and receipt of payment.

Enterprise zone A specific geographic area in which government tries to attract business investment by offering lower taxes and other government support.

Entrepreneur A person who sees a new opportunity for a product or service and risks his or her time and money to start a business to make a profit.

Entrepreneurial team A group of people with different kinds of expertise who form a team to create a new product.

Entrepreneurship The process of taking risks to try to create a new business.

Environmental scanning A look at the wider world around them (by marketing managers), to identify what matters can affect the marketing program.

Equal Employment Opportunity Commission (EEOC) A governmental organization that enforces anti-discrimination and other employment-related laws.

Equity theory This theory focuses on employee perceptions as to how fairly they think they are being treated compared to others.

ETA *Acronym for "estimated time of arrival." In business, it typically refers to the estimated time to completion of a task.*

Ethical dilemma A situation in which people have to decide whether to pursue a course of action that may benefit them or their organization but that is unethical or even illegal.

Ethics The standards of right and wrong that influence behavior.

Ethics officer Employee whose job is to integrate the organization's ethics and values initiatives, compliance activities, and business conduct practices into the company's decision-making processes.

European Union (EU) Consists of 27 trading partners in Europe, covering nearly half a billion consumers.

Event marketing Attempts to direct audience attention to particular athletic, charitable, or cultural events.

Everyday low pricing (EDLP) This is a strategy of continuously setting prices lower than those of competitors and then not doing any other price-cutting tactics such as special sales, rebates, and cents-off coupons.

Exchange-traded fund (ETF) Like a mutual fund, a collection of stocks that is traded on an exchange; however, unlike a mutual fund, it can be traded throughout the trading day.

Exclusive distribution When a product is distributed in only a few locations, as was once the case for Gucci and Prada and is still for luxury cars.

Executive support system (ESS) An easy-to-use decision support system made especially for top managers; it specifically supports strategic decision making.

Expectancy theory This theory suggests that people are motivated by two things: (1) how much they want something, and (2) how likely they think they are to get it.

Expert system A set of interactive computer programs that helps users solve problems that would otherwise require the assistance of a human expert.

Export Assistance Centers Offices located in major metropolitan areas throughout the United States that provide export assistance for small- and medium-sized businesses seeking to market their products to foreign countries.

Exporting When a company produces goods domestically and sells them outside the country.

Export-management companies Also known as *export-trading companies,* consist of international specialists who can help first-time exporters find foreign buyers, complete transaction documents, comply with regulations, and above all get paid.

Express warranty A guarantee of the specific terms stated by the seller.

Expropriation A government's seizure of a domestic or foreign company's assets.

External auditors Public accountants who audit, or review, clients' financial information to see whether it was prepared under generally accepted accounting principles and fairly represent the financial position of the firm.

External expansion When a company merges with or buys another company or companies.

External marketing environment The outside forces that can influence the success of marketing programs.

External recruiting This is what companies do in trying to attract job applicants from outside the organization.

Extranet A private intranet that connects not only internal personnel but also selected suppliers and other strategic parties.

Extrinsic reward The payoff, such as money, a person receives from others for performing a particular task.

Face time *The opportunity to sit down to discuss an issue in person.*

Facility layout The physical arrangement of equipment, offices, rooms, people, and other resources within an organization for producing goods or services.

Facility location Involves the process of selecting a location for company operations.

Factoring accounts receivable When a firm sells its accounts receivable at a discount to a financial institution.

Factors of production Resources to create wealth—natural resources, capital, human resources, and entrepreneurship.

Fair Labor Standards Act Legislation that established the minimum wage and maximum hours for workers in industries engaged in interstate commerce, as well as rules for overtime pay; it also outlawed child labor.

Family brands Where the same brand name is given to all or most of a company's products.

Fear-appeal advertising This type of advertising attempts to stimulate the purchase of a product by motivating consumers through fear of loss or harm.

Featherbedding When workers were paid for unneeded work or for jobs they did not do.

Federal budget deficit, or national debt The amount of money the government owes because federal spending exceeds federal revenue.

Federal Deposit Insurance Corporation (FDIC) An independent agency of the U.S. government that insures bank deposits.

Federal Reserve System Also called *the Fed,* the central bank of the United States, which controls the U.S. money supply.

Federal Trade Commission Act (1914) Legislation that established the Federal Trade Commission, which has the power to define unfair competition and to issue cease and desist orders.

Feeding the gorilla *Making sure the core part of a business is satisfied while one does more important or interesting things.*

Fee-for-service medical plans Allows insured people to choose their physician or hospital, which performs treatment, then presents the person or the insurer with a bill.

Finance Also called *corporate finance,* the business function of obtaining funds for a company and managing them to accomplish the company's objectives.

Finance companies Nondeposit companies that make short-term loans at higher interest rates to individuals or businesses that do not meet the credit requirements of regular banks.

Financial accounting Preparing accounting information and analyses primarily for people outside the organization.

Financial Accounting Standards Board (FASB) A private, self-regulating organization that establishes, evaluates, and enforces the principles used in financial accounting.

Financial budgets Also called *capital budgets* and *cash budgets,* they concentrate on the company's financial goals and the resources needed to achieve them.

Financial control When a company from time to time compares its actual revenues and expenses with those predicted in its budget.

Financial leverage Also simply called *leverage,* the technique of using borrowed funds to increase a firm's rate of return.

Financial management The job of acquiring and managing funds.

Financial managers The people responsible for planning and controlling the acquisition and uses of funds.

Financial plan A firm's strategy for reaching its financial goals. It has three parts: (1) forecasting, (2) budgeting, and (3) financial controls.

Financial planner Someone who would help a person set and reach long-term financial goals, giving advice on investments, diversification, asset allocation, risk management, tax planning, and retirement plans.

Financial statement A summary of all transactions occurring during a particular time period. There are three types of financial statements: (1) *balance sheets*, (2) *income statements,* and (3) *statements of cash flows.*

Firewall A system of hardware and/or software that protects a computer or a network from intruders.

Fiscal policy Represents the U.S. government's attempts to keep the economy stable (1) by raising or lowering taxes or (2) through government borrowing.

Fiscal year The 12-month period designated for annual financial reporting purposes.

Fish or **cut bait** *To be forced to make a decision.*

Fishing expedition *A fact-finding mission.*

Fixed assets Items that are held for a long time and are relatively permanent.

Fixed costs or **total fixed costs** Expenses that do not change regardless of how many products are made or sold.

Fixed-position layout Materials, equipment, and labor are transported to one location.

Flavor of the month *The most recent fad to hit corporate America.*

Flexible manufacturing system (FMS) A facility that can be modified quickly to manufacture different products.

Flextime Also called *flexible time*, consists of flexible working hours, or any schedule that gives one some choices in working hours.

Floating exchange rate system The value of all currencies is determined by supply and demand.

Focus groups Small groups of people who meet with a discussion leader and give their opinions about a product or other matters.

Food chain *An organization's hierarchy.*

For-profit organization A business—an organization formed to make money, or profits, by selling goods or services.

Forced ranking performance review systems Systems in which all employees within a business unit are ranked against one another, and grades are distributed along some sort of bell curve. Top-grade earners are then rewarded with bonuses and promotions, and low-grade earners are warned or dismissed.

Forecasting Predicting revenues, costs, and expenses for a certain period of time.

Foreclosures Banks repossessing and selling homes on which the borrowers could not meet their loan payment obligations.

Foreign licensing A company allows a foreign company to pay it a fee to make or distribute the first company's product or service.

Foreign subsidiary A company in a foreign country that is totally owned and controlled by the parent company.

Forensic accountants They investigate suspected crimes within the field of finance.

Form utility The value that people add in converting resources—natural resources, capital, human resources, entrepreneurship, and knowledge—into finished products.

Formal appraisals Conducted at specific times throughout the year and are based on performance measures that have been established in advance.

Franchise An arrangement in which a business owner allows others the right to use its name and sell its goods or services within a specific geographical area.

Franchisee The buyer of a franchise.

Franchising A company allows another company or individual to pay it a fee and a share of the profit in return for using the first company's brand name and a package of materials and services.

Franchisor A business owner that gives others the rights to sell its products or services.

Free lunch *Something for nothing.*

Free trade The movement of goods and services among nations without political or economic restrictions.

Free-market economy Also commonly called *capitalism.*

Free-rein leaders Also known as *laissez-faire leaders,* leaders who set objectives and employees are relatively free to choose how to achieve them.

Freight forwarder An organization that bundles many small shipments together into a single large shipment for more cost-effective transportation.

Frequency The average number of times each member of the audience is exposed to an ad.

Fringe benefits Examples include vacation pay, sick leave, health benefits, and pension plans, which provide benefits beyond base wages.

From scratch *Creating something from the outset or beginning.*

Full-court press *A term (borrowed from basketball) that is used to describe a maximum effort.*

Full-service merchant wholesaler An independently owned firm that takes title to—that is, becomes owner of—the manufacturer's products and that performs all sales and distribution, as well as provides credit and other services.

Full-service, or **traditional, brokers** Offer, generally through the client's own personal broker, a wide range of investment-related services, not only execution of trades but also investment research, advice, and tax planning.

Functional division People with similar occupational specialties are put together in formal groups.

Futures contract Making an agreement with a seller or broker to buy a specific amount of a commodity at a certain price on a certain date.

Gainsharing The distribution of savings or "gains" to groups of employees that reduced costs and increased measurable productivity.

Gantt chart A kind of time schedule—a specialized bar chart that shows the relationship between the kind of work tasks planned and their scheduled completion data.

Gatekeeper *A person within an organization who controls the flow of information to and from managers.*

General Agreement on Tariffs and Trade (GATT) An international accord first signed by 23 nations in 1947, which helped to reduce worldwide tariffs and other barriers.

General partnership When two or more partners are responsible for the business and share profits, liabilities, and management responsibilities.

Generally accepted accounting principles (GAAP) A set of accounting standards used in the preparation of summaries of financial statements to ensure that they are (1) relevant, (2) reliable, (3) consistent, and (4) comparable.

Generic product A nonbranded product.

Geographic divisions Activities are grouped around defined regional locations.

Geographic segmentation Categorizes customers according to geographic location.

Get the axe *To be fired.*

Givebacks When a union agrees to give up previous wage or benefit gains in return for something else.

Glass ceiling *The invisible barrier to career progression that primarily refers to and affects minorities and women.*

Global climate change An increase in the average temperature of the earth's atmosphere.

Global Compact A voluntary agreement established in 2000 by the United Nations that promotes human rights, good labor practices, environmental protection, and anticorruption standards for businesses.

Global corporate social responsibility pyramid Suggests the obligations of an organization in the global economy are to be a good global corporate citizen, to be ethical, to obey the law, and to be profitable.

Global economy The increasing interaction of the world's economies with one another as a single market instead of in many national markets.

Global outsourcing Sometimes called *offshoring,* using suppliers outside the United States to provide labor, goods, or services.

Global warming Also known as global *climate change,* an increase in the average temperature of the earth's atmosphere.

Globalization The increasing connectivity and interdependence of the world's economies, societies, and cultures because of advances in communication, technology, trade, international investment, movement of currency, and migration.

Goal A broad, long-range target that an organization wishes to attain.

Goal-setting theory Suggests that employees can be motivated by goals that are specific and challenging but achievable.

Go for the gold *To attempt to achieve the maximum result or reward (an allusion to the gold in sports).*

Going off the deep end *In business, doing something involving very high risk, or out of desperation.*

"Going public" The term means that a privately owned company becomes a publicly owned company by issuing stock for sale to the public.

Golden parachute An employment agreement that guarantees a key executive lucrative severance benefits if control of the company changes hands followed by management shifts.

Goods Tangible products.

Goodwill An amount paid for a business beyond the value of its other assets.

Government Accountability Office (GAO) The investigative arm of Congress charged with examining matters relating to the receipt and payment of public funds.

Government bonds Bonds sold by the U.S. Treasury; they consist of treasury notes and treasury bonds.

Governmental regulators Government agencies that establish rules and regulations under which organizations may operate.

Green businesses Those that adapt practices for the use of renewable resources and otherwise operate in ways that solve, rather than cause, both environmental and social problems.

Grievance A complaint by an employee that management has violated the terms of the labor-management agreement.

Gross domestic product (GDP) The total value of all the goods and services that a country produces within its borders in one year.

Gross profit Also called *gross margin,* the amount remaining after the cost of goods sold is subtracted from the net sales.

Growth stage The period in which customer demand increases, the product's sales grow, and later competitors may enter the market.

Growth stocks Stocks issued by small, innovative new companies in hot industries.

Guerrilla marketing Consists of innovative, low-cost marketing schemes that try to get customers' attention in unusual ways.

Hackers (1) Computer enthusiasts, people who enjoy learning programming languages and computer systems, but also (2) people who gain unauthorized access to computers or networks, sometimes just for the challenge of it but also for malicious purposes.

Hard copy *A printout of data stored in a computer.*

Hardware Consists of all the machinery and equipment in a computer system. In a desktop or laptop computer, the hardware consists of the processing device itself (the microprocessor or chip), the screen, keyboard, hard drive (storage), printer, and any communications device.

Hawthorne effect The name given to a Harvard research group's conclusion that employees worked harder if they received added attention, if they thought managers cared about their welfare and that supervisors paid special attention to them.

Heads-up *Refers to a request for a report/update as in "Give me a heads-up on this."*

Health insurance Insurance that provides coverage for medical expenses due to sickness or injuries, as well as health maintenance and tests.

Health maintenance organization (HMO) In return for a fixed monthly fee, patients are allowed to choose from a restricted list of salaried doctors and other health professionals.

Health savings accounts (HSAs) Accounts created for individuals covered under high-deductible health plans to encourage them to set aside money for their medical expenses.

Heavy lifting *The hard work.*

Hero A person whose accomplishments embody the values of the organization.

Hierarchy of authority, or **chain of command** An arrangement for making sure that work specialization actually happens—that the right people do the right things at the right time.

Hiring hall A union-operated placement office where jobs are assigned according to seniority, rotation, or other set formula.

Home office policy (HOP) A combination of homeowner's policy and business insurance that eliminates duplicate coverage or gaps.

Homeowner's insurance Insurance that will cover the loss of not only any contents in the event of fire or theft but also the structure itself.

Horizontal merger Two companies merge that are in the same industry and perform the same activity.

Hostile takeovers Situations in which an outsider—often called a "corporate raider"—buys enough shares in a company to be able to take control of it against the will of the corporation's top management and directors.

Human capital The economic or productive potential of employee knowledge, experience, and actions.

Human relations movement Proposed that better human relations could increase worker productivity.

Human resource (HR) management This consists of the activities managers perform to plan for, attract, develop, and retain an effective workforce.

Human resources Consists of labor, the physical and intellectual contributions of a company's employees.

Human skills The ability to work well in cooperation with other people to get things done.

Hybrid structure A situation in which an organization uses functional and divisional structures in different parts of the same organization.

Hygiene factors Factors associated with job *dissatisfaction*—such as salary, working conditions, interpersonal relationships, and company policy—all of which affect the job environment in which people work.

Idea generation The generation of new product ideas, ideally by collecting ideas from as many sources as possible.

Identity theft A crime in which thieves hijack a person's name and identity and use that person's good credit rating to get cash or buy things.

If it isn't broken, don't fix it *If a system or method works well, there is no reason to change it.*

Implied warranties Warranties dictated by law that are based on two premises: (a) the product or service should deliver the promises advertised, and (b) it should serve the purpose for which it was created and sold.

Import quota A trade barrier in the form of a limit on the numbers of a product that can be imported. Its intent is to protect domestic industry by restricting the availability of foreign products.

Importing When a company buys goods outside the country and resells them domestically.

Incentives Commissions, bonuses, profit-sharing plans, and stock options to induce employees to be more productive or to attract and retain top performers.

Income statement Once known as the *profit-and-loss statement,* shows a firm's revenues and expenses for a particular time period and the resulting profit or loss.

Incubator A facility that offers small businesses low-cost offices with basic services.

Indenture terms The terms of the lending agreement.

Independent audits Done by firms that are independent of the company being audited and therefore are presumed to provide outsiders with unbiased opinion about the truth of the financial data being reviewed.

Individual brands When different brand names are given to different company products.

Industrial goods Also known as *business goods,* products used to produce other products.

Industrial unions Unions that organize workers not by skill but by industry.

Inflation When prices rise, a general increase in the prices of most goods and services.

Infomercials Extended TV commercials ranging from 2 (short form) to 28.5 (long form) minutes that are devoted exclusively to promoting a product in considerable detail.

Informal appraisals Conducted on an unscheduled basis and consist of less rigorous indications of employee performance.

Information Data that has been summarized or otherwise manipulated for use in decision making.

Information technology (IT) Technology that helps to produce, manipulate, store, communicate, and disseminate information.

Informational advertising Provides consumers with straightforward knowledge about the features of the product offered.

Infrastructure The physical facilities that form the basis for its level of economic development.

Initial public offering (IPO) When a corporation's stock is offered for sale for the first time.

Injunction A court order requiring someone to do or stop something.

Innovation A product that customers perceive as being newer or better than existing products.

Input Hardware that consists of devices that translate data into a form the computer can process.

Insider trading The illegal use of private company information to further one's own fortunes or those of family or friends.

Insourcing *The practice of looking within one's company for someone with required skills.*

Institutional advertising This consists of presentations that promote a favorable image for an organization.

Institutional investors Large and powerful organizations such as pension funds and insurance companies, which invest their own or others' funds.

Insurable interest The policyholder must demonstrate that he or she stands to suffer a loss from the specific risk that is being insured.

Insurable risk A pure risk that meets an insurer's requirements for coverage.

Insurance companies Nondeposit companies that accept payments (called *premiums)* from policyholders—individuals or firms that have purchased insurance policies that guarantee financial protection in the event something goes wrong.

Insurance policies Written contracts between insurer and insured that, in return for regular payments, promises to pay for all or part of a loss.

Intangible assets These are assets that are not physical objects but are nonetheless valuable, such as patents, trademarks, and goodwill.

Intangible personal property Nonphysical property in the form of written documentation.

Integrated marketing communication Combines four promotional tools to execute a comprehensive, unified promotional strategy.

Integrity-based ethics codes Attempt to enable responsible employee conduct by creating an environment that supports ethically desirable behavior.

Intellectual property Items that are the creations of the mind.

Intensive distribution When a product is distributed among as many locations as possible.

Intentional tort A willful act resulting in injury.

Interest groups Also known as *special-interest groups—* groups whose members try to influence businesses and governments on specific issues.

Interest rate The price paid for the use of money over a certain period of time.

Intermediaries Also known as *marketing intermediaries,* the people or firms that move products between producer and customers.

Intermittent process A production process in which finished goods or services are turned out in a series of short production runs and the machines are changed frequently to make different products.

Intermodal shipping Shipping that combines use of several different modes of transportation.

Intern A student or a recent graduate who undergoes supervised practical training in a business setting.

Internal expansion A way for a company to grow, namely, by increasing sales and capital investment.

Internal recruiting What companies do when they make employees already working for the organization aware of job openings.

International law Laws that govern activities between nations.

International Monetary Fund (IMF) Consists of 185 nations, and is designed to assist in smoothing the flow of money between nations.

Internet Also called *"the Net,"* the global network of independently operating but interconnected computers.

Internship An opportunity for college students—and even out-of-work professionals—to obtain career-related experience by doing supervised work in their future fields.

In the cards *A likely outcome.*

In the black *Profitable; the opposite of "in the red."*

In the red *Failure to make a profit; circumstance where costs exceed revenues.*

Intranet An organization's internal private network that uses the infrastructure and standards of the Internet and the World Wide Web.

Intrapreneur Someone who works inside an existing organization who sees an opportunity for a product or service and mobilizes the organization's resources to try to realize it.

Intrinsic reward The satisfaction, such as a feeling of accomplishment, a person receives from performing the particular task itself.

Introduction stage The stage in the product life cycle in which a new product is introduced into the marketplace.

Inventory The name given to goods kept in stock to be used for the production process or for sales to customers.

Inventory control The system for determining the right quantity of resources and keeping track of their location and use.

Investment bank A financial institution that deals primarily with raising capital, structuring corporate mergers and acquisitions, and handling securities.

Investment bankers Companies that engage in buying and reselling new securities.

Investment-grade bonds Bonds that are relatively safe, with a low probability of default; they have a bond rating of BBB or above.

"Invisible hand" Economist Adam Smith's idea that, with individuals' drive for prosperity, needed goods and services would be produced that would provide economic and social benefits to all.

Involuntary bankruptcy Type of bankruptcy in which creditors file papers with a federal bankruptcy court seeking to have debtors declared bankrupt because of their inability to pay.

IOU *Abbreviation for "I owe you." A promise to pay a debt, or symbolically, an obligation.*

ISO 9000 series Quality-control procedures companies must install—from purchasing to manufacturing to inventory to shipping—that can be audited by independent quality-control experts, or "registrars."

Job analysis Conducted to determine the basic elements of a job, using observation and analysis.

Job description Summarizes what the holder of the job does and how and why he or she does it.

Job enlargement Increasing the number of tasks in a job to improve employee satisfaction, motivation, and quality of production.

Job enrichment Building into a job such motivating factors as responsibility, achievement, recognition, stimulating work, and advancement.

Job postings Placing information about job vacancies on company websites, break-room bulletin boards, and newsletters.

Job rotation Rotating employees through different assignments in different departments to give them a broader picture of the organization.

Job sharing When two people divide one full-time job.

Job simplification Reducing the number of tasks a worker performs.

Job specification The minimum qualifications a person must have to perform the job successfully.

Joint venture Also known as a *strategic alliance,* an agreement with a foreign company to share the risks and rewards of starting a new enterprise together in a foreign country.

Journal A record book or computer program containing the daily record of the firm's transactions.

Judiciary The branch of government that oversees the court system.

Jump headfirst *To do something without hesitation.*

Just-in-time (JIT) inventory control A concept in which only minimal supplies are kept on the organization's premises and others are delivered by the suppliers on an as-needed basis.

Keogh plan Retirement plan that allows you to set aside up to $40,000 a year, and the funds and their increases are not taxed until withdrawal.

Key player(s) *The most important person(s) in an organization, event, or strategy.*

Kid gloves *Handled with extraordinary care and delicacy.*

Killer app *A piece of software that excites the industry in ways that it's never known.*

Knights of Labor Formed by six Philadelphia tailors in 1869; this was the first truly national union.

Knockoff brands Illegal imitations of national brand-name products.

Know-how *Knowledge of how to do something effectively; expertise.*

Knowledge workers People who work primarily with information or who develop and use knowledge in the workplace.

Kudos *Congratulations.*

Labor unions Organizations of employees formed to protect and advance their members' interests by bargaining with management over job-related issues.

Landrum-Griffin Act or **Labor Management Reporting and Disclosure Act** Legislation that forced unions (1) to revise their election procedures to promote honesty, (2) provided a bill of rights for union members, and (3) required unions to file financial disclosure statements with the U.S. secretary of labor.

Law of adverse selection The principle that groups that are more apt to need insurance are also those that are more apt to want it.

Law of large numbers A principle that says that the future probability of a loss can be predicted from a large number of past occurrences.

Laws Rules of conduct or action formally recognized as binding or enforced by a controlling authority.

Lead balloon *A complete failure.*

Leading Motivating, directing, and otherwise influencing people to work hard to achieve the organization's goals.

Lean manufacturing The production of products by eliminating unnecessary steps and using the fewest resources, as well as continually striving for improvement.

Ledger A specialized record book or computer program that contains summaries of all journal transactions, accumulated into specific categories.

Less-developed countries Also known as *developing countries,* third-world countries, those nations with low economic development and low average incomes.

Level playing field *A situation or competition that is fair to all participants or companies.*

Leverage *To utilize a resource.*

Leveraged buyout (LBO) One firm borrows money to buy another firm. The purchaser uses the assets of the company being acquired as security for the loan being used to finance the purchase.

Liability A debt owed by a firm to an outside individual or organization.

Liability insurance Insurance that protects against financial losses resulting from harm caused to others for which the business is responsible.

Limit order Telling a broker to buy a particular security only if it is less than a certain price or to sell it only if it is above a certain price.

Limited liability company (LLC) Combines the tax benefits of a sole proprietorship or partnership—one level of tax— with the limited liability of a corporation.

Limited liability partnership (LLP) The liability of each partner—and the risk of losing personal assets—is limited to just his or her own acts and omissions and those of his or her directly reporting employees.

Limited partnership A type of partnership that has one or more general partners plus other limited partners who contribute only an investment but do not have any management responsibility or liability.

Limited-function merchant wholesaler An independently owned firm that takes title to—becomes owner of—the manufacturer's products but performs only selected services, such as storage only.

Line managers Employees who have authority to make decisions and usually have people reporting to them.

Line of credit A bank specifies how much it is willing to lend the borrower during a specified period of time.

Lipstick on a pig *An attempt to put a favorable spin on a negative situation or result.*

Liquidity The essential feature of current assets, as they are easily converted into cash.

Liquidity ratios Measure of a firm's ability to meet its short-term obligations when they become due.

Load funds Funds in which the purchaser pays a commission every time shares are purchased.

Local area network (LAN) Connects computers and devices in a limited geographic area, such as one office, one building, or a group of buildings. LANs are the basis for most office networks.

Lockout A management tactic to put pressure on the union by closing the company and not paying workers.

Logistics Planning and implementing the details of moving raw materials, finished goods, and related information along the supply chain, from origin to points of consumption to meet customer requirements.

Long-term forecast A prediction about how money will come into and go out of a firm during the next 1, 5, or 10 years.

Long-term liabilities Obligations in which payments are due in one year or more.

Loss The opposite of profit; it occurs when business expenses are larger than revenues.

Loss leaders Products priced at or below cost in order to attract customers.

Low-ball *A very low quote.*

Low-hanging fruit *Markets in which customers can be easily found.*

M1 The narrowest definition of the money supply, money that can be accessed quickly and easily.

M2 A broader definition of the money supply: (1) money that can be accessed quickly and easily (that is, M1) and (2) money that takes more time to access.

Macroeconomics The study of large economic units, such as the operations of a nation's economy and the effect on it of government policies and allocation of resources.

Magic bullet *The perfect solution to a given business problem.*

Make waves *To cause conflict or argument.*

Malcolm Baldrige National Quality Award An award created by Congress in 1987 that is intended to be the most prestigious recognition of quality in the United States.

Malware Malicious software that attacks computer systems.

Managed care Health care providers limit the fees they charge in return for controlling the use of medical services.

Management The pursuit of organizational goals effectively and efficiently through (1) planning, (2) organization, (3) leading, and (4) controlling the organization's resources.

Management advisory services Specialized accounting services that CPAs offer business managers to resolve different kinds of problems.

Management by objectives (MBO) A four-step process in which (1) managers and employees jointly set objectives for the employee, (2) managers develop action plans, (3) managers and employees periodically review the employee's performance, and (4) the manager makes a performance appraisal and rewards the employee according to results.

Managerial accounting Preparing accounting information and analyses for managers and other decision makers inside an organization.

Manufacturer's branch office An office that is owned and managed by a manufacturer that not only has offices for sales representatives but also carries an inventory from which the staff can fill orders.

Manufacturer's brands Also called *national* or *producer brands*, or even *global brands* when extended worldwide; brands are those attached to products by companies that distribute nationwide or even worldwide.

Manufacturer-owned wholesaler A wholesale business that is owned and operated by a product's manufacturer.

Manufacturer's sales office An office that is owned and managed by a manufacturer and that has offices for sales representatives who sell products that are delivered at a later time.

Manufacturing franchise Franchisees are given the right to manufacture and distribute a certain product, following a formula or using supplies purchased from the franchisor.

Market coverage Product distribution among locations.

Market order Telling a broker to buy or sell a particular security at the best available price.

Market price Also known as *equilibrium price*, determined by the interaction of demand and supply.

Market segmentation Dividing a market into groups whose members have similar characteristics or wants and needs.

Market share The percentage of the market of total sales for a particular product or good.

Market value The price at which a stock is currently selling.

Marketable securities Stocks, bonds, government securities, and money market certificates that can be easily converted to cash.

Marketing The activity, set of institutions, and processes for creating, communicating, delivering, and exchanging offerings that have value for customers, clients, partners, and society at large.

Marketing concept Focuses on customer satisfaction, service, and profitability.

Marketing mix The four key strategy considerations called the "four Ps": *product, pricing, place,* and *promotion* strategies.

Marketing research The systematic gathering and analyzing of data about problems relating to the marketing of goods and services.

Marketing strategy A plan for (1) identifying the *target market* among market segments, (2) creating the right marketing mix to reach that target market, and (3) dealing with important forces in the external marketing environment.

Maslow's hierarchy of needs theory Proposes that people are motivated by five levels of needs, ranging from low to high: (1) physiological, (2) safety, (3) social, (4) esteem, and (5) self-actualization.

Mass customization Use of mass-production techniques to produce customized goods and services.

Mass production The production of uniform goods in great quantities.

Master budgets Budgets that tie together operating, capital, and cash budgets to present the company's overall plan of action for a particular time period.

Master limited partnership (MLP) A partnership that acts like a corporation, selling stock on a stock exchange, but it is taxed like a partnership, paying a lesser rate than the corporate income tax.

Materials handling The physical handling of goods to and from and within warehouses.

Materials requirement planning (MRP) A computer-based method of delivering the right amounts of supplies to the right place at the right time for the production of goods; however, it uses what is known as a *bill of materials*, which is essentially a list of materials that go into the finished product.

Matrix structure Combines, in grid form, the functional chain of command and the divisional chain of command—usually product—so that there is a vertical command structure and a horizontal command structure.

Maturity date The issuing organization is legally required to repay the bond's principal in full to the bondholder.

Maturity stage In the product life cycle, the period in which the product starts to fall out of favor and sales and profits diminish.

MBA Oath A voluntary student-led pledge of intention to serve the greater good. Signers promise to act responsibly and ethically and refrain from advancing their "own narrow ambitions" at the expense of others.

Measuring stick *A tool or reference for measuring or evaluating results.*

Meat and potatoes *Basic or traditional.*

Mechanization The use of machines to do the work formerly performed by people.

Media planning This is the process of choosing the exact kinds of media to be used for an advertising campaign.

Mediation The process in which a neutral third party, a *mediator,* listens to both sides in a dispute, makes suggestions, and encourages them to agree on a solution.

Medium of exchange Using money makes economic transactions easier and eliminates the need to barter.

Mentor An experienced person who coaches and guides lesser-experienced people by helping them understand an industry or organization's culture and structure.

Mentoring This describes the process in which an experienced employee, the *mentor,* supervises, teaches, and provides guidance for a less-experienced employee, the *mentee* or *protégé.*

Merchandise inventory Merchandise that is being held for resale to customers.

Mercosur The largest common market in Latin America; it has four core members—Argentina, Brazil, Paraguay, and Uruguay, with Venezuela scheduled to become a full member—and five associate members, Bolivia, Chile, Colombia, Ecuador, and Peru.

Merger Occurs when two firms join to form a new firm.

Microeconomics The study of small economic units, the operations of particular groups of people, businesses, organizations, and markets.

Micropreneurs Those who take the risk of starting and managing a business that remains small, lets them do the kind of work they want to do, and offers them a balanced lifestyle.

Middle managers Managers who implement the policies and plans of the top managers above them and supervise and coordinate the activities of the supervisory managers below them.

Mission statement A statement of the organization's fundamental purposes.

Mixed economies Some resources are allocated by the free market and some resources are allocated by the government, resulting in a somewhat better balance between freedom and economic equality.

Modem or **dial-up modem** A device that converts digital signals into the analog signals of the standard copper-wire telephone line.

Modular structure A firm assembles pieces, or modules, of a product provided by outside contractors.

Mom-and-pop *A small-time operation.*

Monday morning quarterback *A person who offers perspective and criticism only after something negative has occurred.*

Monetary policy The U.S. government's attempts to manage the money supply and interest rates in order to influence economic activity.

Money Any medium of value that is generally accepted as payment for goods and services.

Money market accounts Bank accounts that offer interest rates competitive with those of brokerage firm money market funds, but they require higher minimum balances and limit check writing to as few as three per month.

Money supply The amount of money the Federal Reserve System makes available for people to buy goods and services. The money supply is customarily referred to in two ways—as M1, the narrowest measure, or M2, a more generous and more commonly used measure.

Money-market instruments Cash investments (short-term IOUs, debt securities that mature within one year) that are issued by governments, large corporations, and financial institutions.

Monopolistic competition The market has many sellers who sell similar products, but they have found ways to distinguish among them or buyers have perceived their products as being different.

Monopoly A market in which there is only one seller, and no competition.

More than meets the eye *Things underneath or hidden that may be more important than what is visible.*

Mortgage pass-through securities Bonds sold by financial institutions that are backed by a pool of mortgages whose monthly mortgage payments are "passed" from mortgagers "through" the issuers to the investors in the security.

Motivating factors, or simply **motivators** Factors associated with job satisfaction—such as achievement, recognition, responsibility, and advancement—all of which affect the rewards of work performance.

Motivation The psychological processes that induce people to pursue goals.

Muddy the water *Making a situation or things more complex, difficult, or less clear.*

Multilevel marketing (MLM) Independent businesspeople, or distributors, sell products both on their own and by recruiting, motivating, supplying, and training others to sell those products, with the distributors' compensation being based on both their personal sales and the group's sales.

Multinational corporations Organizations with multinational management and ownership that manufacture and market products in many different countries.

Municipal bonds Bonds issued by state and local governments and agencies, and consist of revenue bonds and general obligation bonds.

Mutual fund A fund operated by an investment company that brings together money from many people and invests it in an array of diversified stocks, bonds, or other securities.

Mutual insurance companies Nonprofit private insurers owned by their insurance policyholders.

Mutual savings banks Financial institutions similar to savings and loans, except that they are owned by their depositors rather than by shareholders.

Narrow span of control A manager has a limited number of people reporting.

Narrowband Used for regular telephone communications.

NASDAQ The second-largest stock market in the world; a nationwide electronic communications system that enables member securities dealers to buy and sell securities online.

NASDAQ Composite Index Tracks not only domestic but also foreign common stocks traded on the NASDAQ exchange.

National Credit Union Administration (NCUA) An independent federal agency that provides up to $250,000 insurance coverage per individual per credit union.

National Labor Relations Board The National Labor Relations Board (NLRB) enforces procedures whereby employees may vote to have a union and for collective bargaining.

Natural resources Production inputs that are useful just as they appear in nature.

Necessity entrepreneurs People who suddenly must earn a living and are simply trying to replace lost income.

Need-satisfaction presentation Determining customer needs and then tailoring a presentation to address those needs; a preferred approach these days.

Negligence An unintentional act that results in injury.

Negotiable instrument A document representing an unconditional promise to pay that is transferable among individuals and businesses.

Negotiated labor-management contract Sets the general tone and terms under which labor and management agree to work together during the contract period.

Net income The firm's profit or loss after paying income taxes is determined by subtracting expenses from revenues.

Net period The length of time for which the supplier (seller) extends credit.

Net worth The difference between assets and liabilities.

Network or **communications network** A system of interconnected computers, phones, or other communications devices that can communicate with one another and share applications and data.

Networking The process of interacting with others outside and inside the organization in order to build relationships.

Neuromarketing The study of how people's brains respond to advertising and other brand-related messages by scientifically monitoring brainwave activity, eye-tracking, and skin response.

New product A product that either (1) is a significant improvement over existing products and/or (2) performs a new function for the consumer.

New York Stock Exchange (NYSE) The world's largest stock exchange; it is a floor-based exchange that has been in existence since 1792.

Niche marketing Dividing market segments even further to microsegments for which sales may be profitable.

No-load funds Funds in which the investor pays no sales charges at all when purchasing shares.

Nondeposit institutions or **nonbanks** Financial institutions that do not accept deposits but offer some of the services that banks provide.

Nonprofit organization Its purpose is to provide products or services to clients, rather than to make a profit for owners and managers.

Nonstore retailers Companies who sell merchandise in ways other than through retail stores.

Nonverbal communication Messages sent outside of the written or spoken word.

Norris-LaGuardia Act Legislation that (1) limited courts in issuing injunctions against nonviolent union activities, such as strikes, and (2) outlawed yellow dog contracts.

North American Free Trade Agreement (NAFTA) Formed in 1994, a common market consisting of the United States, Canada, and Mexico.

Notes payable Money owed on a loan based on a promise (either short-term or long-term) the firm made.

Not-for-profit accountants Those who work for governments and nonprofit organizations, perform services as for-profit accountants—except they are concerned with efficiency, not profits.

NOW (for "negotiable order of withdrawal) account An account that pays interest and allows a person to write an unlimited number of checks, but the person has to maintain a minimum monthly balance.

Objective A specific, short-term target designed to achieve the organization's goals.

Objective appraisals Also called *results appraisals,* based on facts and are often numerical. In these kinds of appraisals, a manager keeps track of numbers.

Offline *Used in business meetings to mean a later discussion or conversation, in private.*

Off-the-job training Training that consists of classroom programs, videotapes, workbooks, online distance learning programs, and the like.

Old boys club *A tight network of long-standing business relationships.*

Oligopoly The market has a few sellers offering similar but not identical products to many small buyers.

On-the-job training Training that takes place in the work setting while employees are performing job-related tasks.

One-to-one marketing Market segmentation that is reduced to the smallest part—individual customers.

Online networking or social networking The use of online communities that allow members to share personal or professional interests, photos, videos, stories, and ideas with other members.

Online retailing Also known as *electronic retailing*, this is non-store retailing of products directly to consumers using the Internet.

On shaky ground *Idea, proposal, or strategy based on a questionable or risky premise.*

On the cheap *To do something at a low cost.*

Open shop Workers may choose to join or not join a union.

Open-market operations A more commonly used money tool in which the Federal Reserve controls the money supply by buying and selling U.S. Treasury securities, or government bonds, to the public.

Operating budget Budget that identifies a firm's sales and production goals and specifies the costs required to meet those goals.

Operating expenses Selling and administrative expenses.

Operational planning The process of determining how to accomplish specific tasks with available resources within the next 1-week to 1-year period.

Operations management The process of transforming materials, labor, and other resources into goods and/or services.

Opportunities Situations that present possibilities for exceeding existing goals.

Opportunity entrepreneurs Those who are ambitious and start their own businesses in a voluntary pursuit of opportunity.

Order processing Receiving customer orders and seeing that they are handled correctly and that the product is delivered.

Organization A group of people who work together to achieve some specific purpose.

Organization chart A box-and-lines kind of illustration showing the formal lines of authority and the organization's official positions or work specializations.

Organization marketing An attempt to induce people to contribute to, use the services of, or agree with the goals of a specific not-for-profit organization.

Organizational culture Sometimes called *corporate culture*, the shared beliefs and values that develop within an organization and guide the behavior of its members.

Organizing Arranging tasks, people, and other resources to accomplish the work.

Orientation A process in which the newcomer is helped to fit smoothly into the job and the organization.

Out of the loop *Not having knowledge or awareness of something; uninformed.*

Output Hardware that consists of devices that translate information processed by the computer into a form that humans can understand. Common examples are the *monitor* (or display screen) and the *printer*.

Outside the box *A creative solution that avoids a traditional or common approach.*

Outsourcing Also known as *contract manufacturing*, using suppliers outside the company to provide goods and services.

Over-the-counter (OTC) market An organization of several thousand securities brokers that trade stocks that are not listed on the organized stock exchanges.

Owners All those who can claim the organization as their legal property.

Owners' equity Also called *stockholders' equity*, represents the value of a firm if its assets were sold and its debts paid.

Packaging The covering or wrapping around a product that protects and promotes the product.

Paradigm shift *A significant change in thinking or approach.*

Par value The face value of a share of stock, an arbitrary figure set by the issuing corporation's board of directors.

Participative leaders Also called *democratic leaders*, leaders who delegate authority and involve employees in their decisions.

Partnership A business owned and operated by two or more persons as a voluntary legal association.

Part-time work Any work done on a schedule less than the standard 40-hour workweek.

Password A secret word or string of characters that enable a person to connect to a network.

Patent A document that protects ownership rights for the inventors of machines, manufacturing processes, chemical substances, and similar matters.

Pay for performance Bases pay on one's results.

Payday lender A firm that offers short-term loans, in advance of payday, at high rates of interest.

Pave the way *To prepare the way for something to occur.*

Pay the piper *To settle a debt.*

Peer-to-peer (P2P) network A network in which all microcomputers on the network communicate directly with one another without relying on a central server.

Penetration pricing Setting a low price to attract many customers and deter competition.

Penny ante *Something insignificant.*

Pension funds Nondeposit institutions that provide retirement benefits to workers and their families.

People marketing Also called *person marketing*, attracting an audience's attention to a particular person.

Perfect competition A market that has many small sellers who sell interchangeable products to many informed buyers, and no seller is large enough to dictate the price of the product.

Performance appraisal When a manager assesses an employee's performance and provides feedback.

Perks *Short for* perquisites; *employee benefits other than salary.*

Personal finance The application of economic principles to a person's well-being.

Personal selling Face-to-face communication and promotion to influence customers to buy goods and services.

Persuasive advertising A type of advertising that is used to develop a desire among consumers for the product.

PERT chart *PERT* stands for *program evaluation and review technique*. This is a diagram for determining the best sequencing of production activities.

Pharming Thieves implant malicious software on a victim's computer that redirects the user to an impostor Web page, even when the individual types the correct address into his or her browser.

Philanthropy Making charitable donations to benefit humankind.

Phishing Pronounced "fishing" and short for *password harvesting fishing;* the (1) sending of a forged email that (2) directs recipients to a replica of an existing Web page, both of which pretend to belong to a legitimate company. The purpose of the fraudulent sender is to "phish" for, or entice people to share, their personal, financial, or password data.

Physical distribution All the activities required to move products from the manufacturer to the final buyer.

Picketing When workers march in front of their employer's place of business with signs explaining their grievances.

Piece of the action *To get a share of some business or market.*

Piece rate When employees are paid according to how much output they produce.

Pink slip *A notice of termination of employment.*

Place marketing Attracting an audience's attention to a particular geographical area.

Planning Setting goals and deciding how to achieve them.

Pledging accounts receivable When a firm uses its accounts receivable as collateral, or security, to obtain a short-term loan.

Poison pill In a hostile takeover attempt, the term for when managers take actions designed to make the stock less attractive to the potential buyer.

Ponzi scheme Illegal scheme using cash from newer investors to pay off older ones.

Pop-up ads On a computer screen, new windows that open, or "pop up," to display advertisements.

Portfolio The collection of securities representing a person's investments.

Poster child *A person who is a prominent example of something.*

Post-mortem *The meeting, report, or process that addresses project results, assessing what was successful and/or unsuccessful.*

Precedents The decisions judges made in past court cases in similar areas, which become guides to handling new cases.

Predatory pricing A company cuts its prices below its costs to force competitors out of business.

Preferred provider organization (PPO) This type of health provider agrees to treat members of a sponsoring organization, such as an employer or union, at a discount but for a higher fee allows access to outside physicians.

Preferred stock Stockholders are not able to vote on major company decisions, but they get (1) preferred, or first, claim on the company's dividends and (2) first claim on any remaining assets if the firm goes bankrupt and its assets are sold.

Premium The fee that the insured pays the insurer to maintain the insurance policy.

Prepaid debit card Works on the old idea of a regular debit card except it is not linked to a regular bank checking account but rather to an account created by the lender into which a person has deposited funds in advance.

Press conference This involves calling media representatives to a press briefing at which they announce new information.

Press release Also called a *news release* or *publicity release*, a brief statement written in the form of a news story or a video program that is released to the mass media to try to get favorable publicity for a firm or its products.

Price fixing Occurs when supposedly competing firms unite to determine prices on their goods or services.

Price skimming Setting a high price to make a large profit; it can work when there is little competition.

Pricing Figuring out how much to charge for a product—the price, or exchange value, for a good or service.

Pricing objectives Goals that product producers—as well as retailers and wholesalers—hope to achieve in pricing products for sale.

Primary data Data derived from original research.

Primary securities market The financial market in which new security issues are first sold to investors.

Principle of catastrophic hazard Principle that insurers must spread their risks so that no single disaster or catastrophe forces them to satisfy all the claims by all the insured at the same time.

Principle of indemnity Principle that insurers will not pay the insured more in damage claims than the dollar loss actually sustained.

Principle of motion economy System developed by industrial engineers in which every job is broken down into a series of elementary motions.

Privacy The right of people not to reveal information about themselves.

Private accountants Also called *corporate accountants*, in-house accountants working for a single organization.

Private placements Selling stock to only a small group of large investors, such as insurance companies and pension funds.

Private-label brands Also known as *private*, *store*, and *dealer brands;* those attached to products distributed by one store or a chain.

Problems Difficulties that inhibit the achievement of goals.

Process divisions Activities are grouped around work processes.

Process layout Allows for similar work to be grouped by function.

Process manufacturing The name given to production processes that chemically or physically changes materials.

Processor The device that contains millions of electronic circuits used to process raw data into information.

Producer price index (PPI) A measure of prices at the wholesale level.

Product A good (which is tangible) or service (intangible) that can satisfy customer needs.

Product analysis Doing cost estimates to calculate the product's possible profitability.

Product development The production of a prototype of a product, a preliminary version, so the company can see what the product will look like.

Product differentiation The attempt to design a product in a way that will make it be perceived differently enough from competitors' products that it will attract consumers.

Product divisions Activities are grouped around similar products or services.

Product layout Equipment and tasks are arranged into an assembly line—a sequence of steps for producing a single product.

Product liability cases Cases in which a company may be held responsible for injuries caused by negligence in the design, production, sale, and use of its products.

Product liability insurance Insurance to protect a business in case someone claims its product caused damage, injury, or death.

Product life cycle A model that graphs the four stages that a product or service goes through during the "life" of its marketability: (1) introduction, (2) growth, (3) maturity, and (4) decline.

Product line A collection of products designed for a similar market or that are physically similar.

Product mix The combination of all product lines that a firm offers.

Product placement When sellers of a product pay to have that product prominently placed in a TV show or film so that many people will see it.

Product screening Elimination of product ideas that are not feasible.

Product-distribution franchise Also known as a *distributorship,* a franchise situation in which a franchisee is given the right to sell trademarked products purchased from the franchisor.

Production or **operations** Any process that takes basic resources and converts them into finished products—inputs into outputs.

Production concept Emphasizes producing as many goods as possible because there is an unlimited demand.

Productivity The amount of goods and services a person or organization produces given the resources needed to produce them.

Product-use-based segmentation Categorizes business customers according to how they will use the seller's product.

Professional liability insurance Insurance to protect the business when someone claims its professional services caused injury or harm.

Profit The amount of money a business makes after paying for its salaries and all other costs—that is, revenue minus expenses.

Profit sharing The distribution to employees of a percentage of the company's profits.

Profitability ratios Used to measure how well profits are doing in relation to the firm's sales, assets, or owner's equity.

Promissory note A written contract prepared by the buyer who agrees to pay the seller a certain amount by a certain time.

Promotion All the techniques companies use to motivate consumers to buy their products—techniques such as advertising, public relations, publicity, personal selling, and other kinds of sales.

Promotion mix The combination of tools that a company uses to promote a product, selecting from among four promotional tools: (1) advertising, (2) public relations, (3) personal selling, and (4) sales promotion.

Property Anything of value for which a person or organization has sole right of ownership.

Property insurance Insurance that protects against damage to real estate and other property.

Pros and cons *Various arguments in favor of or against something.*

Prospecting For salespeople, the process of identifying potential customers, who are called *prospects.*

Prospects Potential customers.

Prospectus A detailed written description of a new security, including information about the issuing company and its top management.

Prototype A preliminary version of a new product.

Proxy fight The outsider contacts shareholders and urges them to vote for the raider's hand-picked candidates for the board of directors.

Psychographic segmentation Categorizing people according to lifestyle, values, and psychological characteristics.

Psychological pricing Sometimes called *odd-even pricing*, the technique of pricing products or services in odd rather than even amounts to make products seem less expensive.

Public accountants Professionals who provide accounting services to clients on a fee basis.

Public insurance agencies Federal or state governmental units that provide specialized insurance that private insurers are often unwilling to provide.

Public liability insurance Insurance to protect a business against business risks associated with the company's property or employees.

Public offerings Selling stock to the general public in securities markets.

Public relations (PR) Creating and maintaining a favorable image of a firm, its products, and its action with the mass media, consumers, and public at large.

Public service advertising Presentations, usually sponsored by nonprofit organizations, that are concerned with the welfare of the community in general.

Publicity Unpaid coverage by the mass media about a firm or its products.

Pull promotional strategy Aimed directly at consumers, to try to get them to demand the product from retailers.

Purchasing The activity of finding the best resources for the best price from the best suppliers in order to produce the best goods and services.

Pure risk Involves a chance for either loss or no loss; there is no possibility of gain.

Push promotional strategy Aimed at wholesalers and retailers to try to encourage them to market the product to consumers.

Qualifying For a salesperson, the process of determining if a prospect has the authority to buy and the ability to pay.

Quality The total ability of a product or service to meet customer needs.

Quality control The process of minimizing errors by managing each stage of production.

Quality of life Expresses a society's general well-being as measured by standard of living, freedom, happiness, art, environmental health, and innovation.

Quid pro quo Latin. *One thing in return for another.*

Rack jobber A limited-function wholesaler who furnishes products and display racks or shelves in retail stores and shares profits with retailers.

Ratification The union members vote whether or not to accept the contract negotiated by the union's leaders.

Ratio analysis Uses one of a number of financial ratios—such as liquidity, efficiency, leverage, and profitability—to evaluate variables in a financial statement.

Reach The number of people within a given population that an ad will reach at least once.

Recession Two or more consecutive quarters (a quarter is three months) of decline in the gross domestic product.

Recruiting The process by which companies locate and attract qualified applicants for open jobs.

Red flag *Warning sign.*

Referral sales prospecting technique Asking satisfied customers to provide names of potential customers and to contact them on behalf of the salesperson.

Reinforcement Anything that causes a given behavior to be repeated or inhibited.

Reinforcement theory Suggests that behavior with positive consequences tends to be repeated whereas behavior with negative consequences tends not to be repeated.

Reinsurance A general insurer shares the risks and premiums associated with a specific policy with another company, the reinsurer.

Reinventing the wheel *To duplicate a basic method that has already previously been created or optimized by others.*

Reliability The degree to which a test measures the same thing consistently.

Reminder advertising Advertising to remind consumers of the existence of a product.

Renter's insurance Insurance that will protect a renter against financial loss if the contents of the rented dwelling are damaged or destroyed by fire or theft.

Repurpose *To redefine how an item is used in an attempt to leverage or salvage any remaining value.*

Reregulation The enactment of new or additional regulations after industries have been deregulated.

Reserve requirement The percentage of total checking and savings deposits that a bank must keep as cash in its vault or in a non–interest-bearing deposit at its regional Federal Reserve Bank.

Resource development The study of how to develop the resources for creating and best utilizing goods and services.

Responsibility The obligation a person has to perform the tasks assigned to that person.

Retailers Intermediaries who sell products directly to customers.

Retained earnings Net profits minus dividend payments made to stockholders; they are earnings retained by a firm for its own use.

Revenue The total amount of money that the selling of goods or services produces for a business during a defined period of time.

Revolving credit agreement Resembles a line of credit, except that the bank guarantees the loan and is obligated to loan funds up to the credit limit.

Right-sizing *A euphemistic way of saying downsizing (firing).*

Right-to-work laws Statutes that prohibit employees from being required to join a union as a condition of employment.

Risk In the business realm, the possibility that the owner or owners of a business may invest time and money in the enterprise and fail—that is, not make a profit.

Risk avoidance The practice of avoiding risk by not participating in risky activity.

Risk management The process of protecting a company's assets and earning power by reducing or avoiding the threats posed by pure risks.

Risk reduction The practice of reducing risk by removing hazards or taking preventative measures.

Risk transfer The practice whereby a company transfers its risk to an insurance company, in return for a fee.

Risk-return trade-off The activity in which financial managers continually try to balance the firm's investment risk with the expected return, or payoffs, from its investments.

Rites and rituals The activities and ceremonies, planned and unplanned, that celebrate important occasions and accomplishments in the organization's life.

Robinson-Patman Act (1936) Legislation that prohibits price discrimination—selling the same product to different customers at different prices.

Robotics Field that involves the use of programmable machines or robots to manipulate materials and tools to perform a variety of tasks.

Robots Automatic devices that perform functions ordinarily performed by human beings.

Roth IRA An investment vehicle that does not provide a current-year deduction whenever a person makes a contribution, but earnings grow tax free, and when the person makes withdrawals they are also tax free.

Royalties A percentage of sales that a franchisee pays a franchisor.

Rubber stamp *To give a perfunctory approval or endorsement.*

Rules of the road *A set of customary practices followed in operating a business.*

Run it up the flagpole *To find out what colleagues think of a new idea.*

S corporation A corporation with no more than 100 owners (shareholders), but, like a partnership, the owners are taxed only at the personal (not corporate) level.

Sales commission Compensation in which salespeople are paid a percentage of the earnings the company made from their sales.

Sales promotion Short-term marketing incentives to stimulate (1) dealer interest and (2) consumer buying.

Sales revenues Funds received from the sale of goods and services during a certain period.

Sales support Consists not of selling products but of facilitating the sale by providing supportive services, such as finding new customers, building goodwill, and providing follow-up services after the sale.

Sandbag *To downplay or misrepresent something or one's capabilities in an attempt to deceive or mislead.*

Sarbanes–Oxley Act of 2002 Often known simply as *SOX* or *SarbOx;* law that established protections for whistleblowers and requirements for proper financial record keeping for public companies and penalties for noncompliance.

Savings account Otherwise known as a *time deposit,* a bank account that pays low interest and does not allow check writing.

Savings and loan associations (S&Ls) Financial institutions that accept deposits and were originally intended to make loans primarily for home mortgages.

Savings Association Insurance Fund (SAIF) Now part of the FDIC, insures depositors with accounts in savings and loan associations.

Scheduling The act of determining time periods for each task in the production process.

Scientific management A management theory that emphasized the scientific study of work methods to improve the productivity of individual workers.

SCORE or **Service Corps of Retired Executives** Retired executives who volunteer as consultants to advise small-business people.

Scratch the surface *To investigate or treat something superficially.*

Sea of information *Abundance of information that may make its use difficult.*

Secondary data Information acquired and published by others.

Secondary securities market The financial market in which existing stocks and bonds are bought and sold by investors.

Secured bonds Bonds that are backed by some form of the firm's collateral, such as real estate or equipment.

Secured loan The borrower pledges some sort of asset, such as personal property, that is forfeited if the loan is not repaid.

Securities Financial instruments such as stocks and bonds.

Securities and Exchange Commission (SEC) A federal agency that regulates the various stock exchanges.

Securitization A process of distributing risks by packaging loans together into mortgage-backed securities that can be sold to many kinds of investors.

Security The system of safeguards for protecting information technology against unauthorized access and systems failures that can result in damage or loss.

Selection process A process that screens job applicants to hire the best candidate.

Selective distribution When a product is distributed in selected locations, where it will get special attention.

Self-insurance The practice in which a company sets aside money to cover losses with its own funds.

Self-sufficient A country that is able to produce by itself all the products and services it needs or that its people want.

Seller's market A market in which there is more demand for products than there is supply.

Selling The exchange of goods or services for an agreed sum of money.

Selling concept Period in U.S. marketing history that emphasized high-powered sales techniques to sell products.

SEP-IRA plan *SEP plan*—short for *Simplified Employee Pension plan*—allows a person every year to save either about 13% of income or $20,870, whichever is less.

Serial bonds Bonds that mature at different dates.

Server A central computer that holds data and programs for connecting or supplying services to other computers and devices.

Services Intangible products.

Sexual harassment Unwanted sexual attention that creates an adverse work environment.

Shadowing An employee being trained on the job learns skills by watching more experienced employees.

Shareholders Owners of stock—shares of ownership—in a company.

Sherman Antitrust Act (1890) Legislation designed to prohibit contracts, combinations, or conspiracies in restraint of trade or commerce, as well as restrict monopolies from stifling competition.

Shoestring budget *A small or minimal budget.*

Shop steward A union official elected by the union membership who works at the company and represents the interests of unionized employees on a daily basis.

Shopping goods and services More expensive products that people buy after comparing for value, price, quality, and style.

Short-term forecast A prediction about how money will come into and go out of a firm during the next 4 to 12 months.

Shotgun approach *A wide, untargeted strategy.*

Sickout When large numbers of employees call in sick and do not report for work.

Silver bullet *An infallible business solution.*

SIMPLE retirement plan SIMPLE stands for *Savings Incentive Match Plan for Employees*—for companies with 100 or fewer employees.

Sine qua non Latin. *An essential element or condition.*

Sinking-fund bonds Also known as *prefunded bonds*, bonds in which the issuer makes annual deposits to a bank to accumulate funds for paying off the bonds on maturity.

Sit-down strikes When workers refuse to leave the workplace until a settlement is reached; now illegal.

Six Sigma A rigorous statistical analysis process that reduces defects in manufacturing and service-related processes.

Skunkworks A team whose members are separated from the normal operation of an organization and asked to produce a new, innovative project.

Small business A business that is (a) independently owned and operated, (b) is not dominant in its field of operation, and meets certain criteria set by the SBA for (c) number of employees and (d) annual sales revenue.

Small Business Administration (SBA) The principal U.S. Government agency charged with aiding small businesses by providing help in financing, management training, and support in securing government contracts.

Smart card A plastic card with built-in microprocessor and memory chips that can combine the functions of credit, debit, phone, and bridge tolls.

Smell test *An informal method for determining the appropriateness or authenticity of something.*

Social audit A systematic assessment of a company's performance in implementing socially responsible programs, often based on predefined goals.

Social entrepreneurship Innovative, social value–creating activity that can occur within or across for-profit or nonprofit sectors.

Social networking services Attempts to build online communities of people sharing interests and activities.

Social Security The social welfare program that provides workers and their dependents with retirement income, disability payments, some unemployment insurance, and other benefits.

Socialism An economic system in which some major industries are owned by the government, but smaller businesses are owned by individuals. Any wealth or surplus of income is redistributed by the government through social programs.

Software suites Integrated programs combining word processing, spreadsheet, database, presentation graphics, e-mail, and personal information management software.

Software or **programs** Consists of all the electronic instructions that tell the computer how to perform a task.

Sole proprietorship A business owned, and typically managed, by one person.

Soup to nuts *From the beginning to the end of a project, in reference to the first and last courses of a meal.*

Spam Refers to unsolicited e-mail, or junk mail, in the form of advertising or chain letters.

Span of control Refers to the number of people reporting directly to a given manager.

Special courts Courts that hear certain specialized types of cases such as probate, taxes, bankruptcy, or international trade.

Specialty goods and services Usually much more expensive products that buyers seldom purchase or that have unique characteristics that require people to make a special effort to obtain.

Speculative risk Involves a chance of either gain or loss.

Speculative-grade bonds or **junk bonds** High-risk bonds with a greater probability of default; they have a bond rating of BB or lower, but in exchange for the higher risk, they pay about 50% more than investment-grade bonds.

Spoofing The forgery of an e-mail sender name so that the message appears to have originated from someone or somewhere other than the actual source.

Spyware Deceptive software that is surreptitiously installed on a computer via the Web; once installed on the hard disk it allows an outsider to harvest confidential information.

Staff personnel Employees who have advisory functions; they provide advice, recommendations, and research to line managers.

Staffing The recruitment, hiring, motivating, and retention of valuable employees.

Stakeholders The people whose interests are affected by an organization's activities.

Standard & Poor's 500 (S&P 500) An index of stock prices for 500 major corporations in a range of industries.

Standard of living Defined by how many goods and services people can buy with the money they have.

Standard of value Money acts as a standard of value or *unit of account,* meaning that it can be used as a common standard to measure the values of goods and services.

Standardization The use of uniform parts that could be easily interchanged with similar parts.

Statement of cash flows This reports, first, the firm's cash receipts and, second, disbursement related to the firm's (1) operating, (2) investing, and (3) financing activities, which leads to the bottom line of (4) the cash balance.

State-of-the-art *The most contemporary technique, strategy, product, or device.*

Statistical process control A statistical technique that uses periodic random samples from production runs to see if quality is being maintained within a standard range of acceptability.

Statutory laws Written laws, called *statutes,* that are created by legislative bodies.

Staying afloat *Staying in business under challenging circumstances.*

Stock certificate A paper certificate that indicates the shareholder's name, the name of the issuing company, the number of shares held, and the type of stock being issued.

Stock insurance companies Private insurers providing insurance to policyholders and earning profits for shareholders.

Stock market indicators Indexes of stock market prices of groups of stocks that are related in some way.

Stock market or stock exchange A financial marketplace where members buy and sell stocks.

Stock options Options giving certain employees the opportunity to buy stock in the firm at a future date for a discounted price; the purpose of the policy is to motivate and retain key employees.

Stock split A company increases the number of shares of ownership that each stock represents.

Stockholders Owners of *stock*—shares of ownership—in a company.

Stocks Shares of ownership in a company.

Storage Hardware that consists of devices that permanently hold data and information, as well as computer programs. On a personal computer, storage.

Storage warehouses Warehouses that provide storage of products for long periods of time. Example: This type of warehouse is used by producers of seasonal products, such as agricultural items, garden furniture, or Christmas merchandise.

Store of wealth Money acts as a store of wealth, meaning that people can save it until they need to make new purchases.

Story A narrative based on true events, which is repeated—and sometimes embellished upon—to emphasize a particular value.

Strategic planning A process of determining what the organization's long-term goals should be for the next 1–5 years with the resources that are expected to be available.

Strict product liability The company may be assigned legal responsibility for harm or injury caused by its product regardless of whether negligence can be proved.

Strike Also called a *walkout*, the union tactic of temporarily stopping work until a dispute is settled.

Strikebreakers Hiring workers who are willing to cross the picket line and fill the jobs of striking employees.

Structured interview The interviewer asks each applicant the same identical, fixed questions and rates their responses according to some standard measure.

Subjective appraisals Based on a manager's perceptions of an employee's traits or behaviors.

Subprime loans Loans for people with blemished or limited credit histories, which carry a higher rate of interest than prime loans to compensate for increased credit risk.

Subprime mortgage loans Loans to borrowers who do not qualify with mainstream lenders—borrowers with low credit scores and incomes insufficient to repay the loans.

Supervisory managers Managers who make short-term operating decisions, directing the daily tasks of nonmanagerial personnel.

Supplier Also called a *vendor,* a person or an organization that supplies raw materials, services, equipment, labor, or energy to other organizations.

Supply The quantity of products that people are willing to sell at various prices at a given time.

Supply chain The sequence of suppliers that contribute to creating and delivering a product, from raw materials to production to final buyers.

Supply chain management The strategy of planning and coordinating the movement of materials and products along the supply chain, from raw materials to final buyers.

Supreme courts The highest level of American courts, which hear cases from appellate courts; the U.S. Supreme Court also hears cases appealed from state supreme courts.

Sustainability Economic development that meets the needs of the present without compromising the ability of future generations to meet their own needs.

Sweatshop A shop, factory, or farm in which employees work long hours at low wages—or no wages; in the case of prison, slave, and some child labor—usually the work is conducted under environmentally, physically, and/or mentally abusive conditions.

SWOT analysis A search for the strengths (S), weaknesses (W), opportunities (O), and threats (T) affecting the organization.

Symbol An object, act, quality, or event that conveys meaning to others.

Sympathy strike or **secondary strike** A work stoppage initiated by a second union in support of a strike launched by another union.

Synergy *Two or more things working together to produce a result not obtainable independently.*

Synthetic transformation The process in which resources are combined to create finished products.

System software Software that enables the application software to interact with the computer and helps the computer manage its internal and external resources. Examples: Microsoft's Windows XP, Vista, or 7; Apple's Mac OS.

Tactical planning A process that determines what contributions departments or similar work units can make with their given resources during the next six months to two years.

Taft-Hartley Act or **Labor-Management Relations Act** Legislation that defined certain union practices as unfair and illegal.

Tangible personal property Movable physical items that can be owned.

Tangible real property Land and anything attached to it.

Target costing A company starts with the price it wants to charge, figures out the profit margin it wants, then determines what the costs must be to produce the product to meet the desired price and profit goals.

Target marketing strategy Concept of marketing, in which a company markets to a particular market segment, whose members have similar characteristics or wants and needs.

Target return on investment Fancy language for making a profit, a specified yield on the investment.

Tariff A trade barrier in the form of a customs duty, or tax, levied mainly on imports.

Tax accounting A form of accounting in which a CPA, trained in tax law, concentrates on preparing tax returns and doing tax planning.

Tax deferred In retirement planning, the concept of paying no current taxes on any gains, but the gains will be taxed as regular income when a withdrawal is made.

Taxes The means by which governments raise revenues.

Team A small group of people with complementary skills who are committed to common performance goals and approach for which they hold themselves mutually accountable.

Technical skills The job-specific knowledge needed to perform well in a specialized field.

Technology This is not just computer technology; it is any machine or process that enables an organization to gain a competitive advantage in changing materials used to produce a finished product.

Telecom *Short for telecommunications.*

Telecommuting Working at home with telecommunications between office and home.

Telemarketing Using the telephone to sell products directly to customers.

Tender offer An outsider seeking to take over a company directly contacts the company's shareholders and offers to buy their stock at a price that exceeds the present market price.

Term insurance Offers a specified amount of coverage for a specified number of years, after which it expires and the policyholder has no more coverage.

Term-loan agreement A promissory note indicating specific installments, such as monthly or yearly, for repayment.

Terms of trade The conditions a supplier or seller gives a buyer when offering short-term credit.

Test marketing The introduction of a new product in a limited form to selected geographical markets to test consumers' reactions.

Theory X Point of view posed by Douglas McGregor in which managers assume workers to be irresponsible, resistant to change, lacking in ambition, hating work, and preferring to be led rather than to lead.

Theory Y Point of view posed by Douglas McGregor in which managers assume that workers are capable of accepting responsibility, self-direction, and self-control and of being imaginative and creative.

Theory Z A motivation approach proposed by William Ouchi that emphasizes involving employees at all levels, giving them long-term job security, allowing collective decision making, emphasizing slow evaluation and promotion procedures, and treating workers like family.

Thorny issue *An issue or problem that is difficult to resolve.*

Through the grapevine *Communication or information that travels informally.*

Time deposits Bank funds that cannot be withdrawn without notice or transferred by check.

Time to market The length of time it takes from a product being conceived until it is available for sale.

Time-motion studies A system developed by Frederick W. Taylor, in which he broke down each worker's job into basic physical motions and then trained workers to use the methods of their best-performing coworkers.

To be effective To achieve results, to realize the firm's goals by making the right decisions and executing them successfully.

To be efficient To use people, money, raw materials, and other resources wisely and cost effectively.

Top managers The highest level of management, professionals who make long-term decisions about the overall direction of the organization and establish the objectives, strategies, and policies for it.

Tort A civil—that is, noncriminal—wrongful act that results in injury to people or property.

Tort law Laws applying to wrongful injuries in business relationships *not* covered by contract law and *not* covered by criminal law.

Total product offer Also known as the *value package,* all the factors that potential buyers evaluate in a product when considering whether to buy it.

Total quality management (TQM) A comprehensive approach—led by top management and supported throughout the organization—dedicated to continuous quality improvement, training, and customer satisfaction.

Totalitarian political systems Systems that are ruled by a dictator, a single political party, or a special-membership group.

Touch base *To contact or establish communication.*

Trade association Consists of individuals and companies in a specific business or industry organized to promote common interests.

Trade credit Short-term financing by which a firm buys a product, and then receives a bill (an invoice) from the supplier, then pays it later.

Trade deficit An unfavorable balance of trade, which exists when the value of a country's total imports exceeds the value of its total exports.

Trade promotion Also known as *business-to-business (B2B) sales promotion;* the promotional activity of trying to stimulate dealer interest in a product through such means as trade shows, conventions, catalogs, and special printed materials for salespeople.

Trade protectionism The use of government regulations, tariffs, quotas, and embargos to limit the import of goods and services.

Trade show A gathering of manufacturers in the same industry who display their products to their distributors and dealers.

Trade surplus Also called a *favorable balance of trade,* exists when the value of a country's total exports exceeds the value of its total imports. Countries prefer to export more than they import because then they have money left over to spend on other things.

Trademarks Brand names and brand marks, and even slogans that have been given exclusive legal protection.

Trading floor exchanges Buying and selling of securities conducted face to face on a trading floor or in a big room.

Traditional IRA A tax-deferred individual retirement account for individuals—and spouses, if they choose—that allows them to save for retirement and to deduct the amount of the contribution from their income taxes in the year in which the contribution was made.

Training and development Steps taken by the organization to increase employee performance and productivity.

Transaction loan Credit extended by a bank for a specific purpose.

Transactional leadership Focuses on creating a smooth-running organization, motivating employees to meet performance goals.

Transformational leadership Focuses on inspiring long-term vision, creativity, and exceptional performance in employees.

Treasury bills (T-bills) Short-term obligations of the U.S. Treasury with a maturity period of one year or less (typically three months), may be purchased directly from the U.S. government.

Trial balance In bookkeeping, making a summary of all the data in the ledgers to see if the figures are accurate or balanced.

Trial balloon *A tentative statement or action designed to test reaction to a plan, strategy, or project.*

Trial close For salespeople, use of a question or statement that tests the prospect's willingness to buy.

Trial courts The lowest level of courts, general courts that hear criminal or civil cases not specifically assigned to other courts.

Trojan horse A program that pretends to be a useful program, usually free, such as a game, but carries viruses, or destructive instructions, that perpetrate mischief without one's knowledge.

Turn a blind eye *Refusal to acknowledge something of importance.*

Two-factor theory Frederick Herzberg's concept that work dissatisfaction and satisfaction arise from two different factors—work satisfaction from higher-level needs called *motivating factors,* and work dissatisfaction from lower-level needs called *hygiene factors.*

Two-tier wage contracts Contracts in which new employees are paid less than veteran employees.

Underemployed workers Those who hold jobs below their level of qualification or are working part time but want to work full time.

Underwriting The activity of buying new issues of stocks or bonds from issuing corporations and reselling them to the public.

Unemployment insurance Provides financial benefits to people who are involuntarily unemployed and also offers job counseling and placement services.

Unemployment rate The level of joblessness among people actively seeking work.

Uniform Commercial Code (UCC) A comprehensive commercial law designed to provide uniformity in sales and other commercial law and describing the rights of buyers and sellers in transactions.

Uninsurable risk A risk that an insurance company will not cover.

Union security clause The part of the labor-management agreement that states that employees who receive union benefits must join the union, or at least pay dues to it.

Union shop Workers are not required to be union members when hired for a job, but they must join the union within a specified period of time.

Universal product codes (UPCs) Bar codes printed on the package that can be read by bar code scanners.

Unlimited liability Any debts or damages incurred by the business become the responsibility of the business owner.

Unsecured bonds, or debenture bonds Bonds backed only by the reputation of the firm issuing the bonds.

Unsecured loan A loan in which the borrower does not pledge some sort of asset as collateral.

Unsought goods and services Those that people have little interest in, are unaware of, or did not think they needed.

Unstructured interview The interviewer simply asks applicants probing questions in a conversational way; there are no identical, fixed questions asked of all applicants and no systematic scoring of answers.

Upside *Potential for a positive financial outcome.*

User-rate segmentation Categorizing people according to volume or frequency of usage.

Utility The value intermediaries add to products by making them more useful or accessible to consumers.

Validity The test measures what it purports to measure and is free of bias.

Value A customer's perception that a certain product offers a better relationship between costs and benefits than competitors' products do.

Values The relatively permanent and deeply held underlying beliefs and attitudes that help determine people's behavior.

Variable costs Expenses that vary depending on the numbers of products produced.

Variable life insurance Insurance providing coverage for the individual's entire life, but the cash value part is invested in stocks or other high-yield securities and is managed by the policyholder.

Venture capital Funds acquired from wealthy individuals and institutions that are invested in promising start-ups or emerging companies in return for their giving up some ownership.

Venture capitalists Generally companies, not individuals, that invest in new enterprises in return for part ownership of them.

Vertical merger Two companies merge that are in the same industry but each performs a different activity.

Vestibule training Off-the-job training in a simulated environment.

Video marketing Marketing to consumers on television, either through special cable TV channels or through certain programs on regular TV channels.

Viral marketing When companies pay people to promote their products to others, as through Internet chat rooms and blogs.

Virtual Something is created, simulated, or carried on by means of a computer or a computer network.

Virtual organization or **networked organization** A company with a central core that is linked by computer network, usually the Internet, to outside independent firms, which help the core firm achieve its purpose.

Virtual private networks (VPNs) Secure private networks that use a public network (usually the Internet) to connect remote sites.

Virus A "deviant" program, stored on a computer hard drive or CD, that can cause unexpected and often undesirable effects, such as destroying or corrupting data.

Vision A long-term goal describing what the organization wants to become. It is a clear sense of the future and the actions needed to get there.

Voluntary bankruptcy Debtors file papers with a federal bankruptcy court seeking to be declared bankrupt in order to obtain relief from creditors.

Wage reopener clause In union contracts, a clause that allows wage rates to be renegotiated at certain stated times during the life of the contract.

Wagner Act or **National Labor Relations Act** Legislation that gave workers the right (1) to form unions, (2) to bargain collectively, and (3) to engage in such union activities as strikes, picketing, and boycotts; it also (4) formed the *National Labor Relations Board* to oversee union elections and investigate labor practices.

Warehousing The element of physical distribution that is concerned with storage of goods.

Warranty A seller's promise to stand by its products or services—a guarantee that buyers will find the products acceptable for the purposes for which they were designed.

Web 2.0 A move toward a more social, collaborative, interactive, and responsive version of the Web.

Web browser Software that enables one to find and access the various parts of the World Wide Web.

Welfare state Government social services to give citizens economic security by providing for them when they are unemployed, ill, or elderly and, in some countries, providing subsidized college educations and child care.

Whistleblower An employee who reports organizational misconduct to the government or the public.

Whiteboard *To convey information by writing it out on a presentation surface.*

White knight For managers in a firm facing a hostile takeover, a technique that finds a buyer for the company who is more acceptable to management.

Whole life insurance Provides coverage for the individual's whole lifetime rather than for just a specified term, and it builds a form of savings, called *cash value*.

Wholesalers Also known as *middlemen*, these are intermediaries who sell products (1) to other businesses for resale to ultimate customers or (2) to institutions and businesses for use in their operations.

Wide area network (WAN) Covers a wide geographic area, such as a country or the world.

Wide span of control Occurs when a manager has several people reporting.

Wildcat strike A strike that is not authorized by the union during the period covered by the contract.

Win–win situation *A mutually beneficial arrangement for two parties.*

Wired network A computer network that connects the various parts via physical means, such as twisted-pair (telephone) wiring, coaxial cable, or fiber-optic cable.

Wireless network A computer network that connects the various parts via through-the-air means, such as infrared, microwave, or broadcast-radio wave.

Word-of-mouth marketing A promotional technique in which people tell others about products they have purchased or firms they have used.

Work rules Descriptions of the type of work unionized employees may do and the conditions under which they will work.

Work slowdown Employees continue to do their job but at a much slower pace.

Workers' compensation insurance Type of insurance that provides financial benefits as well as coverage of medical care and rehabilitation services to workers who are injured on the job.

World Bank International institution whose purpose is to provide low-interest loans to developing nations for improving transportation, education, health, and telecommunications.

World Trade Organization (WTO) International institution designed to monitor and enforce trade agreements.

World Wide Web An interconnected system of Internet computers called *servers* that support specially formatted documents in multimedia form.

Worm A program that copies itself repeatedly into a computer's memory or onto a disk drive.

Yellow-dog contracts Contracts imposed by employers requiring employees not to join a union.

Yield Income from securities, calculated by dividing dividend or income by the market price.

Zero-sum game *A situation where if one person wins, someone else must lose.*

REFERENCES

CHAPTER 1

1. "On the Road with Rick Steves," CBS News, 60 Minutes, May 26, 2005, www.cbsnews.com/stories/2005/05/25/60II/main697745.shtml; "Europe Through the Back Door: A Gateway to Europe," press release, Europe Through the Back Door, www.ricksteves.com/about/pressroom/aboutetbd.htm; and "Rick's Biography," press release, Europe Through the Back Door, www.ricksteves.com/about/pressroom/rickbio.htm (all accessed April 18, 2011).

2. Adapted from G. Fabrikant and D. Carvajal, "Troubled Story at Golden Books: A Fairy-Tale Pay Package, but Publisher's Losses Grow," *New York Times,* August 10, 1998, www.nytimes.com/1998/08/10/business/troubled-story-golden-books-fairy-tale-pay-package-but-publisher-s-losses-grow.html (accessed April 18, 2011); M. Shnayerson, "Dick Snyder's Tarnished Crown," *Vanity Fair,* May 1999, pp. 110–129; and from A. Kinicki and B. K. Williams, *Management: A Practical Introduction,* 2nd ed. (New York: McGraw-Hill, 2006), p. 151.

3. L. Buchanan, "The Art and Business of Motivational Speaking," *Inc.,* December 2010/January 2011, pp. 124–132.

4. Remarks delivered by U.S. Secretary of Labor Elaine L. Chao to Labor and Human Rights Officers Joint Training Conference, U.S. Department of State, Washington, DC, Wednesday, July 19, 2006, www.dol.gov/_sec/media/speeches/20060719_humanrights.htm (accessed April 18, 2011).

5. J. Zumbrun and S. Chandra, "A U.S. Recovery Built on Low-Paying Jobs," *Bloomberg Businessweek,* February 28–March 6, 2011, pp. 14–15.

6. *NACE Salary Survey,* Spring 2011, National Association of Colleges and Employers, www.aug.edu/career_center/Spring_2011_Salary_Survey.pdf (accessed August 11, 2011).

7. A. P. Carnevale, N. Smith, and J. Strohl, *Help Wanted: Projections of Jobs and Education Requirements through 2018,* June 2010, Center on Education and the Workforce, Georgetown University, http://cew.georgetown.edu/JOBS2018/ (accessed April 18, 2011).

8. M. El-Erian, *When Markets Collide: Investment Strategies for the Age of Global Economic Change* (New York: McGraw-Hill, 2008).

9. D. Barton, "Capitalism for the Long Term," *Harvard Business Review,* March 2011, pp. 85–91.

10. Adapted from "Quality of Life," Dictionary.LaborlawTalk.com, http://encyclopedia.laborlawtalk.com/quality_of_life (accessed April 18, 2011).

11. Food and Agricultural Organization of the United Nations, reported in World Hunger Education Service, "2011 World Hunger and Poverty Facts and Statistics," www.worldhunger.org/articles/Learn/world%20hunger%20facts%202002.htm (accessed April 20, 2011).

12. Public Policy Institute, *A Fair Share—At Least!* March 2003, using data on total New York state revenues from *New York State Executive Budget, 2003–04* (projections for FY '03–'04); local tax total based on extrapolations from Office of the State Comptroller, New York City budget; property tax shares from New York State Office for Real Property Services; and calculations of business share based on data from New York State Division of the Budget, Department of Taxation & Finance,

and other sources; www.ppinys.org/reports./2003/fairshare03.pdf (accessed April 25, 2011).

13. T. J. Stanley and W. D. Danko, *The Millionaire Next Door: The Surprising Secrets of America's Wealthy* (Atlanta: Longstreet Press, 1996), pp. 1–2, 227.

14. Stanley and Danko, 1996, pp. 239, 254–258.

15. Stanley and Danko, 1996, p. 238.

16. Peter Drucker, interviewed by P. Schwartz, "Post-Capitalist," *Wired,* July/August 1993, www.wired.com/wired/archive/1.03/drucker.html (accessed April 25, 2011).

17. L. W. Cheek, "Finding New Life (and Profit) in Doomed Trees," *New York Times,* August 8, 2010, Business section, pp. 1, 6. See also Nick Visser, "Reclaimed Trees Find New Life in Modern Furniture," *Seattle Times,* March 5, 2011, http://o.seattletimes.nwsource.com/html/businesstechnology/2014393560_meyerwells06.html (accessed April 25, 2011).

18. This could be expanded to include other stakeholders such as unions, business allies, and competitors. See, for example, Figure 3.1 in A. Kinicki and B. K. Williams, *Management: A Practical Introduction,* 4th ed. (New York: McGraw-Hill/Irwin, 2009), p. 73.

19. P. Hopkins, "How to Use Facebook Pages for Customer Support—Part 1," *Customer Futurology,* January 16, 2011, www.customerfuturology.com/2011/01/16/facebook-pages-customer-support (accessed August 11, 2011).

20. UTest review by 600 software professionals, reported in B. Acohido, "Study: Amazon Most User Friendly," *USA Today,* December 7, 2009, p. 2B. See also UTest, "Software Testing Leader Holds Competition to Compare E-Tailers Based on Pricing, Usability, Product Search and Other Feature Sets," December 7, 2009, www.utest.com/press/utest-%E2%80%9Cbattle-e-tailers%E2%80%9D-uncovers-more-500-bugs-amazoncom-walmartcom-and-targetcom (accessed April 25, 2011).

21. J. Nocera, "Put Buyers First? What a Concept," *New York Times,* January 5, 2008, pp. B1, B9.

22. Jeff Bezos, quoted in Nocera, 2008, p. B9.

23. J. Pfeffer, *The Human Equation: Building Profits by Putting People First* (Cambridge, MA: Harvard Business School Press, 1996).

24. J. Pfeffer, in A. M. Webber, "Danger: Toxic Company," *Fast Company,* November 1998, pp. 152–161.

25. D. Barboza, "Clues in an iPhone Autopsy," *New York Times,* July 6, 2010, pp. B1, B7.

26. "Hard-Hit Town Can't Salvage DHL Jobs," *CBS News,* April 17, 2009, www.cbsnews.com/stories/2009/04/17/business/main4952111.shtml?source=RSSattr=Business_4952111 (accessed April 25, 2011).

27. Office of Technology Assessment, *Gauging Control Technology and Regulatory Impacts in Occupational Safety and Health: An Appraisal of OSHA's Analytic Approach,* September 1995, http://govinfolibrary.unt.edu/ota/Ota_1/DATA/1995/9531.PDF (accessed August 14, 2010).

28. B. Horovitz, "Domino's Nightmare Holds Lessons for Marketers," *USA Today,* April 16, 2009, p. 3B; S. Clifford, "Video Prank at Domino's Goes Sour," *New York Times,* April 16, 2009,

pp. B1, B6; and B. Levisohn and E. Gibson, "An Unwelcome Delivery," *BusinessWeek*, May 4, 2009, p. 15.

29. A. Hartocollis, "Peaceful Clinic Flooded with Patients with Their Own Fiscal Crises," *New York Times*, January 31, 2009, p. A15.

30. P. H. Rubin, "Instant Info Is a Two-Edged Sword," *Wall Street Journal*, December 31, 2008, p. A9.

31. M. J. Mandel and R. D. Hof, "Rethinking the Internet," *Business-Week*, March 26, 2001, p. 118. See also B. Powell, "The New World Order," *Fortune*, May 14, 2001, pp. 134, 136.

32. Among the many press reports on climate change, see C. Dean, "Marine Life Gravely Threatened by Rising Ocean Acidity, Panel Warns," *San Francisco Chronicle*, January 31, 2009, p. A4; reprinted from the *New York Times*; D. Perlman, "Antarctica's Climate Rapidly Changing—Penguins on Move as Food Chain Shifts," *San Francisco Chronicle*, March 13, 2009, pp. A1, A11; D. Perlman, "Ice in Arctic Getting Thinner and Fading Fast," *San Francisco Chronicle*, April 7, 2009, pp. A1, A13; J. Kay, "Greenhouse Gases Must Be Cut Now, Obama Aide Says," *San Francisco Chronicle*, April 9, 2009, pp. A1, A10; D. Cappiello, "Threat of Climate Change May Yield First Major Pollution Laws in Years," *San Francisco Chronicle*, April 19, 2009, p. A10; T. Fuller, "Study Says Warming Poses Peril to Asia," *New York Times*, April 27, 2009, p. A4; and P. Fimrite, "Major Shifts in Bird Species Predicted in Next 60 Years," *San Francisco Chronicle*, September 2, 2009, pp. A1, A17.

33. K. Dick, "Green Businesses Stick to the 3 P's: Profit, People, and Planet," *Reno Gazette-Journal*, April 22, 2009, pp. 9A, 10A.

34. Study by D. Roland-Holst, Center for Energy, Resources, and Economic Sustainability, University of California, Berkeley, reported in F. Barringer, "Green Policies in California Generated Jobs, Study Finds," *New York Times*, October 20, 2008, p. B2.

35. T. Beaumont and D. Piller, "Obama Calls for New Energy Era," *Reno Gazette-Journal*, April 23, 2009, p. 1B; reprinted from *Des Moines Register*; and M. Duan, "Obama's Green Light for Green Jobs," *U.S. News & World Report*, May 2009, p. 30.

36. J. C. Ramo, *The Age of the Unthinkable: Why the New World Disorder Constantly Surprises Us and What We Can Do about It* (Boston: Little, Brown, 2009).

37. S. Manning, "U.S. Manufacturing Isn't Dead or Dying—It's Moving Upscale," *San Francisco Chronicle*, February 17, 2009, p. C4.

38. T. L. Friedman, *The World Is Flat: A Brief History of the Twenty-First Century* (New York: Farrar, Straus and Giroux, 2005).

39. B. C. Greenwald and J. Kahn, *Globalization: The Irrational Fear That Someone in China Will Take Your Job* (New York: Wiley, 2008).

40. M. M. Phillips, "More Work Is Outsourced to U.S. Than Away from It, Data Show," *Wall Street Journal*, March 15, 2004, p. A2.

41. N. Lieber, "Suddenly, Made in USA Looks Like a Strategy," *Bloomberg Businessweek*, March 28, 2011, pp. 57–58.

42. D. Morgan quoted in A. Bruzzese, "There Are Opportunities Overseas for Young U.S. Jobseekers," *Reno Gazette-Journal*, February 20, 2009, p. 9A.

43. G. Allred, quoted in S. Armour, "Facing a Tough Choice: Your Ethics or Your Job," *USA Today*, September 21, 1998, p. B1.

44. Judge William Alsup, quoted in K. Chu, "Judge Tells Wells Fargo to Repay Customers $203M," *USA Today*, August 12, 2010, p. 1B.

45. Alsup, quoted in A. Martin and R. Lieber, "Wells Fargo Loses Ruling on Overdraft Fees," *New York Times*, August 10, 2010, www.nytimes.com/2010/08/11/business/11wells.html?_r=1& scp=1&sq=August%2011%20Wells%20Fargo%20overdraft& st=cse (accessed April 24, 2011).

46. E. J. Foss, interviewed in W. J. Holstein, "Diversity Is Even More Important in Hard Times," *New York Times*, February 14, 2009, p. B2.

47. S. E. Page, interviewed in C. Dreifus, "In Professor's Model, Diversity = Productivity," *New York Times*, January 8, 2008, p. D2. Page is author of *The Difference: How the Power of Diversity Creates Better Groups, Firms, Schools, and Societies* (Princeton, NJ: Princeton University Press, 2008).

48. Pew Research Center data, reported in S. Roberts, "Birthrate Falls for Whites to about Half," *New York Times*, May 6, 2010, p. A18.

49. U.S. Census Bureau, reported in "Stirring the Pot," *Newsweek*, January 26, 2009, p. 70.

50. Research by Pew Research Center, reported in M. Kuruvila, "Survey Finds 53% of Americans Have Changed Faiths," *San Francisco Chronicle*, April 28, 2009, pp. A1, A14.

51. American Religious Identification Survey, reported in C. L. Grossman, "15% Now Check No Religion," *USA Today*, September 22, 2009, p. 7D.

52. Research by Pew Forum on Religion & Public Life, reported in C. L. Grossman, "Mixing Their Religion," *USA Today*, December 10, 2009, pp. 1A, 2A.

53. LifeWay Research, reported in C. L. Grossman, "Young Adults Less Devoted to Faith," *USA Today*, April 27, 2010, p. 1A.

54. Research by Pew Research Center, reported in M. B. Marcus, "Marriages More Mixed Than Ever," *USA Today*, June 4, 2010, p. 1A.

55. Research by Pew Research Center, reported in D. Crary, "Men See Economic Boost from Marriage," *Reno Gazette-Journal*, January 19, 2010, p. 5A.

56. K. Riddle, "Kids First, Marriage Later—If Ever," *NPR*, July 4, 2010, www.npr.org/templates/story/story.php?storyId=128265730 (accessed April 24, 2011).

57. Data from U.S. Department of Housing and Urban Development, reported in F. Eltman, "Suburban Homelessness on the Rise," *Reno Gazette-Journal*, February 17, 2010, p. 4B.

58. S. Armour, "More Families Move in Together," *USA Today*, February 3, 2009, pp. 1B, 2B.

59. C. Dougherty, "Working Poor Feel the Pinch," *Wall Street Journal*, September 29, 2009, p. A3; H. Yen, "Revised Formula Puts 1 in 6 Americans in Poverty," *San Francisco Chronicle*, October 21, 2009, p. A6; C. Dugas, "Financial Worries Dog Older Workers," *USA Today*, September 30, 2009, p. 2B; H. Yen, "Number of Poor Older Americans on the Rise," *Reno Gazette-Journal*, September 8, 2009, p. 7A; R. Wolf, "Social Security Recipients Up by 19%," *USA Today*, October 2, 2009, p. 1A; and J. DeParle, "49 Million Americans Report a Lack of Food," *New York Times*, November 17, 2009, p. A14.

60. These three skills are adapted from the classic article by R. L. Katz, "Skills of an Effective Administrator," *Harvard Business Review*, September–October, 1974, p. 94. Katz categorized the skills as technical, conceptual, and human skills.

61. D. Heath and C. Heath, "Tase the Haze," *Fast Company*, September 2010, pp. 46–48.

62. W. Gallagher, quoted in book review, D. G. Myers, "Please Pay Attention," *Wall Street Journal*, April 20, 2009, p. A13. Gallagher is author of *Rapt* (New York: Penguin Press, 2009).

63. J. Tierney, "Ear Plugs to Lasers: The Science of Concentration," *New York Times*, May 5, 2009, p. D2.

64. Psychiatrist E. M. Hallowell, quoted in A. Tugend, "Multitasking Can Make You Lose . . . Um . . . Focus," *New York Times*, October 25, 2008, p. B7. Hallowell is the author of *CrazyBusy: Overstretched, Overbooked, and About to Snap!* (New York: Ballantine, 2006).

65. W. Gallagher, cited in blog by J. Tierney, "Attention Must Be Paid—but How?" *New York Times–Tierney Lab,* May 4, 2009, http://tierneylab.blogs.nytimes.com/ (accessed August 14, 2010). Gallagher is author of *Rapt* (New York: Penguin Press, 2009).

66. W. Gallagher, quoted in blog by J. Tierney, 2009.

67. G. Edmunds, "Booker T. Washington's Words Ring True for All Entrepreneurs," *USA Today,* February 20, 2010, www.usatoday.com/money/smallbusiness/columnist/edmunds/2010-02-09-booker-t-washington-entrepreneurs_N.htm (accessed March 26, 2011).

68. K. Whitelaw, "Defining Diversity: Beyond Race and Gender," *NPR,* January 13, 2010, www.npr.org/templates/story/story.php?storyId=122327104 (accessed March 27, 2011).

69. "Corporate Responsibility—Definitions," Motorola, http://responsibility.motorola.com/index.php/suppliers/suppldiversity/definitions (accessed March 27, 2011).

70. "U.S. Diversity and Inclusion Programs," Abbott Laboratories, www.abbott.com/global/url/content/en_US/50.30.10:10/general_content/General_Content_00466.htm (accessed March 27, 2011).

71. E. Cho, "Black Friday vs. Buy Nothing Day," Eugene Cho blog, November 25, 2010, http://eugenecho.wordpress.com/2010/11/25/reservations-about-buy-nothing-day (accessed April 20, 2011).

72. "Buy Nothing Day," www.teddave.com/nothingcontents.html (accessed January 31, 2011).

73. "Quality of Life," Dictionary.LaborlawTalk.com, www.encyclopedia.laborlawtalk.com/quality_of_life (accessed August 22, 2011).

74. P. Burrows, "Apple vs. Google," *Bloomberg Businessweek,* January 14, 2010, www.businessweek.com/magazine/content/10_04/b4164028483414.htm (accessed March 27, 2011).

75. D. Caolo, "NY Times Details Google/Apple Relationship Sorrowing," The Unofficial Apple Weblog, www.tuaw.com/2010/03/15/ny-times-details-google-apple-relationship-souring (accessed March 26, 2011).

76. Burrows, "Apple vs. Google," 2010.

77. B. Solis, "Mobile Internet Market to Eclipse Desktop Internet," Brian Solis, February 3, 2010, www.briansolis.com/2010/02/mobile-internet-market-to-eclipse-desktop-internet (accessed April 23, 2011).

78. Burrows, "Apple vs. Google," 2010.

79. G. Tsurilnik, "$1B Mobile Ad Revenue May Mean Shot at Top for Google," Mobile Marketer, October 18, 2010, www.mobilemarketer.com/cms/news/advertising/7772.html (accessed April 23, 2011).

80. J. E. Vascellaro and Y. I. Kane, "Apple to Tighten Control on Content," *Wall Street Journal Online,* February 2, 2011, http://online.wsj.com/article/SB10001424052748704477560457612 0531458250932.html#ixzz1CrEvpzB0 (accessed February 2, 2011).

81. Vascellaro and Kane, 2011.

CHAPTER 2

1. P. Rogers, "Douglas Durand Blew the Whistle on Hi Drug Firm—and Got $79 Million," *People,* May 6, 2002, www.people.com/people/archive/article/0,,20136933,00.html (accessed April 25, 2011); C. Haddad and A. Barrett, "A Whistle-Blower Rocks an Industry," *BusinessWeek,* June 24, 2002, pp. 126, 128; D. Lavole, "Drug Firm Sales Reps Go on Trial," *San Francisco Chronicle,* April 13, 2004, pp. C1, C5; and N. Weinberg, "The Dark Side of Whistleblowing," *Forbes.com,* March 14, 2005, www.forbes.com/forbes/2005/0314/090_print.html (accessed April 25, 2011).

2. W. H. Swanson, quoted in S. Taub, "Raytheon Chief Punished for Plagiarism," *CFO.com,* May 3, 2006, www.cfo.com/article

.cfm/68**78423?f=rsspage (accessed April 25, 2011). See also news release, "Raytheon Chairman & CEO Comments Regarding 'Unwritten Rules,'" Raytheon, April 24, 2006, www.prnewswire.com/cgi-bin/micro_stories.pl?ACCT=149999&TICK=RTN&STORY=/www/story/04-24-2006/0004346311&EDATE=Apr+24,+2006 (accessed April 25, 2011).

3. L. Wayne, "Chief's Pay Is Docked by Raytheon," *New York Times,* May 4, 2006, pp. C1, C4. See also D. Leonhardt, "Rule No. 35: Reread Rule on Integrity," *New York Times,* May 3, 2006, pp. C1, C7; and D. Hatch, "Denny Hatch's Business Common Sense," *Target Marketing Group Publication,* May 9, 2006, http://napco.com/enewsletters/stories/commonsense/commonsense/286047060488046.html (accessed April 25, 2011).

4. B. Worthen and J. S. Lublin, "Mark Hurd Neglected to Follow H-P Code," *Wall Street Journal,* August 9, 2010, pp. B1, B5.

5. A. B. Carroll, "Managing Ethically with Global Stakeholders: A Present and Future Challenge," *Academy of Management Executive,* May 2004, p. 118. Also see B. W. Husted and D. B. Allen, "Corporate Social Responsibility in the Multinational Enterprise: Strategic and Institutional Approaches," *Journal of International Business Studies,* November 2006, pp. 838–849.

6. B. Carey, "Stumbling Blocks on the Path of Righteousness," *New York Times,* May 5, 2009, p. D5.

7. Bruce Silverglade, quoted in B. Horovitz, "Pepsi Is Dropping Out of Schools," *USA Today,* March 17, 2010, p. 1A.

8. A. B. Carroll, "Managing Ethically with Global Stakeholders: A Present and Future Challenge," 2004, pp. 117–118.

9. B. Egelko, "Damages for Gallery Owners Reinstated Against Kinkade," *San Francisco Chronicle,* June 18, 2009, p. B2.

10. Carey, "Stumbling Blocks on the Path of Righteousness," 2009.

11. N. Epley and D. Dunning, "Feeling 'Holier Than Thou': Are Self-Serving Assessments Produced by Errors in Self- or Social Protection?" *Journal of Personality and Social Psychology* 79 (2000), pp. 861–875.

12. Carey, "Stumbling Blocks on the Path of Righteousness," 2009.

13. D. Tankersley, C. J. Stowe, and S. A. Huettel, "Altruism Is Associated with an Increased Neural Response to Agency," *Nature Neuroscience* advance online edition, January 21, 2007, www.nature.com/neuro/journal/vaop/ncurrent/abs/nn1833.html (accessed April 25, 2011).

14. Scott Huettel, quoted in "Why Do Good? Brain Study Offers Clues," *Forbes.com,* January 22, 2007, www.forbes.com/forbeslife/health/feeds/hscout/2007/01/22/hscout601147.html (accessed April 25, 2011).

15. L. Wayne, "A Promise to Be Ethical in an Era of Immorality," *New York Times,* May 30, 2009, pp. B1, B4.

16. L. Jennings, "Anything to Get Ahead: The New American Norm?" *The Futurist,* September–October 2004, pp. 60–61. D. Callahan is the author of *The Cheating Culture: Why More Americans Are Doing Wrong to Get Ahead* (New York: Harcourt, 2004).

17. T. Dokoupil, "America's Top Liars," *Newsweek,* April 25, 2011, pp. 54–55. J. B. Stewart is the author of *Tangled Webs: How False Statements Are Undermining America: From Martha Stewart to Bernie Madoff* (New York: Penguin Press, 2011).

18. M. H. Bazerman and A. E. Tenbrunsel, "Stumbling into Bad Behavior," *New York Times,* April 21, 2011, p. A2. The two are authors of *Blind Spots: Why We Fail to Do What's Right and What to Do About It* (Princeton, NJ: Princeton University Press, 2011).

19. M. Hinman, "How to Fight College Cheating," *Washington Post,* September 3, 2004, p. A19; N. A. Stanlick, "Ethics and Integrity

in Education: The Problem of Academic Dishonesty," http://pegasus.cc.ucf.edu/~stanlick/gtaacinteg081303.ppt (accessed April 25, 2011); and S. B. Blum, *My Word! Plagiarism and College Cheating* (Ithaca, NY: Cornell University Press, 2009).

20. Josephson Institute survey, *2008 Report Card on Ethics of American Youth,* reported in "The Ethics of American Youth—2008 Summary," Josephson Institute Center for Youth Ethics, http://charactercounts.org/programs/reportcard (accessed April 25, 2011); and Nationwide poll by Benenson Strategy Group for Common Sense Media, reported in "35% of Teenagers Report Using Cell Phones to Cheat," Common Sense Media, June 18, 2009, www.commonsensemedia.org/about-us/press-room/hi-tech-cheating-poll (accessed April 25, 2011). See also G. Topo, "Many Teens Use Phones in Class," *USA Today,* June 18, 2009, p. 13B; and J. Tucker, "Tech-Savvy Students Invent New Ways to Cheat," *San Francisco Chronicle,* June 19, 2009, pp. A1, A16.

21. *Converting Data into Action: Expanding the Boundaries of Institutional Improvement.* National Survey of Student Engagement: The College Student Report, 2003 Annual Report, sponsored by the Carnegie Foundation for the Advancement of Teaching, 2003, http://nsse.iub.edu/2003_annual_report/index.htm (accessed April 25, 2011). See also D. L. McCabe, L. K. Trevino, and K. D. Butterfield, "Cheating in Academic Institutions: A Decade of Research," *Ethics & Behavior* 11 (2001), pp. 219–232. For more on high-tech cheating, see C. Said, "Are Camera Phones Too Revealing?" *San Francisco Chronicle,* May 16, 2004, pp. A1, A2; B. Read, "Wired for Cheating," *Chronicle of Higher Education,* July 16, 2004, pp. A27–A28; M. A. Walker, "High-Tech Crib: Camera Phones Boost Cheating," *Wall Street Journal,* September 10, 2004, pp. B1, B4; S. McAndrew, "Cellular Cheating?" *Reno Gazette-Journal,* September 11, 2004, pp. 1E, 8E; and J. D. Glater, "Colleges Chase as Cheats Shift to High Tech," *New York Times,* May 18, 2006, pp. A1, A20.

22. D. L. McCabe, K. D. Butterfield, and L. K. Trevino, "Academic Dishonesty in Graduate Business Programs: Prevalence, Causes, and Proposed Action," *Academy of Management Learning & Education,* September 2006, pp. 294–305.

23. B. Staples, "Cutting and Pasting: A Senior Thesis by (Insert Name)," *New York Times,* July 12, 2010, www.nytimes.com/2010/07/13/opinion/13tue4.html (accessed April 25, 2011).

24. D. J. Palazzo, Y.-J. Lee, R. Warnakulasooriya, and D. E. Pritchard, "Patterns, Correlates, and Reduction of Homework Copying," *Physical Review Special Topics,* March 2010, http://prst-per.aps.org/abstract/PRSTPER/v6/i1/e010104 (accessed April 25, 2011).

25. M. Jennings and S. Happel, W. P. Carey School of Business, cited in "College Cheating Is Bad for Business," *Knowledge@W.P. Carey,* September 24, 2008, http://knowledge.wpcarey.asu.edu/article.cfm?articleid=1679 (accessed April 25, 2011).

26. B. Carey, "Our Cheating Psyches," *New York Times,* April 17, 2011, Week in Review section, pp. 1, 5.

27. J. Drucker and M. Maremont, "CEOs of Bailed-Out Banks Flew to Resorts on Firms' Jets," *Wall Street Journal,* June 19, 2009, http://online.wsj.com/article/SB124536271699529031.html (accessed April 25, 2011).

28. V. O'Connell, "Test for Dwindling Retail Jobs Spawns a Culture of Cheating," *Wall Street Journal,* January 7, 2009, pp. A1, A10.

29. W. M. Welch, "Employee Screenings See Growth," *USA Today,* June 24, 2009, p. 3A.

30. P. Bernard, "BlackBerry @ Work: The Decline of Manners," letters, *New York Times,* June 26, 2009, p. A22.

31. Reported in Bernard, "BlackBerry @ Work: The Decline of Manners," 2009.

32. B. Stone and A. Vance, "Apple Obsessed with Secrecy on Products and Top Executives," *New York Times,* June 23, 2009, pp. B1, B5.

33. R. Kim, "Jobs Reportedly Had Liver Transplant 2 Months Ago," *San Francisco Chronicle,* June 21, 2009, pp. A1, A13; and D. Grady and B. Meier, "A Transplant That Is Raising Many Questions," *New York Times,* June 23, 2009, pp. B1, B5.

34. A. O. Patrick and V. Bauerlein, "Coke Teams Up with Socially Responsible Smoothie," *Wall Street Journal,* April 8, 2009, p. B6.

35. B. Berkrot, "Pfizer Whistleblower's Ordeal Reaps Big Rewards," Reuters, September 2, 2009, www.reuters.com/article/newsOne/idUSN021592920090902 (accessed April 25, 2011).

36. Study by C. C. Masten, inspector general, U.S. Department of Labor, reported in R. Pear, "Whistleblowers Likely to Get Stronger Federal Protections," *New York Times,* March 15, 1999, pp. A1, A17.

37. B. Levisohn, "How to Make a Madoff," *BusinessWeek,* December 16, 2008, www.businessweek.com/investor/content/dec2008/pi20081215_232943.htm?chan=investing_investing+index+page_top+stories (accessed April 25, 2011). See also D. Gross, "Membership Has Its Penalties," *Newsweek,* January 12, 2009, p. 18; and M. Hosenball, "Made Money with Madoff? Don't Count on Keeping It," *Newsweek,* January 12, 2009, p. 9.

38. D. R. Henriques, "Madoff, Apologizing, Is Given 150 Years," *New York Times,* June 30, 2009, pp. A1, B4.

39. For a debate on the pros and cons of corporate social responsibility, see "Corporate Social Responsibility: Good Citizenship or Investor Rip-off?" *Wall Street Journal,* January 9, 2006, pp. R6–R7.

40. Sir Nicholas Stern, head of Britain's Government Economic Service, who wrote a report on the economic consequences of climate change. See J. Cassidy, "High Costs," *New Yorker,* November 13, 2006, pp. 35–36.

41. P. A. Samuelson, "Love That Corporation," *Mountain Bell Magazine,* Spring 1971.

42. M. Friedman, "The Social Responsibility of Business Is to Increase Its Profits," *New York Times Magazine,* September 13, 1970, pp. 17–20.

43. A. G. Robinson and D. M. Schroeder, "Greener and Cheaper," *Wall Street Journal,* March 23, 2009, p. R4.

44. R. Farzad, "The Scrappiest Car Manufacturer in America," *Bloomberg Businessweek,* June 6, 2011, pp. 68–74.

45. J. Emerson, quoted in C. Dahle, "60 Seconds with Jeb Emerson," *Fast Company,* March 2004, p. 42.

46. J. Emerson, "The Nature of Returns: A Social Capital Markets Inquiry into Elements of Investment and the Blended Value Proposition," *Social Enterprise Series No. 17* (Boston: Harvard Business School Press, 2000), p. 36.

47. J. Wicks, quoted in G. Rifkin, "Making a Profit and a Difference," *New York Times,* October 5, 2006, p. C5.

48. "What Shall We Drink To? How about Progressive Manufacturing Techniques?" *Inc. Magazine,* November 2006, pp. 83–84.

49. "Not Playing Around: A Skateboard Company with a Mission," *Inc. Magazine,* November 2006, p. 83.

50. J. Austin, H. Stevenson, and J. Wei-Skillern, "Social and Commercial Entrepreneurship: Same, Different, or Both?" *Entrepreneurship Theory and Practice,* January 2006, pp. 1–22, www.blackwell-synergy.com/doi/pdf/10.1111/j.1540-6520.2006.00107 (accessed April 25, 2011).

51. P. Garcia, P. Lesova, J. Swindler, and K. Tuggle, "Class of '07: The Fast Company/Monitor Group Social Capitalist Award Winners," *Fast Company,* December 2006–January 2007, p. 70.

52. M. May, "Nonprofit's Tiny Loans Make Big Difference," *San Francisco Chronicle,* April 13, 2009, pp. B1, B3.

53. This definition of sustainability was developed in 1987 by the World Commission on Environment and Development.

54. T. Howard, "Being Eco-Friendly Can Pay Economically," *USA Today,* August 15, 2005, p. 7B; D. Fonda, "G.E.'s Green

Awakening," *Time Inside Business,* August 2005, pp. A10–A16; "The Business of Green" [special section], *New York Times,* May 17, 2006, pp. E1–12; G. Raine, "Good for Earth, Good for Business," *San Francisco Chronicle,* December 12, 2008, pp. C1, C2; and D. Cogan, M. Good, G. Kantor, and E. McAteer, *Corporate Governance and Climate Change: Consumer and Technology Companies,* Ceres, December 2008, www.ceres.org/Page.aspx?pid=1002 (accessed April 25, 2011).

55. R. Todd, "If You Believe Ray Anderson, We Are at the Dawn of the New Industrial Revolution," *Inc. Magazine,* November 2006, pp. 80–81.

56. J. Markoff and S. Lohr, "Gates to Reduce Microsoft Role as Era Changes," *New York Times,* June 16, 2006, pp. A1, C8; and J. Guynn, "He's Opening Windows to Philanthropy," *San Francisco Chronicle,* June 16, 2006, pp. F1, F5.

57. S. Banjo and R. A. Guth, "U.S. Super Rich Vow to Share Wealth," *Wall Street Journal,* August 5, 2010, http://online.wsj.com/article/SB2000142405274870401790457540919379033716 2.html (accessed April 25, 2011).

58. K. Peterson and M. Pfitzer, "Lobbying for Good," *Stanford Social Innovation Review,* Winter 2009, www.ssireview.org/articles/entry/lobbying_for_good (accessed April 25, 2011); and The Mary Kay Foundation website, www.mkacf.org/Pages/Home.aspx (accessed April 25, 2011).

59. W. Buffett, quoted in N. Hertz, "New Ethic: Just Do It Right," *San Francisco Chronicle,* May 15, 2005, http://articles.sfgate.com/2005-05-15/opinion/17371943_1_ethical-tobacco-control-framework-convention (accessed April 25, 2011).

60. J. Lipman, "Are Ethics for Suckers?" *Newsweek,* April 18, 2011, p. 8; H. W. Jenkins Jr., "Warren Buffett, Softie," *Wall Street Journal,* April 30, 2011, p. A15; and S. Ovide and S. Ng, "Buffett Doesn't Expect Controversy to Dent Reputation," *Wall Street Journal,* May 1, 2011, http://online.wsj.com/article/SB10001424052748704436004576297392368003436.html?mod=googlenews_wsj (accessed May 1, 2011).

61. *2010 Report to the Nations on Occupational Fraud & Abuse,* Association of Certified Fraud Examiners, www.acfe.com/rttn/rttn-2010.pdf (accessed April 25, 2011).

62. 2003 survey by Wirthlin Worldwide, cited in *The Hidden Costs of Unethical Behavior,* p. 2.

63. W. Davison, D. Worrell, and C. Lee, "Stock Market Reactions to Announced Corporate Illegalities," *Journal of Business Ethics,* December 1994, pp. 979–988.

64. D. M. Long and S. Rao, "The Wealth Effects of Unethical Business Behavior," *Journal of Economics and Finance,* Summer 1995, pp. 65–73.

65. M. Baucus and D. Baucus, "Paying the Piper: An Empirical Examination of Longer-Term Financial Consequences of Illegal Corporate Behavior," *Academy of Management Journal* 40 (1997), pp. 129–151.

66. 2003 survey by Wirthlin Worldwide, cited in *The Hidden Costs of Unethical Behavior* (Los Angeles: Josephson Institute of Ethics, 2004), p. 2, http://josephsoninstitute.org/business/resources/hidden_costs.html (accessed April 25, 2011).

67. Caravan survey from Opinion Research developed by LRN of 2,037 adults, reported in "Ethics vs. Price," *USA Today,* June 14, 2006, p. 1B.

68. Roper Starch Worldwide Inc. and Cone Communications 1996 survey, reported in R. D. Schatz and C. Poole, "The Two Bottom Lines: Profits and People," *BusinessWeek,* December 7, 1998, pp. ENT 4, ENT 6.

69. R. Gildea, "Consumer Survey Confirms Corporate Social Action Affects Buying Decisions," *Public Relations Quarterly,* Winter 1994, pp. 20–21.

70. A discussion of ethics and financial performance is provided by R. M. Fulmer, "The Challenge of Ethical Leadership," *Organizational Dynamics,* August 2004, pp. 307–317.

71. C. C. Verschoor, "Corporate Performance Is Closely Linked to a Strong Ethical Commitment," *Business and Society Review* 104(1998), pp. 407–415.

72. "Hooked on Junk Food," editorial, *USA Today,* March 31, 2010, p. 10A.

73. P. G. Bailey, "Don't Blame Us," *USA Today,* March 31, 2010, p. 10A.

74. E. Olson, "From a Food Giant, a Broad Effort to Feed Hungry Children," *New York Times,* March 21, 2011, p. B2.

75. 2003 National Business Ethics Survey, cited in *The Hidden Costs of Unethical Behavior,* p. 3. See also D. Turban and G. Greening, "Corporate Social Performance and Organizational Attractiveness to Prospective Employees," *Academy of Management Journal* 40 (1997), pp. 658–672.

76. B. Grow, S. Hamm, and L. Lee, "The Debate Over Doing Good," *BusinessWeek,* August 15, 2005, pp. 76–78.

77. Results can be found in "Tarnished Employment Brands Affect Recruiting," *HR Magazine,* November 2004, pp. 16, 20.

78. F. X. Mullen Jr., "Employers Often Exploit Illegal Immigrants, Who Can't Speak Up," *Reno Gazette-Journal,* November 8, 2008, p. 6A.

79. K. Hafner and C. H. Deutsch, "When Good Will Is Also Good Business," *New York Times,* September 14, 2005, pp. C1, C5.

80. N. Hertz, "New Ethic: Just Do It Right," *San Francisco Chronicle,* May 15, 2005, p. C2.

81. P. Engardio, "Beyond the Green Corporation," *BusinessWeek,* January 29, 2007, pp. 50–64.

82. V. Collier, "Green Good for Business," *San Francisco Chronicle,* June 3, 2005, pp. C1, C6; "U.N. Global Compact Ejects a Further 203 Companies," *Environmental Finance,* January 5, 2007, www.environmental-finance.com/onlinews/0104com.htm (accessed April 25, 2011); and E. D. Lederer, "U.N. Official: We Have Business Goals," *Forbes.com,* January 11, 2007, www.forbes.com/feeds/ap/2007/01/11/ap3321340.html (accessed April 25, 2011).

83. P. Kareiva, S. Watts, R. McDonald, and T. Boucher, "Domesticated Nature: Shaping Landscapes and Ecosystems for Human Welfare," *Science,* June 29, 2007, pp. 1866–869; see also V. Klindenborg, "The 17 Percent Problem and the Perils of Domestication," *New York Times,* August 13, 2007, p. A22.

84. "The Issue of Our Time," editorial, *San Francisco Chronicle,* September 9, 2007, p. F4.

85. Nicholas Stern, *The Economics of Climate Change: The Stern Review* (Cambridge: Cambridge University Press, 2006).

86. J. Eilperin, "Global Warming Threatens Public Lands," *San Francisco Chronicle,* September 7, 2007, p. A5; M. Crenson, "The Tide Turns on Climate Change," *Reno Gazette-Journal,* January 28, 2007, p. 1C; and "Two-Thirds of Polar Bears Extinct in 50 Years as Sea Ice Shrinks," *Environment News Service,* September 11, 2007, www.ens-newswire.com/ens/sep2007/2007-09-11-01.asp (accessed April 25, 2011).

87. D. Vergano and P. O'Driscoll, "Is Earth Near Its 'Tipping Points'?" *USA Today,* April 4, 2007, pp. 1D, 2D; J. M. Broder, "Government Study Warns of Climate Change Effects," *New York Times,* June 16, 2009, p. A12; S. Begley, "Climate-Change Calculus," *Newsweek,* August 3, 2009, p. 30; and D. Perman, "Arctic Warmest in 2,000 Years," *San Francisco Chronicle,* September 4, 2009, pp. A1, A14.

88. A. White, "EU Ministers Agree to 20 Percent Cut in Greenhouse Gas Emissions," *San Francisco Chronicle,* February 21, 2007, p. C5.

89. J. Kahn and J. Yardley, "As China Roars, Pollution Reaches Deadly Extremes," *New York Times*, August 26, 2007, front section, pp. 1, 6; J. Hellprin, "China Making Major Push to Cut Greenhouse Gases," *San Francisco Chronicle*, September 22, 2009, p. A4; J. Weisman and J. Lauria, "U.S. Seeks China's Support in Climate Fight," *Wall Street Journal*, September 23, 2009, p. A5; A. S. Ross, "China Leads Way on Solar Energy," *San Francisco Chronicle*, September 29, 2009, pp. D1, D2; and J. Ball and S. Oster, "China, U.S. Square Off on Climate Proposals," *Wall Street Journal*, November 27, 2009, pp. A1, A8.

90. J. Saseen, "Who Speaks for Business?" *BusinessWeek*, October 19, 2009, pp. 22–24.

91. A. S. Ross, "Apple Heats Up Climate Battle," *San Francisco Chronicle*, October 6, 2009, pp. D1, D3; and D. R. Baker, "Shifting Alliances in Debate," *San Francisco Chronicle*, October 9, 2009, C1, C2.

92. S. Lohr, "The Cost of an Overheated Planet," *New York Times*, December 12, 2006, pp. C1, C5; B. Walsh, "How Business Saw the Light," *Time*, January 15, 2007, pp. 56–57; and J. Ball, "In Climate Controversy, Industry Cedes Ground," *Wall Street Journal*, January 23, 2007, pp. A1, A17.

93. N. G. Mankiw, "One Answer to Global Warming: A New Tax," *New York Times*, September 16, 2007, p. BU-6.

94. N. Skinner and M. Uden, "'Green' Work Can Grow Corporate Bottom Lines," *San Francisco Chronicle*, April 5, 2007, p. B7.

95. This is the opinion of M. Winograd and M. Hais, authors of *Millennial Makeover: MySpace, YouTube, & the Future of American Politics*, cited in A. Stone, "Millennials a Force for Change," *USA Today*, April 14, 2009, pp. 1E, 2E.

96. S. Ryst, "Bringing in the Green," *Philadelphia Inquirer*, June 23, 2009, pp. C1, C8.

97. B. Horovitz, "Helping Out Is All in a (Free) Day's Work," *USA Today*, April 30, 2009, pp. 1B, 2B.

98. K. Yaros, quoted in Stone, "Millennials a Force for Change," 2009.

99. "Oprah Winfrey's Official Biography," Oprah.com, www.oprah.com/pressroom/Oprah-Winfreys-Official-Biography/6 (accessed April 28, 2011).

100. R. Shillingford, "Oprah Winfrey 1954—I Knew There Was a Way Out," The History of the World's Greatest Entrepreneurs, www.thehistoryoftheworldsgreatestentrepreneurs.com/blog/?p=92 (accessed April 28, 2011).

101. Shillingford, 2011.

102. "Oprah Winfrey," NNDB, www.nndb.com/people/466/000022400 (accessed April 28, 2011).

103. "Oprah Winfrey Profile," *Forbes*, www.forbes.com/profile/oprah-winfrey (accessed April 28, 2011).

104. M. Conlin, "The Top Givers," *BusinessWeek*, November 29, 2004, www.businessweek.com/magazine/content/04_48/b3910401.htm (accessed April 28, 2011).

105. Conlin, 2004.

106. L. Mirabella, "Cash Donations, Benefit Concerts, Celebrity Auctions and Celebrity Volunteers to Benefit Victims of Hurricanes Katrina and Rita," *LA Starz*, June 22, 2008, http://web.archive.org/web/20080622181458/http://www.la-starz.com/HurricaneKatrina_CelebrityEfforts.html (accessed April 28, 2011).

107. A. Samuels, "Oprah Goes to School," *Newsweek*, January 8, 2007, www.newsweek.com/2007/01/07/oprah-goes-to-school.html (accessed April 28, 2011).

108. "Oprah Winfrey Quotes," Power-of-giving.com, www.power-of-giving.com/oprah-winfrey-quotes.html (accessed April 28, 2011).

CHAPTER 3

1. "A-List" and "Ulmer Scale," Wikipedia, http://en.wikipedia.org/wiki/A-list (accessed July 12, 2010).

2. Box Office Mojo, reported in "Top-Grossing Film Franchises," *USA Today*, April 3, 2009, p. 1D.

3. M. Scott, "Why Hollywood Loves to Repeat Itself," *BusinessWeek*, November 30, 2009, p. 20.

4. "Shooting Stars' Crash Landings," *The Age*, December 28, 2006, www.theage.com.au/news/film/shooting-stars-crash-landings/2006/12/25/1166895241389.html (accessed May 10, 2011).

5. "Box Office Bomb," Wikipedia, http://en.wikipedia.org/wiki/Box_office_bomb (accessed May 10, 2011).

6. "Sleeper Hit," Wikipedia, http://en.wikipedia.org/wiki/Sleeper_hit (accessed May 10, 2011).

7. A. De Vany, cited in J. Surowiecki, "The Science of Success," *New Yorker*, July 9 & 16, 2007, p. 40.

8. Surowiecki, "The Science of Success," 2007.

9. F. Norris, "No Profit without Risk," *New York Times*, August 22, 2008, pp. C1, C4. See also J. Nocera, "Swept Up by Insanity of Markets," *New York Times*, October 11, 2008, pp. B1, B8; and T. L. Friedman, "Start Up the Risk-Takers," *New York Times*, February 22, 2009, Week in Review section, p. 10.

10. D. W. Dockery and P. H. Stone, "Cardiovascular Risks from Fine Particulate Air Pollution," *New England Journal of Medicine*, February 1, 2007, pp. 511–513.

11. For a debate about the use of the word *scarcity* in the definition of *economics*, see the thread in M. Mandel, "Should 'Scarcity' Be Part of the Definition of Economics?" *BusinessWeek online*, January 16, 2007, www.businessweek.com/the_thread/economicsunbound/archives/2007/01/should_scarcity.html (accessed May 10, 2011).

12. L. Jenkins, "On a Cap in a Faraway Place, Today's Losers Will Be Champs," *New York Times*, February 4, 2007, sec. 1, pp. 1, 23.

13. M. Gladwell, "The Formula," *New Yorker*, October 16, 2006, pp. 138–149.

14. "2011 Index of Economic Freedom," product of the *Wall Street Journal* and the Heritage Foundation, reported in T. Miller, "The U.S. Loses Ground on Economic Freedom," *Wall Street Journal*, January 12, 2011, http://online.wsj.com/article/SB10001424052748703777704576074193214999486.html (accessed May 11, 2011).

15. V. Burnett, "In Shifting Economy, Cubans Savor Working for Themselves," *New York Times*, February 4, 2011, pp. A1, A3; "Communist Party in Cuba OKs Changes," *Reno Gazette-Journal*, April 19, 2011, p. 3B; R. C. Archibold, "Cuba Lays Foundation for a Post-Castro Leader," *New York Times*, April 20, 2011, p. A11; P. Haven, "313 Ways to Open Up Economy," *San Francisco Chronicle*, May 10, 2011, p. A3; and R. C. Archibold, "Cuban Government Outlines Steps Toward a Freer Market," *New York Times*, May 10, 2011, p. A6.

16. B. Snyder, "Vietnam's Market Economy Leaving the Poor Behind," *San Francisco Chronicle*, December 8, 2008, p. A12.

17. B. Powell, "Wanted: A New Miracle," *Time*, January 12, 2009, pp. 40–42; and Y. Tan, "China's Unemployment Rate Climbs," *China Daily*, January 21, 2009 (accessed May 14, 2011).

18. Organisation for Economic Co-operation and Development (OECD). Directorate for Employment, Labour and Social Affairs, *Social Expenditure Database*, 2007, May 11, 2011, www.oecd.org/document/9/0,3343,en_2649_34637_38141385_1_1_1_1,00.html (accessed May 11, 2011).

19. Organisation for Economic Co-operation and Development, Centre for Tax Policy and Administration, *OECD Revenue Statistics 1965–2007, 2008 Edition*, October 15, 2008, Table A, Total tax revenue as percentage of GDP, www.oecd.org/document/4/

0,3343,en_2649_34533_41407428_1_1_1_1,00.html (accessed May 10, 2011).

20. Bureau of Economic Analysis data, reported in D. Cauchon, "Americans' Tax Burden at Lowest Level Since 1958," *Reno Gazette-Journal,* May 6, 2011, p. 1B.

21. World Values Survey, reported in "Denmark 'World's Happiest Nation,'" BBC News, July 3, 2008, http://news.bbc.co.uk/2/hi/in_depth/7487143.stm (accessed May 10, 2011). See also World Values Survey, www.worldvaluessurvey.org.

22. C. Dougherty, "Denmark Feels the Pinch as Young Workers Flee to Lands of Lower Taxes," *New York Times,* December 26, 2007, p. C7.

23. "Budget Deficit % of GDP 2011 Country Ranks, by Rank," *CIA World Fact Book 2011,* www.photius.com/rankings/economy/budget_deficit_pct_of_gdp_2011_0.html (accessed May 10, 2011).

24. Data from Equilar, executive compensation firm, reported in R. Beck, "AP Impact: CEO Pay Exceeds Pre-recession Level," *Houston Chronicle,* May 6, 2011, www.chron.com/disp/story.mpl/ap/business/7553568.html (accessed May 13, 2011). See also J. S. Lublin, "CEO Pay in 2010 Jumped 11%," *Wall Street Journal,* May 9, 2011, pp. B1, B6.

25. World Economic Forum, *The Global Competitiveness Report 2010–2011,* September 9, 2010, www.weforum.org/en/initiatives/gcp/Global%20Competitiveness%20Report/index.htm (accessed May 10, 2011).

26. R. Alonso-Zaldivar, "Competition Absent among Private Insurers," *Reno Gazette-Journal,* August 23, 2009, pp. 1B, 2B.

27. C. Mankowitz, "Mixed Feelings about Health Reform" [letter], *New York Times,* July 28, 2009, p. A20.

28. "Giant Rabbits," *The Week,* February 16, 2007, p. 8.

29. R. J. Shiller, "Everybody Calm Down. A Government Hand in the Economy Is as Old as the Republic," *Washington Post,* September 28, 2008, p. B1.

30. L. Uchitelle, "Encouraging More Reality in Economics," *New York Times,* January 6, 2007, pp. B1, B4.

31. See R. J. Shiller, "An Echo Chamber of Boom and Bust," *New York Times,* August 30, 2009, Business section, p. 5.

32. J. Lehrer, *How We Decide* (Boston: Houghton Mifflin Harcourt, 2009), quoted in S. Johnson, "Mind Matters," *New York Times Book Review,* March 22, 2009, p. 9.

33. U.S. Chamber of Commerce, "Free Enterprise Campaign Announced," *U.S. Chamber Magazine,* June 15, 2009, http://www.uschambermagazine.com/content/090615y.htm (accessed September 4, 2010).

34. Tita Freeman, quoted in P. Coy, "Capitalism, No. Free Enterprise, Yes," *BusinessWeek,* August 17, 2009, p. 18.

35. Rich Thau, president of Presentation Testing, quoted in Coy, 2009.

36. Robert J. Barbera, reported in D. Leonhardt, "Theory and Morality in the New Economy," *New York Times Book Review,* August 23, 2009, p. BR-23.

37. A. B. Krueger, quoted in Leonhardt, 2009.

38. Representative Henry Waxman, quoted in "Out Loud," *U.S. News & World Report,* February 11, 2007, p. 11.

39. "How Much Is a Million? Billion? Trillion?" tysknews.com, www.tysknews.com/Depts/Taxes/million.htm (accessed May 11, 2011).

40. M. Landler, "I.M.F. Puts Bank Losses from Global Financial Crisis at $4.1 Trillion," *New York Times,* April 22, 2009, p. A6.

41. National Bureau of Economic Research, "U.S. Business Cycle Expansions and Contractions," www.nber.org/cycles.html (accessed May 11, 2011).

42. F. Norris, "Time to Say It: Double Dip Recession May Be Happening," *New York Times,* August 4, 2011, http://www.nytimes.com/2011/08/05/business/economy/double-dip-recession-may-be-returning.html (accessed August 11, 2011).

43. J. Deal, "A Dragon Named Inflation," *Brazilbrazil,* August 2004, http://brazilbrazil.com/inflat.html (accessed May 10, 2011).

44. "Employment Situation Summary," July 2011, Bureau of Labor Statistics, August 5, 2011, www.bls.gov/news.release/empsit.nr0.htm (accessed August 12, 2011).

45. J. Welch, quoted in T. A. Stewart, "U.S. Productivity: First but Fading," *Fortune,* October 1992, p. 54.

46. S. Allen, "Entrepreneur Success Story: Brian Scudamore of 1-800-GOT-JUNK?" *About.com: Entrepreneurs,* http://entrepreneurs.about.com/od/casestudies/a/1800gotjunk.htm (accessed May 11, 2011).

47. R. H. Price, quoted in M. Duenwald, "Coping with the Spiral of Stress That Layoffs Create," *New York Times,* October 29, 2002, p. E3.

48. R. H. Price, J. N. Choi, and A. D. Vinokur, "Links in the Chain of Adversity Following Job Loss: How Financial Strain and Loss of Personal Control Lead to Depression, Impaired Functioning, and Poor Health," *Journal of Occupational Health Psychology* 5(1), 2002, 32–47.

49. P. Voydanoff, "Economic Distress and Family Relations: A Review of the Eighties." In A. Booth, ed. *Contemporary Families: Looking Forward, Looking Back* (Minneapolis: National Council on Family Relations, 1991); J. D. Teachman, R. Vaughn, A. Call, and K. P. Carver, "Marital Status and Duration of Joblessness among White Men," *Journal of Marriage and the Family* 56(2), 1994, 415–428; K. Macmillan and R. Gartner, "When She Brings Home the Bacon: Labor-Force Participation and the Risk of Spousal Violence Against Women," *Journal of Marriage and the Family* 61, 2000, 947–958; B. Marsh, "Jobless, Sleepless, Hopeless," *New York Times,* September 6, 2009, Week in Review section, p. 4; and S. Winston, "Losing a Job, Mourning a Lifestyle," *New York Times,* December 12, 2010, Business section, p. 12.

50. J. Zaslow, "Who's the New Guy at Dinner? It's Dad; Laid-off Fathers Face Tough Job at Home," *Wall Street Journal,* October 1, 2002, p. D1.

51. H. Boerner, "Volunteering Yourself into a Job," *San Francisco Chronicle,* March 28, 2010, p. D1.

52. S. McDonald, "Matthews Advises Temple Graduates with 'Card for Life,'" *Newsworks,* May 12, 2011, www.newsworks.org/index.php/the-feed/item/19342-matthews-advises-temple-graduates-with-card-for-life (accessed May 13, 2011).

53. L. Uchitelle, "Productivity Finally Shows the Impact of Computers," *New York Times,* March 12, 2000, sec. 3, p. 4; J. Reingold, M. Stepanek, and D. Brady, "Why the Productivity Revolution Will Spread," *BusinessWeek,* February 14, 2000, pp. 112–118; G. S. Becker, "How Skeptics Missed the Power of Productivity," *BusinessWeek,* January 1, 2004, p. 26; H. R. Varian, "Information Technology May Have Been What Cured Low Service-Sector Productivity," *New York Times,* February 12, 2004, p. C2; J. Aversa, "Bernanke Bullish on Productivity Gains," *BusinessWeek Online,* August 31, 2006, www.businessweek.com/ap/financialnews/D8JRJTJOO.htm?chan=search (accessed May 25, 2011); Bureau of Labor Statistics, "United States—Quarterly Data," Economy at a Glance, September 3, 2010, www.bls.gov/eag/eag.us.htm (accessed May 25, 2011); and Bureau of Labor Statistics, "Major Sector Productivity and Costs Index," September 6, 2010. http://data.bls.gov/PDQ/servlet/SurveyOutputServlet?series_id=PRS85006092&data_tool=XGtable (accessed May 25, 2011).

54. T. Barkley, "Productivity Leaps as Companies Reduce Costs," *Wall Street Journal,* August 12, 2009, p. A2; and S. Matthews,

"Jobless Producing U.S. Profit on Higher Productivity," *Bloomberg Businessweek,* June 28, 2010, www.businessweek .com/news/2010-06-28/jobless-producing-u-s-profit-on-higher-productivity.html (accessed May 25, 2011).

55. World Economic Forum, *Global Competitiveness Report 2010–2011,* 2010.

56. R. J. Samuelson, "The Great Escape," *Newsweek,* October 12, 2009, p. 25.

57. M. Lewis, "The End," *Portfolio,* December 2008/January 2009, pp. 114–123, 154–159.

58. Estimates by Stanford University economist James B. Taylor, cited in V. Postrel, "Macroegonomics," *The Atlantic,* April 2009, pp. 32–34.

59. B. Kiviat, "Sunk by Securitization," *Time,* February 9, 2009, pp. Global 1–Global 5.

60. John Garvey, head of U.S. financial services practice at PricewaterhouseCoopers, quoted in A. Shell, "Collapse Upended Economic Supports," *USA Today,* September 11, 2009, pp. 1B, 2B.

61. L. Belsie, "Unemployment Rate Falls, but Recession's Toll Is Worst Since the '30s," *Christian Science Monitor,* February 5, 2010, www.csmonitor.com/Business/new-economy/2010/0205/Unemployment-rate-falls-but-recession-s-toll-is-worst-since-the-30s (accessed May 25, 2011).

62. C. Lochhead, "U.S. Mortgage Meltdown Has Gone Global," *San Francisco Chronicle,* February 22, 2009, pp. A1, A11.

63. Samuelson, "The Great Escape," 2009.

64. P. Gogoi, "Where Were Regulators When Banks Were Failing?" *USA Today,* June 16, 2009, pp. 1B, 2B.

65. "Tracking the Bailout Bucks," *Newsweek,* September 28, 2009, p. 19.

66. A. Sloan with D. Burke, "Surprise! The Big Bad Bailout Is Paying Off," *Fortune,* July 25, 2011, pp. 65–69.

67. See G. Morgenson, "But Who Is Watching Regulators?" *New York Times,* September 13, 2009, pp. B1, B4; and *Sold Out: How Wall Street and Washington Betrayed America,* March 2009, Essential Information and Consumer Education Foundation, www.wallstreetwatch.org/reports/sold_out.pdf (accessed May 10, 2011). See also J. Cassidy, *How Markets Fail: The Logic of Economic Calamities* (New York: Farrar, Straus & Giroux, 2009); J. B. Stewart, "Eight Days," *New Yorker,* September 21, 2009, pp. 58–81; R. A. Posner, *The Crisis of Capitalist Democracy* (Boston: Harvard University Press, 2010); R. Foroohar, "May the Best Theory Win," *Newsweek,* February 1, 2010, pp. 42–44; A. R. Sorkin, "Preparing for the Next Big One," *New York Times,* June 29, 2010, pp. B1, B8; N. M. Barofsky, "Where the Bailout Went Wrong," *New York Times,* March 30, 2011, p. A25; and M. Powell and A. Martin, "Foreclosure Aid Fell Short, and Is Fading Away," *New York Times,* March 30, 2011, pp. A1, A17.

68. Mary Anne, "David Geffen: The Ultimate Power Player," Yahoo Contributor Network, November 9, 2006, www.associatedcontent.com/article/81973/david_geffen_the_ultimate_power_player.html (accessed May 3, 2011).

69. "Happiness (and How to Measure It)," *The Economist,* December 23, 2006, www.economist.com/node/8450035?story_id=E1_RQVDDPV (accessed May 3, 2011).

70. "Food Truck Trend Puts Roach Coach Makers in High Demand," *Huffington Post,* May 10, 2011, www.huffingtonpost.com/2011/05/10/food-truck-trend-roach-coach-demand_n_859427.html (accessed October 3, 2011).

71. "Food Truck Trend Puts Roach Coach Makers in High Demand," 2011.

72. Ruggless, 2011.

73. R. Ruggless, "Food Truck Trend Still Cruising," *Nation's Restaurant News,* May 23, 2011, www.nrn.com/article/food-truck-trend-still-cruising (accessed October 3, 2011).

74. S. Buck, "The Rise of the Social Food Truck Trend," *Mashable .com* website, August 14, 2011, www.mashable.com/2011/08/04/food-truck-history-infographic/ (accessed October 3, 2011).

75. Ruggless, 2011.

76. A. Caldwell, "Will Tweet for Food. The Impact of Twitter and New York City Food Trucks, Online, Offline, and Inline." *Appetite,* 56(2), 522.

77. "Homepage," Fresher Than Fresh Snow Cones website, www .ftfsnowcones.com/ (accessed October 3, 2011).

78. "Cocoa," Thefreedictionary, www.thefreedictionary.com/cocoa (accessed April 29, 2011).

79. P. Bax, "Ivory Coast Cocoa Farmers Fail to Find Buyers After Export Ban," *Bloomberg Businessweek,* February 8, 2011, www.businessweek.com/news/2011-02-08/ivory-coast-cocoa -farmers-fail-to-find-buyers-after-export-ban.html (accessed May 3, 2011).

80. C. Prentice and I. Almeida, "Cocoa Jumps to One-Year High as Ivory Coast Leader Bans Exports," *Bloomberg Businessweek,* January 24, 2011, www.businessweek.com/news/2011-01-24/cocoa-jumps-to-one-year-high-as-ivory-coast-leader-bans -exports.html (accessed February 8, 2011).

81. N. Rai, "Shipping Firms Say Ivory Coast Cocoa Exports Resume," *Wall Street Journal,* April 26, 2011, http://online.wsj .com/article/SB1000142405274870377810457628687206047550 8.html?KEYWORDS=cocoa (accessed April 29, 2011).

82. "Global Cocoa Prices: 2010–2011 Forecast," Euromonitor Blog, August 5, 2010, http://blog.euromonitor.com/2010/08/global -cocoa-prices-20102011-forecast.html (accessed April 29, 2011).

83. Rai, 2011.

84. L. Josephs, "Cocoa Grindings Gained Despite Supply Break, *Wall Street Journal,* April 15, 2011, http://online.wsj.com/article/SB10001424052748704547604576263381470050712 .html?KEYWORDS=cocoa (accessed April 29, 2011).

85. C. Henshaw, "Cocoa Slump Looks Likely to Continue," *Wall Street Journal,* April 4, 2011, http://online.wsj.com/article/SB10001424052748703712504576236712926406424 .html?KEYWORDS=cocoa+farming (accessed April 29, 2011).

86. C. Cui, "Cocoa Futures Surge on Signs of Shortage," *Wall Street Journal,* April 27, 2010, http://online.wsj.com/article/SB10001424052748704464704575208612324532150.html?mod=WSJ_topics_obama&mg=com-wsj (accessed May 3, 2011).

CHAPTER 4

1. E. Iwata, "Companies Find Gold Inside Melting Pot," *USA Today,* July 9, 2007, pp. 1B, 2B.

2. "Globe Trotting–Overseas Business Opportunities for the U.S. Food Industry," *Prepared Foods,* April 1993, http://findarticles .com/p/articles/mi_m3289/is_n4_v162/ai_14123269/ (accessed August 15, 2011).

3. A. Kline, "Rich Products Acquiring Taste Overseas," *Buffalo Business First,* October 8, 2009, http://buffalo.bizjournals.com/buffalo/stories/2009/10/05/daily38.html (accessed August 15, 2011).

4. N. Groom, "Campbell to Start Russia, China Soup Sales," Reuters, July 9, 2007, www.reuters.com/article/companyNewsAndPR/idUSN0928240820070709 (accessed August 15, 2011).

5. J. Jargon, "Can M'm, M'm Good Translate?" *Wall Street Journal,* July 9, 2007, p. A16.

6. "Campbell Outlines Entry Strategy and Product Plans for Russia and China," *Food Industry News,* September 7, 2007, www .flexnews.com/pages/9712/Campbell/campbell_outlines_entry_strategy_product_plans_russia_china.html (accessed August 15, 2011). See also B. Horowitz, "CEO Nears 10-Year Goal to Clean Up a Soupy Mess," *USA Today,* January 26, 2009, pp. 1B, 2B; and J. N. DiStefano, "Can Campbell Soup Translate

for China, Russia?" *PhillyDeals,* July 13, 2010, www.philly .com/philly/blogs/inq-phillydeals/Can_Campbell_Soup_ translate_for_China_Russia.html (accessed August 15, 2011); and B. Dorftman and M. Geller, "Update 3–Campbell Soup in Joint Deal to Expand in China," Reuters, January 12, 2011, http://in.reuters.com/article/2011/01/12/campbellsoup-swire -china-idINN1219071820110112 (accessed August 15, 2011).

7. D. A. McIntyre, "Campbell Goes to China," *Speeple News,* July 20, 2007, www.bloggingstocks.com/2007/07/09/campbell -goes-to-china (accessed August 15, 2011).

8. B. Dorfman and M. Geller, "Campbell Soup in Joint Venture to Expand in China," Reuters, January 12, 2011, www.reuters .com/article/2011/01/12/us-campbellsoup-swire-china -idUSTRE70B46620110112 (accessed August 15, 2011).

9. R. C. Carter, senior vice president for human resources at A&E Television Networks, quoted in H. Chura, "A Year Abroad (or 3) as a Career Move," *New York Times,* February 25, 2006, p. B5.

10. P. McDonald, quoted in M. L. Levin, "Global Experience Makes Candidates More Marketable," *Wall Street Journal,* September 11, 2007, p. B6.

11. M. Hamori and B. Koyuneu, "Career Advancement in Large Organizations: Do International Assignments Add Value?" working paper presented at August 7–11, 2009 meeting of Academy of Management, reported in "Why That Plum Job Abroad Could Be a Rotten Move," *BusinessWeek,* August 24 & 31, 2009, p. 10.

12. T. Mohn, "The Dislocated Americans," *New York Times,* December 2, 2008, p. B4.

13. T. Mohn, "Overseas without the Family," *New York Times,* September 15, 2009, p. B6.

14. H. Seligson, "New Graduates Finding Jobs in China (Mandarin Optional)," *New York Times,* August 11, 2009, pp. B1, B5.

15. S. Stapleton, quoted in R. Erlich, "Going Far in the East," *San Francisco Chronicle,* June 24, 2006, pp. C1, C2.

16. The first three of these events were described in K. Maney, "Economy Embraces Truly Global Workplace," *USA Today,* December 31, 1998, pp. 1B, 2B. Portions of this discussion were adapted from A. Kinicki and B. K. Williams, *Management: A Practical Introduction,* 4th ed. (New York: McGraw-Hill, 2009), pp. 106–112.

17. "European Mobile Broadband Penetration Nearly Twice the Americas," *February 2011 Broadband Report,* WebSiteOptimization.com, www.websiteoptimization.com/bw/1102 (accessed August 15, 2011).

18. "Over 2 Billion Internet Users Worldwide," *March 2011 Bandwidth Report,* WebSiteOptimization.com, www.websiteoptimization.com/bw/1103/ (accessed August 15, 2011).

19. "Quarterly Retail E-Commerce Sales 2nd Quarter 2011," *U.S. Census Bureau News,* August 16, 2011, http://www.census.gov/ retail/mrts/www/data/pdf/ec_current.pdf (accessed August 16, 2011).

20. D. Croasdell, "Web 2.0: The New 'Culture of Availability' Will Enhance Business," *Reno Gazette-Journal,* August 26, 2009, p. 9A.

21. D. Barboza, "Clues in an iPhone Autopsy," *New York Times,* July 6, 2010, pp. B1, B7.

22. T. Williams, "Costly Hairstyle Is a Beauty Trend That Draws Thieves' Notice," *New York Times,* May 17, 2011, pp. A1, A3.

23. R. Richmond, "Entrepreneurs with Big Dreams Tap Global Market," *Wall Street Journal,* April 17, 2007, p. B6.

24. Thomas Runiewicz, economist with HIS Global Insight, quoted in "What's Made in the USA," *Parade,* April 19, 2009, p. 10.

25. Paul W. Aho, quoted in C. Krauss, "A Taste for Chicken Feet May Keep American Poultry in Chinese Pots," *New York Times,* September 16, 2009, pp. B1, B5.

26. Maney, "Economy Embraces Truly Global Workplace," 1998.

27. Nancy Birdsall, quoted in C. Kleiman, "Global Knowledge Helps in Making Career Decisions," *San Jose Mercury News,* September 24, 1995, p. 1PC.

28. D. J. Lynch, "Developing Nations Poised to Challenge USA as King of the Hill," *USA Today,* February 8, 2007, pp. 1B, 2B.

29. V. Smith, "Last U.S. Dinnerware Companies Struggle," *San Francisco Chronicle,* September 20, 2009, pp. A17, A18.

30. L. Aldrich, "Times Hit Wood Industry Hard," *Wall Street Journal,* August 25, 2009, p. B5.

31. M. Corkery, "Homeowner Problems with Chinese-Made Drywall Spread," *Wall Street Journal,* April 17, 2009, p. A4; and L. Wayne, "The Enemy at Home," *New York Times,* October 8, 2009, pp. B1, B8.

32. D. M. Smick, *The World Is Curved: Hidden Dangers to the Global Economy* (New York: Portfolio/Penguin, 2008). See also F. Norris, "The Upside to Resisting Globalization," *New York Times,* February 6, 2009, pp. B1, B4.

33. C. Lochhead, "U.S. Mortgage Meltdown Has Gone Global," *San Francisco Chronicle,* February 22, 2009, pp. A1, A11.

34. D. J. Lynch, "Global Slump Crimps U.S. Exports," *USA Today,* February 12, 2009, p. B1; and F. Norris, "All Around the World, Trade Is Shrinking," *New York Times,* February 28, 2009, p. B3.

35. C. Smadja, "Living Dangerously," *Time,* February 22, 1999.

36. N. Negroponte, quoted in K. Maney, "Economy Embraces Truly Global Workplace," *USA Today,* December 31, 1998, pp. 1B, 2B.

37. T. Abate, "Offshoring for the Smaller Firms," *San Francisco Chronicle,* April 23, 2010, pp. D1, D4.

38. J. Lahart, "For Small Business, Big World Beckons," *Wall Street Journal,* January 27, 2011, pp. B1, B4.

39. B. Fink, "The Spin Cycle of Outsourcing," *San Francisco Chronicle Magazine,* January 14, 2007, pp. 14–15, 19.

40. H. Tabuchi, "China Urged to Resume Rare-Earth Shipments," *New York Times,* October 25, 2010, p. B3; H. Tabuchi, "The Hunt for Rare Earths," *New York Times,* November 25, 2010, p. B7; M. Ramsey, "Toyota Tries to Break Reliance on China," *Wall Street Journal,* January 14, 2011, pp. B1, B2; J. Clenfield, M. Yasu, and S. Biggs, "Rare Earths from Japan's Junk Pile," *Bloomberg Businessweek,* January 10–January 16, 2011, pp. 9–10; and M. L. Wald, "Scientists Call for New Sources of Critical Elements," *New York Times,* February 19, 2011, p. B5.

41. J. Christoffersen, "In a Changing World, GE Spreads Globally," *Reno Gazette-Journal,* January 13, 2007, p. 8D.

42. U.S. Census Bureau, "U.S. International Trade in Goods & Services," www.census.gov/foreign-trade/Press-Release/current_ press_release (accessed August 15, 2011).

43. AllBusiness.com, "Third Parties Can Help Importers Navigate Through the Legal Maze," *San Francisco Chronicle,* April 25, 2007, p. C4.

44. C. Rampell, "Once a Dynamo, the Tech Sector Is Slow to Hire," *New York Times,* September 7, 2010, pp. A1, A3.

45. D. Wessel, "Big U.S. Firms Shift Hiring Abroad," *Wall Street Journal,* April 19, 2011, pp. B1, B2.

46. J. Throttam, "Is Your Job Going Abroad?" *Time,* March 1, 2004, pp. A1, A5.

47. F. Levy, quoted in D. Wessel, "The Future of Jobs: New Ones Arise, Wage Gap Widens," *Wall Street Journal,* April 2, 2004, pp. A1, A5.

48. A. M. Chaker, "Where the Jobs Are," *Wall Street Journal,* March 18, 2004, pp. D1, D3; J. Shinal, "Which Types of Jobs Will Be in Demand?" *San Francisco Chronicle,* March 24, 2004, pp. C1, C4; and D. Wessel, "The Future of Jobs: New Ones Arise, Wage Gap Widens," *Wall Street Journal,* April 2, 2004, pp. A1, A5.

49. L. Uchitelle, "College Degree Still Pays, but It's Leveling Off," *New York Times,* January 17, 2005, pp. C1, C2.

50. J. Spohrer, quoted in Shinal, "Which Types of Jobs Will Be in Demand?" 2004.

51. Drucker, quoted in Schlender, "Peter Drucker Sets Us Straight," 2004.

52. P. Drucker, quoted in B. Schlender, "Peter Drucker Sets Us Straight," *Fortune*, January 12, 2004, pp. 115–118.

53. Research by Matthew Slaughter, cited by W. S. Cohen, "Obama and the Politics of Outsourcing," *Wall Street Journal*, October 12, 2010, p. A21.

54. L. Brainerd and R. E. Litan, "'Offshoring' Service Jobs: Bane or Boon and What to Do?" Brookings Policy Brief Series #131, April 2004, www.brookings.edu/papers/2004/04macroeconomics_brainard.aspx (accessed August 15, 2011).

55. Yan Lili, quoted in J. S. Pocha, "In China, Buicks Mean Status," *Boston Globe*, August 20, 2005, www.boston.com/business/articles/2005/08/20/in_china_buicks_mean_status/ (accessed August 15, 2011).

56. J. Gopwani and M. Szczepanski, "Buick Remains Popular with China's Upper-Middle Class," *Detroit Free Press*, August 30, 2009, www.allbusiness.com/automotive/motor-vehicle-models-new-car/12783271-1.html (accessed August 15, 2011).

57. M. Thorneman, B. Lannes, and N. Palmer, "Resurrecting the China Joint-Venture," *Far Eastern Economic Review*, October 2008, www.feer.com/economics/2008/october/Resurrecting-the-China-Joint-Venture (accessed August 15, 2011).

58. G. Stoller, "How to Mind Your Manners Abroad," *USA Today*, March 29, 2011, p. 3B.

59. A. M. Sabath, quoted in Stoller, 2011.

60. J. S. Lublin, "Cultural Flexibility in Demand," *Wall Street Journal*, April 11, 2011, pp. B1, B9.

61. This list is based on E. T. Hall, "The Silent Language in Overseas Business," *Harvard Business Review*, May–June 1960, pp. 87–96; and R. Knotts, "Cross-Cultural Management: Transformations and Adaptations," *Business Horizons*, January–February 1989, pp. 29–33.

62. Harris Poll, National Foreign Language Center, reported in "Lingua Franca?" *USA Today*, February 23, 1999, p. 1A.

63. L. Martinez-Fernandez, "Just Like Us? Not Likely," *Chronicle of Higher Education*, December 8, 2006, p. B20.

64. P. Dvorak, "Plain English Gets Harder in Global Era," *Wall Street Journal*, November 5, 2007, pp. B1, B3.

65. D. Arthur, "The Importance of Body Language," *HRFocus*, June 1995, pp. 22–23; and N. M. Grant, "The Silent Should Build Bridges, Not Barriers," *HRFocus*, April 1995, p. 16.

66. S. Khalaf, cited in H. M. Fattah, "Why Arab Men Hold Hands," *New York Times*, May 1, 2005, sec. 4, p. 2.

67. Anthropologist Edward Hall, quoted in "How Cultures Collide," *Psychology Today*, July 1976, p. 14.

68. C. Woodward, "AP Poll Paints Portrait of Impatient American," *Reno Gazette-Journal*, May 29, 2006, pp. 1C, 7C.

69. C. Salazar, "Time Is of the Essence in Peru's Punctuality Effort," *San Francisco Chronicle*, March 2, 2007, p. A16.

70. R. Wartzman, "In the Wake of NAFTA, a Family Firm Sees the Business Go South," *Wall Street Journal*, February 23, 1999, pp. A1, A10.

71. S. R. Safranski and I.-W. Kwon, "Religious Groups and Management Value Systems," in *Advances in International Comparative Management*, vol. 3, eds. R. N. Farner and E. G. McGoun (Greenwich, CT: JAI Press, 1988), pp. 171–183.

72. S. Arnquist, "In Rural Africa, a Fertile Market for Mobile Phones," *New York Times*, October 6, 2009, p. D4.

73. C. Bryan-Low, "New Frontiers in Cellphone Service," *Wall Street Journal*, February 13, 2007, pp. B1, B5; D. Kohanski, "Poorer Nations Get Big Lift from a Little High Tech," *San Francisco Chronicle*, August 19, 2007, p. E6; J. Ewing, "Upwardly Mobile in Africa," *BusinessWeek*, September 13, 2007, www.businessweek.com/globalbiz/content/sep2007/gb20070913_705733.htm?chan=top+news_top+news+index_businessweek+exclusives (accessed August 15, 2011); and L. Lakschman, "India's Cell-Phone Ride Out of Poverty," *BusinessWeek*, September 24, 2007, www.businessweek.com/magazine/content/07_39/b4051058.htm?chan=top+news_top+news+index_global+business (accessed August 15, 2011).

74. M. Mendenhall, B. J. Punnett, and D. Ricks, *Global Management* (Cambridge, MA: Blackwell, 1995).

75. U.S. Central Intelligence Agency, "Country Comparison: Total Fertility Rate," *The World Factbook*, https://www.cia.gov/library/publications/the-world-factbook/rankorder/2127rank.html (accessed August 15, 2011).

76. J. Papier, "The Incredible Shrinking Dollar," PWJohnson Wealth Management, www.pwjohnson.com/resources/articles/falling_dollar.pdf (accessed March 20, 2011).

77. Cost of Living Comparison between New York City (United States) and London (United Kingdom), Expatistan, August 15, 2011, www.expatistan.com/cost-of-living/comparison/london/new-york-city (accessed August 15, 2011).

78. "Japanese Housewives Sweat in Secret as Markets Reel," *Business Times*, September 19, 2007, www.btimes.com.my/Current_News/BT/Wednesday/Corporate/20070918222928/Article (accessed August 15, 2011).

79. J. Hookway and A. Frangos, "Vietnam's Devaluation Alarms Rival Exporters," *Wall Street Journal*, November 27, 2009, p. A8.

80. Reuters, "Chavez Moves to Nationalize Food Companies," CNBC.com, March 5, 2009, www.cnbc.com/id/29523863 (accessed August 15, 2011).

81. D. Searcey, "To Combat Overseas Bribery, Authorities Make It Personal," *Wall Street Journal*, October 8, 2009, p. A13.

82. Portions adapted from S. P. Robbins and M. Coulter, *Management*, 9th ed. (Upper Saddle River, NJ: Pearson, 2007), pp. 94–96; Kinicki and Williams, *Management*, 2009, pp. 118–121; and R. W. Griffin, *Management*, 10th ed. (Mason, OH: South-Western Cengage Learning, 2011), pp. 147–151.

83. K. Bradsher, "China Moves to Beat Back a Tire Tariff," *New York Times*, September 14, 2009, pp. A1, A3; S. Greenhouse, "Tire Tariffs Are Cheered by Labor," *New York Times*, September 14, 2009, pp. B1, B4; and D. J. Lynch, "China-U.S. Trade Tensions Grow," *USA Today*, September 15, 2009, p. 3B.

84. "Mexico Sets 2009 Sugar Import Quota at 900,000 T," *Flexnews*, September 21, 2009, www.flex-news-food.com/pages/25970/Mexico/Sugar/mexico-sets-2009-sugar-import-quotas-900000.html; and "Mexico Sets 250,000 Tonne 2010 Sugar Import Quota," Reuters, February 7, 2010, www.reuters.com/article/idUSN0716673520100207 (both accessed August 14, 2011).

85. J. Jordan, "The Cuban Cigar Embargo," *Ezine Articles*, http://ezinearticles.com/?The-Cuban-Cigar-Embargo&id=297423 (accessed August 15, 2011).

86. J. Bhagwati, *Protectionism* (Cambridge, MA: MIT Press, 1988).

87. "East Asia and Pacific: World Bank Teams at Work in the Aftermath of Disasters," *The World Bank*, October 14, 2009, http://web.worldbank.org/WBSITE/EXTERNAL/COUNTRIES/EASTASIAPACIFICEXT/0,,contentMDK:22351658~pagePK:146736~piPK:146830~theSitePK:226301,00.html (accessed August 15, 2011).

88. E. Malkin, "NAFTA's Promise, Unfulfilled," *New York Times*, March 24, 2009, pp. B1, B4.

89. World Bank study, cited in Lynch, 2007, 1B.

90. N.-H. Tseng, "Three Challenges to McDonald's Growth," *Fortune*, January 21, 2011, http://money.cnn.com/2011/01/21/news/companies/mcdonalds_slowing_growth.fortune/index.htm (accessed May 22, 2011).

91. "Microlending Explained," *Globalvision.com*, May 12, 2006, www.globalenvision.org/library/4/1073 (accessed May 22, 2011).

92. P. M. Shrestha, "A Microcredit Success Story from Nepal," *Poverty News Blog*, January 26, 2009, http://povertynewsblog.blogspot.com/2009/01/microcredit-success-story-from-nepal.html (accessed May 22, 2011).

93. D. Roberts and P. Engardio, "Secrets, Lies, and Sweatshops," *BusinessWeek*, November 22, 2006, www.businessweek.com/magazine/content/06_48/b4011001.htm (accessed May 22, 2011).

94. C. Fishman, "Message in a Bottle," *Fast Company*, July 1, 2007, www.fastcompany.com/magazine/117/features-message-in-a-bottle.html (accessed May 22, 2011).

95. L. Klessig, "Bottled Water Industry," Academic Computing at Evergreen University, http://academic.evergreen.edu/g/grossmaz/klessill (accessed May 22, 2011).

96. Klessig, "Bottled Water Industry."

97. "Electronic Hazardous Waste (E-Waste)," California Department of Toxic Substances Control, www.dtsc.ca.gov/hazardouswaste/ewaste (accessed May 22, 2011).

98. "E-Cycling," United States Environmental Protection Agency website, www.epa.gov/osw/conserve/materials/ecycling (accessed May 22, 2011).

99. "The History of the Mini," *JohnCooperWorks.net*, www.johncooperworks.net/fun-facts-forum-mini-f1-mclaren-cooper.html (accessed May 22, 2011).

100. "Fun Facts—Day Trippers: The Beatles and the Mini," *JohnCooperWorks.net*, www.johncooperworks.net/fun-facts-forum-mini-f1-mclaren-cooper.html (accessed May 22, 2011).

101. "The History of the Mini," 2011.

102. "The Used-to-Be Big Three," *CBC News*, June 3, 2008, www.cbc.ca/news/business/story/2009/02/17/f-bigthreeupdate.html (accessed May 22, 2011).

103. K. Anderson, "Mini Mania Big in U.S.," *BBC News*, June 21, 2002, http://news.bbc.co.uk/2/hi/business/2052620.stm (accessed May 22, 2011).

104. N. F. Fieleke, "The Automobile Industry," *Annals of the American Academy of Political and Social Science*, ANNALS, AAPSS, 460, March 1982, www.ann.sagepub.com/content/460/1/83 (accessed August 8, 2011).

105. Fieleke, 1982.

106. H. Elliot, "Fifty Years of Mini-Love," *Forbes*, July 29, 2009, www.forbes.com/2009/07/29/bmw-mini-cooper-lifestyle-vehicles-mini-car-50.html (accessed May 6, 2011).

107. T. Gresham, "The Rover Mini Cooper and U.S. Emissions Standards," ehow.com, www.ehow.com/facts_7928805_rover-mini-cooper-emissions-standards.html (accessed May 6, 2011).

108. B. Einhorn, "India Company's Medical-Tourism Push," *Bloomberg Businessweek*, March 12, 2010, www.businessweek.com/blogs/eyeonasia/archives/2010/03/india_hospital.html (accessed February 11, 2011).

109. Einhorn, 2010.

110. M. P. McQueen, "More Americans Traveling Abroad for Medical Treatment," *Wall Street Journal*, May 17, 2009, http://online.wsj.com/article/SB124251750976927298.html?KEYWORDS=medical+tourism (accessed February 11, 2011).

111. Z. Galland, "Medical Tourism: The Insurance Debate," *Bloomberg Businessweek*, November 9, 2008, www.businessweek.com/globalbiz/content/nov2008/gb2008119_571910.htm (accessed February 11, 2011).

112. B. Einhorn, "Hannaford's Medical-Tourism Experiment," *Bloomberg Businessweek*, November 9, 2008, www.businessweek.com/globalbiz/content/nov2008/gb2008119_505319.htm (accessed February 11, 2011).

113. A. Poon, "Taiwan Wants to Touch Your Heart," *Wall Street Journal*, December 10, 2010, http://blogs.wsj.com/chinarealtime/2010/12/07/taiwan-wants-to-touch-your-heart/?KEYWORDS=medical+tourism (accessed February 11, 2011).

CHAPTER 5

1. S. Allen, "Wayne Huizenga Biography," About.com: Entrepreneurs, http://entrepreneurs.about.com/od/famousentrepreneurs/p/waynehuizenga.htm (accessed May 24, 2011). See also R. Sandomir, "Entrepreneurs; Wayne Huizenga's Growth Complex," *New York Times*, June 9, 1991, http://query.nytimes.com/gst/fullpage.html?res=9D0CE3DD1730F93AA35755C0A9679582 60&n=Top%2fNews%2fBusiness%2fCompanies%2fBlockbuster%20Inc%2e (accessed May 24, 2011).

2. D. Shook, "AOL Time Warner's Unfinished Revolution," *BusinessWeek*, February 1, 2002, www.businessweek.com/technology/content/feb2002/tc2002021_8004.htm (accessed May 24, 2011).

3. A. Serwer, "How Much Has AOL Really Cost Time Warner?" *Fortune*, February 23, 2004, http://money.cnn.com/magazines/fortune/fortune_archive/2004/02/23/362215/index.htm (accessed May 24, 2011).

4. D. Rushkoff, "Signs of the Times," *The Guardian*, July 25, 2002, www.guardian.co.uk/technology/2002/jul/25/onlinesupplement.newmedia (accessed May 24, 2011).

5. Shook, 2002; T. Mullaney, "Lies, Damn Lies, Statistics and the AOL–Time Warner Merger," *BusinessWeek*, August 1, 2008, www.businessweek.com/the_thread/dealflow/archives/2006/08/lies_damn_lies.html (accessed May 24, 2011).

6. S. Case, "It's Time to Take It Apart," *Washington Post*, December 11, 2005, p. B1.

7. D. Stires, "The Two Faces of Case," *Fortune*, December 12, 2005.

8. A. Field, "Making a Little Company Look Big," *New York Times*, July 12, 2007, p. C5.

9. J. Mehring, "The Real Job Engines," *BusinessWeek SmallBiz*, Spring 2006, p. 42.

10. AllBusiness.com, "Why Sole Proprietorship Is Most Common, Simplest Business Type," *San Francisco Chronicle*, May 30, 2007, p. C4.

11. J. Hopkins, "African-American-Owned Firms Increase," *USA Today*, August 18, 2005, p. 3B.

12. J. M. Rosenberg, "Small-Business Owners Have Trouble Finding Time to Take Off," *San Francisco Chronicle*, June 13, 2007, p. C4.

13. AllBusiness.com, "Partner Can Be a Big Help with Pooling Finances for Purchase," *San Francisco Chronicle*, January 24, 2007, p. C4.

14. AllBusiness.com, "How Couples Run a Home Business without Running Each Other Down," *San Francisco Chronicle*, April 18, 2007, p. C4.

15. L. Petrecca, "Business Partners Can Enrich or Ditch a Start-up," *USA Today*, October 5, 2009, pp. 1B, 2B.

16. AllBusiness.com, "How Couples Run a Home Business without Running Each Other Down," 2007.

17. I. DeBare, "Couples in Business Together Need to Define Roles, Set Limits," *San Francisco Chronicle*, April 11, 2007, pp. C1, C4.

18. AllBusiness.com, "How to Choose the Right Type of Structure for Your Business," *San Francisco Chronicle*, October 3, 2007, p. C4.

19. I. Debare, "Consider Structure of Business Before Forming a Corporation," *San Francisco Chronicle*, January 3, 2007, pp. C1, C4.

20. AllBusiness.com, "Why Forming an LLC Might Be a Useful Setup for Many Startups," *San Francisco Chronicle,* March 14, 2007, p. C4.

21. I. Lapowsky, "B Corporations," *Inc.,* May 2011, p. 78; "About B Corp: Who Certifies?" B Lab, www.bcorporation.net/index .cfm/fuseaction/content.page/nodeID/08c9dc4d-6064-48cb-af04 -4fd9d4ced055 (accessed May 24, 2011); and "B Corporation," Wikipedia, April 12, 2011, http://en.wikipedia.org/wiki/B_corporation (accessed May 24, 2011).

22. The Company Corporation, *Incorporating Your Business for Dummies* (New York: Hungry Minds, 2001), p. 1.

23. D. Carpenter, "Ace More Than Holds Its Own," *USA Today,* January 19, 2007, p. 5B; and "Ace Hardware Reports Second Quarter 2009 Results," http://ourcompany.acehardware.com/ news/index.asp (accessed May 25, 2011).

24. E. H. Shur, "Garnet Mercantile's First-Day Sales Double Projection," *Reno Gazette-Journal,* November 14, 2004, pp. 1E, 7E; A. Batdorff, "Powell Mercantile Serves as Model for Others," *Billings Gazette,* November 16, 2004, www.casperstartribune.net/articles/2004/11/16/news/wyoming/c1d16119668 eeda987256f4e0011b15a.txt (accessed May 25, 2011); and M. Tady, "Communities That Create Their Own Stores," *Yes! Magazine,* www.yesmagazine.org/article.asp?ID=1231 (accessed May 25, 2011).

25. First Prize Franchise, "Popular Franchises and Minorities," www.firstprizefranchise.com/popular-franchises-and-minorities (accessed May 25, 2011).

26. Study by Pricewaterhouse Coopers for International Franchise Association Educational Foundation, "Franchise Business Economic Outlook: 2011," January 3, 2011, www.franchise.org/ uploadedFiles/Franchise%20Business%20Outlook%20 Report%202011%20final.pdf (accessed May 25, 2011).

27. P. Cancro, as told to P. R. Olsen, "Lessons from the Sub Shop," *New York Times,* June 6, 2010, Business section, p. 9.

28. D. Jones, "A Dirty Job, but Someone Has to Get Rich Doing It," *USA Today,* October 11, 2007, pp. 1B, 2B.

29. AllBusiness, "How Much Does a Franchise Cost?" www .allbusiness.com/buying-selling-businesses/franchising -franchise-fee/2182-1.html (accessed May 25, 2011).

30. DoodyCalls, "Franchise Opportunities," www.doodycalls.com/ franchise_opportunities_overview.asp (accessed May 25, 2011).

31. E. Maltby, "Want to Buy a Franchise? The Requirements Went Up," *Wall Street Journal,* November 15, 2010, p. R9.

32. "How Much Does a Franchise Cost?" 2007.

33. AllBusiness, "The Disadvantages of Franchises," www.allbusiness .com/buying-exiting-businesses/franchising-franchises/1425-1 .html (accessed May 24, 2011).

34. "The Disadvantages of Franchises," 2011.

35. T. Bates, "Survival Patterns Among Newcomers to Franchising," *Journal of Business Venturing,* March 1998, pp. 113–130.

36. AllBusiness, "How Much Money Can You Make from a Franchise?" www.allbusiness.com/buying-exiting-businesses/ franchising-franchises/2183-1.html (accessed May 25, 2011).

37. A. Lanford and J. Lanford, "Top 10 Work at Home and Home-Based Business Scams," Scambusters.org, www.scambusters .org/work-at-home.html (accessed May 30, 2011).

38. First Prize Franchise, "Popular Franchises and Minorities," www.firstprizefranchise.com/popular-franchises-and-minorities (accessed May 20, 2011).

39. Data from table "50 Top Franchises for Minorities," selected by the National Minority Franchising Initiative, reported in R. Bond and L. Yu, "50 Top Franchises for Minorities," *USA Today,* November 5, 2010, p. 7B.

40. E. Maltby, "In Search of Good Bets," *Wall Street Journal,* November 15, 2010, p. R9.

41. J. McGregor, "Room & Board Plays Impossible to Get," *BusinessWeek,* October 1, 2007, p. 80.

42. "Google to Buy YouTube for $1.65 Billion," *BusinessWeek,* October 10, 2006, www.businessweek.com/investor/content/oct2006/ pi20061010_297582.htm?chan=search (accessed May 20, 2011).

43. Stephen Beggar, quoted in "What Financial Services Consolidation Means for Investors," *BusinessWeek Online,* September 13, 2000, www.businessweek.com/investor/content/eemi/emi0913a .html?chan=search#top (accessed May 20, 2011).

44. P. Elstrom, "The Sky-High Costs of a Satellite Deal," *BusinessWeek,* October 1, 2007, p. 11.

45. P. Gogoi, "No Wild Oats for Whole Foods?" *BusinessWeek,* June 6, 2007, www.businessweek.com/bwdaily/dnflash/content/ jun2007/db20070606_903061.htm?chan=search (accessed May 20, 2011).

46. D. Bartz, "Whole Foods, FTC Settle on Wild Oats Merger," *Reuters,* March 6, 2009, http://www.reuters.com/article/innovation News/idUSTRE5253AL20090306 (accessed May 20, 2011).

47. J. Lipen, "Concentration: Corporations' Dreams Converge in One Idea: It's Time to Do a Deal," *Wall Street Journal,* February 26, 1997, pp. A1, A8.

48. M. Geniella, "Pacific Lumber Files for Bankruptcy," *Press Democrat* (Santa Rosa, CA), January 20, 2007, www.pressdemocrat.com/ apps/pbcs.dll/article?AID=/20070120/NEWS/701200303/1033/ NEWS01; D. Cobb, "Wall Street vs. Main Street," *Eureka Times Standard* (Eureka, CA), February 1, 2007, www.times-standard .com/davidcobb/ci_5133393 (both accessed May 20, 2011).

49. P. Demarzio, "Bayer as White Knight Edges Out Merck in Bid for Schering," ABCMoney.co.uk, March 25, 2006, www .abcmoney.co.uk/news/2520062226.htm (accessed May 25, 2011).

50. E. Woyke and D. Henry, "The Buyout Boom's Dark Side," *BusinessWeek,* August 13, 2007, pp. 40–42; D. Henry, "Sometimes Merger Math Doesn't Add Up," *BusinessWeek,* August 13, 2007, p. 42.

51. L. M. Holson and S. Waxman, "Los Angeles Times Faces New Questions about the Future," *New York Times,* April 3, 2007, pp. C1, C5; D. Carr, "A New Owner Who Is Hedging His Bets," *New York Times,* April 3, 2007, pp. C1, C4; L. Uchitelle, "Employee Owners Don't Necessarily Have a Say in Management," *New York Times,* April 3, 2007, C4; and J. Nocera, "A Lifeline of Sorts to Newspapers," *New York Times,* June 23, 2007, pp. B1, B8.

52. "Domino's Pizza 2Q Net Income Rises, Revenue Up," *USA Today,* July 26, 2011, www.usatoday.idmanagedsolutions.com/ news/story.idms?ID_NEWS=198895008 (accessed August 24, 2011).

53. "History of Domino's Pizza," Recipe Pizza website, www .recipepizza.com/the_history_of_dominos_pizza.htm (accessed August 25, 2011).

54. "Domino's Pizza 2Q Net Income Rises, Revenue Up," 2011; "History of Domino's Pizza," 2011).

55. "Domino's Pizza," New York Stock Exchange website, www .nyse.com/about/listed/dpz.html (accessed August 25, 2011).

56. B. Horovitz, "Domino's Pizza Delivers Change in Its Core Pizza Recipe," *USA Today,* December 16, 2009, www.usatoday.com/ money/industries/food/2009-12-16-dominos16_ST_N.htm (accessed August 24, 2011).

57. Horovitz, 2009.

58. Horovitz, 2009.

59. "Celebrating Its 50th Year, Domino's Gives Itself a Makeover," *PR Newswire,* December 16, 2009, www.prnewswire.com/

news-releases/celebrating-50th-year-dominos-pizza-gives-itself -a-makeover-79408147.html (accessed August 25, 2011).

60. "Celebrating Its 50th Year, Domino's Gives Itself a Makeover," 2009.

61. "Domino's Pizza Announces 2010 Results," *PR Newswire*, March 1, 2011, www.prnewswire.com/news-releases/dominos -pizza-announces-2010-financial-results-117142383.html (accessed August 25, 2011).

62. "Operator to Owner," Domino's website, www.dominosbiz.com/ Biz-Public-EN/Site+Content/Secondary/Franchise/Operate+ to+Own/ (accessed August 24, 2011).

63. P. Hruby, "The Right Way? The Green Bay Way," ESPN.com, January 31, 2011, http://sports.espn.go.com/espn/commentary/ news/story?page=hruby/110131 (accessed February 19, 2011).

64. "Super Bowls & Championships," packers.com, www.packers .com/history/super-bowls-and-championships.html (accessed May 10, 2011).

65. D. Harding, "America's Only Non-Profit, Community-Owned Franchise in Professional Sports Major Leagues Wins Super Bowl," ProgressOhio.com, February 7, 2011, www.progressohio .org/blog/2011/02/americas-only-only-non-profit-community -qwned-franchise-in-professional-sports-major-leagueswins-sup .html (accessed May 10, 2011).

66. D. Zirin, "Those Non-Profit Packers," *New Yorker*, January 25, 2011, www.newyorker.com/online/blogs/sportingscene/2011/01/ those-non-profit-packers.html (accessed February 19, 2011).

CHAPTER 6

1. J. Cassidy, "Me Media," *New Yorker*, May 15, 2006, pp. 50–59.

2. V. Vara, "Facebook Gets Help from Its Friends," *Wall Street Journal*, June 22, 2007, pp. B1, B2; and B. Stone, "In Facebook, Investing in a Theory," *New York Times*, October 4, 2007, pp. C1, C2.

3. E. Lee, "Making Amends," *San Francisco Chronicle*, September 12, 2006, pp. D1, D7.

4. J. Swartz, "Tech Giants Poke Around Facebook," *USA Today*, October 3, 2007, pp. 1B, 2B.

5. E. Lee and R. Kim, "Microsoft's Big Bet," *San Francisco Chronicle*, October 25, 2007, pp. A1, A10.

6. R. Kim, "He's 23, Rich, and Seems Unfazed," *San Francisco Chronicle*, October 25, 2007, pp. C1, C6.

7. P. Kafka, "Friendster's Cautionary Tale Ends in $100 Million Sale," *D/All Things Digital*, December 10, 2009, http:// mediamemo.allthingsd.com/20091210/friendsters-cautionary -tale-ends-in-100-million%20sale/ (accessed May 31, 2011).

8. M. Arrington, "The Friendster Tell-All Story," *TechCrunch*, October 15, 2006, www.techcrunch.com/2006/10/15/the-friendster -tell-all-story; and M. Chafkin, "How to Kill a Great Idea!" *Inc.*, June 2007, www.inc.com/magazine/20070601/features-how-to -kill-a-great-idea.html (accessed May 31, 2011).

9. G. Rivlin, "Wallflower at the Web Party," *New York Times*, October 15, 2006, www.nytimes.com/2006/10/15/business/your money/15friend.html?ex=1318564800&en=3e9438ed349f7ce 7&ei=5090&partner=rssuserland&emc=rss (accessed May 31, 2011).

10. "Top 15 Most Popular Social Networking Websites," *eBizMBA*, August 15, 2011, www.ebizmba.com/articles/social-networking -websites (accessed August 23, 2011).

11. A. Das and A. Afrati, "Cash Keeps Facebook's Status Private," *Wall Street Journal*, January 4, 2011, http://online.wsj.com/ article/SB10001424052748704111504576059490038639856 .html (accessed May 31, 2011).

12. Survey by Decipher, Inc., of Fresno, CA, for Intuit, reported in R. Abrams, "Study: 72% of Workers Would Rather Work for

Themselves," *USA Today*, October 16, 2007, www.usatoday .com/money/smallbusiness/columnist/abrams/2007-10-11 -workers-survey_N.htm (accessed May 31, 2011).

13. Survey by Decipher, Inc., for Intuit, reported in "Intuit Survey Finds American Dream Alive and Well," March 1, 2006, press release, http://web.intuit.com/about_intuit/press_releases/2006/03-01 .html (accessed May 31, 2011).

14. Survey by Citibank, cited in "Entrepreneurial Spirit Thrives Despite Recession," *USA Today*, July 15, 2010, p. 1B.

15. A. M. Webber, "Danger: Toxic Company," *Fast Company*, November 1998, pp. 152–161.

16. M. Bond, "Stamp Hobby Blossoms in Home-Based Business," *Reno Gazette-Journal*, October 23, 2007, pp. 6A, 7A.

17. Investor Dictionary, www.investordictionary.com/definition/ micropreneur; and A. Robertson, "Are You a Micropreneur?" *WebProNews*, August 17, 2006, www.webpronews.com/ expertarticles/2006/08/17/are-you-a-micropreneur (both accessed May 31, 2011).

18. K. Fagan, "Gold Fever Spikes as Prices Rise," *San Francisco Chronicle*, October 25, 2009, pp. A1, A14.

19. Paula Wolfert, quoted in A. Gold, "Aziza's Chef Has Always Carved a Unique Path," *San Francisco Chronicle*, October 25, 2009, pp. A1, A15.

20. Survey by Decipher, reported in Abrams, "Study: 72% of Workers Would Rather Work for Themselves," 2007.

21. R. Kim, "Jobs Tops Oprah in Teen Poll," *San Francisco Chronicle*, October 14, 2009, pp. C1, C2.

22. P. F. Drucker, *Innovation and Entrepreneurship* (New York: Harper & Row, 1986), pp. 27–28.

23. M. Jewell, "Startup Hopes to Create Online Marketplace for Open Parking Spaces," *Reno Gazette-Journal*, February 20, 2007, p. 2D; and "The Dreaded Hunt and the SpotScout Solution," *Living Labs Global Mobility Report*, September 1, 2009, www.livinglabs-global.com/blog/?p=145 (accessed May 31, 2011).

24. D. Takahashi, "Reinventing the Intrapreneur," *Red Herring Magazine*, September 2000, www.utdallas.edu/~chasteen/Reinvent ing%20the%20intrapreneur.htm (accessed May 31, 2011).

25. J. D. Rey, "A Hot-Tub Maker's Business Was Decimated by the Recession. Will New Products Revive His Company?" *Inc.*, November 2009, pp. 68–72.

26. Global Entrepreneurship Monitor, 2002 study by London Business School and Babson College, reported in J. Bailey, "Desire— More Than Need—Builds a Business," *Wall Street Journal*, May 21, 2002, p. B4.

27. L. Petrecca, "Tough Times Drive Start-ups," *USA Today*, September 14, 2009, pp. 1B, 2B.

28. Small Business Administration, July 2009 report, cited in T. Abate, "Unemployed? Try Starting a Business," *San Francisco Chronicle*, August 12, 2009, pp. C1, C3.

29. Eving Marion Kauffman Foundation, reported in L. Petrecca, "Recession Inspires Business Start-Ups," *USA Today*, March 7, 2011, p. 4B.

30. Chun, quoted in Petrecca, 2011.

31. This section was adapted from A. Kinicki and B. K. Williams, *Management: A Practical Introduction*, 4th ed. (New York: McGraw-Hill/Irwin, 2009), pp. 25–26, relying on the following sources: D. C. McClelland, *The Achieving Society* (New York: Van Nostrand, 1961); D. C. McClelland, *Human Motivation* (Glenview, IL: Scott, Foresman, 1985); D. L. Sexton and N. Bowman, "The Entrepreneur: A Capable Executive and More," *Journal of Business Venturing*, vol. 1, 1985, pp. 129–140; D. Hisrich, "Entrepreneurship/Intrapreneurship," *American Psychologist*, February 1990, p. 218; T. Begley and D. P. Boyd,

"Psychological Characteristics Associated with Performance in Entrepreneurial Firms and Smaller Businesses," *Journal of Business Venturing,* vol. 2, 1987, pp. 79–93; and C. R. Kuehl and P. A. Lambing, *Small Business: Planning and Management* (Fort Worth, TX: Dryden Press, 1994).

32. Z. Kanin, "Deskside," *New Yorker,* September 20, 2010, pp. 50–51.

33. U.S. Small Business Administration, "Frequently Asked Questions," www.sba.gov/advocacy/7495 (accessed May 31, 2011).

34. R. Randazzo, "Sky Is Limit at Tahoe Hotel Aimed at Snowboarders," *Reno Gazette-Journal,* January 14, 2007, pp. 1E, 5E.

35. National Federation of Independent Business, "Small Business Facts."

36. D. Fost, "Where Neo-Nomads' Ideas Percolate," *San Francisco Chronicle,* March 11, 2007, pp. A1, A8.

37. *Inc.* magazine Inc. 500, reported in AllBusiness.com, "Starting a Small Business Depends More on Fortitude Than a Fortune," *San Francisco Chronicle,* June 6, 2007, p. C4.

38. C. Lum, "Birth of Baby Carrier Came After New Son Arrived in '01," *USA Today,* October 17, 2007, p. 4B; reprinted from the *Honolulu Advertiser.*

39. G. Chon, "Compass to Acquire Ergo Baby Carrier," *Wall Street Journal,* September 17, 2010, http://online.wsj.com/article/SB10001424052748704394704575496222162050434.html (accessed May 31, 2011).

40. S. E. Needleman, "Negotiating the Freelance Economy," *Wall Street Journal,* May 6, 2009, pp. D1, D2; and R. Flandez, "Small Businesses, Working from Home," *Wall Street Journal,* June 2, 2009, pp. B1, B6.

41. K. Komando, "Earn Money at Home Via the Internet," *Reno Gazette-Journal,* August 20, 2007, p. 5D.

42. "Working at Home? Get Disciplined," *Reno Gazette-Journal,* March 31, 2007, p. 1E.

43. J. M. Rosenberg, "Trolling the Internet Can Yield a Big Catch for Small Businesses," *San Francisco Chronicle,* October 25, 2006, p. C4.

44. T. Abate, "'Ultralight' Startups Require Little Capital, Just a Computer," *San Francisco Chronicle,* September 7, 2010, pp. D1, D4.

45. W. M. Bulkeley, "Technology for the Solo Entrepreneur," *Wall Street Journal,* May 15, 2010, p. R8.

46. K. Komando, "How Online Businesses Can Best Use Google Ads," *Reno Gazette-Journal,* April 10, 2011, p. 5F.

47. J. Graham, "Facebook Has Tools for Small Businesses," *USA Today,* May 25, 2011, p. 3B.

48. SunTrust study of 201 business owners with annual revenues of $10 million or more, reported in "Majority of Business Owners Start from Scratch," *USA Today,* October 18, 2007, p. 1B.

49. J. Guynn, "Dot-Com on the Cheap," *San Francisco Chronicle,* January 21, 2007, pp. A1, A15.

50. Guynn, 2007.

51. B. Dempsey, "Tools of Running a Business, at Tag-Sale Prices," *New York Times,* September 17, 2007, sec. 3, p. 6.

52. B. Bottoset, "Finding a Business to Buy Can Be Frustrating," *Reno Gazette-Journal,* September 26, 2006, p. 5D.

53. J. Wortham, "Once Just a Site with Funny Cat Pictures, and Now a Web Empire," *New York Times,* June 14, 2010, pp. B1, B8.

54. Quantcast, "Cheezburger Network," June 1, 2011, www.quantcast.com/p-75z9nhQwNH4Ek (accessed June 2, 2011).

55. "10 Ways to Know It's Time to Sell Your Business," *BizLinkIn.com,* www.bizlinkin.com/10-ways-know-its-time-sell-your-business (accessed May 31, 2011).

56. G. Rifkin, "Making a Profit and a Difference," *New York Times,* October 5, 2006, p. C5.

57. R. Abrams, "Find and Keeping Your Niche Is a Key to a Successful Small Business," *Reno Gazette-Journal,* April 10, 2007, p. 7A.

58. L. Gomes, "PlentyOfFish Owner Has the Perfect Bait for a Huge Success," *Wall Street Journal,* May 23, 2007, p. B1; and M. Chafkin, "And the Money Comes Rolling In," *Inc.,* January 1, 2009, www.inc.com/magazine/20090101/and-the-money-comes-rolling-in.html (accessed May 31, 2011).

59. Judy Wicks, reported in Rifkin, "Making a Profit and a Difference," 2006.

60. J. L. Wright, "Art, food, music," *Reno Gazette-Journal,* August 2, 2006, pp. 1E, 4E.

61. R. Abrams, "Outside Resources Exist to Make a Venture Successful," *Reno Gazette-Journal,* August 18, 2009, p. 7A.

62. J. Kellner, "17-Year-Old Entrepreneur Writes Own Business Plan," *Reno Gazette-Journal,* January 29, 2007, p. 8E.

63. Study by S. Shane, cited in K. K. Spors, "Do Start-Ups Really Need Formal Business Plans?" *Wall Street Journal,* January 9, 2007, p. B9.

64. Definition from InvestorWords, www.investorwords.com/629/business_model.html (accessed May 31, 2011).

65. Spors, "Do Start-Ups Really Need Formal Business Plans?" 2007.

66. Study by Amar Bhide, cited in Spors, "Do Start-Ups Really Need Formal Business Plans?" 2007.

67. J. W. Mullins, "Why Business Plans Don't Deliver," *Wall Street Journal,* June 22, 2009, R3; and R. Abrams, "A Business Plan Is the Path to Success," *Reno Gazette-Journal,* October 27, 2009, p. 8A.

68. M. C. Hirshberg, "Brother, Can You Spare a Dime?" *Inc.,* November 2009, pp. 45–46.

69. L. Petrecca, "Big Decision: How Do You Fund Your Venture," *USA Today,* September 29, 2009; R. Abrams, "Finding Cash for Your Startup Can Be Daunting," *Reno Gazette-Journal,* October 6, 2009, p. 7A.; and V. Harnish, "Has Your Bank Turned Its Back on You?" *Fortune,* October 18, 2010, p. 70.

70. B. Hindo, "Money from Home," *BusinessWeek SmallBiz,* Spring 2005, p. 30.

71. A. Piore, "Latest Immigrant Wave: Indian Hotel Developers," *The Real Deal,* February 2007, www.therealdeal.net/issues/FEBRUARY_2007/1170192101.php (accessed May 31, 2011).

72. D. Gleiter, "Indian Families Find Niche in Hotel Industry," *USA Today,* February 18, 2004, www.usatoday.com/travel/hotels/2004-02-18-indian-hotels_x.htm (accessed May 31, 2011).

73. J. Martin, "Fair Trade," *FSB,* June 2009, pp. 76–79; and S. Dominus, "Seeking Goods and Services, No Money Necessary," *New York Times,* July 14, 2009, p. A18.

74. S. Medintz, "Getting the Loan Officer on Your Side," *New York Times,* May 28, 2009, p. B8; and S. Brown, as told to M. Zouhali-Worrall, "Tend to Your Lender," *FSB,* September 2009, p. 53. See also P. Davidson, "This Recession Isn't Being Kind to Entrepreneurs," *USA Today,* June 8, 2009, p. 1B; K. Chu and S. Block, "As Lenders Clamp Down, Credit Scores Take a Hit," *USA Today,* September 22, 2009, pp. 1A, 2A; and P. S. Goodman, "Clamps on Credit Tighten," *New York Times,* October 13, 2009, pp. B1, B4.

75. Abrams, "Outside Resources Exist to Make a Venture Successful," 2009. See also interview with SBA Administrator Karen Mills, in J. Quittner, "Throwing Lifelines to Small Business," *BusinessWeek,* August 3, 2009, pp. 52–53.

76. See H. Plotkin, "So, You Want to Be an Angel Investor?" *Silicon Valley Insider,* August 30, 1999, http://plotkin.com/cnbcs024.htm (accessed September 29, 2010).

77. T. McMahan, "Perfecting the Pitch," *Wall Street Journal,* July 13, 2009, p. R4.

78. Pepperdine Private Capital Markets survey of 185 venture capitalists, reported in "Where Venture-Capital Firms Invest," *USA Today,* October 1, 2009, p. 1B.

79. R. Flandez, "Entrepreneurs Take Second Jobs to Stay Afloat," *Wall Street Journal,* June 16, 2009, p. B4.

80. J. Farwell, "Web Breathing New Life into Lending between Strangers," *Reno Gazette-Journal,* November 30, 2007, p. 10A; and T. Abate, "Microloans Give Small Firms a Leg Up," *San Francisco Chronicle,* October 12, 2009, pp. A1, A7.

81. H. Olen, "Good Neighbors," *FSB,* October 2009, pp. 81–83.

82. A. Field, "Business Incubators Are Growing Up," *BusinessWeek,* November 16, 2009, p. 76.

83. S. Hauge, "Help Small Businesses" [letter to the editor], *San Francisco Chronicle,* October 19, 2007, p. B12.

84. "Learn the Facts," Let's Move website, www.letsmove.gov/learn-facts/epidemic-childhood-obesity (accessed August 26, 2011).

85. "Physical Activity Leading Trend at American International Toy Fair: Toy Manufacturers Respond to First Lady's *Let's Move* Initiative to Combat Childhood Obesity," Wild Planet Toys website, www.wildplanet.com/press/wp_release_single_print.php?prid=161 (accessed August 26, 2011).

86. "Wild Planet Toys, Inc.," Hoovers, www.hoovers.com/company/Wild_Planet_Toys_Inc/rfyhsyi-1.html (accessed August 26, 2011).

87. "Physical Activity Leading Trend at American International Toy Fair," 2011).

88. "Physical Activity Leading Trend at American International Toy Fair," 2011).

89. "Physical Activity Leading Trend at American International Toy Fair," 2011).

90. "Danny Grossman: CEO Mixes Toys and Social Commitments," *San Francisco Chronicle*, June 25, 2003, www.articles.sfgate.com/2003-06-25/business/17495567_1_wild-planet-toys-spy-gear-spy-vision-goggles (accessed August 26, 2011).

91. A. Krueger, "Today's Million-Dollar Idea: Group Dating Site So Women Don't Have to Meet Strangers Alone," *Business Insider,* October 6, 2010, www.businessinsider.com/todays-million-dollar-idea-group-dating-site-so-women-dont-have-to-meet-strangers-alone-2010-10 (accessed February 26, 2011).

92. H. Seligson, "Jilted in the U.S., a Site Finds Love in India," *New York Times,* February 19, 2011, www.nytimes.com/2011/02/20/business/20ignite.html?_r=1&dlbk (accessed February 26, 2011).

93. D. Carta, "A New Way to Date: 6 Online Resources for Group Dating," Mashable.com, August 20, 2008, www.mashable.com/2008/08/20/group-dating-sites (accessed February 27, 2011).

CHAPTER 7

1. A. Lashinsky, "The Decade of Steve," *Fortune,* November 23, 2009, pp. 93–100.

2. L. Ellison, interviewed by A. Lashinsky, "All about Steve," *Fortune,* November 23, 2009, p. 124.

3. Lashinsky, "The Decade of Steve," 2009.

4. D. Lyons, "The Lost Decade: Why Steve Ballmer Is No Bill Gates," *Newsweek,* November 9, 2009, p. 27. See also N. Wingfield, "Microsoft Seeks to Take a Bite Out of Apple with New Stores," *Wall Street Journal,* October 15, 2009, pp. B1, B2; A. Vance, "Forecast for Microsoft: Partly Cloudy," *New York Times,* October 18, 2009, business section, pp. 1, 7; N. Wingfield, "Ballmer Tries Bringing Back Microsoft's Mojo," *Wall Street Journal,* October 22, 2009, pp. B1, B5; J. M. O'Brien, "Microsoft Reboots," *Fortune,* October 26, 2009, pp. 98–108; G. Rivlin,

"The Problem with Microsoft," *Fortune,* March 29, 2011, http://tech.fortune.cnn.com/2011/03/29/the-problem-with-microsoft (accessed June 9, 2011); R. Farzad, "Microsoft Looks Cheap—as Usual," *Bloomberg Businessweek,* April 28, 2011, www.businessweek.com/magazine/content/11_19/b4227039760959.htm (accessed June 9, 2011); and "David Einhorn Loves Microsoft, Hates Steve Ballmer," *Wall Street Journal,* May 25, 2011, http://blogs.wsj.com/deals/2011/05/25/david-einhorn-buy-delta-lloyd-group-microsoft (accessed June 9, 2011).

5. M. P. Follett, quoted in J. F. Stoner and R. E. Freeman, *Management,* 5th ed. (Englewood Cliffs, NJ: Prentice-Hall, 1992), p. 6.

6. M. Zouhali-Worrall, "People Power," *Fortune Small Business,* June 2009, pp. 64–66.

7. A. Deutschman, "Inside the Mind of Jeff Bezos," *Fast Company,* December 19, 2007, www.fastcompany.com/magazine/85/bezos_2.html (accessed November 15, 2009).

8. S. E. Ante, "How Amazon Is Turning Opinions into Gold," *BusinessWeek,* October 26, 2009, pp. 47–48.

9. D. Jones and M. Krantz, "Companies, Investors Tend to Prosper When Founders Remain at the Helm," *USA Today,* August 22, 2007, pp. 1B, 2B.

10. Bezos, quoted in Deutschman, "Inside the Mind of Jeff Bezos," 2007.

11. Salary.com survey reported in "Salary.com Survey Finds Median Pay for Small-Biz CEOs," *Boston Business Journal,* November 29, 2007, www.bizjournals.com/boston/stories/2007/11/26/daily42.html (accessed June 8, 2011).

12. Study by Equilar, reported in D. Costello, "The Drought Is Over (at Least for CEO's)," *New York Times,* April 9, 2011, www.nytimes.com/2011/04/10/business/10comp.html (accessed June 8, 2011).

13. W. Buffett, quoted by Robert A. Iger, CEO of the Walt Disney Company, in interview by A. Bryant, "He Was Promotable After All," *New York Times,* May 3, 2009, business section, p. 2.

14. Based on details from Funding University, "Amazon.com, Inc.," www.fundinguniverse.com/company-histories/Amazoncom-Inc-company-History.html (accessed November 15, 2009).

15. C. Ferran and S. Watts, "Videoconferencing in the Field: A Heuristic Processing Model," *Management Science,* September 2008, pp. 1565–1578.

16. Kishore Sengupta, quoted in P. Dvorak, "Dangers Can Lurk in Clinging to Solutions of the Past," *Wall Street Journal,* March 2, 2009, p. B4.

17. M. Skapinker, "Diversity Fails to End Boardroom Groupthink," *Financial Times,* May 25, 2009, www.ft.com/cms/s/0/433ed210-4954-11de-9e19-00144feabdc0.html?catid=136&SID=google (accessed November 23, 2009).

18. R. L. Keeney, reported in D. Murphy, "When to Make Decisions—or Delay Them," *San Francisco Examiner,* December 6, 1998, p. J-2.

19. O. Pollar, "Six Steps for Making Tough Choices," *San Francisco Examiner and Chronicle,* April 4, 1999, p. J-3.

20. N. T. Sheehan and G. Vaidyanathan, "The Path to Growth," *Wall Street Journal,* March 3–4, 2007, p. R8.

21. D. Leider, "Purposeful Work," *Utne Reader,* July/August 1988, p. 52; excerpted from *On Purpose: A Journal about New Lifestyles & Workstyles,* Winter 1986.

22. T. A. Stewart, "A Refreshing Change: Vision Statements That Make Sense," *Fortune,* September 30, 1996, pp. 195–196.

23. P. J. Below, G. L. Morrisey, and B. L. Acomb, *The Executive Guide to Strategic Planning* (San Francisco: Jossey-Bass, 1987), p. 2.

24. D. Kiley, "Putting Ford on Fast-Forward," *BusinessWeek,* October 26, 2009, pp. 56–57.

25. D. Welch and I. Rowley, "Toyota Gets Stuck in a Pair of Ruts," *BusinessWeek,* November 30, 2009, p. 60; M. Ramsey and C. Dawson, "Toyota, Honda Lose U.S. Edge," *Wall Street Journal,* November 15, 2010, pp. B11, B2; M. Ramsey, "Toyota Expands Prius into a Brand," *Wall Street Journal,* January 11, 2011, p. B4; C. Woodyard, "Prius Gets Big Brother, Little Sis," *USA Today,* January 11, 2011, p. 1B; D. Leinwand and C. Woodyard, "No Flaws Found in Toyota Electronics," *USA Today,* February 9, 2011, p. 1B; "J. D. Power and Associates Reports: While Vehicle Dependability Continues to Improve, New Technologies and Features Pose Challenges for Automakers," press release, J. D. Power and Associates, March 17, 2011, http://business center.jdpower.com/news/pressrelease.aspx?ID=2011029 (accessed June 2, 2011); and "Small SUV: Toyota RAV4," *ConsumerReports.org,* April 2011, www.consumerreports.org/cro/cars/new-cars/cr-recommended/top-picks/small-suv/index.htm (accessed June 2, 2011).

26. D. McGinn, "Managing Along the Cutting Edge," *Newsweek,* February 9, 2009, pp. 46–47.

27. E. Lawler, reported in S. Ross, "Worker Involvement Pays Off," *San Francisco Examiner,* November 15, 1998, p. J-2.

28. R. L. Katz, "Skills of an Effective Administrator," *Harvard Business Review,* September–October 1974, p. 94. This section also adapted from Kinicki and Williams, *Management,* 2009, pp. 4, 27–28.

29. T. Lowry, "Can MTV Stay Cool?" *BusinessWeek,* February 20, 2006, pp. 19–24.

30. Sarah Levinson, quoted in Lowry, 2006.

31. J. P. Kotter, "What Leaders Really Do," *Harvard Business Review,* December 2001, pp. 85–96.

32. D. Rooke and W. R. Torbert, "Transformations of Leadership," *Harvard Business Review,* April 2005, pp. 67–76.

33. R. Tannenbaum and W. H. Schmidt, "How to Choose a Leadership Pattern," *Harvard Business Review,* May 1, 1973, pp. 162–164.

34. "Autocratic Leadership," *Money-Zine.com,* www.money-zine .com/Career-Development/Leadership-Skill/Autocratic-Leader ship (accessed June 8, 2011).

35. "Participative Management," *Encyclopedia Britannica,* www .britannica.com/EBchecked/topic/445024/participative -management (accessed June 8, 2011).

36. S. Bennett, quoted in C. Hymowitz, "Business Is Personal, So Managers Need to Harness Emotions," *Wall Street Journal,* November 13, 2006, p. B1.

37. Jeff Rich, quoted in D. Jones, "Autocratic Leadership Works— Until It Fails," *USA Today,* June 5, 2003, www.usatoday.com/news/nation/2003-06-05-raines-usat_x.htm (accessed June 8, 2011).

38. J. McNerney, quoted in M. Arndt, "3M's Rising Star," *BusinessWeek,* April 12, 2004, p. 65.

39. J. Antonakis and R. J. House, "The Full-Range Leadership Theory: The Way Forward," in B. J. Avolio and F. J. Yammarino, eds., *Transformational and Charismatic Leadership: The Road Ahead* (New York: JAI Press, 2002), pp. 3–34.

40. M. R. Barrick, M. K. Mount, and T. A. Judge, "Personality and Performance at the Beginning of the New Millennium: What Do We Know and Where Do We Go Next?" *Personality and Performance,* March/June 2001, pp. 9–30; and S. N. Kaplan, M. M. Klebanov, and M. Sorensen, "Which CEO Characteristics and Abilities Matter?" *NBR Working Paper,* No. 14195, Issued June 2008, National Bureau of Economic Research. See also D. Brooks, "In Praise of Dullness," *New York Times,* May 19, 2009, p. A23.

41. J. Kosecoff, interviewed by A. Bryant in "The Divine, Too, Is in the Details," *New York Times,* June 21, 2009, business section, p. 2.

42. R. Kark, B. Shamir, and C. Chen, "The Two Faces of Transformational Leadership: Empowerment and Dependency," *Journal of Applied Psychology,* April 2003, pp. 246–255. Parts of this section adapted from G. R. Jones and J. M. George, *Contemporary Management,* 6th ed. (New York: McGraw-Hill/Irwin, 2009), pp. 573–76; Kinicki and Williams, *Management,* 2009, pp. 455–56; and R. L. Daft, *Management,* 9th ed. (Mason, OH: South-Western Cengage, 2010), p. 524.

43. M. Borden, "iPhone Envy? You Must Be Jöking," *Fast Company,* September 2009, pp. 66–73, 106.

44. L. Whitney, "Apple, Android Surge in 2010; Nokia, RIM Slip," *CNET News,* February 7, 2011, http://news.cnet.com/8301-13579_3-20030831-37.html (accessed June 8, 2011); and C. Lawton and Y.-H. Kim, "Nokia Updates Smartphones," *Wall Street Journal,* August 25, 2011, p. B5.

45. D. Koeppel, "Strange Brew," *Fortune Small Business,* June 2009, p. 68.

46. "CEO Mark Parker Upgrades His Footprint," *Fast Company,* March 2009, p. B1.

47. W. Taylor, "Control in an Age of Chaos," *Harvard Business Review,* November–December 1994, pp. 64–70.

48. B. Horovitz, "Starbucks' Growth Strategy Thinks Outside the Cup," *USA Today,* March 24, 2011, p. 1B.

49. Data from Pacific Gas & Electric's Food Service Technology Center, reported in B. Horovitz, "Can Restaurants Go Green, Earn Green?" *USA Today,* May 19, 2008, www.usatoday.com/money/industries/environment/2008-05-15-green-restaurants -eco-friendly_N.htm (accessed June 8, 2011).

50. Horovitz, 2008.

51. B. Ocohido, "Citigroup Latest to Report Data Breach," *USA Today,* June 10, 2011, p. 1A.

52. Study by Insurance Institute for Highway Safety, reported in J. O'Donnell and R. Roubein, "Deaths Plunge for SUV Drivers," *USA Today,* June 9, 2011, p. 1A.

53. V. O'Connell, "Reversing Field, Macy's Goes Local," *Wall Street Journal,* March 6, 2008, pp. B1, B8.

54. G. Hamel, with B. Breen, *The Future of Management* (Boston: Harvard Business School Press, 2007).

55. L. Gratton, "The End of the Middle Manager," *Harvard Business Review,* January–February 2011, www.hbr.org/2011/01/column -the-end-of-the-middle-manager/ar/1 (accessed June 25, 2011).

56. S. Davie, "Gen Y @ work," *Straits Times,* www.asiaone.com/Business/Office/Learn/Story/A1Story20080511-64480.html (accessed March 7, 2011).

57. M. Bower, "Thoughts on Enterprise 2.0 and Corporate Culture Change," Mark Bower website, June 11, 2009, markbower.com/2009/06/11/thoughts-on-enterprise-2-0-and-corporate-culture -change/ (accessed March 7, 2011).

CHAPTER 8

1. Adapted from N. Byrnes, "The Art of Motivation," *BusinessWeek,* May 1, 2006, pp. 296–312.

2. Both quotes from N. Byrnes, P. Burrows, and L. Lee, "Dark Days at Dell," *BusinessWeek,* September 4, 2006, pp. 26–29.

3. G. A. Moore, quoted in Byrnes, Burrows, and Lee, 2006, p. 27. Moore is author of *Dealing with Darwin: How Great Companies Innovate at Every Phase of Their Evolution* (New York: Portfolio/Penguin, 2006).

4. C. Edwards, "Dell's Do-Over," *BusinessWeek,* October 26, 2009, pp. 37–40; and A. Vance, "Though Dell's Profit Slips, Its Outlook Turns Brighter," *New York Times,* November 20, 2009, p. B4.

5. E. Cornish, "Foresight Conquers Fears of the Future," *Futurist,* January–February 2010, pp. 50–51.

6. P. Drucker, "The Future That Has Already Happened," *Futurist,* November 1998, pp. 16–18; L. Jennings and J. Minerd, "Cybertrends Shaping Tomorrow's Marketplace," *Futurist,* March 1999, pp. 12–14; and M. Richarme, "Ten Forces Driving Business Futures," *Futurist,* July–August 2009, pp. 40–43.

7. J. Collins, "How the Mighty Fall," *BusinessWeek,* May 24, 2009, pp. 26–38.

8. J. Collins, *How the Mighty Fall: And Why Some Companies Never Give In* (New York: HarperCollins, 2009).

9. Based on Collins, "How the Mighty Fall," 2009.

10. Gregory Q. Brown, co-chief executive, Motorola, interviewed by R. O. Crockett, "What They Learned on the Way Down," *BusinessWeek,* May 25, 2009, p. 33.

11. Survey by Robert Half Technology, reported in B. Evangelista, "Social Sites Invade Corporate Culture," *San Francisco Chronicle,* November 7, 2009, pp. D1, D2.

12. Kailash Ambwani, CEO of FaceTime Communications Inc., quoted in Evangelista, 2009.

13. M. Gunther, "Best Buy Wants Your Junk," *Fortune,* December 7, 2009, pp. 96–100.

14. E. H. Schein, "Organizational Culture," *American Psychologist,* vol. 45, 1990, pp. 109–119; E. H. Schein, *Organizational Culture and Leadership* (San Francisco: Jossey-Bass, 1985); and E. H. Schein, "The Role of the Founder in Creating Organizational Culture," *Organizational Dynamics,* Summer 1983, pp. 13–28.

15. Collins, "How the Mighty Fall," 2009, pp. 36, 38.

16. B. Donahue, "You Do It for Family," *Inc.,* June 2009, pp. 70–76. Facts updated in personal telephone conversation by Brian Williams with Dave Dahl on August 25, 2011.

17. M. Gunther, "Nothing Blue about This Airline," *Fortune,* September 14, 2009, pp. 114–118.

18. D. Grossman, "Business Meetings Take to the High Seas," *USA Today,* February 26, 2006, www.usatoday.com/travel/columnist/grossman/2006-02-20-grossman_x.htm (accessed October 9, 2010).

19. D. Anfuso, "3M's Staffing Strategy Promotes Productivity and Pride," *Personnel Journal,* February 1995, pp. 28–34.

20. J. C. Collins and J. I. Porris, *Built to Last: Successful Habits of Visionary Companies* (New York: HarperBusiness, 1994).

21. Dahle, "Fast Start: Your First 60 Days," 1998; Murphy, 1998; S. Gruner, "Lasting Impressions," *Inc.,* July 1998, p. 126; and M. Nemko, "Smart Ways to Give Your Career a Boost," *U.S. News & World Report,* May 2009, p. 27.

22. R. Ailes, in "Your First Seven Seconds," *Fast Company,* June–July 1998, p. 184. Some of this box material was adapted from Kinicki and Williams, *Management,* 2009, p. 275.

23. Nemko, "Smart Ways to Give Your Career a Boost," 2009.

24. L. P. Frankel, in "Your First Impression," *Fast Company,* June–July 1998, p. 188.

25. M. Tutton, *CNN.com,* quoted in "How to Manage Your Boss," *The Week,* December 18, 2009, p. 40.

26. C. L. Potter, "5 Ways to Wow Your Boss," *San Francisco Chronicle,* December 27, 2009, p. F1.

27. A. Bruzzese, citing K. Elster and K. Crowley, in "Learning How to Manage the Boss Can Ease Work Blues," *Reno Gazette-Journal,* October 8, 2009, p. 9A.

28. P. Burrows, "Cisco's Extreme Ambitions," *BusinessWeek,* November 30, 2009, pp. 26–27.

29. P. Burrows and J. Galante, "Cisco Revises Unpopular Management Structure," *San Francisco Chronicle,* May 6, 2011, p. D2.

30. "About UTC," United Technologies, www.utc.com/About+UTC (accessed September 22, 2011).

31. E. Marzec, "Types of Global Organizational Structure," *eHow,* January 22, 2010, www.ehow.com/list_5899634_types-global-organizational-structure.html (accessed June 14, 2011).

32. "Piece by Piece: The Suppliers Behind the New BlackBerry Torch Smartphone," *Wall Street Journal,* August 17, 2010, p. B1.

33. J. R. Katzenbach and D. K. Smith, "The Discipline of Teams," *Harvard Business Review,* March–April 1995, p. 112.

34. J. R. Katzenbach and D. K. Smith, *The Wisdom of Teams: Creating the High-Performance Organization* (Boston: Harvard Business School Press, 1993), p. 45.

35. B. Bettinger, "Toy Story 3 is Now the Highest Grossing Animated Film of All Time," Collider.com website, www.collider.com/toy-story-3-highest-grossing-animated-film-disney-pixar-lee-unkrich-john-lasseter/43811/ (accessed August 15, 2011).

36. "How Pixar Fosters Collective Creativity," *Harvard Business Review*, September 2008, hbr.org/2008/09/how-pixar-fosters-collective-creativity/ar/1 (accessed March 13, 2011).

37. "Definition: Corporate Silo," Gary Eckstein Blog, eckstein.id.au/?s=corporate+culture+silo&cat=plus-5-results (accessed June 28, 2011).

38. R. Cross, *Harvard Business Review Blog,* posted March 8, 2011, blogs.hbr.org/cs/2011/03/the_most_valuable_people_in_yo.html (accessed March 13, 2011).

39. A. M. Wilkinson, "On Leadership: BP, Dell, Wall Street—Where Have the Corporate Heroes Gone?" *Washington Post*, August 1, 2010, www.washingtonpost.com/wp-dyn/content/article/2010/07/31/AR2010073100036.html (accessed June 28, 2011).

40. "Herman Miller History," Funding Universe Website, www.fundinguniverse.com (accessed March 15, 2011).

41. P. Stott, "Office Romance Survey 2010," Vault Career Intelligence Website, www.vault.com/wps/portal/usa/vcm/detail/Career-Advice/Office-Romance/Office-Romance-Survey-2010?id=5519 (accessed March 13, 2011).

42. K. E. Klein, "How Employers Should Handle Workplace Romance," *Bloomberg Businessweek*, February 10, 2010, www.businessweek.com/print/smallbiz/content/feb2010/sb2010211_326976.htm (accessed March 13, 2011).

43. S. Shellenbarger, "For Office Romance, the Secret's Out," *Wall Street Journal*, February 10, 2010, online.wsj.com/article/SB10001424052748704182004575055191587179832.html (accessed March 13, 2011).

44. Klein, "How Employers Should Handle Workplace Romance," 2010.

45. M. Selvin, "'Love Contract,' It's Office Policy," *Los Angeles Times*, February 13, 2007, articles.latimes.com/2007/feb/13/business/fi-love 13 (accessed March 13, 2011).

CHAPTER 9

1. R. O. Crockett, "Keeping Ritz Carlton at the Top of Its Game," *BusinessWeek Online,* May 29, 2006, www.businessweek.com/magazine/content/06_22/b3986130.htm?chan=search (accessed June 16, 2011); C. Gallo, "How Ritz-Carlton Maintains Its Mystique," *BusinessWeek,* February 13, 2007, www.businessweek.com/smallbiz/content/feb2007/sb20070213_171606.htm?chan=search (accessed June 16, 2011); and J. McGregor, "Customer Service Champs," *BusinessWeek,* March 5, 2007, pp. 52–64.

2. D. Wakabayashi, "'Toyota Way' Retains Management Followers," *Wall Street Journal,* February 26, 2010, p. B4.

3. Y. Takahashi, "Toyota Accelerates Its Cost-Cutting Efforts," *Wall Street Journal,* December 23, 2009, p. B4; C. Woodyard, "Toyota's Reputation Needs Some TLC," *USA Today,* December 31, 2009, pp. 1B, 2B; M. Maynard and H. Tabuchi, "Rapid Growth Has Its Perils, Toyota Learns," *New York Times,* January 28,

2010, pp. A1, B4; K. Linebaugh and N. Shirouzu, "Toyota Heir Faces Crisis at the Wheel," *Wall Street Journal,* January 28, 2010, pp. A1, A8; and M. Dolan, "Supplier Perplexed by Toyota's Action," *Wall Street Journal,* January 28, 2010, p. A9.

4. J. R. Healey and A. DeBarros, "Toyota Tops Speed Control Complaints," *USA Today,* March 26, 2010, pp. 1B, 2B.

5. N. Bunkley, "Toyota Halts Production of 8 Models," *New York Times,* January 27, 2010, pp. B1, B2; J. R. Healey, "Toyota Halts U.S. Sales of 8 Models," *USA Today,* January 27, 2010, p. 1A; C. Said, "Reports on Priuses Add to Toyota's Woes," *San Francisco Chronicle,* February 4, 2010, pp. D1, D2; and M. Ramsey, "Toyota Fixes Five Million Recalled Cars," *Wall Street Journal,* October 5, 2010, p. B4.

6. James P. Womack, quoted in Maynard and Tabuchi, 2010.

7. Toyota Motor president Akio Toyoda, quoted in A. Ohnsman, J. Green, and K. Inoue, "The Humbling of Toyota," *Bloomberg BusinessWeek,* March 22 & 29, 2010, pp. 32–36.

8. S. Godin, blog, "Music Lessons," January 8, 2008, www.sethgodin .typepad.com (accessed June 16, 2011).

9. P. Steel, "The Nature of Procrastination: A Meta-Analytic and Theoretical Review of Quintessential Self-Regulatory Failure," *Psychological Bulletin,* January 2007, pp. 65–94. See also S. Borenstein, "Study: More Americans Doing Less," *San Francisco Chronicle,* January 12, 2007, p. A2.

10. Researcher Clifford Nass, quoted in "The Truth about Multitasking," *The Week,* September 11, 2009, p. 22.

11. A. Gawande, "The Checklist Manifesto," *The Week,* January 15, 2010, pp. 40–41.

12. A. Lakwete, *Inventing the Cotton Gin: Machine and Myth in Antebellum America* (Baltimore: Johns Hopkins University Press, 2003).

13. K. C. Arabe, "The Car Factory of the Future: Lean, Fast, and Flexible," *Industrial Market Trends,* August 13, 2003, http:// news.thomasnet.com/IMT/archives/2003/08/the_car_factory. html?t=archive; and E. Garsten, "Flexible and Profitable, GM Lansing Shoots to Top," *Detroit News,* February 22, 2004, http:// detnews.com/2004/specialreport/0402/22/a14-70492.htm (both accessed June 16, 2011).

14. A. Markels, "Dishing It Out in Style," *U.S. News & World Report,* April 23, 2007, pp. 52–55.

15. G. Rifkin, "Designing Tools for Designers," *New York Times,* June 18, 1992, p. C6.

16. D. Welch, "How Nissan Laps Detroit," *BusinessWeek,* December 22, 2003, pp. 58–60.

17. S. F. Brown, "Wresting New Wealth from the Supply Chain," *Fortune,* November 9, 1998, pp. 204[C]–204[Z]; N. Shirouzu, "Gadget Inspector: Why Toyota Wins Such High Marks on Quality Surveys," *Wall Street Journal,* March 15, 2001, pp. A1, A11; and M. Maynard, "Toyota Shows Big Three How It's Done," *New York Times,* January 13, 2006, pp. C1, C4.

18. T. Aeppel and J. Lahart, "Lean Factories Find It Hard to Cut Jobs Even in a Slump," *Wall Street Journal,* March 9, 2009, pp. A1, A15.

19. J. Jargon, "Latest Starbucks Buzzword: 'Lean' Japanese Techniques," *Wall Street Journal,* August 4, 2009, pp. A1, A10.

20. J. Jargon, "At Starbucks, Baristas Told No More Than Two Drinks," *Wall Street Journal,* October 13, 2010, pp. B1, B2.

21. E. Schonfeld, "The Customized, Digitized, Have-It-Your-Way Economy," *Fortune,* September 28, 1998, pp. 114–120.

22. J. Kaufman, "A Cookbook of One's Own from the Internet," *New York Times,* November 12, 2007, p. C7.

23. J. Markoff and S. Hansell, "Hiding in Plain Sight, Google Seeks More Power," *New York Times,* June 14, 2006, www.nytimes .com/2006/06/14/technology/14search.html; and D. Terdiman,

"Jostling to Get Inside Google's Oregon Outpost," L. Rosencrance, "Top-Secret Google Data Center Almost Completed," *ComputerWorld,* June 16, 2006, www.computerworld.com/action/ article.do?command=viewArticleBasic&articleId=9001262; and CNET News, June 29, 2006, www.news.com/2100-1030_3 -6089518.html (all accessed June 16, 2011).

24. K. Bradsher, "G.M. Sees China, and the Chinese, in a Chevrolet," *New York Times,* January 11, 2007, www.nytimes.com/ 2007/01/11/business/worldbusiness/11sinochevy.html (accessed June 16, 2011).

25. K. Bradsher, 2007.

26. G. A. Garrett, "Integrated Supply Chain Management Outsourcing: Challenges and Opportunities," Supply Chain Networks, Lucent Technologies, 2004, www.acq.osd.mil/dpap/about/ Procurement2004/presentations/11G_Garrett-R.pdf (accessed June 16, 2011).

27. R. A. Bruce, "A Case Study of Harley-Davidson's Business Practices," *Little Shack,* http://stroked.virtualave.net/casestudy .shtml (accessed June 16, 2011).

28. For more about the quality movement and its tools, see S. P. Robbins and M. Coulter, *Management,* 7th ed. (Upper Saddle River, NJ: Pearson/Prentice Hall, 2007), pp. 579–80; A. Kinicki and B. K. Williams, *Management: A Practical Introduction,* 4th ed. (New York: McGraw-Hill/Irwin, 2009), pp. 522–523, 528–530; R. Kreitner and A. Kinicki, *Organizational Behavior,* 9th ed. (New York: McGraw-Hill/Irwin, 2010), pp. 10–11; and R.W. Griffin, *Management,* 10th ed. (Mason, OH: Cengage Learning, 2011), pp. 695–700.

29. H. Menzies, "Quality Counts When Wooing Overseas Clients," *Fortune,* June 1, 1997, www.fortune.com/fortune/subs/article/ 0,15114,378797,00.html (accessed June 16, 2011).

30. B. Ekeler, quoted in Menzies, 1997.

31. A. Fisher, "Rules for Joining the Cult of Perfectability," *Fortune,* February 7, 2000, p. 206.

32. D. Jones, "Firms Aim for Six Sigma Efficiency," *USA Today,* July 21, 1998, pp. 1B, 2B.

33. J. E. Morehouse, quoted in C. H. Deutsch, "Six Sigma Enlightenment," *New York Times,* December 7, 1998, pp. C1, C7.

34. L. Clifford, "Why You Can Safely Ignore Six Sigma," *Fortune,* January 22, 2001, www.fortune.com/fortune/investing/ articles/0,15114,367825,00.html (accessed June 16, 2011).

35. E. Rosenthal, "Partying Helps Power a Dutch Nightclub That Harnesses the Energy of Youth," *New York Times,* October 24, 2008, p. A11.

36. D. R. Baker, "Field with a Future," *San Francisco Chronicle,* February 10, 2009, p. C1.

37. M. Kimes, "Get a Green Job in Two Years," *Fortune,* November 23, 2009, p. 32.

38. J. Berman, "Sustainability Could Secure a Good Future," *USA Today,* August 3, 2009, p. 7D.

39. M. Brant and M. Ohtake, "A Growth Industry," *Newsweek,* April 14, 2008, p. 64.

40. Levi Strauss website, http://store.levi.com/waterless (accessed March 24, 2011).

41. Blackbird Guitars website www.blackbirdguitars.com/technology .html (accessed August 31, 2011).

42. Blackbird Guitars, 2011.

43. M. Hinkley, "Robots in Car Manufacturing," eHow.com website, www.ehow.com/about_4678910_robots-car-manufacturing .html#ixzz1HT61dmXO (accessed March 23, 2011).

44. J. Markoff, "The Boss Is Robotic, and Rolling up Behind You," September 4, 2010, *New York Times,* www.nytimes.com/2010/ 09/05/science/05robots.html (accessed March 22, 2011).

45. D. Bartz, "Toyota Sees Robotic Nurses in Your Lonely Final Years," *Wired,* January 19, 2010, www.wired.com/gadgetlab/2010/01/toyota-sees-robotic-nurses-in-your-lonely-final-years/ (accessed March 22, 2011); and J. Markoff, "Opening Doors on the Way to a Personal Robot," June 9, 2009, *New York Times,* www.nytimes.com/2009/06/09/science/09robot.html?scp=1&sq=Opening%20doors%20on%20the%20Way%20to%20a%20Personal%20Robot&st=cse (accessed March 22, 2011).

CHAPTER 10

1. A. T. Gajilan, "Scrap Mettle," *FSB,* December 2005/January 2006, pp. 95–96.

2. J. Greenberg, "Who Stole the Money, and When? Individual and Situational Determinants of Employee Theft," *Organizational Behavior and Decision Processes,* September 2002, pp. 985–1003.

3. T. Shulman, quoted in M. Keating, "Why Do Employees Steal from Their Workplace?" *The Guardian,* October 8, 2005, www.guardian.co.uk/money/2005/oct/08/careers.work1 (accessed June 23, 2011).

4. S. Westcott, "Are Your Staffers Stealing?" *Inc.,* October 2006, pp. 33–35.

5. E. Nelson, "Work Week: A Special News Report about Life on the Job—and the Trends Taking Shape There," *Wall Street Journal,* February 6, 1996, p. A1. For a list of reasons why employees cheat and steal, see T. W. Singleton, A. J. Singleton, G. J. Bologna, and R. J. Lindquist, *Fraud Auditing and Forensic Accounting,* 3rd ed. (New York: Wiley, 2006).

6. D. A. Kaplan, "The Best Company to Work For," *Fortune,* February 8, 2010, pp. 57–64.

7. K. Barr, "Mind Game," *Inc.,* March 2010, p. 66.

8. R. Gold, "Investment Dollars Flow to Green Energy Start-Ups," *Wall Street Journal,* February 4, 2010, pp. B1, B11.

9. Paul Holland of Foundation Capital, quoted in C. Tuna, "Putting Green Technology into Bricks," *Wall Street Journal,* November 4, 2009, p. B4. See also S. S. Muñoz, "Ratings Proliferate for 'Green' Builders," *Wall Street Journal,* November 8, 2007, pp. D1, D3; N. Buhayar, "Old Wine, New Bottles," *Wall Street Journal,* September 21, 2009, p. R5; and W. Koch, "Green Homes Growing Red-Hot," *USA Today,* December 4, 2009, p. 1A.

10. Survey for Panetta Institute for Public Policy, reported in "Socially Responsible Jobs Most Popular," *USA Europe,* May 15, 2009, p. 10B. See also P. Korkki, "Taking a Break from the Idea of Making a Buck," *New York Times,* January 4, 2009, Business section, p. 2.

11. J. Schmit, "As Colleges Add Green Studies, Classes Fill," *USA Today,* December 28, 2009, p. 1B; N. Roberts, "Making a Difference at Work—Is a Green MBA Right for You?" *Causes & News,* February 6, 2010, www.care2.com/causes/education/blog/making-a-difference-at-work-is-a-green-mba-right-for-you/ (accessed June 23, 2011); and A. Dizik, "Sustainability Is a Growing Theme," *Wall Street Journal,* March 4, 2010, p. B10.

12. Michael Richmond, quoted in "Green Jobs Under Your Nose," *The Futurist,* September–October 2009, pp. 36–37.

13. D. R. Baker, "Green Jobs Just 1% of Total in California," *San Francisco Chronicle,* December 9, 2009, pp. D1, D4; T. Hsu, "Corporate Eco-Managers Turning Companies Green," *San Francisco Chronicle,* January 2, 2010, p. D2, reprinted from *Los Angeles Times*; and Dizik, "Sustainability Is a Growing Theme," 2010.

14. P. Slim, "Is This the Time to Follow Your Bliss?" *New York Times,* April 19, 2009, Business section, p. 10. See also K. Hannon, "Find Your Purpose and Thrive," *USA Today,* February 16, 2009, p. 6B.

15. D. Katz and R. L. Kahn, *The Social Psychology of Organizations* (New York: Wiley, 1966); A. Kinicki and B. K. Williams, *Management: A Practical Introduction,* 4th ed. (New York: McGraw-Hill/Irwin, 2009), p. 371; and T. S. Bateman and S. A. Snell, *Management: Leading & Collaborating in a Competitive World,* 9th ed. (New York: McGraw-Hill/Irwin, 2011), p. 454.

16. C. Crossen, "Early Industry Expert Soon Realized a Staff Has Its Own Efficiency," *Wall Street Journal,* November 6, 2006, p. B1.

17. S. Monson, "Maid to Order," *Seattle Times,* April 16, 2006, http://blog.marketplace.nwsource.com/careercenter/maid_to_order.html (accessed June 23, 2011).

18. A. Maslow, "A Theory of Human Motivation," *Psychological Review,* July 1943, pp. 370–396.

19. D. E. Meyerson, *Tempered Radicals: How Everyday Leaders Inspire Change at Work* (Boston: Harvard Business School Press, 2003). For examples of the need for achievement, see M. R. della Cava, "Answering Their Calling," *USA Today,* March 13, 2006, pp. 1D, 2D.

20. C. Conley, *Peak: How Great Companies Get Their Mojo from Maslow* (San Francisco: Jossey-Bass, 2007).

21. C. C. Pinder, *Work Motivation: Theory, Issues, and Applications* (Glenview, IL: Scott, Foresman, 1984), p. 52.

22. F. Herzberg, B. Mausner, and B. B. Snyderman, *The Motivation to Work* (New York: John Wiley & Sons, 1959); and F. Herzberg, "One More Time: How Do You Motivate Employees?" *Harvard Business Review,* January–February 1968, pp. 53–62.

23. Susan Gramatges, CEO of Pierpont Communications, quoted in J. M. Rosenberg, "An Extra Day Off in Summertime Is Great Motivator for Small Staffs," *San Francisco Chronicle,* July 25, 2007, p. C4.

24. Spherion survey of 1,996 employed adults 18 and older, reported in "Why Workers Change Jobs," *USA Today,* March 8, 2007, p. 1B.

25. G. Thompson, "The Job You Won't Do: Try Working a Season in the Lettuce Fields of Yuma," *Arizona Republic,* March 14, 2010, http://www.azcentral.com/arizonarepublic/viewpoints/articles/2010/03/14/20100314thompson14.html (accessed October 18, 2010). Thompson was doing research in preparation for his book *Working in the Shadows: A Year of Doing the Jobs (Most) Americans Won't Do* (New York: Nation Books, 2009).

26. P. Dvorak, "Hotelier Finds Happiness Keeps Staff Checked In," *Wall Street Journal,* December 17, 2007, p. B3.

27. D. McGregor, *The Human Side of Enterprise* (New York: McGraw-Hill, 1960).

28. Kaplan, "The Best Company to Work For," 2010.

29. B. F. Skinner, *Walden Two* (New York: Macmillan, 1948); *Science and Human Behavior* (New York: Macmillan, 1953); and *Contingencies of Reinforcement* (New York: Appleton-Century-Crofts, 1969).

30. H. Benson, "In an Era of High Technology, Low Commitment, One Man Says He's Found a Way to Measure Integrity," *San Francisco Chronicle,* June 21, 2006, pp. E1, E3. See also LinkUp Central, http://linkupcentral.com; and Kinicki and Williams, *Management,* 2009, p. 374.

31. V. H. Vroom, *Work and Motivation* (New York: Wiley, 1964).

32. Kevin Volpp, quoted in L. Szabo, "Financial Incentives Can Help Smokers Quit," *USA Today,* December 12, 2009, p. 6D. See the study in K. G. Volpp, A. B. Troxel, M. V. Pauly, et al., "Trial of Financial Incentives for Smoking Cessation," *New England Journal of Medicine,* February 12, 2009, pp. 699–709.

33. J. Stacey Adams, "Toward an Understanding of Inequity," *Journal of Abnormal and Social Psychology,* November 1963, pp. 422–436; and J. Stacey Adams, "Injustice in Social Exchange," in L. Berkowitz, ed., *Advances in Experimental Social Psychology,* 2nd ed. (New York, Academic Press, 1965), pp. 267–300.

34. E. Nelson, "Work Week: A Special News Report about Life on the Job—and the Trends Taking Shape There," *Wall Street Journal,* February 6, 1996, p. A1. See also S. Greenhouse,

"Shoplifters? The Statistics Say Stores Should Watch Workers," *New York Times,* December 30, 2009, pp. A1, B2; and J. Lambe, "In Tough Economy, Employee Theft Becomes a Bigger Challenge," *Kansas City Star,* March 1, 2010, www.mcclatchydc.com/2010/03/01/89569/in-tough-economy-employee-theft.html (accessed June 23, 2011).

35. E. A. Locke and G. P. Latham, *Goal Setting: A Motivational Technique that Works!* (Englewood Cliffs, NJ: Prentice-Hall, 1984); and E. A. Locke, K. N. Shaw, L. A. Saari, and G. P. Latham, "Goal Setting and Task Performance," *Psychological Bulletin,* August 1981, pp. 125–152.

36. P. F. Drucker, *The Practice of Management* (New York: Harper & Row, 1954).

37. R. Rodgers and J. E. Hunter, "Impact of Management by Objectives on Organizational Productivity," *Journal of Applied Psychology,* April 1991, pp. 322–336.

38. PricewaterhouseCoopers survey, reported in S. Shellenbarger, "What Job Candidates Really Want to Know: Will I Have a Life?" *Wall Street Journal,* November 17, 1999, p. B1. Also see Kinicki and Williams, *Management,* 2009, p. 394.

39. Pippa Dunn, brand marketing director for U.K. Orange, the mobile phone unit, quoted in J. S. Lublin, "Keeping Clients by Keeping Workers," *Wall Street Journal,* December 20, 2004, p. B3.

40. K. Lingle, quoted in C. Kleiman, "Work-Life Rewards Grow," *San Francisco Examiner,* January 16, 2000, p. J-2; reprinted from *Chicago Tribune.*

41. C. Kleiman, "CEO of Family-Friendly Firm Tells Others to 'Just Do It,'" *San Jose Mercury News,* September 19, 1999, p. PC-1; and D. Dallinger, "Battling for a Balanced Life," *San Francisco Chronicle,* November 14, 1999, Sunday section, p. 9.

42. Walker Information survey, reported in D. E. Lewis, "Employees Need to Be Appreciated," *San Francisco Chronicle,* May 26, 2000, p. B4; reprinted from *Boston Globe.*

43. Spherion and Louis Harris Associates 1999 survey, reported in A. Zipkin, "The Wisdom of Thoughtfulness," *New York Times,* May 31, 2000, p. C5.

44. A. J. Kinicki, F. M. McKee-Ryan, C. A. Schriesheim, and K. P. Carson, "Assessing the Construct Validity of the Job Descriptive Index: A Review and Meta-Analysis," *Journal of Applied Psychology,* February 2002, pp. 14–32.

45. B. Moses, quoted in Lewis, "Employees Need to Be Appreciated," 2000.

46. E. White, "How Surveying Workers Can Pay Off," *Wall Street Journal,* June 18, 2007, p. B3.

47. S. McKnight, "Workplace Gossip? Keep It to Yourself," *New York Times,* November 15, 2009, Business section, p. 9.

48. Bob Nelson, reported in J. Zaslow, "The Most-Praised Generation Goes to Work," *Wall Street Journal,* April 20, 2007, pp. W1, W7.

49. C. R. Rogers and F. J. Roethlisberger, "Barriers and Gateways to Communication," *Harvard Business Review,* July–August 1952, pp. 46–52.

50. Rogers and Roethlisberger, 1952, p. 47.

51. A. Bruzzese, "Communication Is Critical to Coping with Workplace Stress," *Reno Gazette-Journal,* September 4, 2008, p. 6A.

52. L. Seltzer, in a blog for *Psychology Today,* reported in A. Tugend, "For Best Results, Take the Sting Out of Criticism," *New York Times,* August 29, 2009, p. B6.

53. Darren Gurney, described in Tugend, 2009.

54. E. Bernstein, "Why Do Compliments Cause So Much Grief?" *Wall Street Journal,* May 4, 2010, pp. D1, D6.

55. Bernstein, 2010.

56. A. Tugend, "An Attempt to Revive the Lost Art of Apology," *New York Times,* January 30, 2010, p. B5. See also E. Bernstein, "Who's Sorry Now? Nearly Everyone," *Wall Street Journal,* January 12, 2010, pp. D1, D3.

57. H. Weeks, quoted in Tugend, "An Attempt to Revive the Lost Art of Apology," 2010.

58. Jerry Pounds, reported in J. Zaslow, "In Praise of Less Praise," *Wall Street Journal,* May 3, 2007, p. D1.

59. Zaslow, "The Most-Praised Generation Goes to Work," 2007.

60. Data from Jack Morton Worldwide Experiential Marketing Global Consumer Response survey, conducted by Sponsorship Research International, in "What Employees Want," *USA Today,* December 20, 2006, p. 1B.

61. M. Chafkin, "The Zappos Way of Managing," *Inc.,* May 1, 2009, www.inc.com/magazine/20090501/the-zappos-way-of-managing.html (accessed March 28, 2011).

62. T. Hsieh, "Why I Sold Zappos," *Inc.,* June 1, 2010, www.inc.com/magazine/20100601/why-i-sold-zappos_pagen_2.html (accessed March 28, 2011).

63. A. Sorkin, "Tensions Simmered in Zappos Sale to Amazon," *New York Times,* June 7, 2010, http://dealbook.nytimes.com/2010/06/07/tensions-simmered-in-zappos-sale-to-amazon/?scp=1&sq=zappos&st=cse (accessed March 28, 2011).

64. Hsieh, "Why I Sold Zappos," 2010.

65. W. Naylor, "Why Zappos Pays New Employees to Quit—and You Should Too," *Harvard Business Review* Blog Network, May 19, 2008, blogs.hbr.org/taylor/2008/05/why_zappos_pays_new_employees.html (accessed July 5, 2011).

66. K. McFarland, "Why Zappos Offers New Hires $2,000 to Quit," *BusinessWeek,* September 16, 2008, www.businessweek.com/smallbiz/content/sep2008/sb20080916_288698.htm (accessed July 5, 2011).

67. "American Dog Population Rises to 77.5 Million," ohmidog.com, www.ohmidog.com/2009/08/11/american-dog-population-rises-to-77-5-million (accessed March 27, 2011).

68. M. Mackety, "Pet Economy: Americans Feed the Beast and Then Some," *Fiscal Times,* June 26, 2010, www.thefiscaltimes.com/Articles/2010/06/26/The-Pet-Economy-Americans-Feed-the-Beast-and-Then-Some.aspx (accessed July 4, 2011).

69. "One in Five U.S. Companies Allow Pets at Work," FoxNews.com, June 21, 2006, www.foxnews.com/story/0,2933,200460,00.html (accessed March 27, 2011).

70. "Recent National Study Shows That Pets Provide More Benefits to Companies than Management Classes," March 27, 2011, www.dogandkennel.com website, courtesy of APPMA (American Pet Products Manufacturers Association), www.petpublishing.com/dogken/news/appma01.shtml (accessed March 28, 2011).

71. "One in Five U.S. Companies Allow Pets at Work," 2006.

CHAPTER 11

1. "Costco Wholesale Salaries," *Glassdoor.com,* June 12, 2011, www.glassdoor.com/Salary/Costco-Wholesale-Salaries-E2590.htm# (accessed June 24, 2011).

2. S. Greenhouse, "How Costco Became the Anti-Wal-Mart," *New York Times,* July 17, 2005, sec. 7, p. 1. See also J. Flanigan, "Costco Sees Value in Higher Pay," *Los Angeles Times,* February 15, 2004, www.latimes.com/business/la-fi-flan15feb15,1,61048 (accessed June 23, 2011); and C. Frey, "Costco's Love of Labor: Employees' Well-being Key to Its Success," *Seattle Post-Intelligencer,* March 29, 2004, http://seattlepi.nwsource.com/business/166680_costco29.html (accessed June 23, 2011).

3. A. Zimmerman, "Costco's Dilemma: Be Kind to Its Workers, or Wall Street," *Wall Street Journal,* March 26, 2004, pp. B1, B3.

4. RetailSails, "Walmart," April 30, 2011, http://retailsails.com/monthly-sales-summary/wmt/ (accessed June 24, 2011).

5. "Hourly Rate for Employer: Wal-Mart Stores Inc.," *PayScale*, June 22, 2011, www.payscale.com/research/US/Employer=Wal-Mart_Stores,_Inc/Hourly_Rate (accessed June 24, 2011).

6. C. Connolly, "At Wal-Mart, a Health-Care Turnaround," *Washington Post*, February 13, 2009, www.washingtonpost.com/wp-dyn/content/story/2009/02/13/ST2009021300507.html (accessed June 23, 2011).

7. M. Bustillo, "Wal-Mart Is Sued Over Care," *Wall Street Journal*, July 21, 2010, pp. B1, B2.

8. J. Unseem, "Should We Admire Wal-Mart?" *Fortune*, March 8, 2004, pp. 118–120.

9. "Store Wars: When Wal-Mart Comes to Town," *PBS*, February 24, 2007, www.pbs.org/itvs/storewars/ (accessed June 24, 2011).

10. Parts of this section adapted from A. Kinicki and B. K. Williams, *Management: A Practical Introduction*, 4th ed. (New York: McGraw-Hill/Irwin, 2009), pp. 72–73.

11. T. Gutner, "Graduating with a Major in Go-Getting," *Wall Street Journal*, March 31, 2009, p. D6; and J. Marte, "Boom Times for Young Workers," *Wall Street Journal*, April 20, 2010, p. D4.

12. A. Bruzzese, "College Graduates Can Still Find Good Jobs, Despite Market," *Reno Gazette-Journal*, May 7, 2009, pp. 5A, 6A; P. Korkki, "Graduates' First Job: Marketing Themselves," *New York Times*, May 23, 2010, Business section, p. 10.

13. A. Levit, quoted in C. M. L. Potter, "New Grads: What to Do When You Can't Get the Jobs You Want," *San Francisco Chronicle*, July 12, 2009, p. D1. Levit is the author of *They Don't Teach Corporate in College: A Twenty-Something's Guide to the Business World*, 2nd ed. (Pompton Plains, NJ: Career Press, 2009).

14. S. Meisinger, "Taking the Measure of Human Capital," *HR Magazine*, January 2003, p. 10.

15. M. Brewster and F. Dalzell, *Driving Change: The UPS Approach to Business* (New York: Hyperion, 2007).

16. J. Levitz, "UPS Thinks Outside the Box on Driver Training," *Wall Street Journal*, April 6, 2010, pp. B1, B2.

17. C. Said, "Green MBA Degrees Sprout on Campuses," *San Francisco Chronicle*, April 21, 2010, pp. D1, D5; and T. Hughes, "More Colleges Using Green as Selling Tool," *USA Today*, July 9, 2010, p. 3A.

18. Equal Employment Opportunity Commission, reported in S. Hananel, "More Men File Claims of Sexual Harassment," *Reno Gazette-Journal*, March 5, 2010, p. 2C; and D. Mattioli, "More Men Make Harassment Claims," *Wall Street Journal*, March 23, 2010, p. D4. See also C. M. Blow, "Don't Tickle Me, Bro!" *New York Times*, March 13, 2010, p. A17.

19. Survey in 2007 by Novations Group, Boston, reported in D. Stead, "Is the Workplace Getting Raunchier?" *BusinessWeek*, March 17, 2008, p. 19.

20. Survey in 2007 by Zogby International, reported in T. Parker-Pope, "When the Bully Sits in the Next Cubicle," *New York Times*, March 25, 2008, p. D5. See also J. A. Segal, "'I Did It, but . . . ,'" *HR Magazine*, March 2008, pp. 91–93.

21. B. Egelko, "Former Fed Ex Worker Given New Trial to Seek Damages," *San Francisco Chronicle*, June 21, 2010, p. C4.

22. L. Katz, cited in A. Tugend, "Getting Hired, Never a Picnic, Is Increasingly a Trial," *New York Times*, October 10, 2009, p. B6.

23. T. Abate, "Experts Dissect Decade's Job Losses," *San Francisco Chronicle*, August 1, 2010, pp. A1, A16; and R. Reich, "Profits Mean Jobs? You're Living on Another Planet," *San Francisco Chronicle*, August 1, 2010, p. E5.

24. K. Brooks, University of Texas, Austin, quoted in Korkki, "Graduates' First Job: Marketing Themselves," 2010.

25. B. Schneider and N. Schmitt, *Staffing Organizations*, 2nd ed. (Glenview, IL: Scott, Foresman, 1986).

26. J. Linder and C. Zoller, "Recruiting Employees for Small Businesses: A Little Planning Goes a Long Way," *Ohio State University Fact Sheet*, CDFS-1382-97, http://ohioline.osu.edu/cd-fact/1382.html; E. Sweeten, "Attracting the Best and Brightest: How Small Businesses Can Recruit—and Keep—Stellar Employees," *Utah Business*, October 1, 2005, www.allbusiness.com/business-planning/870645-1.html; "Would You Ever Use Facebook to Recruit Employees?" *My Focus*, www.focus.com/questions/human-resources/would-you-ever-use-facebook-recruit-employees (all accessed June 23, 2011).

27. M. Jewell, "Tech Helps, but Face Time Is Best," *San Francisco Chronicle*, February 23, 2009, p. C2.

28. Nielsen research, reported in J. Swartz, "Time Spent on Facebook, Twitter, YouTube Grows," *USA Today*, August 2, 2010, p. 2B.

29. J. De Avila, "Beyond Job Boards: Targeting the Source," *Wall Street Journal*, July 2, 2009, pp. D1, D5.

30. D. LaGesse, "Turning Social Networking into a Job Offer," *U.S. News & World Report*, May 2009, pp. 44–45; E. Garone, "A Web Presence from Scratch," *Wall Street Journal*, May 19, 2009, p. D5; and D. Koeppel, "HR by Twitter," *FSB*, September 2009, p. 57.

31. L. Weber, quoted in A. Bruzzese, "Cultivate Your Online Reputation for Best Results," *Reno Gazette-Journal*, August 13, 2009, p. 5A.

32. C. Choi, "Be Smart about What You Include in Profile," *San Francisco Chronicle*, January 11, 2009, p. C4; E. Zimmerman, "All Is Not Lost for the Class of 2009," *New York Times*, April 12, 2009, Business section, p. 12; V. Kopytoff, "OMG! Do You Really Want to Post That?" *San Francisco Chronicle*, April 27, 2009, pp. A1, A6; and T. Wayne, "Managing Reputations on Social Sites," *New York Times*, June 14, 2010, p. B2.

33. S. Allen, quoted in J. S. Lublin, "Networking? Here's How to Stand Out," *Wall Street Journal*, November 4, 2008, p. D4.

34. R. Burt, reported in E. Zlomek, "Turns Out Whom You Know Is Not Key," *Arizona Republic*, December 27, 2009, p. D5.

35. A. Tugend, "When Job Hunting, Be Your Own Salesman," *New York Times*, October 11, 2008, p. B6.

36. J. O'Connor, quoted in L. Buhl, "Is Your Network Helping or Hurting Your Career?" *San Francisco Chronicle*, May 23, 2010, p. D12.

37. Survey by National Association of Colleges and Employers, 2008, reported in H. Stout, "The Coveted but Elusive Summer Internship," *New York Times*, July 4, 2010, Style section, pp. 1, 7.

38. Internships.com, reported in H. Chura, "Hiring Is Rising in One Area: Low-Paid Interns," *New York Times*, November 28, 2009, p. B5.

39. J. Walker, "Getting Creative to Land an Internship," *Wall Street Journal*, June 8, 2010, p. D7.

40. A. Bruzzese, "Demonstrate Your Worth to Land an Internship," *Reno Gazette-Journal*, April 8, 2010, p. 8A; and J. Marte, "Creating Internships Out of Thin Air," *Wall Street Journal*, May 18, 2010, p. D10.

41. S. Steinberg, "All Work, No Pay for Some," *USA Today*, July 27, 2010, p. 5D.

42. S. E. Needleman, "Starting Fresh with an Unpaid Internship," *Wall Street Journal*, July 14, 2009, pp. D1, D6; C. M. L. Potter, "Intern at Any Age," *San Francisco Chronicle*, October 19, 2009, p. D8.

43. Study of 498 members by Society for Human Resource Management, reported in E. Zlomek, "What Job Interviewers Deem Important," *Arizona Republic*, December 30, 2009, p. CL-1.

44. D. Chang and P. Meehan, *Momofuku* (New York: Clarkson Potter, 2009), pp. 19–20.

45. D. Brox, "Making a Transition Job Work for You," *San Francisco Chronicle,* August 1, 2010, p. D12.

46. Report by the Society for Human Resource Management, 2003, cited in "When Do Exaggerations and Misstatements Cross the Line?" *Knowledge@Wharton,* June 23, 2010, http://knowledge.wharton.upenn.edu/article.cfm?articleid=2522 (accessed June 23, 2011).

47. Survey by Society for Human Resource Management, reported in C. Tuna and K. J. Winstein, "Economy Promises to Fuel Résumé Fraud," *Wall Street Journal,* November 17, 2008, p. B8.

48. C. W. Nevius, "If You Like Fiction, Read the Job Resumes," *San Francisco Chronicle,* February 28, 2006, pp. B1, B2. See also D. Koeppel, "That Padded Résumé Won't Help Break Your Fall," *San Francisco Chronicle,* April 23, 2006, p. F5, reprinted from *New York Times.*

49. Report by Automatic Data Processing, Roseland, NJ, cited in J. L. Seglin, "Lies Can Have a (Long) Life of Their Own," *New York Times,* June 16, 2002, sec. 3, p. 4. See also S. Armour, "Security Checks Worry Workers," *USA Today,* June 19, 2004, p. 1B.

50. J. S. Lublin, "Job Hunters with Gaps in Their Résumés Need to Write Around Them," *Wall Street Journal,* May 6, 2003, p. B1.

51. M. Conlin, "Don't Hedge Your Age," *BusinessWeek,* October 6, 2003, p. 14. See also C. Dahle, "A Nip and Tuck for the Résumé," *New York Times,* April 17, 2005, sec. 3, p. 10.

52. S. McManis, "Little White-Collar Lies," *San Francisco Chronicle,* October 1, 1999, pp. B1, B3; J. Schwartz, "Résumés Made for Fibbing," *New York Times,* May 13, 2010, Week in Review section, p. 5; J. S. Schultz, "On Lying about Your Salary," *New York Times,* June 19, 2010, p. B5.

53. P. Korkki, "A Cover Letter Is Not Expendable," *New York Times,* February 15, 2009, Business section, p. 10. See also C. Cadwell, "Making the Cover Letter Better," *San Francisco Chronicle,* January 13, 2008, p. H1; H. Boerner, "Cover Letters That Catch the Eye," *San Francisco Chronicle,* July 26, 2009, p. D6; and S. E. Needleman, "Standout Letters to Cover Your Bases," *Wall Street Journal,* March 9, 2010, p. D4.

54. To make references work for you, see T. Lindstrom, "The Right References," *San Francisco Chronicle,* November 9, 2008, p. H1; and J. S. Lublin, "Bulletproofing Your References in the Hunt for a New Job," *Wall Street Journal,* April 7, 2009, pp. B1, B12.

55. Jason Morris, quoted in "Can Bad Credit Keep You from Being Hired?" *Parade,* October 4, 2009, p. 6.

56. B. Roberts, "Close-Up on Screening," February 1, 2011, SHRM.org website, www.shrm.org/Publications/hrmagazine/Editorial Content/2011/0211/Pages/0211roberts.aspx (accessed April 14, 2011).

57. A. Martin, "As a Hiring Filter, Credit Checks Draw Questions," *New York Times,* April 10, 2010, pp. B1, B4; and J. Rideout, "Time to End Job Hunters' Credit History Catch-22," *San Francisco Chronicle,* July 6, 2010, p. A10.

58. College Board, Trends in Student Aid study, reported in R. Lieber, "Placing the Blame as Students Are Buried in Debt," *New York Times,* May 29, 2010, pp. B1, B5.

59. See E. Krell, "Unmasking Illegal Workers," *HR Magazine,* December 2007, pp. 49–52; and S. Berfield, "Illegals and Business: A Glimpse of the Future?" *BusinessWeek,* January 14, 2008, pp. 52–54.

60. W. M. Welch, "Employee Screenings See Growth," *USA Today,* June 24, 2009, p. 3A; and L. Radnofsky and M. Jordan, "Illegal Workers Slip by System," *Wall Street Journal,* February 25, 2010, p. A6.

61. D. Belkin, "More Job Seekers Scramble to Erase Their Criminal Past," *Wall Street Journal,* November 11, 2009, pp. A1, A16.

62. B. Bergstein, "Ex-Wiki Exec's Criminal History," *San Francisco Chronicle,* December 27, 2007, pp. C1, C2.

63. D. Stamps, "Cyberinterviews Combat Turnover," *Training,* August 1995, p. 16.

64. M. P. Cronin, "This Is a Test," *Inc.,* August 1993, pp. 64–68.

65. P. Korkki, "Workers May Lie about Drug Use, but Hair Doesn't," *New York Times,* December 13, 2009, Business section, p. 2.

66. Development Dimensions International survey of 1,910 interviewers, reported in "How to Blow Your Interview," *USA Today,* March 10, 2009, p. 1B.

67. J. S. Lublin, "The New Job Is in the Details," *Wall Street Journal,* January 5, 2010, p. D5.

68. A. Arredondo, "Prepare Yourself for the Behavioral Interview," *Arizona Republic,* March 2, 2008, p. EC1; "Preparation Key to Snaring Job," *Arizona Republic,* April 15, 2009, p. EC1; and "4 Keys to Interview Success," *Arizona Republic,* April 4, 2010, p. EC1.

69. Zlomek, "What Job Interviewers Deem Important," 2009.

70. Brandi Britton, quoted in C. M. L. Potter, "Interview Insights: 10 Ways to Make the Most of the First 10 Minutes," *San Francisco Chronicle,* June 28, 2009, p. D1.

71. "Preparation Key to Snaring Job," 2009.

72. T. Lindstrom, "Managing Multiple Interviews," *San Francisco Chronicle,* April 13, 2008, p. H1.

73. J. S. Lublin, "Notes to Interviewers Should Go beyond a Simple Thank You," *Wall Street Journal,* February 15, 2008, p. B1.

74. MCI Communications surveys, reported in S. Shellenbarger, "Companies Are Finding It Really Pays to Be Nice Employees," *Wall Street Journal,* July 22, 1998, p. B1.

75. G. R. Jones, "Organizational Socialization as Information Processing Activity: A Life History Analysis," *Human Organization,* vol. 42, no. 4, 1983, pp. 314–320.

76. Development Dimension International (DDI) Global Leadership Forecast of 4,561 respondents from 42 countries, reported in "Mentoring Impact," *USA Today,* March 22, 2006, p. 1B.

77. M. Cottle, "Minding Your Mentors," *New York Times,* March 7, 1999, sec. 3, p. 8; C. Dahle, "HP's Mentor Connection," *Fast Company,* November 1998, pp. 78–80; and I. Abbott, "If You Want to Be an Effective Mentor, Consider These Tips," *San Francisco Examiner,* October 18, 1998, p. J-3; D. A. Thomas, "The Truth about Mentoring Minorities—Race Matters," *Harvard Business Review,* April 2001, pp. 366–391; S. A. Mehta, "Best Companies for Minorities: Why Mentoring Works," *Fortune,* July 9, 2001, www.fortune.com/fortune/-diversity/articles/0,15114,370475,00.html (accessed June 23, 2011); F. Warner, "Inside Intel's Mentoring Movement," *Fast Company,* April 2002, p. 116; B. Raabe and T. A. Beehr, "Formal Mentoring versus Supervisor and Coworker Relationships: Differences in Perceptions and Impact," *Journal of Organizational Behavior* 24 (2003), pp. 271–293; and A. Fisher, "A New Kind of Mentor," *Fortune,* July 2004, www.fortune.com/fortune/annie/0,15704,368863,00.html (accessed June 23, 2011). Parts of this section adapted from Kinicki and Williams, *Management,* 2009, p. 251.

78. Anne Hayden, quoted in Cottle, 1999.

79. D. Tapscott, *Grown Up Digital: How the Net Generation Is Changing Your World* (New York: McGraw-Hill, 2009), pp. 73–96.

80. Survey of workers at Ernst & Young, reported in B. Hite, "Employers Rethink How They Give Feedback," *Wall Street Journal,* October 13, 2008, p. B5.

81. L. B. Combings and D. P. Schwab, *Performance in Organizations: Determinants and Appraisal* (Glenview, IL: Scott, Foresman, 1973). Parts of this section adapted from Robbins and Coulter, *Management,* 2007, pp. 337–338; Kinicki and Williams, *Management,* 2009, pp. 294–297; Bateman and Snell, *Management,* 2011, pp. 360–364; and Griffin, *Management,* 2011, pp. 450–454.

82. S. A. Culbert and L. Rout, *Get Rid of Performance Reviews! How Companies Can Stop Intimidating, Start Managing—and Focus on What Really Matters* (New York: Business Plus, 2010).

83. S. A. Culbert, "Yes, Everyone Really Does Hate Performance Reviews," *Wall Street Journal,* April 19, 2010, http://finance.yahoo.com/career-work/article/109343/yes-everyone-really-does-hate-performance-reviews (accessed June 23, 2011). See also S. A. Culbert, "Get Rid of the Performance Review!" *Wall Street Journal,* October 20, 2008, p. R4.

84. J. Pfeffer, "Low Grades for Performance Reviews," *BusinessWeek,* August 3, 2009, p. 68.

85. G. Namie, director of the Workplace Bullying Institute in Bellingham, WA, cited in T. Parker-Pope, "Time to Review Workplace Reviews?" *New York Times,* May 18, 2010, p. D5.

86. M. Steen, "How to Prepare for a Performance Review," *San Francisco Chronicle,* April 12, 2009, p. L-8.

87. J. S. Civitelli, quoted in Steen, "How to Prepare for a Performance Review," 2009.

88. R. I. Sutton, cited in Parker-Pope, "When the Bully Sits in the Next Cubicle," 2010.

89. Salesman quoted in D. Robinson, "The Importance of Accurate Self-Assessments," *San Francisco Chronicle,* June 21, 2009, p. L7.

90. J. McGregor, "Job Review in 140 Keystrokes," *BusinessWeek,* March 23 & 30, 2009, p. 58.

91. M. Boyle, "Performance Reviews: Perilous Curves Ahead," *Fortune,* May 15, 2001, www.fortune.com/fortune/subs/print/0,15935,374010,00.html (accessed April 19, 2010); C. M. Ellis, G. B. Moore, and A. M. Saunier, "Forced Ranking: Not So Fast," *Perspectives,* June 30, 2003, www.imakenews.com/eletra/mod_print_view.cfm?this_id=162170&u=sibson&issue_id=000034313 (accessed June 23, 2011); and A. Meisler, "Dead Man's Curve," *Workforce Management,* July 2003, pp. 45–49.

92. S. Scherreik, "Your Performance Review: Make It Perform," *BusinessWeek Online,* December 17, 2001, www.businessweek.com/magazine/content/01_51/b3762136.htm?chan=search (accessed June 23, 2011); and J. McGregor, "The Struggle to Measure Performance," *BusinessWeek Online,* January 9, 2006, www.businessweek.com/magazine/content/06_02/b3966060.htm?chan=search (accessed June 23, 2011). See also criticism of forced ranking in J. Pfeffer and R. I. Sutton, *Hard Facts, Dangerous Half-Truths & Total Nonsense: Profiting from Evidence-Based Management* (Boston: Harvard Business School Press, 2006).

93. F. Cordaro, quoted in T. Parker-Pope, "When the Bully Sits in the Next Cubicle," 2010.

94. P. Shrivastava, quoted in M. Villano, "'Your Performance Has Come Up Short,'" *New York Times,* November 30, 2008, Business section, p. 9.

95. T. Hires, quoted in Villano, "Your Performance Has Come Up Short," 2008.

96. J. Robinson, quoted in A. Bruzzese, "Evaluations: Dreadful Event or Time for Career Rebirth," *Reno Gazette-Journal,* July 9, 2009, p. 5A.

97. R. Mitchell, quoted in Villano, "Your Performance Has Come Up Short," 2008.

98. M. Boyle, "Cutting Costs without Cutting Jobs," *BusinessWeek,* March 9, 2009, p. 55; and G. Colvin, "Layoffs Cost More Than You Think," *Fortune,* March 30, 2009, p. 24.

99. L. Petrecca, "Employee Benefits Squeezed," *USA Today,* April 7, 2009, pp. 1B, 2B.

100. *Employee Benefits Study, 2007* (Washington, DC: U.S. Chamber of Commerce, 2008).

101. "Take Stock of Stock Options," *Human Resource Executive Magazine,* June 3, 2004, www.workindex.com/editorial/hre/hre0406-03.asp (accessed June 23, 2011).

102. "Percentage of Business That Have Gainsharing," *Zunaif.net,* May 12, 2011, http://zunaif.net/archives/550 (accessed June 23, 2011).

103. Based on L. Buhl, "6 Soft Skills Everyone Needs," *San Francisco Chronicle,* July 11, 2010, p. D12.

104. Colvin, "Layoffs Cost More Than You Think," 2009.

105. Boyle, "Cutting Costs without Cutting Jobs," 2009, citing Peter Cappelli, director of the Center for Human Resources, Wharton School of Business.

106. Roberts, "Close-Up on Screening," 2011.

107. R. Zupek, "Infamous Resume Lies," Careerbuilder.com website, July 7, 2010, msn.careerbuilder.com/Article/MSN-1154-Cover-Letters-Resumes-Infamous-R%C3%A9sum%C3%A9-Lies/ (accessed April 15, 2011).

108. "Fact Sheet on Employee Tests and Selection Procedures," Equal Employment Opportunity Commission, www.eeoc.gov/policy/docs/factemployment_procedures.html (accessed July 9, 2011).

109. "Sexual Harassment Charges, EEOC & FEPAs Combined: FY 1997–FY 2010," www.eeoc.gov/eeoc/statistics/enforcement/sexual_harassment.cfm (accessed April 12, 2011).

110. M. Velasquez, "A New Era in Sexual Harassment," Sexual Harassment Prevention Center, www.stopharass.com/article-sexual-harassment.htm (accessed August 24, 2011).

111. "About Page," Chipconley.com website (accessed April 14, 2011).

112. "About Page," Chipconley.com website.

113. "Beasley Replaces Chip Conley as Joie de Vivre CEO," *San Francisco Business Times*, September 20, 2010, www.bizjournals.com/sanfrancisco/stories/2010/09/20/daily13.html (accessed April 14, 2011).

114. L. Fishman, "Employee's Tattoos Leads to Title VII Suit against Starbucks," February 16, 2010. www.houstonemploymentlawsblog.com/2010/02/employees-tattoos-lead-to-suit-against-starbucks.html (accessed August 24, 2011).

115. M. Feldstein, "Piercing, Tattoos Create Workplace Issues," Rense.com website, www.rense.com/general11/plac.htm (accessed July 9, 2011).

116. "Tattoo Lady: Is a No-Tattoo Dress Code Policy Out of Step with the Times?" *Blogher Ad Network,* funnybusiness.typepad.com/funnybusiness/2005/07/tattoo_lady.html (accessed April 15, 2011).

117. M. J. Feldstein, "Piercing, Tattoos Create Workplace Issues," 2010.

118. "Why Tattoos and Piercings Cause Discrimination in the Workplace," www.helium.com/items/820340-why-tattoos-and-piercings-cause-discrimination-in-the-workplace (accessed July 9, 2011).

119. "Three in Ten Americans with a Tattoo Say Having One Makes Them Feel Sexier or More Artsy," Harris Interactive website www.harrisinteractive.com (accessed April 15, 2011).

CHAPTER 12

1. M. Helft and A. Vance, "Apple Is No. 1 in Tech, Overtaking Microsoft," *New York Times,* May 27, 2010, pp. B1, B4; Y. I. Kane and C. Rohwedder, "Apple Strives for Global Markets," *Wall Street Journal,* June 9, 2010, p. B5; I. Sherr, "Apple Seeks Growth beyond Consumers," *Wall Street Journal,* July 22, 2010, p. B6; and "Apple Gains on Exxon as Most Valuable Firm," *San Francisco Chronicle,* October 4, 2010, p. E4.

2. R. Kim, "IPhone Antenna Sends Bad Memories," *San Francisco Chronicle,* July 13, 2010, pp. A1, A7.

3. D. Lyons, "Apple's Shuffle," *Newsweek,* September 13, 2010, p. 22.

4. N. Wingfield, "At Apple, Secrecy Complicates Life but Maintains Buzz," *Wall Street Journal,* June 28, 2006, pp. A1, A11; and

J. Guynn, "Behind the iPhone Hype," *San Francisco Chronicle,* June 28, 2007, pp. A1, A14.

5. F. Maharg-Bravo and R. Cyran, "Downside of Secrecy," *New York Times,* July 14, 2010, p. B2; M. Helft, "Will Apple's Culture Hurt the iPhone?" *New York Times,* October 18, 2010, pp. B1, B4.

6. J. Greene, "Why Apple Will Survive the iPhone Glitch," *Wall Street Journal,* July 29, 2010, p. A11.

7. S. Jobs, quoted in Greene, 2010.

8. N. Wingfield, "Microsoft Legal Salvo Seeks to Slow Google," *Wall Street Journal,* October 2, 2010, pp. A1, A2.

9. W. S. Mossberg, "Microsoft's New Windows Phone 7: Novel but Lacking," *Wall Street Journal,* October 21, 2010, pp. D1, D4.

10. R. Jaroslovsky, "Windows Phone 7 Too Little, Too Late," *San Francisco Chronicle,* October 25, 2010, pp. D1, D5.

11. Greene, 2010.

12. C. Woodyard, "Outlander Goes Online with Virtual Test Drive," *USA Today,* November 15, 2010, p. 3B.

13. American Marketing Association, "AMA Adopts New Definition of Marketing," *Marketing Power,* October 2007, www.marketingpower.com/aboutama/pages/definitionofmarketing.aspx (accessed June 25, 2011).

14. D. Agren, "Mexico's Boom Industry: Bulletproof Cars," *USA Today,* November 15, 2010, p. 8A.

15. Matt Thornill, founder of specialty research firm the Boomer Project, quoted in B. Horovitz, "Big-Spending Boomers Bend Rules of Marketing," *USA Today,* November 16, 2010, pp. 1A, 2A.

16. Forester Research, reported in Horovitz, 2010, p. 2A.

17. Alloy Media + Marketing/College Explorer study, reported in B. Horovitz, "Marketers Pull an Inside Job on College Campuses," *USA Today,* October 4, 2010, pp. 1B, 2B.

18. Horovitz, "Marketers Pull an Inside Job on College Campuses," 2010.

19. L. W. Foderaro, "In a Digital Age, Students Still Cling to Paper Textbooks," *New York Times,* October 20, 2010, pp. A18, A19.

20. M. Higgins, "In Board Sports, Credibility Sells Along with Gear," *New York Times,* pp. A1, C13. See also P. Glader, "Avid Boarders Bypass Branded Gear," *Wall Street Journal,* July 27, 2007, pp. B1, B2.

21. Cited in B. Carey, "$2.50 Placebo Gives More Relief Than a 10¢ One," *New York Times,* March 5, 2008, p. A12.

22. R. L. Waber, B. Shiv, Z. Carmon, and D. Ariely, "Commercial Features of Placebo and Therapeutic Efficacy," *Journal of the American Medical Association,* March 5, 2008, pp. 1016–1017.

23. Daniel Ariely, quoted in Carey, 2008. Ariely is the author of *Predictably Irrational: The Hidden Forces That Shape Our Decisions* (New York: HarperCollins, 2008).

24. C. Krauss, "Women, Hear Them Roar," *New York Times,* July 25, 2007, pp. C1, C9.

25. S. Simon, "The Secret to Turning Consumers Green," *Wall Street Journal,* October 18, 2010, pp. R1, R2.

26. L. Petrecca, "Ouidad Builds Business on Good Hair Days," *USA Today,* September 16, 2007, p. 3B.

27. S. Banjo, "Attention, Bloggers," *Wall Street Journal,* March 17, 2008, p. R5. See also C. Choi, "Food Companies Target Popular Blogs to Gain Cheap Publicity," *Reno Gazette-Journal,* March 21, 2008, p. 10A.

28. E. K. Clemons, P. F. Nunes, and M. Reilly, "Six Strategies for Successful Niche Marketing," *Wall Street Journal,* May 24, 2010, p. R6.

29. General Mills careers website, http://generalmills.com/careers.aspx (accessed October 22, 2011).

30. M. S. Olson, D. van Bever, and S. Verry, "When Growth Stalls," *Harvard Business Review,* March 2008, pp. 50–61.

31. N. Wingfield and E. Smith, "Disney Cuts, Revamps Videogame Operations," *Wall Street Journal,* January 26, 2011, p. B9.

32. E. Byron, "Revlon's Makeup Test," *Wall Street Journal,* March 13, 2008, pp. B1, B6.

33. J. Crown and G. Coleman, *No Hands: The Rise and Fall of the Schwinn Bicycle Company, an American Institution* (New York: Henry Holt and Company, 1996).

34. N. Bunkley, "Plug-In Cars Are Almost Here, but Charging Stations Lag," *New York Times,* October 22, 2009, p. B6; C. Sweet, "Preparing for Electric Cars," *Wall Street Journal,* December 23, 2009, p. B7; T. Woody and C. Krauss, "Ready, Set, Charge," *New York Times,* February 15, 2010, pp. B1, B3; T. Abate, "Long Road Left before Electric Car Is Common," *San Francisco Chronicle,* May 23, 2010, pp. A1, A12; A. Ohnsman, "Charging Can Be a Challenge for Electric Cars," *San Francisco Chronicle,* June 7, 2010, pp. D1, D3; G. F. Seib, "Time to Plug in Electric Cars," *Wall Street Journal,* June 18, 2010, p. A2; and R. Smith, "Scouting Sites for an Electric Future," *Wall Street Journal,* October 20, 2010, pp. B1, B2.

35. A. K. Pradeep, quoted in J. Guthrie, "Mining the Brain for Marketing," *San Francisco Chronicle,* November 17, 2010, pp. E1, E3. Pradeep is author of *The Buying Brain: Secrets for Selling to the Subconscious Mind* (New York: Wiley, 2010).

36. M. Lindstrom, quoted in S. Brown, "A Peek Inside Buyers' Heads," *USA Today,* October 27, 2008, p. 7B. Lindstrom is author of *Buyology: Truth and Lies about Why We Buy* (New York: Doubleday Business, 2008).

37. A. A. Newman, "Using Appeals to Emotions to Sell Paint," *New York Times,* June 8, 2010, p. B3.

38. USA Today/Gallup Poll, reported in E. C. Baig, "Internet Users Say: Don't Track Me," *USA Today,* December 14, 2010, p. 1B.

39. Newman, "Using Appeals to Emotions to Sell Paint," 2010.

40. M. Gottfried, "A Taste for Hotter, Mintier, Fruitier," *Wall Street Journal,* May 26, 2010, pp. D1, D6.

41. S. Jayson, "Tired of the Baby Boomers," *USA Today,* November 18, 2010, pp. 1D, 2D.

42. M. Bustillo and A. Zimmerman, "Phone-Wielding Shoppers Strike Fear into Retailers," *Wall Street Journal,* December 16, 2010, pp. A1, A19.

43. T. Zeller Jr. and K. Bradsher, "Wind-Tossed Worries," *New York Times,* December 16, 2010, pp. B1, B4.

44. S. Yager, "Food Safety Act: The New Law Will Mean (Big Food) Business as Usual—Or Will It?" *Huffington Post,* December 25, 2010, www.huffingtonpost.com/susan-yager/the-food-safety-bill-mean_b_800189.html (accessed June 25, 2011).

45. L. Storey, "To Aim Ads, Web Is Keeping Closer Eye on What You Click," *New York Times,* March 10, 2008, pp. A1, A14.

46. Susana Martinez Vidal, quoted in C. Passariello, K. Johnson, and S. Vranica, "A New Force in Advertising—Protest by Email," *Wall Street Journal,* March 22, 2007, pp. B1, B2.

47. M. Barbaro, "Unbound, Wal-Mart Tastemakers Write a Blunt and Unfiltered Blog," *New York Times,* March 3, 2008, pp. C1, C8.

48. C. Choi, "Food Companies Target Popular Blogs to Gain Cheap Publicity," *Reno Gazette-Journal,* March 21, 2008, p. 10A.

49. D. Fost, "On the Internet, Everyone Can Hear You Complain," *New York Times,* February 25, 2008, p. C6.

50. "The Top Five Social Media Ad Campaigns," Searchenginepeople.com website, www.searchenginepeople.com/blog/top-social-media-campaigns.html (accessed October 2, 2011).

51. "Official about Jones Soda Company," www.jonessoda.com, www.jonessoda.com/files_4/about.php (accessed October 2, 2011).

52. M. Alison, "Seattle Soda Maker Ends the Sweet Talk, Opts for Sugar," *Seattle Times,* February 5, 2007, http://seattletimes.nwsource

.com/html/businesstechnology/2003557096_sugar05.html (accessed July 12, 2011).

53. "My Jones," www.myjones.com jonessoda.com website (accessed April 9, 2011).

54. "Jones Snags $10 Million in Financing," June 14, 2010, *Puget Sound Business Journal,* www.bizjournals.com/seattle/stories/2010/06/14/daily2.html (accessed April 7, 2011).

55. "The Stats on Soft Drinks," The Vice Busting Diet, www.vicebusting diet.com/blog/soft-drinks-are-the-1-reason-for-obesity-and-overweight.html (accessed July 12, 2011).

56. C. Cowles, "Denim Ads Too 'Crude' for the *Wall Street Journal*," New York Fashion, October 12, 2010, http://nymag.com/daily/fashion/2010/10/denim_ads_are_using_crude_lang.html (accessed July 12, 2011).

57. Cowles, 2010.

58. A. Odell, "The Resurrected A&F Quarterly Contains More Male Nudity than Female Nudity," *New York Magazine*, July 19, 2010, http://nymag.com/daily/fashion/2010/07/the_af_quarterly_contains_more.html (accessed July 12, 2011).

59. "Calvin Klein: A Case Study," Media Awareness Network website, www.media-awareness.ca/english/resources/educational/handouts/ethics/calvin_klein_case_study.cfm (accessed July 12, 2011).

60. R. Smith, "Jean Ads Get Risque," LocalNet360.com, www.localnet360.com/jeans-ads-get-risque/ (accessed July 12, 2011).

61. Smith, 2011.

62. Smith, 2011.

63. "Calvin Klein: A Case Study," 2011.

64. M. Barnett, "When Ads Go Strange. Calvin Klein Conducts Kiddie Porn Auditions," June 11, 2010, www.minyanville.com/special-features/articles/strange-ads-calvin-klein-target-macys/6/11/2010/id/27861 (accessed July 12, 2011).

CHAPTER 13

1. "Back in the Day . . . ," Mint.com, www.mint.com/company (accessed July 4, 2011).

2. V. Kopytoff, "The Award Goes to . . . Mint," *San Francisco Chronicle,* September 18, 2007, www.sfgate.com/cgi-bin/blogs/techchron/detail?entry_id=20409; D. Caruso, "Securing Very Important Data: Your Own," *New York Times,* October 7, 2007, www.nytimes.com/2007/10/07/technology/07frame.html (both accessed July 4, 2011).

3. E. Zimmerman, "How Six Companies Failed to Survive 2010," *New York Times,* January 6, 2011, p. B7.

4. M. Hedlund, "Why Wesabe Lost to Mint," Marc Hedlund's Blog, October 1, 2010, http://blog.precipice.org/why-wesabe-lost-to-mint (accessed July 4, 2011).

5. J. McGregor, "How Failure Breeds Success," *BusinessWeek,* July 10, 2006, pp. 42–46.

6. S. Ogawa and F. T. Piller, "Reducing the Risks of New Product Development," *MIT Sloan Management Review,* Winter 2006, pp. 65–71.

7. C. Woodyard, "Prius Gets Big Brother, Little Sis," *USA Today,* January 11, 2011, p. 1B.

8. M. Puente, "Those $45,000 Bags Are a Sellout," *USA Today,* March 15, 2007, p. 1D; and E. Pfanner, "Vuitton Is Embracing Medium of the Masses," *New York Times,* January 30, 2008, p. C8.

9. "A World Transformed: What Are the Top Innovations of the Last 30 Years?" *Knowledge@Wharton,* February 18, 2009, http://knowledge.wharton.upenn.edu/article.cfm?articleid=2163 (accessed July 4, 2011).

10. M. R. Solomon, G. W. Marshall, and E. W. Stuart, *Marketing: Real People, Real Choices,* 5th ed. (Upper Saddle River, NJ: Pearson, 2008), Table 8.3, p. 247.

11. D. Canedy, "After 102 Years, Campbell Alters Soup Labels," *New York Times,* August 26, 1999, pp. C1, C7.

12. M. McCarthy, "A Revolutionary Sneaker, or Overhyped Gimmick?" *USA Today,* June 30, 2010, pp. A1, A2.

13. C. Cain Miller and N. Bilton, "Cellphone Payments Offer Alternative to Cash," *New York Times,* April 28, 2010, www.nytimes.com/2010/04/29/technology/29cashless.html (accessed July 4, 2011).

14. R. King, "Wells Tests Paying by Smart Phone," *San Francisco Chronicle,* January 5, 2011, pp. D1, D2.

15. P. Svensson, "Google Tries to Replace Wallets with Smartphone," *ABC News,* May 26, 2011, http://abcnews.go.com/Technology/wireStory?id=13695281 (accessed July 5, 2011).

16. O. Kharif, "Google's Search for a Digital Wallet," *Bloomberg Businessweek,* January 10–January 16, 2011, pp. 33–34.

17. "What's the Kindle Worth to Amazon?" *New York Times,* January 9, 2009, p. B2.

18. MediaMorph, reported in G. A. Flower and J. A. Trachtenberg, "Barnes & Noble Soups Up Its E-Reader," *Wall Street Journal,* October 27, 2010, p. B6.

19. W. S. Mossberg, "Find the Best Way to Read Books on an iPad," *Wall Street Journal,* September 16, 2010, pp. D1, D2.

20. Data from survey by ChangeWave Research, reported in A. Yoskowitz, "Kindle Losing E-reader Market Share to iPad," *AfterDawn,* December 1, 2010, www.afterdawn.com/news/article.cfm/2010/12/02/kindle_losing_e-reader_market_share_to_ipad (accessed July 4, 2011).

21. M. Malone and T. Hayes, "Bye-Bye, PCs and Laptops," *Wall Street Journal,* January 7, 2011, p. A13.

22. F. Gillette, "The Rise and Inglorious Fall of Myspace," *Bloomberg Businessweek,* June 27–July 3, 2011, pp. 52–59.

23. "Why Did They Cancel ER?" Yahoo Answers, April 6, 2009, http://answers.yahoo.com/question/index?qid=20090406170900AAKGQyh (accessed July 4, 2011).

24. P. Vitello, "More Americans Are Giving Up Golf," *New York Times,* February 21, 2008, www.nytimes.com/2008/02/21/nyregion/21golf.html?pagewanted=all; and M. Fitzpatrick, "Golf's Decline in America: Work/Life Balance Is the True Culprit," *Tour Report: PGA Tour News, Insight and Analysis,* March 31, 2011, www.thetourreport.com/uncategorized/golfs-decline-america-worklife-balance-true-culpri (both accessed July 4, 2011).

25. J. Connell, G. C. Edgar, B. Olex, R. Scholl, et al., "Troubling Successes and Good Failures: Successful New Product Development Requires Five Critical Factors," *Engineering Management Journal,* December 2001, http://findarticles.com/p/articles/mi_qa5394/is_200112/ai_n21465594 (accessed July 4, 2011).

26. S. Elliott, "Not Ready to Pay for TV Time, a Mexican Beer Goes Online," *New York Times,* February 27, 2008, p. C6.

27. B. Nussbaum, "The Power of Design," *BusinessWeek,* May 17, 2004, pp. 86–94.

28. M. Ray and R. Myers, *Creativity in Business* (Garden City, NY: Doubleday, 1986), p. 40.

29. Ray and Myers, 1986, pp. 40, 42.

30. C. S. Dweck, *Mindset: The New Psychology of Success* (New York: Ballantine Books, 2006).

31. E. J. Langer, *Mindfulness* (Reading, MA: Addison-Wesley, 1989). See also D. J. Siegel, *The Mindful Brain: Reflection and Attunement in the Cultivation of Well-Being* (New York: W.W. Norton, 2007); and M. Landau, "When Doctors Negotiate Uncertainty," *Focus Online: News from Harvard Medical, Dental, and Public Health Schools,* May 4, 2007, http://focus.hms.harvard.edu/2007/050407/education.shtml (accessed July 4, 2011).

32. E. J. Langer, *The Power of Mindful Learning* (Reading, MA: Addison-Wesley, 1997), p. 4.

33. Langer, *Mindfulness,* 1989, p. 69.

34. J. L. Adams, *Conceptual Blockbusting* (Stanford, CA: The Portable Stanford, 1974), pp. 52–53.

35. Twitter spokesman Matt Graves, quoted in E. Spitznagel, "Companies in a Twitter over Finding Monikers," *San Francisco Chronicle,* October 25, 2010, pp. D1, D4.

36. Naseem Javed, founder of ABC Namebank, reported in Spitznagel, 2010.

37. A. A. Newman, "Turning 30, an Office Product Works at Home," *New York Times,* July 28, 2010, p. B3.

38. Tim Sproul, creative director for Razorfish, Portland, Ore., quoted in S. Elliott, "Coors Light Uses Cold to Turn Up Heat on Rivals," *New York Times,* April 27, 2009, www.nytimes.com/2009/04/27/business/media/27adnewsletter1.html (accessed July 4, 2011).

39. Elliott, 2009.

40. B. Stone, "The Fight Over Who Can Determine Prices at the Online Mall," *New York Times,* February 8, 2010, pp. B1, B4.

41. E. Ruppel Shell, *Cheap: The High Cost of Discount Culture* (New York: Penguin, 2009).

42. Ruppel Shell, quoted in D. Leonard, "What's Beyond Those Bargains," *New York Times,* July 5, 2009, Business section, p. 5.

43. Leonard, 2009.

44. Study by B. Shiv and colleagues at California Institute of Technology, reported in J. O'C. Hamilton, "This Is Your Brain on Bargains," *Stanford Magazine,* November/December 2008, pp. 70–74.

45. A. Martin, "Have They Got a Deal for You," *New York Times,* May 31, 2010, pp. B1, B2.

46. S. Rosenbloom, "Stores Sweeten the Discounts with Add-Ons," *New York Times,* December 27, 2009, pp. A1, A10.

47. Manoj Thomas, quoted in J. Clements, "Price Fixing: In This Market, Selling a Home Requires Savvy," *Wall Street Journal,* February 27, 2008, p. D1.

48. Cornell University business school study, cited in P. B. Brown, "An American Portrait," *New York Times,* February 23, 2008, p. B5.

49. M. Roth, "For Sellers, a Penny Shaved Is More Than a Penny Earned," *San Francisco Chronicle,* December 23, 2006, pp. C1, C2; J. Clements, "Price Fixing: In This Market Selling a Home Requires Savvy," *Wall Street Journal,* February 27, 2008, p. D1; and J. Hough, "Selling a House? Try to Avoid Zeros," *Smart-Money,* April 16, 2010, www.smartmoney.com/personal-finance/real-estate/selling-a-house-try-to-avoid-zeros (accessed July 4, 2011).

50. V. Bajaj, "Tata's Nano, the Car That Few Want to Buy," *New York Times,* December 9, 2010, www.nytimes.com/2010/12/10/business/global/10tata.html?pagewanted=1&_r=1# (accessed April 20, 2011).

51. G. Kumparak, "Microsoft Employees Leave the Windows Phone 7 Team to Make Windows Phone 7 Apps," *Tech Crunch Website,* March 15, 2010, http://techcrunch.com/2010/03/15/microsoft-employees-leave-the-windows-phone-7-team-to-make-windows-phone-7-apps/ (accessed July 14, 2011).

52. "Welcome to Cupidtino," *www.cupidtino.com website,* www.cupidtino.com/about (accessed May 14, 2011).

53. I. Steiner, "eBay and Amazon Release Mobile Apps," *Auction-Bytes.com,* November 23, 2010, www.auctionbytes.com/cab/cab/abn/y10/m11/i23/s01 (accessed May 14, 2011).

54. C. Cain Miller, "Ad Revenue on the Web? No Sure Bet," *New York Times,* May 24, 2009, www.nytimes.com/2009/05/25/technology/start-ups/25startup.html (accessed May 14, 2011).

55. "Main Menu," *Smashburger website,* www.smashburger.com/menu_main.php (accessed May 15, 2011).

56. A. Tugend, "Too Many Choices: A Problem That Can Paralyze," *New York Times,* February 26, 2010, www.nytimes.com/2010/02/27/your-money/27shortcuts.html (accessed May 18, 2011).

57. B. Schwartz, *The Paradox of Choice: Why More Is Less* (New York: Harper Collins, 2003).

58. D. Lee Yohn, "Why Too Much Choice Is a Bad Thing," *Wall Street Journal,* February 1, 2011, www.businessinsider.com/the-fundamentals-of-choice-2011-2?utm_source=feedburner&utm_medium=feed&utm_campaign=Feed%3A+business insider%2Fwarroom+%28War+Room%29#ixzz1MkpknQNo (accessed May 18, 2011).

59. "You Choose," *The Economist,* December 16, 2010, www.economist.com/node/17723028/ (accessed May 18, 2011).

60. P. Thompson, "Shopping Optimized," *The Hub,* March/April 2010, www.hrcpinsights.com/growth-insights/articles/upload/Shopping_Optimized_the_hub35_rak.pdf (accessed May 18, 2011).

61. G. Brown, "1000% Increase in Sales. Do Less Choices Increase Conversions?" *Evolution Website,* February 8, 2010, www.evolution-internet.com/blog/do-less-choices-mean-more-sales.html (accessed May 18, 2011).

62. P. Graves, "Too Much Choice," *PhilipGraves.net,* April 2, 2009, www.philipgraves.net/discussion/too-much-choice.htm (accessed May 18, 2011).

CHAPTER 14

1. Michael Pacher, Wedbush Morgan Securities analyst, quoted in R. Stross, "Why Bricks and Clicks Don't Always Mix," *New York Times,* September 19, 2010, Business section, p. 3.

2. Stross, 2010.

3. J. Surowiecki, "The Next Level," *New Yorker,* October 18, 2010, p. 28.

4. Stross, "Why Bricks and Clicks Don't Always Mix," 2010.

5. Surowiecki, "The Next Level," 2010.

6. B. Stelter, "Customers Angry Over Revamped Pricing Are Deserting Netflix," *New York Times,* September 16, 2011, p. B3; Associated Press, "Netflix and Quikster: Will People Pay Twice?" *Reno Gazette-Journal,* September 20, 2011, pp. 7A, 8A; J. Wortham and B. Stelter, "Latest Move Gets Netflix More Wrath," *New York Times,* September 20, 2011, pp. B1, B2; and B. Stelter, "NetFlix Reverses Course on a Breakup Plan," *New York Times,* October 11, 2011, pp. B1, B6.

7. Surowiecki, "The Next Level," 2010.

8. Jeff Bezos, quoted in K. Mayo and P. Newcomb, "An Oral History of the Internet: How the Web Was Won," *Vanity Fair,* July 2008, p. 110.

9. I. DeBare, "Sales Reps, Trade Shows Help to Get Gift Products in Stores," *San Francisco Chronicle,* April 18, 2007, pp. C1, C4.

10. D. Thomas, *Deluxe: How Luxury Lost Its Luster* (New York: Penguin Press, 2007), reported in H. Hurt III, "Luxury, and How It Became Common," *New York Times,* August 19, 2007, Business section, p. 6.

11. M. Locke, "Vendor Sells Chocolate-Covered Bacon," *Reno Gazette-Journal,* August 9, 2008, p. 4B.

12. S. Finz, "Big Growers Give Produce a Pedigree," *San Francisco Chronicle,* June 4, 2010, pp. A1, A16. See also California Giant Berry Farms, "Company Story," at company website, www.calgiant.com/consumers/company-story.php (accessed July 7, 2011).

13. R. Abrams, "Weigh Multilevel Marketing Option Carefully before Jumping into It," *Reno Gazette-Journal,* May 12, 2009, p. 5A.

14. Abrams, 2009.

15. J. O'Donnell, "Direct Sales Raises Questions," *USA Today,* October 15, 2010, pp. 1B, 6B.

16. L. Petrecca and T. Howard, "Eco-Marketing a Hot Topic for Advertisers at Cannes," *USA Today,* June 22, 2007, p. 4B; and "Fashion or Strategy? Why Firms Are Jumping on the Sustainability Bandwagon," *Knowledge@Wharton,* January 19, 2011, http://

knowledge.wharton.upenn.eduj/article.cfm?articleid=2677 (accessed July 7, 2011).

17. G. Bounds, "What Do Labels Really Tell You?" *Wall Street Journal,* April 2, 2009, pp. D1, D2; T. Watson, "Eco-Friendly Claims Go Unchecked," *USA Today,* June 22, 2009, p. 1A; V. O'Connell, "'Green' Goods, Red Flags," *Wall Street Journal,* April 24–25, 2010, p. A3; and T. Vega, "Agency Seeks to Tighten Rules for 'Green' Labeling," *New York Times,* October 7, 2010, p. B4. See also TerraChoice, www.terrachoice.com.

18. B. Walsh, "Eco-Buyer Beware," *Time,* September 22, 2008, pp. 71–72.

19. Tony Baca, quoted in M. Walker, "The Bad Boys of Aviation," *The Week,* April 18, 2008, pp. 40–41. Adapted from a longer article in *Men's Vogue,* March 2008.

20. See "The Journey of the Couch," Ted Koppel on Discovery Channel, http://dsc.discovery.com/convergence/koppel/koppel.html "Changes in China: Koppel Investigates," CNN.com, July 7, 2008, http://www.cnn.com/2008/SHOWBIZ/TV/07/06/koppel.china.ap; and F. R. Lee, "Ted Koppel Tours a China Brimming with Dreams and Consumerism," *New York Times,* July 8, 2008, www.nytimes.com/2008/07/08/arts/television/08kopp.html?n=Top/Reference/Times%20Topics/Organizations/C/Council%20on%20Foreign%20Relations (both accessed July 7, 2011).

21. L. Rohter, "Shipping Costs Start to Crimp Globalization," *New York Times,* August 3, 2008, News section, pp. 1, 10.

22. Based on Canadian Association of Logistics Management, www.calm.org/calm/AboutCALM/AboutCALM.html, 12 February 23, 1998 (accessed July 7, 2011).

23. U.S. Ton-Miles of Freight (BTS Special Tabulation), October 10, 2008, Bureau of Transportation Statistics, www.bts.gov/publications/national_transportation_statistics/html (accessed July 7, 2011).

24. For standard dimensions of ocean containers, see www.foreign-trade.com/reference/ocean.cfm.

25. A. A. Newman, "The Body as Billboard: Your Ad Here," *New York Times,* February 18, 2009, p. B3.

26. J. Gluck, "NASCAR's Extensive Research to Shape New Marketing, Communications Approach for Sport," *SB Nation,* July 2, 2011.

27. AllBusiness.com, "Business Cards Are Often Effective Tools—Don't Be Stingy with Them," *San Francisco Chronicle,* August 6, 2008, p. C2; and H. Barovick, "The Return of the Calling Card," *Time,* August 11, 2008, p. 57.

28. For a history of the infomercial industry, see R. Stern, *But Wait . . . There's More! Tighten Your Abs, Make Millions, and Learn How the $100 Billion Infomercial Industry Sold Us Everything but the Kitchen Sink* (New York: HarperCollins, 2009).

29. M. Puente, "Pop Culture Embraces the Snuggie," *USA Today,* January 28, 2009, p. 1D.

30. M. Lindstrom, quoted in "Should You 'Buy This Now!'?" *Consumer Reports,* February 2010, pp. 16–17.

31. "Should You 'Buy This Now!'?" 2010.

32. R. San Juan, "Push-Pull Marketing," Gaebler Ventures Resources for Entrepreneurs, www.gaebler.com/Push-Pull-Marketing.htm (accessed July 7, 2011).

33. S. Clifford, "Before Hiring Actors, Filmmakers Cast Products," *New York Times,* April 5, 2010, pp. A1, A11.

34. E. Porter, "Would You Buy a New Car from Eva Longoria?" *New York Times,* July 10, 2008, p. A22; S. Clifford, "Product Placements Acquire a Life of Their Own on Shows," *New York Times,* July 14, 2008, pp. C1, C4; and S. Clifford, "A Product's Place Is on the Set," *New York Times,* July 22, 2008, pp. C1, C6.

35. Clifford, 2010.

36. Data from The Nielsen Company, AdAcross, "Share of Ad Spending by Medium, December 2009," Marketing Charts, March 22, 2010, www.marketingcharts.com/print/share-of-ad-spending-by-medium-december-2009-12352 (accessed July 7, 2011).

37. "The Big Fight over Your Local Advertising Dollars," Chase New Media, www.chasenewmedia.com/articles/local-online-advertising.html (accessed July 7, 2011).

38. V. Letang, "Google Expands Lead in Search Ad in 2010," *iSupply Screen Digest,* January 18, 2011, www.isuppli.com/Media-Research/News/Pages/Google-Expands-Lead-in-Search-Advertising-Market-in-2010.aspx (accessed July 7, 2011).

39. Lieberman, "New Media Expected to Get More Ad Dollars," 2008.

40. E. Steel, "Web vs. TV: Research Aims to Gauge Ads," *Wall Street Journal,* March 19, 2008, p. B3. See also S. Clifford and M. Helft, "Online Search Ads Faring Better Than Expensive Displays," *New York Times,* May 19, 2008, pp. C1, C6; and R. Abrams, "Online Advertising Could Help Your Small Business Succeed," *Reno Gazette-Journal,* July 15, 2008, p. 6A.

41. B. Tedeschi, "Small Merchants Gain Large Presence on Web," *New York Times,* December 3, 2007, p. C8; A. Zipkin, "An Online Comfort Zone," *New York Times,* February 14, 2008, p. C6; S. Clifford, "The Web as a Store Window," *New York Times,* August 24, 2010, pp. B1, B5.

42. K. Komando, "Websites Make It Easy to Sell Crafts," *Reno Gazette-Journal,* May 2, 2010, p. 5E.

43. J. Gill, "Contagious Commercials: How to Get in on the YouTube Craze," *Inc.,* November 2006, pp. 31–32; A. Jesdanun, "Companies Get in Your Facebook," *San Francisco Chronicle,* November 7, 2007, p. C3; Elliott, 2007; and K. J. Delaney, E. Steel, V. Vara, "Social Sites Don't Deliver Big Ad Gains," *Wall Street Journal,* February 5, 2008, pp. B1, B2; S. E. Needleman, "Merchants Push Sales through Social Media," *Wall Street Journal,* June 1, 2010, p. B6; B. Evangelista, "Retailer, Social Media a Good Fit," *San Francisco Chronicle,* July 7, 2010, pp. D1, D6; S. Vranica, "Social Media Draws a Crowd," *Wall Street Journal,* July 19, 2010, p. B7; B. Abrams, "Social Media Can Work, but You Really Have to Work at It," *Reno Gazette-Journal,* July 20, 2010, p. 8A; J. Swartz, "More Small Businesses Use Twitter, Facebook," *Reno Gazette-Journal,* July 25, 2010, p. 5E; S. Vranica, "Tweeting to Sell Cars," *Wall Street Journal,* November 15, 2010, p. B12; E. Olson, "Restaurants Reach Out to Customers with Social Media," *New York Times,* January 20, 2011, p. B4.

44. M. Alboher, "Blogging as a Low-Cost, High-Return Marketing Tool," *New York Times,* December 27, 2007; and S. Banjo, "Attention, Bloggers," *Wall Street Journal,* March 17, 2008, p. R5.

45. AllBusiness.com, "E-Mail Newsletters an Effective Way to Promote Your Business," *San Francisco Chronicle,* September 6, 2006, p. C4; and AllBusiness.com, "With Help, You Can Create Successful E-Mail Marketing," *San Francisco Chronicle,* June 11, 2008, p. C3.

46. S. Elliott, "Web Videos Stealing TV Viewers, and Marketers," *New York Times,* November 6, 2007, p. C6; and D. Lieberman, "Promoters of All Kinds Take a Shot at Online Video," *USA Today,* March 9, 2009, p. 1B.

47. R. Flandez, "Calling All Customers," *Wall Street Journal,* April 30, 2007, p. R7; D. Ho, "Cell Phone Ads Get a New Life—as Long as They Can Avoid Spam," *San Francisco Chronicle,* August 20, 2007, p. C6; A. Jesdanun, "Ads on the Go," *Reno Gazette-Journal,* December 31, 2007, p. 7A; O. Kharif, "Smart Phones Make Mobile Radio Ads Hum," *San Francisco Chronicle,* July 18, 2010, p. D7; N. Sheth, "Newest Cellphone Ads Crave Entire Screen," *Wall Street Journal,* August 6, 2010, p. B7; and K. Pattison, "Geolocation Services: Find a Smartphone, Find a Customer," *New York Times,* October 7, 2010, p. B10.

48. A. Barber, "Christopher Gardner," *aTrader,* December 2006/January 2007, www.atrader.com/Christopher_Gardner.html; and

"Chris Gardner," Wikipedia, July 19, 2008, http://en.wikipedia
.org/wiki/Christopher_Gardner (both accessed July 7, 2011).

49. Chris Gardner, quoted in C. Gallo, "From Homeless to Multimil-lionaire," *BusinessWeek,* July 23, 2007, www.businessweek.com/smallbiz/content/jul2007/sb20070723_608918.htm?campaign_id=rss_daily (accessed July 7, 2011).

50. M. Sunnafrank and A. Ramirez Jr., "At First Sight: Persistent Relational Effects of Get-Acquainted Conversations," *Journal of Social and Personal Relationships,* June 1, 2004, pp. 361–379. See also J. Zaslow, "First Impressions Get Faster," *Wall Street Journal,* February 16, 2006, p. D4.

51. R. Ailes, in "Your First Seven Seconds," *Fast Company,* June–July 1998, p. 184.

52. See J. Gitomer, "Strength of Opening Line Dictates Success of Sales Pitch," *Journal Record,* Oklahoma City, August 22, 1996, http://findarticles.com/p/articles/mi_qn4182/is_19960822/ai_n10095215 (accessed July 7, 2011).

53. T. Audi, "Loyalty Points That Buy a Night with Travolta," *Wall Street Journal,* December 26, 2007, pp. D1, D2.

54. AllBusiness.com, "Trade Shows Bring Together Rivals—and Potential Partners," *San Francisco Chronicle,* July 25, 2007, p. C4.

55. D. R. Baker, "Hyping 'Free Gas' to Fuel Sales," *San Francisco Chronicle,* June 22, 2008, pp. C1, C4.

56. B. Barnes, "It Seemed Like a Good Idea . . . ," *Wall Street Journal,* April 30, 2007, p. R7; L. Stern, "Ads That Stay with You," *Newsweek,* November 19, 2007, p. E2; and V. Tong, "Tattoos, No Longer Rebel Badges, Have Become a Marketing Tool," *San Francisco Chronicle,* November 27, 2007, p. C6.

57. F. Manjoo, "Branded," *New York Times Book Review,* July 27, 2008, p. 7, reviewing Rob Walker, *Buying In: The Secret Dialogue between What We Buy and Who We Are* (New York: Random House, 2008).

58. S. Barlyn, "Talk Is Cheap," *Wall Street Journal,* November 26, 2007, p. R6. See also J. Bennett, "The New World of Marketing: Word-of-Mouth Campaigns Replace Traditional Tools," *Wall Street Journal,* February 6, 2006, p. B7; and D. Fost, "Viral Campaign Spreading," *San Francisco Chronicle,* June 9, 2007, pp. C1, C2.

59. A. Tokik, "Subaru Forester: Reunion," *AutoGuide.com,* October 25, 2010, www.youtube.com/watch?v=n5UwvFbi5PE (accessed July 7, 2011).

60. D. Castillo, "Transformer Movie Incorporates the Strongest Product Placement in Film History," *Product Placement News* website, July 17, 2007, http://productplacement.biz/200707172249/news/transformer-movie-incorporates-the-strongest-product-placement-in-film-history.html (accessed July 16, 2011).

61. D. Castillo, "Auto Product Placement in Transformers: Dark of the Moon," *Product Placement News* website, August 25, 2011, http://productplacement.biz/200707172249/news/transformer-movie-incorporates-the-strongest-product-placement-in-film-history.html (accessed July 16, 2011).

62. R. Moore, "Greatest Movie Ever Sold Explains the Art of Product Placement," *Detroit Free Press*, May 19, 2011.

63. D. Munger, "Product Placements in Movies: When They Work, and When They Don't," Science Blogs website, October 28, 2009, http://scienceblogs.com/cognitivedaily/2009/10/product_placements_in_movies_w.php (accessed May 22, 2011).

64. S. Newman, "Michael Vick Needs to Score PR Victory, Experts Say," npr.org website, May 20, 2009, www.npr.org/templates/story/story.php?storyId=104346013 (accessed May 22, 2011).

65. Newman, 2009.

66. D. Hamilton, "How Drug Reps Do That Thing They Do," *Venture Beat,* April 23, 2007, www.venturebeat.com/2007/04/23/how-drug-reps-do-that-thing-they-do/ (accessed May 22, 2011).

67. S. Church and E. Pettersson, "Bristol Myers Doctors in Drug Scheme, California Commissioner Says," March 18, 2011, www.bloomberg.com/news/2011-03-18/bristol-myers-bribed-doctors-in-drug-scheme-california-commissioner-says.html (accessed May 22, 2011).

68. "Buy Online and Reduce Your Carbon Footprint," Creative Citizen website, www.creativecitizen.com/solutions/1181 (accessed May 22, 2011).

69. "Product Lines," Pet Food Express website, www.petfoodexpress.com/products/product-lines/ (accessed August 29, 2011).

70. "Pet Wash," Pet Food Express website, www.petfoodexpress.com/products/pet-wash/ (accessed September 6, 2011).

71. "Who We Are," Pet Food Express website, www.petfoodexpress.com/about/who-we-are/ (accessed August 29, 2011).

72. "Product Lines," Pet Food Express website, 2011.

73. "Awards," Pet Food Express website, www.petfoodexpress.com/about/awards/ (accessed August 29, 2011).

74. "Greening the Supply Chain: Businesses Unlock Hidden Value," atkearney.com website, January 26, 2011, www.atkearney.com/index.php/News-media/greening-the-supply-chain-businesses-unlock-hidden-value.html (accessed May 25, 2011).

75. B. C. Upham, "Are Wal-Mart's Sustainability Efforts Heavy Handed?" July 2, 2010, triplepundit.com website, www.triplepundit.com/2010/07/are-walmarts-sustainability-efforts-unfair-to-suppliers-and-customers/?dhiti=1 (accessed May 25, 2011).

76. Upham, 2010.

77. "Our Work," Environmental Defense Fund website, www.edf.org/page.cfm?tagID=51528 (accessed July 17, 2011).

78. "The Chemical Industry Welcomes Walmart's New Goal to Cut Greenhouse Gas Emissions in Its Supply Chain," icis.com website, May 5, 2010, www.icis.com/Articles/2010/05/10/9356545/walmarts-green-goals-will-impact-chemical-supply-chain.html (accessed May 25, 2011).

79. Upham, "Are Wal-Mart's Sustainability Efforts Heavy Handed?" 2010.

80. Upham, 2010.

81. "The Chemical Industry Welcomes Walmart's New Goal to Cut Greenhouse Gas Emissions in Its Supply Chain," 2010.

82. "Reducing Greenhouse Gas (GHG) Emissions from Our Global Supply Chain," walmart.com annual report, http://walmartstores.com/sites/ResponsibilityReport/2011/environment_products_ReducingGHG.aspx (accessed May 25, 2011).

83. M. Visser, "Reducing Packaging by Concentrating Product," Design-4-sustainability.com, July 12, 2010, www.design-4-sustainability.com/case_studies/13-reducing-packaging-by-concentrating-product (accessed May 25, 2011).

84. Visser, 2010.

85. "2011 Global Responsibility Report," Walmart website, http://walmartstores.com/sites/ResponsibilityReport/2011/environment_products_ReducingGHG.aspx (accessed July 17, 2011).

CHAPTER 15

1. David Leuthold, quoted in A. Loten, "Audits Add Shine to Firms," *Wall Street Journal,* January 13, 2011, p. B5.

2. M. Minnis, "The Value of Financial Statement Verification in Debt Financing: Evidence from Private U.S. Firms," *Journal of Accounting Research,* May 2011 (in press), http://onlinelibrary.wiley.com/doi/10.1111/j.1475-679X.2011.00411.x/abstract (accessed July 9, 2011).

3. Loten, "Audits Add Shine to Firms," 2011.

4. John Rose, quoted in Loten, 2011.

5. B. Levisohn, "How to Make a Madoff," *BusinessWeek,* December 16, 2008, www.businessweek.com/investor/content/dec2008/pi20081215_232943.htm?chan=investing_investing+index+

page_top+stories (accessed July 11, 2011). See also D. Gross, "Membership Has Its Penalties," *Newsweek,* January 12, 2009, p. 18; and M. Hosenball, "Made Money with Madoff? Don't Count on Keeping It," *Newsweek,* January 12, 2009, p. 9.

6. F. Norris, "Victims Who Deserve Their Fate," *New York Times,* February 11, 2011, pp. B1, B6.

7. D. B. Henriques, "Madoff Says from Prison That Banks 'Had to Know,'" *New York Times,* February 16, 2011, pp. B1, B5.

8. Henriques, 2011.

9. S. Gandel, "The Madoff Fraud: How Culpable Were the Auditors?" *Time,* December 17, 2008, www.time.com/time/business/article/0,8599,1867092,00.html (accessed July 11, 2011).

10. Christopher Wells, quoted in Gandel, 2008.

11. See, for example, AllBusiness.com, "Keep Track of Accounts Receivable to Keep Business on an Even Keel," *San Francisco Chronicle,* July 18, 2007, p. C4; and R. D. Hershey Jr., "For Entrepreneurs, a Crash Course in Accounting," *New York Times,* December 11, 2007, sec. 3, p. 11.

12. S. Thurm, "Now, It's Business by Data, but Numbers Still Can't Tell Future," *Wall Street Journal,* July 23, 2007, p. B1.

13. J. Case, *The Open-Book Experience: Lessons from over 100 Companies Who Successfully Transformed Themselves* (New York: Basic Books, 1998).

14. T. Howard, "Experts: Admission Could Have Aided Andersen," *USA Today,* March 29, 2002, p. 1B.

15. G. L. Dodaro, "30 Steps to Better Government," *New York Times,* February 16, 2011, p. A23.

16. S. Freeman, "How Forensic Accounting Works," *How Stuff Works,* http://science.howstuffworks.com/forensic-accounting2.htm (accessed July 11, 2011).

17. S. Ward, "Top 5 Accounting Software for Small Business," *About.com,* 2008, http://sbinfocanada.about.com/od/accountin1/tp/accountsoft.htm (accessed July 11, 2011).

18. T. Gray, "Tasting 3 Flavors of Software," *New York Times,* February 13, 2011, Business section, p. 11.

19. J. M. Rosenberg, "Choosing the Right CPA Is a Big Decision," *San Francisco Chronicle,* January 17, 2007, p. C4.

20. F. Norris, "U.S. Moves Step Closer to Universal Accounting," *New York Times,* August 28, 2008, p. C3.

21. Based on "Double Entry Bookkeeping," *QuickMBA.com,* © 1999–2010, www.quickmba.com/accounting/fin/double-entry (accessed July 11, 2011).

22. M. Press, "How to Read an Annual Report," *EzineArticles.com,* June 15, 2005, http://ezinearticles.com/?How-to-Read-an-Annual -Report&id=43523 (accessed July 11, 2011).

23. J. B. Quinn, "How to Read an Annual Report," http://209.85.173 .104/search?q=cache:R9ULKHK0u9EJ:cc.pkg.msu.edu/How% 2520to%2520read%2520an%2520annual%2520report.pdf+ Jane+Bryant+Quinn,+How+to+Read+an+Annual+Report &hl=en&ct=clnk&cd=1&gl=us (accessed July 11, 2011). See also M. Schiffres, "All the Good News That Fits," *U.S. News & World Report,* April 14, 1986, pp. 50–51.

24. Press, "How to Read an Annual Report," 2005.

25. S. Thurm, "Now, It's Business by Data, but Numbers Still Can't Tell the Future," *Wall Street Journal,* July 23, 2007, http://online .wsj.com/article/SB118514369308274339.html (accessed October 2, 2011).

26. C. Said, "Firm to Give Even More Back," *San Francisco Chronicle,* February 14, 2011, pp. E1, E4.

27. U.S. Securities and Exchange Commission, "Beginners' Guide to Financial Statements," www.sec.gov/investor/pubs/begfinstmt guide.htm (accessed July 11, 2011).

28. "What Is a Bean Counter?" wisegeek.com website, www.wisegeek .com/what-is-a-bean-counter.htm (accessed May 29, 2011).

29. A. Hamilton, "Why Circuit City Busted While Best Buy Boomed," *Time,* November 11, 2008, www.time.com/time/business/article/0,8599,1858079,00.html (accessed May 29, 2011).

30. "About Open Book Accounting," Sabah Karimi, ehow.com web-site, www.ehow.com/about_4571747_open-book-accounting. html (accessed May 29, 2011).

31. J. Van Baren, "Human Asset Accounting," ehow.com website, August 10, 2010, www.ehow.com/list_6825717_human-asset -accounting-methods.html (accessed May 29, 2011).

32. "Route 66 Icon Celebrates Milestone," POPS website, August 4, 2008, www.pops66.com/fileadmin/images/PDFs/BIRTHDAY RELEASE.8.08.pdf (accessed August 28, 2011).

33. "Landmark," POPS website, www.pops66.com (accessed August 29, 2011).

34. "New Route 66 Site Is Bound to Be Pop-ular," www.route66 .com/fileadmin/user_upload/Tulsa_World_7.21.07.pdf (accessed August 27, 2011).

35. "New Route 66 Site Is Bound to Be Pop-ular," 2011.

36. "New Route 66 Site Is Bound to Be Pop-ular," 2011.

37. "New Route 66 Site Is Bound to Be Pop-ular," 2011.

38. "Mother Road Icons Bring Travelers Enjoyment," *Edmond Sun* website, February 2, 2008, www.edmondsun.com/columns/x519225838/Mother-Road-icons-bring-travelers-enjoyment (accessed August 27, 2011).

39. "Accounting the Language of Business," Educating for Success website, www.educatingforsuccess.com/public/department3.cfm (accessed August 28, 2011).

40. "Why Is Accounting Often Referred to as the Language of Busi-ness?" eHow website, www.ehow.com/about_5254886_accounting -referred-language-business.html (accessed August 28, 2011).

41. "Management Accounting and Decision Making," Micro Busi-ness Publication website, www.microbuspub.com/pdfs/chapter2 .pdf (accessed August 28, 2011).

42. "Management Accounting and Decision Making," 2011.

43. "Management Accounting and Decision Making," 2011.

44. L. Munoz, "Hanks Sues over Profit on 'Greek Wedding,'" *Los Angeles Times,* August 8, 2007, http://articles.latimes.com/keyword/gold-circle-films (accessed June 2, 2011).

45. V. Mancini, "Hollywood Accounting Explained," filmdrunk .com website, http://filmdrunk.uproxx.com/2010/07/hollywood -accounting-explained (accessed June 2, 2011).

46. Mancini, 2011.

47. M. Cieply, "Michael Moore Sues Weinsteins over 'Fahrenheit 911,'" *New York Times,* February 7, 2011, http://artsbeat.blogs .nytimes.com/2011/02/07/michael-moore-sues-weinsteins/ (accessed June 3, 2011).

48. Cieply, 2011.

49. J. Hart and P. Hacker, "Less than Zero Studio Accounting Practices in Hollywood," Hollywood Law Cybercenter website, www.hollywoodnetwork.com/Law/Hart/columns/ (accessed June 3, 2011).

50. Hart and Hacker, 2011.

51. G. Susman, "We Call It Martian Accounting," *The Guardian,* August 31, 2001, www.guardian.co.uk/film/2001/aug/31/artsfeatures (accessed June 3, 2011).

CHAPTER 16

1. M. Litchenberger, quoted in E. Maltby, "Entrepreneurs Find Success with Specialty Lenders," *Wall Street Journal,* April 26, 2010, p. B8.

2. Maltby, 2010.

3. M. Cohen, "A Bank Idea, with Ancient Roots, for Helping Small Businesses," *New York Times,* December 24, 2009, p. B5.

4. National Small Business Administration, "Top Ten SBA Lenders for First Quarter 2010," February 2, 2010, www.nsba.biz/content/printer.2845.shtml (accessed July 14, 2011).

5. G. Fabrikant, "Risky Loans Hurt Lender in California," *New York Times,* September 6, 2008, pp. B1, B6.

6. See, for example, N. D. Schwartz and V. Bajaj, "Credit Time Bomb Ticked, but Few Heard," *New York Times,* August 19, 2007, news section, pp. 1, 17; E. Dash and N. D. Schwartz, "Bankers Ignored Signs of Trouble on Foreclosures," *New York Times,* October 14, 2010, pp. A1, A4; and S. Chan, "Financial Crisis Was Avoidable, Inquiry Finds," *New York Times,* January 26, 2011, pp. A1, A3.

7. A. Loten, "Figuring Things Out: Mistakes Start-Ups Make," *Wall Street Journal,* February 24, 2011, p. B4.

8. J. M. Rosenberg, "Small-Business Owners Who Can't Pay Taxes Still Have a Few Options," *San Francisco Chronicle,* March 7, 2007, p. C4.

9. I. DeBare, "Having Big Order May Demand Big Changes in Your Processing," *San Francisco Chronicle,* July 18, 2007, pp. C1, C4.

10. Remo Belli, quoted in M. Lacter, "Remo Belli," *Inc.,* March 2011, pp. 79–80.

11. J. O'Donnell, "Borrowing from Friends, Family?" *USA Today,* September 24, 2010, p. 3B.

12. Eileen Fisher, quoted in L. Welch, "Eileen Fisher: It's Not Always Easy to Keep It Simple," *Inc.,* November 2010, pp. 97–98.

13. E. Maltby, "Saying No to Plastic's Fees," *Wall Street Journal,* August 19, 2010, p. B5.

14. A. Barrett, "Robin Sauve Picked Up the Pieces of Her Employer's Failed Logistics Company. Could Her Bid to Relaunch the Business Backfire?" *Inc.,* March 2011, pp. 51–53.

15. AllBusiness.com, "Don't Borrow Trouble When Applying for a Business Loan," *San Francisco Chronicle,* August 22, 2007, p. C5.

16. A. Zipkin, "Making a Business of Family Loans," *New York Times,* September 6, 2008, p. B2.

17. P. Renton, "The Demise of Virgin Money US," *Social Lending Network,* November 24, 2010, www.sociallending.net/direct-p2p/the-demise-of-virgin-money-us (accessed July 14, 2011).

18. B. Baker, "Fan-Funding and Donation Sites: 9 Ways to Raise Money for Your Next Music Project," *Music Think Tank,* www.musicthinktank.com/blog/fan-funding-donation-sites-9-ways-to-raise-money-for-your-ne.html (accessed July 14, 2011).

19. I. Lapowsky, "A Good Fit: When Banks Won't Lend, Customers Try Customer Financing," *Inc.,* November 2010, pp. 31–32.

20. Lapowsky, 2010.

21. C. Richards, "Investing with the Herd," *New York Times,* January 22, 2011, p. B5.

22. M. Meece, "The Cash-Strapped Turn to Barter," *New York Times,* November 13, 2008, pp. F1, F4. See also B. Mattox, "Salon Lets Clients Barter for Services," *Reno Gazette-Journal,* September 23, 2010, pp. 7A, 8A, reprinted from the *Arizona Republic.*

23. C. M. Bradley and L. Shibut, "The Liability Structure of FDIC-Insured Institutions: Changes and Implications," *FDIC Banking Review,* Vol. 18, No. 2 (2006), www.fdic.gov/bank/analytical/banking/2006sep/article1/article1.pdf (accessed July 14, 2011). See also "Loopholes Swallow Bank $ Reserve Requirements," *Sidetalk,* February 2, 2008, http://acheson.wordpress.com/2008/02/02/loopholes-swallow-bank-reserve-requirements (accessed July 14, 2011).

24. K. Blumenthal, "The Holdup at Online Banks," *Wall Street Journal,* October 22, 2008, p. D3.

25. P. Svensson, "Tickets, Contacts among Tap-to-Pay Phone Uses," *Reno Gazette-Journal,* February 27, 2011, p. 5E. See also P. Eichenbaum and M. Collins, "Smart Phones May Threaten Credit Cards," *San Francisco Chronicle,* August 3, 2010, p. D3;

and J. Temple, "Google CEO Sees Phones Replacing Credit Cards," *San Francisco Chronicle,* November 16, 2010, pp. D1, D6.

26. J. S. Gordon, "A Short Banking History of the United States," *Wall Street Journal,* October 10, 2008, p. A17.

27. Federal Reserve Statistical Release, *Large Commercial Banks,* September 30, 2010, www.federalreserve.gov/releases/lbr/current/default.htm (accessed July 14, 2011).

28. Michael Poulos, quoted in D. Enrich, "Banks Wage a Rate War to Attract Depositors," *Wall Street Journal,* November 14, 2008, pp. A1, A14.

29. A. Martin and R. Lieber, "Alternative to Banks, Now Playing Offense," *New York Times,* June 12, 2010, pp. B1, B5.

30. R. Kuttner, the *Boston Globe,* described in "It's Time to Make Banking Simple Again," *The Week,* October 24, 2008, p. 38.

31. A. Geller, "Lessons to Be Learned from Great Depression," *San Francisco Chronicle,* October 5, 2008, p. C5.

32. R. Wiles, "When Banks Fail, Uninsured Deposit Losses Can Vary Widely," *Reno Gazette-Journal,* September 20, 2008, p. 8A. See also M. Gordon, "FDIC to Double Bank Premiums to Replenish Diminished Reserves," *San Francisco Chronicle,* October 8, 2008, p. C5.

33. S. Block, "If Your Cash Is FDIC Insured, You Can Relax," *USA Today,* September 30, 2008, p. 3B.

34. C. Said, "Learning the Hard Way about FDIC Insurance," *San Francisco Chronicle,* October 12, 2008, pp. D1, D5.

35. C. Said, "The Great Depression—How Close Are We?" *San Francisco Chronicle,* October 20, 2008, pp. A1, A8, A9.

36. Gordon, "FDIC to Double Bank Premiums to Replenish Diminished Reserves," 2008.

37. E. Lipson and S. Labaton, "A Deregulator Looks Back, Unswayed," *New York Times,* November 17, 2008, pp. A1, A12.

38. S. Labaton, "Agency's '04 Rule Let Banks Pile Up New Debt, and Risk," *New York Times,* October 3, 2008, pp. A1, A23.

39. T. Cowen, "Three Trends and a Train Wreck," *New York Times,* October 19, 2008, Business section, p. 6.

40. "Wall Street's Hidden Time Bombs," *The Week,* October 10, 2008, p. 11; and J. Hidalgo, "The 4 Horsemen of the Financial Apocalypse," *Reno Gazette-Journal,* October 12, 2008, pp. 9A, 10A.

41. L. Gomes, "Computing Our Way into the Collapse," *Forbes,* November 17, 2008, p. 44.

42. D. Akst, "Expensive Mistakes," *Wall Street Journal,* September 24, 2008, p. A27.

43. Lawrence Krzanowski, quoted in "What Goes Up Must Come Down," *The Week,* October 31, 2008, p. 14.

44. J. Waggoner and D. J. Lynch, "Red Flags in Bear Stearns' Collapse," *USA Today,* March 19, 2008, www.usatoday.com/money/industries/banking/2008-03-17-bear-stearns-bailout_N.htm (accessed July 14, 2011).

45. "A Wild Week Transforms Wall Street," *The Week,* September 26, 2008, p. 4.

46. D. J. Lynch, "World Markets Fall as U.S. Ills Spread," *USA Today,* October 7, 2008, pp. 1B, 2B.

47. N. D. Schwartz, "U.S. Missteps Are Evident, but Europe Is Implicated," *New York Times,* October 13, 2008, pp. B1, B8.

48. M. Fackler, "Trouble without Borders," *New York Times,* October 24, 2008, pp. B1, B4.

49. N. Pender, "Europe Is Following U.S. Tactic of Aid for Credit Institutions at Risk," *San Francisco Chronicle,* October 7, 2008, pp. A1, A12.

50. David M. Smick, quoted in "Book of the Week," *The Week,* October 24, 2008, p. 22, in review of Smick's *The World Is Curved: Hidden Dangers to the Global Economy.*

51. R. J. Samuelson, "The Great Confidence Game," *Newsweek,* September 29, 2008, p. 31.

52. Paul Slovic, quoted in J. Nocera, "Swept Up by Insanity of Markets," *New York Times,* October 11, 2008, pp. B1, B8.

53. Robert Shiller, quoted in Nocera, 2008.

54. Nocera, 2008.

55. "Code of Ethics for Financial Executives," Walgreen Co., www .files.shareholder.com/downloads/WAG/1331474338x0x 145598/33b1a553-fad2-46c2-94f1-e0272e1a40b9/sfo_ethics .pdf (accessed July 20, 2011).

56. S. Algar, "Plastic's Now off the Menu," *New York Post,* August 16, 2010, www.nypost.com/p/news/local/plastic_now_ off_the_menu_MysBpYobRgR3wD1fvCv0WO (accessed June 4, 2011).

57. "How Banks Work," www.money.howstuffworks.com/personal -finance/banking/bank4.htm (accessed August 27, 2011); "Reserve Requirements," Federal Reserve website, www.federal reserve.gov/monetarypolicy/reservereq.htm (accessed August 30, 2011).

58. "How Banks Work," 2001; and "Reserve Requirements," 2011.

59. L. Moyer, "How to Pick the Best Bank," January 16, 2010, www .forbes.com/2010/01/16/banking-fees-fdic-business-wall-street -banks.html (accessed August 27, 2011).

60. "Money Supply," Reference for Business website, www.reference forbusiness.com/encyclopedia/Mor-Off/Money-Supply.html (accessed August 30, 2011).

61. "Alternative Currencies/Barter Systems," New Earth Cyber School website, http://newearthcyberschool.com/node/25 (accessed August 27, 2011).

62. T. Ray, "TARP: Mixed Success, Hugely Unpopular," *Barron's,* September 16, 2010, http://blogs.barrons.com/stockstowatch today/2010/09/16/tarp-mixed-success-hugely-unpopular/ (accessed August 27, 2011).

63. J. Seidell, "Rich and Poor Pawn for Cash; Shops Provide Alternative to Bank Loans, Credit," *Seattle Times,* May 2, 2010, www .seattletimes.nwsource.com/html/living/2011749726_pawn shop03.html (accessed June 7, 2011).

64. "Pawning," Something Awful forums, www.forums.something awful.com/showthread.php?threadid=3235228 (accessed July 21, 2011).

65. "Pawning," 2011.

66. Seidell, "Rich and Poor Pawn for Cash; Shops Provide Alternative to Bank Loans, Credit," 2010.

67. Fields, "Plan B Borrowing," *Wall Street Journal,* March 2009, www.wsjclassroom.com/cre/articles/09mar_natl_pawnshop.htm (accessed June 6, 2011).

68. T. McMahan, "Taking Stock of Being in Hock," *Wall Street Journal,* May 7, 2010, www.pawnonomics.com/tag/wall-street -journal/ (accessed June 8, 2011).

69. G. Hoffman, "Pawnbroking—The Oldest Credit Business in the World," moneymuseum.com, www.moneymuseum.com/ moneymuseum/library/texts/text.jsp?lang=en&pid=349&i=3 (accessed June 7, 2011).

70. "Pawnbroking Industry Overview: Meeting the Needs of America's Working Families," National Pawnbrokers website, www.assets.nationalpawnbrokers.org/2010/10/Industry-Over view-7-7-09.pdf (accessed June 7, 2011).

71. "Pawnbroking Industry Overview: Meeting the Needs of America's Working Families," 2011.

72. M. Orndorff, "Pawn Shops Fret New Regulations, Donate to New Rep, Spencer Bachus," *Birmingham News,* April 22, 2010, www.blog.al.com/spotnews/2010/04/pawn_shops_fret_new_ regulation.html (accessed June 6, 2011).

73. G. Rivlin, "It's a Hot Time to Be a Pawn Star," *Newsweek,* June 19, 2011, www.newsweek.com/2011/06/19/it-s-a-hot-time -to-be-a-pawn-star.html (accessed July 19, 2011).

74. "Pawn Stars—New Episodes," History Channel website, www .history.com/shows/pawn-stars/articles/about-pawn-stars (accessed June 7, 2011).

75. "Living without a Bank Account," Corporation for Enterprise Development website, www.blogs.cfed.org/cfed_news_clips/2010/ 10/living-without-a-bank-account.html (accessed June 10, 2011).

CHAPTER 17

1. J. Schonberger, "Parnassus Small-Cap Fund Blends Ethics with Success," *Kiplinger.com,* November 24, 2010, www.kiplinger .com/columns/fundwatch/archive/parnassus-small-cap-fund- blends-ethics-with-success.html (accessed July 15, 2011). © 2010 The Kiplinger Washington Editors Inc. All rights reserved.

2. "Parnassus Small Cap Fund," *Best Mutual Funds, U.S. News,* February 3, 2011, http://money.usnews.com/funds/parnassus -small-cap-fund/parsx (accessed March 3, 2011).

3. "Parnassus Small Cap," *Morningstar,* March 3, 2011, http:// quote.morningstar.com/fund/f.aspx?t=PARSX (accessed July 15, 2011).

4. Benzinga staff, "Dubious Chinese Companies in America," *Benzinga,* December 21, 2010, www.benzinga.com/trading -ideas/short-ideas/10/12/720853/dubious-chinese-companies-in -america-zstn-rino-cvvt-liwa (accessed July 15, 2011).

5. G. Weiss, "China Small Caps Are Ridiculously Risky," *The Street,* February 10, 2011, www.businessinsider.com/with-china -small-caps-its-shorts-vs-auditors-2011-2 (accessed July 15, 2011).

6. A. Markels, "Built to Make Billions?" *U.S. News & World Report,* August 6, 2007, pp. 51–52. See also A. Markels, "How to Make Money the Buffett Way," *U.S. News & World Report,* August 6, 2007, pp. 46–51.

7. "The World's Billionaires: #3 Warren Buffett," *Forbes.com,* March 10, 2010, www.forbes.com/lists/2010/10/billionaires-2010_Warren -Buffett_C0R3.html (accessed July 15, 2011).

8. Markels, "Built to Make Billions?" 2007.

9. J. M. Coates and J. Herbert, "Endogenous Steroids and Financial Risk Taking on a London Trading Floor," *Proceedings of the National Academy of Sciences of the USA 105*(16): 6167–6172. See also J. H. Dobrzynski, "Maybe the Meltdown's a Guy Thing," *New York Times,* November 16, 2008, Week in Review section, p. 5.

10. L. DiCosmo, "Warren Buffett Invests Like a Girl," *Motley Fool,* March 20, 2008, www.fool.com/investing/value/2008/03/20/ warren-buffett-invests-like-a-girl.aspx (accessed July 15, 2011).

11. D. Mitchell, "At Last, Buffett's Key to Success," *New York Times,* April 5, 2008, p. B5. See also J. Clements, "He Invests, She Invests: Who Gets the Better Returns?" *Wall Street Journal,* February 6, 2008, p. D1.

12. B. M. Barber and T. Odean, "Boys Will Be Boys: Gender, Overconfidence, and Common Stock Investment," *Quarterly Journal of Economics,* February 2001, pp. 261–292, http://faculty.haas .berkeley.edu/odean/papers/gender/BoysWillBeBoys.pdf (accessed July 15, 2011).

13. B. Sisario, "Investors Are Drawn Anew to Digital Music," *New York Times,* March 11, 2011, pp. B1, B2.

14. J. Swartz, "Tech Start-Ups Not Eager for IPOs," *USA Today,* October 29, 2010, pp. 1B, 2B.

15. A. Shell, "How Crazy Is a No-Stock Portfolio?" *USA Today,* January 14, 2011, p. 3B.

16. A. Taylor, "Credit Raters Admit They Succumbed to Pressure," *San Francisco Chronicle,* October 23, 2008, p. C3; J. Surowiecki, "Greasing the Slide," *New Yorker,* November 3, 2008,

p. 50; G. Morgenson and L. Story, "Rating Agencies Shared Data, and Wall St. Seized Advantage," *New York Times,* April 24, 2010, pp. A1, A9; H. Dixon and C. Swann, "Ratings Agencies Are Overrated," *New York Times,* April 29, 2010, p. B2; P. Wiseman, "Buffett Comes to Defense of Credit-Rating Agencies," *USA Today,* June 3, 2010, p. 1B; and G. Morgenson, "BB? AAA? Disclosure Tells Us More," *New York Times,* September 5, 2010, Business section, pp. 1, 2.

17. Christopher Shays, quoted in P. Gogoi, "Credit Raters' Judgment Questioned," *USA Today,* October 23, 2008, p. 3B.

18. R. Beales, A. T. Crane, and R. Cox, "Rating Agencies Still Influential," *New York Times,* February 2, 2011, p. B2.

19. E. Petroff, "Callable Bonds Lead a Double Life," *Forbes,* May 29, 2007, www.forbes.com/investoreducation/2007/05/29/callable-bonds-pf-education-in_ep_0529investopedia_inl.html (accessed July 15, 2011).

20. L. G. Crovitz, "Exporting Wall Street," *Wall Street Journal,* February 28, 2011, p. A17.

21. C. Kowalski, "Top Reasons Why Commodity Traders Lose Money," *About.com,* http://commodities.about.com/od/gettingstarted/a/commoditylosses.htm (accessed July 15, 2011).

22. J. Waggoner, "How Rational Is Stock Market?" *USA Today,* February 15, 2011, pp. 1B, 2B.

23. K. D. Daniel, D. Hirshleifer, and A. Subrahmanyam, "Investor Psychology and Security Market Under- and Over-Reactions," *Journal of Finance* 53:6(1998), pp. 1839–1886.

24. Study by Jon Lukomnik for IRRC Institute, reported in J. Zweig, "High Trading Is Bad News for Investors," *Wall Street Journal,* February 13, 2010, http://online.wsj.com/article/SB1000142405 2748704337004575059960489864970.html (accessed July 15, 2011).

25. Waggoner, "How Rational Is Stock Market?" 2011.

26. Based on data from Morgan Stanley, reported in A. Shell, "How Crazy Is a No-Stock Portfolio?" *USA Today,* January 14, 2011, p. 3B.

27. "Introduction to Socially Responsible Investing," Social Funds website, www.socialfunds.com/page.cgi/article1.html (accessed June 12, 2011); and "The Benefit of Socially Responsible Investing," *U.S. News* website, July 8, 2009, www.money.usnews .com/money/blogs/alpha-consumer/2009/07/08/the-benefits-of -socially-responsible-investing (accessed June 13, 2011).

28. J. Unger, "Can Monkeys Pick Stocks Better than Experts?" Automatic Finances website, August 17, 2009, www.automatic finances.com/monkey-stock-picking/ (accessed June 13, 2011).

29. Unger, 2009.

30. "Our Philosophy—A Tactical Approach," Capital Advisors website, www.capitaladv.com/philosophy.html (accessed August 23, 2011).

31. "Our Philosophy—A Tactical Approach," 2011.

32. "Putting It All Together," Capital Advisors website, www.capitaladv .com/putting_it_all_together.html (accessed August 21, 2011).

33. M. Kolakowski, "Financial Assets," About.com website, www .financecareers.about.com/od/glossary/g/finassets.htm (accessed August 21, 2011).

34. "Day Trading," Encyclopedia.com, www.encyclopedia.com/topic/Day_trading.aspx (accessed June 14, 2011).

35. R. Heakal, "What Is Market Efficiency?" Investopedia.com, www .investopedia.com/articles/02/101502.asp#axzz1SrFWV17N (accessed July 22, 2011).

36. A. Keown, *Personal Finance Turning Money into Wealth* (Upper Saddle River, NJ: Prentice Hall, 2010), p. 375.

37. "Day Trading," 2011.

38. "Currency Day Trading," Forexmastercourse.com, www.forex mastercourse.com/currency-trading-information/currency-day -trading_4.html (accessed June 17, 2011).

39. "Day Trading," 2011.

40. D. Barboza, "Day Trading Still Alive, Outsourced to China," *New York Times,* December 9, 2010, www.nytimes.com/2010/12/10/business/global/10daytrade.html?scp=1&sq=%22day%20trading%22&st=cse (accessed June 14, 2011).

41. "Day Trading: Your Dollars at Risk," Securities and Exchange Commission website, www.sec.gov/investor/pubs/daytips.htm (accessed June 18, 2011).

Name, Organization, & Brand Index

Page references with "n" refer to endnotes cited by number.

Closets By Design, 145
Club Watt, 277
CNN, 103
CNN.com, 233
Coates, J. M., 530n9
Cobb, D., 142n48
Coca-Cola, 36, 41, 146, 156, 250, 305, 380, 385, 420, 423, 530, 546
"Cocoa," 95n78
Cogan, D., 48n54
Cohen, M., 489n3
Cohen, W. S., 112n53
Coke, 36, 128, 380
Coldwell Banker, 426
Coleman, G., 368n33
Colgate, 400
College Hunks Hauling Junk, 144
College Student Report, 38n21
Collier, V., 52n82
Collins, Jim, 226–228, 226nn7–9, 231n15, 232n20, 244, 248
Collins, M., 510n25
Colvin, G., 340n98, 344n104
Combings, L. B., 334n81
Comcast, 228
Comet Skateboards, 47
Comfort Company, 136
Community Owned Mercantile Project Inc., 143
Companion Global Healthcare, 129
Company Corporation, The, 141n22
Compass Diversified Holdings, 169
Complaints.com, 377
Computer Associates, 467
Con Edison, 75
ConAgra Foods, 50
CondéNet, 265
Cone Communications, 50n68
Conley, Chip, 292, 292n20, 348–349, 348n111, 349nn112–113
Conlin, M., 58nn104–105, 328n51
Connell, J., 395n25
Connolly, C., 315n6
Conoco, 104
Consumer Capital Partners, 412
Consumer Reports, 203, 402
Consumerist, The, 17
ConsumerReports.org., 203n25
Contractor South Mountain Company, 192
Coors, 402
Coors Light, 402
Cordaro, Frank, 339, 339n93
CorelCAD, 263
Corkery, M., 104n31
Cornell University, 408
Cornish, Edward, 226, 226n5
Corporate Social Responsibility, 44n39
Corporation for Enterprise Development, 525n75
Costco, 316, 408, 425, 426, 427
Costco Wholesale, 315
"Costco Wholesale Salaries," 315n1
Costello, D., 194n12
Cottle, M., 333nn77–78
Coulter, M., 274n28

Council of Economic Advisors, 87
Courvoisier, 379–380
Cover Girl, 368
Cowen, T., 318n39
Cowles, C., 381nn56–57
Cox, R., 537n18
Coy, P., 78n34, 78n35
CPC International/Best Foods, 99
Craftsman, 399
Craft, 327
Craigslist, 188, 324, 359
Crane, A. T., 537n18
Crary, D., 22n55
Crawford, Fred, 203
Creative Citizen, 455n68
Credle, Susan, 381
CREDO Mobile, 47
Crenson, M., 53n86
Croasdell, D., 101n20
Crockett, R. O., 227n10, 255n1
Cronin, M. P., 330n64
Cross, Rob, 249, 250n38
Crossen, C., 289n16
Crovitz, L. Gordon, 542, 542n29
Crow, Sheryl, 364
Crowe, Russell, 61
Crowley, K., 233n27
Crown, J., 368n33
Crown Prince Abdullah of Saudi Arabia, 115
Cruise Planners, 148
Crutchfield, Dean, 381
CSA movement, 502
Cui, C., 95n86
Culbert, S. A., 334nn82–83
Cupidtino, 411
Cupidtino.com website, 411n52
"Currency Day Trading," 555n38
Currier, James, 172
Curves, 110
Cyran, R., 353n5

D

Daft, R. L., 211n42
Dahl, Dave, 231, 231n16, 233n21
Dahl, Glenn, 231
Dahle, C., 46n45, 328n51, 333n77
Dallinger, D., 306n41
Dalzell, F., 318n15
Damato, Gina, 357
Daniel, K. D., 550n23
Danko, William, 9–10, 9nn13–15
Das, A., 161n11
Das, Sanjiv, 40
Dasani, 128
Dash, E., 489n6
Dave Matthews Band, 364
Dave, Ted, 27
Dave's Killer Bread, 231
Davidson, P., 181n74
Davie, S., 221n57
Davison, W., 49n63
Dawson, C., 203n25
De Avila, J., 325n29

De Beers Diamonds, 92
De Vany, A., 61n7
Deal, Christian, 306
Deal, John, 81, 81n43
Deal, Josiane, 306
Dean, C., 18n32
Dean Witter, 544
Dean Witter Reynolds, 444
DeBare, Ilana, 139, 139n17, 140n19, 420, 420n9, 495n9
DeBarros, A., 255n4
Decipher, Inc., 162nn12–13, 164n20
Def Jam Records, 379
Delaney, K. J., 443n43
del.icio.us, 385
Dell Computer, 49, 377, 420, 542
Dell Inc., 225
Dell, Michael, 225
della Cava, M. R., 292n19
Deloitte Touche, 465
Delta, 74
Demarzio, P., 153n49
Deming, W. Edwards, 274–275
Dempsey, B., 172n51
Denny's, 144, 148
Deparle, J., 22n59
Department of Motor Vehicles, 115
Depp, Johnny, 61
DeskJet, 407
Deutsch, C. H., 51n79, 277n33
Deutsche Boerse, 541
Deutschman, A., 193n7, 194n10
DeVany, Arthur, 61
Development Dimensions International survey, 331n66, 333n76
DHL, 440
DHL Express, 17
Diamond Motors, 409
DiCaprio, Leonardo, 61
Dick, K., 18n33
DiCosmo, LouAnn, 530, 530n10
Diehard, 399
Dienst, Daniel, 257
Dimension One Spas, 166
DiStefano, J. N., 99n6
Dixon, H., 537n16
Dizik, A., 288n11, 288n13
DKNY, 450
Dobrzynski, J. H., 530n9
DocBase Direct, 276
Dockery, D. W., 62n10
Dodaro, Gene, 466, 466n15
Dodson, Jerome, 529
Dogandkennel.com, 311n70
Dogster, 312
Dokoupil, T., 38n17
Dolan, M., 255n3
Dolce & Gabbana, 440
Dollar Stores, 408, 427
Dollar Tree, 427
Dominick's, 157
Domino's Pizza, 17, 110, 157–158
Domino's website, 158n62
Donahue, B., 231n16
DoodyCalls, 145, 147, 147n30

U.S. Small Business Administration, 168n33
U.S. Treasury Department, 89, 355, 505, 509
U.S. Treasury securities, 532, 535, 552
U.S. Weekly, 206
USA Today, 33, 50nn72–73, 99, 157n52, 516
USM. *See* United Scrap Metal
UTC Fire & Security, 241
UTC Power, 241

V

Vaidyanathan, G., 198n20
Valspar, 373–374
Van Baren, J., 484n31
van Bever, D., 367n30
van der Rohe, Ludwig Mies, 385
Vance, A., 41n32, 191n4, 225n4, 353n1
Vanguard, 547
Vara, V., 161n2, 443n43
Varian, H. R., 85n53
Vascellaro, J. E., 29n80, 29n81
Vaughn, A., 84n49
Vault Career Services, 251
Vauxhall Motors, 113
Vega, T., 430n17
Velasquez, M., 348n110
Velcro, 390
Velocity Micro, 421
Vergano, D., 53n87
Verhoeven, Paul, 61
Verizon, 354, 397, 407
Vermont Maple Syrup, 402
Verry, S., 367n30
Verschoor, C. C., 50n71
Veterans Administration, 246
Viacom, 133
Viagra, 92
Vice Busting Diet, 381n55
Victoria's Secret, 427
Vidal, Susana Martinez, 377n46
VietinBank. *See* Vietnam Bank for Industry
    and Trade
Vietnam Bank for Industry and Trade
    (VietinBank), 510
Villlano, M., 339nn94–95, 97
Vinokur, A. D., 84n48
Virgin Group, 502
Virgin Money USA, 502
Visa, 78, 393, 399, 498
Visser, M., 457nn83–84
Vista, 191
VistaPrint, 172
Vitale, Guy, 258
Vitello, P., 394n24
Volkswagen, 104, 129, 203
Volpp, Kevin, 300n32
Volvo, 102
Voydanoff, P., 84n49
Vranica, S., 377n46, 443n43
Vroom, Victor, 299, 299n31

W

Waber, R. L., 361n22
Waggoner, Jason, 418n44, 550, 550n22,
    550n25

Waggoner, Rick, 540
Wakabayashi, D., 255n2
Waksal, Sam, 37
Wald, L., 107n40
Walgreen Co., 427, 522, 522n55
Walker, J., 326n39
Walker, M. A., 38n21, 431n19
Walker, Rob, 450n57
Wall Drug, 437
Wall Street Journal, 33, 65, 99, 191n4,
    245n32, 342, 381, 393, 413, 449, 489,
    490, 525n67, 542, 546, 554
"Wall Street's Hidden Time Bombs," 518n40
Walmart, 3, 51, 103, 128, 142, 270, 315,
    316, 349, 377, 380, 404, 408, 413,
    417, 427, 457, 495, 541
Walmart Supercenters, 427
Walmart.com, 16, 457n82, 457n85
Walsh, B., 53n92, 430n18
Walt Disney Company, 156, 191, 226, 306,
    368, 546
Ward, S., 467n17
Warhol, Andy, 211
Warnakulasooriya, R., 38n24
Warner Bros., 133
Warner, F., 333n77
Warner Lambert, 156
Warner Music Group, 364
Wartzman, R., 116n70
Washington, Booker T., 27
Washington, Denzel, 486
Washington, George, 77
Washington Mutual, Wachovia, 511, 518
Waste Management Inc. (WMI), 133–134
Watkins, Sharron, 20
Watson, T., 430n17
Watts, S., 52n83, 197n15
Waxman, Henry, 79n38
Waxman, S., 154n51
Wayne, L., 33n3, 37n15
Wayne, T., 326n32
Webber, A. M., 162n15
Weber, Larry, 325, 325n31
Weblistic, 443
WebVisible, 443
Weeks, Holly, 307, 307n57
Wegmans Food Markets, 317
Wei-Skillern, J., 47n50
Weinberg, N., 33n1
Weiner, Russell, 157
Weinstein brothers, 486
Weisman, J., 53n89
Weiss, G., 529n5
Welch, D., 203n25, 263n16
Welch, Jack, 82, 250
Welch, L., 497n12
Welch, W. M., 40n29, 328n69
Wells, Christopher, 461n10
Wells Fargo, 20–21, 31, 393, 398, 498,
    509, 510
Wells, John, 11
Wendy's, 74, 146
Wesabe, 385
Wesleyan University, 100

Wessel, D., 111n45, 111n48
West Edmonton Mall, 428
Westcott, S., 285n4
Western Electric, 290
Western Reserve University, 177
Westin, 290
Wharton School, 134
Wheaties, 398, 402
Wheaton, 400
White, A., 53n88
White Castle, 74
White Dog Café, 46, 175
White, E., 306n46
Whitelaw, K., 27n68
Whitney, Eli, 261
Whitney, L., 211n44
Whole Foods Market, 151, 215, 427
Whopper, 74
"Why Tattoos and Piercings Cause
    Discrimination in the Workplace,"
    349n118
Wicks, J., 46n47
Wicks, Judy, 46, 175, 176n59
WikiLoan, 502
Wikipedia, 221, 329
Wild Oats Market, 151
Wild Planet Entertainment, 187
Wild Planet Toys, 187
Wild Planet Toys website, 187nn85–89
Wiles, R., 516n32
Wilkinson, A. M., 250n39
Williams, B. K., 3n2, 15n18, 101n16,
    122n82, 167n31, 211n42, 215n55,
    231n16, 233n22, 274n28, 288n15,
    298n30, 304n38, 315n10, 334n81
Williams, Tom, 102n22, 349
Willliams-Sonoma, 427
Willow Garage, 281
Wilpon, Fred, 461
Wilshire 500, 544, 546, 553
WIND (Wednesday Is Networking Day), 84
Windows 7, 191, 353
Windows Mobile, 191, 353
Windows Phone 7, 353
Winfrey, Oprah, 57–58, 164
Wingfield, N., 191n4, 353nn4, 8, 368n31
Winn-Dixie, 427
Winograd, M., 54n95
Winstein, K. J., 328n47
Winston, S., 84n49
Wirthlin Worldwide, 49n62, 59n66
Wise, Ouidad, 364
Wisegeek.com, 484n28
Wiseman, P., 537n16
Witherspoon, Reese, 61
W.L. Gore & Associates, 305
WMI. *See* Waste Management Inc.
Wokai, 47
Wolf, R., 22n59
Wolfe, Kyle, 280
Wolfert, Paula, 164n19
Womack, James P., 255n6
Women's Initiative for
    Self-Employment, 182

SUBJECT INDEX

Key terms/glossary terms are **bolded**.

Automation, 262, 278
Autonomy, 295

B

B corporations ("benefit corporations"), 134, 140–141
B2B market. *See* Business-to-business (B2B) market
B2C market. *See* Business-to-consumer (B2C) market
Baby boomers, 27
    marketing technology to, 356
Bad Sports: How Owners Are Ruining the Games We Love (Zirin), 158
Bahamas, 110
Bailout money, 39
Balance, between life and work, 304
Balance of payments, 106, 108, 126
Balance-of-payments deficit, 108
Balance-of-payments surplus, 108
Balance of trade, 106, 108–109, 126
Balance sheets, 460, 471, 472–475, 483
Balanced books, 470
Bank fees, 513, 521
Bank runs, 516
Banking system, 511–516
    commercial banks, 511–513, 521
    credit unions, 511, 513, 521
    investment banks, 511, 515, 521
    money protection governmental agencies, 511, 515–516, 521
    nonbanks, 511, 514–515, 521
    savings institutions, 511, 513, 521
Bankruptcy, 3, 203, 227, 519, 534
Banks, 181, 498
    offshore, 34
    types of, 524
    See also Banking system; Commercial banks
Bar codes, 432
Barbershop (film), 61
Bargain retailers, 427
Barriers to trade, 122–123, 127
    See also Trade protectionism
BARS. *See* Behavioral anchored rating scale
Bartering for goods and services (countertrading), 108–109, 172, 181, 503
Base pay, 340, 347
Basic Instinct (film), 61
Basic Instinct 2 (film), 61
Batman movies, 61
Bear market, 551
Bed and breakfasts, 183
Beer producers, 176
Beer promotion, 450
Behaving badly, 37
Behaving well, 37
Behavior modification, 289, 298–299, 309
    See also Reinforcement theory (Thorndike & Skinner)
Behavioral anchored rating scale (BARS), 336
Behavioral appraisals, 336
Behavioral-description interviews, 330
    See also Structured interviews

Behavioral economics, 78
Behaviors
    consumer buying, 359–361
    motivation and, 286–287
    See also Consumer buying behavior
Being nice, 306
Belgium, 67, 69
Beliefs, 35
    buying decisions and, 361
Believability, 300
Bell curve, for performance appraisals, 337, 347
Benchmarking, 275
Benefit segmentation, 362, 364, 378
Benefits, 8, 25, 293, 297, 315, 340–341, 347
    legally required, 341
    legislation affecting, 319, 320
    nonmonetary, 304–307, 340–341, 347
    orientation and, 332
    See also Compensation; Nonmonetary motivation methods; Perks
"Best Companies to Work For" (*Fortune*), 286
Biases, 197
    performance appraisals and, 330, 335
Bicycles, 368
Big Board, 541
Big-box retailers, 457
Big Four international accounting and professional services, 465
Bill of materials, 271
Bill payments, 491
Billing, fraudulent, 49
Billionaires, young, 9
Birth rates, high in less-developed countries, 117–118
Black markets, 64
Blair Witch Project, The (film), 61
Blended value, 32, 44, 46
Blogging services, inexpensive, 172
Blogs
    advertising and, 443
    for customer feedback, 377
Blue-chip stocks, 551
BND. *See* Buy Nothing Day
Board of directors, 153
Board of Governors (Fed), 506
Body art lawsuit, 349–350
Body movements, 115
Body piercings, 349–350
Body work shop, 268
Bolivia, Mercosur and, 125
Bond ratings, 536–537, 552
Bonds, 528, 534, 535–538, 552
    advantages and disadvantages of issuing bonds vs. stocks, 538
    callable, 537, 552
    convertible, 538, 552
    corporate, 535, 552
    for debt financing, 500, 520
    government, 535, 552
    mortgage pass-through securities, 536–537, 552
    municipal, 535, 552
    ratings for, 536–537, 552

serial, 537, 552
    sinking-fund, 537–538, 552
Bonds payable, 475
Bonuses, 341–342, 347
Book failures, 61
Book printing, quality control and, 276
Book sales, 64
Book translations, licensing, 110
Book value, of a stock, 539, 552
Bookkeeping, 462
Booms and busts, 79–80
    See also Depression; Great Depression; Great Recession; Recession
Borrow-and-buy strategies, 153–154
    See also Employee buyouts; Leveraged buyouts
Borrowing, by government, 85–86
Borrowing money, 488, 494–495, 520
Boss-centered leadership, 208, 209
    See also Leading
Bottom line, 478
Boutique hotels, 348–349
Box-and-lines illustration, 204
    See also Organization chart
Box office bombs, 61
Box office grosses, 61
Box office hits, 61
Brain drain, 68
Brainstorming, 195
Branch sales managers, 195
Brand, 397, 398, 410
Brand advertising, 438–439, 453
Brand awareness, 397, 400, 410
Brand equity, 397, 400, 410
Brand failure rate, 372
Brand insistence, 397, 401, 410
Brand loyalty, 397, 400, 410
Brand manager, 398, 410
Brand marks, 397, 398, 410
Brand names, 397, 398, 410
Brand preference, 397, 400, 410
Branding, 384, 397–401, 410
    brand awareness, 397, 400, 410
    brand equity, 397, 400, 410
    brand insistence, 397, 401, 410
    brand loyalty, 397, 400, 410
    brand marks, 397, 398, 410
    brand names, 397, 398, 410
    brand preference, 397, 400, 410
    co-branding, 399, 410
    to differentiate the company's product from competitors, 397, 399–400, 410
    family brands, 399, 410
    to get repeat sales, 397, 400, 410
    individual brands, 399, 410
    to make entering new markets easier, 397, 400, 410
    manufacturer's brands, 398, 410
    private-label brands, 398–399, 410
    to publicize the company name and build trust, 397, 399, 410
    trademarks, 397, 398, 410
Brazil, 52, 72, 104, 117
    inflation in, 81
    Mercosur and, 125

Computer-aided design. *See* CAD
Computer-aided manufacturing. *See* CAM
Computer engineers, 267
Computer-integrated manufacturing.
    See CIM
Computer repair franchise, 147
Computerized design and manufacturing.
    See CAD; CAM; CIM
Computers, accounting and, 467, 482
Concept testing, 370
Conceptual skills, 204, 206
Confidence, economy and, 519, 521
Conglomerate mergers, 149, 151, 155
Conglomerate structure, 241, 248, 249
Conglomerates, 241
Consolidated Omnibus Budget
    Reconciliation Act (COBRA), 320
Consolidations, 150
    See also Mergers and acquisitions
Construction, 299
Construction contractors, 202
Construction subcontractors, 202
Consumer blogs, for reviewing
    products, 377
Consumer buying behavior, 352, 378,
    384, 385
    culture and subculture and, 359, 360, 378
    personal image and, 359, 361, 378
    reference groups and, 359, 360, 378
    situational matters and, 359, 361, 378
    social class and, 359, 360, 378
    step 1. problem recognition, 359, 378
    step 2. information search, 359, 378
    step 3. evaluating alternatives, 359, 378
    step 4. purchase decision, 359, 360, 378
    step 5. postpurchase evaluation, 359,
      360, 378
    See also Consumer markets; Customers
Consumer finance companies, 514
Consumer fraud, 34
Consumer-friendly behavior, 34
Consumer goods, export of, 102
Consumer markets, 363, 384, 386,
    387–389, 409
    convenience products, 387, 409
    distribution channels for, 418,
      420–421, 452
    shopping products, 388, 409
    specialty products, 388, 409
    unsought products, 388–389, 409
Consumer-oriented sales promotion
    techniques, 449
Consumer price index (CPI), 63, 79, 82,
    91, 508
Consumer sovereignty, 77, 78
Consumers
    for-profit marketing to, 362,
      363–366, 378
    See also Consumer buying behavior;
      Consumer markets; Customers
Consumption, 62
Containerization, 434, 452
Contingency planning, 198, 203, 217
Contingent workers, 327
    See also Temporary workers

Continuity, of ads, 442
Continuous improvement (*kaizen*), 255
Continuous innovation, 390–391, 409
Continuous processes, 254, 259, 260, 278
Continuous quality improvement,
    274–275, 279
Contract enforcement, 12
Contract manufacturing, 110
    See also Global outsourcing;
      Outsourcing
Contraction, in the business cycle, 80
Contributions, 301
Control process, 215
Control standards, 215
Controller, 490
Controlling, 190, 192, 194, 213–216, 218
    1. establishing standards, 213, 215, 218
    2. performance monitoring, 213,
      216, 218
    3. comparing performance against
      standards, 213, 216, 218
    4. taking corrective action, 213, 216, 218
    becoming aware of opportunities,
      213–214, 218
    dealing with changes and uncertainties
      and, 213, 218
    dealing with complexity, 214–215, 218
    decentralizing decision making and
      facilitating teamwork, 215, 218
    detecting errors and irregularities,
      214, 218
    increasing productivity, eliminating
      waste, reducing costs, adding
      value, 214, 218
    span of control: narrow vs. wide, 235–236
Convenience goods and services, 387, 409
Convertible bonds, 538, 552
COO. *See* Chief operating officer
Cooperative department store, 142–143
Cooperatives (co-ops), 132, 142–143
Coordinating activities, 199
    See also Planning
Copycat social networking, 161
Corner cutting, 38
Corporate blogs, for comments, 377
Corporate bonds, 500, 520, 535, 552
    See also Bonds
Corporate citizenship, 34–35
Corporate culture, 224, 230
    motivating employees through, 310–311
    See also Organizational cultures
      (informal)
Corporate finance, 490
Corporate policy, 47
Corporate raiders, 152–154
    See also Hostile takeovers
Corporate social responsibility (CSR), 32,
    36, 44–46, 55–56
    case against, 45
    case for, 44
    companies ranking high in, 47
    payoffs for good business practice, 50–52
    See also Ethical behavior
Corporations, 132, 134, 155
    applying for incorporation, 141

B, 134, 140–141
    benefits of, 141
    C, 134, 139–140
    cooperatives, 142–143
    drawbacks of, 141–142
    glossary of, 140
    limited liability company (LLC),
      134, 140
    S, 134, 140
    See also Multinational corporations
Corrective action, 213, 216
Corruption, 12, 49, 119–121
    anticorruption, 52
    See also Bribery
Cost of capital, 496, 501, 520
Cost of goods sold, 476–477, 483
Cost per thousand (CPM) of ads, 442
Cost pricing, 403, 406, 410
Costs
    from employee fraud, 49
    reducing, 214
    reducing through mergers and
      acquisitions, 150
Cotton gin, 261
Countertrading, 106, 108–109
    See also Bartering
Countries, top 15 livable, 8
Coupons, 64, 449
Courage, vs. cheating, 33
Cover letters, 323, 328
    for business plan, 179
Coworkers, performance appraisals by, 334,
    336, 347
CPI. *See* Consumer price index
CPM. *See* Cost per thousand (CPM)
    of ads
Creative selling, 445, 453
    See also Personal selling
Creativity
    emotional blocks to, 396
    promoting, 211–212
      See also Transformational leaders
Credit
    easy, 517–518, 521
    extending, 494–495
    lack of, 183
Credit card phone, 392, 510
Credit cards, 78
    for financing, 180, 498, 520
    vs. cash, 77
Credit checks, job applicants and,
    328–329, 346
Credit default swaps, 515, 518
Credit ratings, 498–500
Credit risk, 517–518
Credit unions, 181, 511, 513, 521
    National Credit Union Administration
      (NCUA) protection and, 511,
      516, 521
Crisis planning, 203
    See also Contingency planning
Critical path, 273
Criticism, 307
    performance appraisals and,
      338–339, 347

CRM. *See* Customer relationship management

Cross-functional, 247

Cross-functional self-managed teams, 244, 246, 247, 249

CSA. *See* Community-supported agriculture

CSR. *See* Corporate social responsibility

Cuba, 66, 119

Cuban cigars, embargo on, 123

Cuisine, international, 375

Cultural differences, 99, 126
ethics and legalities, 35
keys to, 116
religion, 116
time orientation: segmented vs. flexible, 115–116
verbal and nonverbal communication, 114–115

Culture
buying behavior and, 359, 360, 361, 378
cheating, 38, 114
See also Cultural differences; Organizations

Culture shock, 114

Currency, 505, 507

Currency Converter, 118

Currency devaluation, 119

Currency exchange rates, 118–119

Currency shifts, 116, 118, 126

Currency traders, 119

Current assets, 474

Current liabilities, 475

Current ratio, 479–480

Custom sales pitch, 365
See also One-to-one marketing

Customer-based segmentation, 362, 365, 378

Customer-centric companies, 193

Customer characteristics, 365

Customer complaints, on the Web, 377

Customer divisions, 240, 248

Customer experience, 15–16

Customer feedback, websites for, 377

Customer friendly, 317

Customer lifetime value (CLV), 361

Customer loyalty, 292, 353

Customer relationship era (1990s–present), 354, 357, 378

Customer relationship management (CRM), 357

Customer relationships, 352
See also Marketing

Customer satisfaction, 220, 274–277, 356
See also Quality assurance

Customer-satisfaction ad, 356

Customer service, 356
social media and, 228
websites for, 170

Customers, 13
benefits to for good business practice, 50
customers' experience, 15–16
difficult, 183
employee appraisals, 336, 347
facility location and, 267–268
happy employees and, 305

involvement of in the production process, 255
marketing technology to baby boomers, 356
online dating site, 175
personalized cookbooks, 265
social media for targeting students' wants and needs, 357
staying in tune with, 184
total quality management (TQM) and, 275
See also Consumer buying behavior; Consumer markets

Customhouse brokers, 109

Customization, 265

Cutting-edge jobs, 318

Cybercriminals, 214

Cybermalls, 430

Cyclical unemployment, 83

Czech Republic, 106

D

Data
analyzing, 374, 379
collecting, 373, 379
primary, 373, 379
secondary, 373, 379

Data analysis, 374, 379

Data mining, 373, 379

Data warehouses, 373

Databases, 373, 379

Dating websites, 175, 187–188

Day trading, 545, 555–556

Dealer brands, 398
See also Private-label brands

Debenture bonds, 500, 535, 552
See also Unsecured bonds

Debit cards, 510

Debt, national, 86

Debt financing, 496, 500, 520

Debt instruments, 518

Debt-rating services, 500

Debt to owners' equity ratios, 479, 481, 483

Decentralization, decision making and, 213, 215

Decentralized authority, 234, 237–238, 248

Decision, 195

Decision making, 195–197, 213
decentralizing, 215
See also Management

Decline stage, of products, 390, 393, 410

Deficits
in nonsocialist states, 68
in socialist states, 68

"Defining Diversity: Beyond Race and Gender" (National Public Radio), 27

Deflation, 79, 80, 81–82, 91, 508

Deflationary economy, 82

Delegation, 208–209, 234, 247
dos and don'ts for, 237
line vs. staff positions, 236–237, 248
See also Leading

Delivering Happiness: A Path to Profits, Passion, and Purpose (Hsieh), 310

Deluxe: How Luxury Lost Its Luster (Thomas), 423

Demand, 60, 63, 76
See also Demand and supply model

Demand and supply model, 75–78
See also Demand; Supply

Demand curve, 76

Demand deposits, 505

Democratic administrations, macroeconomics in, 63

Democratic leaders. *See* Participative (democratic) leaders

Democratic political systems, international business and, 119

Demographic segmentation, 362, 363, 378

Demographics, 13
changes in U.S., 21–22, 27

Demonstrations, 447, 449

Denial of Risk and Peril (Collins), 227, 248

Denim marketing strategies, 381

Denmark, 65, 67, 68, 69, 72

Denominations, of bonds, 535

Densitometers, 276

Department heads, 195

Department store sales, 407

Departmentalization, 239–243, 248

Depression, 80
See also Great depression

Deregulation, 90, 488, 517–518, 521

Derivatives, 517, 518, 521

Design restraint, 385

Designer jeans makers, 367

Devaluation, 119

Developed countries, 117

Developing countries, 117–118

Development, 332
See also Training and development

Differential rate system, 289

Differentiation
branding and, 399–400
packaging and, 402
See also Product differentiation

Digital mapmakers, 258

Digital reputation, 325

Digital storefronts, 430

Digital textbooks, vs. paper, 357

Direct-action advertising, 438, 440–441, 453

Direct channel, 420

Direct exports, 109

Direct mail advertising, 438, 441

Direct mail marketing, 429

Direct marketing, 424, 429, 452

Direct sales, website for, 170

Direct selling, 424, 428, 452

Disassembly line, 261

Disciplining, job, 314, 344, 347

Discontinuous innovation, 390, 391, 392, 409

Discount brokers, 544–545, 552

Discount rate, 503, 509, 521

Discount stores, 315

Discounting, 403, 407–408, 410

HIPAA. *See* Health Insurance Portability and Accountability Act
Hiring practices, 40
Hispanics, population of, 13
Historical production processes, 260–262, 278
   See also Production processes
Holding companies, 530
Holding hands, Middle East culture and, 115
Holier-than-thou effect, 37
Holland, 277
Hollywood accounting, 486
Hollywood Economics (DeVany), 61
Home-based businesses, 135, 160, 169–170, 185
   websites for, 170
   See also Small-business entrepreneurs
Home work, 343
Homelessness, suburban, 22
Honesty
   during job interviews, 331
   on résumés, 328
Hong Kong, 65
Horizontal mergers, 149, 151, 155
Horizontal specialization, 204–205
   See also Organizing
Hostile environment sexual harassment, 322
Hostile takeovers, 132, 149, 151–153, 155
Hosting services, inexpensive, 172
Hot List, The, 61
Hotel housecleaning, 290
Hotel job retention, 294–295
Hotel management, 23
Hotel promotions, 448
Hourly wages, 319
House-party sales, 428
House (TV show), 394
How the Mighty Fall and Why Some Companies Never Give In (Collins), 226
How We Decide (Lehrer), 77
HR. *See* Human resource (HR) management
Hubris Born of Success (Collins), 227, 248
Human capital, 314, 316–318, 346
Human development measures (UN Human Development Index), 8
Human relations movement, 291
   See also Hierarch of needs theory (Maslow)
Human resource (HR) management, 314–351
   compensation, 314, 340–343, 347
   determining the human resources needed, 314, 317–318, 346
   development, 314, 323, 332–333, 346
   disciplining, 314, 344, 347
   dismissal, 314, 344–345, 347
   employment tests, 323, 330, 346
   human capital, 314, 346
   interviewing, 323, 329–330, 346
   laws affecting, 314, 319–322, 346
   mentoring, 333, 346
   orientation, 314, 323, 332, 346
   performance appraisals, 314, 334–338, 346–347

promotion, 314, 340, 343, 347
recruiting, 314, 323, 324–327, 346
selection process, 314, 323, 327–330, 346
training, 314, 323, 332–333, 346
transferring, 340, 344, 347
Human resources, 9, 64, 257, 259
Human rights, 52
Human Side of Enterprise, The (McGregor), 296
Human skills, 204, 205
Hungary, 67, 106
Hurricane Katrina, 51
Hybrid cars, 387
Hybrid structure, 239, 242, 248
Hygiene factors theory (Herzberg), 289, 292–293, 309
Hyperchanging world, 224, 244
   See also Change; Networked organizations; Organizations; Teamwork
Hyperinflation, 81

I

Iceland, 8, 104
   financial crisis in, 519
   geothermal plants in, 376
Idea generation, 390, 395, 396, 410
Ideas, 174–175
Identity, organizational, 232, 248
IMF. *See* International Monetary Fund
Immigration Reform and Control Act (1986), 320
Imperfect information, 77
Implementation, 196
Import companies, 109
Import quotas, 122–123
Imports, 102
   balance of trade and, 108
   entering foreign markets and, 109
   top 10 nations U.S. imports from, 107
   See also International trade
Impulse buying, 361
Inbound logistics, 433
Incentives
   in free-market economies, 69
   job, 340, 341–342, 347
   lack of in communism, 66
   lack of in socialism, 68
   See also Motivating employees; Motivation theories; Nonmonetary motivation methods
Income
   in capitalist countries, 69–70
   investing for, 550–551, 553
   as measure of human development, 8
Income inequality, capitalism and, 70
Income statements, 460, 471, 475–477, 483
Incomplete buyer-seller information, 77
Incubators, 182, 186
Indenture terms, 500
Independent audits, 465
Independent booksellers, 196
Independent contractors, 327

India, 6, 19, 71, 105, 110, 117, 267, 376, 420
   Americans working in, 100
   dating websites in, 187–188
   growing economy of, 125
   hair extension imports, 102
Indian Americans, lodging industry and, 181
Indirect exports, 109
Individual brands, 397, 399, 410
Indonesia, 119
Industrial goods, 389, 409
Industrial production, growth in, 63
Industrial supplies, exports of, 102
Industry divisions (conglomerates), 241, 248
Inflation, 79, 81, 86, 91, 97, 508
Infomercials, 436–437
Informal appraisals, 334, 335, 346–347
Informal organizational cultures. *See* Organizational cultures (informal)
Information search, 359, 378
Information technology, 31, 228
   accounting and, 467, 482
   social media and, 173, 228
   See also Technology
Information utility, 421, 422
Informational advertising, 435, 436, 438, 440, 453
Infrastructure, international business and, 116–118, 126
Initial public offering (IPO), 500, 531, 552
Innovation, 19, 168, 384, 390–392, 409
   continuous, 390–391, 409
   discontinuous, 390, 391, 392, 409
   dynamically continuous, 390, 391, 409
   examples of, 390
   level of, 291
   top 30 of the last three decades, 392
   See also Small-business entrepreneurs
Inputs, 256
Inquiry into the Nature and Causes of the Wealth of Nations, An (Smith), 69
Insider trading, 37, 543
Installations, 389
Institutional advertising, 438, 439, 453
Institutional investors, 531
Instrumentality, 299
Insurance companies, 511, 514, 521
Intangible assets, 474
Intangible products, 5, 84
   See also Service industry
Intangible services, 358
Intangibility, 255
Integrated marketing communication, 416, 435–436, 453
Integrity, 212, 298
Integrity-based ethics codes, 41
Intensive distribution, 418, 423, 452
Interaction, 23
Interchangeable gun parts, 261
Interdependency, 52–53
Interest groups, 17
Interest on loans (banks), 513, 521
Interest-rate wars, 512

Mortgage-backed securities, 88–89, 518–519, 521, 537, 552
Mortgage guarantees, indirect, 90
Mortgage lenders, 39–40
Mortgage loans
  overvalued (subprime bubble), 88–89, 91, 104
  See also Subprime bubble
Mortgage pass-through securities, 536, 552
"Most Admired Companies" (*Fortune*), 315
Motivated blindness, 38
Motivating employees, 284–288, 304–313
  extrinsic rewards, 286, 287, 308
  five reasons for, 286, 288
  how it works and importance of, 286–288, 308
  intrinsic rewards, 286, 288, 308
  nonmonetary methods, 304–307
  through company culture, 310–311
  See also Motivation theories; Nonmonetary motivation methods
Motivating factors, 292
Motivating factors theory (Herzberg), 289, 292–293, 309
Motivation, 193–194
  importance of, 288
  reasons for, 288
  transformational leaders and, 211–212
  See also Leading; Motivating employees; Motivation theories; Nonmonetary motivation methods
Motivation theories, 289–303, 308–309
  equity theory (Adams), 289, 300–301, 309
  expectancy theory (Vroom), 289, 299–300, 309
  goal-setting theory (Locke & Latham), 302–303, 309
  "Hawthorne effect" (Mayo), 289, 290–291, 309
  hierarchy of needs (Maslow), 289, 291–292, 309
  job enrichment, 289, 293–296, 309
  management by objectives (Drucker), 289, 303, 309
  motivating factors and hygiene factors (Herzberg), 289, 292–293, 309
  principle of motion economy (Gilbreth & Gilbreth), 290
  reinforcement theory/behavior modification (Thorndike & Skinner), 289, 298–299, 309
  scientific management; studying work methods (Taylor), 289–290, 309
  Theory X/Theory Y: treating employees differently (McGregor), 289, 296–297, 309
  Theory Z: combining Japanese and American management approaches (Ouchi), 289, 297, 309
Motivational mind game for success, 286–287
Motivators, 292
Motorcycle parts, 271

Movie budgets, 61
Movies, predicting hits, 61, 64, 96
MRP. *See* Materials requirement planning
Mt. Kilimanjaro, 53
Muda (eliminating waste), 255
Multilevel marketing (MLM), 428–429
Multinational corporations, 98, 102, 104, 111, 126
  See also Corporations
Multiple job interviews, 331
Multitasking, 258
Municipal bonds, 535, 552
Mutual funds, 528, 547–548, 553
Mutual savings banks, 511, 513, 521
My Big Fat Greek Wedding (film), 61, 486

N

NAFTA. *See* North American Free Trade Agreement
Narrow span of control, 235–236, 248
National brands, 398
  See also Manufacturer's brands
National Business Ethics Survey, 50–51
National communities, benefits to for good business practice, 51
National debt, 86
  See also Federal budget deficit
National debt clock, 86
National Do Not Call Registry, 429
National stability, 13
Natural resources, 9, 10, 64, 257, 259
  international trade and, 107
Nearby communities, 17
Necessity entrepreneurs, 166–167, 185
Need-satisfaction presentations, 447
Needs
  motivation and, 286
  See also Hierarchy of needs theory (Maslow)
Negative effects
  of bad business behavior, 49–50
  of globalization, 103–104
Negative performance appraisals, 334, 338–339, 347
Negative reinforcement, 298
Net Generation, 375
Net income, 477, 483
Net period, 496
Net profit, 486
Net sales, 476
Netherlands, 8, 65, 69, 72
Networked organizations, 244–245, 249
Networking, 170, 206, 224
  for jobs, 325
  online connections for small-business people, 170
  See also Organizations
Neuromarketing, 372, 373, 379
New media marketing, 442, 443
New product development, 367–368, 378, 384, 390, 394–395, 410
  1. idea generation, 390, 395, 410
  2. product screening, 390, 395, 410
  3. product analysis, 390, 395, 410
  4. product development, 390, 395, 410

  5. test marketing, 390, 395, 410
  6. commercialization, 390, 395, 410
  to continue to expand revenues and profits, 367–368, 378
  to fill out a product line, 368, 378
  to stay ahead/match the competition, 367, 378
  to take advantage of an opportunity, 368, 378
New Zealand, 8, 117
News releases, 442
Newspapers, for advertising, 438, 441
Newsweek, 10
Niche marketing, 362, 364–365, 378
Niger, birth rate in, 117–118
Nigeria, 107, 117
No-load funds, 548
Non-Hispanic whites, population in U.S., 21
Nonbanks, 488, 511, 514–515, 521
Nondisclosure agreements, 41
Nonmanagerial employees, 195, 201, 247
Nonmonetary motivation methods, 304–308, 309, 340–341, 347
  being nice, 306
  learning opportunities, 305
  listening, 306, 307
  pets in the workplace, 311–312
  praise, 306, 307
  treating employees well, 304–305
  work-life benefits, 305–306
  See also Benefits; Motivating employees; Motivation theories; Perks
Nonprofit organizations, 2, 4–5, 25, 27, 158
  advertising and, 439
  credit unions, 511, 513, 521
  See also Not-for-profit organizations
Nonprofit professional football team owned by the fans (Green Bay Packers), 158
Nonstore retailers, 424, 428–430, 452
Nonverbal communication, 115
North American Free Trade Agreement (NAFTA), 124
North Korea, 66, 75
Norway, 8, 65, 67
Not-for-profit accountants, 462, 466–467, 482
Not-for-profit marketing, 362, 366, 378
Not-for-profit organizations, 2, 4–5, 354–355
  See also Nonprofit organizations
Notes payable, 475
NOW (negotiable order of withdrawal) accounts, 512, 521

O

Objections, handling, 444, 447–448
Objective appraisals, 334, 335, 346–347
Objectives, 202
Obsolescence, 390
Obsolete inventory, 480
Occupational Safety and Health Act (OSHA), 320, 321, 346

Reminder advertising, 435, 437, 438, 440, 453
Republican administrations, macroeconomics in, 63
Research
  preparing for a job interview, 331
  See also Marketing research
Resentment, cheating and, 38
Reserve requirement, 503, 508, 521
Resource development, 64
Resources
  arranging, 193
  enterprise resource planning (ERP) for managing, 272, 279
  facility location and, 266–267
  materials requirement planning (MRP) for managing, 271, 278–279
  outsourcing and, 112
  suppliers and, 269–271
  transforming into finished products, 256–258
  See also Organizing
Responsibility, 234–235, 248, 295
Restoration, using green materials, 175
Restraint, vs. freedom, 12, 25
Restrictive monetary policy, 86
Résumé checking, 329
Résumés, 323, 328, 346
Retail banks, 524
Retailers, 418, 419, 452
  bargain, 427
  product-line, 427
  See also Nonstore retailers; Shopping centers; Store retailers
Retained earnings, 475, 500, 520
Retirees, 9
Retirement, 22
Retirement plans, canceling, 34
Return on assets, 481
Return on investment, 61
Return on owners' equity, 482
Return on sales, 481
Returns, 301, 533
Revenue bonds, 535, 552
Revenues, 2, 5, 27
  expanding through new product development, 367–368
Reverse logistics, 433
Revolving credit agreement, 498, 520
Rewards
  extrinsic, 286, 287, 308
  in free-market economies, 69
  intrinsic, 286, 287, 308
  linked to performance, 299–300
  motivation and, 286–287
Right and wrong standards, 35
Right to compete, 73
Right to free choice, 73
Right to make and keep profits, 73
Right to own property, 72
Risk, 2, 10, 25, 461
  buying a successful business and, 173
  day trading and, 555–556
  of default on bonds, 536, 552

denial of, 227
entering foreign markets and, 109–113
entrepreneurship and, 167
in free-market economies, 69
investing and, 550–551, 553
of multilevel marketing, 429
political stability and, 120
securitization and, 88
sole proprietorships and, 136
subprime bubble and, 517–518, 521
Risk management, 554–555
Risk-return trade-off, 491, 520
Rites and rituals, in organizational culture, 230, 232
Road transport, 431, 432, 433, 452
Robotics, 262
Robots, 262, 281
Romania, 106
Royalties, 147
Russia, 99, 104
  bribery (*vzyatka*), 120

S

S corporations, 134, 140
Safety
  higher-level needs and, 291–292
  workplace health and safety, 319, 320, 321, 346
Safety needs (Maslow), 291
Salaried employees, 319
  vs. self-employed, 9, 25
Salaries, 5, 340
  entry-level pay for business college graduates, 6
Sales, vs. profits, 356
Sales commissions, 341
Sales growth, bad business behavior and, 49
Sales promotion, 416, 435, 444, 448–449, 453
Sales reports, 3
Sales representatives, 365–366
Sales returns, 476
Sales revenue, 476, 483
Sales support, 444, 445, 453
Samples, 449
Sarbanes-Oxley Reform Act, 39, 42–43, 55, 320, 465, 532
SarbOx. *See* Sarbanes-Oxley Reform Act
Satisfied employees, 292–296
Saudi Arabia, 107
Savings accounts, 512, 521
  See also Time deposits
Savings and loan associations (S&Ls), 16, 513, 521
  Savings Association Insurance Fund (SAIF) protection and, 511, 516, 521
Savings and loans, 181
SBA. *See* Small Business Administration
Scarcity, 60–63
Scheduling, 272, 279
Scheduling tools, 266
  Gantt charts, 272, 279
  PERT charts, 273, 279

Scientific management theory of motivation (Taylor), 289–290, 309
Scuffy the Tugboat, 3
Seafood market, 419
Seasonal businesses, 183
Seasonal unemployment, 83
Seasonal workers, 327
Second Great Depression (almost), 7, 60, 91
  See also Great Recession
Second jobs, 182
Second mortgages, for financing, 180
Secondary data, 373, 379
Secondary securities market, 528, 530, 532, 552
Secretaries, eliminating, 19
Secured bonds, 500, 520, 535, 552
Secured loans, 497, 520
Securities, 530, 552
  mortgage-backed, 88
  See also Securities markets
Securities Act, 543
Securities and Exchange Commission, 543, 552
Securities investment dealers, 514
  See also Brokerage firms
Securities markets, 528–557
  bonds, 528, 534, 535–538, 552
  buying and selling securities, 528, 544–545, 552–553
  commodities, 547, 549, 553
  exchange-traded funds, 547, 548–549, 553
  investment postures, 533
  investment strategies, 528, 550–551, 553
  investment styles by gender, 530
  money market instruments, 534, 552
  mutual funds, 547–548, 553
  primary, 528, 530, 531–532, 552
  regulating: the Securities and Exchange Commission (SEC), 543, 552
  secondary, 528, 530, 532, 552
  stock indicators, 544, 545–546, 553
  stock markets, 534, 541–543, 552
  stocks, 534, 538–540, 552
  See also Bonds; Stocks
Securitization, 88
Security, 13
Segmentation. *See* Market segmentation
Segmented time orientation, 115
Selected markets, 395
  See also Test marketing
Selection process for jobs, 314, 327–330, 346
  checks on legal status, 329, 346
  cover letters, 328
  credit checks, 328–329, 346
  reference checks, 328, 346
  résumés, 323, 328, 346
Selective distribution, 418, 423, 452
Self-actualization needs (Maslow), 291
Self-appraisals, 334, 336–337, 347
Self-confidence, 167
Self-development, 22–23, 26

Sweepstakes, 449
Switzerland, 8, 65, 107
SWOT analysis (**S**trengths, **W**eaknesses, **O**pportunities, **T**hreats), 198, 202–203, 217
Symbols, in organizational culture, 230, 231–232
Syndicates, 531
Synthetic transformation, 260

T

T-bills. *See* Treasury bills
T-shirt startup business, 170–171
Tablet computers, 394
Taco trucks, 10
Tactical planning (middle managers), 190, 200–201, 217
Tactics, 432
Taft-Hartley Act (1947), 319
Taiwan, 65
Taking action, 374
Tall span of control, 235–236
Tangible products, 5, 84, 358
Tangled Webs (Stewart), 38
Target costing, 403, 406, 410
Target marketing strategy, 362, 369–370, 374, 375, 378
Target return on investment, 403, 410
See also Profits
Tariffs, 122
Task identity, 295
Task management, 273
See also PERT charts
Task significance, 295
Tasking, 24, 193
See also Organizing
Tattoo advertisement, 435
Tattoos, employees with, 349–350
Tax accounting, 465
Tax benefits, 90
Tax credits, 182
Tax planning, 465
Tax returns, 465
Taxation, 12
Taxes, 8, 25
avoiding on U.S. revenues using offshore banks, 34
cash payments to avoid, 34
corporations and, 139–143
by country, 67
facility location and, 268
fiscal policy and, 85
high in welfare states, 67, 68
investments and, 533
mergers and acquisitions and, 150
minimizing, 491
risk-return trade-off and, 491
See also Tariffs
Team leaders, 195
Teams, 245, 249
action, 246, 249
advice, 246, 249
cross-functional self-managed, 244, 247, 249

production, 246, 249
project, 246, 249
See also Teamwork
Teamwork, 220, 224, 244, 245–247, 264
facilitating, 213, 215, 244, 245–247
importance/improvements, 246
organizations using, 245
See also Organizations; Teams
Tech startups, financing, 531–532
Technical skills, 204, 205
Technological forces, 12–13, 25
marketing and, 375–376, 379
Technology
improving services and, 85
international trade and, 107
marketing to baby boomers, 356
organizational change and, 228, 248
for predicting hit movies, 64
productivity and, 25–26
world economy and, 101
Technology stocks, overvalued, 87–88
Teens, cheating and, 195
Teen's Guide to World Domination, The: Advice on Life, Liberty, and the Pursuit of Awesomeness (Shipp), 5
Telecommuting, 343, 347
Telemarketing, 429
Telephone job interviews, 330
Telepresence robots, 281
Teleradiology, 106
Television, for advertising, 438, 441
"Tempered radical," 292
Temporary job dismissals, 344, 347
Temporary workers, 327
See also Contingent workers
Tender offer, 152–153
Term-loan agreement, 499, 520
Terms of trade, 496
Test marketing, 370, 390, 395, 410
Testimonials, 447
Tests, for employment, 323, 330, 346
Textbooks, digital vs. paper, 357
Thailand, 420
Theft, in the workplace, 38
Theory X/Theory Y: treating employees differently (McGregor), 289, 296–297, 309
Theory Z: combining Japanese and American management approaches (Ouchi), 289, 297, 309
Think Pink campaign, 366
Third-world countries, 117–118
Threats, 202–203
See also SWOT analysis
Three Sigma, 277
360-degree assessment, 337, 347
Time deposits, 505–506, 512
See also Savings accounts
Time-motion studies, 289–290
See also Scientific management theory of motivation (Taylor)
Time orientation, 115–116
Time to market, 267
Time utility, 421, 422

Timing, buying decisions and, 361
Tipping, vs. bribery, 35
Tipping-point approach, 166
Titanic (film), 61
Title VII (Civil Rights Act), 320, 321, 349
Tombstones, 531
Toning shoes, 391
Top managers (strategic planners), 190, 194, 198, 200, 206, 217, 303
ethics and, 39–40, 55
Total asset turnover ratios, 480
Total fixed costs, 405
Total product offer, 384, 386–387, 409
components of, 387
Total quality management (TQM), 274–275, 279
Totalitarian political systems, 119–120
Touch, 115
Toys, 187
TQM. *See* Total quality management
Trade, 13
See also International trade
Trade agreements. *See* International trade
Trade associations, 176
Trade barriers, 122–123, 127
See also Trade protectionism
Trade credit, 496, 496–497, 520
Trade deficit, 108
Trade facilitators
International Monetary Fund (IMF), 124
World Bank, 124
World Trade Organization (WTO), 123
Trade promotion, 444, 449
Trade protectionism
embargoes, 123, 127
import quotas, 122–123, 127
tariffs, 122, 127
Trade shows, 449
Trade surplus, 108
Trademarks, 397, 398, 410, 474
Trading, stocks, 541
Trading floor exchanges, 541, 552
Traditional brokers. *See* Full-service brokers
Training and development, job, 323, 332–333, 346
Training programs, 274, 276
ethics codes and, 40–42
for green jobs, 277
Trait appraisals, 336
Transaction loans, 498, 520
Transactional leaders, 207, 210–211, 218
Transcription, websites for, 170
Transfers, job, 340, 344, 347
Transformation
analytic, 259
efficiency and, 258
of resources into finished products, 254, 256–257, 259–260, 278
synthetic, 560
See also Operations management; Operations management planning; Production processes; Quality assurance